Keeping you safely on the m…

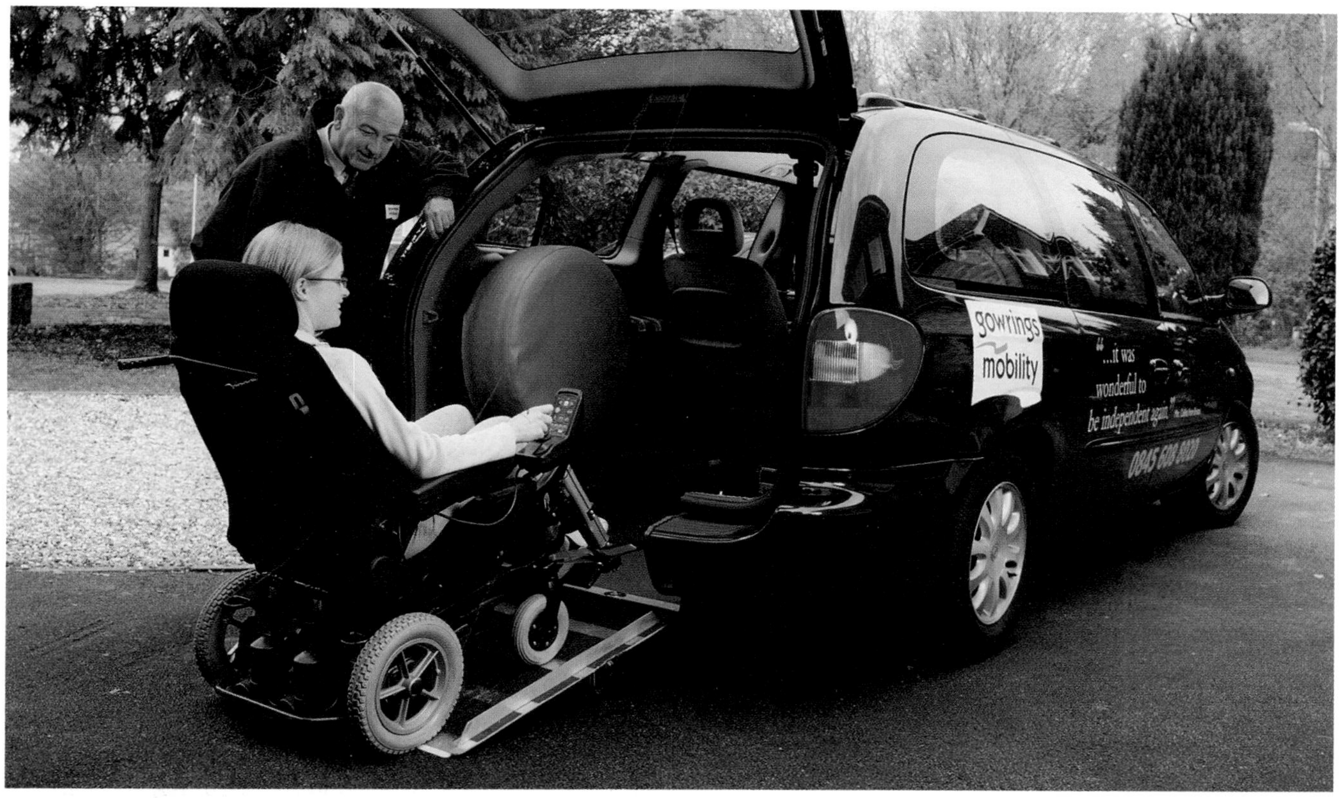

"It has transformed our lives!"

Mandy, Steven & Emily Johnson in Berkshire

Emily was diagnosed at birth with microcephaly. This means her brain has not grown in size with the rest of her body causing severe developmental delay. Consequently she has little control of movement and no natural balance.

Transport has always been an issue for us, because as a family, we like to get out and about whenever we want. Our previous vehicle, a 4 by 4, was suitable for Emily at a younger age. We could lift her into a child's booster seat like any other child, then dismantle her wheelchair and fold it into the boot.

As Emily grew with increased weight, we started to find this procedure increasingly difficult. As soon as Emily is lifted her body will go rigid, making it very difficult to manoeuvre her into a car seat. As a result, Steven and I were suffering with muscular back pains. We realised that it was only a matter of time before we did ourselves a serious, permanent injury.

Simply popping out to the shops would be near impossible. At every stop, we would have to unload her wheelchair, lift her out of the car seat and into her chair. Then we would do the reverse every time we returned to the car. It would make us think twice about going out, and often on weekends, I would go shopping alone leaving Emily with Steve at home.

It was at this point that we decided to invest in a specially adapted car.

With the Gowrings Mobility car, it is just a matter of wheeling Emily in, which takes a few minutes. It's so quick and convenient, and we can just nip out to the supermarket with Emily whenever we feel like it. The best thing is that we can make spur of the moment decisions and be a lot more spontaneous.

Car swivel seats

Discreet, effective yet solidly built, our range of swivel seats is ideal for anyone who needs some help getting in and out of cars. They are compatible with most makes of car on the driver or front passenger side, and, if you are thinking of buying a new car, installing a swivel seat can make a new car entirely VAT free.

We are also a national supplier of the AutoAdapt Turny Seat range. The Turny HD offers manual swivelling using a release lever plus the benefit of electrically operated lifting and lowering, whereas the Turny Orbit offers the additionally benefit of motorised swivelling.

4 IN 4 power chair

Superior comfort, advanced technical features and its elegant design gives the Gowrings Mobility 4 IN 4 power chair distinction over any other power chair in the UK.

Designed for travelling in cars, the 4 IN 4 power chair is a successfully crash-tested solution for your added security. With an extra low sitting height, making it ideal for travelling and at standard desks or tables; an orthopaedically designed Recaro seating system and the ability to fully recline with your legs extended, the Gowrings Mobility 4 IN 4 power chair is perfect for any customer who demands quality and excellence from a trusted name.

Wheelchair Passenger Vehicles

If you want the simplicity of a wheelchair passenger vehicle, it makes sense to choose the UK's leading manufacturer. We enjoy a close working relationship with the major car manufacturers on all aspects, from initial design to technical support, ensuring that you receive the highest standards possible.

Our cars are ideal for anyone who finds it difficult to transfer into a car seat. Wheelchair access is at the rear and the chair is then safely secured using a 4-point tie down restraint system with a lap & diagonal belt for the passenger. All our cars benefit from a built-in lightweight ramp to allow quick and easy access and the lowered floor enables the passenger to travel at a similar height to the other passengers to aid communication.

Please call for your free information brochure

Lo-Call **0845 608 8020** **www.gowringsmobility.co.uk**

gowrings mobility

Information
Support
Guidance
All routes lead to MAGIC 0800 240 241

gowrings mobility

Gowrings Mobility UK Road Atlas

Foreword by Dame Tanni Grey-Thompson

Tanni Triumphant in Sydney's Olympic Stadium

As a wheelchair user and a keen motorist, I was thrilled to be asked to write a few words about this unique motoring and parking guide.

Being independent is something that's really important to me. Had I not been able to drive all over the UK to get to some really 'out of the way' race venues, I would never have been able to pursue my dream of becoming a wheelchair racer. My car has enabled me to do everyday things like getting to work, doing the shopping and taking my daughter to school, as well as exciting things such as going on holiday and maintaining a social life!

For many disabled people, there's nothing more annoying than arriving at a venue and not being able to find a disabled parking spot, or stopping at a petrol station that doesn't have an accessible toilet.

For the first time, this atlas provides all the important, practical information that disabled people need in one handy guide. It's perfect to keep in the car and I hope it encourages more disabled motorists to attempt journeys they may well have avoided in the past.

Happy and safe motoring!

Tanni

Collins

Specially produced for PIE Enterprises Ltd by Collins, a subsidiary of HarperCollins*Publishers* Ltd.

Tel: 01242 258155

www.collins.co.uk/businessmaps

Mapping generated from Collins Bartholomew digital databases

The grid on this map is the National Grid taken from the Ordnance Survey map with the permission of the Controller of Her Majesty's Stationery Office.

The representation of a road, track or footpath is no evidence of a right of way.

Information specific for the Blue Badge user supplied by PIE Enterprises Ltd © 2006

General Enquires & Trade Sales
Telephone: 0870 444 5434, Fax: 0870 444 5437

email: enquires@thePIEguide.com

WWW.thePIEguide.com

ISBN 0-9951711-0-5 ISBN-13 978-0-9551711-0-9

Printed in Great Britain by NJP Ltd

Special thanks to the help & support from:

Mike Hudson
Operations & Content Manager

Information Providers:
Tourism for All, English, Scottish and Welsh Tourist Boards, DDA/DDMC, Blue Badge Network, National Federation of Shopmobility, Motability, Wheelyboat Trust, Caravan Site-finder

Publishers/Cartographers:
Collins Maps & Atlases, Robert Talbot, Jackie McGeough & Sonia Dawkins

Our team of surveyors:
Adnan Khan, Nigel Lockhart

Advertising Sales:
Jackie Ouko, Liam Fair, Magnus Cole

Layout & Design:
Neil Forrest & Arthur Noel

www.thePIEguide.com

Contents

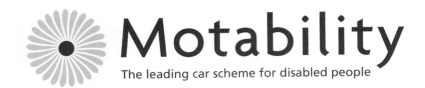

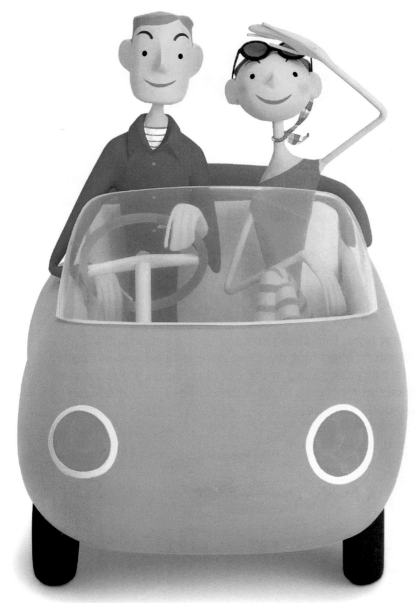

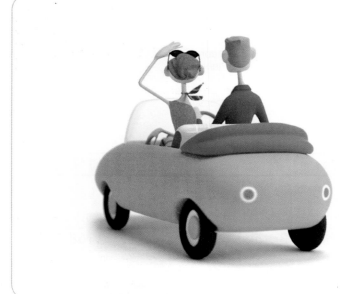

Key to map pages

28-29	Road mapping
(grey box)	Urban area maps
LONDON	City centre map
Oxford	City and town centre plans

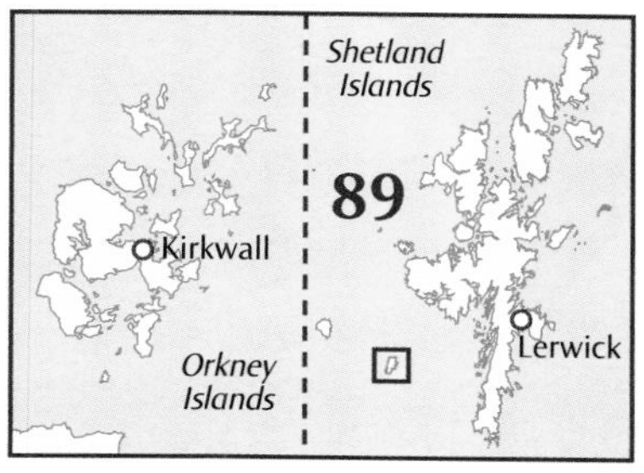

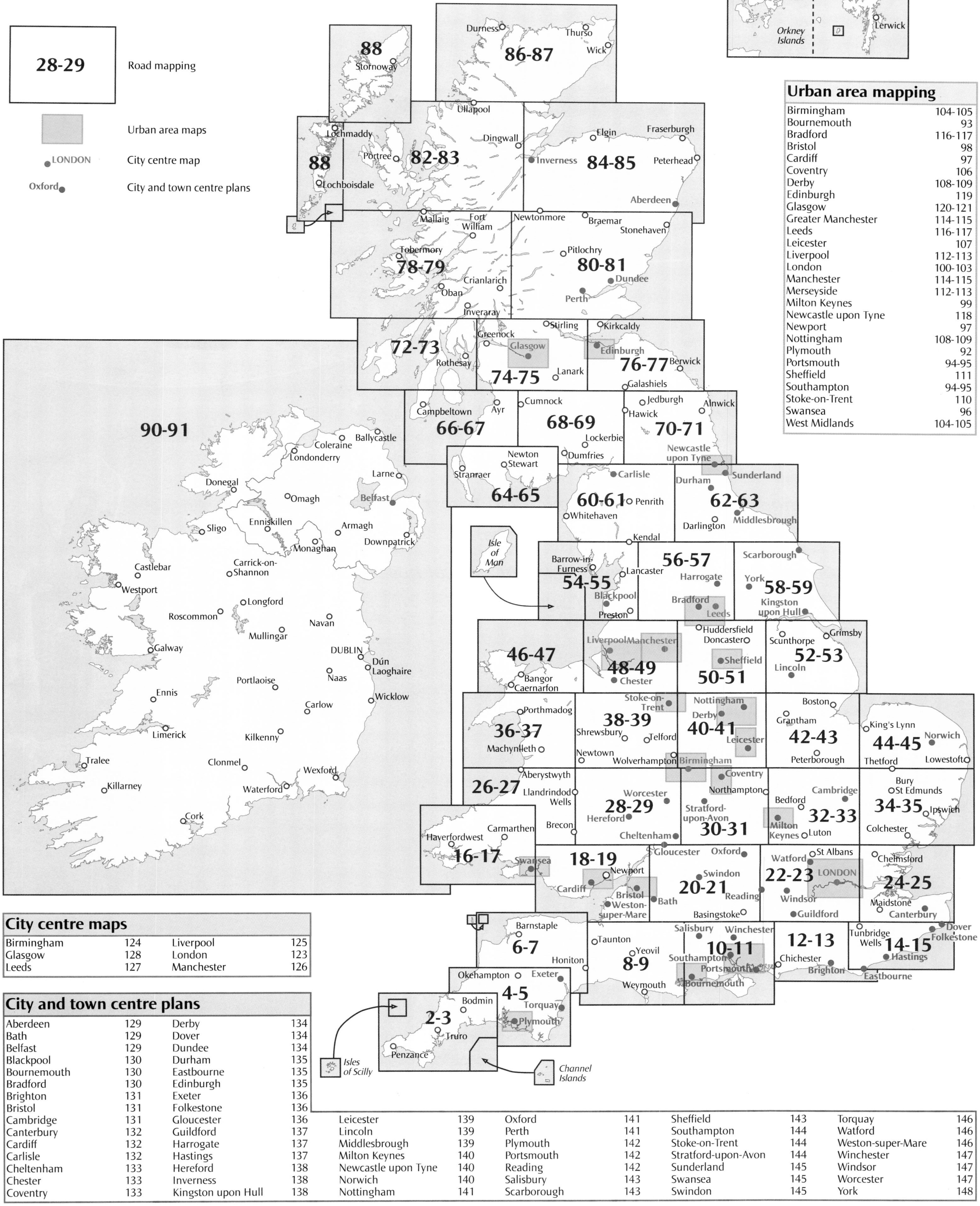

Urban area mapping

Birmingham	104-105
Bournemouth	93
Bradford	116-117
Bristol	98
Cardiff	97
Coventry	106
Derby	108-109
Edinburgh	119
Glasgow	120-121
Greater Manchester	114-115
Leeds	116-117
Leicester	107
Liverpool	112-113
London	100-103
Manchester	114-115
Merseyside	112-113
Milton Keynes	99
Newcastle upon Tyne	118
Newport	97
Nottingham	108-109
Plymouth	92
Portsmouth	94-95
Sheffield	111
Southampton	94-95
Stoke-on-Trent	110
Swansea	96
West Midlands	104-105

City centre maps

Birmingham	124	Liverpool	125
Glasgow	128	London	123
Leeds	127	Manchester	126

City and town centre plans

Aberdeen	129	Derby	134						
Bath	129	Dover	134						
Belfast	129	Dundee	134						
Blackpool	130	Durham	135						
Bournemouth	130	Eastbourne	135						
Bradford	130	Edinburgh	135						
Brighton	131	Exeter	136						
Bristol	131	Folkestone	136						
Cambridge	131	Gloucester	136	Leicester	139	Oxford	141	Sheffield	143	Torquay	146
Canterbury	132	Guildford	137	Lincoln	139	Perth	141	Southampton	144	Watford	146
Cardiff	132	Harrogate	137	Middlesbrough	139	Plymouth	142	Stoke-on-Trent	144	Weston-super-Mare	146
Carlisle	132	Hastings	137	Milton Keynes	140	Portsmouth	142	Stratford-upon-Avon	144	Winchester	147
Cheltenham	133	Hereford	138	Newcastle upon Tyne	140	Reading	142	Sunderland	145	Windsor	147
Chester	133	Inverness	138	Norwich	140	Salisbury	143	Swansea	145	Worcester	147
Coventry	133	Kingston upon Hull	138	Nottingham	141	Scarborough	143	Swindon	145	York	148

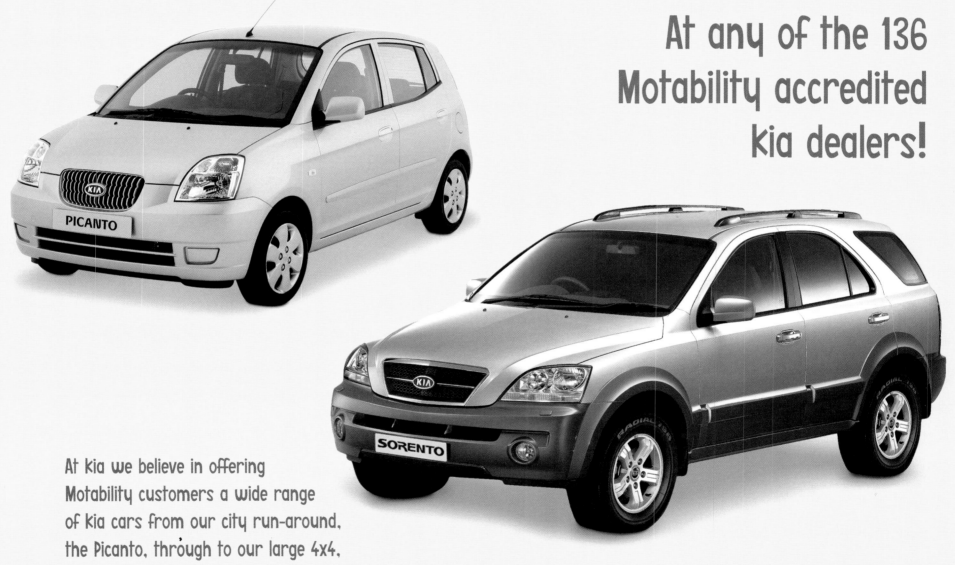

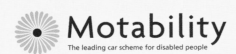

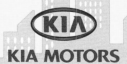

Key to map symbols

www.thePIEguide.com

Blue Badge symbols

- Shopmobility
- Accessible beach
- Accessible beach with disabled car parking
- Accessible accommodation (see page 148)
- Motability dealer
- Forum of Mobility Centres
- Discount — Toll with discount for Blue Badge holders
- Disabled friendly caravan site
- Mobility shop
- Wheelchair accessible boat
- Mobility vehicle servicing
- Vehicle adaptations
- Mobility exhibition
- Petrol station
- Petrol station with service call
- Petrol station with accessible toilet for the disabled
- Petrol station with service call and disabled accessible toilet
- Wheelchair accessible public toilet

Blue Badge parking bay -

- Maximum stay 3 hours
- Maximum stay 4 hours
- Maximum stay unlimited
- Check local limits
- Car park (number within square refers to the accessibility of the car park)
- Car park free or discounted for Blue Badge holders
- Car park with height restriction of 2.20m or less
- Car park with height restrictions free or discounted for Blue Badge holders

Red Box parking bay -

- Maximum stay 3 hours
- Maximum stay 4 hours
- Maximum stay unlimited
- Check local limits

Definition of accessibility grading used for car parks

- **1** - Accessible to a wheelchair-user travelling independently
- **2** - Accessible to a wheelchair-user travelling with assistance
- **3** - Accessible to a wheelchair-user or someone with limited mobility, able to walk a few paces and up a max of three steps

Road maps

Pages 2-89

- M5 — Motorway
- M6Toll — Toll motorway
- 8 9 — Motorway junction with full / limited access
- Maidstone, Birch, Sarn — Motorway service area with off road / full / limited access
- A556 — Primary route with dual / single carriageway
- **Peterhead** — Primary route destination

Primary route destinations are places of major traffic importance linked by the primary route network. They are shown on a green background on direction signs.

- A30 — 'A' road dual / single carriageway
- B1403 — 'B' road dual / single carriageway
- Minor road
- Road with restricted access
- Roads with passing places
- Road proposed or under construction
- 24 — Multi-level junction (occasionally with junction number)
- Roundabout
- 4 — Road distance in miles between markers
- Road tunnel
- Steep hill (arrows point downhill)
- Toll — Level crossing / Toll
- St. Malo 8hrs(10hrs) — Car ferry route with journey times; daytime and (night-time)
- Railway line / station / tunnel
- South Downs Way — National Trail / Long Distance Route
- Airport with scheduled services
- Heliport
- Park and Ride site (operates at least 5 days a week)
- Built up area
- Town / Village / Other settlement
- Hythe — Seaside destination
- National boundary
- KENT — County / Unitary Authority boundary and name
- National / Regional park
- Forest park boundary
- Woodland
- Danger Zone — Military range
- 468 ▲941 — Spot / Summit height (in metres)
- Lake / Dam / River / Waterfall
- Canal / Dry canal / Canal tunnel
- Lighthouse
- Beach
- SEE PAGE 108 — Area covered by urban area map

Tourist information

Tourist sites have not been assessed for full accessibility yet the majority have made adequate provision. It is advisable to check with the tourist information centre regarding facilities available.

- Tourist information centre (open all year)
- Tourist information centre (open seasonally)
- Ancient monument
- Aquarium
- 1643 — Battlefield
- Camp site / Caravan site
- Castle
- Country park
- Ecclesiastical building
- Garden
- Golf course
- Historic house
- Major football club
- Major shopping centre / Outlet village
- Major sports venue
- Motor racing circuit
- Museum / Art gallery
- Nature reserve
- Preserved railway
- Racecourse
- Spotlight Nature Reserve
- Theme park
- University
- Wildlife park / Zoo
- Other interesting feature
- (NT) (NTS) — National Trust / National Trust for Scotland property

Urban area maps

Pages 92-121

- 12 13 — Motorway junctions with full access
- 14 15 — Motorway junctions with limited access
- LEICESTER SERVICES — Motorway service area
- M6Toll — Toll motorway
- A316 — Primary route dual / single carriageway
- A4054 — 'A' road dual / single carriageway
- B7078 — 'B' road dual / single carriageway
- Minor road dual / single carriageway
- Road proposed or under construction
- Road tunnel
- Roundabout
- T — Toll
- One way street
- Level crossing
- Park and Ride site (operates at least 5 days a week)
- Dublin 8hrs — Car ferry with destination
- Airport with scheduled services
- Railway line / Railway tunnel
- Railway station / Light rail station
- London underground / Glasgow Subway station
- Congestion charging zone
- Public building
- 362 ▲ — Spot height in metres
- Built up area
- Woodland / Park
- National Park
- BRISTOL — County / Unitary Authority boundary and name
- SEE PAGE 131 — Area covered by town plan

City centre maps

Pages 123-128

- M8 — Motorway
- A4 — Primary route dual / single carriageway
- A40 — 'A' road dual / single carriageway
- B507 — 'B' road
- Other road
- One way street
- Access restriction
- Pedestrian street
- Street market
- Track/Footpath
- Main / other National Rail station
- London Underground / Glasgow Subway / Manchester Metro / Birmingham Metro station
- Bus/Coach station
- Vehicle / Pedestrian ferry
- Car park
- Tourist information centre
- Theatre
- Major hotel
- Pol — Police station
- PO — Post office
- Lib — Library
- JAPAN — Embassy
- Cinema
- Church
- Mosque
- Synagogue
- Mormon — Other place of worship
- Leisure & tourism
- Shopping
- Administration & law
- Health & welfare
- Education
- Industry & commerce
- Park / Garden / Sports ground
- Cemetery
- Central London congestion charging zone

City and town centre plans

Pages 129-148

- M8 — Motorway
- A40 — Primary route dual / single carriageway
- A4119 — 'A' road dual / single carriageway
- B4632 — 'B' road dual / single carriageway
- Other road dual / single carriageway
- Restricted access street
- Pedestrian street
- Path / Footbridge
- One way street
- Car park
- Park and Ride site (operates at least 5 days a week)
- Railway line / station
- Underground station
- Metro station
- Light rail station
- Ecclesiastical building
- Tourist information centre (open all year / seasonally)
- Tourist building
- Important building
- Higher Education building
- Hospital
- Cemetery
- Recreational area / Open space

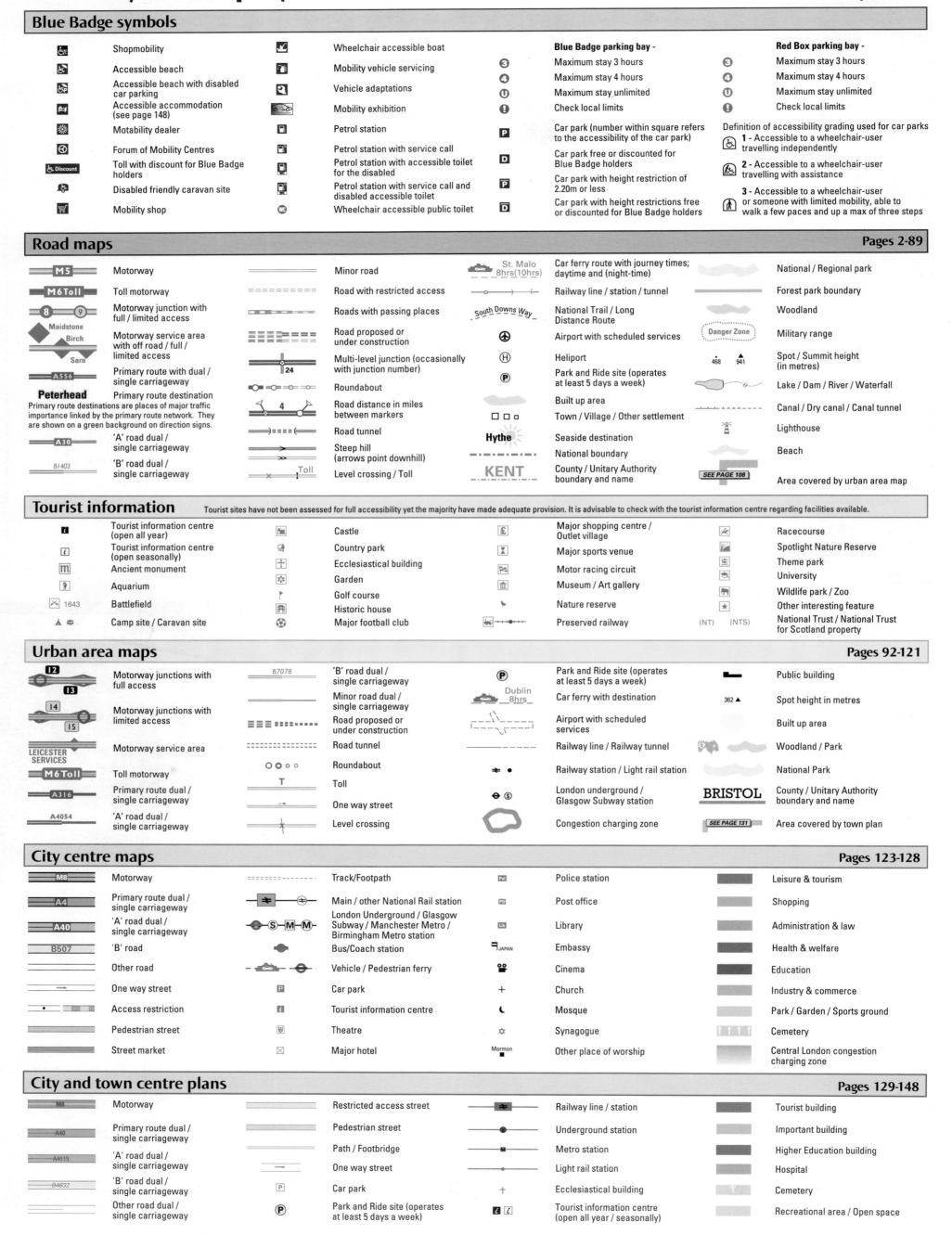

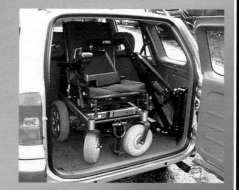

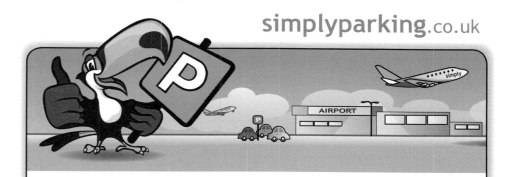

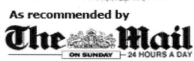

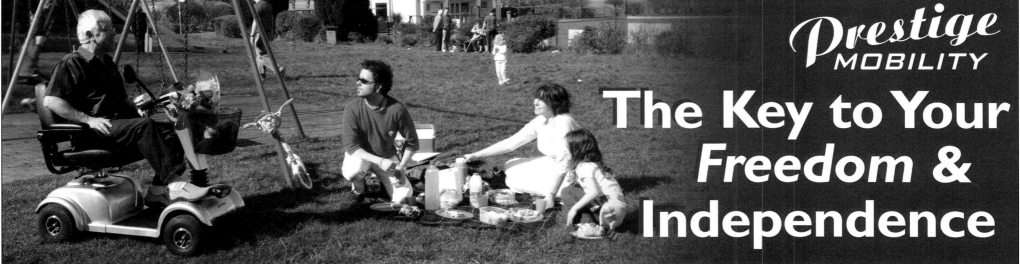

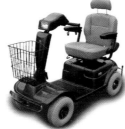

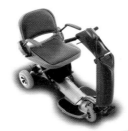

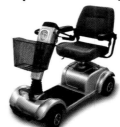

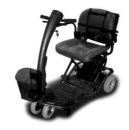

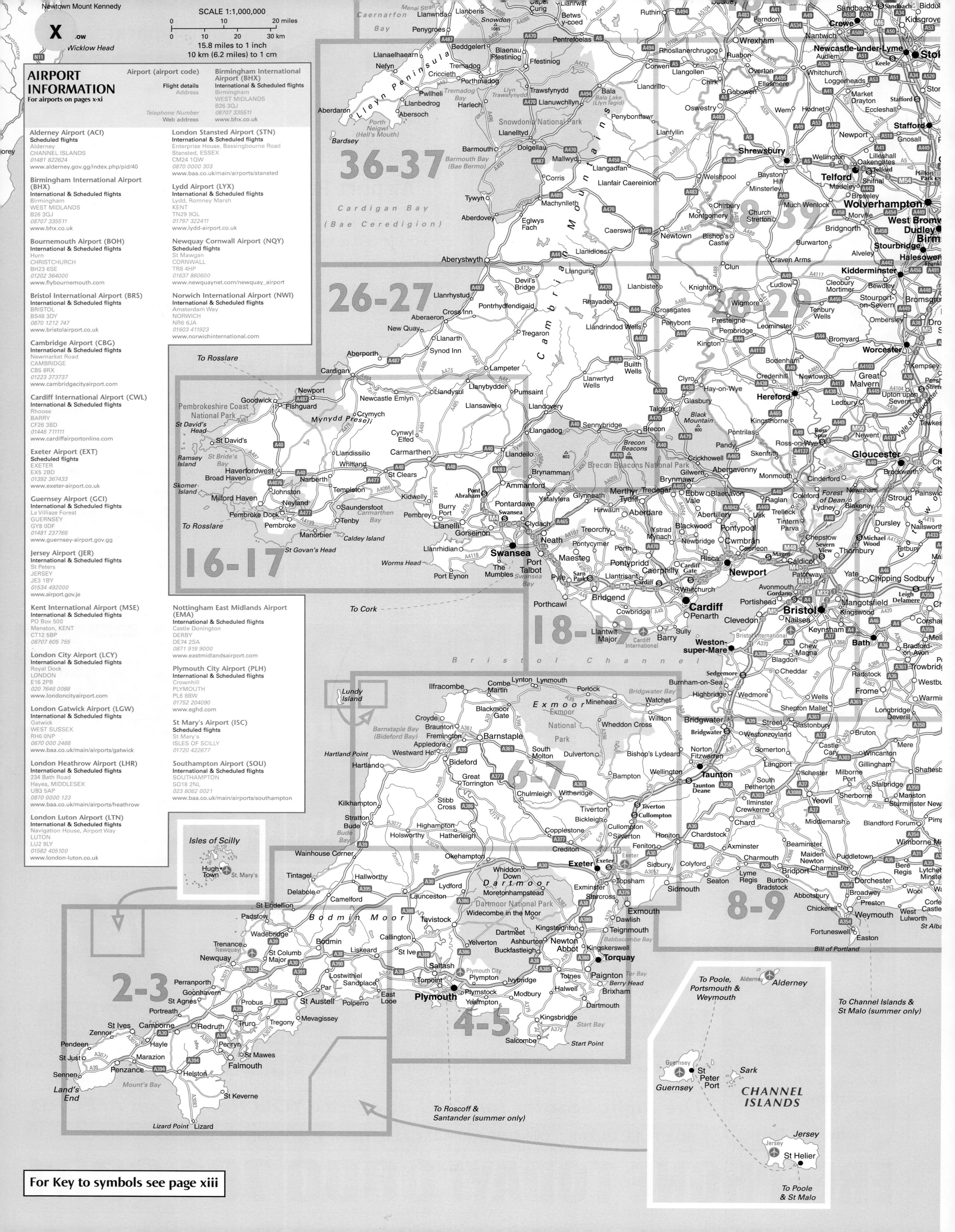

AIRPORT INFORMATION

For airports on pages x-xi

Airport (airport code)	Birmingham International Airport (BHX)
Flight details	International & Scheduled flights
Address	Birmingham WEST MIDLANDS B26 3QJ
Telephone Number	*08707 335511*
Web address	www.bhx.co.uk

Alderney Airport (ACI)
Scheduled flights
Alderney
CHANNEL ISLANDS
01481 822624
www.alderney.gov.gg/index.php/pid/40

Birmingham International Airport (BHX)
International & Scheduled flights
Birmingham
WEST MIDLANDS
B26 3QJ
08707 335511
www.bhx.co.uk

Bournemouth Airport (BOH)
International & Scheduled flights
Hurn
CHRISTCHURCH
BH23 6SE
01202 364000
www.flybournemouth.com

Bristol International Airport (BRS)
International & Scheduled flights
BRISTOL
BS48 3DY
0870 1212 747
www.bristolairport.co.uk

Cambridge Airport (CBG)
International & Scheduled flights
Newmarket Road
CAMBRIDGE
CB5 8RX
01223 373737
www.cambridgecityairport.com

Cardiff International Airport (CWL)
International & Scheduled flights
Rhoose
BARRY
CF26 3BD
01446 711111
www.cardiffairportonline.com

Exeter Airport (EXT)
Scheduled flights
EXETER
EX5 2BD
01392 367433
www.exeter-airport.co.uk

Guernsey Airport (GCI)
International & Scheduled flights
La Villiaze Forest
GUERNSEY
GY8 0DF
01481 237766
www.guernsey-airport.gov.gg

Jersey Airport (JER)
International & Scheduled flights
St Peters
JERSEY
JE3 1BY
01534 492000
www.airport.gov.je

Kent International Airport (MSE)
International & Scheduled flights
PO Box 500
Manston, KENT
CT12 5BP
08707 605 755

London City Airport (LCY)
International & Scheduled flights
Royal Dock
LONDON
E16 2PB
020 7646 0088
www.londoncityairport.com

London Gatwick Airport (LGW)
International & Scheduled flights
Gatwick
WEST SUSSEX
RH6 0NP
0870 000 2468
www.baa.co.uk/main/airports/gatwick

London Heathrow Airport (LHR)
International & Scheduled flights
234 Bath Road
Hayes, MIDDLESEX
UB3 5AP
0870 0000 123
www.baa.co.uk/main/airports/heathrow

London Luton Airport (LTN)
International & Scheduled flights
Navigation House, Airport Way
LUTON
LU2 9LY
01582 405100
www.london-luton.co.uk

London Stansted Airport (STN)
International & Scheduled flights
Enterprise House, Bassingbourne Road
Stansted, ESSEX
CM24 1QW
0870 0000 303
www.baa.co.uk/main/airports/stansted

Lydd Airport (LYX)
International & Scheduled flights
Lydd, Romney Marsh
KENT
TN29 9QL
01797 322411
www.lydd-airport.co.uk

Newquay Cornwall Airport (NQY)
Scheduled flights
St Mawgan
CORNWALL
TR8 4HP
01637 860600
www.newquaynet.com/newquay_airport

Norwich International Airport (NWI)
International & Scheduled flights
Amsterdam Way
NORWICH
NR6 6JA
01603 411923
www.norwichinternational.com

Nottingham East Midlands Airport (EMA)
International & Scheduled flights
Castle Donington
DERBY
DE74 2SA
0871 919 9000
www.eastmidlandsairport.com

Plymouth City Airport (PLH)
International & Scheduled flights
Crownhill
PLYMOUTH
PL6 8BW
01752 204090
www.eghd.com

St Mary's Airport (ISC)
Scheduled flights
St Mary's
ISLES OF SCILLY
01720 422677

Southampton Airport (SOU)
International & Scheduled flights
SOUTHAMPTON
SO18 2NL
023 8062 0021
www.baa.co.uk/main/airports/southampton

For Key to symbols see page xiii

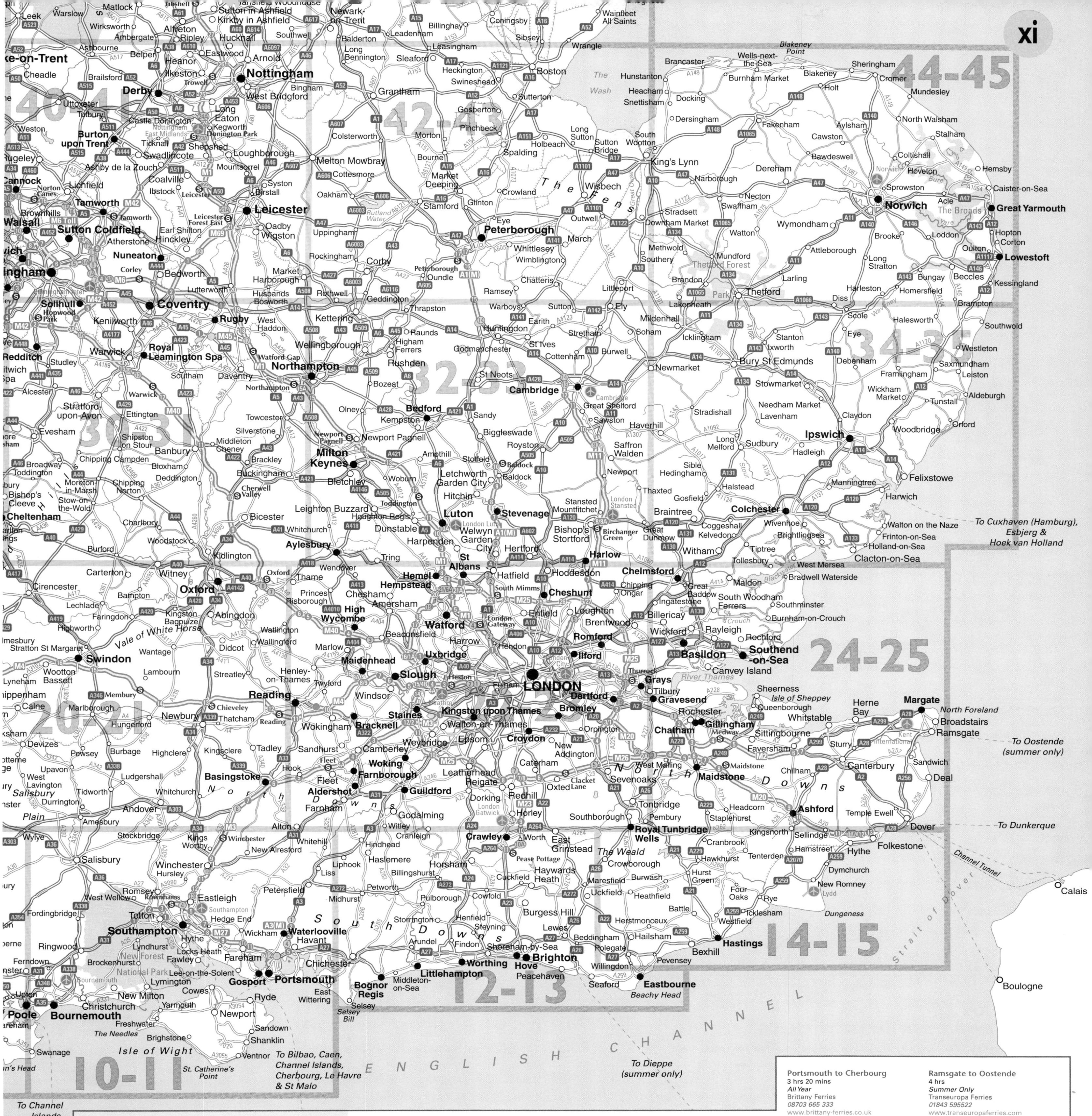

FERRY INFORMATION

For routes on pages x-xi

Route	Duration	Season	Operator	Telephone Number	Web address
Dover to Calais	1 hr 15 mins	All Year	P&O Ferries	08705 980 333	www.poferries.com
Dover to Boulogne	50 mins	All Year	Speed Ferries	0870 220 0570	www.speedferries.com
Dover to Calais	1 hr 15 mins	All Year	P&O Ferries	08705 980 333	www.poferries.com
Dover to Calais	1 hr 10 mins - 1 hr 30 mins	All Year	SeaFrance	08705 711 711	www.seafrance.com
Dover to Calais	1 hr	All Year	Hoverspeed	0870 240 8070	www.hoverspeed.co.uk
Dover to Dunkerque	2 hrs	All Year	Norfolk Line Ferries	0870 870 1020	www.norfolkline.com
Fishguard to Rosslare	1 hr 50 mins - 3 hrs 30 mins	All Year	Stena Line	08705 707070	www.stenaline.co.uk
Guernsey to Jersey	1 hr	All Year	Condor Ferries	0845 345 2000	www.condorferries.co.uk
Harwich to Cuxhaven (Hamburg)	20 hrs	All Year	DFDS Seaways	08705 333 111	www.dfdsseaways.co.uk
Harwich to Esbjerg	19 hrs	All Year	DFDS Seaways	08705 333 111	www.dfdsseaways.co.uk
Harwich to Hoek van Holland	3 hrs 40 mins	All Year	Stena Line	08705 707070	www.stenaline.co.uk
Jersey to St Malo	1 hr 15 mins	All Year	Emeraude Lines	01534 766566	www.emeraude.co.uk
Lymington to Yarmouth	30 mins	All Year	Wightlink	0870 582 7744	www.wightlink.co.uk
Newhaven to Dieppe	4 hrs	Summer Only	Transmanche Ferries	0800 917 1201	www.transmancheferries.com
Pembroke to Rosslare	3 hrs 45 mins	All Year	Irish Ferries	08705 171717	www.irishferries.com
Plymouth to Roscoff	6 hrs - 7 hrs 30 mins	All Year	Brittany Ferries	08703 665 333	www.brittany-ferries.co.uk
Plymouth to Santander	24 hrs	Summer Only	Brittany Ferries	08703 665 333	www.brittany-ferries.co.uk
Poole to Cherbourg	2 hrs 15 mins	Summer Only	Condor Ferries	0845 345 2000	www.condorferries.co.uk
Poole to Cherbourg	2 hrs 15 mins - 4 hrs 15 mins	All Year	Brittany Ferries	08703 665 333	www.brittany-ferries.co.uk
Poole to Guernsey	2 hrs 30 mins	Summer Only	Condor Ferries	0845 345 2000	www.condorferries.co.uk
Poole to Jersey	3 hrs - 3 hrs 45 mins	Summer Only	Condor Ferries	0845 345 2000	www.condorferries.co.uk
Poole to St Malo (via Guernsey or Jersey)	4 hrs 35 mins	Summer Only	Condor Ferries	0845 345 2000	www.condorferries.co.uk
Portsmouth to Bilbao	35 hrs	All Year	P&O Ferries	08705 980 333	www.poferries.com
Portsmouth to Caen	6 hrs - 6 hrs 15 mins	All Year	Brittany Ferries	08703 665 333	www.brittany-ferries.co.uk
Portsmouth to Cherbourg	3 hrs 20 mins	All Year	Brittany Ferries	08703 665 333	www.brittany-ferries.co.uk
Portsmouth to Fishbourne	35 mins	All Year	Wightlink	0870 582 7744	www.wightlink.co.uk
Portsmouth to Guernsey	6 hrs 30 mins	All Year	Condor Ferries	0845 345 2000	www.condorferries.co.uk
Portsmouth to Jersey	10 hrs	All Year	Condor Ferries	0845 345 2000	www.condorferries.co.uk
Portsmouth to Le Havre	2 hrs 45 mins - 5 hrs	All Year	P&O Ferries	08705 980 333	www.poferries.com
Portsmouth to St. Malo	8 hrs 45 mins - 10 hrs 30 mins	All Year	Brittany Ferries	08703 665 333	www.brittany-ferries.co.uk
Ramsgate to Oostende	4 hrs	Summer Only	Transeuropa Ferries	01843 595522	www.transeuropaferries.com
Southampton to East Cowes	1 hr	All Year	Red Funnel Ferries	0870 444 8898	www.redfunnel.co.uk
Swansea to Cork	10 hrs	All Year	Swansea Cork Ferries	01792 456116	www.swansea-cork.ie
Weymouth to Guernsey	2 hrs - 2 hrs 15 mins	All Year	Condor Ferries	0845 345 2000	www.condorferries.co.uk
Weymouth to Jersey	3 hrs 15 mins - 3 hrs 35 mins	All Year	Condor Ferries	0845 345 2000	www.condorferries.co.uk
Weymouth to St. Malo	4 hrs 30 mins	Summer Only	Condor Ferries	0845 345 2000	www.condorferries.co.uk

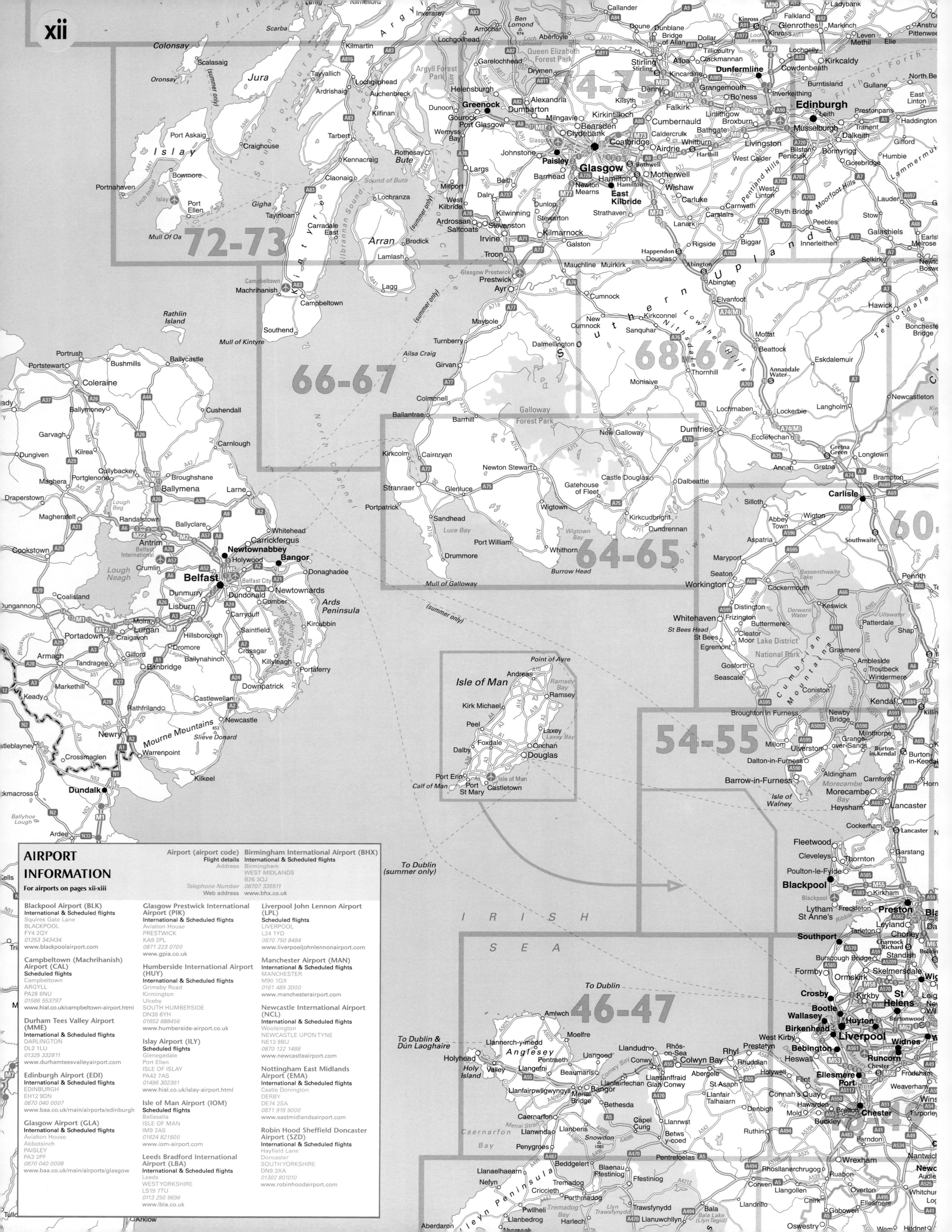

AIRPORT INFORMATION

For airports on pages xii-xiii

Airport (airport code)	Birmingham International Airport (BHX)
Flight details	International & Scheduled flights
Address	Birmingham WEST MIDLANDS B26 3QJ
Telephone Number	*08707 335511*
Web address	www.bhx.co.uk

Blackpool Airport (BLK)
International & Scheduled flights
Squires Gate Lane
BLACKPOOL
FY4 2QY
01253 343434
www.blackpoolairport.com

Campbeltown (Machrihanish) Airport (CAL)
Scheduled flights
Campbeltown
ARGYLL
PA28 6NU
01586 553797
www.hial.co.uk/campbeltown-airport.html

Durham Tees Valley Airport (MME)
International & Scheduled flights
DARLINGTON
DL2 1LU
01325 332811
www.durhamteesvalleyairport.com

Edinburgh Airport (EDI)
International & Scheduled flights
EDINBURGH
EH12 9DN
0870 040 0007
www.baa.co.uk/main/airports/edinburgh

Glasgow Airport (GLA)
International & Scheduled flights
Aviation House
Abbotsinch
PAISLEY
PA3 2PF
0870 040 0008
www.baa.co.uk/main/airports/glasgow

Glasgow Prestwick International Airport (PIK)
International & Scheduled flights
Aviation House
PRESTWICK
KA9 2PL
0871 223 0700
www.gpia.co.uk

Humberside International Airport (HUY)
International & Scheduled flights
Grimsby Road
Kirmington
Ulceby
SOUTH HUMBERSIDE
DN39 6YH
01652 688456
www.humberside-airport.co.uk

Islay Airport (ILY)
Scheduled flights
Glenegedale
Port Ellen
ISLE OF ISLAY
PA42 7AS
01496 302361
www.hial.co.uk/islay-airport.html

Isle of Man Airport (IOM)
Scheduled flights
Ballasalla
ISLE OF MAN
IM9 2AS
01624 821600
www.iom-airport.com

Leeds Bradford International Airport (LBA)
International & Scheduled flights
Leeds
WEST YORKSHIRE
LS19 7TU
0113 250 9696
www.lbia.co.uk

Liverpool John Lennon Airport (LPL)
Scheduled flights
LIVERPOOL
L24 1YD
0870 750 8484
www.liverpooljohnlennonairport.com

Manchester Airport (MAN)
International & Scheduled flights
MANCHESTER
M90 1QX
0161 489 3000
www.manchesterairport.com

Newcastle International Airport (NCL)
International & Scheduled flights
Woolsington
NEWCASTLE UPON TYNE
NE13 8BU
0870 122 1488
www.newcastleairport.com

Nottingham East Midlands Airport (EMA)
International & Scheduled flights
Castle Donington
DERBY
DE74 2SA
0871 919 9000
www.eastmidlandsairport.com

Robin Hood Sheffield Doncaster Airport (SZD)
International & Scheduled flights
Hayfield Lane
Doncaster
SOUTH YORKSHIRE
DN9 3XA
01302 801010
www.robinhoodairport.com

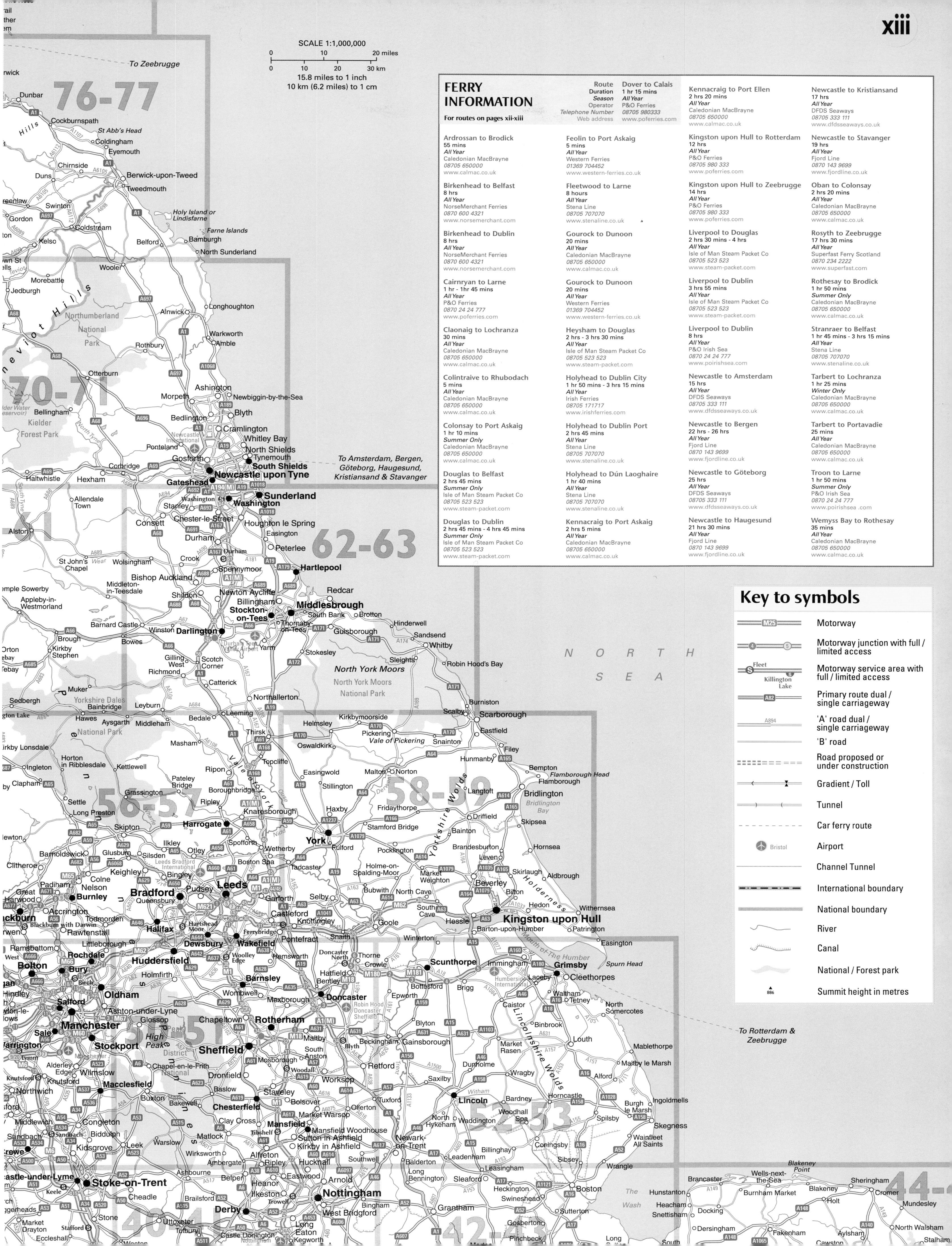

FERRY INFORMATION

For routes on pages xii-xiii

Route	Duration	Season	Operator	Telephone Number	Web address
Dover to Calais	1 hr 15 mins	All Year	P&O Ferries	08705 980333	www.poferries.com
Ardrossan to Brodick	55 mins	All Year	Caledonian MacBrayne	08705 650000	www.calmac.co.uk
Birkenhead to Belfast	8 hrs	All Year	NorseMerchant Ferries	0870 600 4321	www.norsemerchant.com
Birkenhead to Dublin	8 hrs	All Year	NorseMerchant Ferries	0870 600 4321	www.norsemerchant.com
Cairnryan to Larne	1 hr - 1hr 45 mins	All Year	P&O Ferries	0870 24 24 777	www.poferries.com
Claonaig to Lochranza	30 mins	All Year	Caledonian MacBrayne	08705 650000	www.calmac.co.uk
Colintraive to Rhubodach	5 mins	All Year	Caledonian MacBrayne	08705 650000	www.calmac.co.uk
Colonsay to Port Askaig	1 hr 10 mins	Summer Only	Caledonian MacBrayne	08705 650000	www.calmac.co.uk
Douglas to Belfast	2 hrs 45 mins	Summer Only	Isle of Man Steam Packet Co	08705 523 523	www.steam-packet.com
Douglas to Dublin	2 hrs 45 mins - 4 hrs 45 mins	Summer Only	Isle of Man Steam Packet Co	08705 523 523	www.steam-packet.com
Feolin to Port Askaig	5 mins	All Year	Western Ferries	01369 704452	www.western-ferries.co.uk
Fleetwood to Larne	8 hours	All Year	Stena Line	08705 707070	www.stenaline.co.uk
Gourock to Dunoon	20 mins	All Year	Caledonian MacBrayne	08705 650000	www.calmac.co.uk
Gourock to Dunoon	20 mins	All Year	Western Ferries	01369 704452	www.western-ferries.co.uk
Heysham to Douglas	2 hrs - 3 hrs 30 mins	All Year	Isle of Man Steam Packet Co	08705 523 523	www.steam-packet.com
Holyhead to Dublin City	1 hr 50 mins - 3 hrs 15 mins	All Year	Irish Ferries	08705 171717	www.irishferries.com
Holyhead to Dublin Port	2 hrs 45 mins	All Year	Stena Line	08705 707070	www.stenaline.co.uk
Holyhead to Dún Laoghaire	1 hr 40 mins	All Year	Stena Line	08705 707070	www.stenaline.co.uk
Kennacraig to Port Askaig	2 hrs 5 mins	All Year	Caledonian MacBrayne	08705 650000	www.calmac.co.uk
Kennacraig to Port Ellen	2 hrs 20 mins	All Year	Caledonian MacBrayne	08705 650000	www.calmac.co.uk
Kingston upon Hull to Rotterdam	12 hrs	All Year	P&O Ferries	08705 980 333	www.poferries.com
Kingston upon Hull to Zeebrugge	14 hrs	All Year	P&O Ferries	08705 980 333	www.poferries.com
Liverpool to Douglas	2 hrs 30 mins - 4 hrs	All Year	Isle of Man Steam Packet Co	08705 523 523	www.steam-packet.com
Liverpool to Dublin	3 hrs 55 mins	All Year	Isle of Man Steam Packet Co	08705 523 523	www.steam-packet.com
Liverpool to Dublin	8 hrs	All Year	P&O Irish Sea	0870 24 24 777	www.poirishsea.com
Newcastle to Amsterdam	15 hrs	All Year	DFDS Seaways	08705 333 111	www.dfdsseaways.co.uk
Newcastle to Bergen	22 hrs - 26 hrs	All Year	Fjord Line	0870 143 9699	www.fjordline.co.uk
Newcastle to Göteborg	25 hrs	All Year	DFDS Seaways	08705 333 111	www.dfdsseaways.co.uk
Newcastle to Haugesund	21 hrs 30 mins	All Year	Fjord Line	0870 143 9699	www.fjordline.co.uk
Newcastle to Kristiansand	17 hrs	All Year	DFDS Seaways	08705 333 111	www.dfdsseaways.co.uk
Newcastle to Stavanger	19 hrs	All Year	Fjord Line	0870 143 9699	www.fjordline.co.uk
Oban to Colonsay	2 hrs 20 mins	All Year	Caledonian MacBrayne	08705 650000	www.calmac.co.uk
Rosyth to Zeebrugge	17 hrs 30 mins	All Year	Superfast Ferry Scotland	0870 234 2222	www.superfast.com
Rothesay to Brodick	1 hr 50 mins	Summer Only	Caledonian MacBrayne	08705 650000	www.calmac.co.uk
Stranraer to Belfast	1 hr 45 mins - 3 hrs 15 mins	All Year	Stena Line	08705 707070	www.stenaline.co.uk
Tarbert to Lochranza	1 hr 25 mins	Winter Only	Caledonian MacBrayne	08705 650000	www.calmac.co.uk
Tarbert to Portavadie	25 mins	All Year	Caledonian MacBrayne	08705 650000	www.calmac.co.uk
Troon to Larne	1 hr 50 mins	Summer Only	P&O Irish Sea	0870 24 24 777	www.poirishsea .com
Wemyss Bay to Rothesay	35 mins	All Year	Caledonian MacBrayne	08705 650000	www.calmac.co.uk

Key to symbols

- M25 Motorway
- 4 5 Motorway junction with full / limited access
- Fleet, Killington Lake: Motorway service area with full / limited access
- A82 Primary route dual / single carriageway
- A894 'A' road dual / single carriageway
- 'B' road
- Road proposed or under construction
- Gradient / Toll
- Tunnel
- Car ferry route
- Bristol: Airport
- Channel Tunnel
- International boundary
- National boundary
- River
- Canal
- National / Forest park
- 886: Summit height in metres

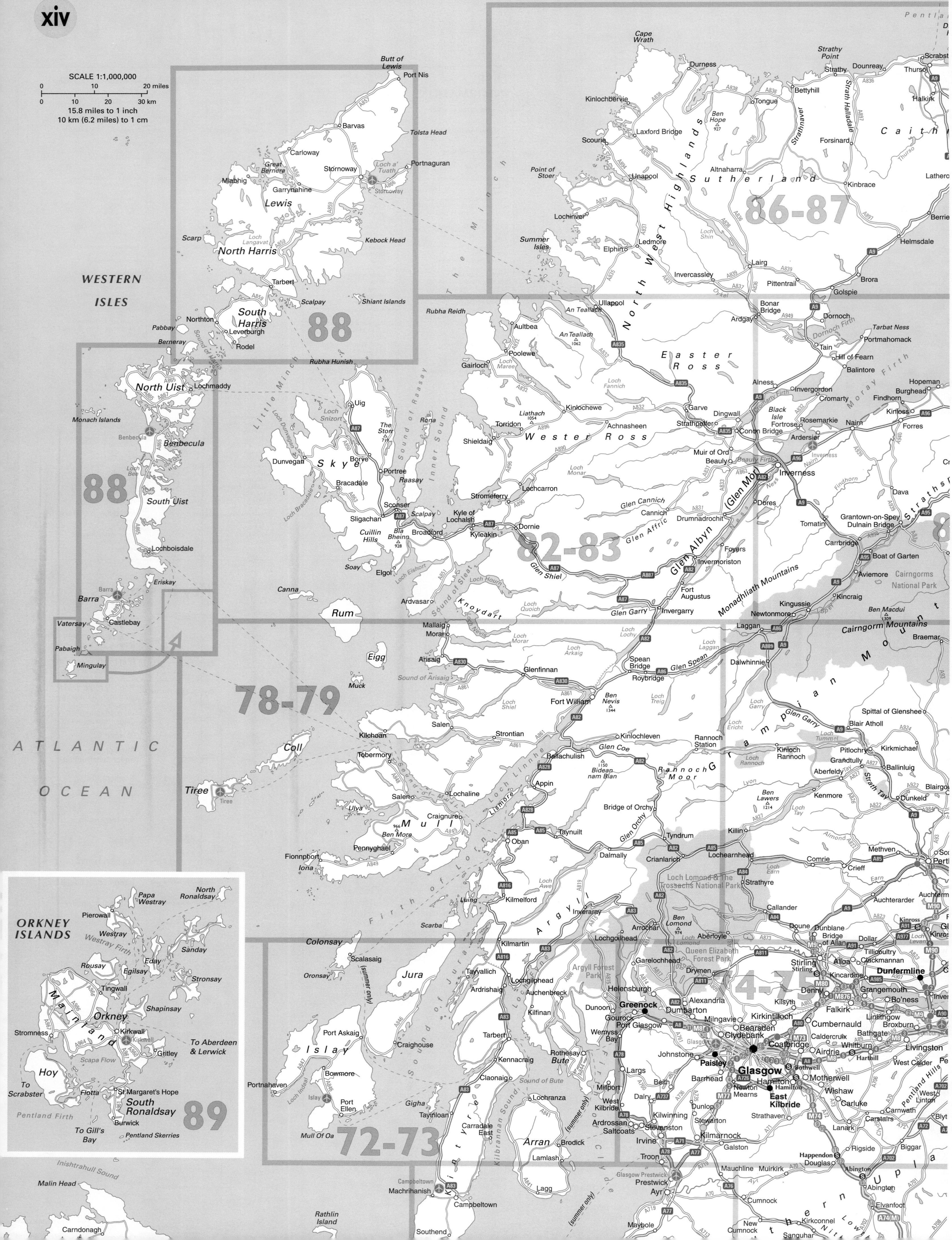
SCALE 1:1,000,000
0 10 20 miles
0 10 20 30 km
15.8 miles to 1 inch
10 km (6.2 miles) to 1 cm
WESTERN ISLES
ATLANTIC OCEAN
ORKNEY ISLANDS
88
86-87
82-83
78-79
74-75
72-73
89
Butt of Lewis
Port Nis
Barvas
Tolsta Head
Carloway
Great Bernera
Stornoway
Loch a' Tuath
Portnaguran
Miabhig
Garrynahine
Lewis
Scarp
Loch Langavat
North Harris
Kebock Head
Tarbert
Scalpay
Shiant Islands
South Harris
Northton
Leverburgh
Rodel
Pabbay
Berneray
Sound of Harris
Rubha Hunish
North Uist
Lochmaddy
Monach Islands
Benbecula
Loch Bee
South Uist
Lochboisdale
Eriskay
Barra
Castlebay
Vatersay
Pabaigh
Mingulay
Little Minch
The Minch
Uig
Loch Snizort
Loch Dunvegan
Dunvegan
Skye
Borve
Portree
The Storr
Raasay
Sound of Raasay
Rona
Inner Sound
Bracadale
Loch Bracadale
Sconser
Sligachan
Scalpay
Cuillin Hills
Bla Bheinn
Broadford
Kyle of Lochalsh
Kyleakin
Soay
Elgol
Loch Eishort
Canna
Rum
Ardvasar
Sound of Sleat
Knoydart
Loch Hourn
Mallaig
Morar
Loch Morar
Loch Nevis
Arisaig
Eigg
Sound of Arisaig
Muck
Coll
Tiree
Kilchoan
Tobermory
Salen
Mull
Ulva
Craignure
Ben More
Pennyghael
Fionnphort
Iona
Lochaline
Sound of Mull
Lismore
Loch Linnhe
Oban
Taynuilt
Firth of Lorn
Scarba
Luing
Kilmelford
Colonsay
Oronsay
Scalasaig
Jura
Sound of Jura
Islay
Port Askaig
Craighouse
Bowmore
Port Ellen
Portnahaven
Loch Indaal
Mull Of Oa
Gigha
Tayinloan
Kintyre
Kilbrannan Sound
Carradale East
Machrihanish
Campbeltown
Southend
Rathlin Island
Inishtrahull Sound
Malin Head
Carndonagh
Arran
Brodick
Lamlash
Lagg
Lochranza
Claonaig
Kennacraig
Tarbert
Sound of Bute
Bute
Rothesay
Ardrishaig
Lochgilphead
Tayvallich
Kilmartin
Kilfinan
Auchenbreck
Dunoon
Argyll
Inveraray
Loch Fyne
Argyll Forest Park
Lochgoilhead
Arrochar
Ben Lomond
Loch Lomond
Loch Lomond & The Trossachs National Park
Queen Elizabeth Forest Park
Aberfoyle
Drymen
Garelochhead
Helensburgh
Greenock
Gourock
Port Glasgow
Wemyss Bay
Alexandria
Dumbarton
Milngavie
Bearsden
Clydebank
Kirkintilloch
Glasgow
Paisley
Johnstone
Barrhead
Newton Mearns
East Kilbride
Hamilton
Motherwell
Wishaw
Coatbridge
Airdrie
Cumbernauld
Kilsyth
Largs
Millport
West Kilbride
Dalry
Beith
Kilwinning
Stevenston
Ardrossan
Saltcoats
Irvine
Troon
Kilmarnock
Stewarton
Dunlop
Galston
Strathaven
Prestwick
Glasgow Prestwick
Ayr
Mauchline
Muirkirk
Cumnock
Maybole
New Cumnock
Kirkconnel
Sanquhar
Douglas
Happendon
Abington
Elvanfoot
Lanark
Carluke
Carstairs
Carnwath
Rigside
Biggar
West Linton
Pentland Hills
Livingston
West Calder
Bathgate
Whitburn
Harthill
Linlithgow
Broxburn
Falkirk
Grangemouth
Bo'ness
Denny
Stirling
Bridge of Allan
Dunblane
Doune
Callander
Alloa
Clackmannan
Tillicoultry
Dollar
Kincardine
Dunfermline
Kinross
Auchterarder
Crieff
Comrie
Methven
Perth
Dunkeld
Blairgowrie
Strathyre
Lochearnhead
Killin
Loch Earn
Loch Tay
Ben Lawers
Kenmore
Aberfeldy
Grandtully
Ballinluig
Pitlochry
Kirkmichael
Blair Atholl
Spittal of Glenshee
Strath Tay
Loch Rannoch
Kinloch Rannoch
Rannoch Station
Rannoch Moor
Loch Tummel
Loch Ericht
Glen Garry
Grampian Mountains
Dalwhinnie
Loch Laggan
Laggan
Newtonmore
Kingussie
Kincraig
Aviemore
Boat of Garten
Carrbridge
Cairngorms National Park
Cairngorm Mountains
Ben Macdui
Braemar
Dulnain Bridge
Grantown-on-Spey
Tomatin
Dava
Forres
Kinloss
Findhorn
Nairn
Burghead
Hopeman
Moray Firth
Ardersier
Inverness
Beauly
Beauly Firth
Muir of Ord
Fortrose
Rosemarkie
Black Isle
Cromarty
Cromarty Firth
Invergordon
Alness
Dingwall
Conon Bridge
Strathpeffer
Garve
Achnasheen
Kinlochewe
Loch Fannich
Liathach
Torridon
Shieldaig
Wester Ross
Loch Monar
Lochcarron
Stromeferry
Dornie
Glen Shiel
Glen Affric
Glen Cannich
Cannich
Drumnadrochit
Dores
Glen Albyn (Glen Mor)
Loch Ness
Foyers
Invermoriston
Fort Augustus
Monadhliath Mountains
Invergarry
Glen Garry
Loch Quoich
Loch Lochy
Loch Arkaig
Spean Bridge
Roybridge
Glen Spean
Glenfinnan
Loch Shiel
Fort William
Ben Nevis
Loch Treig
Strontian
Kinlochleven
Glen Coe
Ballachulish
Bidean nam Bian
Appin
Bridge of Orchy
Glen Orchy
Tyndrum
Crianlarich
Dalmally
Loch Awe
Gairloch
Loch Maree
Poolewe
Aultbea
Rubha Reidh
An Teallach
Ullapool
Easter Ross
North West Highlands
Sutherland
Caithness
Summer Isles
Elphin
Ledmore
Lochinver
Point of Stoer
Unapool
Scourie
Laxford Bridge
Kinlochbervie
Cape Wrath
Durness
Tongue
Ben Hope
Altnaharra
Loch Shin
Lairg
Invercassley
Oykel
Bonar Bridge
Ardgay
Pittentrail
Golspie
Brora
Helmsdale
Berriedale
Kinbrace
Forsinard
Strathnaver
Strath Halladale
Bettyhill
Strathy
Strathy Point
Dounreay
Thurso
Scrabster
Halkirk
Latheron
Dornoch
Dornoch Firth
Tain
Tarbat Ness
Portmahomack
Hill of Fearn
Balintore
Pentland Firth
Papa Westray
North Ronaldsay
Westray
Westray Firth
Sanday
Eday
Rousay
Egilsay
Stronsay
Mainland
Tingwall
Shapinsay
Orkney
Kirkwall
Stromness
Scapa Flow
Hoy
Gritley
To Aberdeen & Lerwick
Flotta
St Margaret's Hope
South Ronaldsay
Burwick
To Scrabster
To Gill's Bay
Pentland Skerries

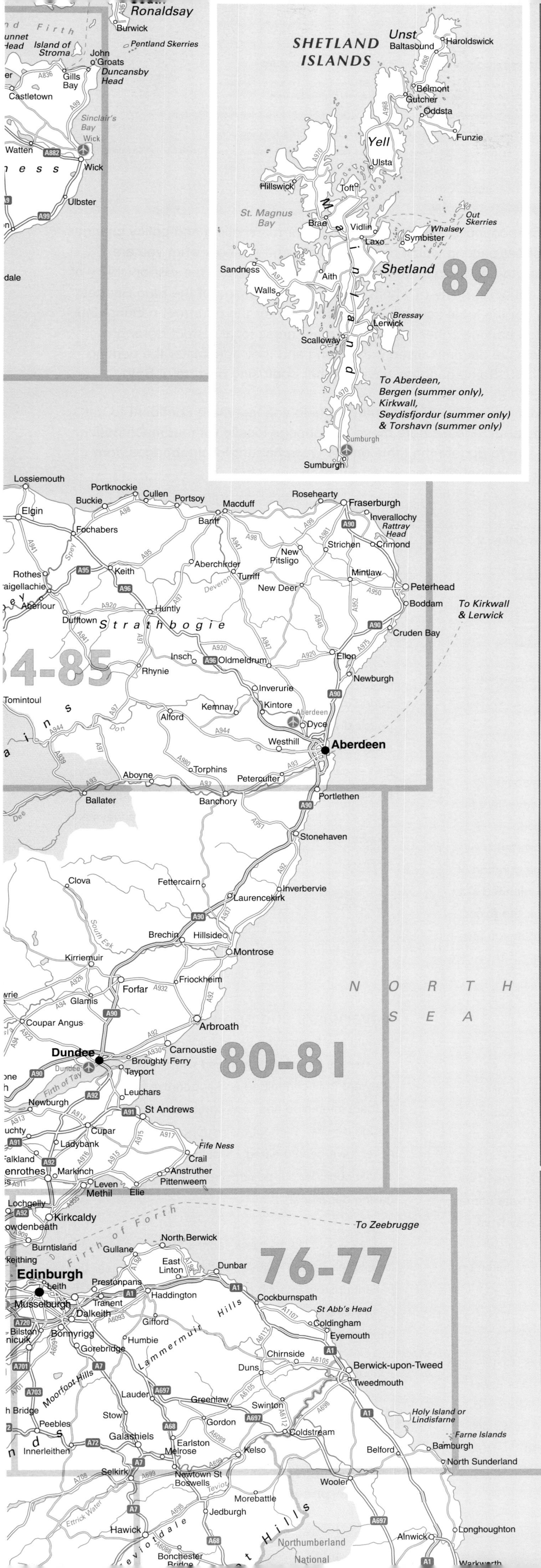

FERRY INFORMATION

For routes on pages xiv-xv

Route	Dover to Calais
Duration	1 hr 15 mins
Season	*All Year*
Operator	P&O Stena Line
Telephone Number	*08705 980333*
Web address	www.posl.com

Aberdeen to Kirkwall
6 hrs 30 mins
All Year
North Link Ferries
0845 6000 449
www.northlinkferries.co.uk

Aberdeen to Lerwick
12-14 hrs
All Year
North Link Ferries
0845 6000 449
www.northlinkferries.co.uk

Ardrossan to Brodick
55 mins
All Year
Caledonian MacBrayne
08705 650000
www.calmac.co.uk

Barra to Eriskay
40 mins
All Year
Western Isles Council
01851 701702
www.w-isles.gov.uk/harbourmaster/barratimetable.htm

Belmont to Gutcher
10 mins
All Year
Shetland Islands Council
01426 986763
www.shetland.gov.uk/ferryinfo/ferry.htm

Belmont to Oddsta
30 mins
All Year
Shetland Islands Council
01426 986763
www.shetland.gov.uk/ferryinfo/ferry.htm

Castlebay to Lochboisdale
1 hr 50 mins
All Year
Caledonian MacBrayne
08705 650000
www.calmac.co.uk

Claonaig to Lochranza
30 mins
All Year
Caledonian MacBrayne
08705 650000
www.calmac.co.uk

Coll to Tiree
1 hr 10 mins
All Year
Caledonian MacBrayne
08705 650000
www.calmac.co.uk

Colonsay to Port Askaig
1 hr 10 mins
Summer Only
Caledonian MacBrayne
08705 650000
www.calmac.co.uk

Eday to Sanday
20 mins
All Year
Orkney Ferries
01856 872044
www.orkneyferries.co.uk

Eday to Stronsay
35 mins
All Year
Orkney Ferries
01856 872044
www.orkneyferries.co.uk

Egilsay to Rousay
20 mins
All Year
Orkney Ferries
01856 872044
www.orkneyferries.co.uk

Egilsay to Wyre
20 mins
All Year
Orkney Ferries
01856 872044
www.orkneyferries.co.uk

Gill's Bay to St. Margaret's Hope
1 hr
All Year
Pentland Ferries
01856 831226
www.pentlandferries.com

Gourock to Dunoon
20 mins
All Year
Caledonian MacBrayne
08705 650000
www.calmac.co.uk

Gourock to Dunoon
20 mins
All Year
Western Ferries
01369 704452
www.western-ferries.co.uk

Gutcher to Oddsta
25 mins
All Year
Shetland Islands Council
01426 986763
www.shetland.gov.uk/ferryinfo/ferry.htm

Houton to Flotta
15 mins
All Year
Orkney Ferries
01856 872044
www.orkneyferries.co.uk

Houton to Lyness
35 mins
All Year
Orkney Ferries
01856 872044
www.orkneyferries.co.uk

Kennacraig to Port Askaig
2 hrs 5 mins
All Year
Caledonian MacBrayne
08705 650000
www.calmac.co.uk

Kennacraig to Port Ellen
2 hrs 20 mins
All Year
Caledonian MacBrayne
08705 650000
www.calmac.co.uk

Kirkwall to Eday
1 hr 15 mins
All Year
Orkney Ferries
01856 872044
www.orkneyferries.co.uk

Kirkwall to North Ronaldsay
3 hrs
All Year
Orkney Ferries
01856 872044
www.orkneyferries.co.uk

Kirkwall to Papa Westray
1 hr 50 mins
All Year
Orkney Ferries
01856 872044
www.orkneyferries.co.uk

Kirkwall to Sanday
1 hr 25 mins
All Year
Orkney Ferries
01856 872044
www.orkneyferries.co.uk

Kirkwall to Shapinsay
25 mins
All Year
Orkney Ferries
01856 872044
www.orkneyferries.co.uk

Kirkwall to Stronsay
1 hr 35 mins
All Year
Orkney Ferries
01856 872044
www.orkneyferries.co.uk

Kirkwall to Westray
1 hr 25 mins
All Year
Orkney Ferries
01856 872044
www.orkneyferries.co.uk

Largs to Cumbrae Slip
10 mins
All Year
Caledonian MacBrayne
08705 650000
www.calmac.co.uk

Laxo to Symbister
30 mins
All Year
Shetland Islands Council
01426 986763
www.shetland.gov.uk/ferryinfo/ferry.htm

Lerwick to Bergen
12 hrs 30 mins
Summer Only
Smyril Line
01595 690845
www.smyril-line.com

Lerwick to Bressay
5 mins
All Year
Shetland Islands Council
01426 986763
www.shetland.gov.uk/ferryinfo/ferry.htm

Lerwick to Kirkwall
5 hrs 30 mins
All Year
North Link Ferries
0845 6000 449
www.northlinkferries.com.uk

Lerwick to Seydisfjordur
31 hrs
Summer Only
Smyril Line
01595 690845
www.smyril-line.com

Lerwick to Skerries
2 hrs 30 mins
All Year
Shetland Islands Council
01426 986763
www.shetland.gov.uk/ferryinfo/ferry.htm

Lerwick to Torshavn
13 hrs
Summer Only
Smyril Line
01595 690845
www.smyril-line.com

Leverburgh to Berneray
1 hr 10 mins
All Year
Caledonian MacBrayne
08705 650000
www.calmac.co.uk

Lochaline to Fishnish
15 mins
All Year
Caledonian MacBrayne
08705 650000
www.calmac.co.uk

Longhope to Flotta
25 mins
All Year
Orkney Ferries
01856 872044
www.orkneyferries.co.uk

Longhope to Lyness
25 mins
All Year
Orkney Ferries
01856 872044
www.orkneyferries.co.uk

Lyness to Flotta
25 mins
All Year
Orkney Ferries
01856 872044
www.orkneyferries.co.uk

Mallaig to Armadale
25 mins
All Year
Caledonian MacBrayne
08705 650000
www.calmac.co.uk

Oban to Castlebay
5 hrs 10 mins
All Year
Caledonian MacBrayne
08705 650000
www.calmac.co.uk

Oban to Coll
2 hrs 45 mins
All Year
Caledonian MacBrayne
08705 650000
www.calmac.co.uk

Oban to Colonsay
2 hrs 20 mins
All Year
Caledonian MacBrayne
08705 650000
www.calmac.co.uk

Oban to Craignure
45 mins
All Year
Caledonian MacBrayne
08705 650000
www.calmac.co.uk

Oban to Lismore
50 mins
All Year
Caledonian MacBrayne
08705 650000
www.calmac.co.uk

Oban to Lochboisdale
5-7 hrs
All Year
Caledonian MacBrayne
08705 650000
www.calmac.co.uk

Oban to Tiree
3 hrs 30 mins - 4 hrs 15 mins
All Year
Caledonian MacBrayne
08705 650000
www.calmac.co.uk

Otternish to Berneray
5 mins
All Year
Caledonian MacBrayne
08705 650000
www.calmac.co.uk

Rosyth to Zeebrugge
17 hrs 30mins
All Year
Superfast Ferry Scotland
0800 0681 676
www.superfast.com

Rothesay to Brodick
1 hr 50 mins
Summer Only
Caledonian MacBrayne
08705 650000
www.calmac.co.uk

Rousay to Wyre
5 mins
All Year
Orkney Ferries
01856 872044
www.orkneyferries.co.uk

Sconser to Raasay
15 mins
All Year
Caledonian MacBrayne
08705 650000
www.calmac.co.uk

Scrabster to Stromness
1 hr 30 mins
All Year
North Link Ferries
0845 6000 449
www.northlinkferries.co.uk

Stromness to Graemsay
15 mins
All Year
Orkney Ferries
01856 872044
www.orkneyferries.co.uk

Tarbert to Lochranza
1 hr 25 mins
Winter Only
Caledonian MacBrayne
08705 650000
www.calmac.co.uk

Tarbert to Portavadie
25 mins
All Year
Caledonian MacBrayne
08705 650000
www.calmac.co.uk

Tayinloan to Gigha
20 mins
All Year
Caledonian MacBrayne
08705 650000
www.calmac.co.uk

Tingwall to Rousay
25 mins
All Year
Orkney Ferries
01856 872044
www.orkneyferries.co.uk

Tobermory to Kilchoan
35 mins
Summer Only
Caledonian MacBrayne
08705 650000
www.calmac.co.uk

Toft to Ulsta
20 mins
All Year
Shetland Islands Council
01426 986763
www.shetland.gov.uk/ferryinfo/ferry.htm

Troon to Larne
1 hr 50 mins
Summer Only
P&O Ferries
0870 24 24 777
www.poferries.com

Uig to Lochmaddy
1 hr 45 mins
All Year
Caledonian MacBrayne
08705 650000
www.calmac.co.uk

Uig to Tarbert
1 hr 40 mins
All Year
Caledonian MacBrayne
08705 650000
www.calmac.co.uk

Ullapool to Stornoway
2 hrs 45 mins
All Year
Caledonian MacBrayne
08705 650000
www.calmac.co.uk

Vidlin to Skerries
1 hr 30 mins
All Year
Shetland Islands Council
01426 986763
www.shetland.gov.uk/ferryinfo/ferry.htm

Vidlin to Symbister
40 mins
All Year
Shetland Islands Council
01426 986763
www.shetland.gov.uk/ferryinfo/ferry.htm

Wemyss Bay to Rothesay
35 mins
All Year
Caledonian MacBrayne
08705 650000
www.calmac.co

Westray to Papa Westray
40 mins
All Year
Orkney Ferries
01856 872044
www.orkneyferries.co.uk

Wyre to Tingwall
25 mins
All Year
Orkney Ferries
01856 872044
www.orkneyferries.co.uk

AIRPORT INFORMATION

For airports on pages xiv-xv

Airport (airport code)	Birmingham International Airport (BHX)
Flight details	International & Scheduled flights
Address	Birmingham WEST MIDLANDS B26 3QJ
Telephone Number	*08707 335511*
Web address	www.bhx.co.uk

Aberdeen Airport (ABZ)
International & Scheduled flights
Farburn Terrace
Dyce
ABERDEEN
AB21 7DU
0870 040 0006
www.baa.co.uk/main/airports/aberdeen

Barra Airport (BRR)
Scheduled flights
Eoligarry
Castlebay
ISLE OF BARRA
HS9 5YD
01871 890212
www.hial.co.uk/barra-airport.html

Benbecula Aerodrome (BEB)
Scheduled flights
Benbecula
WESTERN ISLES
HS7 5LA
01870 602310
www.hial.co.uk/benbecula-airport.html

Campbeltown (Machrihanish) Airport (CAL)
Scheduled flights
Campbeltown
ARGYLL
PA28 6NU
01586 553797
www.hial.co.uk/campbeltown-airport.html

Dundee Airport (DND)
Scheduled flights
Riverside Drive
DUNDEE
DD2 1UH
01382 662200
www.dundeecity.gov.uk/airport

Edinburgh Airport (EDI)
International & Scheduled flights
EDINBURGH
EH12 9DN
0870 040 0007
www.baa.co.uk/main/airports/edinburgh

Glasgow Airport (GLA)
International & Scheduled flights
Abbotsinch
PAISLEY
PA3 2PF
0870 040 0008
www.baa.co.uk/main/airports/glasgow

Glasgow Prestwick International Airport (PIK)
International & Scheduled flights
Aviation House
PRESTWICK
KA9 2PL
0871 223 0700
www.gpia.co.uk

Inverness Airport (INV)
International & Scheduled flights
INVERNESS
IV2 4BD
01667 464000
www.hial.co.uk/inverness-airport.html

Islay Airport (ILY)
Scheduled flights
Glenegedale
Port Ellen
ISLE OF ISLAY
PA42 7AS
01496 302361
www.hial.co.uk/islay-airport.html

Kirkwall Airport (KOI)
International & Scheduled flights
Kirkwall
ORKNEY
KW15 1TH
01856 872421
www.hial.co.uk/kirkwall-airport.html

Stornoway Airport (SYY)
Scheduled flights
Melbost
Stornoway
ISLE OF LEWIS
HS2 OBN
01851 702256
www.hial.co.uk/stornoway-airport.html

Sumburgh Airport (KOI)
Scheduled flights
Sumburgh
SHETLAND
ZE3 9JP
01950 461000
www.hial.co.uk/sumburgh-airport.html

Tiree Airport (TRE)
Scheduled flights
TIREE
TA77 6UW
01879 220456
www.hial.co.uk/tiree-airport.html

Wick Airport (WIC)
Scheduled flights
Wick
CAITHNESS
01955 602215
www.hial.co.uk/wick-airport.html

Editor's Notes

Welcome to the first national atlas for Blue Badge drivers. This is more than just a road atlas. Your feedback and need for more information and independence has encouraged us to collate essential day to day information and deliver this geographically and in a manner that is easy to understand.

We have contacted over 450 county/district/unitary councils in the country and collated parking information relevant to Blue Badge holders. This information has been collated into a comprehensive table of the varying parking rules that apply for pay and display, time restrictions for the standard single and double yellow lines, and parking concessions in residents bays/areas.

We have colour coded the city maps and council rule table with one of seven colour options. These colours reflect the parking concessions on the street. The cities/councils that support the Blue Badge Scheme parking concessions are shaded in yellow. Any variances to these rules are shown with a different background colour on the map and table.

Background map shades to reflect the Blue Badge parking concessions

Free parking on Single & Double Yellow lines (3hrs max) except where loading and unloading restrictions apply, Pay & Display, Shared Use, Residents and Blue Badge Bays
Free parking in most places (Single & Double Yellow lines (3hrs max) & Pay & Display) except Residents Bays
Free parking in Blue badge bays, Single & Double Yellow lines (3hrs max) & Residents Bays
Free parking in most places (Single & Double Yellow lines (3hrs max) & Pay & Display) except Shared Use and Residents Bays
Free parking in Blue badge bays and Single & Double Yellow lines (3hrs max) only
Free parking in Blue badge bays with limited concessions on Pay & Display
Free parking in Blue badge bays only

Many local councils are now responsible for marshalling and policy changes for on-street parking which can make it difficult to know what you are permitted to do. In some areas the on-street parking is the responsibility of county councils, many of whom administer the issuing of the Blue Badges as well, yet the local councils are responsible for the off-street parking and controlled parking zones (CPZ's). In other areas local district/borough councils have decriminalised the parking and they administer the parking regulations. Some counties have a rather confusing mixture of both.

I hope our table and contact numbers help you feel more confident to get out and about. Please note these can change locally without much notice. We will aim to update the table on the **www.parkingforbluebadges.com** website as we get the changes from each council.

How to use the atlas

This may seem a bit obvious but it is worth a mention. All the icons on the map such as the Mobility shops, Accessible accommodation sites, Car adaptation companies, Motability dealers represent a business of possible interest to any Blue Badge holder. If you want to contact any of these businesses they are listed in the Directory **(starting on page 148)**. This listing is based on city/town name; the actual atlas page number and grid square is next to each entry.

Listing by location (city/town)

Page ref. *Town/Name* *Services*

62 B5 **Darlington East Greystone Farm Cottages** GB SC
East Greystone Farm Cottages, Gainford, T 01325 730236
www.holidayfarmcottages.co.uk
Two quality barn conversions; one level. Set in open countryside with lovely views, peaceful and relaxing. Ideal location for local amenities, attractions; The Dales .

Page & Grid Reference

City Maps

We have also surveyed the many car parks and petrol stations to determine accessibility of car parks and whether a petrol station offers Service Call. You will see from the key that we have had to create a new range of symbols which I hope are straightforward.

For car parks, the key criteria are:

- **Accessibility:**

Accessibility category 1:

Accessible to a wheelchair-user travelling independently.

P1 P1 D1 D1

Accessibility category 2:

Accessible to a wheelchair-user travelling with assistance.

P2 P2 D2 D2

Accessibility category 3:

Accessible to a wheelchair-user or someone with limited mobility, able to walk a few paces and up a maximum of three steps.

P3 P3 D3 D3

- **For Car Parks with height restrictions below 2.20m**

P1 D1 P2 D2 P3 D3

- **Free Car park or discounted for Blue Badge holders**

D1 D1 D2 D2 D3 D3

- **Car parks that have received no access rating**

P D

The Bays

We have marked the Blue Badge bays where available. Please note some councils have very few as they declare there are sufficient parking concessions on the street. We have inserted a symbol within the bay icon to reflect the duration of stay. **Note; U U U represents unlimited stay and ! ! ! requires you to check the exact conditions of use on the plate.** In London you are permitted to use bays on the Red Routes. These are marked out but with a red background:

3 4 U !

Accommodation sites

The atlas contains information on locations of accessible accommodation supported by Tourism for All and the various national Tourist Boards. We have written to every single property, but as you know, things do change and in particular some properties have been bought and converted into private homes and changes in the accessibility levels may have improved. We always recommend that you call in advance of any stay to ensure that your requirements can be accommodated.

Airport parking

You may be aware that Blue Badge rules do not apply at airports. We have mapped out the major airports and the parking options at these sites. More and more services are being provided, such as a valet service, which can save a lot of time and inconvenience. We will list these businesses on the www.parkingforbluebadges.com site.

Activities

One of the major requests and challenges was to identify locations to get out and about. We found that most mainstream tourist attractions are accessible and these sites have been left on the map. We have added accessible beaches (defined by where it is physically possible with ramps or board walks to allow easy access to the beach for wheelchairs) and also shown those with disabled parking. Why not try to visit one of the many disabled friendly caravan sites, or go fishing, or simply enjoy the waterways and lakes at some of The Wheelyboat Trust locations shown on the map.

If you have other useful suggestions please let us know and we can put them on the www.parkingforbluebadges.com website as well as in future editions of our Blue Badge maps.

Advertisers and sponsors

I would like to mention the importance of the businesses that have advertised within this atlas. They are truly committed and supportive businesses that are interested and care particularly for Blue Badge drivers. Without their support the atlas would never have been created. I would like to ask that you simply consider our advertisers when you make those buying decisions.

Lastly I would like to thank Tanni & Gowrings Mobility for all their support with this atlas and in particular the patient customers who have pre-ordered the atlas. I hope you enjoy and value this atlas as it certainly has been an enjoyable challenge pulling this altogether.

Happy motoring

Freddie Talberg
Chief Executive
PIE Enterprises Ltd

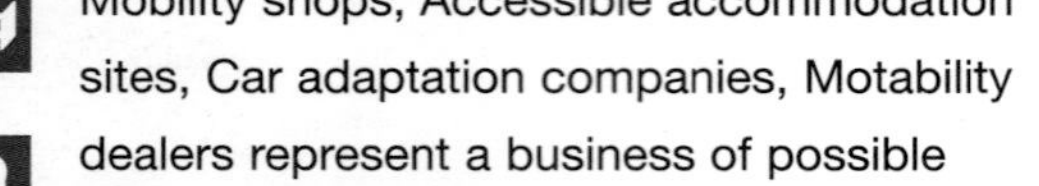

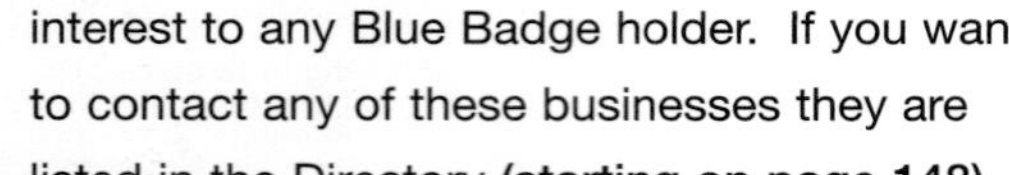

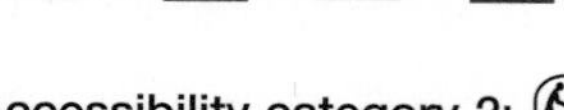

Neon

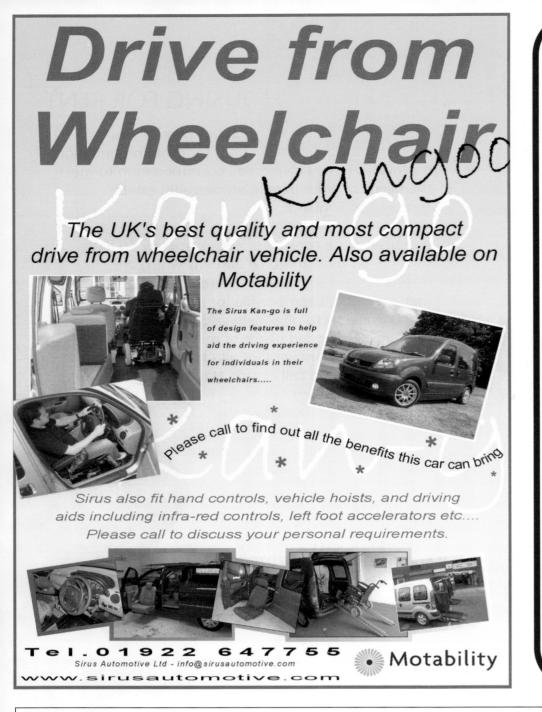

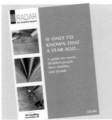

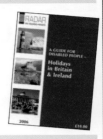

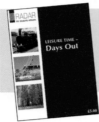

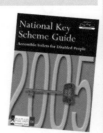

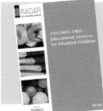

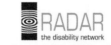

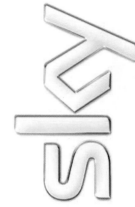

Restricted motorway junctions are shown on the mapping as

Restricted motorway junctions

A1(M) LONDON TO NEWCASTLE
2
Northbound : No access
Southbound : No exit
3
Southbound : No access
5
Northbound : No exit
Southbound : No access
: No exit
44
Northbound : No exit to M1 westbound
Junction of A1(M), A1 & A63
Northbound : Access only from A1
Southbound : Exit only to A1
Dishforth
Southbound : No access from A168 Eastbound
57
Northbound : No access
: Exit only to A66(M) Northbound
Southbound : Access only from A66(M)
: No exit
65
Northbound : No access from A1
Southbound : No exit to A1

A3(M) PORTSMOUTH
1
Northbound : No exit
Southbound : No access
4
Northbound : No access
Southbound : No exit

A38(M) BIRMINGHAM
Victoria Road
Northbound : No exit
Southbound : No access

A48(M) CARDIFF
Junction with M4
Westbound : No access from M4 29 Eastbound
Eastbound : No exit to M4 29 Westbound
29A
Westbound : No exit to A48 Eastbound
Eastbound : No access from A48 Westbound

A57(M) MANCHESTER
Brook Street
Westbound : No exit
Eastbound : No access

A58(M) LEEDS
Westgate
Southbound : No access
Woodhouse Lane
Westbound : No exit

A64(M) LEEDS
Claypit Lane
Eastbound : No access

A66(M) DARLINGTON
Junction with A1(M)
Northbound : No access from A1(M) Southbound
: No exit
Southbound : No access
: No exit to A1(M) Northbound

A74(M) LOCKERBIE
18
Northbound : No access
Southbound : No exit

A167(M) NEWCASTLE
Campden Street
Northbound : No exit
Southbound : No access
: No exit

M1 LONDON TO LEEDS
2
Northbound : No exit
Southbound : No access
4
Northbound : No exit
Southbound : No access
6A
Northbound : Access only from M25 21
: No exit
Southbound : No access
: Exit only to M25 21
7
Northbound : Access only from M10
: No exit
Southbound : No access
: Exit only to M10
17
Northbound : No access
: Exit only to M45
Southbound : Access only from M45
: No exit
19
Northbound : Exit only to M6
Southbound : Access only from M6
21A
Northbound : No access
Southbound : No exit
23A
Northbound : No access from A453
Southbound : No exit to A453
24A
Northbound : No exit
Southbound : No access
35A
Northbound : No access
Southbound : No exit
43
Northbound : No access
: Exit only to M621
Southbound : No exit
: Access only from M621
48
Northbound : No exit to A1 Southbound
: Access only from A1 Northbound
Southbound : Exit only to A1 Southbound
: No access

M2 ROCHESTER TO CANTERBURY
1
Westbound : No exit to A2 Eastbound
Eastbound : No access from A2 Westbound

M3 LONDON TO WINCHESTER
8
Westbound : No access
Eastbound : No exit
10
Northbound : No access
Southbound : No exit
13
Southbound : No exit to A335 Eastbound
: No access
14
Westbound : No access
Eastbound : No exit

M4 LONDON TO SWANSEA
1
Westbound : No access from A4 Eastbound
Eastbound : No exit to A4 Westbound
2
Westbound : No access from A4 Eastbound
: No exit to A4 Eastbound
Eastbound : No access from A4 Westbound
: No exit to A4 Westbound
21
Westbound : No access from M48 Eastbound
Eastbound : No exit to M48 Westbound
23
Westbound : No exit to M48 Eastbound
Eastbound : No access from M48 Westbound
25
Westbound : No access
Eastbound : No exit
25A
Westbound : No access
Eastbound : No exit
29
Westbound : No access
: Exit only to A48(M)
Eastbound : Access only from A48(M) Eastbound
: No exit
38
Westbound : No access
39
Westbound : No exit
Eastbound : No access
: No exit
41
Westbound : No exit
Eastbound : No access
42
Westbound : No exit to A48
Eastbound : No access from A48

M5 BIRMINGHAM TO EXETER
10
Northbound : No exit
Southbound : No access
11A
Northbound : No access from A417 Eastbound
Southbound : No exit to A417 Westbound

M6 COVENTRY TO CARLISLE
Junction with M1
Northbound : No access from M1 19 Southbound
Southbound : No exit to M1 19 Northbound
3A
Northbound : No access from M6 Toll
Southbound : No exit to M6 Toll
4
Northbound : No exit to M42 Northbound
: No access from M42 Southbound
Southbound : No exit to M42
: No access from M42 Southbound
4A
Northbound : No access from M42 8 Northbound
: No exit
Southbound : No access
: Exit only to M42 8
5
Northbound : No access
Southbound : No exit
10A
Northbound : No access
: Exit only to M54
Southbound : Access only from M54
: No exit
11A
Northbound : No exit to M6 Toll
Southbound : No access from M6 Toll
24
Northbound : No exit
Southbound : No access
25
Northbound : No access
Southbound : No exit
30
Northbound : Access only from M61 Northbound
: No exit
Southbound : No access
: Exit only to M61 Southbound
31A
Northbound : No access
Southbound : No exit

M6 Toll BIRMINGHAM
T1
Northbound : Exit only to M42
: Access only from A4097
Southbound : No exit
: Access only from M42 Southbound
T2
Northbound : No exit
: No access
Southbound : No access
T5
Northbound : No exit
Southbound : No access
T7
Northbound : No access
Southbound : No exit
T8
Northbound : No access
Southbound : No exit

M8 EDINBURGH TO GLASGOW
8
Westbound : No access from M73 2 Southbound
: No access from A8 Eastbound
: No access from A89 Eastbound
Eastbound : No access from A89 Westbound
: No exit to M73 2 Northbound
9
Westbound : No exit
Eastbound : No access
13
Westbound : Access only from M80
Eastbound : Exit only to M80
14
Westbound : No exit
Eastbound : No access
16
Westbound : No access
Eastbound : No exit
17
Eastbound : Access only from A82, not central Glasgow
: Exit only to A82, not central Glasgow
18
Westbound : No access
Eastbound : No access
19
Westbound : Access only from A814 Eastbound
Eastbound : Exit only to A814 Westbound, not central Glasgow
20
Westbound : No access
Eastbound : No exit
21
Westbound : No exit
Eastbound : No access
22
Westbound : No access
: Exit only to M77 Southbound
Eastbound : Access only from M77 Northbound
: No exit
23
Westbound : No access
Eastbound : No exit
25
Westbound : No access from A739 Northbound
: No exit to A739 Southbound
Eastbound : No access from A739 Northbound
: No exit to A739 Southbound
25A
Eastbound : No exit
Westbound : No access
28
Westbound : No access
Eastbound : No exit
28A
Westbound : No access
Eastbound : No exit

M9 EDINBURGH TO STIRLING
1A
Westbound : No access
Eastbound : No exit
2
Westbound : No exit
Eastbound : No access
3
Westbound : No access
Eastbound : No exit
6
Westbound : No exit
Eastbound : No access
8
Westbound : No access
Eastbound : No exit

M10 ST ALBANS
Junction with M1
Northbound : No access
: Exit only to M1 7 Northbound
Southbound : Access only from M1 7 Southbound
: No exit

M11 LONDON TO CAMBRIDGE
4
Northbound : No access from A1400 Westbound
: No exit
Southbound : No access
: No exit to A1400 Eastbound
5
Northbound : No access
Southbound : No exit
8A
Northbound : No access
Southbound : No exit
9
Northbound : No access
Southbound : No exit
13
Northbound : No access
Southbound : No exit
14
Northbound : No access from A428 Eastbound
: No exit to A428 Westbound
: No exit to A1307
Southbound : No access from A428 Eastbound
: No access from A1307
: No exit

M20 LONDON TO FOLKESTONE
2
Westbound : No exit
Eastbound : No access
3
Westbound : No access
: Exit only to M26 Westbound
Eastbound : Access only from M26 Eastbound
: No exit
11A
Westbound : No exit
Eastbound : No access

M23 LONDON TO CRAWLEY
7
Northbound : No exit to A23 Southbound
Southbound : No access from A23 Northbound
10A
Southbound : No access from *B2036*
Northbound : No exit to *B2036*

M25 LONDON ORBITAL MOTORWAY
1B
Clockwise : No access
Anticlockwise : No exit
5
Clockwise : No exit to M26 Eastbound
Anticlockwise : No access from M26 Westbound
Spur of M25 5
Clockwise : No access from M26 Westbound
Anticlockwise : No exit to M26 Eastbound
19
Clockwise : No access
Anticlockwise : No exit
21
Clockwise : No access from M1 6A Northbound
: No exit to M1 6A Southbound
Anticlockwise : No access from M1 6A Northbound
: No exit to M1 6A Southbound
31
Clockwise : No exit
Anticlockwise : No access

M26 SEVENOAKS
Junction with M25 5
Westbound : No exit to M25 Anticlockwise
: No exit to M25 spur
Eastbound : No access from M25 Clockwise
: No access from M25 spur
Junction with M20
Westbound : No access from M20 3 Eastbound
Eastbound : No exit to M20 3 Westbound

M27 SOUTHAMPTON TO PORTSMOUTH
4 West
Westbound : No exit
Eastbound : No access
4 East
Westbound : No access
Eastbound : No exit
10
Westbound : No access
Eastbound : No exit
12 West
Westbound : No exit
Eastbound : No access
12 East
Westbound : No access from A3
Eastbound : No exit

M40 LONDON TO BIRMINGHAM
3
Westbound : No access
Eastbound : No exit
7
Eastbound : No exit
8
Northbound : No access
Southbound : No exit
13
Northbound : No access
Southbound : No exit
14
Northbound : No exit
Southbound : No access
16
Northbound : No exit
Southbound : No access

M42 BIRMINGHAM
1
Northbound : No exit
Southbound : No access
7
Northbound : No access
: Exit only to M6 Northbound
Southbound : Access only from M6 Northbound
: No exit
7A
Northbound : No access
: Exit only to M6 Eastbound
Southbound : No access
: No exit
8
Northbound : Access only from M6 Southbound
: No exit
Southbound : Access only from M6 Southbound
: Exit only to M6 Northbound

M45 COVENTRY
Junction with M1
Westbound : No access from M1 17 Southbound
Eastbound : No exit to M1 17 Northbound
Junction with A45
Westbound : No exit
Eastbound : No access

M48 CHEPSTOW
M4
Westbound : No exit to M4 Eastbound
Eastbound : No access from M4 Westbound

M49 BRISTOL
18A
Northbound : No access from M5 Southbound
Southbound : No access from M5 Northbound

M53 BIRKENHEAD TO CHESTER
11
Northbound : No access from M56 15 Eastbound
: No exit to M56 15 Westbound
Southbound : No access from M56 15 Eastbound
: No exit to M56 15 Westbound

M54 WOLVERHAMPTON TO TELFORD
Junction with M6
Westbound : No access from M6 10A Southbound
Eastbound : No exit to M6 10A Northbound

M56 STOCKPORT TO CHESTER
1
Westbound : No access from M60 Eastbound
: No access from A34 Northbound
Eastbound : No exit to M60 Westbound
: No exit to A34 Southbound
2
Westbound : No access
Eastbound : No exit
3
Westbound : No exit
Eastbound : No access
4
Westbound : No access
Eastbound : No exit
7
Westbound : No access
Eastbound : No exit
8
Westbound : No exit
Eastbound : No access
9
Westbound : No exit to M6 Southbound
Eastbound : No access from M6 Northbound
15
Westbound : No access
: No access from M53 11
Eastbound : No exit
: No exit to M53 11

M57 LIVERPOOL
3
Northbound : No exit
Southbound : No access
5
Northbound : Access only from A580 Westbound
: No exit
Southbound : No access
: Exit only to A580 Eastbound

M58 LIVERPOOL TO WIGAN
1
Westbound : No access
Eastbound : No exit

M60 MANCHESTER
2
Westbound : No exit
Eastbound : No access
3
Westbound : No access from M56 1
: No access from A34 Southbound
: No exit to A34 Northbound
Eastbound : No access from A34 Southbound
: No exit to M56 1
: No exit to A34 Northbound
4
Westbound : No access
Eastbound : No exit to M56
5
Westbound : No access from A5103 Southbound
: No exit to A5103 Southbound
Eastbound : No access from A5103 Northbound
: No exit to A5103 Northbound
14
Westbound : No access from A580
: No exit to A580 Eastbound
Eastbound : No access from A580 Westbound
: No exit to A580
16
Westbound : No access
Eastbound : No exit
20
Westbound : No access
Eastbound : No exit
22
Westbound : No access
25
Westbound : No access
26
Eastbound : No access
: No exit
27
Westbound : No exit
Eastbound : No access

M61 MANCHESTER TO PRESTON
2
Northbound : No access from A580 Eastbound
: No access from A666
Southbound : No exit to A580 Westbound
3
Northbound : No access from A580 Eastbound
: No access from A666
Southbound : No exit to A580 Westbound
Junction with M6
Northbound : No exit to M6 30 Southbound
Southbound : No access from M6 30 Northbound

M62 LIVERPOOL TO HULL
23
Westbound : No exit
Eastbound : No access

M65 BURNLEY
9
Westbound : No exit
Eastbound : No access
11
Westbound : No access
Eastbound : No exit

M66 MANCHESTER TO EDENFIELD
1
Northbound : No access
Southbound : No exit
Junction with A56
Northbound : Exit only to A56 Northbound
Southbound : Access only from A56 Southbound

M67 MANCHESTER
1
Westbound : No exit
Eastbound : No access
2
Westbound : No access
Eastbound : No exit

M69 COVENTRY TO LEICESTER
2
Northbound : No exit
Southbound : No access

M73 GLASGOW
1
Northbound : No access from A721 Eastbound
Southbound : No exit to A721 Eastbound
2
Northbound : No access from M8 8 Eastbound
Southbound : No exit to M8 8 Westbound
3
Northbound : No exit to A80 Southbound
Southbound : No access from A80 Northbound

M74 GLASGOW
2
Westbound : No access
Eastbound : No exit
3
Westbound : No exit
Eastbound : No access
7
Northbound : No exit
Southbound : No access
9
Northbound : No access
: No exit
Southbound : No access
10
Southbound : No exit
11
Northbound : No exit
Southbound : No access
12
Northbound : Access only from A70 Northbound
Southbound : Exit only to A70 Southbound

M77 GLASGOW
Junction with M8
Northbound : No exit to M8 22 Westbound
Southbound : No access from M8 22 Eastbound
4
Northbound : No exit
Southbound : No access
Junction with A77
Northbound : No access from A77 Southbound
Southbound : No exit to A77 Northbound

M80 STIRLING
3
Southbound : No access
5
Northbound : No access
: No access from M876
Southbound : No exit
: No exit to M876

M90 EDINBURGH TO PERTH
2A
Northbound : No access
Southbound : No exit
7
Northbound : No exit
Southbound : No access
8
Northbound : No access
Southbound : No exit
10
Northbound : No access from A912
: No exit to A912 Southbound
Southbound : No access from A912 Northbound
: No exit to A912

M180 SCUNTHORPE
1
Westbound : No exit
Eastbound : No access

M606 BRADFORD
Straithgate Lane
Northbound : No access

M621 LEEDS
2A
Northbound : No exit
Southbound : No access
4
Southbound : No access
5
Northbound : No access
Southbound : No exit
6
Northbound : No exit
Southbound : No access

M876 FALKIRK
Junction with M80
Westbound : No exit to M80 5 Northbound
Eastbound : No access from M80 5 Southbound
Junction with M9
Westbound : No access
Eastbound : No exit
2
Northbound : No access
Southbound : No exit

M25 orbital map

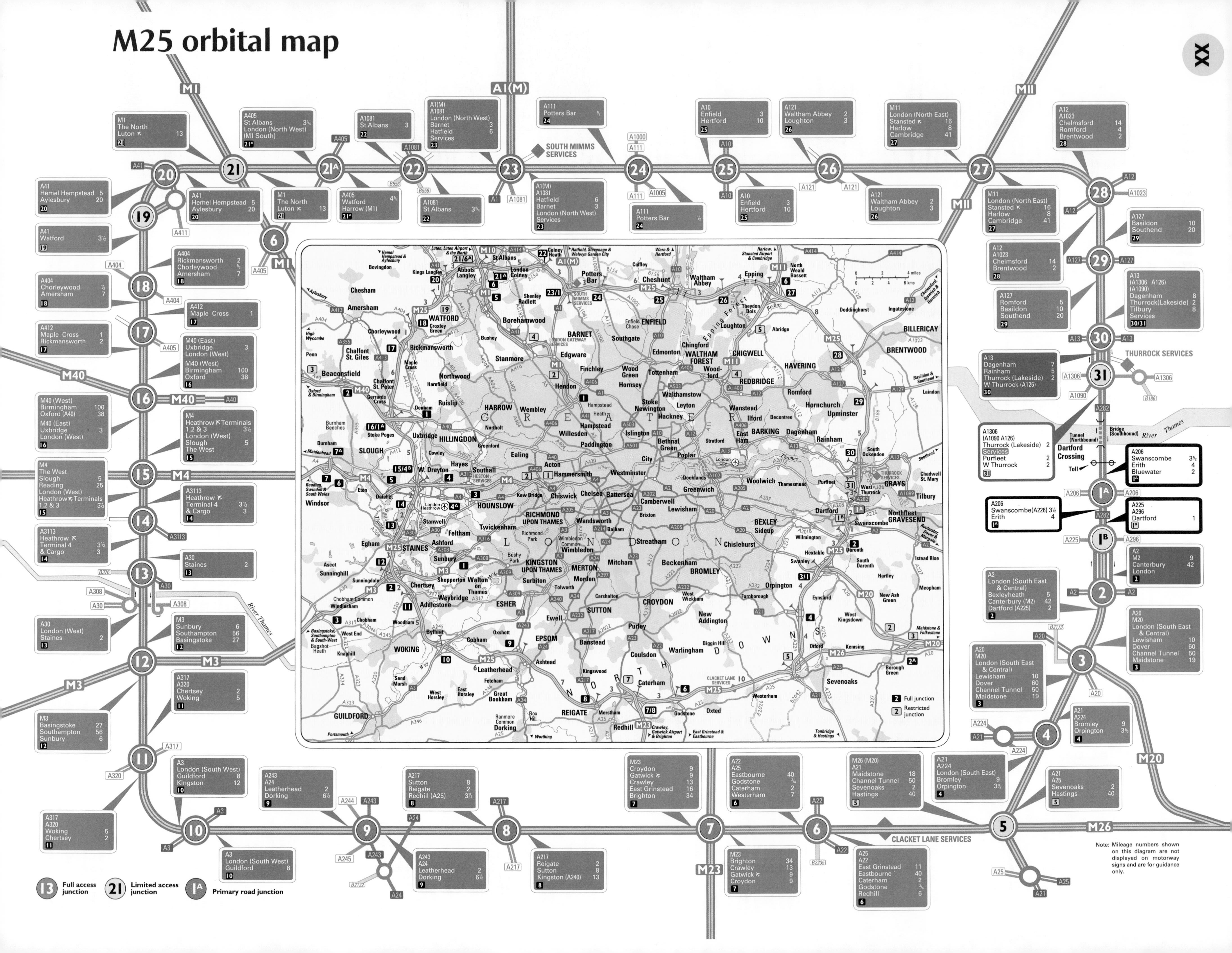

SOUTH MIMMS SERVICES
THURROCK SERVICES
CLACKET LANE SERVICES
Dartford Crossing
Tunnel (Northbound)
Bridge (Southbound)
River Thames
Toll
Full access junction
Limited access junction
Primary road junction
Full junction
Restricted junction
Note: Mileage numbers shown on this diagram are not displayed on motorway signs and are for guidance only.

Birmingham motorway map

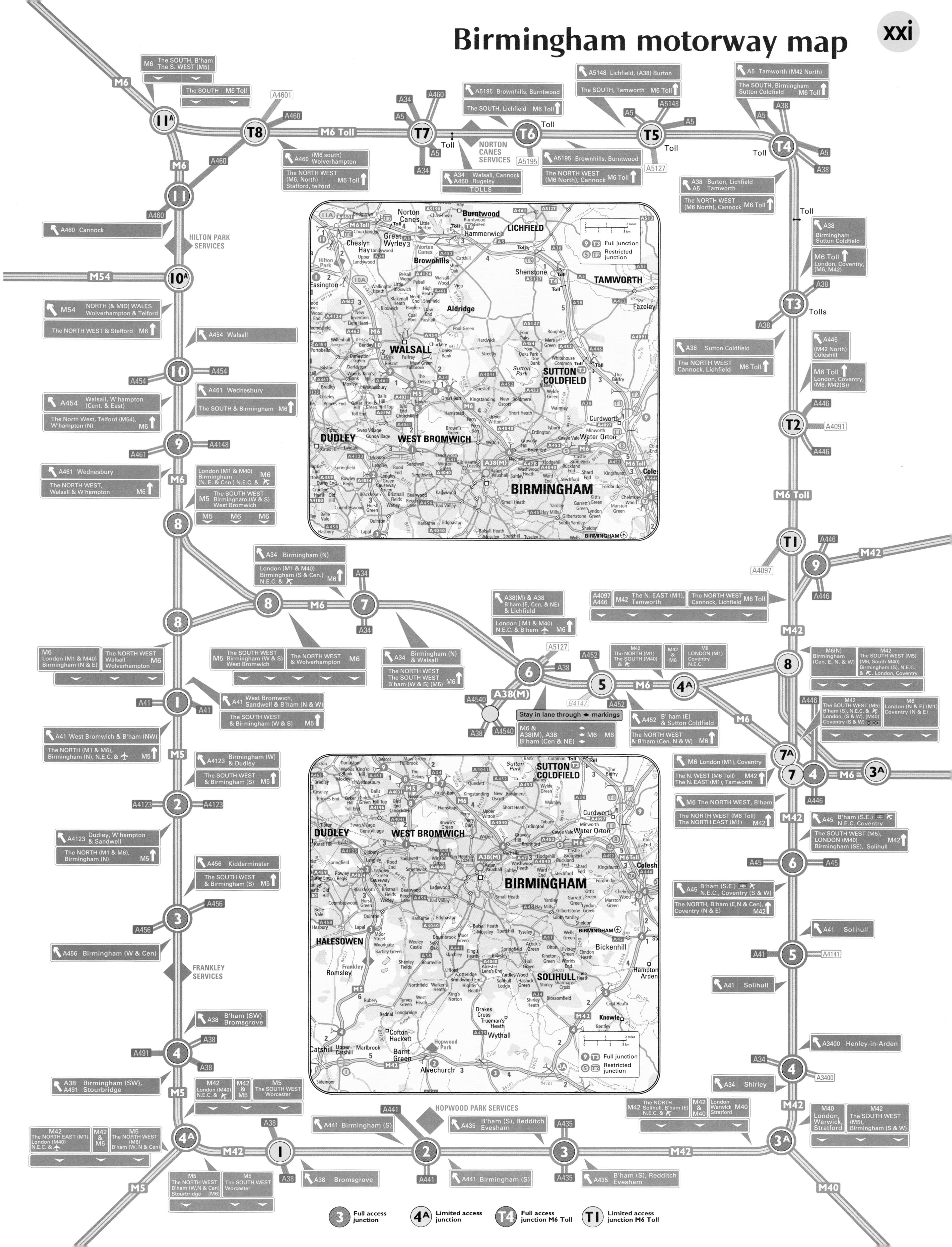

Full access junction
Limited access junction
Full access junction M6 Toll
Limited access junction M6 Toll
HILTON PARK SERVICES
FRANKLEY SERVICES
HOPWOOD PARK SERVICES
NORTON CANES SERVICES
Stay in lane through markings

M60 orbital map

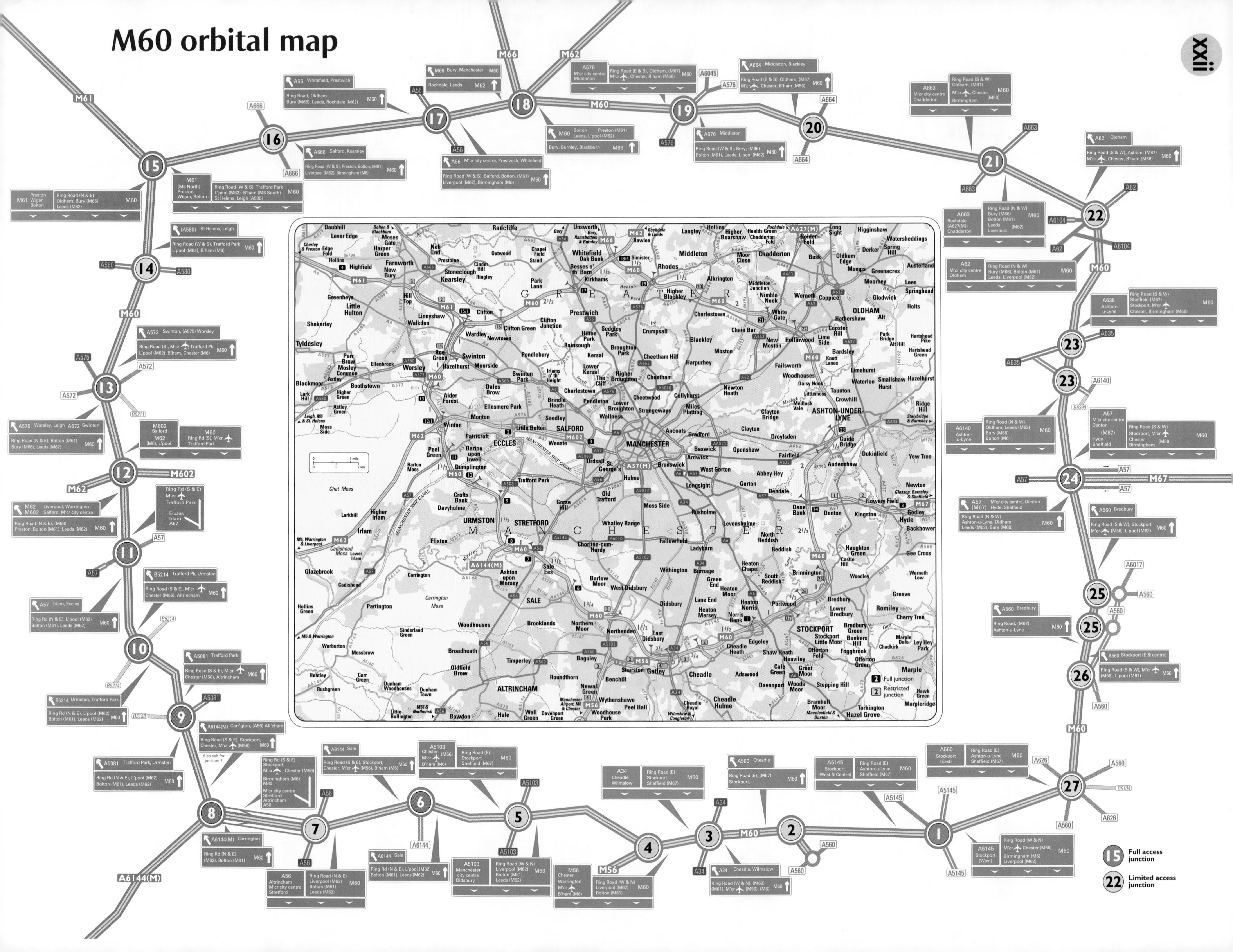

Full access junction
Limited access junction
Full junction
Restricted junction
MANCHESTER
SALFORD
STOCKPORT
OLDHAM
ASHTON-UNDER-LYNE
STRETFORD
SALE
ALTRINCHAM
URMSTON
ECCLES
MANCHESTER SHIP CANAL

Motorway services information

There are three major operators of motorway service areas in Britain; **RoadChef**, **Welcome Break** and **Moto**; as well as a small number of **independent** operators. All motorway service areas are required by law to provide fuel, free toilets and free short term parking 24 hours a day.

As part of its *Think, don't drive tired* road safety campaign the Government has the following tips for drivers:

- If you are feeling tired, opening the window or turning up the radio does not work, instead find a safe place to stop.
- On long journeys take a 15 minute break every 2 hours.
- If feeling tired, a 15 minute nap will help as will drinking 2 cups of coffee or other high caffeine drink. The most effective solution is to have some caffeine and then take a short sleep which gives the caffeine time to kick in.
- Avoid making long trips between midnight and 6am when you are most susceptible to sleepiness.
- Don't begin a journey if you are already feeling tired.

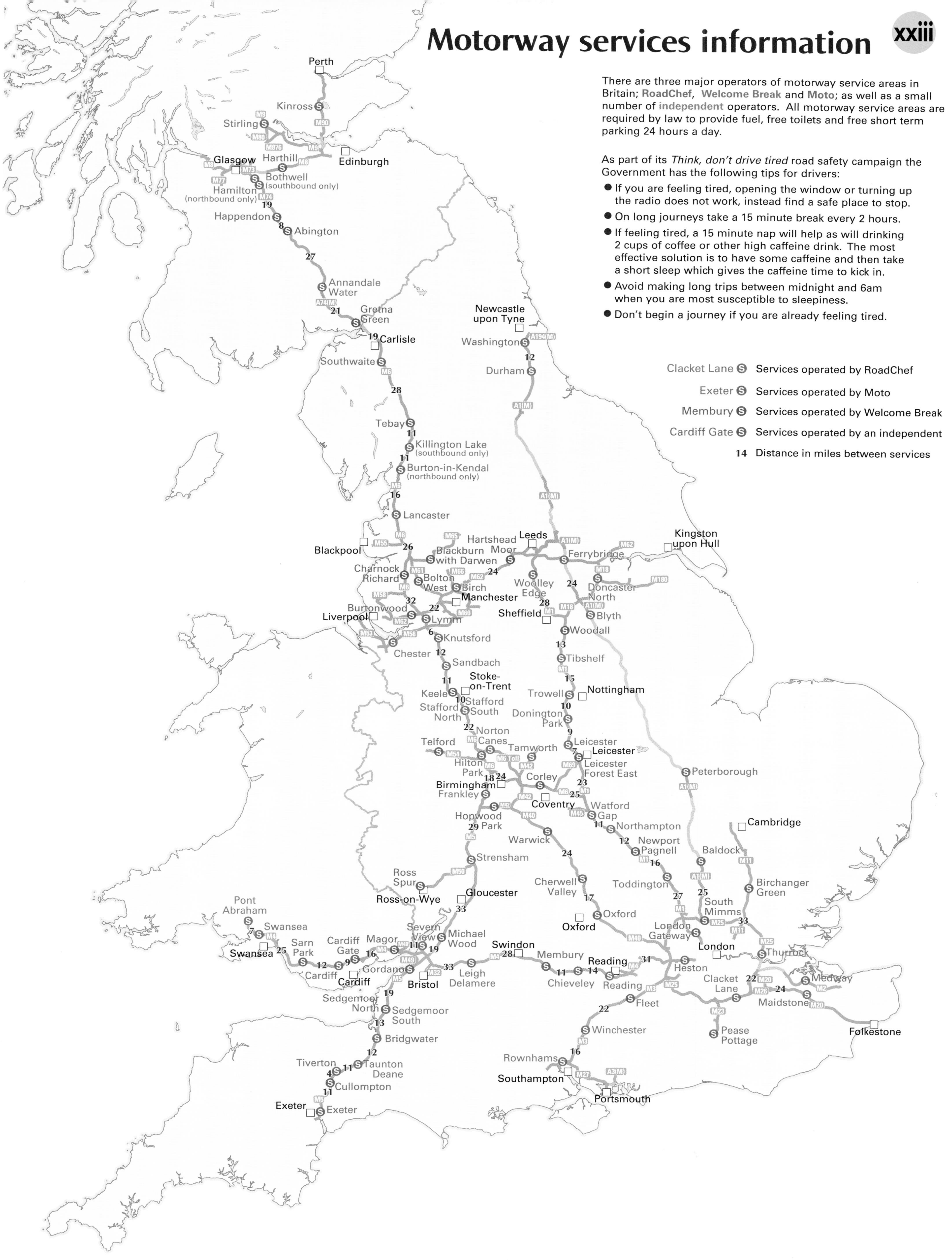

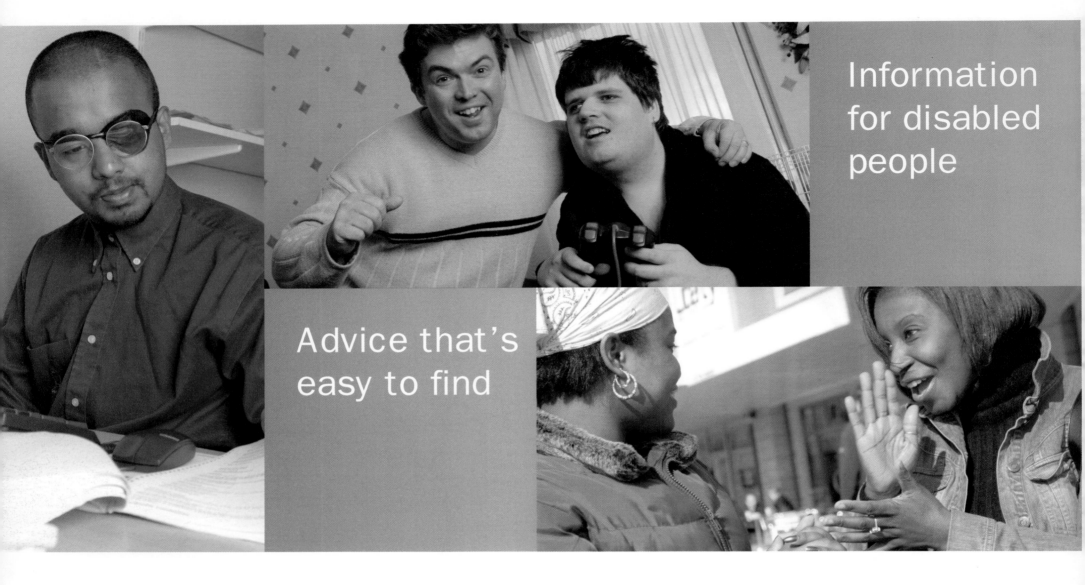

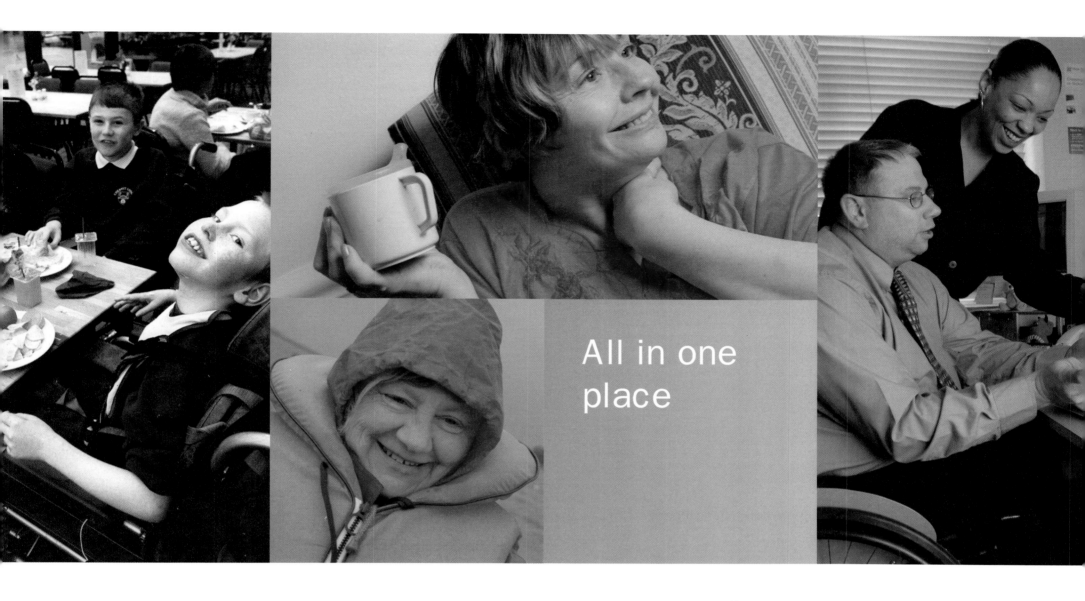

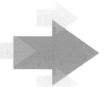

Blue Badge Parking Rules & Useful Information

The Blue Badge Scheme offers special parking concessions for some people with disabilities. It allows badge holders to park close to their destination. The concessions typically apply only to on-street parking but some concessions apply in select Car Parks. This Guide illustrates the various concessions throughout the UK and will detail the specific on-street parking options as well as detailing any other concession available close to your destination. Please remember the Blue Badge is a concession and not a licence to park anywhere.

Blue Badge holders are entitled to parking concessions in other EU member states, and in some other European countries. A useful leaflet is available from Department for Transport that explains the concessions and lists all the countries.

On-street parking concessions

Listed below are the various on-street parking options for Blue Badge holders. As you may already be aware some of the concessions vary across the London authorities/areas and various cities across the UK. Some local authorities operate their own local parking concession scheme and you should always check local street signs to ascertain if such a scheme is in operation. This Guide illustrates where on-street parking is available and what the concessions are so you can check your destination point before you leave.
(see the council table on page xxvii - xxix)

The on-street parking options include:

Single & double Yellow Lines

A Blue Badge Holder is usually permitted to park on single or double yellow lines in most areas up to 3 hours except where loading restrictions apply or a local scheme is in operation. You must ensure you are not causing an obstruction. Use your clock to indicate your arrival time. Clocks are not required in Scotland where no time limit exists. Blue Badge holders living in Scotland who intend to visit England or Wales should be able to obtain a clock from their local Council.

Red Route Box Bays

Red Routes mark out London's important roads identified by the red no-stopping lines or signs along the route. No stopping is permitted on these routes. Red boxes marked on the road indicate that parking, or loading is permitted during the off-peak times, normally between 10am and 4 pm. Special conditions apply to Blue Badge holders, typically a maximum of 3 hours. Ensure you check this time limit and try not to use these during the rush hours.

Pay & display or metered parking

Badge holders may park free of charge and without time limit at parking meters on-street and pay-and-display on-street parking unless a local time limit is in force. Payment for parking on Pay & Display or meters does apply in some areas. Certain Borough's provide a period of time free of charge once an initial payment has been made.

Please note Pay & Display machines often do not give any information on the concessions for Blue Badge holders and if your disability prevents you reaching the slot to put your money in you will need to write to the council to explain this if you get a ticket. Many authorities, especially coastal authorities, will only offer parking concessions to Blue Badge holders who also display a tax disc indicating their vehicle is taxed in the disabled class and the vehicle is exempt from road fund licence.

Blue Badge parking bays

You may park without time restriction in free parking bays which have a maximum stay, unless the signs show a time limit.

Residents Parking

You may not park on a residents parking bay, unless signs to the contrary are displayed. Residents' parking provides a large area of parking spaces in some borough. Not all residents' spaces are free to use for Blue Badge holders.

Shared Use Bay

Shared use bays operate in some Boroughs and are a combination of Pay & Display as well as residents parking. The Borough of Redbridge is the tricky one as you are permitted to park in Pay & Display but not in Residents and Shared Use bays.

'Off-street' disabled parking bays

The majority of disabled persons' parking bays in off-street car parks such as supermarket car parks, privately and council owned car parks are not covered by the Blue Badge scheme regulations.

Car parks and parking bays like these are usually privately owned and managed by the individual business or councils. Many such car parks offer free or discounted parking to blue badge holders, but this does not apply in all cases and some owners will only allow the concessions if parked in the designated bays. Some councils only offer free parking in Pay and Display Car Parks and not where the car parks operate an automated barrier system.

If people are unfairly parking in disabled bays you should write to the owner of the car park. 'Baywatch' is a partnership between several major supermarkets and disability organisations who's campaign aims to end the abuse of disabled parking bays. For more information visit www.baywatchcampaign.org

Where NOT to park

Red Routes

Red Routes prohibit parking for Blue Badge holders within the controlling hours. You can only stop briefly to set down or pick up the badge holder. Stopping to set down other non-disabled passengers is not permitted. Taxis are also permitted to drop down and pick up on Red Routes. There are loading and parking bays available on these routes for parking. Please check the signs for times.

Loading Bans

Loading bans are shown by a single or double stripe on the kerb. Please ensure you do not park here. You are permitted to pick up or set down a passenger only. Loading bans are typically on junctions, corners and the entrance or exit of streets. The double stripes indicate no loading at any time yet the single stripe should have a post mounted plate indicating the times no loading/unloading is permitted. If there is an arrow on the sign, it indicates the direction in which the prohibition starts.

Pedestrian Areas

Please note in pedestrian areas; waiting and loading restrictions may be in force even where there are no yellow lines shown on the road or stripes on the kerb. The restrictions in force should be shown on plates displayed at the kerbside.

Clearways

Some areas are protected by clearway restrictions at certain times (please check the plate). On clearways stopping is not permitted and there is no concession for Blue Badge holders. You must also not park where there are double white lines in the centre of the road even if one of the lines is broken.

Others areas NOT permitted to park include:

- Bus Lanes and Bus Stops during the hours of operation
- Cycle Lanes or pavements, footways or verges (except in areas where there are signs showing it is legal).
- On any pedestrian crossing which includes Zebra, Pelican, Toucan (for bicycles) and Puffin crossings.
- Next to any dropped footway either across a driveway or where the kerb has been lowered for pedestrians to cross.
- On zigzag markings used typically before and after pedestrian crossings or school entrances and on markings where is it is written KEEP CLEAR.
- The Blue Badge scheme does not apply on the road system at some airports. You should therefore check car parking arrangements before traveling.

Other Bay types NOT permitted to park

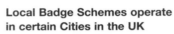

Do not park in suspended bays (shown by a yellow no parking sign or cones) or business, trader, doctor, police, diplomat, ambulance, motorcycle, or similar bays including taxi ranks. Blue Badge holders are not permitted to use dedicated disabled badge holder bays (indicated by a sign or painted on the street), often with a permit number painted by it.

Local Badge Schemes operate in certain Cities in the UK

You may be aware that within Central London the following boroughs have their registered disabled badge scheme for residents as well as their business residents; Westminster (white badge), Corporation of London (red badge), Kensington and Chelsea (purple badge) and Camden (green badge). Some other cities within the UK also operate their own local schemes. Always check the signs to see if a local scheme is in operation.

Congestion Charge Schemes

London congestion charge

Blue Badge holders are eligible for a 100% discount from congestion charging after registering and making a one-off payment of **£10**. If your vehicle is exempt from excise duty (road tax) you do not need to register for your discount. For more information contact Transport for London on: **0845 900 1234** or visit www.tfl.gov.uk

Durham congestion charge

The Durham Road User Charge applies to vehicles accessing the historic city centre and the approach to Durham's cathedral and castle. A charge of **£2** per vehicle applies between 10am and 4pm, Monday to Saturday. Disabled people can be issued with exemption permits by the establishments they choose to visit or can reserve a permit in advance by contacting the NCP Parking Shop on **0191 3846633**, provided they have pre-arranged a parking space. Permits are not available where the purpose of the journey is to set down or pick up passengers.

Bristol, Cardiff, Leeds & the Peak District National Park proposed congestion charging

These city councils and the Peak District National Park are all evaluating congestion charging options for the future. As yet no details are available for charging for Blue Badge drivers.

Hazardous places where you should NOT park:

You must also ensure you do NOT park where it would be obstructive or cause danger to others.

For example:

- On a bend in a road
- Near the brow of a hill
- Hump back bridge
- Close to junctions where it would make it difficult for others to see clearly
- By a traffic island, road works etc. where you would make the road much narrower
- Blocking vehicle entrances, particularly emergency vehicles. For further guidance consult **The Highway Code**.

Important to know

Your vehicle cannot legally be wheel clamped on the public highway for parking offences provided a valid Blue Badge is correctly displayed. Be aware that if you park improperly on privately-owned land you may risk having your vehicle clamped. If you park where it would cause an obstruction or be a danger to other road users your vehicle could be removed. You could also be prosecuted and your badge withdrawn.

From May 2005 clamping vehicles without a licence from the Security Industry Authority (SIA) became a criminal offence. In addition to holding a valid SIA licence, vehicle immobilisers must NOT clamp, blocked or tow a vehicle if a valid disabled badge is displayed on the vehicle

What to do if?

Blue Badge gets stolen – report the theft immediately to the Police and the issuing authority. The crime reference is likely to be required before a replacement badge can be issued.

Towed away or clamped – If your Blue Badge is displayed you should not be clamped or towed away even if you park illegally. If the vehicle is causing an obstruction it may be repositioned, but usually to a nearby street.

Car is missing – If your vehicle is missing in the London area call the **TRACE** service **020 7747 4747** (24 hours). They will be able to confirm if it has been towed away and where it has been removed to. Outside of London we recommend you contact the local police as the first point on contact.

If you get a parking ticket (Penalty Charge Notices - PCN) – do not ignore it. You may have to pay more if you do not either pay or contest the ticket promptly. If you want to contest the ticket write to the council concerned.

Fixed Penalty Notices (FPN) are issued by the Police. If you want to contest the ticket you must ask for a court hearing by typically writing to the address on the back of the ticket.

Your duties as a Badge Holder

It is your responsibility to ensure that the badge is used properly. It is in your own interest that the badge should retain the respect of other motorists. Please play your part. Do not allow others to use your Blue Badge – this is a criminal offence. To reduce the risk of this happening accidentally, you should remove the badge whenever you are not using the parking concessions. You must ensure that the details on the front of the badge remain legible. If they become unreadable, the badge must be returned to the local authority to be re-issued. To combat fraudulent use, the powers exist to allow for the inspection of the photograph on the badge.

Ensure you set your clock and display your badge and clock clearly and read the signs.

Vehicle Excise Duty (VED)

If you receive the Higher Mobility Component of the Disability Living allowance (DLA) or War Pensioners Mobility Supplement, you can apply for exemption from Vehicle Excise Duty (road tax). This can either be for a vehicle you drive yourself or have driven for you but the vehicle must be registered in the name of the person with the disability or a nominee and must only be used by or for the purposes of the disabled person named. The exemption certificate V188 can be obtained from the Benefits Agency. Apart from the exemption for road tax you will also qualify for other savings such as on tolls, congestion charging and benefit from additional parking benefits in certain areas.

Blue Badge parking concessions by local Councils

We hope that the table below will help to simplify the Blue Badge Parking Rules in all of the council boroughs and districts in England, Scotland, Wales and Northern Ireland.

Who administers the regulations is not always clear. The highways are often administered by the county councils or unitary authorities, however many councils have opted to decriminalise the parking regulations in well populated areas or areas with a high number of visitors and they now administer the parking enforcement. This provides a complex overview for Blue Badge parking.

We have contacted all of the councils in the UK, many of whom have embraced this unique publication; sadly not all have been as helpful. The table shows all the council areas and we have shown the rules that apply in each of these areas, in some cases the rules will be administered by the County Council and we have shown these rules as applicable for the District Council.

More and more councils are opting to decriminalise the parking in their area, several are looking to simplify their parking regulations for Blue Badge holders and abolish old Green Badge schemes that have been unpopular.

If you are aware of any changes please let us know. We hope that with the councils continued co-operation and feedback from Blue Badge holders we can keep this rules table updated on www.parkingforbluebadges.com

Key
- ! The rules may vary locally
- Ref DC Refer to District Council for rulings
- Ref CC Refer to County Council for rulings
- B C Borough Council
- C C County Council
- D C District Council
- – Not applicable

County	Council	Blue Badge Park FREE with no time restrictions	Pay & Display (On street only) Park FREE with No time restrictions during the enforced time period	Shared Use Bays (Pay & Display and Resident) Park FREE with No time restrictions during the enforced time period	Resident Bays Park with no time restrictions during the enforced time period	Single & Double Yellow Lines Park for a maximum 3 hrs on a Single or Double Yellow Line	Council Owned Car Parks Free or Discounted parking for the Blue Badge Holders	Council Specific Contact Number For the Blue Badge Scheme
England								
Bedfordshire	Bedfordshire C C	✔	✔	✔	✔	✔	Ref DC	01234 228557
Bedfordshire	Bedford B C	✔	✔	✔	✔	✔	✔ Unlimited	01234 228557
Bedfordshire	Luton B C	✔ Max stay !	✔	–	✘	✔	✔ Unlimited	01582547516
Bedfordshire	Mid Bedfordshire D C	✔	–	–	–	✔	✘	01234 228557
Bedfordshire	South Bedfordshire D C	✔ Except when signs display the limit	–	–	✘	✔	✔	01582 472222
Berkshire	Bracknell Forest B C	✔	✔	–	✘	✔	✔ in P&D Car Parks only	01344 351465
Berkshire	Reading B C	✔ Max stay 4hrs	–	–	✘	✔	✔ Unlimited	
Berkshire	Slough B C	✔ Max stay !	✔	–	✘	✔	✔ Unlimited	01753 690400
Berkshire	West Berkshire C	✔		–	✘	✔	✔ Unlimited	01635 50 30 90
Berkshire	Windsor & Maidenhead Royal B C	✔	✔	–	✘	✔	✔ Unlimited	01628 683711
Berkshire	Wokingham D C	✔	✔	–	✘	✔	✔ Unlimited	0118 974 6800
Bristol	Bristol City C	✔ Max stay !	✔	–	✘	✔	✔ Unlimited	0117 922 2198
Buckinghamshire	Buckinghamshire C C	✔	✔	✔	✔	✔	Ref DC	01296 382902
Buckinghamshire	Aylesbury Vale D C	✔	✔	–	✔	✔	✔ Unlimited	01296 382902
Buckinghamshire	Chiltern D C	✔	–	–	✔	✔	✔ Unlimited	01296 382902
Buckinghamshire	Milton Keynes B C	✔	✔	–	✔	✔	✔ Unlimited	01908 253449
Buckinghamshire	South Bucks D C	✔	✔	–	✔	✔	✔ Unlimited	01296 382902
Buckinghamshire	Wycombe D C	✔	✔ Max stay 2hrs	Ref CC	Ref CC	✔	✔ Unlimited	01296 382902
Cambridgeshire	Cambridgeshire C C	✔ Max stay !	✔ Max stay 3hrs	Ref DC	✔	✔	✔ Max stay 3hrs!	0845 045 5204
Cambridgeshire	Cambridge City C	✔	✔	–	✔	✔	✔ Max stay 3hrs	0845 045 5204
Cambridgeshire	East Cambridgeshire D C	✔	–	–	✔	✔	✔ Unlimited	0845 045 5204
Cambridgeshire	Fenland D C	✔	–	–	✔	✔	✔ Unlimited	0845 045 5204
Cambridgeshire	Huntingdonshire D C	✔	✔	–	✔	✔	✔ Unlimited	0845 045 5204
Cambridgeshire	Peterborough City C	✔	✔	–	✔	✔	✔ Unlimited	0845 045 5204
Cambridgeshire	South Cambridgeshire D C	✔ Max stay !	✔ Max stay 3hrs	–	✔	✔	✔ Unlimited	0845 045 5204
Cheshire	Cheshire C C	✔ Max stay 4hrs	✔ Max stay 4hrs	–	✔ Max stay 24hrs	✔	✔ !	0845 1131133
Cheshire	Chester City C	✔ Max stay 4hrs	✔ Max stay 4hrs	–	✔ Max stay 24hrs	✔	✔ !	0845 1131133
Cheshire	Congleton B C	✔	✔	✔	✔	✔	✔ Unlimited	0845 1131133
Cheshire	Crewe & Nantwich B C	✔	✔	–	–	✔	✔ Unlimited	0845 1131133
Cheshire	Ellesmere Port & Neston B C	✔ Max stay 4hrs	✔ Max stay 4hrs	–	✔ Max stay 24hrs	✔	✔ !	0845 1131133
Cheshire	Halton B C	✔	✔	–	–	✔	✔ Unlimited	0845 1131133
Cheshire	Macclesfield B C	✔	✔	–	–	✔	✘	0845 1131133
Cheshire	Vale Royal B C	✔ Max stay 4hrs	✔ Max stay 4hrs	–	✔ Max stay 24hrs	✔	✔ Unlimited	0845 1131133
Cheshire	Warrington B C	✔	✔	–	✘	✔	✔ Unlimited !	01925 444 239
Cornwall	Cornwall C C	Ref DC	Ref DC	–	✔	✔	Ref DC	
Cornwall	Caradon D C	✔	✔	–	✘	✔	✘	01579 342919
Cornwall	Carrick D C	✔ (Require Vehicle Exeption Tax)	✔ (Tax)	–	✘	✔	✘	01872 278533
Cornwall	Kerrier D C	✔	✔	–	✔	✔	✔ Max stay rules apply	01209 614000
Cornwall	North Cornwall D C	✔	✔	None	None	✔	✔ If Tax Exempt	
Cornwall	Penwith D C	✔ Max stay 3hrs	✔ Max stay 3hrs	–	–	✔	✔ Unlimited	
Cornwall	Restormel B C	✔	–	–	✘	✔	✘	01872 323658
Cumbria	Cumbria C C	Ref DC	Ref DC	Ref DC	Ref DC	✔	Ref DC	01228 607080
Cumbria	Carlisle City C	✔ Except when signs display the limit	–	–	✔	✔	✔ Unlimited Unless specified	01228 607080
Cumbria	Allerdale B C	✔ Max stay !	✔	✔	✔	✔	✔ Unlimited	01900 325348
Cumbria	Barrow-in-Furness B C	✔	✔	–	✔	✔	✔ Unlimited	01229 894894
Cumbria	Copeland B C	✔	✔ Max stay 4 hrs	✔	✘	✔	✔ Unlimited	01228 607000
Cumbria	Eden D C	✔	✔ !	–	✔	✔	✔ Unlimited	
Cumbria	South Lakeland D C	✔	–	–	✘	✔	✔ Max stay 3hrs	01539 77 33 77
Derbyshire	Derbyshire C C	Ref DC	Ref DC	Ref DC	Ref DC	✔	Ref DC	
Derbyshire	Derby City C	✔ Max stay 3hrs	✔ Max stay 3hrs	–	✔	✔	✔ Unlimited if Tax Exempt	01824 715032
Derbyshire	Amber Valley B C	✔ Max stay 3hrs	✔ Max stay 3hrs	–	✔	✔	✔ Unlimited	
Derbyshire	Bolsover D C	✔	–	–	–	✔	✘	01629 772220
Derbyshire	Chesterfield B C	✔	✔	–	✔	✔	✔ Unlimited	
Derbyshire	Derbyshire Dales D C	✔	✔	–	✘	✔	✔ Unlimited	01629 772233
Derbyshire	Erewash B C	✔	✔	–	✘	✔	✔ Unlimited	01159 072244
Derbyshire	High Peak B C	✔	✔	–	✘	✔	✔ Unlimited	08456 058058
Derbyshire	North East Derbyshire D C	✔ Max stay !	✔	–	✘	✔	✔ Unlimited	01629 580000 ext 2222
Derbyshire	South Derbyshire D C	✔	–	–	✔	✔	✔ Unlimited	
Devon	Devon C C	Ref DC	Ref DC	Ref DC	Ref DC	✔	Ref DC	0800 444000
Devon	Torbay C	✔	–	–	–	✔	✔ 1 hr free once payment made	0800 444000
Devon	East Devon D C	✔ Except when signs display the limit	✔	–	–	✔	✘	01392 381300
Devon	Exeter City C	✔	✔	–	✘	✔	✔ Unlimited	01392 382000
Devon	Mid Devon D C	✔ Max stay 3hrs	–	–	–	✔	✘	01884 255 255
Devon	North Devon D C	✔	–	–	–	✔	✘	0800 444000
Devon	Plymouth City C	✔	✔	–	✔ Max stay 3 hrs	✔	✔ Unlimited	01752 308686
Devon	South Hams D C	✔ Max stay !	✔	✔	✔	✔	✘	0800 444000
Devon	Teignbridge D C	✔ Max stay 3hrs	✔	✔	✘	✔	✘	0800 444000
Devon	Torridge D C	Ref CC	–	–	–	✔	✘	0800 444000
Devon	West Devon B C	✔	–	–	–	✔	✔ 1 hrs free once payment made	0800 444000
Dorset	Dorset C C	✔ Max stay !	✔	–	✔ Max stay 3 hrs	✔	Ref DC	01305 224321
Dorset	Borough of Poole	✔ Max stay !	✔ Max stay 3hrs!	–	✔	✔	✔ If Tax Exempt	01202 633605
Dorset	Bournemouth B C	✔ Max stay !	✔ Max stay 3hrs	✔	✘	✔	✘	01202 458774
Dorset	Christchurch B C	✔ Max stay !	✔ (Tax)	–	✔	✔	✔ If Tax Exempt	01305 251000
Dorset	East Dorset D C	✔ Max stay !	✔	–	✔ Max stay 3 hrs	✔	✔ !	01305 224321
Dorset	North Dorset D C	✔ Max stay !	✔	–	✔ Max stay 3 hrs	✔	✘	01305 224321
Dorset	Purbeck D C	✔	–	–	–	✔	–	01305 224321
Dorset	West Dorset D C	✔	–	–	–	✔	✔ If Tax Exempt Max 3hrs	01305 224321
Dorset	Weymouth & Portland B C	✔	✔	✔	✔	✔	✘	01305 224321
Durham	Durham C C	Ref DC	Ref DC	–	✔	✔	Ref DC	0191 3836001
Durham	Darlington B C	✔ Max stay !	✔ Max stay 3hrs	–	✔ !	✔	✔ Max stay 3hrs	01325 346200
Durham	Chester-le-Street D C	✔ !	✔	–	–	✔	✘	0191 3836001
Durham	Derwentside D C	✔ Except when signs display the limit	–	✔	✔	✔	✔ Unlimited	0191 3836001
Durham	Durham City C	✔	–	–	–	✔	✘	0191 3836001
Durham	Easington D C	Ref CC	Ref CC	Ref CC	Ref CC	✔	✔ Except Automated Car parks	0845 850 5010
Durham	Hartlepool B C	✔	✔ Max stay 3hrs	–	✔ Max stay 3 hrs	✔	✔ Max stay 3hrs	01429 523369
Durham	Sedgefield B C	✔	✔	–	✔	✔	✔ Unlimited	0845 850 5010
Durham	Stockton-on-Tees B C	✔	✔	–	✔	✔	✔ Unlimited	01642 528499
Durham	Teesdale D C	✔ Max stay 3hrs	✔ !	–	✘	✔	✔ Unlimited	0191 3836001
Durham	Wear Valley D C	✔	✔	–	✔	✔	✔ Unlimited	0191 383 6001
East Sussex	East Sussex C C	✔	✔ Except when signs display a limit	✔ Except when signs display a limit	✔	✔	✔	01323 466680
East Sussex	Brighton & Hove City C	✔	✔	✔	✘	✔	✔ Unlimited	01273 296270
East Sussex	Eastbourne B C	✔	✔	✔	✔	✔	✔	01323 466680
East Sussex	Hastings B C	✔	✔ Max stay 3hrs	✔	✘	✔	✔ 3hrs Max (Disabled Bay Only)	0845 608 0191
East Sussex	Lewes D C	✔ Max stay 3hrs	✔	–	–	✔	✔ Unlimited	0845 608 0191
East Sussex	Rother D C	✔	–	–	–	✔	✔ Permit required	01424 787507
East Sussex	Wealden D C	✔ Max stay 3hrs	✔ Max stay 3hrs!	✔ Max stay 3hrs	✔	✔	✔ Unlimited	01323 443 322
East Yorkshire	East Riding of Yorkshire C	✔	!	–	✔	✔	✘	01482 393939
East Yorkshire	Kingston upon Hull City C	✔	✔	✔	✔	✔	✔ Unlimited	01482 374137
Essex	Essex C C	Ref DC	✔	Ref DC	Ref DC	✔	Ref DC	
Essex	Basildon D C	✔	✔	✔ Max stay 3hrs	✔ Max stay 3 hrs	✔	✔ Unlimited	01268 643333
Essex	Braintree D C	✔	✔	–		✔	✔ Unlimited	0208 227 2334
Essex	Brentwood B C	✔	✔	–	✔	✔	✔ Unlimited	0845 603 7630
Essex	Castle Point B C	✔	–	–	✔	✔	✔ Unlimited	
Essex	Chelmsford B C	✔ Max stay !	✔ Max stay 3hrs !	✔ Max stay 3hrs	✔ Max stay 3 hrs	✔	✔ Unlimited	01245 434090
Essex	Colchester B C	✔ Max stay !	✔ Max stay 3hrs	–	✘	✔	✔ Except Automated Car parks	01255 253423
Essex	Epping Forest D C	✔	✔	✔	✔	✔	✔ Unlimited	
Essex	Harlow D C	✔	✔	–	✔	✔	✔ Unlimited	
Essex	Maldon D C	✔	✔	–	✘	✔	✔ Unlimited	
Essex	Rochford D C	✔ Max stay 3hrs	–	–	–	✔	✔ If Tax Exempt	
Essex	Southend-on-Sea B C	✔	✔	✔	✔	✔	✔ Unlimited	01702 534261
Essex	Tendring D C	✔	–	–	✘	✔	✔ Max stay 3hrs Pay for extra time	01255 686 868
Essex	Thurrock C	✔	✔ Max stay Displayed by Plate	–	✔	✔	✔ Max stay Displayed by Car Park	01375 652 652
Essex	Uttlesford D C	✔	✔	–	✘	✔	✔ Unlimited	01799 510 510
Gloucestershire	Gloucestershire City C	Ref DC	Ref DC	Ref DC	Ref DC	✔	Ref DC	*1
Gloucestershire	Cheltenham B C	✔ Max stay !	✔ Max stay 2hrs	✔ Max stay 3hrs	✔ Max stay 2hrs	✔ Max 2 hrs	✔ Max stay 2hrs	01242 5325000
Gloucestershire	Cotswold D C	✔	✔ !	–	✘	✔	✔ Unlimited	01452 426000
Gloucestershire	Forest of Dean D C	✔	–	–	–	✔	✔ Unlimited	01594 820500
Gloucestershire	Gloucester City C	✔ Max stay !	✔ Max stay 3hrs	✔ Max stay 3hrs	✔	✔	✔ Max stay 3hrs	01452 426868
Gloucestershire	South Gloucestershire C	✔	–	–	–	✔	✔ Unlimited !	01454 865994
Gloucestershire	Stroud D C	✔	✔	✔	✘	✔	✔ Unlimited	01453 760500
Gloucestershire	Tewkesbury B C	✔	✔	–	✔	✔	✔ Unlimited	01453 760500
Greater London	Hillingdon London B C	✔	✔	✔	✔	✔	Ref DC	01453 760500
Greater London	Barking & Dagenham London B C	✔ Max stay 4hrs	✔ Max stay 4hrs	–	✔ Max stay 4hrs	✔	✔ Unlimited	020 8227 2334
Greater London	Barnet London B C	✔ Max stay !	✔	✔	✔	✔	✔ Max stay 3hrs	020 8359 4131
Greater London	Bexley London B C	✔	✔	✔	✔	✔	✔ Unlimited	020 8836 7436
Greater London	Brent London B C	✔	✔	✔	✔	✔	✔ Unlimited	020 8937 4097
Greater London	Bromley London B C	✔ !	✔ !	✔ !	✘	✔	✔ Unlimited	020 8461 7629
Greater London	Camden London B C	✔	✘ 1 hr free once payment made	✘	✘	✘	✘	020 7974 4646 *2
Greater London	Camden London B C	✔	✔	✔	✔	✔	✘	020 7974 4646 *3
Greater London	Corporation of London	✔ Max stay 3hrs	✘ 1 hr free once payment made	–	✘	✘	✘	020 7332 1548 *4
Greater London	Croydon London B C	✔	✔	✔	✔	✔	✔	020 8825 6677
Greater London	Ealing London B C	✔	✔ Max stay 3hrs!	✔ Max stay 3hrs	✔	✔	✔ Unlimited	020 8825 6677
Greater London	Enfield London B C	✔	✔	✔	✔	✔	✔ Unlimited	020 8379 1000
Greater London	Greenwich London B C	✔	✔	✔	✘	✔	✘	020 8921 2388
Greater London	Hackney London B C	✔	✔	✔	✘	✔	✔ Unlimited	020 8356 8370
Greater London	Hammersmith & Fulham London B C	✔	✔	✔	✔	✔	✔ Unlimited	020 8753 5133/4
Greater London	Haringey London B C	✔	✔	✔	✔	✔	✔ Unlimited	020 8489 1865
Greater London	Harrow London B C	✔	✔	✔	✔	✔	✔ Unlimited	020 8863 5611
Greater London	Havering London B C	✔	✔	✔	✔	✔	✘	01708 432 797
Greater London	Hounslow London B C	✔ Max stay 3hrs	✔	✔	✘	✔	✘	020 8583 3073
Greater London	Islington London B C	✔	✔	✔	✔	✔	✘	020 7527 6108
Greater London	Kensington & Chelsea Royal B C	✔ Max stay 4hrs Mon–Fri	✘ 1 hr free once payment made	✘	✘	✘ 20 mins to unload/load	✘	020 7361 3108 *5
Greater London	Lambeth London B C	✔ Max stay 3hrs	✔	✔	✘	✔	✘	020 7926 9000
Greater London	Lewisham London B C	✔	✔	✔	✘	✔	✘	020 8314 8129
Greater London	Merton London B C	✔	✔	✔	✔	✔	✔ Unlimited	020 8545 4661
Greater London	Newham London B C	✔ !	✔	✔	✘	✔	✔ Unlimited	020 8430 2000
Greater London	Redbridge London B C	✔	✔	✘	✘	✔	✔ Unlimited	020 8708 3636
Greater London	Richmond upon Thames London B C	✔	✔	✔	✔	✔	✔ Pass Required	020 8831 6096 / 6312

*1 Gloucester City Council is exempt from the Blue Badge Scheme and they operate their own GREEN Badge Scheme

*2 Part of Camden Borough Council is exempt from the Blue Badge Scheme and they operate their own GREEN Badge Scheme

*3 An area of Camden Borough Council that operates the Blue Badge Scheme

*4 Corporation of London is exempt from the Blue Badge Scheme and they operate their own RED Badge Scheme

*5 The Royal Borough of Kensington & Chelsea is exempt from the Blue Badge Scheme and they operate their own PURPLE Badge Scheme

- Free parking on Single & Double Yellow lines (3hrs max) except where loading and unloading restrictions apply, Pay & Display, Shared Use, Residents and Blue Badge Bays
- Free parking in most places (Single & Double Yellow lines (3hrs max) & Pay & Display) except Residents Bays
- Free parking in Blue badge bays, Single & Double Yellow lines (3hrs max) & Residents Bays
- Free parking in most places (Single & Double Yellow lines (3hrs max) & Pay & Display) except Shared Use and Residents Bays
- Free parking in Blue badge bays and Single & Double Yellow lines (3hrs max) only
- Free parking in Blue badge bays with limited concessions on Pay & Display
- Free parking in Blue badge bays only

Users should be aware that this information may change at any time. This information was correct as of January 2006. Compiled by PIE Enterprises Ltd

Key
- ! The rules may vary locally
- Ref DC Refer to District Council for rulings
- Ref CC Refer to County Council for rulings
- B C Borough Council
- C C County Council
- D C District Council
- – Not applicable

County	Council	Blue Badge Park FREE with no time restrictions	Pay & Display (On street only) Park FREE with No time restrictions during the enforced time period	Shared Use Bays (Pay & Display and Resident) Park FREE with No time restrictions during the enforced time period	Resident Bays Park with no time restrictions during the enforced time period	Single & Double Yellow Lines Park for a maximum 3 hrs on a Single or Double Yellow Line	Council Owned Car Parks Free or Discounted parking for the Blue Badge Holders	Council Specific Contact Number For the Blue Badge Scheme
Greater London	Royal Borough of Kingston upon Thames	✔ Max stay 3hrs	✔ Max stay 3hrs	–	✔	✔	✔ Unlimited	020 8547 6600
Greater London	Southwark London B C	✔ Except when signs display the limit	✔	✔	✘	✔	✔	0870 600 6768
Greater London	Sutton London B C	✔	✔	✔	✔	✔	✘	020 8770 5341
Greater London	Tower Hamlets London B C	✔ Max stay 3hrs !	✔	✔	✘	✔	✔ In Blue Badge Bays Only	020 7364 3788
Greater London	Waltham Forest London Borough	✔ Max stay 3hrs	✔	✔	✔	✔	✔ Unlimited	020 8496 1659
Greater London	Wandsworth B C	✔	✔	✔	✔	✔	✘	020 8871 7709
*6 Greater London	Westminster City C	✔ Max stay 4hrs	✘ 1 hr free once payment made	✔ 1 hr free once payment made	✘	✘	✘	020 7823 4567
Greater Manchester	Salford City C	✔	✔	–	✔	✔	✔ Unlimited	0161 909 6508
Greater Manchester	Trafford Metropolitan Borough	✔ Max stay 3hrs !	✔	✔	✘	✔	✔ !	0161 912 1388
Greater Manchester	Wigan Metropolitan B C	✔	✔	–	✘	✔	✔ Unlimited	01942 244991
Greater Manchester	Bolton Metropolitan B C	✔	✔	–	✘	✔	✔ Unlimited	01204 337266
Greater Manchester	Bury Metropolitan B C	✔	✔ Max 3 hrs unless signs displays otherwise	–	✘	✔	✔ In Blue Badge Bays Only	0161 2536855
Greater Manchester	Manchester City C	✔	✔	✔	✔	✔	✔ Unlimited	0161 819 1993
Greater Manchester	Oldham Metropolitan B C	✔	✔ Max stay 3hrs !	–	✔ Max stay 3 hrs	✔	✔ Unlimited	0161 911 3000
Greater Manchester	Rochdale Metropolitan B C	✔ !	✔ Max stay 3hrs	✔	✘	✔	✘	01706 644106
Greater Manchester	Stockport Metropolitan B C	✔ Max stay 3hrs	✔ Max stay 3hrs	–	✘	✔	✔ Max stay 3hrs	0161 427 7011
Greater Manchester	Tameside Metropolitan B C	✔	–	–	–	✔	✔ Unlimited	0161 3422462
Hampshire	Hampshire C C	Ref DC	Ref DC	Ref DC	Ref DC	✔	Ref DC	01962 847650
Hampshire	Basingstoke & Deane B C	✔ Max stay 3hrs	✔	✔	✔	✔	✘	01962 845117
Hampshire	East Hampshire D C	✔	✔	–	✘	✔	✔ Unlimited	01962 841841
Hampshire	Eastleigh B C	✔	✔	–	✔	✔	✔ Unlimited	01962 841841
Hampshire	Fareham B C	✔	✔	–	–	✔	✔ Unlimited	01962 841841
Hampshire	Gosport B C	✔	✔	–	✘	✔	✔ Unlimited	01962 841841
Hampshire	Hart D C	✔	✔	✔	✔	✔	✔ Unlimited	01962 847650
Hampshire	Havant B C	✔	✔	–	–	✔	✔ Unlimited	01962 841841
Hampshire	New Forest D C	✔	–	–	✘	✔	✔ Unlimited	01962847747
Hampshire	Portsmouth City C	✔	✔	✔ Max stay 3hrs	✔	✔	✔ Unlimited!	02392841176
Hampshire	Rushmoor B C	✔	✔ Max stay 3hrs	–	✘	✔	✔ Unlimited !	01962 847650
Hampshire	Southampton City C	✔	✔	✔	✔	✔	✔ Except Automated Car parks	023 8022 3855
Hampshire	Test Valley B C	✔ Max stay 3hrs	✔ Max stay 3hrs	–	✔	✔	✔ Unlimited	01962 847650
Hampshire	Winchester City C	✔	✔	✔	✔	✔	✔ in P&D Car Parks only	01962 840 222
Herefordshire	Herefordshire C C	✔	Ref DC	Ref DC	✔	✔	Ref DC	
Hertfordshire	Hertfordshire C C	Ref DC	Ref DC	Ref DC	✔	✔	Ref DC	
Hertfordshire	Broxbourne B C	✔	–	–	–	✔	✔ Unlimited	01992 555555
Hertfordshire	Dacorum B C	✔	✔	–	✘	✔	✘	01923 471400
Hertfordshire	East Hertfordshire D C	✔	–	✔	–	✔	✔ Unlimited	01438 737400
Hertfordshire	Hertsmere B C	✔ Max stay !	✔	–	✘	✔	✔ Unlimited	01438 737400
Hertfordshire	North Hertfordshire D C	✔ Max stay 3hrs	✔	–	✔	✔	✔ Unlimited	
Hertfordshire	St Albans D C	✔	✔ Max stay 3hrs	✔ Max stay 3hrs	✘	✔	✔ Unlimited	01438 737 400
Hertfordshire	Stevenage B C	✔ Max stay 3hrs !	–	–	–	✔	✔ With Season Discount Card	
Hertfordshire	Three Rivers D C	✔	✔	–	✔	✔	✘	
Hertfordshire	Watford B C	✔	✔	✔	✘	✔	✘	01923 471400
Hertfordshire	Welwyn Hatfield D C	✔ Max stay 3hrs !	–	–	–	✔	!	
Isle of Man	Douglas B C	✔	–	–	✘	✔	✔ Unlimited	01624 686325
Isle of Man	Isle of Man Government	✔	–	–	✘	✔	✔ Unlimited	01624 686325
Isle of Wight	Isle of Wight C	✔	✔	–	✘	✔	✔ Unlimited	01983 821000
Isles of Scilly	Isle of Scilly C	✔	–	–	–	✔	✔	01720 422148
Kent	Kent C C	✔ Max stay !	Ref DC	Ref to DC	✘	✔	✘	01622 605020
Kent	Ashford B C	✔	✔	–	✘	✔	✔ Max stay 3hrs Pay for extra time	01622 605020
Kent	Canterbury City C	✔ Max stay 3hrs	✔	✔ Max stay 3hrs	✔	✔	✔ Unlimited	01622 605020
Kent	Dartford B C	✔ Max stay 3hrs	✔ Max stay 3hrs	–	✘	✔	✘	01622 605020
Kent	Dover D C	✔	✔	–	✔	✔	✔ Max stay 3hrs	01622 605020
Kent	Gravesham B C	✔	✔	✔ !	✔	✔	✔ Unlimited	01622 605020
Kent	Maidstone B C	✔	✔	–	✔	✔	✔ Unlimited	01622 605020
Kent	Medway C	✔ Max stay 3hrs	–	–	✔	✔	✔ Except Automated Car parks	01634 306000
Kent	Sevenoaks D C	✔	✔	–	✔	✔	✔ Unlimited	01622 605020
Kent	Shepway D C	✔	✔ Max stay 3hrs	–	✔	✔	✔ Unlimited	01303 853380
Kent	Swale B C	✔	✔ Max stay 3hrs	✔ Max stay 3hrs	✔	✔	✔ Max stay 4hrs	01795 417204
Kent	Thanet D C	✔	✔	–	✔	✔	✔ Unlimited	01622 605020
Kent	Tonbridge & Malling B C	✔	✔ Max 3hrs	–	✔	✔	✔ Unlimited in BB Bay Max stay 3hrs if not BB Bay	01622 605020
Kent	Tunbridge Wells B C	✔	✔	✔	✔	✔	✔ Unlimited	01622 605020
Lancashire	Lancashire C C	Ref DC	Ref DC	Ref DC	Ref DC	✔	Ref DC	0845 053 0049
Lancashire	Blackburn with Darwen BC	✔	✔	–	✘	✔	✔ Unlimited	01254 585381
Lancashire	Blackpool B C	✔ Max stay !	✔	–	✘	✔	✔ Unlimited	01253 477752
Lancashire	Burnley B C	✔ Max stay 12hrs	✔ Max stay 3hrs	–	✘	✔	✔ Max stay 3hrs Pay for extra time	0845 053 0049
Lancashire	Chorley B C	✔ Max stay 3hrs	✔ Max stay 3hrs	–	✘	✔	✔ Unlimited	0845 053 0049
Lancashire	Fylde B C	✔	✔ Max stay 3hrs	–	✔	✔	✔ Max stay 3hrs Pay for extra time	0845 053 0049
Lancashire	Hyndburn B C	✔ Max stay 3hrs	✔	–	✔	✔	✔ Unlimited	0845 053 0049
Lancashire	Lancaster City C	✔	✔	✔	✘	✔	✔ Unlimited	01524 66246
Lancashire	Pendle B C	✔	–	–	With Permit or in BB Bay	✔	✔ Unlimited in BB Bay Limited if not BB Bay	01772 533689
Lancashire	Preston City C	✔	✔	–	✘	✔	✔ Unlimited	01772 533689
Lancashire	Ribble Valley B C	✔	✔	–	✔	✔	✔ Unlimited	01772 533689
Lancashire	Rossendale B C	✔	–	–	–	✔	✔ Unlimited	01706 211221
Lancashire	South Ribble B C	✔	✔	–	✔	✔	✔ Unlimited	01772 533689
Lancashire	West Lancashire D C	✔	✔	–	✔	✔	✔ Unlimited	01695 577177
Lancashire	Wyre B C	✔ Max stay 3hrs	–	–	✘	✔	✘	0845 053 0049
Leicestershire	Leicestershire C C	✔ Max stay !	–	✔ Max stay 2hrs	✔ Max stay 3 hrs	✔	Ref DC	0116 265 7584
Leicestershire	Leicester City C	✔ Max stay 3hrs	✔	–	✔	✔	✔ Unlimited	0116 252 7000
Leicestershire	Blaby D C	✔	–	–	–	✔	✔ Unlimited	0116 2657584
Leicestershire	Charnwood B C	✔	–	✔ limits apply without resident permit (shown by time plate)	✔ limits apply without resident permit (shown by time plate)	✔	✔	0116 265 7584

*6 City of Westminster is exempt from the Blue Badge Scheme and they operate their own WHITE Badge Scheme

Free parking on Single & Double Yellow lines (3hrs max) except where loading and unloading restrictions apply, Pay & Display, Shared Use, Residents and Blue Badge Bays

Free parking in most places (Single & Double Yellow lines (3hrs max) & Pay & Display) except Residents Bays

Free parking in Blue badge bays, Single & Double Yellow lines (3hrs max) & Residents Bays

Free parking in most places (Single & Double Yellow lines (3hrs max) & Pay & Display) except Shared Use and Residents Bays

Key
- ! The rules may vary locally
- Ref DC Refer to District Council for rulings
- Ref CC Refer to County Council for rulings
- B C Borough Council
- C C County Council
- D C District Council
- – Not applicable

County	Council	Blue Badge Park FREE with no time restrictions	Pay & Display (On street only) Park FREE with No time restrictions during the enforced time period	Shared Use Bays (Pay & Display and Resident) Park FREE with No time restrictions during the enforced time period	Resident Bays Park with no time restrictions during the enforced time period	Single & Double Yellow Lines Park for a maximum 3 hrs on a Single or Double Yellow Line	Council Owned Car Parks Free or Discounted parking for the Blue Badge Holders	Council Specific Contact Number For the Blue Badge Scheme
Leicestershire	Harborough D C	✔	✔	–	✘	✔	✔ Unlimited	0116 265 7584
Leicestershire	Hinckley & Bosworth B C		✔	–	✘	✔	✔ Unlimited	0116 265 7584
Leicestershire	Melton B C	✔ Max stay !	✔ Max stay 3hrs	✔ Max stay 3hrs	✔	✔	✘	0116 265 7523
Leicestershire	North West Leicestershire D C	✔	–	–	✘	✔	✔ Unlimited	0116 265 7523
Leicestershire	Oadby & Wigston B C	✔ Max stay 3hrs	✔ Max stay 3hrs	–	✔	✔	✔ Unlimited	0116 265 7523
Lincolnshire	Lincolnshire C C	✔ Max stay 3hrs !	✔	✔	✘	✔	Ref DC	01522 552 222
Lincolnshire	Boston B C	✔	✔	–	–	✔	✔ Unlimited	0845 030536
Lincolnshire	East Lindsey D C	✔	✘	–	✘	✔	✘	0845 030536
Lincolnshire	Lincoln City C	✔ Max stay 3hrs	✔	–	–	✔	✔	01522 552 222
Lincolnshire	North Kesteven D C	✔	–	–	–	✔	✔ Unlimited	01529 414155 01522 699699
Lincolnshire	South Holland D C	✔	–	–	–	✔	✘	0845 603 0536
Lincolnshire	South Kesteven D C	✔	✔	–	–	✔	✘	01522 550 711
Lincolnshire	West Lindsey D C	✔	–	–	–	✔	✔ Unlimited	0845 603 0536
Lincolnshire (part of)	North East Lincolnshire C	✔	✔ !	–	✔	✔	✔ Unlimited	01472325435
Lincolnshire (part of)	North Lincolnshire C	✔	✔ !	–	✔	✔	✔ Unlimited	01724 297979
Merseyside	Wirral Metropolitan B C	✔	✔	✔	✔	✔	✔ Unlimited	None Supplied
Merseyside	Knowsley Metropolitan B C	✔	✔	–	✘	✔	✔ Unlimited	0151 4433841
Merseyside	Liverpool City C	✔	✔	✔	✘	✔	✔ Unlimited	0151 233 3000
Merseyside	Sefton C	✔	✔	–	✘	✔	✔ Unlimited	0845 140 0845
Merseyside	St Helens Metropolitan B C	✔ Max stay 2hrs		–	✘	✔	✘	01744 456000
Norfolk	Norfolk C C	✔	–	–	–	✔	Ref DC	0844 800 8020
Norfolk	Norwich City C	✔ !	✔	✔	✔	✔	✔ Unlimited !	0844 800 8014
Norfolk	Breckland D C	✔	✔	–	–	✔	✔ Unlimited	0844 800 8014
Norfolk	Broadland D C	✔	–	–	–	✔	✔ Unlimited	0844 800 8014
Norfolk	Great Yarmouth B C	✔	✔	–		✔	✔ Unlimited	0844 800 8020
Norfolk	King's Lynn & West Norfolk B C	✔	✔	✔	Ref CC	✔	✔ Unlimited	0844 800 8020
Norfolk	North Norfolk D C	✔	✔ !	–	–	✔	✘	0844 800 8014
Norfolk	South Norfolk C	Ref CC	–	–	–	✔	✔	01508 533853
North Yorkshire	North Yorkshire C C	Ref DC	Ref DC	Ref DC	Ref DC	✔	Ref DC	01609 779999
North Yorkshire	York City C	✔	✔	✔	✔	✔	✔ Max stay rules apply	01609 779999 *7
North Yorkshire	Craven D C	✔ Max stay 3hrs !	✔	–	✘	✔	✔ Unlimited	01609 779999
North Yorkshire	Hambleton D C	✔	✔	✔	✔	✔	✘	01609 779999
North Yorkshire	Harrogate B C	✔	✔	–	✔ !	✔	✔ Unlimited	01609 779999
North Yorkshire	Richmondshire D C	✔ Max stay 3hrs	✔	–	✔	✔	✔ !	01609 779999
North Yorkshire	Ryedale D C	✔	–	–	–	✔	✘ but allowed an additional hour free	01609 779999
North Yorkshire	Scarborough B C	✔ Max stay 3hrs	✔	–	✔	✔	✘	01609 779999
North Yorkshire	Selby D C	✔	✔	–	–	✔	✔ Unlimited	01609 779999
Northamptonshire	Northamptonshire C C	✔ Max stay 3hrs	✔	–	–	✔	Ref DC	01604 236236
Northamptonshire	Corby B C	✔	–	–	–	✔	✘	01604 236236
Northamptonshire	Daventry D C	✔	✔	–	–	✔	✔ Unlimited	01604 654364
Northamptonshire	East Northamptonshire D C	✔	–	–	–	✔	✔ Unlimited	01604 654364
Northamptonshire	Kettering B C	✔	✔	–	✘	✔	✔ Unlimited	01604 654365
Northamptonshire	Northampton B C	✔ Max stay 3hrs	✔	–	✔	✔	✔ Unlimited	01604 654 364
Northamptonshire	South Northamptonshire C	✔ Max stay 3hrs	✔ Max stay 3hrs	–	–	✔	✔ Unlimited	01604 654363
Northamptonshire	Wellingborough B C	✔	✔	–	–	✔	✔ Unlimited	01604 654 364
Northumberland	Northumberland C C	Ref DC	Ref DC	Ref DC	Ref DC	✔	Ref DC	01670 533000
Northumberland	Alnwick D C	✔ !	✔ !	–	–	✔	✔ Unlimited	01665 510505
Northumberland	Berwick–upon–Tweed B C	✔	✔	–	–	✔	✔ Unlimited	01670 533000
Northumberland	Blyth Valley B C	✔	–	–	–	✔	✔ Unlimited	01670 354316
Northumberland	Castle Morpeth B C	✔	–	–	✘	✔	✔ In Blue Badge Bays Only	01670 533000
Northumberland	Tynedale C	✔ Max stay !	✔ Max stay 2hrs !	–	✘	✔	✔ Unlimited	01434 603582
Northumberland	Wansbeck D C	✔	✔	–	✔	✔	✔ Unlimited	01670 533000
Nottinghamshire	Nottinghamshire C C	✔	–	–	✘	✔	Ref DC	0115 982 3823
Nottinghamshire	Ashfield D C	✔	✔	✔	✘	✔	✔ Unlimited	01623 405300
Nottinghamshire	Bassetlaw D C	✔	✘	–	✘	✔	✔ only in BB Bays, With Car Park's Time Limit	01909 535602
Nottinghamshire	Broxtowe B C	✔	–	–	✘	✔	✔ Unlimited	0115 917 5800
Nottinghamshire	Gedling B C	✔	–	–	✘	✔	✔ In Blue Badge Bays Only: max 3hrs otherwise	0115 982 3823
Nottinghamshire	Mansfield D C	✔ Max stay 3hrs	✔	–	✔	✔	✔ Except Automated Car parks	01623 433433
Nottinghamshire	Newark & Sherwood D C	✔ !	–	–	✘	✔	✔ Unlimited	01636 682700
Nottinghamshire	Nottingham City C	✔	✔	–	✘	✔	✔ Unlimited	0115 915 9835 *8
Nottinghamshire	Rushcliffe B C	✔ Max stay 3hrs	✔	–	✔	✔	✔ Except Automated Car parks	0115 914 1500
Oxfordshire	Oxfordshire C C	✔	✔	–	✔	✔	✘	01865 854409
Oxfordshire	Cherwell D C	✔	✔	–	–	✔	✔ Unlimited	01865 854409
Oxfordshire	Oxford City C	✔	✔	✔	✔	✔	✘	01865 854409
Oxfordshire	South Oxfordshire D C	✔	✔	–	–	✔	✔ Unlimited	01865 854409
Oxfordshire	Vale of White Horse D C	✔	✔	–	✔	✔	✔ Unlimited	01235 520202
Oxfordshire	West Oxfordshire D C	✔	✔	–	–	✔	✔ Unlimited	01865 854409
Rutland	Rutland C C	✔	–	✔	✔	✔	✔ in P&D Car Parks only	01572 758375
Shropshire	Shropshire C C	✔ Max stay 3hrs	✔ Max stay 3hrs	–	–	✔	Ref DC	01743 460093
Shropshire	Telford & Wrekin B C	✔ Max stay 3hrs	✘ Double Time once payment made	–	✘	✔	✘	01952 202016
Shropshire	Bridgnorth D C	✔	–	–	–	✔	✔ Max stay 3hrs	01743 460093
Shropshire	North Shropshire D C	✔	✔ Max stay 3hrs	–	✔	✔	✔ Unlimited	01743 460093
Shropshire	Oswestry B C	Ref CC	–	–	–	✔	✘	01691 671111
Shropshire	Shrewsbury & Atcham B C	✔	✔ Max 3hrs	✔ Max 3hrs	–	✔	✘ discounted by car parks	01743 460093
Shropshire	South Shropshire D C	✔ Max stay 3hrs	✔ Max stay 3hrs	–	–	✔	✔ Max stay 3hrs	01743 460093
Somerset	Somerset C C	Ref DC	Ref DC	Ref DC	Ref DC	✔	Ref DC	08453459133
Somerset	North Somerset D C	✔ Max stay 2hrs	–	–	–	✔	✘	01934 634725
Somerset	Bath & North East Somerset C	✔	✔	–	✔	✔	✔ Unlimited	01225 394147
Somerset	Mendip D C	✔	✔	✔	✔	✔	✔ Unlimited	0845 345 9133
Somerset	Sedgemoor D C	✔	✔	–	–	✔	✔ Unlimited	0845 345 9133
Somerset	South Somerset D C	✔	✔	–	✘	✔	✔ Unlimited	0845 345 9133
Somerset	Taunton Deane D C	✔	✔ Max stay 3hrs	–	✘	✔	✔ Unlimited	0845 345 9133
Somerset	West Somerset D C	✔ Max stay 3hrs	✔ Max stay 3hrs	✔	✘	✔	✘	0845 345 9133
South Yorkshire	Barnsley Metropolitan B C	✔ Max stay !	✔	–	✘	✔	✔ Unlimited	01226 772163

*7 Blue badge holders can obtain a permit to enter and park in the pedestrian zone for a 2hr Max Stay

*8 Special Permit to access City Centre pedestrian zones

Free parking in Blue badge bays and Single & Double Yellow lines (3hrs max) only

Free parking in Blue badge bays with limited concessions on Pay & Display

Free parking in Blue badge bays only

Key
- ! The rules may vary locally
- Ref DC Refer to District Council for rulings
- Ref CC Refer to County Council for rulings
- B C Borough Council
- C C County Council
- D C District Council
- – Not applicable

County	Council	Blue Badge Park FREE with no time restrictions	Pay & Display (On street only) Park FREE with No time restrictions during the enforced time period	Shared Use Bays (Pay & Display and Resident) Park FREE with No time restrictions during the enforced time period	Resident Bays Park with no time restrictions during the enforced time period	Single & Double Yellow Lines Park for a maximum 3 hrs on a Single or Double Yellow Line	Council Owned Car Parks Free or Discounted parking for the Blue Badge Holders	Council Specific Contact Number For the Blue Badge Scheme
South Yorkshire	Doncaster Metropolitan B C	✔	✔	✔ Max 3 hrs	✔ Max 3hrs	✔	✔ In Blue Badge Bays Only	01302 737711
South Yorkshire	Rotherham Metropolitan B C	✔ Max stay !	✔	✔	✘	✔	✔ Unlimited !	01709 382121
South Yorkshire	Sheffield City C	✔ Max stay 4hrs	✔	–	✘	✔	✔ Unlimited	01142 734897
Staffordshire	Staffordshire C C	✔	✔	–	–	✔	✘	01785 276950
Staffordshire	Cannock Chase D C	✔	✔	–	–	✔	✔ Unlimited	01785 276950
Staffordshire	East Staffordshire B C	✔	✔	–	–	✔	✔ Unlimited	01283 239888
Staffordshire	Lichfield D C	✔	✔	–	–	✔	✔ Unlimited	01543 510800
Staffordshire	Newcastle under Lyme B C	✔ Max stay 3hrs	–	–	✘	✔	✔ Unlimited	01785 276950
Staffordshire	South Staffordshire C	✔	✔	–	–	✔	✔ Unlimited	01785 276950
Staffordshire	Stafford B C	✔	✔	–	✘	✔	✔ Unlimited	01785 276950
Staffordshire	Staffordshire Moorlands D C	✔	✔	–	✘	✔	✔ !	01785 276950
Staffordshire	Stoke on Trent City C	✔ Max stay 3hrs	✔ Max stay 3hrs	–	✘	✔	✔ Unlimited	01782 234 567
Staffordshire	Tamworth B C	✔	✔	–	✘	✔	✘	01827 709709
Suffolk	Suffolk C C	Ref DC	Ref DC	Ref DC	Ref DC	✔	Ref DC	0845 602 3023
Suffolk	Babergh D C	✔	✘	–	✘	✔	✔ Unlimited! Max 3hrs in very few	0845 602 3023
Suffolk	Forest Heath D C	✔	✔	–	✔ !	✔	✔ Unlimited	0845 023 023
Suffolk	Ipswich B C	✔ !	✔	–	✔	✔	✔ Unlimited !	01773 583000
Suffolk	Mid Suffolk D C	✔ Max stay 3hrs	✔ Max stay 3hrs	–	✔	✔	✔ Unlimited	0845 602 3023
Suffolk	St Edmundsbury B C	✔ !	✔	✔	✘	✔	✔ Unlimited	01284 763233
Suffolk	Suffolk Coastal D C	✔	–	–	–	✔	✔ Unlimited !	0845 602 3023
Suffolk	Waveney D C	✔ Max stay 3hrs	–	–	✔	✔	✔ Unlimited	08456 023 023
Surrey	Surrey C C	Ref DC	Ref DC	Ref DC	Ref DC	✔	Ref DC	08456 009 009
Surrey	Elmbridge B C	✔ Max stay 3hrs	✔	–	✔	✔	✔ Unlimited	0208 541 8981
Surrey	Epsom & Ewell B C	✔	✔	–	✔	✔	✔ Unlimited	08456 009 009
Surrey	Guildford B C	✔ !	✔	✔	✔	✔	✔ in P&D Car Parks only	08456 009 009
Surrey	Mole Valley D C	✔	✔	–	✔	✔	✔ Unlimited	01306 885001
Surrey	Reigate & Banstead B C	✔	–	–	–	✔	✔ Unlimited	01737 276000
Surrey	Runnymede B C	✔	–	–	–	✔	✔ Unlimited	01932 838383
Surrey	Spelthorne B C	✔	–	–	✘	✔	✘	08456 009 009
Surrey	Surrey Heath B C	✔	✔	✔	✘	✔	✔ in P&D Car Parks only	08456 009 009
Surrey	Tandridge D C	✔ Max stay 3hrs	✔ !	–	–	✔	✔ After 9.30am	08456 009 009
Surrey	Waverley B C	✔ Max stay 3hrs	✔ !	–	✔	✔	✔ Unlimited	01483 523333
Surrey	Woking B C	✔	✔	✔	✔	✔	✔ Unlimited	None Supplied
Tyne & Wear	Gateshead Metropolitan B C	✔	✔	–	✘	✔	✔ Unlimited	0191 4332429
Tyne & Wear	Newcastle upon Tyne City C	✔	✔	✔	✔	✔	✔ Unlimited	01912116111
Tyne & Wear	North Tyneside Metropolitan B C	✔	✔	–	✔	✔	✔ Unlimited	0191 2005308
Tyne & Wear	South Tyneside Metropolitan B C	✔ Max stay 3hrs	✔ Max stay 3hrs	✔	✘	✔	✔ Unlimited	0191 4230200
Tyne & Wear	Sunderland City C	✔	✔	–	✘	✔	✔ Unlimited	0191 5661202
Warwickshire	Warwickshire C C	✔ Max stay 3hrs	✔ Max stay 3hrs	✔	✔	✔	Ref DC	01926 410410
Warwickshire	North Warwickshire B C	✔ Max stay 3hrs !	✔ Max stay 3hrs	✔	✔	✔	✘	01926 410410
Warwickshire	Nuneaton & Bedworth B C	✔	✔	✔	–	✔	✔ Unlimited	01926 410410
Warwickshire	Rugby B C	✔ Max stay 3hrs	✔ !	✔	✔	✔	✔ Unlimited	01926 410410
Warwickshire	Stratford on Avon D C	✔	✔	–	✔	✔	✔ Unlimited	01926 410410
Warwickshire	Warwick D C	✔	✔	✔	✔	✔	✔ Unlimited	01926 410410
West Midlands	Birmingham City C	✔	✔	✔	✘	✔	✔ Unlimited	0121 303 6644
West Midlands	Sandwell Metropolitan B C	✔ Max stay !	✔	✔	✔ Max stay 3 hrs	✔	✔ Unlimited	0121 520 0201
West Midlands	Coventry City C	✔	✔	–	✔	✔	✔ Unlimited	0276 785210
West Midlands	Dudley Metropolitan B C	✔	✔	–	–	✔	✔ Unlimited	01384 815822
West Midlands	Solihull Metropolitan B C	✔ Max stay 3hrs	–	–	–	✔	✔ Unlimited	01217 046000
West Midlands	Walsall Metropolitan B C	✔ Max stay 3hrs	✔	–	✘	✔	✔ Unlimited !	01922 653560
West Midlands	Wolverhampton City C	✔ Max stay 3hrs	✔	–	✔	✔	✘	
West Sussex	West Sussex C C	✔	✔	–	✘	✔	Ref DC	01243 756759
West Sussex	Adur D C	✔	✔	–	✘	✔	✔ Unlimited	01243 756759
West Sussex	Arun D C	✔	✔	✘	✘	✔	✔ Unlimited	01243 756759
West Sussex	Chichester D C	✔	✔ (Voucher Parking)	–	✘	✔	✔ Unlimited	01243 756759
West Sussex	Crawley B C	✔	✔	–	–	✔	✔ Unlimited	01243 756759
West Sussex	Horsham D C	✔ Max stay !	✔	–	✘	✔	✔ Unlimited !	01243 777653
West Sussex	Mid Sussex D C	✔	✔	–	✘	✔	✔ Unlimited	01243 756759
West Sussex	Worthing B C	✔	✔	–	✘	✔	✔ Unlimited	01243 756759
West Yorkshire	City of Bradford Metropolitan D C	✔ Max stay !	✔	–	✘	✔	✔ Unlimited	
West Yorkshire	Calderdale Metropolitan B C	✔	✔	–	✘	✔	✘	01422 363561
West Yorkshire	City of Wakefield Metropolitan D C	✔	✔	–	✘	✔	✔ Unlimited	0800 1696520
West Yorkshire	Kirklees Metropolitan B C	✔	✔	–	–	✔	✔ Unlimited	01924 325070
West Yorkshire	Leeds City C	✔	✔	–	✘	✔	✔ Unlimited	0113 398 4700
Wiltshire	Wiltshire C C	✔ Except when signs display the limit	✘	✘	✔	✔	Ref DC	01225 713000
Wiltshire	Swindon B C	✔ Max stay 3hrs	✔	–	✔	✔	✔ in P&D Car Parks only	01793 463725
Wiltshire	Kennet D C	✔ Max stay !	✔	–	–	✔	✔ Max stay 3hrs Pay for extra time	01225 713000
Wiltshire	North Wiltshire D C	✔ Max stay !	✔ Max stay 3hrs	–	✘	✔	✔ Unlimited	01225 713000
Wiltshire	Salisbury D C	✔ Max stay 3hrs	✔	–	✔	✔	✔ Max stay rules apply	01225 713000
Wiltshire	West Wiltshire D C	✔ Max stay !	✔	–	✔	✔	✔ Max stay 3hrs	01225 713 000
Worcestershire	Worcestershire C C	Ref DC	Ref DC	Ref DC	Ref DC	✔	Ref DC	01905 763763
Worcestershire	Bromsgrove D C	✔	✔	–	–	✔	✔ Unlimited	01527 881288
Worcestershire	Malvern Hills D C	✔	–	–	–	✔	✔ Unlimited !	01684 862 151
Worcestershire	Redditch B C	✔	✔	–	✘	✔	✔ Unlimited	01527 534123
Worcestershire	Worcester City C	✔ Max stay 3hrs	✔ Max stay 3hrs	–	✘	✔	✔ Max stay 3hrs in Short stay Unlimited in Long stay!	01905 722233
Worcestershire	Wychavon D C	✔	✔	–	✔	✔	✔ Unlimited	01386 565000
Worcestershire	Wyre Forest D C	✔	✔	–	–	✔	✔ Unlimited	01562 732 928
Yorkshire (parts of)	Middlesbrough C	✔	✔	✔	✘	✔	✔ Unlimited	01642 726004
Yorkshire (parts of)	Redcar & Cleveland B C	✔ Max stay 3hrs	✔ Max stay 3hrs!	✔	✘	✔	✔ Max stay 3hrs!	01642 771500
Northern Ireland								
	Antrim B C	✔ Max stay 3hrs	–	–	✔	✔	✘	028 6634 3700
	Ards B C	✔ Max stay 3hrs	–	–	–	✔	✘	028 6634 3700
	Armagh City & D C	✔ Max stay 3hrs	✔	–	✔	✔	✘	028 6634 3700
	Ballymena B C	✔ Max stay 3hrs	✔	–	✔	✔	✘	028 6634 3700
	Ballymoney B C	✔ Max stay 3hrs	✔	✔	✔	✔	✘	028 2766 1810
	Banbridge B C	✔ Max stay 3hrs	✔	–	✔	✔	✘	028 6634 3700

*9 The council operates Blue Badge scheme and operates their own GREEN Badge Policy

County	Council	Blue Badge Park FREE with no time restrictions	Pay & Display (On street only) Park FREE with No time restrictions during the enforced time period	Shared Use Bays (Pay & Display and Resident) Park FREE with No time restrictions during the enforced time period	Resident Bays Park with no time restrictions during the enforced time period	Single & Double Yellow Lines Park for a maximum 3 hrs on a Single or Double Yellow Line	Council Owned Car Parks Free or Discounted parking for the Blue Badge Holders	Council Specific Contact Number For the Blue Badge Scheme
	Belfast City C	✔ Max stay 3hrs	✔	–	✔	✔	✘	028 6634 3730
	Carrickfergus B C	✔ Max stay 3hrs	✔	–	✔	✔	✘	028 6634 3700
	Castlereagh B C	✔ Max stay 3hrs	✔	–	✔	✔	✔ Unlimited	028 6634 3700
	Coleraine B C	✔ Max stay 3hrs Unless signs says otherwise	✔	✔	✔	✔	✘	028 6634 3700
	Cookstown D C	✔ Max stay 3hrs	✔ Max stay 3hrs	✔	✔	✔	✔ Max stay 3hrs Pay for extra time	028 6634 3700
	Craigavon B C	✔ Max stay 3hrs	✔	–	✔	✔	✘	028 6634 3700
	Derry City C	✔ Max stay 3hrs	✔	–	✔	✔	✘	None Supplied
	Down D C	✔ Max stay 3hrs Unless signs says otherwise	✔	–	–	✔	✘	028 6634 3700
	Dungannon & South Tyrone B C	✔ Max stay 3hrs	✔	–	✔	✔	✘	028 6634 3700
	Fermanagh D C	✔ Max stay 3hrs	✔	–	✔	✔	✘	028 6634 3700
	Larne B C	✔ Max stay 3hrs	✔	–	✔	✔	✘	028 6634 3700
	Limavady B C	✔ Max stay 3hrs	✔	–	✔	✔	✘	028 6634 3700
	Lisburn City C	✔ Max stay 3hrs	✔	–	✔	✔	✘	028 6634 3700
	Londonderry City C	✔ Max stay 3hrs	✔	–	✔	✔	✘	028 6634 3700
	Magherafelt D C	✔ Max stay 3hrs	✔	–	✔	✔	✘	028 6634 3700
	Moyle D C	✔ Max stay 3hrs	✔	–	✔	✔	✘	028 6634 3700
	Newry & Mourne D C	✔ Max stay 3hrs	✔	–	✔	✔	✘	028 6634 3700
	Newtownabbey B C	✔ Max stay 3hrs	✔	–	✔	✔	✘	028 6634 3700
	North Down B C	✔ Max stay 3hrs	✔	–	✔	✔	✘	028 6634 3700
	Omagh D C	✔ Max stay 3hrs	✔	–	✔	✔	✘	028 6634 3700
	Strabane D C	✔ Max stay 3hrs	✔	–	✔	✔	✘	028 6634 3700
Scotland								
	Aberdeen City C	✔	✔	✔	✔ !	✔ Unlimited	✔ Unlimited	01224 522599 *9
	Aberdeenshire C	✔	Ref DC	Ref DC	Ref DC	✔ Unlimited	✘	
	Angus C	✔	✔	✔	✔	✔ Unlimited	✔ Unlimited	01241 435093
	Argyll & Bute C	✔	✔	–	✔	✔ Unlimited	✔ Unlimited	
	Clackmannanshire C	✔	–	–	✘	✔ Unlimited	✔ Unlimited	01529 452542
	Dumfries & Galloway C	✔	–	–	–	✔ Unlimited	✔ Unlimited	01387 26 0000
	Dundee City C	✔	✔	–	✔	✔ Unlimited	✔ Unlimited	01382 438310
	East Ayrshire C	✔ Max stay !	✔	–	–	✔ Unlimited	✔ Unlimited	01563 576000
	East Dunbartonshire C	✔	✔	–	–	✔ Unlimited	✔ Unlimited	0141 7751311
	East Lothian D C	✔	✔	✔	✘	✔ Unlimited	✔ Unlimited	0162 082 7367
	East Renfrewshire C	✔	–	–	–	✔ Unlimited	✔ Unlimited	0141 5773001
	Edinburgh City C	✔	✔	–	✘	✔ Unlimited	✘	0131 200 2351
	Falkirk C	✔	✔	–	✘	✔ Unlimited	✔ Unlimited	01324 504725
	Fife C	✔	✔	–	–	✔ Unlimited	✔ Unlimited	
	Glasgow City C	✔	✔	✔ !	✘	✔ Unlimited	✔ Unlimited (P & D Only)	
	Highland C	Ref DC	Ref DC	Ref DC	Ref DC	✔ Unlimited	Ref DC	01463 702142
	Inverclyde C	✔	–	–	–	✔ Unlimited	✔ Unlimited	01475 714100
	Midlothian C	✔	–	–	–	✔ Unlimited	✔ Unlimited	0131 271 3522
	Moray C	✔ Max stay 3hrs	✔	–	✔	✔ Unlimited	✘	01343551339
	North Ayrshire C	✔	–	–	✔	✔ Unlimited	✘	01294 317700
	North Lanarkshire C	✔	–	–	–	✔ Unlimited	✔	01698 332000
	Orkney Islands C	✔	✔	–	✔	✔ Unlimited	✔ Unlimited	01856 873535
	Perth & Kinross C	✔	✔	–	✘	✔ Unlimited	✔ Unlimited	01738 476868
	Renfrewshire C	✔	✔	✔	✔	✔ Unlimited	✔ Unlimited	0141 842 5000
	Scottish Borders C	✔	✔	–	✔	✔ Unlimited	✔ Unlimited	
	Shetland Islands C	✔	–	–	–	✔ Unlimited	✔ Unlimited	01595 74 4319
	South Ayrshire C	✔	✔	–	✔	✔ Unlimited	✔ Unlimited	
	South Lanarkshire C	✔	✔	✔	✔	✔ Unlimited	✔ If Not automated	01698 454444
	Stirling C	✔	✔	✔	✘	✔ Unlimited	✔ Unlimited	0845 277 7000 *10
	West Dunbartonshire C	✔	–	–	–	✔ Unlimited	✔ Unlimited	01389 737000
	West Lothian C	✔ Max stay !	✔	–	–	✔ Unlimited	✔ Unlimited	01506 775287
	Western Isles / Comhairle nan Eilean Siar	✔	–	–	–	✔ Unlimited	✔ Unlimited	01851 709611
Wales								
	Blaenau Gwent C C B C	✔ Max stay 3hrs	✔	–	✔	✔	✔ Unlimited	
	Bridgend County B C	✔ Max stay !	✔	–	–	✔ Unlimited	✔ Unlimited	01656 642200
	Caerphilly County B C	✔	–	–	✘	✔ Unlimited	–	0808 100 2500
	Cardiff C C	✔	✔	–	✔ Max stay 3 hrs	✔ Unlimited	Ref DC	02920 521855
	Carmarthenshire C C	✔ Max stay !	✔ Max stay 3hrs	–	✔	✔	✔ Max stay 3 hrs Pay for extra time	01267 224401
	Ceredigion C C	✔	✘	–	–	✔	✘	01545 574000
	Conwy County B C	✔	✔	–	–	✔ Unlimited	✔ In Blue Badge Bays Only	01492 574000
	Denbighshire C C	Ref DC	Ref DC	–	–	✔ Unlimited	Ref DC	
	Flintshire C C	Ref DC	Ref DC	–	Ref DC	✔ Unlimited	Ref DC	01352 701304
	Gwynedd C C	✔	✔	–	Ref DC	✔ Unlimited	Ref DC	01386 682646
	Isle of Anglesey C C	✔	✔	–	–	✔	✔ Unlimited	01248 750157
	Merthyr Tydfil County B C	✔	✔	✔	✘	✔ Unlimited	✘	01685 724500
	Monmouthshire C C	✔	✔	✔	✘	✔ Unlimited	Ref DC	01873 735394
	Neath Port Talbot County B C	✔	–	–	–	✔ Unlimited	Ref DC	
	Newport City C	✔	✔	✔	✘	✔	✔ Unlimited if surface Car Park	01633 656656
	Pembrokeshire C C	✔ Max stay !	–	–	✘	✔ Unlimited	✔ Max stay 3hrs	01437 760999
	Powys C C	✔	✔	✔	✘	✔ Unlimited	Ref DC	01597 826000
	Rhondda Cynon Taff County B C	✔	✔	–	✘	✔	✔ Unlimited	01443 431513
	Swansea City & B C	✔ Max stay !	–	–	–	✔ Unlimited	Ref DC	
	Torfaen County B C	✔	✔	–	✔	✔	✔ Unlimited	01495 762200
	Vale of Glamorgan C	✔	–	–	✔ Max stay 3 hrs	✔	✔ Unlimited	01446 730 402
	Wrexham County Borough	✔	✔	✔	–	✔	✔ Unlimited	01978 292042
Channel Islands								
	The States of Guernsey	✔	✔	✔	✘	✔ Unlimited	✘	01481 243400
	The States of Jersey	✔ Max stay !	✔	✔	✔	✔ Unlimited	✔ Max stay 12hrs	01534 603000

*10 RED Badge scheme in operation but due for review/termination

- Free parking on Single & Double Yellow lines (3hrs max) except where loading and unloading restrictions apply, Pay & Display, Shared Use, Residents and Blue Badge Bays
- Free parking in most places (Single & Double Yellow lines (3hrs max) & Pay & Display) except Residents Bays
- Free parking in Blue badge bays, Single & Double Yellow lines (3hrs max) & Residents Bays
- Free parking in most places (Single & Double Yellow lines (3hrs max) & Pay & Display) except Shared Use and Residents Bays
- Free parking in Blue badge bays and Single & Double Yellow lines (3hrs max) only
- Free parking in Blue badge bays with limited concessions on Pay & Display
- Free parking in Blue badge bays only

Airport car parking maps

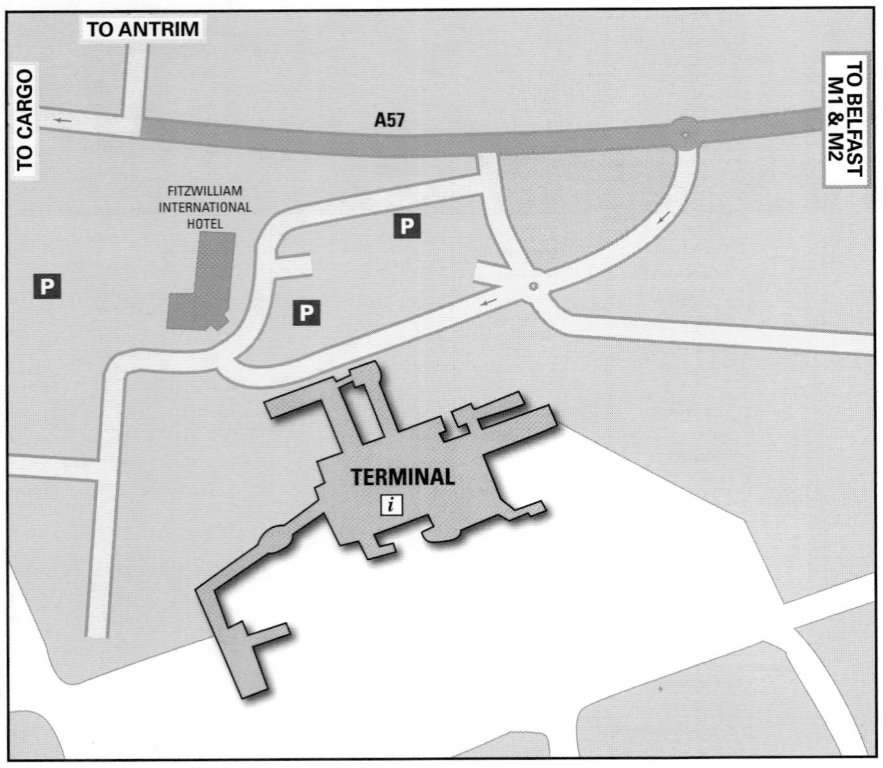

BELFAST INTERNATIONAL

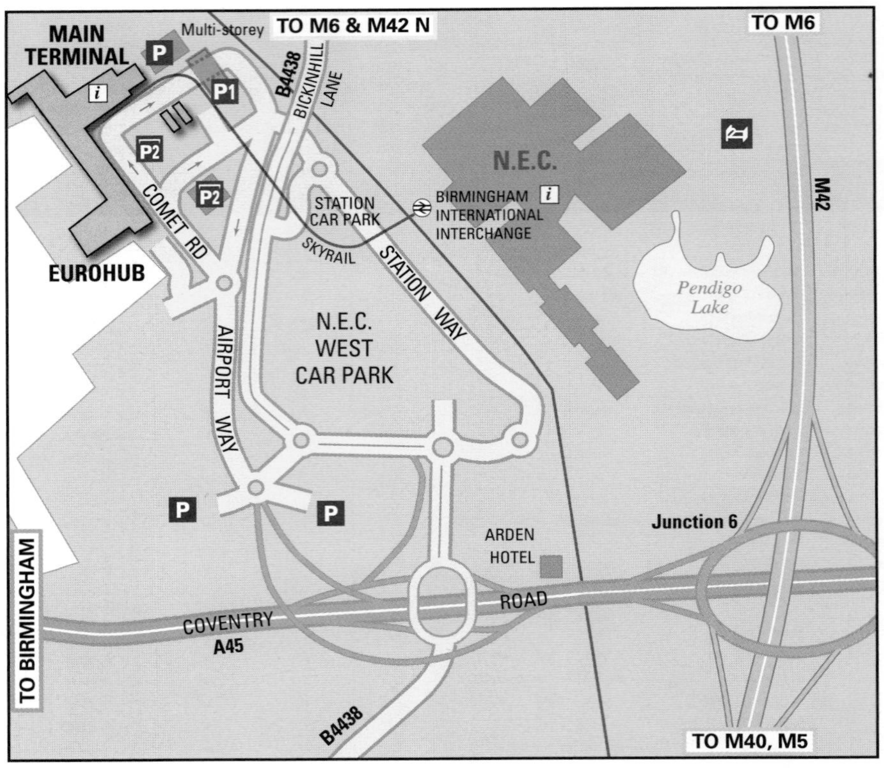

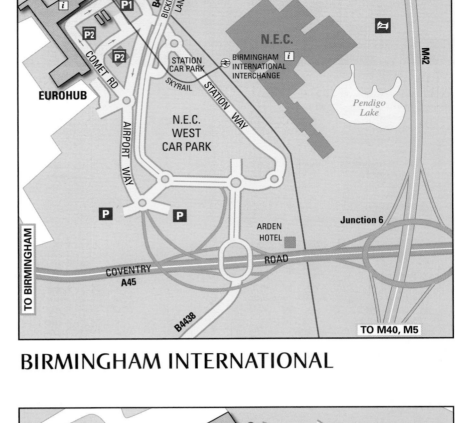

BIRMINGHAM INTERNATIONAL

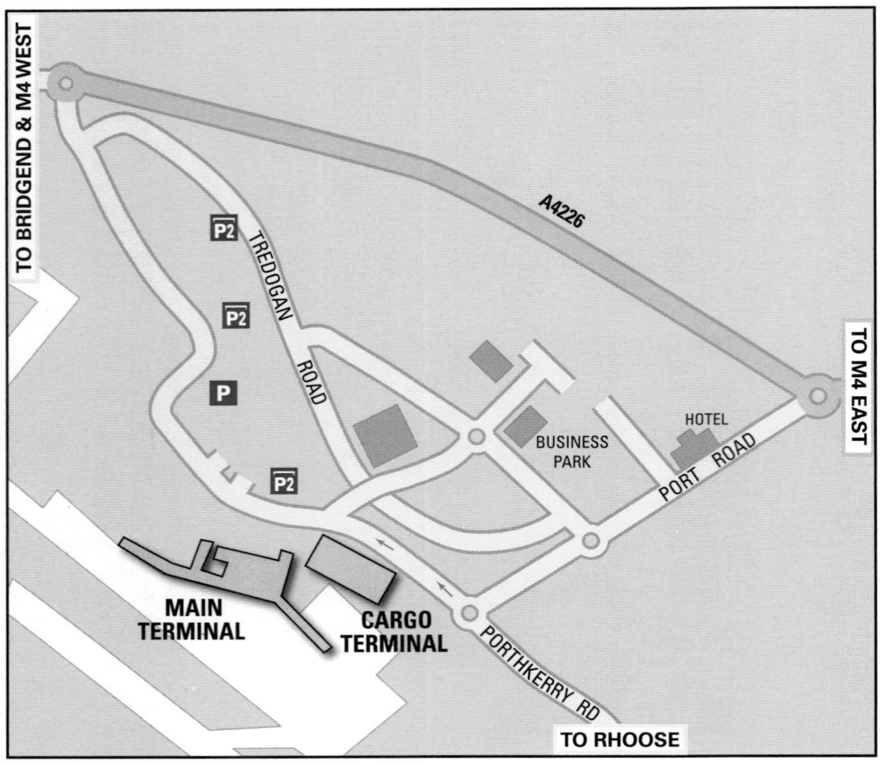

CARDIFF INTERNATIONAL

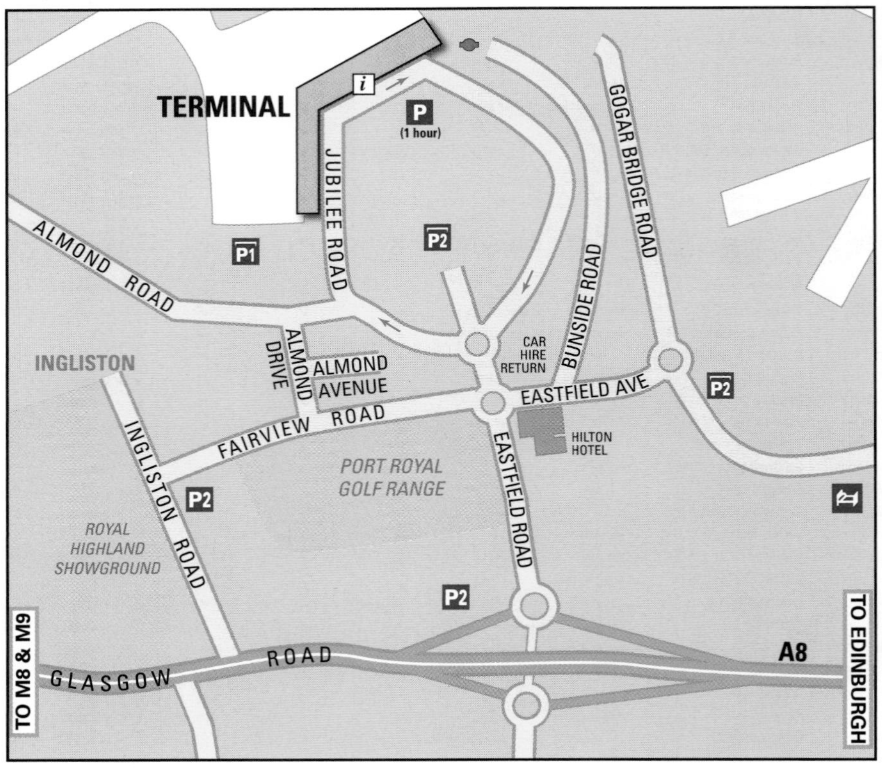

EDINBURGH

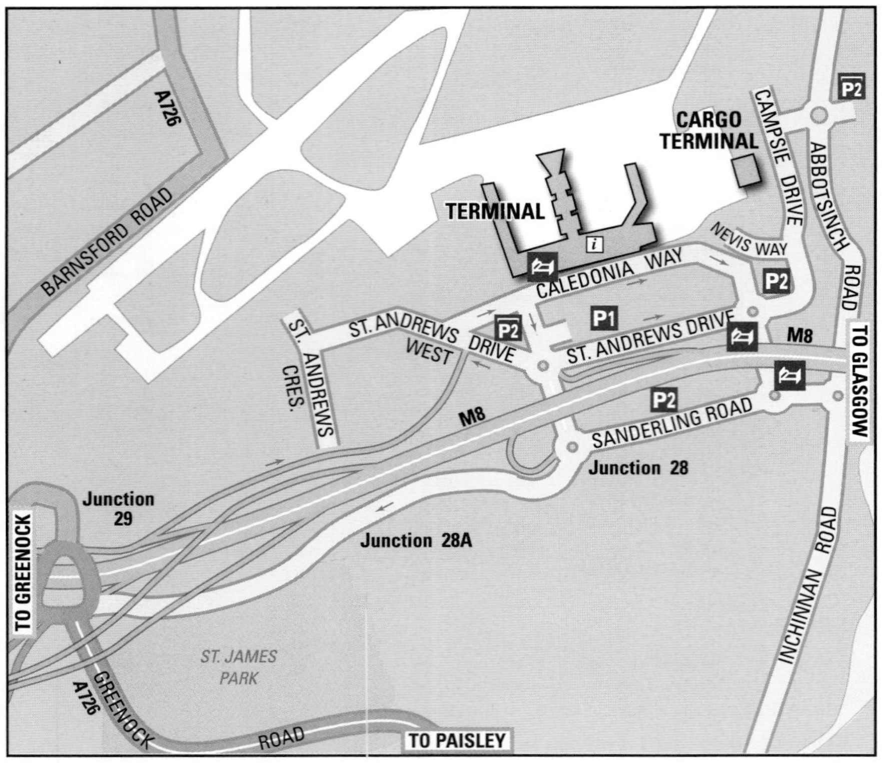

GLASGOW

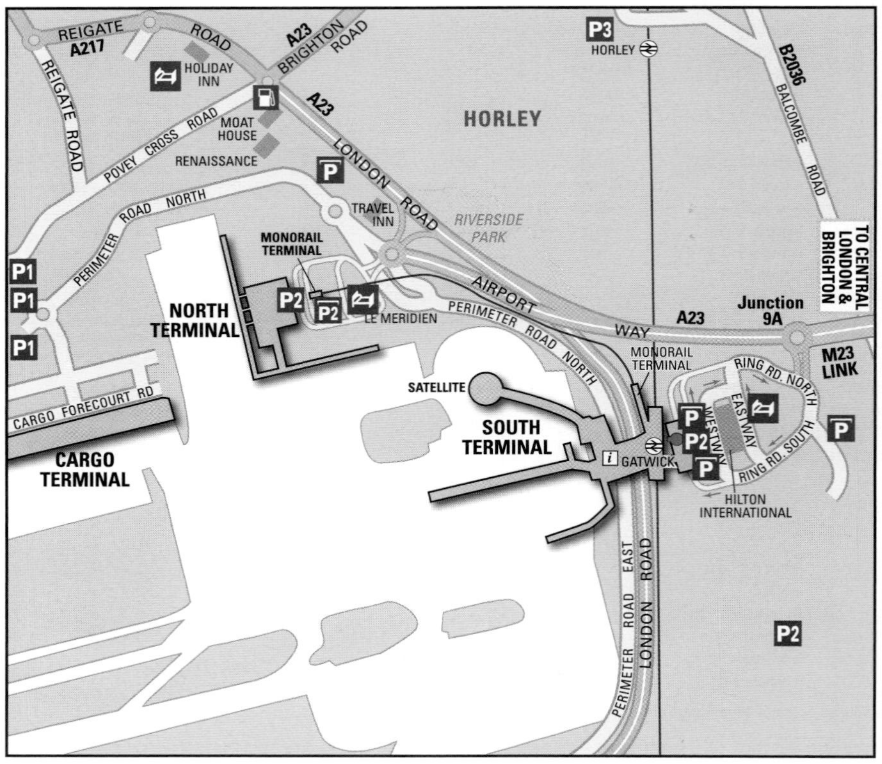

LONDON GATWICK

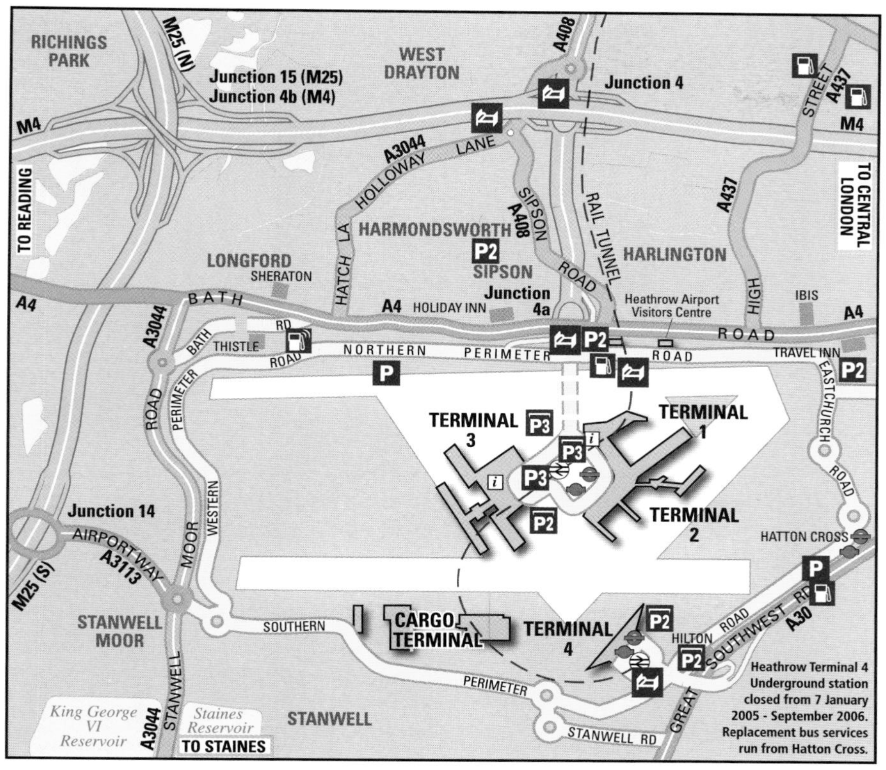

LONDON HEATHROW

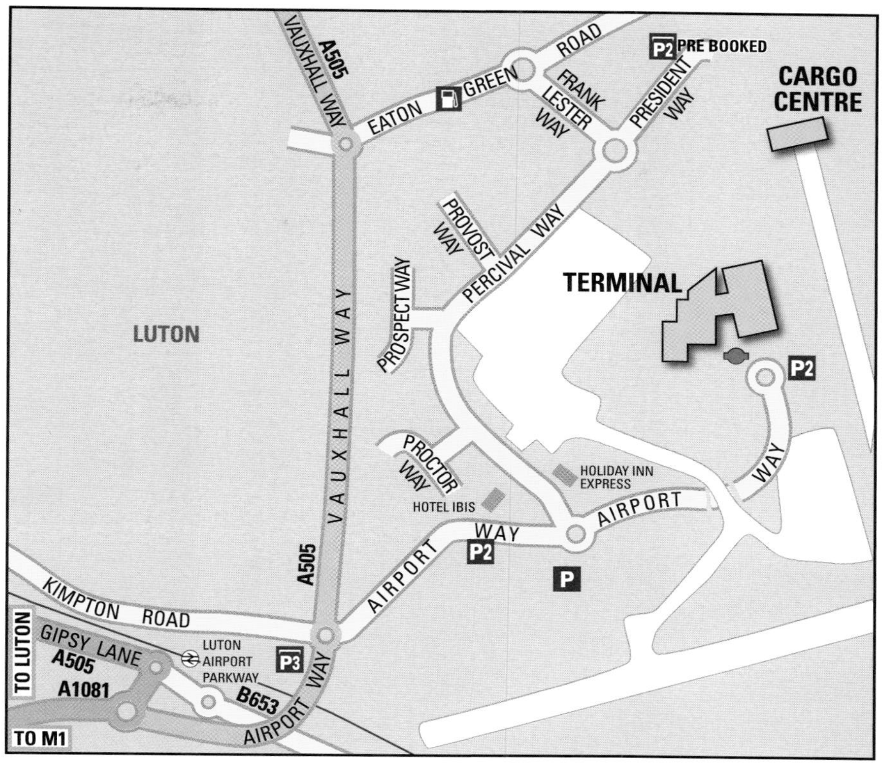

LONDON LUTON

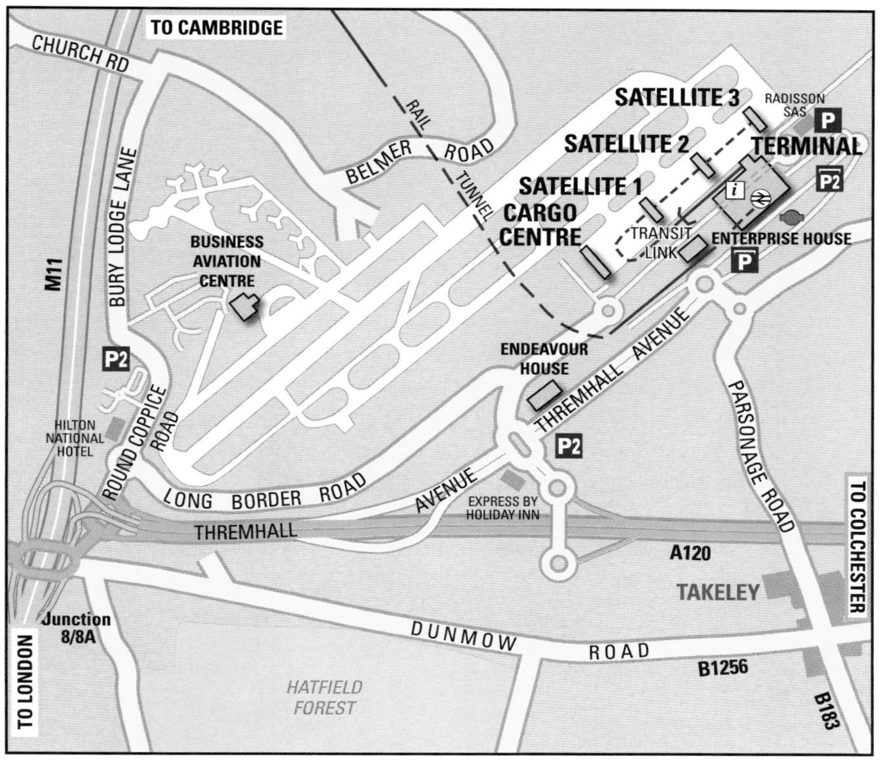

LONDON STANSTED

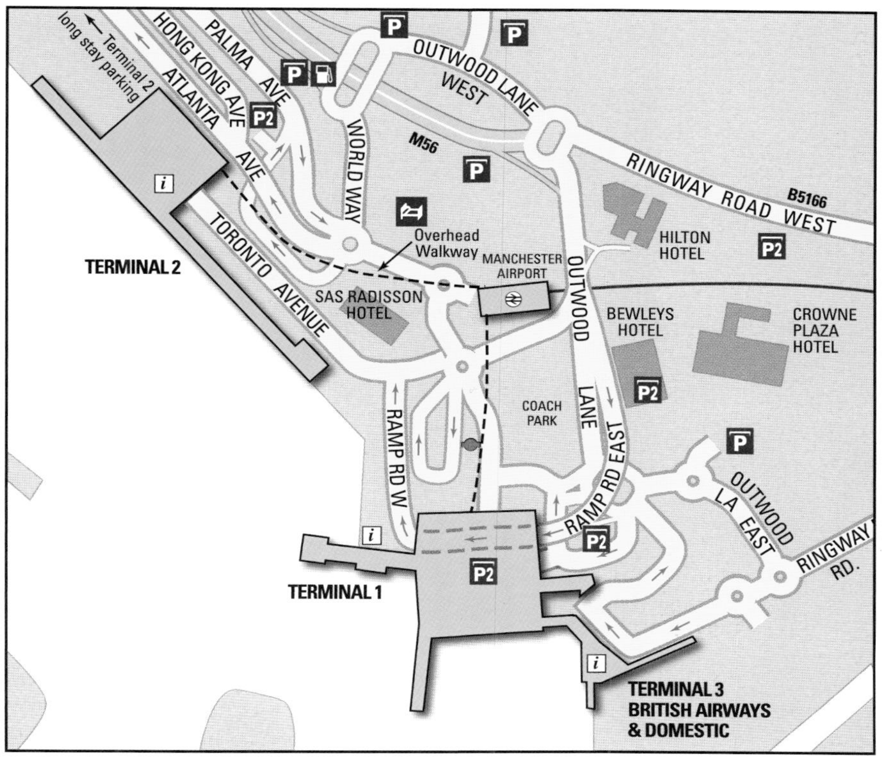

MANCHESTER

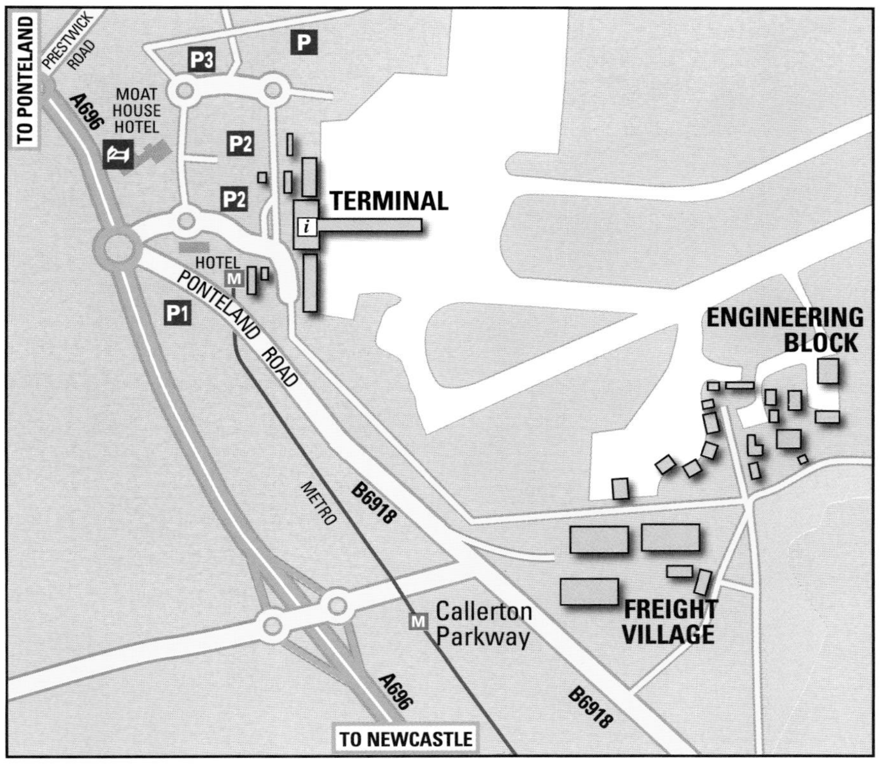

NEWCASTLE INTERNATIONAL

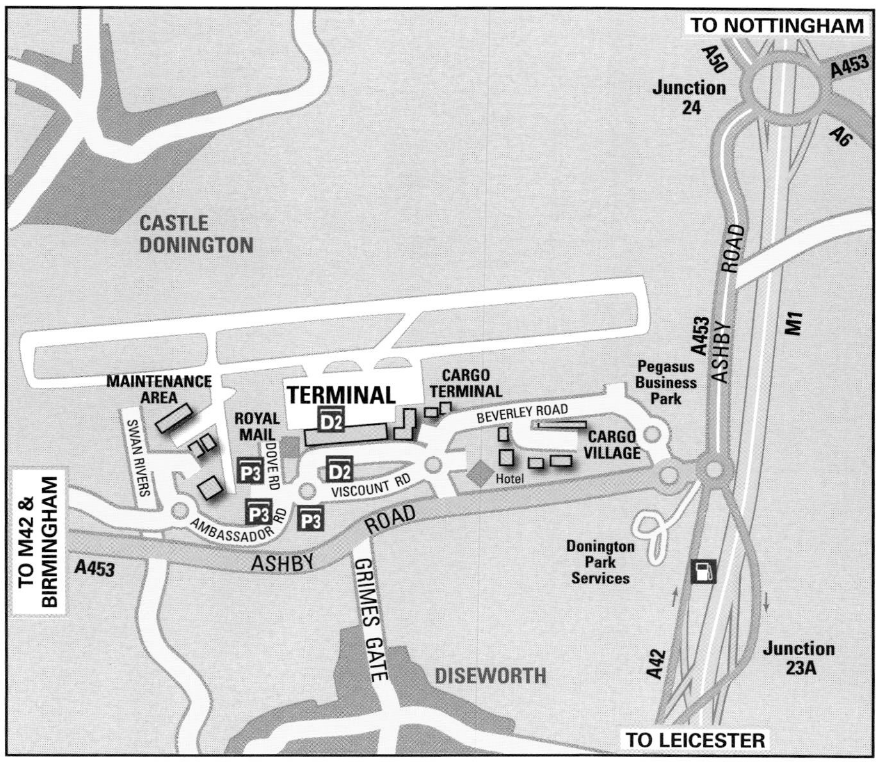

NOTTINGHAM EAST MIDLANDS

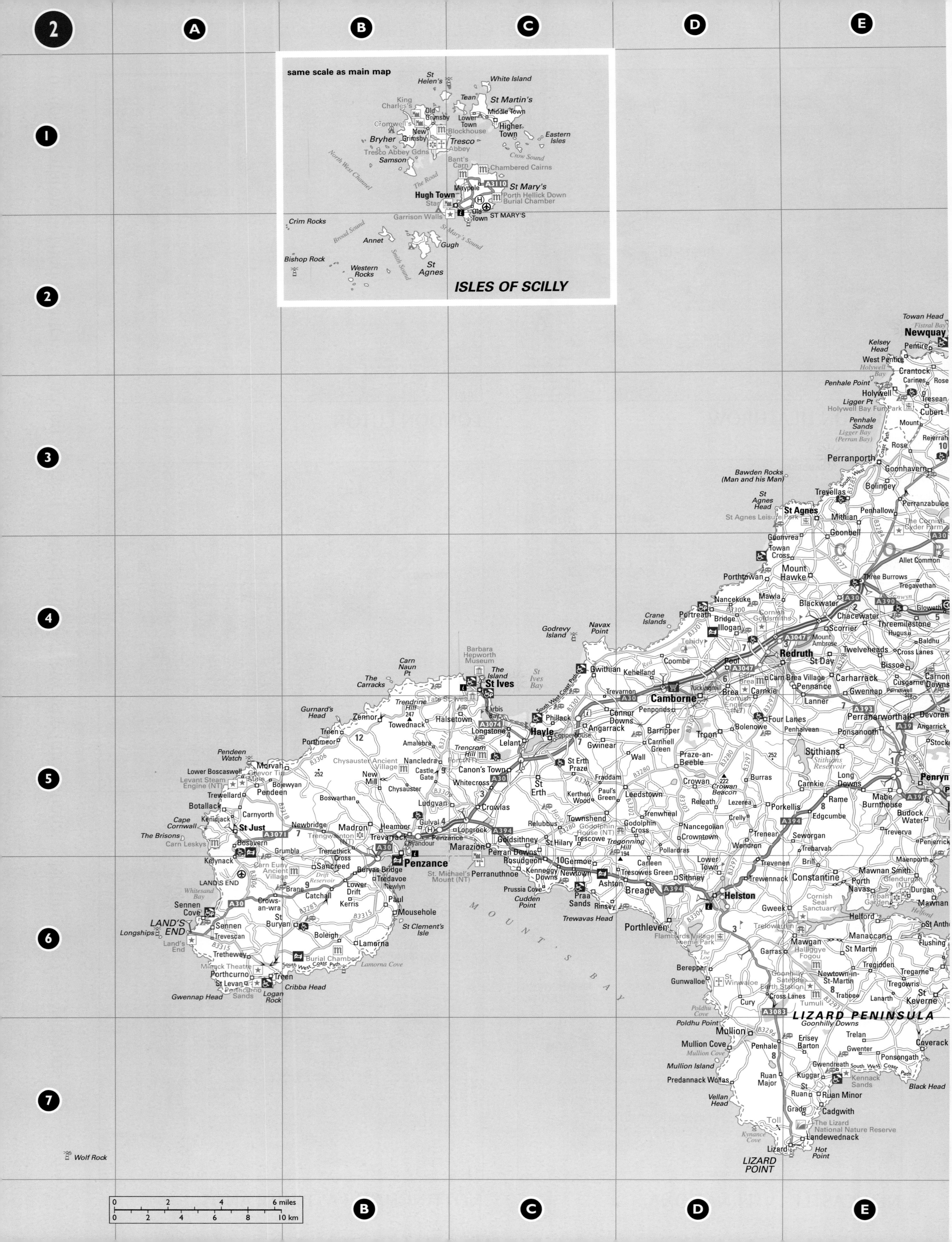
A
B
C
D
E
1
2
3
4
5
6
7
same scale as main map
St Helen's
White Island
King Charles's
Tean
St Martin's
Middle Town
Old Grimsby
Lower Town
Cromwell's
New Grimsby
Blockhouse
Higher Town
Eastern Isles
Bryher
Tresco
Abbey
Tresco Abbey Gdns
Crow Sound
North West Channel
Samson
Bant's Carn
Chambered Cairns
The Road
A3110
St Mary's
Maypole
Hugh Town
Porth Hellick Down Burial Chamber
Star
Garrison Walls
Old Town
ST MARY'S
Crim Rocks
Broad Sound
Annet
St Mary's Sound
Gugh
Bishop Rock
Western Rocks
Smith Sound
St Agnes
ISLES OF SCILLY
Towan Head
Fistral Bay
Newquay
Kelsey Head
Pentire
West Pentire
Crantock
Holywell Bay
Carines
Rose
Penhale Point
Holywell
Tresean
Ligger Pt
Holywell Bay Fun Park
Cubert
Penhale Sands
Mount
Ligger Bay (Perran Bay)
Rose
Rejerrah
Perranporth
Goonhavern
Bawden Rocks (Man and his Man)
Bolingey
Trevellas
St Agnes Head
Perranzabuloe
St Agnes
Penhallow
Mithian
St Agnes Leisure Park
The Cornish Cyder Farm
Goonbell
Goonvrea
Towan Cross
Allet Common
Mount Hawke
Porthtowan
Three Burrows
Tregavethan
Nancekuke
Mawla
Blackwater
A30
A390
Gloweth
Portreath
Cornish Goldsmiths
Chacewater
Crane Islands
Bridge
Illogan
Scorrier
Threemilestone
Godrevy Island
Navax Point
Tehidy
Mount Ambrose
Twelveheads
Cross Lanes
A3047
Baldhu
Redruth
St Day
Bissoe
Coombe
Pool
Carn Brea Village
Carharrack
Carnon Downs
Gwithian
Kehelland
Cusgarne
Carn Brea
Pennance
Gwennap
Perranwell
Trevarnon
Camborne
Tuckingmill
Brea
Carnkie
Cornish Engines (NT)
Lanner
Penponds
Four Lanes
A393
Perranarworthal
Devoran
Connor Downs
Barripper
Bolenowe
Penhalvean
A39
Angarrick
Phillack
Angarrack
Troon
Ponsanooth
Stockl
Copperhouse
Hayle
Gwinear
Carnhell Green
Stithians
Stithians Reservoir
Wall
Praze-an-Beeble
St Erth Praze
Fraddam
Crowan
Long Downs
Penryn
St Erth
Burras
Carnkie
Mabe Burnthouse
Kerthen Wood
Paul's Green
Leedstown
Crowan Beacon
Rame
Releath
Lezerea
Porkellis
Budock Water
Townshend
Trenwheal
Crelly
Edgcumbe
Relubbus
Godolphin House (NT)
Godolphin Cross
Nancegollan
Treverva
St Hilary
Trescowe
Tregonning Hill
Crowntown
Seworgan
Trenear
Penjerrick
Goldsithney
Wendron
Trebarvah
Perran Downs
Pollardras
Maenporth
Rosudgeon
Germoe
Carleen
Lower Town
Trevenen
Brill
Kenneggy Downs
Newtown
Tresowes Green
Sithney
Trewennack
Constantine
Mawnan Smith
Porth Navas
Glendurgan (NT)
Prussia Cove
Ashton
Breage
Helston
Durgan
Cudden Point
Praa Sands
Rinsey
Trebah Garden
Mawnan
Gweek
Cornish Seal Sanctuary
Helford
Trewavas Head
Porthleven
Flambards Village Theme Park
Trelowarren
St Anthony
Manaccan
The Loe
Mawgan
Halliggye Fogou
St Martin
Flushing
Garras
Tregidden
Bereppe
Tregarne
Goonhilly Satellite Earth Station
Newtown-in-St-Martin
Gunwalloe
St Winwaloe
Tregowris
Trabboe
Cross Lanes
Lanarth
St Keverne
Cury
Tumuli
Poldhu Cove
A3083
LIZARD PENINSULA
Poldhu Point
Goonhilly Downs
Mullion
Erisey Barton
Trelan
Mullion Cove
Penhale
Coverack
Gwenter
Ponsongath
Mullion Island
Gwendreath
South West Coast Path
Predannack Wollas
Kuggar
Kennack Sands
Black Head
Ruan Major
St Ruan
Ruan Minor
Vellan Head
Grade
Cadgwith
Toll
The Lizard National Nature Reserve
Kynance Cove
Landewednack
Lizard
Hot Point
LIZARD POINT
Carn Naun Pt
Barbara Hepworth Museum
The Carracks
The Island
St Ives
St Ives Bay
Tate St Ives
Gurnard's Head
Zennor
Trendrine Hill 247
Towednack
Halsetown
Carbis Bay
A3074
Lelant
Treen
Porthmeor
Amalebra
Trencrom Hill
Longstone
Pendeen Watch
Morvah
Chysauster Ancient Village
Nancledra
Lower Boscaswell
Geevor Tin Mine
252
Castle Gate
Fort (NT)
Canon's Town
Levant Steam Engine (NT)
Bojewyan
New Mill
Chysauster
Whitecross
Trewellard
Pendeen
Botallack
Carnyorth
Boswarthan
Ludgvan
Crowlas
Cape Cornwall
Kenidjack
St Just
Newbridge
Madron
Heamoor
Gulval
A3071
Trengwainton (NT)
Trevarrack
Chyandour
Longrock
The Brisons
Carn Lesky
Bosavern
Penzance
A394
Grumbla
Tremethick Cross
Marazion
Kelynack
Carn Euny Ancient Village
Sancreed
Buryas Bridge
St. Michael's Mount (NT)
Perranuthnoe
LAND'S END
Drift Reservoir
Tredavoe
Newlyn
Whitesand Bay
Brane
Lower Drift
Crows-an-wra
Catchall
Kerris
Paul
Sennen Cove
St Buryan
Mousehole
Longships
LAND'S END
Sennen
Trevescan
Boleigh
St Clement's Isle
Land's End
Lamorna
Trethewey
Burial Chamber
Minack Theatre
Lamorna Cove
Porthcurno
St Levan
Treen
South West Coast Path
Cribba Head
Porthcurno Sands
Logan Rock
Gwennap Head
MOUNT'S BAY
Wolf Rock
0
2
4
6 miles
0
2
4
6
8
10 km

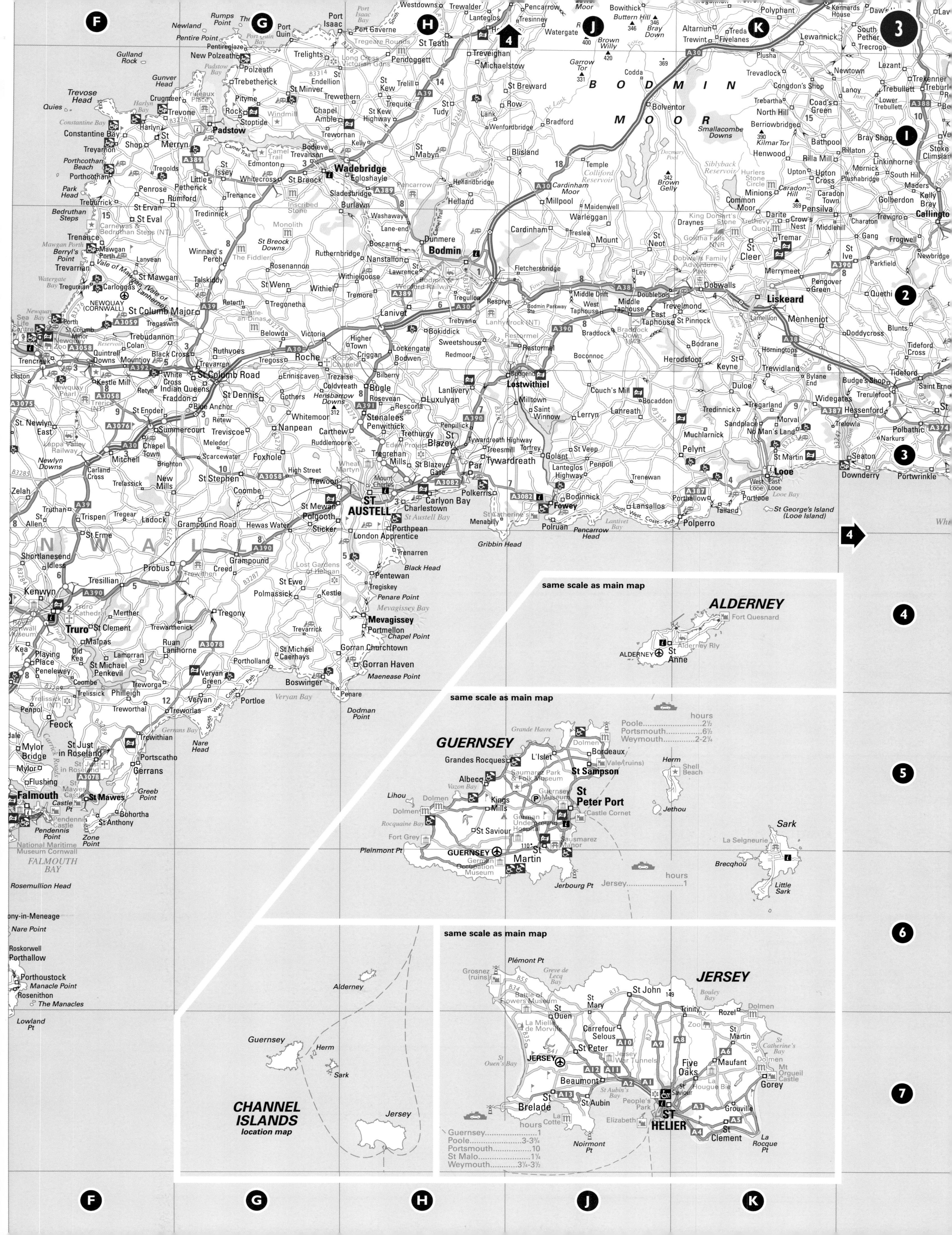
F
G
H
J
K
3
4
I
2
5
6
7
BODMIN MOOR
Padstow
Wadebridge
Bodmin
Lostwithiel
Liskeard
Looe
Fowey
ST AUSTELL
Truro
Falmouth
St Mawes
Newquay
St Columb Major
St Columb Road
Indian Queens
Camelford
Port Isaac
Polzeath
New Polzeath
Trevose Head
Constantine Bay
St Merryn
Harlyn
Trevone
Porthcothan
Bedruthan Steps
Mawgan Porth
St Mawgan
NEWQUAY (CORNWALL)
Trencreek
Quintrell Downs
Mitchell
Summercourt
St Stephen
St Dennis
Roche
Bugle
Lanivet
Luxulyan
Par
Tywardreath
Polkerris
Charlestown
Mevagissey
Gorran Haven
Dodman Point
Tregony
Probus
Grampound
Veryan
Portloe
St Just in Roseland
Gerrans
Portscatho
St Anthony
Zone Point
Pendennis Point
National Maritime Museum Cornwall
FALMOUTH BAY
Rosemullion Head
Nare Point
Porthallow
Porthoustock
Manacle Point
The Manacles
Lowland Pt
Mylor Bridge
Feock
Kenwyn
Malpas
St Clement
St Michael Penkevil
Polperro
Lansallos
Polruan
Gribbin Head
Pencarrow Head
St George's Island (Looe Island)
Seaton
Downderry
Portwrinkle
St Martin
Widegates
Hessenford
Menheniot
Dobwalls
St Cleer
Minions
St Neot
Cardinham
Blisland
St Breward
St Tudy
St Mabyn
St Kew
St Teath
Delabole
Trewarmett
Altarnun
Five Lanes
Bolventor
Callington
Pensilva
Upton Cross
Same scale as main map
ALDERNEY
Fort Quesnard
Alderney Rly
ALDERNEY
St Anne
GUERNSEY
Grande Havre
Grandes Rocques
L'Islet
St Sampson
Bordeaux
Vale (ruins)
Saumarez Park & Folk Museum
Albecq
Vazon Bay
Kings Mills
St Peter Port
Castle Cornet
Lihou
Rocquaine Bay
Fort Grey
Pleinmont Pt
St Saviour
German Underground Hospital
GUERNSEY
German Occupation Museum
St Martin
Sausmarez Manor
Jerbourg Pt
Herm
Shell Beach
Jethou
Sark
La Seigneurie
Brecqhou
Little Sark
hours
Poole 2½
Portsmouth 6½
Weymouth 2-2¼
Jersey 1
CHANNEL ISLANDS location map
Alderney
Guernsey
Herm
Sark
Jersey
JERSEY
Plémont Pt
Grosnez (ruins)
Greve de Lecq Bay
Bouley Bay
St John
Trinity
Rozel
St Mary
St Ouen
La Mielle de Morville
St Ouen's Bay
Carrefour Selous
St Peter
Jersey War Tunnels
St Martin
St Catherine's Bay
Mt Orgueil Castle
Gorey
Five Oaks
Maufant
Hougue Bie
St Saviour
Beaumont
St Aubin's Bay
St Brelade
St Aubin
La Cotte
Elizabeth
People's Park
ST HELIER
St Clement
Grouville
La Rocque Pt
Noirmont Pt
hours
Guernsey 1
Poole 3-3¾
Portsmouth 10
St Malo 1¼
Weymouth 3¼-3½

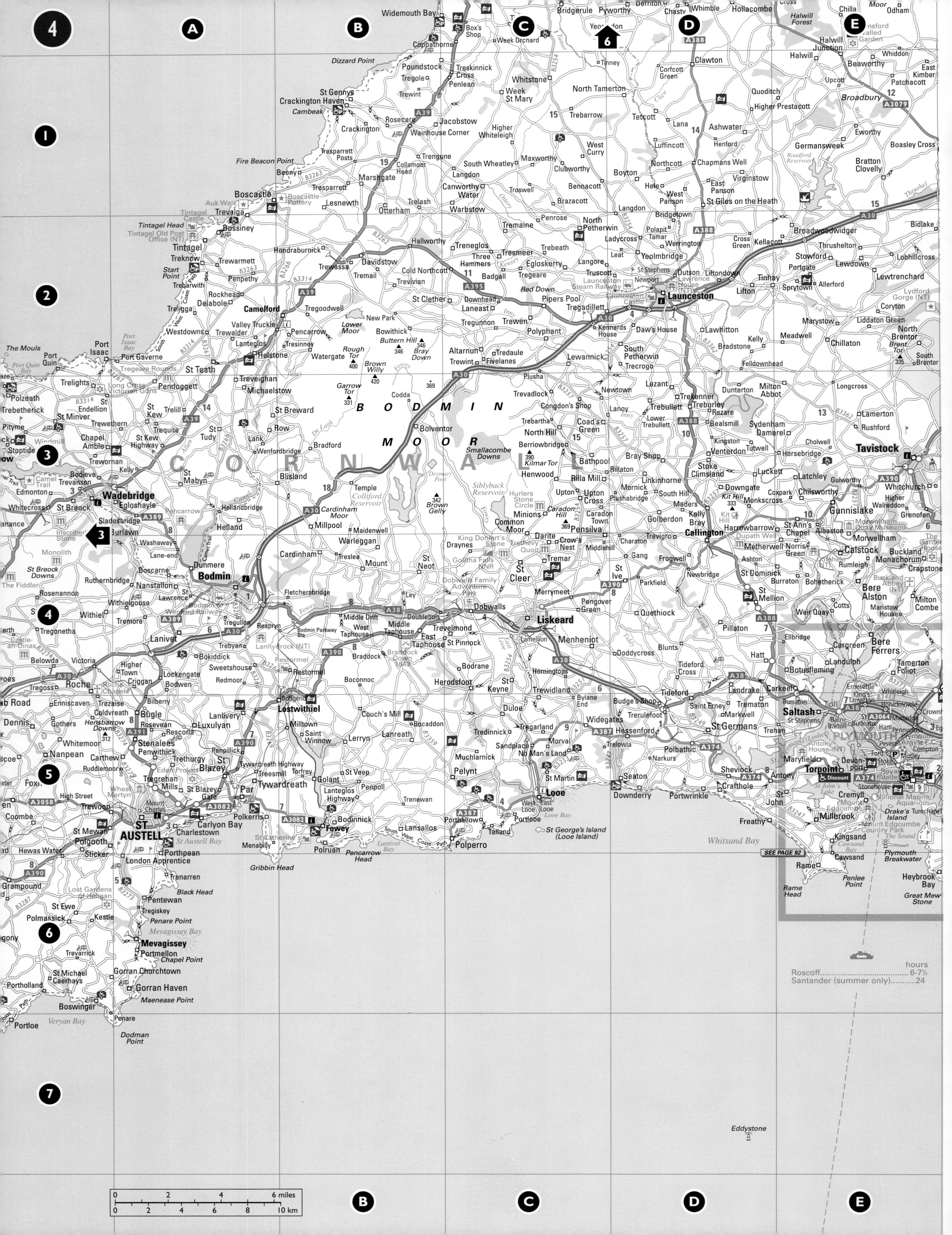

4
A
B
C
D
E
1
2
3
4
5
6
7
Widemouth Bay
Box's Shop
Coppathorne
Bridgerule
Pyworthy
Derriton
Chasty
Whimble
Holsworthy
Hollacombe
Halwill Forest
Chilla
Moor
Odham
Week Orchard
Halwill Junction
Halwill
Beaworthy
Whiddon
East Kimber
Patchacott
Upcott
Dizzard Point
Poundstock
Treskinnick Cross
Tregole
Penlean
Trewint
Whitstone
Week St Mary
North Tamerton
Clawton
Corfcott Green
Quoditch
Higher Prestacott
Broadbury
A3079
St Gennys
Crackington Haven
Cambeak
Rosecare
Jacobstow
Wainhouse Corner
Crackington
Higher Whiteleigh
Trebarrow
Tetcott
Lana
Ashwater
Henford
Germansweek
Eworthy
Boasley Cross
Roadford Reservoir
Bratton Clovelly
West Curry
Luffincott
Northcott
Chapmans Well
Virginstow
Fire Beacon Point
Beeny
Tresparrett Posts
Trengune
Collamoor Head
South Wheatley
Maxworthy
Clubworthy
Langdon
Canworthy Water
Boyton
Hele
East Panson
West Panson
St Giles on the Heath
Boscastle
Boscastle Pottery
Tresparrett
Marshgate
Lesnewth
Trelash
Otterham
Warbstow
Troswell
Bennacott
Brazacott
Langdon
Bridgetown
Thrushel
Auk Walk
Tintagel Castle
Trevalga
Bossiney
Tintagel Head
Tintagel Old Post Office (NT)
Tintagel
Treknow
Start Point
Trebarwith
Trewarmett
Penpethy
Rockhead
Delabole
Treligga
Hendraburnick
Hallworthy
Treneglos
Tremaine
Penrose
North Petherwin
Polapit Tamar
Werrington
Ladycross
Yeolmbridge
Broadwoodwidger
Bidlake
Kellacott
Cross Green
Thrushelton
Stowford
Portgate
Lewdown
Lobhillcross
Allerford
Lewtrenchard
Davidstow
Trewassa
Tremail
Cold Northcott
Trevivian
Three Hammers
Tresmeer
Badgall
Trebeath
Egloskerry
Tregeare
Langore
Leat
Truscott
St Stephens
Launceston Steam Railway
Newport
Launceston Castle
Launceston
Dutson
Lawrence House (NT)
Liftondown
Lifton
Tinhay
Sprytown
Lydford Gorge (NT)
Coryton
Camelford
Tregoodwell
St Clether
Downhead
Laneast
Red Down
Pipers Pool
Tregadillett
Kennards House
Daw's House
Lawhitton
Marystow
Liddaton Green
North Brentor
Brent Tor
South Brentor
The Mouls
Port Quin
Port Quin Bay
Port Isaac
Port Isaac Bay
Port Gaverne
Westdowns
Valley Truckle
Trewalder
Lanteglos
Helstone
Pencarrow
Tresinney
Watergate
Lower Moor
Rough Tor
New Park
Bowithick
Buttern Hill
Bray Down
Tregunnon
Treween
Polyphant
Altarnun
Trewint
Tredaule
Fivelanes
Lewannick
South Petherwin
Trecrogo
Bradstone
Kelly
Meadwell
Chillaton
Felldownhead
Trelights
Long Cross Victorian Gdns
Tregeare Rounds
St Teath
Treveighan
Michaelstow
Brown Willy
Garrow Tor
Codda
Plusha
Newtown
Lezant
Trekenner
Treburley
Dunterton
Milton Abbot
Longcross
Polzeath
Trebetherick
St Endellion
St Minver
Pityme
Trewethern
Pendoggett
St Kew
Trelill
Trequite
St Breward
B O D M I N
M O O R
Bolventor
Trevadlock
Congdon's Shop
Lanoy
Trebullett
Lower Trebullett
Rezare
Bealsmill
Sydenham Damerel
Lamerton
Rushford
Stoptide
Chapel Amble
St Kew Highway
St Tudy
Lank
Row
Wenfordbridge
Bradford
Smallacombe Downs
Trebartha
North Hill
Coad's Green
Berriowbridge
Kilmar Tor
Kingston
Venterdon
Tutwell
Cholwell
Horsebridge
Tavistock
Treworder
Kelly
Bodieve
Camel Trail
Trevanson
Edmonton
St Mabyn
C O R N W A L L
Blisland
Dozmary Pool
Siblyback Reservoir
Henwood
Bathpool
Rillaton
Bray Shop
Linkinhorne
Stoke Climsland
Luckett
Latchley
Gulworthy
Whitchurch
Wadebridge
Egloshayle
Whitecross
St Breock
Sladesbridge
Burlawn
Pencarrow
Hellandbridge
Temple
Colliford Reservoir
Cardinham Moor
Brown Gelly
Hurlers Stone Circle
Upton
Upton Cross
Rilla Mill
Mornick
Plushabridge
South Hill
Downgate
Kit Hill
Coxpark
Chilsworthy
Monkscross
Higher Walreddon
Gunnislake
Grenofen
Inscribed Stone
Helland
Millpool
Maidenwell
Minions
Caradon Hill
Caradon Town
Common Moor
Pensilva
Golberdon
Maders
Kelly Bray
Callington
Kit Hill CP
Harrowbarrow
St Ann's Chapel
Albaston
Morwellham Quay Museum
Morwellham
Monolith
Washaway
Lane-end
Camel Trail
Cardinham
Warleggan
Treslea
Mount
King Doniert's Stone
Draynes
Trethevy Quoit
Darite
Crow's Nest
Middlehill
Charaton
Trevigro
Dupath Well
Metherwell
Norris Green
Calstock
Buckland Monachorum
St Breock Downs
Boscarne
Dunmere
Bodmin
St Neot
Golitha Falls NNR
Tremar
St Cleer
Gang
Frogwell
Ashton
Cotehele (NT)
Rumleigh
Crapstone
The Fiddler
Ruthernbridge
Nanstallon
St Lawrence
Fletchersbridge
Dobwalls Family Adventure Park
St Ive
Parkfield
Newbridge
St Dominick
Burraton
Bohetherick
Buckland Abbey (NT)
Rosenannon
Withielgoose
Bodmin & Wenford Railway
Ley
Merrymeet
Pengover Green
St Mellion
Bere Alston
Milton Combe
Withiel
Tregonetha
Tremore
Lanivet
Middle Drift
Respryn
Bodmin Parkway Sta
West Taphouse
Middle Taphouse
Doublebois
Dobwalls
Liskeard
Quethiock
Weir Quay
Cotts
Maristow House
Trebyan
Tregullon
Lanhydrock (NT)
East Taphouse
Trevelmond
St Pinnock
Lamellion
Menheniot
Pillaton
Blunts
Ellbridge
Cargreen
Bere Ferrers
Belowda
Victoria
Bokiddick
Braddock
Braddock Down 1643
Restormel
Bodrane
Doddycross
Hatt
Landulph
Tamerton Foliot
Higher Town
Sweetshouse
Redmoor
Restormel
Boconnoc
Herodsfoot
Hornningtops
Tideford Cross
Botusfleming
Tregoss
Roche
Roche Chapel
Criggan
Lockengate
Bodwen
Lostwithiel
Bridgend
St Keyne
Trewidland
Bylan End
Tideford
Landrake
Carkeel
Whitleigh
Enniscaven
Treziase
Coldvreath
Bilberry
Bugle
Lanlivery
Couch's Mill
Duloe
Budge's Shop
Saint Erney
Trematon
Saltash
Burraton
Dennis
Gothers
Hensbarrow Downs
Rosevean
Luxulyan
Milltown
Saint Winnow
Lerryn
Lanreath
Bocaddon
Tredinnick
Tregarland
Widegates
Trerulefoot
Hessenford
St Germans
Trehan
St Stephens
Whitemoor
Stenalees
Penwithick
Rescorla
Tywardreath Highway
Treesmill
Torfrey
Sandplace
Morval
No Man's Land
Polbathic
Narkurs
Antony House (NT)
Maryfield
Devonport
Stoke
Plymouth
Nanpean
Carthew
Trethurgy
Penpillick
St Blazey
Tywardreath
Golant
St Veep
Muchlarnick
Pelynt
Trelowia
Seaton
Sheviock
Crafthole
Antony
Torpoint
Ruddlemoor
Eden Project
Tregrehan Mills
St Blazey Gate
Par
Lanteglos Highway
Penpoll
St Martin
Looe
Downderry
Portwrinkle
Cremyll
Mount Edgcumbe
Millbrook
National Marine Aquarium
Drake's Island
High Street
Trewoon
Wheal Martyn
Mount Charles
Carlyon Bay
Polkerris
Bodinnick
Trenewan
Porthallow
West Looe
East Looe
Looe Bay
Portlooe
St John
Freathy
Mount Edgcumbe Country Park
The Sound
St Mewan
St Austell
Charlestown
St Austell Bay
St Catherine's
Fowey
Lansallos
Talland
St George's Island (Looe Island)
Whitsand Bay
Kingsand
Cawsand Bay
Cawsand
Hewas Water
Polgooth
Sticker
Porthpean
Menabilly
Polruan
Pencarrow Head
Lantivet Bay
South West Coast Path
Polperro
SEE PAGE 92
Plymouth Breakwater
Rame
Rame Head
Penlee Point
Heybrook Bay
Great Mew Stone
London Apprentice
Gribbin Head
Trenarren
Grampound
Lost Gardens of Heligan
Black Head
Pentewan
St Ewe
Tregiskey
Polmassick
Kestle
Penare Point
Mevagissey Bay
Mevagissey
Portmellon
Chapel Point
Trevarrick
Gorran Churchtown
St Michael Caerhays
Gorran Haven
Portholland
Maenease Point
Boswinger
Veryan Bay
Portloe
Penare
Dodman Point
hours
Roscoff.. 6-7½
Santander (summer only)...........24
Eddystone
0 2 4 6 miles
0 2 4 6 8 10 km
A30
A39
A38
A388
A389
A390
A391
A395
A386
A3058
A3082
A374
A387
A3064
B3254
B3257
B3263
B3266
B3314
B3267
B3262
B3268
B3269
B3273
B3287
B3359
B3247
B3252
B3253
B3362

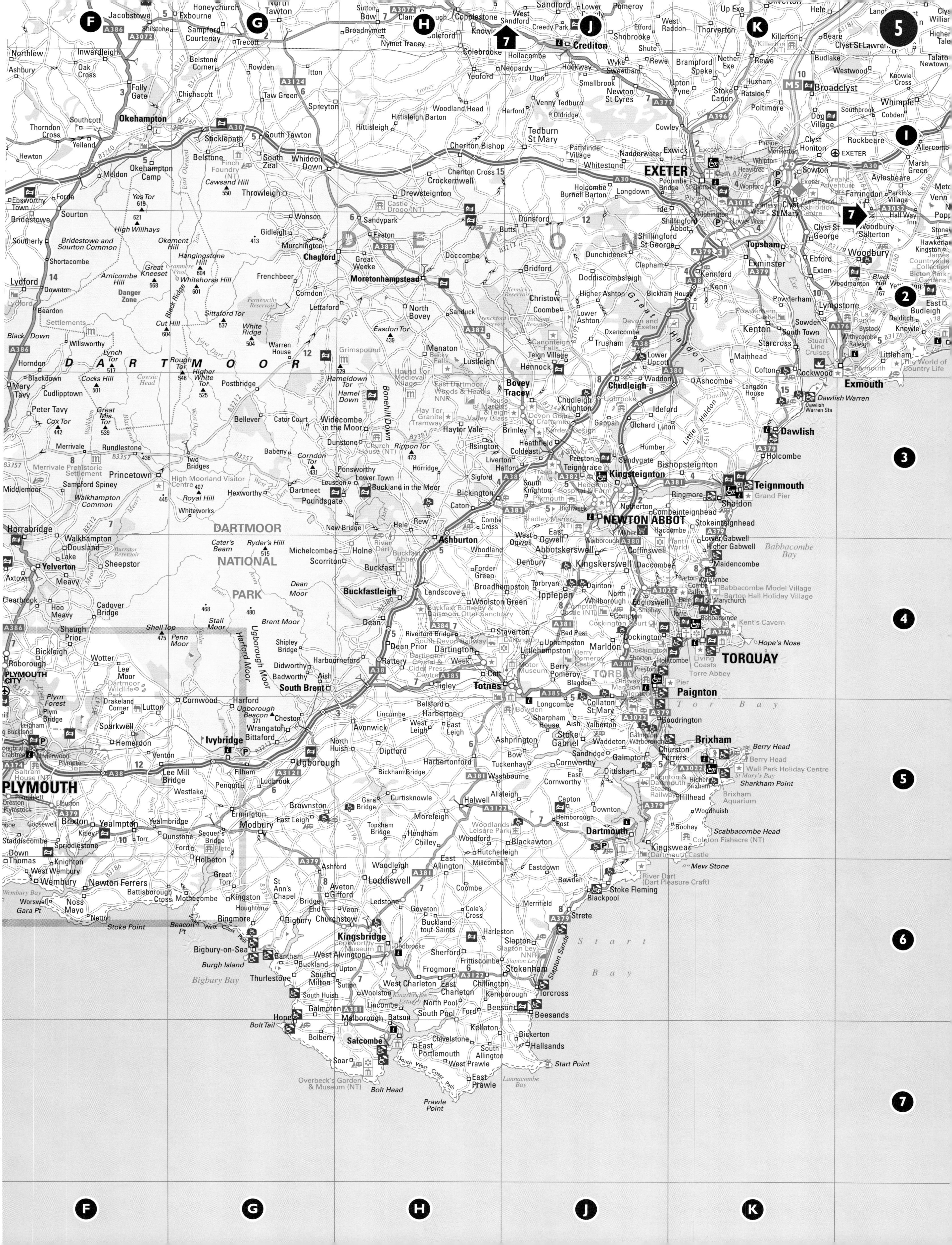

5
F
G
H
J
K
1
2
3
4
5
6
7
Jacobstowe
Honeychurch
Exbourne
North Tawton
Sampford Courtenay
Shilstone
Trecott
Sutton
Bow
Broadnymett
Nymet Tracey
Clannaborough
Coleford
Copplestone
West Sandford
Knowle
Colebrooke
Hollacombe
Sandford
Lower Creedy
Creedy Park
Crediton
Pomeroy
Efford
Shobrooke
West Raddon
Thorverton
Up Exe
Killerton (NT)
Hele
Beare
Clyst St Lawrence
Northlew
Ashbury
Inwardleigh
Oak Cross
Folly Gate
Belstone Corner
Rowden
Itton
Chichacott
Taw Green
Spreyton
Yeoford
Neopardy
Uton
Hookway
Wyke
Sweetham
Shute
Rewe
Brampford Speke
Nether Exe
Upton Pyne
Huxham
Stoke Canon
Ratsloe
Budlake
Westwood
Knowle Cross
Broadclyst
Poltimore
Whimple
Smallbrook
Newton St Cyres
Woodland Head
Hittisleigh Barton
Hittisleigh
Harford
Venny Tedburn
Oldridge
Tedburn St Mary
Cowley
Southbrook
Dog Village
Cobden
Rockbeare
Clyst Honiton
EXETER
Thorndon Cross
Southcott
Okehampton
Yelland
Sticklepath
South Tawton
South Zeal
Whiddon Down
Hewton
Meldon
Okehampton Camp
Belstone
Finch Foundry (NT)
Cawsand Hill
Cheriton Bishop
Cheriton Cross
Crockernwell
Pathfinder Village
Whitestone
Nadderwater
Exwick
Pinhoe
Monkerton
Allercombe
Marsh Green
Aylesbeare
Sowton
Ebsworthy Town
Forda
Bridestowe
Sourton
Yes Tor
High Willhays
Throwleigh
Drewsteignton
Castle Drogo (NT)
Holcombe Burnell Barton
Longdown
Pocombe Bridge
St Thomas
Heavitree
Wonford
Farringdon
Perkin's Village
Clyst St Mary
Westpoint Exhibition Centre
Woodbury Salterton
Half Way Inn
Southerly
Bridestowe and Sourton Common
Okement Hill
Wonson
Gidleigh
Sandypark
Easton
Murchington
Chagford
DEVON
Dunsford
Butts
Ide
Shillingford Abbot
Shillingford St George
Alphington
Topsham
Clyst St George
Woodbury
Hangingstone Hill
Great Kneeset
Cranmere Pool
Whitehorse Hill
Great Weeke
Doccombe
Bridford
Dunchideock
Clapham
Exminster
Ebford
Exton
Shortacombe
Lydford
Downton
Amicombe Hill
Danger Zone
Black Ridge
Frenchbeer
Moretonhampstead
Kennick Reservoir
Christow
Doddiscombsleigh
Higher Ashton
Bickham House
Kennford
Kenn
Woodmanton
Black Hill
Lympstone
Beardon
Settlements
Sittaford Tor
Fernworthy Reservoir
Corndon
Lettaford
North Bovey
Sanduck
Trenchford Reservoir
Tottiford Reservoir
Coombe
Lower Ashton
Devon and Exeter
Powderham Castle
Powderham
Sowden
A La Ronde
Dalditch
Budleigh
Black Down
Cut Hill
White Ridge
Easdon Tor
Oxencombe
Trusham
Kenton
South Town
Bystock
Knowle
Willsworthy
Warren House
Grimspound
Manaton
Becky Falls
Lustleigh
Canonteign Falls
Teign Village
Starcross
Stuart Line Cruises
Withycombe Raleigh
Littleham
The World of Country Life
Horndon
Lynch Tor
Rough Tor
DARTMOOR
Hound Tor Medieval Village
Hennock
Lower Upcott
Mamhead
Cofton
Cockwood
Exmouth
Mary Tavy
Blackdown
Cocks Hill
Higher White Tor
Postbridge
Hameldown Tor
Hamel Down
Bonehill Down
East Dartmoor Woods & Heaths NNR
Bovey Tracey
Chudleigh
Waddon
Ashcombe
Langdon House
Dawlish Warren
Cudlipptown
Cowsic Head
Peter Tavy
Great Mis Tor
Cox Tor
Bellever
Cator Court
Widecombe in the Moor
Hay Tor Granite Tramway
Haytor Vale
House of Marbles
Valley Glass
Devon Guild of Craftsmen
Chudleigh Knighton
Ugbrooke
Gappah
Olchard
Ideford
Luton
Little Haldon
Dawlish
Merrivale
Rundlestone
Dunstone
Church House (NT)
Rippon Tor
Brimley
Heathfield
Ilsington
Coldeast
Humber
Holcombe
Merrivale Prehistoric Settlement
Princetown
Two Bridges
Babeny
Corndon Tor
Liverton
Halford
Stover
Preston
Sandygate
Bishopsteignton
Middlemoor
Sampford Spiney
High Moorland Visitor Centre
Royal Hill
Hexworthy
Dartmeet
Poundsgate
Ponsworthy
Lower Town
Leusdon
Buckland in the Moor
Horridge
Sigford
Teigngrace
Kingsteignton
Teignmouth
Shaldon
Grand Pier
Ringmore
Walkhampton Common
Whiteworks
South Knighton
Hedgehog Hospital & Farm
Bickington
Caton
Netherton
Combeinteignhead
Horrabridge
Walkhampton
Dousland
Burrator Reservoir
DARTMOOR NATIONAL PARK
Cater's Beam
Ryder's Hill
New Bridge
Hele
Rew
Ashburton
Combe Cross
Bradley Manor (NT)
NEWTON ABBOT
Highweek
Stokeinteignhead
Lake
Yelverton
Sheepstor
Michelcombe
Holne
River Dart
Scorriton
Buckfast Abbey
Buckfast
Woodland
West Ogwell
East Ogwell
Abbotskerswell
Haccombe
Milber
Wolborough
Plant World
Coffinswell
Lower Gabwell
Higher Gabwell
Babbacombe Bay
Maidencombe
Axtown
Meavy
Dean Moor
Buckfastleigh
Denbury
Forder Green
Broadhempston
Torbryan
Dainton
Kingskerswell
Daccombe
Clearbrook
Hoo Meavy
Cadover Bridge
PARK
Landscove
Woolston Green
Ipplepen
North Whilborough
Edginswell
Barton
Watcombe
Babbacombe Model Village
Barton Hall Holiday Village
St Marychurch
Shaugh Prior
Shell Top
Penn Moor
Stall Moor
Brent Moor
Dean
Buckfast Butterfly & Dartmoor Otter Sanctuary
Staverton
Compton Castle (NT)
Compton
Shiphay
Kent's Cavern
Cockington Court
Cockington
Red Post
Bickleigh
Harford Moor
Ugborough Moor
Shipley Bridge
Riverford Bridge
South Devon Railway
Dartington
Dean Prior
Rattery
Week
Littlehempston
Uphempston
Marlborough
Berry Pomeroy Castle
Hope's Nose
TORQUAY
Roborough
Wotter
Lee Moor
Didworthy
Harbourneford
Berry Pomeroy
Motor Museum
Living Coasts
Torre Abbey
PLYMOUTH CITY
Dartmoor Wildlife Park
Badworthy
Aish
Dartington Crystal & Cider Press Centre
Tigley
Cott
Totnes
Blagdon
TORBAY
Oldway Mansion
Paignton
Pier
Plym Forest
Cornwood
Drakeland Corner
Lutton
Harford
Ugborough Beacon
South Brent
Belsford
Harberton
Bowden
Longcombe
Collaton St Mary
Tor Bay
Plym Bridge
Sparkwell
Cheston
Wrangaton
Bittaford
Lincombe
West Leigh
East Leigh
Avonwick
Sharpham House
Aish
Yalberton
Goodrington
Leigham
Hemerdon
Ivybridge
North Huish
Diptford
Ashprington
Bow
Stoke Gabriel
Waddeton
Galmpton Warborough
Churston Ferrers
Brixham
Berry Head
Longbridge
Underwood
Plympton
Venton
Filham
Ugborough
Harbertonford
Tuckenhay
Cornworthy
Sandridge
Galmpton
Wall Park Holiday Centre
St Mary's Bay
Saltram House (NT)
Lee Mill Bridge
Penquit
Ludbrook
Bickham Bridge
Washbourne
East Cornworthy
Dittisham
Paignton & Dartmouth Steam Railway
Higher Brixham
Sharkham Point
PLYMOUTH
Westlake
Curtisknowle
Allaleigh
Capton
Hillhead
Brixham Aquarium
Oreston
Plymstock
Elburton
Brownston
Gara Bridge
Halwell
Downton
Woodhuish
Hooe
Goosewell
Brixton
Yealmpton
Yealmbridge
Ermington
East Leigh
Modbury
Topsham Bridge
Moreleigh
Woodlands Leisure Park
Hemborough Post
Dartmouth
Boohay
Scabbacombe Head
Staddiscombe
Kitley
Torr
Dunstone
Sequer's Bridge
Flete
Hendham
Chilley
Woodford
Blackawton
Coleton Fishacre (NT)
Kingswear
Dartmouth Castle
Down Thomas
Spriddlestone
Ford
Holbeton
Knighton
Ashford
Hutcheleigh
Millcombe
Eastdown
Mew Stone
West Wembury
Wembury
Newton Ferrers
Great Torr
Woodleigh
East Allington
Bowden
River Dart (Dart Pleasure Craft)
Wembury Bay
Worswell
Noss Mayo
Gara Pt
Battisborough Cross
Mothecombe
Kingston
St Ann's Chapel
Aveton Gifford
Loddiswell
Coombe
Stoke Fleming
Blackpool
Houghton
Bridge End
Venn
Ledstone
Goveton
Cole's Cross
Merrifield
Strete
Netton
Stoke Point
Beacon Pt
Bingmore
Bigbury
Churchstow
Buckland-tout-Saints
Harleston
South West Coast Path
Kingsbridge
Cookworthy Museum
Dodbrooke
Slapton
Slapton Ley NNR
Start Bay
Bigbury-on-Sea
Burgh Island
Bantham
West Alvington
Buckland
Upton
South Milton
Sherford
Frittiscombe
Frogmore
Stokenham
Slapton Sands
Bigbury Bay
Thurlestone
Sutton
West Charleton
East Charleton
Chillington
South Huish
Woolston
Kingsbridge Estuary
North Pool
Kernborough
Torcross
Galmpton
Lincombe
Malborough
Batson
South Pool
Ford
Beeson
Beesands
Hope
Bolt Tail
Kellaton
Bolberry
Salcombe
Chivelstone
Bickerton
Hallsands
East Portlemouth
South Allington
Start Point
Soar
West Prawle
East Prawle
Lannacombe Beach
Overbeck's Garden & Museum (NT)
Bolt Head
Prawle Point

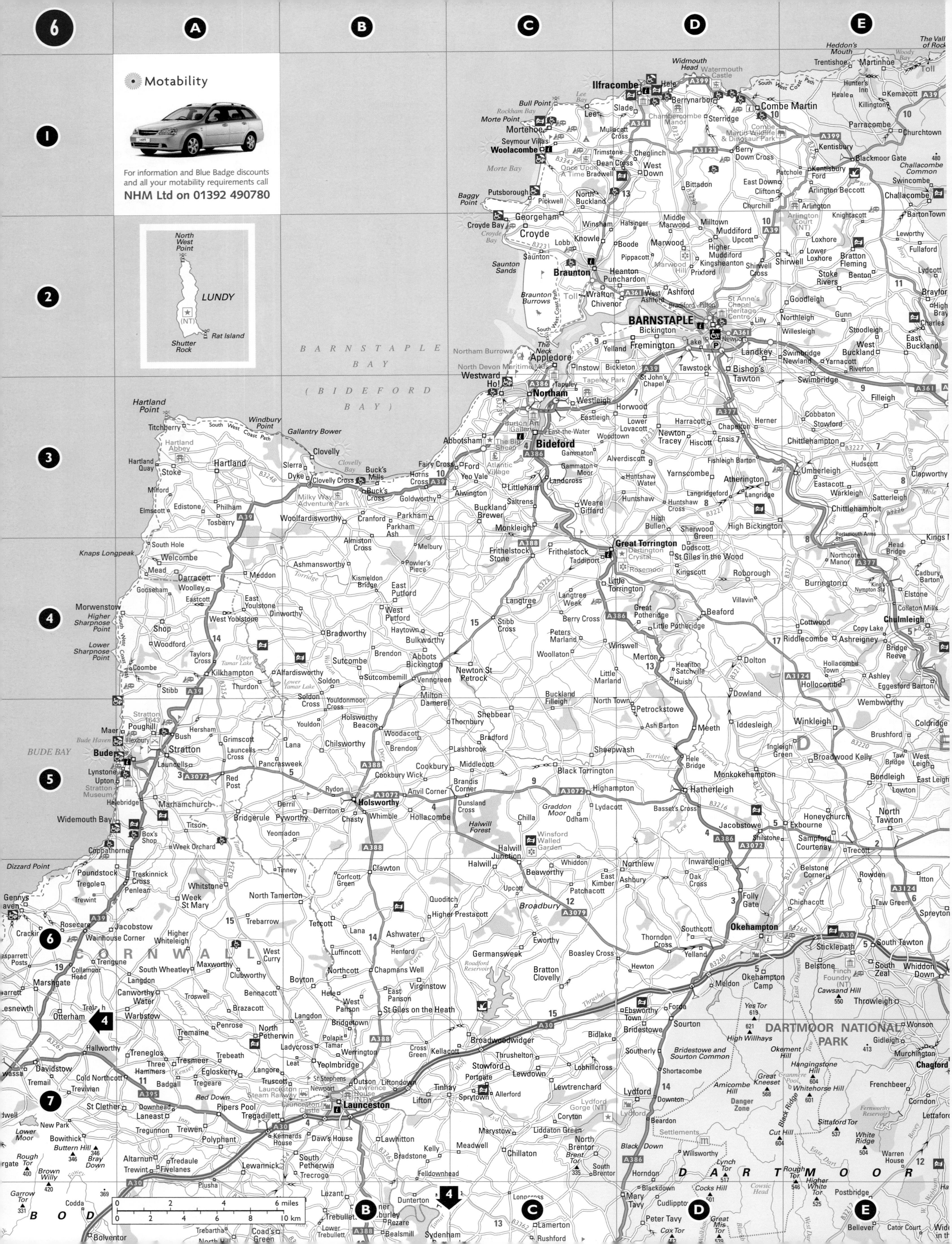

6
A
B
C
D
E
1
2
3
4
5
6
7
Motability
For information and Blue Badge discounts and all your motability requirements call
NHM Ltd on 01392 490780
North West Point
LUNDY
Rat Island
Shutter Rock
BARNSTAPLE BAY
(BIDEFORD BAY)
BUDE BAY
Ilfracombe
Combe Martin
Woolacombe
Mortehoe
Morte Point
Morte Bay
Croyde
Braunton
BARNSTAPLE
Fremington
Appledore
Westward Ho!
Northam
Bideford
Hartland Point
Hartland
Clovelly
Great Torrington
Holsworthy
Bude
Stratton
Hatherleigh
Okehampton
Launceston
Chulmleigh
South Molton
Lydford
Chagford
Widemouth Bay
Dizzard Point
CORNWALL
DARTMOOR NATIONAL PARK
DARTMOOR
Yes Tor
High Willhays
Mary Tavy
Peter Tavy
Sydenham
BODMIN
0 2 4 6 miles
0 2 4 6 8 10 km

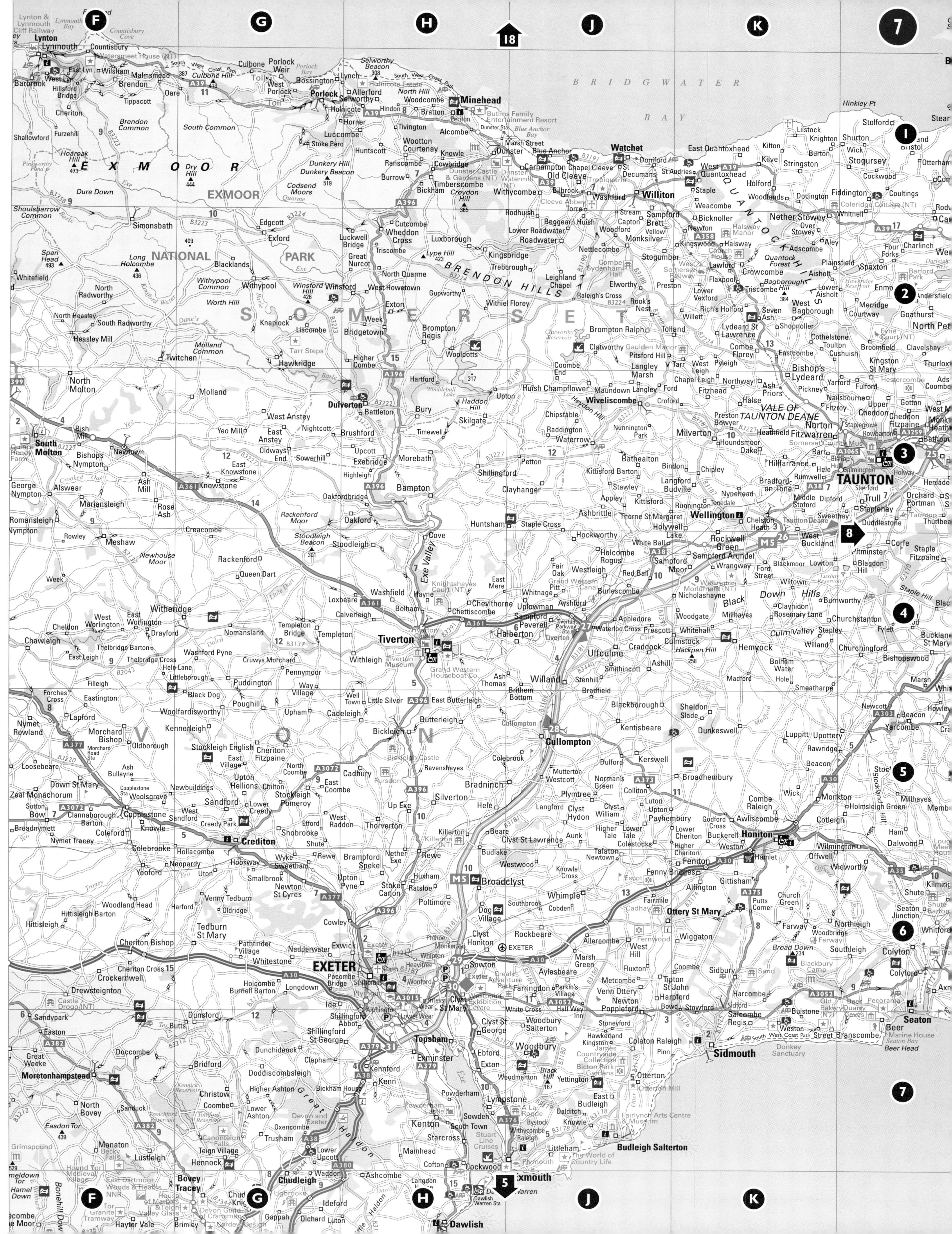
F
G
H
18
J
K
7
Lynton & Lynmouth Cliff Railway
Lynmouth Bay
Countisbury Cove
Lynton
Lynmouth
Countisbury
Watersmeet House (NT)
Barbrook
East Lyn
West Lyn
Wilsham
Malmsmead
Brendon
Hillsford Bridge
Tippacott
Oare
Culbone Hill
Culbone
Porlock Weir
Porlock Bay
Porlock
Bossington
West Porlock
Selworthy Beacon
Lynch
Holnicote Estate
Allerford
Selworthy
Holnicote
Horner
North Hill
Minehead
Butlins Family Entertainment Resort
Dunster Sta
Blue Anchor Bay
Woodcombe
Hindon
Bratton
Alcombe
Tivington
Luccombe
Stoke Pero
Cheriton
Furzehill
Shallowford
Brendon Common
South Common
Hoaroak Hill
Pinkworthy Pond
EXMOOR
Dry Hill
EXMOOR
Dure Down
Wootton Courtenay
Huntscott
Ranscombe
Dunkery Hill
Dunkery Beacon
Codsend Moors
Quarme
Knowle
Cowbridge
Timberscombe
Burrow
Dunster
Marsh Street
Blue Anchor
Dunster Castle & Gardens (NT)
Dunster Watermill (NT)
Croydon Hill
Bickham
Withycombe
Carhampton
Chapel Cleeve
Old Cleeve
Bilbrook
Watchet
Doniford
St Decumans
Washford
Cleeve Abbey
Torre
Tropiquaria
Williton
BRIDGWATER BAY
Hinkley Pt
Stolford
Lilstock
Knighton
Shurton
Burton
Wick
Kilton
Kilve
Stringston
Stogursey
East Quantoxhead
West Quantoxhead
St Audries
Staple
Weacombe
Holford
Woodlands
Dodington
Fiddington
Cockwood
Coultings
Coleridge Cottage (NT)
Nether Stowey
Over Stowey
Whitnell
Bicknoller
Halsway Manor
Sampford Brett
Capton
Stream
Yellow
Monksilver
Woodford
Newton
Kingswood
Halsway
Nettlecombe
Church House
Stogumber
Lawford
Crowcombe
QUANTOCK HILLS
Quantock Forest
Bagborough Hill
Triscombe
Adscombe
Aley
Four Forks
Charlinch
Plainsfield
Spaxton
Aisholt
Lower Aisholt
Hawkridge Reservoir
Durleigh Reservoir
Barford Park
Enmore
Merridge
Courtway
Goathurst
Andersfield
North Petherton
Shoulsbarrow Common
Simonsbath
Edgcott
Exford
Cutcombe
Wheddon Cross
Luxborough
Luckwell Bridge
Triscombe
Lype Hill
Kingsbridge
Treborough
Rodhuish
Beggearn Huish
Lower Roadwater
Roadwater
Combe Sydenham Hall
West Somerset Railway
Flaxpool
Elworthy
Leighland Chapel
Raleigh's Cross
Rook's Nest
Lower Vexford
Preston
Seven Ash
Rich's Holford
Willett
West Bagborough
Shopnoller
Span Head
Long Holcombe
NATIONAL
PARK
Blacklands
Great Nurcot
North Quarme
BRENDON HILLS
Whitefield
North Radworthy
Withypool Common
Withypool
Winsford Hill
Winsford
West Howetown
Gupworthy
Withiel Florey
Worth Hill
North Heasley
South Radworthy
Heasley Mill
SOMERSET
Exton
Week
Knaplock
Liscombe
Bridgetown
Brompton Regis
Clatworthy Reservoir
Brompton Ralph
Tolland
Lydeard St Lawrence
Cothelstone
Toulton
Cushuish
Broomfield
Clavelshay
Fyne Court (NT)
Twitchen
Molland Common
Tarr Steps
Hawkridge
Higher Combe
Woolcotts
Clatworthy
Gaulden Manor
Pitsford Hill
Combe Florey
Eastcombe
Kingston St Mary
Thurloxton
North Molton
Molland
Hartford
Wimbleball Lake
Haddon Hill
Upton
Coombe End
Huish Champflower
Maundown
Langley Marsh
Langley
Tarr
West Leigh
Chapel Leigh
Pyleigh
Northway
Bishop's Lydeard
Yarford
Fulford
Hestercombe
Dulverton
Battleton
Bury
Skilgate
Heydon Hill
Wiveliscombe
Croford
Fitzhead
Ash Priors
Pickney
Halse
Nailsbourne
Fitzroy
Upper Cheddon
Cheddon Fitzpaine
VALE OF TAUNTON DEANE
Preston Bowyer
Norton Fitzwarren
Heathfield
Staplegrove
Rowbarton
Bathpool
Monkton Heathfield
South Molton
Bish Mill
West Anstey
East Anstey
Yeo Mill
Nightcott
Brushford
Timewell
Chipstable
Raddington
Waterrow
Nunnington Park
Milverton
Houndsmoor
Oake
Somerset County Museum
Quince Honey Farm
Bishops Nympton
Newtown
Oldways End
Sowerhill
Upcott
Exebridge
Morebath
Petton
Shillingford
Kittisford Barton
Bathealton
Bindon
Chipley
Hillfarrance
Barr
Bishop's Hull
Galmington
Hele
Rumwell
TAUNTON
Holway
Henlade
Sherford
George Nympton
Alswear
East Knowstone
Ash Mill
Knowstone
Highleigh
Bampton
Clayhanger
Stawley
Langford Budville
Bradford-on-Tone
Nynehead
Middle Stoford
Dipford
Trull
Orchard Portman
Mariansleigh
Rose Ash
Oakfordbridge
Appley
Kittisford
Runnington
Tonedale
Staplehay
Romansleigh
Rackenford Moor
Oakford
Huntsham
Staple Cross
Ashbrittle
Thorne St Margaret
Wellington
Chelston Heath
Taunton Deane
Sweethay
Taunton Racecourse
Thurlbear
Duddlestone
Nympton
Rowley
Meshaw
Creacombe
Stoodleigh Beacon
Stoodleigh
Cove
Hockworthy
Holywell Lake
Rockwell Green
West Buckland
Corfe
Staple Fitzpaine
8
Newhouse Moor
Rackenford
Exe Valley
White Ball
Holcombe Rogus
Sampford Moor
Sampford Arundel
Wrangway
Blackmoor
Lowton
Pitminster
Blagdon Hill
Week
Queen Dart
Knightshayes Court (NT)
East Mere
Fair Oak
Westleigh
Grand Western Canal
Red Ball
Wellington Monument (NT)
Ford Street
Luxhay Reservoir
Witheridge
Washfield
Hayne
Bolham
Whitnage
Pitt
Burlescombe
Nicholashayne
Black Down Hills
Wiltown
Burnworthy
Staple Hill
Clayhidon
Rosemary Lane
West Worlington
East Worlington
Drayford
Loxbeare
Calverleigh
Chevithorne
Chettiscombe
Uplowman
Ayshford
Sampford Peverell
Tiverton Parkway Sta
Appledore
Woodgate
Millhayes
Churchstanton
Cheldon
Chawleigh
Nomansland
Templeton Bridge
Templeton
Tiverton
Tiverton Castle
Halberton
Waterloo Cross
Prescott
Whitehall
Culm Valley
Stapley
Fyfett
Buckland St Mary
Thelbridge Barton
Thelbridge Cross
East Leigh
Dalch
Washford Pyne
Cruwys Morchard
Withleigh
Tiverton Museum
Grand Western Houseboat Co.
Uffculme
Craddock
Culmstock
Hackpen Hill
Hemyock
Wellsland
Churchingford
Bishopswood
Hele Lane
Littleborough
Pennymoor
Filleigh
Puddington
Way Village
Ash Thomas
Willand
Smithincott
Ashill
Bolham Water
Hole
Madford
Smeatharpe
Marsh
Forches Cross
Eastington
Black Dog
Poughill
Well Town
Little Silver
East Butterleigh
Brithem Bottom
Stenhill
Bradfield
Sheldon
Blackborough
Slade
Nymet Rowland
Lapford
Woolfardisworthy
Kennerleigh
Upham
Cadeleigh
Butterleigh
Cullompton
Kentisbeare
Dunkeswell
Luppitt
Upottery
Newcott
Beacon
Yarcombe
Morchard Bishop
Morchard Road Sta
Oldborough
Stockleigh English
Cheriton Fitzpaine
Bickleigh
Bickleigh Castle
Colebrook
Rawridge
Loosebeare
Ash Bullayne
East Village
North Coombe
Cadbury
Fursdon
Ravenshayes
Kerswell
Dulford
Broadhembury
Beacon
Stockland
Down St Mary
Copplestone Sta
Woolsgrove
Newbuildings
Upton Hellions
Chilton
Stockleigh Pomeroy
East Coombe
Bradninch
Mutterton
Westcott
Norman's Green
Colliton
Zeal Monachorum
Copplestone
Sandford
Lower Creedy
Up Exe
Silverton
Hele
Plymtree
Luton
Combe Raleigh
Wick
Monkton
Millhayes
Holmsleigh Green
Sutton
Bow
Clannaborough Barton
West Sandford
Creedy Park
West Raddon
Langford
Clyst Hydon
Clyst William
Upton
Payhembury
Awliscombe
Cotleigh
Broadnymett
Coleford
Knowle
Shobrooke
Efford
Thorverton
Killerton
Killerton (NT)
Beare
Higher Tale
Lower Tale
Godford Cross
Buckerell
Lower Cheriton
Honiton
Ham
Nymet Tracey
Colebrooke
Crediton
Shute
Rewe
Clyst St Lawrence
Aunk
Colestocks
Weston
Dalwood
Hollacombe
Brampford Speke
Nether Exe
Bradninch
Budlake
Talaton
Newtown
Higher Cheriton
Wilmington
Yeoford
Neopardy
Hookway
Wyke
Sweetham
Westwood
Knowle Cross
Feniton
Hamlet
Offwell
Widworthy
Uton
Smallbrook
Newton St Cyres
Upton Pyne
Stoke Canon
Huxham
Rewe
Broadclyst
Fenny Bridges
Escot
Alfington
Gittisham
Venny Tedburn
Oldridge
Harford
Ratsloe
Poltimore
Whimple
Cobden
Fairmile
Putts Corner
Church Green
Kilmington
Woodland Head
Hittisleigh Barton
Cowley
Southbrook
Dog Village
Cadhay
Ottery St Mary
Shute Barton
Seaton Junction
Hittisleigh
Tedburn St Mary
Pathfinder Village
Exwick
Rockbeare
Fernwood
Wiggaton
Farway
Northleigh
Woodbridge
Whitford
Cheriton Bishop
Nadderwater
Whitestone
Exeter
Pinhoe
Monkerton
Clyst Honiton
EXETER
Allercombe
West Hill
Broad Down
Southleigh
Colyton
Blackbury Camp
Cheriton Cross
Crockernwell
Heavitree
Whipton
Sowton
Aylesbeare
Marsh Green
Fluxton
Sidbury
Colyford
EXETER
Pocombe Bridge
Holcombe Burnell Barton
Longdown
Wonford
Crealy Adventure Park
Farringdon
Perkin's Village
Metcombe
Tipton St John
Venn Ottery
Coombe
Sand
Harcombe
Axmouth
Drewsteignton
Castle Drogo (NT)
Ide
Alphington
Clyst St Mary
Westpoint Exhibition Centre
White Cross
Half Way Inn
Newton Poppleford
Harpford
Bowd
Stowford
Sidford
Bulstone
Old Beer Quarry Caves
Pecorama
Seaton
Sandypark
Dunsford
Butts
Shillingford Abbot
Lower Wear
Clyst St George
Woodbury Salterton
Stoneyford
Salcombe Regis
Weston
Beer
Marine House
Seaton Bay
Beer Head
Easton
Shillingford St George
Topsham
Hawkerland
Kingston
Colaton Raleigh
South West Coast Path
Street
Branscombe
Great Weeke
Doccombe
Dunchideock
Clapham
Exminster
Ebford
Woodbury
Countryside Collection
James Countryside Collection
Bicton Park Gardens
Pinn
Sidmouth
Donkey Sanctuary
Moretonhampstead
Bridford
Doddiscombsleigh
Kennford
Exton
Woodmanton
Black Hill
Kennick Reservoir
Christow
Higher Ashton
Great Haldon
Bickham House
Kenn
Powderham
Yettington
Otterton
Otterton Mill
7
North Bovey
Sanduck
Trenchford Reservoir
Tottiford Reservoir
Coombe
Lower Ashton
Devon and Exeter Racecourse
Powderham Castle
Lympstone
East Budleigh
Easdon Tor
Oxencombe
Kenton
Sowden
A La Ronde
Bystock
Dalditch
Knowle
Fairlynch Arts Centre & Museum
Manaton
Becky Falls
Canonteign Falls
Teign Village
Trusham
Lower Upcott
Starcross
South Town
Stuart Line Cruises
Withycombe Raleigh
Littleham
The World of Country Life
Budleigh Salterton
Grimspound
Lustleigh
Hennock
Mamhead
Cockwood
Exmouth
Hound Tor Medieval Village
Bovey Tracey
Chudleigh
Waddon
Ashcombe
Cofton
Dawlish Warren
Dawlish Warren Sta
East Dartmoor Woods & Heaths NNR
House of Marbles & Teign Valley Glass
Devon Guild of Craftsmen
Ugbrooke
Haldon
Langdon
Ideford
Luton
Gappah
Olchard
Brimley
Haytor Vale
Dawlish
Bonehill Down
F
G
H
5
J
K
1
2
3
4
5
6
7

8
A
B
C
D
E
1
2
3
4
5
6
7
19
7
QUANTOCK HILLS
SOMERSET
POLDEN HILLS
VALE OF TAUNTON DEANE
Black Down Hills
Culm Valley
DEVON
D
LYME BAY
Williton
Watchet
Nether Stowey
Bridgwater
BRIDGWATER
Glastonbury
Street
Wiveliscombe
Milverton
TAUNTON
Wellington
North Petherton
Langport
Somerton
Ilchester
Martock
YEOVIL
South Petherton
Ilminster
Crewkerne
Chard
Honiton
Axminster
Ottery St Mary
Sidmouth
Seaton
Beer
Lyme Regis
Charmouth
Bridport
Beaminster
Budleigh Salterton
Uffculme
Hemyock
Tiverton
Cullompton
Kentisbeare
Wootton Fitzpaine
West Bay
Abbotsbury
Chesil
Beer Head
Golden Cap
South West Coast Path
Marine Aquarium
The World of Country Life
0
2
4
6 miles
0
2
4
6
8
10 km
B
C
D
E

F
G
H
J
K
9
20
East Compton
East Town
Street on the Fosse
Prestleigh
Royal Bath & West Showground
Higher Alham
Weston Town
Wanstrow
Witham Friary
East Somerset Rly
Longleat House
Newbury
Horningsham
Pottle Street
Sutton Veny
Longbridge Deverill
Tytherington
Tytherington Hill
176
Heytesbury
Knook
Corton
Boyton
Codford St Peter
Codford St Mary
Sherrington
Stockton
Fisherton de la Mere
Deptford
Wylye
Bapton
Wylye Valley
Stonehenge
Winterbourne Stoke
Berwick St James
Steeple Langford
Hanging Langford
Little Langford
Serrington
Stapleford
Little Wishford
Great Wishford
Wilsford
Lake
Great Durnford
Upper Woodford
Heale House & Garden
Netton
Lower Woodford
Middle Woodford
Stoford
Winterbourne Dauntsey
Grovely Wood
South Newton
Old Sarum
Chilhampton
Fugglestone St Peter
Wilton Carpet Factory Shop
Ugford
Wilton
Wilton House
Bemerton
Stratford sub Castle
Netherhampton
Mompesson (NT)
West Harnham
Harnham
East Harnham
Salisbury
SALISBURY
Stoney Stratton
Batcombe
Westcombe
Upton Noble
Gare Hill
Hill Deverill
Brixton Deverill
Monkton Deverill
Maiden Bradley
Kingston Deverill
Keysley Down
Evercreech
Milton Clevedon
Ditcheat
Wraxall
Lamyatt
Bruton
North Brewham
South Brewham
Kilmington
Kilmington Common
Norton Ferris
White Sheet Hill
246
Stourhead (NT)
Stourton
Alhampton
Wyke Champflower
Cole
Hardway
Redlynch
Stoney Stoke
Pitcombe
Hadspen
Shepton Montague
Ansford
Castle Cary
Alford
Hadspen House
Barrow
Charlton Musgrove
Bratton Seymour
Penselwood
Southmarsh
Queen Oak
White Cross
Zeals
Mere
Burton
Wolverton
White Hill
West Knoyle
Upton
The Green
Barrow Street
East Knoyle
Hindon
Chicklade
Berwick St Leonard
Fonthill Bishop
Fonthill Gifford
Chilmark
Ridge
Teffont Magna
Teffont Evias
Lower Chicksgrove
Upper Chicksgrove
Philipps House (NT)
Dinton
Baverstock
Barford St Martin
Burcombe
Galhampton
North Barrow
Yarlington
Wincanton
Riding Gate
Leigh Common
Bayford
Stoke Trister
Cucklington
West Bourton
Bourton
Huntingford
Milton on Stour
Sedgehill
Pythouse
Newtown
Tisbury
East Hatch
Fovant
Compton Chamberlayne
North Cadbury
Sparkford
South Cadbury
Blackford
Compton Pauncefoot
Holton
Maperton
Lattiford
North Cheriton
Horsington Marsh
Buckhorn Weston
Peacemarsh
Bay
Gillingham
Coppleridge
Ham Common
Wyke
Madjeston
Motcombe
North End
West Hatch
Semley
Old Wardour Castle
Swallowcliffe
Ansty
Ansty Coombe
Sutton Mandeville
Donhead St Andrew
Donhead St Mary
White Sheet Hill
West End
Alvediston
Fifield Bavant
Mount Sorrel
Ebbesborne Wake
Broad Chalke
Mead End
Stoke Farthing
Bishopstone
Croucheston
Faulston
Stratford Tony
Coombe Bissett
Homington
Odstock
Odsto Down
Cadbury Castle
Weston Bampfylde
Sutton Montis
South Cheriton
Horsington
Charlton Horethorne
Corton Denham
Abbas Combe
Kington Magna
Higher Nyland
Lower Nyland
West Stour
East Stour
Knap Corner
Shaftesbury
Ludwell
Birdbush
Misselfore
Bowerchalke
Woodminton
Berwick St John
Stowell
Templecombe
Yenston
Henstridge
Henstridge Marsh
Gartell Light Railway
Fifehead Magdalen
Stour Provost
Stour Row
Guy's Marsh
Cann
West Melbury
Cann Common
Charlton
277
Rimpton
Sandford Orcas
Poyntington
Milborne Wick
Henstridge Bowden
Ash
Milborne Port
The Manor
Todber
Moorside
Margaret Marsh
Twyford
Melbury Abbas
Chase
Tollard Royal
New Town
Deanland
Woodyates
Pentridge
185
Pentridge Hill
Martin Drove End
Martin
East Martin
Tidpit
Whitsbury
Rockbourne
Wick Down
Rockbourne Down
Breamore
Upper Street
Oborne
Old Castle
Sherborne
Sherborne Castle
Goathill
Purse Caundle
Stalbridge
Stalbridge Weston
Marnhull
Walton Elm
Hartgrove
East Orchard
West Orchard
Compton Abbas
Bedchester
East Compton
Ashmore
Fontmell Magna
Larmer Tree Gardens
Woodcutts
Dean
Farnham
Sixpenny Handley
Tollard Farnham
North End
Rockbourne Roman Villa
Damerham
South End
Sandleheath
Fordingbridge
Haydon
North Wootton
Abbey
Alweston
Bishop's Caundle
Stourton Caundle
Hinton St Mary
Manston
Sturminster Newton
Hammoon
Fontmell Parva
Sutton Waldron
Iwerne Minster
Cranborne
Stubhampton
Minchington
Gussage St Andrew
Cashmoor
Monkton Up Wimborne
Boveridge
Cranborne Manor
Cranborne
Crendell
Ashford
Cripplestyle
Daggons
Alderholt
Bickton
Stuckton
Thornford
Folke
Longburton
Caundle Marsh
Lydlinch
Bagber
Fiddleford Manor
Fiddleford
Gold Hill
Child Okeford
Shroton (Iwerne Courtney)
Tarrant Gunville
Chettle
Chettle House
Beer Hackett
Lillington
Knighton
Woodbridge
Holwell
Sturminster Common
Fifehead Neville
Hanford
Hod Hill
143
Shillingstone
Tarrant Hinton
Pimperne Down
Gussage All Saints
Gussage St Michael
Wimborne St Giles
Edmondsham House
Edmondsham
Charing Cross
Cranborne Common
Harbridge Green
Sandhills
Pleck
King's Stag
Woodrow
Okeford Fitzpaine
Ash
Long Crichel
Church & Earthworks
Sutton Holms
Romford
Verwood
Harbridge
Ibsley
Holnest
Boys Hill
Crouch Hill
East Pulham
Kingston
Fifehead St Quintin
Belchalwell
Belchalwell Street
Stourpaine
Pimperne
Tarrant Launceston
Knowlton
Whitmore
Ringwood Forest
Hamlet
Leigh
Chetnole
Pulham
Glanvilles Wootton
West Pulham
Hazelbury Bryan
Droop
Ibberton
Durweston
Tarrant Monkton
Manswood
Moor Crichel
Horton Inn
Horton
Woodlands
Ellingham
Hermitage
Middlemarsh
Brockhampton Green
Woolland
Turnworth
Blandford Forum
Blandford Camp
Tarrant Rawston
Witchampton
Chalbury
Chalbury Common
Horton Common
Blashford
Lyon's Gate
Buckland Newton
Duntish
Mappowder
Stoke Wake
Bulbarrow Hill
Bryanston
Blandford St Mary
Langton Long Blandford
Tarrant Rushton
New Town
Hinton Martell
Holt Wood
Mannington
Three Legged Cross
Moors Valley Country Park
Ashley Heath
Ring
Hilfield
Sharnhill Green
Henley
Winterborne Stickland
Tarrant Keyneston
Hinton Parva
Gaunt's Common
Lower Mannington
Moors Valley Railway
Minterne Magna
Minterne
Minterne Parva
Batcombe
Ansty Cross
Higher Ansty
Hilton
Winterborne Houghton
Charlton on the Hill
Charlton Marshall
Tarrant Crawford
Badbury Rings (NT)
Stanbridge
Holt
Holt Heath
Highbury
St Leonards
St Ives
Crow
Up Cerne
Alton Pancras
Melcombe Bingham
Milton Abbas
Milton Abbey
Winterborne Clenston
Thornicombe
Spetisbury
Shapwick
Broom Hill
West Moors
Ameysford
Kingston
Frome St Quintin
Up Sydling
The Giant (NT)
Plush
Bingham's Melcombe
Higher Whatcombe
Charlton Down
Tadden
Hillbutts
Furzehill
Colehill
Stapehill Abbey Crafts & Gardens
Ferndown
Trickett's Cross
Avon Heath
Bisterne
Cerne Abbas
Winterborne Whitechurch
Kingston Lacy (NT)
Pamphill
Priest's House
Leigh
Canford Bottom
Knoll Gardens
Parley Common
Sydling St Nicholas
Piddletrenthide
White Lackington
Cheselbourne
Lower Street
Sturminster Marshall
Wimborne Minster
Little Canford
Hampreston
East Parley
Ripley
Maiden Newton
Nether Cerne
Piddlehinton
Puddletown Down
122
Dewlish
Mapperton
Almer
Oakley
Merley
Canford Magna
Longham
Dudsbury
Parley Cross
Avon
BOURNEMOUTH
Godmanstone
Dewlish
Milborne St Andrew
Winterborne Kingston
Winterborne Zelston
SEE PAGE 93
Corfe Mullen
East End
West Parley
Hurn
Sopley
Forston
Anderson
Lytchett Matravers
POOLE
Canford Heath
Parley Green
Alice in Wonderland Family Park
Muscliff
Holdenhurst
Winkton
Burton
Frampton
Athelhampton House
Puddletown
Burleston
Tolpuddle
Bere Regis
West Morden
Morden
East Morden
Hill View
Broadstone
Kinson
East Howe
West Howe
Grimstone
Stratton
Athelhampton
Affpuddle
Bloxworth
Whitefield
Beacon Hill
Wallisdown
Moordown
Muckleford
Charminster
Hardy's Cottage (NT)
Briantspuddle
Turners Puddle
Slepe
Lytchett Minster
Upton
Waterloo
Talbot Village
Bradford Peverell
Frome Whitfield
Wolfeton
Tutankhamun Exhibition
Stinsford
Dorset County Mus
Ilsington
Tincleton
Throop
Lane End
Wareham Forest
Organford
Upton Park
Rossmore
Bournemouth
Winton
Christchurch
Winterbourne Abbas
Kingston Maurward
Kingston Maurward Park
Dinosaur Mus
Gallows Hill
Bloxworth Heath
Gore Heath
Hamworthy
Longfleet
Parkstone
Branksome
Boscombe
Southbourne
Wick
Winterbourne Steepleton
Poundbury
Dorchester
Higher Woodsford
Woodsford
Clouds Hill (NT)
Moreton Sta
Moreton
Bovington Camp
Trigon Hill
Holton Heath
Holton Heath Sta
Sandford
Poole
Guildhall
The Lighthouse
Westbourne
Branksome Park
Lilliput
Russell-Cotes Art Gallery & Museum
Nine Stones
Maiden Castle
Martinstown
Winterborne Came
West Stafford
Whitcombe
Tank Museum
Monkey World
Northport
Wareham
Arne
Poole Harbour
Pottery
Compton Acres
Canford Cliffs
Hardy Monument (NT)
Bronkham Hill
237
205
Black Down
Winterborne Monkton
Winterborne Herringston
West Knighton
Crossways
East Burton
Stokeford
Worgret
Stoborough
Brownsea Island
(NT)
Sandbanks
Portesham
South West Coast Path
Broadmayne
Warmwell
Winfrith Heath
Giddy Green
Wool
Bindon Abbey
East Stoke
East Holme
Ridge
Stoborough Green
West Holme
Hartland Moor
Poole Bay
Upwey
Bincombe
White Horse
Poxwell
Owermoigne
Watercombe
East Knighton
Coombe Keynes
Grange Heath
Middlebere Heath
Wytch Heath
Newton Heath
Studland & Godlington Heath National Nature Reserve
Rodden
Broadwey
Sutton Poyntz
Nottington
Littlemoor
Osmington
Upton
Winfrith Newburgh
Norden
Corfe Castle (NT)
Isle of Purbeck
Studland Bay
Studland
Langton Herring
Buckland Ripers
Jordan Hill Roman Temple
Radipole
Preston
Holworth
West Chaldon
Chaldon Herring (East Chaldon)
Lulworth Castle
East Lulworth
Danger Zone
Purbeck Hills
199
Church Knowle
Creech
Corfe Castle
Woolgarston
Nine Barrow Down
Ballard Down
The Foreland (Handfast Point)
Ballard Point
Chickerell
Sea Life Centre
Overcombe
Osmington Mills
Chaldon Down
Lulworth Camp
Steeple
Corfe Castle Museum
Harman's Cross
Ulwell
Swanage Railway
Swanage Bay
Bennetts Water Garden
Melcombe Regis
Weymouth Bay
Ringstead Bay
South West Coast Path
West Lulworth
Tyneham
Lutton
Kingston
Langton Matravers
Swanage
Peveril Point
Beach
Chafesbrook
Westham
WEYMOUTH
Brewers Quay
Nothe Fort
Durdle Door
Lulworth Cove & Heritage Centre
Worbarrow Bay
Kimmeridge
Toll
Smedmore
Acton
Putlake Adventure Farm
Durlston
Durlston Bay
Wyke Regis
East Fleet
Broad Bench
Worth Matravers
Durlston Head
Tilly Whim Caves
Ferry Bridge
Portland Harbour
Portland Castle
Seacombe Cliff
Durlston Country Park Visitor Centre
St Aldhelm's Head (St Alban's Head)
Fortuneswell
Castletown
Grove
Easton
Isle of Portland
Weston
Southwell
Bill of Portland
W I L T S
D O R S E T
B L A C K M O O R V A L E
Cranborne Chase
hours
Guernsey 2-2¼
Jersey 3¼-3½
St Malo (summer only) 4½
hours
Cherbourg 2¼-4¼
Guernsey 2½
Jersey 3-3¼
St Malo (summer only) 4½
1
2
3
4
5
6
7
10
A303
A350
A30
A357
A354
A35
A31
A338
A36
A37
A352
A353
A3030
A359
A371
A348
A349
A341
A347
A3049
A3060
A3040
A3094
A345
A351
B3081
B3092
B3095
B3089
B3078

10
A
B
C
D
E
1
2
3
4
5
6
7
20
9
WILTSHIRE
DORSET
HAM
NEW FOREST
NATIONAL PARK
Heytesbury
Knook
Sutton Veny
Longbridge Deverill
Tytherington
Codford St Peter
Codford St Mary
Corton
Boyton
Sherrington
Stockton
Fisherton de la Mere
Deptford
Wylye
Berwick St James
Steeple Langford
Hanging Langford
Little Langford
Stapleford
Winterbourne Stoke
Stonehenge
Amesbury
West Amesbury
Wilsford
Lake
Great Durnford
Upper Woodford
Middle Woodford
Lower Woodford
Netton
Little Durnford
Heale House & Garden
Cholderton
Newton Tony
Allington
Boscombe
Idmiston
Porton
Gomeldon
Winterbourne Dauntsey
Winterbourne Gunner
Winterbourne Earls
Grateley
Palestine
Over Wallop
Middle Wallop
Nether Wallop
Danebury Ring
Danger Zone
Lopcombe Corner
Longstock
Leckford
Stockbridge
Chilbolton
Wherwell
Cottonworth
Fullerton
Middle Winterslow
East Winterslow
Whiteshoot Hill
Firsdown
Winterslow
The Common
West Winterslow
Pitton
Broughton
North Houghton
Houghton
Houghton Lodge
Little Somborne
King's Somborne
Ashley
Bossington
Horsebridge
Farley
West Tytherley
East Tytherley
Farley Down
Brook
East Grimstead
West Dean
West Grimstead
Lockerley
Mottisfont
Mottisfont Abbey Gardens (NT)
Dunbridge
Michelmersh
Kimbridge
Braishfield
Timsbury
Awbridge
Sir Harold Hillier Gardens & Arboretum
Abbottswood
Romsey
Romsey Abbey
Kent's Oak
Newton
Upper Ratley
Sherfield English
Plaitford Green
Whiteparish
Cowesfield Green
Dean Hill
East Dean
Butt's Green
Carter's Clay
Kingston Deverill
Hill Deverill
Brixton Deverill
Monkton Deverill
Great Ridge
Chicklade
Berwick St Leonard
Hindon
Fonthill Bishop
Chilmark
Ridge
Teffont Magna
Teffont Evias
Dinton
Baverstock
Barford St Martin
Philipps House (NT)
Fonthill Gifford
West Knoyle
Upton
The Green
East Knoyle
Barrow Street
Lower Chicksgrove
Upper Chicksgrove
Tisbury
Newtown
East Hatch
Pythouse
West Hatch
Sedgehill
Sutton Mandeville
Swallowcliffe
Ansty
Semley
Old Wardour Castle
Donhead St Andrew
Donhead St Mary
Ludwell
Birdbush
West End
White Sheet Hill
Alvediston
Ebbesborne Wake
Fifield Bavant
Mount Sorrel
Broad Chalke
Mead End
Bowerchalke
Misselfore
Woodminton
Berwick St John
Fovant
Compton Chamberlayne
Burcombe
Wilton
Wilton House
Netherhampton
Ugford
Groveley Wood
South Newton
Great Wishford
Little Wishford
Stoford
Chilhampton
Fugglestone St Peter
Bemerton
Stratford sub Castle
Old Sarum
SALISBURY
Salisbury Cath
Laverstock
Petersfinger
Britford
Mompesson (NT)
West Harnham
Harnham
East Harnham
Stratford Tony
Coombe Bissett
Homington
Odstock
Odstock Down
Nunton
Alderbury
Bodenham
Whaddon
Stoke Farthing
Bishopstone
Faulston
Croucheston
Charlton-All-Saints
Downton
Wick
Redlynch
Woodfalls
Lover
Bohemia
Newhouse
Morgan's Vale
Hamptworth
Landford
Wick Down
Rockbourne Down
Martin Drove End
East Martin
Tidpit
Martin
Shaftesbury
Cann
Cann Common
Charlton
Melbury Abbas
Twyford
Compton Abbas
East Compton
Ashmore
Cranborne Chase
Tollard Royal
New Town
Deanland
Woodyates
Pentridge
Pentridge Hill
Whitsbury
Breamore
North Charford
Hale
Rockbourne
Upper Street
Woodgreen
Fontmell Magna
East Orchard
West Orchard
Bedchester
Larmer Tree Gardens
Tollard Farnham
Woodcutts
Dean
Farnham
Sixpenny Handley
Gussage St Andrew
Minchington
Iwerne Minster
Stubhampton
Chettle
Chettle House
Cashmoor
Monkton Up Wimborne
Boveridge
Cranborne
Cranborne Manor
Damerham
North End
South End
Rockbourne Roman Villa
Sandleheath
Fordingbridge
Ashford
Alderholt
Upper Burgate
Lower Burgate
Godshill
Criddlestyle
Stuckton
Blissford
Frogham
Hungerford
Bickton
North Gorley
South Gorley
Mockbeggar
Ibsley
Linwood
Shroton (Iwerne Courtney)
Child Okeford
Tarrant Gunville
Tarrant Hinton
Pimperne
Stourpaine
Durweston
Gussage All Saints
Gussage St Michael
Long Crichel
Tarrant Launceston
Tarrant Monkton
Tarrant Rawston
Wimborne St Giles
Edmondsham
Edmondsham House
Cripplestyle
Crendell
Daggons
Charing Cross
Cranborne Common
Harbridge Green
Harbridge
Sutton Holms
Church & Earthworks
Knowlton
Romford
Verwood
Ringwood Forest
Whitmore
Woodlands
Horton
Horton Inn
Moor Crichel
Manswood
Witchampton
Chalbury
Chalbury Common
Horton Common
Hinton Martell
Blandford Forum
Blandford Camp
Bryanston
Langton Long Blandford
Tarrant Rushton
Tarrant Keyneston
Tarrant Crawford
Charlton Marshall
Charlton on the Hill
Spetisbury
Thornicombe
Winterborne Stickland
Winterborne Clenston
Winterborne Whitechurch
Charlton Down
Hinton Parva
Badbury Rings (NT)
Stanbridge
Gaunt's Common
Holt
Holt Heath
Mannington
Lower Mannington
Three Legged Cross
Moors Valley Country Park
Moors Valley Railway
Ashley Heath
Ellingham
Rockford
Blashford
Linford
Shobley
Picket Post
Ringwood
Hightown
Crow
Burley Street
Burley
Bisterne Close
Kingston
North Kingston
Bisterne
St Leonards
St Ives
West Moors
Highbury
Broom Hill
Furzehill
Colehill
Ferndown
Stapehill Abbey Crafts & Gardens
Ameysford
Avon Heath
Trickett's Cross
Parley Common
Tadden
Hillbutts
Kingston Lacy (NT)
Shapwick
Pamphill
Wimborne Minster
Leigh
Canford Bottom
Little Canford
Hampreston
Knoll Gardens
Oakley
Merley
Longham
Dudsbury
Canford Magna
Knighton
Parley Cross
West Parley
East Parley
Hurn
Bournemouth Airport
Sturminster Marshall
Mapperton
Almer
Winterborne Kingston
Winterborne Zelston
Anderson
Lower Street
Corfe Mullen
East End
Lytchett Matravers
West Morden
Morden
East Morden
Slepe
Whitefield
Bloxworth
Bere Regis
Turners Puddle
Wareham Forest
Bloxworth Heath
Lane End
Gallows Hill
Bovington Camp
Lytchett Minster
Organford
Gore Heath
Holton Heath
Upton
Upton Park
Beacon Hill
Hill View
Broadstone
Waterloo
Canford Heath
Oakdale
Stanley Green
Longfleet
Hamworthy
POOLE
Parkstone
Branksome
Branksome Park
West Howe
Wallisdown
Kinson
East Howe
Talbot Village
Moordown
Winton
Muscliff
Holdenhurst
Alice in Wonderland Family Park
Bournemouth Uni
Rossmore
Westbourne
Boscombe
Southbourne
Tuckton
Iford
Jumpers Common
CHRISTCHURCH
Wick
Mudeford
Christchurch Priory
Purewell
Hengistbury Head
Tumuli
BOURNEMOUTH
Russell-Cotes Art Gallery & Museum
The Lighthouse
Guildhall
Lilliput
Canford Cliffs
Compton Acres
Pottery
Sandbanks
Poole Harbour
Brownsea Island (NT)
Poole Bay
Avon
Sopley
Winkton
Burton
Bransgore
Ripley
Shirley
Neacroft
Thorney Hill
Avon Tyrrell
Macpenny's
Middle Bockhampton
South Bockhampton
Hinton Admiral
Hinton
Highcliffe
Walkford
Old Milton
Barton on Sea
New Milton
Ashley
Hordle
Bashley
Tiptoe
Wootton
Sway
Mount Pleasant
Brockenhurst
Setley
Boldre
Pilley
Battramsley
Upper Pennington
Pennington
Lymington
Lymington Pier
Everton
Downton
Lymore
Keyhaven
Milford on Sea
Christchurch Bay
Woodside
Lower Pennington
Walhampton
Buckland
Portmore
Norleywood
East End
South Baddesley
Spinners
Beaulieu
Beaulieu Heath
Beaulieu Palace House
National Motor Museum
Furzey Lodge
East Boldre
Buckler's Hard
Maritime Museum
Hamstead
Yarmouth
Norton
Fort Victoria Country Park
Colwell Bay
Totland
Totland Bay
Norton Green
Freshwater
Yarmouth Castle
Afton
Thorley Street
Wellow
Bouldnor
Cranmore
Hurst
Sconce Point
Needles Pleasure Park
Alum Bay
The Needles
The Needles Old Battery (NT)
Freshwater Bay
Compton Bay
Brook Down
Hulverstone
Brook
The Undercliff
Easton
Lyndhurst
New Forest Museum & Information Centre
Bank
Emery Down
Clayhill
Pikeshill
Balmerlawn
Ashurst
Ashurst New Forest Sta
Colbury
Woodlands
Netley Marsh
Bartley
Minstead
London Minstead
Newtown
Furzey
Stoney Cross
Bolderwood
Fritham
Brook
Newbridge
Cadnam
Copythorne
Winsor
Calmore
Totton
Eling
Hounsdown
Marchwood
Rushington
Pooksgreen
Bramshaw
Brook Hill
Nomansland
Furzley
Canada
Deadman Hill
West Wellow
East Wellow
Paulton's Park
Ower
Wigley
Nursling
Rownhams
Toothill
Lee
Upton
Hill Street
Testwood
Lord's Hill
Hillyfields
Shirley Warren
North Baddesley
Broadlands
Woodington
Heritage & Visitor Centre
Millbrook
Bellevue
Sandford
Northport
Wareham
Stoborough
Stoborough Green
Ridge
Arne
Worgret
Stokeford
Wool
Bindon
East Stoke
East Holme
West Holme
Holme
Monkey World
Coombe Keynes
Grange Heath
Trigon Hill
Hartland Moor
Middlebere Heath
Wytch Heath
Norden
Newton Heath
Isle of Purbeck
Studland
Studland Bay
Studland & Godlingston Heath National Nature Reserve
The Foreland (Handfast Point)
Ballard Down
Ballard Point
Nine Barrow Down
Ulwell
Swanage
Swanage Bay
Swanage Railway
Peveril Point
Durlston Bay
Durlston
Durlston Head
Durlston Country Park Visitor Centre
Tilly Whim Caves
Church Knowle
East Creech
Creech
Corfe Castle
Corfe Castle (NT)
Corfe Castle Museum
Woolgarston
Harman's Cross
Langton Matravers
Kingston
Acton
Putlake Adventure Farm
Worth Matravers
Seacombe Cliff
South West Coast Path
St Aldhelm's Head (St Alban's Head)
Kimmeridge
Steeple
Tyneham
Smedmore
Broad Bench
Worbarrow Bay
Lutton
Purbeck Hills
Danger Zone
East Lulworth
West Lulworth
Lulworth Castle
Toll
SEE PAGE 93
hours
Cherbourg........................2¼-4¼
Guernsey..................................2½
Jersey.................................3-3¼
St Malo (summer only)...........4½
½ hr
0 2 4 6 miles
0 2 4 6 8 10 km

	hours
Bilbao	35
Caen	6-6¼
Cherbourg	3¼
Guernsey	6½
Jersey	10
Le Havre	2¾-5
St. Malo	8¾-10½

F G H J K

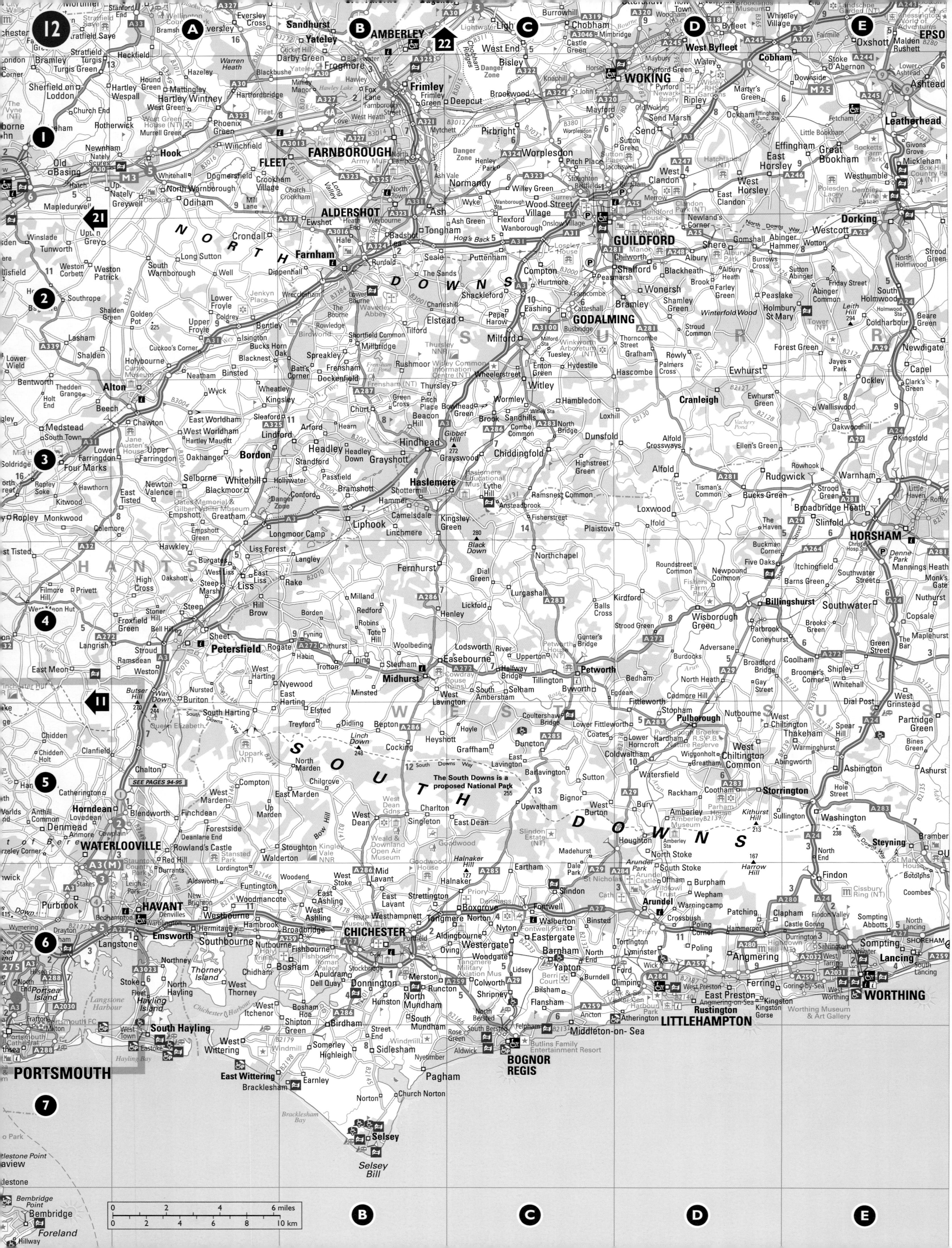
12
A
B
C
D
E
1
2
3
4
5
6
7
22
21
11
SEE PAGES 94-95
Sandhurst
Yateley
AMBERLEY
Eversley
Chobham
West Byfleet
Byfleet
Cobham
Oxshott
WOKING
Frimley
FARNBOROUGH
FLEET
Hook
Old Basing
Odiham
ALDERSHOT
Farnham
Ash
Tongham
Pirbright
Worplesdon
Normandy
Wood Street Village
GUILDFORD
Shalford
Chilworth
GODALMING
Milford
Witley
Haslemere
Hindhead
Grayshott
Headley
Bordon
Alton
Four Marks
Chawton
Medstead
Liphook
Liss
Petersfield
Midhurst
Petworth
Pulborough
Billingshurst
Horsham
Dorking
Leatherhead
Ashtead
Ripley
Send
East Horsley
West Horsley
Shere
Gomshall
Cranleigh
Ewhurst
Alfold
Rudgwick
Warnham
Slinfold
Fernhurst
Northchapel
Kirdford
Wisborough Green
Storrington
Washington
Steyning
Findon
WORTHING
Lancing
Sompting
Angmering
Rustington
LITTLEHAMPTON
Arundel
Amberley
Bury
Fontwell
Barnham
Yapton
BOGNOR REGIS
Middleton-on-Sea
Felpham
Pagham
Selsey
Selsey Bill
East Wittering
West Wittering
CHICHESTER
Bosham
Emsworth
HAVANT
WATERLOOVILLE
Horndean
Purbrook
South Hayling
Hayling Island
PORTSMOUTH
Bembridge
Bembridge Point
Foreland
Singleton
Charlton
Goodwood
Boxgrove
Tangmere
Westhampnett
Lavant
Compton
Rogate
Easebourne
Cocking
Heyshott
Graffham
Duncton
Sutton
Bignor
Upwaltham
Slindon
Eartham
Halnaker
Houghton
North Stoke
South Stoke
Burpham
Wepham
NORTH DOWNS
SOUTH DOWNS
HANTS
WEST SUSSEX
SURREY
The South Downs is a proposed National Park
Black Down
Butser Hill
Harrow Hill
Kithurst Hill
Leith Hill
Gibbet Hill
Hog's Back
Langstone Harbour
Chichester Harbour
Thorney Island
Bracklesham Bay
Portsea Island
Chichester Harbour
Queen Elizabeth Country Park
M3
M25
A3
A3(M)
A27
A29
A24
A272
A286
A283
A281
A31
A32
0
2
4
6 miles
0
2
4
6
8
10 km

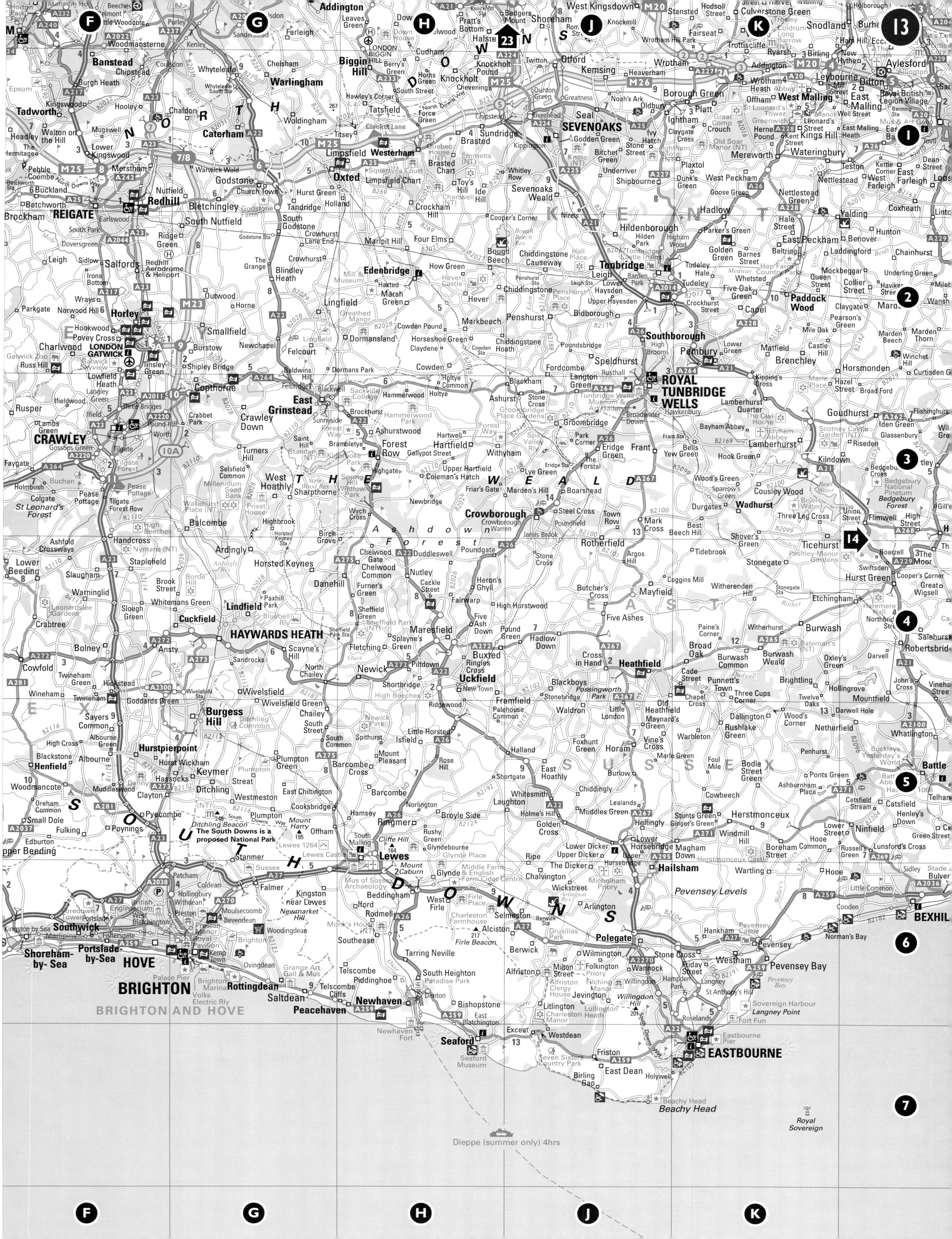
13
F
G
H
J
K
1
2
3
4
5
6
7
14
23
NORTH DOWNS
THE WEALD
ASHDOWN FOREST
KENT
EAST SUSSEX
SOUTH DOWNS
REIGATE
Redhill
Horley
LONDON GATWICK
CRAWLEY
East Grinstead
Oxted
Westerham
Caterham
Biggin Hill
SEVENOAKS
Edenbridge
Tonbridge
Southborough
ROYAL TUNBRIDGE WELLS
Crowborough
Paddock Wood
Wadhurst
Ticehurst
Mayfield
Heathfield
Uckfield
HAYWARDS HEATH
Cuckfield
Lindfield
Burgess Hill
Hurstpierpoint
Henfield
Ditchling
Lewes
Hailsham
Polegate
Battle
Burwash
BEXHILL
EASTBOURNE
Seaford
Newhaven
Peacehaven
BRIGHTON
HOVE
Shoreham-by-Sea
Southwick
Portslade-by-Sea
BRIGHTON AND HOVE
Rottingdean
Pevensey
Pevensey Bay
Beachy Head
Royal Sovereign
Dieppe (summer only) 4hrs
The South Downs is a proposed National Park
Aylesford
West Malling
Snodland
Kings Hill
Wrotham
Kemsing
Otford
Shoreham
Tadworth
Banstead
Epsom
Warlingham
Godstone
Lingfield
Forest Row
Hartfield
Frant
Lamberhurst
Goudhurst
Brenchley
Horsmonden
Pembury
Speldhurst
Penshurst
Fordcombe
Groombridge
Withyham
Rotherfield
Nutley
Maresfield
Ringmer
Newick
Wivelsfield
Keymer
Hassocks
Alfriston
Jevington
Herstmonceux
Ninfield
Catsfield

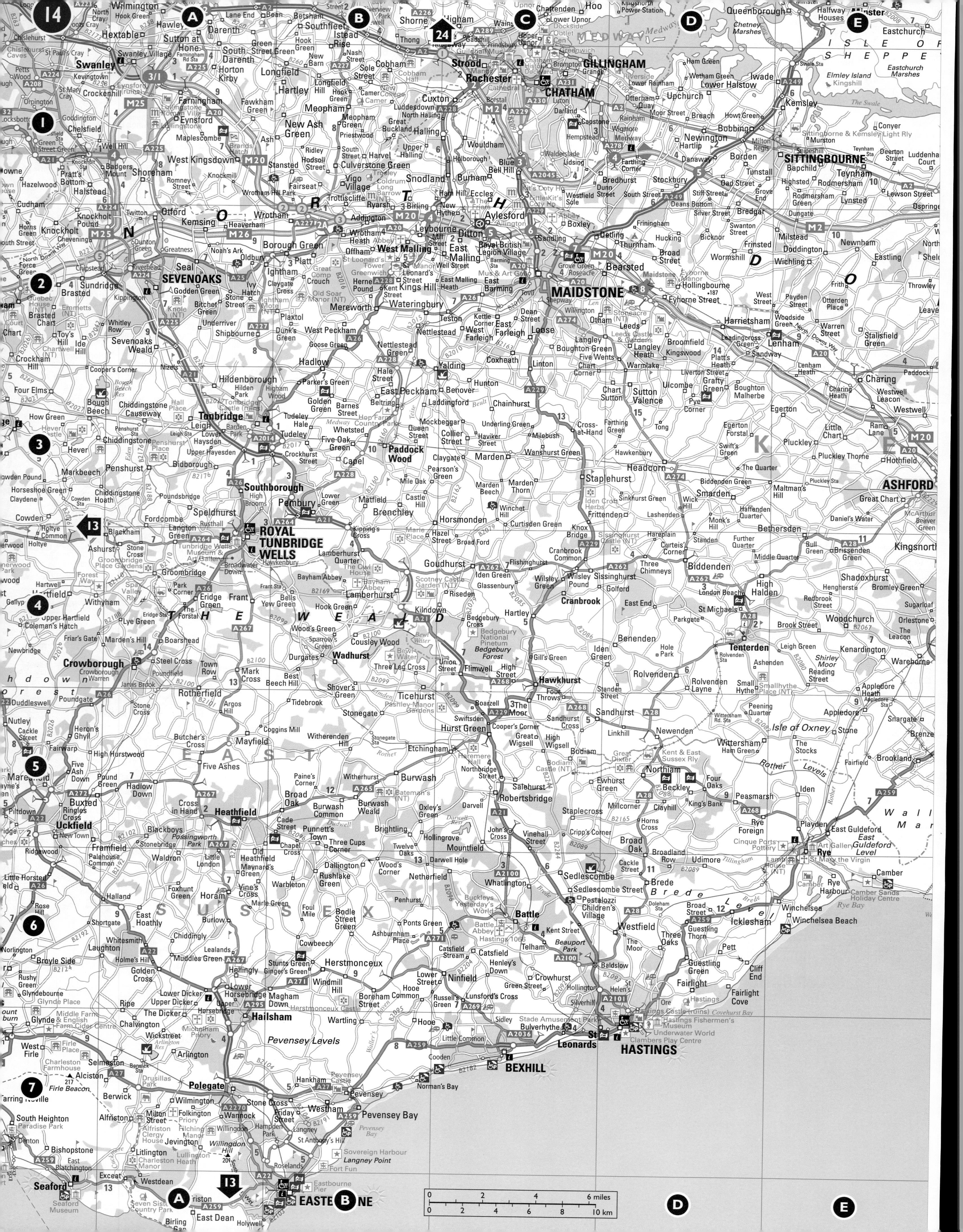

24
13
13
Swanley
Sevenoaks
Tonbridge
Royal Tunbridge Wells
Southborough
Crowborough
Uckfield
Heathfield
Hailsham
Polegate
Seaford
Eastbourne
Pevensey
Pevensey Bay
Pevensey Levels
Bexhill
Hastings
St Leonards
Battle
Robertsbridge
Rye
Winchelsea
Camber
Tenterden
Cranbrook
Hawkhurst
Goudhurst
Lamberhurst
Wadhurst
Mayfield
Paddock Wood
Staplehurst
Headcorn
Maidstone
Aylesford
West Malling
Snodland
Rochester
Strood
Chatham
Gillingham
Sittingbourne
Ashford
Charing
Lenham
Biddenden
Northiam
Burwash
Herstmonceux
Westfield
Icklesham
Fairlight
Isle of Sheppey
Isle of Oxney
North Downs
The Weald
East Sussex
Rother Levels
Brede Level
Walland Marsh
Beachy Head
0 2 4 6 miles
0 2 4 6 8 10 km

Channel Tunnel terminal map

Eurotunnel: Access from the UK

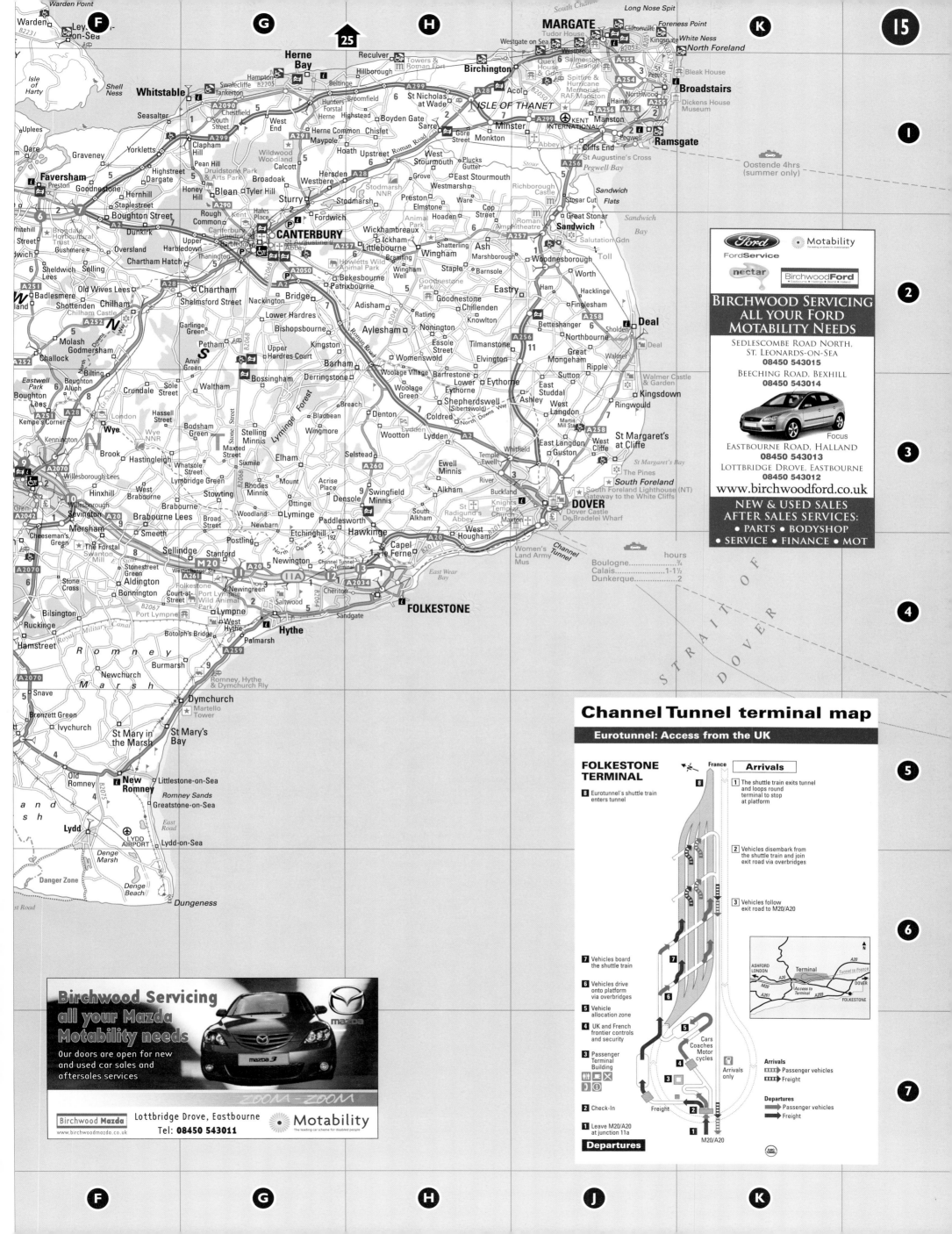

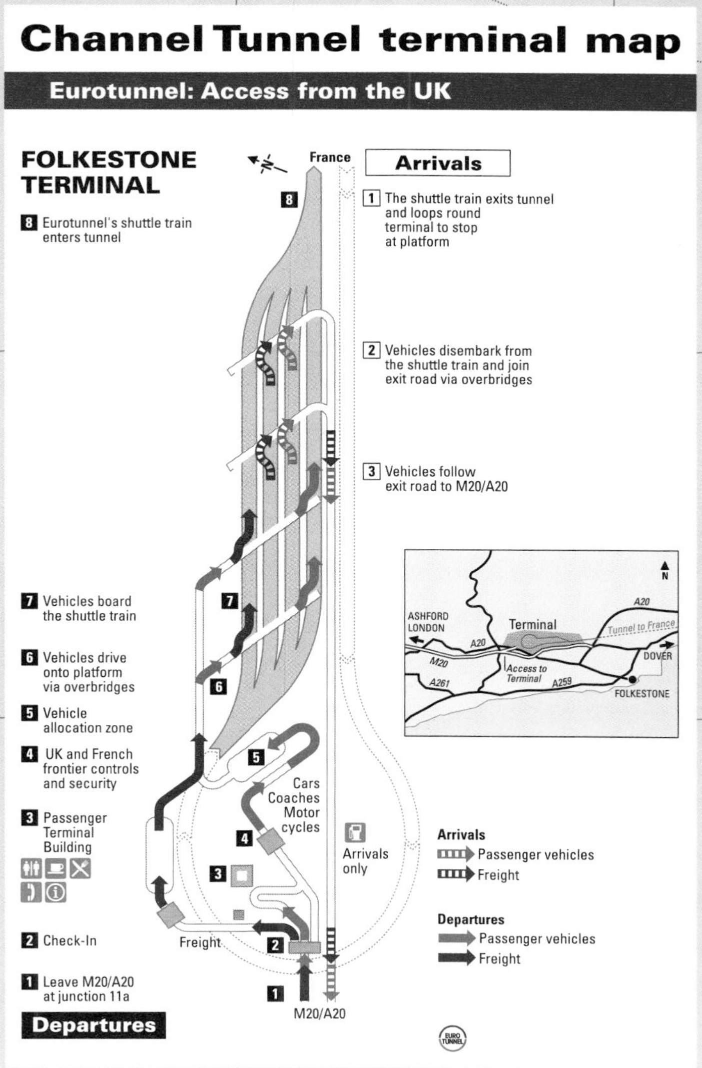

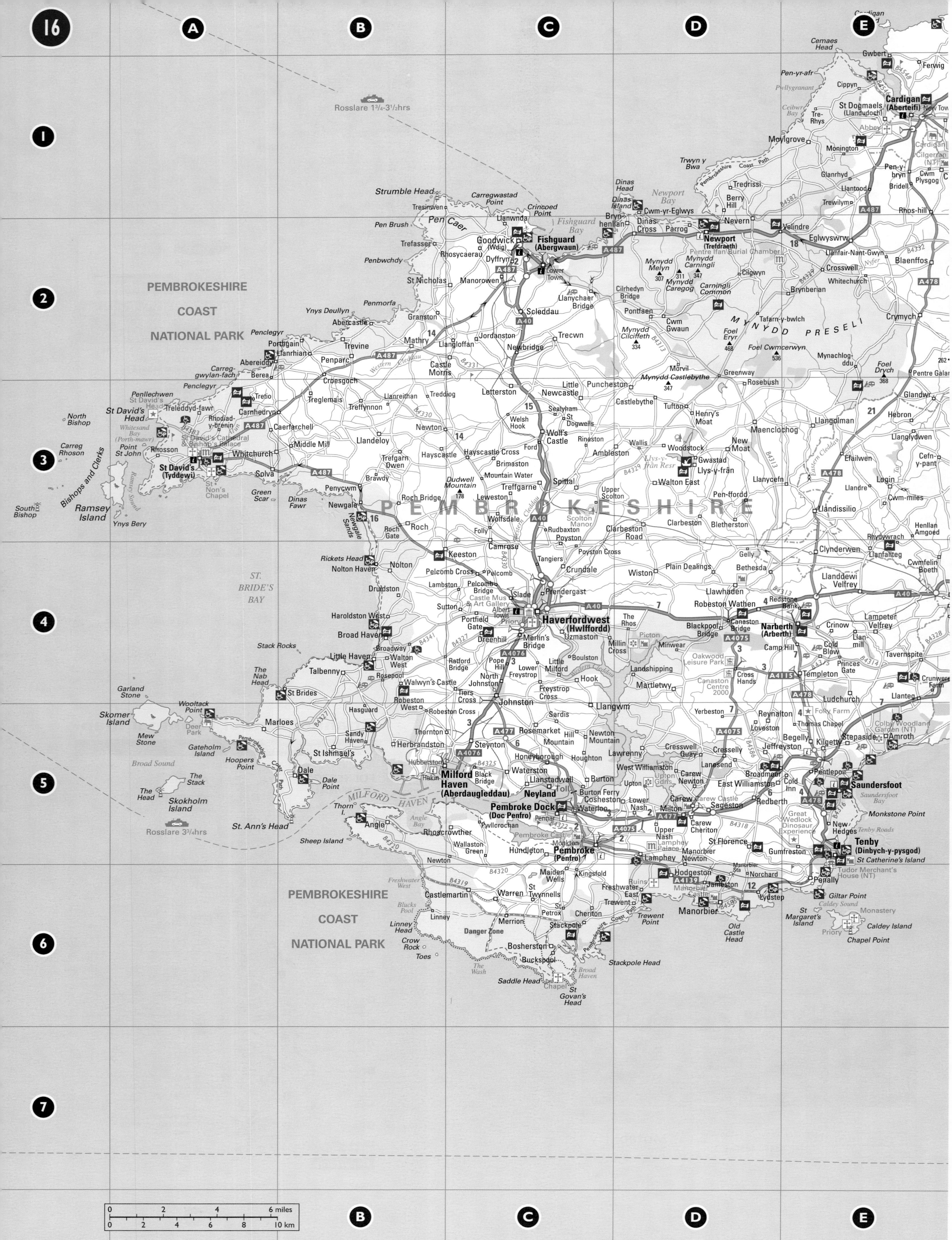
A
B
C
D
E
1
2
3
4
5
6
7
Rosslare 1¾-3½hrs
Cardigan
Cemaes Head
Gwbert
Ferwig
Pen-yr-afr
Cippyn
Cardigan (Aberteifi)
St Dogmaels (Llandudoch)
Tre-Rhys
Abbey
Moylgrove
Monington
Cilgerran
Pen-y-bryn
Cwm Plysgog
Trwyn y Bwa
Pembrokeshire Coast Path
Glanrhyd
Llantood
Bridell
Tredrissi
Berry Hill
Trewilym
Rhos-hill
Dinas Head
Dinas Island
Newport Bay
Cwm-yr-Eglwys
Strumble Head
Carregwastad Point
Crincoed Point
Tresinwen
Pen Caer
Llanwnda
Fishguard Bay
Pen Brush
Bryn-henllan
Dinas Cross
Parrog
Nevern
Velindre
Eglwyswrw
Goodwick (Wdig)
Fishguard (Abergwaun)
Trefasser
Rhosycaerau
Dyffryn
Lower Town
Newport (Trefdraeth)
Pentre Ifan Burial Chamber
Llanfair-Nant-Gwyn
Pencwbchdy
Mynydd Melyn
Mynydd Carningli
Mynydd Caregog
Cilgwyn
Crosswell
Blaenffos
Whitechurch
St Nicholas
Manorowen
Cilrhedyn Bridge
Carningli Common
Brynberian
Penmorfa
Llanychaer Bridge
Ynys Deullyn
Granston
Scleddau
Pontfaen
Cwm Gwaun
Tafarn-y-bwlch
Crymych
Abercastle
Mynydd Preseli
PEMBROKESHIRE COAST NATIONAL PARK
Penclegyr
Mathry
Jordanston
Trecwn
Mynydd Cilciffeth
Foel Eryr
Foel Cwmcerwyn
Porthgain
Llanrhian
Trevine
Llangloffan
Newbridge
Mynachlog-ddu
Abereiddy
Penparc
Castle Morris
Morvil
Foel Drych
Carreg-gwylan-fach
Berea
Croesgoch
Mynydd Castlebythe
Greenway
Rosebush
Pentre Galar
Penclegyr
Little Newcastle
Puncheston
Penllechwen
Trefin
Llanreithan
Treddiog
Letterston
Castlebythe
Tufton
Glandwr
St David's Head
Treleddyd-fawr
Treglemais
Treffynnon
Henry's Moat
Hebron
North Bishop
Whitesand Bay (Porth-mawr)
Rhodiad-y-brenin
Carnhedryn
Welsh Hook
Sealyham
St Dogwells
Maenclochog
Llangolman
Carreg Rhoson
Point St John
Caerfarchell
Newton
Wolf's Castle
Rinaston
Wallis
Woodstock
New Moat
Llanglydwen
St David's Cathedral & Bishop's Palace
Middle Mill
Llandeloy
Ford
Ambleston
Gwastad
Rhosson
Whitchurch
Trefgarn Owen
Hayscastle
Hayscastle Cross
Brimaston
Llys-y-frân Resr
Efailwen
Cefn-y-pant
St David's (Tyddewi)
Solva
Mountain Water
Spittal
Walton East
Llanycefn
Login
St Non's Chapel
Ramsey Sound
Bishops and Clerks
Green Scar
Dinas Fawr
Brawdy
Dudwell Mountain
Treffgarne
Upper Scolton
Pen-ffordd
Llandre
Cwm-miles
South Bishop
Ramsey Island
Ynys Bery
Penycwm
Newgale
Roch Bridge
Leweston
PEMBROKESHIRE
Llandissilio
Newgale Sands
Roch Gate
Roch
Wolfsdale
Scolton Manor
Clarbeston
Clarbeston Road
Bletherston
Henllan Amgoed
Folly
Rudbaxton
Poyston
Rhydywrach
Camrose
Poyston Cross
Clynderwen
Llanfallteg
Rickets Head
Nolton Haven
Keeston
Tangiers
Gelly
Cwmfelin Boeth
Nolton
Pelcomb Cross
Pelcomb
Crundale
Wiston
Plain Dealings
Bethesda
Llanddewi Velfrey
St. Bride's Bay
Druidston
Lambston
Pelcomb Bridge
Prendergast
Llawhaden
Castle Mus & Art Gallery
Slade
Robeston Wathen
Redstone Bank
Sutton
Albert Town
Haroldston West
Portfield Gate
Priory
Haverfordwest (Hwlffordd)
The Rhos
Blackpool Bridge
Canaston Bridge
Narberth (Arberth)
Crinow
Lampeter Velfrey
Broad Haven
Uzmaston
Picton
Merlin's Bridge
Greenhill
Millin Cross
Stack Rocks
Broadway
Walton West
Boulston
Minwear
Camp Hill
Cold Blow
Llan-mill
Tavernspite
Little Haven
Ratford Bridge
Pope Hill
Little Milford
Oakwood Leisure Park
Princes Gate
The Nab Head
Talbenny
Lower Freystrop
Landshipping
Cross Hands
Templeton
Garland Stone
Rosepool
Walwyn's Castle
North Johnston
Hook
Martletwy
Canaston Centre 2000
Crunwere Farm
Wooltack Point
St Brides
Robeston West
Tiers Cross
Freystrop Cross
Ludchurch
Llanteg
Skomer Island
Deer Park
Hasguard
Robeston Cross
Johnston
Llangwm
Yerbeston
Reynalton
Folly Farm
Marloes
Sardis
Loveston
Thomas Chapel
Colby Woodland Garden (NT)
Mew Stone
Sandy Haven
Thornton
Rosemarket
Hill Mountain
Newton Mountain
Begelly
Stepaside
Amroth
Gateholm Island
St Ishmael's
Herbrandston
Steynton
Cresswell Quay
Cresselly
Jeffreyston
Kilgetty
Hoopers Point
Hubberston
Honeyborough
Lawrenny
Houghton
Broad Sound
Dale
Hakin
Milford Haven (Aberdaugleddau)
Black Bridge
Waterston
West Williamston
Lanesend
Broadmoor
Pentlepoir
The Stack
Dale Point
Llanstadwell
Burton
Upton
Upton Gdns
Carew Newton
East Williamston
Cold Inn
Saundersfoot
The Head
Skokholm Island
Milford Haven
Neyland
Burton Ferry
Cosheston
Lower Nash
Redberth
Saundersfoot Bay
Thorn I.
Angle Bay
Pembroke Dock (Doc Penfro)
Waterloo
Carew
Carew Castle
Sageston
Monkstone Point
Rosslare 3¾hrs
St. Ann's Head
Angle
Pwllcrochan
Pennar
Milton
Carew Cheriton
Great Wedlock Dinosaur Experience
Rhoscrowther
Upper Nash
New Hedges
Tenby Roads
Sheep Island
Wallaston Green
Pembroke Castle
Monkton
Lamphey Palace
St Florence
Tenby (Dinbych-y-pysgod)
Hundleton
Pembroke (Penfro)
Manorbier Newton
Gumfreston
St Catherine's Island
Newton
Lamphey
Freshwater West
Maiden Wells
Kingsfold
Hodgeston
Norchard
Tudor Merchant's House (NT)
Penally
PEMBROKESHIRE COAST NATIONAL PARK
Castlemartin
Warren
St Twynnells
Freshwater East
Jameston
Manorbier Castle
Lydstep
Giltar Point
Caldey Sound
Blucks Pool
Trewent
Manorbier
Monastery
Linney Head
Linney
Merrion
St Petrox
Cheriton
Trewent Point
St Margaret's Island
Caldey Island
Danger Zone
Stackpole
Old Castle Head
Priory
Chapel Point
Crow Rock
Bosherston
Toes
Stackpole Head
The Wash
Buckspool
Broad Haven
Saddle Head
Chapel
St Govan's Head
A487
A40
A477
A4076
A4075
A4115
A478
A4139
B4330
B4331
B4329
B4313
B4341
B4327
B4325
B4320
B4319
B4584
B4582
B4546
B4548
B4332
B4314
B4328
B4318
B4316
B4585
B4322
0 2 4 6 miles
0 2 4 6 8 10 km

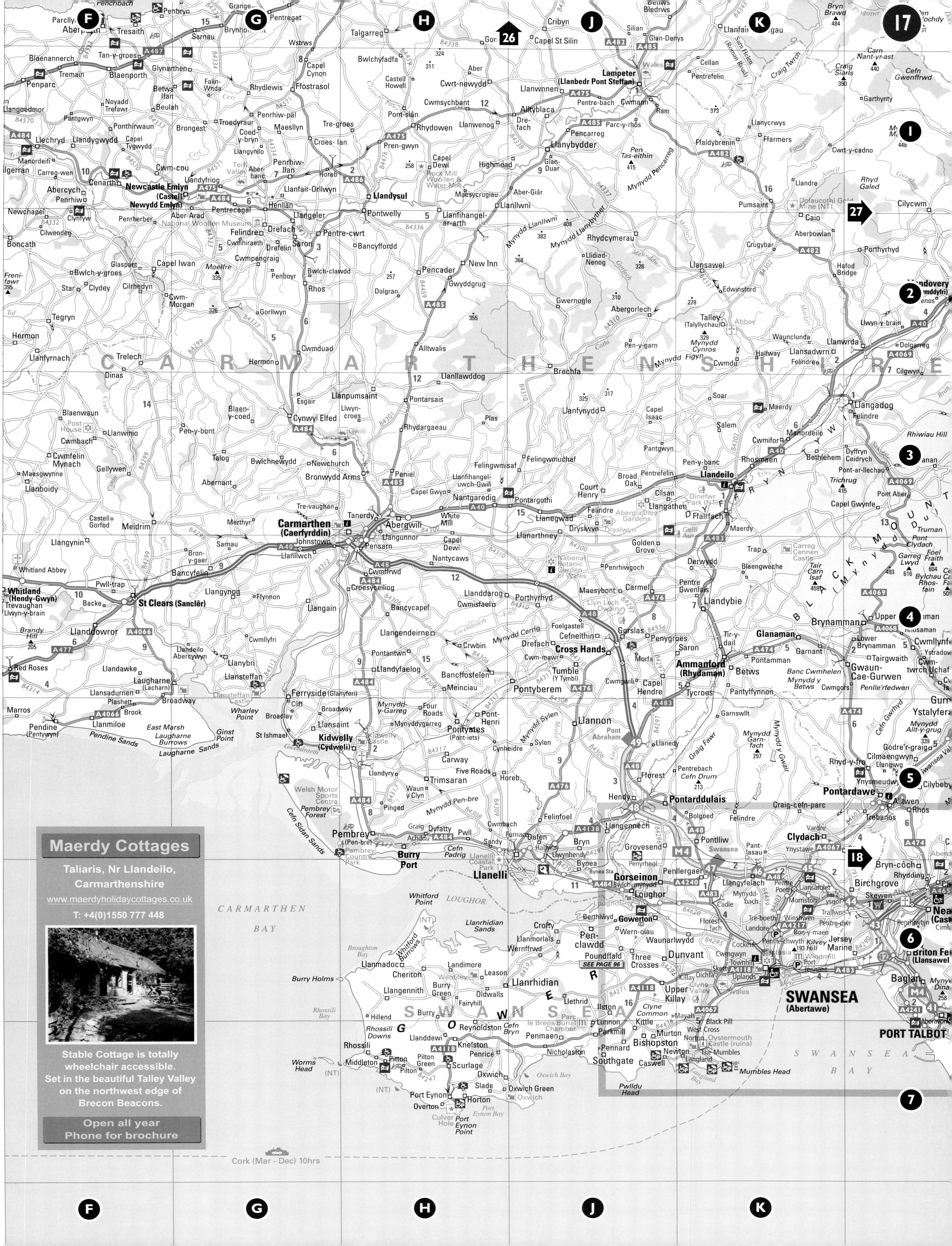
F
G
H
J
K
26
27
18
2
3
4
5
6
7
CARMARTHENSHIRE
Carmarthen (Caerfyrddin)
Newcastle Emlyn (Castell Newydd Emlyn)
Lampeter (Llanbedr Pont Steffan)
Llandysul
Llandeilo
Ammanford (Rhydaman)
St Clears (Sancler)
Whitland (Hendy-Gwyn)
Kidwelly (Cydweli)
Llanelli
Burry Port
Pembrey (Pen-bre)
Pontarddulais
Gorseinon
Gowerton
Loughor
Pontardawe
Clydach
SWANSEA (Abertawe)
PORT TALBOT
Cross Hands
Llangadog
Llandovery
Brynamman
Glanaman
Talley (Talyllychau)
Brechfa
Pencader
Llanybydder
GOWER
SWANSEA
CARMARTHEN BAY
SWANSEA BAY
Pendine (Pentywyn)
Laugharne (Lacharn)
Ferryside (Glanyferi)
Mumbles Head
Port Eynon
Rhossili
Worms Head
Burry Holms
Whitford Point
Llanrhidian Sands
Cefn Sidan Sands
Pendine Sands
BLACK MOUNTAIN (Mynydd Du)
Cork (Mar - Dec) 10hrs
SEE PAGE 96

27
17
SWANSEA
(Abertawe)
NEATH
PORT TALBOT
AFAN FOREST PARK
RHONDDA
CYNON
TAFF
MERTHYR TYDFIL
BRIDGEND
(Pen-y-Bont ar Ogwr)
CAERPHILLY
CARDIFF
VALE OF GLAMORGAN
BARRY
Penarth
Dinas Powys
Pontypridd
Aberdare
Maesteg
Porthcawl
Cowbridge
Llantwit Major
Neath
(Castell-nedd)
Merthyr Tydfil
Ebbw Vale
(Glynebwy)
Tredegar
Rhymney
Bargoed
Blackwood
Caerphilly
Ystradgynlais
Pontardawe
Clydach
Swansea Bay
Mumbles Head
Cork (Mar-Dec) 10hrs
SEE PAGE 96
BRISTOL CHANNEL
BRIDGWATER BAY
DEVON
SOMERSET
EXMOOR NATIONAL PARK
EXMOOR
QUANTOCK HILLS
Lynton
Lynmouth
Porlock
Minehead
Watchet
Williton
Dunster
Foreland Point
Countisbury
Selworthy Beacon
Dunkery Beacon
Sully Island
Barry Island
Whitmore Bay
CARDIFF INT
7
A
B
C
D
E
1
2
3
4
5
6
7
0 2 4 6 miles
0 2 4 6 8 10 km

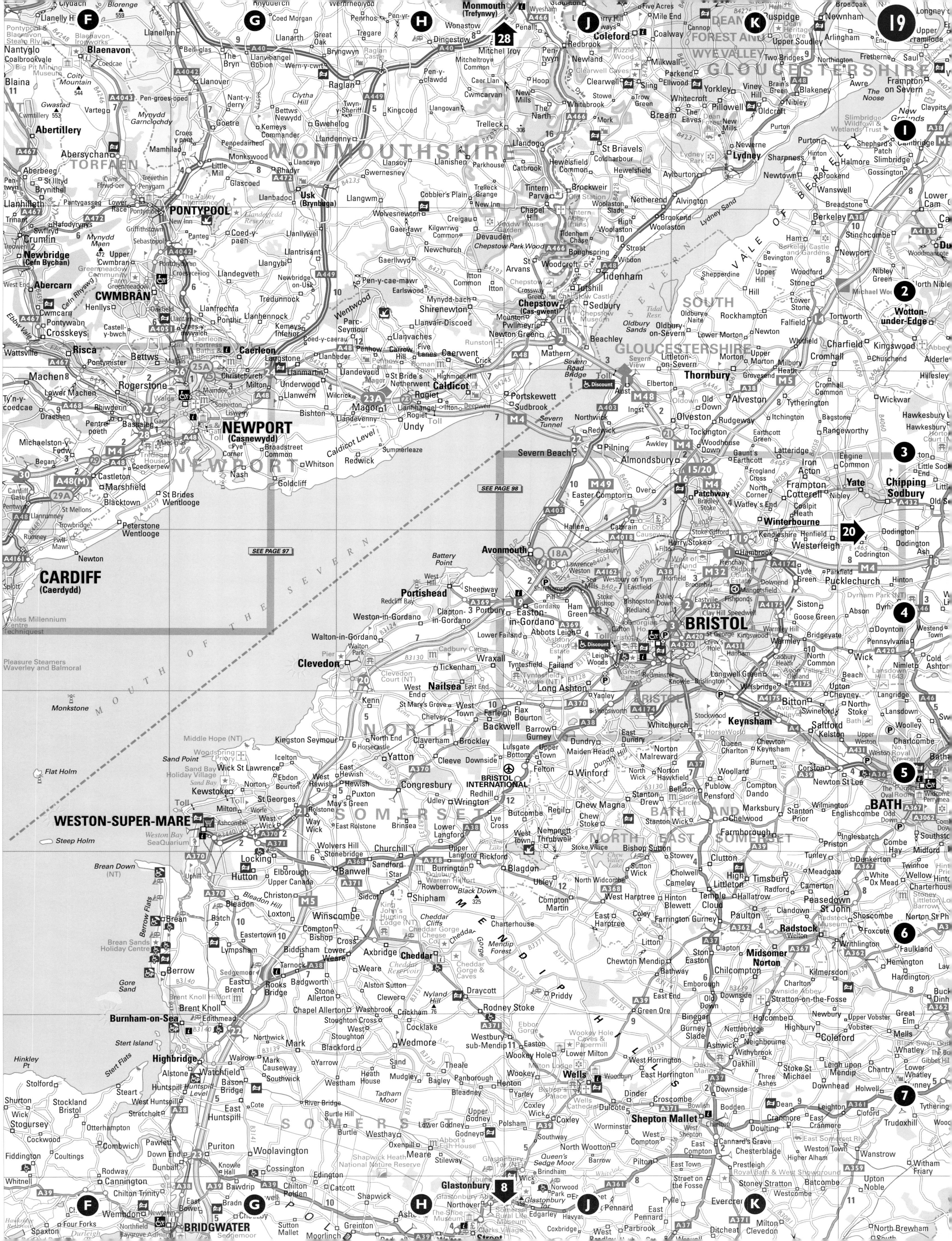
F
G
H
J
K
28
Monmouth (Trefynwy)
Blaenavon
Nantyglo
Abertillery
Abersychan
TORFAEN
PONTYPOOL
Crumlin
Newbridge (Cefn Bychan)
Abercarn
CWMBRAN
Crosskeys
Risca
Caerleon
Usk (Brynbuga)
Raglan
MONMOUTHSHIRE
Chepstow (Cas-gwent)
Coleford
DEAN FOREST AND WYE VALLEY
GLOUCESTERSHIRE
Lydney
Newnham
Cinderford
Berkeley
VALE OF BERKELEY
SOUTH GLOUCESTERSHIRE
Thornbury
Wotton-under-Edge
Chipping Sodbury
Yate
Winterbourne
Patchway
Severn Beach
Avonmouth
Portishead
Clevedon
Nailsea
NEWPORT (Casnewydd)
NEWPORT
Caldicot
Magor
Rogerstone
CARDIFF (Caerdydd)
Wales Millennium Centre
Techniquest
Flat Holm
Steep Holm
MOUTH OF THE SEVERN
SEE PAGE 97
SEE PAGE 98
BRISTOL
BRISTOL INTERNATIONAL
Keynsham
BATH
NORTH SOMERSET
BATH AND NORTH EAST SOMERSET
WESTON-SUPER-MARE
Congresbury
Yatton
Wrington
Chew Magna
Burnham-on-Sea
Highbridge
Cheddar
MENDIP HILLS
Wells
Shepton Mallet
Midsomer Norton
Radstock
Paulton
Glastonbury
BRIDGWATER
SOMERSET
20
8
1
2
3
4
5
6
7
M4
M5
M48
M49
M32
A38
A48
A370
A37
A39

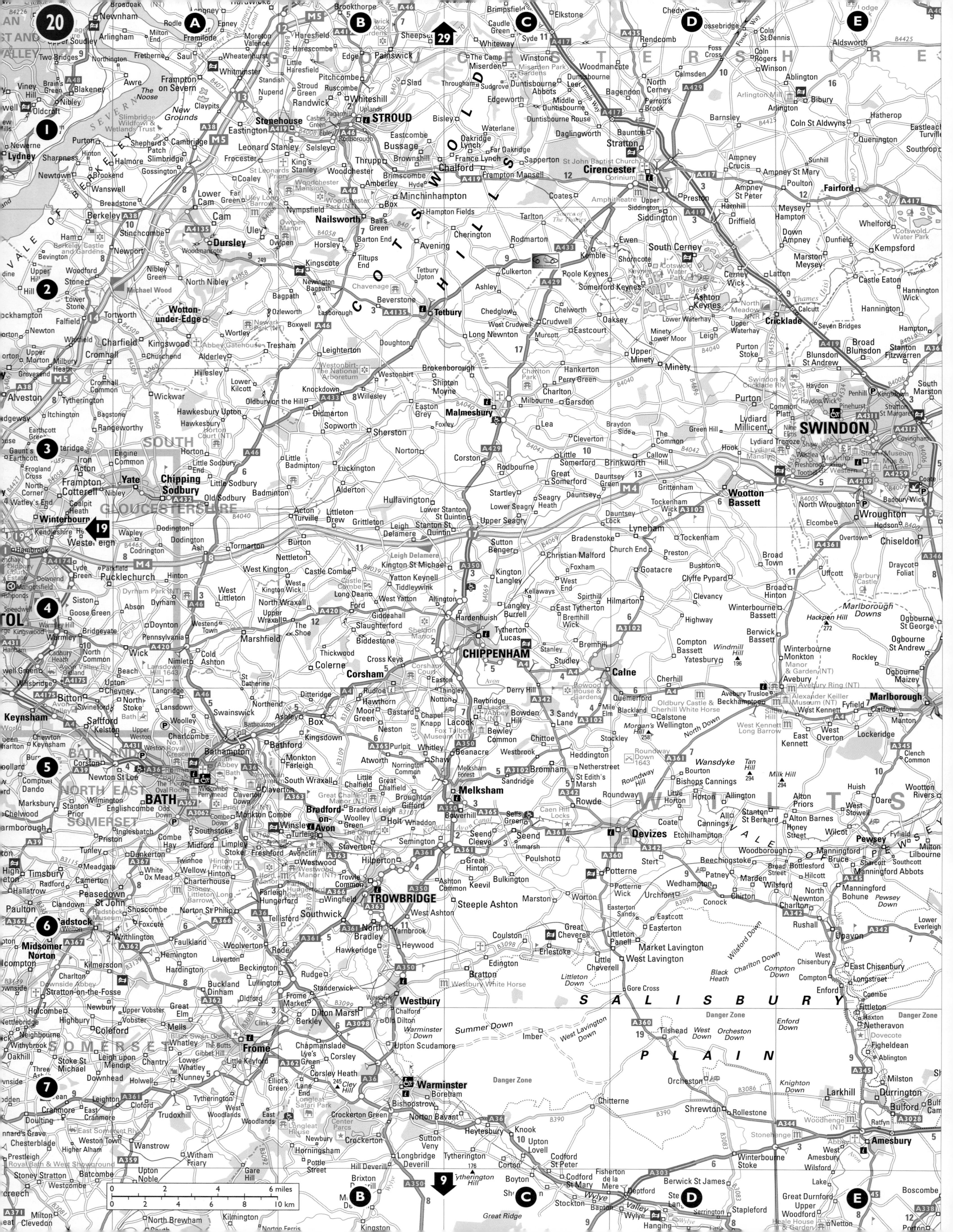

A
B
C
D
E
1
2
3
4
5
6
7
29
19
9
Newnham
Arlingham
Framilode
Frampton on Severn
Whitminster
Stonehouse
STROUD
Painswick
Miserden
Cirencester
Corinium
Bibury
Fairford
Lydney
Sharpness
Berkeley
Cam
Dursley
Nailsworth
Minchinhampton
Chalford
Tetbury
Wotton-under-Edge
Kingswood
Charfield
Cromhall
Wickwar
Hawkesbury Upton
Chipping Sodbury
Yate
Winterbourne
Pucklechurch
Marshfield
Keynsham
BATH
Bathampton
Box
Corsham
CHIPPENHAM
Calne
Malmesbury
Sherston
Hullavington
Lyneham
Wootton Bassett
SWINDON
Cricklade
Ashton Keynes
South Cerney
Kemble
Purton
Wroughton
Chiseldon
Marlborough
Avebury
Devizes
Melksham
Bradford-on-Avon
TROWBRIDGE
Westbury
Warminster
Frome
Radstock
Midsomer Norton
Peasedown St John
Timsbury
Paulton
Coleford
Steeple Ashton
Market Lavington
West Lavington
Potterne
Pewsey
Upavon
Durrington
Bulford
Amesbury
Larkhill
Shrewton
Tilshead
Heytesbury
Codford St Peter
Wylye
Stockton
Boyton
Sutton Veny
Longbridge Deverill
Horningsham
Crockerton
Bishopstrow
Boreham
Imber
Edington
Bratton
Erlestoke
Urchfont
Bishops Cannings
Rowde
Seend
Semington
Hilperton
Holt
Lacock
Sandy Lane
Derry Hill
Studley
Cherhill
Compton Bassett
Broad Hinton
Winterbourne Bassett
Ogbourne St George
Ogbourne St Andrew
Overton
Lockeridge
Fyfield
Manton
Woodborough
Alton Barnes
Manningford Bruce
Milton Lilbourne
Burbage
Netheravon
Enford
Figheldean
Ablington
Milston
Great Durnford
Boscombe
Berwick St James
Winterbourne Stoke
Chitterne
Orcheston
Rollestone
COTSWOLD HILLS
GLOUCESTERSHIRE
WILTSHIRE
SOMERSET
BATH AND NORTH EAST SOMERSET
SOUTH GLOUCESTERSHIRE
SALISBURY PLAIN
VALE OF PEWSEY
VALE OF BERKELEY
Danger Zone
Stonehenge
Longleat Safari Park
Westonbirt The National Arboretum
Cotswold Water Park
Marlborough Downs
Hackpen Hill
Cley Hill
Wansdyke
M4
M5
A46
A417
A419
A429
A350
A36
A361
A342
A345
A303
A4
A420
A39
A37
A367
A362
A3102
A338
A38
A4135
A433
A436
A3098
A363
A365
A366
0
2
4
6 miles
0
2
4
6
8
10 km

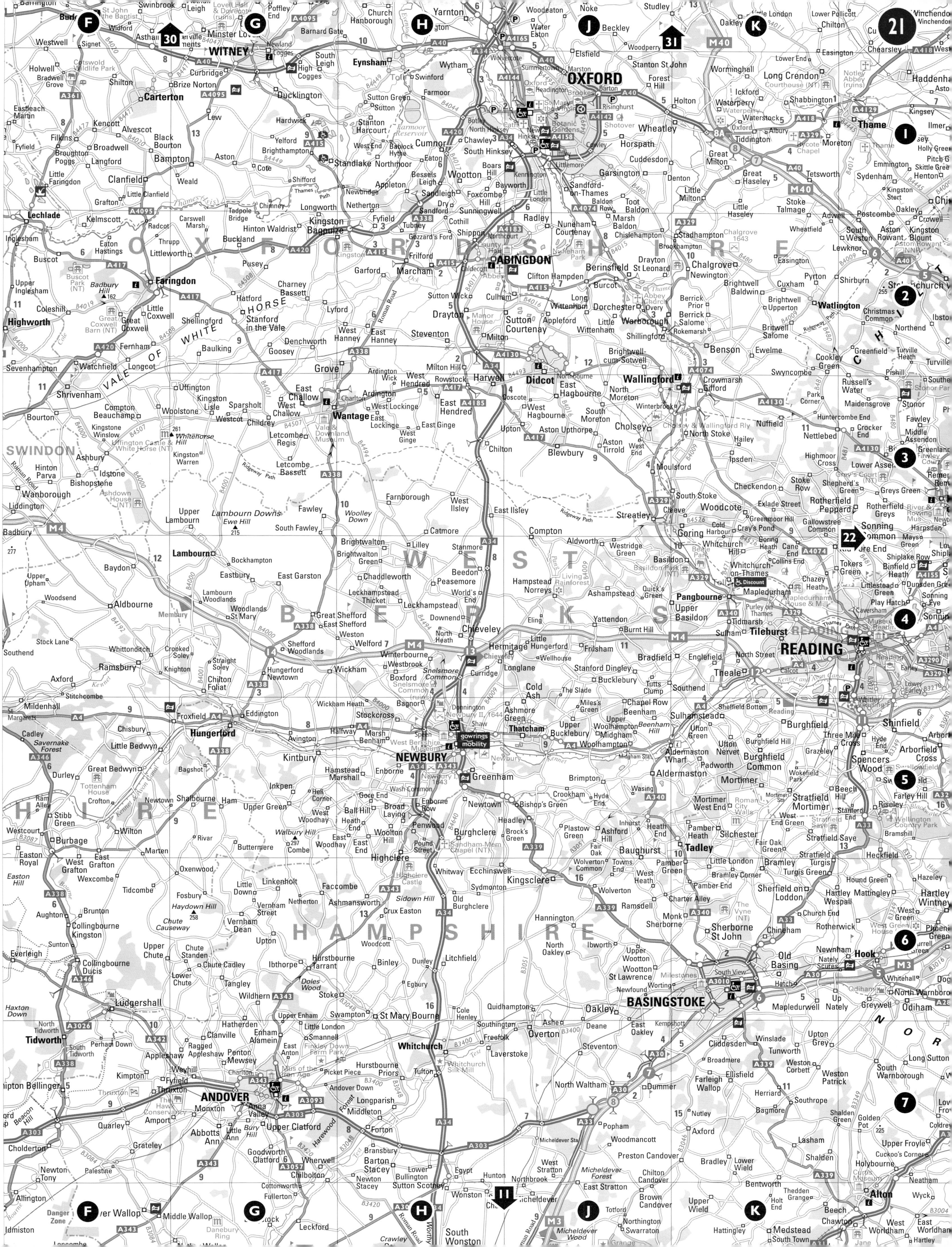
OXFORDSHIRE
WEST BERKS
HAMPSHIRE
SWINDON
CHILTERN
VALE OF WHITE HORSE
OXFORD
WITNEY
Carterton
Faringdon
Highworth
Lechlade
Bampton
ABINGDON
Didcot
Wantage
Wallingford
Thame
Watlington
Henley
READING
NEWBURY
Hungerford
Lambourn
Thatcham
Tadley
BASINGSTOKE
Hook
Alton
ANDOVER
Whitchurch
Ludgershall
Tidworth
Overton
Kingsclere
Goring
Pangbourne
Theale
Burghfield
Mortimer
Aldermaston
Tilehurst
Wheatley
Cumnor
Eynsham
Kidlington
Great Milton
Benson
Cholsey
Blewbury
Chieveley
Compton
Aldbourne
Shrivenham
Wanborough
Oakley
Stockbridge
Middle Wallop
Over Wallop
Danger Zone
Sutton Scotney
South Wonston
Micheldever
Bramley
Sherfield on Loddon
Old Basing
Odiham
Long Sutton
Newnham
Highclere
Burghclere
Kintbury
Ramsbury
Great Bedwyn
Savernake Forest
Vale of White Horse
Ridgeway Path
Lambourn Downs
Kennet and Avon Canal
M4
M40
M3
A34
A4
A339
A303
30
31
22
11
F
G
H
J
K

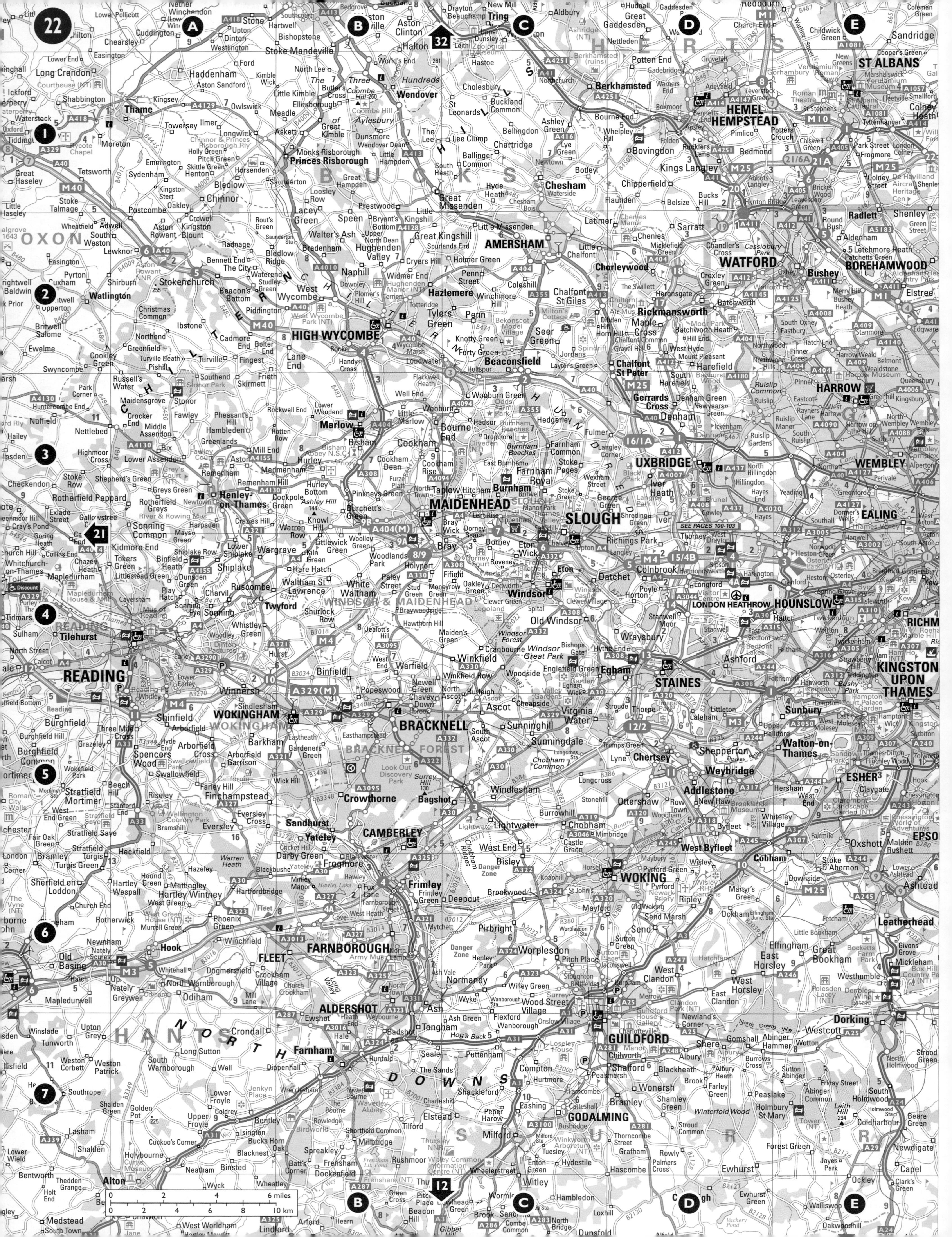
OXON
BUCKS
HERTS
HANTS
NORTH DOWNS
CHILTERN HILLS
WINDSOR & MAIDENHEAD
BRACKNELL FOREST
WOKINGHAM
READING
SLOUGH
Thame
Princes Risborough
Wendover
Aylesbury
Tring
Berkhamsted
HEMEL HEMPSTEAD
ST ALBANS
Chesham
AMERSHAM
HIGH WYCOMBE
Beaconsfield
Marlow
Henley-on-Thames
WATFORD
BOREHAMWOOD
Rickmansworth
Chalfont St Peter
Gerrards Cross
UXBRIDGE
HARROW
WEMBLEY
EALING
MAIDENHEAD
Windsor
Eton
LONDON HEATHROW
HOUNSLOW
Egham
STAINES
KINGSTON UPON THAMES
Tilehurst
WOKINGHAM
BRACKNELL
Ascot
Crowthorne
Sandhurst
Yateley
CAMBERLEY
Frimley
FARNBOROUGH
FLEET
Hook
Odiham
ALDERSHOT
Farnham
WOKING
Chertsey
Weybridge
Addlestone
Walton-on-Thames
ESHER
Cobham
Leatherhead
Dorking
GUILDFORD
GODALMING
Alton
Watlington
Stokenchurch
Twyford
Burnham
Denham
Sunbury
SEE PAGES 100-103
32
21
12
A
B
C
D
E
1
2
3
4
5
6
7
0 2 4 6 miles
0 2 4 6 8 10 km

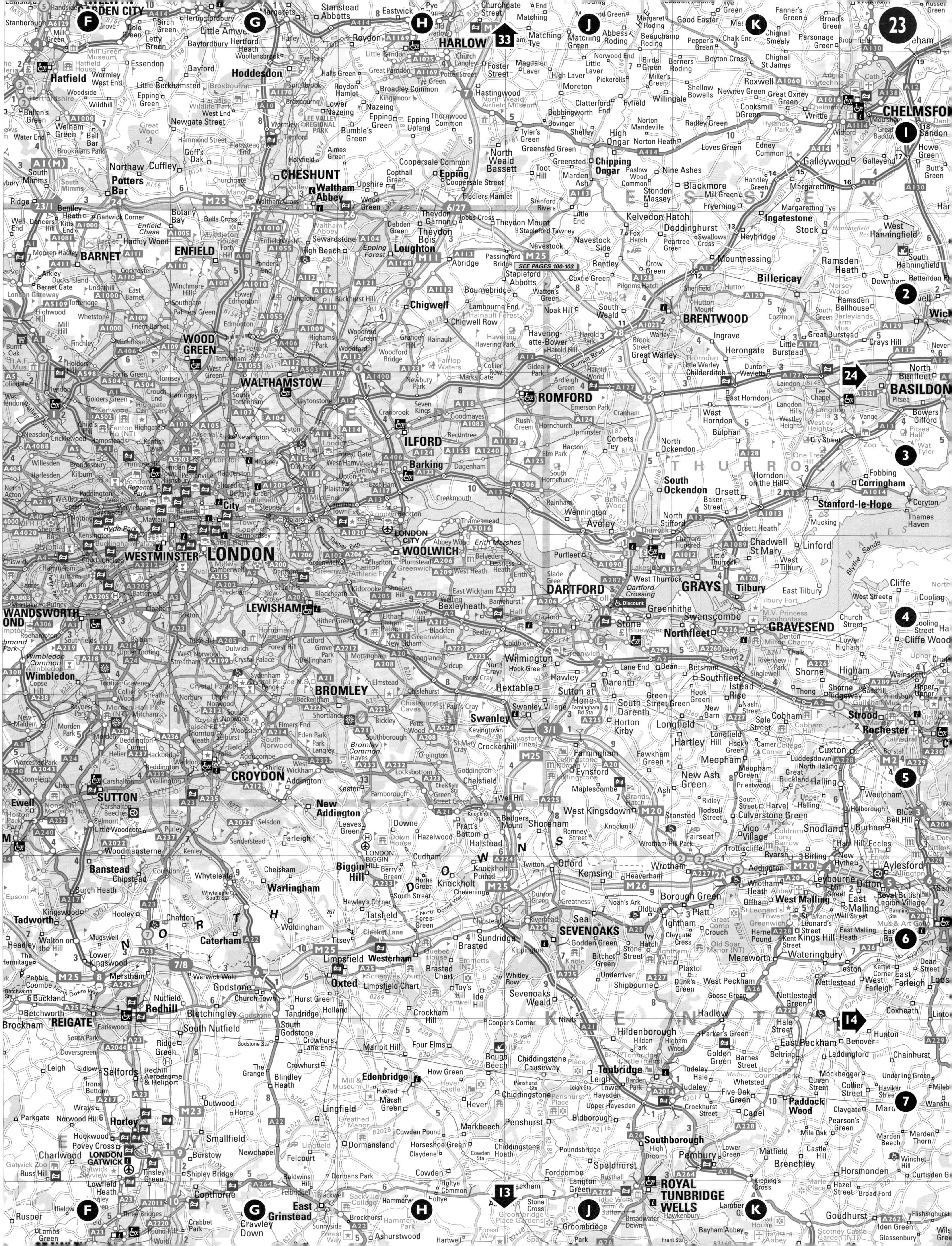

F
G
H
J
K
1
2
3
4
5
6
7
33
24
14
13
HARLOW
Hatfield
Hoddesdon
CHESHUNT
Waltham Abbey
Epping
Chipping Ongar
CHELMSFORD
Potters Bar
BARNET
ENFIELD
Loughton
Chigwell
BRENTWOOD
Billericay
WOOD GREEN
WALTHAMSTOW
ROMFORD
ILFORD
Barking
BASILDON
City
WESTMINSTER
LONDON
WOOLWICH
LONDON CITY
DARTFORD
GRAYS
Tilbury
GRAVESEND
Northfleet
WANDSWORTH
LEWISHAM
Wimbledon
BROMLEY
Swanley
Strood
Rochester
CROYDON
SUTTON
Ewell
New Addington
Biggin Hill
Warlingham
Caterham
SEVENOAKS
Westerham
Oxted
Aylesford
West Malling
REIGATE
Redhill
Edenbridge
Tonbridge
Horley
LONDON GATWICK
ROYAL TUNBRIDGE WELLS
East Grinstead
ESSEX
THURROCK
KENT
NORTH DOWNS
M25
M11
M20
M26
M23
M2
A12
A13
A127
SEE PAGES 100-103

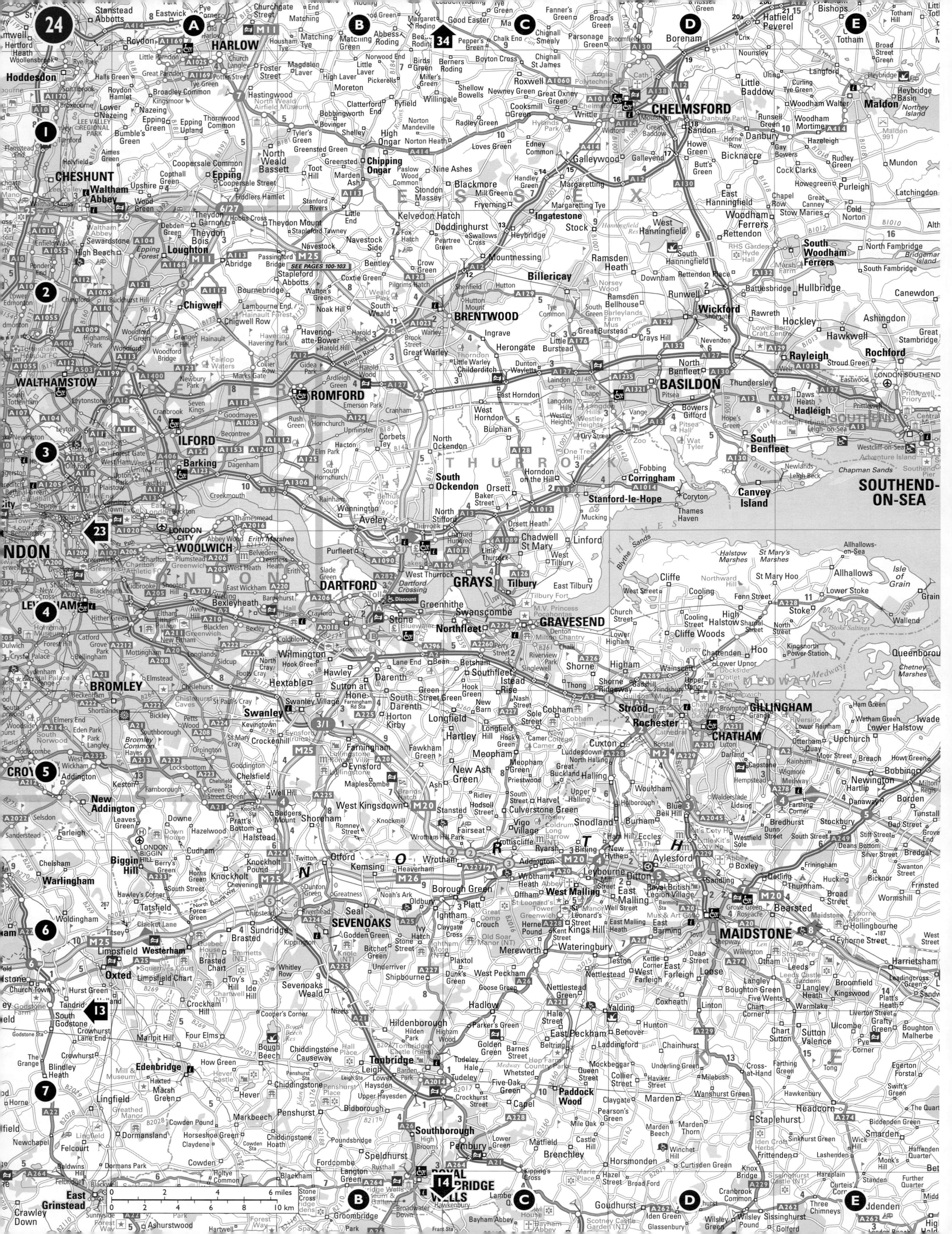
HARLOW
CHESHUNT
Waltham Abbey
Epping
Loughton
Chigwell
Chipping Ongar
CHELMSFORD
Maldon
BRENTWOOD
Billericay
Wickford
BASILDON
Rayleigh
Rochford
Hadleigh
South Benfleet
Canvey Island
SOUTHEND-ON-SEA
South Woodham Ferrers
Ingatestone
ROMFORD
ILFORD
Barking
WALTHAMSTOW
WOOLWICH
LONDON CITY
DARTFORD
GRAYS
Tilbury
GRAVESEND
Northfleet
South Ockendon
Stanford-le-Hope
Corringham
BROMLEY
Swanley
Strood
Rochester
CHATHAM
GILLINGHAM
MAIDSTONE
West Malling
Aylesford
SEVENOAKS
Westerham
Oxted
Edenbridge
East Grinstead
Tonbridge
Southborough
Paddock Wood
ROYAL TUNBRIDGE WELLS
Biggin Hill
Warlingham
New Addington
Hoddesdon
ESSEX
GREATER LONDON
THURROCK
NORTH KENT
THAMES
MEDWAY
SEE PAGES 100-103
M11
M25
M20
M26
M2
A12
A13
A127
A2
A20
A21
A228
A229
A130
A414
34
23
13
14
A
B
C
D
E
1
2
3
4
5
6
7
0
2
4
6 miles
8
10 km

F
G
H
J
K
35
15
1
2
3
4
5
6
7
Tolleshunt D'Arcy
Tollesbury
West Mersea
Cobmarsh Island
Great Cob Island
Virley Channel
Colne Point
Gunfleet
Goldhanger
Bradwell Waterside
Sales Point
St Peter's Flat
East End
Bradwell- on-Sea
Osea Island
Blackwater
Ramsey Island
St Lawrence
Steeple
Tillingham
Dengie Flat
Maylandsea
Dengie
Mayland
Asheldham
Dengie Marshes
Southminster
Ray Sand
Mangapps Railway Museum
Eves Corner
Stoneyhills
Old Montsale
Ostend
Burnham-on-Crouch
Deal Hall
Holliwell Point
Foulness Sands
Crouch
Foulness Point
Paglesham Churchend
Wallasea Island
Courtsend
Ballards Gore
Churchend
Paglesham Eastend
Potton Island
Foulness Island
Barling
Havengore Island
Little Wakering
Maplin Sands
Great Wakering
Southchurch
North Shoebury
Thorpe Bay
Shoeburyness
Shoebury Ness
Sheerness
Marine Town
Mile Town
East End
West Minster
Minster
Halfway Houses
Warden Point
Warden
Eastchurch
Leysdown-on-Sea
ISLE OF SHEPPEY
Elmley Island
Kingshill
Eastchurch Marshes
Isle of Harty
Shell Ness
The Swale
Kemsley
Conyer
Sittingbourne & Kemsley Light Rly
Murston
Uplees
SITTINGBOURNE
Bapchild
Teynham
Deerton Street
Luddenham Court
Oare
Graveney
Faversham
Preston
Goodnestone
Rodmersham
Lynsted
Lewson Street
Ospringe
Whitstable
Swalecliffe
Tankerton
Chestfield
Seasalter
South Street
Yorkletts
Clapham Hill
Pean Hill
Highstreet
Dargate
Hernhill
Staplestreet
Boughton Street
Dunkirk
Herne Bay
Hampton
Beltinge
Reculver
Towers & Roman Fort
Hillborough
Herne
Broomfield
Highstead
St Nicholas at Wade
Herne Common
Chislet
Boyden Gate
Sarre
Birchington
Acol
ISLE OF THANET
Minster
Monkton
KENT INTERNATIONAL
Manston
MARGATE
Tudor House
Westgate on Sea
Westbrook
Salmestone Grange
Quex House & Gdns
Spitfire & Hurricane Memorial, RAF Manston
Cliftonville
Kingsgate
Foreness Point
Long Nose Spit
White Ness
North Foreland
Bleak House
Broadstairs
Dickens House Museum
Northwood
Haine
Ramsgate
Pegwell
Cliffs End
St Augustine's Cross
Pegwell Bay
Oostende 4hrs (summer only)
Sandwich Flats
Stonar Cut
Great Stonar
Sandwich
Sandwich Bay
Salutation Gdn
Richborough Castle
Roman Amphitheatre
West End
Maypole
Hoath
Upstreet
Roman Road
West Stourmouth
Plucks Gutter
Wildwood Woodland
Calcott
Broadoak
Blean
Tyler Hill
Hersden
Westbere
Stodmarsh NNR
Stodmarsh
Grove
East Stourmouth
Westmarsh
Preston
Elmstone
Ware
Cop Street
Sturry
Fordwich
CANTERBURY
Canterbury Cathedral
Harbledown
Upper Harbledown
Thanington
St Augustine's Abbey
Wickhambreaux
Ickham
Littlebourne
Bramling
Shatterling
Ash
Marshborough
Wingham
Wingham Well
Staple
Barnsole
Woodnesborough
Worth
Toll
Howletts Wild Animal Park
Bekesbourne
Patrixbourne
Goodnestone Park
Goodnestone
Chillenden
Eastry
Ham
Hackling
Finglesham
Deal
Sholden
Adisham
Ratling
Knowlton
Betteshanger
Northbourne
Aylesham
Nonington
Easole Street
Tilmanstone
Elvington
Great Mongeham
Ripple
Walmer
Walmer Castle & Garden
Kingsdown
Ringwould
Sutton
East Studdal
Ashley
West Langdon
Martin Mill Sta
St Margaret's at Cliffe
West Cliffe
East Langdon
Guston
St Margaret's Bay
The Pines
South Foreland
South Foreland Lighthouse (NT)
Gateway to the White Cliffs
DOVER
Dover Castle
De Bradelei Wharf
Whitfield
Temple Ewell
River
Buckland
Knights Templar Church
Maxton
Womenswold
Woolage Village
Woolage Green
Barfrestone
Lower Eythorne
Eythorne
Shepherdswell (Sibertswold)
North Downs Way
Coldred
Denton
Wootton
Lydden
Ewell Minnis
Alkham
St Radigund's Abbey
South Alkham
West Hougham
Capel le Ferne
Women's Land Army Mus
Channel Tunnel
Channel Tunnel Terminal
East Wear Bay
Hawkinge
Paddlesworth
Swingfield Minnis
Densole
Acrise Place
Selstead
Etchinghill
Bridge
Nackington
Lower Hardres
Bishopsbourne
Kingston
Upper Hardres Court
Barham
Derringstone
Breach
Bladbean
Wingmore
Lyminge Forest
Elham
Stelling Minis
Bossingham
Stone Street
Waltham
Petham
Garlinge Green
Chartham
Shalmsford Street
Chartham Hatch
Oversland
Selling
Sheldwich Lees
Sheldwich
Gushmere
North Street
Brogdale Horticultural Trust
Whitehill
Old Wives Lees
Chilham
Chilham Castle
Shottenden
Badlesmere
Leaveland
Throwley
Eastling
Newnham
Doddington
Milstead
Dungate
Wichling
Frith
Payden Street
Otterden Place
Woodside Green
Warren Street
Stalisfield Green
Molash
Godmersham
Challock
Bilting
Crundale
Sole Street
Anvil Green
Lenham Heath
Charing
Charing Heath
Westwell Leacon
Westwell
Eastwell Park
Boughton Aluph
Boughton Lees
Kempe's Corner
Wye
Wye NNR
Hassell Street
Bodsham Green
Hastingleigh
Brook
Kennington
Little Chart
Pluckley
Pluckley Thorne
Hothfield
Ram Lane
Egerton
Pluckley Sta
ASHFORD
Willesborough Lees
Willesborough
Sevington
Great Chart
McArthur Glen
Beaver Green
Daniel's Water
Maltman's Hill
Bethersden
Bull Green
Brissenden
Shadoxhurst
Kingsnorth
Cheeseman's Green
Mersham
Smeeth
Sellindge
Stanford
Postling
Newington
Hinxhill
West Brabourne
Brabourne
Brabourne Lees
Broad Street
Stowting
Rhodes Minnis
Whatsole Street
Lymbridge Green
Sixmile
Maxted Street
Mount
Woodland
Ottinge
Lyminge
Newbarn
Stonestreet Green
Aldington
Westenhanger Sta
Tunnel
DOWNS
M2
M20
A2
A28
A299
A20
A256
A258
Boulogne ¾
Calais 1-1½
Dunkerque 2
hours

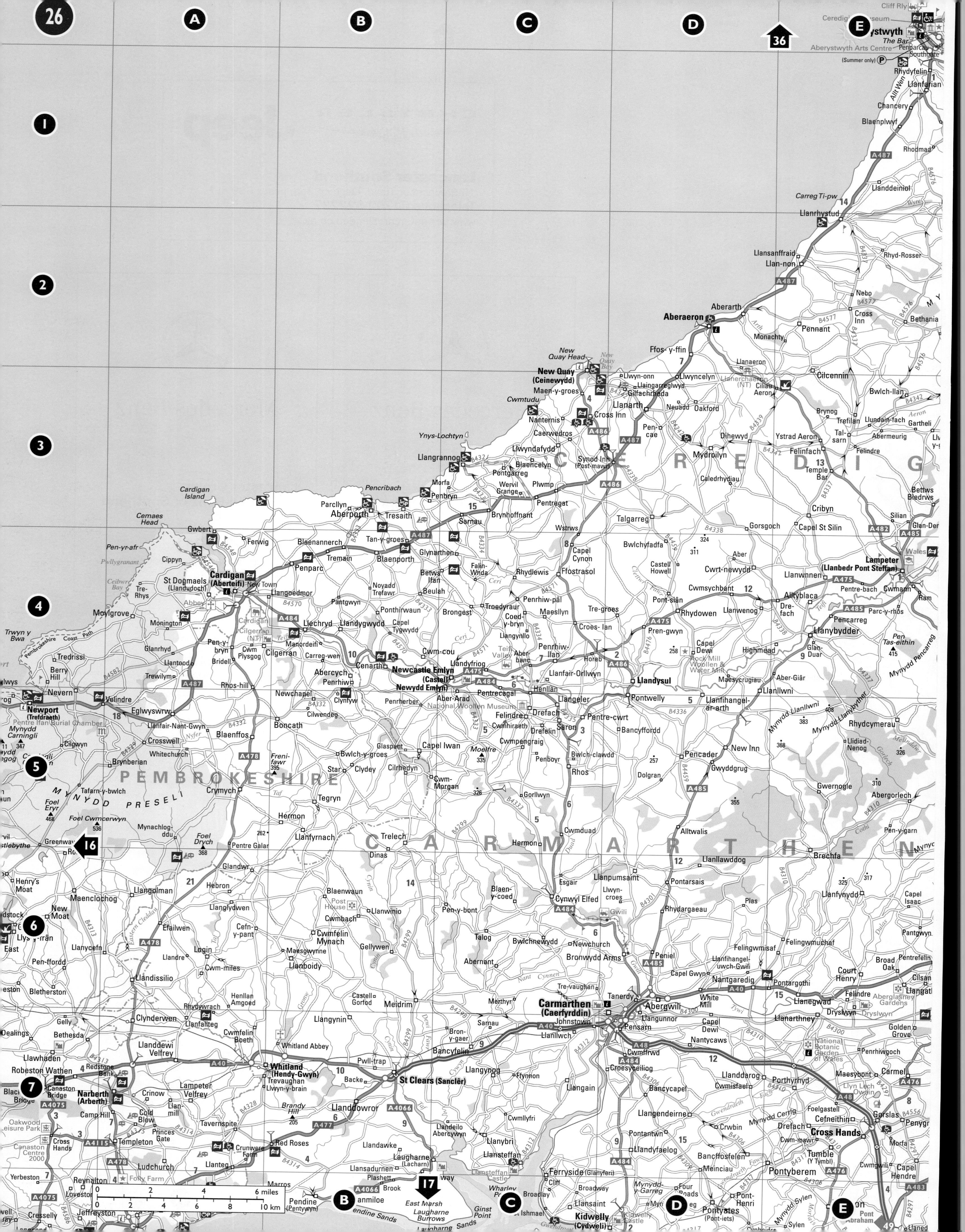
A
B
C
D
E
1
2
3
4
5
6
7
36
16
17
Aberystwyth
Ceredigion Museum
Cliff Rly
The Bar
Aberystwyth Arts Centre
Penparcau
Southgate
(Summer only)
Rhydyfelin
Llanfarian
Allt Wen
Chancery
Blaenplwyf
Rhodmad
A487
B4576
Llanddeiniol
Carreg Ti-pw
Wyre
Llanrhystud
Llansanffraid
Llan-non
Rhyd-Rosser
B4337
Nebo
B4577
Cross Inn
Bethania
Aberarth
Aberaeron
Pennant
Monachty
Arth
Ffos-y-ffin
New Quay Head
New Quay
(Ceinewydd)
New Quay Bay
Llwyn-onn
Llwyncelyn
Llaingarreglwyd
Gilfachrheda
Llanerchaeron (NT)
Cilcennin
Ciliau Aeron
Maen-y-groes
Cwmtudu
Llanarth
Neuadd
Oakford
Bwlch-llan
B4342
Nanternis
Cross Inn
A486
Pen-cae
Dihewyd
Brynog
Trefilan
Llundain-fach
Gartheli
Aeron
Caerwedros
Ystrad Aeron
Tal-sarn
Abermeurig
Ynys-Lochtyn
Llwyndafydd
Synod Inn
(Post-mawr)
Mydroilyn
Felinfach
Felindre
Llangrannog
Blaencelyn
Pontgarreg
C E R E D I G
13
Temple Bar
Caledrhydiau
Cardigan Island
Pencribach
Morfa
Penbryn
Wervil Grange
Plwmp
Bettws Bledrws
Cemaes Head
Parcllyn
Aberporth
Tresaith
15
Sarnau
Brynhoffnant
Pentregat
Talgarreg
Cribyn
Gwbert
Ferwig
Blaenannerch
Tan-y-groes
Glynarthen
Wstrws
Gorsgoch
Capel St Silin
Silian
Glan-Dery
Pen-yr-afr
Pwllygranant
Cippyn
Tremain
Blaenporth
8
Capel Cynon
Bwlchyfadfa
324
311
Aber
A482
A485
Ceibwr Bay
St Dogmaels
(Llandudoch)
Cardigan
(Aberteifi)
New Town
Penparc
Betws Ifan
Falin-Wnda
Rhydlewis
Ffostrasol
Castell Howell
Cwrt-newydd
Lampeter
(Llanbedr Pont Steffan)
Tre-Rhys
Llangoedmor
Noyadd Trefawr
Beulah
Ceri
Cwmsychbant
12
Llanwnnen
A475
Pentre-bach
Cwmann
Moylgrove
Abbey
Pantgwyn
Ponthirwaun
Brongest
Troedyraur
Penrhiw-pâl
Pont-siân
Alltyblaca
Drefach
Ram
Monington
Cardigan
Cilgerran (NT)
B4570
A484
Llechryd
Llandygwydd
Capel Tygwydd
Coed y-bryn
Maesllyn
Tre-groes
Croes-lan
Rhydowen
Llanwenog
A485
Pencarreg
Parc-y-rhôs
Trwyn y Bwa
Pembrokeshire Coast Path
Glanrhyd
Pen-y-bryn
Manordeifi
Llangynllo
Pren-gwyn
Llanybydder
Pen Tas-eithin
415
Tredrissi
Llantood
Cwm Plysgog
Cilgerran
Carreg-wen
10
Cwm-cou
Penrhiw-llan
Teifi Valley
Aber-banc
7
Horeb
2
Capel Dewi
258
Rock Mill Woollen & Water Mill
Highmead
Glan-Duar
9
Berry Hill
Bridell
Trewilyme
Abercych
Cenarth
Newcastle Emlyn
(Castell Newydd Emlyn)
Llandyfriog
A475
A484
6
Llanfair-Orllwyn
Llandysul
Maesycrugiau
Aber-Giâr
Mynydd Pencarreg
Nevern
Velindre
A487
Rhos-hill
Penrhiw
Newchapel
Clynfyw
Penrherber
Aber-Arad
Pentrecagal
Henllan
Llangeler
Pontwelly
Llanllwni
Newport
(Trefdraeth)
Eglwyswrw
National Woollen Museum
Drefach
Felindre
5
Pentre-cwrt
Llanfihangel-ar-arth
Mynydd Llanllwni
Mynydd Llanybydder
Rhydcymerau
Pentre Ifan Burial Chamber
18
Llanfair-Nant-Gwyn
Boncath
Cilwendeg
B4332
Cwmhiraeth
Saron
Drefelin
3
Bancyffordd
383
408
Llidiad-Nenog
Mynydd Carningli
347
Crosswell
Blaenffos
Nyfer
Whitechurch
Glaspant
Capel Iwan
Moelfre
335
Cwmpengraig
Bwlch-clawdd
257
Pencader
New Inn
368
326
Cilgwyn
A478
Freni-fawr
395
Bwlch-y-groes
Penboyr
Rhos
Gwyddgrug
Brynberian
Star
Clydey
Cilrhedyn
Dolgran
PEMBROKESHIRE
Cwm-Morgan
Gwernogle
310
Tafarn-y-bwlch
Crymych
Gorllwyn
Foel Eryr
468
MYNYDD PRESELI
Taf
Tegryn
326
355
Abergorlech
Hermon
B4333
6
Foel Cwmcerwyn
536
Mynachlog-ddu
Alltwalis
Pen-y-garn
262
5
Foel Drych
368
Greenway
Pentre Galar
Llanfyrnach
Trelech
Cwmduad
C A R M A R T H E N
Brechfa
Dinas
Hermon
12
Llanllawddog
Mynydd
Glandwr
B4299
Henry's Moat
21
Hebron
14
Esgair
Llanpumsaint
Pontarsais
325
317
Maenclochog
Llangolman
Blaenwaun
Blaen-y-coed
Cynwyl Elfed
Llwyn-croes
Llanfynydd
Capel Isaac
New Moat
Llangydwen
Post House
Llanwinio
Pen-y-bont
A484
Gwili
Rhydargaeau
Plas
B4313
Cwmbach
B4301
Efailwen
Cefn-y-pant
Cwmfelin Mynach
6
Pantgwyn
A478
Gellywen
Talog
Bwlchnewydd
Newchurch
Felingwmisaf
Felingwmuchaf
Llys-y-frân
East
Llanycefn
Login
Abernant
Bronwydd Arms
Peniel
Llanfihangel-uwch-Gwili
Broad Oak
Pentrefelin
Pen-ffordd
Llandre
Maesgwynne
Court Henry
Cwm-miles
Llanboidy
Nant Cynnen
Capel Gwyn
A485
Nantgaredig
Pontargothi
Cilsan
Llangathen
Llandissilio
Tre-vaughan
A40
15
Felindre
Bletherston
Henllan Amgoed
Castell Gorfod
Meidrim
Merthyr
Carmarthen
(Caerfyrddin)
Tanerdy
Abergwili
White Mill
Llanegwad
Aberglasney Gardens
Rhydywrach
Llangynin
Sarnau
Johnstown
Llangunnor
Dryslwyn
Gelly
Clynderwen
Llanfallteg
Cwmfelin Boeth
Pensarn
Llanarthney
Golden Grove
Dealings
Bethesda
Whitland Abbey
Bron-y-gaer
Llanllwch
Capel Dewi
Nantycaws
Llanddewi Velfrey
B4299
Bancyfelin
9
A48
National Botanic Garden of Wales
Penrhiwgoch
Llawhaden
Redstone Bank
A40
Whitland
(Hendy-Gwyn)
Pwll-trap
Cwmffrwd
12
Robeston Wathen
Trevaughan
10
Llangynog
Croesyceiliog
Llanddarog
Porthyrhyd
Maesybont
Carmel
Canaston Bridge
Narberth
(Arberth)
Llwyn-y-brain
Backe
St Clears (Sanclêr)
Ffynnon
Cwmisfael
A476
Lampeter Velfrey
Llangain
Bancycapel
Llyn Llech Owain
A48
Crinow
Llan-mill
A4066
B4310
8
Cold Blow
Brandy Hill
205
Llanddowror
Cwmllyfri
Llangendeirne
Foelgastell
Cefneithin
Gorslas
Camp Hill
Taf
Gwendraeth
Crwbin
Mynydd Cerrig
Drefach
Penygroes
Oakwood Leisure Park
Tavernspite
6
Llandeilo Abercywyn
Llanybri
Pontantwn
Cross Hands
3
Princes Gate
A477
9
Cwm-mawr
A4115
Templeton
Cross Hands
Crunwere Farm
Red Roses
Llandawke
Llansteffan
Llandyfaelog
15
Bancffosfelen
Tumble
(Y Tymbl)
Morfa
Canaston Centre 2000
Laugharne
(Lacharn)
Meinciau
Pontyberem
Cwmgwili
Capel Hendre
A478
Ludchurch
Llanteg
4
Llansadurnen
Llansteffan Castle
Ferryside (Glanyferi)
Cliff
Yerbeston
Reynalton
Folly Farm
Plashett
Brook
Marros
Broadway
A476
A4075
Lovesto
A4066
Pendine
(Pentywyn)
Amroth
East Marsh
Laugharne Burrows
Wharley Point
Broadlay
Llansaint
Mynydd-y-Garreg
Four Roads
Pont-Henri
Mynydd Sylen
Cresselly
Jeffreyston
Pendine Sands
Laugharne Sands
Ginst Point
St Ishmael
Kidwelly
(Cydweli)
Kidwelly Castle
Pontyates
(Pont-iets)
Sylen
Pont Abraham
Llanedi
0 2 4 6 miles
0 2 4 6 8 10 km

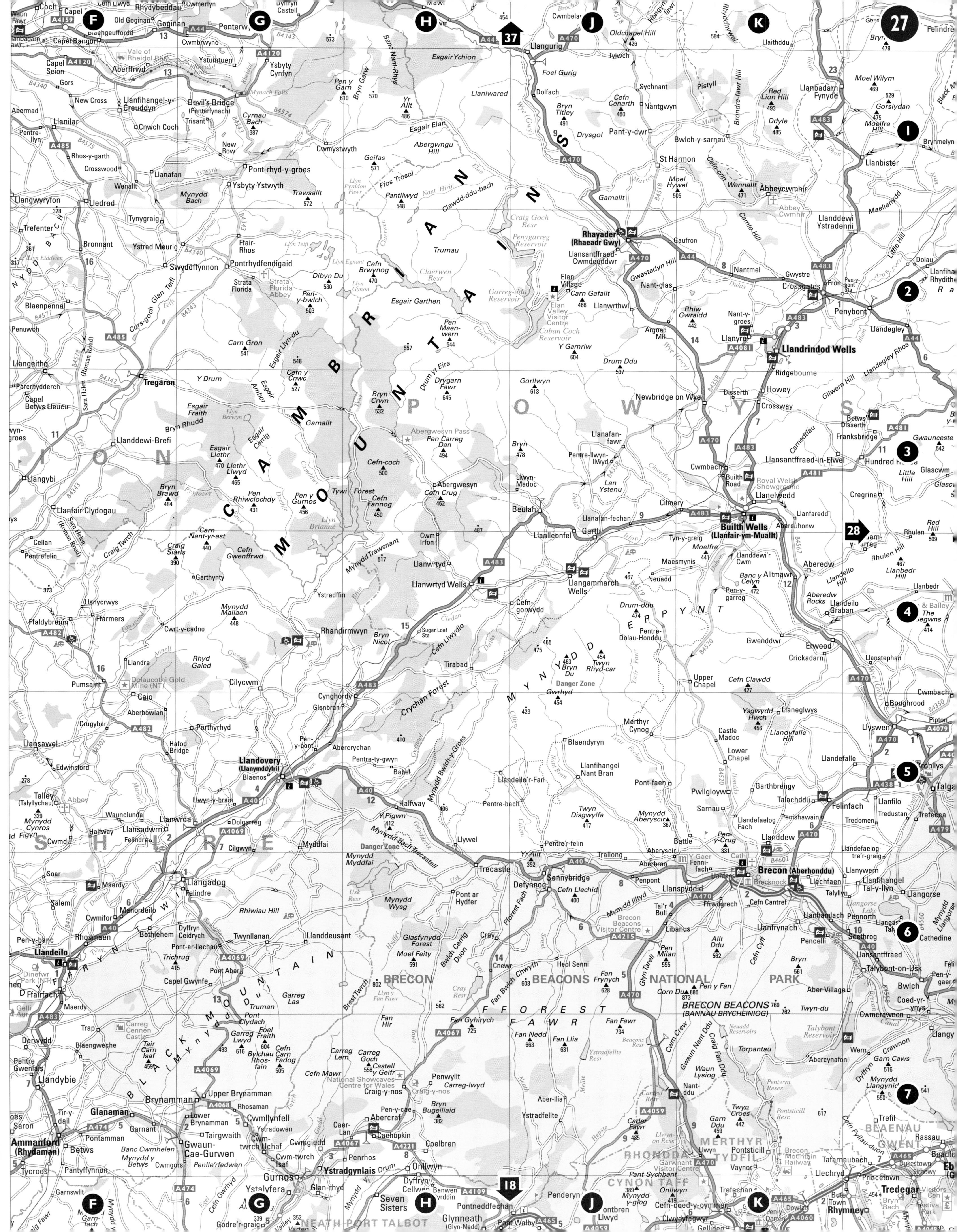

F
G
H
J
K
37
Capel Bangor
Goginan
Ponterwyd
Aberffrwd
Devil's Bridge (Pontarfynach)
Cwmystwyth
Llangurig
Rhayader (Rhaeadr Gwy)
Abbeycwmhir
Llanbadarn Fynydd
Llanbister
Llanddewi Ystradenni
Penybont
Llandrindod Wells
Crossgates
Newbridge on Wye
Builth Wells (Llanfair-ym-Muallt)
Llanwrtyd Wells
Llangammarch Wells
Beulah
Garth
Abergwesyn
Tregaron
Llanddewi-Brefi
Lampeter
Pontrhydfendigaid
Strata Florida
Ysbyty Ystwyth
Pont-rhyd-y-groes
Llanafan
Lledrod
Bronnant
Elan Village
Elan Valley Visitor Centre
Caban Coch Reservoir
Garreg-ddu Reservoir
Penygarreg Reservoir
Craig Goch Resr
Claerwen Resr
Llyn Brianne
CAMBRIAN MOUNTAINS
POWYS
Rhandirmwyn
Cilycwm
Pumsaint
Dolaucothi Gold Mine (NT)
Caio
Llansawel
Talley (Talyllychau)
Llandovery (Llanymddyfri)
Llangadog
Llandeilo
Ffairfach
Llandybie
Ammanford (Rhydaman)
Glanaman
Brynamman
Gwaun-Cae-Gurwen
Ystalyfera
Ystradgynlais
Abercraf
Craig-y-nos
Sennybridge
Trecastle
Defynnog
Brecon (Aberhonddu)
Llanfaes
Talgarth
Bronllys
Llyswen
Erwood
Felinfach
Libanus
Llanfrynach
Pencelli
Talybont-on-Usk
Bwlch
Llangorse
Talyllyn
Llanhamlach
Scethrog
Llansantffraed
Storey Arms
Pen y Fan
Corn Du
Cribyn
Fan Fawr
Fan Gyhirych
Fan Nedd
Fan Llia
Fan Brycheiniog
Fan Hir
Carmarthen Fan
BRECON BEACONS NATIONAL PARK
BRECON BEACONS (BANNAU BRYCHEINIOG)
FFOREST FAWR
BLACK MOUNTAIN (Mynydd Du)
MYNYDD EPPYNT
Danger Zone
Usk Resr
Cray Resr
Llwyn-on Resr
Talybont Reservoir
Neuadd Reservoirs
Brecon Beacons Visitor Centre
Brecon Mountain Railway
National Showcaves Centre for Wales
Merthyr Tydfil
Pontsticill
Penderyn
Glynneath (Glyn-Nedd)
Pontneddfechan
Seven Sisters
Tredegar
Rhymney
Princetown
Dukestown
Llechryd
BLAENAU GWENT
RHONDDA CYNON TAFF
MERTHYR TYDFIL
NEATH PORT TALBOT
CARMARTHENSHIRE
CEREDIGION
18
28
A44
A470
A483
A485
A482
A40
A4069
A4067
A4059
A465
A479
A438
A4215
A4120
A4081
A481
A4109
A4221
A4068
A474
A4159

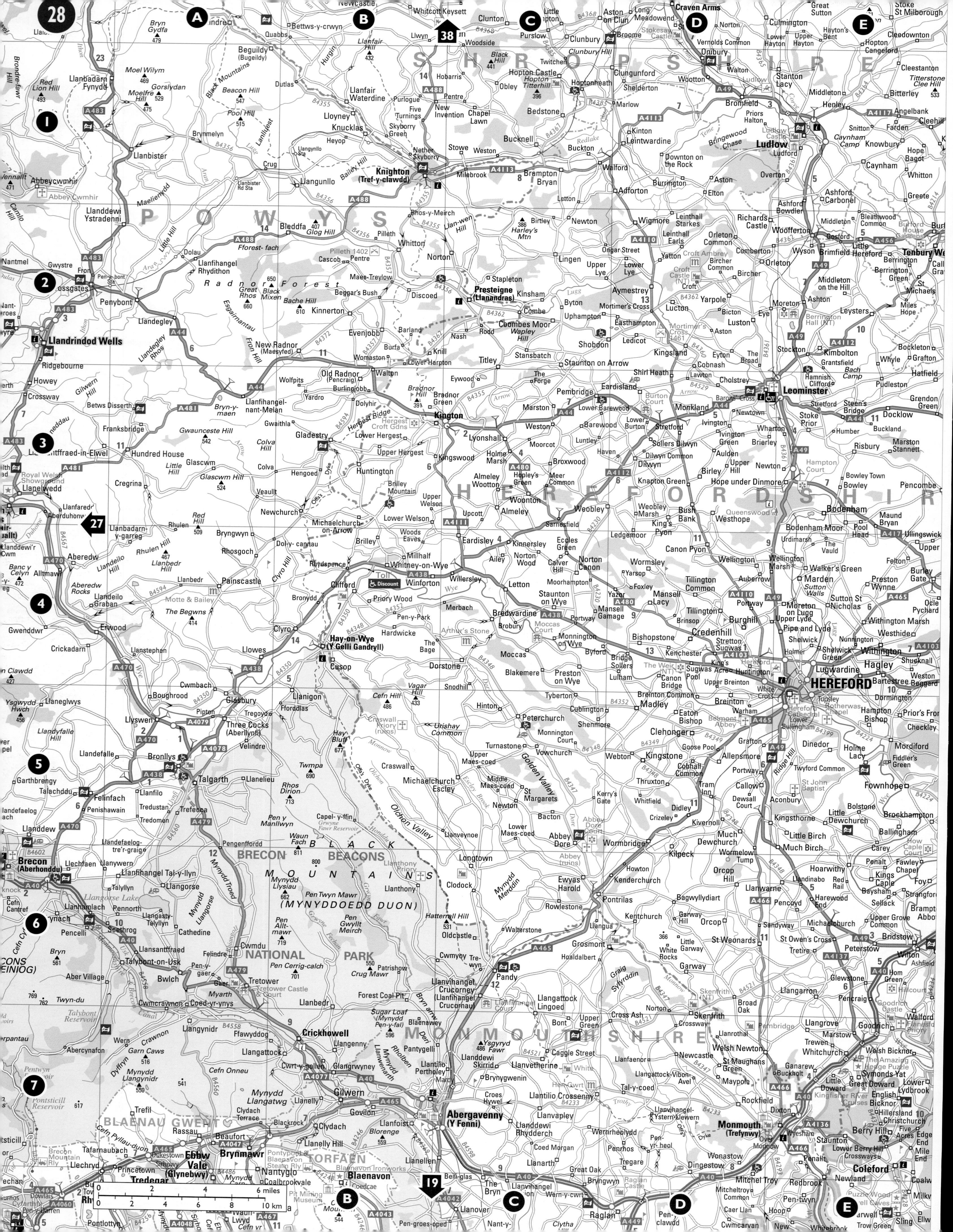
A
B
C
D
E
1
2
3
4
5
6
7
38
27
19
SHROPSHIRE
POWYS
HEREFORDSHIRE
MONMOUTHSHIRE
BLAENAU GWENT
TORFAEN
BRECON BEACONS NATIONAL PARK
BLACK MOUNTAINS (MYNYDDOEDD DUON)
Radnor Forest
Newcastle
Whitcott Keysett
Clunton
Purslow
Clunbury
Aston on Clun
Craven Arms
Onibury
Bromfield
Ludlow
Knighton (Tref-y-clawdd)
Beguildy (Bugeildy)
Llanbister
Abbeycwmhir
Llandrindod Wells
Penybont
Crossgates
Presteigne (Llanandras)
New Radnor (Maesyfed)
Old Radnor (Pencraig)
Kington
Pembridge
Leominster
Tenbury Wells
Bodenham
Hereford
Weobley
Eardisley
Hay-on-Wye (Y Gelli Gandryll)
Clifford
Whitney-on-Wye
Builth Wells (Llanfair-ym-Muallt)
Llanelwedd
Brecon (Aberhonddu)
Talgarth
Bronllys
Glasbury
Three Cocks (Aberllynfi)
Crickhowell
Abergavenny (Y Fenni)
Gilwern
Govilon
Blaenavon
Brynmawr
Ebbw Vale (Glynebwy)
Tredegar
Nantyglo
Raglan
Monmouth (Trefynwy)
Pandy
Pontrilas
Kilpeck
Madley
Ross-on-Wye
Coleford
Goodrich
Mordiford
Fownhope
Tupsley
Credenhill
Burghill
Wellington
Marden
Dinmore
Moccas
Peterchurch
Dorstone
Longtown
Llanthony
Golden Valley
Olchon Valley
Talybont-on-Usk
Bwlch
Llangorse
Llangorse Lake
Pennorth
Llangynidr
Pen y Fan
Toll
Discount
Welsh Newton
Skenfrith
Grosmont
Garway
St Weonards
Llangarron
Much Dewchurch
Much Birch
Kingsthorne
Orcop
Kentchurch
Ewyas Harold
Kenderchurch
Abbey Dore
Vowchurch
Kingstone
Allensmore
Clehonger
Belmont Abbey
Ludlow Castle
Croft Castle (NT)
Berrington Hall (NT)
Hergest Croft Gdns
Arthur's Stone
Tretower Castle & Court
Llanvihangel Crucorney
Llantilio Crossenny
Blaenavon Ironworks
Pontypool & Blaenavon Steam Rly
The Amazing Hedge Puzzle
Kingfisher River Cruises
0 2 4 6 miles
0 2 4 6 8 10 km

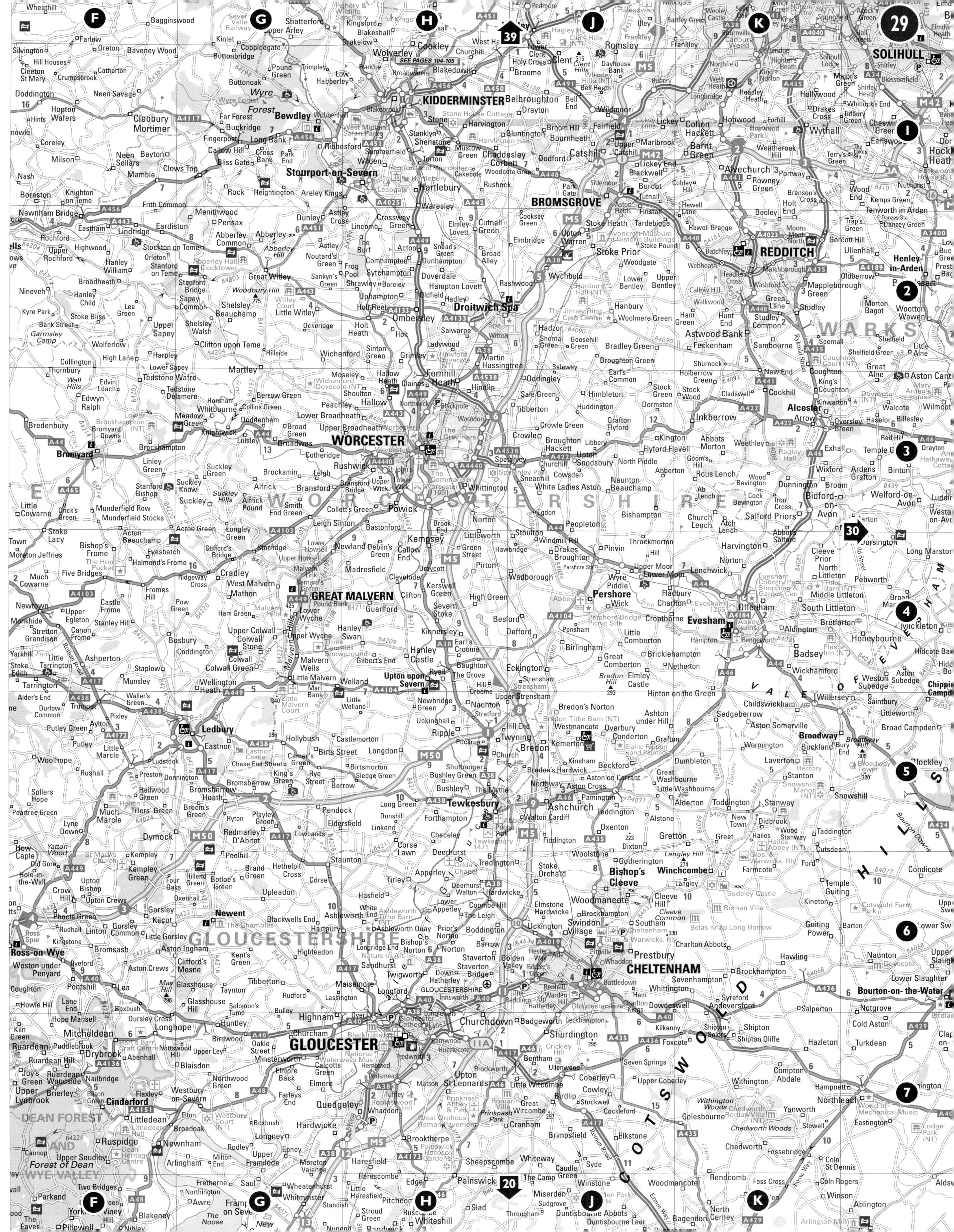
F
G
H
J
K
39
SEE PAGES 104-105
SOLIHULL
KIDDERMINSTER
Bewdley
Wyre Forest
Cleobury Mortimer
Stourport-on-Severn
BROMSGROVE
REDDITCH
Henley-in-Arden
Droitwich Spa
WARKS
Alcester
Bromyard
WORCESTER
WORCESTERSHIRE
Pershore
Evesham
Bidford-on-Avon
30
GREAT MALVERN
Ledbury
Upton upon Severn
Tewkesbury
Ashchurch
Broadway
VALE OF EVESHAM
Bishop's Cleeve
Winchcombe
Newent
GLOUCESTERSHIRE
Ross-on-Wye
CHELTENHAM
Bourton-on-the-Water
GLOUCESTER
Cinderford
DEAN FOREST AND Forest of Dean
WYE VALLEY
COTSWOLD HILLS
COTSWOLD
Painswick
Northleach
20
M5
M50
M42
A38
A44
A46
A417
A435
A40
A449
A456

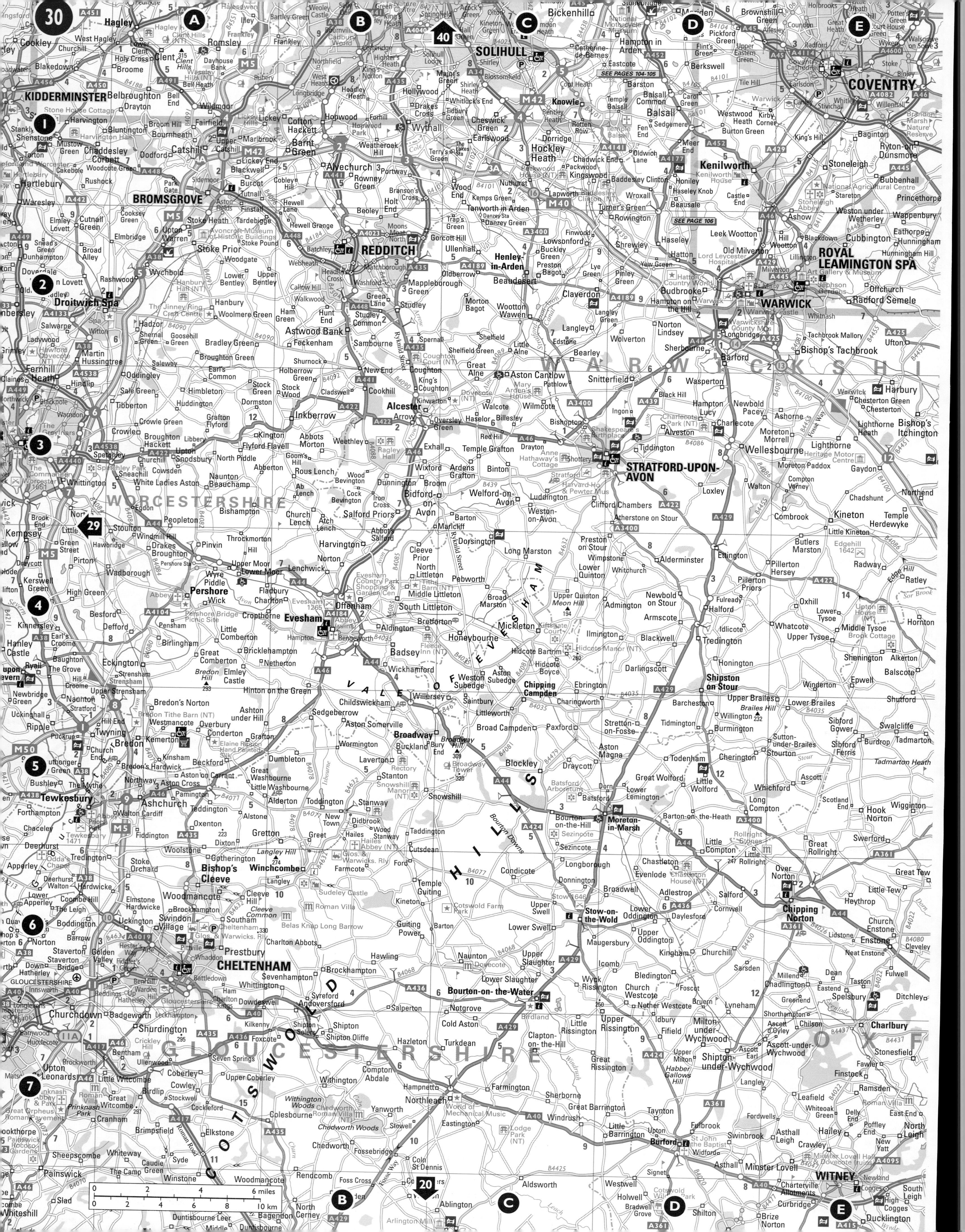
A
B
C
D
E
40
20
29
KIDDERMINSTER
BROMSGROVE
Droitwich Spa
REDDITCH
SOLIHULL
COVENTRY
Kenilworth
WARWICK
ROYAL LEAMINGTON SPA
STRATFORD-UPON-AVON
Alcester
Evesham
Pershore
Tewkesbury
CHELTENHAM
Winchcombe
Broadway
Chipping Campden
Moreton-in-Marsh
Shipston on Stour
Stow-on-the-Wold
Bourton-on-the-Water
Chipping Norton
Charlbury
Burford
WITNEY
Henley-in-Arden
Hagley
WORCESTERSHIRE
WARWICKSHIRE
GLOUCESTERSHIRE
VALE OF EVESHAM
COTSWOLD HILLS
COTSWOLDS
SEE PAGES 104-105
SEE PAGE 106
M5
M42
M40
M50
A44
A46
A429
A40
A435
A38
A422
A3400
A361
A424
A436
A417
A4019
A445
A452
0 2 4 6 miles
0 2 4 6 8 10 km

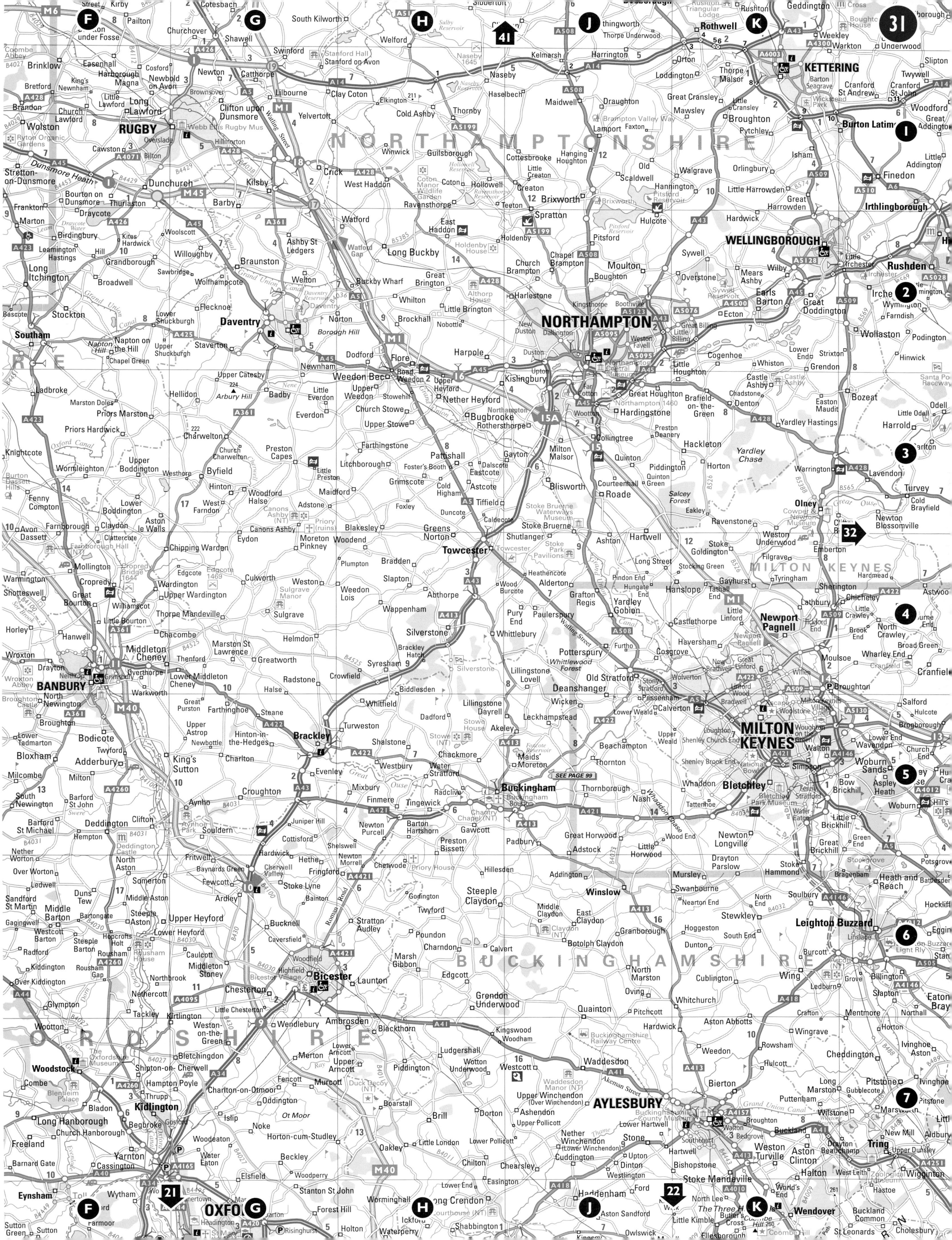
NORTHAMPTONSHIRE
BUCKINGHAMSHIRE
OXFORDSHIRE
MILTON KEYNES
F
G
H
J
K
I
2
3
4
5
6
7
41
32
21
22
SEE PAGE 99
M6
M1
M40
M45
A5
A14
A43
A45
A428
A421
A422
A413
A41
A34
A4260
RUGBY
Brinklow
Long Lawford
Newbold on Avon
Clifton upon Dunsmore
Dunchurch
Thurlaston
Southam
Stockton
Long Itchington
Daventry
Braunston
Welton
Norton
Crick
Kilsby
Barby
Yelvertoft
Swinford
South Kilworth
Welford
Naseby
Kelmarsh
Harrington
Rothwell
Orton
KETTERING
Barton Seagrave
Burton Latimer
Finedon
Broughton
Pytchley
Isham
Orlingbury
Guilsborough
West Haddon
Cottesbrooke
Creaton
Brixworth
Spratton
Holdenby
Long Buckby
East Haddon
Watford
Great Brington
Little Brington
Harlestone
Church Brampton
Chapel Brampton
Moulton
Boughton
Pitsford
Hannington
Walgrave
Overstone
Sywell
Mears Ashby
Wilby
WELLINGBOROUGH
Irthlingborough
Rushden
Great Doddington
Earls Barton
Ecton
Wollaston
NORTHAMPTON
Duston
Kingsthorpe
Weston Favell
Great Billing
Little Houghton
Great Houghton
Hardingstone
Collingtree
Milton Malsor
Blisworth
Gayton
Kislingbury
Harpole
Nether Heyford
Bugbrooke
Rothersthorpe
Weedon Bec
Flore
Dodford
Newnham
Badby
Everdon
Church Stowe
Upper Stowe
Farthingstone
Pattishall
Litchborough
Maidford
Preston Capes
Byfield
Charwelton
Priors Marston
Priors Hardwick
Woodford Halse
Adstone
Canons Ashby
Moreton Pinkney
Eydon
Chipping Warden
Wardington
Culworth
Sulgrave
Weedon Lois
Towcester
Greens Norton
Blakesley
Tiffield
Roade
Courteenhall
Stoke Bruerne
Shutlanger
Hartwell
Ashton
Hanslope
Yardley Gobion
Grafton Regis
Potterspury
Paulerspury
Silverstone
Whittlebury
Deanshanger
Old Stratford
Wicken
Akeley
Leckhampstead
Olney
Emberton
Sherington
Newport Pagnell
Lathbury
Chicheley
North Crawley
Moulsoe
Broughton
MILTON KEYNES
Wolverton
Stony Stratford
Bletchley
Woburn Sands
Woburn
Great Brickhill
Soulbury
Leighton Buzzard
Linslade
Wing
Stewkley
Winslow
Swanbourne
Mursley
Great Horwood
Nash
Thornborough
Buckingham
Maids Moreton
Tingewick
Finmere
Padbury
Steeple Claydon
East Claydon
Middle Claydon
Granborough
Quainton
Waddesdon
Whitchurch
Aston Abbotts
Bierton
AYLESBURY
Stone
Bishopstone
Stoke Mandeville
Wendover
Weston Turville
Aston Clinton
Halton
Tring
Wigginton
Marsworth
Pitstone
Cheddington
Ivinghoe
Haddenham
Long Crendon
Brill
Ludgershall
Grendon Underwood
Edgcott
Marsh Gibbon
Bicester
Launton
Ambrosden
Blackthorn
Arncott
Piddington
Merton
Charlton-on-Otmoor
Islip
Oddington
Noke
Beckley
Kidlington
Woodstock
Bladon
Long Hanborough
Church Hanborough
Freeland
Yarnton
Cassington
Eynsham
Wytham
OXFORD
Headington
Begbroke
Shipton-on-Cherwell
Bletchingdon
Weston-on-the-Green
Kirtlington
Chesterton
Middleton Stoney
Upper Heyford
Lower Heyford
Steeple Aston
Middle Aston
Somerton
Ardley
Fritwell
Souldern
Aynho
Croughton
Evenley
Brackley
Turweston
Westbury
Kings Sutton
Charlton
Hinton-in-the-Hedges
Farthinghoe
BANBURY
Middleton Cheney
Bodicote
Adderbury
Bloxham
Milcombe
Deddington
Barford St Michael
Hempton
Hanwell
Drayton
Wroxton
Horley
Cropredy
Mollington
Farnborough
Fenny Compton
Wormleighton
Avon Dassett
Ladbroke
Napton on the Hill
Bourton on Dunsmore
Draycote
Marton
Birdingbury
Leamington Hastings
Grandborough
Willoughby
Wolfhampcote
Flecknoe
Staverton
Hellidon
Catesby
Arbury Hill

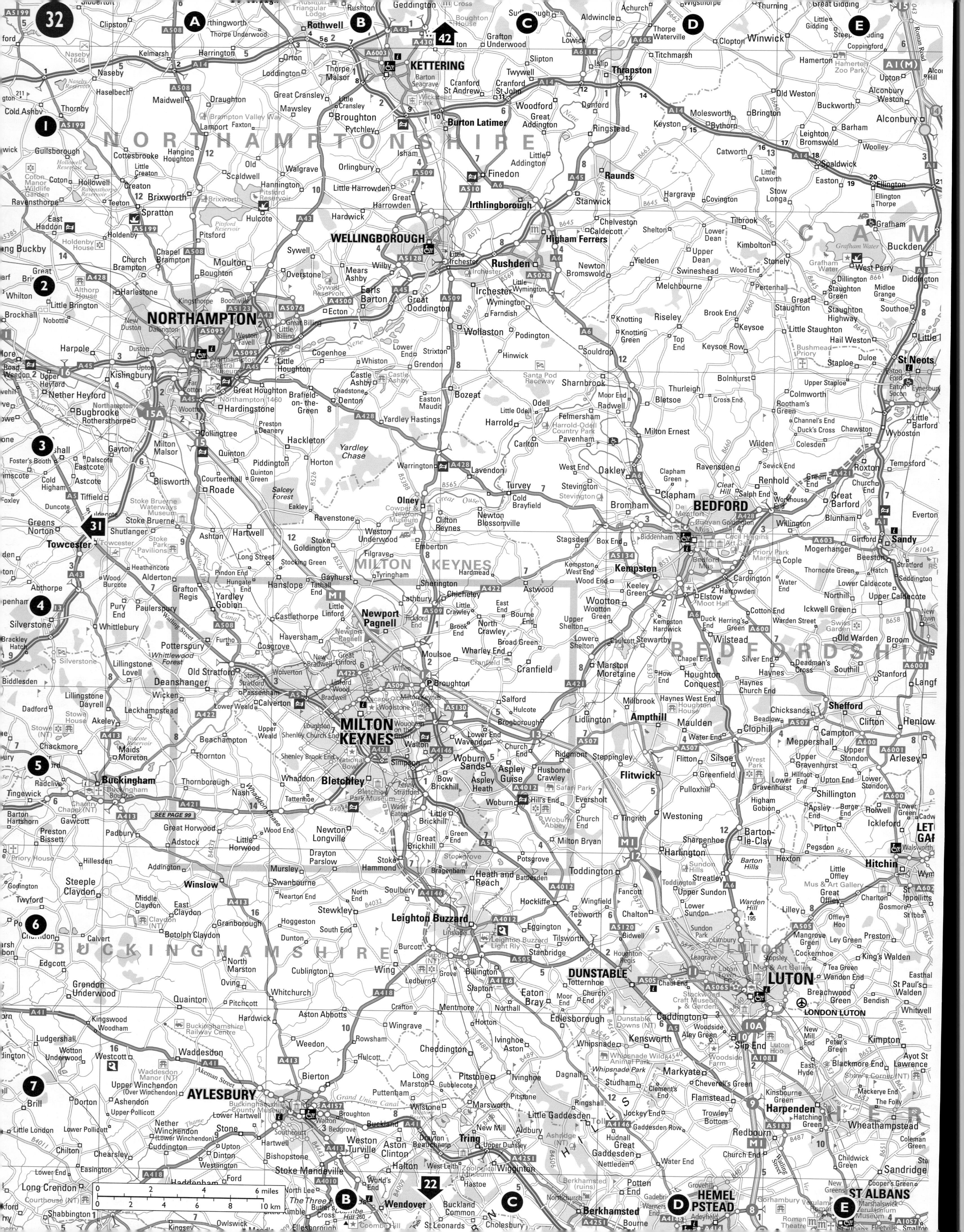

NORTHAMPTONSHIRE
BUCKINGHAMSHIRE
BEDFORDSHIRE
MILTON KEYNES
KETTERING
Rothwell
Burton Latimer
Thrapston
Raunds
Finedon
Irthlingborough
Higham Ferrers
Rushden
WELLINGBOROUGH
NORTHAMPTON
Towcester
Olney
Newport Pagnell
MILTON KEYNES
Bletchley
Buckingham
Winslow
Leighton Buzzard
DUNSTABLE
LUTON
LONDON LUTON
Harpenden
ST ALBANS
HEMEL HEMPSTEAD
Berkhamsted
Tring
Wendover
AYLESBURY
BEDFORD
Kempston
Ampthill
Flitwick
Shefford
Sandy
St Neots
Hitchin
Woburn
Toddington
Yardley Chase
Salcey Forest
Whittlewood Forest
Grafham Water
Brixworth
Long Buckby
Brackley
Silverstone
Stony Stratford
Olney
Wing
Brill
SEE PAGE 99
0 2 4 6 miles
0 2 4 6 8 10 km

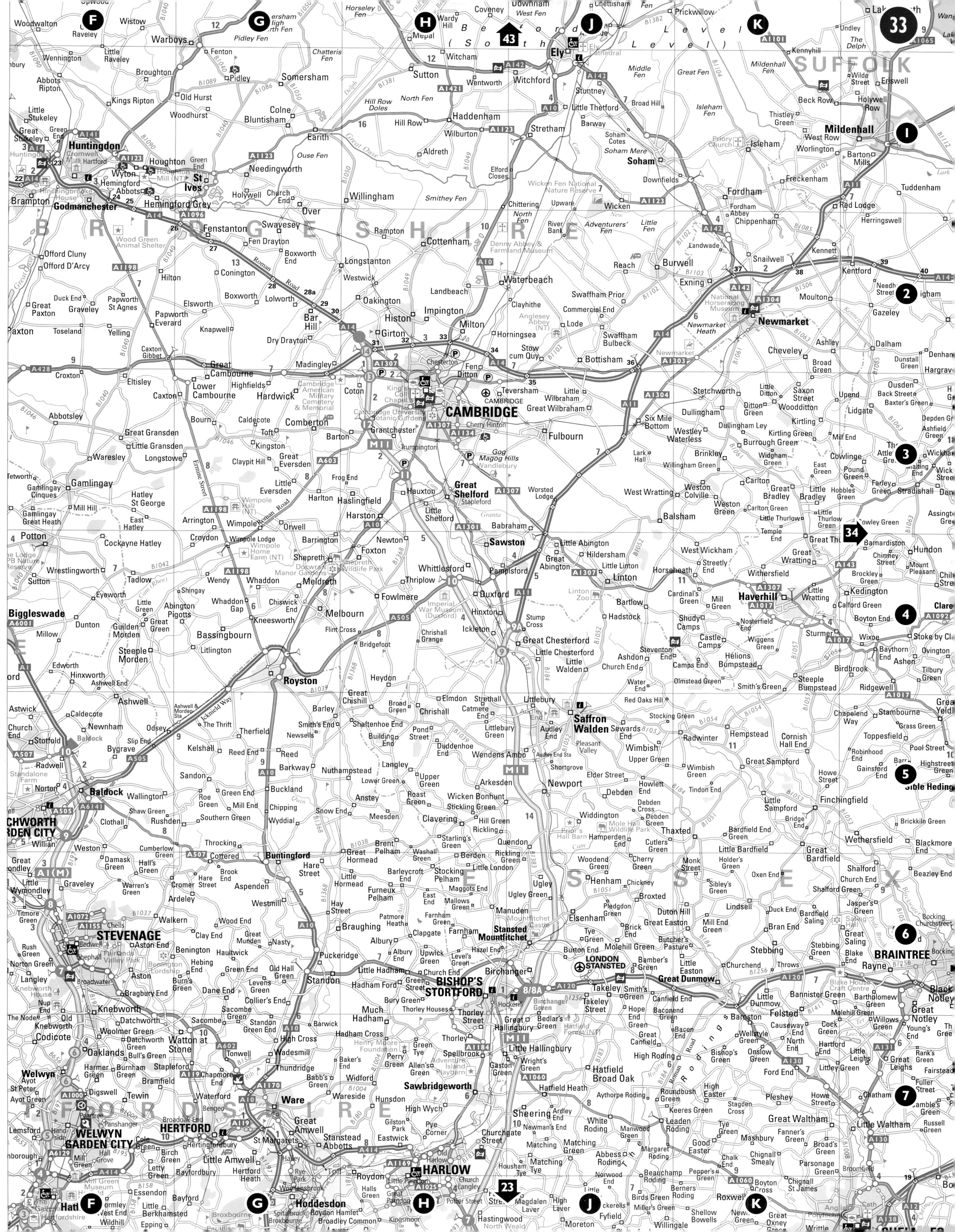

F
G
H
J
K
43
SUFFOLK
CAMBRIDGESHIRE
HERTFORDSHIRE
ESSEX
Bedford Level (South Level)
Huntingdon
Godmanchester
St Ives
Warboys
Somersham
Ely
Witchford
Sutton
Haddenham
Stretham
Soham
Mildenhall
Isleham
Fordham
Chippenham
Burwell
Newmarket
Exning
Kentford
Moulton
Cheveley
Willingham
Over
Cottenham
Waterbeach
Histon
Girton
Impington
Milton
Bottisham
CAMBRIDGE
Cherry Hinton
Fulbourn
Teversham
Grantchester
Trumpington
Comberton
Barton
Great Shelford
Sawston
Linton
Haverhill
Balsham
Great Abington
Duxford
Whittlesford
Melbourn
Meldreth
Bassingbourn
Royston
Gamlingay
Biggleswade
Potton
Baldock
Letchworth Garden City
Ashwell
Buntingford
Saffron Walden
Newport
Thaxted
Great Dunmow
Stansted Mountfitchet
Bishop's Stortford
London Stansted
Sawbridgeworth
Harlow
Ware
Hertford
Hoddesdon
Stevenage
Knebworth
Welwyn
Welwyn Garden City
Hatfield
Braintree
Great Bardfield
Finchingfield
Steeple Bumpstead
Clare
Great Sampford
Felsted
Great Waltham
Little Waltham
Great Notley
Standon
Puckeridge
Much Hadham
Sheering
Hatfield Broad Oak
Great Cambourne
Papworth Everard
Bar Hill
Fenstanton
Hemingford Grey
Brampton
Wood Green Animal Shelter
Wicken Fen National Nature Reserve
Anglesey Abbey (NT)
Imperial War Museum (Duxford)
National Horseracing Museum
Wimpole Hall (NT)
Wimpole Home Farm (NT)
Shepreth Wildlife Park
Linton Zoo
Mole Hall Wildlife Park
34
23

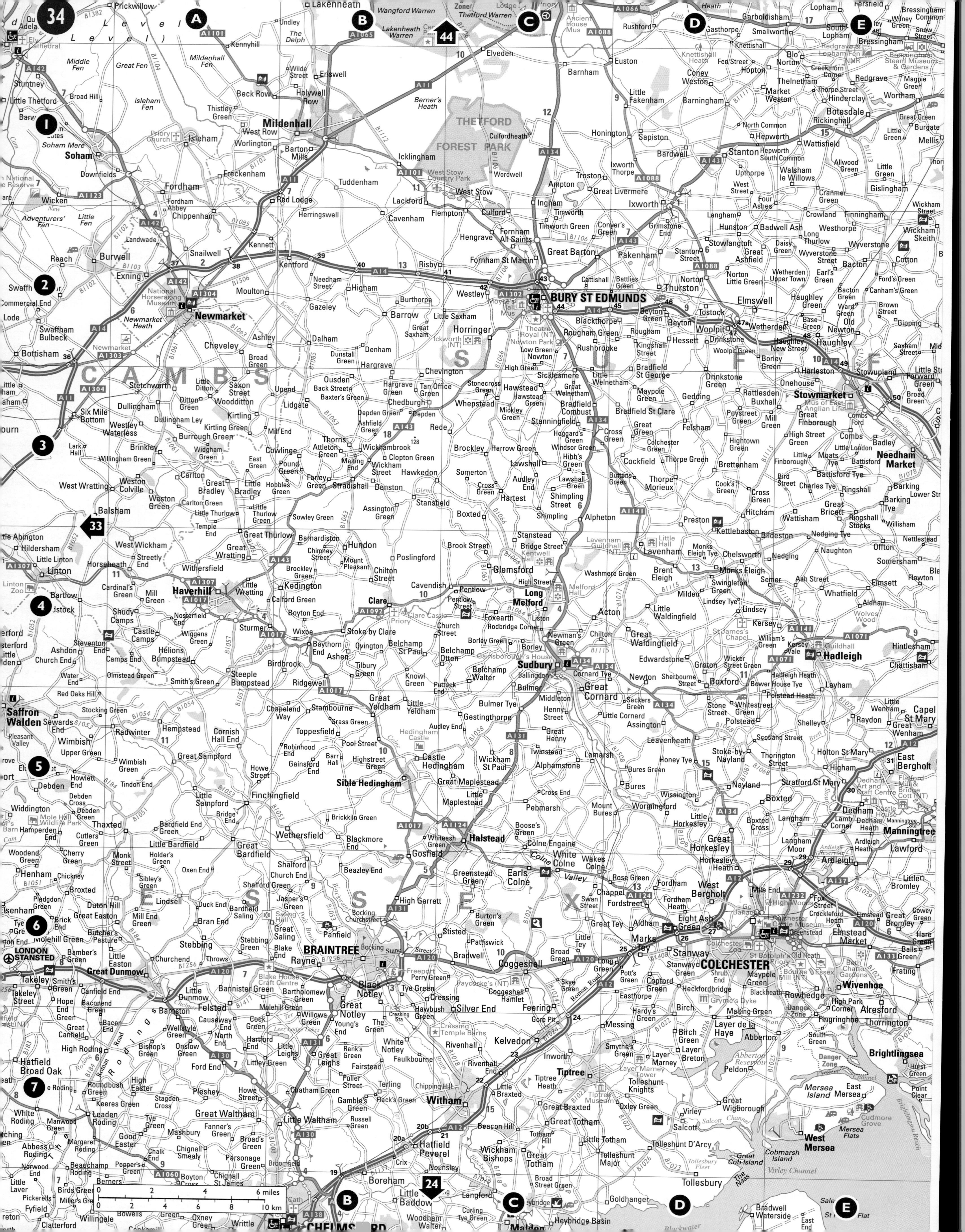

A
B
C
D
E
44
Prickwillow
Lakenheath
Wangford Warren
Lakenheath Warren
Thetford Warren
Elveden
Rushford
Garboldisham
Gasthorpe
Lopham
South Lopham
Bressingham
Fersfield
Ely Cathedral
Middle Fen
Great Fen
Mildenhall Fen
Kennyhill
Undley
The Delph
Wilde Street
Eriswell
Euston
Knettishall
Coney Weston
Hopton
Thelnetham
Blo' Norton
Redgrave
Market Weston
Hinderclay
Botesdale
Rickinghall
Wortham
Stuntney
Little Thetford
Broad Hill
Isleham Fen
Thistley Green
Beck Row
Holywell Row
Berner's Heath
Barnham
Little Fakenham
Barningham
THETFORD FOREST PARK
Culfordheath
Mildenhall
West Row
Isleham
Worlington
Barton Mills
Icklingham
Honington
Sapiston
Hepworth
Wattisfield
North Common
Soham Mere
Soham
Downfields
Freckenham
Tuddenham
West Stow Country Park
Wordwell
Bardwell
Stanton
Walsham le Willows
Ixworth Thorpe
Troston
Ampton
Great Livermere
Fordham
Red Lodge
Lackford
West Stow
Culford
Flempton
Ingham
Timworth
Ixworth
Wicken
Adventurers' Fen
Little Fen
Chippenham
Herringswell
Cavenham
Hengrave
Fornham All Saints
Conyer's Green
Pakenham
Langham
Badwell Ash
Hunston
Finningham
Westhorpe
Wyverstone
Reach
Burwell
Landwade
Snailwell
Kennett
Kentford
Risby
Fornham St Martin
Great Barton
Stowlangtoft
Great Ashfield
Bacton
Cotton
Swaffham Bulbeck
Exning
Newmarket
Newmarket Heath
Moulton
Needham Street
Higham
Gazeley
Barrow
Burthorpe
Little Saxham
Westley
BURY ST EDMUNDS
Thurston
Norton
Elmswell
Tostock
Beyton
Woolpit
Wetherden
Haughley
Bottisham
Cheveley
Ashley
Dalham
Denham
Great Saxham
Ickworth (NT)
Horringer
Blackthorpe
Rougham Green
Rushbrooke
Hessett
Drinkstone
Harleston
Stowupland
CAMBS
Stetchworth
Saxon Street
Woodditton
Upend
Ousden
Hargrave
Chevington
Hawstead
Sicklesmere
Bradfield St George
Bradfield Combust
Bradfield St Clare
Rattlesden
Buxhall
Onehouse
Stowmarket
Six Mile Bottom
Dullingham
Westley Waterless
Kirtling
Lidgate
Chedbrugh
Whepstead
Stanningfield
Felsham
Great Finborough
Combs
Burrough Green
Brinkley
Cowlinge
Wickhambrook
Rede
Brockley
Cockfield
Hightown Green
Brettenham
Needham Market
Barking
Carlton
Great Bradley
Little Bradley
Stradishall
Denston
Hawkedon
Somerton
Lawshall
Hartest
Thorpe Morieux
Cross Green
West Wratting
Weston Colville
Weston Green
Balsham
33
Little Thurlow
Great Thurlow
Sowley Green
Stansfield
Boxted
Shimpling
Alpheton
Preston
Hitcham
Wattisham
Ringshall
Bildeston
Nedging Tye
Little Abington
Hildersham
Linton
Horseheath
West Wickham
Great Wratting
Withersfield
Barnardiston
Hundon
Poslingford
Brook Street
Glemsford
Lavenham
Brent Eleigh
Monks Eleigh
Chelsworth
Naughton
Offton
Somersham
Bartlow
Haverhill
Kedington
Little Wratting
Chilton Street
Cavendish
Clare
Long Melford
Acton
Swingleton Green
Milden
Whatfield
Aldham
Castle Camps
Sturmer
Stoke by Clare
Wixoe
Belchamp St Paul
Foxearth
Liston
Little Waldingfield
Kersey
Great Waldingfield
Hintlesham
Ashdon
Helions Bumpstead
Birdbrook
Ashen
Ovington
Tilbury Green
Borley
Sudbury
Chilton
Edwardstone
Groton
Boxford
Hadleigh
Chattisham
Steeple Bumpstead
Ridgewell
Knowl Green
Belchamp Walter
Bulmer
Great Cornard
Newton
Layham
Saffron Walden
Wimbish
Radwinter
Hempstead
Cornish Hall End
Great Yeldham
Little Yeldham
Stambourne
Toppesfield
Gestingthorpe
Henny Street
Little Cornard
Assington
Leavenheath
Shelley
Raydon
Capel St Mary
Great Wenham
Debden
Great Sampford
Finchingfield
Castle Hedingham
Sible Hedingham
Wickham St Paul
Alphamstone
Lamarsh
Bures
Nayland
Stoke-by-Nayland
Higham
Holton St Mary
East Bergholt
Stratford St Mary
Thaxted
Little Sampford
Wethersfield
Halstead
Pebmarsh
Wormingford
Boxted
Langham
Dedham
Manningtree
Lawford
Great Bardfield
Little Bardfield
Shalford
Gosfield
Colne Engaine
White Colne
Wakes Colne
Earls Colne
Great Horkesley
West Bergholt
Ardleigh
Little Bromley
Lindsell
Great Easton
Stebbing
Braintree
Bocking
High Garrett
Panfield
Rayne
Coggeshall
Marks Tey
Stanway
COLCHESTER
Elmstead Market
Wivenhoe
LONDON STANSTED
Great Dunmow
Takeley
Felsted
Black Notley
Great Notley
Silver End
Feering
Kelvedon
Messing
Rowhedge
Alresford
Thorrington
High Roding
Hatfield Broad Oak
Pleshey
Great Waltham
Little Waltham
Terling
Witham
Tiptree
Layer de la Haye
Abberton
Peldon
Brightlingsea
White Roding
Leaden Roding
Good Easter
Hatfield Peverel
Wickham Bishops
Great Totham
Tolleshunt D'Arcy
Tollesbury
West Mersea
Mersea Island
East Mersea
Boreham
Little Baddow
24
Langford
Maldon
Heybridge Basin
Goldhanger
Bradwell Waterside
CHELMSFORD
Writtle
Willingale
Fyfield
0 2 4 6 miles
0 2 4 6 8 10 km

F
G
H
J
K
1
2
3
4
5
6
7
45
25
Diss
Scole
Eye
Halesworth
Southwold
Walberswick
Blythburgh
Wenhaston
Blyford
Wangford
Reydon
Stradbroke
Framlingham
Saxmundham
Leiston
Sizewell
Thorpeness
Aldeburgh
Snape
Wickham Market
Debenham
Woodbridge
Melton
Orford
Orford Ness
Rendlesham Forest
Tunstall Forest
Martlesham
IPSWICH
Felixstowe
Harwich
Walton on the Naze
Frinton- on-Sea
CLACTON-ON-SEA
Jaywick
St Osyth
Manningtree
Mistley
Brantham
Holbrook
Shotley Gate
Landguard Point
Hollesley Bay
Aldeburgh Bay
Gunfleet Sand
Colne Point
Sandy Point
Stone Point
The Naze
hours
Cuxhaven (Hamburg)......20
Esbjerg............................19
Hoek van Holland..........3¾

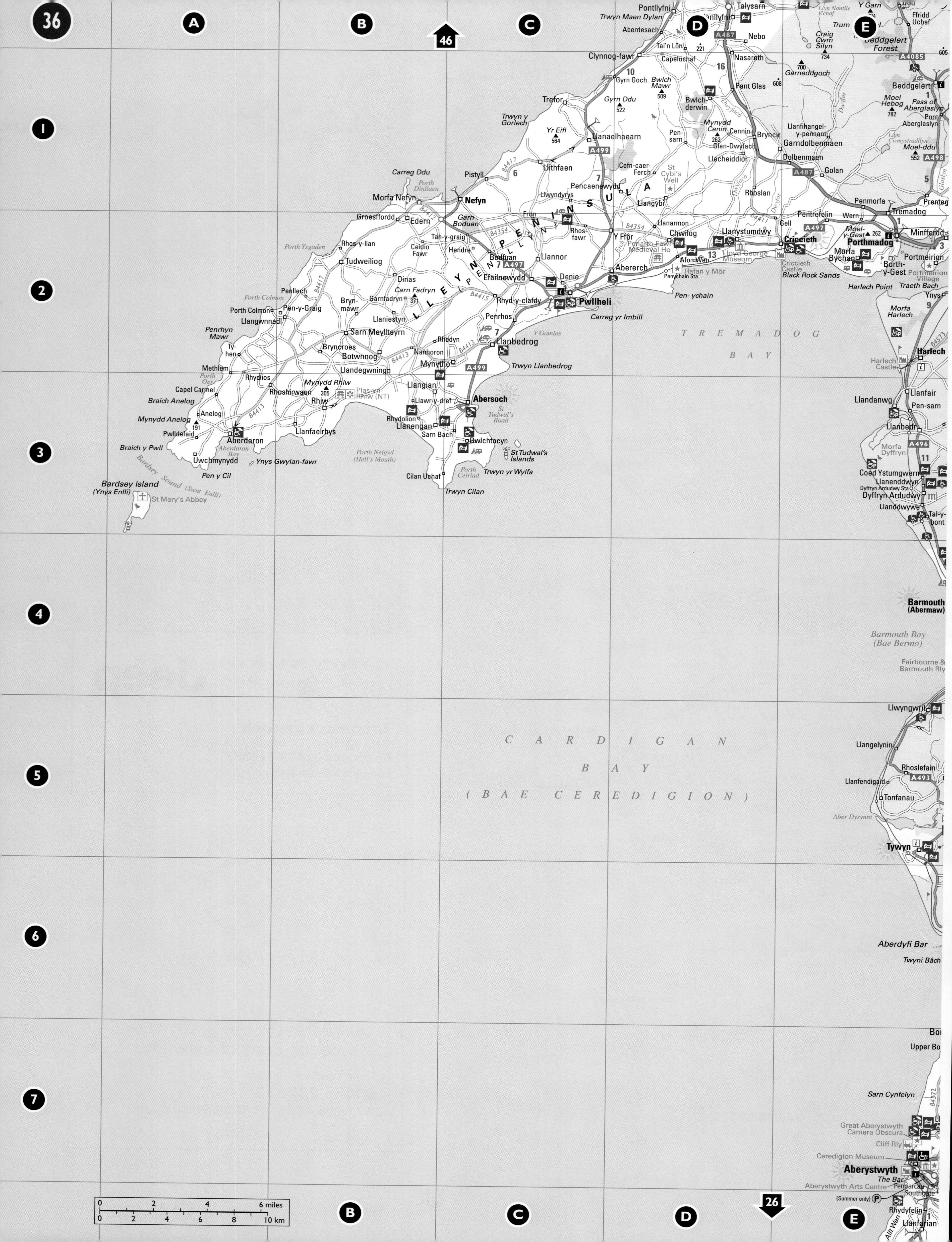
A
B
C
D
E
46
26
1
2
3
4
5
6
7
Pontllyfni
Trwyn Maen Dylan
Aberdesach
Talysarn
Llanllyfni
Tai'n Lôn
Nebo
Clynnog-fawr
Capeluchaf
Nasareth
Llyn Nantlle Uchaf
Y Garn
Trum
Craig Cwm Silyn
Ffridd Uchaf
Beddgelert Forest
Garneddgoch
Gyrn Goch
Bwlch Mawr
Pant Glas
Beddgelert
Moel Hebog
Pass of Aberglaslyn
Pont Aberglaslyn
Trefor
Gyrn Ddu
Bwlch-derwin
Trwyn y Gorlech
Yr Eifl
Llanaelhaearn
Mynydd Cenin
Pen-sarn
Cennin
Bryncir
Llanfihangel-y-pennant
Garndolbenmaen
Glan-Dwyfach
Llecheiddior
Dolbenmaen
Moel-ddu
Llithfaen
Cefn-caer-Ferch
St Cybi's Well
Golan
Carreg Ddu
Porth Dinllaen
Pistyll
Pencaenewydd
Llwyndyrys
Llangybi
Rhoslan
Morfa Nefyn
Nefyn
Penmorfa
Tremadog
Prenteg
Groesffordd
Edern
Garn Boduan
Fron
Rhos-fawr
Llanarmon
Pentrefelin
Wern
Gell
Tan-y-graig
Y Ffôr
Chwilog
Llanystumdwy
Criccieth
Moel-y-Gest
Minffordd
Porthmadog
Porth Ysgaden
Rhos-y-llan
Ceidio Fawr
Hendre
Penarth Fawr Medieval Ho
Lloyd George Museum
Morfa Bychan
Portmeirion
Tudweiliog
Bodfuan
Llannor
Abererch
Afon Wen
Criccieth Castle
Black Rock Sands
Borth-y-Gest
Portmeirion Village
Hafan y Môr
Penychain Sta
LLEYN PENINSULA
(PENRHYN LLŶN)
Efailnewydd
Denio
Dinas
Harlech Point
Traeth Bach
Carn Fadryn
Penllech
Porth Colmon
Garnfadryn
Rhyd-y-clafdy
Pwllheli
Pen- ychain
Ynys
Porth Colmon
Pen-y-Graig
Bryn-mawr
Llangwnnadl
Llaniestyn
Carreg yr Imbill
Morfa Harlech
Penrhos
Penrhyn Mawr
Sarn Meyllteyrn
Y Gamlas
TREMADOG BAY
Bryncroes
Rhedyn
Ty-hen
Botwnnog
Nanhoron
Llanbedrog
Harlech
Harlech Castle
Methlem
Mynytho
Trwyn Llanbedrog
Porth Oer
Rhydlios
Llandegwning
Capel Carmel
Mynydd Rhiw
Llangian
Llanfair
Rhoshirwaun
Plas-yn-Rhiw (NT)
Braich Anelog
Rhiw
Abersoch
Llandanwg
Pen-sarn
Llawr-y-dref
St Tudwal's Road
Anelog
Mynydd Anelog
Rhydolion
Llanengan
Llanbedr
Pwlldefaid
Aberdaron
Llanfaelrhys
Sarn Bach
Bwlchtocyn
Morfa Dyffryn
Braich y Pwll
Aberdaron Bay
Uwchmynydd
Ynys Gwylan-fawr
Porth Neigwl (Hell's Mouth)
St Tudwal's Islands
Coed Ystumgwern
Bardsey Sound (Swnt Enlli)
Pen y Cil
Porth Ceiriad
Trwyn yr Wylfa
Llanenddwyn
Dyffryn Ardudwy Sta
Dyffryn Ardudwy
Bardsey Island (Ynys Enlli)
Cilan Uchaf
Trwyn Cilan
St Mary's Abbey
Llanddwywe
Tal-y-bont
Barmouth (Abermaw)
Barmouth Bay (Bae Bermo)
Fairbourne & Barmouth Rly
Llwyngwril
Llangelynin
CARDIGAN BAY
(BAE CEREDIGION)
Rhoslefain
Llanfendigaid
Tonfanau
Aber Dysynni
Tywyn
Aberdyfi Bar
Twyni Bâch
Upper Bo
Sarn Cynfelyn
Great Aberystwyth Camera Obscura
Cliff Rly
Ceredigion Museum
Aberystwyth
The Bar
Aberystwyth Arts Centre
Penparcau
Southgate
(Summer only)
Rhydyfelin
Llanfarian
Allt Wen
A487
A497
A499
A4085
A498
A496
A493
B4417
B4412
B4354
B4411
B4413
B4415
B4573
B4572
0 2 4 6 miles
0 2 4 6 8 10 km

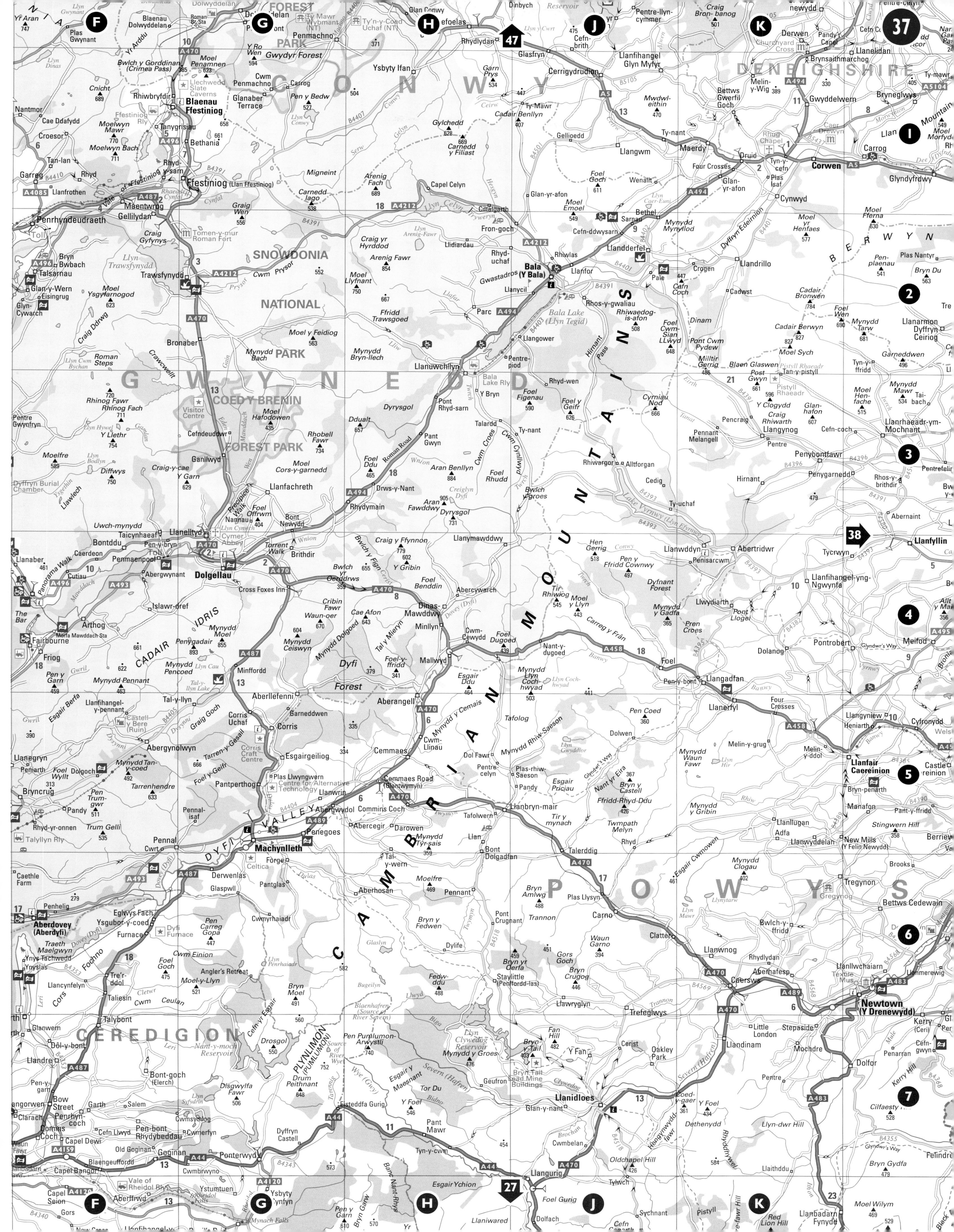
CONWY
DENBIGHSHIRE
GWYNEDD
POWYS
CEREDIGION
BERWYN
SNOWDONIA NATIONAL PARK
CAMBRIAN MOUNTAINS
COED Y BRENIN FOREST PARK
Gwydyr Forest
Dyfi Forest
CADAIR IDRIS
DYFI VALLEY
PLYNLIMON (PUMLUMON)
47
38
27
Blaenau Ffestiniog
Ffestiniog (Llan Ffestiniog)
Penrhyndeudraeth
Maentwrog
Gellilydan
Trawsfynydd
Talsarnau
Harlech
Bronaber
Tomen-y-mur Roman Fort
Llechwedd Slate Caverns
Tanygrisiau
Bethania
Rhiwbryfdir
Penmachno
Ysbyty Ifan
Glan Conwy
Pentrefoelas
Rhydlydan
Glasfryn
Cerrigydrudion
Llanfihangel Glyn Myfyr
Pentre-llyn-cymmer
Derwen
Clawdd-newydd
Melin-y-Wig
Bettws Gwerfil Goch
Gwyddelwern
Bryneglwys
Corwen
Carrog
Glyndyfrdwy
Cynwyd
Llandrillo
Druid
Maerdy
Llangwm
Ty-nant
Four Crosses
Glan-yr-afon
Bethel
Sarnau
Llandderfel
Frongoch
Capel Celyn
Llyn Celyn
Bala (Y Bala)
Llanfor
Rhiwlas
Llanycil
Parc
Bala Lake (Llyn Tegid)
Llangower
Rhos-y-gwaliau
Llanuwchllyn
Pentre-piod
Rhyd-wen
Hirnant Pass
Llanarmon Dyffryn Ceiriog
Cadair Berwyn
Moel Sych
Pistyll Rhaeadr
Tan-y-pistyll
Llanrhaeadr-ym-Mochnant
Llangynog
Pennant Melangell
Penybontfawr
Pentrefelin
Lake Vyrnwy (Llyn Efyrnwy)
Llanwddyn
Abertridwr
Llanfyllin
Llanfihangel-yng-Ngwynfa
Pont Llogel
Dolanog
Pontrobert
Meifod
Llangadfan
Foel
Llanerfyl
Llanfair Caereinion
Cyfronydd
Heniarth
Llangyniew
Melin-y-ddol
Castle Caereinion
Manafon
New Mills (Y Felin Newydd)
Adfa
Llanllugan
Tregynon
Bettws Cedewain
Bwlch-y-ffridd
Newtown (Y Drenewydd)
Aberhafesp
Caersws
Llanwnog
Clatter
Carno
Talerddig
Llanbrynmair
Trefeglwys
Llandinam
Llanidloes
Llangurig
Cwmbelan
Oldchapel Hill
Tylwch
Kerry (Ceri)
Dolfor
Penarran
Mochdre
Stepaside
Little London
Kerry Hill
Llanbadarn Fynydd
Dolgellau
Llanelltyd
Cymer Abbey
Llanfachreth
Ganllwyd
Penmaenpool
Arthog
Fairbourne
Friog
Barmouth
Bontddu
Taicynhaeaf
Cross Foxes Inn
Brithdir
Rhydymain
Drws-y-Nant
Dinas-Mawddwy
Mallwyd
Minllyn
Cwm-Cewydd
Aberangell
Llanymawddwy
Minffordd
Aberllefenni
Corris
Corris Uchaf
Corris Craft Centre
Esgairgeiliog
Cemmaes
Cemmaes Road (Glantwymyn)
Commins Coch
Darowen
Abercegir
Penegoes
Machynlleth
Centre for Alternative Technology
Pennal
Aberdyfi
Abergynolwyn
Tal-y-llyn
Llanegryn
Bryncrug
Tywyn
Talyllyn Rly
Aberdovey (Aberdyfi)
Eglwys Fach
Furnace
Taliesin
Talybont
Tre'r-ddol
Bow Street
Comins Coch
Capel Bangor
Goginan
Ponterwyd
Devil's Bridge
Ysbyty Ystwyth
Vale of Rheidol Rly
Eisteddfa Gurig
Pant Mawr
Staylittle
Llyn Clywedog
Clywedog Reservoir
Bryn Tail Lead Mine Buildings
Glan-y-nant
Nant-y-moch Reservoir
Cwmystwyth
Bont-goch (Elerch)
Forge
Derwenlas
Glaspwll
Pennant
Pont Crugnant
Trannon
Dylife
Llanbrynmair
Cwmyrhaiadr
Celtica
Snowdonia
Pant Gwyn
Aran Fawddwy
Aran Benllyn
Arenig Fawr
Rhobell Fawr
Moel Hebog
Bwlch Oerddrws
Bwlch y Groes
Cwm Cynllwyd
Glyndŵr's Way
Dyffryn Ardudwy
Llanenddwyn
Llanaber

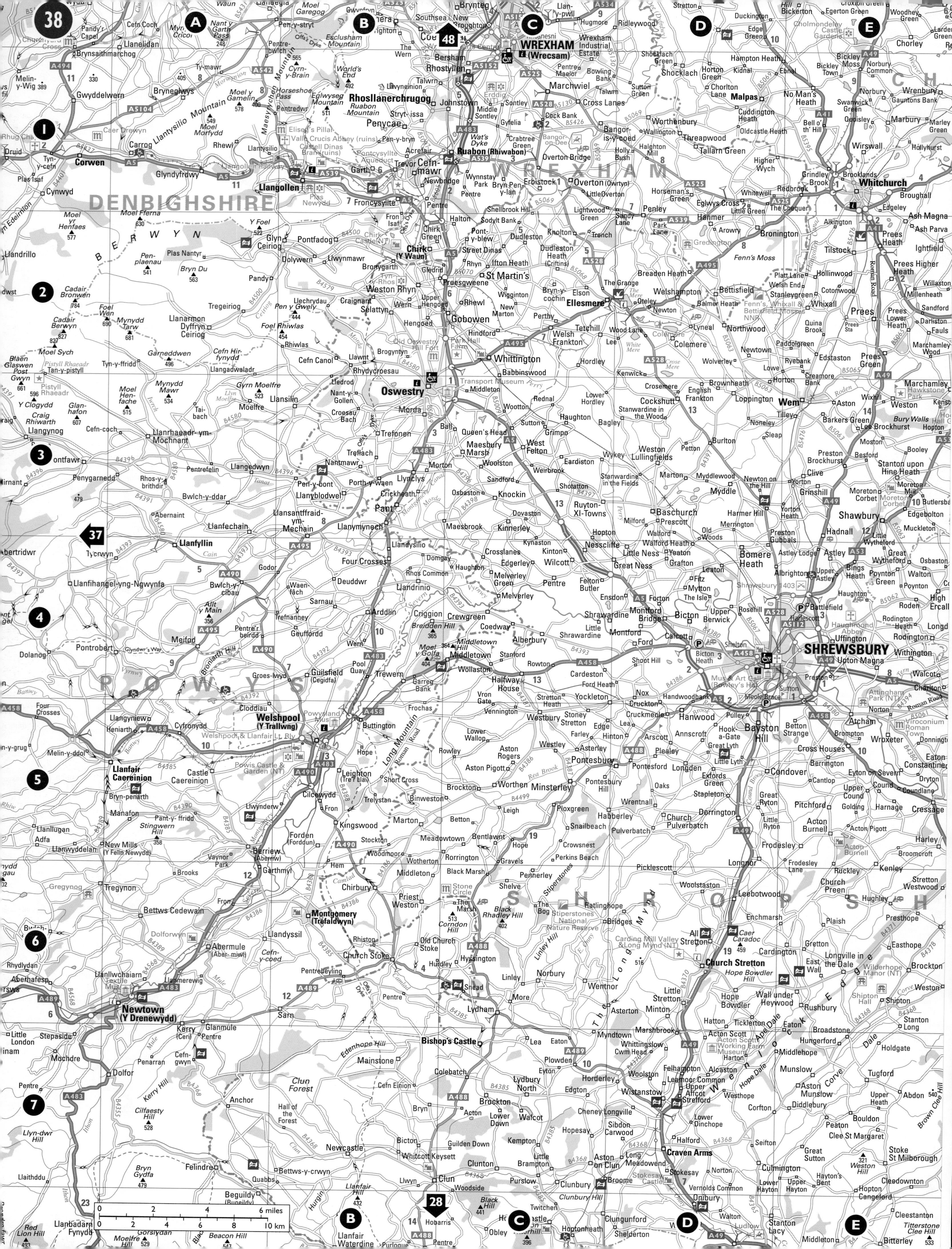

48
37
28
WREXHAM (Wrecsam)
DENBIGHSHIRE
BERWYN
WREXHAM
POWYS
SHROPSHIRE
Corwen
Llangollen
Rhosllanerchrugog
Ruabon (Rhiwabon)
Cefn-mawr
Chirk (Y Waun)
Oswestry
St Martin's
Ellesmere
Overton (Owrtyn)
Malpas
Whitchurch
Wem
Shawbury
SHREWSBURY
Welshpool (Y Trallwng)
Llanfyllin
Llanfair Caereinion
Montgomery (Trefaldwyn)
Newtown (Y Drenewydd)
Bishop's Castle
Church Stretton
Craven Arms
Clun
Ludlow
Pontesbury
Minsterley
Bayston Hill
Whittington
Gobowen
Knockin
Baschurch
Hanwood
Clun Forest
Long Mountain
The Long Mynd
Wenlock Edge
Stiperstones
Offa's Dyke
Valle Crucis Abbey (ruins)
Pontcysyllte Aqueduct
Llangollen Railway
Chirk Castle (NT)
Powis Castle & Garden (NT)
Welshpool & Llanfair Lt Rly
Transport Museum
Stokesay Castle
Carding Mill Valley & Long Mynd (NT)
Acton Scott Working Farm Museum
Attingham Park (NT)
Viroconium Roman Town
Haughmond Abbey
Mus & Art Gall (Rowley's Ho)
Fenn's, Whixall & Bettisfield Mosses NNR
Fenn's Moss
Moel Fferna 630
Cadair Berwyn 827
Moel Sych 827
Pistyll Rhaeadr
Corndon Hill 513
Black Rhadley Hill 402
Moel y Golfa 404
Breidden Hill 365
0 2 4 6 miles
0 2 4 6 8 10 km

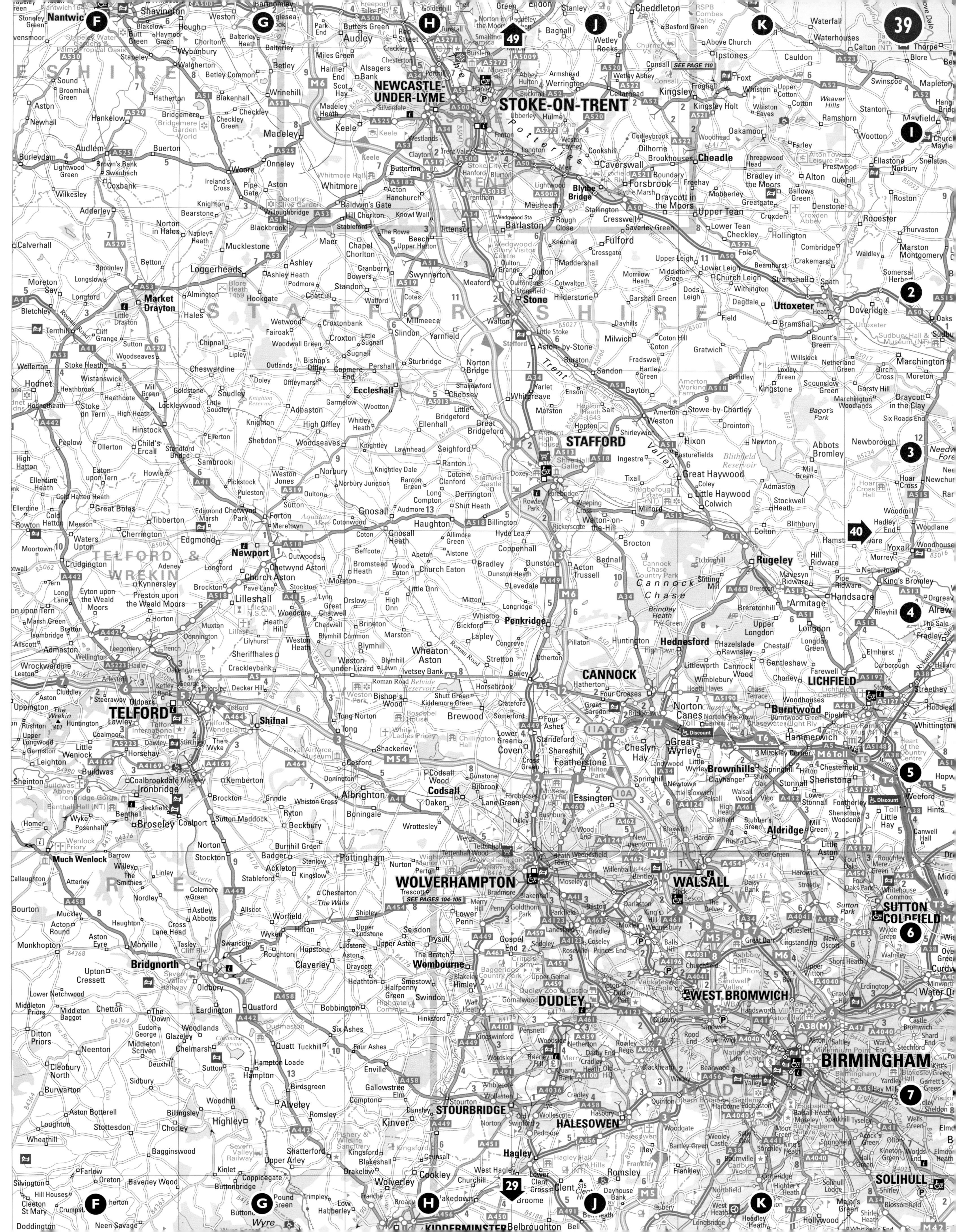

STOKE-ON-TRENT
NEWCASTLE-UNDER-LYME
STAFFORD
STAFFORDSHIRE
TELFORD & WREKIN
TELFORD
CANNOCK
LICHFIELD
WOLVERHAMPTON
WALSALL
WEST BROMWICH
DUDLEY
STOURBRIDGE
HALESOWEN
BIRMINGHAM
SUTTON COLDFIELD
SOLIHULL
KIDDERMINSTER
Market Drayton
Newport
Stone
Uttoxeter
Rugeley
Cheadle
Bridgnorth
Ironbridge
Shifnal
Penkridge
Hednesford
Burntwood
Eccleshall
Much Wenlock
Broseley
Codsall
Albrighton
Wombourne
Kinver
Hagley
Cannock Chase
Trent Valley
SEE PAGE 110
SEE PAGES 104-105
49
40
29
F
G
H
I
J
K
2
3
4
5
6
7

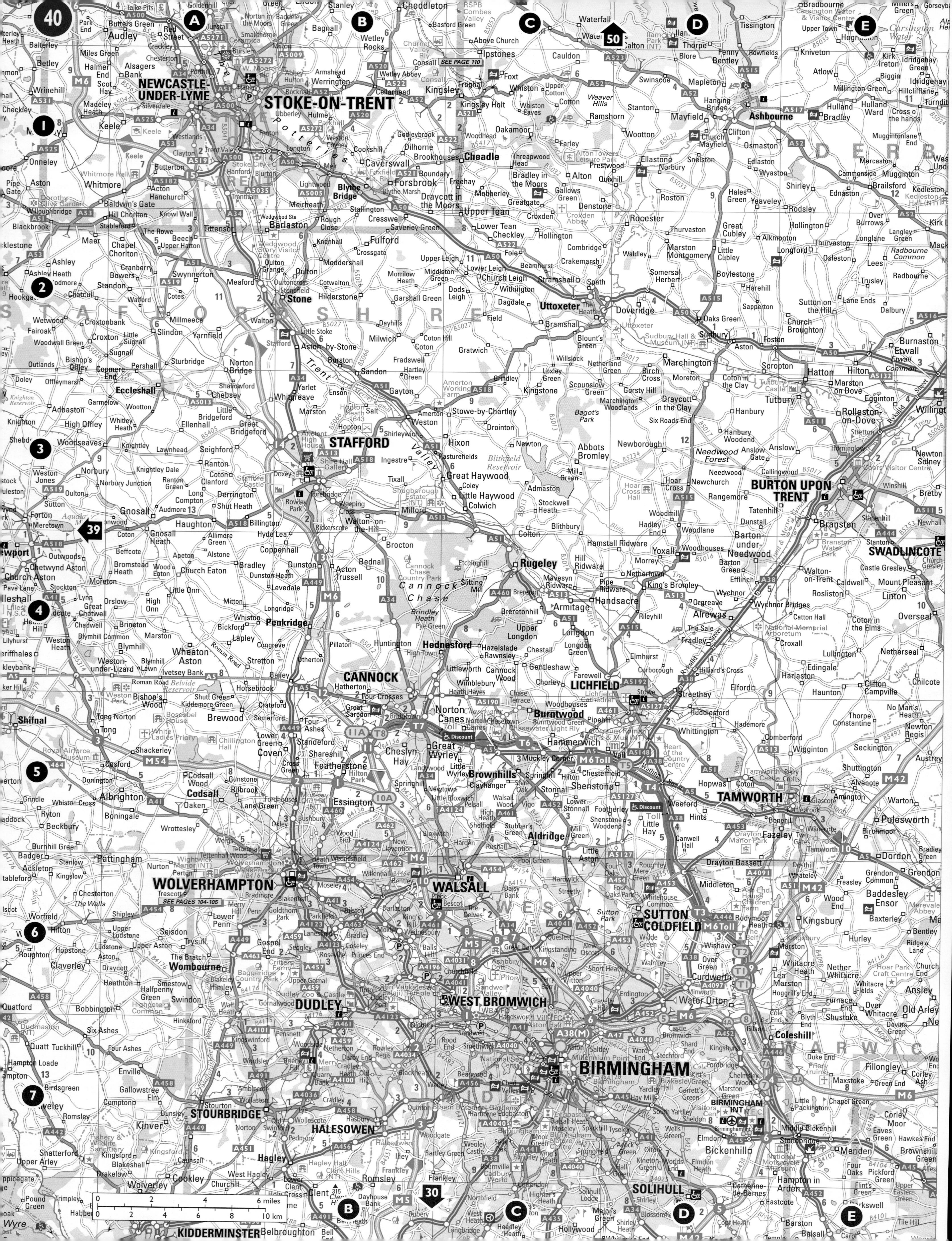

STOKE-ON-TRENT
NEWCASTLE-UNDER-LYME
STAFFORDSHIRE
STAFFORD
Stone
Uttoxeter
Cheadle
Ashbourne
Eccleshall
Penkridge
CANNOCK
Hednesford
Rugeley
Cannock Chase
LICHFIELD
BURTON UPON TRENT
SWADLINCOTE
TAMWORTH
Burntwood
Brownhills
Aldridge
WALSALL
WOLVERHAMPTON
SEE PAGES 104-105
SEE PAGE 110
WEST BROMWICH
DUDLEY
SUTTON COLDFIELD
BIRMINGHAM
BIRMINGHAM INT
SOLIHULL
HALESOWEN
STOURBRIDGE
KIDDERMINSTER
Coleshill
Hagley
Kinver
Wombourne
Codsall
Albrighton
Shifnal
Tutbury
Uttoxeter
Alton Towers Leisure Park
Cannock Chase Country Park
Shugborough Estate
Weston Park
Boscobel House
Royal Airforce Museum
National Memorial Arboretum
Discount
50
39
30
0 2 4 6 miles
0 2 4 6 8 10 km
A B C D E
1 2 3 4 5 6 7

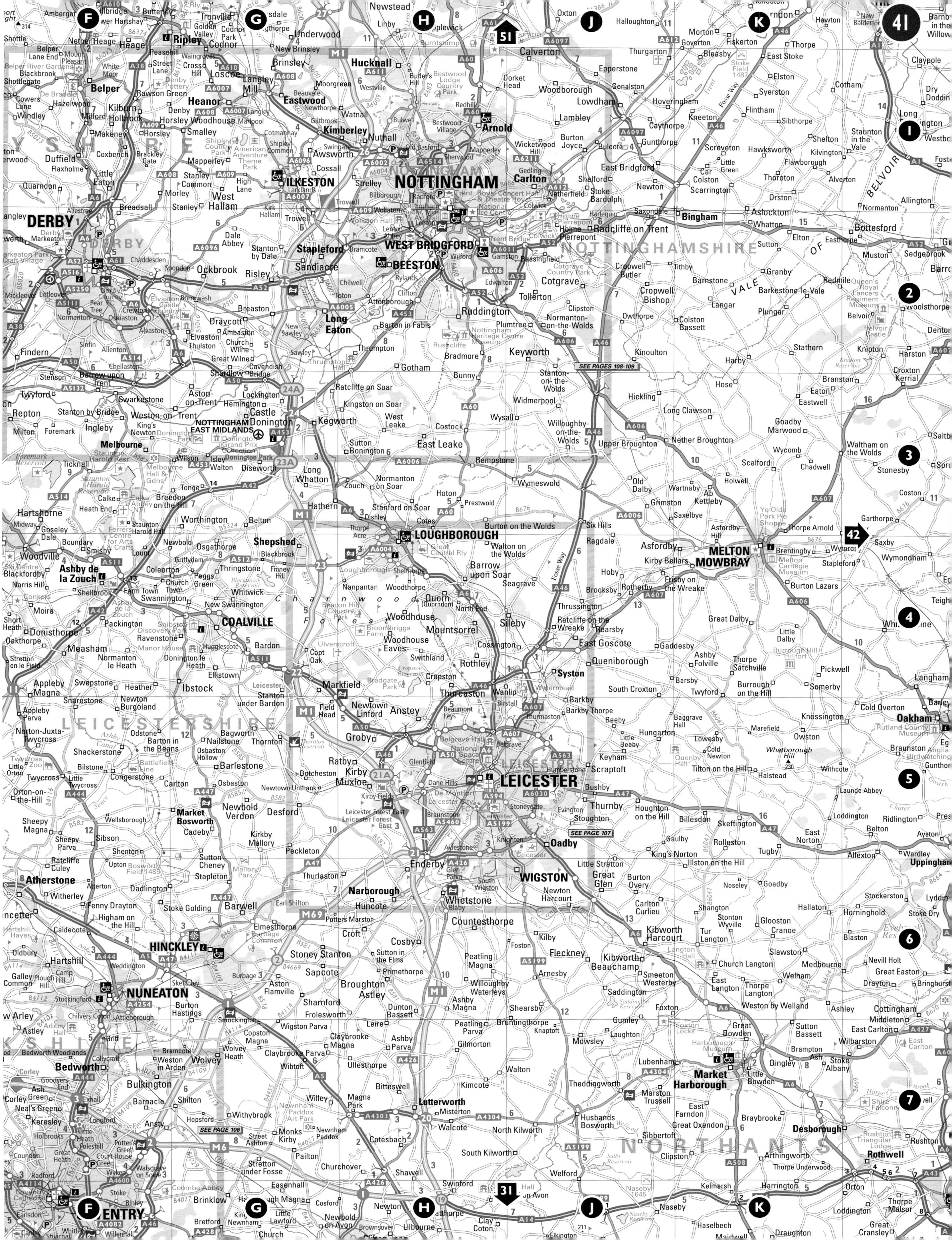
NOTTINGHAM
DERBY
LEICESTER
LOUGHBOROUGH
COALVILLE
HINCKLEY
NUNEATON
ILKESTON
MELTON MOWBRAY
NOTTINGHAMSHIRE
LEICESTERSHIRE
NORTHANTS
Charnwood Forest
VALE OF BELVOIR
WEST BRIDGFORD
BEESTON
NOTTINGHAM EAST MIDLANDS
Market Harborough
Lutterworth
Market Bosworth
Ashby de la Zouch
Melbourne
Oakham
Uppingham
Bottesford
Bingham
Radcliffe on Trent
Carlton
Arnold
Hucknall
Calverton
Eastwood
Heanor
Ripley
Belper
Kimberley
Stapleford
Long Eaton
Castle Donington
Kegworth
Shepshed
Syston
Oadby
Wigston
Narborough
Whetstone
Enderby
Groby
Anstey
Rothley
Sileby
Quorn
Mountsorrel
Ibstock
Atherstone
Bedworth
Rothwell
Desborough
Keyworth
Ruddington
Cotgrave
East Leake
Barrow upon Soar
Countesthorpe
Broughton Astley
Great Glen
Kibworth Harcourt
Kibworth Beauchamp
Fleckney
Earl Shilton
Barwell
SEE PAGES 108-109
SEE PAGE 107
SEE PAGE 106
51
42
31
F
G
H
J
K
1
2
3
4
5
6
7
M1
M6
M69
A46
A6
A47
A52
A60
A606
A607
A453
A5
A42
A50
A511
A444
A426
A14

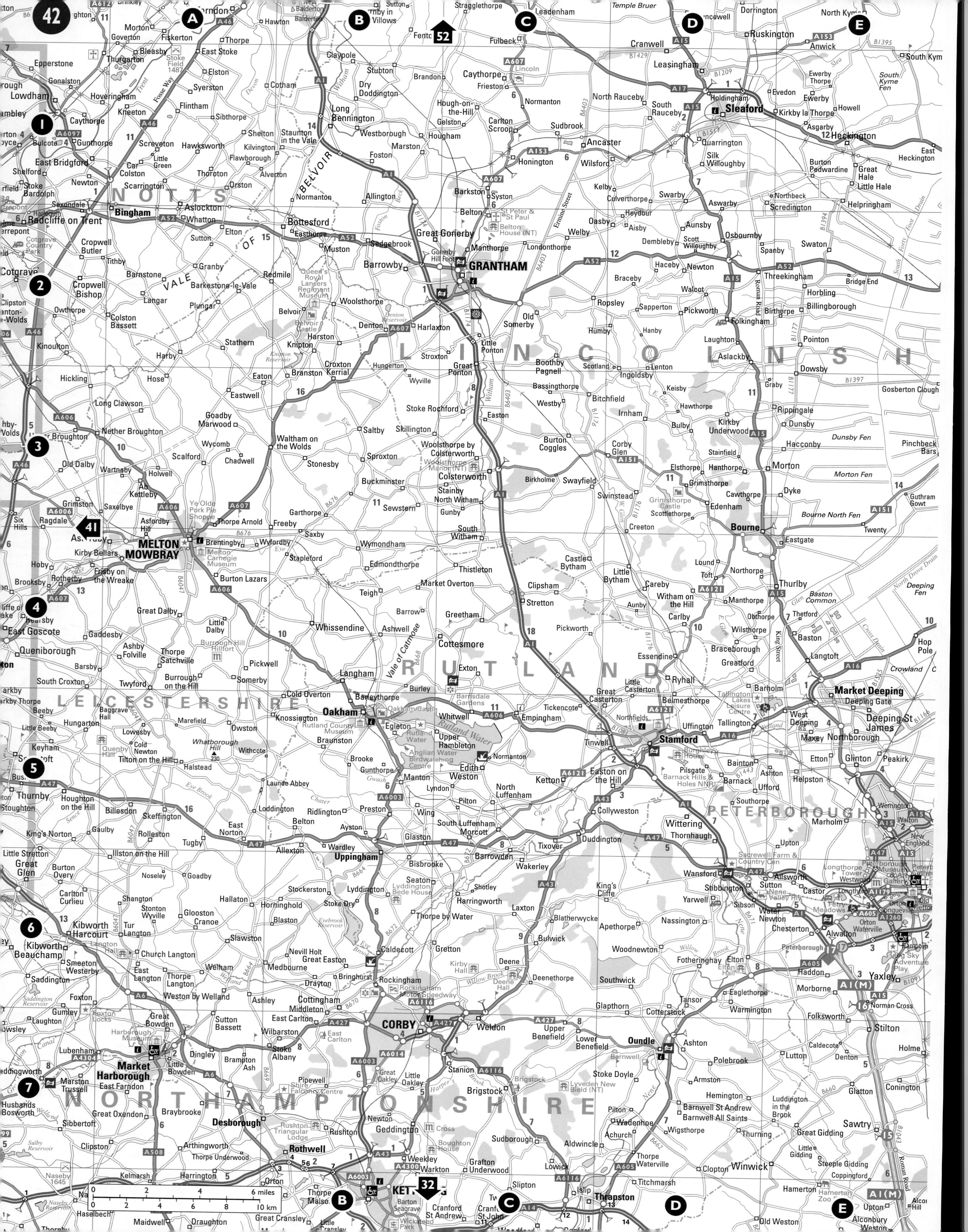
A
B
C
D
E
52
41
32
NOTTS
VALE OF BELVOIR
LINCOLNSHIRE
RUTLAND
LEICESTERSHIRE
NORTHAMPTONSHIRE
PETERBOROUGH
Sleaford
GRANTHAM
Bingham
Radcliffe on Trent
Lowdham
Cotgrave
MELTON MOWBRAY
Oakham
Uppingham
Stamford
Bourne
Market Deeping
Deeping St James
Oundle
CORBY
Market Harborough
Desborough
Rothwell
Geddington
Thrapston
Peterborough
Yaxley
Stilton
Sawtry
Heckington
Ancaster
Colsterworth
Cottesmore
Rutland Water
Corby Glen
Bottesford
Belvoir Castle
Belton House (NT)
Oakham Castle
Rockingham Motor Speedway
Deene Park
Lyveden New Bield (NT)
Rutland County Museum
Melton Carnegie Museum
Harborough Museum
Burghley House
Barnack Hills & Holes NNR
Sacrewell Farm & Country Centre
Peterborough Museum & Art Gallery
Rushton Triangular Lodge
Boughton House
Stoke Field 1487
Naseby 1645
Witham
Welland
Nene
Eye Brook
Chater
Gwash
Fosse Way
Ermine Street
Roman Road
King Street
Deeping Fen
Morton Fen
Dunsby Fen
Bourne North Fen
Baston Common
A1
A1(M)
A15
A17
A52
A46
A47
A43
A6
A606
A607
A6003
A6116
A427
A16
A153
A14
0 2 4 6 miles
0 2 4 6 8 10 km

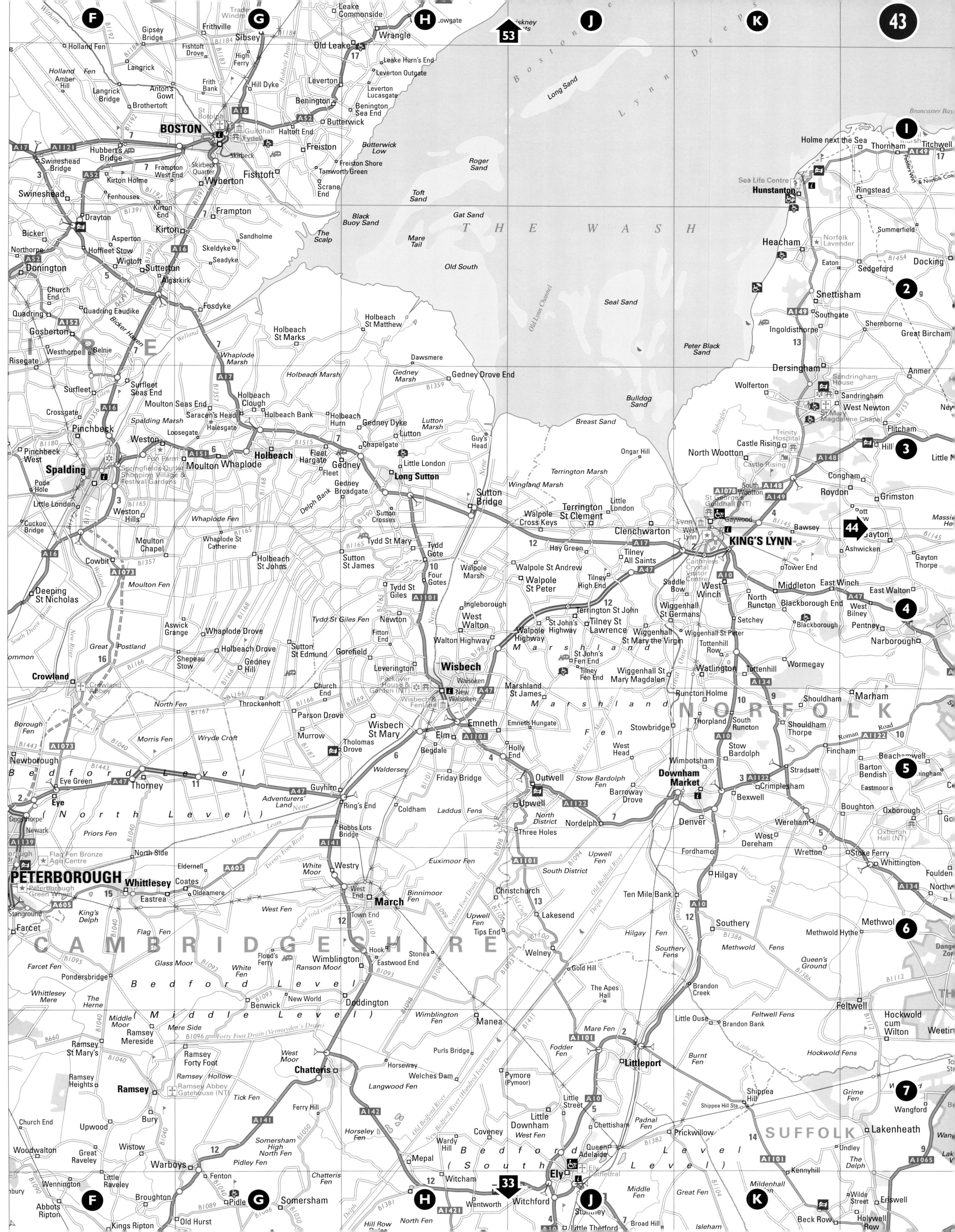

F
G
H
J
K
I
53
44
33
BOSTON
Frithville
Sibsey
Gipsey Bridge
Leake Commonside
Old Leake
Wrangle
Lowgate
Holland Fen
Fishtoft Drove
High Ferry
Langrick
Amber Hill
Langrick Bridge
Anton's Gowt
Frith Bank
Brothertoft
Hill Dyke
Leverton
Leake Hurn's End
Leverton Outgate
Leverton Lucasgate
Benington
Benington Sea End
Butterwick
Haltoft End
Freiston
Freiston Shore
Tamworth Green
Fishtoft
Skirbeck
Skirbeck Quarter
Wyberton
Frampton
Frampton West End
Kirton Holme
Kirton
Kirton End
Hubbert's Bridge
Swineshead Bridge
Swineshead
Fenhouses
Drayton
Bicker
Asperton
Hoffleet Stow
Northorpe
Donington
Wigtoft
Sutterton
Algarkirk
Sandholme
Skeldyke
Seadyke
Fosdyke
Church End
Quadring
Quadring Eaudike
Gosberton
Westhorpe
Belnie
Risegate
Surfleet
Surfleet Seas End
Crossgate
Pinchbeck
Pinchbeck West
Spalding
Springfields Outlet Shopping Village & Festival Gardens
Pode Hole
Little London
Cuckoo Bridge
Weston
Weston Hills
Moulton
Moulton Chapel
Moulton Seas End
Whaplode
Holbeach
Saracen's Head
Halesgate
Loosegate
Spalding Marsh
Whaplode Marsh
Holbeach Clough
Holbeach Bank
Holbeach Hurn
Holbeach Marsh
Holbeach St Marks
Holbeach St Matthew
Dawsmere
Gedney Marsh
Gedney Drove End
Gedney Dyke
Lutton
Lutton Marsh
Chapelgate
Fleet Hargate
Fleet
Gedney
Gedney Broadgate
Little London
Long Sutton
Sutton Bridge
Sutton Crosses
Delph Bank
Guy's Head
Whaplode Fen
Whaplode St Catherine
Holbeach St Johns
Tydd St Mary
Tydd Gote
Sutton St James
Four Gotes
Tydd St Giles
Tydd St Giles Fen
Newton
Fitton End
Cowbit
Moulton Fen
Deeping St Nicholas
Aswick Grange
Whaplode Drove
Holbeach Drove
Shepeau Stow
Gedney Hill
Sutton St Edmund
Gorefield
Leverington
Peckover House & Garden (NT)
Wisbech
Wisbech & Fenland Museum
Walsoken
New Walsoken
Church End
Parson Drove
Throckenholt
Great Postland
Crowland
Crowland Abbey
North Fen
Borough Fen
Morris Fen
Wryde Croft
Murrow
Tholomas Drove
Wisbech St Mary
Emneth
Elm
Begdale
Emneth Hungate
Newborough
Bedford Level
Eye Green
Thorney
Eye
Dogsthorpe
Newark
(North Level)
Guyhirn
Ring's End
Adventurers' Land
Waldersey
Friday Bridge
Coldham
Laddus Fens
Hobbs Lots Bridge
Priors Fen
Flag Fen Bronze Age Centre
North Side
Eldernell
PETERBOROUGH
Peterborough Green Wheel
Whittlesey
Coates
Eastrea
Oldeamere
Stanground
King's Delph
Farcet
White Moor
Westry
March
West End
Town End
Binnimoor Fen
Euximoor Fen
West Fen
Flag Fen
CAMBRIDGESHIRE
Farcet Fen
Pondersbridge
Glass Moor
White Fen
Flood's Ferry
Wimblington
Ranson Moor
Hook
Stonea
Eastwood End
Whittlesey Mere
The Herne
Bedford Level
Benwick
New World
Doddington
Middle Moor
(Middle Level)
Mere Side
Ramsey Mereside
Ramsey St Mary's
Forty Foot Drain (Vermuyden's Drain)
Ramsey Forty Foot
Ramsey Hollow
Ramsey Heights
Ramsey
Ramsey Abbey Gatehouse (NT)
Tick Fen
West Moor
Chatteris
Horseway
Welches Dam
Langwood Fen
Purls Bridge
Manea
Wimblington Fen
Church End
Upwood
Bury
Wistow
Great Raveley
Woodwalton
Warboys
Somersham High North Fen
Pidley Fen
Ferry Hill
Horseley Fen
Chatteris Fen
Wennington
Little Raveley
Fenton
Broughton
Pidley
Somersham
Abbots Ripton
Kings Ripton
Old Hurst
Mepal
Witcham
Wentworth
Witchford
Wardy Hill
Coveney
Little Downham
West Fen
Pymore (Pymoor)
Hill Row
North Fen
Ely
Ely Cathedral
Queen Adelaide
Chettisham
Little Street
Littleport
Fodder Fen
Mare Fen
Stuntney
Little Thetford
Broad Hill
Middle Fen
Great Fen
Isleham
Padnal Fen
Prickwillow
(South Level)
Boston Deeps
Lynn Deeps
Long Sand
Roger Sand
Toft Sand
Black Buoy Sand
Gat Sand
THE WASH
The Scalp
Mare Tail
Old South
Seal Sand
Old Lynn Channel
Peter Black Sand
Bulldog Sand
Breast Sand
Ongar Hill
Terrington Marsh
Wingland Marsh
Terrington St Clement
Little London
Walpole Cross Keys
Clenchwarton
Hay Green
Tilney All Saints
Walpole Marsh
Walpole St Andrew
Walpole St Peter
Tilney High End
Ingleborough
West Walton
Walton Highway
Walpole Highway
Terrington St John
St John's Highway
Tilney St Lawrence
Wiggenhall St Mary the Virgin
Marshland
St John's Fen End
Tilney Fen End
Wiggenhall St Mary Magdalen
Marshland St James
Fen
West Head
Holly End
Outwell
Upwell
North District
Three Holes
Nordelph
Stow Bardolph Fen
Barroway Drove
Upwell Fen
South District
Christchurch
Lakesend
Upwell Fen
Tips End
Welney
Gold Hill
The Apes Hall
Hilgay Fen
Ten Mile Bank
Southery Fens
Brandon Creek
Little Ouse
Brandon Bank
Burnt Fen
Shippea Hill
Shippea Hill Sta
SUFFOLK
Holme next the Sea
Thornham
Titchwell
Brancaster Bay
Norfolk Coast Path
Peddars Way
Ringstead
Sea Life Centre
Hunstanton
Heacham
Norfolk Lavender
Summerfield
Docking
Sedgeford
Eaton
Snettisham
Southgate
Ingoldisthorpe
Shernborne
Great Bircham
Dersingham
Anmer
Sandringham House
Sandringham
Wolferton
West Newton
St Mary Magdalene Chapel
Castle Rising
Trinity Hospital
North Wootton
Castle Rising
Flitcham
Hillington
Congham
Roydon
Grimston
South Wootton
Gaywood
St George's Guildhall (NT)
West Lynn
KING'S LYNN
Bawsey
Gayton
Ashwicken
Gayton Thorpe
Tower End
Caithness Crystal Visitor Centre
Middleton
East Winch
East Walton
West Winch
Saddle Bow
North Runcton
Blackborough End
West Bilney
Wiggenhall St Germans
Setchey
Blackborough
Pentney
Narborough
Wiggenhall St Peter
Tottenhill Row
Tottenhill
Wormegay
Watlington
Runcton Holme
Shouldham
Marham
NORFOLK
Thorpland
South Runcton
Shouldham Thorpe
Stowbridge
Stow Bardolph
Wimbotsham
Downham Market
Fincham
Roman Road
Beachamwell
Stradsett
Barton Bendish
Eastmoor
Crimplesham
Bexwell
Denver
Wereham
Boughton
Oxborough
Oxburgh Hall (NT)
West Dereham
Fordham
Wretton
Stoke Ferry
Whittington
Foulden
Hilgay
Southery
Methwold Hythe
Methwold
Methwold Fens
Queen's Ground
Feltwell
Feltwell Fens
Hockwold cum Wilton
Hockwold Fens
Grime Fen
Wangford
Lakenheath
Undley
The Delph
Kennyhill
Mildenhall
Wilde Street
Eriswell
Beck Row
Holywell Row

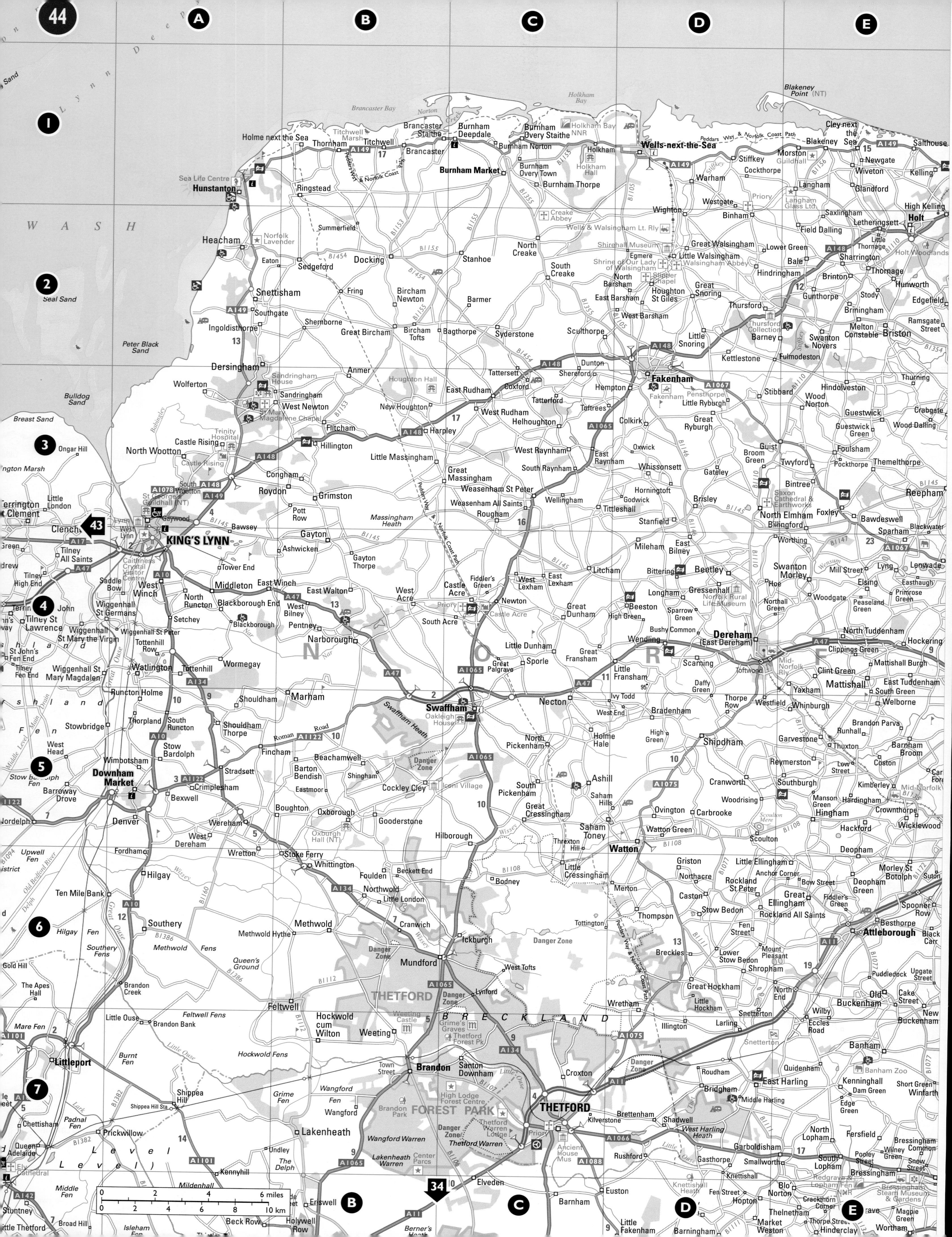
A
B
C
D
E
1
2
3
4
5
6
7
Lynn Deeps
The Wash
Seal Sand
Peter Black Sand
Bulldog Sand
Breast Sand
Brancaster Bay
Holkham Bay
Blakeney Point (NT)
Holme next the Sea
Titchwell Marsh
Thornham
Titchwell
Brancaster Staithe
Brancaster
Burnham Deepdale
Burnham Overy Staithe
Holkham Bay NNR
Holkham
Holkham Hall
Wells-next-the-Sea
Peddars Way & Norfolk Coast Path
Stiffkey
Morston
Blakeney
Cley next the Sea
Salthouse
Newgate
Wiveton
Kelling
Glandford
Cockthorpe
Langham
Langham Glass Ltd
Burnham Norton
Burnham Market
Burnham Overy Town
Burnham Thorpe
Sea Life Centre
Hunstanton
Ringstead
Warham
Wighton
Westgate
Binham
Priory
Saxlingham
Letheringsett
Holt
High Kelling
Field Dalling
Creake Abbey
Wells & Walsingham Lt. Rly
Summerfield
Heacham
Norfolk Lavender
North Creake
Shirehall Museum
Great Walsingham
Little Walsingham
Walsingham Abbey
Egmere
Shrine of Our Lady of Walsingham
Slipper Chapel
Lower Green
Bale
Hindringham
Sharrington
Thornage
Little Thornage
Holt Woodlands
Brinton
Hunworth
Eaton
Sedgeford
Docking
Stanhoe
South Creake
North Barsham
Houghton St Giles
Great Snoring
Thursford
Gunthorpe
Stody
Edgefield
Snettisham
Fring
Bircham Newton
Barmer
East Barsham
West Barsham
Thursford Collection
Briningham
Melton Constable
Briston
Ramsgate Street
Southgate
Shernborne
Ingoldisthorpe
Great Bircham
Bircham Tofts
Bagthorpe
Syderstone
Sculthorpe
Little Snoring
Barney
Swanton Novers
Kettlestone
Fulmodeston
Dersingham
Anmer
Sandringham House
Houghton Hall
Tattersett
Dunton
Shereford
Fakenham
Pensthorpe
Stibbard
Thurning
Wolferton
Sandringham
West Newton
New Houghton
East Rudham
Coxford
Tatterford
Hempton
Little Ryburgh
Wood Norton
Hindolveston
St Mary Magdalene Chapel
Flitcham
Harpley
West Rudham
Helhoughton
Toftrees
Colkirk
Great Ryburgh
Guestwick
Guestwick Green
Crabgate
Wood Dalling
Trinity Hospital
Castle Rising
North Wootton
Ongar Hill
Hillington
Little Massingham
West Raynham
East Raynham
Oxwick
Guist
Broom Green
Twyford
Foulsham
Themelthorpe
Pockthorpe
Congham
Great Massingham
South Raynham
Whissonsett
Gateley
Bintree
Roydon
South Wootton
Weasenham St Peter
Horningtoft
Godwick
Saxon Cathedral & Earthworks
Reepham
Little London
Terrington St Clement
Grimston
Weasenham All Saints
Wellingham
Tittleshall
Brisley
North Elmham
Foxley
Bawdeswell
St George's Guildhall (NT)
Gaywood
Pott Row
Massingham Heath
Rougham
Stanfield
Billingford
Sparham
Blackwater
Clenchwarton
43
Lynn
West Lynn
KING'S LYNN
Bawsey
Gayton
Ashwicken
Mileham
East Bilney
Worthing
Tilney All Saints
Tilney High End
Caithness Crystal Visitor Centre
Tower End
Gayton Thorpe
Litcham
Bittering
Beetley
Swanton Morley
Mill Street
Lyng
Lenwade
Saddle Bow
West Winch
Middleton
East Winch
East Walton
West Acre
Castle Acre
Fiddler's Green
West Lexham
East Lexham
Longham
Gressenhall
Norfolk Rural Life Museum
Hoe
Elsing
Easthaugh
Primrose Green
Wiggenhall St Germans
North Runcton
Blackborough End
West Bilney
Newton
Great Dunham
Beeston
Northall Green
Woodgate
Peaseland Green
Tilney St Lawrence
Terrington St John
Setchey
Blackborough
Pentney
South Acre
Castle Acre Priory
High Green
Sparrow Green
Bushy Common
Wiggenhall St Peter
Wiggenhall St Mary the Virgin
Narborough
Wendling
Dereham (East Dereham)
North Tuddenham
Hockering
St John's Fen End
Tilney Fen End
Tottenhill Row
Wormegay
Little Dunham
Great Fransham
Sporle
Scarning
Mid-Norfolk Rly
Toftwood
Clippings Green
Mattishall Burgh
Wiggenhall St Mary Magdalen
Watlington
Tottenhill
Great Palgrave
Little Fransham
Clint Green
Mattishall
East Tuddenham
South Green
Runcton Holme
Shouldham
Marham
Swaffham
Swaffham Heath
Necton
Ivy Todd
Daffy Green
Yaxham
Whinburgh
Welborne
Thorpe Row
Westfield
Stowbridge
Thorpland
South Runcton
Shouldham Thorpe
Oakleigh House
West End
Bradenham
Brandon Parva
Runhall
West Head
Stow Bardolph
Fincham
Roman Road
North Pickenham
Holme Hale
High Green
Shipdham
Garvestone
Thuxton
Barnham Broom
Wimbotsham
Downham Market
Stradsett
Beachamwell
Barton Bendish
Shingham
Danger Zone
Reymerston
Coston
Low Street
Stow Bardolph Fen
Barroway Drove
Crimplesham
Bexwell
Eastmoor
Cockley Cley
Iceni Village
South Pickenham
Ashill
Cranworth
Southburgh
Kimberley
Mid-Norfolk
Denver
Boughton
Oxborough
Gooderstone
Great Cressingham
Saham Hills
Woodrising
Manson Green
Hardingham
Hingham
Crownthorpe
Nordelph
Wereham
Oxburgh Hall (NT)
Hilborough
Saham Toney
Ovington
Carbrooke
Scoulton Mere
Hackford
Wicklewood
West Dereham
Watton Green
Scoulton
Fordham
Wretton
Stoke Ferry
Threxton Hill
Watton
Deopham
Upwell Fen
Whittington
Beckett End
Foulden
Little Cressingham
Bodney
Griston
Northacre
Little Ellingham
Anchor Corner
Rockland St Peter
Bow Street
Morley St Botolph
Deopham Green
Suton
Hilgay
Northwold
Little London
Merton
Caston
Great Ellingham
Fiddler's Green
Spooner Row
Ten Mile Bank
Old Bedford River
Delph
Stow Bedon
Thompson
Rockland All Saints
Besthorpe
Southery
Cranwich
Tottington
Fen Street
Attleborough
Hilgay Fen
Methwold Hythe
Methwold
Ickburgh
Lower Stow Bedon
Breckles
Mount Pleasant
Black Carr
Southery Fens
Methwold Fens
Queen's Ground
Danger Zone
Mundford
West Tofts
Shropham
Puddledock
Upgate Street
Gold Hill
The Apes Hall
Brandon Creek
Great Hockham
Little Hockham
North End
Old Buckenham
Cake Street
Thetford
Lynford
Feltwell
Wretham
Snetterton
Wilby
Eccles Road
New Buckenham
Little Ouse
Brandon Bank
Feltwell Fens
Hockwold cum Wilton
Weeting
Weeting Castle
Grime's Graves
Breckland
Illington
Larling
Mare Fen
Thetford Forest Pk
Littleport
Burnt Fen
Hockwold Fens
Banham
Town Street
Brandon
Santon Downham
Croxton
Danger Zone
Roudham
Quidenham
Banham Zoo
Kenninghall
Short Green
Dam Green
Winfarthing
Shippea Hill
Shippea Hill Sta
Grime Fen
Wangford
Brandon Park
High Lodge Forest Centre
FOREST PARK
Bridgham
East Harling
Middle Harling
Edge Green
Chettisham
Padnal Fen
Prickwillow
Lakenheath
Wangford Warren
Danger Zone
Thetford Warren Lodge
Thetford Warren
Priory
THETFORD
Brettenham
Kilverstone
Shadwell
West Harling Heath
North Lopham
Fersfield
Queen Adelaide
Ely
Cathedral
Level
Undley
The Delph
Kennyhill
Lakenheath Warren
Center Parcs
Ancient House Mus
Rushford
Gasthorpe
Garboldisham
Smallworth
South Lopham
Bressingham Common
Pooley Street
Wilney Green
Snow Street
Bressingham
Middle Fen
Mildenhall
Stuntney
Little Thetford
Broad Hill
Isleham Fen
Beck Row
Eriswell
Holywell Row
34
Elveden
Berner's Heath
Barnham
Euston
Little Fakenham
Knettishall Heath
Knettishall
Fen Street
Hopton
Barningham
Blo' Norton
Redgrave & Lopham Fen NNR
Bressingham Steam Museum & Gardens
Crackthorn Corner
Thelnetham
Thorpe Street
Market Weston
Hinderclay
Magpie Green
Wortham
0 2 4 6 miles
0 2 4 6 8 10 km
N
O
R
F

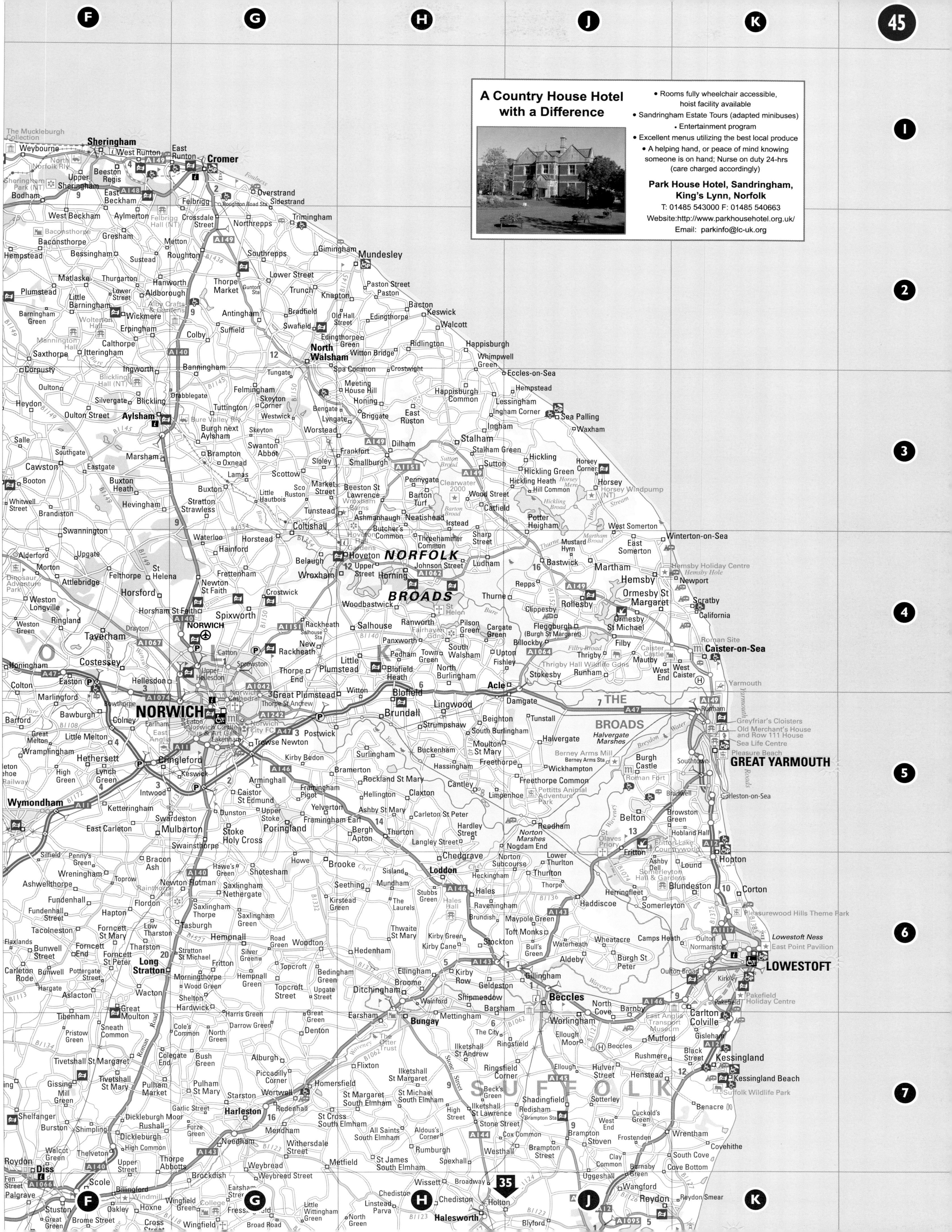
F
G
H
J
K
I
2
3
4
5
6
7
The Muckleburgh Collection
Sheringham
Weybourne
West Runton
East Runton
Cromer
North Norfolk Rly
Beeston Regis
Upper Sheringham
Sheringham Park (NT)
Bodham
East Beckham
Felbrigg
Overstrand
Sidestrand
Roughton Road Sta
West Beckham
Aylmerton
Felbrigg Hall (NT)
Crossdale Street
Trimingham
Northrepps
Baconsthorpe
Gresham
Metton
Roughton
Southrepps
Gimingham
Mundesley
Hempstead
Bessingham
Sustead
Matlaske
Thurgarton
Hanworth
Thorpe Market
Gunton Sta
Lower Street
Trunch
Paston Street
Paston
Knapton
Plumstead
Little Barningham
Lower Street
Aldborough
Alby Crafts & Gardens
Barningham Green
Wickmere
Antingham
Bradfield
Bacton
Keswick
Old Hall Street
Edingthorpe
Walcott
Wolterton Hall
Erpingham
Suffield
Swafield
Edingthorpe Green
Mannington Hall
Calthorpe
Colby
North Walsham
Ridlington
Happisburgh
Saxthorpe
Itteringham
Witton Bridge
Whimpwell Green
Corpusty
Ingworth
Banningham
Tungate
Spa Common
Crostwight
Eccles-on-Sea
Blickling Hall (NT)
Oulton
Meeting House Hill
Hempstead
Felmingham
Happisburgh Common
Heydon
Silvergate
Blickling
Drabblegate
Skeyton Corner
Honing
Lessingham
Oulton Street
Aylsham
Bure Valley Rly
Tuttington
Westwick
Bengate
East Ruston
Ingham Corner
Sea Palling
Burgh next Aylsham
Skeyton
Lyngate
Briggate
Salle
Worstead
Ingham
Waxham
Southgate
Marsham
Brampton
Swanton Abbot
Frankfort
Dilham
Stalham
Stalham Green
Oxnead
Sloley
Smallburgh
Sutton Broad
Hickling
Horsey Corner
Cawston
Eastgate
Lamas
Scottow
Sutton
Hickling Green
Horsey
Booton
Buxton Heath
Buxton
Sco Ruston
Market Street
Beeston St Lawrence
Pennygate
Clearwater 2000
Hickling Heath
Horsey Mere
Hill Common
Horsey Windpump (NT)
Little Hautbois
Barton Turf
Wood Street
Whitwell Street
Hevingham
Stratton Strawless
Wroxham Barns
Hickling Broad
Catfield
Brandiston
Tunstead
Ashmanhaugh
Neatishead
Barton Broad
Potter Heigham
Coltishall
Irstead
West Somerton
Swannington
Hoveton Common
Butcher's Common
Threehammer Common
Sharp Street
Martham Broad
Winterton-on-Sea
Waterloo
Horstead
Thurne
Mustard Hyrn
East Somerton
Alderford
Upgate
Hainford
Hoveton Hall Gardens
Hoveton
NORFOLK
Bastwick
Martham
Belaugh
Upper Street
Johnson Street
Ludham
Morton
St Helena
Frettenham
Wroxham
Horning
Hemsby Holiday Centre
Hemsby Hole
Dinosaur Adventure Park
Felthorpe
Newton St Faith
Repps
Hemsby
Newport
Attlebridge
BROADS
Thurne
Ormesby St Margaret
Scratby
Horsford
Crostwick
Woodbastwick
St Helen
Rollesby
California
Weston Longville
Horsham St Faith
Spixworth
Clippesby
Ringland
NORWICH
Rackheath
Salhouse
Ranworth
Pilson Green
Cargate Green
Fleggburgh (Burgh St Margaret)
Ormesby St Michael
Weston Green
Taverham
Drayton
Salhouse Sta
Fairhaven Gdns
Panxworth
Billockby
Filby
Roman Site
Caister-on-Sea
New Rackheath
South Walsham
Upton
Filby Broad
Thrigby
Caister Castle
Costessey
Catton
Sprowston
Little Plumstead
Pedham
Town Green
Fishley
Thrigby Hall Wildlife Gdns
Mautby
West Caister
Honingham
Hellesdon
Upper Hellesdon
Thorpe End
Blofield Heath
North Burlingham
Stokesby
Runham
West End
Colton
Easton
Norwich Cathedral
Great Plumstead
Witton
Blofield
Acle
Yarmouth
Marlingford
Bowthorpe
Thorpe St Andrew
Lingwood
Damgate
THE BROADS
Barford
Bawburgh
NORWICH
Norwich City FC
Brundall
Beighton
Tunstall
Runham
Colney
Earlham
Eaton
Norwich Castle Mus & Art Gall
Postwick
Strumpshaw
South Burlingham
Greyfriar's Cloisters
Old Merchant's House and Row 111 House
Great Melton
Little Melton
East Anglia
Lakenham
Trowse Newton
Moulton St Mary
Halvergate
Halvergate Marshes
Breydon Water
Sea Life Centre
Wramplingham
Hethersett
Cringleford
Kirby Bedon
Surlingham
Buckenham
Hassingham
Freethorpe
Berney Arms Mill
Berney Arms Sta
Wickhampton
Burgh Castle
Pleasure Beach
Southtown
GREAT YARMOUTH
High Green
Lynch Green
Keswick
Bramerton
Rockland St Mary
Cantley
Freethorpe Common
Roman Fort
Wymondham
Intwood
Arminghall
Framingham Pigot
Claxton
Limpenhoe
Pettitts Animal Adventure Park
Bradwell
Gorleston-on-Sea
Ketteringham
Caistor St Edmund
Hellington
Swardeston
Dunston
Upper Stoke
Yelverton
Ashby St Mary
Carleton St Peter
Browston Green
Belton
East Carleton
Mulbarton
Stoke Holy Cross
Poringland
Framingham Earl
Bergh Apton
Thurton
Hardley Street
Reedham
Norton Marshes
Nogdam End
St Olaves Priory
Hobland Hall
Swainsthorpe
Langley Street
Chedgrave
Fritton
Fritton Lake Countryworld
Silfield
Penny's Green
Bracon Ash
Howe
Brooke
Sisland
Loddon
Norton Subcourse
Lower Thurlton
Ashby Dell
Lound
Hopton
Wreningham
Hawe's Green
Shotesham
Heckingham
Thurlton
Somerleyton Hall & Gardens
Ashwellthorpe
Toprow
Newton Flotman
Saxlingham Nethergate
Seething
Mundham
Hales
Thorpe
Blundeston
Fundenhall
Rainthorpe Hall
Kirstead Green
The Laurels
Stubbs Green
Hales Hall
Raveningham
Herringfleet
Haddiscoe
Corton
Fundenhall Street
Hapton
Flordon
Saxlingham Thorpe
Somerleyton
Pleasurewood Hills Theme Park
Tasburgh
Saxlingham Green
Thwaite St Mary
Kirby Green
Brundish
Maypole Green
Toft Monks
Tacolneston
Forncett St Mary
Low Tharston
Hempnall
Road Green
Woodton
Kirby Cane
Stockton
Wheatacre
Camps Heath
Oulton
Lowestoft Ness
East Point Pavilion
Flaxlands
Bunwell Street
Forncett End
Tharston
Stratton St Michael
Silver Green
Hedenham
Bull's Green
Waterheath
Normanston
Forncett St Peter
Long Stratton
Fritton
Topcroft
Ellingham
Kirby Row
Aldeby
Burgh St Peter
LOWESTOFT
Carleton Rode
Bunwell
Pottergate Street
Morningthorpe
Hempnall Green
Bedingham Green
Broome
Geldeston
Gillingham
Oulton Broad
Kirkley
Hargate
Wood Green
Topcroft Street
Upgate Street
Ditchingham
Shipmeadow
Beccles
Pakefield
Pakefield Holiday Centre
Wacton
Shelton
Wainford
North Cove
Barnby
Aslacton
Hardwick
Great Moulton
Harris Green
Great Green
Earsham
Bungay
Mettingham
Barsham
Worlingham
East Anglia Transport Museum
Carlton Colville
Tibenham
Sneath Common
Cole's Common
Darrow Green
Denton
The City
Ellough Moor
Mutford
Gisleham
Pristow Green
North Green
The Otter Trust
Ilketshall St Andrew
Ringsfield
Beccles
Rushmere
Black Street
Kessingland
Colegate End
Bush Green
Alburgh
Flixton
Ilketshall St Margaret
Ringsfield Corner
Ellough
Hulver Street
Henstead
Kessingland Beach
Tivetshall St Margaret
Tivetshall St Mary
Pulham Market
Pulham St Mary
Piccadilly Corner
Homersfield
St Margaret South Elmham
St Michael South Elmham
Beck's Green
SUFFOLK
Suffolk Wildlife Park
Gissing
Mill Green
Starston
Wortwell
Ilketshall St Lawrence
Shadingfield
Sotterley
Benacre
Shelfanger
Dickleburgh Moor
Garlic Street
Harleston
Redenhall
St Cross South Elmham
High Street
Redisham
Brampton Sta
Cuckold's Green
Burston
Shimpling
Rushall
Dickleburgh
Gorze Green
Mendham
All Saints South Elmham
Aldous's Corner
Stone Street
Cox Common
Brampton
West End
Frostenden
Wrentham
High Common
Needham
Withersdale Street
Rumburgh
Brampton Street
Stoven
South Cove
Covehithe
Walcot Green
Thelveton
Roydon
Diss
Upper Street
Thorpe Abbotts
Weybread
Metfield
St James South Elmham
Spexhall
Westhall
Clay Common
Barnaby Green
Cove Bottom
Fen Street
Scole
Brockdish
Weybread Street
Wissett
Broadway
Uggeshall
Wangford
Palgrave
Billingford
Windmill
Wingfield Green
Earsham Street
Chediston
Holton
Reydon
Reydon Smear
Stuston
Oakley
Hoxne
College
Fressingfield
Little Wittingham Green
Linstead Parva
North Green
Halesworth
Great Green
Brome Street
Cross Street
Wingfield
Broad Road
Blyford
35
A149
A148
A140
A1151
A1062
A1064
A47
A1074
A1067
A1042
A1242
A11
A146
A143
A144
A145
A1117
A12
A140
A1066
A1095
B1149
B1145
B1150
B1354
B1436
B1152
B1140
B1108
B1172
B1135
B1332
B1527
B1113
B1134
B1062
B1136
B1074
B1375
B1385
B1123
B1124
B1127
B1126
B1118

A
B
C
D
E
1
2
3
4
5
6
7
The Skerries
West Mouse
Middle Mouse
Carmel Head
Cemlyn Bay
Cemaes Bay
Llanbadrig
Porth Wen Bay
Bull Bay (Porth Llechog)
Point Lynas
Cemaes
Neuadd
Amlwch
Amlwch Port
Llaneilian
(NT)
Tregele
Burwen
Pengorffwysfa
Llanfechell
Llanfairynghornwy
Bodewryd
Pen-y-sarn
Ynys Dulas
Mynyddmechell
Nebo
Rhos-goch
Parys Mountain
Dulas
Llanrhyddlad
Carreglefn
A5025
Rhyd-wyn
Llanfflewyn
Rhos-y-bol
Dulas Bay
HOLYHEAD BAY
Church Bay
17
8
Llaneuddog
ISLE OF
City Dulas
Lligwy Bay
Llanfaethlu
Llanbabo
Capel Parc
Brynrefail
Din Lligwy
Capel Lligwy
Dublin 1¾-3¼
Dún Laoghaire 1¾
hours
Rhoslligwy
Moelfre
A5025
Windmill
Gwredog
Llyn Alaw
Ceidio
Llandyfrydog
Llanallgo
Lligwy Burial Chamber
North Stack
Llanfwrog
Llanddeusant
Elim
Llannerch-y-medd
Maenaddwyn
Holyhead Mountain
220
Holyhead (Caergybi)
Stryd y Facsen
Llantrisant
Bachau
Marian-glas
South Stack Cliffs
Roman Fort
Tregwehelydd Standing Stone
Salt Island
Llanfachraeth
Llanfigael
ANGLESEY
Bryn-teg
Tyn-y-gongl
Benllech
South Stack
Llaingoch
Pen-llyn
Carmel
Capel Coch
Red Wharf Bay
St Seiriol's Well
Puffin Island (Priestholm)
Hut Circles
Kingsland
Penrhos
Llanynghenedl
Llyn Llywenan
ANGLESEY
Llechcynfarwy
Mariandyrys
Standing Stones
A5
Burial Chambers
B5109
Llanbedrgoch
Red Wharf Bay (Traeth Coch)
Glan-yr-afon
Cim
Penmon Priory (ruins)
Bodedern
Penmon
CONWY BAY
Penrhyn Mawr
Burial Chamber
Trearddur
Valley
Trefor
Llangwyllog
Tregaian
Mynydd Llwydiarth
Llangoed
(YNYS MÔN)
Llanddyfnan
Llanddona
Caergeiliog
Llynfaes
Rhosmeirch
Pentraeth
HOLY ISLAND
Four Mile Bridge
Bryngwran
Llyn Frogwy
Cefni Res.
Llan-faes
Dutchman Bank
B4545
Bodior
Llanfihangel-yn-Nhywyn
Bodffordd
Talwrn
10
B5109
Beaumaris Castle
Rhoscolyn
Llanfair-yn-neubwll
Gwalchmai
Llangefni
Capel Gwyn
Heneglwys
A5025
Llansadwrn
Beaumaris (Biwmares)
Penmaen Swatch
Tywyn Trewan
A4080
A55
A5
Rhostrehwfa
Lavan Sands
Cymyran Bay
Ty Newydd Burial Chamber
6
Ceint
Pen-mynydd
Llandegfan
Llanfairfechan
A4080
Rhosneigr
Pencarnisiog
Cerrigceinwen
A545
Port Penrhyn
Pandy
Nant-y-
Llanfaelog
Burial Chamber
Llangristiolus
7
Llanfairpwllgwyngyll
Bangor
Penrhyn Castle (NT)
Gorddinog
Garreg Fawr
Ty Croes Sta
Capel Mawr
Pentre Berw
Gaerwen
Menai Bridge (Porthaethwy)
Garth
Abergwyngregyn
Barclodiad y Gawres Chambered Cairn
Bethel
Malltraeth Marsh
7A
Llanddaniel Fab
A4087
Llandygai
Crymlyn
Coedydd Aber
Trefdraeth
Penrhos-garnedd
Minffordd
Tal-y-bont
Aber Falls
Aberffraw
Llangadwaladr
Bryn Celli Ddu Burial Chamber
Plas Newydd (NT)
Moel Wnion
580
849
Hermon
Malltraeth
Capel-y-graig
Glasinfryn
Llanllechid
Llwytmor
Llangaffo
Bodowyr Burial Chamber
Waen-wen
Rachub
Drosgl 758
Foel-Fras 942
Aberffraw Bay
Bodorgan
Malltraeth Sands
Castell Bryn-gwyn
Brynsiencyn
Y Felinheli
Rhyd-y-groes
Tal-y-Cae
Tregarth
Bethesda
Gerlan
Garnedd Uchaf 926
A4080
Newborough (Niwbwrch)
Dwyran
Seion
Pentir
Coed-y-parc
Saron
Llanddeiniolen
Rhiwlas
Braichmelyn
SNOWD
Malltraeth Bay
Pen-lôn
Anglesey Sea Zoo
Menai Strait
Plas Menai National Watersports Centre
Bethel
Penisa'r Waun
Mynydd Llandygai
Foel Grach 976
Newborough Warren
A4244
12
Carnedd Llywelyn 1064
Llanddwyn Island
Newborough Warren
Waterloo Port
Caernarfon
Pont-rug
Llanrug
Deiniolen
Nant Ffrancon
Carnedd Dafydd 1044
Llanddwyn Bay
Royal Welch Fusiliers Regiment Mus
Caeathro
Brynrefail
Clwt-y-bont
Gallt-y-foel
Fachwen
Mynydd Perfedd 812
Elidyr Fawr 923
Foel Goch 831
Abermenai Point
Caernarfon Castle
Segontium Roman Mus
Brynbras
Cwm-y-glo
Llyn Padarn
Dinorwig
Padarn
Llyn Ogwen
NATIO
The Bar
Llanfaglan
Bontnewydd
A4085
Ceunant
Llanberis Lake Railway
Llanberis
Electric Mountain
Foryd Bay
Croesywaun
Groeslon
Dolbadarn
Welsh Slate Museum
Y Garn 946
Pont Pen-y-benglog
314
Saron
Welsh Highland Rly
Waunfawr
Snowdon Mountain Rly
Cwm Idwal
Glyder Fach 994
Dinas
Rhostryfan
Llyn Peris
Glyder Fawr 999
CAERNARFON BAY
Llanwnda
Rhosgadfan
Betws Garmon
Moel Eilio 726
Nant Peris
Gwastadnant
A4086
Dinas Dinlle
Penyffridd
Moel Tryfan
GWYNEDD
Salem
SNOWDONIA (ERYRI)
Pass of Llanberis
Pen-y-Pass 356
Pen-y-Gwryd Hotel
Nantygwryd
PAR
Llandwrog
Groeslon
Bwlchyllyn
13
Siop y Fron (Upper Llandwrog)
Mynydd Mawr 698
Llyn Cwellyn
1085
Glaslyn
Glynllifon Park
Carmel
Snowdon (Yr Wyddfa) 898
Llyn Llydaw
Carnedd y Cribau 591
Penygroes
Nantlle
Llyn Nantlle Uchaf
Y Garn 634
Rhyd-Ddu
Llyn Diwaunedd
Pontllyfni
Talysarn
B4418
A498
Trwyn Maen Dylan
Llanllyfni
Ffridd Uchaf
Llyn Gwynant
Trum y Ddysgl 709
747 Yr Aran
Blaenau Dolwyddelan
Aberdesach
A499
A487
Craig Cwm Silyn 734
Beddgelert Forest
Plas Gwynant
221
Nebo
605
Clynnog-fawr
Tai'n Lôn
36
Capeluchaf
Nasareth
700
Garnedd-goch
A4085
Llyn Dinas
Yr Arddu
Bwlch y Gorddinan (Crimea Pass)
0 2 4 6 miles
0 2 4 6 8 10 km
10
Gyrn Goch
Bwlch Mawr 509
Pant Glas
608
Beddgelert
Trefor
Gyrn Ddu
Bwlch-
Moel Hebog
Pass of
Rhiwbryfdir

F
G
H
J
K
Birkenhead to hours
Belfast 8
Dublin 8
Liverpool to hours
Douglas 2½-4
Dublin 4-8
I
Southport
Ainsdale Sand Dunes National Nature Reserve
Formby Red Squirrel Reserve (NT)
Mad Wharf
Formby Point
2
LIVERPOOL BAY
3
Mockbeggar
East Hoyle Bank
48
Meols Sta
Moreton
Manor Road Sta
Hoylake Sta
Saughall Massie
West Hoyle Bank
Hilbre Island
West Kirby Sta
West Kirby
Grange
Frankby
Caldy
Irby
Thurstaston
Welsh Channel
Point of Ayr
Talacre
Prestatyn Sands Holiday Centre
Llawndy
Mostyn Bank
The Wirral (NT)
Pensby
Dawpool Bank
Heswall
Gayton
4
Great Ormes Head
Great Orme Cabin Lift
North Wales Theatre
Great Orme Country Park
Toll
Llandudno
Little Ormes Head
Gogarth
Great Orme Tramway
Penrhyn-side
Penrhyn Bay (Bae Penrhyn)
Conwy Sands
Glanwydden
Rhôs-on-Sea
Colwyn Bay (Bae Colwyn)
Deganwy
Aberconwy House (NT)
Llandudno Junction
Esgyryn
Mochdre
Welsh Mountain Zoo
Old Colwyn
Penmaen Rhos
Llanddulas
Llysfaen
Abergele Roads
Abergele
Pensarn
Kinmel Bay (Bae Cinmel)
Towyn
Plas Llwyd
Morfa Rhuddlan
Rhyl
Sky Tower
SeaQuarium
Ocean Beach Amusement Park
Prestatyn
Ffrith
Meliden (Gallt Melyd)
Gronant
Gwespyr
Ffynnongroyw
Llanasa
Gwaenysgor
Gop Hill
Pen-y-ffordd
Trelogan
Mostyn Quay
Mostyn
Glan-y-don
Llannerch-y-Môr
Holywell Bank
Greenfield Valley
Greenfield
Basingwerk Abbey
St Winefride's Holy Well & Chapel
Whelston
Bagillt
Walwen
Holywell (Treffynnon)
Tan-yr-allt
Trelawnyd
Axton
Rhuddlan
Rhuddlan Castle & Twt Hill
Dyserth
Cwm
Marian Cwm
Llyn Helyg
Maen Achwyfaen
Lloc
Gorsedd
Carmel
Pantasaph
Conwy
Dwygyfylchi
Capelulo
Penmaenmawr
Penmaenan
Conwy Castle
Suspension Bridge (NT)
Llansanffraid Glan Conwy
Llanelian-yn-Rhos
Bryn-y-maen
Pentrefelin
Foel Lus
Moelfre 435
Henryd
Tal-y-fan 610
Rowen
Ty'n-y-groes
Caerhun
Bodnant Gardens (NT)
Graig
Moel Gyffylog 341
Tal-y-cafn
Eglwysbach
Dolwen
Betws-yn-Rhos
Mynydd Llanelian 336
Dawn
Trofarth
Moelfre Isaf 317
Moelfre Uchaf 396
Mynydd Bodrochwyn
Mynydd Branar 324
Rhyd-y-foel
St George
Bodelwyddan
Pengwern
St Asaph (Llanelwy)
Groesffordd Marli
Tremeirchion
Cefn Meiriadog
Llannefydd
Plas-yn-Cefn
Bont-newydd
Cefn Berain
Llannerch Hall
Trefnant
Pen-y-cefn
Rhuallt
Offa's Dyke
Sodom
Caerwys
Babell
Brynford
Dolphin
Pentre Halkyn
Flint (Y Fflint)
Flint (ruins)
Mount Pleasant
Oakenholt
Halkyn
Flint Mountain
5
Afon-wen
Ysceifiog
Lixwm
Walwen
Rhes-y-cae
Halkyn Mountain
Afonwen Craft and Antique Centre
Nannerch
Moel y Parc 398
Bodfari
Waen Aberwheeler
Rhosesmor
The Green
Northop (Llaneurgain)
Soughton
Northop Hall
Drum 770
Llanbedr-y-cennin
Castell
Tal-y-bont
Dulyn Reservoir
Dolgarrog
Dolgarrog Sta
Pont Dolgarrog
Llyn Eigiau Reservoir
Pen Llithrig y-wrach 799
Llyn Cowlyd Reservoir
Pentre'r Felin
Mwdwl Eithin 389
Gell
Llangernyw
Hafodunos
Rhos-y-mawn
Wenlli
Llanfair Talhaiarn
Pentre Isaf
Tre-pys-llygod
Pen y Mwdwl
Llansannan
Plasisaf
Deunant
Rhydgaled
Tan-y-fron
Henllan
Denbigh (Dinbych)
Denbigh Castle
Gwaynynog
Friary (ruins)
Brookhouse
Waen
Llangwyfan
Llandyrnog
Moel Llys-y-coed 465
Cilcain
Pantymwyn
Gwernaffield
Ffordd-las
Moel Famau
Moel Famau 554
Loggerheads
Mold (Yr Wyddgrug)
Cadole
6
Llangynhafal
Gellifor
Hirwaen
Tafarn-y-Gelyn
Gwernymynydd
Moel Findeg
Nercwys
Maeshafn
Llanferres
Stryt-cae-rhedyn
Leeswood
Pontybodkin
CONWY
DENBIGHSHIRE
FLINTSHIRE
VALE OF CLWYD
CLWYDIAN RANGE
Vale of Conwy
Llanddoged
Pandy Tudur
Trefriw
Trefriw Woollen Mill
Llanrwst
Gwydir
Gwydir Uchaf Chapel
Pentre-tafarn-y-fedw
Melin-y-coed
Oerfa 396
Gwytherin
Bylchau
Pen-cae-cwm
Groes
Waen
Nantglyn
Llanrhaeadr
Pant-pastynog
Llanynys
Rhewl
Cader
Pentre Saron
Ffridd Fawr 344
Meifod
Gorsedd Bran 518
Sportsman's Arms
Bryn Trillyn 496
Llyn Aled Isaf Reservoir
Moel Seisiog 468
Moel Llyn 448
Llyn Aled
Llanbedr-Dyffryn-Clwyd
Ruthin (Rhuthun)
Ruthin Craft Centre
Cyffylliog
Bontuchel
Llanfwrog
Llanfair Dyffryn Clwyd
Eryrys
Treuddyn
Rhyd-y-ceirw
Pantyffordd
Graianrhyd
Llanarmon-yn-Ial
Efenechtyd
Capel Curig
Ty-Hyll
Swallow Falls
Glyn
Pont Cyfyng
Llynnau Mymbyr
Betws-y-coed
Conwy Valley Railway Museum
Mynydd Cribau 345
GWYDYR FOREST PARK
Oaklands
Capel Garmon
Nebo
Mynydd Hiraethog
Llyn Brenig
Chambered Long Cairn
Pont-y-pant
Dolwyddelan
Roman Br Sta
Pentre-bont
Ty Mawr Wybrnant (NT)
Fairy Glen
Rhydlanfair
Ty'n-y-Coed Uchaf (NT)
Glan Conwy
Pentrefoelas
Penmachno
Hafod-Dinbych
Alwen Reservoir
Llyn Brenig Visitor Centre
Pentre-llyn-cymmer
Pont yr Alwen
Cefn-brith
Nilig
Cefn Du 422
Clocaenog
Clocaenog Forest
Craig Bron-banog 501
Clawdd-newydd
Pwll-glas
Graig-fechan
Pentre-celyn
Gelli Gynan
Moel y Waun
Llandegla
Moel Garegog
Bwlchgwyn
Gwynfryn
Minera
Pen-y-stryt
Esclusham Mountain
Brighton
7
Rhydlydan
Glasfryn
Cerrigydrudion
Llanfihangel Glyn Myfyr
37
Derwen
Churchyard Cross
Brynsaithmarchog
Pandy'r Capel
Llanelidan
Cefn Coch
Mynydd Cricor
Nant y Garth Pass 248
Pentre-bwlch
Cyrn-y-Brain 565
World's End 492
Horseshoe Pass
Moel y Gamelin
Eglwyseg Mountain
Rhosllanerchrugog
Gwyddelwern
Betws Gwerfil Goch
Bryneglwys
Ysbyty Ifan
Garn Prys 534
Ty-Mawr
Mwdwl-eithin
Moel Penamnen 623
Glanaber Terrace
Llechwedd Slate Caverns
Pen y Bedw
Gwydyr Forest
Yr Ro Wen 594
Carrog
8

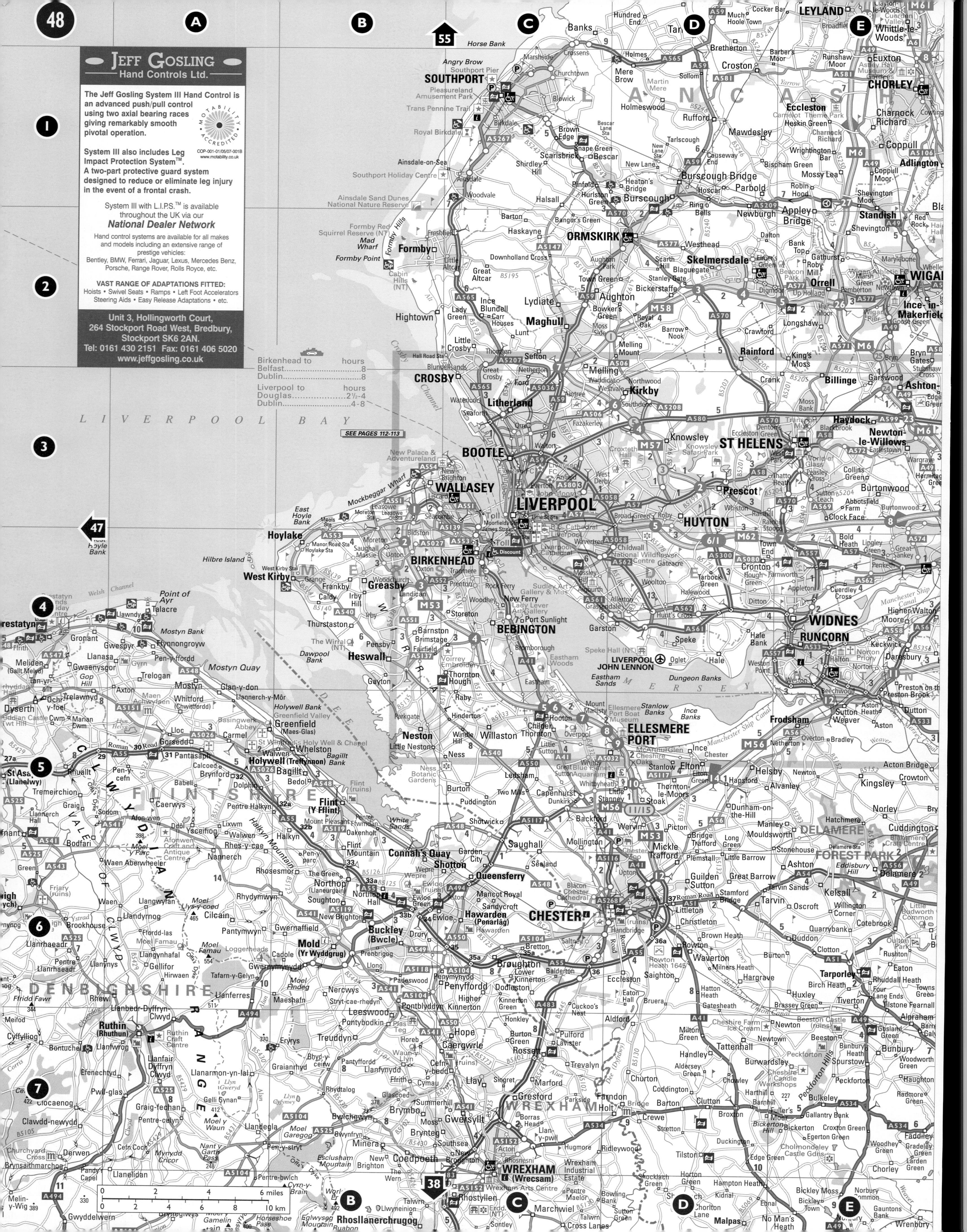
55
47
38
SEE PAGES 112-113
Birkenhead to hours
Belfast....8
Dublin....8
Liverpool to hours
Douglas....2½-4
Dublin....4-8
LIVERPOOL BAY
SOUTHPORT
Formby
CROSBY
Litherland
BOOTLE
WALLASEY
LIVERPOOL
BIRKENHEAD
Hoylake
West Kirby
Greasby
Heswall
BEBINGTON
Neston
ELLESMERE PORT
CHESTER
HUYTON
ST HELENS
Prescot
WIDNES
RUNCORN
Frodsham
Helsby
ORMSKIRK
Skelmersdale
Maghull
Kirkby
Burscough
LEYLAND
CHORLEY
WIGAN
Orrell
Haydock
Newton-le-Willows
Flint (Y Fflint)
Holywell (Treffynnon)
Connah's Quay
Shotton
Queensferry
Hawarden (Penarlâg)
Buckley (Bwcle)
Mold (Yr Wyddgrug)
Ruthin (Rhuthun)
WREXHAM (Wrecsam)
Rhosllanerchrugog
Tarporley
FLINTSHIRE
DENBIGHSHIRE
CLWYDIAN RANGE
VALE OF CLWYD
WIRRAL
MERSEYSIDE
LANCASHIRE
CHESHIRE
WREXHAM
DELAMERE FOREST PARK
LIVERPOOL JOHN LENNON
Mersey
Dee
Manchester Ship Canal
0 2 4 6 miles
0 2 4 6 8 10 km

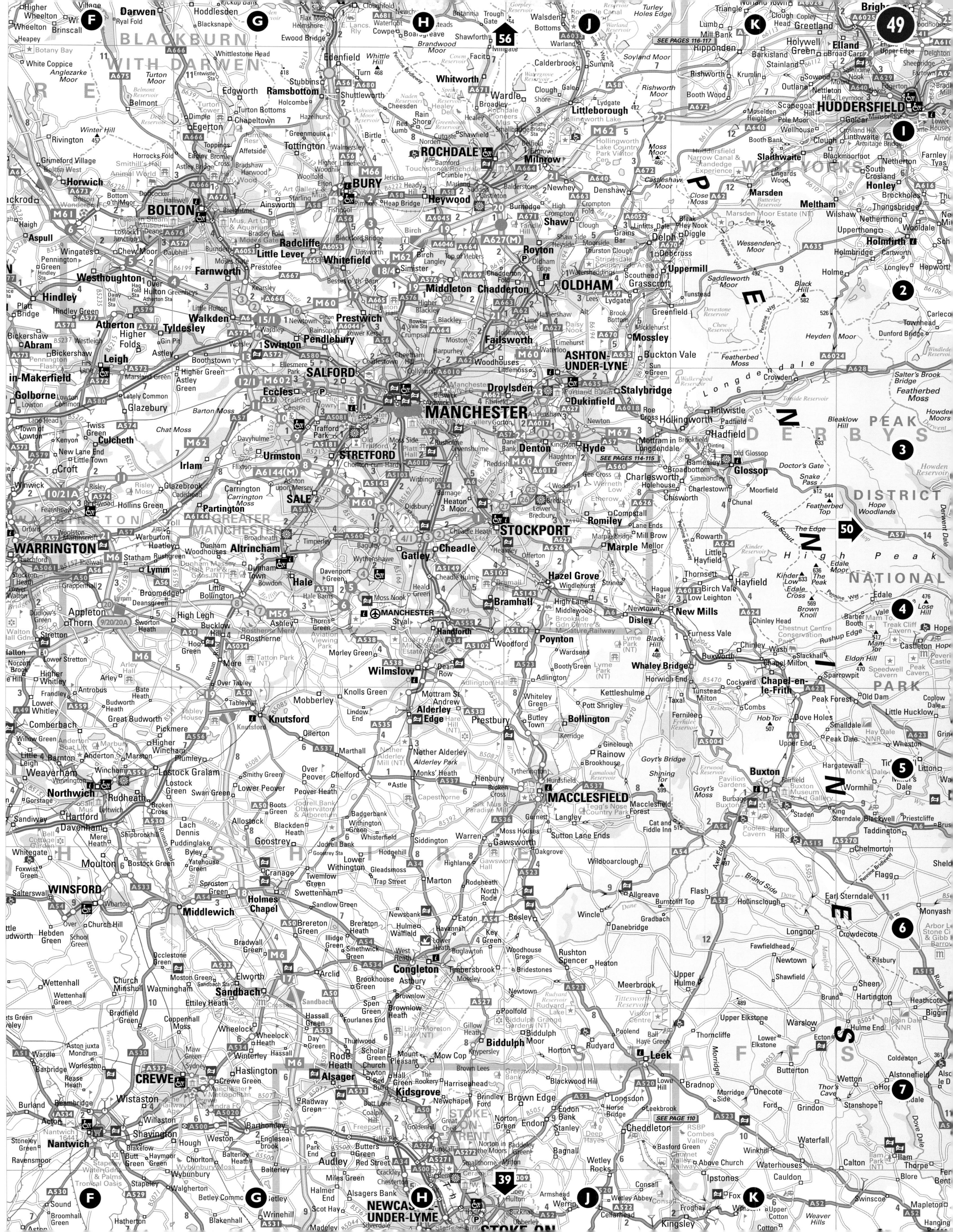
F
G
H
J
K
56
SEE PAGES 116-117
BLACKBURN WITH DARWEN
Darwen
BOLTON
BURY
ROCHDALE
HUDDERSFIELD
OLDHAM
SALFORD
MANCHESTER
ASHTON-UNDER-LYNE
STOCKPORT
WARRINGTON
GREATER MANCHESTER
SEE PAGES 114-115
50
PEAK DISTRICT NATIONAL PARK
DERBYS
PENNINES
WEST YORKS
High Peak
MACCLESFIELD
CHESHIRE
CONGLETON
WINSFORD
CREWE
STAFFS
SEE PAGE 110
STOKE-ON-TRENT
NEWCASTLE-UNDER-LYME
39
Wigan
Leigh
Altrincham
Sale
Stretford
Eccles
Wilmslow
Knutsford
Northwich
Middlewich
Sandbach
Nantwich
Buxton
Leek
Glossop
Hyde
Stalybridge
Marple
Hazel Grove
Poynton
Biddulph
Kidsgrove
Alsager
Holmfirth
Marsden
Meltham
Whaley Bridge
Chapel-en-le-Frith
New Mills
Hayfield
Edale
Castleton
Horwich
Farnworth
Walkden
Radcliffe
Heywood
Middleton
Prestwich
Whitefield
Ramsbottom
Littleborough
Milnrow
Royton
Shaw
Failsworth
Droylsden
Denton
Dukinfield
Mossley
Cheadle
Gatley
Hale
Lymm
Irlam
Urmston
Partington
Atherton
Tyldesley
Hindley
Westhoughton
Golborne
Holmes Chapel
Alderley Edge
Bollington
Prestbury
Wincle
M6
M56
M60
M61
M62
M66
M67
M602
A6
A34
A50
A523
A537
A54
A628
A635
A57
1
2
3
4
5
6
7

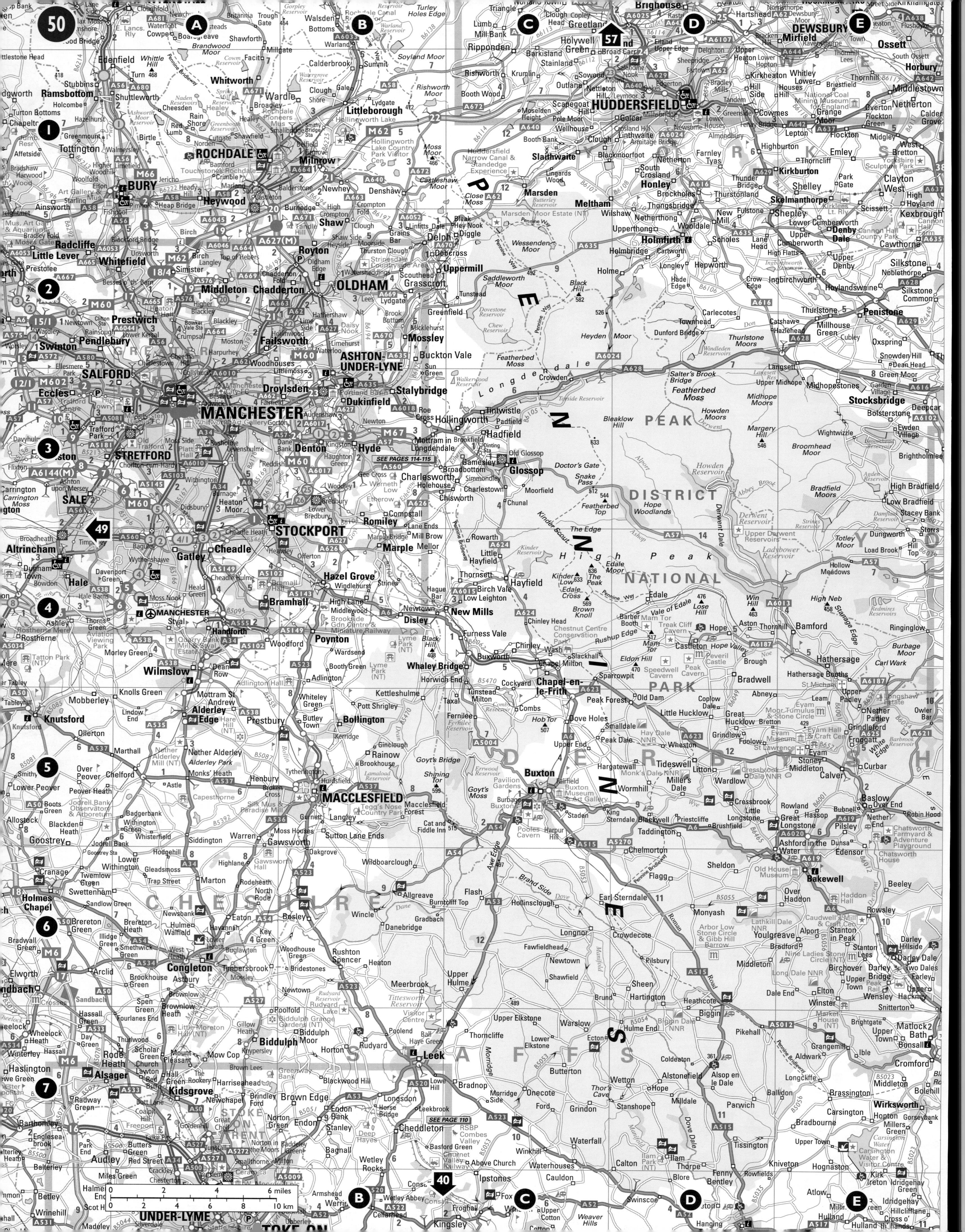
A
B
C
D
E
1
2
3
4
5
6
7
57
49
40
SEE PAGES 114-115
SEE PAGE 110
Brighouse
DEWSBURY
Mirfield
Ossett
Horbury
HUDDERSFIELD
Holmfirth
Penistone
Stocksbridge
ROCHDALE
Littleborough
Milnrow
BURY
Heywood
Ramsbottom
Radcliffe
Whitefield
Middleton
OLDHAM
Chadderton
Shaw
Royton
Prestwich
Swinton
Pendlebury
SALFORD
Eccles
MANCHESTER
Droylsden
Failsworth
ASHTON-UNDER-LYNE
Stalybridge
Dukinfield
Mossley
Hyde
Denton
Glossop
STRETFORD
SALE
Altrincham
Hale
Cheadle
STOCKPORT
Marple
Hazel Grove
Bramhall
Poynton
New Mills
Disley
Whaley Bridge
Chapel-en-le-Frith
Wilmslow
Alderley Edge
Knutsford
Bollington
MACCLESFIELD
Buxton
Bakewell
Holmes Chapel
Congleton
Alsager
Kidsgrove
Biddulph
Leek
Cheddleton
Sandbach
Matlock
Wirksworth
Hathersage
MANCHESTER
PEAK DISTRICT NATIONAL PARK
High Peak
PENNINES
CHESHIRE
DERBYSHIRE
STAFFS
STOKE ON TRENT
NEWCASTLE-UNDER-LYME
0 2 4 6 miles
0 2 4 6 8 10 km

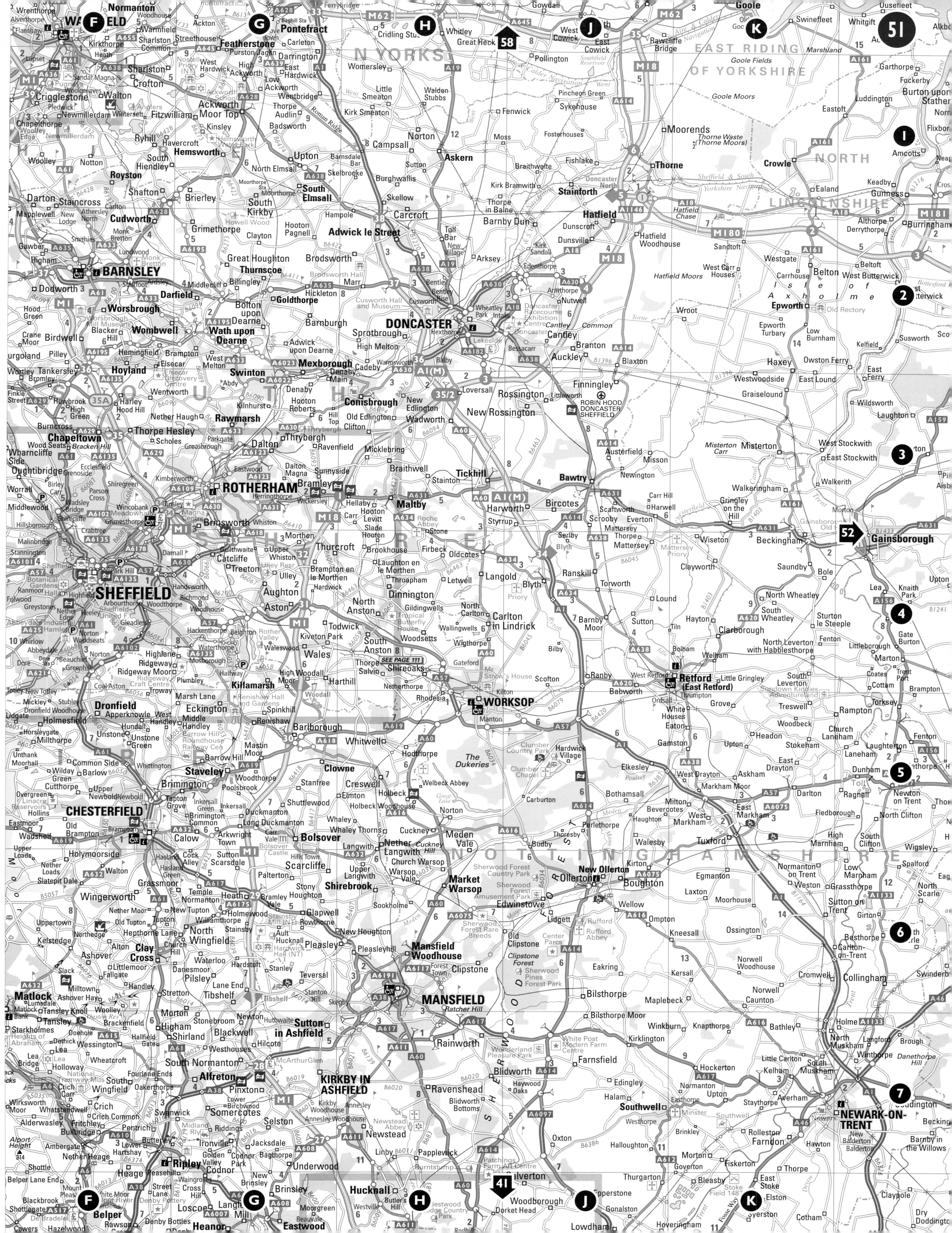

51
58
52
41
F
G
H
J
K
I
1
2
3
4
5
6
7
Wakefield
Normanton
Pontefract
Featherstone
Ackworth Moor Top
Hemsworth
South Elmsall
Askern
Thorne
Crowle
Goole
N YORKS
EAST RIDING OF YORKSHIRE
NORTH LINCOLNSHIRE
Hatfield
Stainforth
Adwick le Street
BARNSLEY
Darfield
Wombwell
Worsbrough
Goldthorpe
DONCASTER
Mexborough
Conisbrough
Swinton
Hoyland
Rawmarsh
Chapeltown
ROTHERHAM
Maltby
Tickhill
Bawtry
Harworth
Bircotes
Epworth
Isle of Axholme
Misterton
Gainsborough
SOUTH YORKSHIRE
SHEFFIELD
Thurcroft
Dinnington
North Anston
Aston
Aughton
Killamarsh
Eckington
Dronfield
WORKSOP
Retford (East Retford)
Barlborough
Clowne
Staveley
CHESTERFIELD
Bolsover
Shirebrook
Market Warsop
New Ollerton
Ollerton
Boughton
Tuxford
Clay Cross
North Wingfield
Mansfield Woodhouse
MANSFIELD
Sutton in Ashfield
KIRKBY IN ASHFIELD
Alfreton
Matlock
Belper
Ripley
Heanor
Eastwood
Hucknall
Southwell
NEWARK-ON-TRENT
NOTTINGHAMSHIRE
SHERWOOD FOREST
The Dukeries
Clumber Country Park
Rufford Abbey
Sherwood Pines Forest Park
ROBIN HOOD DONCASTER SHEFFIELD
SEE PAGE 111
M1
M18
M62
M180
A1(M)
A1
A57
A60
A61
A614
A616
A617
A619
A631
A638

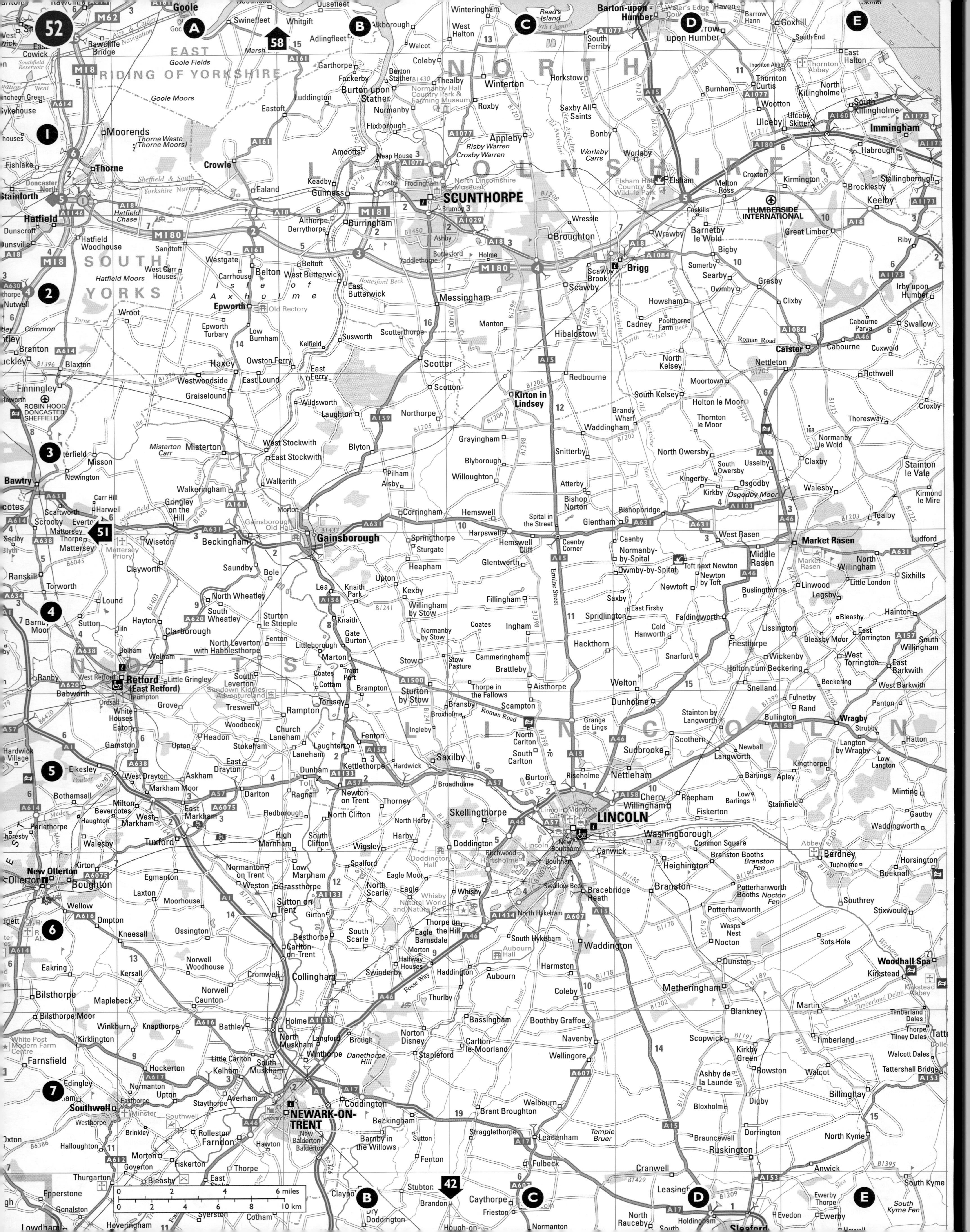
A
B
C
D
E
Goole
Swinefleet
Whitgift
58
Ousefleet
Alkborough
Winteringham
Read's Island
Barton-upon-Humber
Haven
Barrow Haven
Goxhill
EAST
RIDING OF YORKSHIRE
Goole Fields
Marsh
Adlingfleet
Walcot
West Halton
South Ferriby
Barrow upon Humber
South End
East Halton
Cowick
Rawcliffe Bridge
M62
M18
Garthorpe
Fockerby
Burton Stather
Burton upon Stather
Coleby
Thealby
Normanby Hall Country Park & Farming Museum
NORTH
Winterton
Horkstow
Thornton Abbey Sta
Thornton Abbey
Thornton Curtis
North Killingholme
Burnham
Wootton
Goole Moors
Luddington
Eastoft
Normanby
Roxby
Saxby All Saints
Ulceby
Ulceby Skitter
South Killingholme
Immingham
Moorends
Thorne Waste (Thorne Moors)
Flixborough
Appleby
Risby Warren
Crosby Warren
Bonby
Worlaby Carrs
Worlaby
Habrough
Amcotts
Neap House
Fishlake
Thorne
Crowle
LINCOLNSHIRE
Doncaster North
Stainforth
Sheffield & South Yorkshire Navigation
Ealand
Keadby
Gunness
Crosby
Frodingham
North Lincolnshire Museum
SCUNTHORPE
Elsham Hall Country & Wildlife Park
Elsham
Croxton
Melton Ross
Kirmington
Brocklesby
Stallingborough
HUMBERSIDE INTERNATIONAL
Keelby
Hatfield
Hatfield Chase
Althorpe
Derrythorpe
Burringham
Brumby
Ashby
Wressle
Broughton
Wrawby
Barnetby le Wold
Great Limber
Riby
Dunscroft
Dunsville
Hatfield Woodhouse
M180
Sandtoft
Bottesford
Yaddlethorpe
Holme
Bigby
SOUTH
YORKS
Westgate
West Carr Houses
Carrhouse
Belton
Beltoft
West Butterwick
East Butterwick
Bottesford Beck
Scawby Brook
Brigg
Somerby
Searby
Owmby
Grasby
Irby upon Humber
Hatfield Moors
Isle of Axholme
Epworth
Old Rectory
Messingham
Scawby
Howsham
Clixby
Nutwell
Wroot
Epworth Turbary
Low Burnham
Scotterthorpe
Susworth
Manton
Hibaldstow
Cadney
Poolthorpe Farm
North Kelsey
Cabourne Parva
Swallow
Branton
Common
Torne
Kelfield
Owston Ferry
Haxey
Scotter
Caistor
Cabourne
Cuxwold
Blaxton
Westwoodside
East Lound
East Ferry
Scotton
Redbourne
North Kelsey
Nettleton
Rothwell
Finningley
Graiselound
Wildsworth
Kirton in Lindsey
South Kelsey
Moortown
ROBIN HOOD DONCASTER SHEFFIELD
Laughton
Northorpe
Brandy Wharf
Holton le Moor
Thornton le Moor
Croxby
Thoresway
Waddingham
Grayingham
Misterton Carr
Misterton
West Stockwith
East Stockwith
Blyton
North Owersby
Normanby le Wold
Austerfield
Misson
Blyborough
Snitterby
South Owersby
Usselby
Claxby
Stainton le Vale
Bawtry
Newington
Pilham
Aisby
Willoughton
Atterby
Kingerby
Osgodby
Walesby
Kirmond le Mire
Carr Hill
Walkeringham
Walkerith
Bishop Norton
Kirkby
Osgodby Moor
Harwell
Gringley on the Hill
Morton
Corringham
Hemswell
Bishopbridge
Tealby
Scaftworth
Everton
Scrooby
Mattersey
Mattersey Thorpe
Chesterfield Canal
Gainsborough Old Hall
Spital in the Street
Glentham
West Rasen
Ludford
Serlby
51
Wiseton
Beckingham
Gainsborough
Springthorpe
Sturgate
Harpswell
Hemswell Cliff
Caenby Corner
Caenby
Normanby-by-Spital
Market Rasen
Mattersey Priory
Middle Rasen
North Willingham
Ranskill
Clayworth
Saundby
Bole
Heapham
Glentworth
Owmby-by-Spital
Toft next Newton
Newton by Toft
Sixhills
Torworth
Upton
Newtoft
Linwood
Little London
North Wheatley
Lound
South Wheatley
Sturton le Steeple
Lea
Knaith Park
Kexby
Fillingham
Buslingthorpe
Legsby
Willingham by Stow
Saxby
East Firsby
Spridlington
Faldingworth
Bleasby
Hainton
Barnby Moor
Sutton
Hayton
Clarborough
Knaith
Gate Burton
Normanby by Stow
Coates
Ingham
Ermine Street
Cold Hanworth
Lissington
East Torrington
South Willingham
Tiln
Fenton
North Leverton with Habblesthorpe
Littleborough
Hackthorn
Friesthorpe
Bleasby Moor
Bolham
Welham
Marton
Stow
Stow Pasture
Cammeringham
Snarford
Wickenby
West Torrington
East Barkwith
Ranby
West Retford
Retford (East Retford)
Little Gringley
South Leverton
Coates
Trent Port
Brattleby
Holton cum Beckering
Beckering
Babworth
Thrumpton
Sundown Kiddies Adventureland
Cottam
Brampton
Sturton by Stow
Thorpe in the Fallows
Aisthorpe
Welton
Snelland
West Barkwith
Ordsall
Grove
Treswell
Rampton
Torksey
Bransby
Broxholme
Roman Road
Scampton
Dunholme
Fulnetby
Rand
Panton
White Houses
Eaton
Woodbeck
Church Laneham
Ingleby
Grange de Lings
Stainton by Langworth
Bullington
Wragby
Strubby
Hardwick Village
Gamston
Headon
Upton
Stokeham
Laughterton
Fenton
North Carlton
South Carlton
Sudbrooke
Scothern
Newball
Langton by Wragby
Hatton
Laneham
Kettlethorpe
Hardwick
Saxilby
Langworth
Low Langton
Elkesley
West Drayton
Askham
East Drayton
Dunham
Burton
Riseholme
Nettleham
Barlings
Apley
Kingthorpe
Bothamsall
Markham Moor
Darlton
Toll
Ragnall
Newton on Trent
Thorney
Broadholme
Cherry Willingham
Reepham
Low Barlings
Stainfield
Minting
Milton
Bevercotes
West Markham
East Markham
Fledborough
North Clifton
North Harby
Skellingthorpe
Lincoln
LINCOLN
Fiskerton
Gautby
Waddingworth
Haughton
Perlethorpe
Walesby
Tuxford
High Marnham
South Clifton
Harby
Doddington
Washingborough
Common Square
Abbey
Bardney
Horsington
Ollerton
New Ollerton
Kirton
Boughton
Egmanton
Normanton on Trent
Low Marnham
Spalford
Doddington Hall
Birchwood
Hartsholme
New Boultham
Boultham
Canwick
Branston Booths
Branston Fen
Heighington
Tupholme
Bucknall
Laxton
Weston
Grassthorpe
Eagle Moor
Eagle
North Scarle
Whisby
Whisby Natural World and Nature Park
Swallow Beck
Bracebridge Heath
Branston
Potterhanworth Booths
Nocton Fen
Southrey
Wellow
Ompton
Moorhouse
Sutton on Trent
Girton
Thorpe on the Hill
North Hykeham
Potterhanworth
Stixwould
Kneesall
Ossington
Besthorpe
Eagle Barnsdale
South Scarle
South Hykeham
Wasps Nest
Nocton
Sots Hole
Carlton-on-Trent
Aubourn Hall
Waddington
Eakring
Norwell Woodhouse
Morton
Halfway Houses
Swinderby
Fosse Way
Haddington
Aubourn
Harmston
Dunston
Woodhall Spa
Kirkstead
Kersall
Cromwell
Collingham
Norwell
Caunton
Thurlby
Coleby
Metheringham
Kirkstead Abbey
Bilsthorpe
Maplebeck
Blankney
Martin
Timberland Delph
Timberland Dales
Bilsthorpe Moor
Winkburn
Knapthorpe
Bathley
Holme
Bassingham
Boothby Graffoe
Thorpe Tilney Dales
White Post Modern Farm Centre
Kirklington
North Muskham
Langford
Brough
Norton Disney
Carlton-le-Moorland
Navenby
Scopwick
Kirkby Green
Timberland
Farnsfield
Hockerton
Little Carlton
South Muskham
Winthorpe
Danethorpe Hill
Stapleford
Wellingore
Walcott Dales
Kelham
Rowston
Walcot
Tattershall Bridge
Edingley
Normanton
Upton
Ashby de la Launde
Southwell
Easthorpe
Minster
Staythorpe
Averham
Coddington
Welbourn
Billinghay
Westhorpe
NEWARK-ON-TRENT
Beckingham
Brant Broughton
Digby
Bloxholm
Brinkley
Rolleston
Farndon
New Balderton
Balderton
Barnby in the Willows
Sutton
Stragglethorpe
Leadenham
Temple Bruer
Brauncewell
Dorrington
North Kyme
Halloughton
Hawton
Ruskington
Morton
Goverton
Fiskerton
Thorpe
Fenton
Fulbeck
Cranwell
Anwick
Thurgarton
Bleasby
East Stoke
Stubton
Brandon
42
Caythorpe
Leasingham
South Kyme
Epperstone
Claypole
Dry Doddington
Friesthorpe
Evedon
Ewerby Thorpe
Ewerby
South Kyme Fen
Gonalston
Syerston
Cotham
Hough-on-the-Hill
Normanton
North Rauceby
Holdingham
Sleaford
Lowdham
Hoveringham
0 2 4 6 miles
0 2 4 6 8 10 km

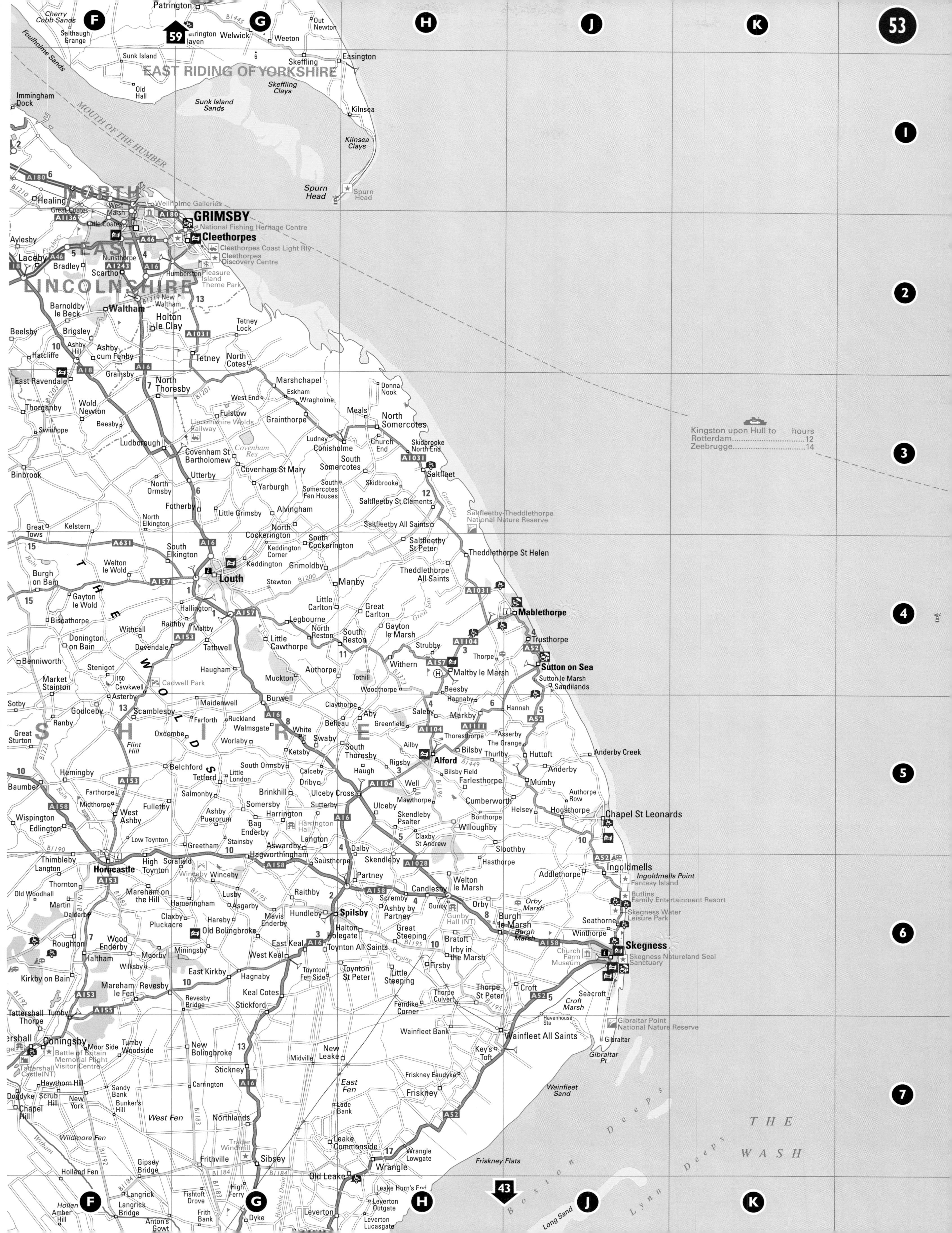

F
G
H
J
K
59
43
1
2
3
4
5
6
7
Patrington
Cherry Cobb Sands
Salthaugh Grange
Foulholme Sands
Patrington Haven
Welwick
Weeton
Out Newton
Easington
Skeffling
Sunk Island
EAST RIDING OF YORKSHIRE
Skeffling Clays
Old Hall
Sunk Island Sands
Immingham Dock
MOUTH OF THE HUMBER
Kilnsea
Kilnsea Clays
Spurn Head
NORTH EAST LINCOLNSHIRE
Healing
Great Coates
West Marsh
Wellholme Galleries
GRIMSBY
National Fishing Heritage Centre
Little Coates
Cleethorpes
Cleethorpes Coast Light Rly
Cleethorpes Discovery Centre
Aylesby
Laceby
Bradley
Nunsthorpe
Scartho
Humberston
Pleasure Island Theme Park
New Waltham
Barnoldby le Beck
Waltham
Holton le Clay
Tetney Lock
Beelsby
Brigsley
Ashby Hill
Ashby cum Fenby
Hatcliffe
Tetney
North Cotes
East Ravendale
Grainsby
North Thoresby
Marshchapel
Eskham
Wragholme
Donna Nook
Thorganby
Wold Newton
West End
Fulstow
Grainthorpe
Beesby
Swinhope
Lincolnshire Wolds Railway
Meals
North Somercotes
Ludborough
Covenham Res
Ludney
Conisholme
Church End
Skidbrooke North End
Covenham St Bartholomew
South Somercotes
Saltfleet
Binbrook
Covenham St Mary
Utterby
North Ormsby
Yarburgh
South Somercotes Fen Houses
Skidbrooke
Saltfleetby St Clements
Fotherby
Little Grimsby
Alvingham
Great Eau
Saltfleetby-Theddlethorpe National Nature Reserve
Great Tows
Kelstern
North Elkington
North Cockerington
Saltfleetby All Saints
South Cockerington
Saltfleetby St Peter
Keddington Corner
Theddlethorpe St Helen
South Elkington
Welton le Wold
Keddington
Grimoldby
Burgh on Bain
Louth
Stewton
Manby
Theddlethorpe All Saints
THE WOLDS
LINCOLNSHIRE
Gayton le Wold
Little Carlton
Great Carlton
Mablethorpe
Hallington
Legbourne
Gayton le Marsh
Biscathorpe
Raithby
Maltby
North Reston
South Reston
Trusthorpe
Withcall
Donington on Bain
Dovendale
Tathwell
Little Cawthorpe
Strubby
Thorpe
Sutton on Sea
Benniworth
Withern
Maltby le Marsh
Stenigot
Haugham
Authorpe
Tothill
Sutton le Marsh
Sandilands
Market Stainton
Cawkwell
Cadwell Park
Muckton
Woodthorpe
Beesby
Asterby
Hagnaby
Hannah
Sotby
Goulceby
Scamblesby
Maidenwell
Burwell
Claythorpe
Aby
Saleby
Markby
Ranby
Farforth
Ruckland
Walmsgate
White Pit
Belleau
Greenfield
Thoresthorpe
Asserby
Great Sturton
Oxcombe
Swaby
Ailby
The Grange
Flint Hill
Worlaby
Ketsby
South Thoresby
Alford
Bilsby
Thurlby
Huttoft
Anderby Creek
Belchford
South Ormsby
Calceby
Haugh
Rigsby
Bilsby Field
Anderby
Hemingby
Tetford
Little London
Driby
Farlesthorpe
Mumby
Baumber
Farthorpe
Salmonby
Brinkhill
Ulceby Cross
Well
Authorpe Row
Midthorpe
West Ashby
Fulletby
Somersby
Sutterby
Mawthorpe
Cumberworth
Helsey
Hogsthorpe
Wispington
Edlington
Ashby Puerorum
Harrington
Harrington Hall
Ulceby
Skendleby Psalter
Bonthorpe
Chapel St Leonards
Bag Enderby
Willoughby
Low Toynton
Langton
Claxby St Andrew
Stainsby
Aswardby
Sloothby
Greetham
Hagworthingham
Dalby
Skendleby
Hasthorpe
Ingoldmells
Thimbleby
Langton
High Toynton
Scrafield
Sausthorpe
Horncastle
Winceby 1643
Winceby
Partney
Welton le Marsh
Addlethorpe
Ingoldmells Point
Fantasy Island
Thornton
Old Woodhall
Mareham on the Hill
Lusby
Raithby
Candlesby
Butlins Family Entertainment Resort
Martin
Dalderby
Hameringham
Asgarby
Scremby
Ashby by Partney
Gunby
Orby
Orby Marsh
Claxby Pluckacre
Hareby
Mavis Enderby
Hundleby
Spilsby
Gunby Hall (NT)
Burgh le Marsh
Skegness Water Leisure Park
Seathorne
Old Bolingbroke
Halton Holegate
Great Steeping
Burgh Marsh
Winthorpe
Roughton
Wood Enderby
East Keal
Toynton All Saints
Bratoft
Irby in the Marsh
Skegness
Church Farm Museum
Skegness Natureland Seal Sanctuary
Haltham
Moorby
Miningsby
West Keal
Steeping
Firsby
Wilksby
East Kirkby
Toynton Fen Side
Toynton St Peter
Little Steeping
Kirkby on Bain
Hagnaby
Mareham le Fen
Revesby
Keal Cotes
Thorpe Culvert
Thorpe St Peter
Croft
Seacroft
Croft Marsh
Tattershall Thorpe
Tumby
Revesby Bridge
Stickford
Fendike Corner
Havenhouse Sta
Gibraltar Point National Nature Reserve
Coningsby
Moor Side
Tumby Woodside
Battle of Britain Memorial Flight Visitor Centre
New Bolingbroke
Wainfleet Bank
Wainfleet All Saints
Gibraltar
Tattershall Castle (NT)
Key's Toft
Gibraltar Pt
Midville
New Leake
Hawthorn Hill
Stickney
Carrington
Friskney Eaudyke
East Fen
Wainfleet Sand
Sandy Bank
Bunker's Hill
Dogdyke
Scrub Hill
New York
Lade Bank
Friskney
Chapel Hill
West Fen
Northlands
Boston Deeps
THE WASH
Wildmore Fen
Trader Windmill
Leake Commonside
Wrangle Lowgate
Frithville
Sibsey
Wrangle
Friskney Flats
Lynn Deeps
Holland Fen
Gipsey Bridge
Old Leake
Leake Hurn's End
Langrick
Fishtoft Drove
High Ferry
Hobhole Drain
Leverton Outgate
Hollan Amber Hill
Langrick Bridge
Frith Bank
Leverton
Leverton Lucasgate
Anton's Gowt
Dyke
Long Sand
Witham
Bain
Freshney
Kingston upon Hull to hours
Rotterdam..............................12
Zeebrugge...............................14
A180
A1136
A46
A1243
A16
A18
A1031
A631
A157
A153
A158
A1104
A1111
A52
A1028
A155
B1210
B1445
B1219
B1201
B1203
B1200
B1373
B1449
B1196
B1195
B1225
B1190
B1191
B1183
B1192
B1184
B1172

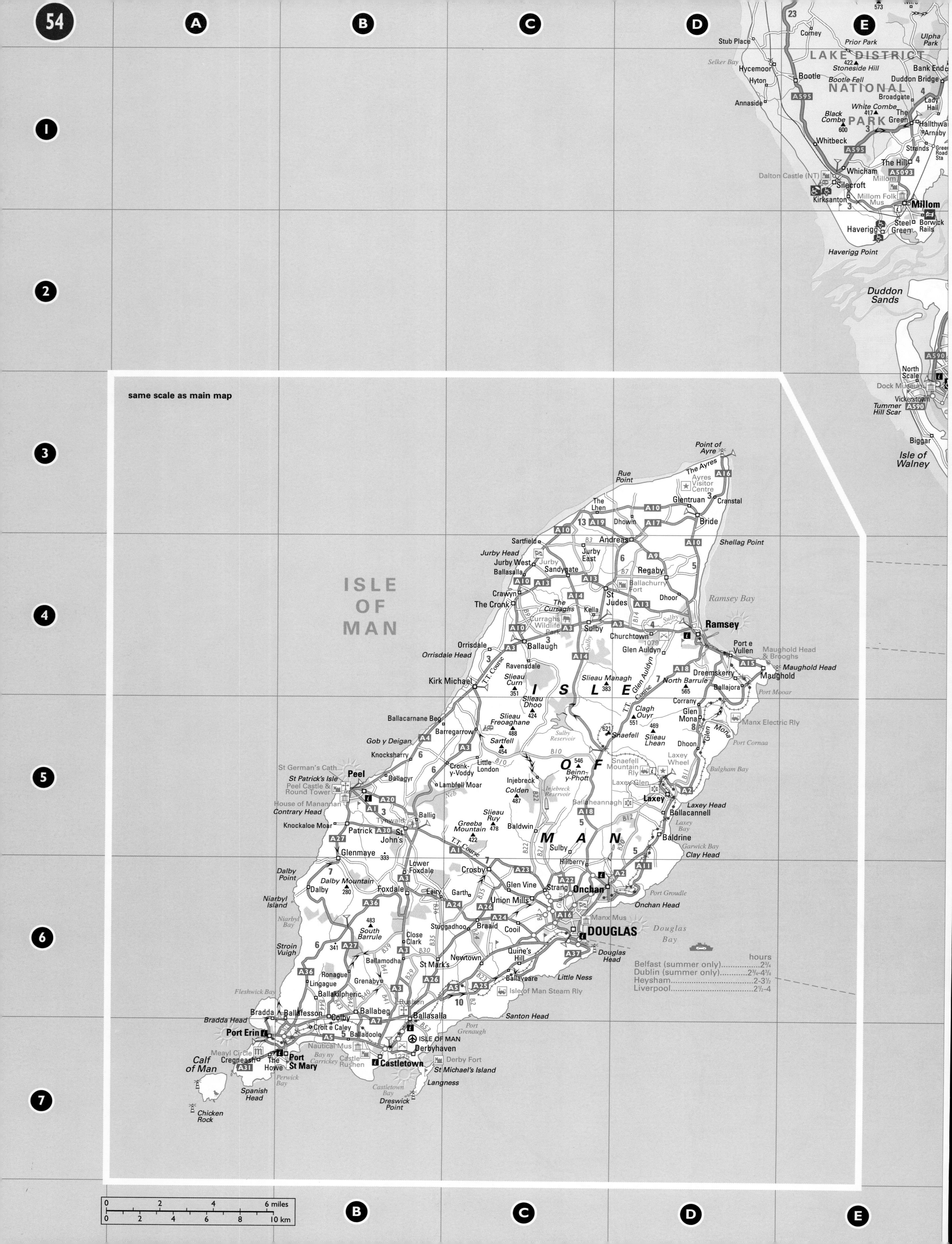

A
B
C
D
E
1
2
3
4
5
6
7
same scale as main map
ISLE OF MAN
ISLE OF MAN
Point of Ayre
The Ayres
Ayres Visitor Centre
Rue Point
Glentruan
Cranstal
The Lhen
Dhowin
Bride
Sartfield
Andreas
Shellag Point
Jurby Head
Jurby West
Jurby East
Ballasalla
Sandygate
Regaby
Crawyn
The Cronk
The Curraghs
Curraghs Wildlife Park
St Judes
Kella
Ballachurry Fort
Dhoor
Ramsey Bay
Ramsey
Sulby
Churchtown
Glen Auldyn
Orrisdale
Orrisdale Head
Ballaugh
Ravensdale
Port e Vullen
Maughold Head & Brooghs
Maughold Head
Maughold
Dreemskerry
Ballajora
North Barrule
Kirk Michael
Slieau Curn
Slieau Dhoo
Slieau Managh
Port Mooar
Corrany
Glen Mona
Clagh Ouyr
Slieau Lhean
Manx Electric Rly
Ballacarnane Beg
Barregarrow
Slieau Freoaghane
Snaefell
Sulby Reservoir
Dhoon
Port Cornaa
Gob y Deigan
Sartfell
Knocksharry
Cronk-y-Voddy
Little London
Beinn-y-Phott
Snaefell Mountain Rly
Laxey Wheel
Bulgham Bay
St German's Cath
St Patrick's Isle
Peel Castle & Round Tower
Peel
Ballagyr
Lambfell Moar
Injebreck
Colden
Injebreck Reservoir
Laxey Glen
Laxey
House of Manannan
Contrary Head
Ballig
Tynwald
Ballaheannagh
Laxey Head
Ballacannell
Knockaloe Moar
Patrick
St John's
Slieau Ruy
Greeba Mountain
Baldwin
Laxey Bay
Baldrine
Garwick Bay
Clay Head
Glenmaye
T.T. Course
Sulby
Hillberry
Dalby Point
Dalby Mountain
Dalby
Lower Foxdale
Crosby
Glen Vine
Strang
Onchan
Port Groudle
Onchan Head
Niarbyl Island
Niarbyl Bay
Foxdale
Eairy
Garth
Union Mills
South Barrule
Stuggadhoo
Braaid
Cooil
Manx Mus
DOUGLAS
Douglas Bay
Strooin Vuigh
Close Clark
Newtown
Quine's Hill
Douglas Head
Ballamodha
St Mark's
hours
Belfast (summer only)..............2¾
Dublin (summer only)..........2¾-4¾
Heysham..................................2-3½
Liverpool.................................2½-4
Ronague
Lingague
Grenaby
Little Ness
Fleshwick Bay
Ballakilpheric
Ballaveare
Isle of Man Steam Rly
Bradda
Ballafesson
Ballabeg
Rushen
Bradda Head
Colby
Ballasalla
Santon Head
Port Erin
Croit e Caley
Balladoole
Port Grenaugh
ISLE OF MAN
Meayl Circle
Nautical Mus
Derbyhaven
Calf of Man
Cregneash
The Howe
Port St Mary
Bay ny Carrickey
Castle Rushen
Castletown
Derby Fort
St Michael's Island
Perwick Bay
Langness
Spanish Head
Castletown Bay
Dreswick Point
Chicken Rock
Stub Place
Corney
Prior Park
Ulpha Park
Selker Bay
Hycemoor
Hyton
LAKE DISTRICT NATIONAL PARK
Stoneside Hill
Bootle
Bootle Fell
Bank End
Duddon Bridge
Broadgate
Annaside
White Combe
Lady Hall
Black Combe
The Green
Hallthwaites
Arnaby
Whitbeck
Strands
Green Road Sta
The Hill
Whicham
Dalton Castle (NT)
Silecroft
Millom
Kirksanton
Millom Folk Mus
Millom
Steel Green
Borwick Rails
Haverigg
Haverigg Point
Duddon Sands
North Scale
Dock Museum
Vickerstown
Tummer Hill Scar
Biggar
Isle of Walney
0 2 4 6 miles
0 2 4 6 8 10 km

60
56
48
CUMBRIA
LANCASHIRE
MORECAMBE BAY
Forest of Bowland
BLACKBURN WITH DARWEN
Broughton in Furness
Ulverston
Dalton-in-Furness
BARROW-IN-FURNESS
Askam in Furness
Newbiggin
Roosebeck
Rampside
Roa Island
Piel Island
Foulney Island
Hilpsford Point
Cartmel
Grange-over-Sands
Flookburgh
Cartmel Sands
Arnside
Silverdale
Levens
Kendal
Oxenholme
Natland
Sedbergh
Dent
Dentdale
Garsdale
Kirkby Lonsdale
Casterton
Barbon
Ingleton
Clapham
High Bentham
Low Bentham
Burton-in-Kendal
Milnthorpe
Carnforth
Warton
Bolton-le-Sands
Morecambe
Heysham
LANCASTER
Halton
Caton
Galgate
Glasson
Cockerham
Forton
Garstang
Slaidburn
Chipping
Longridge
Clitheroe
Whalley
Fleetwood
Knott End-on-Sea
Cleveleys
Thornton
Poulton-le-Fylde
BLACKPOOL
Kirkham
Wesham
LYTHAM ST ANNE'S
Freckleton
PRESTON
Penwortham
Bamber Bridge
Leyland
BLACKBURN
Darwen
Oswaldtwistle
Great Harwood
Clayton-le-Moors
Rishton
ACCRINGTON
CHORLEY
Eccleston
Croston
Tarleton
Banks
SOUTHPORT
Douglas 2-3½hrs
Larne 8hrs
Ribble Estuary
Banks Sands
Horse Bank
Clougha Pike 413
Ward's Stone 560
Fair Snape Fell 520
Parlick 432
Whernside 736
Ingleborough Common
M6
M55
M65
M61
A6
A59
A65
A683
A590
A591
A595
A583
A584
A585
A586
A588

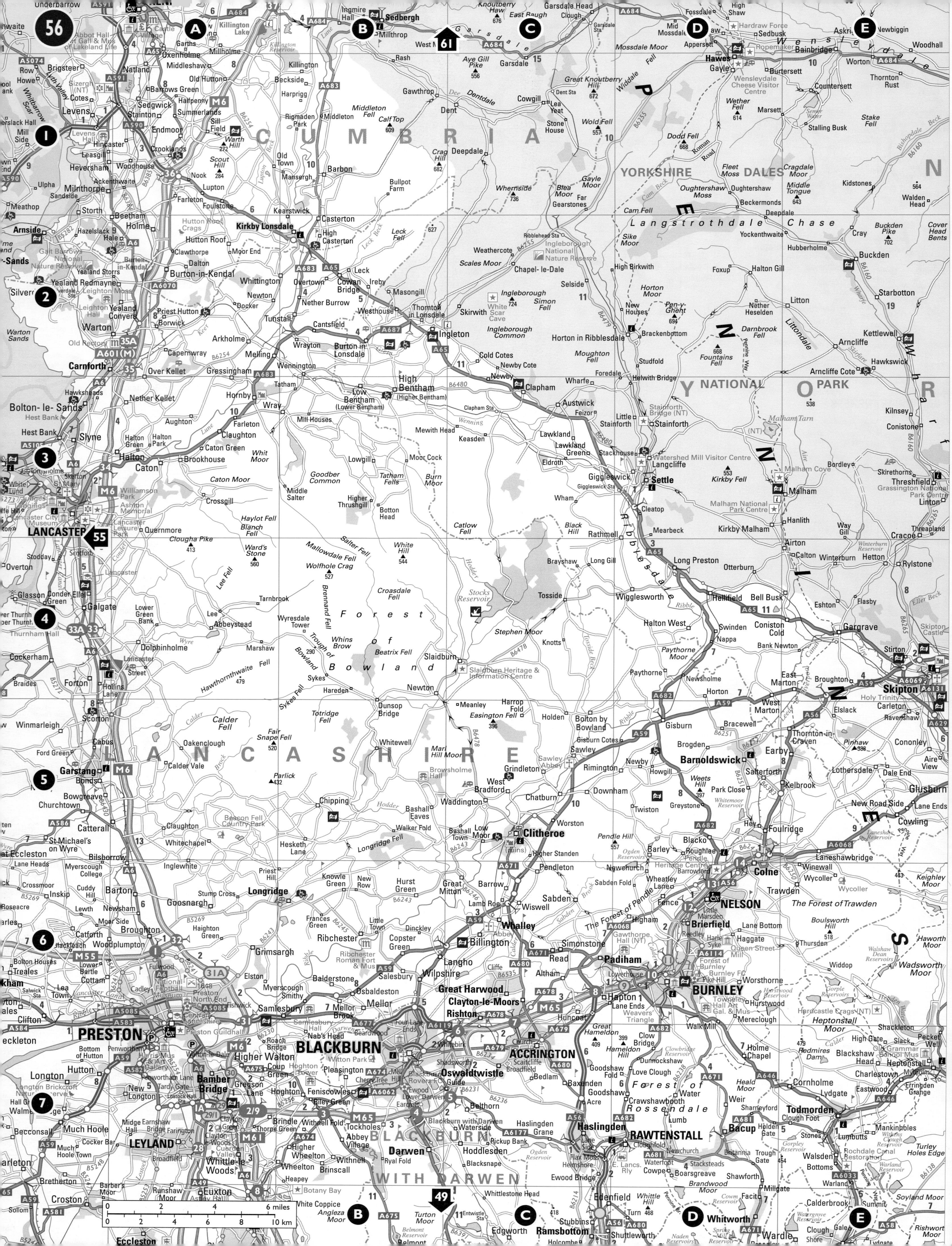
A
B
C
D
E
61
C U M B R I A
YORKSHIRE DALES
N A T I O N A L   P A R K
L A N C A S H I R E
Forest of Bowland
Langstrothdale Chase
Wensleydale
Ribblesdale
The Forest of Pendle
Forest of Rossendale
BLACKBURN WITH DARWEN
Sedbergh
Hawes
Kirkby Lonsdale
Ingleton
Settle
Skipton
LANCASTER
55
Garstang
Clitheroe
Colne
NELSON
BURNLEY
Padiham
PRESTON
BLACKBURN
ACCRINGTON
Darwen
LEYLAND
RAWTENSTALL
Haslingden
Bacup
Todmorden
Ramsbottom
Whitworth
Carnforth
Morecambe Bay
Longridge
Barnoldswick
Whalley
Great Harwood
Oswaldtwistle
Bamber Bridge
Chorley
49
1
2
3
4
5
6
7
0 2 4 6 miles
0 2 4 6 8 10 km

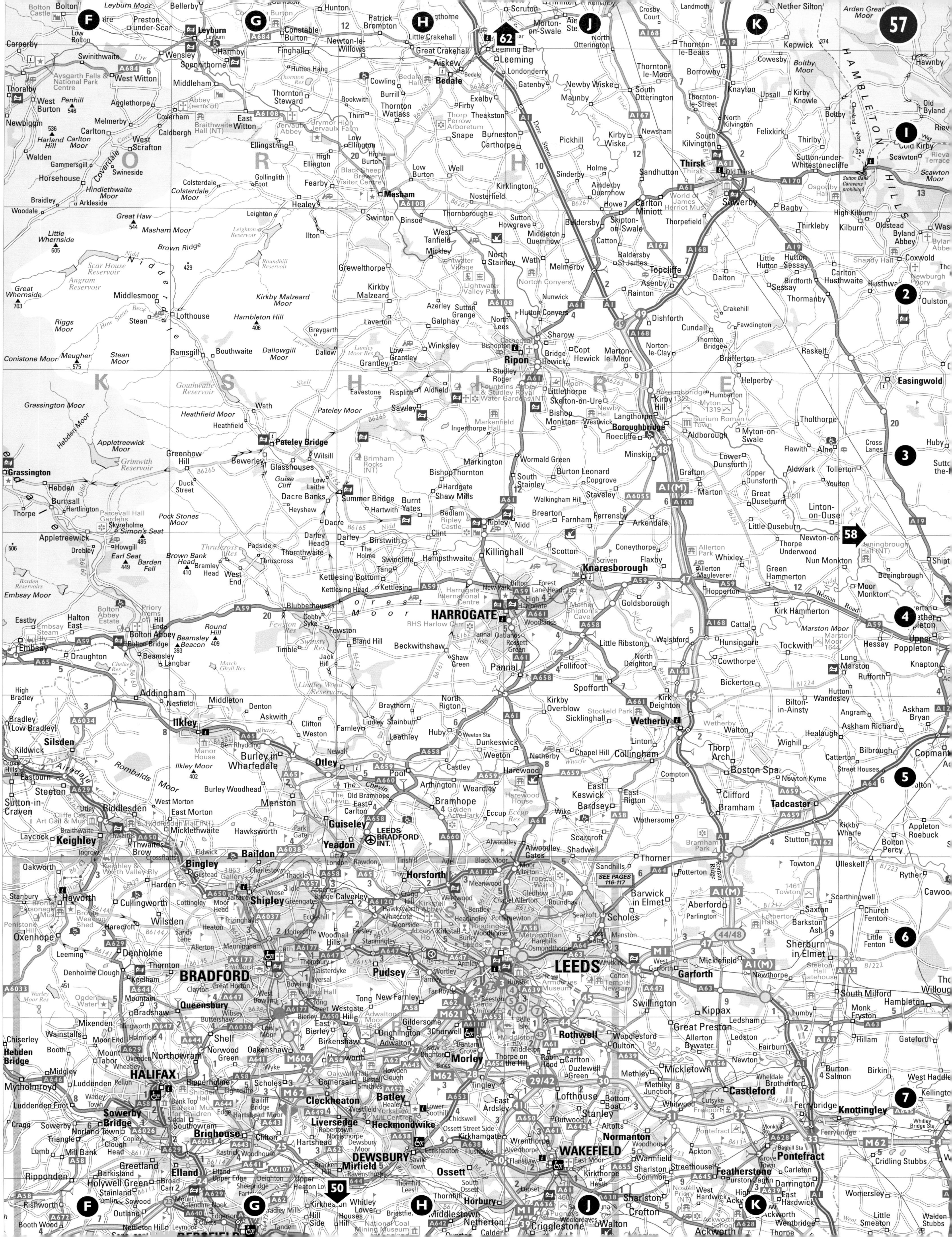

F
G
H
J
K
62
58
50
I
2
3
4
5
6
7
Leyburn
Bedale
Leeming
Thirsk
Masham
Ripon
Easingwold
Pateley Bridge
Boroughbridge
Knaresborough
HARROGATE
Wetherby
Ilkley
Otley
Tadcaster
Keighley
Bingley
Shipley
Horsforth
BRADFORD
LEEDS
Pudsey
Morley
Garforth
Queensbury
HALIFAX
Brighouse
Cleckheaton
Batley
Castleford
Knottingley
Pontefract
Featherstone
WAKEFIELD
DEWSBURY
Ossett
Elland
Mirfield
Rothwell
Normanton
Sowerby Bridge
Grassington
Haworth
Yeadon
Guiseley
Baildon
Heckmondwike
Liversedge
Horbury
LEEDS BRADFORD INT.
SEE PAGES 116-117

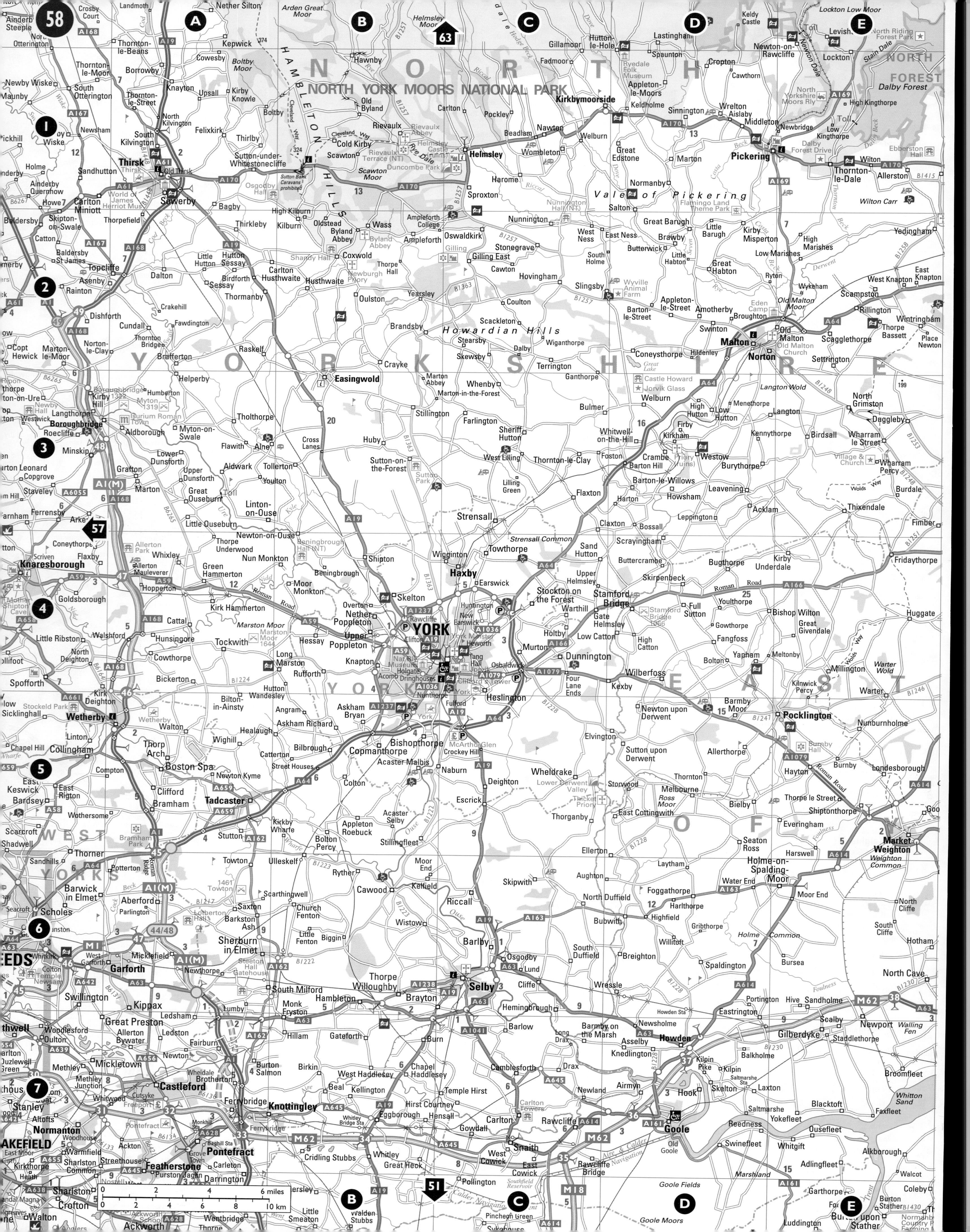
NORTH YORK MOORS NATIONAL PARK
N O R T H
Y O R K S H I R E
E A S T
O F
W E S T
Y O R K S
Howardian Hills
Vale of Pickering
HAMBLETON HILLS
NORTH FOREST
Dalby Forest
Thirsk
Sowerby
Helmsley
Kirkbymoorside
Pickering
Thornton-le-Dale
Malton
Norton
Easingwold
Boroughbridge
Knaresborough
Wetherby
Haxby
YORK
Tadcaster
Selby
Pocklington
Market Weighton
Howden
Goole
Castleford
Pontefract
Knottingley
Garforth
Normanton
Featherstone
Strensall
Dunnington
Stamford Bridge
Heslington
Bishopthorpe
Copmanthorpe
Sherburn in Elmet
Brayton
Gilberdyke
Snaith
Castle Howard
Kirkby Hill
Helmsley Castle
Rievaulx Abbey
Byland Abbey
Newburgh Priory
Sutton Park
Beningbrough Hall (NT)
Nunnington Hall (NT)
Flamingo Land Theme Park
North Yorkshire Moors Rly
York Minster
Marston Moor 1644
Stamford Bridge 1066
Towton 1461
A1(M)
A19
A59
A64
A166
A1079
A163
A614
A63
A645
M62
M18
A170
A169
A168
A61
A1
63
57
51
0 2 4 6 miles
0 2 4 6 8 10 km

F
G
H
J
K
SCARBOROUGH
Scalby
Cayton
Filey
Filey Bay
Hunmanby
Reighton
Speeton
Flamborough
Flamborough Head
Bempton
Buckton
Sewerby
Bridlington
BRIDLINGTON BAY
Carnaby
Fraisthorpe
Barmston
Skipsea
Atwick
Hornsea
Mappleton
Aldbrough
Withernsea
Patrington
Easington
Driffield
Nafferton
THE WOLDS
RIDING
YORKSHIRE
BEVERLEY
Cottingham
Hessle
KINGSTON UPON HULL
Hedon
Humber
Barton-upon-Humber
NORTH LINCOLNSHIRE
52
53
Sunk Island
Skeffling
Holmpton
Keyingham
Leven
Brandesburton
A165
A1033
A164
A1079
A614
A166
A1035
Dixon - where all your Motability needs are met.
Motability is a registered charity which helps disabled people and their families in the UK to become more mobile. Dixon are delighted to support this charity and offer a wide range of Motability vehicles starting from Nil Advance Payment. Why not contact our Motability Specialist on 0845 838 3426 to find whether you are eligible for our scheme.
Motability
The leading car scheme for disabled people
DIXON
Motability
The leading car scheme for disabled people
Nil Advance Payment
available on a wide selection of Motability vehicles at Dixon.
Contact our Motability specialist on 0845 838 3426
DIXON

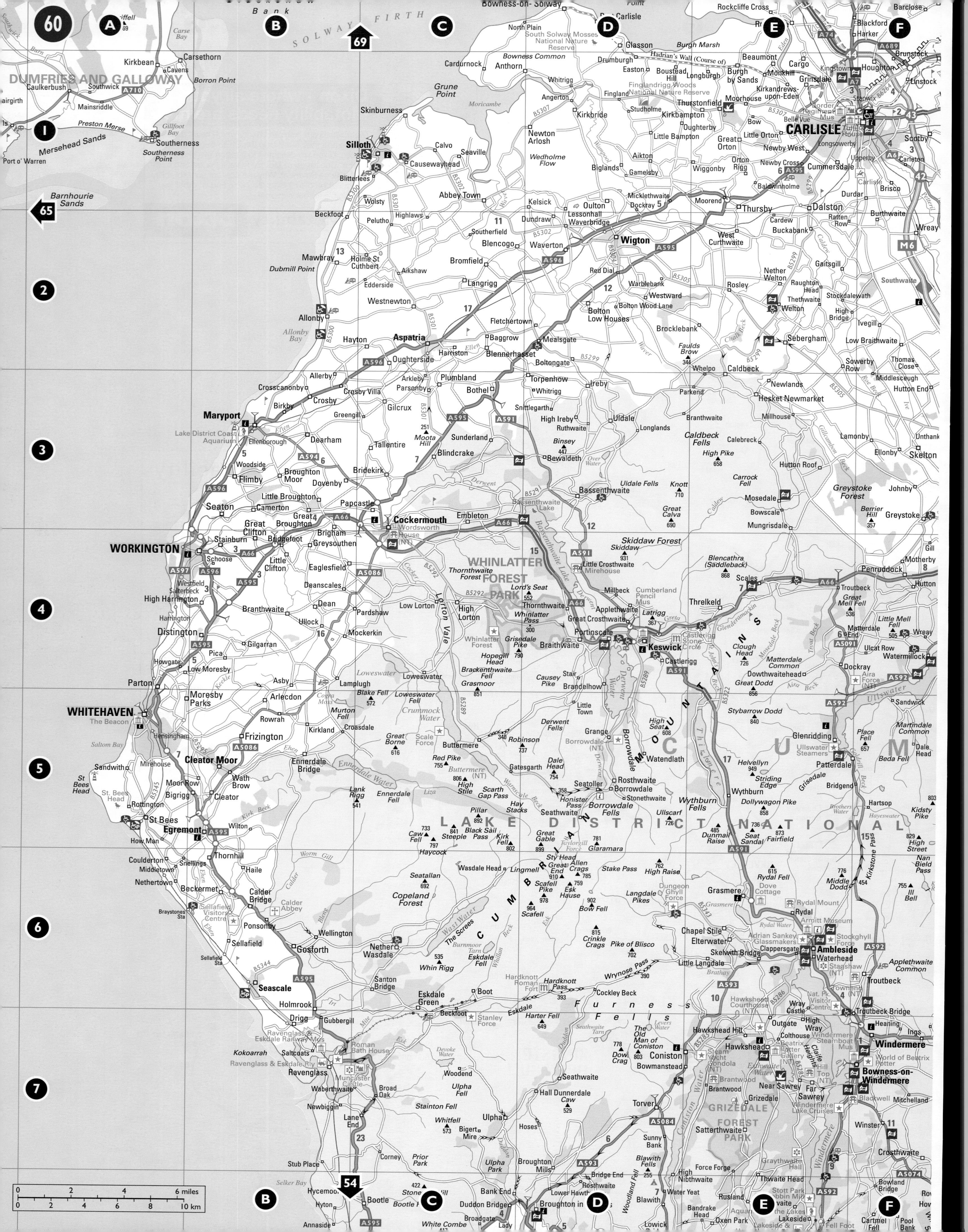
A
B
C
D
E
F
69
65
54
SOLWAY FIRTH
Bank
Bowness-on-Solway
Port Carlisle
Rockcliffe Cross
Barclose
Blackford
Harker
Carse Bay
Kirkbean
Carsethorn
Cavens
Borron Point
DUMFRIES AND GALLOWAY
Caulkerbush
Southwick
Mainsriddle
Preston Merse
Gillfoot Bay
Southerness
Southerness Point
Mersehead Sands
Port o' Warren
Barnhourie Sands
North Plain
South Solway Mosses National Nature Reserve
Glasson
Burgh Marsh
Cardurnock
Bowness Common
Anthorn
Drumburgh
Hadrian's Wall (Course of)
Easton
Boustead Hill
Longburgh
Burgh by Sands
Beaumont
Cargo
Monkhill
Kirkandrews-upon-Eden
Grinsdale
Kingstown
Houghton
Linstock
Grune Point
Moricambe
Whitrigg
Finglandrigg Woods National Nature Reserve
Fingland
Angerton
Studholme
Thurstonfield
Moorhouse
Kirkbride
Kirkbampton
Oughterby
Border Regiment Mus
Belle Vue
Skinburness
Newton Arlosh
Little Bampton
Great Orton
Little Orton
CARLISLE
Bow
Stanwix
Scotby
Silloth
Calvo
Seaville
Wedholme Flow
Aikton
Newby West
Longsowerby
Upperby
Carleton
Causewayhead
Biglands
Gamelsby
Wiggonby
Orton Rigg
Newby Cross
Cummersdale
Carlisle
Blitterlees
Baldwinholme
Brisco
Abbey Town
Micklethwaite
Dockray
Moorend
Durdar
Wolsty
Kelsick
Oulton
Lessonhall
Waverbridge
Thursby
Dalston
Beckfoot
Pelutho
Highlaws
Dundraw
Cardew
Ratten Row
Buckabank
Burnthwaite
Wreay
Southerfield
Wigton
West Curthwaite
Mawbray
Holme St Cuthbert
Blencogo
Waverton
Dubmill Point
Aikshaw
Bromfield
Red Dial
Nether Welton
Gaitsgill
Edderside
Langrigg
Warblebank
Rosley
Raughton Head
Southwaite
Westward
Thethwaite
Stockdalewath
Westnewton
Bolton Wood Lane
Bolton Low Houses
Welton
High Bridge
Ivegill
Allonby
Allonby Bay
Fletchertown
Brocklebank
Hayton
Aspatria
Baggrow
Mealsgate
Faulds Brow
Sebergham
Low Braithwaite
Oughterside
Harriston
Blennerhasset
Boltongate
Whelpo
Caldbeck
Sowerby Row
Thomas Close
Allerby
Arkleby
Parsonby
Plumbland
Torpenhow
Middlesceugh
Crosscanonby
Crosby Villa
Bothel
Whitrigg
Ireby
Parkend
Newlands
Hutton End
Birkby
Crosby
Gilcrux
Snittlegarth
Hesket Newmarket
Maryport
Greengill
High Ireby
Ruthwaite
Uldale
Longlands
Branthwaite
Millhouse
Lake District Coast Aquarium
Ellenborough
Dearham
Tallentire
Moota Hill
Sunderland
Binsey
Caldbeck Fells
Calebreck
Lamonby
Unthank
Woodside
Broughton Moor
Bridekirk
Blindcrake
Bewaldeth
High Pike
Ellonby
Skelton
Flimby
Dovenby
Over Water
Uldale Fells
Knott
Carrock Fell
Hutton Roof
Little Broughton
Papcastle
Derwent
Bassenthwaite
Mosedale
Greystoke Forest
Johnby
Seaton
Camerton
Great Clifton
Great Broughton
Cockermouth
Embleton
Bassenthwaite Lake
Great Calva
Bowscale
Berrier Hill
Greystoke
Stainburn
Bridgefoot
Brigham
Wordsworth House (NT)
Mungrisdale
WORKINGTON
Greysouthen
Schoose
Little Clifton
Eaglesfield
WHINLATTER FOREST PARK
Skiddaw Forest
Skiddaw
Little Crosthwaite
Mirehouse
Blencathra (Saddleback)
Motherby
Penruddock
Westfield
Salterbeck
Deanscales
Thornthwaite Forest
Lord's Seat
Millbeck
Cumberland Pencil Mus
Scales
Troutbeck
Hutton
High Harrington
Dean
Lorton Vale
High Lorton
Thornthwaite
Applethwaite
Threlkeld
Great Mell Fell
Harrington
Branthwaite
Low Lorton
Whinlatter Pass
Great Crosthwaite
Latrigg
Glenderamackin
Little Mell Fell
Distington
Ullock
Pardshaw
Mockerkin
Portinscale
Castlerigg Stone Circle
Matterdale End
Wreay
Gilgarran
Whinlatter Forest
Grisedale Pike
Braithwaite
Keswick
Clough Head
Ulcat Row
Watermillock
Howgate
Pica
Hopegill Head
Brackenthwaite Fell
Castlerigg
Matterdale Common
Dockray
Low Moresby
Loweswater
Grasmoor
Causey Pike
Stair
Dowthwaitehead
Aira Force (NT)
Parton
Asby
Lamplugh
Brandelhow
Great Dodd
Ullswater
Moresby Parks
Arlecdon
Blake Fell
Loweswater Fell
Little Town
Sandwick
WHITEHAVEN
The Beacon
Cogra Moss
Murton Fell
Crummock Water
Stybarrow Dodd
Martindale Common
Rowrah
Derwent Fells
High Seat
Hensingham
Kirkland
Croasdale
Great Borne
Scale Force
Robinson
Grange
Borrowdale (NT)
Glenridding
Place Fell
Frizington
Ullswater Steamers
Dale Head
Saltom Bay
Buttermere
Watendlath
Thirlmere
Beda Fell
Cleator Moor
Ennerdale Bridge
Red Pike
Gatesgarth
Helvellyn
Patterdale
Sandwith
Mirehouse
Ennerdale Water
Dale Head
Striding Edge
Bridgend
St Bees Head
Wath Brow
High Stile
Seatoller
Rosthwaite
Moor Row
Lank Rigg
Ennerdale Fell
Scarth Gap Pass
Honister Pass
Borrowdale
Wythburn
Grisedale
Bigrigg
Cleator
Liza
Stonethwaite
Wythburn Fells
Dollywagon Pike
Hartsop
St Bees Head
Rottington
Pillar
Hay Stacks
Borrowdale Fells
Brothers Water
Kidsty Pike
St Bees
Kirk Beck
Seathwaite
Ullscarf
Hayeswater
Egremont
Wilton
Caw Fell
Steeple
Black Sail Pass
Kirk Fell
Great Gable
LAKE DISTRICT NATIONAL PARK
Dunmail Raise
Seat Sandal
Fairfield
High Street
How Man
Haycock
Glaramara
Thornhill
Worm Gill
Sty Head
Allen Crags
Stake Pass
High Raise
Rydal Fell
Nan Bield Pass
Coulderton
Snellings
Haile
Wasdale Head
Lingmell
Great End
Middleton
Seatallan
Scafell Pike
Esk Hause
Langdale Pikes
Dungeon Ghyll Force
Grasmere
Dove Cottage
Middle Dodd
Kirkstone Pass
Ill Bell
Nethertown
Beckermet
Calder Bridge
Copeland Forest
Scafell
Bow Fell
Rydal Mount
Rydal
Braystones Sta
Sellafield Visitors Centre
Calder Abbey
Ponsonby
Wast Water
The Screes
CUMBRIAN MOUNTAINS
Wellington
Crinkle Crags
Pike of Blisco
Chapel Stile
Elterwater
Armitt Museum
Adrian Sankey Glassmakers
Stockghyll Force
Sellafield
Gosforth
Nether Wasdale
Burnmoor Tarn
Eskdale Fell
Skelwith Bridge
Clappersgate
Ambleside
Waterhead
Sellafield Sta
Whin Rigg
Hardknott Roman Fort
Hardknott Pass
Wrynose Pass
Little Langdale
Brathay
Stagshaw (NT)
Applethwaite Common
Troutbeck
Seascale
Santon Bridge
Eskdale Green
Boot
Cockley Beck
Furness Fells
Hawkshead Courthouse (NT)
Wray Castle
Townend (NT)
Nat. Pk. Visitor Centre
Troutbeck Bridge
Holmrook
Beckfoot
Eskdale
Harter Fell
Seathwaite Tarn
Levers Water
Outgate
High Wray
Hawkshead Hill
Colthouse
Windermere
Drigg
Gubbergill
Stanley Force
The Old Man of Coniston
Hawkshead
Windermere Steamboat Mus
Ings
Ravenglass & Eskdale Railway Mus
Roman Bath House
Dow Crag
Coniston
Steam Yacht Gondola
Beatrix Potter Gallery (NT)
Claife Heights
World of Beatrix Potter
Kokoarrah
Saltcoats
Devoke Water
Bowmanstead
Esthwaite Water
Bowness-on-Windermere
Ravenglass & Eskdale Rly
Ravenglass
Muncaster Castle
Woodend
Seathwaite
Brantwood
Hill Top (NT)
Waberthwaite
Broad Oak
Ulpha Fell
Hall Dunnerdale Caw
Brantwood
Near Sawrey
Far Sawrey
Blackwell
Mitchelland
Newbiggin
Stainton Fell
Torver
Grizedale
GRIZEDALE FOREST PARK
Windermere Lake Cruises
Lane End
Whitfell
Ulpha
Hoses
Satterthwaite
Winster
Bigert Mire
Sunny Bank
Coniston Water
Windermere
Crosthwaite
Corney
Prior Park
Ulpha Park
Broughton Mills
Blawith Fells
Force Forge
Graythwaite Hall
Stub Place
Bridge End
High Nibthwaite
Thwaite Head
Bowland Bridge
Selker Bay
Hycemoor
Hyton
Bootle
Stone
Bootle
Bank End
Duddon Bridge
Lower Hawthwaite
Rosthwaite
Woodland Fell
Water Yeat
Rusland
Stott Park Bobbin Mill
Broughton in Furness
Blawith
Bandrake Head
Lakeside
Oxen Park
Lakeside & Haverthwaite Rly
Fell Foot
Cartmel Fell
Pool Bank
Annaside
White Combe
Broadgate
Lady
Lowick
Aquarium
0 2 4 6 miles
0 2 4 6 8 10 km
A710
A74
A689
A7
A6
A595
A596
A591
A594
A597
A66
A5086
A5091
A592
A593
A5084
A5074
A590
B5300
B5301
B5302
B5307
B5299
B5305
B5291
B5292
B5289
B5322
B5343
B5286
B5285
B5345
B5295
B5344
M6
1
2
3
4
5
6
7
44
43
42

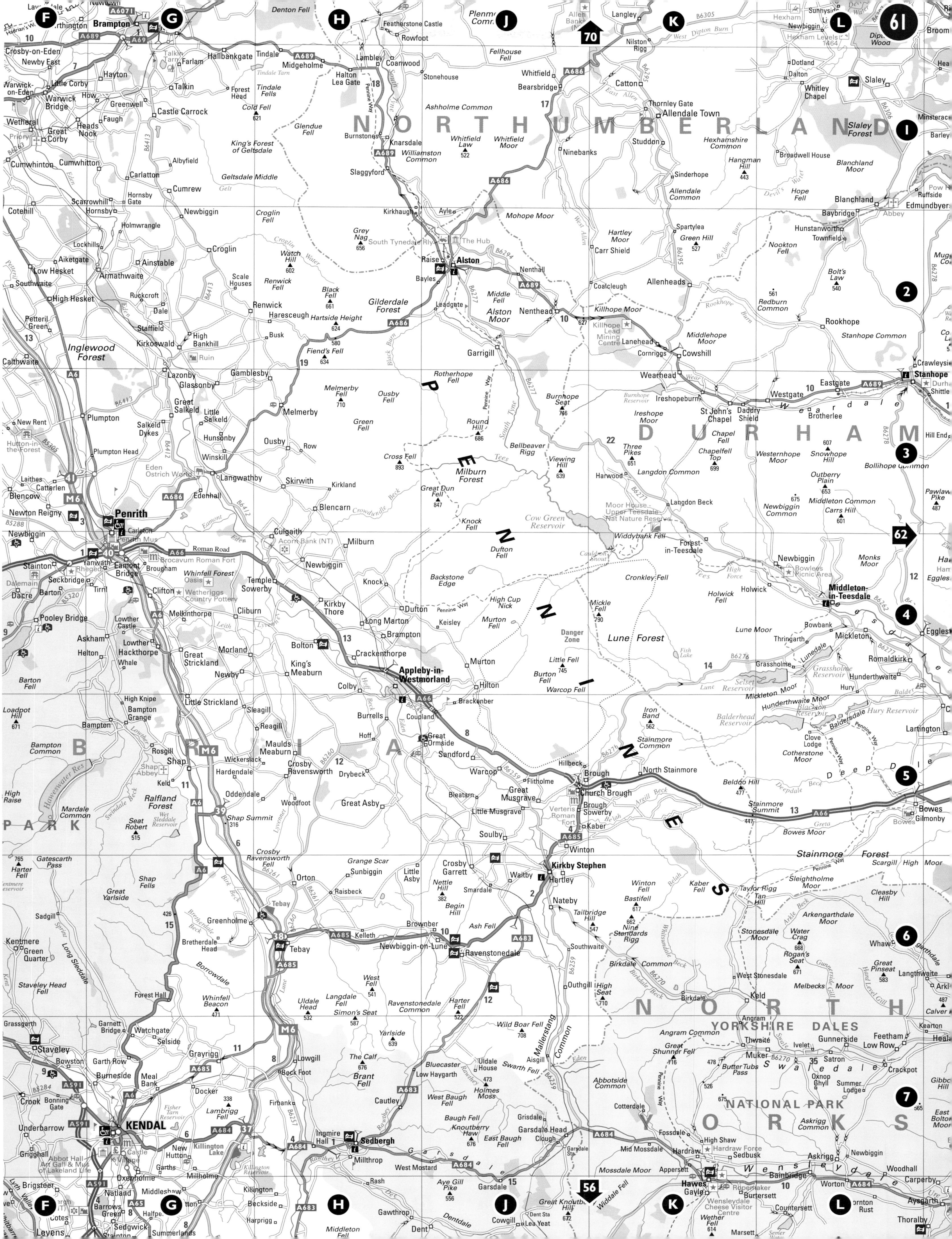
F
G
H
J
K
L
70
62
56
2
3
4
5
6
7
I
NORTHUMBERLAND
DURHAM
PENNINES
NORTH YORKSHIRE DALES
NATIONAL PARK
YORKS
PARK
Brampton
Newtown
A6071
A689
A69
Hadrian's Wall
Crosby-on-Eden
Newby East
Hayton
Little Corby
Warwick-on-Eden
Warwick Bridge
How
Talkin Tarn
Talkin
Farlam
Hallbankgate
Tindale
Tindale Tarn
Tindale Fells
Midgeholme
Halton Lea Gate
Lambley
Coanwood
Featherstone Castle
Rowfoot
Denton Fell
Stonehouse
Fellhouse Fell
Whitfield
Bearsbridge
A686
Langley
Nilston Rigg
Allen Banks
Catton
Thornley Gate
Allendale Town
East Allen
West Dipton Burn
B6305
B6295
Hexham
Newbiggin
Hexham Levels
Sunnyside
Slaley
Whitley Chapel
Dotland
Dalton
Diptoo Wood
Broom
Minsteracres
Barley
Slaley Forest
Forest Head
Greenwell
Castle Carrock
Cold Fell
621
Ashholme Common
Wetheral
Great Corby
Heads Nook
Faugh
Priory
Glendue Fell
Burnstones
Knarsdale
King's Forest of Geltsdale
Williamston Common
Whitfield Law
522
Whitfield Moor
Ninebanks
Studdon
Hexhamshire Common
Hangman Hill
443
Broadwell House
Blanchland Moor
Cumwhinton
Cumwhitton
Albyfield
Carlatton
Geltsdale Middle
Slaggyford
Cumrew
Gelt
Sinderhope
Allendale Common
Devil's Water
Hope Fell
Blanchland
Baybridge
Abbey
Pow Hill
Ruffside
Edmundbyers
Scarrowhill
Hornsby Gate
Hornsby
Cotehill
Newbiggin
Croglin Fell
Kirkhaugh
Ayle
Mohope Moor
West Allen
Hartley Moor
Carr Shield
Spartylea
Green Hill
527
Beldon Burn
Hunstanworth
Townfield
Nookton Fell
Holmwrangle
Lockhills
Croglin
Croglin Water
Watch Hill
602
Grey Nag
656
South Tynedale Rly
The Hub
Alston
Raise
Bayles
B6294
Nenthall
A689
Aiketgate
Low Hesket
Ainstable
Armathwaite
Southwaite
High Hesket
Ruckcroft
Dale
Scale Houses
Renwick Fell
Black Fell
661
B6413
Renwick
Harescaugh
Hartside Height
624
Gilderdale Forest
Leadgate
Middle Fell
Alston Moor
Nenthead
10
Killhope Moor
627
Coalcleugh
Allenheads
Rookhope
Redburn Common
561
Bolt's Law
540
Rookhope
Stanhope Common
Petteril Green
Staffield
High Bankhill
Busk
Kirkoswald
Inglewood Forest
Fiend's Fell
634
580
Killhope Lead Mining Centre
Lanehead
Cornriggs
Cowshill
Middlehope Moor
Calthwaite
Ruin
Lazonby
Glassonby
Gamblesby
Garrigill
Black Burn
Rotherhope Fell
Pennine Way
Melmerby Fell
710
Ousby Fell
Wearhead
Wear
Ireshopeburn
Burnhope Seat
746
Burnhope Reservoir
St John's Chapel
Daddry Shield
Westgate
Eastgate
Weardale
Brotherlee
Stanhope
Crawleyside
Durham
Shittle
New Rent
Plumpton
Great Salkeld
Little Salkeld
Salkeld Dykes
Melmerby
Green Fell
Round Hill
686
South Tyne
Ireshope Moor
Chapel Fell
Hill End
Hutton-in-the-Forest
Plumpton Head
Hunsonby
Ousby
Row
Bellbeaver Rigg
Three Pikes
651
Chapelfell Top
699
Westernhope Moor
Snowhope Hill
607
Bollihope Common
Eden Ostrich World
Winskill
Langwathby
Cross Fell
893
Tees
Milburn Forest
Viewing Hill
639
Harwood
Langdon Common
Outberry Plain
653
Laithes
Catterlen
Blencow
Skirwith
Kirkland
Great Dun Fell
847
Crowdundle Beck
Langdon Beck
Newbiggin Common
675
Middleton Common
Carrs Hill
601
Pawlaw Pike
487
Newton Reigny
Penrith
Edenhall
Blencarn
Moor House-Upper Teesdale Nat Nature Reserve
Cow Green Reservoir
Knock Fell
Newbiggin
Carleton
Penrith Mus
Culgaith
Acorn Bank (NT)
Milburn
Dufton Fell
Widdybank Fell
Forest-in-Teesdale
Cauldron Snout
Newbiggin
Bowlees Picnic Area
Monks Moor
Stainton
Yanwath
Rheged
Eamont Bridge
Brougham
Brocavum Roman Fort
Roman Road
Dalemain
Sockbridge
Tirril
Whinfell Forest
Oasis
Temple Sowerby
Newbiggin
Knock
Backstone Edge
Cronkley Fell
High Force
Middleton-in-Teesdale
Holwick
Holwick Fell
Eggleston
Dacre
Barton
Clifton
Wetheriggs Country Pottery
Kirkby Thore
Dufton
High Cup Nick
Mickle Fell
790
Pooley Bridge
Lowther Castle
Melkinthorpe
Cliburn
Long Marton
Keisley
Murton Fell
Danger Zone
Lune Forest
Lune Moor
Bowbank
Thringarth
Mickleton
Askham
Lowther
Hackthorpe
Morland
Bolton
Brampton
Crackenthorpe
Helton
Whale
Great Strickland
King's Meaburn
Newby
Appleby-in-Westmorland
Murton
Little Fell
745
Burton Fell
Warcop Fell
Fish Lake
Grassholme
Grassholme Reservoir
Lunedale
Romaldkirk
Hunderthwaite
Selset Reservoir
Mickleton Moor
Hury
Barton Fell
Colby
Hilton
Brackenber
A66
High Knipe
Bampton Grange
Little Strickland
Sleagill
Burrells
Coupland
Iron Band
562
Hunderthwaite Moor
Blackton Reservoir
Balderhead Reservoir
Baldersdale
Hury Reservoir
Lartington
Loadpot Hill
671
Bampton
Reagill
Hoff
Great Ormside
Stainmore Common
Clove Lodge
Bampton Common
Maulds Meaburn
Sandford
Cotherstone Moor
Haweswater Res
Rosgill
Shap
Shap Abbey
Wickersiack
Crosby Ravensworth
Hardendale
Drybeck
Warcop
Hillbeck
Brough
North Stainmore
Deepdale
Keld
Flitholme
Church Brough
Belldoo Hill
477
Bowes
Gilmonby
High Raise
Ralfland Forest
Oddendale
Great Musgrave
Bleatarn
Verteris Roman Fort
Brough Sowerby
Argill Beck
Stainmore Summit
447
Greta
Mardale Common
Swindale Beck
Woodfoot
Great Asby
Little Musgrave
Belah
Kaber
Bowes Moor
Seat Robert
515
Wet Sleddale Reservoir
Shap Summit
316
Soulby
Winton
Stainmore Forest
Scargill High Moor
Crosby Ravensworth Fell
Grange Scar
Sunbiggin
Little Asby
Crosby Garrett
Waitby
Kirkby Stephen
Hartley
765
Harter Fell
Gatescarth Pass
Shap Fells
Orton
Raisbeck
Nettle Hill
382
Smardale
Winton Fell
Bastifell
617
Kaber Fell
Tan Hill
Taylor Rigg
Sleightholme Moor
Cleasby Hill
Great Yarlside
Birk Beck
Tebay
Begin Hill
Nateby
Tailbridge Hill
547
Nine Standards Rigg
662
Arkengarthdale Moor
Sadgill
Bretherdale Beck
Greenholme
Brownber
Ash Fell
Stonesdale Moor
Water Crag
668
Whaw
Kentmere
Green Quarter
Bretherdale Head
Kelleth
A685
Newbiggin-on-Lune
Ravenstonedale
A683
Southwaite
Rogan's Seat
671
Great Pinseat
583
Long Sleddale
Borrowdale
West Fell
541
Birkdale Common
Whitsundale Beck
West Stonesdale
Langthwaite
Staveley Head Fell
Forest Hall
Whinfell Beacon
471
Uldale Head
532
Langdale Fell
Simon's Seat
587
Ravenstonedale Common
Harter Fell
522
Outhgill
High Seat
710
Birkdale
Keld
Melbecks Moor
Arkle
Calver Hill
Grassgarth
Garnett Bridge
Watchgate
Selside
Mallerstang Common
Wild Boar Fell
708
Angram
Angram Common
Kearton
Staveley
Bowston
Garth Row
Grayrigg
Lowgill
Yarlside
639
The Calf
676
Aisgill
Great Shunner Fell
716
Thwaite
Ivelet
Gunnerside
Feetham
Low Row
Healaugh
Burneside
Meal Bank
Beck Foot
Brant Fell
Bluecaster
Low Haygarth
Uldale House
Swarth Fell
Muker
Butter Tubs Pass
478
Satron
Swaledale
Crackpot
Crook
Bonning Gate
Docker
Fisher Tarn Reservoir
Lambrigg Fell
338
Firbank
Cautley
West Baugh Fell
Holmes Moss
473
Abbotside Common
526
Oxnop Ghyll
Summer Lodge
Gibbon Hill
Underbarrow
KENDAL
Killington Lake
Ingmire Hall
Sedbergh
Baugh Fell
Knoutberry Haw
676
East Baugh Fell
Grisdale
Garsdale Head
Cotterdale
675
East Bolton Moor
Grigghall
Abbot Hall Art Gall & Mus of Lakeland Life
Castle
New Hutton
Millthrop
Garsdale
Clough
Fossdale
High Shaw
Askrigg Common
Askrigg
Newbiggin
Garths
Killington Reservoir
West Mostard
Mid Mossdale
Hardraw
Hardraw Force
Sedbusk
Wensleydale
Oxenholme
Millholme
Rash
Ayle Gill Pike
556
Mossdale Moor
Appersett
Hawes
Gayle
Ropemaker
Bainbridge
Woodhall
Worton
Carperby
Brigsteer
Natland
Middleshaw
Killington
Dee
Garsdale
Widdale Fell
Burtersett
Aysgarth
Barrows Green
Becksíde
Great Knoutberry Hill
672
Dent Sta
Wensleydale Cheese Visitor Centre
Countersett
Thoralby
Sedgwick
Halfpenny
Harprigg
Gawthrop
Dent
Dentdale
Cowgill
Lea Yeat
Wether Fell
614
Marsett
Levens
Summerlands
Middleton Fell
Semer Water
M6
A6
A591
A684
A683
A65
B6259
B6260
B6261
B6276
B6277
B6278
B6412
B6413
B5288
B5305
B5320
B5284
B6542
B6270
B6306
Sizergh Castle
Cotes
Lyth Valley
Nunnington Rust
Dent
Mardale Common
Pennine Way
Eamont

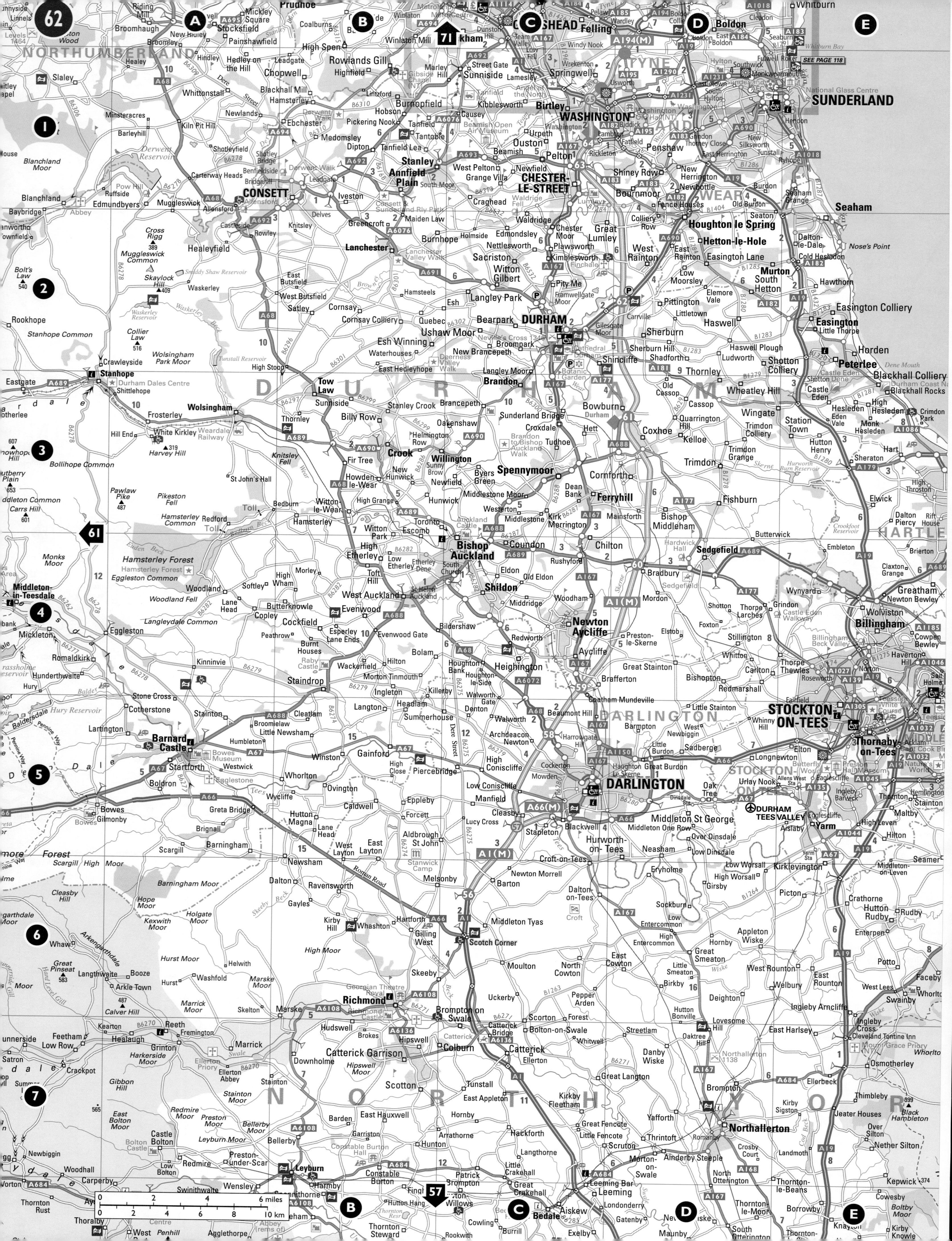
NORTHUMBERLAND
Prudhoe
GATESHEAD
Felling
Boldon
Whitburn
SUNDERLAND
SEE PAGE 118
National Glass Centre
71
Whickham
Stocksfield
Rowlands Gill
Chopwell
Burnopfield
Sunniside
Springwell
Birtley
WASHINGTON
Usworth
Hetton
Stanley
Annfield Plain
Pelton
CHESTER-LE-STREET
Penshaw
Shiney Row
Seaham
CONSETT
Allensford
Blanchland
Blanchland Moor
Derwent Reservoir
Edmundbyers
Muggleswick
Healeyfield
Lanchester
Burnhope
Sacriston
Great Lumley
West Rainton
Houghton le Spring
Hetton-le-Hole
Easington Lane
Murton
South Hetton
Nose's Point
Easington Colliery
Easington
Horden
Peterlee
Blackhall Colliery
Blackhall Rocks
DURHAM
Bearpark
Ushaw Moor
Esh Winning
Brandon
Sherburn
Shincliffe
Thornley
Wheatley Hill
Wingate
Station Town
Rookhope
Stanhope Common
Stanhope
Durham Dales Centre
Eastgate
Crawleyside
Wolsingham
Frosterley
Tow Law
Crook
Willington
Spennymoor
Coxhoe
Trimdon
Bowburn
Cornforth
Ferryhill
Fishburn
Sedgefield
HARTLEPOOL
Bishop Auckland
Shildon
Newton Aycliffe
Chilton
Hamsterley
Hamsterley Forest
61
Middleton-in-Teesdale
Eggleston
Romaldkirk
Mickleton
Cotherstone
Barnard Castle
Startforth
Bowes
Staindrop
Gainford
Piercebridge
Heighington
Billingham
Wolviston
STOCKTON-ON-TEES
Thornaby-on-Tees
DARLINGTON
DURHAM TEES VALLEY
Middleton St George
Yarm
Hurworth-on-Tees
Croft-on-Tees
Eaglescliffe
Greta Bridge
Scotch Corner
Middleton Tyas
Gilling West
Richmond
Brompton on Swale
Catterick
Catterick Garrison
Colburn
Reeth
Leyburn
Middleham
Bedale
Leeming
Northallerton
Brompton
Osmotherley
Ingleby Cross
Kirklevington
Hutton Rudby
57
DURHAM
DARLINGTON
NORTH YORKSHIRE
A1(M)
A19
A66
A167
A68
A688
A689
A690
A693
A692
A691
A6108
A684
0 2 4 6 miles
0 2 4 6 8 10 km

F
G
H
J
K
1
2
3
4
5
6
7
National Nature Reserve
Hartlepool Historic Ships
The Headland
Jackson's Landing
Hartlepool Bay
Historic Quay & Museum of Hartlepool
HARTLEPOOL
Tees Bay
Seaton Carew
Teesmouth National Nature Reserve
Seal Sands
Coatham
Redcar
Warrenby
Dormanstown
Westfield
Marske-by-the-Sea
Saltburn Inclined Railway
Saltburn-by-the-Sea
Port Clarence
MIDDLESBROUGH
Kirkleatham Old Hall Mus
Kirkleatham
Grangetown
South Bank
Lazenby
Yearby
Wilton
New Marske
Upleatham
Dunsdale
Warsett Hill
Brotton
Skelton
Skinningrove
Tom Leonard Mining Museum
Boulby
Staithes
Carlin How
Loftus
North Skelton
Kilton
Easington
Port Mulgrave
Dalehouse
Hinderwell
Kettle Ness
Runswick Bay
Kettleness
Roxby
Borrowby
Newton Mulgrave
Ellerby
Goldsborough
Cleveland Way
Sandsend Ness
Sandsend
Lythe
East Barnby
West Barnby
Mickleby
Whitby Lifeboat Museum
Whitby
St Mary's
Saltwick Bay
Whitby Abbey
REDCAR AND CLEVELAND
Eston
Normanby
Ormesby Hall (NT)
Ormesby
Flatts Lane Woodland Country Park
Margrove Park
Boosbeck
Lingdale
Kilton Thorpe
Charltons
Stanghow
Liverton
Handale
Guisborough
Priory
Pinchinthorpe
Nunthorpe
Marton
Stewart Park
Coulby Newham
Tollesby
Moorsholm
Lockwood Beck Reservoir
Freebrough Hill
Newton under Roseberry
Roseberry Topping
Gisborough Moor
Commondale Moor
Commondale
Moorsholm Moor
Scaling
Roxby Low Moor
Scaling Reservoir
Roxby High Moor
Lealholm Moor
Danby Beacon
Danby Low Moor
Moors Centre
Danby
Ainthorpe
Castleton
Houlsyke
Lealholm
Stonegate
Ugthorpe
Dunsley
Newholm
East Row
Hutton Mulgrave
Aislaby
Briggswath
Ruswarp
Whitby Mus
Captain Cook Memorial Museum
Stainsacre
Egton Low Moor
Sleights
Egton
North Yorkshire Moors Rly
Ugglebarnby
Sneaton
Sneatonthorpe
Low Hawsker
High Hawsker
Ness Point (North Cheek)
Robin Hood's Bay
Fylingthorpe
Raw
Newby
Tanton
Langbaurgh
Great Ayton
Little Ayton
Easby Moor
Stokesley
Kildale
Kildale Moor
Easby
Battersby
Baysdale Beck
Baysdale
Brawith
Great Broughton
Ingleby Greenhow
Kirkby
Great Busby
Carlton-in-Cleveland
Westerdale
Baysdale Moor
NORTH YORK MOORS
NATIONAL PARK
CLEVELAND HILLS
Castleton Ridge
Street
Glaisdale
Egton Bridge
Grosmont
Littlebeck
Low Moor
Sleights Moor
Falling Foss
Beck Hole
Goathland
Thomason Foss
Mallyan Spout
Egton High Moor
Pike Hill Moss
Glaisdale Moor
Danby High Moor
Westerdale Moor
Farndale Moor
Glaisdale Rigg
Urra
Round Hill
Seave Green
Chop Gate
Cockayne Ridge
Cockayne
Rosedale Moor
Ravenscar Coastal Centre (NT)
Ravenscar
Old Peak (South Cheek)
Wellington Lodge Llama Trekking
Staintondale Shire Horse Centre
Staintondale
Flask Inn
Fylingdales Moor
Burn Howe Rigg
Hunt House
Wheeldale Moor
Wheeldale Moor Roman Road
Snilesworth Moor
Bilsdale West Moor
Arnsgill Ridge
Cow Ridge
Bilsdale East Moor
Farndale
Church Houses
Hill Cottages
Thorgill
Rosedale
Rosedale Abbey
Low Mill
Blakey Ridge
Rudland Rigg
Bransdale
Hodge Beck
Lockton High Moor
Allerston High Moor
Cloughton Newlands
Harwood Dale
Cloughton
Burniston
Cromer Point
Cropton Forest
NORTH RIDING FOREST PARK
Spaunton Moor
Hartoft End
Saltergate
Lockton Low Moor
Black Beck
Broxa Forest
Silpho
Suffield
Broxa
Hackness
Scalby
Scalby Ness
Sea Life Centre
North Bay
Fangdale Beck
Arden Great Moor
Helmsley Moor
Keldy Castle
Levisham
North Riding Forest Park
Langdale End
Everley
Wrench Green
Newton-on-Rawcliffe
Lockton
Stain Dale
Newton Dale
Gillamoor
Hutton-le-Hole
Ryedale Folk Museum
Spaunton
Lastingham
Fadmoor
Appleton-le-Moors
Cawthorn
Hawnby
Old Byland
Kirkbymoorside
Keldholme
Wrelton
North Yorkshire Moors Rly
High Kingthorpe
Dalby Forest
Irton Moor
Bird of Prey & Conservation Centre
Barrowcliff
Falsgrave
South Bay
Spa Complex
East
58
A1049
A178
A1042
A1085
A66
A174
A171
A172
A173
A169
A170
A165
A64
B1269
B1366
B1266
B1257
B1416
B1447
B1380
B1277

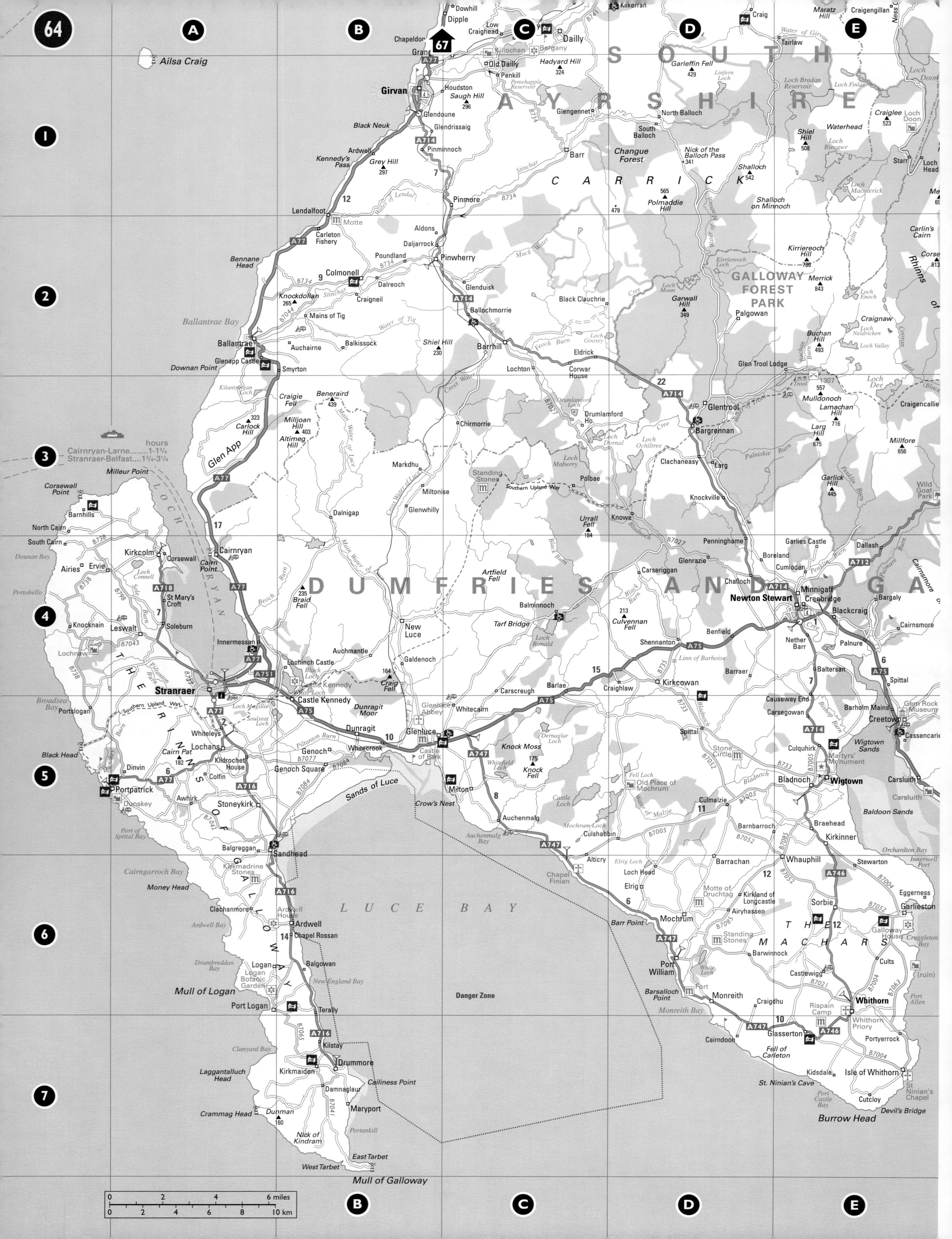
A
B
C
D
E
1
2
3
4
5
6
7
67
SOUTH AYRSHIRE
CARRICK
GALLOWAY FOREST PARK
DUMFRIES AND GA
THE RINNS OF GALLOWAY
THE MACHARS
LUCE BAY
LOCH RYAN
Ailsa Craig
Dowhill
Dipple
Kilkerran
Craig
Maratz Hill
Craigengillan
Chapeldonan
Low Craighead
Dailly
Bargany
Tairlaw
Water of Girvan
Killochan
Old Dailly
Hadyard Hill 324
Garleffin Fell 429
Linfern Loch
Loch Bradan Reservoir
Loch Finlas
Loch Doon
Penkill
Penwhapple Reservoir
Girvan
Houston
Saugh Hill 296
Glendoune
Glendrissaig
Glengennet
North Balloch
Craiglee 523
Black Neuk
South Balloch
Shiel Hill 508
Waterhead
Loch Riecawr
Ardwell
Pinminnoch
Barr
Changue Forest
Nick of the Balloch Pass 341
Kennedy's Pass
Grey Hill 297
Stinchar
Starr
Loch Head
Shalloch 542
Loch Macaterick
Polmaddie Hill 565
Pinmore
Lendalfoot
Water of Lendal
Shalloch on Minnoch
Motte
479
Carleton Fishery
Aldons
Carlin's Cairn
Daljarrock
Kirriereoch Hill 786
Bennane Head
Poundland
Pinwherry
Muck Water
Kirriereoch Loch
Colmonell
Dalreoch
Glenduisk
Loch Moan
Merrick 843
Rhinns of
Knockdolian 265
Craigneil
Black Clauchrie
Garwall Hill 349
Loch Enoch
Mains of Tig
Ballochmorrie
Palgowan
Craignaw
Loch Neldricken
Ballantrae Bay
Ballantrae
Auchairne
Balkissock
Shiel Hill 230
Barrhill
Feoch Burn
Loch Goosey
Eldrick
Buchan Hill 493
Loch Valley
Glenapp Castle
Downan Point
Smyrton
Lochton
Corwar House
Glen Trool Lodge
Loch Dee
Loch Trool
Kilantringan Loch
Craigie Fell
Beneraird 439
Drumlamford Loch
Drumlamford Ho.
Glentrool
1307
Mulldonoch 557
Lamachan Hill 716
Craigencallie
323
Carlock Hill
Milljoan Hill 403
Altimeg Hill
Chirmorrie
Bargrennan
Loch Dornal
Loch Ochiltree
Larg Hill 675
Millfore 656
Cairnryan-Larne........1-1¾ hours
Stranraer-Belfast....1¾-3¼
Glen App
Loch Maberry
Clachaneasy
Larg
Pulniskie Burn
Milleur Point
Markdhu
Standing Stones
Polbae
Garlick Hill 445
Corsewall Point
Miltonise
Southern Upland Way
Cross Water of Luce
Wild Goat Park
Barnhills
Dalnigap
Glenwhilly
Knockville
North Cairn
Knowe
Urrall Fell 184
South Cairn
Cairnryan
Penninghame
Garlies Castle
Dallash
Kirkcolm
Corsewall
Cairn Point
Boreland
Dounan Bay
Airies
Ervie
Loch Connell
Carseriggan
Glenrazie
Cumloden
Artfield Fell
Cairnsmore
Portobello
St Mary's Croft
Braid Fell 235
Challoch
Newton Stewart
Minnigaff
Creebridge
Bargaly
Balminnoch
213
Culvennan Fell
Blackcraig
Knocknain
Leswalt
Soleburn
New Luce
Tarf Bridge
Benfield
Cairnsmore
Lochnaw
Loch Ronald
Innermessan
Auchmantle
Shennanton
Linn of Barhoise
Nether Barr
Palnure
Galdenoch
Lochinch Castle
Black Loch
Baltersan
Castle Kennedy
Craig Fell 164
Barlae
Barraer
Spittal
Stranraer
White Loch
Carscreugh
Craighlaw
Kirkcowan
Broadsea Bay
Portslogan
Loch Magillie
Dunragit Moor
Glenluce Abbey
Whitecairn
Causeway End
Carsegowan
Barholm Mains
Gem Rock Museum
Soulseat Loch
Creetown
Whiteleys
Dunragit
Cassencarie
Lochans
Pilnatton Burn
Glenluce
Dernaglar Loch
Culquhirk
Wigtown Sands
Black Head
Cairn Pat 182
Genoch
Knock Moss
Castle of Park
Kildrochet House
Whitecrook
Whitefield Loch
Stone Circle
Martyrs' Monument
Dinvin
Colfin
Genoch Square
Knock Fell 175
Fell Loch
Old Place of Mochrum
Bladnoch
Wigtown
Portpatrick
Sands of Luce
Milton
Carsluith
Dunskey
Awhirk
Stoneykirk
Crow's Nest
Castle Loch
Culmalzie
Carsluith
Baldoon Sands
Port of Spittal Bay
Auchenmalg
Water of Malzie
Braehead
Mochrum Loch
Auchenmalg Bay
Culshabbin
Barnbarroch
Kirkinner
Balgreggan
Sandhead
Orchardton Bay
Cairngarroch Bay
Kirkmadrine Stones
Elrig Loch
Alticry
Barrachan
Whauphill
Stewarton
Innerwell Port
Money Head
Chapel Finian
Loch Head
Elrig
Motte of Druchtag
Kirkland of Longcastle
Eggerness
Clachanmore
Ardwell House
Sorbie
Garlieston
Ardwell
Mochrum
Airyhassen
Ardwell Bay
Chapel Rossan
Barr Point
Galloway House
Standing Stones
Cruggleton Bay
Drumbreddan Bay
Balgowan
Port William
Barwinnock
Cults
Logan
Logan Botanic Garden
New England Bay
White Loch
Castlewigg
(ruin)
Mull of Logan
Danger Zone
Barsalloch Point
Fort
Monreith
Craigdhu
Whithorn
Port Allen
Port Logan
Terally
Monreith Bay
Rispain Camp
Whithorn Priory
Cairndoon
Glasserton
Portyerrock
Clanyard Bay
Kilstay
Fell of Carleton
Drummore
Kirkmaiden
Laggantalluch Head
Kidsdale
Isle of Whithorn
Cailiness Point
St. Ninian's Cave
Damnaglaur
St Ninian's Chapel
Port Castle Bay
Maryport
Crammag Head
Dunman 160
Cutcloy
Devil's Bridge
Burrow Head
Portankill
Nick of Kindram
East Tarbet
West Tarbet
Mull of Galloway
A77
A714
A751
A75
A716
A747
A718
A712
A746
B741
B734
B7044
B7027
B738
B798
B7043
B7077
B7084
B7042
B7065
B7041
B733
B735
B7005
B7052
B7085
B7004
B7021
B7063
0 2 4 6 miles
0 2 4 6 8 10 km

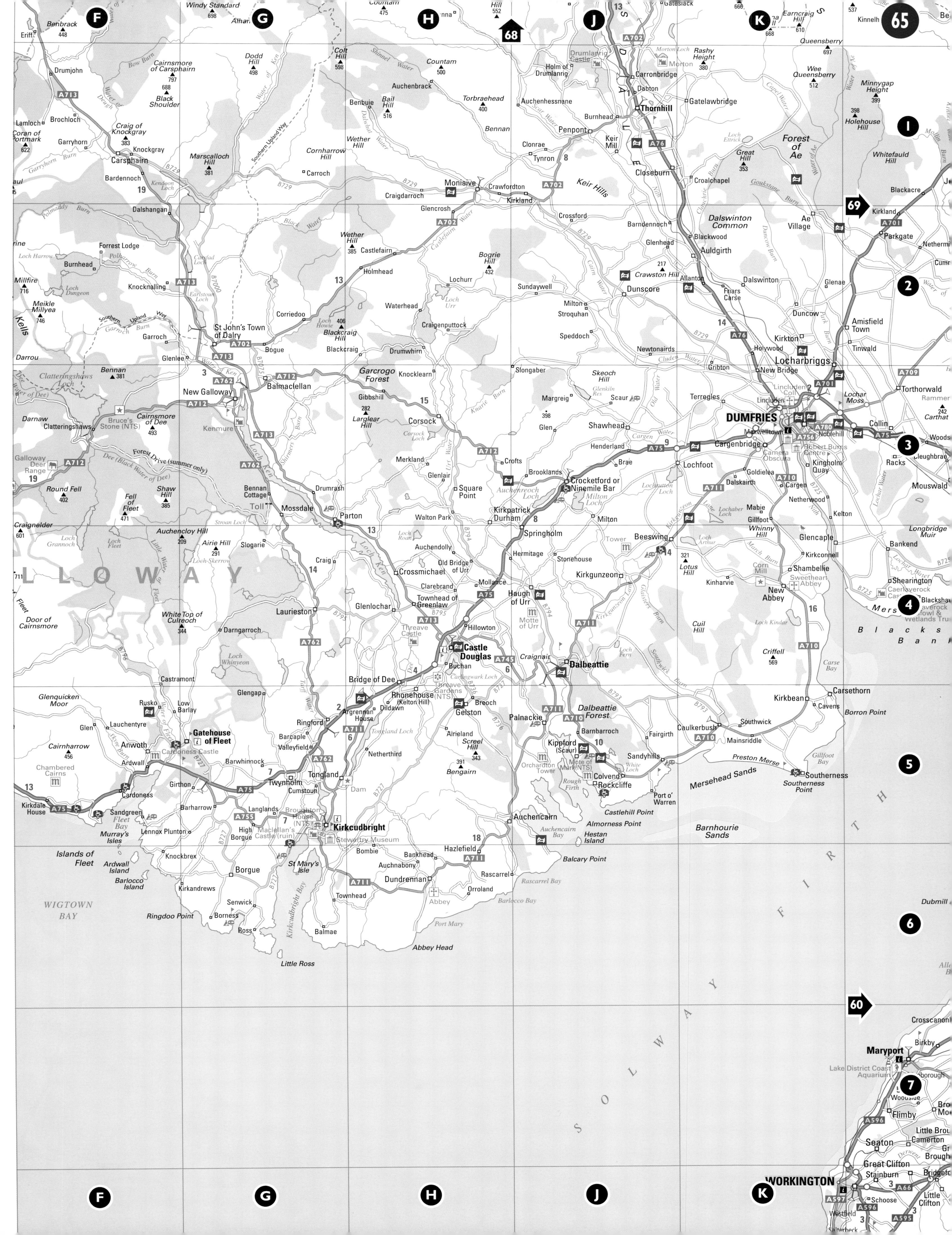
F
G
H
J
K
68
Windy Standard
698
Benbrack
448
Eriff
Drumjohn
A713
Cairnsmore of Carsphairn
797
688
Black Shoulder
Dodd Hill
498
Colt Hill
598
Countam
500
Auchenbrack
Benbuie
Bail Hill
516
Torbrachead
400
Bennan
Wether Hill
Cornharrow Hill
Carroch
Lamloch
Brochloch
Coran of Portmark
622
Craig of Knockgray
383
Garryhorn
Knockgray
Carsphairn
Marscalloch Hill
381
Southern Upland Way
Bardennoch
19
B729
Kendoon Loch
Dalshangan
Moniaive
Crawfordton
Kirkland
Craigdarroch
Glencrosh
A702
Wether Hill
385
Castlefairn
Holmhead
13
Bogrie Hill
432
Lochurr
Sundaywell
Forrest Lodge
Loch Harrow
Burnhead
Knocknalling
A713
Earlstoun Loch
B7000
Millfire
716
Loch Dungeon
Meikle Millyea
746
Kells
Corriedoo
Loch Howie
406
Blackcraig Hill
Blackcraig
Waterhead
Craigenputtock
Drumwhirn
St John's Town of Dalry
A702
Bogue
Garroch
Glenlee
A713
Darrou
Clatteringshaws Loch
Bennan
381
3
New Galloway
A762
A712
Balmaclellan
Garcrogo Forest
Knocklearn
Gibbshill
282
Larglear Hill
15
Corsock
Corsock Loch
Darnaw
Clatteringshaws
Bruce's Stone (NTS)
Cairnsmore of Dee
493
Kenmure
A713
Galloway Deer Range
A712
19
Forest Drive (summer only)
A762
Round Fell
402
Fell of Fleet
471
Shaw Hill
385
Bennan Cottage
Toll
Mossdale
Drumrash
Parton
13
Merkland
Glenlair
Square Point
A712
Crofts
Brooklands
Auchenreoch Loch
Craignelder
601
Auchencloy Hill
209
Airie Hill
291
Loch-Skerrow
Loch Grannoch
Loch Fleet
Slogarie
Stroan Loch
Craig
14
Walton Park
Auchendolly
Crossmichael
Old Bridge of Urr
Clarebrand
Townhead of Greenlaw
B795
A713
LLOWAY
Fleet
Door of Cairnsmore
White Top of Culreoch
344
Darngarroch
Laurieston
B795
Glenlochar
Threave Castle
A762
Hillowton
Castle Douglas
A745
Buchan
Carlingwark Loch
Threave Gardens
Loch Whinyeon
B796
Castramont
Glengap
Bridge of Dee
4
Rhonehouse (Kelton Hill)
Dildawn
Glenquicken Moor
Rusko
Low Barlay
Glen
Lauchentyre
Gatehouse of Fleet
Anwoth
Cairnharrow
456
Cardoness Castle
Ardwall
Chambered Cairns
Ringford
Argrennan House
A711
Barcaple
Valleyfield
6
A762
Tongland Loch
Netherthird
Barwhinnock
7
Twynholm
Cumstoun
Tongland
Dam
13
Girthon
Cardoness
A75
Kirkdale House
A75
Sandgreen
Fleet Bay
Murray's Isles
Barharrow
Langlands
A755
Lennox Plunton
High Borgue
B727
Maclellan's Castle (ruin)
Broughton House (NTS)
Kirkcudbright
Stewartry Museum
Bombie
Islands of Fleet
Ardwall Island
Barlocco Island
Knockbrex
Borgue
St Mary's Isle
Kirkandrews
Senwick
Borness
Ross
Kirkcudbright Bay
Ringdoo Point
WIGTOWN BAY
Little Ross
Balmae
Townhead
A711
Dundrennan
Abbey
Auchnabony
Bankhead
Hazlefield
18
A711
Rascarrel
Rascarrel Bay
Orroland
Barlocco Bay
Port Mary
Abbey Head
Gelston
Breoch
B736
B727
Airieland
Screel Hill
343
391
Bengairn
Palnackie
A711
A710
Dalbeattie Forest
Dalbeattie
Craignair
Barnbarroch
Kippford (Scaur)
10
Orchardton Tower
Mote of Mark (NTS)
Rough Firth
Colvend
Rockcliffe
White Loch
Sandyhills
Port o' Warren
Castlehill Point
Almorness Point
Auchencairn
Auchencairn Bay
Hestan Island
Balcary Point
Fairgirth
Caulkerbush
Southwick
Mainsriddle
A710
Preston Merse
Mersehead Sands
Southerness
Southerness Point
Gillfoot Bay
Barnhourie Sands
SOLWAY FIRTH
Drumlanrig Castle
Holm of Drumlanrig
Carronbridge
A702
Morton Loch
Morton
Rashy Height
380
Dabton
Thornhill
Gatelawbridge
Auchenhessnane
Burnhead
Penpont
Keir Mill
A76
Clonrae
Tynron
8
Keir Hills
Closeburn
A702
Crawfordton
Loch Ettrick
Great Hill
353
Forest of Ae
Croalchapel
Wee Queensberry
512
Queensberry
697
Minnygap Height
399
398
Holehouse Hill
Whitefauld Hill
Blackacre
69
Kirkland
A701
Parkgate
Nethermi
Crossford
B729
Barndennoch
Dalswinton Common
Ae Village
Blackwood
Glenhead
Auldgirth
217
Crawston Hill
Allanton
Dalswinton
Friars Carse
Glenae
Dunscore
Milton
Stroquhan
Duncow
Amisfield Town
Speddoch
B729
14
A76
Kirkton
Holywood
Tinwald
Newtonairds
Cluden Water
Gribton
New Bridge
Locharbriggs
A709
Slongaber
Skeoch Hill
Glenkiln Res
Scaur
Margreig
398
Glen
Shawhead
Terregles
Lincluden Coll
Lincluden
A701
Torthorwald
Lochar Moss
Rammer
242
Carthat
DUMFRIES
Maxwelltown
A780
A756
Noblehill
Collin
A75
Woods
Henderland
Cargen Water
9
A75
Cargenbridge
Camera Obscura
Robert Burns Centre
Racks
Cleughbrae
Brae
Lochfoot
Kingholm Quay
Crocketford or Ninemile Bar
Milton Loch
Lochrutton Loch
Goldielea
Dalskairth
A710
Cargen
B725
Mouswald
A711
Netherwood
Kirkpatrick Durham
8
Milton
Lochaber Loch
Mabie
Gillfoot
Kelton
Springholm
Tower
Beeswing
14
Loch Arthur
Whinny Hill
Glencaple
Longbridge Muir
Bankend
Hermitage
Stonehouse
321
Lotus Hill
Kirkconnell
B725
Kirkgunzeon
Corn Mill
Shambellie
Sweetheart Abbey
Shearington
Mollance
A75
Haugh of Urr
B794
Kinharvie
New Abbey
B725
Caerlaverock Castle
Blackshaw
Motte of Urr
A711
16
Cuil Hill
Loch Kindar
Merse
Blackshaw Bank
A710
Criffell
569
Loch Fern
Carse Bay
B793
Kirkbean
Carsethorn
Cavens
Borron Point
I
2
3
4
5
6
7
Dubmill
60
Crosscanonby
Birkby
Maryport
Lake District Coast Aquarium
Ewanrigg
Flimby
A596
Seaton
Camerton
Great Clifton
Stainburn
Bridgefoot
WORKINGTON
A66
A597
A596
Schoose
Little Clifton
Westfield
A595
Salterbeck

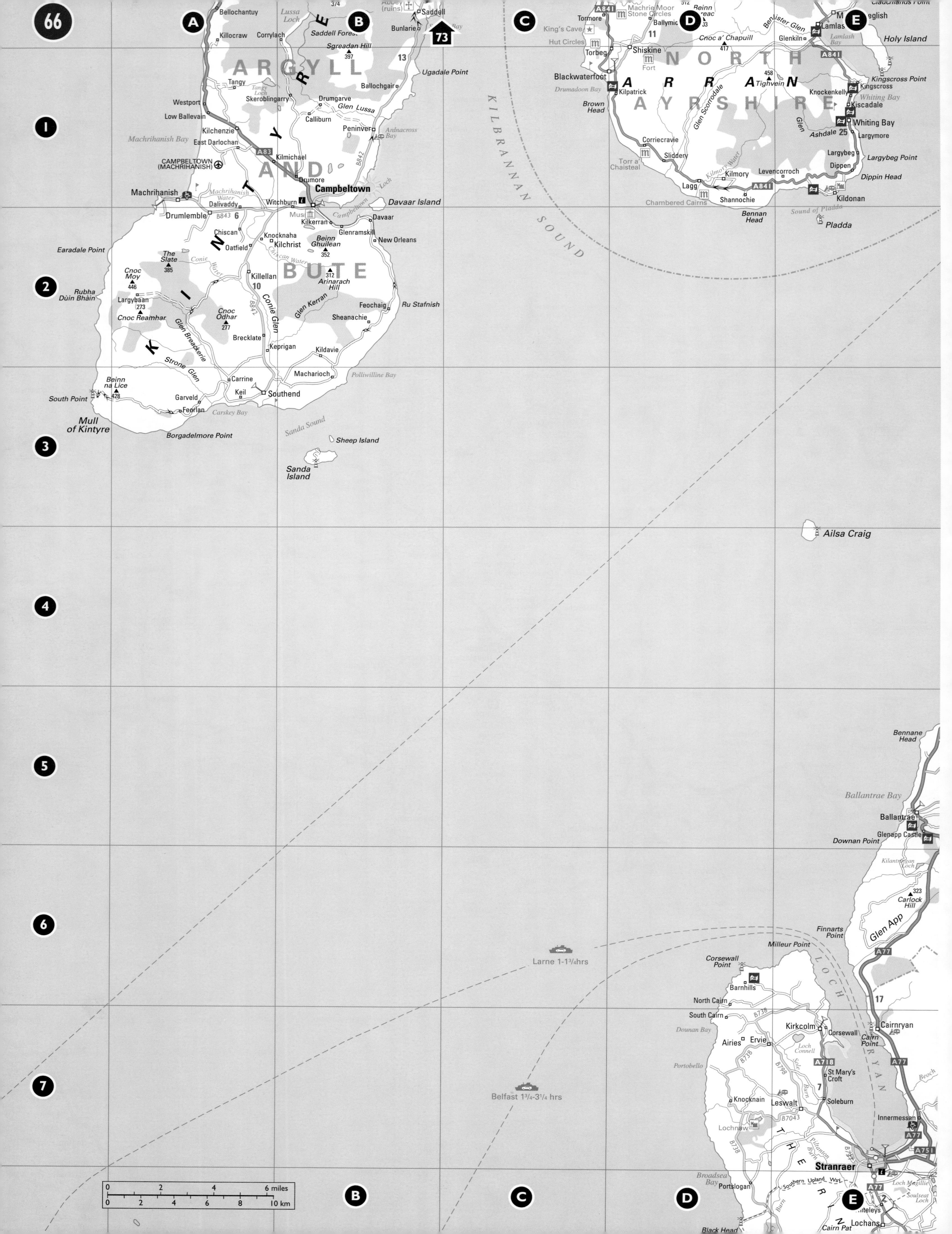

ARGYLL AND BUTE
KINTYRE
NORTH AYRSHIRE
ARRAN
Bellochantuy
Killocraw
Corrylach
Saddell Forest
Saddell
Bunlarie
73
Sgreadan Hill
397
Ugadale Point
Ballochgair
Tangy
Westport
Skeroblingarry
Drumgarve
Glen Lussa
Low Ballevain
Calliburn
Kilchenzie
Peninver
Ardnacross Bay
Machrihanish Bay
East Darlochan
A83
Kilmichael
CAMPBELTOWN (MACHRIHANISH)
Drumore
Campbeltown
Machrihanish
Witchburn
Davaar Island
Dalivaddy
Drumlemble
B843
Kilkerran
Davaar
Chiscan
Glenramskill
Knocknaha
New Orleans
Earadale Point
Oatfield
Kilchrist
Beinn Ghuilean
352
The Slate
385
Conie Water
Cnoc Moy
446
Killellan
312
Arinarach Hill
Rubha Dùin Bhàin
Largybaan
273
Glen Kerran
Feochaig
Ru Stafnish
Cnoc Reamhar
Cnoc Odhar
277
Sheanachie
Glen Breackerie
Brecklate
Conie Glen
B842
Keprigan
Kildavie
Strone Glen
Macharioch
Polliwilline Bay
Beinn na Lice
428
Carrine
South Point
Keil
Southend
Garveld
Feorlan
Carskey Bay
Mull of Kintyre
Borgadelmore Point
Sanda Sound
Sheep Island
Sanda Island
Tormore
A841
Machrie Moor Stone Circles
Beinn Bhreac
Ballymichael
King's Cave
Benlister Glen
Lamlash
Holy Island
Hut Circles
Cnoc a' Chapuill
417
Glenkiln
Lamlash Bay
Torbeg
Shiskine
Fort
458
Tighvein
Kingscross Point
Kingscross
Blackwaterfoot
Kilpatrick
Drumadoon Bay
Glen Scorrodale
Knockenkelly
Whiting Bay
Brown Head
Kiscadale
Whiting Bay
Ashdale
Largymore
Corriecravie
Largybeg
Largybeg Point
Sliddery
Torr a' Chaisteal
Kilmory Water
Dippen
Kilmory
Levencorroch
Dippin Head
Lagg
Kildonan
Chambered Cairns
Shannochie
Sound of Pladda
Pladda
Bennan Head
KILBRANNAN SOUND
Ailsa Craig
Bennane Head
Ballantrae Bay
Ballantrae
Glenapp Castle
Downan Point
Kilantringan Loch
323
Carlock Hill
Glen App
Finnarts Point
Millieur Point
Larne 1-1¾hrs
A77
Corsewall Point
Barnhills
LOCH RYAN
North Cairn
South Cairn
B738
Kirkcolm
Corsewall
Cairnryan
Dounan Bay
Airies
Ervie
Loch Connell
Cairn Point
Portobello
A718
St Mary's Croft
Beoch
Knocknain
Leswalt
Soleburn
Belfast 1¾-3¼ hrs
B7043
Innermessan
Lochnaw
RHINNS OF GALLOWAY
A751
Stranraer
Broadsea Bay
Portslogan
Southern Upland Way
Loch Magillie
Soulseat Loch
Black Head
Whiteleys
Cairn Pat
Lochans
0 2 4 6 miles
0 2 4 6 8 10 km

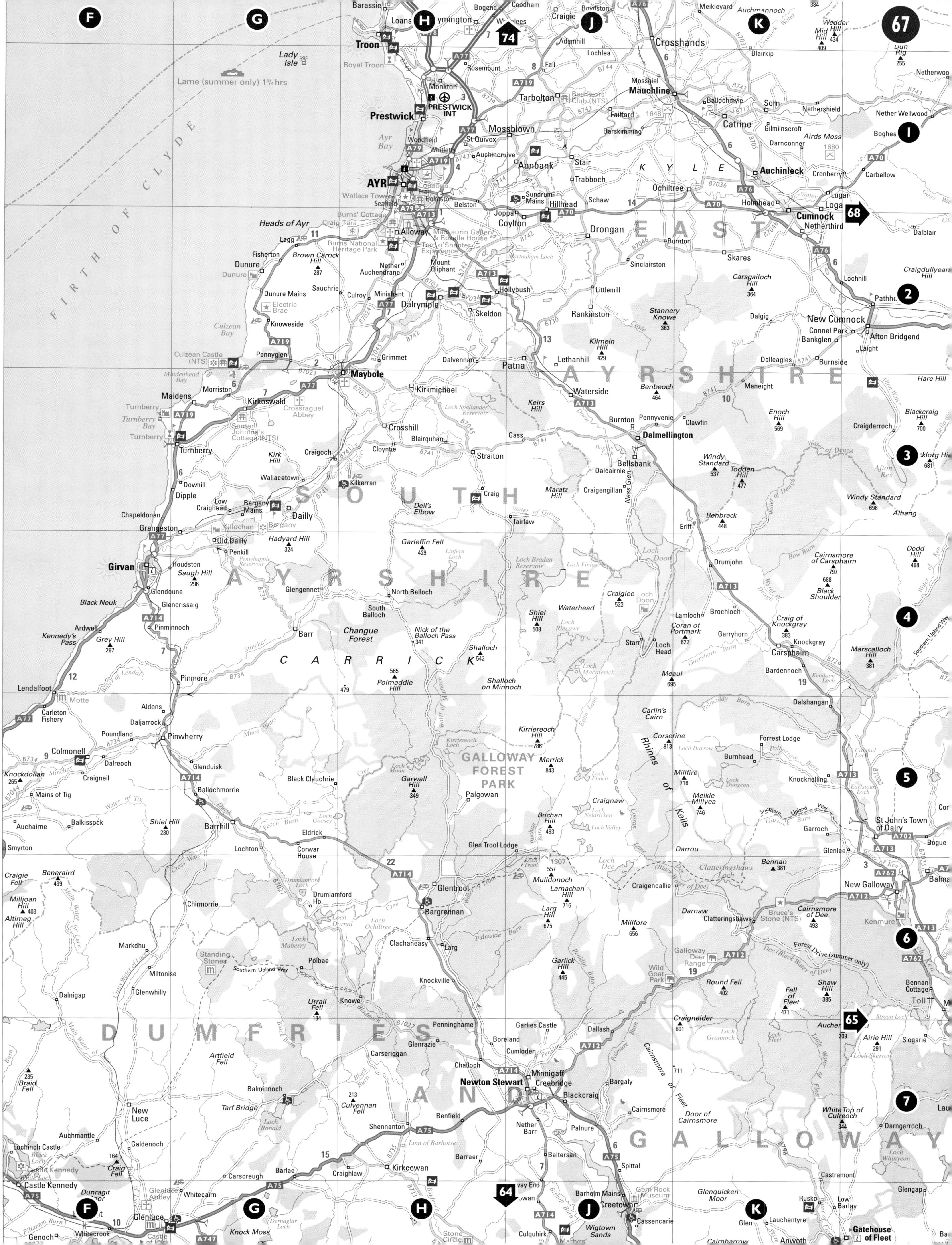

FIRTH OF CLYDE
Larne (summer only) 1¾ hrs
Lady Isle
Troon
Royal Troon
Loans
Barassie
Prestwick
PRESTWICK INT
Monkton
Ayr Bay
AYR
Heads of Ayr
Burns' Cottage
Alloway
Burns National Heritage Park
Tam o' Shanter Experience
Dunure
Fisherton
Brown Carrick Hill
Electric Brae
Knoweside
Culzean Bay
Culzean Castle (NTS)
Maidenhead Bay
Maidens
Turnberry
Turnberry Bay
Kirkoswald
Crossraguel Abbey
Souter Johnnie's Cottage (NTS)
Maybole
Kirkmichael
Crosshill
Dalrymple
Hollybush
Skeldon
Minishant
Culroy
Sauchrie
Grimmet
Patna
Rankinston
Littlemill
Drongan
Coylton
Joppa
Hillhead
Sundrum Mains
Annbank
Mossblown
St Quivox
Auchincruive
Tarbolton
Bachelors' Club (NTS)
Failford
Barskimming
Stair
Trabboch
Mauchline
Mossgiel
Crosshands
Lochlea
Craigie
Fail
Rosemount
Catrine
Sorn
Ballochmyle
Auchinleck
Ochiltree
Cumnock
Netherthird
Lugar
Logan
Holmhead
Skares
Sinclairston
Burnton
K Y L E
EAST AYRSHIRE
New Cumnock
Connel Park
Bankglen
Afton Bridgend
Pathhead
Dalmellington
Bellsbank
Dalcairnie
Waterside
Burnton
Pennyvenie
Benbeoch 464
Keirs Hill
Loch Spallander Reservoir
Straiton
Blairquhan
Cloyntie
Craigoch
Kirk Hill
Kilkerran
Wallacetown
Dipple
Dowhill
Low Craighead
Bargany Mains
Dailly
Chapeldonan
Grangeston
Killochan
Girvan
Old Daily
Penkill
Houdston
Saugh Hill 296
Hadyard Hill 324
SOUTH AYRSHIRE
Craig
Tairlaw
Deil's Elbow
Garleffin Fell 429
Loch Bradan Reservoir
Loch Finlas
Loch Doon
Craiglee 523
Glendoune
Glendrissaig
Black Neuk
Ardwell
Kennedy's Pass
Grey Hill 297
Pinminnoch
Barr
Glengennet
North Balloch
South Balloch
Changue Forest
Nick of the Balloch Pass 341
Shalloch 542
C A R R I C K
Polmaddie Hill 565
Shalloch on Minnoch
Lendalfoot
Carleton Fishery
Pinmore
Aldons
Daljarrock
Pinwherry
Poundland
Colmonell
Dalreoch
Craigneil
Knockdolian 265
Mains of Tig
Auchairne
Balkissock
Glenduisk
Ballochmorrie
Barrhill
Shiel Hill 230
Black Clauchrie
Smyrton
Eldrick
Lochton
Corwar House
Garwall Hill 349
GALLOWAY FOREST PARK
Kirriereoch Hill 786
Merrick 843
Palgowan
Glen Trool Lodge
Buchan Hill 493
Craignaw
Mulldonoch 557
Lamachan Hill 716
Larg Hill 675
Glentrool
Bargrennan
Drumlamford Ho.
Chirmorie
Beneraird 439
Craigie Fell
Milljoan Hill 403
Altimeg Hill
Markdhu
Standing Stones
Southern Upland Way
Miltonise
Glenwhilly
Dalnigap
Polbae
Clachaneasy
Larg
Knockville
Knowe
Urrall Fell 184
Penninghame
Garlies Castle
Boreland
Cumloden
Glenrazie
Carseriggan
Challoch
Minnigaff
Creebridge
Newton Stewart
Blackcraig
Bargaly
Cairnsmore
Cairnsmore of Fleet
Door of Cairnsmore
Palnure
Nether Barr
Benfield
Shennanton
Culvennan Fell 213
Balminnoch
Tarf Bridge
New Luce
Artfield Fell
Braid Fell 235
Auchmantle
Galdenoch
Lochinch Castle
Castle Kennedy
Craig Fell 164
Dunragit
Glenluce
Whitecairn
Carscreugh
Barlae
Craighlaw
Kirkcowan
Barraer
Baltersan
Spittal
Knock Moss
Genoch
Whitecrook
Barholm Mains
Creetown
Gem Rock Museum
Cassencarie
Wigtown Sands
Culquhirk
Glenquicken Moor
Glen
Lauchentyre
Rusko
Low Barlay
Gatehouse of Fleet
Anwoth
Cairnharrow
Castramont
Glengap
Darngarroch
White Top of Culreoch 344
Loch Whinyeon
Airie Hill 291
Slogarie
Craignelder 601
Dallash
Loch Grannoch
Loch Fleet
Fell of Fleet 471
Round Fell 402
Shaw Hill 385
Bennan Cottage
Galloway Deer Range
Wild Goat Park
Garlick Hill 445
Millfore 656
Darnaw
Clatteringshaws
Bruce's Stone (NTS)
Cairnsmore of Dee 493
Kenmure
New Galloway
Balmaclellan
Glenlee
Craigencallie
Clatteringshaws Loch
Bennan 381
Darrou
Garroch
St John's Town of Dalry
Bogue
Meikle Millyea 746
Millfire 716
Rhinns of Kells
Corserine 813
Carlin's Cairn
Burnhead
Forrest Lodge
Knocknalling
Loch Dungeon
Earlstoun Loch
Dalshangan
Bardennoch
Kendoon Loch
Carsphairn
Knockgray
Craig of Knockgray 383
Garryhorn
Meaul 695
Coran of Portmark 622
Lamloch
Brochloch
Loch Head
Starr
Shiel Hill 508
Waterhead
Drumjohn
Eriff
Benbrack 448
Windy Standard 537
Todden Hill 477
Windy Standard 698
Cairnsmore of Carsphairn 797
Black Shoulder 688
Marscalloch Hill 381
Dodd Hill 498
Blackcraig Hill 700
Craigdarroch
Enoch Hill 569
Clawfin
Maneight
Dalleagles
Burnside
Laight
Dalgig
Stannery Knowe 363
Kilmein Hill 429
Lethanhill
Dalvennan
Carsgailoch Hill 364
Craigdullyeart Hill
Lochhill
Hare Hill
Netherwood
Nether Wellwood
Nethershield
Gilmilnscroft
Darnconner
Airds Moss
Cronberry
Carbellow
Dalblair
Blairkip
Auchmannoch
Meikleyard
Wedder Hill 434
Mid Hill 409
Dun Rig 255
Adamhill
Bogend
Coodham
Galloway
DUMFRIES AND GALLOWAY

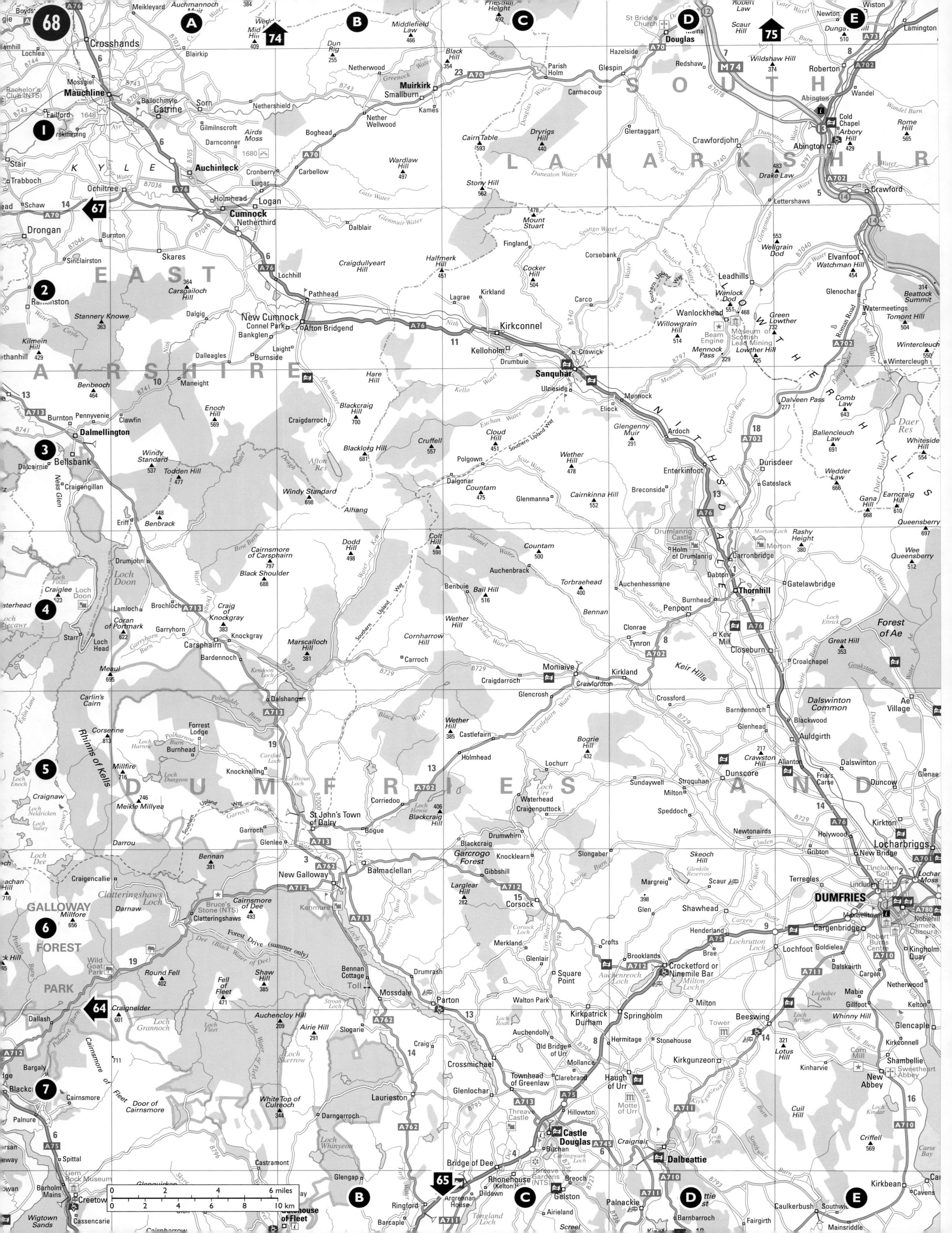
A
B
C
D
E
74
75
67
64
65
1
2
3
4
5
6
7
EAST
AYRSHIRE
SOUTH
LANARKSHIRE
DUMFRIES AND
KYLE
LOWTHER HILLS
NITHSDALE
GALLOWAY FOREST PARK
Rhinns of Kells
Boydston
Meikleyard
Auchmannoch Muir
Weddar Law
Mid Hill
Middlefield Law
Priesthill Height
St Bride's Church
Douglas
Robert Law
Scaur Hill
Newton
Wiston
Lamington
Crosshands
Blairkip
Dun Rig
Black Hill
Parish Holm
Hazelside
Glespin
Redshaw
Wildshaw Hill
Roberton
Lochlea
Mossgiel
Bachelor's Club (NTS)
Mauchline
Ballochmyle
Catrine
Sorn
Netherwood
Muirkirk
Smallburn
Carmacoup
Abington
Cold Chapel
Wandel
Nethershield
Kames
Nether Wellwood
Failford
Gilmilnscroft
Darnconner
Airds Moss
Boghead
Cairn Table
Dryrigs Hill
Glentaggart
Crawfordjohn
Arbory Hill
Rome Hill
Stair
Trabboch
Auchinleck
Cronberry
Carbellow
Wardlaw Hill
Lugar
Ochiltree
Holmhead
Logan
Stony Hill
Duneaton Water
Drake Law
Crawford
Schaw
Cumnock
Netherthird
Mount Stuart
Lettershaws
Drongan
Burnton
Dalblair
Fingland
Wellgrain Dod
Elvanfoot
Watchman Hill
Sinclairston
Skares
Craigdullyeart Hill
Halfmerk Hill
Corsebank
Cocker Hill
Leadhills
Beattock Summit
Glenochar
Lochhill
Carsgailoch Hill
Pathhead
Lagrae
Kirkland
Carco
Wanlock Dod
Wanlockhead
Watermeetings
Tomont Hill
Rankinston
Stannery Knowe
Dalgig
New Cumnock
Connel Park
Afton Bridgend
Bankglen
Laight
Burnside
Kirkconnel
Kelloholm
Drumbuie
Crawick
Willowgrain Hill
Beam Engine
Museum of Scottish Lead Mining
Mennock Pass
Green Lowther
Lowther Hill
Wintercleuch
Kilmein Hill
Dalleagles
Hare Hill
Sanquhar
Ulzieside
Mennock
Eliock
Dalveen Pass
Comb Law
Benbeoch
Maneight
Enoch Hill
Blackcraig Hill
Craigdarroch
Euchan Water
Burnton
Pennyvenie
Clawfin
Dalmellington
Glengenny Muir
Ardoch
Daer Res
Whiteside Hill
Ballencleuch Law
Windy Standard
Todden Hill
Blacklorg Hill
Afton Res
Cruffell
Cloud Hill
Wether Hill
Bellsbank
Dalcairnie
Ness Glen
Craigengillan
Polgown
Dalgonar
Countam
Enterkinfoot
Durisdeer
Gateslack
Wedder Law
Breconside
Glenmanna
Cairnkinna Hill
Windy Standard
Alhang
Gana Hill
Earncraig Hill
Eriff
Benbrack
Queensberry
Drumlanrig Castle
Holm of Drumlanrig
Morton
Rashy Height
Carronbridge
Cairnsmore of Carsphairn
Dodd Hill
Colt Hill
Countam
Wee Queensberry
Drumjohn
Loch Doon
Black Shoulder
Auchenbrack
Dabton
Thornhill
Gatelawbridge
Craiglee
Loch Finlas
Benbuie
Bail Hill
Torbraehead
Auchenhessnane
Burnhead
Penpont
Lamloch
Brochloch
Craig of Knockgray
Coran of Portmark
Garryhorn
Wether Hill
Bennan
Clonrae
Forest of Ae
Starr
Loch Head
Carsphairn
Knockgray
Cornharrow Hill
Marscalloch Hill
Tynron
Keir Mill
Closeburn
Great Hill
Bardennoch
Carroch
Keir Hills
Croalchapel
Meaul
Kendoon Loch
Moniaive
Kirkland
Craigdarroch
Crawfordton
Carlin's Cairn
Dalshangan
Glencrosh
Crossford
Dalswinton Common
Ae Village
Corserine
Forrest Lodge
Burnhead
Wether Hill
Castlefairn
Bogrie Hill
Barndennoch
Glenhead
Blackwood
Auldgirth
Holmhead
Lochurr
Crawston Hill
Allanton
Dalswinton
Millfire
Knocknalling
Loch Dungeon
Sundaywell
Stroquhan
Dunscore
Friars Carse
Duncow
Glenae
Craignaw
Meikle Millyea
Corriedoo
Waterhead
Craigenputtock
Milton
Speddoch
St John's Town of Dalry
Blackcraig Hill
Kirkton
Garroch
Bogue
Newtonairds
Holywood
Locharbriggs
Darrou
Glenlee
Blackcraig
Drumwhirn
Gribton
New Bridge
Loch Dee
Bennan
Garcrogo Forest
Knocklearn
Slongaber
Skeoch Hill
Glenkiln Reservoir
Lincluden Coll
Terregles
Lochar Moss
Craigencallie
New Galloway
Balmaclellan
Gibbshill
Margreig
Scaur
DUMFRIES
Clatteringshaws Loch
Bruce's Stone (NTS)
Cairnsmore of Dee
Laglear Hill
Corsock
Glen
Shawhead
Maxwelltown
Nobleh
Camera Obscura
Darnaw
Millfore
Clatteringshaws
Kenmure
Henderland
Cargenbridge
Robert Burns Centre
Merkland
Crofts
Lochrutton Loch
Lochfoot
Goldielea
Kingholm Quay
Forest Drive (summer only)
Wild Goat Park
Round Fell
Shaw Hill
Bennan Cottage
Glenlair
Square Point
Brooklands
Crocketford or Ninemile Bar
Dalskairth
Cargen
Fell of Fleet
Toll
Mossdale
Drumrash
Auchenreoch Loch
Milton Loch
Mabie
Netherwood
Craignelder
Dallash
Auchencloy Hill
Airie Hill
Slogarie
Parton
Walton Park
Kirkpatrick Durham
Springholm
Beeswing
Milton
Gillfoot
Kelton
Loch Grannoch
Lochaber Loch
Whinny Hill
Glencaple
Cairnsmore of Fleet
Loch Skerrow
Craig
Auchendolly
Old Bridge of Urr
Hermitage
Stonehouse
Tower
Lotus Hill
Kirkconnell
Corn Mill
Shambellie
Bargaly
Crossmichael
Mollance
Kirkgunzeon
Kinharvie
New Abbey
Sweetheart Abbey
Glenlochar
Townhead of Greenlaw
Clarebrand
Haugh of Urr
Motte of Urr
Blackcraig
Cairnsmore
Door of Cairnsmore
White Top of Culreoch
Laurieston
Threave Castle
Hillowton
Cuil Hill
Loch Kindar
Palnure
Darngarroch
Castle Douglas
Loch Whinyeon
Craignair
Criffell
Carse Bay
Spittal
Castramont
Bridge of Dee
Buchan
Carlingwark Loch
Dalbeattie
Gem Rock Museum
Glengap
Rhonehouse (Kelton Hill)
Threave Gardens (NTS)
Breoch
Barholm Mains
Creetown
Ringford
Argrennan House
Dildawn
Gelston
Palnackie
Kirkbean
Cavens
Airieland
Wigtown Sands
Cassencarie
Gatehouse of Fleet
Barcaple
Tongland Loch
Screel
Barnbarroch
Caulkerbush
Southwick
Fairgirth
Mainsriddle
A76
A70
M74
A702
A713
A712
A762
A75
A711
A745
A710
A780
A701
B741
B729
B794
B7000
0 2 4 6 miles
0 2 4 6 8 10 km

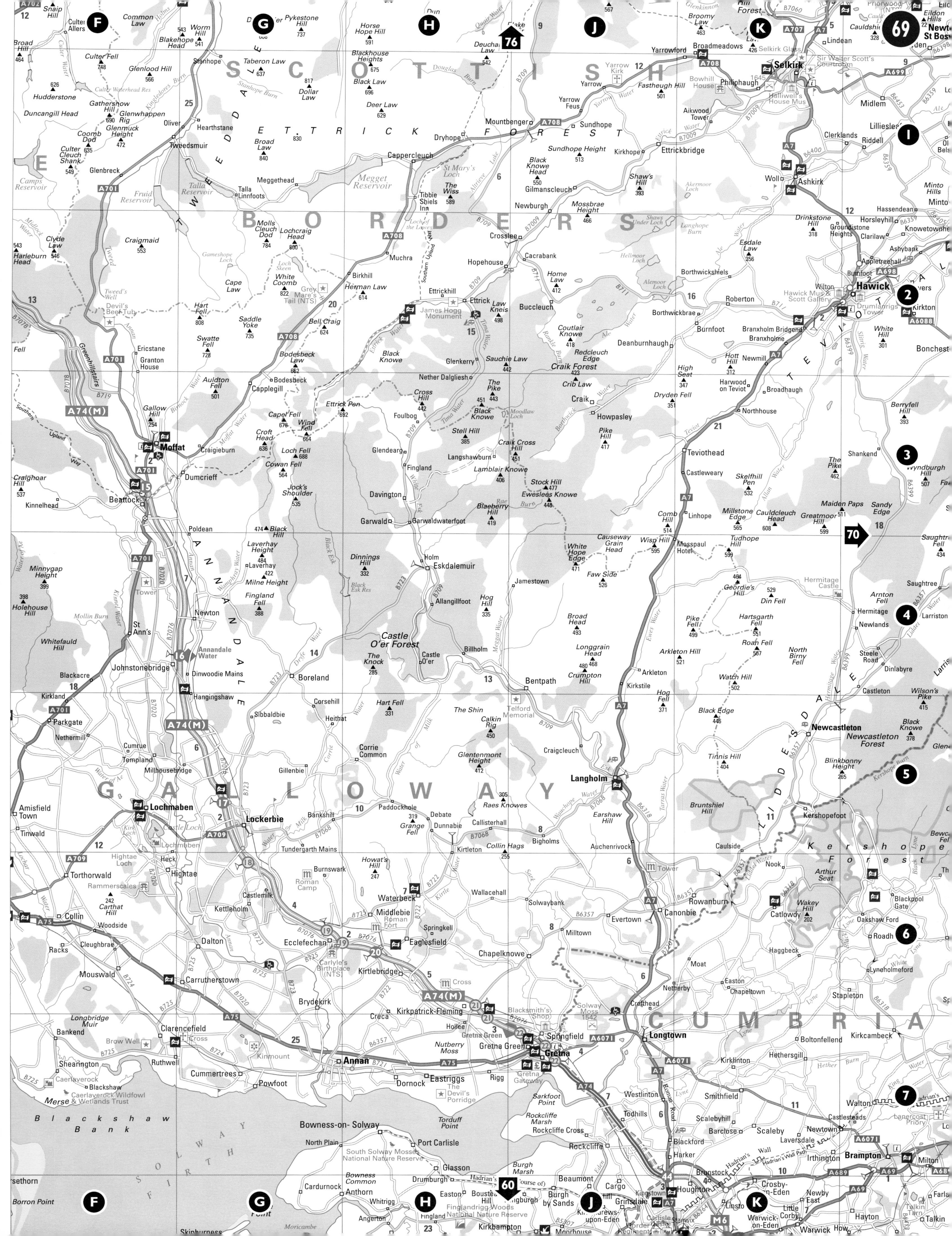
69
76
70
60
SCOTTISH BORDERS
ETTRICK FOREST
TWEEDDALE
TEVIOTDALE
ANNANDALE
DUMFRIES AND GALLOWAY
LIDDESDALE
CUMBRIA
Kershope Forest
SOLWAY FIRTH
Blackshaw Bank
Selkirk
Hawick
Moffat
Lockerbie
Lochmaben
Langholm
Annan
Gretna
Gretna Green
Longtown
Brampton
Newcastleton
Ecclefechan
Eskdalemuir
Tweedsmuir
Ettrickbridge
Ashkirk
Philiphaugh
Yarrowford
Broadmeadows
Yarrow
Mountbenger
Cappercleuch
Tibbie Shiels Inn
Talla Reservoir
Fruid Reservoir
Megget Reservoir
St Mary's Loch
Craik Forest
Craik
Teviothead
Castle O'er Forest
Johnstonebridge
Beattock
Boreland
Bentpath
Canonbie
Springfield
Kirkpatrick-Fleming
Clarencefield
Ruthwell
Cummertrees
Powfoot
Eastriggs
Dornock
Bowness-on-Solway
Port Carlisle
Glasson
Drumburgh
Burgh by Sands
Rockcliffe
Westlinton
Smithfield
Scaleby
Irthington
Walton
Crosby-on-Eden
Houghton
Kingstown
Grey Mare's Tail (NTS)
James Hogg Monument
Telford Memorial
Carlyle's Birthplace (NTS)
Caerlaverock Wildfowl & Wetlands Trust
South Solway Mosses National Nature Reserve
Hermitage Castle
Halliwell's House Mus
Hawick Mus & Scott Gallery
Sir Walter Scott's Courtroom
Bowhill House
Selkirk Glass
A7
A74(M)
A701
A708
A709
A75
A6071
A69
A698
A699
M6
F
G
H
J
K
I
2
3
4
5
6
7

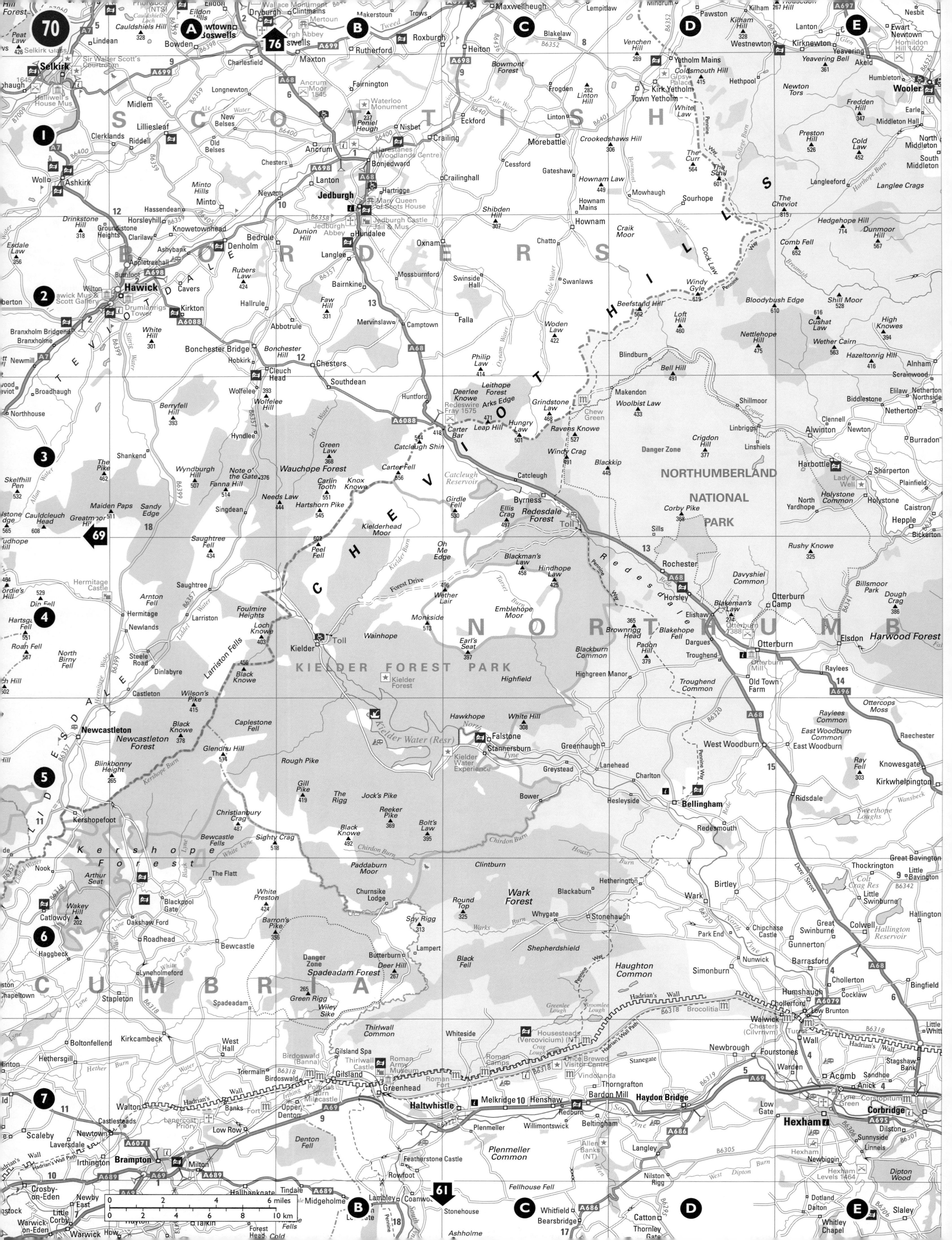
A
B
C
D
E
1
2
3
4
5
6
7
76
69
61
SCOTTISH
BORDERS
CHEVIOT HILLS
TEVIOTDALE
NORTHUMBERLAND NATIONAL PARK
NORTH
NORTHUMB
KIELDER FOREST PARK
CUMBRIA
LIDDESDALE
Kershope Forest
Wauchope Forest
Redesdale Forest
Kielder Water (Resr)
Spadeadam Forest
Wark Forest
Harwood Forest
Selkirk
Newtown St Boswells
Jedburgh
Hawick
Kelso
Wooler
The Cheviot
815
Otterburn
Bellingham
Kielder
Newcastleton
Haltwhistle
Hexham
Corbridge
Haydon Bridge
Brampton
Greenhead
Hadrian's Wall
Yetholm Mains
Kirk Yetholm
Town Yetholm
Carter Bar
Byrness
Rochester
Falstone
Stannersburn
Kielder Water Experience
Housesteads (Vercovicium) (NT)
Vindolanda
Danger Zone
Pennine Way
A7
A68
A69
A697
A698
A699
A6088
A6079
A696
A6071
A689
A686
A695
0 2 4 6 miles
0 2 4 6 8 10 km

F
G
H
J
K
77
62
1
2
3
4
5
6
7
Doddington
East Horton
West Horton
Bradford
Adderstone
Lucker
Bellshill
New Shoreston
Seahouses
& Fishing Museum
North Sunderland
East Fleetham
Beadnell
Elford
Greendykes
Wandon
Chatton
Warenford
Newham Hall
Newham
Benthall
Beadnell Bay
Swinhoe
West Fleetham
Twizell House
Newstead
Rosebrough
Haugh Head
Chillingham
Chillingham Park
Newtown
Lilburn Tower
Hepburn
East Lilburn
Hepburn Bell
Old Bewick
Cateran Hill
Bewick Moor
Ilderton
Roseden
Roddam
Chathill
Ellingham
Preston
Tughall
High Newton-by-the-Sea
Snook Point
Newton Haven (St Mary's)
Low Newton-by-the-Sea
Embleton Bay
Embleton
Dunstanburgh Castle (NT)
Dunstan Steads
Wandylaw
Brownieside
Middle Moor
Preston Tower
Brunton
Christon Bank
North Charlton
South Charlton
West Ditchburn
Harehope
Eglingham
Wooperton
New Bewick
Beanley
Rock
Stamford
Rennington
Dunstan
Craster
Cullernose Point
Howick Hall Gardens
Howick
Howick Haven
Longhoughton Steel
Brandon
Reaveley
Ingram
Powburn
Branton
East Bolton
Shipley
Hulne Priory
Titlington
Littlehoughton
Cochrane Pike
Glanton
Glanton Pyke
Hulne Park
Alnwick Abbey
Alnwick
Denwick
Alnwick Castle & Garden
Longhoughton
Boulmer
Boulmer Haven
Great Ryle
Prendwick
Whittingham
Bolton
Abberwick
Broome Wood
Barter Books
Hawkhill
Lesbury
Alnmouth Sta
Hipsburn
Thrunton
Little Ryle
Yetlington
Callaly Castle
Alnwick Moor
Edlingham Castle
Bilton
Alnmouth
Callaly
Thrunton Wood
Edlingham
Alnmouth Bay
Shilbottle
High Buston
Lorbottle Hall
Netherton Burnfoot
Long Crag
Lorbottle
Bigges' Pillar
Low Buston
Birling
High Trewhitt
Newton-on-the-Moor
Eastfield Hall
Warkworth Castle
Warkworth
Gloster Hill
Coquet Island
Cartington
Shirlaw Pike
Forest
Hazon
Amble
Swarland
Guyzance
Morwick Hall
High Hauxley
Warton
Snitter
National Park Visitor Centre
Cragside (NT)
Old Swarland
North Togston
Hauxley Haven
Flotterton
Nelly's Moss Lakes
North End
Acklington
Radcliffe
Thropton
Rothbury
Tosson
Little Tosson
Newtown
Whitton
Longframlington
Felton
West Thirston
Broomhill
Togston
Hadston Carrs
Great Tosson
Low Town
Hadston
Thirston New Houses
South Broomhill
Chevington Drift
Tosson Hill
Simonside
Pauperhaugh
East Thirston
Red Row
Druridge Bay Country Pk
Druridge Bay
Rothbury
Hesleyhurst
Low
Brinkburn Priory
Eshott
Forestburn Gate
West Chevington
Widdrington
Coldrife
Wingates
Causey Park
Druridge
Longhorsley
Widdrington Station
Widdrington Sta
Cresswell
The Scars
Fontburn Reservoir
Earsdon Moor
Fenrother
Snab Point
Nunnykirk
Tritlington
Ulgham
Ellington
Lynemouth
Espley Hall
Cockle Park
Harwood
Rothley Lakes
Stanton
Beacon Point
Netherwitton
Todd Hill
Hebron
Longhirst
Queen Elizabeth II
Woodhorn
Hartington Hall
Longwitton
Pegswood
Rothley
Pigdon
ASHINGTON
Newbiggin-by-the-Sea
Scots' Gap
Newton Underwood
Northumbria Craft Centre
Bothal
Hirst
Thropbill
Hartburn
Mitford
Morpeth Chantry
Sheepwash
Wansbeck
North Seaton
Cambo
Middleton
Morpeth
Shadfen
Stakeford
Guide Post
High Angerton
Wallington (NT)
Meldon
Molesden
Choppington
Cambois
Low Angerton
Kirkharle
Middleton Bank Top
Bolam Lake
Bolam
West Edington
Tranwell
Clifton
Hepscott
East Sleekburn
Nedderton
Whalton
Bedlington
Bebside
BLYTH
Cowpen
Capheaton
Saltwick
Plessey Woods
Newsham
Bradford
Belsay
Ogle
Stannington
East Hartford
Kirkheaton
Belsay Hall Castle & Gardens
Shankhouse
Shotton
Nelson Village
New Hartley
Seaton Delaval Hall
Seaton Sluice
Kearsley Fell
Black Heddon
Cramlington
Seaton
Hartley
Milbourne
Westgate
Berwick Hill
East Cramlington
Seaton Delaval
St Mary's Island (Bait Island)
Higham Dykes
Ryal
Ingoe
Horton Grange
Brenkley
Seghill
Holywell
Dudley
Dinnington
Seaton Burn
Spanish City
Grindstonelaw
Fenwick
Heugh
Whitley Bay
Stamfordham
Brunswick Village
Wide Open
Burradon
Earsdon
Prestwick
Campdown
Backworth
Monkseaton
Matfen
Hawkwell
Dalton
Ponteland
Darras Hall
Hazlerigg
Killingworth
Shiremoor
Cullercoats
Eachwick
NEWCASTLE INTERNATIONAL
New York
Marden
Great Whittington
Ouston
High Callerton
Black Callerton
Tynemouth
Callerton Lane End
Forest Hall
Benton Square
Wall Houses
Harlow Hill
Hadrian's Wall Path
Kenton
Longbenton
Willington
Chirton
North Shields
SOUTH SHIELDS
Halton
Vindobala
Heddon-on-the-Wall
Gosforth
Rudchester
Newcastle United FC
WALLSEND
Westerhope
Throckley
Jesmond
Aydon
Stephenson's Birthplace (NT)
Newburn
Walbottle
NEWCASTLE UPON TYNE
Bede's World
Westoe
Horsley
Lemington
Heaton
Marsden Bay
Newton
Wylam
Clara Vale
Ryton
Stella
Benwell
Walker
Byker
Hebburn
Jarrow
Simonside
Harton
Marsden
Ovingham
Blaydon
Ovington
Crawcrook
Metro Centre
Monkton
Whitburn
Riding Mill
Mickley Square
Prudhoe
Metrocentre
Pelaw
Cleadon
Broomhaugh
Bywell
Stocksfield
Coalburns
Greenside
Barlow
Whickham
Winlaton
GATESHEAD
Felling
Wardley
Boldon Colliery
Boldon
East Boldon
Painshawfield
Dunston Hill
Winlaton Mill
Team Valley
Windy Nook
West Boldon
Whitburn Bay
Seaburn
Broomley
New Ridley
Leadgate
Healey
Hindley
Hedley on the Hill
High Spen
Rowlands Gill
Low Fell
Wrekenton
Hylton
Fulwell
Southwick
Roker
Monkwearmouth
Sunderland AFC
Chopwell
Sunniside
Street Gate
Springwell
Usworth
Whittonstall
High Spen
Marley Hill
Lamesley
Tanfield
Blackhall Mill
Burnopfield
Kibblesworth
Birtley
WASHINGTON
South Hylton
National Glass Centre
SUNDERLAND
Hamsterley
Lintzford
SEE PAGE 118
Discount
Hours
Bergen 22-26
Göteborg 25
Haugesund 21½
Kristiansand 17
Stavanger 19
Amsterdam 15hrs
A1
A697
A68
A69
A696
A1068
A189
A197
A192
A193
A19
A1056
A1058
A186
A187
A191
A194
A167(M)
A184
A185
A1300
A183
A1018
A1290
A1231
A195
A692
A694
A695
A6085
A1147
A1061
A1171
A1148
A196
B6348
B6346
B6341
B6347
B1340
B1339
B6342
B6344
B6345
B1330
B6343
B6524
B1331
B1337
B1334
B6318
B6321
B6309
B6528
B6317
B6395
B6315
B6530
B1505
B1426
B1296
B1298
B1291
B1301
B1405
B6309
B6918
B6324
B1325
1464
1093
315
257
308
429
440
244
223
1640

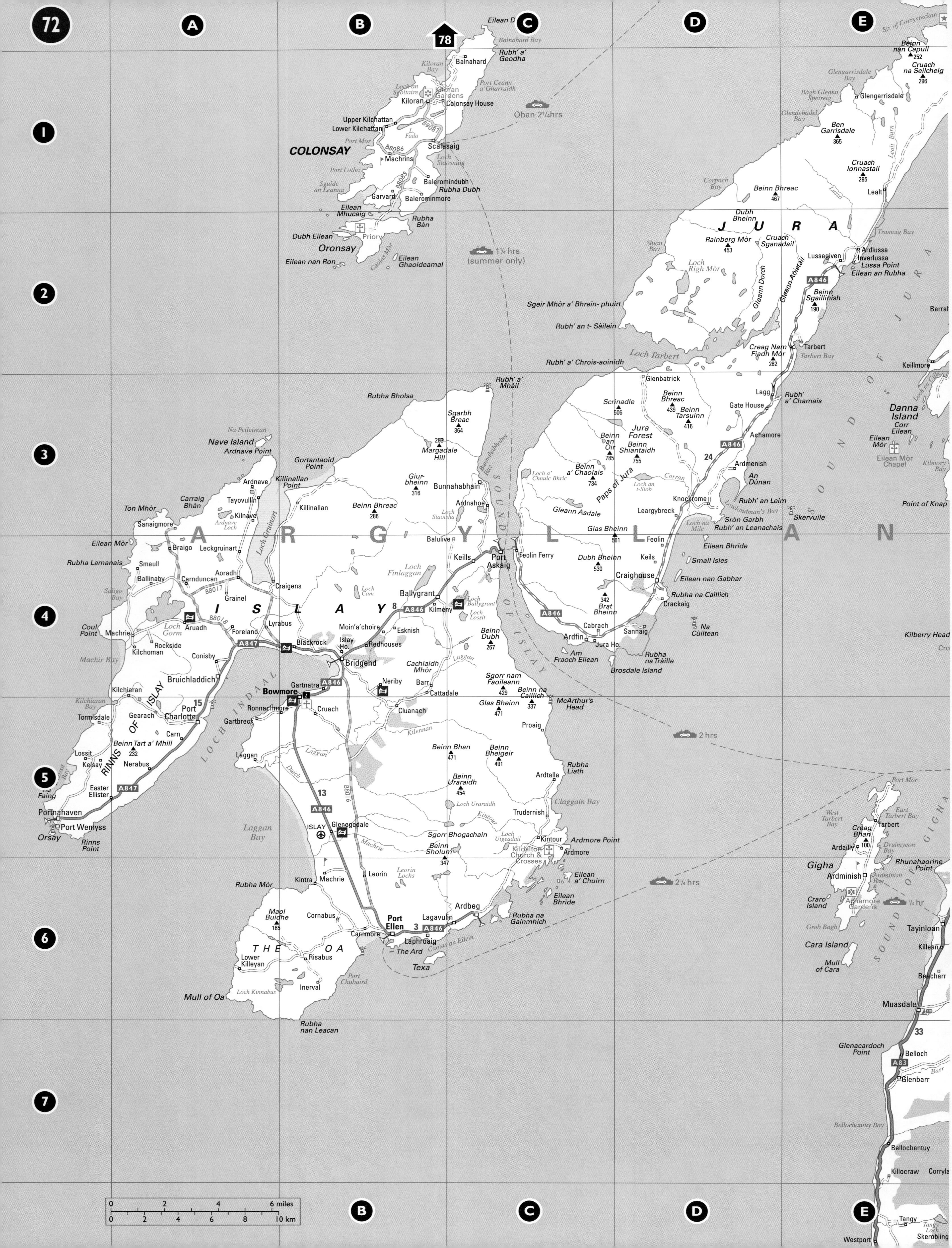
A
B
C
D
E
1
2
3
4
5
6
7
78
Eilean Dubh
Balnahard Bay
Rubh' a' Geodha
Balnahard
Kiloran Bay
Port Ceann a' Gharraidh
Loch an Sgoltaire
Kiloran Gardens
Kiloran
Colonsay House
Oban 2¼hrs
Upper Kilchattan
Lower Kilchattan
Port Mòr
L. Fada
B8087
COLONSAY
B8086
Scalasaig
Loch Staosnaig
Machrins
Port Lotha
Sguide an Leanna
B8085
Baleromindubh
Rubha Dubh
Garvard
Balerominmore
Eilean Mhucaig
Rubha Bàn
Dubh Eilean
Priory
Oronsay
1¼ hrs (summer only)
Caolas Mòr
Eilean Ghaoideamal
Eilean nan Ron
Str. of Corryvreckan
Beinn nan Capull
252
Cruach na Seilcheig
296
Glengarrisdale Bay
Bàgh Gleann Speireig
Glengarrisdale
Glendebadel Bay
Ben Garrisdale
365
Cruach Ionnastail
295
Lealt Burn
Lealt
Corpach Bay
Beinn Bhreac
467
Lussa
Dubh Bheinn
JURA
Tramaig Bay
Shian Bay
Rainberg Mòr
453
Cruach Sganadail
Loch Righ Mòr
Gleann Dorch
Gleann Aoistail
Lussagiven
Ardlussa
Inverlussa
Lussa Point
Eilean an Rubha
A846
Beinn Sgaillinish
190
Sgeir Mhòr a' Bhrein- phuirt
Rubh' an t- Sàilein
Barrah
Creag Nam Fiadh Mòr
262
Tarbert
Tarbert Bay
Loch Tarbert
Rubh' a' Chrois-aoinidh
Keillmore
Glenbatrick
Beinn Bhreac
439
Beinn Tarsuinn
416
Scrinadle
506
Lagg
Rubh' a' Chamais
Rubh' a' Mhàil
Rubha Bholsa
Gate House
Sgarbh Breac
364
Danna Island
Corr Eilean
Jura Forest
Beinn Shiantaidh
755
Beinn an Oir
785
Achamore
Eilean Mòr
Eilean Mòr Chapel
Kilmory Bay
Na Peileirean
Nave Island
Ardnave Point
283
Margadale Hill
Bunnahabhainn Bay
24
Ardmenish
Gortantaoid Point
Killinallan Point
Giur-bheinn
316
Bunnahabhain
Beinn a' Chaolais
734
Loch a' Chnuic Bhric
Paps of Jura
Corran
Loch an t-Siob
An Dùnan
Ardnave
Carraig Bhàn
Tayovullin
Kilnave
Ardnave Loch
Killinallan
Beinn Bhreac
286
Ardnahoe
Loch Staoisha
Gleann Asdale
Leargybreck
Knockrome
Rubh' an Leim
Lowlandman's Bay
Sròn Garbh
Rubh' an Leanachais
Skervuile
Point of Knap
Ton Mhòr
Sanaigmore
Loch Gruinart
SOUND OF ISLAY
Loch na Mile
Glas Bheinn
561
Feolin
ARGYLL AND BUTE
Eilean Mòr
Braigo
Leckgruinart
Balulive
Feolin Ferry
Eilean Bhride
Keills
Port Askaig
Dubh Bheinn
530
Keils
Small Isles
Rubha Lamanais
Smaull
Aoradh
Loch Finlaggan
Craighouse
Eilean nan Gabhar
Saligo Bay
Ballinaby
Carnduncan
B8017
Craigens
Loch Cam
Ballygrant
342
Brat Bheinn
Rubha na Caillich
Crackaig
Grainel
ISLAY
8
Loch Ballygrant
A846
Kilmeny
Loch Lossit
Coul Point
Machrie
Loch Gorm
Aruadh
B8018
Lyrabus
Foreland
Moin'a'choire
Esknish
Cabrach
Sannaig
Na Cùiltean
Kilberry Head
Rockside
A847
Blackrock
Islay Ho.
Redhouses
Beinn Dubh
267
Ardfin
Jura Ho.
Kilchoman
Am Fraoch Eilean
Rubha na Tràille
Brosdale Island
Machir Bay
Conisby
Bridgend
Cachlaidh Mhòr
Laggan
Bruichladdich
Loch Indaal
Kilchiaran
Gartnatra
A846
Neriby
Barr
Sgorr nam Faoileann
429
Beinn na Caillich
337
McArthur's Head
Kilchiaran Bay
Rinns of Islay
15
Bowmore
Port Charlotte
Ronnachmore
Cruach
Cattadale
Glas Bheinn
471
Tormisdale
Gearach
Cluanach
Gartbreck
Proaig
Carn
Kilennan
2 hrs
Beinn Tart a' Mhill
232
Lossit
Kelsay
Lossit Bay
Nerabus
Laggan
Beinn Bhan
471
Beinn Bheigeir
491
Rubha Liath
Duich
B8016
Port Mòr
Na Faing
Easter Ellister
A847
13
Beinn Uraraidh
454
Ardtalla
Loch Uraraidh
Claggain Bay
West Tarbert Bay
East Tarbert Bay
Portnahaven
A846
Kintour
Trudernish
Creag Bhan
100
Tarbert
Port Wemyss
Laggan Bay
ISLAY
Glenegedale
Loch Uigeadail
Sgorr Bhogachain
Ardmore Point
Ardailly
Druimyeon Bay
Orsay
Rinns Point
Machrie
Beinn Sholum
347
Kildalton Church & Crosses
Kintour
Ardmore
Gigha
Ardminish
Ardminish Bay
Rhunahaorine Point
Rubha Mòr
Kintra
Machrie
Leorin
Leorin Lochs
Eilean a' Chuirn
2¼ hrs
Craro Island
Achamore Gardens
¼ hr
Eilean Bhride
Maol Buidhe
165
Cornabus
Ardbeg
Port Ellen
Lagavulin
Rubha na Gainmhich
3
A846
Grob Bagh
Tayinloan
SOUND OF GIGHA
Carnmore
Laphroaig
THE OA
The Ard
Caolas an Eilein
Cara Island
Killean
Lower Killeyan
Risabus
Texa
Mull of Cara
Port Chubaird
Beacharr
Inerval
Loch Kinnabus
Mull of Oa
Muasdale
Rubha nan Leacan
33
Glenacardoch Point
Belloch
A83
Barr
Glenbarr
Bellochantuy Bay
Bellochantuy
Killocraw
Corrylach
0
2
4
6 miles
0
2
4
6
8
10 km
Tangy
Tangy Loch
Westport
Skerobling

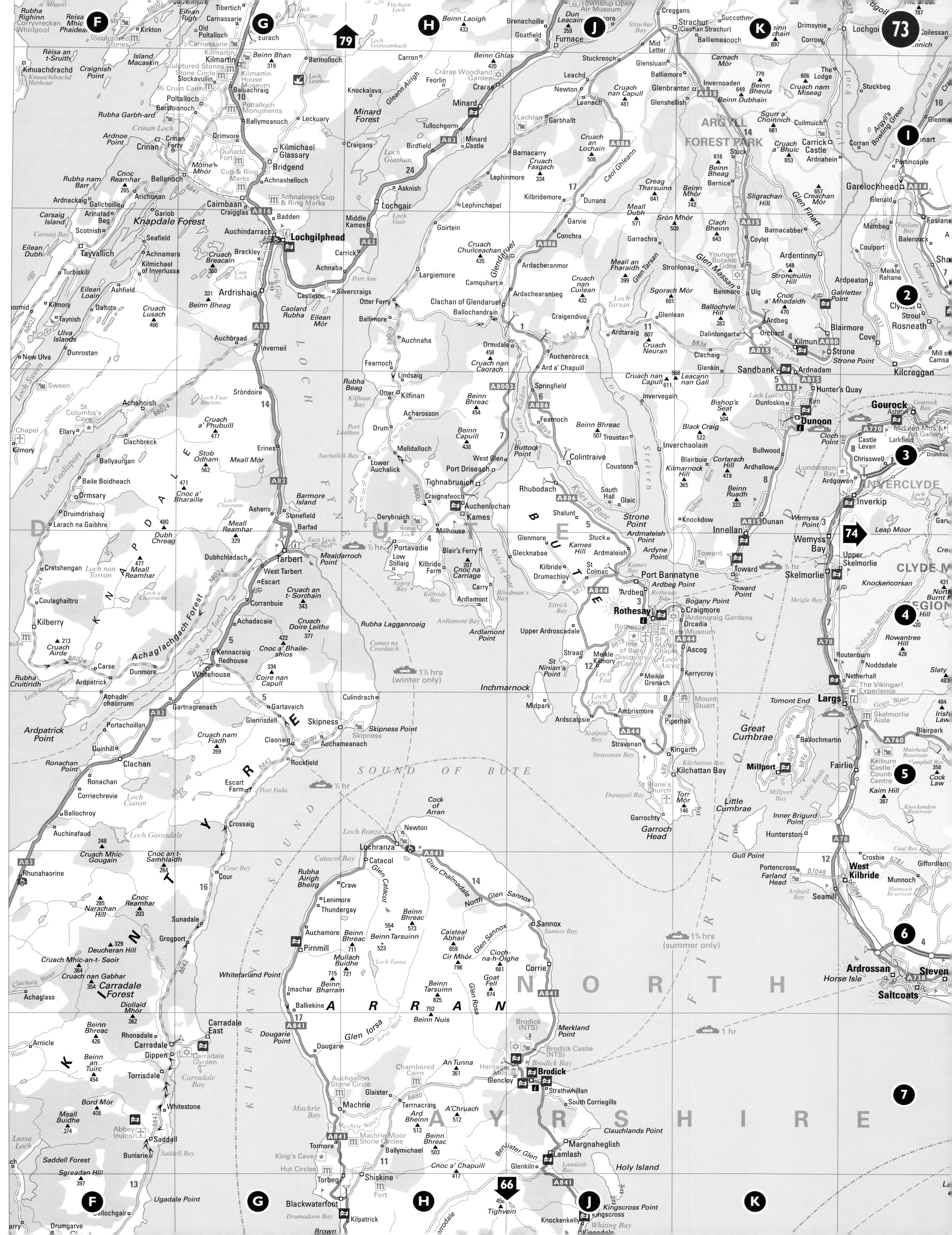

F
G
H
J
K
79
74
66
Rubha Righinn
Corryvreckan Whirlpool
Reisa Mhic Phaidean
Kirkton
Eilean Righ
Tibertich
Carnassarie
Old Poltalloch
Carnassarie
Eurach
Loch Gainneamhach
Fincharn Loch
Beinn Laoigh
433
Dun Leacainn
359
Furnace
Township Open Air Museum
Brenachoille
Goatfield
Strachur Bay
Strachur
(Clachan Strachur)
Creggans
Succothmore
Balliemeanoch
Mid Letter
Beinn Lochain
697
Drimsynie
Lochgoil
Corrow
Colessan
Sculptured Stones
Rèisa an t-Sruith
Island Macaskin
Kilmartin
Beinn Bhan
319
Barmolloch
Carron
Beinn Ghlas
420
Sculptured Stones
Stone Circle
Slockavullin
Kilmartin House Museum
Ri Cruin Cairn
Baluachraig
Loch Leathan
Crarae Woodland Garden
Crarae
Feorlin
Knockalava
Gleann Airigh
Stuckreoch
Glensluain
Carnach Mòr
Leachd
Balliemore
Newton
Leanach
Cruach nan Capull
481
Glenbranter
Glenshellish
Invernoaden
649
Beinn Bheula
779
Beinn Dubhain
A815
The Lodge
606
Cruach nam Miseag
Stuckbeg
Kinuachdrachd
Kinuachdrachd Harbour
Craignish Point
Poltalloch
Barsloisnoch
Poltalloch Monuments
Ballymeanoch
Leckuary
Minard Forest
Minard
Tullochgorm
A83
Minard Castle
Lachlan
Garbhallt
ARGYLL FOREST PARK
Stuck
Sgurr a' Choinnich
661
Cuilmuich
Argyll's Bowling Green
Corran
Rubha Garbh-ard
Crinan Loch
Drimvore
Ardnoe Point
Crinan
Crinan Ferry
Dunadd Fort
Kilmichael Glassary
Craigans
Bridgend
Moine Mhòr
Cup & Ring Marks
Achnashelloch
Loch Glashan
24
Birdfield
Barnacarry
Cruach Fasgach
334
Cruach an Lochain
508
A886
Caol Ghleann
618
Beinn Bheag
Bernice
Cruach a' Bhuic
653
Carrick Castle
Ardnahein
Portincaple
Rubha nam Barr
Cnoc Reamhar
265
Bellanoch
Crinan Canal
B841
Achnabreck Cup & Ring Marks
Asknish
Lephinmore
17
Creag Tharsuinn
641
Beinn Mhòr
742
Sligrachan Hill
657
Creachan Mòr
Garelochhead
A814
Glenald
Ardnackaig
Gallchoille
Arichonan
Cairnbaan
Lochgair
Lephinchapel
Dunans
Kilbridemore
Carsaig Island
Arinafad Beg
Gariob
Knapdale Forest
Craiglass
A816
Badden
Middle Kames
Loch Gair
Meall Dubh
571
Sròn Mhòr
509
Clach Bheinn
643
Glen Finart
Mambeg
Faslane Bay
Scotnish
Carsaig Bay
Auchindarrach
Lochgilphead
Goirtein
Garvie
Conchra
A815
Barnacabber
Coylet
Balernock
Eilean Dubh
Tayvallich
Seafield
Achnamara
Brackley
Carrick
A83
Cruach Chuilceachan
435
A886
Garrachra
Younger Botanic Gdns
Coulport
Turbiskill
Kilmichael of Inverlussa
Cruach Breacain
360
Cam Loch
Loch Gilp
Achnaba
Port Ann
Largiemore
Glendaruel
Ardacheranmor
Meall an Fharaidh
399
Glen Tarsan
Stronlonag
Glen Massan
Ardentinny
548
Stronchullin Hill
Meikle Rahane
Ardpeaton
Gare Loch
Eilean Loain
Ashfield
331
Beinn Bheag
Ardrishaig
Castleton
Silvercraigs
Camquhart
Ardachearanbeg
Cruach an Cuilean
432
Loch Tarsan
Sgorach Mòr
601
Benmore
Uig
Cnoc a' Mhadaidh
470
Gairletter Point
Clynder
2
Kilmory
Taynish
Daltote
Cruach Lusach
466
Caolard Rubha
Eilean Mòr
Otter Ferry
Ballimore
Clachan of Glendaruel
Ballochandrain
Craigendive
Glenlean
Ballochyle Hill
382
Ardbeg
Orchard
Blairmore
Stroul
Rosneath
Cove
Ulva Islands
Auchbraad
Inverneil
Auchnaha
Ormidale
458
Cruach nan Caorach
B836
Ardtaraig
607
Cruach Neuran
Dalinlongart
Kilmun
A880
Strone
Strone Point
Kilcreggan
New Ulva
Dunrostan
Loch Sween
Fearnoch
Lindsaig
Auchenbreck
Ard a' Chapuill
Clachaig
Glenkin
Sandbank
Ardnadam
Holy Loch
Mill of Camsa
Sween
Sròndoire
Rubha Beag
Kilfinan Bay
Otter
Kilfinan
A8003
Springfield
Cruach nan Capull
611
568
Leacann nan Gall
A815
Hunter's Quay
Achahoish
Loch Fuar Bheinne
14
Beinn Bhreac
454
Loch Riddon
A886
Invervegain
Bishop's Seat
504
Loch Loskin
Dunloskin
Kirn
Dunoon
Gourock
Gourock Bay
Ashton
St Columba's Cave
Cruach a' Phubuill
477
Acharosson
Fearnoch
Beinn Bhreac
507
Troustan
Black Craig
522
A770
McLean Mus & Art Gallery
Chapel
Ellary
Port Leathan
Drum
Beinn Capuill
438
Cloch Point
Castle Levan
Larkfield
Kilmory
Clachbreck
Erines
Auchalick Bay
Melldalloch
West Glen
Buttock Point
Colintraive
Inverchaolain
Bullwood
Chrisswell
3
Drumfrochar
Ballyaurgan
Stob Odham
562
Meall Mòr
Lower Auchalick
Port Driseach
Coustonn
Blairbuie
Kilmarnock Hill
365
Corlarach Hill
419
Ardhallow
Lunderston Bay
Ardgowan
Loch Caolisport
Baile Boidheach
471
Cnoc a' Bharaille
A83
Tighnabruaich
Rhubodach
South Hall
Glaic
Beinn Ruadh
323
INVERCLYDE
Ormsary
Loch Chaorunn
Barmore Island
Ashens
Craignafeoch
Auchenlochan
Kames
Kyles of Bute
Strone Point
Inverkip
Loch Thom
Druimdrishaig
480
Dubh Chreag
Meall Reamhar
329
Stonefield
Barfad
Derybruich
Asgog Loch
Millhouse
Shalunt
Ardmaleish Point
Knockdow
A815
Dunan
Wemyss Point
Garv
Larach na Gaibhre
East Loch Tarbert
½ hr
Portavadie
Blair's Ferry
Glenmore
Stuck
Innellan
Wemyss Bay
Leap Moor
Dubhchladach
Tarbert
Mealdarroch Point
Low Stillaig
Kilbride Farm
207
Cnoc na Carriage
Glecknabae
Kames Hill
Ardmaleish
Ardyne Point
Toward
Upper Skelmorlie
CLYDE M
Cretshengan
Loch nan Torran
477
Meall Reamhar
B8024
West Tarbert
Escart
Asgog Bay
Kilbride Bay
Carry
Kilbride
Drumachloy
St Colmac
Kames Bay
Port Bannatyne
Ardbeg Point
Toward
Skelmorlie
Knockencorsan
431
Loch a' Chaorainn
Cruach an t-Sorchain
343
Ardlamont
Blindman's Bay
Ardbeg
Rothesay Bay
Toward Point
North Burnt Hill
Coulaghailtro
Corranbuie
Etterick Bay
Bogany Point
Craigmore
Ardencraig Gardens
Meigle Bay
REGION
Kilberry
Achaglachgach Forest
Achadacaie
Cruach Doire Leithe
377
Rubha Lagganroaig
Ardlamont Bay
Rothesay
Bute Museum
Orcadia
4
Hill
420
Cruach Airde
213
Kennacraig
Redhouse
West Loch Tarbert
422
Cnoc a' Bhaile-shios
Camas na Ceardaich
Ardlamont Point
Upper Ardroscadale
Isle of Bute Discovery Centre
St Mary's Chapel
Loch Ascog
Ascog
A844
A78
Rowantree Hill
428
Carse
Dunmore
Whitehouse
334
Coire nan Capull
1½ hrs (winter only)
Straad
Meikle Kilmory
Loch Fad
Kerrycroy
Routenburn
Noddsdale
Slaty
Rubha Cruitiridh
Ardpatrick
Loch Stornoway
St Ninian's Point
Meikle Grenach
Netherhall
The Vikingar! Experience
483
Achadh-chaorrunn
Inchmarnock
Loch Quien
Mount Stuart
Largs
Gogo Water
484
Tomont End
Gartnagrenach
Gartavaich
Culindrach
Midpark
Ardscalpsie
Ambrismore
Piperhall
Skelmorlie Aisle
Irish Law
Ardpatrick Point
Portachoillan
Glenrisdell
Skipness
Skipness Point
Scalpsie Bay
A844
Great Cumbrae
Blairpark
Quinhill
Cruach nam Fiadh
269
Claonaig
Auchameanach
Stravanan
Stravanan Bay
Kingarth
Ballochmartin
A760
Muirhead Reservoir
Camphill Res
Ronachan Point
Clachan
Rockfield
SOUND OF BUTE
Kilchattan Bay
Millport
Fairlie
Kelburn Castle Country Centre
5
358
Cock Law
Ronachan
Escart Farm
Port Fada
½ hr
St Blane's Church
Millport Bay
Kaim Hill
387
Corriechrevie
Loch Ciaran
Cock of Arran
Dunagoil Bay
Torr Mòr
146
Little Cumbrae
Knockendon Reservoir
Ballochroy
Crossaig
Garrochty
Inner Brigurd Point
Garroch Head
Hunterston
Auchinafaud
248
Loch Garasdale
Loch Ranza
Newton
Lochranza
A841
Catacol Bay
Gull Point
Caaf Res
A83
Cruach Mhic-Gougain
Cnoc an t-Samhlaidh
264
Cour Bay
Cour
Catacol
Glen Catacol
Glen Chalmadale
14
Crosbie
Giffordland
Portencross
B7048
West Kilbride
Rhunahaorine
Rubha Airigh Bheirg
Craw
Farland Head
Munnoch
16
Lenimore
North Glen Sannox
Ardneil Bay
Seamill
Munnoch Reservoir
285
Narachan Hill
Cnoc Reamhar
203
Thundergay
Beinn Bhreac
573
Sannox
Sannox Bay
Sunadale
554
Auchamore
Beinn Bhreac
711
Beinn Tarsuinn
523
Caisteal Abhail
859
Glen Sannox
1¾ hrs (summer only)
6
329
Deucheran Hill
Grogport
Pirnmill
Cir Mhòr
798
Cìoch-na-h-Oighe
661
Corrie
Cruach Mhic-an-t-Saoir
Loch Tanna
Ardrossan
Mullach Buidhe
721
715
364
Cruach nan Gabhar
Whitefarland Point
Goat Fell
874
Horse Isle
A738
Stevenston
354
Carradale Forest
Beinn Tarsuinn
825
Glen Rosa
NORTH
Clachaig Water
Achaglass
Imachar
Beinn Bharrain
A841
Saltcoats
Diollaid Mhòr
362
Balliekine
ARRAN
792
Beinn Nuis
Carradale East
Brodick
Merkland Point
Beinn Bhreac
426
Rhonadale
Glen Iorsa
Dougarie Point
Iorsa Water
1 hr
Arnicle
Carradale
Dougarie
Brodick Castle (NTS)
Dippen
Carradale Garden
Beinn an Tuirc
454
Torrisdale
Carradale Bay
Chambered Cairn
An Tunna
361
Heritage Mus
Brodick Bay
Glencloy
Strathwhillan
Auchgallon Stone Circle
Glaister
South Corriegills
7
Bord Mòr
408
Meall Buidhe
374
Whitestone
Machrie Bay
Machrie
Tarrnacraig
B880
A' Chruach
512
Ard Bheinn
512
AYRSHIRE
Abbey (ruins)
Saddell
B842
Machrie Water
Machrie Moor Stone Circles
Beinn Bhreac
503
Clauchlands Point
Lussa Loch
Bunlarie
Saddell Bay
Tormore
A841
Ballymichael
Benlister Glen
Margnaheglish
Lamlash
King's Cave
Saddell Forest
Hut Circles
11
Cnoc a' Chapuill
417
Glenkiln
Holy Island
Sgreadan Hill
397
Lamlash Bay
13
Torbeg
Shiskine
A841
Ugadale Point
Fort
Ballochgair
Blackwaterfoot
Drumadoon Bay
Tighvein
456
Kingscross Point
Kingscross
Knockenkelly
Kilpatrick
Drumgarve
Brown
Whiting Bay
Kingsdale

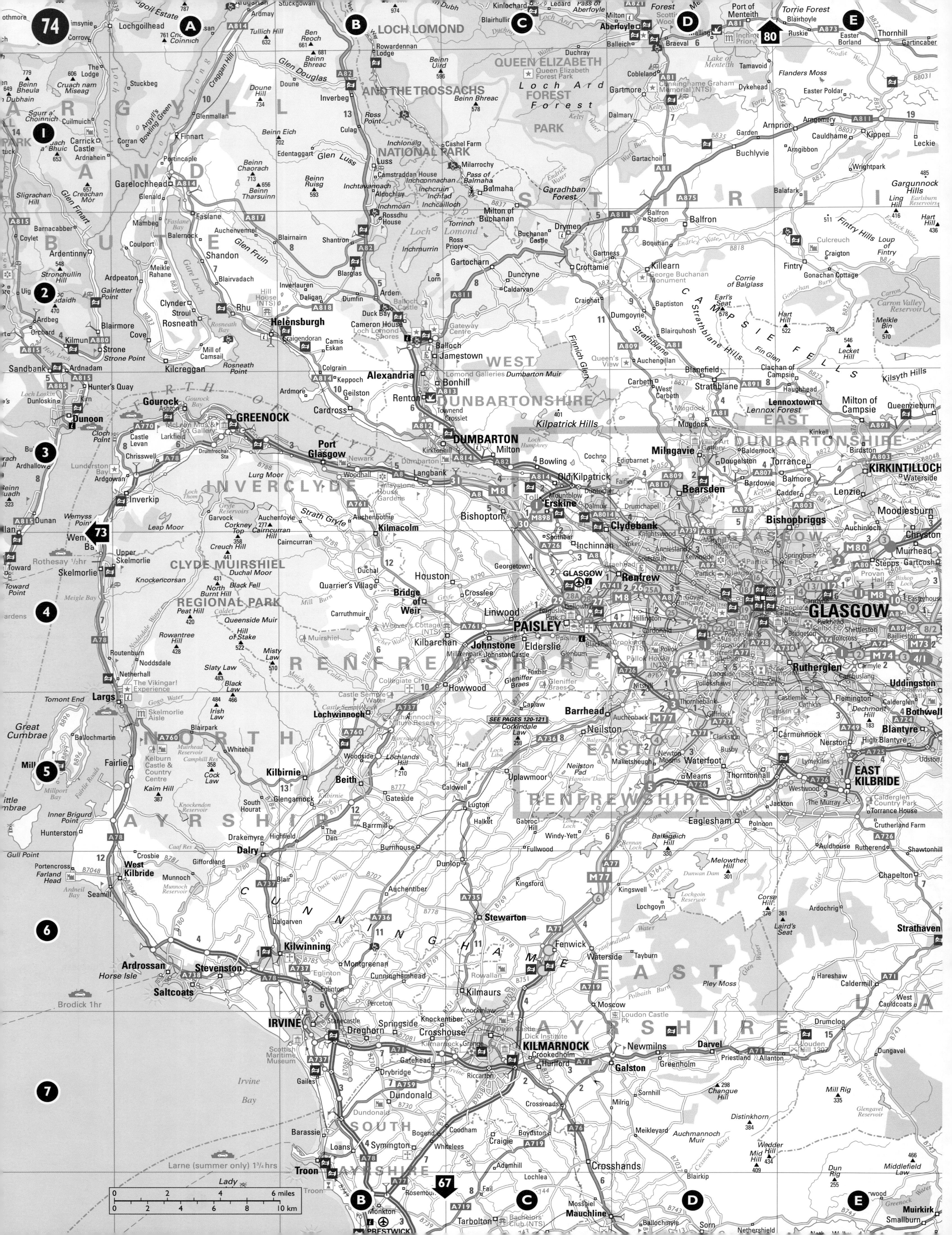

74
LOCH LOMOND
QUEEN ELIZABETH FOREST PARK
AND THE TROSSACHS NATIONAL PARK
Loch Ard Forest
80
73
67
ARGYLL AND BUTE
STIRLING
WEST DUNBARTONSHIRE
EAST DUNBARTONSHIRE
INVERCLYDE
RENFREWSHIRE
EAST RENFREWSHIRE
NORTH AYRSHIRE
EAST AYRSHIRE
SOUTH AYRSHIRE
CUNNINGHAME
CAMPSIE FELLS
CLYDE MUIRSHIEL REGIONAL PARK
FIRTH OF CLYDE
Kilpatrick Hills
Lochgoilhead
Aberfoyle
Port of Menteith
Thornhill
Kippen
Arnprior
Buchlyvie
Balfron
Drymen
Killearn
Fintry
Strathblane
Lennoxtown
Milton of Campsie
Kilsyth Hills
Garelochhead
Helensburgh
Rhu
Rosneath
Kilcreggan
Dunoon
Sandbank
Gourock
GREENOCK
Port Glasgow
Balloch
Alexandria
Jamestown
Bonhill
Renton
DUMBARTON
Milngavie
Bearsden
KIRKINTILLOCH
Bishopbriggs
Clydebank
Erskine
Bishopton
Kilmacolm
Inverkip
Wemyss Bay
Skelmorlie
Largs
Fairlie
Great Cumbrae
Millport
West Kilbride
Ardrossan
Saltcoats
Stevenston
Kilwinning
IRVINE
Troon
PRESTWICK
Houston
Bridge of Weir
Linwood
PAISLEY
Johnstone
Elderslie
Renfrew
GLASGOW
Rutherglen
Barrhead
Neilston
Newton Mearns
EAST KILBRIDE
Blantyre
Uddingston
Eaglesham
Lochwinnoch
Kilbirnie
Beith
Dalry
Howwood
Stewarton
Kilmaurs
Fenwick
KILMARNOCK
Galston
Newmilns
Darvel
Strathaven
Mauchline
Tarbolton
Symington
Dundonald
Crosshouse
Dreghorn
SEE PAGES 120-121
Larne (summer only) 1¾ hrs
Brodick 1hr
Rothesay ½hr
Irvine Bay
0 2 4 6 miles
0 2 4 6 8 10 km

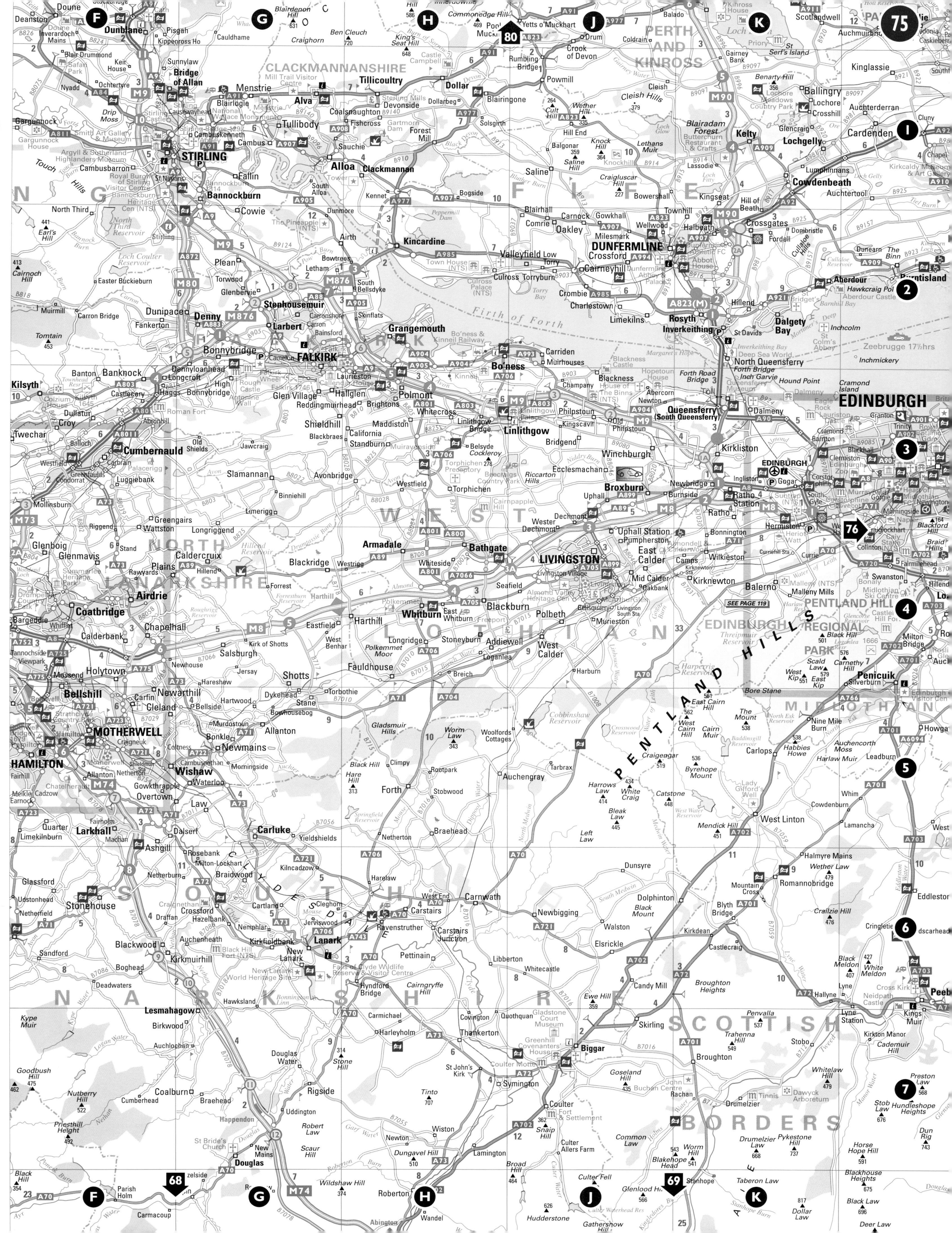
PERTH AND KINROSS
CLACKMANNANSHIRE
FIFE
FALKIRK
WEST LOTHIAN
NORTH LANARKSHIRE
SOUTH LANARKSHIRE
MIDLOTHIAN
SCOTTISH BORDERS
EDINBURGH
PENTLAND HILLS
PENTLAND HILLS REGIONAL PARK
CLYDESDALE
Firth of Forth
Doune
Dunblane
Bridge of Allan
STIRLING
Bannockburn
Tillicoultry
Alva
Dollar
Menstrie
Tullibody
Alloa
Clackmannan
Kincardine
Dunfermline
Kelty
Cowdenbeath
Lochgelly
Cardenden
Ballingry
Kinglassie
Kirkcaldy Museum & Art Gallery
Burntisland
Aberdour
Dalgety Bay
Inverkeithing
Rosyth
North Queensferry
Queensferry (South Queensferry)
Kirkliston
Ratho
Ratho Station
Newbridge
Broxburn
Uphall
Winchburgh
Linlithgow
Bo'ness
Grangemouth
FALKIRK
Larbert
Stenhousemuir
Denny
Bonnybridge
Banknock
Kilsyth
Cumbernauld
Croy
Airdrie
Coatbridge
Chapelhall
Holytown
Bellshill
MOTHERWELL
HAMILTON
Wishaw
Newmains
Carluke
Larkhall
Stonehouse
Lanark
New Lanark
Carstairs
Carnwath
Forth
Shotts
Harthill
Whitburn
Blackburn
Bathgate
Armadale
LIVINGSTON
East Calder
Mid Calder
West Calder
Kirknewton
Balerno
Currie
Penicuik
West Linton
Carlops
Biggar
Symington
Lesmahagow
Douglas
Abington
Peebles
Tinto
Culter Fell
Zeebrugge 17½hrs
SEE PAGE 119
80
76
68
69
A9
M9
M90
M80
M876
M8
M74
A70
A71
A72
A701
A702
A703
A90
A720
A985
A904
A905
A801
A89
A73
A721
A706
A743
A707
A721
A823(M)

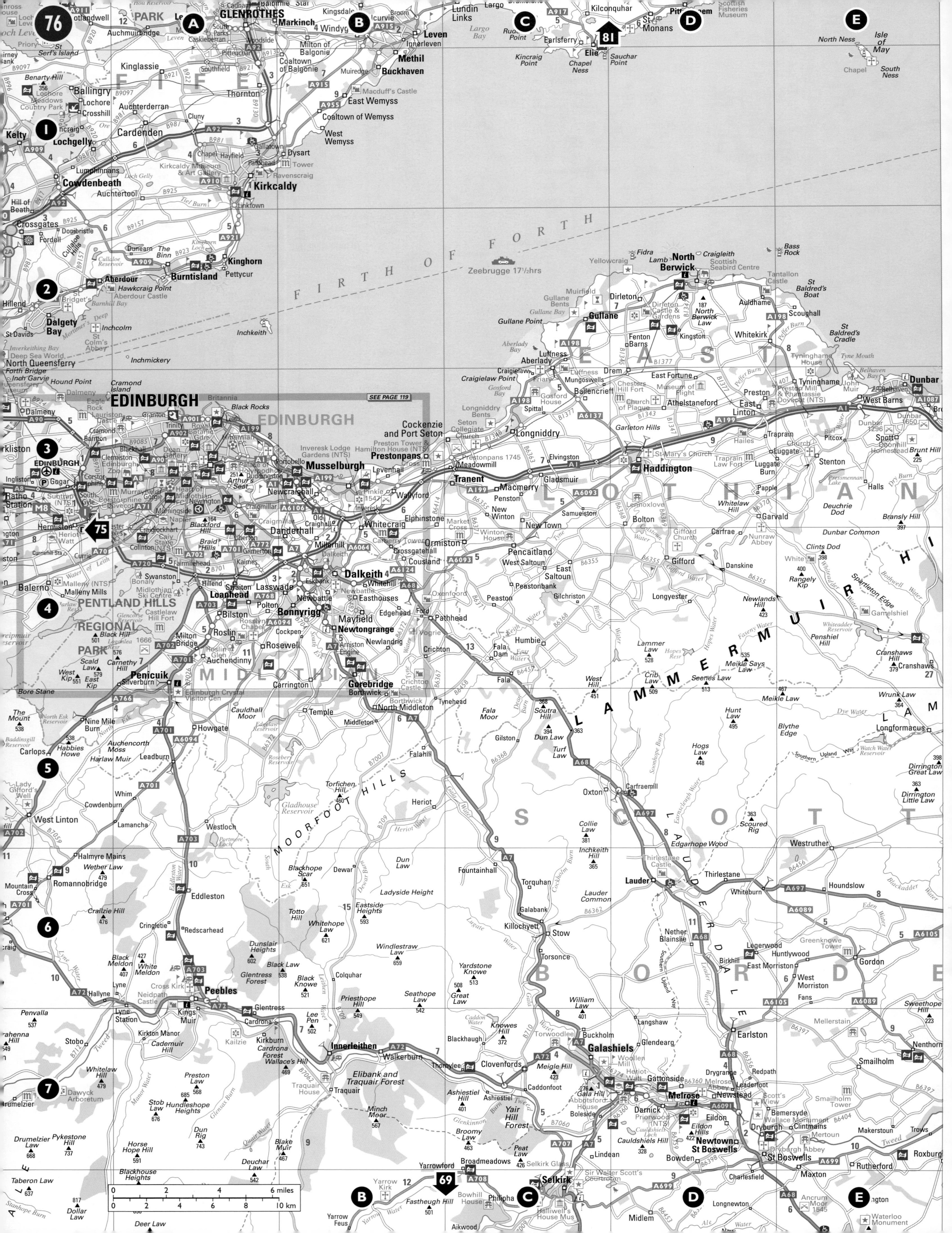
GLENROTHES
Markinch
Windygates
Leven
Lundin Links
Largo Bay
Kilconquhar
Pittenweem
St Monans
Scottish Fisheries Museum
Isle of May
North Ness
South Ness
Chapel
Earlsferry
Elie
Chapel Ness
Sauchar Point
Kincraig Point
Ruddons Point
Innerleven
Methil
Buckhaven
Milton of Balgonie
Coaltown of Balgonie
Macduff's Castle
East Wemyss
Coaltown of Wemyss
West Wemyss
Auchmuirbridge
Scotlandwell
St Serf's Island
Kinglassie
Southfield
Thornton
FIFE
Benarty Hill
356
Ballingry
Lochore Meadows Country Park
Lochore
Crosshill
Auchterderran
Cardenden
Cluny
Kelty
Lochgelly
Dysart
Gallatown
Pathhead
Ravenscraig
Tower
Chapel
Hayfield
Kirkcaldy Museum & Art Gallery
Lumphinnans
Cowdenbeath
Loch Gelly
Kirkcaldy
Linktown
Auchtertool
Tiel Burn
Hill of Beath
Crossgates
Donibristle
Fordell
Cullaloe Hills
Cullaloe Reservoir
Dunearn
The Binn
Kinghorn Loch
Kinghorn
Pettycur
Burntisland
Aberdour
Hawkcraig Point
Aberdour Castle
St Bridget's
Hillend
Dalgety Bay
Inchcolm
St Colm's Abbey
St Davids
Inverkeithing Bay
Deep Sea World
North Queensferry
Forth Bridge
Inchkeith
Inchmickery
FIRTH OF FORTH
Zeebrugge 17½hrs
Fidra
Yellowcraig
Lamb
North Berwick
Craigleith
Bass Rock
Scottish Seabird Centre
Tantallon Castle
St Baldred's Boat
Dirleton
Dirleton Castle & Gardens
Muirfield
Gullane Bents
Gullane Bay
Gullane
Gullane Point
North Berwick Law
187
Kingston
Auldhame
Scoughall
Whitekirk
St Baldred's Cradle
Peffer Burn
Fenton Barns
Aberlady Bay
Luffness
Aberlady
Craigielaw Point
Luffness Mungoswells
Drem
East Fortune
Museum of Flight
Tyninghame House
Tyne Mouth
Tyninghame
Belhaven Bay
Dunbar
Belhaven
John Muir
Gosford Bay
Gosford House
Spittal
Ballencrieff
Chesters Hill Fort
Church of Plague
Athelstaneford
Preston
Preston Mill & Phantassie Dovecot (NTS)
East Linton
West Barns
EAST LOTHIAN
Longniddry Bents
Seton Collegiate Church
Longniddry
Garleton Hills
Cockenzie and Port Seton
Prestonpans
Preston Tower & Hamilton House (NTS)
Prestonpans 1745
Meadowmill
Inveresk Lodge Gardens (NTS)
Traprain
Hailes
Pitcox
Dunbar 1296
Dunbar 1650
Spott
Doonhill Homestead
Brunt Hill
225
St Mary's Church
Haddington
Traprain Law Fort
Luggate
Luggate Burn
Stenton
Elvingston
Gladsmuir
Tranent
Macmerry
Penston
Pressmennan Lake
Papple
Halls
Deuchrie Dod
Bransly Hill
397
Dunbar Common
Whitelaw Hill
Garvald
Lennoxlove
Samuelston
Bolton
New Winton
New Town
Gifford Church
Carfrae
Nunraw Abbey
Gifford
Danskine
Clints Dod
398
Whiteadder Water
Rangely Kip
400
Spartleton Edge
Newlands Hill
423
Gamelshiel
Whiteadder Reservoir
Penshiel Hill
Cranshaws Hill
379
Cranshaws
LAMMERMUIR HILLS
EDINBURGH
Britannia
Black Rocks
Granton
Trinity
Royal Botanic Gdn
Leith
Dalmeny
Eagle Rock
Cramond
Cramond Island
Barnton
Clermiston
Edinburgh Zoo
Corstorphine
Murrayfield
Gorgie
Dean Gallery
Palace of Holyroodhouse
Arthur's Seat
251
Duddingston
Newington
Morningside
Portobello
Musselburgh
Levenhall
Wallyford
Pinkie 1547
Inveresk
Newcraighall
Craigmillar
Danderhall
Whitecraig
Elphinstone
Ormiston
Carberry Tower
Crossgatehall
Cousland
Winton House
Pencaitland
West Saltoun
East Saltoun
Peastonbank
Gilchriston
Longyester
Kirkliston
EDINBURGH
Gogar
Ingliston
Ratho Station
Hermiston
Heriot Watt
Sighthill
Currie
Currie Hill Sta
Balerno
Malleny (NTS)
Malleny Mills
Swanston
Bonaly
Colinton
Fairmilehead
Braid Hills
Blackford Hill
164
Craiglockhart
Gilmerton
Liberton
Hillend
Midlothian Ski Centre
Straiton
Loanhead
Lasswade
Eskbank
Dalkeith
Whitehill
Newbattle
Easthouses
Bonnyrigg
Polton
Bilston
Castlelaw Hill Fort
PENTLAND HILLS REGIONAL PARK
Glencorse Reservoir
Harlaw Res
Black Hill
501
Roslin
Rosslyn Chapel
Rosslyn Glen
Milton Bridge
Cockpen
Mayfield
Newtongrange
Edgehead
Ford
Pathhead
Oxenfoord
Peaston
Newlandrig
Arniston Engine
Vogrie
Crichton
Crichton Castle
Rosewell
Auchendinny
Penicuik
Silverburn
Edinburgh Crystal Visitor Cen
Carnethy Hill
576
Scald Law
579
East Kip
West Kip
551
Bore Stane
1666
MIDLOTHIAN
Gorebridge
Borthwick
Borthwick Castle
North Middleton
Carrington
Tynehead
Keith Water
Humbie
Fala Dam
Fala
Fala Moor
Lammer Law
528
Crib Law
509
Hopes Reservoir
Meikle Says Law
535
Seenes Law
513
Meikle Law
467
West Hill
451
Soutra Hill
368
Dun Law
394
Turf Law
363
Wrunk Law
364
Dye Water
Blythe Edge
Longformacus
Hunt Law
495
Hogs Law
448
Southern Upland Way
Watch Water Reservoir
Dirrington Great Law
398
Dirrington Little Law
363
The Mount
538
North Esk Reservoir
Baddinsgill Reservoir
Nine Mile Burn
Carlops
Habbies Howe
Auchencorth Moss
Harlaw Muir
Leadburn
Howgate
Cauldhall Moor
Temple
Middleton
Gladhouse Reservoir
Rosebery Reservoir
Edgelaw Reservoir
Falahill
Gilston
Lady Gifford's Well
Whim
Cowdenburn
Lamancha
Torfichen Hill
460
MOORFOOT HILLS
Heriot
West Linton
Westloch
Portmore Loch
Halmyre Mains
Wether Law
479
Romannobridge
Mountain Cross
Craigie Hill
476
Cringletie
Redscarhead
Eddleston
Blackhope Scar
651
Dewar
Dun Law
Totto Hill
Eastside Heights
593
Whitehope Law
621
Ladyside Height
Fountainhall
Torquhan
Galabank
Killochyett
Stow
Torsonce
Oxton
Carfraemill
Collie Law
381
Inchkeith Hill
365
Scoured Rig
363
Edgarhope Wood
Westruther
Thirlestane Castle
Lauder
Thirlestane
Lauder Common
Whiteburn
Houndslow
LAUDERDALE
SCOTT
Nether Blainslie
Legerwood
Greenknowe Tower
Gordon
Huntlywood
Birkhill
East Morriston
West Morriston
Fans
Sweethope Hill
223
Mellerstain
Earlston
Langshaw
Glendearg
Nenthorn
Smailholm
Redpath
Drygrange
Leaderfoot
Smailholm Tower
Newstead
Scott's View
Bemersyde
Wallace Monument
Clintmains
Mertoun
Makerstoun
Trows
Dryburgh
Dryburgh Abbey
St Boswells
Newtown St Boswells
Eildon
Eildon Hills
422
Melrose
Melrose Abbey
Darnick
Priorwood (NTS)
Cauldshiels Hill
328
Bowden
Lindean
Gala Hill
276
Abbotsford House
Boleside
Galashiels
Torwoodlee
Buckholm
Gattonside
Clovenfords
Meigle Hill
423
Caddonfoot
Ashiestiel Hill
401
Ashiestiel
Yair Hill Forest
Broomy Law
463
Peat Law
426
Selkirk Glass
Sir Walter Scott's Courtroom
Selkirk
Philiphaugh
Halliwell's House Mus
Broadmeadows
Bowhill House
Yarrowford
Yarrow Kirk
Fastheugh Hill
501
Yarrow Feus
Aikwood
Midlem
Longnewton
Ancrum Moor 1545
Waterloo Monument
Maxton
Charlesfield
Rutherford
Roxburgh
Black Meldon
407
White Meldon
427
Cross Kirk
Neidpath Castle
Peebles
Kings Muir
Glentress
Glentress Forest
Dunslair Heights
602
Black Law
538
Black Knowe
521
Colquhar
Windlestraw Law
659
Yardstone Knowe
513
Great Law
508
Priesthope Hill
549
Seathope Law
542
William Law
401
Caddon Water
Knowes Hill
372
Blackhaugh
Thornylee
Innerleithen
Walkerburn
Cardrona
Kirkburn
Cardrona Forest
Wallace's Hill
469
Traquair House
Traquair
Elibank and Traquair Forest
Minch Moor
567
Lee Pen
502
Kailzie
Hallyne
Lyne
Lyne Station
Kirkton Manor
Cademuir Hill
Penvalla
537
Stobo
Whitelaw Hill
479
Dawyck Arboretum
Drumelzier
Drumelzier Law
668
Pykestone Hill
737
Stob Law
676
Hundleshope Heights
685
Preston Law
568
Horse Hope Hill
591
Dun Rig
743
Blake Muir
467
Deuchar Law
542
Blackhouse Heights
Taberon Law
637
Dollar Law
817
Deer Law
SEE PAGE 119
75
81
69
0 2 4 6 miles
0 2 4 6 8 10 km

F
G
H
J
K
1
2
3
4
5
6
7
Barns Ness
Skateraw
Skateraw Harbour
Thorntonloch
Innerwick
Reed Point
Cove
Pease Bay
Siccar Point
Cocklaw Hill
319
Bilsdean
Dunglass Church
Cockburnspath
Oldhamstocks
Fast
Wheat Stack
Telegraph Hill
174
St Abb's Head
Lumsdaine
Coldingham Loch
St Abb's Head (NTS)
Northfield
St Abbs
Coldingham Bay
A1107
245
Meikle Black Law
Coldingham Moor
Ecclaw
277
Ecclaw Hill
Heart Law
391
Monynut Edge
Southern Upland Way
Blackburn Rig
Grantshouse
13
Coldingham
Priory
Press
Mus
A1107
Eyemouth
Laughing Law
307
Abbey St Bathans
Abbey & Trout Farm
Houndwood
9
Cairncross
Horseley Hill
262
Reston
Ayton
Burnmouth
Ellemford
Cockburn Law
325
Edin's Hall Broch
A6112
Drakemire
Marygold
B6438
Auchencrow
Millerton Hill
132
Ayton Hill
199
Hilton Bay
Lamberton Beach
Preston
Lintlaw
Lamberton
Marshall Meadows
Blanerne
Chirnside
Tithe Barn
Mordington Holdings
Halidon Hill
Needles Eye
Edrom Norman Arch
Edrom
Chirnsidebridge
16
A6105
Fouldon
Clappers
163
Sharper's Head
Duns
Manderston
Allanton
Hutton
Halidon Hill 1333
Highfields
Ravensdowne Barracks
Berwick-upon-Tweed
A6105
A6112
Gavinton
Blackadder
Whitelaw
Sunwick
Paxton
Berwick (ruins)
Tweedmouth
Choicelee
Polwarth
Sinclair's Hill
Fishwick
Paxton House
Union Bridge
East Ord
Spittal
Redshin Cove
Whitsome
Horncliffe
Longridge Towers
A1167
Scremerston
Hule Moss
Greenlaw Moor
Fogo
Fogo Church
Fogorig
Horndean
Lady Kirk Church
Ladykirk
Thornton Park
Norham
Murton
Thornton
Cheswick Black Rocks
A6105
Swinton
Swinton Quarter
12
Upsettlington
A698
Allerdean Burn
Cheswick
Greenlaw
Swintonmill
A6112
Norham
Shoreswood
Shoresdean
West Allerdean
Cheswick Buildings
Goswick
Purves Hall
Simprim
Grindon
Ancroft
Holy Island (Lindisfarne)
Emmanuel Head
10
Leitholm
Felkington
Berrington
Haggerston
Easter Howlaws
Orange Lane
Duddo
Beal
Lindisfarne National Nature Reserve
St Mary
St Aidan's Winery
Lambden
Castle Heaton
Bowsden
West Mains
Holy Island
Castle Point
Hume
Humehall
Hume
Legars
Eccles
The Hirsel
Lennel
Coldstream Museum
Coldstream
Cornhill on Tweed
Etal
Barmoor Lane End
West Kyloe
Holy Island Sands
Fenham
Priory
Lindisfarne (NT)
Burrows Hole
Guile Point
12
Bigham
Carham
Wark
West Learmouth
New Heaton
Pallinsburn House
Crookham Eastfield
Crookham
Lowick
Fenwick
East Kyloe
Kyloe Hills
Fenham Flats
Longstone
Stichill
Ednam
A697
Branxton
Mardon
Ford
Buckton
Farne Islands National Nature Reserve
Farne Islands
Hendersyde Park
A698
Hadden
East Learmouth
Flodden 1513
Holburn
Detchant
Elwick
Ross
Budle Bay
Budle Point
Grace Darling Museum
Staple Sound
Farne Island
Kelso
Sprouston
Pressen
Flodden
Kimmerston
Cockenheugh
211
Middleton
Low Middleton
Easington
Budle
Bamburgh Castle
Inner Sound
Kelso
Kelso Abbey
Maxwellheugh
A699
Mindrummill
Downham
NORTHUMBERLAND
15
Milfield
Fenton
Belford
Waren Mill
Bamburgh
Monks House Rocks
Lempitlaw
Mindrum
Howtel
Housedon Hill
267
North Hazelrigg
Outchester
Spindlestone
Glororum
Burton
Marine Life Centre & Fishing Museum
Pawston
Kilham
Kilham Hill
328
A697
Nesbit
Doddington
South Hazelrigg
Bradford
Shoreston
New
Seahouses
Blakelaw
Lanton
Coupland
Ewart Newtown
East Horton
Roman Road
North Sunderland
8
Venchen Hill
269
Westnewton
Kirknewton
Glen
Homildon Hill 1402
West Horton
10
Warenton
Bellshill
Adderstone
Lucker
Elford
East Fleetham
Beadnell
Heiton
Bowmont Forest
Yetholm Mains
Yeavering Bell
361
Yeavering
Akeld
Greendykes
Newham Hall
Benthall
70
71
Humbleton
Wooler
Chatton
Newham
Swinhoe
Kirk Yetholm
Town Yetholm
Hethpool
Newton Tors
Twizell House
Newstead
West Fleetham
Beadnell Bay
Frogden
282
Linton Hill
Kale Water
Fredden Hill
Earle
Haugh Head
Wandon
Rosebrough
Chillingham
Chathill
LAMMERMUIR HILLS
MERSE
Motability
The leading car scheme for disabled people
Motability at Henry Bros.
If you are looking for a BMW under the Motability Scheme, call our Motability Specialist today.
Henry Bros Kyle Street, Glasgow.
0141 333 0088
www.henrybrosbmw.co.uk
Opening hours: Sales Mon-Fri 9am-6pm Sat 9am-5pm
Henry Bros
BMW
The Ultimate Driving Machine

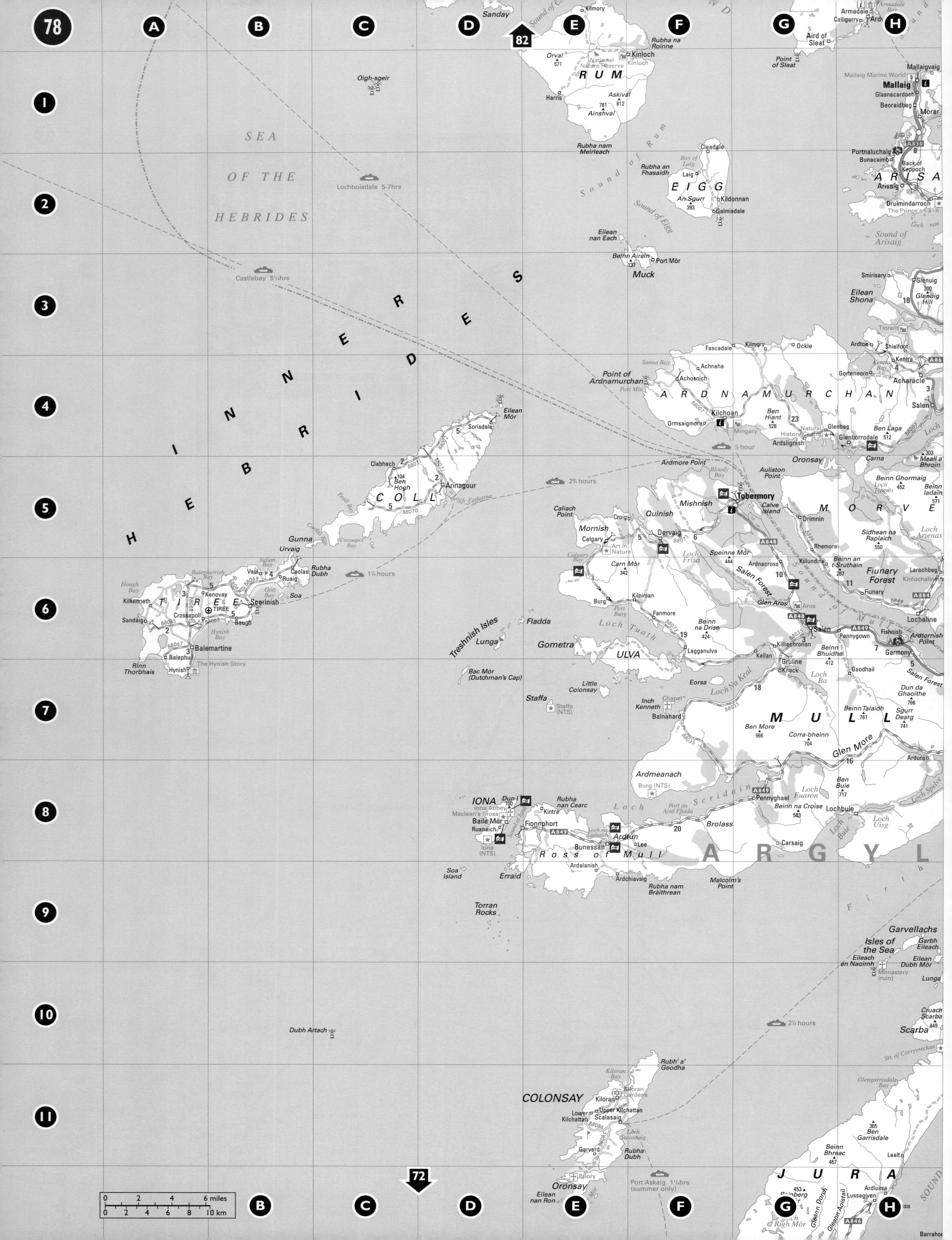
A
B
C
D
E
F
G
H
1
2
3
4
5
6
7
8
9
10
11
82
72
SEA
OF THE
HEBRIDES
H E B R I D E S
I N N E R
Sound of Rum
Sound of Eigg
Sanday
Kilmory
Rubha na Roinne
Orval
571
National Nature Reserve
Kinloch
RUM
Harris
Askival
812
781
Ainshval
Rubha nam Meirleach
Oigh-sgeir
Lochboisdale 5-7hrs
Castlebay 5¼hrs
Aird of Sleat
Point of Sleat
Armadale
Calligarry
Mallaig Marine World
Mallaigvaig
Mallaig
Glasnacardoch
Beoraidbeg
Morar
Portnaluchaig
Bunacaimb
Back of Keppoch
Arisaig
ARISAIG
Druimindarroch
The Prince's Cairn
Sound of Arisaig
Cleadale
Bay of Laig
Laig
Rubha an Fhasaidh
EIGG
An Sgurr
393
Kildonnan
Galmisdale
Eilean nan Each
Beinn Airein
137
Port Mòr
Muck
Smirisary
Glenuig
Glenuig Hill
300
Eilean Shona
Tioram
Fascadale
Kilmory
Ockle
Ardtoe
Shielfoot
Kentra
Kentra Bay
Gorteneorn
Acharacle
Salen
Point of Ardnamurchan
Sanna Bay
Achnaha
Achosnich
Port Mìn
ARDNAMURCHAN
B8007
Kilchoan
Ormsaigmore
Mingary
Ben Hiant
528
Natural History Centre
Glenbeg
Glenborrodale
Ardslignish
Ben Laga
512
Loch
½ hour
Carna
Meall a' Bhroin
303
Oronsay
Eilean Mòr
Sorisdale
5
B8071
B8072
Clabhach
Ben Hogh
104
Arinagour
COLL
Loch Eatharna
Feall Bay
B8070
Crossapol Bay
Gunna
Caolas Bay
Urvaig
2¾ hours
1¼ hours
Ardmore Point
Bloody Bay
Auliston Point
Beinn Ghormaig
452
Beinn Iadain
571
Loch Teacuis
Tobermory
Mishnish
Calve Island
Caliach Point
Quinish
Drimnin
MORVERN
Loch Arienas
Sidhean na Raplaich
550
Mornish
Croig
Calgary
Calgary Bay
Art in Nature
Dervaig
B8073
Loch Frisa
Speinne Mòr
444
A848
Rhemore
Carn Mòr
342
Ardnacross
Killundine
Beinn an t-Sruthain
267
Fiunary Forest
Larachbeg
Kinlochaline
Salen Forest
Sound of Mull
Fiunary
B849
A884
Balephetrish Bay
Salum Bay
Vaul
Caolas
Ruaig
Rubha Dubh
Hough Bay
Kilkenneth
Kenovay
Gott Bay
Scarinish
Soa
TIREE
Crossapol
Sandaig
B8065
B8068
B8069
Baugh
Hynish Bay
B8067
Balemartine
Balephuil
Rinn Thorbhais
Hynish
The Hynish Story
Burg
Kilninian
Port Burg
Fanmore
Loch Tuath
Glen Aros
Aros
A848
Beinn na Drise
424
Salen
A849
Pennygown
Fishnish
Ardtornish Point
Lochaline
Garmony
Treshnish Isles
Fladda
Lunga
Gometra
ULVA
Lagganulva
Killiechronan
Kellan
Gruline
Knock
Beinn Bhuidhe
412
Gaodhail
Salen Forest
Bac Mòr (Dutchman's Cap)
Little Colonsay
Eorsa
Loch Na Keal
Loch Ba
Dun da Ghaoithe
766
Staffa
Staffa (NTS)
Inch Kenneth
Chapel
Balnahard
B8035
18
Beinn Talaidh
761
Sgurr Dearg
741
MULL
Ben More
966
Corra-bheinn
704
Glen More
Ardura
Ardmeanach
Burg (NTS)
Loch Scridain
A849
Pennyghael
Loch Fuaron
Ben Buie
717
Loch Spelve
IONA
Dun-I
100
Iona Abbey
Maclean's Cross
Baile Mòr
Ruanaich
Iona (NTS)
Sound of Iona
Rubha nan Cearc
Kintra
Fionnphort
Port an Aird Fhada
Beinn na Croise
503
Lochbuie
Loch Uisg
Loch Buie
Loch na Lathaich
Ardtun
Lee
Brolass
Bunessan
Ross of Mull
Carsaig
ARGYLL
Ardalanish
Soa Island
Erraid
Ardchiavaig
Rubha nam Bràithrean
Malcolm's Point
Torran Rocks
Firth of Lorn
Garvellachs
Isles of the Sea
Garbh Eileach
Eileach an Naoimh
Eilean Dubh Mòr
Monastery (ruin)
Lunga
Dubh Artach
2¼ hours
Cruach Scarba
449
Scarba
Str. of Corryvreckan
Rubh' a' Geodha
Kiloran Bay
Kiloran
Kiloran Gardens
COLONSAY
Lower Kilchattan
Upper Kilchattan
Scalasaig
B8086
Loch Staoisha
Garvard
Rubha Dubh
Priory
Oronsay
Eilean nan Ron
Port Askaig 1¼hrs (summer only)
Glengarrisdale Bay
Dun da Ghaoithe
Ben Garrisdale
365
Beinn Bhreac
467
Lealt
JURA
453
Beinn Dorch
Glenn Aoistail
Ardlussa
Lussagiven
A846
Loch Righ Mòr
Barrahormid
SOUND
0 2 4 6 miles
0 2 4 6 8 10 km

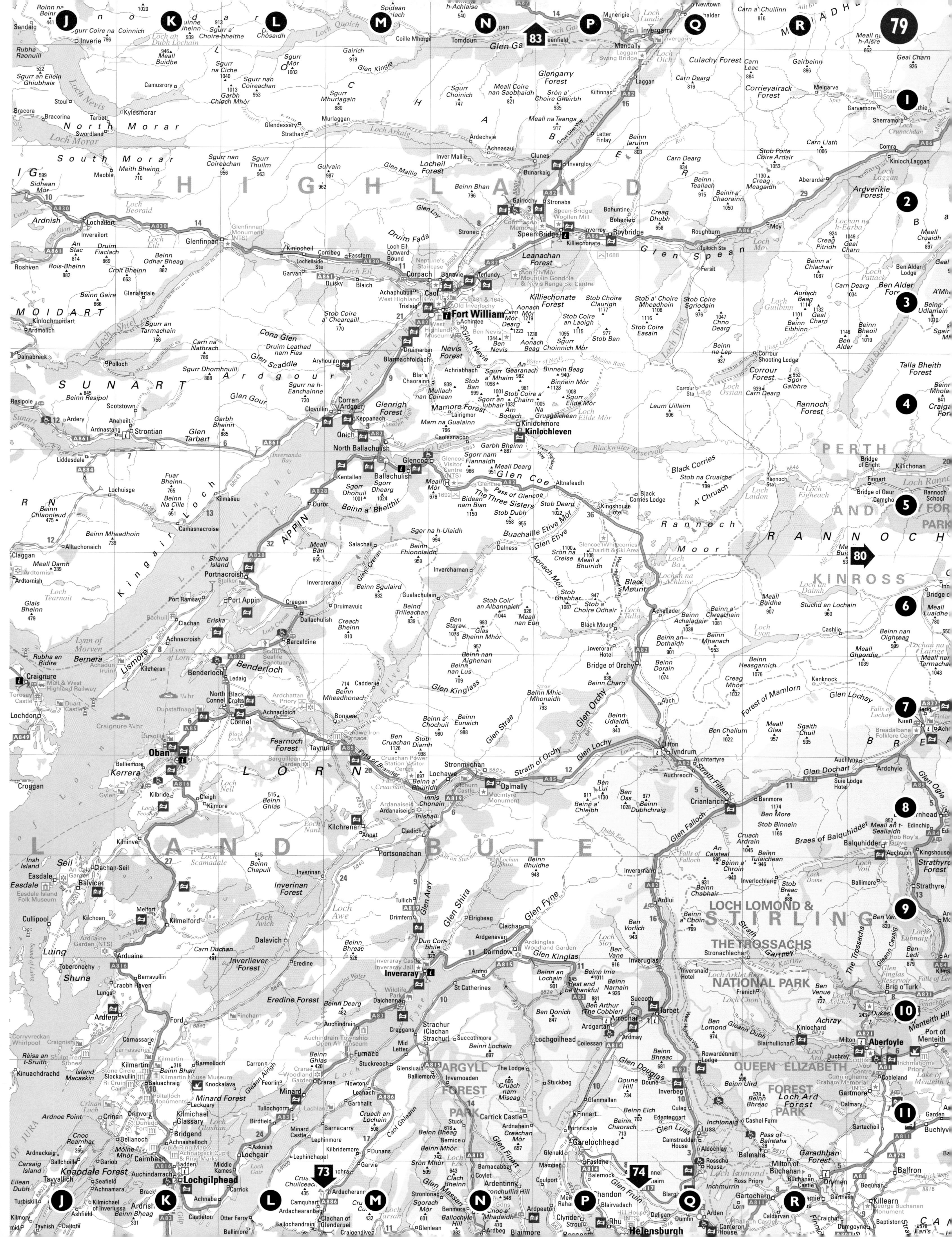
HIGHLAND
LORN
AND BUTE
PERTH AND KINROSS
STIRLING
RANNOCH
83
80
73
74
North Morar
South Morar
MOIDART
SUNART
Ardgour
APPIN
LOCH LOMOND & THE TROSSACHS NATIONAL PARK
QUEEN ELIZABETH FOREST PARK
ARGYLL FOREST PARK
Fort William
Kinlochleven
Oban
Inveraray
Lochgilphead
Helensburgh
Aberfoyle
Glenfinnan
Spean Bridge
Invergarry
Glencoe
Ballachulish
North Ballachulish
Onich
Corran
Strontian
Lochailort
Corpach
Banavie
Caol
Roybridge
Tulloch Sta
Kinloch Laggan
Dalwhinnie
Bridge of Orchy
Tyndrum
Crianlarich
Arrochar
Tarbet
Inveruglas
Luss
Balloch
Drymen
Killin
Balquhidder
Strathyre
Callander
Connel
Benderloch
Taynuilt
Dalmally
Kilmelford
Kilmartin
Ardrishaig
Tighnabruaich
Strachur
Garelochhead
Rhu
Glen Coe
Glen Etive
Glen Orchy
Glen Lochy
Glen Spean
Glen Nevis
Glen Kinglas
Glen Fyne
Glen Shira
Glen Falloch
Glen Dochart
Strath Fillan
Loch Linnhe
Loch Eil
Loch Lochy
Loch Leven
Loch Etive
Loch Awe
Loch Fyne
Loch Long
Loch Lomond
Loch Katrine
Loch Ard
Loch Rannoch
Loch Laggan
Loch Shiel
Loch Morar
Loch Nevis
Loch Arkaig
Rannoch Moor
Black Mount
Ben Nevis 1344
Aonach Mòr
Buachaille Etive Mòr
The Three Sisters
Ben Cruachan 1126
Ben Lui 1130
Ben More 1174
Ben Vorlich 943
Ben Arthur (The Cobbler)
Ben Lomond 974
Ben Alder
Mamore Forest
Blackwater Reservoir
Kerrera
Lismore
Seil
Luing
Shuna
Craignure
Knapdale Forest
Minard Forest
Eredine Forest
Inverliever Forest
Inverinan Forest
A82
A830
A861
A828
A85
A816
A819
A83
A815
A86
A84
A81
A821

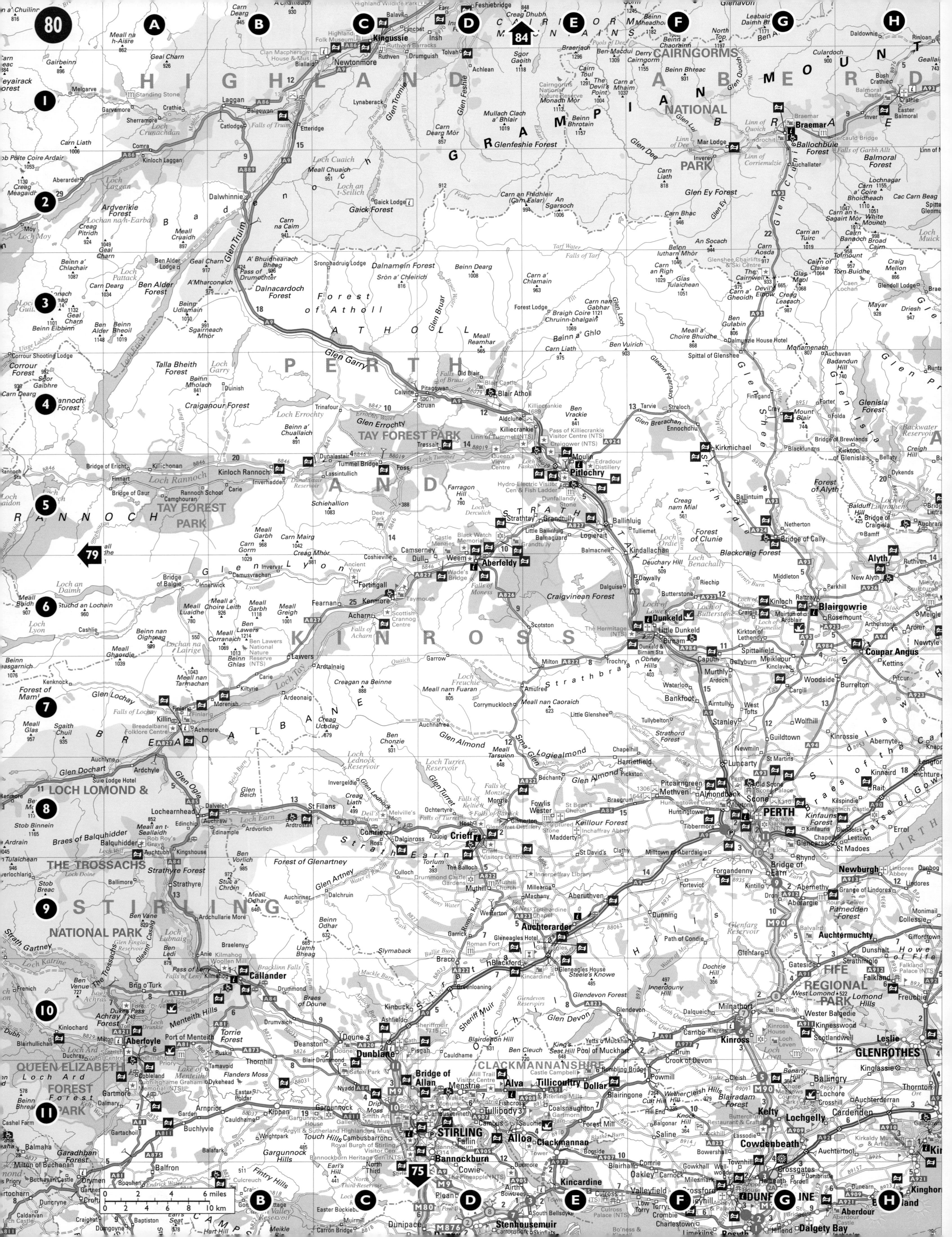

A
B
C
D
E
F
G
H
1
2
3
4
5
6
7
8
9
10
11
84
79
75
HIGHLAND
GRAMPIAN
ABERDEEN
CAIRNGORMS NATIONAL PARK
CAIRNGORM MOUNTAINS
PERTH AND KINROSS
ATHOLL
Forest of Atholl
RANNOCH
TAY FOREST PARK
BREADALBANE
LOCH LOMOND & THE TROSSACHS NATIONAL PARK
STIRLING
QUEEN ELIZABETH FOREST PARK
CLACKMANNANSHIRE
FIFE REGIONAL PARK
Ochil Hills
Sidlaw Hills
Braes of the Carse
Strathearn
Strathallan
Strathbraan
Strath Tay
Strathardle
Glen Shee
Glen Isla
Glen Lyon
Glen Almond
Glen Garry
Glen Errochty
Glen Dochart
Glen Ogle
Glen Artney
Glen Devon
Glen Truim
Glen Feshie
Glen Tromie
Glen Bruar
Glen Dee
Glen Lochay
Loch Rannoch
Loch Tummel
Loch Tay
Loch Earn
Loch Ericht
Loch Laggan
Loch Katrine
Loch Ard
Loch Leven
Kingussie
Newtonmore
Laggan
Dalwhinnie
Braemar
Ballater
Blair Atholl
Pitlochry
Aberfeldy
Dunkeld
Blairgowrie
Alyth
Coupar Angus
PERTH
Crieff
Comrie
St Fillans
Killin
Callander
Aberfoyle
Dunblane
Bridge of Allan
STIRLING
Bannockburn
Alloa
Clackmannan
Alva
Tillicoultry
Dollar
Kinross
Auchterarder
Auchtermuchty
Newburgh
GLENROTHES
Cowdenbeath
Lochgelly
Kelty
Kincardine
DUNFERMLINE
Dalgety Bay
Aberdour
Stenhousemuir
Blackford
Methven
Scone
Kenmore
Fortingall
Kinloch Rannoch
Schiehallion
Ben Lawers
Ben Vorlich
Ben Ledi
Ben Venue
Beinn a' Ghlo
Ben Chonzie
Ben Vrackie
Lochearnhead
Strathyre
Balquhidder
0 2 4 6 miles
0 2 4 6 8 10 km

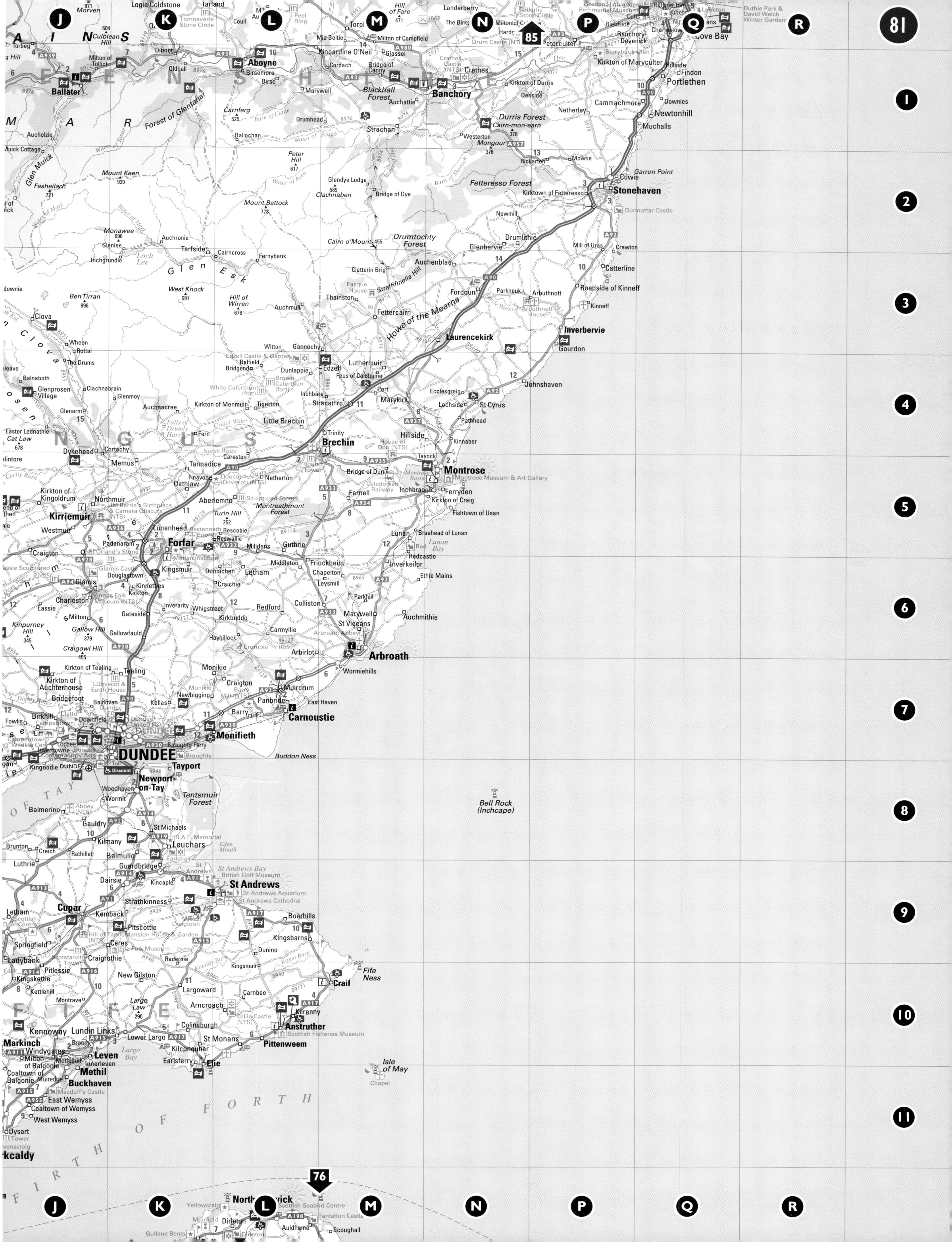
J
K
L
M
N
P
Q
R
1
2
3
4
5
6
7
8
9
10
11
85
76
Morven
Logie Coldstone
Tarland
Coull
Aboyne
Peel Ring
Torphins
Hill of Fare
Landerberry
The Birks
Milton of Campfield
Mid Beltie
Kincardine O'Neil
Glassel
Cordach
Bridge of Canny
Birsemore
Birse
Marywell
Blackhall Forest
Banchory
Auchattie
Crathes
Crathes Castle (NTS)
Drum Castle (NTS)
Peterculter
Kirkton of Maryculter
Kirkton of Durris
Denside
Durris Forest
Cairn-mon-earn
Netherley
Cammachmore
Portlethen
Findon
Hillside
Downies
Newtonhill
Muchalls
Banchory-Devenick
Cove Bay
Duthie Park & David Welch Winter Gardens
Gordon Highlanders Regimental Museum
Storybook Glen
Bieldside
Culter
Tomnaverie Stone Circle
Dinnet
Oldhall
Culblean Hill
Milton of Tullich
Ballater
Torbeg
Forest of Glentanar
Carnferg
Ballochan
Drumhead
Strachan
Westerton
Mongour
Rickarton
Mowtie
Cowie
Garron Point
Stonehaven
Dunnottar Castle
Kirktown of Fetteresso
Fetteresso Forest
Newmill
Drumlithie
Glenbervie
Mill of Uras
Crawton
Catterline
Roadside of Kinneff
Kinneff
Arbuthnott
Arbuthnott House
Parkneuk
Fordoun
Auchenblae
Drumtochty Forest
Cairn o'Mount
Clatterin Brig
Fasque House
Strathfinella Hill
Thainston
Fettercairn
Howe of the Mearns
Laurencekirk
Inverbervie
Gourdon
Johnshaven
Glendye Lodge
Clachnaben
Bridge of Dye
Peter Hill
Mount Keen
Mount Battock
Aucholzie
Muick Cottage
Glen Muick
Fasheilach
Monawee
Auchronie
Glenlee
Inchgrundle
Loch Lee
Tarfside
Cairncross
Fernybank
Glen Esk
West Knock
Hill of Wirren
Ben Tirran
Clova
Wheen
Rottal
The Drums
Balnaboth
Glenprosen Village
Clachnabrain
Glenmoy
Glenarm
Auchnacree
Kirkton of Menmuir
Tigerton
Little Brechin
Witton
Gannochy
Edzell Castle & Garden
Balfield
Bridgend
Dunlappie
Brown Caterthun (fort)
White Caterthun (fort)
Edzell
Luthermuir
Fetus of Caldhame
Inchbare
Stracathro
Pert
Marykirk
Hillside
Ecclesgreig
Lochside
St Cyrus
Pathhead
Kinnaber
Brechin
Trinity
House of Dun (NTS)
Round Tower
Bridge of Dun
Caledonian Railway
Montrose Basin
Montrose
Montrose Museum & Art Gallery
Ferryden
Inchbraoch
Tayock
Kirkton of Craig
Fishtown of Usan
Farnell
Careston
Tannadice
Finavon
Doocot (NTS)
Netherton
Oathlaw
Aberlemno
Sculptured Stones
Montreathmont Forest
Turin Hill
Easter Lednathie
Cat Law
Falls of Drumly Harry
Fern
Dykehead
Cortachy
Memus
Kirkton of Kingoldrum
Northmuir
JM Barrie's Birthplace & Camera Obscura (NTS)
Kirriemuir
Westmuir
Lunanhead
Restenneth Priory
Rescobie
Reswallie
Forfar
Padanaram
St Orland's Stone
Craigton
Glamis Castle
Glamis
Douglastown
Kingsmuir
Meffan Institute
Dunnichen
Letham
Craichie
Milldens
Guthrie
Middleton
Friockheim
Chapelton
Leysmill
Lunan
Braehead of Lunan
Lunan Bay
Red Castle
Redcastle
Inverkeilor
Ethie Mains
Kinnettles
Kirkton
Charleston
Angus Folk Museum (NTS)
Eassie
Milton
Kinpurney Hill
Gallow Hill
Gallowfauld
Craigowl Hill
Gateside
Inverarity
Whigstreet
Kirkbuddo
Redford
Colliston
Parkhill
Marywell
St Vigeans
Arbroath Abbey
Auchmithie
Hayhillock
Carmyllie
Crombie
Arbirlot
Arbroath
Wormiehills
Kirkton of Tealing
Tealing
Kirkton of Auchterhouse
Dovecot & Earth House
Bridgefoot
Baldovan
Birkhill
Downfield
Monikie
Craigton
Newbigging
Barry Mill (NTS)
Muirdrum
Panbride
East Haven
Carnoustie
Kellas
Barry
Monifieth
Broughty Ferry
Broughty Castle
Buddon Ness
Invergowrie
Liff
Fowlis
Lochee
Camperdown
DUNDEE
Kingoodie
Discount
Tayport
Newport-on-Tay
Woodhaven
Wormit
Tentsmuir Forest
Balmerino
Abbey (NTS)
Gauldry
St Michaels
R.A.F. Memorial
Kilmany
Leuchars
Eden Mouth
Brunton
Creich
Rathillet
Balmullo
Luthrie
Guardbridge
St Andrews Bay
British Golf Museum
Dairsie
Kincaple
St Andrews
St Andrews Aquarium
St Andrews Cathedral
Cupar
Strathkinness
Kemback
Letham
Scottish Deer Centre
Pitscottie
Hill of Tarvit Mansion House & Garden (NTS)
Ceres
Fife Folk Museum
Boarhills
Kingsbarns
Dunino
Springfield
Scotstarvit Tower
Craigrothie
Radernie
Kingsmuir
Ladybank
Pitlessie
Kingskettle
Kettlehill
New Gilston
Fife Ness
Crail
Carnbee
Largoward
Montrave
Largo Law
Arncroach
Kellie Castle (NTS)
Kilrenny
Anstruther
Scottish Fisheries Museum
Colinsburgh
Pittenweem
St Monans
Kennoway
Lundin Links
Lower Largo
Kilconquhar
Largo Bay
Elie
Earlsferry
Markinch
Windygates
Milton of Balgonie
Leven
Innerleven
Methil
Coaltown of Balgonie
Buckhaven
Macduff's Castle
East Wemyss
Coaltown of Wemyss
West Wemyss
Dysart
Isle of May
Chapel
Bell Rock (Inchcape)
FIRTH OF FORTH
FIRTH OF TAY
ANGUS
FIFE
ABERDEENSHIRE
North Berwick
Scottish Seabird Centre
Yellowcraig
Dirleton
Tantallon Castle
Auldhame
Scoughall
Gullane Bents
A90
A92
A93
A94
A96
A914
A915
A917
A919
A921
A926
A928
A930
A932
A933
A934
A935
A937
A939
A957
A980
A198

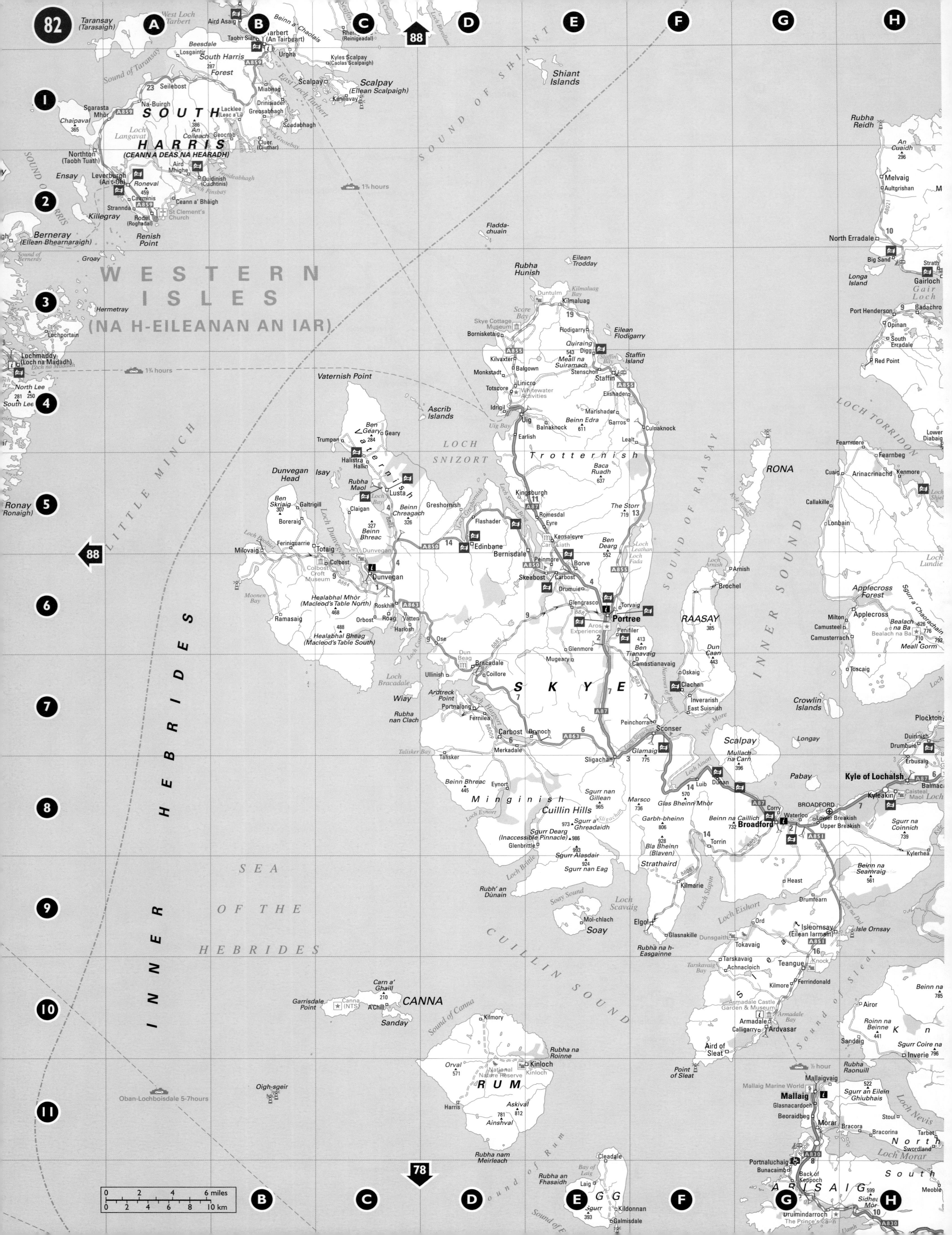

Taransay (Tarasaigh)
West Loch Tarbert
Aird Asaig
Tarbert (An Tairbeart)
Taobh Siar
Urgha
Beinn a' Chaolais
Rhenigidale (Reinigeadal)
Loch Brollum
88
Beesdale
Losgaintir
South Harris
Forest
Kyles Scalpay (Caolas Scalpaigh)
Sound of Taransay
Scalpay
Scalpay (Ellean Scalpaigh)
Kennavay
Shiant Islands
Seilebost
Miabhag
East Loch Tarbert
Na-Buirgh
Drinisiader
Sgarasta Mhòr
Lacklee (Leac a'Li)
Greosabhagh
SOUTH
HARRIS
(CEANN A DEAS NA HEARADH)
Chaipaval
365
Loch Langavat
386
An Coileach
Geocrab
Cluer (Cliuthar)
Scadabhagh
Loch Grosebay
SOUND OF SHIANT
Rubha Reidh
An Cuaidh
296
Northton (Taobh Tuath)
Ensay
Leverburgh (An t-Ob)
Roneval
459
Aird Mhighe
Quidinish (Cuidhtinis)
Fleideabhagh
Loch Finsbay
1¾ hours
Melvaig
Aultgrishan
SOUND OF HARRIS
Strannda
Carminis
Ceann a' Bhàigh
Killegray
Rodel (Roghadal)
St Clement's Church
Renish Point
Berneray (Ellean Bhearnaraigh)
Sound of Berneray
Fladda-chuain
North Erradale
Big Sand
Groay
Eilean Trodday
Rubha Hunish
Longa Island
Gairloch
Gair Loch
WESTERN ISLES
(NA H-EILEANAN AN IAR)
Hermetray
Duntulm
Kilmaluag Bay
Kilmaluag
Score Bay
Port Henderson
Badachro
Opinan
South Erradale
Red Point
Skye Cottage Museum
Borniskeitaig
Flodigarry
Eilean Flodigarry
Lochportain
Lochmaddy (Loch na Madadh)
Loch na Madadh
1¾ hours
Quiraing
Digg
Meall na Suiramach
543
Staffin Bay
Staffin Island
Kilvaxter
Balgown
Monkstadt
Stenscholl
Staffin
Vaternish Point
Totscore
Linicro
Whitewater Activities
Elishader
North Lee
South Lee
281
250
Ascrib Islands
Idrigil
Uig
Uig Bay
Marishader
Beinn Edra
611
Garros
Balnaknock
Earlish
Lealt
Culnaknock
LOCH TORRIDON
Lower Diabaig
LITTLE MINCH
Ben Geary
284
Geary
Trumpan
Vaternish
Halistra
Hallin
LOCH SNIZORT
Trotternish
Fearnmore
Fearnbeg
Dunvegan Head
Isay
Rubha Maol
Lusta
Loch Bay
Baca Ruadh
637
RONA
Cuaig
Arinacrinachd
Kenmore
Ronay (Ronaigh)
Ben Skriaig
307
Galtrigill
Boreraig
Claigan
Beinn Chreagach
326
Greshornish
Loch Greshornish
Flashader
Kingsburgh
Romesdal
Eyre
The Storr
719
Callakille
Kyle Rona
Lonbain
Loch Dunvegan
327
Beinn Bhreac
Loch Snizort Beag
Kensaleyre
Carn Liath
Ben Dearg
552
Loch Leathan
Loch Fada
SOUND OF RAASAY
INNER SOUND
Loch Lundie
88
Loch Pooltiel
Feriniquarrie
Milovaig
Totaig
Dunvegan
Colbost
Colbost Croft Museum
A850
Edinbane
Bernisdale
Peinmore
Borve
Skeabost
Carbost
Loch Arnish
Arnish
Brochel
Applecross Forest
Moonen Bay
Healabhal Mhòr (Macleod's Table North)
468
Roskhill
Drumuie
Glengrasco
Torvaig
Portree
Aros Experience
Penifiler
RAASAY
385
Applecross
Milton
Camusteel
Camusterrach
Bealach na Ba
Bealach na Ba
626
776
710
792
Meall Gorm
Sgurr a' Chaorachain
Ramasaig
Orbost
Roag
Vatten
Harlosh
488
Healabhal Bheag (Macleod's Table South)
Ose
Loch Caroy
Dun Beag
Bracadale
Coillore
Mugeary
Glenmore
413
Ben Tianavaig
Camastianavaig
Dun Caan
443
Toscaig
Loch Bracadale
Ullinish
Wiay
Ardtreck Point
Rubha nan Clach
SKYE
Oskaig
Clachan
Inverarish
East Suisnish
Narrows of Raasay
Crowlin Islands
Portnalong
Fernilea
Loch Harport
Carbost
Drynoch
Peinchorran
Sconser
Loch Sligachan
Kyle More
Talisker Bay
Talisker
Merkadale
Sligachan
Glamaig
775
Scalpay
Mullach na Carn
396
Longay
Plockton
Duirinish
Drumbuie
Erbusaig
Kyle of Lochalsh
Pabay
Beinn Bhreac
445
Eynort
Minginish
Cuillin Hills
Sgurr nan Gillean
965
Marsco
736
Glas Bheinn Mhòr
Loch Ainort
Luib
570
Dunan
BROADFORD
Kyleakin
Caisteal Maol
Loch Eynort
Sgurr a' Ghreadaidh
973
Sgurr Dearg (Inaccessible Pinnacle)
986
Glenbrittle
Garbh-bheinn
806
Beinn na Caillich
732
Broadford
Corry
Waterloo
Lower Breakish
Upper Breakish
Sgurr na Coinnich
739
Kylerhea
928
Bla Bheinn (Blaven)
Torrin
953
Sgurr Alasdair
924
Sgurr nan Eag
Loch Slapin
SEA OF THE HEBRIDES
INNER HEBRIDES
Loch Brittle
Strathaird
Kilmarie
Heast
Beinn na Seamraig
561
Rubh' an Dunain
Soay Sound
Loch Scavaig
Drumfearn
Mol-chlach
Soay
Elgol
Glasnakille
Loch Eishort
Ord
Dunsgaith
Tokavaig
Isleornsay (Eilean Iarmain)
Isle Ornsay
Loch na Dal
CUILLIN SOUND
Rubha na h-Easgainne
Tarskavaig
Tarskavaig Bay
Achnacloich
Teangue
Knock
Sleat
Ferrindonald
Kilmore
Armadale Castle Garden & Museum
Armadale
Armadale Bay
Calligarry
Ardvasar
Sound of Sleat
Beinn na
785
Airor
Roinn na Beinne
441
Sandaig
Sgurr Coire na
796
Inverie
Carn a' Ghaill
210
Garrisdale Point
Canna (NTS)
A'Chill
CANNA
Sanday
Sound of Canna
Kilmory
Rubha na Roinne
Aird of Sleat
Point of Sleat
½ hour
Rubha Raonuill
Orval
571
National Nature Reserve
Kinloch
RUM
Oigh-sgeir
Oban-Lochboisdale 5-7hours
Harris
Askival
781
812
Ainshval
Mallaig Marine World
Mallaigvaig
522
Sgurr an Eilein Ghiubhais
Mallaig
Glasnacardoch
Beoraidbeg
Morar
Stoul
Bracora
Bracorina
Tarbet
Loch Nevis
North Morar
Swordland
Loch Morar
Rubha nam Meirleach
Sound of Rum
Cleadale
Bay of Laig
Laig
Rubha an Fhasaidh
EGG
Sgurr
393
Kildonnan
Galmisdale
Sound of Eigg
78
Portnaluchaig
Bunacaimb
Back of Keppoch
ARISAIG
South Morar
599
Sidhean Mor
Meoble
Druimindarroch
The Prince's Cairn
0 2 4 6 miles
0 2 4 6 8 10 km
A B C D E F G H
1 2 3 4 5 6 7 8 9 10 11

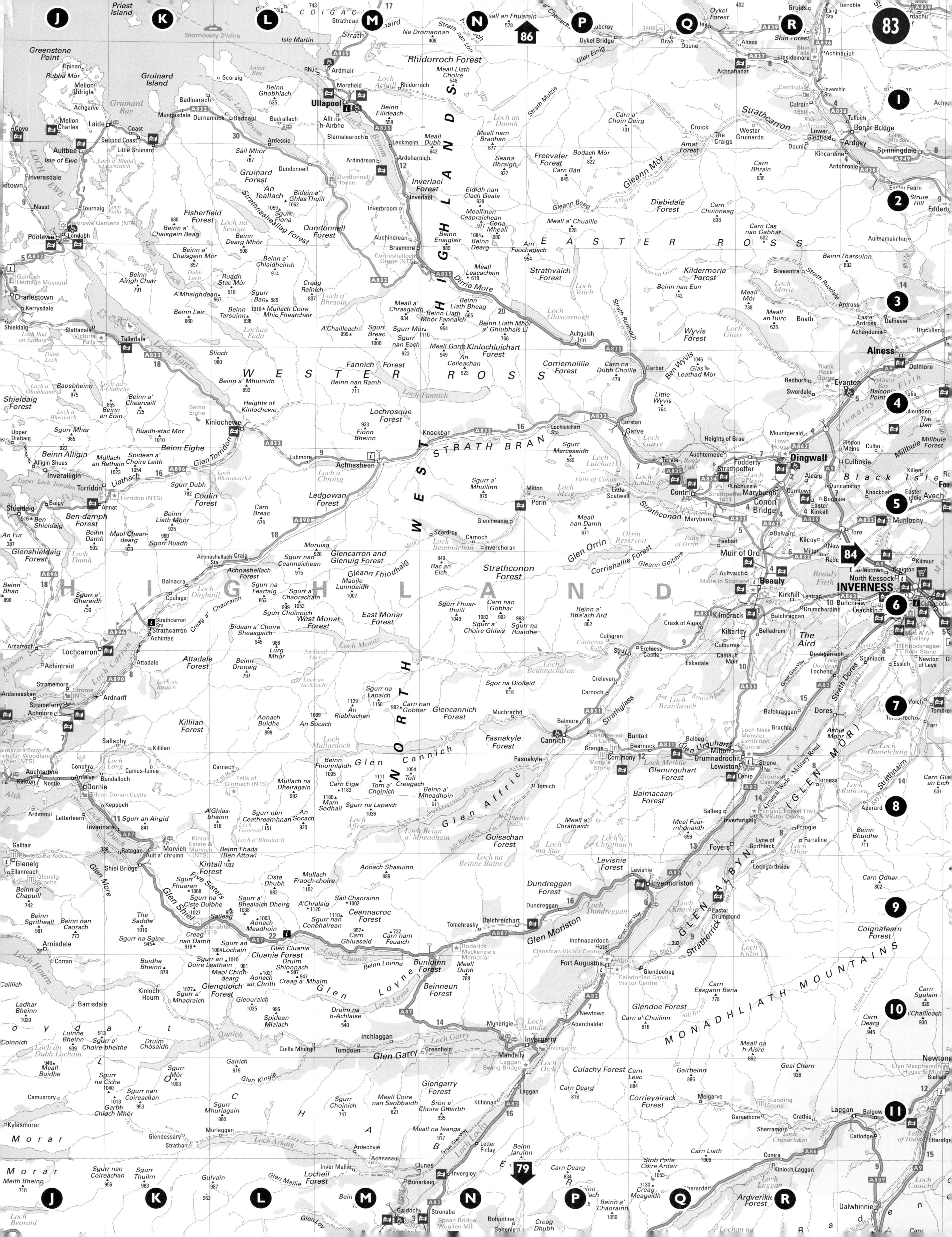

J
K
L
M
N
P
Q
R
86
Priest Island
Stornoway 2¾hrs
Isle Martin
Strathcanaird
Oykel Forest
Oykel Bridge
Shin Forest
Greenstone Point
Gruinard Island
Gruinard Bay
Rhidorroch Forest
Ullapool
Loch Broom
Little Loch Broom
Laide
Aultbea
Isle of Ewe
Loch Ewe
Inverasdale
Poolewe
Inverewe Gardens (NTS)
Gairloch
Gairloch Heritage Museum
Charlestown
Kerrysdale
Shieldaig
Dundonnell
Dundonnell Forest
Gruinard Forest
An Teallach
Fisherfield Forest
Strathnasheallag Forest
Inverlael Forest
Inverlael
Corrieshalloch Gorge (NTS)
Braemore
Dirrie More
Freevater Forest
Glen Einig
Strathcarron
Croick
Amat Forest
The Craigs
Bonar Bridge
Ardgay
Spinningdale
Glenn Mòr
Diebidale Forest
E A S T E R R O S S
Kildermorie Forest
Strathvaich Forest
Loch Vaich
Loch Glascarnoch
Aultguish Inn
Wyvis Forest
Ben Wyvis
Alness
Evanton
Dalmore
Cromarty Firth
Loch Maree
Talladale
Slioch
W E S T E R R O S S
Fannich Forest
Loch Fannich
Kinlochluichart Forest
Corriemoillie Forest
Garbat
Little Wyvis
Shieldaig Forest
Kinlochewe
Heights of Kinlochewe
Beinn Eighe
Lochrosque Forest
Knockban
Garve
Loch Garve
Lochluichart
Gorstan
Glen Torridon
Liathach
Torridon
Torridon (NTS)
Achnasheen
S T R A T H B R A N
Dingwall
Strathpeffer
Contin
Maryburgh
Conon Bridge
Black Isle
Munlochy
Avoch
Upper Loch Torridon
Inveralligin
Alligin Shuas
Beinn Alligin
Ben-damph Forest
Coulin Forest
Ledgowan Forest
Loch Achilty
Loch Luichart
Scatwell
Strathconon
Marybank
Muir of Ord
Beauly
Beauly Firth
INVERNESS
North Kessock
Tore
Kilcoy
84
Glenshieldaig Forest
Achnashellach
Achnashellach Forest
Glencarron and Glenuig Forest
Strathconon Forest
Glen Orrin
Orrin Reservoir
Corriehallie Forest
H I G H L A N D
W E S T
N O R T H
Strathcarron
Lochcarron
Loch Carron
Attadale
Attadale Forest
West Monar Forest
East Monar Forest
Loch Monar
Kilmorack
Kiltarlity
The Aird
Crask of Aigas
Erchless Castle
Struy
Dochgarroch
Lochend
Scaniport
Essich
Strome Ferry
Achmore
Stromemore
Plockton
Ardaneaskan
Strath Dores
Dores
Killilan Forest
Glencannich Forest
Fasnakyle Forest
Cannich
Strathglass
Glen Cannich
Loch Mullardoch
Drumnadrochit
Lewiston
Glen Urquhart
Glenurquhart Forest
Loch Ness Monster Exhibition Centre
Urquhart Castle
Strone
Dornie
Eilean Donan Castle
Kyle of Lochalsh
Conchra
Ardelve
Bundalloch
Glen Affric
Loch Affric
Tomich
Balmacaan Forest
General Wade's Military Road
G L E N M Ò R
Loch Ness
Inverfarigaig
Foyers
Sàil Chaorainn
Kintail Forest
Five Sisters
Morvich
Shiel Bridge
Ratagan
Glenelg
Glen Shiel
Glen More
Ceannacroc Forest
Glen Moriston
Invermoriston
Dundreggan Forest
Levishie Forest
Guisachan Forest
Stratherrick
G L E N A L B Y N
Coignafearn Forest
Fort Augustus
Caledonian Canal
Cluanie Forest
Loch Cluanie
Glen Loyne
Bunloinn Forest
Beinneun Forest
Glendoe Forest
M O N A D H L I A T H M O U N T A I N S
Arnisdale
Loch Hourn
Glenquoich Forest
Kinloch Hourn
Loch Quoich
Invergarry
Glen Garry
Tomdoun
Mandally
Laggan
Culachy Forest
Corrieyairack Forest
Glengarry Forest
Loch Lochy
Loch Arkaig
Glen Kingie
Morar
Newtonmore
Laggan
Kinloch Laggan
Loch Laggan
Ardverikie Forest
Dalwhinnie
Clunes
Invergloy
Bunarkaig
Gairlochy
Spean Bridge
Spean Bridge Woollen Mill
Locheil Forest
Glen Mallie
79
Glen Loy
Stronaba

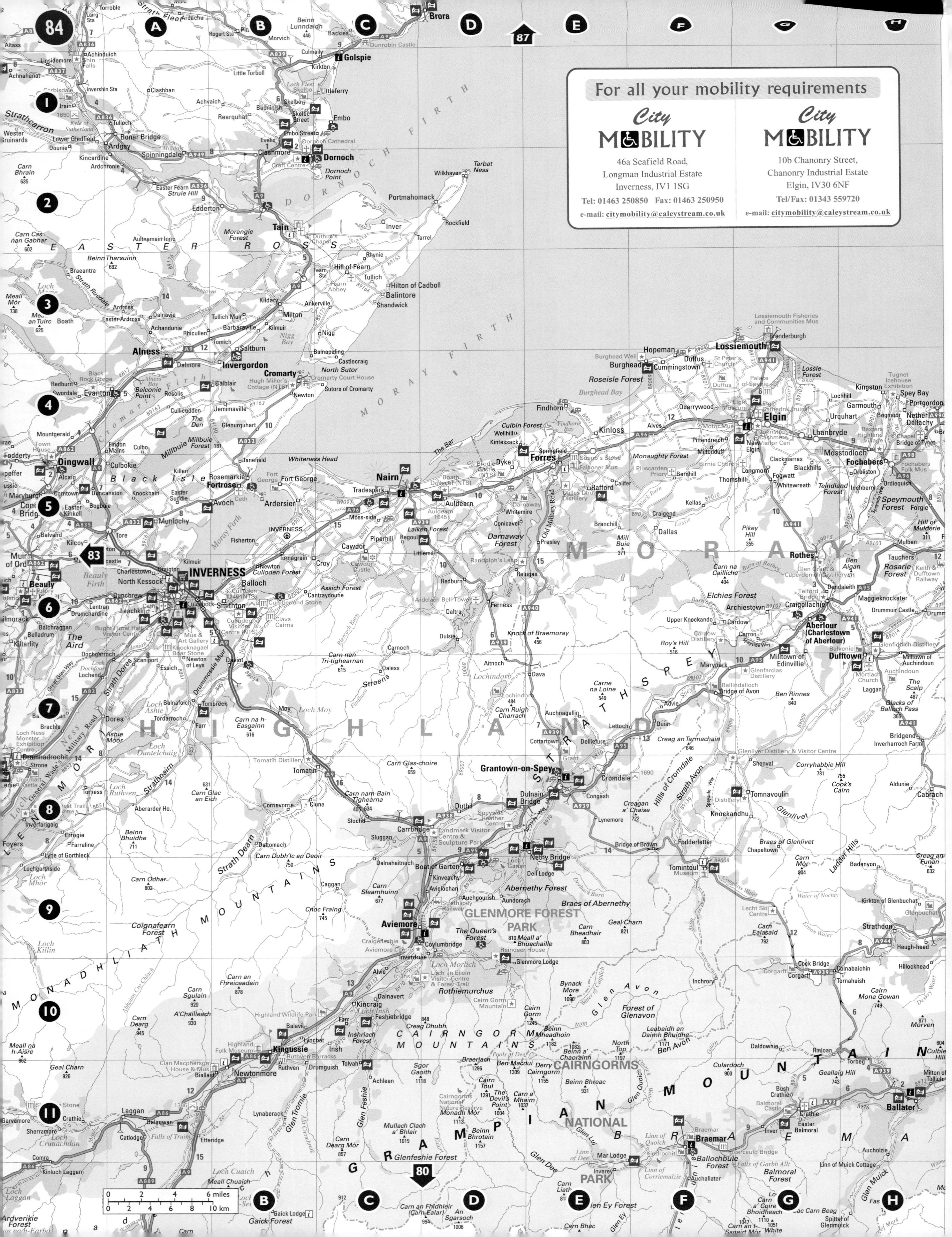
A
B
C
D
E
F
G
H
87
1
2
3
4
5
6
7
8
9
10
11
83
80
Brora
Golspie
Dunrobin Castle
Dornoch
Dornoch Cathedral
Dornoch Point
Embo
Skelbo
Clashmore
Bonar Bridge
Ardgay
Spinningdale
Strathcarron
Kincardine
Ardchronie
Edderton
Tain
Tarbat Ness
Portmahomack
Inver
Rockfield
Tarrel
Hill of Fearn
Hilton of Cadboll
Balintore
Shandwick
Fearn Abbey
Tullich
Rhynie
Ankerville
Kildary
Milton
Nigg
Nigg Bay
Balnapaling
Castlecraig
North Sutor
Cromarty
Cromarty Court House
Hugh Miller's Cottage (NTS)
Sutors of Cromarty
Invergordon
Saltburn
Alness
Dalmore
Evanton
Balblair
Resolis
Jemimaville
Cullicudden
Balcony Point
Dingwall
Culbokie
Black Isle
Rosemarkie
Fortrose
Fort George
Ardersier
Avoch
Munlochy
Tore
Kilcoy
Muir of Ord
Beauly
Beauly Firth
North Kessock
Charlestown
INVERNESS
Culloden Forest
Balloch
Smithton
Culloden Visitor Centre (NTS)
Cumberland Stone
Clava Cairns
Croy
Cawdor
Cawdor Castle
Nairn
Auldearn
Tradespark
Moss-side
Piperhill
Lethen
Conicavel
Forres
Findhorn
Kinloss
Culbin Forest
Darnaway Forest
Sueno's Stone
Falconer Mus
Rafford
Dallas
Dallas Dhu Distillery
Burghead
Burghead Bay
Roseisle Forest
Hopeman
Duffus
Cummingstown
Lossiemouth
Lossiemouth Fisheries and Communities Mus
Branderburgh
Elgin
Lhanbryde
Garmouth
Kingston
Spey Bay
Portgordon
Urquhart
Mosstodloch
Fochabers
Fochabers Folk Mus
Speymouth Forest
Rothes
Glen Grant & Caperdonich Distillery
Dandaleith
Craigellachie
Aberlour (Charlestown of Aberlour)
Dufftown
Glenfiddich Distillery
Balvenie Castle
Mortlach Church
Elchies Forest
Archiestown
Upper Knockando
Cardow
Marypark
Glenfarclas Distillery
Bridge of Avon
Ben Rinnes
The Scalp
Glacks of Balloch Pass
Bridgend
Inverharroch Farm
Cabrach
Corryhabbie Hill
Cook's Cairn
Glenlivet Distillery & Visitor Centre
Tomnavoulin
Knockandhu
Braes of Glenlivet
Chapeltown
Tomintoul
Ladder Hills
Cock Bridge
Corgarff
Strathdon
Colnabaichin
Tornahaish
Lecht Ski Centre
Carn Ealasaid
MORAY
HIGHLAND
STRATHSPEY
Grantown-on-Spey
Cromdale
Hills of Cromdale
Dulnain Bridge
Nethy Bridge
Boat of Garten
Carrbridge
Landmark Visitor Centre & Sculpture Park
Aviemore
Coylumbridge
Inverdruie
Loch Morlich
Glenmore Lodge
GLENMORE FOREST PARK
Abernethy Forest
Braes of Abernethy
Rothiemurchus
Cairn Gorm
CAIRNGORM MOUNTAINS
CAIRNGORMS NATIONAL PARK
Ben Macdui
Braeriach
Cairn Toul
The Devil's Point
Ben Avon
Beinn a' Bhuird
Forest of Glenavon
Glen Avon
Inchrory
Kincraig
Highland Wildlife Park
Feshiebridge
Kingussie
Ruthven Barracks
Newtonmore
Clan Macpherson House & Mus
Highland Folk Museum
Laggan
Glen Feshie
Glen Tromie
Glenfeshie Forest
Gaick Forest
GRAMPIAN MOUNTAINS
MONADHLIATH MOUNTAINS
Tomatin
Tomatin Distillery
Moy
Loch Moy
Daviot
Farr
Dores
Loch Ness
Loch Ashie
Drumnadrochit
Loch Ness Monster Exhibition Centre
Urquhart Castle
Foyers
Inverfarigaig
The Aird
Kiltarlity
Braemar
Braemar Castle
Invercauld Bridge
Ballochbuie Forest
Mar Lodge
Linn of Dee
Linn of Quoich
Ballater
Crathie
Balmoral Castle
Balmoral Forest
Lochnagar
Glen Muick
Loch Laggan
Ardverikie Forest
Kinloch Laggan
Loch Cuaich
Falls of Truim
Dalwhinnie
Cairn Gorm Mountain
Lochindorb
Dava
Ferness
Relugas
Randolph's Leap
Ardclach Bell Tower
Knock of Braemoray
Dulsie
Old Military Road
Strath Dearn
Strathnairn
Whiteness Head
Moray Firth
Dornoch Firth
Cromarty Firth
Easter Ross
0 2 4 6 miles
0 2 4 6 8 10 km

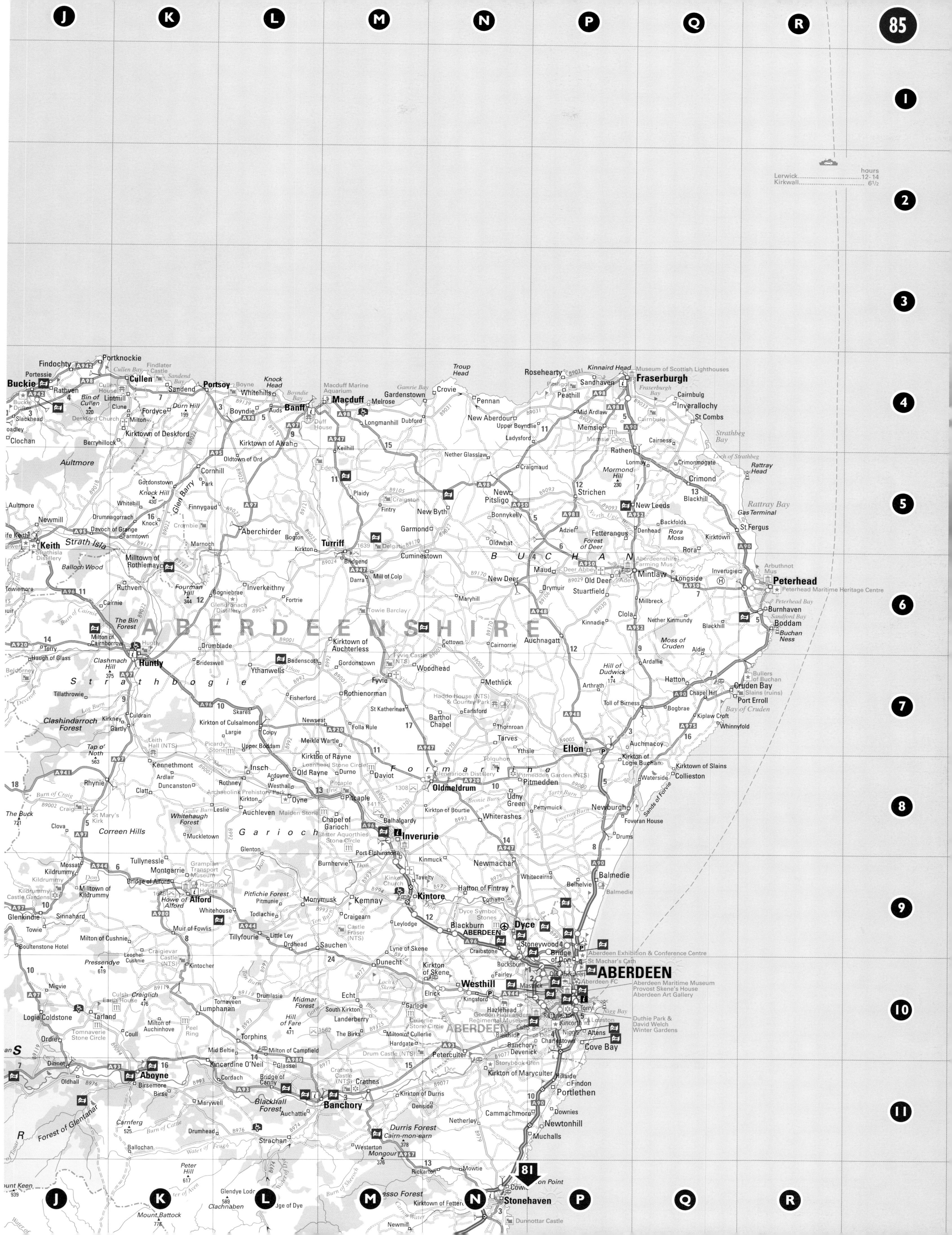
J
K
L
M
N
P
Q
R
1
2
3
4
5
6
7
8
9
10
11
hours
Lerwick 12-14
Kirkwall 6½
Findochty
Portknockie
Portessie
Buckie
Cullen Bay
Findlater Castle
Cullen
Sandend Bay
Sandend
Portsoy
Boyne
Whitehills
Knock Head
Boyndie Bay
Banff
Macduff Marine Aquarium
Macduff
Gamrie Bay
Gardenstown
Crovie
Troup Head
Pennan
Rosehearty
Kinnaird Head
Museum of Scottish Lighthouses
Fraserburgh
Fraserburgh Bay
Sandhaven
Pitsligo
Peathill
Cairnbulg
Inverallochy
St Combs
Rathven
Bin of Cullen
Lintmill
Clune
Fordyce
Durn Hill
Boyndie
Duff House
Melrose
Longmanhill
Dubford
New Aberdour
Upper Boyndie
Mid Ardlaw
Memsie
Memsie Cairn
Strathbeg Bay
Slackhead
Deskford Church
Milton
Kirktown of Deskford
Clochan
Berryhillock
Kirktown of Alvah
Keilhill
Ladysford
Cairness
Rathen
Loch of Strathbeg
Rattray Head
Crimonmogate
Lonmay
Mormond Hill
Crimond
Aultmore
Cornhill
Oldtown of Ord
Eden
Nether Glasslaw
Craigmaud
Strichen
Blackhill
Gordonstown
Park
Knock Hill
Glen Barry
Plaidy
Craigston
Fintry
New Pitsligo
New Byth
Bonnykelly
New Leeds
Rattray Bay
Gas Terminal
Whitehill
Newmill
Drumnagorrach
Finnygaud
Knock
Crombie
Aberchirder
Garmond
Adziel
Fetterangus
Forest of Deer
Denhead
Backfolds
Rora Moss
St Fergus
Keith
Davoch of Grange
Farmtown
Strath Isla
Strathisla Distillery
Marnoch
Bogton
Kirkton
Turriff
Delgatie
Cuminestown
Oldwhat
Kirktown
Rora
Balloch Wood
Milltown of Rothiemay
Bridgend
Darra
Mill of Colp
BUCHAN
Maud
Deer Abbey
Old Deer
Aden
Aberdeenshire Farming Mus
Mintlaw
Longside
Inverugie
Arbuthnot Mus
Peterhead
Peterhead Maritime Heritage Centre
Ruthven
Fourman Hill
Inverkeithny
Bogniebrae
Glendronach Distillery
Fortrie
New Deer
Maryhill
Drymuir
Stuartfield
Millbreck
Peterhead Bay
Burnhaven
Sandford Bay
Boddam
Buchan Ness
Carnie
Burn of Cairnie
The Bin Forest
Towie Barclay
ABERDEENSHIRE
Clola
Kinnadie
Nether Kinmundy
Blackhill
Milton of Cairnborrow
Huntly
Drumblade
Kirktown of Auchterless
Cottown
Cairnorrie
Auchnagatt
Moss of Cruden
Aldie
Torry
Haugh of Glass
Clashmach Hill
Brideswell
Badenscoth
Gordonstown
Fyvie Castle (NTS)
Woodhead
Ardallie
Ythanwells
Fyvie
Methlick
Hill of Dudwick
Hatton
Bullers of Buchan
Cruden Bay
Slains (ruins)
Port Erroll
Bay of Cruden
Strathbogie
Tillathrowie
Rothienorman
Fisherford
Haddo House (NTS) & Country Park
Arthrath
Toll of Birness
Chapel Hill
Bogbrae
Kiplaw Croft
Whinnyfold
Clashindarroch Forest
Culdrain
Kirkney
Gartly
Skares
Kirkton of Culsalmond
Newseat
Folla Rule
St Katherines
Barthol Chapel
Earlsford
Thornroan
Tarves
Ythsie
Auchmacoy
Largie
Colpy
Leith Hall (NTS)
Picardy Stone
Upper Boddam
Meikle Wartle
Kirkton of Rayne
Loanhead Stone Circle
Old Rayne
Durno
Daviot
Tolquhon
Glenbarrioch Distillery
Pitmedden Garden (NTS)
Ellon
Kirkton of Logie Buchan
Kirktown of Slains
Collieston
Waterside
Sands of Forvie
Tap o' Noth
Kennethmont
Ardlair
Duncanston
Insch
Ardoyne
Westhall
Rothney
Formartine
Oldmeldrum
Pitmedden
Udny Green
Rhynie
Clatt
Archaeolink Prehistory Park
Kirkton
Dyne
Pitcaple
Bronie Burn
Tarty Burn
Pettymuick
Newburgh
Foveran House
Burn of Craig
Craig
Leslie
Gadie Burn
Auchleven
Maiden Stone
Chapel of Garioch
Balhalgardy
Kirkton of Bourtie
Whiterashes
Foveran Burn
The Buck
St Mary's Kirk
Clova
Whitehaugh Forest
Correen Hills
Muckletown
Garioch
Easter Aquorthies Stone Circle
Inverurie
Drums
Glenton
Port Elphinstone
Newmachar
Tullynessle
Grampian Transport Museum
Montgarrie
Mossat
Kildrummy
Burnhervie
Don
Kinmuck
Kildrummy Castle Gardens
Bridge of Alford
Haughton House
Kinkell Church
Tavelty
Hatton of Fintray
Whitecairns
Belhelvie
Balmedie
Milton of Kildrummy
Howe of Alford
Alford
Pitfichie Forest
Pitmunie
Monymusk
Kemnay
Kintore
Cothall
Glenkindie
Sinnahard
Whitehouse
Todlachie
Craigearn
Dyce Symbol Stones
Towie
Muir of Fowlis
Castle Fraser (NTS)
Leylodge
Blackburn
ABERDEEN
Dyce
Tillyfourie
Little Ley
Stoneywood
Boultenstone Hotel
Milton of Cushnie
Ordhead
Sauchen
Lyne of Skene
Craibstone
Aberdeen Exhibition & Conference Centre
Bucksburn
Bridge of Don
St Machar's Cath
Craigievar Castle (NTS)
Leochel-Cushnie
Pressendye
Kintocher
Dunecht
Kirkton of Skene
Fairley
Old Aberdeen
ABERDEEN
Westhill
Loch of Skene
Mastrick
Aberdeen FC
Aberdeen Maritime Museum
Provost Skene's House
Aberdeen Art Gallery
Migvie
Cush
Craiglich
Earl's House
Tornaveen
Drumlasie
Midmar Forest
Echt
Elrick
Kingsford
Lumphanan
South Kirkton
Garlogie
Hazlehead
Gordon Highlanders Regimental Museum
Torry
Nigg Bay
Logie Coldstone
Tarland
Hill of Fare
Landerberry
Cullerlie Stone Circle
Loirston
Duthie Park & David Welch Winter Gardens
Milton of Auchinhove
Peel Ring
Torphins
The Birks
Milton of Cullerlie
Bieldside
Cults
Kincorth
Nigg
Altens
Tomnaverie Stone Circle
Coull
Hardgate
Charlestown
Ordie
Banchory-Devenick
Cove Bay
Mid Beltie
Milton of Campfield
Drum Castle (NTS)
Peterculter
Dinnet
Aboyne
Kincardine O'Neil
Glassel
Dee
Storybook Glen
Kirkton of Maryculter
Hillside
Findon
Oldhall
Birsemore
Cordach
Bridge of Canny
Crathes Castle (NTS)
Crathes
Portlethen
Birse
Maryhill
Blackhall Forest
Banchory
Kirkton of Durris
Denside
Auchattie
Cammachmore
Downies
Forest of Glentanar
Carnferg
Burn of Cattie
Netherley
Newtonhill
Drumhead
Strachan
Durris Forest
Cairn-mon-earn
Muchalls
Ballochan
Water of Feugh
Westerton
Mongour
Peter Hill
Rickarton
Mowtie
Cowie
Garron Point
Glendye Lodge
Stonehaven
Clachnaben
Bridge of Dye
Mount Battock
Kirktown of Fetteresso
Fetteresso Forest
Dunnottar Castle
Newmill
Mount Keen
ABERDEEN
81

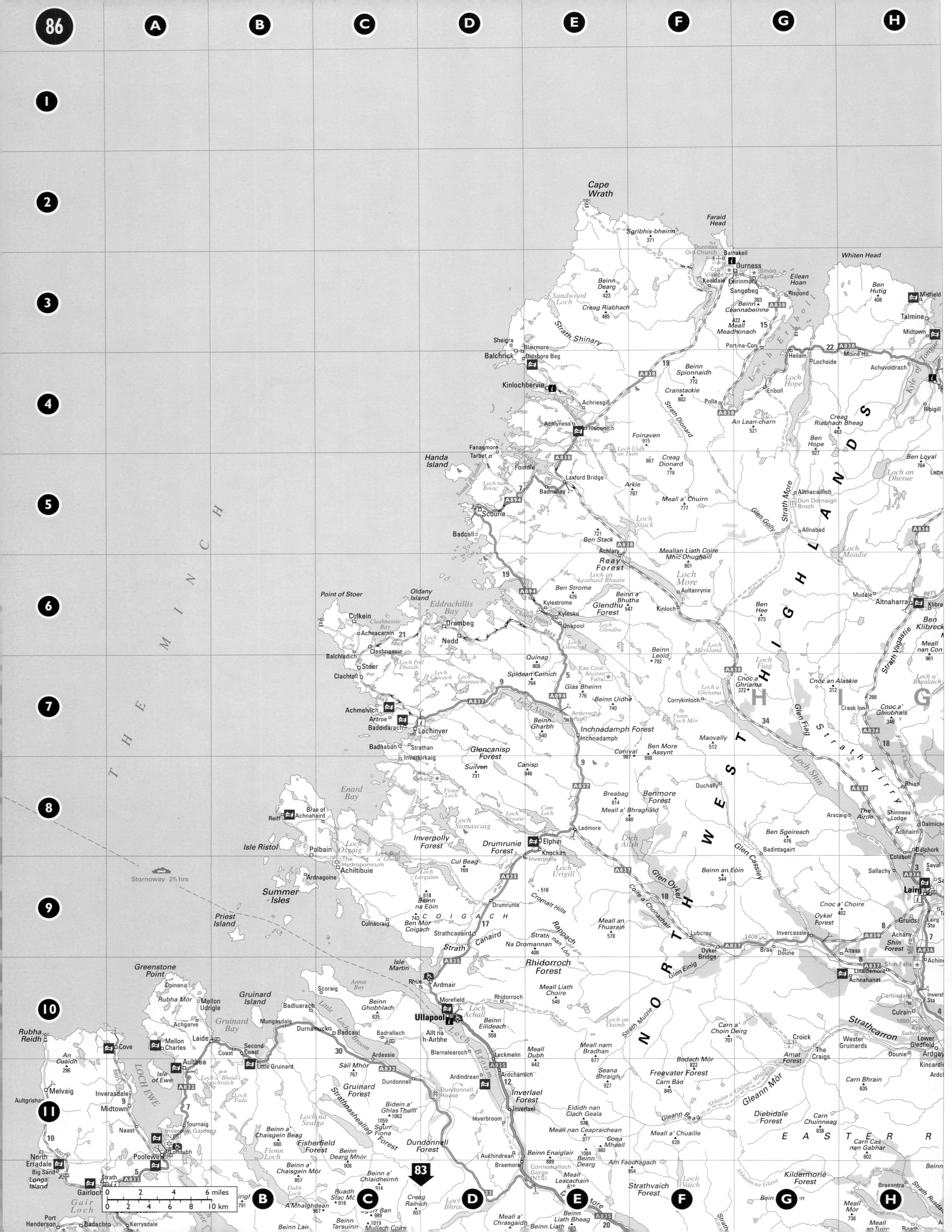
A
B
C
D
E
F
G
H
1
2
3
4
5
6
7
8
9
10
11
Cape Wrath
Faraid Head
Sgribhis-bheinn
371
Durness
Old Church
Balnakeil
Craft Village
Smoo Cave
Keoldale
Leirinmore
Eilean Hoan
Whiten Head
Beinn Dearg
423
Sandwood Loch
Creag Riabhach
485
Strath Shinary
Sangobeg
Rispond
Beinn Ceannabeinne
383
Meall Meadhonach
Ben Hutig
408
Midfield
Talmine
Midtown
Sheigra
Blairmore
Oldshore Beg
Balchrick
Port-na-Con
Loch Eriboll
A838
Heilam
Lochside
Moine Ho.
Achuvoldrach
Kyle of Tongue
Kinlochbervie
B801
Beinn Spionnaidh
772
Cranstackie
802
Polla
Eriboll
Loch Hope
Achriesgill
Achlyness
Rhiconich
Strath Dionard
An Lean-charn
521
Creag Riabhach Bheag
485
Ribigill
Foinaven
911
Fanagmore
Tarbet
Handa Island
Foindle
Creag Dionard
778
Ben Hope
927
Ben Loyal
764
Loch an Dherue
Laxford Bridge
Arkle
787
Badnabay
Meall a' Chuirn
777
Altnacaillich
Dun Dornaigil Broch
Strath More
Glen Golly
Scourie
A894
Loch Stack
Allnabad
A836
Badcall
721
Ben Stack
Achfary
Meallan Liath Coire Mhic Dhughaill
801
Loch Meadie
Reay Forest
THE MINCH
Loch More
Aultanrynie
Ben Strome
426
Beinn a' Bhutha
547
Point of Stoer
Oldany Island
Eddrachillis Bay
Kylestrome
Kylesku
Glendhu Forest
Kinloch
Unapool
Ben Hee
873
Mudale
Altnaharra
Klibreck
Culkein
Clashnessie Bay
Achnacarnin
Drumbeg
21
Nedd
B869
Clashnessie
Balchladich
Stoer
Clachtoll
Quinag
808
Spidean Coinich
764
Beinn Leoid
792
Loch Merkland
Loch Fiag
Ben Klibreck
Meall nan Con
961
Strath Vagastie
Eas Coul Aluinn Falls
Glas Bheinn
776
Loch a' Ghriama
Cnoc a' Ghriama
372
Cnoc an Alaskie
312
Loch a' Bhealaich
Achmelvich
Ardroe
Baddidarach
Lochinver
A837
Loch Assynt
Ardvreck Castle
Beinn Uidhe
740
Corrykinloch
NORTH WEST HIGHLANDS
Crask Inn
266
Cnoc a' Ghiubhais
346
Beinn Gharbh
540
Inchnadamph Forest
Inchnadamph
Glen Fiag
Maovally
512
Strath Tirry
Strathan
Badnaban
Inverkirkaig
Glencanisp Forest
Conival
987
Ben More Assynt
998
Loch Shin
Falls of Kirkaig
Suilven
731
Canisp
846
Duchally
Rhian
Enard Bay
Breabag
814
Benmore Forest
Meall a' Bhraghaid
688
Brae of Achnahaird
Reiff
Loch Sionascaig
Cam Loch
Ledmore
Ben Sgeireach
476
Arscaig
The Airde
Shinness Lodge
Achnairn
Dalmichy
Isle Ristol
Polbain
Inverpolly Forest
Drumrunie Forest
Elphin
Knockan
Loch Ailsh
Glen Cassley
Dalchork
Badintagairt
Colaboll
Stornoway 2¾ hrs
The Hydroponicum
Achiltibuie
Ardnagoine
Cul Beag
769
A835
Loch Urigill
Glen Oykel
Beinn an Eòin
544
Sallachy
Saval
Summer Isles
Loch Lurgainn
618
Beinn na Eòin
516
Cromalt Hills
18
Lairg
Priest Island
743
Ben Mòr Coigach
COIGACH
17
Drumrunie
Culnacraig
Cnoc a' Choire
402
Oykel Forest
Meall an Fhuarain
578
Corrie a Chonachair
Strathcanaird
Strath Canaird
Rappach
Strath nan Lon
Na Dromannan
408
Lubcroy
Oykel Bridge
Invercassley
A839
Gruids
Achany
Shin Forest
Brae
Doune
Altass
Isle Martin
Rhidorroch Forest
Glen Einig
Shin Falls
Greenstone Point
Opinan
Annat Bay
Scoraig
Rhue
Ardmair
Linsidemore
Achnahanat
Gruinard Island
Rubha Mòr
Mellon Udrigle
Badluarach
Little Loch Broom
Beinn Ghobhlach
635
Morefield
Rhidorroch
Meall Liath Choire
548
Strath Mulzie
Carbisdale
Culrain
Strathcarron
Rubha Reidh
Achgarve
Gruinard Bay
Mungasdale
Ullapool
Loch Achall
Beinn Eilideach
558
Loch an Daimh
Carn a' Choin Deirg
701
Wester Gruinards
Kyle of Sutherland
Lower Gledfield
Ardgay
An Cuaidh
296
Cove
Mellon Charles
Laide
Second Coast
Dundonnell
Badcaul
Badrallach
Allt na h-Airbhe
Croick
Aultbea
Coast
30
Ardessie
Blarnalearoch
Leckmelm
Meall Dubh
642
Meall nam Bradhan
677
Amat Forest
The Craigs
Dounie
B8057
LOCH EWE
Isle of Ewe
Little Gruinard
Sàil Mhòr
767
A832
Ardindrean
Ardcharnich
12
Seana Bhraigh
927
Bodach Mòr
822
Freevater Forest
Carn Bàn
845
Carn Bhrain
635
Kincardine
Loch a' Bhaid-luachraich
Gruinard Forest
Dundonnell House
Inverlael Forest
Inverlael
Abhainn a' Ghlinne Mhoir
Gleann Mòr
Aultgrishan
Melvaig
Inverasdale
9
Midtown
Loch Fada
Strathnasheallag Forest
Bidein a' Ghlas Thuill
1062
1059
Sgurr Fiona
Inverbroom
Eididh nan Clach Geala
928
Gleann Beag
Diebidale Forest
Carn Chuinneag
838
Tournaig
Inverewe Gardens (NTS)
Naast
Loch na Sealga
Beinn a' Chaisgein Beag
680
Fisherfield Forest
Dundonnell Forest
Meall nan Ceapraichean
977
Cona' Mheall
980
Meall a' Chuilla
628
EASTER ROSS
Carn Chuinneag
10
North Erradale
Poolewe
Londubh
Fionn Loch
Beinn Dearg Mhòr
908
Auchindrean
Beinn Enaiglair
889
1084
Beinn Dearg
Am Faochagach
954
Carn Cas nan Gabhar
602
Big Sand
Longa Island
Strath
Gairloch
A832
5
Beinn a' Chaisgein Mòr
857
Beinn a' Chlaidheimh
914
83
Braemore
Corrieshalloch Gorge (NTS)
Meall Leacachain
Loch Vaich
Strathvaich Forest
Abhainn na Glasa
Kildermorie Forest
Braeantra
Strath Rusdale
Gair Loch
Dubh Loch
Ruadh Stac Mòr
918
Creag Rainich
807
A'Mhaighdean
967
Sgurr Ban
989
Beinn Liath Bheag
665
Meall a' Chrasgaidh
Meall Mòr
738
Meall an Tuirc
Port Henderson
Badachro
Kerrysdale
Beinn Lair
Beinn Tarsuinn
Mullach Coire
Beinn Liath
A835
20
0 2 4 6 miles
0 2 4 6 8 10 km

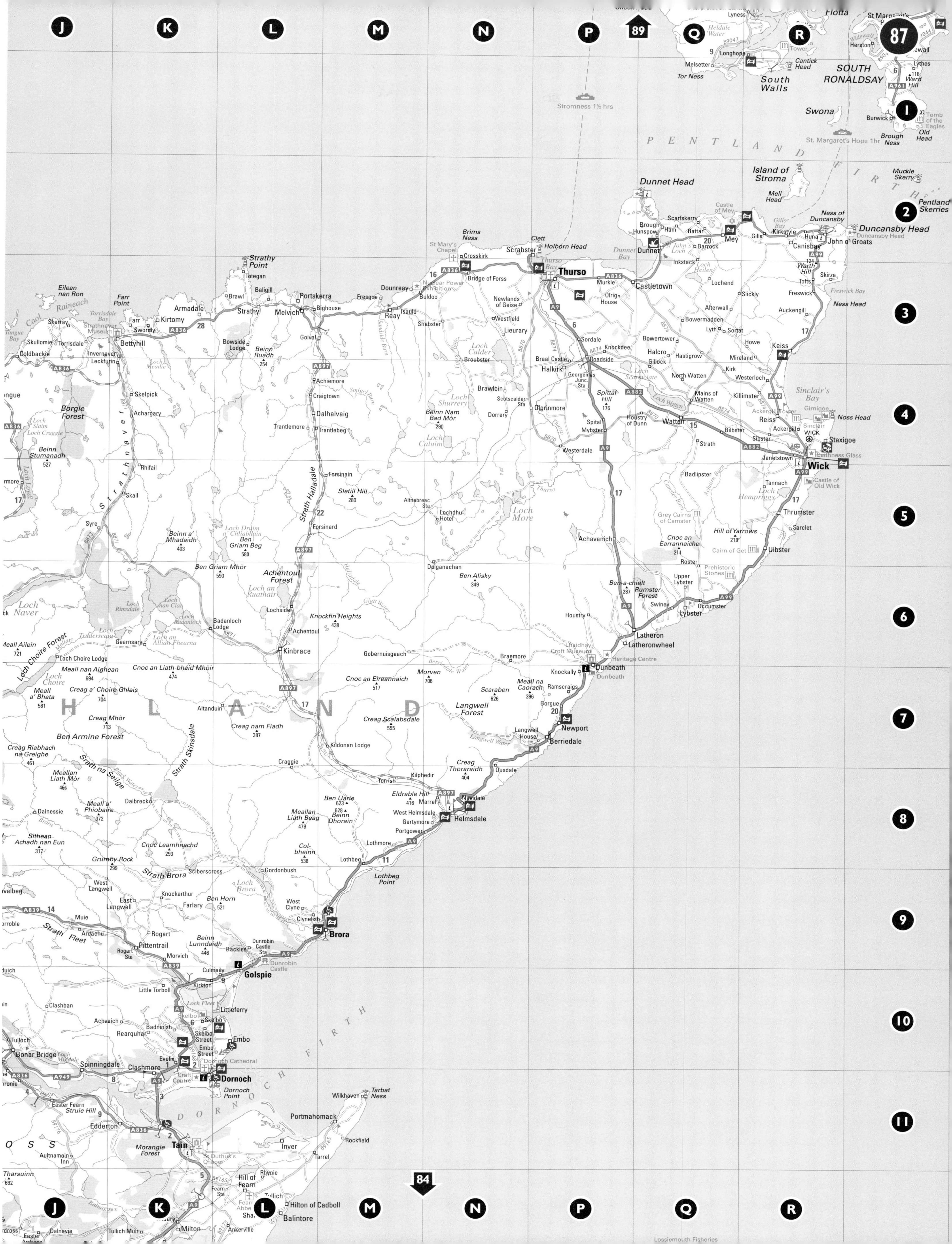
J
K
L
M
N
P
Q
R
89
84
1
2
3
4
5
6
7
8
9
10
11
Flotta
St Margaret's Hope
Heldale Water
Lyness
B9047
Longhope
Tower
Melsetter
Tor Ness
Cantick Head
South Walls
SOUTH RONALDSAY
Herston
Lythes
Ward Hill
Swona
Burwick
Tomb of the Eagles
Old Head
Brough Ness
St. Margaret's Hope 1hr
Stromness 1½ hrs
P E N T L A N D   F I R T H
Island of Stroma
Mell Head
Muckle Skerry
Pentland Skerries
Dunnet Head
Castle of Mey
Ness of Duncansby
Duncansby Head
Scarfskerry
Brough
Ham
Rattar
Mey
Gills
Gills Bay
Kirkstyle
Huna
John o' Groats
Canisbay
Hunspow
Dunnet
Dunnet Bay
Barrock
Inkstack
Loch Heilen
Lochend
Warth Hill
Tofts
Skirza
Freswick
Freswick Bay
Ness Head
Clett
Holborn Head
Scrabster
Brims Ness
St Mary's Chapel
Crosskirk
Thurso Bay
Thurso
Murkle
Castletown
Bridge of Forss
Olrig House
Newlands of Geise
Westfield
Lieurary
Strathy Point
Totegan
Baligill
Brawl
Strathy
Portskerra
Melvich
Bighouse
Dounreay
Nuclear Power Exhibition
Buldoo
Fresgoe
Reay
Isauld
Shebster
Eilean nan Ron
Farr Point
Torrisdale Bay
Caol Raineach
Armadale
Kirtomy
Farr
Swordly
Skerray
Strathnaver Museum
Tongue Bay
Skullomie
Torrisdale
Bettyhill
Coldbackie
Invernaver
Leckfurin
Loch Meadie
Bowside Lodge
Beinn Ruadh 254
Golval
Sandside Burn
Forss Water
Loch Calder
Broubster
Sordale
Knockdee
Bowertower
Halcro
Hastigrow
Gillock
Braal Castle
Halkirk
Roadside
Georgemas Junc. Sta
Loch Scarmclate
North Watten
Slickly
Alterwall
Bowermadden
Lyth
Sortat
Howe
Mireland
Kirk
Keiss
Auckengill
Westerloch
Killimster
Mains of Watten
Loch Watten
Sinclair's Bay
Girnigoe
Noss Head
Ackergill Tower
Reiss
Ackergill
Sinclair
WICK
Staxigoe
Caithness Glass
Bilbster
Sibster
Janetstown
Wick
Watten
Spittal Hill 176
Houstry of Dunn
Spittal
Mybster
Olgrinmore
Brawlbin
Scotscalder Sta
Dorrery
Loch Shurrery
Beinn Nam Bad Mòr 290
Loch Caluim
Westerdale
Strath
Badlipster
Tannach
Castle of Old Wick
Loch Hempriggs
Thrumster
Sarclet
Grey Cairns of Camster
Hill of Yarrows 213
Cnoc an Earrannaiche 211
Cairn of Get
Ulbster
Roster
Prehistoric Stones
Upper Lybster
Lybster
Occumster
Swiney
Ben-a-chielt 287
Rumster Forest
Houstry
Achavanich
Loch More
Altnabreac Sta
Lochdhu Hotel
Sletill Hill 280
Forsinain
Achiemore
Craigtown
Smisel Burn
Dalhalvaig
Trantlemore
Trantlebeg
Strath Halladale
Forsinard
Skelpick
Achargary
Strathnaver
Rhifail
Skail
Syre
Borgie Forest
Loch Slaim
Loch Craggie
Beinn Stumanadh 527
Loch Loyal
Tongue
Loch Naver
Beinn a' Mhadaidh 403
Loch Druim a' Chliabhain
Ben Griam Beg 580
Ben Griam Mhòr 590
Achentoul Forest
Loch an Ruathair
Dalganachan
Ben Alisky 349
Loch Rimsdale
Loch nan Clar
Loch Badanloch
Badanloch Lodge
Lochside
Knockfin Heights 438
Glutt Water
Achentoul
Loch Truderscaig
Gearnsary
Loch an Alltan Fhearna
Kinbrace
Meall Ailein 721
Loch Choire Forest
Loch Choire Lodge
Meall nan Aighean 694
Loch Choire
Cnoc an Liath-bhaid Mhòir 474
Gobernuisgeach
Braemore
Berriedale Water
Laidhay Croft Museum
Latheron
Latheronwheel
Heritage Centre
Dunbeath
Knockally
Morven 706
Cnoc an Eireannaich 517
Meall na Caorach 396
Ramscraigs
Scaraben 626
Meall a' Bhata 581
Creag a' Choire Ghlais 704
H I G H L A N D
Altanduin
Borgue
Langwell Forest
Creag Mhòr 713
Creag nam Fiadh 387
Creag Scalabsdale 555
Newport
Langwell House
Berriedale
Langwell Water
Ben Armine Forest
Kildonan Lodge
Creag Riabhach na Greighe 461
Strath na Seilge
Strath Skinsdale
Craggie
Creag Thoraraidh 404
Ousdale
Kilphedir
Torrish
Meallan Liath Mòr 463
Eldrable Hill 416
Navidale
Marrel
Ben Uarie 623
Beinn Dhorain 628
Helmsdale
West Helmsdale
Gartymore
Portgower
Dalbreck
Dalnessie
Meall a' Phiobaire 372
Meallan Liath Beag 479
Sithean Achadh nan Eun 317
Cnoc Leamhnachd 293
Col-bheinn 538
Lothmore
Lothbeg
Lothbeg Point
Grumby Rock 299
Strath Brora
Sciberscross
Gordonbush
Loch Brora
West Langwell
East Langwell
Knockarthur
Farlary
Ben Horn 521
West Clyne
Clynelish
Brora
Muie
Ardachu
Strath Fleet
Rogart
Beinn Lunndaidh 446
Pittentrail
Dunrobin Castle Sta
Backies
Rogart Sta
Morvich
Dunrobin Castle
Culmaily
Golspie
Kirkton
Little Torboll
Loch Fleet
Littleferry
Clashban
Skelbo
Achvaich
Rearquhar
Badninish
Skelbo Street
Embo Street
Embo
Tulloch
Bonar Bridge
Evelix
Dornoch Cathedral
Spinningdale
Clashmore
Craft Centre
Dornoch
Dornoch Point
D O R N O C H   F I R T H
Easter Fearn
Struie Hill
Edderton
Wilkhaven
Tarbat Ness
Portmahomack
Rockfield
Morangie Forest
Tain
St Duthus's Chapel
Inver
Tarrel
Aultnamain Inn
Tharsuinn 692
Hill of Fearn
Rhynie
Fearn Sta
Tullich
Fearn Abbey
Hilton of Cadboll
Balintore
Shandwick
Milton
Ankerville
Dalnavie
Tullich Muir
Lossiemouth Fisheries
R O S S
A836
A9
A99
A882
A897
A839
A949
A961
B874
B870
B876
B855
B871
B873
B9176
B9165
B9175

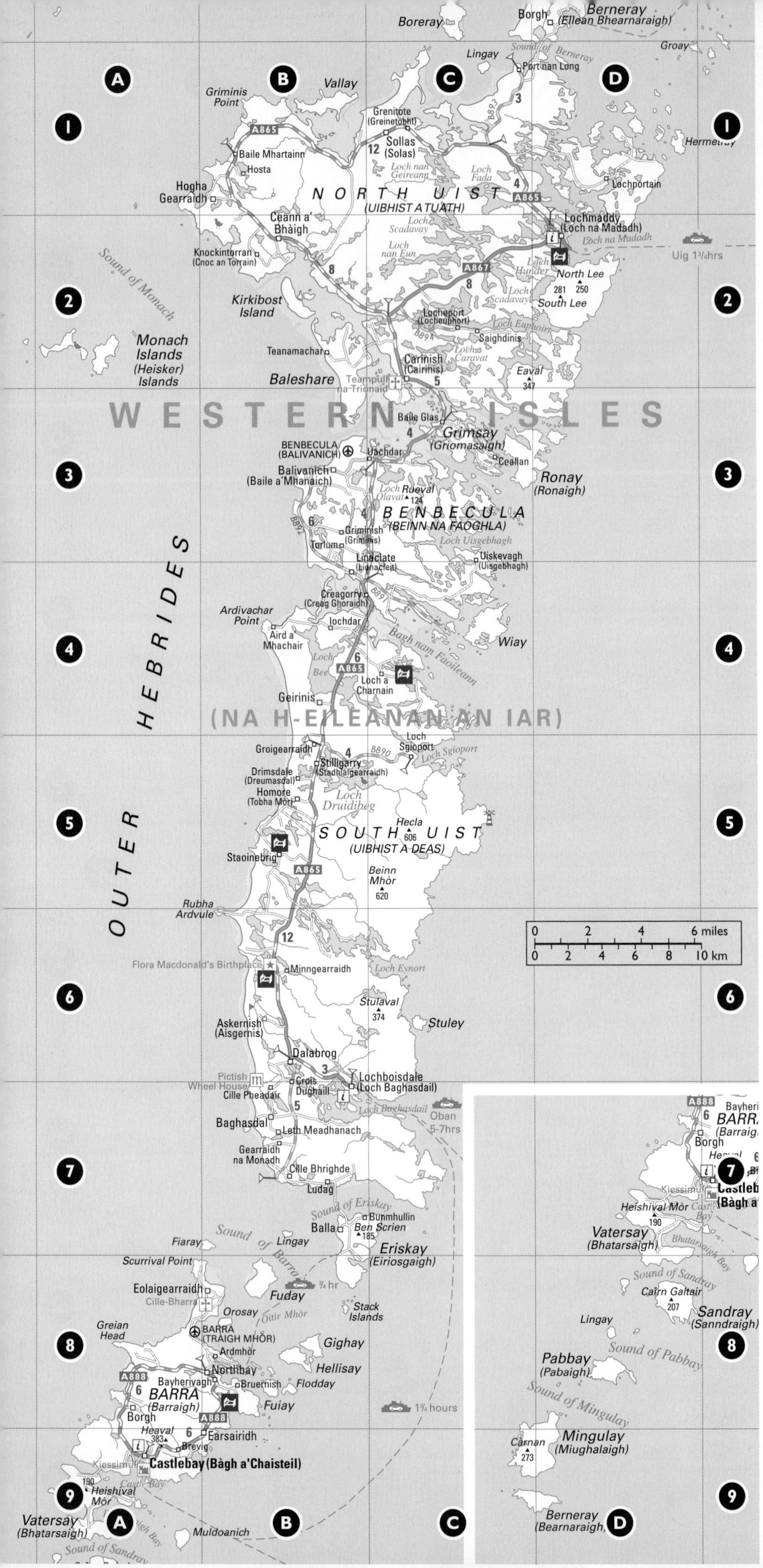
WESTERN ISLES
(NA H-EILEANAN AN IAR)
OUTER HEBRIDES
NORTH UIST
(UIBHIST A TUATH)
BENBECULA
(BEINN NA FAOGHLA)
SOUTH UIST
(UIBHIST A DEAS)
BARRA
(Barraigh)
Lochmaddy
(Loch na Madadh)
Lochboisdale
(Loch Baghasdail)
Castlebay (Bàgh a'Chaisteil)
BENBECULA
(BALIVANICH)
Boreray
Berneray
(Eilean Bhearnaraigh)
Vallay
Griminis Point
Kirkibost Island
Monach Islands
(Heisker)
Islands
Sound of Monach
Baleshare
Grimsay
(Griomasaigh)
Ronay
(Ronaigh)
Wiay
Stuley
Eriskay
(Eiriosgaigh)
Fuday
Gighay
Hellisay
Flodday
Fuiay
Vatersay
(Bhatarsaigh)
Sandray
(Sanndraigh)
Pabbay
(Pabaigh)
Mingulay
(Miughalaigh)
Berneray
(Bearnaraigh)
Lingay
Hecla
606
Beinn Mhòr
620
Eaval
347
Rubha Ardvule
Flora Macdonald's Birthplace
Uig 1¾hrs
Oban 5-7hrs
1¾ hours
0 2 4 6 miles
0 2 4 6 8 10 km

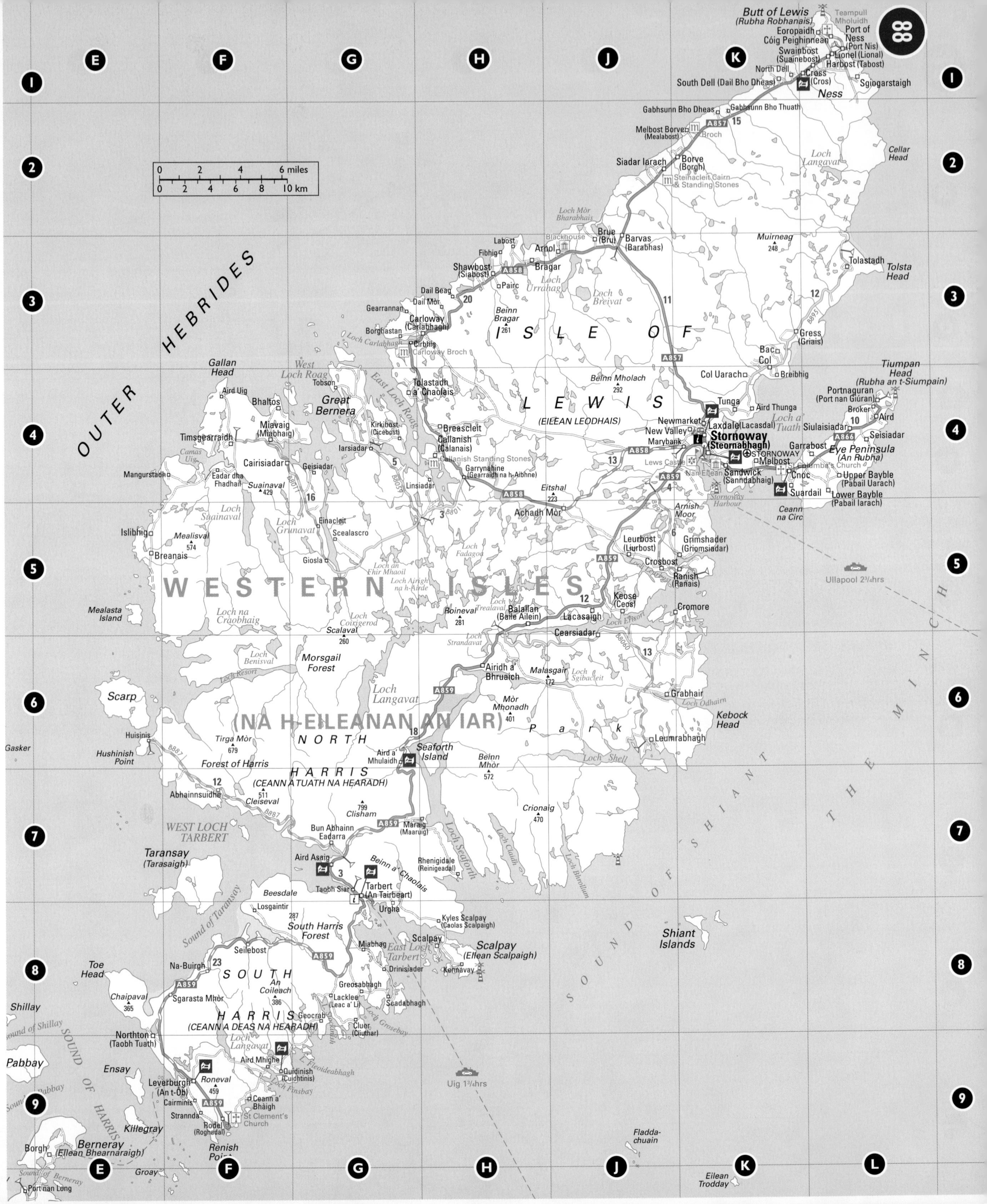
WESTERN ISLES
(NA H-EILEANAN AN IAR)
OUTER HEBRIDES
ISLE OF LEWIS
(EILEAN LEODHAIS)
NORTH HARRIS
(CEANN A TUATH NA HEARADH)
SOUTH HARRIS
(CEANN A DEAS NA HEARADH)
Stornoway
(Steornabhagh)
Butt of Lewis
(Rubha Robhanais)
Ness
Tolsta Head
Tiumpan Head
(Rubha an t-Siumpain)
Eye Peninsula
(An Rubha)
Great Bernera
Gallan Head
Scarp
Taransay
(Tarasaigh)
Scalpay
(Eilean Scalpaigh)
Shiant Islands
Kebock Head
Tarbert
(An Tairbeart)
Leverburgh
(An t-Ob)
Rodel
(Roghadal)
Berneray
(Eilean Bhearnaraigh)
Pabbay
Killegray
Ensay
Toe Head
Mealasta Island
Morsgail Forest
Forest of Harris
South Harris Forest
Park
Loch Seaforth
Loch Langavat
West Loch Tarbert
Clisham
799
Sound of Harris
Sound of Shiant
The Minch
Ullapool 2¾hrs
Uig 1¾hrs
0 2 4 6 miles
0 2 4 6 8 10 km

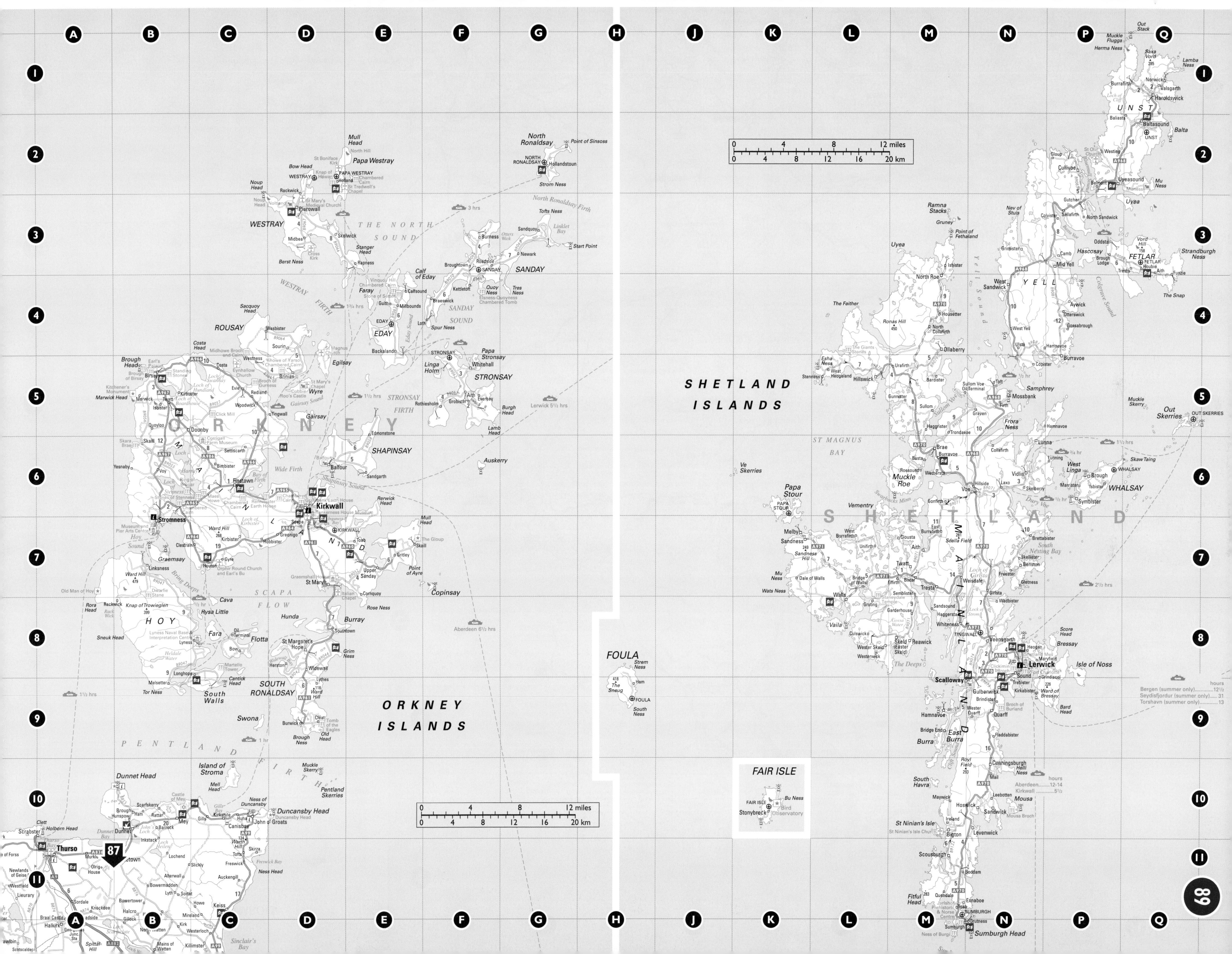

ORKNEY ISLANDS
SHETLAND ISLANDS
ORKNEY
MAINLAND
SHETLAND
FAIR ISLE
FOULA
WESTRAY
Papa Westray
North Ronaldsay
SANDAY
EDAY
STRONSAY
ROUSAY
SHAPINSAY
HOY
SOUTH RONALDSAY
Kirkwall
Stromness
Thurso
Lerwick
Scalloway
UNST
YELL
FETLAR
WHALSAY
Papa Stour
Muckle Roe
SCAPA FLOW
PENTLAND FIRTH
ST MAGNUS BAY
Yell Sound
Sumburgh Head
Duncansby Head
Dunnet Head
Isle of Noss
Bressay
Out Skerries
Bergen (summer only) 12½
Seydisfjordur (summer only) 31
Torshavn (summer only) 13
Aberdeen 12-14
Kirkwall 5½
Lerwick 5½ hrs
Aberdeen 6½ hrs
87

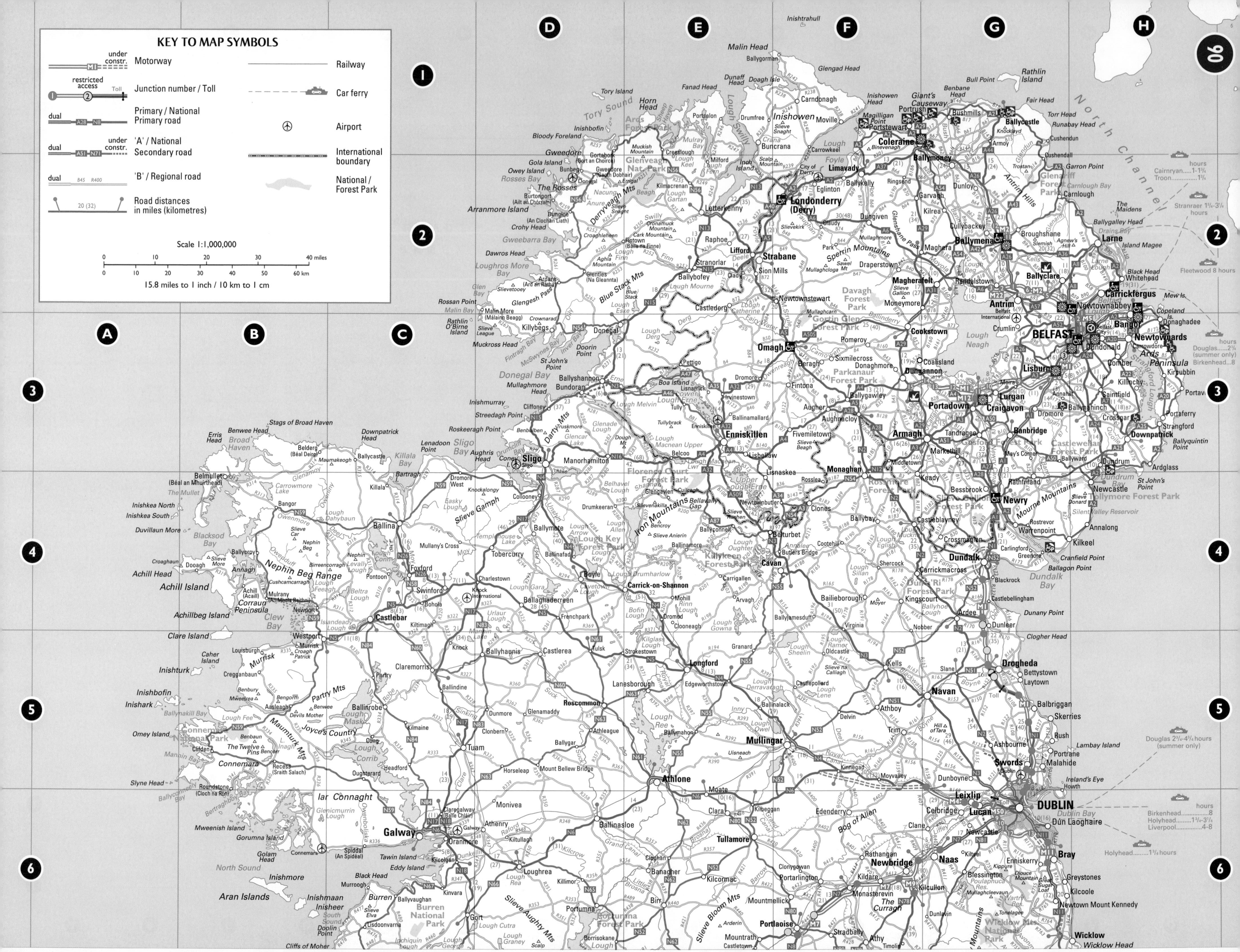
KEY TO MAP SYMBOLS
Motorway
under constr.
Junction number / Toll
restricted access
Primary / National Primary road
dual
'A' / National Secondary road
'B' / Regional road
Road distances in miles (kilometres)
20 (32)
Railway
Car ferry
Airport
International boundary
National / Forest Park
Scale 1:1,000,000
15.8 miles to 1 inch / 10 km to 1 cm
North Channel
Cairnryan......1-1¾ hours
Troon..........1¾
Stranraer 1¾-3¼ hours
Fleetwood 8 hours
Douglas......2¾ (summer only)
Birkenhead...8
Douglas 2¾-4¾ hours (summer only)
Birkenhead..........8
Holyhead.........1¾-3¼
Liverpool..........4-8
Holyhead.........1¾ hours
Malin Head
Inishowen
Londonderry (Derry)
Coleraine
Ballymoney
Ballymena
Antrim
Larne
Carrickfergus
BELFAST
Bangor
Newtownards
Lisburn
Lurgan
Craigavon
Portadown
Armagh
Newry
Downpatrick
Dundalk
Drogheda
DUBLIN
Dún Laoghaire
Bray
Wicklow
Naas
Newbridge
Portlaoise
Tullamore
Athlone
Mullingar
Longford
Navan
Cavan
Monaghan
Enniskillen
Omagh
Strabane
Letterkenny
Donegal
Sligo
Ballina
Castlebar
Westport
Tuam
Galway
Roscommon
Carrick-on-Shannon
Achill Island
Aran Islands
Connemara
Lough Neagh
Sperrin Mountains
Mourne Mountains
Slieve Bloom Mts
Slieve Aughty Mts
Nephin Beg Range
Blue Stack Mts
Derryveagh Mts
Iron Mountains
Antrim Hills
Burren National Park
Cliffs of Moher

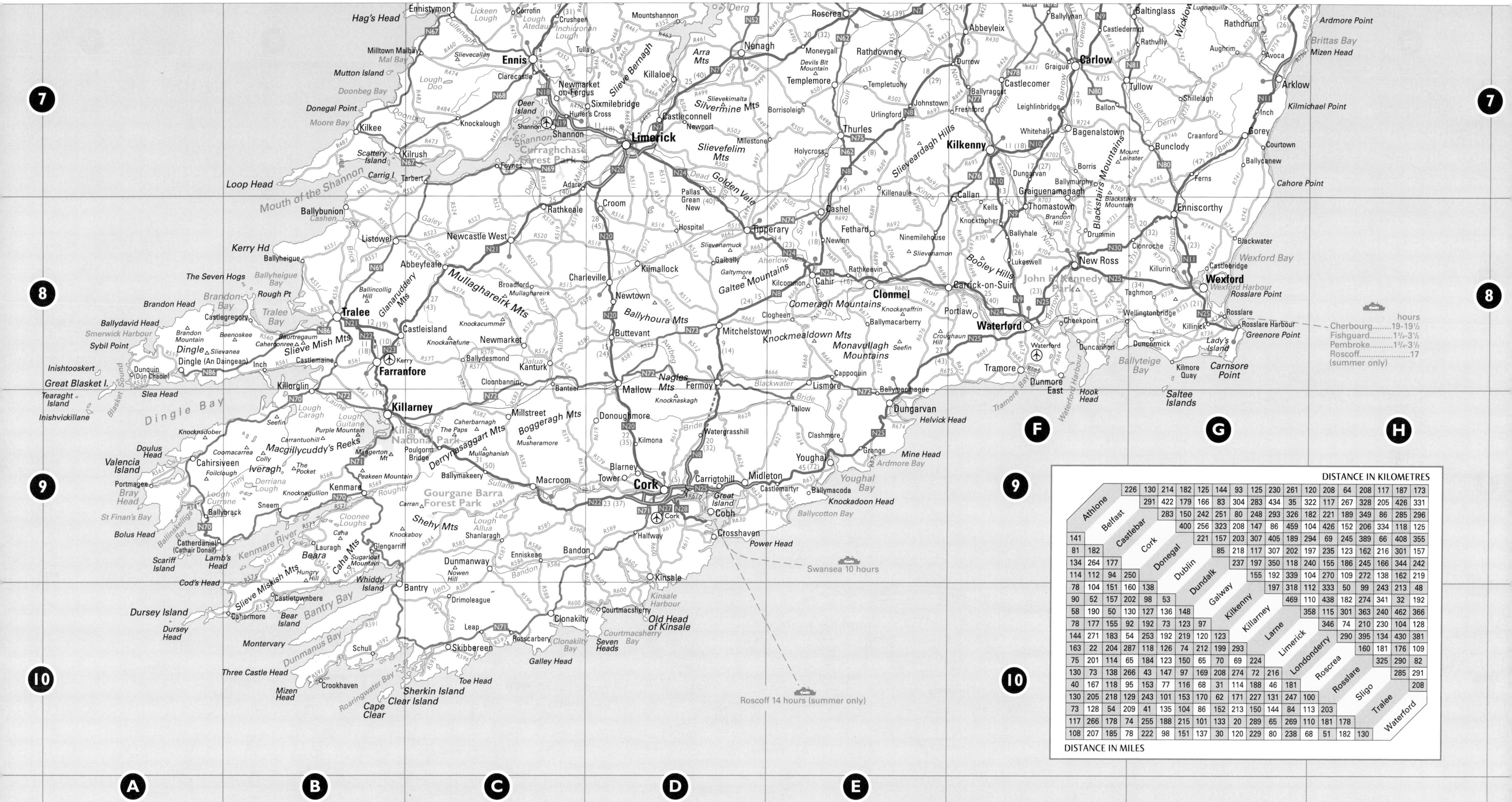

DISTANCE IN KILOMETRES (above the diagonal) / **DISTANCE IN MILES** (below the diagonal)

	Athlone	Belfast	Castlebar	Cork	Donegal	Dublin	Dundalk	Galway	Kilkenny	Killarney	Larne	Limerick	Londonderry	Roscrea	Rosslare	Sligo	Tralee	Waterford
Athlone		226	130	214	182	125	144	93	125	230	261	120	208	64	208	117	187	173
Belfast	141		291	422	179	166	83	304	283	434	35	322	117	267	328	205	426	331
Castlebar	81	182		283	150	242	251	80	248	293	326	182	221	189	349	86	285	296
Cork	134	264	177		400	256	323	208	147	86	459	104	426	152	206	334	118	125
Donegal	114	112	94	250		221	157	203	307	405	189	294	69	245	389	66	408	355
Dublin	78	104	151	160	138		85	218	117	307	202	197	235	123	162	216	301	157
Dundalk	90	52	157	202	98	53		237	197	350	118	240	155	186	245	166	344	242
Galway	58	190	50	130	127	136	148		155	192	339	104	270	109	272	138	162	219
Kilkenny	78	177	155	92	192	73	123	97		197	318	112	333	50	99	243	213	48
Killarney	144	271	183	54	253	192	219	120	123		469	110	438	182	274	341	32	192
Larne	163	22	204	287	118	126	74	212	199	293		358	115	301	363	240	462	366
Limerick	75	201	114	65	184	123	150	65	70	69	224		346	74	210	230	104	128
Londonderry	130	73	138	266	43	147	97	169	208	274	72	216		290	395	134	430	381
Roscrea	40	167	118	95	153	77	116	68	31	114	188	46	181		160	181	176	109
Rosslare	130	205	218	129	243	101	153	170	62	171	227	131	247	100		325	290	82
Sligo	73	128	54	209	41	135	104	86	152	213	150	144	84	113	203		285	291
Tralee	117	266	178	74	255	188	215	101	133	20	289	65	269	110	181	178		208
Waterford	108	207	185	78	222	98	151	137	30	120	229	80	238	68	51	182	130	

FERRY INFORMATION

Route: **Larne to Cairnryan**
Duration: 1 hr - 1 hrs 45 mins
Season: *All year*
Operator: P&O Irish Sea
Telephone number (from UK): *0870 24 24 777*
Web address: www.poirishsea.com

Arranmore to Burtonport
20 mins
All year
Arranmore Island Ferry Service
00353 75 20532
www.littleireland.ie/arranmoreferry

Belfast to Birkenhead
8 hrs
All year
NorseMerchant Ferries
0870 600 4321
www.norsemerchant.com

Belfast to Douglas
2 hrs 45 mins
Summer only
Isle of Man Steam Packet Co
08705 523 523
www.steam-packet.com

Belfast to Stranraer
1 hr 45 mins - 3 hrs 15 mins
All year
Stena Line
08705 707070
www.stenaline.co.uk

Cork to Roscoff
11 hrs
Summer only
Brittany Ferries
0870 366 5333
www.brittany-ferries.ie

Cork to Swansea
10 hrs
All year
Swansea Cork Ferries
01792 456116
www.swansea-cork.ie

Dublin to Birkenhead
8 hrs
All year
NorseMerchant Ferries
0870 600 4321
www.norsemerchant.com

Dublin to Douglas
2 hrs 45 mins - 4 hrs 45 mins
Summer only
Isle of Man Steam Packet Co
08705 523 523
www.steam-packet.com

Dublin City to Holyhead
1 hr 50 mins - 3 hrs 15 mins
All year
Irish Ferries
08705 171717
www.irishferries.com

Dublin Port to Holyhead
2 hrs 45 mins
All year
Stena Line
08705 707070
www.stenaline.co.uk

Dublin to Liverpool
4 hrs
Mar-Dec
Irish Sea Express
0870 112 2222
www.irishseaexpress.com

Dublin to Liverpool
8 hrs
All year
P&O Irish Sea
0870 24 24 777
www.poirishsea.com

Dún Laoghaire to Holyhead
1 hr 40 mins
All year
Stena Line
08705 707070
www.stenaline.co.uk

Larne to Cairnryan
1 hr - 1 hr 45 mins
All year
P&O Irish Sea
0870 24 24 777
www.poirishsea.com

Larne to Fleetwood
8 hrs
All year
Stena Line
08705 707070
www.stenaline.co.uk

Larne to Troon
1 hr 50 mins
Summer only
P&O Irish Sea
0870 24 24 777
www.poirishsea.com

Lough Foyle Ferry
15 mins
All year
Lough Foyle Ferry
00353 74 9381901
www.loughfoyleferry.com

Passage East to Ballyhack
5 mins
All year
Passage East Car Ferry Company
00353 51 382480
homepage.tinet.ie/~passferry/

Rosslare to Cherbourg
19 hrs 30 mins
All year
Irish Ferries
08705 171717
www.irishferries.com

Rosslare to Cherbourg
19 hrs
All year
P&O Irish Sea
0870 24 24 777
www.poirishsea.com

Rosslare to Fishguard
1 hr 50 mins - 3 hrs 30 mins
All year
Stena Line
08705 707070
www.stenaline.co.uk

Rosslare to Pembroke
3 hrs 45 mins
All year
Irish Ferries
08705 171717
www.irishferries.com

Rosslare to Roscoff
17 hrs
Summer only
Irish Ferries
08705 171717
www.irishferries.com

Tarbert to Killimer
20 mins
All year
Shannon Ferry Limited
00353 65 905 3124
www.shannonferries.com

AIRPORT INFORMATION

Airport (airport code): **Dublin Airport (DUB)**
Flight details: International & scheduled flights
Address: Fingal, IRELAND
Telephone number (from UK): *00353 1 8141 111*
Web address: www.dublinairport.com

Belfast City Airport (BHD)
Scheduled flights
Belfast
NORTHERN IRELAND
BT3 9JH
028 9093 9093
www.belfastcityairport.com

Belfast International Airport (BFS)
International & scheduled flights
Aldergrove
Belfast
NORTHERN IRELAND
BT29 4AB
028 9448 4848
www.bial.co.uk

City of Derry Airport (LDY)
International & scheduled flights
Airport Road
Eglinton
NORTHERN IRELAND
028 7181 0784
www.cityofderryairport.com

Connemara Airport (NNR)
Scheduled flights
Inverin
County Galway
IRELAND
00353 91 593034

Cork Airport (ORK)
International & scheduled flights
Cork City
IRELAND
00353 21 4313 131
www.corkairport.com

Donegal Airport (CFN)
International & scheduled flights
Carrickfinn
County Donegal
IRELAND
00353 74 9548232
www.donegalairport.ie

Dublin Airport (DUB)
International & scheduled flights
Fingal
IRELAND
00353 1 8141 111
www.dublinairport.com

Enniskillen (St Angelo) Airport (ENK)
Scheduled flights
Rossahilly
Fermanagh
NORTHERN IRELAND
028 6632 8282
www.enniskillen.com/enniskillen_air.html

Galway Airport (GWY)
International & scheduled flights
Carnmore
County Galway
IRELAND
00353 71 755569
www.galwayairport.com

Kerry Airport (KIR)
International & scheduled flights
Farranfore
Killarney
County Kerry
IRELAND
00353 66 976 4644
www.kerryairport.ie

Knock International Airport (NOC)
International & scheduled flights
Charlestown
County Mayo
IRELAND
00353 94 9367222
www.knockairport.com

Shannon Airport (SNN)
International & scheduled flights
County Clare
IRELAND
00353 61 712000
www.shannonairport.com

Sligo Airport (SXL)
Scheduled flights
Strandhill
County Sligo
IRELAND
00353 71 916 8396
www.sligoairport.com

Waterford Regional Airport (WAT)
Scheduled flights
Killowen
County Waterford
IRELAND
00353 51 875589
www.flywaterford.com

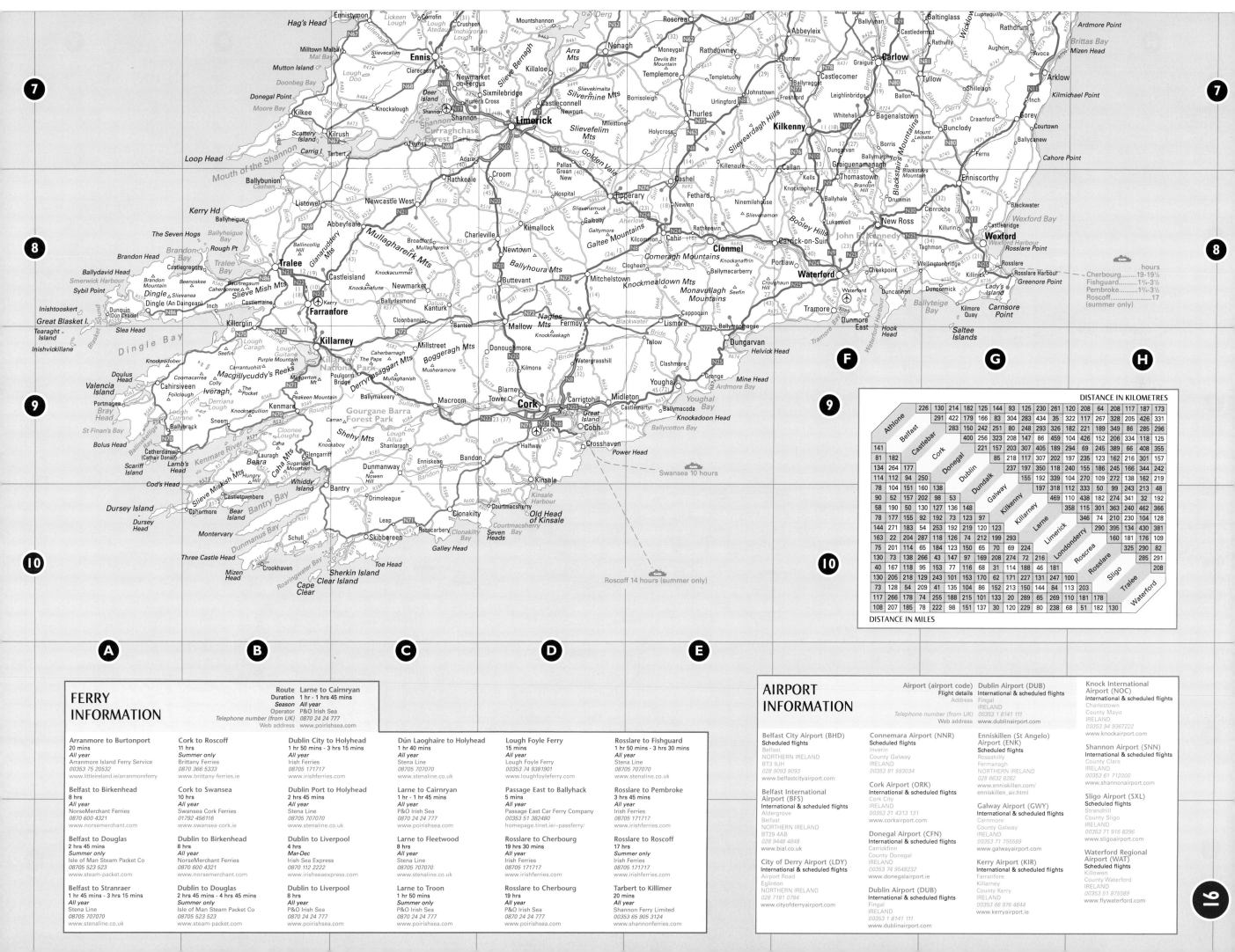

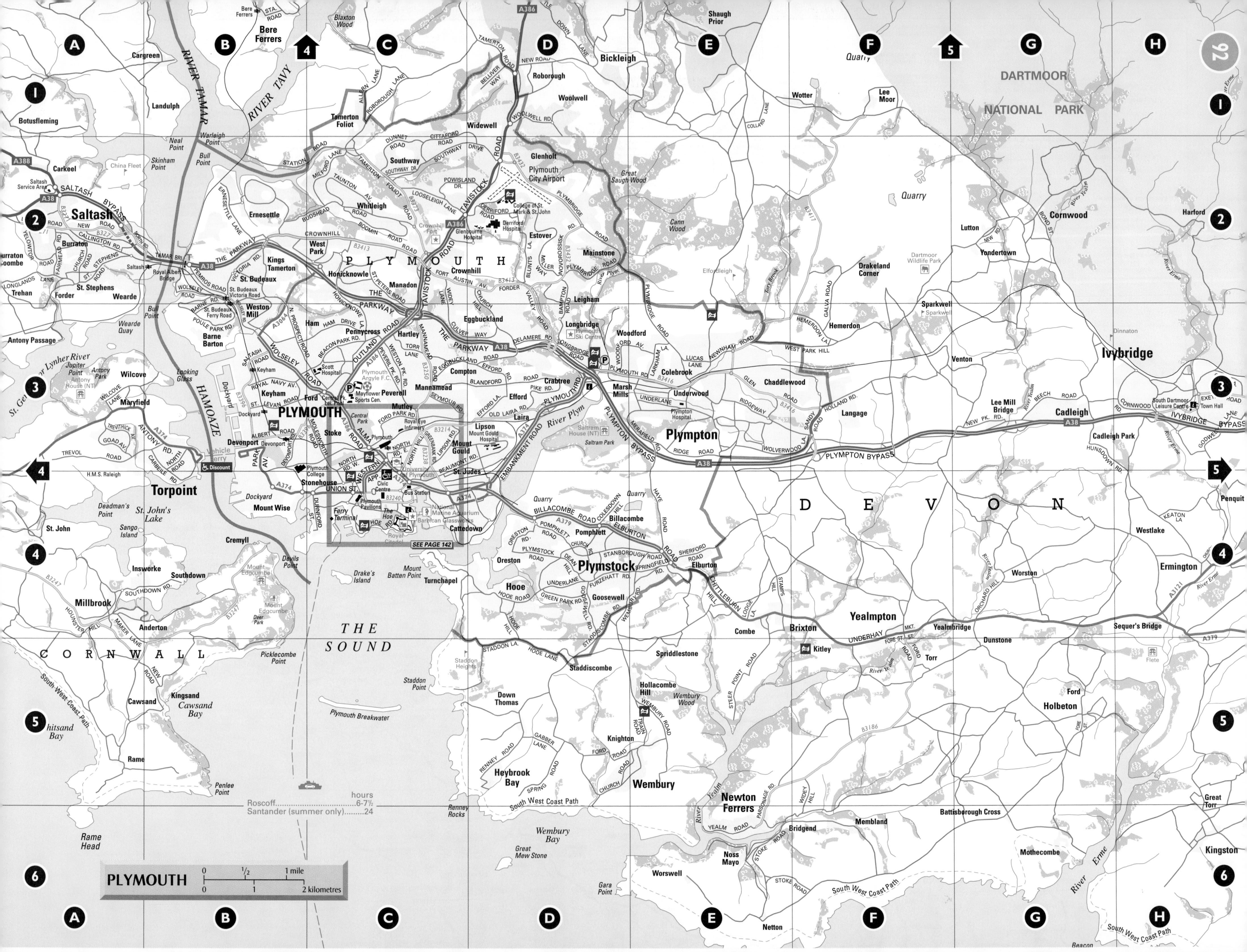
PLYMOUTH
DARTMOOR NATIONAL PARK
D E V O N
C O R N W A L L
THE SOUND
HAMOAZE
RIVER TAMAR
RIVER TAVY
Saltash
Plymouth
Plympton
Plymstock
Ivybridge
Yealmpton
Torpoint
Bere Ferrers
Tamerton Foliot
Bickleigh
Roborough
Woolwell
Widewell
Glenholt
Plymouth City Airport
Estover
Mainstone
Leigham
Crownhill
Southway
Whitleigh
Ernesettle
West Park
Honicknowle
Manadon
Kings Tamerton
St. Budeaux
Weston Mill
Ham
Pennycross
Hartley
Eggbuckland
Longbridge
Woodford
Colebrook
Chaddlewood
Underwood
Marsh Mills
Crabtree
Efford
Laira
Compton
Mannamead
Peverell
Mutley
Keyham
Ford
Stoke
Devonport
Stonehouse
Mount Wise
Lipson
Mount Gould
St. Judes
Cattedown
Turnchapel
Oreston
Hooe
Pomphlett
Billacombe
Elburton
Goosewell
Staddiscombe
Down Thomas
Heybrook Bay
Wembury
Knighton
Hollacombe Hill
Spriddlestone
Combe
Brixton
Kitley
Newton Ferrers
Noss Mayo
Bridgend
Membland
Worswell
Netton
Yealmbridge
Torr
Dunstone
Holbeton
Ford
Mothecombe
Battisborough Cross
Kingston
Great Torr
Sequer's Bridge
Flete
Ermington
Westlake
Worston
Penquit
Cadleigh
Cadleigh Park
Lee Mill Bridge
Langage
Venton
Sparkwell
Hemerdon
Drakeland Corner
Lee Moor
Wotter
Shaugh Prior
Lutton
Yondertown
Cornwood
Harford
Dartmoor Wildlife Park
Cann Wood
Great Saugh Wood
Cremyll
Mount Edgcumbe
Millbrook
Insworke
Southdown
Anderton
Cawsand
Kingsand
Cawsand Bay
Rame
Rame Head
Penlee Point
Picklecombe Point
St. John
St. John's Lake
Maryfield
Wilcove
Antony Passage
Forder
Trehan
St. Stephens
Wearde
Burraton
Carkeel
Botusfleming
Cargreen
Landulph
Plymouth Breakwater
Drake's Island
Mount Batten Point
Staddon Point
Wembury Bay
Great Mew Stone
Gara Point
South West Coast Path
PLYMPTON BYPASS
A38
A386
A374
A379
SEE PAGE 142
Roscoff .... 6-7½ hours
Santander (summer only) 24
0 ½ 1 mile
0 1 2 kilometres

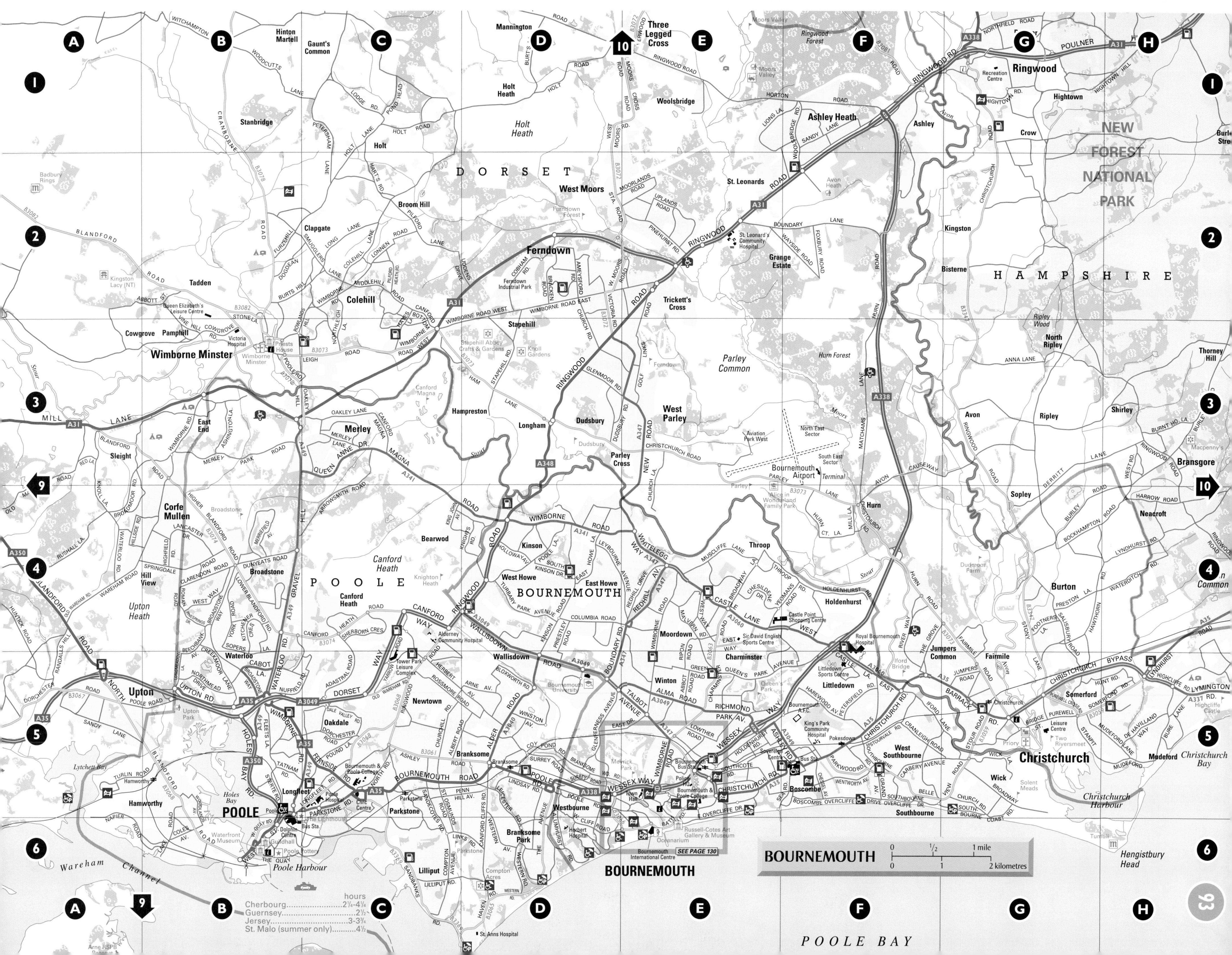
BOURNEMOUTH
0 1/2 1 mile
0 1 2 kilometres
SEE PAGE 130
POOLE BAY
DORSET
HAMPSHIRE
NEW FOREST NATIONAL PARK
POOLE
BOURNEMOUTH
Ringwood
Poulner
Hightown
Crow
Ashley
Ashley Heath
St. Leonards
West Moors
Three Legged Cross
Woolsbridge
Mannington
Holt Heath
Holt
Hinton Martell
Gaunt's Common
Stanbridge
Broom Hill
Clapgate
Colehill
Ferndown
Tadden
Cowgrove
Pamphill
Wimborne Minster
Stapehill
Hampreston
Longham
Dudsbury
West Parley
Parley Cross
Tricketts Cross
Parley Common
Hurn Forest
Bournemouth Airport
Hurn
Kingston
Bisterne
Avon
Ripley
North Ripley
Sopley
Shirley
Bransgore
Neacroft
Burton
Thorney Hill
East End
Merley
Sleight
Corfe Mullen
Hill View
Upton Heath
Upton
Broadstone
Waterloo
Canford Heath
Bearwod
Kinson
West Howe
East Howe
Throop
Holdenhurst
Moordown
Charminster
Winton
Wallisdown
Newtown
Oakdale
Branksome
Parkstone
Lilliput
Branksome Park
Westbourne
Boscombe
Littledown
Jumpers Common
Fairmile
West Southbourne
Southbourne
Wick
Christchurch
Somerford
Mudeford
Hengistbury Head
Christchurch Harbour
Christchurch Bay
Poole Harbour
Holes Bay
Hamworthy
Wareham Channel
Lytchett Bay
Cherbourg 2¼-4¼
Guernsey 2½
Jersey 3-3¾
St. Malo (summer only) 4½
hours

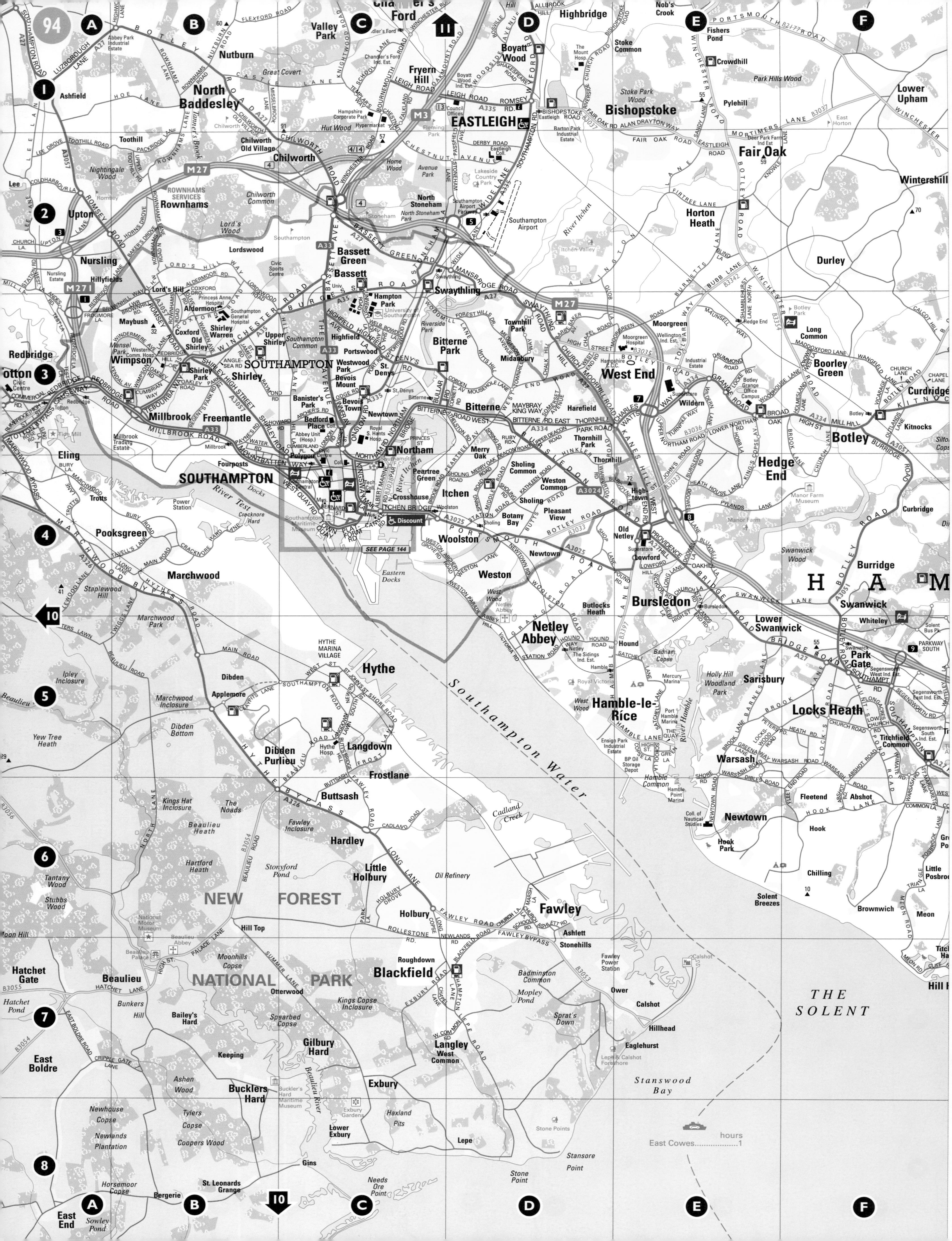

A
B
C
D
E
F
11
Chandler's Ford
Valley Park
Nutburn
Great Covert
North Baddesley
Ashfield
Chilworth Old Village
Chilworth
Toothill
Nightingale Wood
Hut Wood
Fryern Hill
Boyatt Wood
Highbridge
Nob's Crook
Stoke Common
Fishers Pond
Crowdhill
Park Hills Wood
Lower Upham
Pylehill
Bishopstoke
Stoke Park Wood
EASTLEIGH
Fair Oak
East Horton
Wintershill
Home Wood
Avenue Park
Lakeside Country Park
North Stoneham
Southampton Airport
Chilworth Common
Rownhams
Upton
Lee
Nursling
Lord's Wood
Lordswood
Hillyfields
Lord's Hill
Bassett Green
Bassett
Swaythling
Horton Heath
Durley
River Itchen
Itchen Valley
Redbridge
Totton
Maybush
Aldermoor
Coxford
Shirley Warren
Upper Shirley
Southampton Common
Highfield
Portswood
Westwood Park
St. Denys
Bevois Mount
Bevois Town
Riverside Park
Bitterne Park
Townhill Park
Midanbury
Moorgreen
Long Common
Boorley Green
Curdridge
Wimpson
SOUTHAMPTON
Shirley
Millbrook
Freemantle
Banister's Park
Bedford Place
Polygon
Newtown
Northam
Bitterne
Harefield
Thornhill Park
West End
Wildern
Kitnocks
Botley
Hedge End
Eling
Fourposts
Merry Oak
Peartree Green
Sholing Common
Weston Common
Thornhill
Manor Farm Museum
Curbridge
Trotts
Power Station
River Test
Cracknore Hard
Crosshouse
Itchen
Sholing
Pleasant View
Botany Bay
High Town
Pooksgreen
Woolston
Old Netley
Lowford
SEE PAGE 144
Eastern Docks
Newtown
Weston
Swanwick Wood
Burridge
Marchwood
Staplewood Hill
West Wood
Butlocks Heath
Bursledon
H A M
Swanwick
Whiteley
10
Marchwood Park
Netley Abbey
Lower Swanwick
Park Gate
Hythe Marina Village
Hythe
Dibden
Applemore
Southampton Water
Hound
Badnam Copse
Mercury Marina
Holly Hill Woodland Park
Sarisbury
Ipley Inclosure
Marchwood Inclosure
Hamble-le-Rice
Locks Heath
Titchfield Common
Yew Tree Heath
Dibden Bottom
Dibden Purlieu
Langdown
Frostlane
Warsash
Hamble Common
River Hamble
Fleetend
Abshot
Kings Hat Inclosure
The Noads
Buttsash
Cadland Creek
Newtown
Beaulieu Heath
Fawley Inclosure
Hardley
Hook
Hook Park
Hartford Heath
Stonyford Pond
Little Holbury
Oil Refinery
Chilling
Tantany Wood
Stubbs Wood
NEW FOREST
Holbury
Fawley
Solent Breezes
Brownwich
Meon
Hill Top
Ashlett
Stonehills
National Motor Museum
Beaulieu Abbey
Moonhills Copse
Roughdown
Blackfield
Fawley Power Station
Calshot
Badminton Common
Mopley Pond
Hatchet Gate
Beaulieu
NATIONAL PARK
Otterwood
Kings Copse Inclosure
Ower
Calshot
THE SOLENT
Hatchet Pond
Bunkers Hill
Bailey's Hard
Spearbed Copse
Sprat's Down
Hillhead
East Boldre
Keeping
Gilbury Hard
Langley
West Common
Eaglehurst
Lepe & Calshot Foreshore
Stanswood Bay
Ashen Wood
Bucklers Hard
Exbury
Buckler's Hard Maritime Museum
Beaulieu River
Newhouse Copse
Tylers Copse
Exbury Gardens
Haxland Pits
Newlands Plantation
Coopers Wood
Lower Exbury
Lepe
Stone Points
East Cowes hours 1
Stansore Point
Gins
Stone Point
Needs Ore Point
Horsemoor Copse
Bergerie
St. Leonards Grange
East End
Sowley Pond
M27
M271
M3
A27
A33
A35
A335
A3057
A326
A3025
A3024
A334
A3051
B3054
B3053
B3055
B3033
B3035
B3036
B3037
B3342
B3354
B2177

SOUTHAMPTON & PORTSMOUTH
0 1/2 1 mile
0 1 2 kilometres
SEE PAGE 142
hours
Bilbao 35
Caen 6-6¼
Cherbourg 3¼
Fishbourne ½
Guernsey 6½
Jersey 10
Le Havre 2¾-5
St. Malo 8¾-10½
Upham
Corhampton
Exton
Meonstoke
Dean
Droxford
Bishop's Waltham
Swanmore
Hambledon
Clanfield
Horndean
Shirrell Heath
Waltham Chase
Soberton Heath
Newtown
Wickham
Denmead
Lovedean
Cowplain
Waterlooville
Southwick
Purbrook
HAVANT
Bedhampton
FAREHAM
Portchester
Port Solent
Cosham
Drayton
Farlington
Titchfield
Stubbington
Lee-on-the-Solent
GOSPORT
Fleetlands
Rowner
Elson
PORTSMOUTH
Portsmouth Harbour
Langstone Harbour
Southsea
Old Portsmouth
Hilsea
North End
Copnor
Fratton
Milton
Eastney
PORTSEA ISLAND
Whale Island
Horsea Island
Tipner
Stamshaw
Browndown
Gilkicker Point
Stokes Bay
Hayling Bay
Leigh Park
Warren Park
Langstone
West Town
M27
M275
A3(M)

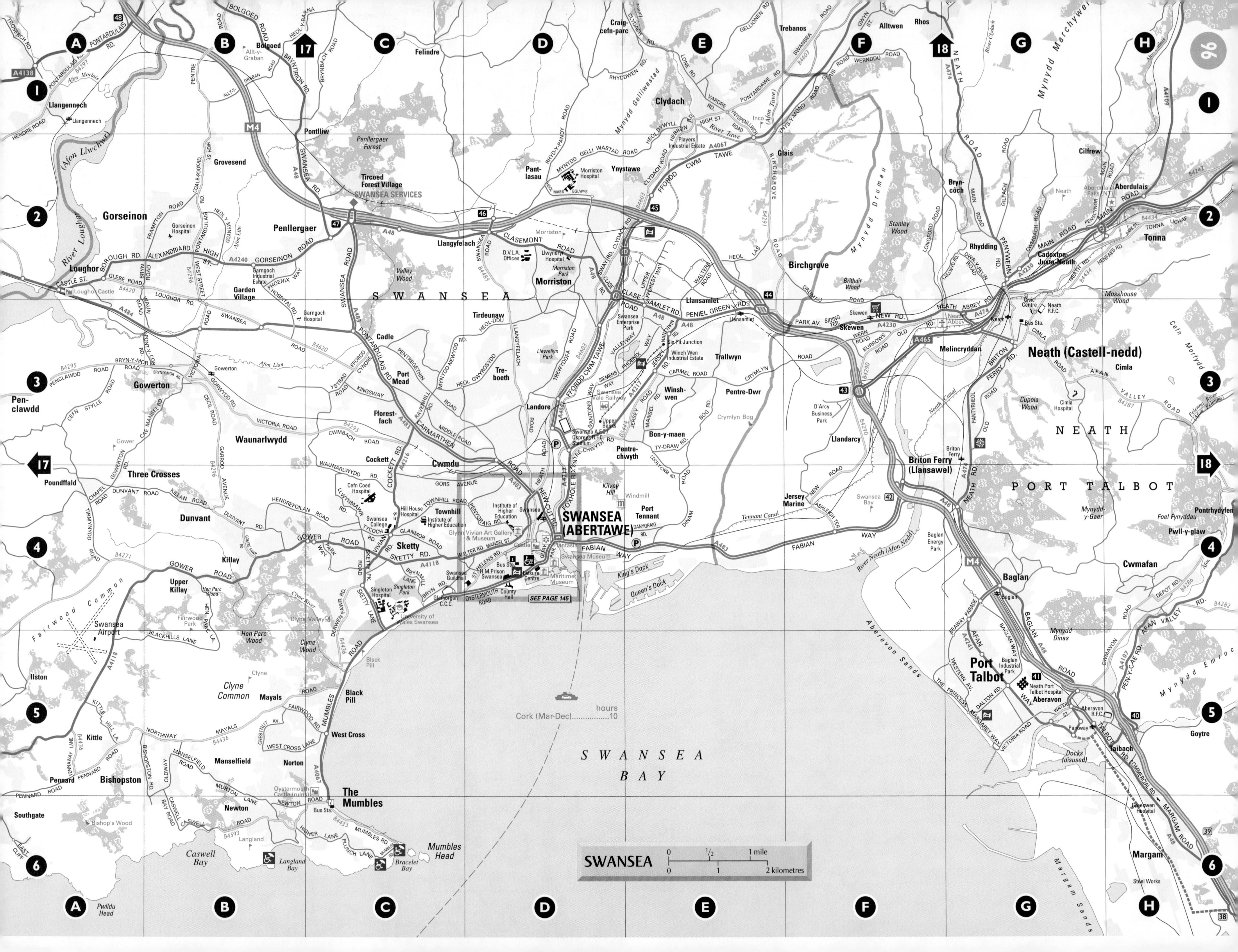
SWANSEA
0 1/2 1 mile
0 1 2 kilometres
SWANSEA (ABERTAWE)
SWANSEA BAY
Cork (Mar-Dec)................10 hours
SEE PAGE 145
Neath (Castell-nedd)
Port Talbot
NEATH
PORT TALBOT
SWANSEA
Morriston
Gorseinon
Penllergaer
Loughor
Llangennech
Gowerton
Waunarlwydd
Three Crosses
Dunvant
Killay
Sketty
Mayals
Bishopston
The Mumbles
West Cross
Black Pill
Mumbles Head
Caswell Bay
Langland Bay
Bracelet Bay
Clyne Common
Fairwood Common
Swansea Airport
Ilston
Kittle
Pennard
Southgate
Pwlldu Head
Newton
Norton
Manselfield
Upper Killay
Pen-clawdd
Poundffald
Cockett
Cwmdu
Townhill
Fforest-fach
Port Mead
Cadle
Tre-boeth
Landore
Tirdeunaw
Llangyfelach
Pant-lasau
Ynystawe
Clydach
Craig-cefn-parc
Felindre
Pontlliw
Grovesend
Garden Village
Tircoed Forest Village
SWANSEA SERVICES
Bolgoed
Llansamlet
Trallwyn
Pentre-Dwr
Winsh-wen
Bon-y-maen
Pentre-chwyth
Port Tennant
Kilvey Hill
Jersey Marine
Llandarcy
Skewen
Birchgrove
Glais
Trebanos
Alltwen
Rhos
Bryn-coch
Rhydding
Cadoxton-Juxta-Neath
Aberdulais
Tonna
Cilfrew
Cimla
Melincryddan
Briton Ferry (Llansawel)
Baglan
Aberavon
Cwmafan
Pontrhydyfen
Pwll-y-glaw
Goytre
Taibach
Margam
King's Dock
Queen's Dock
Aberavon Sands
Margam Sands
River Loughor
Mynydd Drumau
Mynydd Gelliwastad
Mynydd Marchywel
Mynydd Emroch
M4
A48
A483
A4067
A4118
A474
A465

CARDIFF & NEWPORT
1 mile
2 kilometres
BRISTOL CHANNEL
NEWPORT
CARDIFF
CAERPHILLY
TORFAEN
RHONDDA CYNON TAFF
VALE OF GLAMORGAN
Caerleon
Crosskeys
Risca
Cwmfelinfach
Brynawel
Wattsville
Pontymister
Danygraig
Bettws
Malpas
Bryngals
Crindau
Barrack Hill
Allt-yr-yn
Barnardtown
St. Julians
Christchurch
Lawrence Hill
Bishpool
Beechwood
Alway
Somerton
Liswerry
Maindee
Summerhill
Ridgeway
Glasllwch
Stelvio
Gaer
Mendalgief
Maes-glas
Pillgwenlly
Duffryn
Rogerstone
High Cross
Cefn
Garth
Bassaleg
Pye Corner
Pentre-poeth
Rhiwderin
Ty-Sign
Penrhiw
Machen
Chatham
Lower Machen
Draethen
Nant-y-ceisiad
Bedwas
Craig-y-Rhacca
Trethomas
Waterloo
Rudry
Caerphilly
Castle Park
Van
Lansbury Park
Morningtown Meadows
Greenacre
Pwllypant
Energlyn
Trecenydd
Glenfields
Watford Park
Penyrheol
Caledfryn
Abertridwr
Senghenydd
Llanbradach
Hendredenny Park
Groes-wen
Nantgarw
Glan-y-llyn
Thornhill
Ty Rhiw
Taff's Well
Tongwynlais
Morganstown
Pantmawr
Coryton
Radyr
Whitchurch
Llandaff North
Rhiwbina
Llanishen
Lisvane
Parc
Birchgrove
Heath
Mynachdy
Cyncoed
Pontprennau
Pentwyn
Llanedeyrn
Llanrumney
Rumney
St.Mellons
Trowbridge
Roath Park
Pen-y-Lan
Cathays
Maendy
Gabalfa
Llandaff
Blackweir
Pontcanna
Roath
Splott
Tremorfa
Riverside
Canton
Butetown
Grangetown
Fairwater
Pentrebane
St. Fagans
Llanmaes
Ely
Caerau
Cyntwell
Michaelston-y-Fedw
Castleton
Marshfield
Blacktown
Coedkernew
St. Brides Wentlooge
Peterstone Wentlooge
Wentloog
Newton
Pye Corner
Broadstreet Common
Nash
Uskmouth
SEE PAGE 132
M4
A48(M)
CARDIFF GATE SERVICES

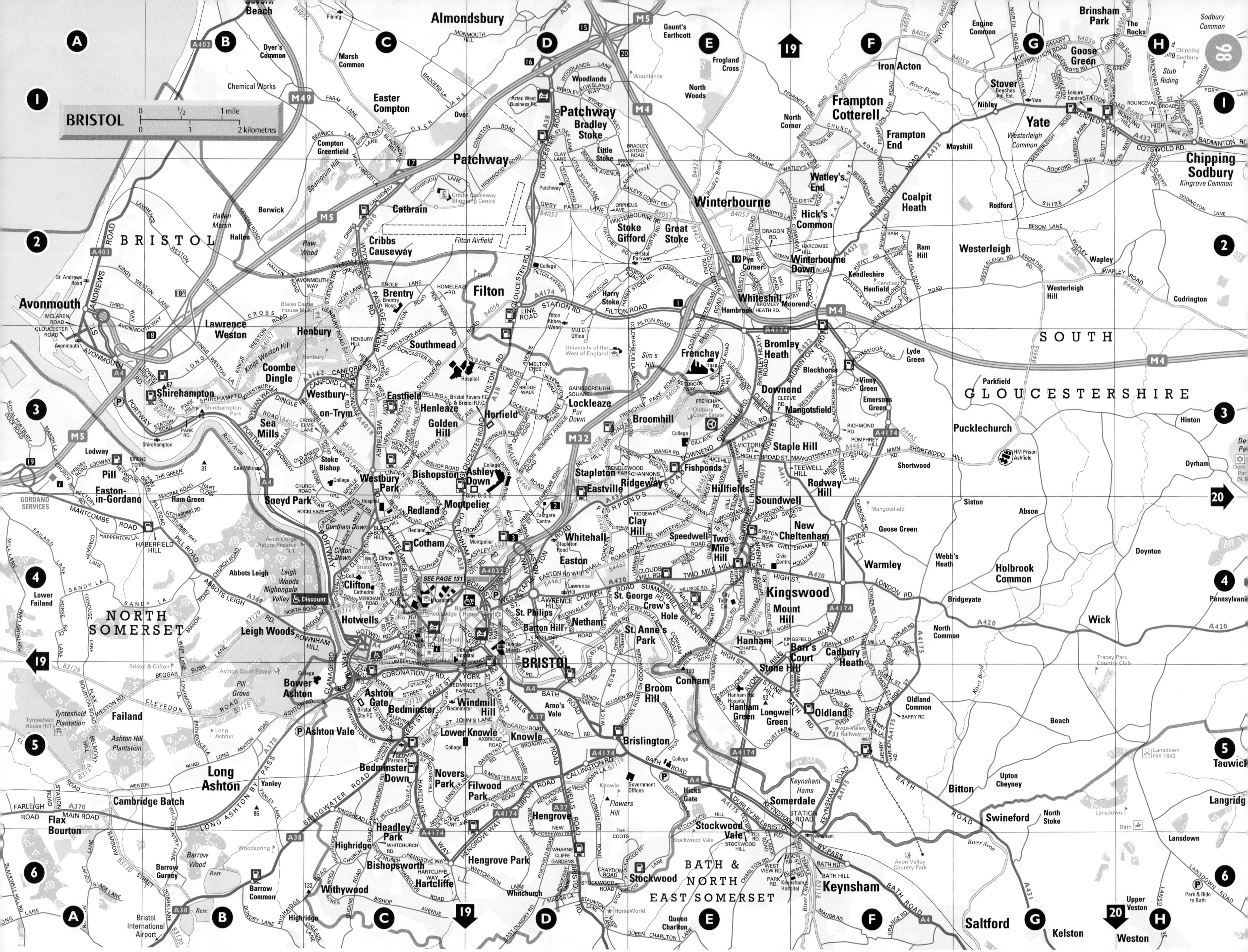
BRISTOL
0 1/2 1 mile
0 1 2 kilometres
Almondsbury
Avonmouth
Shirehampton
Lawrence Weston
Henbury
Patchway
Bradley Stoke
Filton
Winterbourne
Frampton Cotterell
Yate
Chipping Sodbury
Coalpit Heath
Westerleigh
Pucklechurch
SOUTH GLOUCESTERSHIRE
Frenchay
Downend
Staple Hill
Kingswood
Warmley
Soundwell
Hanham
Oldland
Keynsham
Saltford
BATH & NORTH EAST SOMERSET
NORTH SOMERSET
Long Ashton
Failand
Pill
Easton-in-Gordano
Clifton
Hotwells
Redland
Cotham
Montpelier
Westbury-on-Trym
Southmead
Horfield
Lockleaze
Stapleton
Fishponds
Eastville
Easton
St. Philips
BRISTOL
Bedminster
Windmill Hill
Knowle
Brislington
Bishopsworth
Hartcliffe
Withywood
Hengrove Park
Stockwood
Whitchurch
Bristol International Airport
Cambridge Batch
Flax Bourton
SEE PAGE 131
Filton Airfield
Cribbs Causeway
Sea Mills
Stoke Bishop
Sneyd Park
Leigh Woods
Ashton Vale
Bower Ashton
Conham
Broom Hill
St. Anne's Park
St. George
Whitehall
Speedwell
Two Mile Hill
Mount Hill
Cadbury Heath
Longwell Green
Somerdale
Bitton
Swineford
Upton Cheyney
Wick
Doynton
Dyrham
Hinton
Codrington
Iron Acton
Kelston
Weston
Lansdown
Langridge

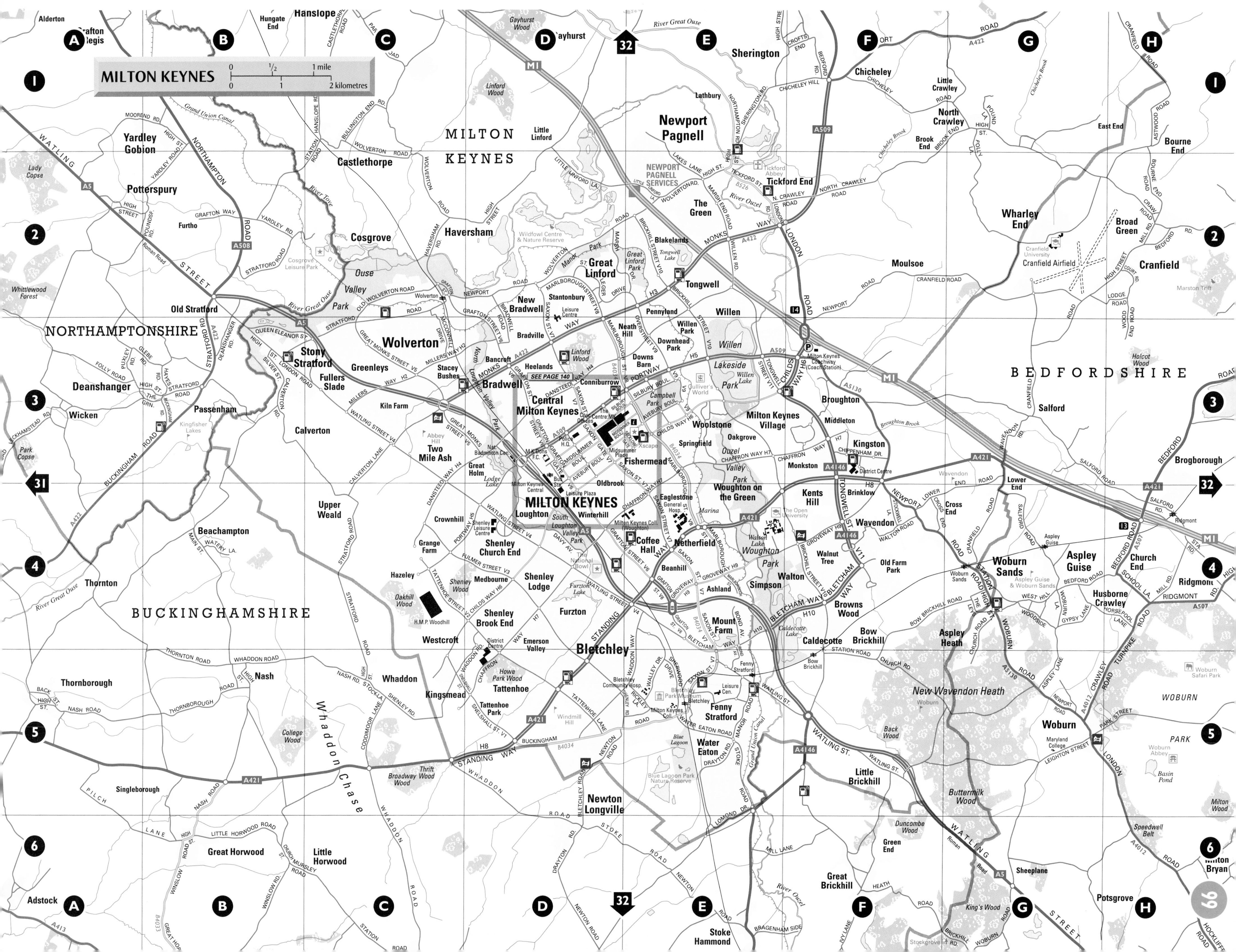
MILTON KEYNES
0 1/2 1 mile
0 1 2 kilometres
MILTON KEYNES
NORTHAMPTONSHIRE
BUCKINGHAMSHIRE
BEDFORDSHIRE
Newport Pagnell
Wolverton
Stony Stratford
Bradwell
Central Milton Keynes
SEE PAGE 140
Bletchley
Fenny Stratford
Woburn Sands
Aspley Guise
Woburn
Cranfield
Cranfield Airfield
Castlethorpe
Haversham
Cosgrove
Great Linford
Tongwell
Willen
Broughton
Kingston
Kents Hill
Wavendon
Walton
Simpson
Netherfield
Coffee Hall
Shenley Church End
Shenley Brook End
Tattenhoe
Westcroft
Whaddon
Nash
Thornborough
Great Horwood
Little Horwood
Newton Longville
Water Eaton
Little Brickhill
Great Brickhill
Bow Brickhill
Caldecotte
Yardley Gobion
Potterspury
Deanshanger
Passenham
Wicken
Old Stratford
Calverton
Upper Weald
Thornton
Beachampton
Sherington
Chicheley
Moulsoe
Salford
Brogborough
Ridgmont
Husborne Crawley
Church End
Aspley Heath
New Wavendon Heath
Whaddon Chase
31
32
99

GREATER LONDON - WEST
0 1/2 1 mile
0 1 2 kilometres
HERTFORDSHIRE
BARNET
HARROW
BRENT
HILLINGDON
CAMDEN
EALING
22
102
NORTH WATFORD
Aldenham
Letchmore Heath
Patchetts Green
BOREHAMWOOD
Elstree
High Barnet
BARNET
Hadley Wood
Monken Hadley
Cockfosters
East Barnet
Osidge
Oakleigh Park
Southgate
New Southgate
FRIERN BARNET
Bowes Park
North Finchley
Whetstone
Totteridge
Arkley
Chipping Barnet
New Barnet
Underhill
Rowley Green
Barnet Gate
Croxley Green
Holywell
Oxhey
South Oxhey
Watford Heath
Carpenders Park
BUSHEY
Bushey Heath
Merry Hill
Batchworth
Batchworth Heath
Moor Park
NORTHWOOD
Eastbury
Hatch End
Pinnerwood Park
Pinner Green
Pinner
Northwood Hills
RUISLIP
Eastcote
Eastcote Village
Ruislip Common
Ruislip Manor
Ruislip Gardens
South Ruislip
Ickenham
North Hillingdon
Hillingdon
Yeading
Hayes End
Northolt
Greenford
Perivale
Alperton
Park Royal
North Acton
Harlesden
Stonebridge
Willesden
Kensal Rise
Kilburn
Maida Vale
PADDINGTON
MARYLEBONE
St. John's Wood
Regent's Park
South Hampstead
Belsize Park
Brondesbury
Kentish Town
Camden Town
Tufnell Park
Upper Holloway
Dartmouth Park
HAMPSTEAD
Hampstead Heath
Highgate
Crouch End
HORNSEY
Muswell Hill
East Finchley
Hampstead Garden Suburb
Golders Green
Childs Hill
Cricklewood
Dollis Hill
Neasden
Tokyngton
WEMBLEY
Wembley Park
North Wembley
Sudbury
South Harrow
HARROW
Harrow on the Hill
West Harrow
North Harrow
Rayners Lane
Headstone
HARROW WEALD
Wealdstone
Kenton
Belmont
Stanmore
Canons Park
EDGWARE
Burnt Oak
Queensbury
Kingsbury
West Hendon
HENDON
Church End
FINCHLEY
MILL HILL
Highwood Hill
LONDON GATEWAY SERVICES

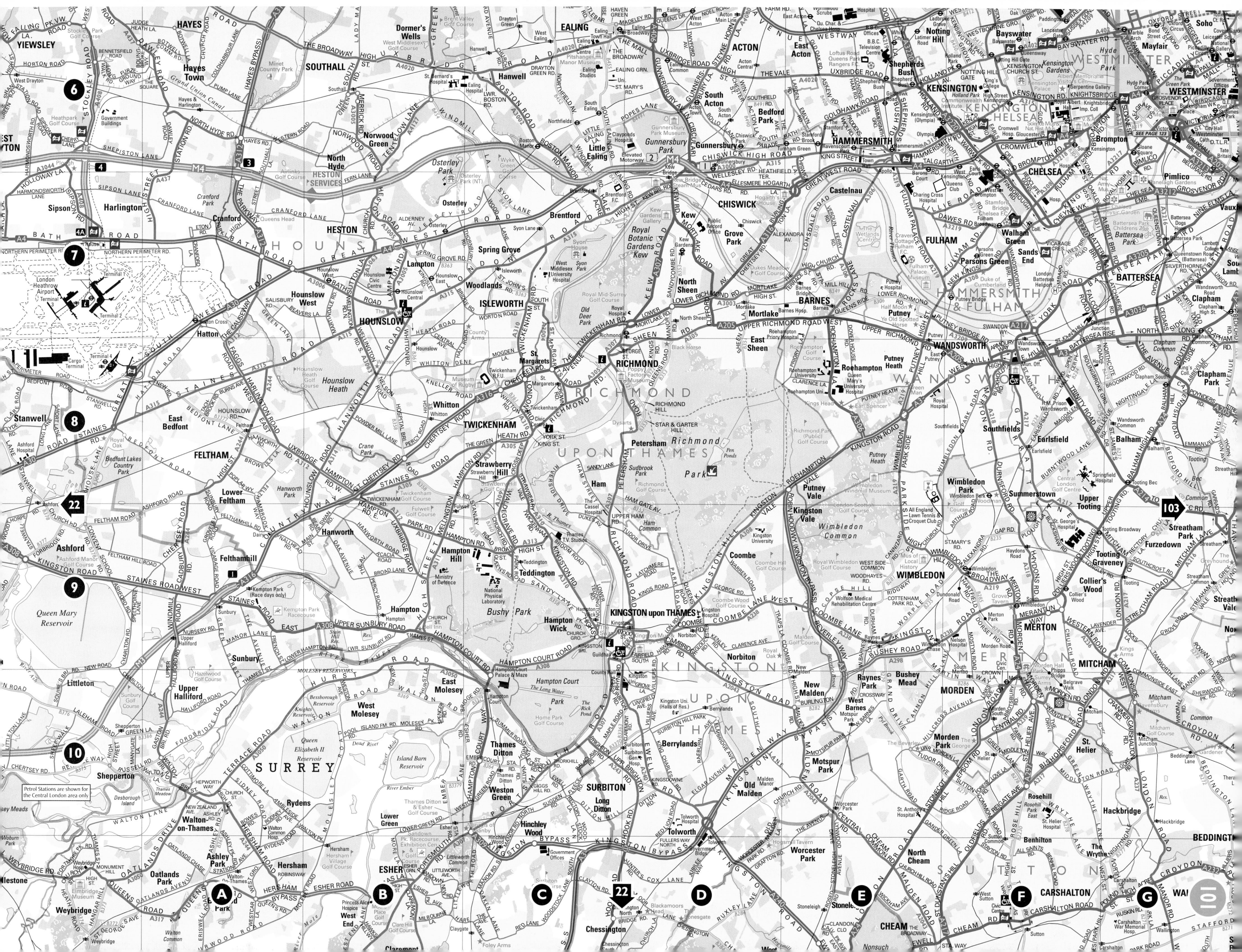

YIEWSLEY
HAYES
Hayes Town
SOUTHALL
Dormer's Wells
Hanwell
EALING
ACTON
East Acton
Notting Hill
Bayswater
Mayfair
Soho
WESTMINSTER
KENSINGTON
Shepherds Bush
HAMMERSMITH
CHISWICK
South Acton
Bedford Park
Gunnersbury
Little Ealing
Brentford
Osterley
North Hyde
Norwood Green
Harlington
Sipson
Cranford
HESTON
Lampton
Spring Grove
HOUNSLOW
Hounslow West
Woodlands
ISLEWORTH
Kew
Grove Park
North Sheen
Mortlake
BARNES
Castelnau
East Sheen
FULHAM
Walham Green
Parsons Green
Sands End
CHELSEA
Brompton
Pimlico
BATTERSEA
Clapham
Clapham Park
Putney
WANDSWORTH
Roehampton
Putney Heath
RICHMOND
St. Margarets
TWICKENHAM
Whitton
Hatton
Stanwell
East Bedfont
FELTHAM
Lower Feltham
Hanworth
Strawberry Hill
Teddington
Hampton Hill
Hampton
Petersham
Ham
Richmond Park
Putney Vale
Kingston Vale
Southfields
Earlsfield
Balham
Wimbledon Park
Summerstown
Upper Tooting
Streatham Park
Furzedown
Tooting Graveney
Collier's Wood
WIMBLEDON
Coombe
KINGSTON upon THAMES
Hampton Wick
Norbiton
MERTON
MITCHAM
MORDEN
Raynes Park
Bushey Mead
West Barnes
New Malden
Berrylands
SURBITON
Long Ditton
Thames Ditton
Weston Green
East Molesey
West Molesey
Hinchley Wood
Tolworth
Old Malden
Motspur Park
Worcester Park
Morden Park
North Cheam
CHEAM
St. Helier
Rosehill
Hackbridge
CARSHALTON
Benhilton
The Wrythe
Chessington
ESHER
Lower Green
Hersham
Rydens
Walton-on-Thames
Ashley Park
Oatlands Park
Weybridge
Shepperton
Littleton
Upper Halliford
Sunbury
Felthamhill
Ashford
Queen Mary Reservoir
SURREY
Petrol Stations are shown for the Central London area only
6
7
8
9
10
A
B
C
D
E
F
G
22
103

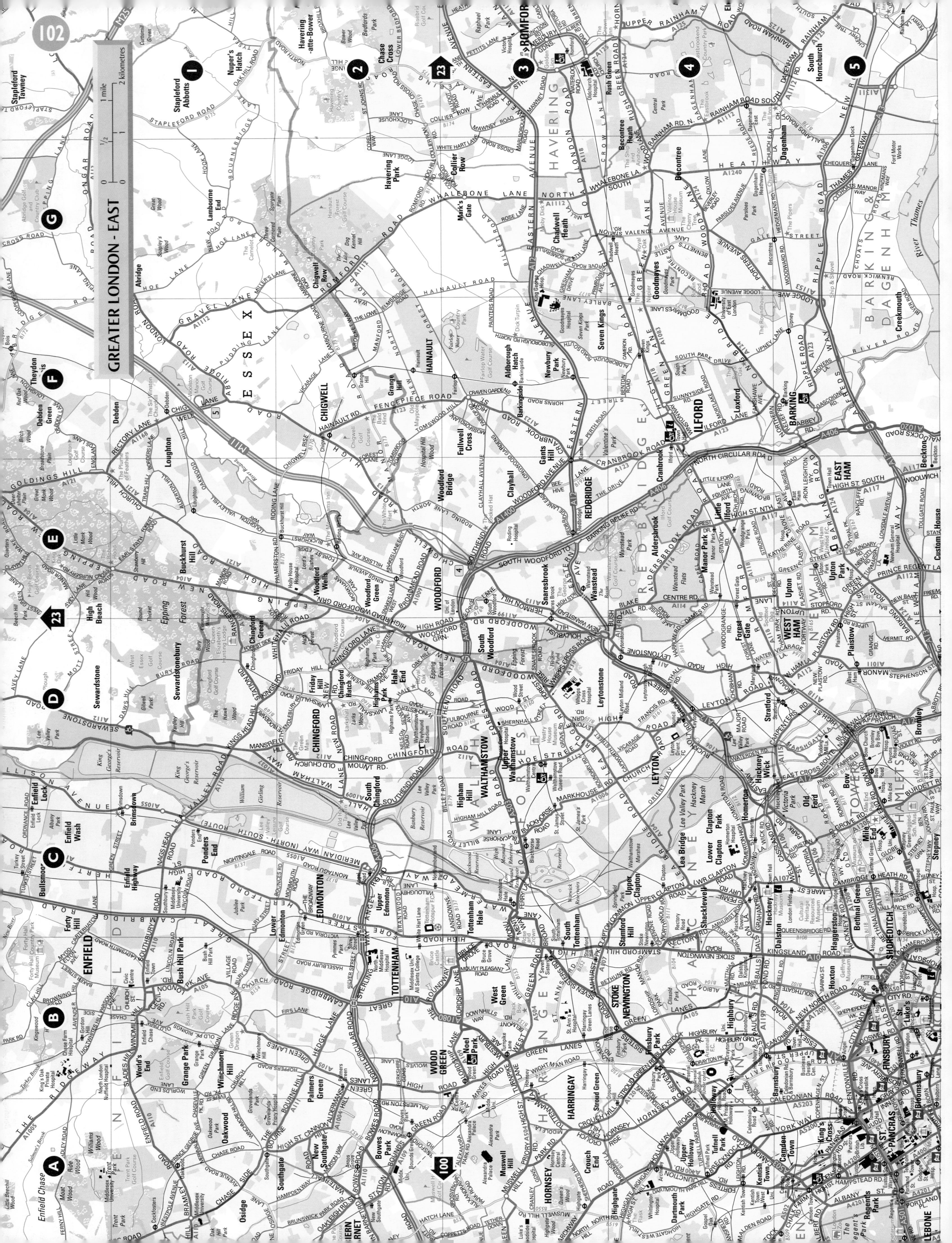
GREATER LONDON - EAST
0 1/2 1 mile
0 1 2 kilometres
A
B
C
D
E
F
G
1
2
3
4
5
ENFIELD
ESSEX
HAVERING
REDBRIDGE
WALTHAM FOREST
HARINGEY
HACKNEY
ISLINGTON
NEWHAM
TOWER HAMLETS
BARKING & DAGENHAM
100
23

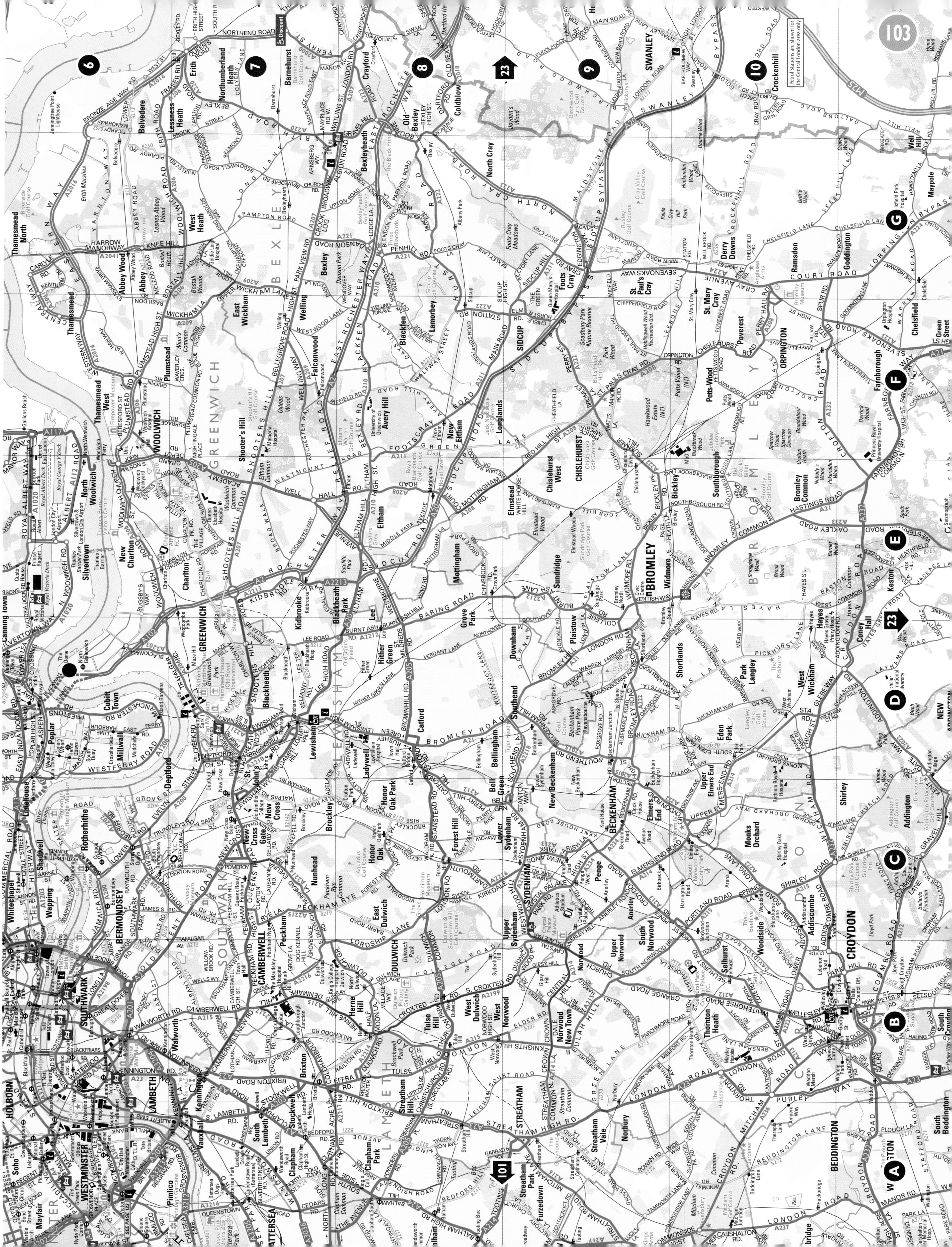
Petrol Stations are shown for the Central London area only
WESTMINSTER
SOUTHWARK
LAMBETH
BERMONDSEY
Rotherhithe
Wapping
Whitechapel
Shadwell
Limehouse
Poplar
Millwall
Cubitt Town
Deptford
GREENWICH
Charlton
New Charlton
Silvertown
North Woolwich
WOOLWICH
Plumstead
Thamesmead
Thamesmead West
Thamesmead North
Abbey Wood
Belvedere
Erith
Northumberland Heath
Barnehurst
Crayford
Old Bexley
Bexleyheath
Welling
Falconwood
Shooter's Hill
East Wickham
Blackheath
Lewisham
Catford
Brockley
Honor Oak
Honor Oak Park
Forest Hill
Nunhead
Peckham
Camberwell
Walworth
Kennington
Vauxhall
Stockwell
Brixton
Clapham
Clapham Park
Tulse Hill
Herne Hill
Dulwich
East Dulwich
West Dulwich
West Norwood
Streatham
Streatham Hill
Streatham Vale
Norbury
Thornton Heath
Selhurst
South Norwood
Upper Norwood
Anerley
Penge
Sydenham
Upper Sydenham
Lower Sydenham
Bellingham
Southend
Downham
Grove Park
Lee
Hither Green
Eltham
Kidbrooke
Mottingham
New Eltham
Avery Hill
Blackfen
Lamorbey
Sidcup
Foots Cray
Longlands
Chislehurst
Chislehurst West
Elmstead
Sundridge
BROMLEY
Widmore
Plaistow
Shortlands
BECKENHAM
New Beckenham
Elmers End
Eden Park
Park Langley
West Wickham
Hayes
Keston
Coney Hall
Addington
Shirley
Monks Orchard
Addiscombe
Woodside
CROYDON
South Croydon
Waddon
Beddington
Mitcham
Bickley
Southborough
Bromley Common
Petts Wood
St. Paul's Cray
St. Mary Cray
Orpington
Poverest
Farnborough
Chelsfield
Green Street Green
Ramsden
Goddington
Derry Downs
Crockenhill
Swanley
North Cray
Coldblow
Maypole
Well Hill
Welling
MAIDSTONE ROAD
SIDCUP BYPASS
ROCHESTER WAY
SEVENOAKS WAY
Thames Barrier
The Dome
SEE PAGE 122

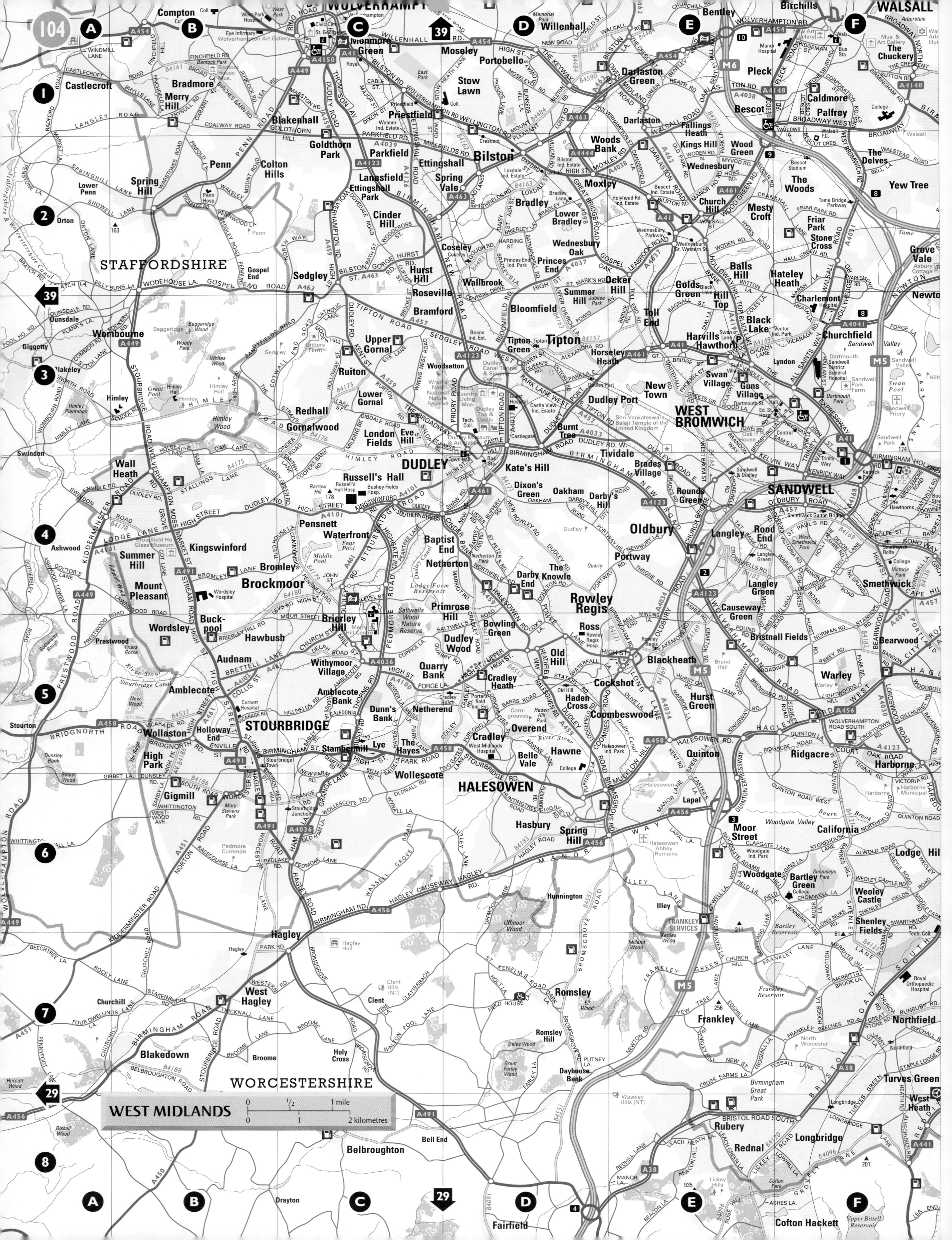
WEST MIDLANDS
0 1/2 1 mile
0 1 2 kilometres
STAFFORDSHIRE
WORCESTERSHIRE
39
29
A B C D E F
1 2 3 4 5 6 7 8
Compton
Willenhall
Bentley
Birchills
WALSALL
Monmore Green
Moseley
Portobello
Castlecroft
Bradmore
Merry Hill
Stow Lawn
Darlaston Green
Pleck
The Chuckery
Caldmore
Palfrey
Bescot
Blakenhall
Priestfield
Darlaston
Fallings Heath
Kings Hill
Wood Green
Goldthorn Park
Parkfield
Woods Bank
Wednesbury
The Delves
Penn
Colton Hills
Bilston
Ettingshall
Spring Hill
Lower Penn
Lanesfield
Spring Vale
Moxley
The Woods
Yew Tree
Ettingshall Park
Bradley
Church Hill
Mesty Croft
Orton
Cinder Hill
Lower Bradley
Friar Park
Stone Cross
Coseley
Wednesbury Oak
Grove Vale
Sedgley
Hurst Hill
Princes End
Balls Hill
Hateley Heath
Gospel End
Wallbrook
Ocker Hill
Golds Green
Hill Top
Charlemont
Roseville
Summer Hill
Bramford
Bloomfield
Toll End
Black Lake
Wombourne
Upper Gornal
Tipton Green
Tipton
Harvills Hawthorn
Churchfield
Giggetty
Swindon
Himley
Ruiton
Woodsetton
Horseley Heath
Swan Village
Guns Village
Lower Gornal
Redhall
Gornalwood
New Town
Dudley Port
WEST BROMWICH
Burnt Tree
Eve Hill
London Fields
Tividale
Wall Heath
DUDLEY
Russell's Hall
Kate's Hill
Brades Village
Dixons Green
Oakham
Darby's Hill
Rounds Green
SANDWELL
Pensnett
Waterfront
Oldbury
Langley
Rood End
Ashwood
Kingswinford
Summer Hill
Baptist End
Netherton
Portway
Bromley
Brockmoor
Mount Pleasant
Darby End
The Knowle
Rowley Regis
Langley Green
Smethwick
Primrose Hill
Buckpool
Wordsley
Brierley Hill
Bowling Green
Ross
Causeway Green
Bristnall Fields
Hawbush
Dudley Wood
Old Hill
Bearwood
Audnam
Withymoor Village
Quarry Bank
Cradley Heath
Blackheath
Warley
Amblecote
Amblecote Bank
Netherend
Haden Cross
Cockshot
Hurst Green
Dunn's Bank
Coombeswood
Stourton
Wollaston
STOURBRIDGE
Holloway End
Cradley
Overend
Lye
The Hayes
Stambermill
High Park
Belle Vale
Hawne
Quinton
Ridgacre
Harborne
Wollescote
Gigmill
HALESOWEN
Lapal
Hasbury
Spring Hill
Moor Street
California
Lodge Hill
Woodgate
Bartley Green
Weoley Castle
Shenley Fields
Hunnington
Illey
Hagley
Frankley Services
Churchill
West Hagley
Clent
Romsley
Frankley
Northfield
Blakedown
Broome
Holy Cross
Romsley Hill
Dayhouse Bank
Turves Green
West Heath
Rubery
Rednal
Longbridge
Bell End
Belbroughton
Drayton
Fairfield
Cofton Hackett
M5
M6

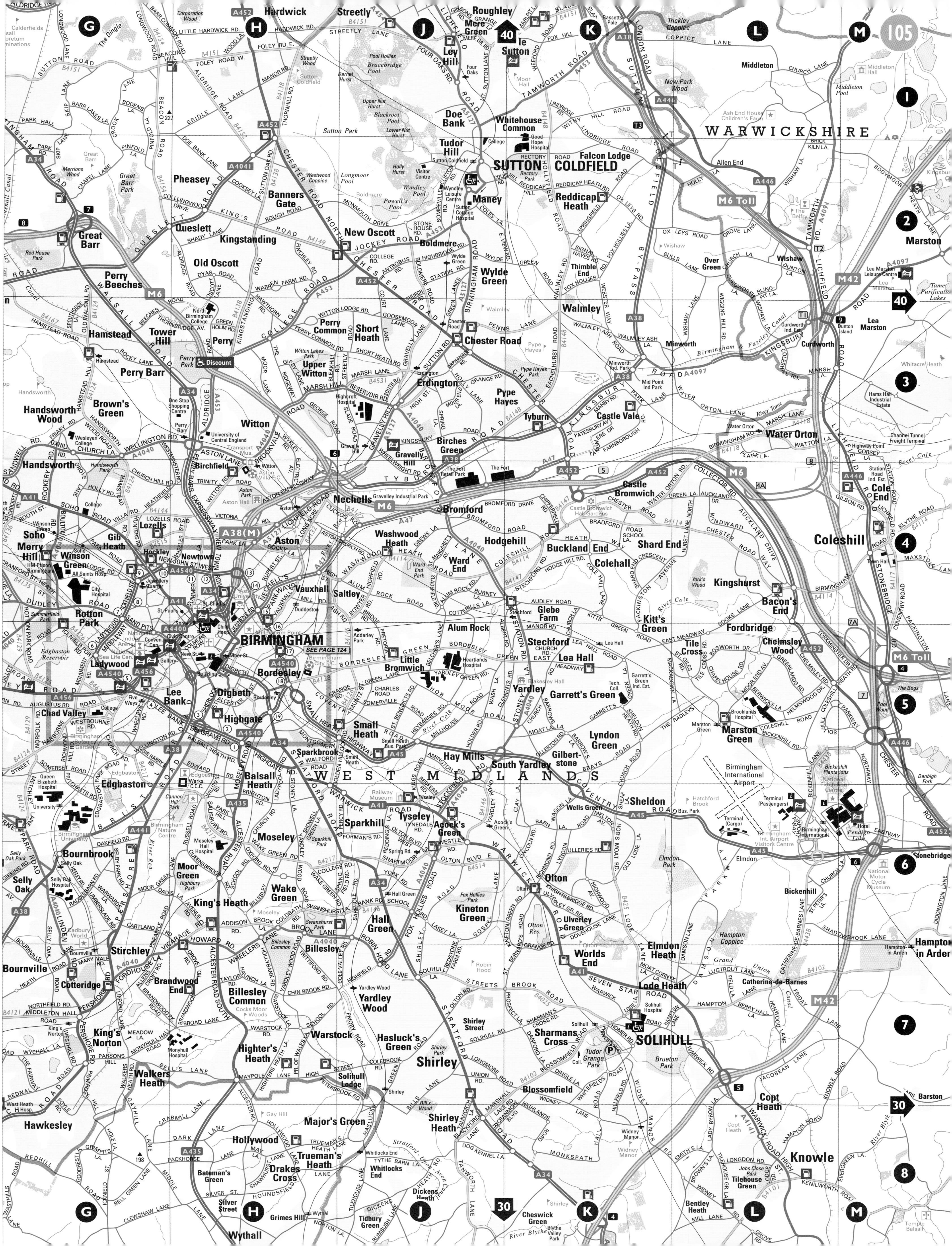

G
H
J
K
L
M
Hardwick
Streetly
Roughley
Mere Green
Ley Hill
Sutton
Middleton
WARWICKSHIRE
Doe Bank
Whitehouse Common
Tudor Hill
SUTTON COLDFIELD
Falcon Lodge
Pheasey
Banners Gate
Maney
Reddicap Heath
Queslett
Kingstanding
New Oscott
Boldmere
Great Barr
Old Oscott
Wylde Green
Marston
Perry Beeches
Walmley
Minworth
Curdworth
Lea Marston
Hamstead
Tower Hill
Perry
Perry Common
Short Heath
Chester Road
Perry Barr
Upper Witton
Erdington
Pype Hayes
Handsworth Wood
Brown's Green
Witton
Castle Vale
Tyburn
Water Orton
Birches Green
Gravelly Hill
Handsworth
Birchfield
Castle Bromwich
Cole End
Nechells
Bromford
Lozells
Aston
Washwood Heath
Hodgehill
Buckland End
Shard End
Coleshill
Soho
Gib Heath
Hockley
Newtown
Ward End
Colehall
Kingshurst
Merry Hill
Winson Green
Vauxhall
Saltley
Bacon's End
Kitt's Green
Rotton Park
Alum Rock
Glebe Farm
Fordbridge
BIRMINGHAM
Stechford
Tile Cross
Chelmsley Wood
Little Bromwich
Lea Hall
Ladywood
Bordesley
Yardley
Garrett's Green
Lee Bank
Digbeth
Chad Valley
Highgate
Small Heath
Lyndon Green
Marston Green
Sparkbrook
Hay Mills
South Yardley
Gilbertstone
WEST MIDLANDS
Edgbaston
Balsall Heath
Sheldon
Birmingham International Airport
Tyseley
Sparkhill
Acock's Green
Wells Green
Moseley
Bournbrook
Selly Oak
Moor Green
Wake Green
Olton
Elmdon
Bickenhill
King's Heath
Hall Green
Kineton Green
Ulverley Green
Stirchley
Elmdon Heath
Worlds End
Bournville
Billesley
Cotteridge
Brandwood End
Billesley Common
Yardley Wood
Lode Heath
Catherine-de-Barnes
King's Norton
Warstock
Shirley Street
Sharmans Cross
SOLIHULL
Hasluck's Green
Higher's Heath
Shirley
Walkers Heath
Solihull Lodge
Blossomfield
Copt Heath
Hawkesley
Shirley Heath
Major's Green
Hollywood
Trueman's Heath
Drakes Cross
Knowle
Whitlocks End
Tilehouse Green
Bentley Heath
Dickens Heath
Silver Street
Grimes Hill
Tidbury Green
Cheswick Green
Wythall
M6 Toll
M42
M6
SEE PAGE 124
40
30
1
2
3
4
5
6
7
8

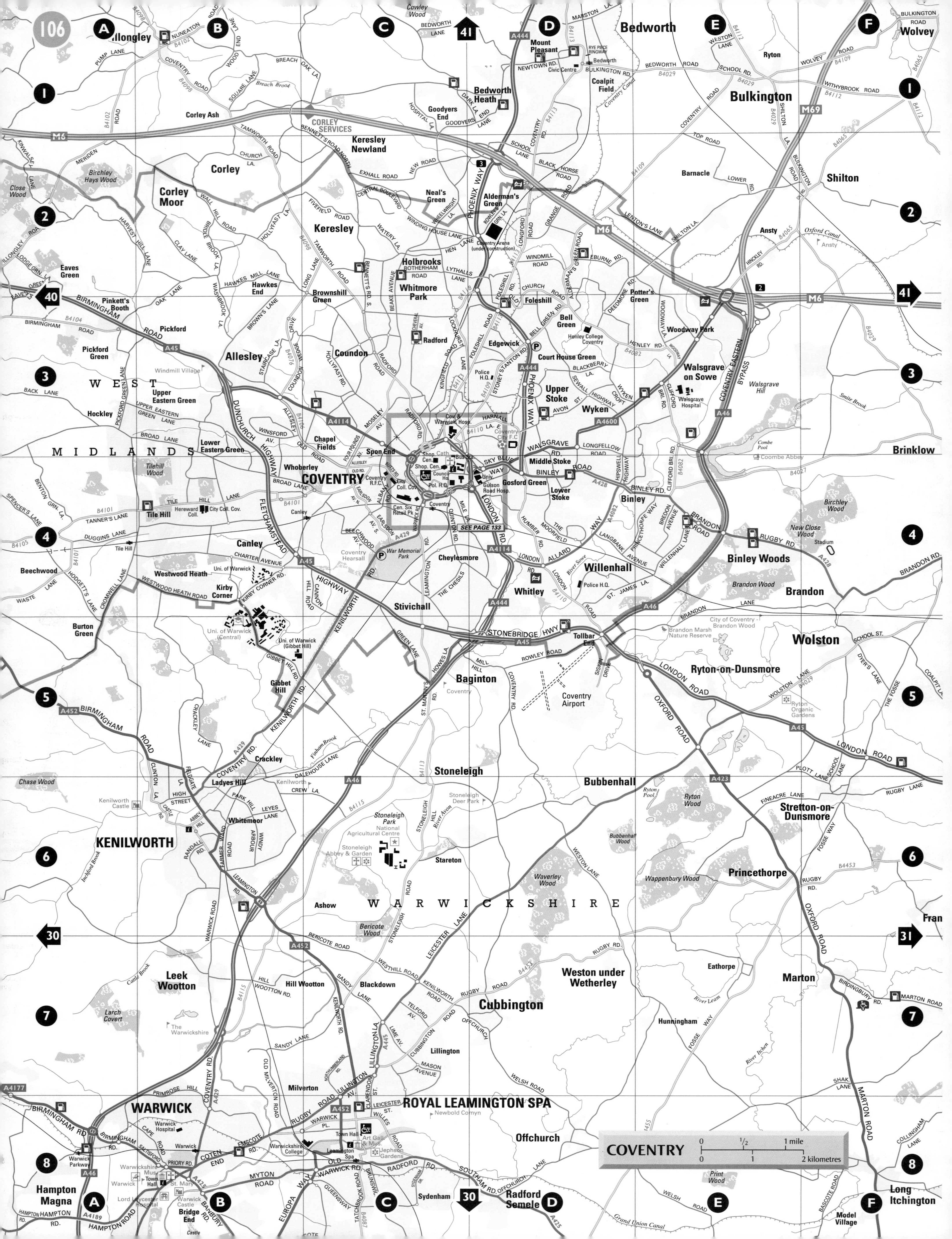

Willongley
Bedworth
Wolvey
Bulkington
Mount Pleasant
Bedworth Heath
Goodyers End
Coalpit Field
Ryton
Corley Ash
Corley Services
Keresley Newland
Corley
Corley Moor
Birchley Hays Wood
Close Wood
Neal's Green
Alderman's Green
Coventry Arena (under construction)
Barnacle
Shilton
Ansty
Oxford Canal
Keresley
Holbrooks
Whitmore Park
Foleshill
Potter's Green
Eaves Green
Hawkes End
Brownshill Green
Pinkett's Booth
Pickford
Pickford Green
Allesley
Coundon
Radford
Edgewick
Bell Green
Henley College Coventry
Court House Green
Woodway Park
Walsgrave on Sowe
Walsgrave Hospital
Walsgrave Hill
Upper Stoke
Wyken
West Midlands
Windmill Village
Upper Eastern Green
Hockley
Lower Eastern Green
Chapel Fields
Spon End
Coventry
Whoberley
Coventry City F.C.
Middle Stoke
Gosford Green
Lower Stoke
Binley
Combe Pool
Coombe Abbey
Brinklow
Tilehill Wood
Tile Hill
Hereward Coll.
City Coll. Cov.
Canley
Coventry R.F.C.
Cen. Six Retail Pk
Coventry Hearsall
War Memorial Park
Cheylesmore
See page 133
Birchley Wood
New Close Wood
Binley Woods
Stadium
Brandon Wood
Brandon
Beechwood
Westwood Heath
Uni. of Warwick
Kirby Corner
Burton Green
Uni. of Warwick (Central)
Uni. of Warwick (Gibbet Hill)
Stivichall
Whitley
Willenhall
Police H.Q.
Tollbar End
City of Coventry - Brandon Wood
Brandon Marsh Nature Reserve
Wolston
Ryton-on-Dunsmore
Gibbet Hill
Baginton
Coventry Airport
Ryton Organic Gardens
Crackley
Finham Brook
Stoneleigh
Bubbenhall
Ryton Pool
Ryton Wood
Chase Wood
Ladyes Hill
Kenilworth Castle
Whitemoor
Stoneleigh Deer Park
Stoneleigh Park National Agricultural Centre
Stoneleigh Abbey & Garden
River Avon
Bubbenhall Wood
Stretton-on-Dunsmore
Kenilworth
Stareton
Waverley Wood
Wappenbury Wood
Princethorpe
Inchford Brook
Ashow
Warwickshire
Bericote Wood
Fran
Leek Wootton
Hill Wootton
Blackdown
Weston under Wetherley
Eathorpe
Marton
Larch Covert
The Warwickshire
Cubbington
River Leam
Hunningham
Lillington
River Itchen
Milverton
Warwick
Royal Leamington Spa
Newbold Comyn
Warwick Hospital
Warwick Parkway
Warwickshire College
Town Hall
Art Gall. & Mus.
Jephson Gardens
Leamington Spa
Warwickshire Mus.
Lord Leycester Hospital
St. Mary
Warwick Castle
Bridge End
Castle
Offchurch
Print Wood
Hampton Magna
Sydenham
Radford Semele
Long Itchington
Model Village
Grand Union Canal
Coventry
0 1/2 1 mile
0 1 2 kilometres
M6
M69
A45
A46
A444
A4114
A4600
A428
A423
A452
A429
A425
A445
A4177
A4189
Phoenix Way
Coventry Eastern Bypass
Kenilworth Road
Birmingham Road
London Road
Oxford Road
Fosse Way
Leicester Lane
Stonebridge Hwy
Fletchamstead Highway
Dunchurch Highway
Holyhead Road
Sky Blue Way
Binley Road
Walsgrave Rd.
Tamworth Road
Warwick Road
Rugby Road
Marton Road
30
31
40
41
A B C D E F
1 2 3 4 5 6 7 8

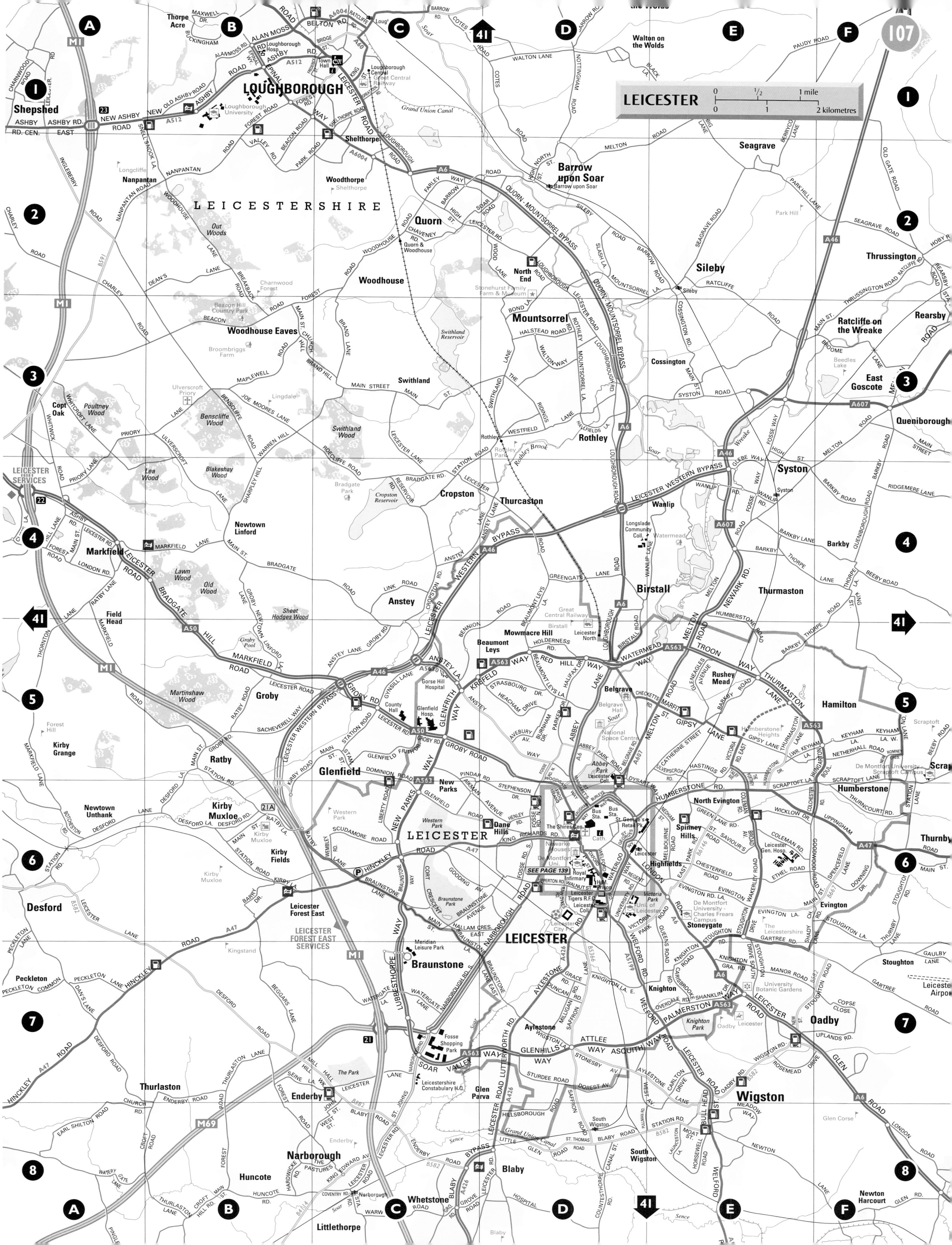
LEICESTER
0 1/2 1 mile
0 1 2 kilometres
LEICESTERSHIRE
LOUGHBOROUGH
LEICESTER
Shepshed
Thorpe Acre
Loughborough University
Shelthorpe
Woodthorpe
Nanpantan
Quorn
Woodhouse
Woodhouse Eaves
Barrow upon Soar
Seagrave
Walton on the Wolds
Sileby
Thrussington
Rearsby
Ratcliffe on the Wreake
Cossington
Mountsorrel
North End
Swithland
Rothley
East Goscote
Queniborough
Syston
Cropston
Thurcaston
Wanlip
Birstall
Barkby
Thurmaston
Copt Oak
Markfield
Newtown Linford
Field Head
Anstey
Beaumont Leys
Mowmacre Hill
Groby
Glenfield
Ratby
Kirby Grange
Kirby Muxloe
Newtown Unthank
Kirby Fields
Desford
Leicester Forest East
New Parks
Dane Hills
Belgrave
Rushey Mead
Hamilton
Humberstone
North Evington
Spinney Hills
Highfields
Evington
Stoneygate
Thurnby
Stoughton
Oadby
Knighton
Aylestone
Braunstone
Glen Parva
Wigston
South Wigston
Peckleton
Thurlaston
Enderby
Narborough
Huncote
Whetstone
Blaby
Littlethorpe
Newton Harcourt
Leicester Forest East Services
Leicester Services
Scraptoft
Glen Corse
Kingstand
M1
M69
A6
A46
A47
A50
A512
A563
A607
A6004
A426
A5199
41
SEE PAGE 139
A B C D E F
1 2 3 4 5 6 7 8

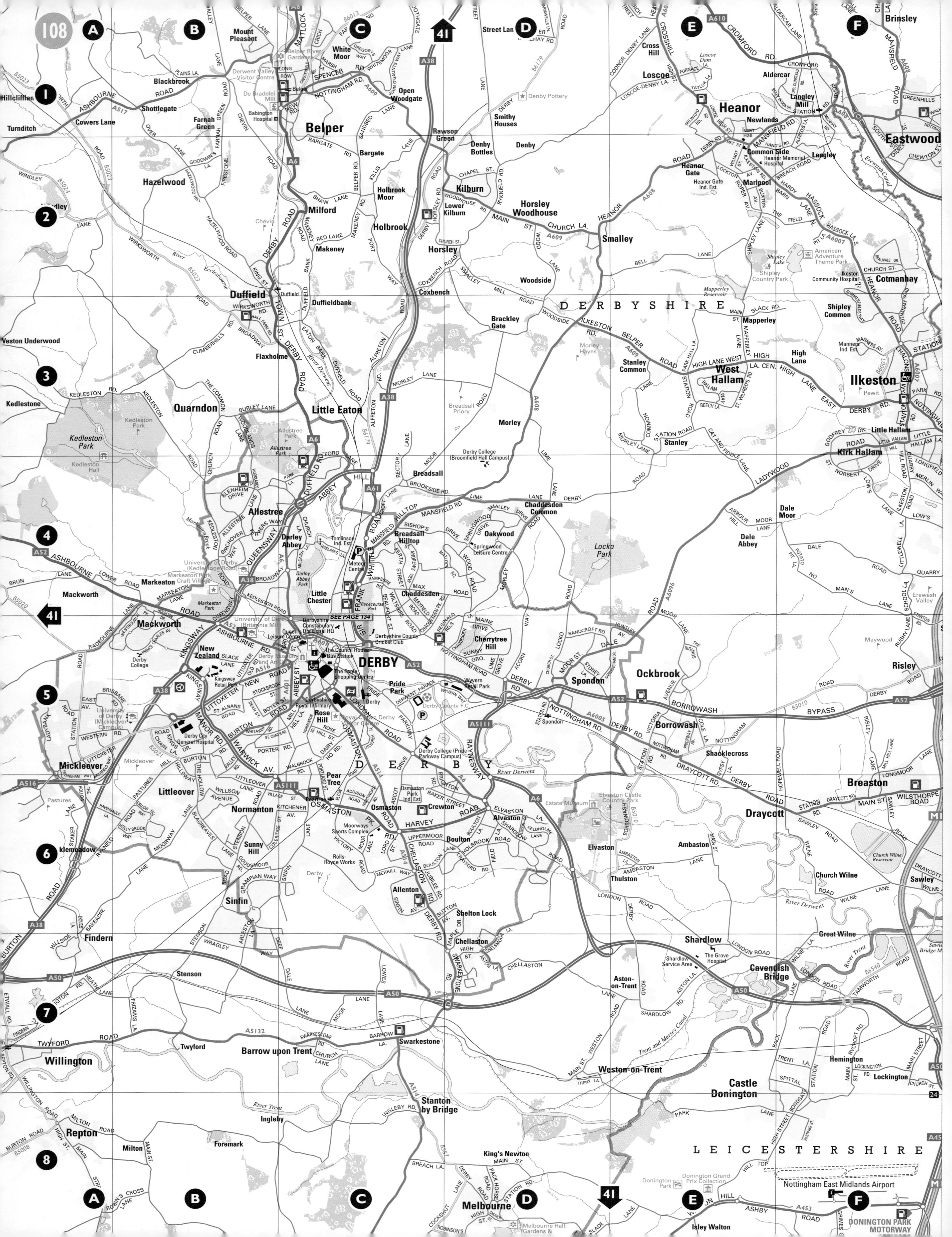
A
B
C
D
E
F
1
2
3
4
5
6
7
8
41
Belper
Heanor
Eastwood
Brinsley
Aldercar
Loscoe
Cross Hill
Langley Mill
Newlands
Heanor Gate
Marlpool
Langley
Street Lane
Denby
Denby Bottles
Smithy Houses
Denby Pottery
Rawson Green
Kilburn
Lower Kilburn
Horsley Woodhouse
Horsley
Smalley
Coxbench
Woodside
Brackley Gate
Holbrook
Holbrook Moor
Bargate
Milford
Makeney
Duffield
Duffieldbank
Flaxholme
Hazelwood
Blackbrook
Shottlegate
Farnah Green
Cowers Lane
Turnditch
Hillclifflan
Mount Pleasant
White Moor
Open Woodgate
Weston Underwood
Kedlestone
Kedleston Park
Kedleston Hall
Quarndon
Little Eaton
Allestree
Allestree Park
Breadsall
Breadsall Priory
Morley
Morley Hayes
Stanley Common
Stanley
West Hallam
Mapperley
Mapperley Reservoir
High Lane
Ilkeston
Shipley Common
Shipley Country Park
American Adventure Theme Park
Cotmanhay
Little Hallam
Kirk Hallam
Dale Moor
Dale Abbey
Locko Park
Erewash Valley
Maywood
Risley
Chaddesden Common
Breadsall Hilltop
Oakwood
Darley Abbey
Markeaton
Mackworth
Little Chester
Chaddesden
Cherrytree Hill
DERBY
New Zealand
Pride Park
Spondon
Ockbrook
Borrowash
Shacklecross
Breaston
Draycott
Sawley
Church Wilne
Great Wilne
Ambaston
Elvaston
Thulston
Alvaston
Crewton
Boulton
Osmaston
Pear Tree
Rose Hill
Normanton
Littleover
Mickleover
Sunny Hill
Sinfin
Allenton
Shelton Lock
Chellaston
Findern
Stenson
Littleover
Aston-on-Trent
Shardlow
Cavendish Bridge
Weston-on-Trent
Swarkestone
Barrow upon Trent
Twyford
Willington
Repton
Milton
Foremark
Ingleby
Stanton by Bridge
King's Newton
Melbourne
Castle Donington
Hemington
Lockington
Isley Walton
Nottingham East Midlands Airport
DONINGTON PARK MOTORWAY
D E R B Y S H I R E
D E R B Y
L E I C E S T E R S H I R E
River Derwent
River Trent
Trent and Mersey Canal
Erewash Canal
SEE PAGE 134
A6
A38
A52
A50
A61
A608
A609
A610
A514
A5111
A516
A5132
A453
B5023
B6179
B5010

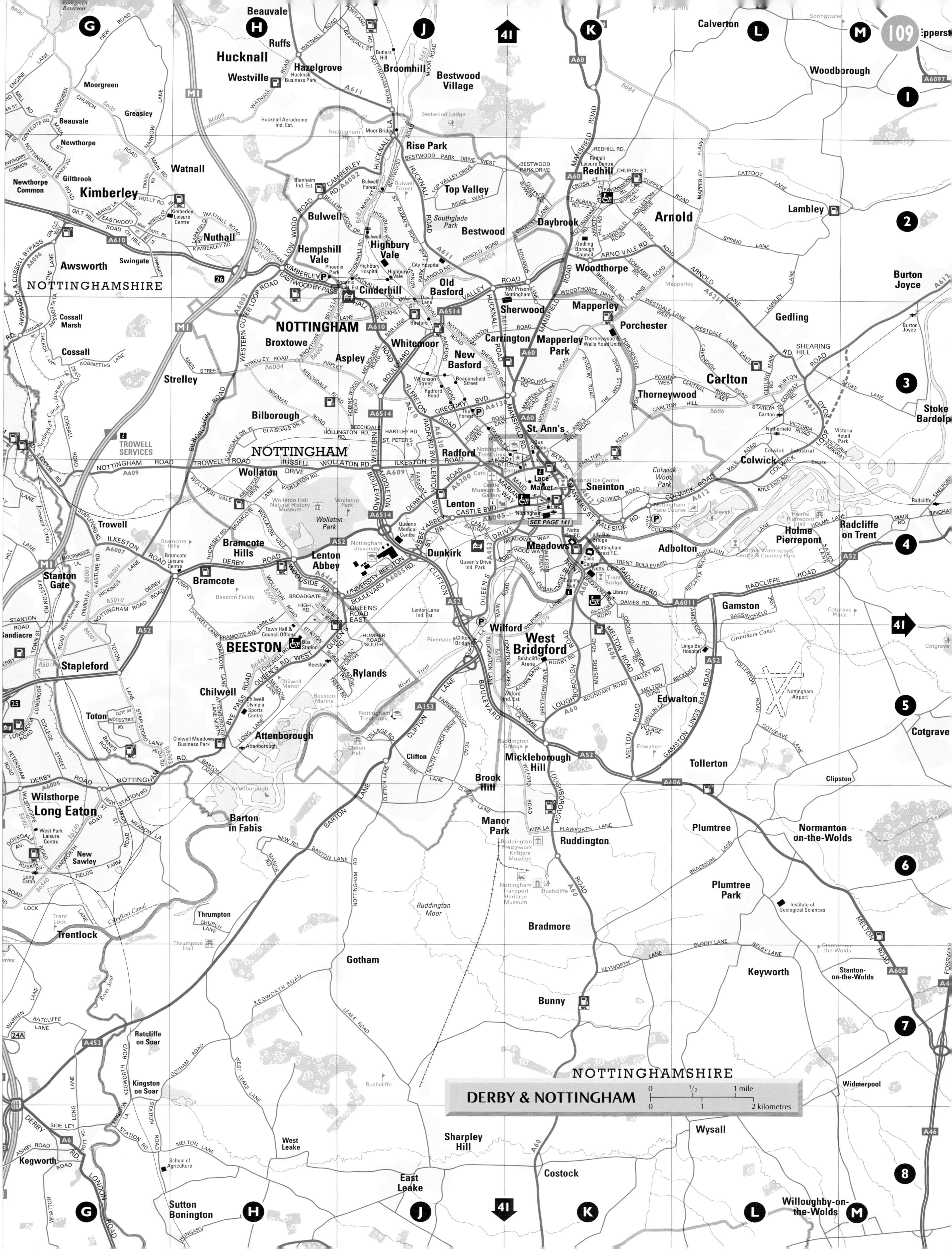
DERBY & NOTTINGHAM
0 1/2 1 mile
0 1 2 kilometres
41
SEE PAGE 141
NOTTINGHAMSHIRE
NOTTINGHAM
Beauvale
Ruffs
Hucknall
Hazelgrove
Westville
Broomhill
Bestwood Village
Calverton
Woodborough
Moorgreen
Greasley
Newthorpe
Newthorpe Common
Giltbrook
Kimberley
Watnall
Nuthall
Rise Park
Top Valley
Redhill
Arnold
Lambley
Daybrook
Bulwell
Bestwood
Hempshill Vale
Highbury Vale
Awsworth
Swingate
Cinderhill
Old Basford
Woodthorpe
Mapperley
Porchester
Burton Joyce
Gedling
Cossall Marsh
Cossall
Broxtowe
Sherwood
Carrington
Mapperley Park
Whitemoor
Aspley
New Basford
Strelley
Carlton
Thorneywood
Stoke Bardolph
Bilborough
St. Ann's
TROWELL SERVICES
Radford
Colwick
Wollaton
Sneinton
Lace Market
Lenton
Trowell
Radcliffe on Trent
Holme Pierrepont
Bramcote Hills
Lenton Abbey
Dunkirk
Meadows
Adbolton
Stanton Gate
Bramcote
Gamston
Wilford
West Bridgford
BEESTON
Stapleford
Rylands
Chilwell
Edwalton
Toton
Attenborough
Cotgrave
Tollerton
Clifton
Mickleborough Hill
Brook Hill
Wilsthorpe
Long Eaton
Barton in Fabis
Manor Park
Clipston
Plumtree
Normanton on-the-Wolds
Ruddington
New Sawley
Plumtree Park
Thrumpton
Trentlock
Bradmore
Gotham
Keyworth
Stanton-on-the-Wolds
Bunny
Ratcliffe on Soar
Kingston on Soar
Widmerpool
West Leake
Sharpley Hill
Wysall
Kegworth
East Leake
Costock
Sutton Bonington
Willoughby-on-the-Wolds
M1
A52
A60
A453
A606
A610
A612
A6514
A46
A6

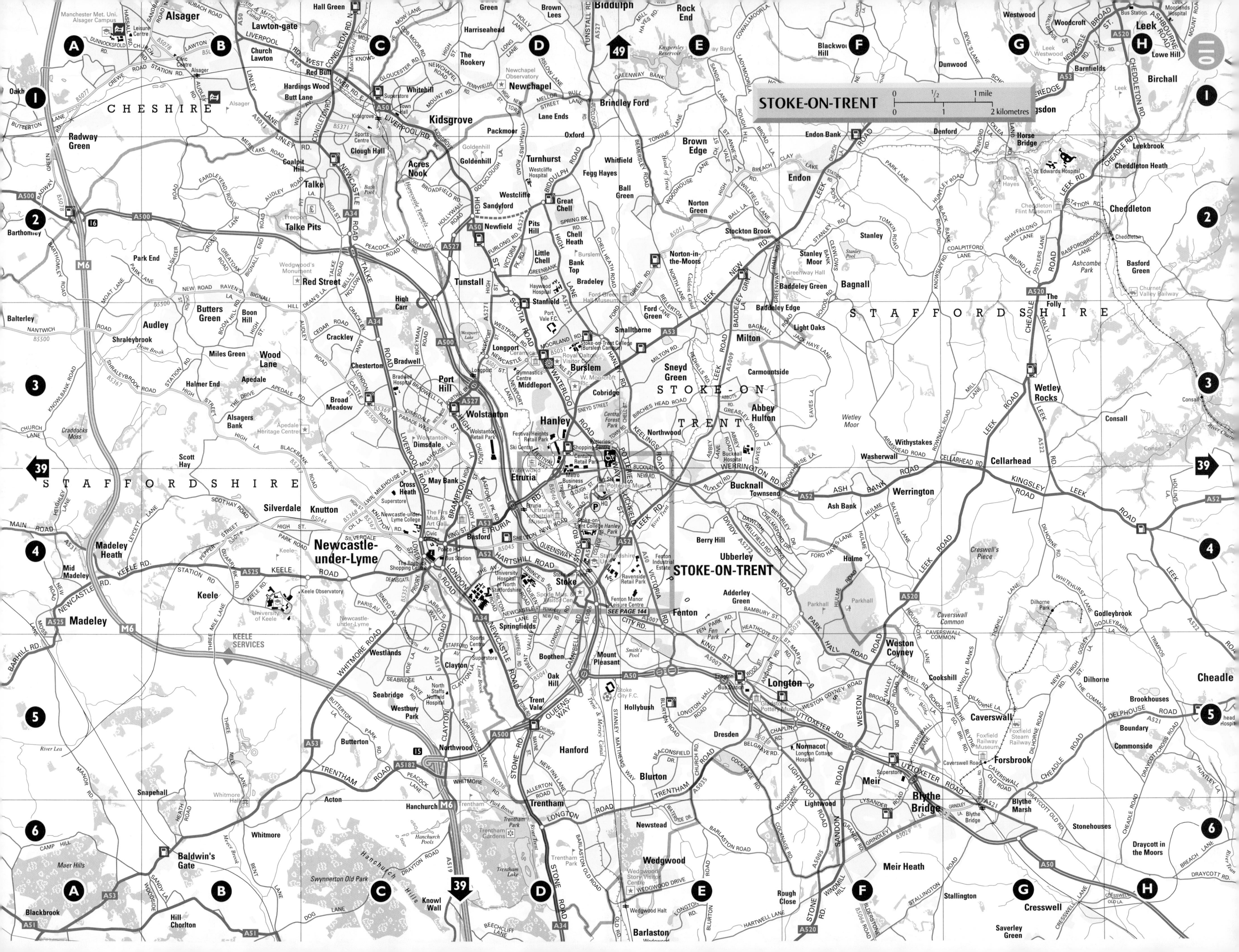
STOKE-ON-TRENT
0 1/2 1 mile
0 1 2 kilometres
CHESHIRE
STAFFORDSHIRE
STAFFORDSHIRE
STOKE-ON-TRENT
STOKE-ON-TRENT
Alsager
Lawton-gate
Church Lawton
Red Bull
Hardings Wood
Butt Lane
Kidsgrove
Newchapel
Biddulph
Rock End
Brindley Ford
Brown Edge
Endon
Leek
Birchall
Cheddleton
Radway Green
Talke
Talke Pits
Red Street
Audley
Tunstall
Burslem
Hanley
Stoke
Etruria
Wolstanton
Newcastle-under-Lyme
Madeley
Keele
KEELE SERVICES
Silverdale
Knutton
Bucknall
Werrington
Cellarhead
Wetley Rocks
Milton
Abbey Hulton
Bagnall
Stanley
Fenton
Longton
Meir
Blythe Bridge
Caverswall
Forsbrook
Cheadle
Trentham
Hanford
Blurton
Wedgwood
Barlaston
Meir Heath
Cresswell
Baldwin's Gate
Whitmore
Clayton
Westlands
Northwood
SEE PAGE 144
39
49
M6
A50
A500
A34
A53
A52
A520
A521
A522
A527

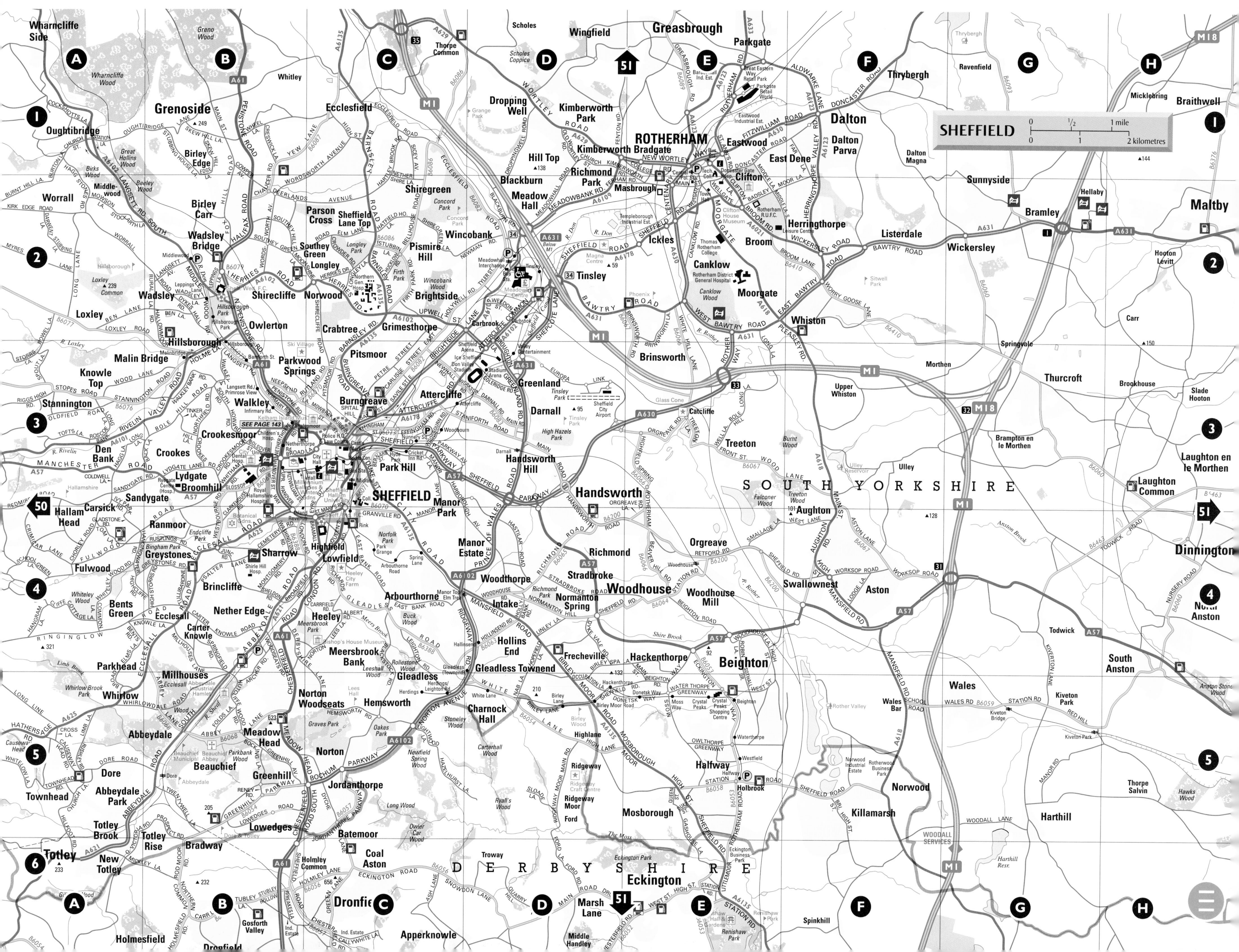

SHEFFIELD
0 1/2 1 mile
0 1 2 kilometres
SOUTH YORKSHIRE
DERBYSHIRE
ROTHERHAM
SHEFFIELD
SEE PAGE 143
50
51
Wharncliffe Side
Oughtibridge
Grenoside
Ecclesfield
Whitley
Thorpe Common
Scholes
Wingfield
Greasbrough
Parkgate
Thrybergh
Ravenfield
Micklebring
Braithwell
Maltby
Dalton
Dalton Parva
Dalton Magna
Sunnyside
Bramley
Hellaby
Wickersley
Listerdale
Hooton Levitt
Worrall
Wadsley Bridge
Wadsley
Loxley
Hillsborough
Malin Bridge
Owlerton
Shirecliffe
Norwood
Longley
Southey Green
Parson Cross
Shiregreen
Wincobank
Pismire Hill
Brightside
Crabtree
Grimesthorpe
Pitsmoor
Parkwood Springs
Burngreave
Attercliffe
Darnall
Greenland
Tinsley
Blackburn
Meadow Hall
Hill Top
Kimberworth Park
Kimberworth
Bradgate
Richmond Park
Masbrough
Ickles
Canklow
Moorgate
Broom
Herringthorpe
East Dene
Eastwood
Clifton
Whiston
Brinsworth
Catcliffe
Treeton
Upper Whiston
Morthen
Thurcroft
Brookhouse
Slade Hooton
Carr
Springvale
Brampton en le Morthen
Laughton en le Morthen
Laughton Common
Dinnington
North Anston
South Anston
Todwick
Ulley
Aughton
Aston
Swallownest
Orgreave
Handsworth
Handsworth Hill
Richmond
Woodhouse
Woodhouse Mill
Stradbroke
Normanton Spring
Woodthorpe
Intake
Manor Estate
Manor Park
Park Hill
Stannington
Walkley
Crookesmoor
Crookes
Den Bank
Lydgate
Broomhill
Sandygate
Carsick
Hallam Head
Ranmoor
Greystones
Sharrow
Highfield
Lowfield
Fulwood
Bents Green
Ecclesall
Nether Edge
Brincliffe
Carter Knowle
Heeley
Arbourthorne
Hollins End
Gleadless Townend
Gleadless
Meersbrook Bank
Parkhead
Millhouses
Whirlow
Abbeydale
Norton Woodseats
Hemsworth
Norton
Charnock Hall
Frecheville
Hackenthorpe
Beighton
Halfway
Holbrook
Mosborough
Ridgeway
Ridgeway Moor
Ford
Eckington
Marsh Lane
Middle Handley
Killamarsh
Norwood
Spinkhill
Wales
Wales Bar
Kiveton Park
Harthill
Thorpe Salvin
Dore
Abbeydale Park
Totley Brook
Totley Rise
Totley
New Totley
Townhead
Beauchief
Meadow Head
Greenhill
Jordanthorpe
Lowedges
Bradway
Batemoor
Coal Aston
Dronfield
Holmesfield
Gosforth Valley
Apperknowle
Troway
Knowle Top
Birley Carr
Birley Edge
Sheffield Lane Top
M1
M18
A57
A61
A631

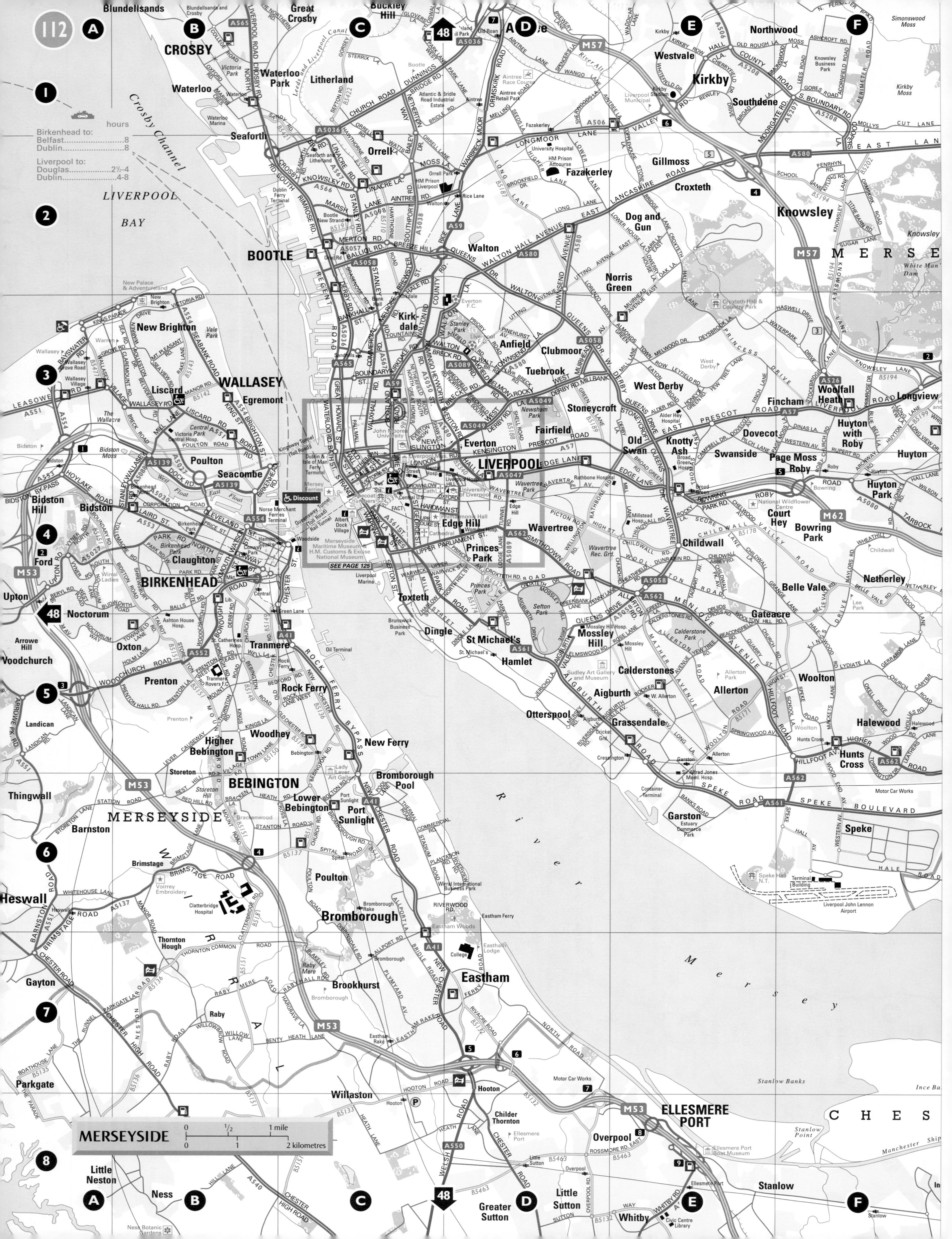
MERSEYSIDE
0 ½ 1 mile
0 1 2 kilometres
Birkenhead to:
Belfast........................8
Dublin..........................8
hours
Liverpool to:
Douglas..................2½-4
Dublin.......................4-8
LIVERPOOL BAY
Crosby Channel
River Mersey
MERSEYSIDE
WIRRAL
CHES
Blundellsands
CROSBY
Great Crosby
Waterloo
Waterloo Park
Litherland
Seaforth
Orrell
Aintree
Fazakerley
Kirkby
Westvale
Northwood
Southdene
Gillmoss
Croxteth
Knowsley
BOOTLE
Walton
Dog and Gun
Norris Green
Kirkdale
Anfield
Clubmoor
Tuebrook
West Derby
Stoneycroft
Everton
Fairfield
LIVERPOOL
Edge Hill
Wavertree
Old Swan
Knotty Ash
Dovecot
Swanside
Page Moss
Roby
Huyton with Roby
Huyton
Huyton Park
Woolfall Heath
Fincham
Longview
Court Hey
Bowring Park
Childwall
Netherley
Belle Vale
Gateacre
Woolton
Halewood
Hunts Cross
Allerton
Calderstones
Mossley Hill
Aigburth
Grassendale
Garston
Speke
Otterspool
Princes Park
Toxteth
Dingle
St Michael's
Hamlet
New Brighton
WALLASEY
Liscard
Egremont
Poulton
Seacombe
Bidston
Bidston Hill
Claughton
BIRKENHEAD
Ford
Upton
Noctorum
Oxton
Tranmere
Rock Ferry
Prenton
Woodchurch
Landican
Higher Bebington
Woodhey
New Ferry
BEBINGTON
Lower Bebington
Port Sunlight
Bromborough Pool
Storeton
Thingwall
Barnston
Brimstage
Heswall
Thornton Hough
Bromborough
Brookhurst
Eastham
Gayton
Raby
Parkgate
Willaston
Hooton
Childer Thornton
Overpool
ELLESMERE PORT
Little Neston
Ness
Greater Sutton
Little Sutton
Whitby
Stanlow
M53
M57
M62
SEE PAGE 125
Liverpool John Lennon Airport
48

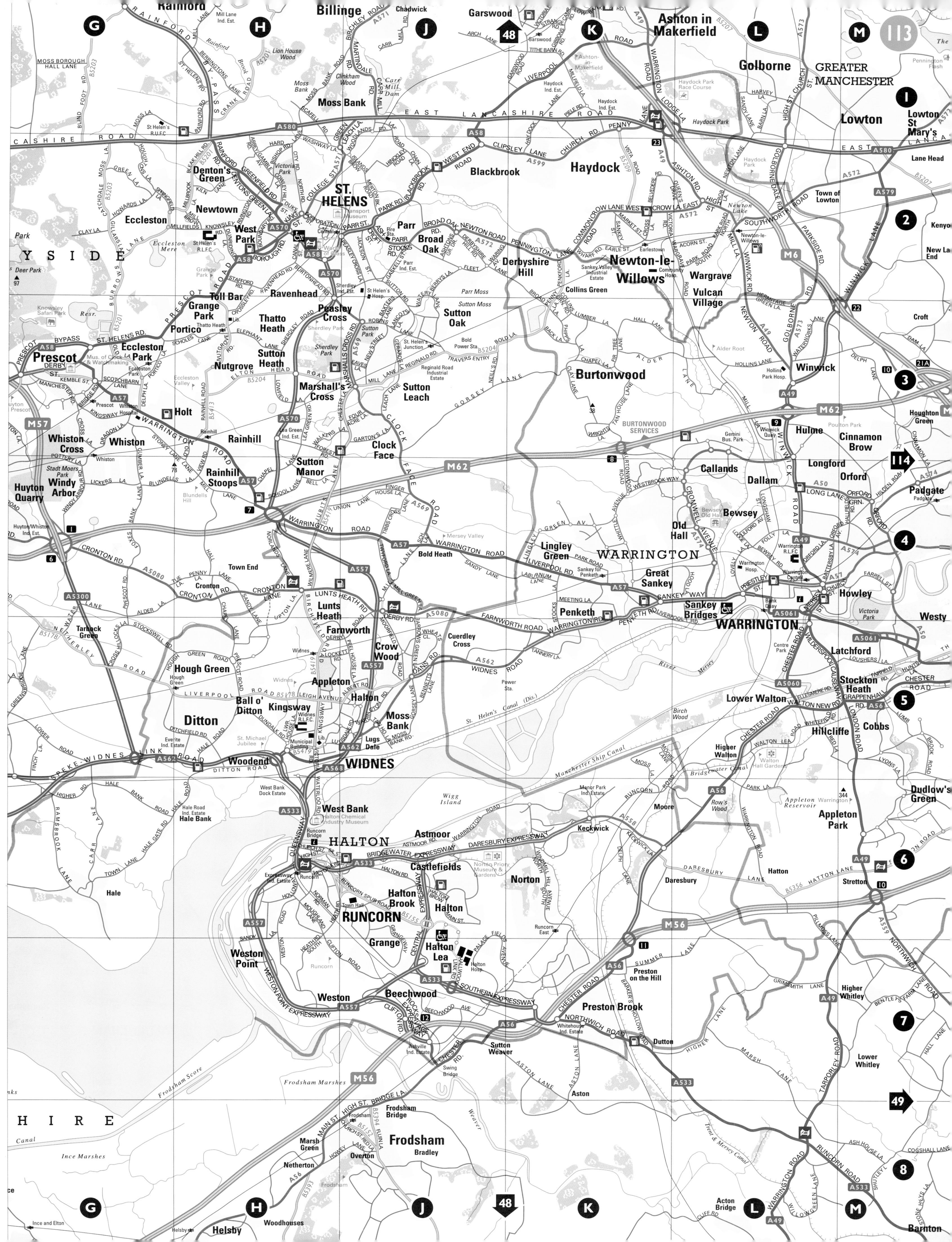

G
H
J
K
L
M
Rainford
Billinge
Chadwick
Garswood
48
Ashton in Makerfield
Golborne
GREATER MANCHESTER
Lowton
Lowton St Mary's
Lane Head
Town of Lowton
Kenyon
New Lane End
Croft
Winwick
Hulme
Cinnamon Brow
Houghton Green
Longford
Orford
Padgate
114
Moss Bank
Haydock
Blackbrook
Denton's Green
ST. HELENS
Newtown
Eccleston
West Park
Parr
Broad Oak
Derbyshire Hill
Newton-le-Willows
Wargrave
Vulcan Village
Collins Green
Ravenhead
Toll Bar
Grange Park
Portico
Thatto Heath
Peasley Cross
Sutton Oak
Sutton Heath
Nutgrove
Eccleston Park
Prescot
Marshall's Cross
Sutton Leach
Burtonwood
BURTONWOOD SERVICES
Holt
Whiston Cross
Whiston
Rainhill
Clock Face
Sutton Manor
Rainhill Stoops
Huyton Quarry
Windy Arbor
Callands
Dallam
Bewsey
Old Hall
Lingley Green
WARRINGTON
Great Sankey
Penketh
Sankey Bridges
Howley
Westy
Latchford
Town End
Cronton
Lunts Heath
Farnworth
Bold Heath
Crow Wood
Cuerdley Cross
Tarbock Green
Hough Green
Appleton
Halton
Ball o' Ditton
Kingsway
Ditton
Moss Bank
Lugs Dale
WIDNES
Woodend
Stockton Heath
Lower Walton
Hillcliffe
Cobbs
Higher Walton
Dudlow's Green
Appleton Park
Hale Bank
West Bank
Wigg Island
HALTON
Astmoor
Keckwick
Moore
Castlefields
Norton
Daresbury
Hatton
Stretton
Halton Brook
RUNCORN
Grange
Halton Lea
Weston Point
Weston
Beechwood
Preston on the Hill
Preston Brook
Higher Whitley
Lower Whitley
Dutton
Sutton Weaver
Aston
Hale
Frodsham Marshes
Frodsham Bridge
Frodsham
Bradley
Marsh Green
Overton
Netherton
Ince Marshes
Woodhouses
Helsby
Acton Bridge
Barnton
49
M6
M62
M57
M56
A580
A58
A57
A49
A56
A533
A557
A562
EAST LANCASHIRE ROAD
River Mersey
Manchester Ship Canal
St. Helen's Canal (Dis.)
Trent & Mersey Canal

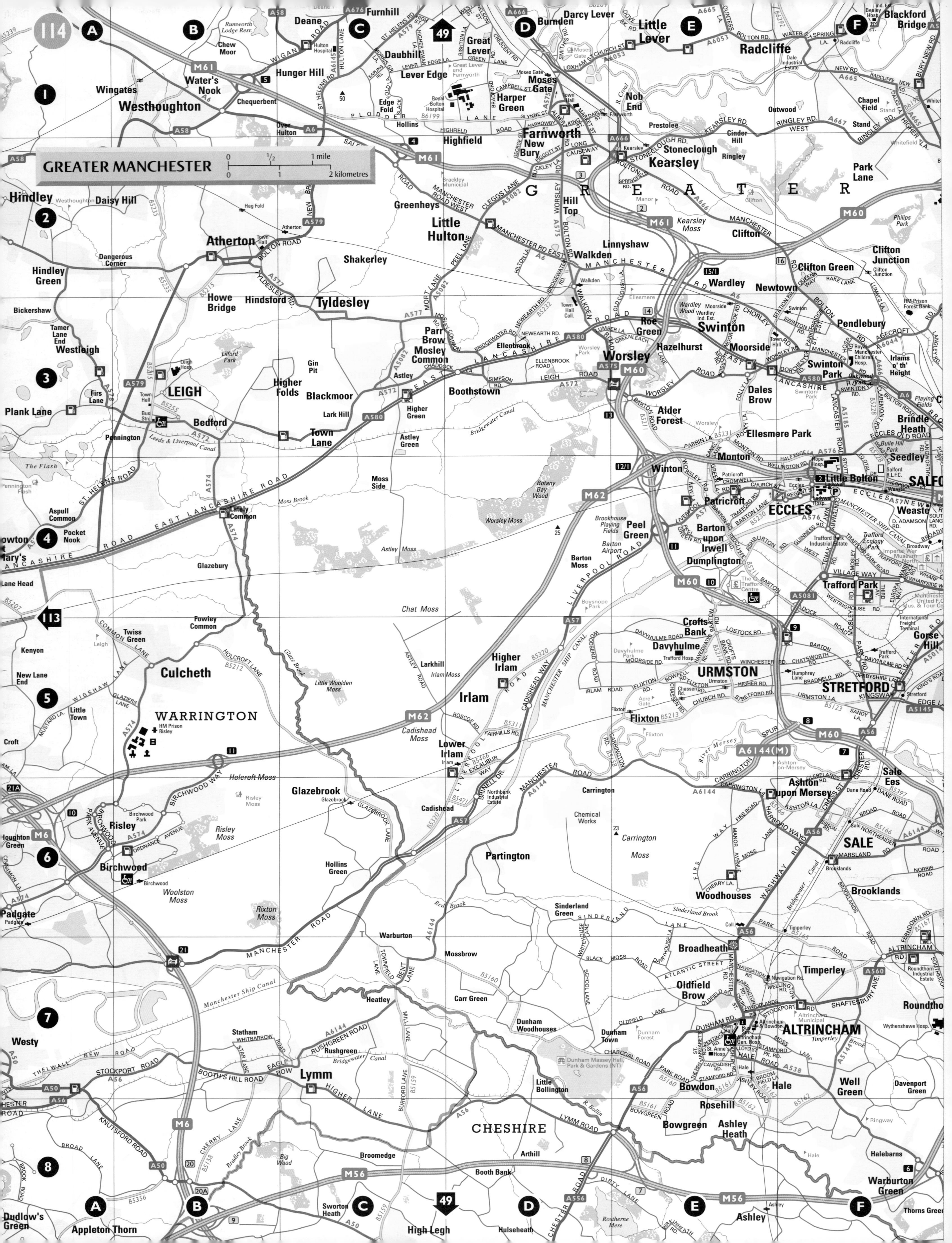
GREATER MANCHESTER
0 ½ 1 mile
0 1 2 kilometres
G R E A T E R
CHESHIRE
WARRINGTON
A B C D E F
1 2 3 4 5 6 7 8
49
113
Deane
Furnhill
Rumworth Lodge Resr.
Chew Moor
Hulton Hospital
Daubhill
Great Lever
Burnden
Darcy Lever
Little Lever
Radcliffe
Blackford Bridge
Hunger Hill
Lever Edge
Moses Gate
Harper Green
Wingates
Westhoughton
Water's Nook
Chequerbent
Edge Fold
Hollins
Highfield
Farnworth
New Bury
Nob End
Prestolee
Outwood
Chapel Field
Stand
Over Hulton
Cinder Hill
Ringley
Stoneclough
Kearsley
Park Lane
Hindley
Daisy Hill
Hag Fold
Greenheys
Little Hulton
Hill Top
Kearsley Moss
Clifton
Philips Park
Atherton
Dangerous Corner
Hindley Green
Shakerley
Linnyshaw
Walkden
Clifton Junction
Clifton Green
Wardley
Newtown
Bickershaw
Howe Bridge
Hindsford
Tyldesley
Ellesmere
Roe Green
Swinton
Pendlebury
Tamer Lane End
Westleigh
Lilford Park
Gin Pit
Higher Folds
Parr Brow
Mosley Common
Ellenbrook
Worsley
Hazelhurst
Moorside
Swinton Park
Irlams o' th' Height
LEIGH
Firs Lane
Astley
Blackmoor
Boothstown
Dales Brow
Plank Lane
Lark Hill
Higher Green
Alder Forest
Ellesmere Park
Brindle Heath
Bedford
Pennington
Town Lane
Astley Green
Monton
Seedley
The Flash
Pennington Flash
Winton
Little Bolton
SALFO
Patricroft
ECCLES
Weaste
Aspull Common
Moss Side
Botany Bay Wood
Lately Common
Worsley Moss
Peel Green
Barton upon Irwell
Pocket Nook
Bowton
Mary's
Astley Moss
Barton Airport
Barton Moss
Dumplington
Trafford Park
Glazebury
Lane Head
Chat Moss
Boysnope Park
Fowley Common
Twiss Green
Kenyon
Leigh
Crofts Bank
Davyhulme
Gorse Hill
New Lane End
Culcheth
Larkhill
Irlam Moss
Higher Irlam
URMSTON
STRETFORD
Little Woolden Moss
Little Town
Irlam
Flixton
HM Prison Risley
Croft
Cadishead Moss
Lower Irlam
Holcroft Moss
Carrington
Ashton upon Mersey
Sale
Ees
Glazebrook
Risley
Risley Moss
Cadishead
Chemical Works
Carrington Moss
SALE
Houghton Green
Birchwood
Partington
Hollins Green
Woodhouses
Brooklands
Woolston Moss
Padgate
Rixton Moss
Sinderland Green
Warburton
Broadheath
Mossbrow
Timperley
Oldfield Brow
Heatley
Carr Green
Roundthorn
Westy
Statham
Dunham Woodhouses
Dunham Town
ALTRINCHAM
Rushgreen
Dunham Massey Hall, Park & Gardens (NT)
Lymm
Little Bollington
Bowdon
Hale
Well Green
Davenport Green
Rosehill
Bowgreen
Ashley Heath
Ringway
Broomedge
Arthill
Halebarns
Big Wood
Booth Bank
Warburton Green
Appleton Thorn
Dudlow's Green
Sworton Heath
High Legh
Hulseheath
Rostherne Mere
Ashley
Thorns Green
Manchester Ship Canal
Bridgewater Canal
Leeds & Liverpool Canal
River Mersey
Glaze Brook
Moss Brook
M61
M60
M62
M6
M56
A6144(M)
EAST LANCASHIRE ROAD
LIVERPOOL ROAD
MANCHESTER ROAD
CADISHEAD WAY
BIRCHWOOD WAY
HOLCROFT LANE
STOCKPORT ROAD
KNUTSFORD ROAD
LYMM ROAD
HIGHER LANE

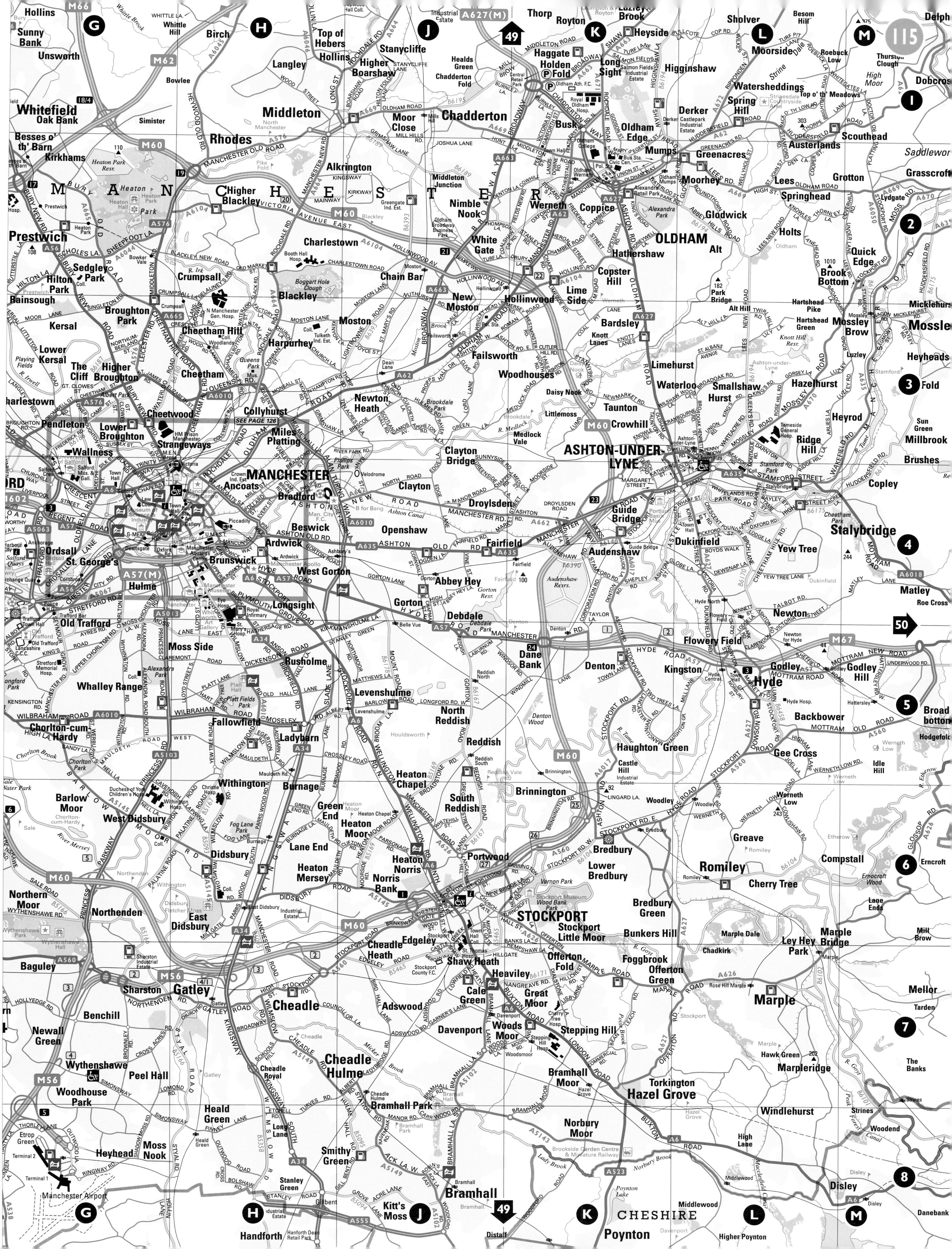

MANCHESTER
Hollins
Sunny Bank
Unsworth
Whitefield
Oak Bank
Besses o' th' Barn
Kirkhams
Prestwich
Heaton Park
Birch
Whittle Hill
Bowlee
Simister
Rhodes
Middleton
Langley
Top of Hebers
Hollins
Stanycliffe
Higher Boarshaw
Moor Close
Chadderton
Heald Green
Chadderton Fold
Thorp
Royton
Heyside
Haggate
Holden Fold
Long Sight
Higginshaw
Sholver
Moorside
Watersheddings
Spring Hill
Derker
Oldham Edge
Busk
Mumps
Greenacres
Scouthead
Austerlands
Grotton
Grasscroft
Lees
Springhead
Moorhey
Alkrington
Middleton Junction
Higher Blackley
Nimble Nook
White Gate
Werneth
Coppice
Glodwick
OLDHAM
Holts
Alt
Quick Edge
Hathershaw
Charlestown
Sedgley Park
Hilton Park
Rainsough
Crumpsall
Blackley
Chain Bar
New Moston
Hollinwood
Copster Hill
Lime Side
Brook Bottom
Park Bridge
Broughton Park
Kersal
Lower Kersal
The Cliff
Higher Broughton
Cheetham Hill
Cheetham
Harpurhey
Moston
Failsworth
Woodhouses
Bardsley
Knott Lanes
Limehurst
Hartshead Pike
Mossley Brow
Heyheads
Fold
Hazelhurst
Smallshaw
Hurst
Waterloo
Daisy Nook
Taunton
Crowhill
Littlemoss
Heyrod
Ridge Hill
Millbrook
Brushes
Copley
Salford
Pendleton
Lower Broughton
Cheetwood
Collyhurst
SEE PAGE 126
Strangeways
Miles Platting
Newton Heath
Clayton Bridge
Clayton
ASHTON-UNDER-LYNE
Wallness
Ancoats
Bradford
Droylsden
Guide Bridge
Stalybridge
Ordsall
St. George's
Hulme
Brunswick
Ardwick
Beswick
Openshaw
Fairfield
Audenshaw
Dukinfield
Yew Tree
Matley
Roe Cross
West Gorton
Abbey Hey
Gorton
Longsight
Debdale
Old Trafford
Moss Side
Rusholme
Dane Bank
Denton
Flowery Field
Newton
Kingston
Godley
Godley Hill
Hyde
Whalley Range
Levenshulme
North Reddish
Backbower
Broadbottom
Chorlton-cum-Hardy
Fallowfield
Ladybarn
Reddish
Haughton Green
Gee Cross
Hodgefold
Idle Hill
Barlow Moor
Withington
Burnage
Heaton Chapel
Brinnington
Woodley
South Reddish
West Didsbury
Green End
Heaton Moor
Lane End
Didsbury
Heaton Mersey
Heaton Norris
Portwood
Bredbury
Greave
Compstall
Erncroft
Lower Bredbury
Romiley
Cherry Tree
Northern Moor
Northenden
Norris Bank
East Didsbury
STOCKPORT
Stockport Little Moor
Bredbury Green
Bunkers Hill
Marple Dale
Marple Bridge
Ley Hey Park
Mill Brow
Baguley
Sharston
Gatley
Cheadle Heath
Edgeley
Shaw Heath
Offerton Fold
Foggbrook
Offerton Green
Chadkirk
Heaviley
Cale Green
Great Moor
Marple
Mellor
Tarden
Benchill
Cheadle
Adswood
Davenport
Woods Moor
Stepping Hill
Newall Green
Wythenshawe
Peel Hall
Cheadle Hulme
Bramhall Moor
Torkington
Hazel Grove
Hawk Green
Marpleridge
The Banks
Woodhouse Park
Bramhall Park
Windlehurst
Strines
Woodend
Heald Green
Moss Nook
Heyhead
Etrop Green
Long Lane
Norbury Moor
High Lane
Smithy Green
Manchester Airport
Stanley Green
Bramhall
Kitt's Moss
Disley
Danebank
Handforth
Poynton
Higher Poynton
Middlewood
CHESHIRE
Distaff
M60
M62
M66
M56
M67
A627(M)
A57(M)
49
50
G
H
J
K
L
M
1
2
3
4
5
6
7
8

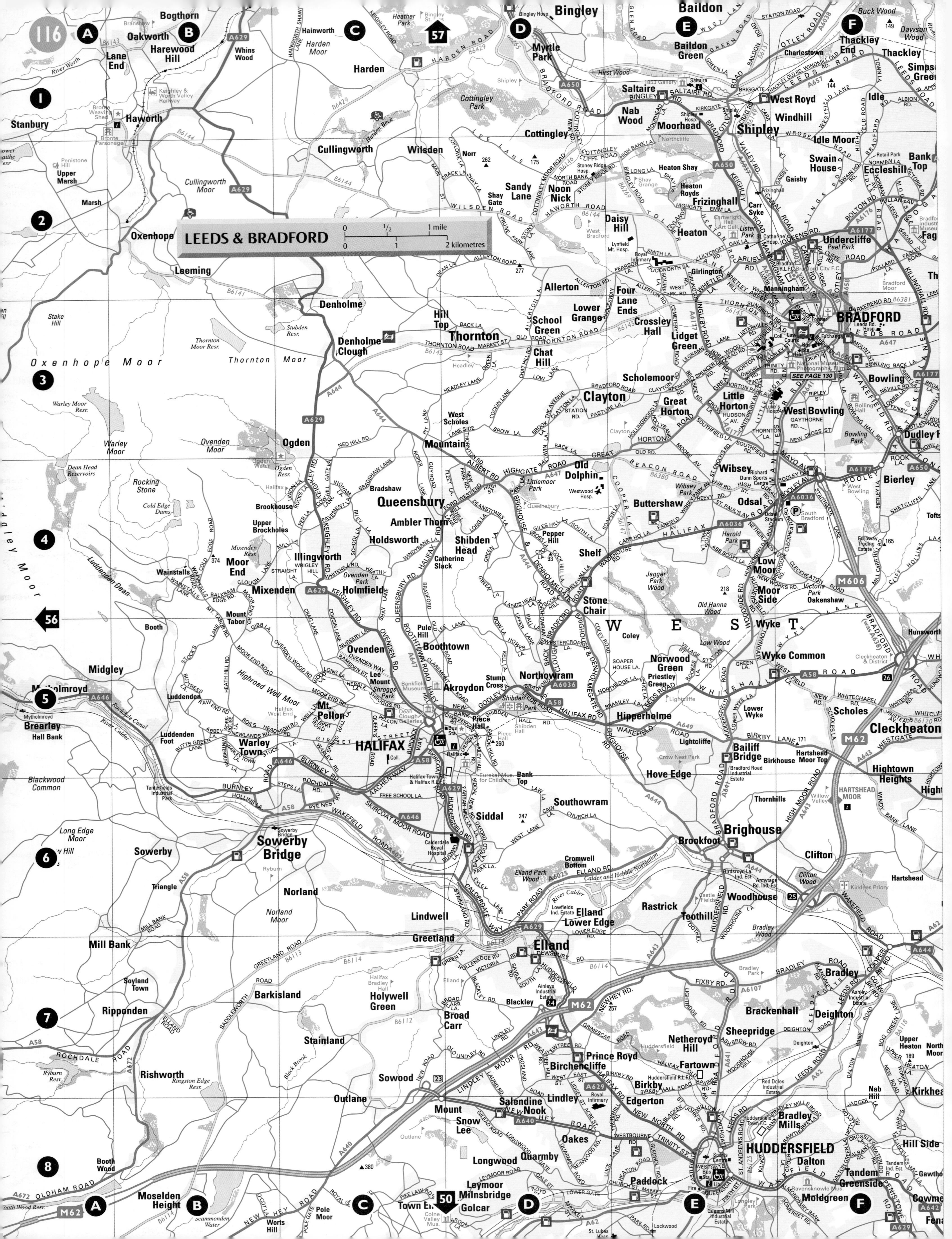
LEEDS & BRADFORD
0 1/2 1 mile
0 1 2 kilometres
A B C D E F
1 2 3 4 5 6 7 8
57
56
50
SEE PAGE 130
Bogthorn
Oakworth
Lane End
Harewood Hill
Whins Wood
Stanbury
Haworth
Keighley & Worth Valley Railway
Bronte Parsonage
Upper Marsh
Marsh
Oxenhope
Cullingworth Moor
Leeming
Stake Hill
Oxenhope Moor
Thornton Moor
Thornton Moor Resr.
Stubden Resr.
Warley Moor Resr.
Warley Moor
Ovenden Moor
Dean Head Reservoirs
Rocking Stone
Cold Edge Dams
Midgley Moor
Luddenden Dean
Wainstalls
Mount Tabor
Booth
Midgley
Mytholmroyd
Brearley
Hall Bank
Blackwood Common
Long Edge Moor
Sowerby
Triangle
Mill Bank
Soyland Town
Ripponden
Rishworth
Ryburn Resr.
Ringston Edge Resr.
Booth Wood
Moselden Height
Scammonden Water
Worts Hill
Pole Moor
Outlane
Sowood
Stainland
Barkisland
Holywell Green
Norland Moor
Norland
Sowerby Bridge
Luddenden Foot
Luddenden
Warley Town
Highroad Well Moor
Mt. Pellon
HALIFAX
Ovenden
Illingworth
Holmfield
Mixenden
Moor End
Upper Brockholes
Brookhouse
Ogden
Denholme
Denholme Clough
Harden
Harden Moor
Hainworth
Heather Park
Cullingworth
Wilsden
Cottingley Park
Cottingley
Bingley
Myrtle Park
Baildon
Baildon Green
Saltaire
Shipley
Nab Wood
Moorhead
Frizinghall
Heaton
Heaton Shay
Heaton Royds
Daisy Hill
Sandy Lane
Shay Gate
Norr
Noon Nick
Allerton
Four Lane Ends
Lower Grange
School Green
Crossley Hall
Lidget Green
Thornton
Hill Top
Chat Hill
Clayton
Scholemoor
Great Horton
Little Horton
West Bowling
Bowling
Bowling Park
Dudley Hill
BRADFORD
Manningham
Girlington
Undercliffe
Peel Park
Eccleshill
Swain House
Idle Moor
Idle
Windhill
West Royd
Thackley
Thackley End
Charlestown
Bank Top
Gaisby
Queensbury
Ambler Thorn
Holdsworth
Bradshaw
Mountain
West Scholes
Shibden Head
Catherine Slack
Old Dolphin
Littlemoor Park
Wibsey
Wibsey Park
Odsal
Buttershaw
Harold Park
Low Moor
Shelf
Pepper Hill
Stone Chair
Jagger Park Wood
Old Hanna Wood
Moor Side
Oakenshaw
Wyke
Coley
Low Wood
Norwood Green
Priestley Green
WEST
Wyke Common
Cleckheaton
Scholes
Lower Wyke
Bierley
Boothtown
Pule Hill
Lee Mount
Shroggs Park
Akroydon
Stump Cross
Northowram
Shibden Park
Hipperholme
Lightcliffe
Bailiff Bridge
Birkhouse
Hartshead Moor Top
Hightown Heights
Hove Edge
Thornhills
Brighouse
Brookfoot
Clifton
Hartshead
Southowram
Bank Top
Siddal
Piece Hall
Elland Park Wood
Cromwell Bottom
Rastrick
Woodhouse
Toothill
Bradley Wood
Lindwell
Greetland
Elland
Lower Edge
Blackley
Broad Carr
Brackenhall
Deighton
Bradley
Sheepridge
Netheroyd Hill
Fartown
Birchencliffe
Prince Royd
Birkby
Edgerton
Lindley
Salendine Nook
Mount
Snow Lee
Oakes
Longwood
Quarmby
Leymoor
Milnsbridge
Golcar
Town End
Paddock
HUDDERSFIELD
Bradley Mills
Dalton
Moldgreen
Tandem
Greenside
Hill Side
Kirkheaton
Upper Heaton
Nab Hill
M62
M606
A629
A646
A58
A644
A647
A650
A6036
A6177
A641
A643
A640
A62
A672
B6144
B6145
B6141
B6113
B6114

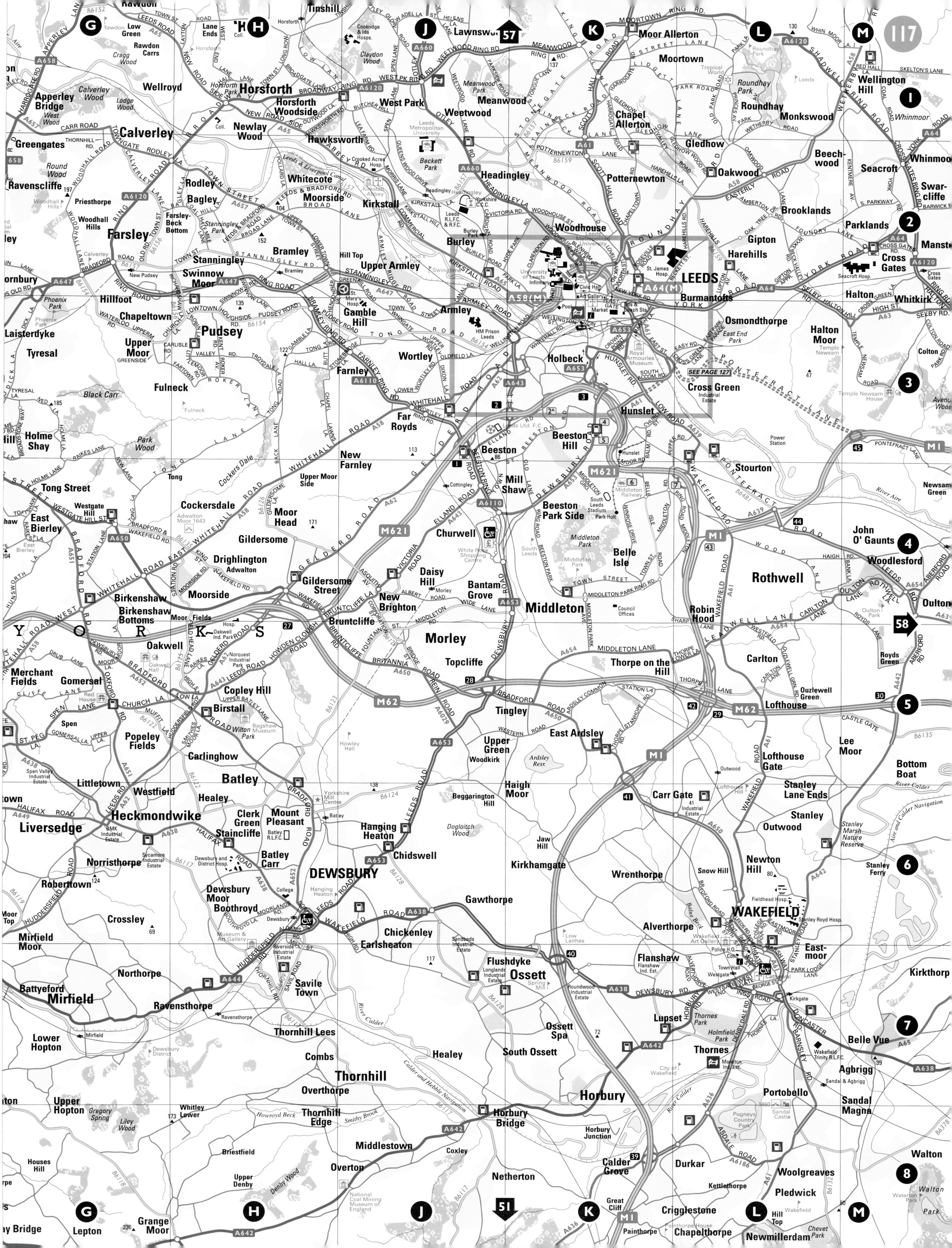
G
H
J
K
L
M
57
Rawdon
Low Green
Lane Ends
Tinshill
Cookridge & Ids Hosps.
Lawnswood
Moor Allerton
Moortown
Rawdon Carrs
Cragg Wood
Clayton Wood
Tropical World
Roundhay Park
Wellington Hill
Apperley Bridge
Calverley Wood
Wellroyd
Horsforth
Horsforth Park
West Park
Meanwood Park
Meanwood
Roundhay
Monkswood
Lodge Wood
West Wood
Horsforth Woodside
Weetwood
Chapel Allerton
Whinmoor
Greengates
Calverley
Newlay Wood
Hawksworth
Leeds Metropolitan University
Gledhow
Beech-wood
Seacroft
Whinmoor
Round Wood
Beckett Park
Oakwood
Swarcliffe
Ravenscliffe
Rodley
Whitecote
Headingley
Potternewton
Bagley
Moorside
Kirkstall
Priesthorpe
Kirkstall Abbey
Yorkshire C.C.C.
Brooklands
Woodhall Hills
Farsley-Beck Bottom
Stanningley Park
Leeds R.L.F.C. & R.F.C.
Parklands
Farsley
Burley Park
Woodhouse
Gipton
Manston
Bramley
Burley
Harehills
Cross Gates
Stanningley
Hill Top
Upper Armley
University of Leeds
St. James Hosp.
LEEDS
Seacroft Hosp.
Swinnow Moor
Civic Hall
Art Gallery
Burmantofts
Halton
Whitkirk
Phoenix Park
Hillfoot
Gamble Hill
Armley
Market
Osmondthorpe
Chapeltown
HM Prison Leeds
Halton Moor
Laisterdyke
Pudsey
Temple Newsam
Colton
Tyresal
Upper Moor
Wortley
Holbeck
Royal Armouries Museum
Farnley
SEE PAGE 127
Cross Green
Fulneck
Cross Green Industrial Estate
3
Black Carr
Temple Newsam House
Far Royds
Hunslet
Holme Shay
Leeds Utd. F.C.
Beeston Hill
Power Station
Park Wood
New Farnley
Beeston
M1
Stourton
Upper Moor Side
Mill Shaw
Tong
Tong Street
Cockersdale
Middleton Railway
Newsam Green
East Bierley
Westgate Hill
Moor Head
South Leeds Stadium
Beeston Park Side
River Aire
Adwalton Moor 1643
Gildersome
Churwell
White Rose Shopping Centre
Middleton Park
John O' Gaunts
4
Drighlington
Adwalton
South Leeds
Belle Isle
Woodlesford
Daisy Hill
Gildersome Street
Bantam Grove
Rothwell
Birkenshaw
Moorside
New Brighton
Oulton
Birkenshaw Bottoms
Middleton
Robin Hood
Council Offices
Oulton Park
58
YORKS
Bruntcliffe
Oakwell
Morley
Oakwell Hall
Merchant Fields
Gomersal
Topcliffe
Thorpe on the Hill
Carlton
Royds Green
Copley Hill
Oulton Green
Birstall
Tingley
Lofthouse
5
Spen
Popeley Fields
Bagshaw Museum
Wilton Park
East Ardsley
Upper Green
Woodkirk
Howley Hall
Ardsley Resr.
Lee Moor
Carlinghow
Lofthouse Gate
Bottom Boat
Spen Valley Industrial Estate
Batley
Outwood
Littletown
Westfield
Haigh Moor
Stanley Lane Ends
Healey
Yorkshire Mill Centre
Carr Gate
River Calder
Liversedge
Heckmondwike
Clerk Green
Mount Pleasant
Beggarington Hill
Stanley
Outwood
BMK Industrial Estate
Staincliffe
Batley R.L.F.C.
Hanging Heaton
Dogloitch Wood
Aire and Calder Navigation
Jaw Hill
Stanley Marsh Nature Reserve
Sycamore Industrial Estate
Batley Carr
Chidswell
Newton Hill
Norristhorpe
Dewsbury and District Hosp.
DEWSBURY
Kirkhamgate
Wrenthorpe
Snow Hill
Stanley Ferry
6
Roberttown
Dewsbury Moor
College
Fieldhead Hosp.
Boothroyd
Gawthorpe
WAKEFIELD
Crossley
Dewsbury
Stanley Royd Hosp.
Moor Top
Alverthorpe
Chickenley
Wakefield Art Gallery
Museum & Art Gallery
Low Laithes
East-moor
Mirfield Moor
Earlsheaton
Riverside Industrial Estate
Sandbeds Industrial Estate
Flanshaw
Flanshaw Ind. Est.
Police H.Q.
Northorpe
Flushdyke
Town Hall
Kirkthorpe
Longlands Industrial Estate
Ossett
Westgate
Spring Mill
Battyeford
Savile Town
Roundwood Industrial Estate
Cathedral
Kirkgate
Mirfield
Ravensthorpe
Ossett Spa
Lupset
Thornes Park
7
River Calder
Holmfield Park
Belle Vue
Lower Hopton
Thornhill Lees
Dewsbury District
South Ossett
Thornes
Wakefield Trinity R.L.F.C.
Combs
Healey
Monkton Ind. Est.
Agbrigg
City of Wakefield
Sandal & Agbrigg
Thornhill
Horbury
River Calder
Portobello
Upper Hopton
Overthorpe
Sandal Magna
Gregory Wood
Whitley Lower
Howroyd Beck
Thornhill Edge
Smithy Brook
Horbury Bridge
Calder and Hebble Navigation
Pugneys Country Park
Sandal Castle
Liley Wood
Horbury Junction
Middlestown
Coxley
Walton
Briestfield
Durkar
Calder Grove
8
Houses Hill
Overton
Woolgreaves
Upper Denby
Netherton
Denby Wood
Kettlethorpe
Pledwick
National Coal Mining Museum of England
Great Cliff
Walton Park
Lepton
51
Crigglestone
Hill Top
Wakefield
Grange Moor
Painthorpe
Painthorpe House
Chapelthorpe
Newmillerdam
Chevet Park

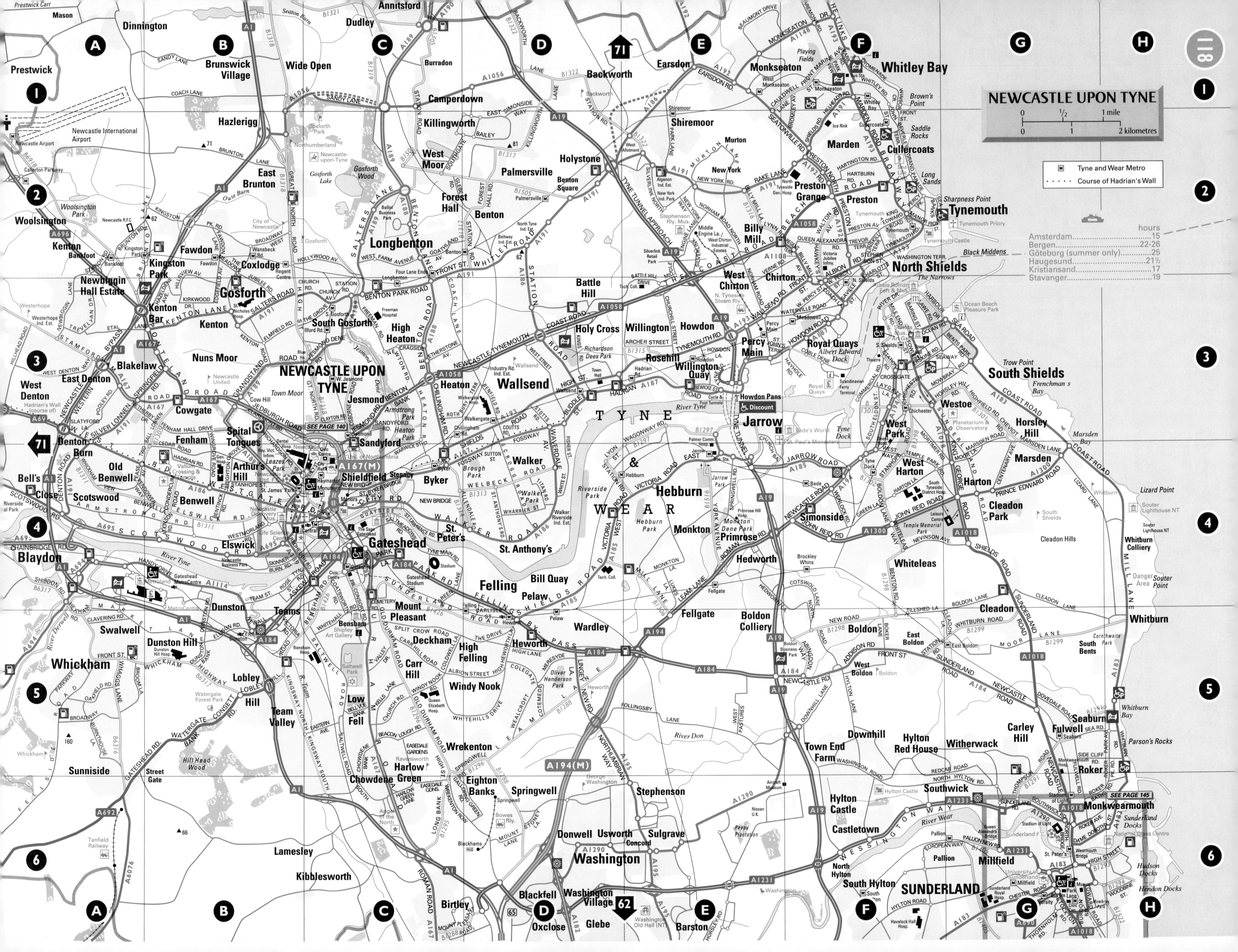
NEWCASTLE UPON TYNE
0 1/2 1 mile
0 1 2 kilometres
Tyne and Wear Metro
Course of Hadrian's Wall
hours
Amsterdam 15
Bergen 22-26
Göteborg (summer only) 25
Haugesund 21½
Kristiansand 17
Stavanger 19
Whitley Bay
Monkseaton
Tynemouth
North Shields
South Shields
Cullercoats
Marden
Preston
Earsdon
Shiremoor
Backworth
Holystone
Killingworth
Camperdown
Longbenton
Forest Hall
Benton
Palmersville
Wallsend
Willington Quay
Howdon
Percy Main
Jarrow
Hebburn
Felling
Gateshead
NEWCASTLE UPON TYNE
Jesmond
Heaton
Byker
Walker
Gosforth
Kenton
Fenham
Benwell
Elswick
Scotswood
Blaydon
Whickham
Dunston
Lobley Hill
Team Valley
Low Fell
Wrekenton
Washington
Boldon
Cleadon
Whitburn
Marsden
Harton
Westoe
Sunderland
Monkwearmouth
Roker
Seaburn
Fulwell
Southwick
Castletown
Hylton Castle
Millfield
Pallion
Birtley
Kibblesworth
Lamesley
Sunniside
Prestwick
Dinnington
Dudley
Annitsford
Wide Open
Brunswick Village
Hazlerigg
Newcastle International Airport
Woolsington
Newbiggin Hall Estate
Blakelaw
West Denton
Denton Burn
Cowgate
River Tyne
River Wear
River Don
TYNE & WEAR
SEE PAGE 140
SEE PAGE 145
71
62

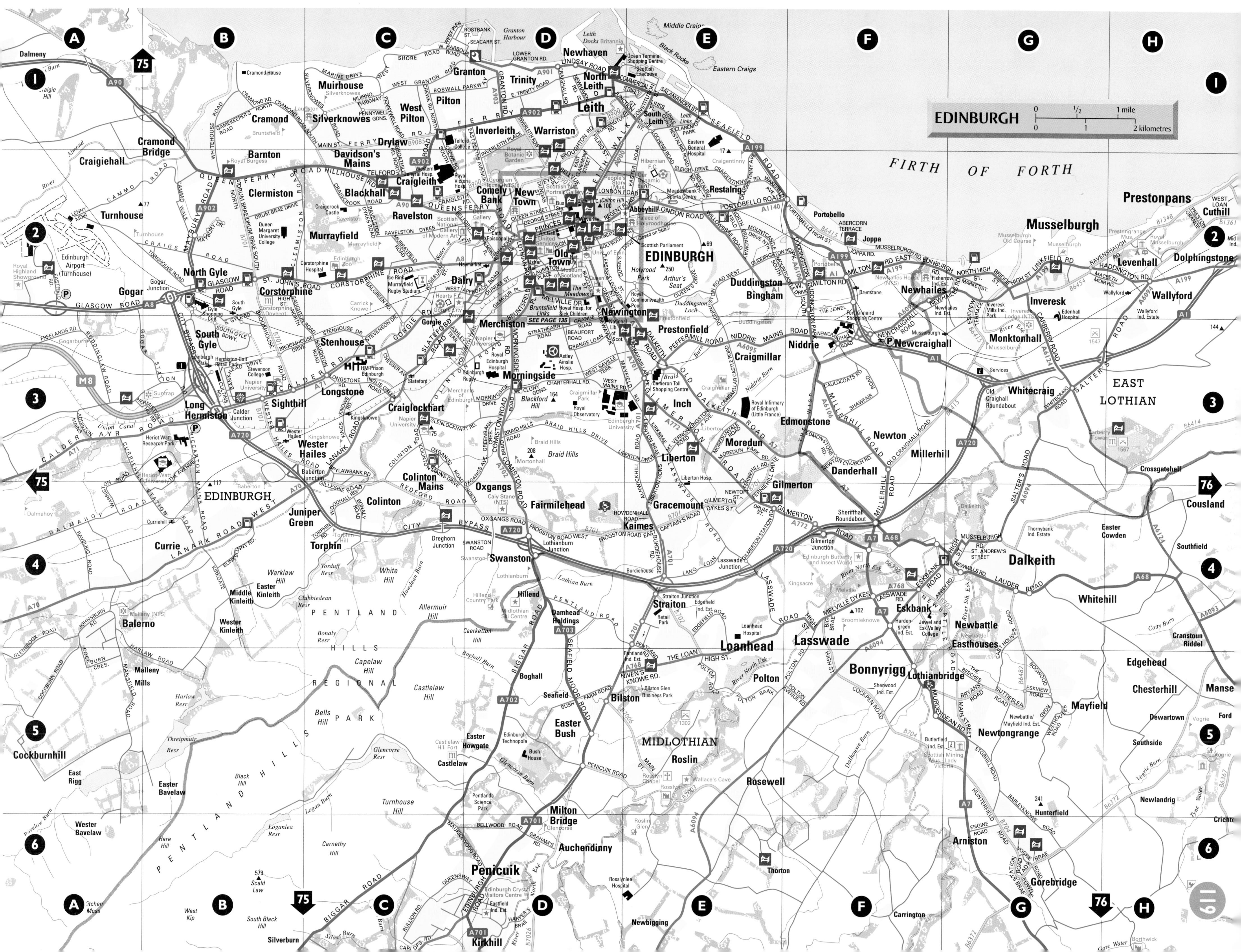
EDINBURGH
0 1/2 1 mile
0 1 2 kilometres
FIRTH OF FORTH
EAST LOTHIAN
MIDLOTHIAN
PENTLAND HILLS REGIONAL PARK
SEE PAGE 135
Dalmeny
Cramond Bridge
Craigiehall
Turnhouse
Edinburgh Airport (Turnhouse)
Gogar
Cramond
Barnton
Clermiston
North Gyle
South Gyle
Corstorphine
Muirhouse
Silverknowes
Davidson's Mains
Blackhall
Murrayfield
Pilton
West Pilton
Drylaw
Craigleith
Ravelston
Granton
Trinity
Inverleith
Warriston
Comely Bank
New Town
Newhaven
North Leith
Leith
South Leith
Restalrig
Abbeyhill
Old Town
EDINBURGH
Dalry
Gorgie
Stenhouse
Merchiston
Morningside
Newington
Prestonfield
Duddingston
Bingham
Craigmillar
Niddrie
Inch
Liberton
Moredun
Gilmerton
Gracemount
Kaimes
Fairmilehead
Oxgangs
Colinton Mains
Colinton
Craiglockhart
Longstone
Sighthill
Wester Hailes
Long Hermiston
Juniper Green
Currie
Torphin
Swanston
Balerno
Malleny Mills
Cockburnhill
Portobello
Joppa
Newcraighall
Newhailes
Musselburgh
Inveresk
Monktonhall
Whitecraig
Prestonpans
Levenhall
Wallyford
Dolphingstone
Cuthill
Edmonstone
Danderhall
Newton
Millerhill
Dalkeith
Eskbank
Newbattle
Easthouses
Bonnyrigg
Lothianbridge
Lasswade
Loanhead
Straiton
Bilston
Polton
Roslin
Rosewell
Easter Bush
Seafield
Boghall
Hillend
Damhead Holdings
Milton Bridge
Auchendinny
Penicuik
Kirkhill
Newbigging
Thorton
Carrington
Newtongrange
Mayfield
Arniston
Gorebridge
Hunterfield
Cousland
Crossgatehall
Whitehill
Edgehead
Chesterhill
Manse
Southfield
Cranstoun Riddel
Easter Cowden
Newlandrig
Silverburn
A90
A902
A8
A720
A70
A71
A702
A703
A701
A7
A68
A1
A199
A6094
A6124
M8
75
76

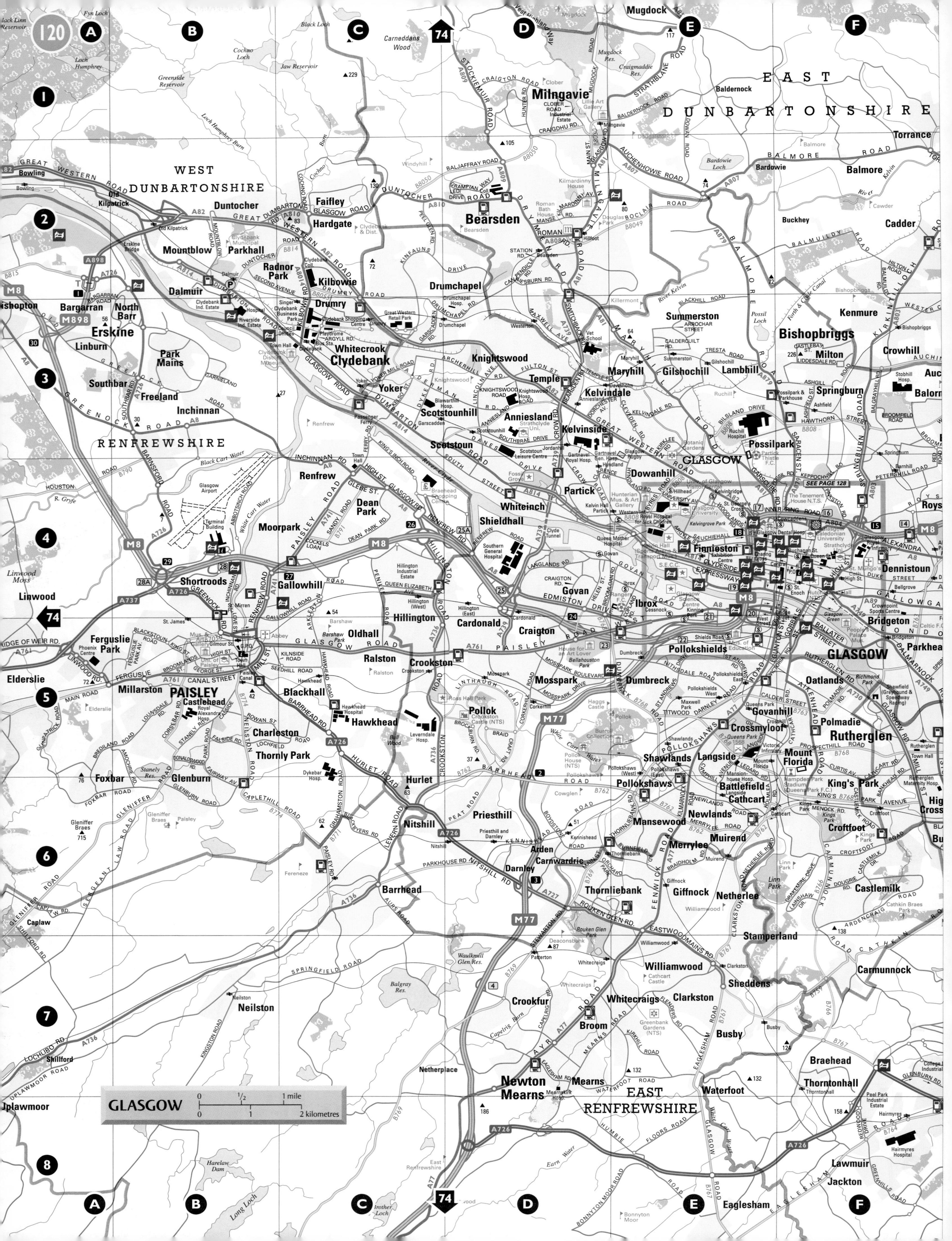
GLASGOW
0 1/2 1 mile
0 1 2 kilometres
WEST DUNBARTONSHIRE
EAST DUNBARTONSHIRE
RENFREWSHIRE
EAST RENFREWSHIRE
GLASGOW
SEE PAGE 128
74
Milngavie
Bearsden
Mugdock
Baldernock
Torrance
Balmore
Bardowie
Cadder
Buckhey
Kenmure
Bishopbriggs
Crowhill
Auchinairn
Balornock
Springburn
Milton
Lambhill
Gilshochill
Summerston
Maryhill
Possilpark
Kelvindale
Kelvinside
Dowanhill
Partick
Knightswood
Temple
Anniesland
Scotstounhill
Scotstoun
Whiteinch
Shieldhall
Yoker
Clydebank
Whitecrook
Kilbowie
Drumry
Drumchapel
Radnor Park
Faifley
Hardgate
Duntocher
Mountblow
Parkhall
Dalmuir
Old Kilpatrick
Bowling
Erskine
Bargarran
North Barr
Linburn
Bishopton
Park Mains
Southbar
Freeland
Inchinnan
Renfrew
Dean Park
Moorpark
Glasgow Airport
Linwood
Linwood Moss
Shortroods
Gallowhill
Ferguslie Park
Elderslie
Millarston
PAISLEY
Castlehead
Charleston
Thornly Park
Foxbar
Glenburn
Blackhall
Hawkhead
Oldhall
Hillington
Cardonald
Ralston
Crookston
Pollok
Hurlet
Nitshill
Priesthill
Barrhead
Darnley
Arden
Carnwadric
Thornliebank
Mosspark
Dumbreck
Craigton
Govan
Ibrox
Finnieston
Pollokshields
Crossmyloof
Govanhill
Shawlands
Langside
Mount Florida
Pollokshaws
Battlefield
Cathcart
Mansewood
Newlands
Merrylee
Muirend
Giffnock
Netherlee
Oatlands
Polmadie
Rutherglen
King's Park
Croftfoot
Castlemilk
Bridgeton
Dennistoun
Parkhead
Stamperland
Carmunnock
Williamwood
Sheddens
Clarkston
Whitecraigs
Crookfur
Broom
Busby
Newton Mearns
Mearns
Waterfoot
Thorntonhall
Braehead
Lawmuir
Jackton
Eaglesham
Netherplace
Neilston
Caplaw
Shillford
Uplawmoor
M8
M77
M898
A82
A726
A737
A736
A761
A77
A8
GREAT WESTERN ROAD
PAISLEY ROAD WEST
GLASGOW ROAD
DUMBARTON ROAD
BALMORE ROAD
MARYHILL ROAD
AYR ROAD
BARRHEAD ROAD
CLYDESIDE EXPRESSWAY
River Clyde
White Cart Water
Black Cart Water
Forth & Clyde Canal
Loch Humphrey
Cochno Loch
Greenside Reservoir
Jaw Reservoir
Black Loch
Fyn Loch
Balgray Res.
Waulkmill Glen Res.
Harelaw Dam
Long Loch
Brother Loch
Linn Park
Rouken Glen Park
Bellahouston Park
Queens Park
Pollok House (NTS)
Hampden Park Stadium
Southern General Hospital
Royal Alexandra Hosp.
A B C D E F
1 2 3 4 5 6 7 8

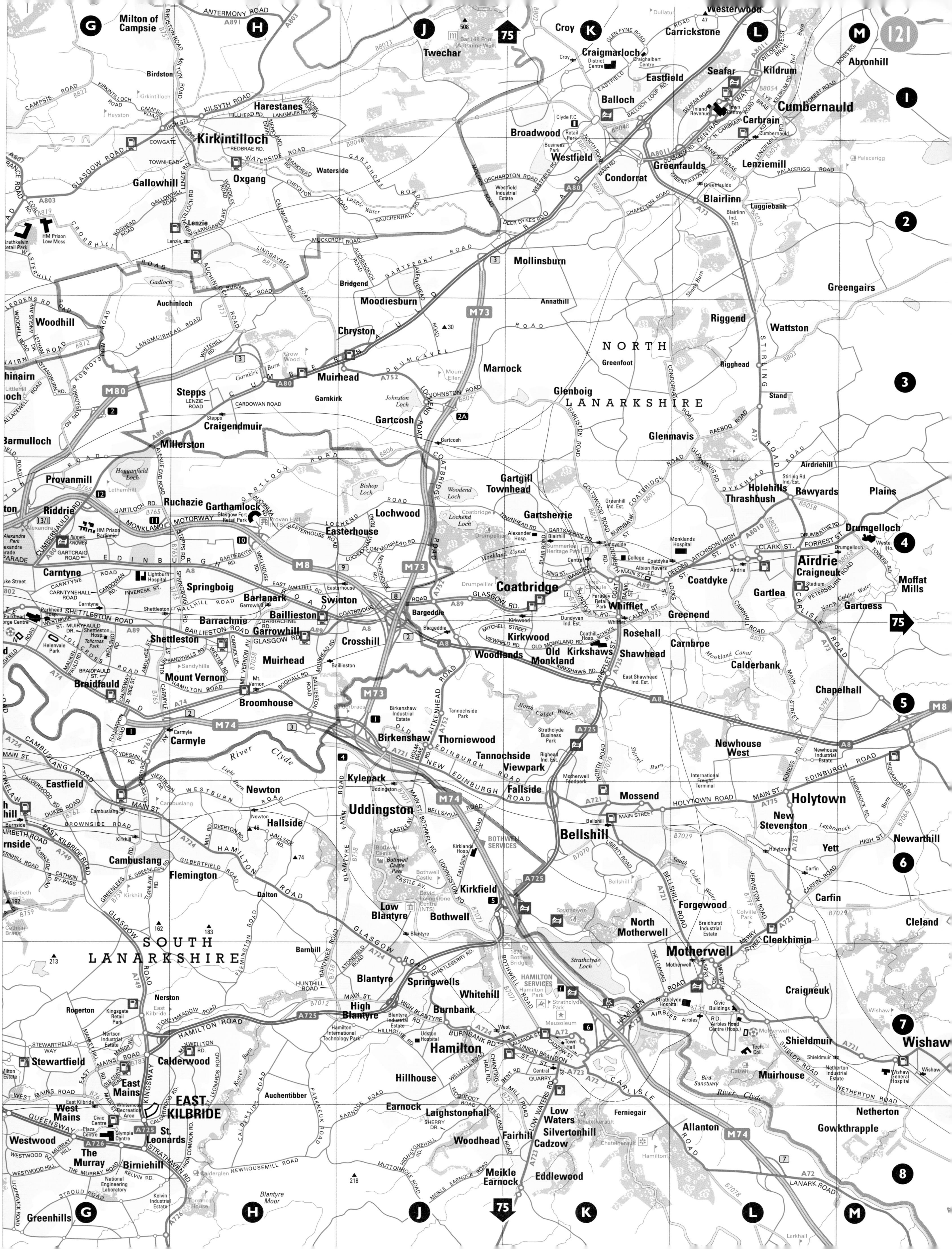

Milton of Campsie
Croy
Craigmarloch
Carrickstone
Westerwood
Twechar
Abronhill
Kildrum
Seafar
Eastfield
Balloch
Cumbernauld
Carbrain
Birdston
Harestanes
Kirkintilloch
Broadwood
Westfield
Condorrat
Greenfaulds
Lenziemill
Waterside
Gallowhill
Oxgang
Blairlinn
Luggiebank
Lenzie
Mollinsburn
Greengairs
Auchinloch
Bridgend
Moodiesburn
Annathill
Woodhill
Chryston
Riggend
Wattston
NORTH LANARKSHIRE
Greenfoot
Rigghead
Muirhead
Marnock
Stepps
Garnkirk
Glenboig
Stand
Craigendmuir
Gartcosh
Glenmavis
Barmulloch
Millerston
Airdriehill
Provanmill
Gartgill
Townhead
Holehills
Bawyards
Plains
Thrashbush
Riddrie
Ruchazie
Garthamlock
Gartsherrie
Lochwood
Drumgelloch
Easterhouse
Carntyne
Springboig
Coatbridge
Airdrie
Craigneuk
Coatdyke
Moffat Mills
Barlanark
Swinton
Gartlea
Whifflet
Gartness
Baillieston
Barrachnie
Bargeddie
Greenend
Garrowhill
Shettleston
Crosshill
Kirkwood
Rosehall
Woodlands
Old Monkland
Kirkshaws
Shawhead
Carnbroe
Muirhead
Calderbank
Mount Vernon
Braidfauld
Broomhouse
Chapelhall
Birkenshaw
Thorniewood
Carmyle
Tannochside
Viewpark
Newhouse West
Eastfield
Newton
Kylepark
Fallside
Mossend
Holytown
Uddingston
New Stevenston
Hallside
Bellshill
Newarthill
Yett
Cambuslang
Flemington
Kirkfield
Forgewood
Carfin
Low Blantyre
Bothwell
North Motherwell
Cleland
Cleekhimin
SOUTH LANARKSHIRE
Motherwell
Barnhill
Blantyre
Springwells
Craigneuk
Whitehill
Nerston
Rogerton
Burnbank
High Blantyre
Shieldmuir
Wishaw
Hamilton
Stewartfield
Calderwood
East Mains
Hillhouse
Muirhouse
Auchentibber
Earnock
West Mains
EAST KILBRIDE
Laighstonehall
Netherton
Low Waters
Ferniegair
Allanton
Gowkthrapple
Westwood
St. Leonards
Woodhead
Fairhill
Silvertonhill
Cadzow
The Murray
Birniehill
Meikle Earnock
Eddlewood
Greenhills
75
M73
M74
M80
M8
A80
A8

Association of London Government

Free parking on Single & Double Yellow lines (3hrs max) except where un/loading restrictions apply, Pay & Display, Shared Used, Residents & Blue Badge Bays	Free parking in most places (single/double yellow line, Pay & Display) **except Residents Parking Bays & where un/loading restrictions apply**	Free parking in most places (single/double yellow line, Pay & Display) **except for Residents Parking & Shared Use Bays & where un/loading restrictions apply**	Free parking in Blue Badge Bays with **limited concessions on Pay & Display**	Free parking in **Blue Badge Bays only**

London Congestion Charge for Blue Badge Holders

Blue Badge holders are eligible for a full discount on the Congestion Charge.
This is available to Blue Badge holders throughout the European Union. After registering and making a one off payment of £10, holders of this discount are not required to pay the congestion charge when they enter the congestion charging zone.

Disabled passenger carrying vehicles and vehicles used by disabled persons that are exempt from Vehicle Excise Duty (road tax), are automatically exempt from the Congestion Charge and do not need to be registered with Transport for London.

Note that you do not need to own a vehicle or drive a vehicle to register for the discount.

The discount applies to the person who is the Blue Badge Holder, not the vehicle that is being used.

Please note that you MUST register a nominated vehicle. This can be done on the day of travel. There are various nomination rules to register for long term and short term vehicles, details of which are explained on the TfL registration form.

The form is available from Transport for London (TfL). It can be obtained in the following ways: Download it from the web: **www.cclondon.com/downloads/DisabledPeople.pdf**

Write to: Congestion Charging, PO Box 2982, Coventry CV7 8WR

Telephone: **0845 900 1234** or from outside the UK **+44 20 7649 9122**

Text phone: **020 7649 9123**

Please note the Congestion Charge boundary is shown in the map pages with the following line style and colour.

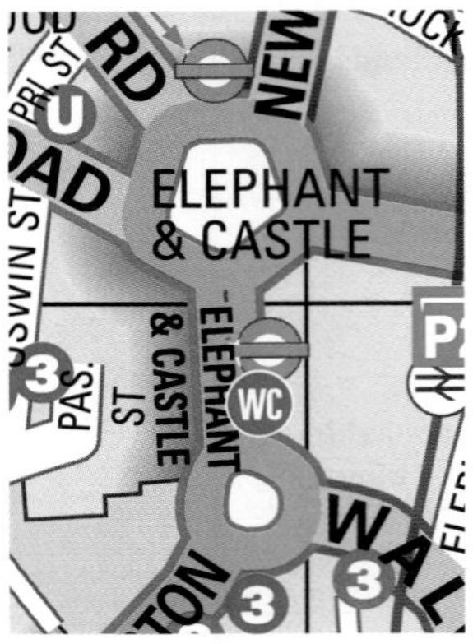

If you need more information on the Congestion Charge you can visit **www.cclondon.com** or call **0845 900 1234.**

Other general information about the Congestion Charge

Congestion Charge Operating Hours are 7am - 6.30pm Monday to Friday, excluding Public Holidays.

The normal daily tariff is £8 which has to be paid by no later than 10pm on the day of travel. A surcharge of £2 is applied when paying between 10pm and midnight. From September 2006, drivers will be able to pay the Charge the day after entering the congestion zone.

Traffic signs and markings on the road should make it clear exactly where the charging zone is. Below are some examples. The London Street map has the congestion zone marked out. The new extended zone (not marked on the map) is scheduled to become operational from 19 February 2007 for details of the extended zone visit www.tfl.gov.uk.

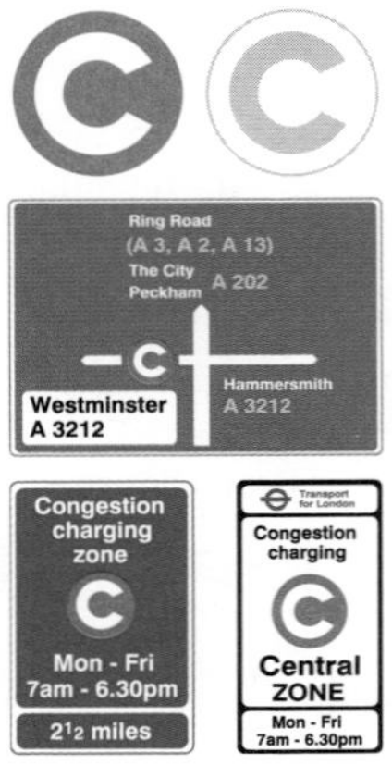

Red Route Box Bays in London

Red Routes mark out London's important roads identified by the red no-stopping lines or signs along the route. No stopping is permitted on these routes. Red boxes marked on the road indicate that parking, or loading is permitted during the off peak times, normally between 10am and 4 pm. Special conditions apply to Blue Badge Holders, typically a maximum of 3 hours. Ensure you check this time limit and try not to use these during the rush hours

In surveying London we have discovered that Blue Badge holders are permitted to park between the standard restriction times (i.e. 10am to 4pm) on the conventional Red Route Parking Box bays. These are different to Red Route **Loading box bays** where you often see a Blue Badge sign typically with a maximum stay of 3 hours. **Red Route parking box bays** do not have any Blue Badge symbols yet you are permitted to park there for most of the day.

This information has been validated by TfL and is particularly good news in the central London area where you are only permitted to park in Blue Badge bays. Again these are all marked on the map.

Useful Information for London

Travel by Bus/Taxi/Tube

Dial-a-ride
Multi occupancy transport service, nominal charge per journey
Tel: 020 7222 1234
www.tfl.gov.uk

Docklands Light Railway
Travel Hotline: 020 7918 4000

Freedom Passes
Free travel on public transport for the elderly and disabled
Tel: 020 7747 4858
www.freedompass.org

London Underground
24 hour London travel information
Tel: 020 7222 1234
Textphone: 020 7918 3015
www.thetube.com

Taxicard Scheme
Travel in licensed London taxis at a reduced rate for the elderly and disabled
Tel: 020 7484 2929
www.taxicard.org.uk

Car Related Issues

BBC London Travel Information
94.9FM Updates every 15/30minutes
If you spot travel incidents:
Text: 07786 200 949

Parking and Traffic Appeals Service
Tel: 020 7747 4700
www.parkingandtrafficappeals.gov.uk

TRACE
Towed Away? Clamped?
24 hour helpline
Tel: 020 7747 4747

CENTRAL LONDON
0 1/4 mile
0 0.25 0.5 kilometres
OXFORD STREET where marked is closed to through traffic (except buses & taxis) from 7a.m. - 7p.m. Monday - Saturday
Free parking on Single & Double Yellow lines (3hrs max) except where un/loading restrictions apply, Pay & Display, Shared Used, Residents & Blue Badge Bays
Free parking in Blue Badge Bays with limited concessions on Pay & Display
Free parking in most places (single/double yellow line, Pay & Display) except Residents Parking Bays & where un/loading restrictions apply
Free parking in Blue Badge Bays only
101
102
103
CLERKENWELL
BLOOMSBURY
BRITISH MUSEUM
HOLBORN
SOHO
STRAND
MAYFAIR
ST. JAMES'S
GREEN PARK
ST. JAMES'S PARK
BUCKINGHAM PALACE
BUCKINGHAM PALACE GDNS
WESTMINSTER
HOUSES OF PARLIAMENT
LAMBETH
WATERLOO
SOUTHWARK
THE BOROUGH
NEWINGTON
BARBICAN
RIVER
TATE MODERN
ST. PAUL'S CATH
OXFORD STREET
REGENT STREET
PICCADILLY
VICTORIA EMBANKMENT
WATERLOO BR
BLACKFRIARS BR
WESTMINSTER BR
TRAFALGAR SQ
PICCADILLY CIRCUS
OXFORD CIRCUS
CHARING CROSS
ELEPHANT & CASTLE
London Eye
County Hall
LAMBETH PALACE GDNS
GERALD. MARY HARMSWORTH PARK

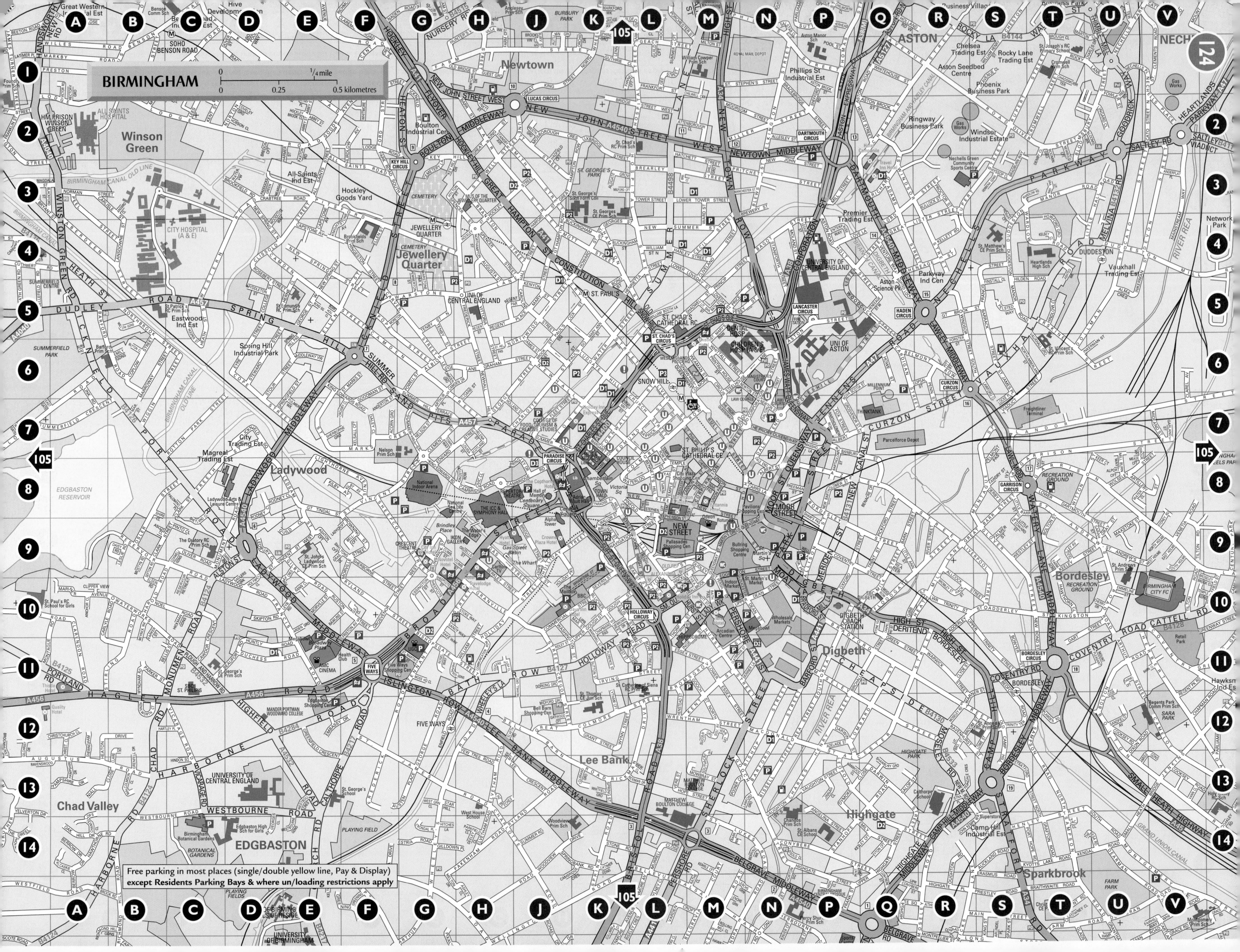
BIRMINGHAM
1/4 mile
0 0.25 0.5 kilometres
Free parking in most places (single/double yellow line, Pay & Display) except Residents Parking Bays & where un/loading restrictions apply
Winson Green
Newtown
Aston
Jewellery Quarter
Ladywood
Edgbaston
Lee Bank
Digbeth
Highgate
Bordesley
Sparkbrook
Chad Valley
Edgbaston Reservoir
Lucas Circus
Key Hill Circus
Dartmouth Circus
Lancaster Circus
Haden Circus
Curzon Circus
Garrison Circus
Bordesley Circus
Holloway Circus
Paradise Circus
St. Chad's Circus
Five Ways
New Street
Moor Street
Snow Hill
St. Philip's Cathedral CE
St. Chad's Cathedral RC
Uni of Aston
University of Central England
City Hospital (A & E)
National Indoor Arena
The ICC & Symphony Hall
Birmingham City FC
Digbeth Coach Station
Bullring Shopping Centre
Middleway
105

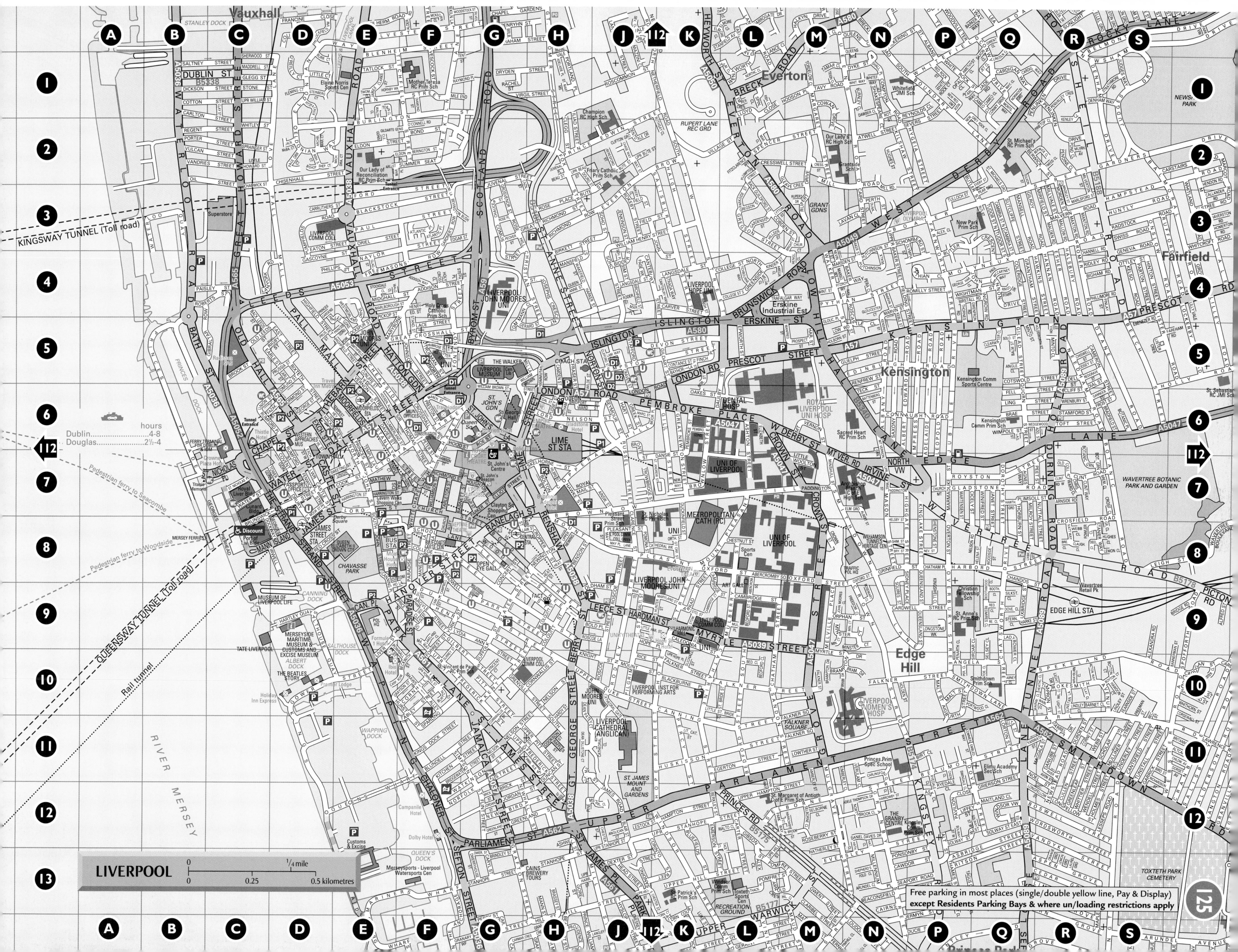

LIVERPOOL
1/4 mile
0 0.25 0.5 kilometres
Free parking in most places (single/double yellow line, Pay & Display) except Residents Parking Bays & where un/loading restrictions apply
125
hours
Dublin.....4-8
Douglas.....2½-4
Pedestrian ferry to Seacombe
Pedestrian ferry to Woodside
QUEENSWAY TUNNEL (Toll road)
KINGSWAY TUNNEL (Toll road)
Rail tunnel
RIVER MERSEY
Vauxhall
Everton
Fairfield
Kensington
Edge Hill
LIME ST STA
EDGE HILL STA
WAVERTREE BOTANIC PARK AND GARDEN
TOXTETH PARK CEMETERY
UNI OF LIVERPOOL
LIVERPOOL CATHEDRAL (ANGLICAN)
METROPOLITAN CATH (RC)
ROYAL LIVERPOOL UNI HOSP
LIVERPOOL WOMEN'S HOSP
MERSEYSIDE MARITIME MUSEUM & CUSTOMS AND EXCISE MUSEUM
TATE LIVERPOOL
THE BEATLES STORY
MUSEUM OF LIVERPOOL LIFE
CHAVASSE PARK
ST JAMES MOUNT AND GARDENS

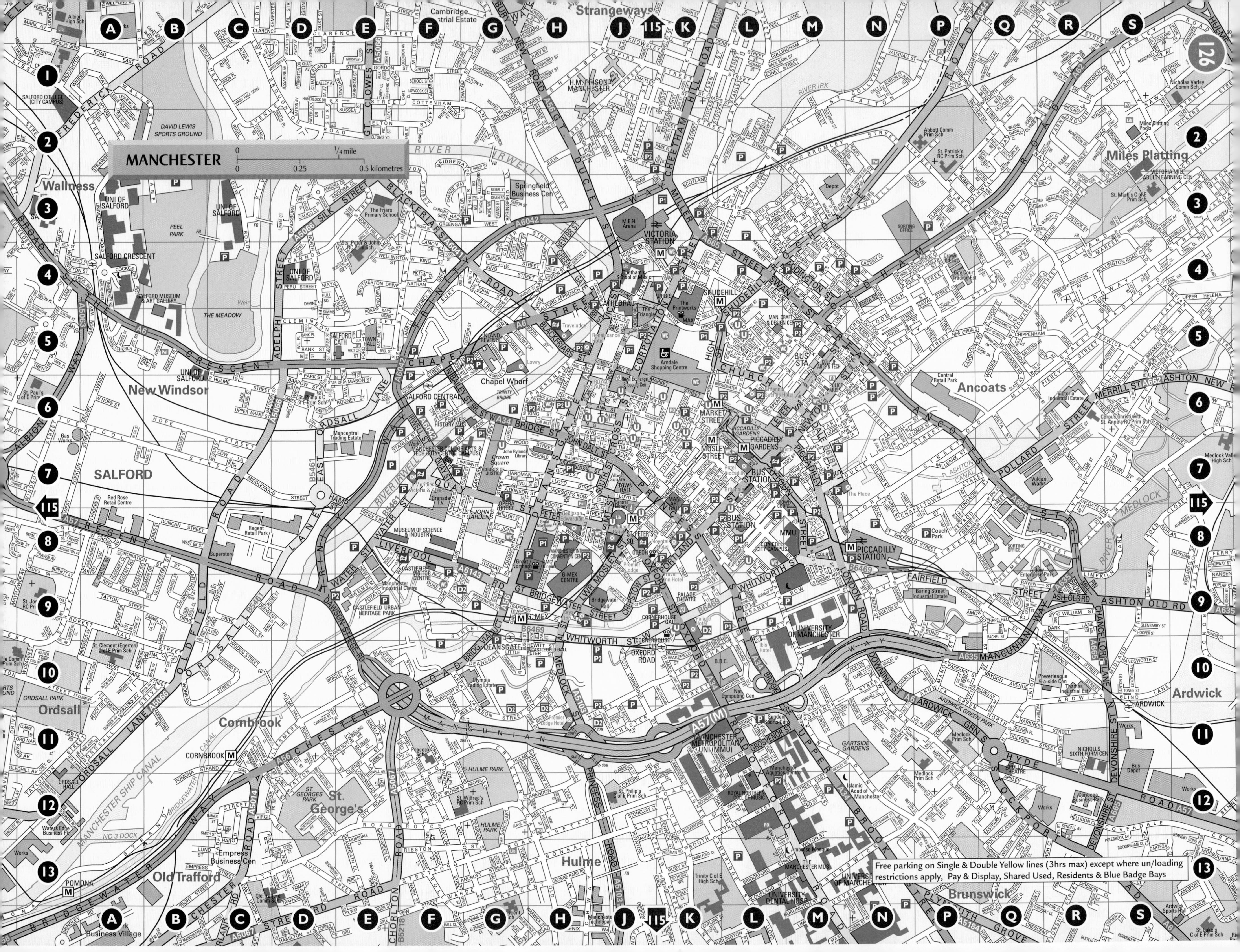
MANCHESTER
0
¼ mile
0
0.25
0.5 kilometres
Free parking on Single & Double Yellow lines (3hrs max) except where un/loading restrictions apply, Pay & Display, Shared Used, Residents & Blue Badge Bays
Strangeways
Miles Platting
Ancoats
Ardwick
Brunswick
Hulme
St. George's
Old Trafford
Cornbrook
Ordsall
SALFORD
New Windsor
Walness
Chapel Wharf
Castlefield Urban Heritage Park
Piccadilly Station
Victoria Station
Arndale Shopping Centre
G-MEX Centre
Museum of Science & Industry
University of Manchester
Manchester Metropolitan Uni (MMU)
Uni of Salford
Peel Park
The Meadow
David Lewis Sports Ground
River Irwell
Manchester Ship Canal
Bridgewater Canal
Rochdale Canal
River Medlock
River Irk
115

Free parking in most places (single/double yellow line, Pay & Display)
except Residents Parking Bays & where un/loading restrictions apply
LEEDS
0
0.25
1/4 mile
0.5 kilometres
Burmantofts
Quarry Hill
Holbeck
Burley
Armley
Wortley
Cross Green
LEEDS CEMETERY
ST. JAMES'S UNIV. HOSP.
UNIVERSITY OF LEEDS
LEEDS GENERAL INFIRMARY
LEEDS DENTAL INSTITUTE
LEEDS MET UNI
LEEDS STATION
RIVER AIRE
LEEDS & LIVERPOOL CANAL
ST. GEORGES PARK
WOODHOUSE MOOR
LOVELL PARK
Kirkgate Market
Victoria Quarter Shop Cen
Merrion Centre
Leeds Shopping Plaza
Royal Armouries Museum
Tetley Brewery
Crown Point Retail Park
Apex Business Park
Leeds City Office Park
Wellington Road Industrial Est
Kirkstall Industrial Park
Scotch Park Trading Est
Gelderd Trading Estate
Latchmore Industrial Park
H.M. PRISON LEEDS
NEW WORTLEY CEMETERY
WORTLEY RECREATION GROUND
BURLEY REC GRD
SPORTS GROUND
Yorkshire TV Studios
Junction 3
Junction 2
117
YORK ROAD
REGENT STREET
SHEEPSCAR STREET SOUTH
INNER RING RD
WOODHOUSE LANE
BLENHEIM WALK
KIRKSTALL ROAD
WELLINGTON ST
WEST ST
WELLINGTON RD
ARMLEY ROAD
CANAL STREET
GELDERD ROAD
DEWSBURY RD
MEADOW LANE
GT WILSON STREET
VICTORIA RD
CROWN POINT RD
HUNSLET RD
BLACK BULL STREET
EAST STREET
SOUTH ACCOMMODATION ROAD
MARSH LANE
DOMESTIC RD
WHITEHALL ROAD
A64(M)
A58(M)
A61
A653
A639
A660
A65
A647
A643
A62
M621
A58
B6154

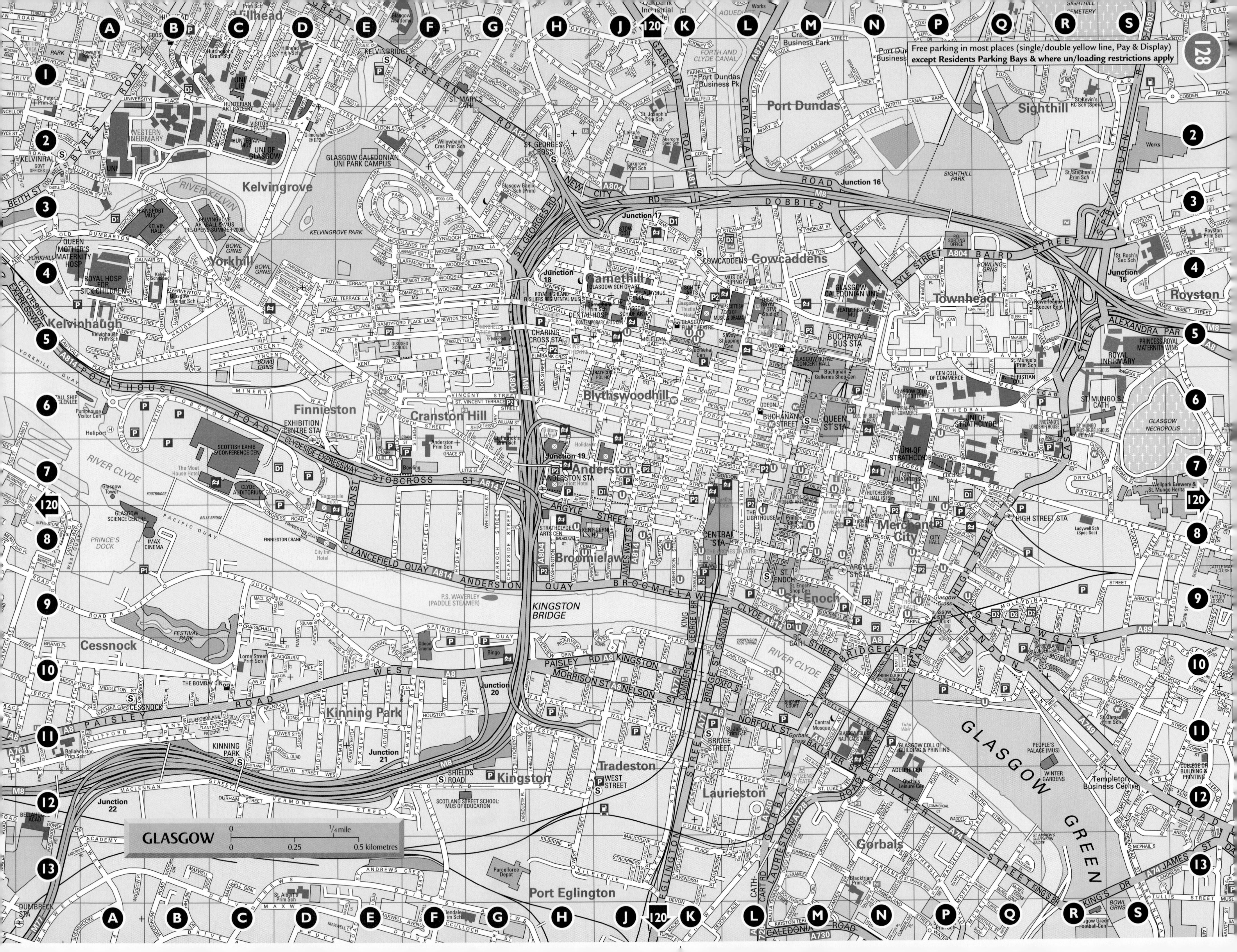
GLASGOW
Free parking in most places (single/double yellow line, Pay & Display) except Residents Parking Bays & where un/loading restrictions apply
0 1/4 mile
0 0.25 0.5 kilometres
Hillhead
Kelvingrove
Yorkhill
Kelvinhaugh
Finnieston
Cranston Hill
Anderston
Broomielaw
Blythswoodhill
Garnethill
Cowcaddens
Port Dundas
Sighthill
Townhead
Royston
Merchant City
St Enoch
Laurieston
Gorbals
Tradeston
Kingston
Kinning Park
Cessnock
Port Eglington
GLASGOW GREEN
RIVER CLYDE
KINGSTON BRIDGE
GLASGOW NECROPOLIS
KELVINGROVE PARK
SIGHTHILL PARK
PRINCE'S DOCK
FESTIVAL PARK
CENTRAL STA
QUEEN ST STA
BUCHANAN BUS STA
HIGH STREET STA
ARGYLE ST STA
ANDERSTON STA
CHARING CROSS STA
EXHIBITION CENTRE STA
SCOTTISH EXHIB & CONFERENCE CEN
CLYDE AUDITORIUM
GLASGOW SCIENCE CENTRE
IMAX CINEMA
ROYAL INFIRMARY
WESTERN INFIRMARY
UNI OF GLASGOW
UNI OF STRATHCLYDE
GLASGOW CALEDONIAN UNI
PEOPLE'S PALACE (MUS)
WINTER GARDENS
P.S. WAVERLEY (PADDLE STEAMER)
Junction 15
Junction 16
Junction 17
Junction 18
Junction 19
Junction 20
Junction 21
Junction 22
M8
A8
A804
A814
A82
A803
A879
A81
A77
A730
A728
A74
A749
A89
A761
M77
A B C D E F G H J K L M N P Q R S
1 2 3 4 5 6 7 8 9 10 11 12 13
120

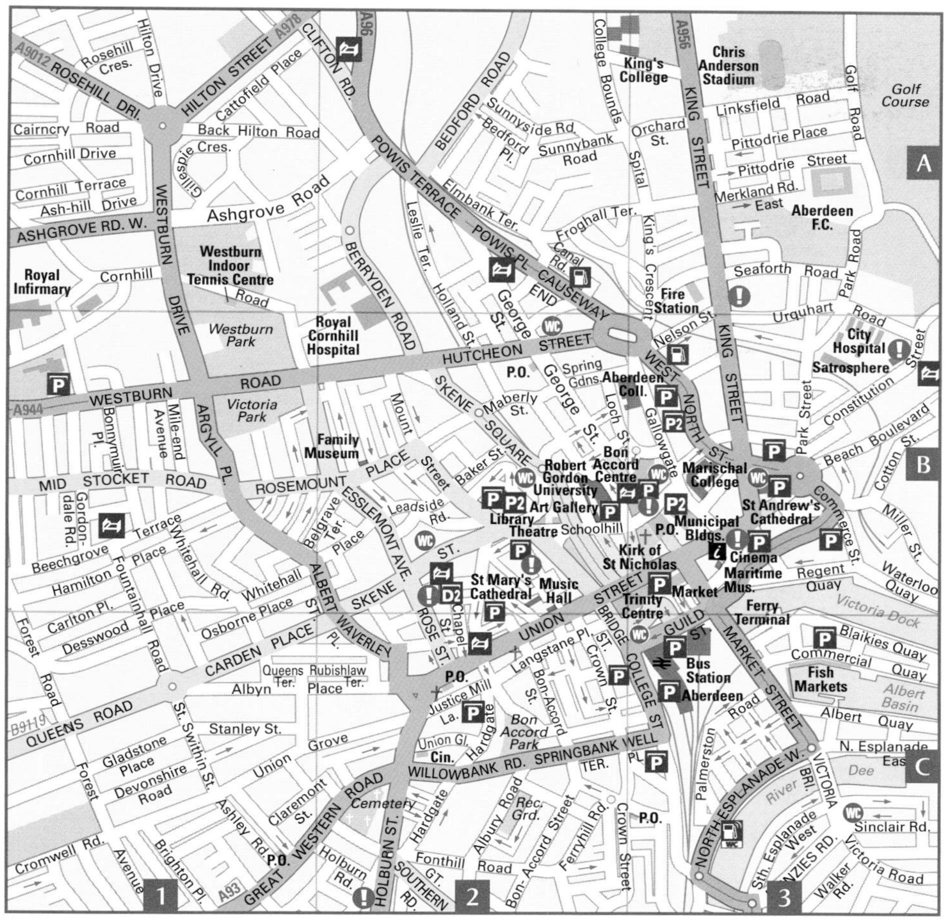

ABERDEEN

0 500 yds
0 500m

INDEX TO STREET NAMES

Albert Quay C3
Albert Street B2
Albury Road C2
Albyn Place C1
Argyll Place B1
Ashgrove Road A1
Ashgrove Road West A1
Ash-hill Drive A1
Ashley Road C1
Back Hilton Road A1
Baker Street B2
Beach Boulevard B3
Bedford Place A2
Bedford Road A2
Beechgrove Terrace B1
Belgrave Terrace B1
Berryden Road A2
Blaikie's Quay C3
Bon-Accord Street C2
Bonnymuir Place B1
Bridge Street B2
Brighton Place C1
Caircry Road A1
Canal Road A2
Carden Place C1
Carlton Place A1
Cattofield Place A1
Causewayend A2
Chapel Street B2
Claremont Street C1
Clifton Road A1
College Bounds A3
College Street C2
Commerce Street B3
Commercial Quay C3
Constitution Street B3
Cornhill Drive A1
Cornhill Road A1
Cornhill Terrace A1
Cotton Street B3
Cromwell Road C1
Crown Street C2
Desswood Place C1
Devonshire Road C1
Elmbank Terrace A2
Esslemont Avenue B2
Ferryhill Road C2
Fonthill Road C2
Forest Road C1
Forest Avenue C1
Fountainhall Road B1
Froghall Terrace A2
Gallowgate B3
George Street A2
Gillespie Crescent A1
Gladstone Place C1
Golf Road A3
Gordondale Road B1
Great Southern Road C2
Great Western Road C1
Guild Street C3
Hamilton Place B1
Hardgate C2
Hilton Drive A1
Hilton Street A1
Holburn Road C2
Holburn Street C2
Holland Street A2
Hutcheon Street B2
Justice Mill Lane C2
King's Crescent A3
King Street A3
Langstane Place C2
Leadside Road B2
Leslie Terrace A2
Linksfield Road A3
Loch Street B2
Maberly Street B2
Market Street C3
Menzies Road C3
Merkland Road East A3
Mid Stocket Road B1
Mile-end Avenue B1
Miller Street B3
Mount Street B2
Nelson Street B3
North Esplanade East C3
North Esplanade West C3
Orchard Street A3
Osborne Place C1
Palmerston Road C3
Park Road A3
Park Street B3
Pittodrie Place A3
Pittodrie Street A3
Powis Place A2
Powis Terrace A2
Queens Road C1
Queens Terrace C1
Regent Quay B3
Rosehill Crescent A1
Rosehill Drive A1
Rosemount Place B1
Rose Street B2
Rubislaw Terrace C2
St. Swithin Street C1
Schoolhill B2
Seaforth Road A3
Sinclair Road C3
Skene Square B2
Skene Street B2
South Esplanade West C3
Spital A3
Springbank Terrace C2
Spring Gardens B2
Stanley Street C1
Sunnybank Road A2
Sunnyside Road A2
Union Glen C2
Union Grove C1
Union Street C2
Urquhart Road B3
Victoria Bridge C3
Victoria Road C3
Walker Road C3
Waterloo Quay B3
Waverley Place C2
Westburn Drive A1
Westburn Road B1
West North Street B3
Whitehall Place B1
Whitehall Road B1
Willowbank Road C2

TOURIST INFORMATION ☎ 01224 288828
23 UNION STREET,
ABERDEEN, AB11 5BP

COUNCIL OFFICE ☎ 01224 522000
TOWN HOUSE, BROAD STREET,
ABERDEEN, AB10 1FY

HOSPITAL A & E ☎ 01224 681818
ABERDEEN ROYAL INFIRMARY, FORESTERHILL,
ABERDEEN, AB25 2ZN

WEB-SITE www.aberdeencity.gov.uk

BATH

0 200 yds
0 200m

INDEX TO STREET NAMES

Ambury C1
Archway Street C3
Argyle Street B2
Avon Street B1
Barton Street B1
Bath Street B2
Bathwick Hill A3
Beau Street B2
Bennett Street A1
Bridge Street B2
Broad Quay C1
Broad Street A2
Broadway C3
Brock Street A1
Chapel Row B1
Charles Street B1
Charlotte Street A1
Cheap Street B2
Claverton Street C2
Corn Street C1
Daniel Street A3
Darlington Street A3
Dorchester Street C2
Edward Street A3
Excelsior Street C3
Ferry Lane B3
Gay Street A1
George Street A1
Grand Parade B2
Great Pulteney Street A3
Green Park Road B1
Green Street A2
Grove Street A2
Henrietta Gardens A3
Henrietta Mews A3
Henrietta Road A2
Henrietta Street A2
Henry Street B2
High Street B2
Holloway C1
James Street West B1
John Street A1
Kingsmead East B1
Lansdown Road A2
Laura Place A2
Lime Grove B3
Lime Grove Gardens B3
Lower Borough Walls B2
Lower Bristol Road C1
Magdalen Avenue C1
Manvers Street C2
Milk Street B1
Milsom Street A2
Monmouth Place A1
Monmouth Street B1
Newark Street C2
New Bond Street B2
New King Street B1
New Orchard Street B2
New Street B1
North Parade B2
North Parade Road B3
Old King Street A1
Orange Grove B2
Paragon A2
Pierrepont Street B2
Pulteney Crescent C3
Pulteney Mews A3
Pulteney Road B3
Queen Street B1
Quiet Street A1
Rossiter Road C2
St. James's Parade B1
St. John's Road A2
St. Marks Road C2
Sawclose B1
Southgate Street C2
Spring Crescent C3
Stall Street B2
Sutton Street A3
Sydney Place A3
The Circus A1
Union Street B2
Upper Borough Walls B1
Walcot Street A2
Wells Road C1
Westgate Buildings B1
Westgate Street B1
Wood Street A1
York Street B2

TOURIST INFORMATION ☎ 0906 711 2000
ABBEY CHAMBERS, ABBEY CHURCH YARD,
BATH, BA1 1LY

COUNCIL OFFICE ☎ 01225 477000
THE GUILDHALL, HIGH STREET,
BATH, BA1 5AW

HOSPITAL A & E ☎ 01225 428331
ROYAL UNITED HOSPITAL, COMBE PARK,
BATH, BA1 3NG

WEB-SITE www.bathnes.gov.uk

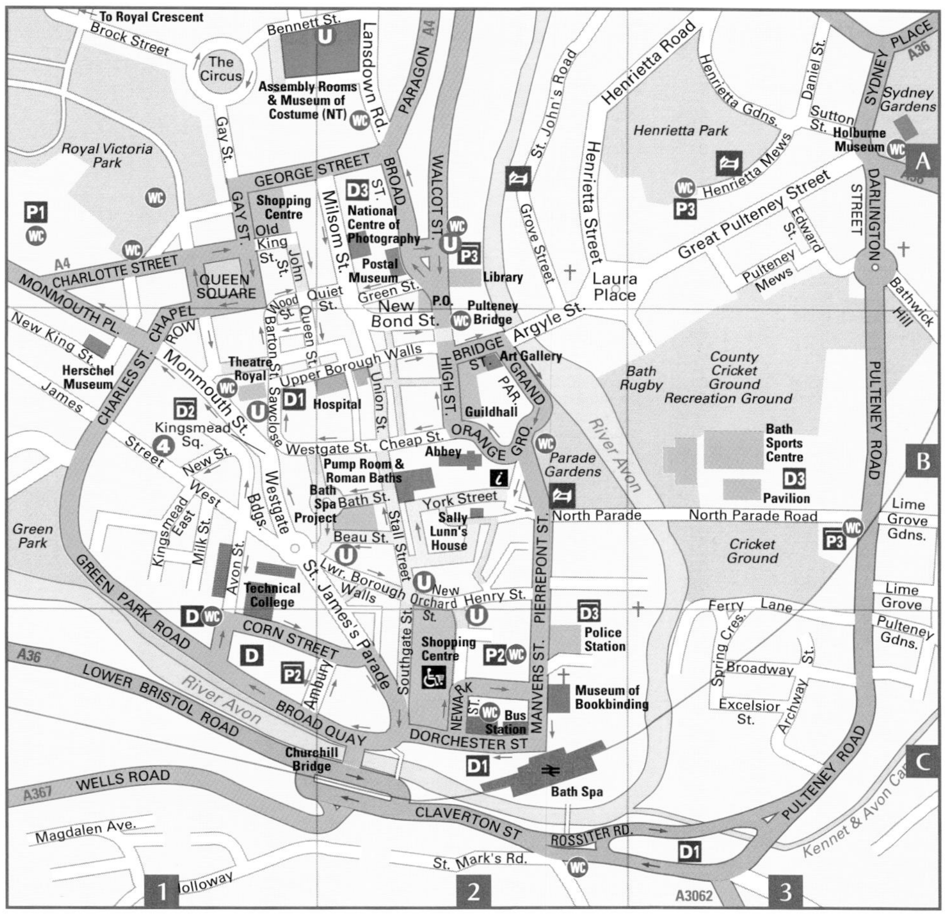

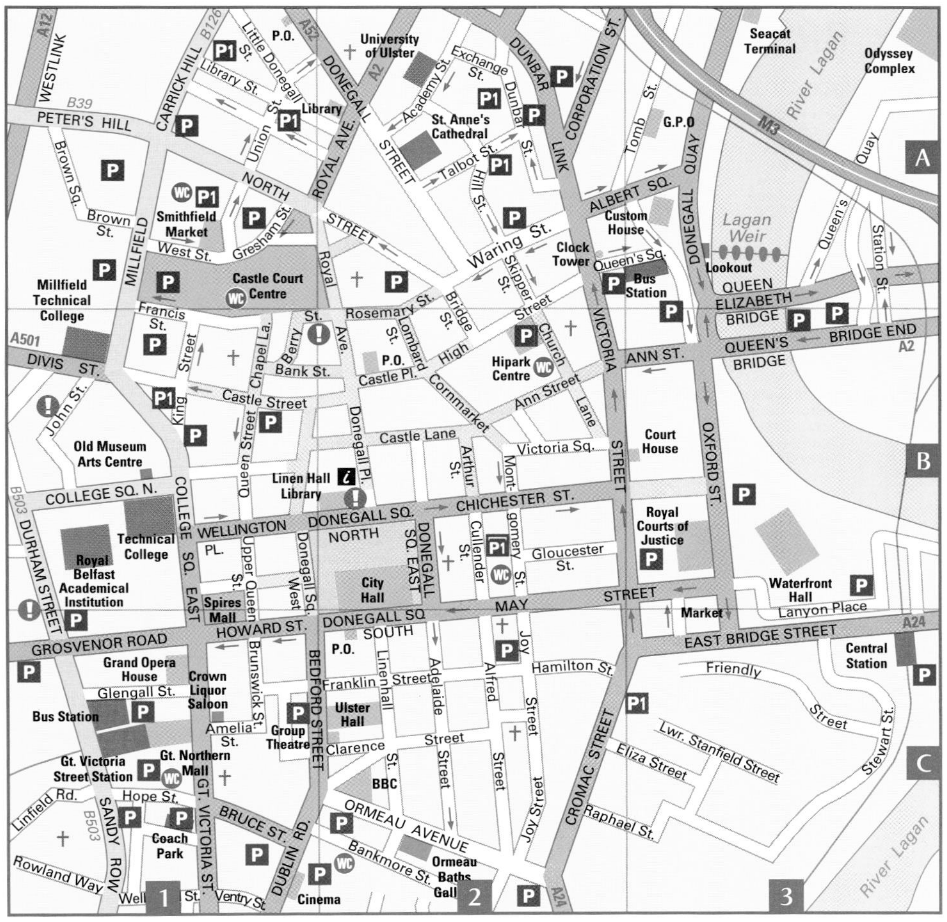

BELFAST

0 200 yds
0 200m

INDEX TO STREET NAMES

Academy Street A2
Adelaide Street C2
Albert Square A2
Alfred Street C2
Amelia Street C1
Ann Street B2
Arthur Street B2
Bankmore Street C2
Bank Street B1
Bedford Street C1
Berry Street B1
Bridge End B3
Bridge Street A2
Brown Square A1
Brown Street A1
Bruce Street C1
Brunswick Street C1
Carrick Hill A1
Castle Lane B2
Castle Place B2
Castle Street B1
Chapel Lane B1
Chichester Street B2
Church Lane B2
Clarence Street C2
College Square East B1
College Square North B1
Cornmarket B2
Corporation Street A2
Cromac Street C2
Cullender Street B2
Divis Street B1
Donegall Place B2
Donegall Quay A3
Donegall Square East B2
Donegall Square North B2
Donegall Square South C2
Donegall Square West B1
Donegall Street A2
Dublin Road C1
Dunbar Link A2
Dunbar Street A2
Durham Street B1
East Bridge Street C3
Eliza Street C2
Exchange Street A2
Francis Street B1
Franklin Street C2
Friendly Street C3
Glengall Street C1
Gloucester Street B2
Great Victoria Street C1
Gresham Street A1
Grosvenor Road C1
Hamilton Street C2
High Street B2
Hill Street A2
Hope Street C1
Howard Street C1
John Street B1
Joy Street C2
King Street B1
Lanyon Place C3
Library Street A1
Linenhall Street C2
Linfield Road C1
Little Donegall Street A1
Lombard Street B2
Lower Stanfield Street C3
May Street B2
Millfield A1
Montgomery Street B2
North Street A1
Ormeau Avenue C2
Oxford Street B3
Peter's Hill A1
Queen Elizabeth Bridge A3
Queen Street B1
Queen's Bridge B3
Queen's Quay A3
Queen's Square A2
Raphael Street C2
Rosemary Street B2
Rowland Way C1
Royal Avenue A2
Sandy Row C1
Skipper Street A2
Station Street A3
Stewart Street C3
Talbot Street A2
Tomb Street A3
Union Street A1
Upper Queen Street B1
Ventry Street C1
Victoria Square B2
Victoria Street B2
Waring Street A2
Wellington Place B1
Wellwood Street C1
Westlink A1
West Street A1

TOURIST INFORMATION ☎ 028 9024 6609
47 DONEGALL PLACE,
BELFAST, BT1 5AD

COUNCIL OFFICE ☎ 028 9032 0202
CITY HALL,
BELFAST, BT1 5GS

HOSPITAL A & E ☎ 028 9032 9241
BELFAST CITY HOSPITAL, 51 LISBURN ROAD,
BELFAST, BT9 7AB

WEB-SITE www.gotobelfast.com

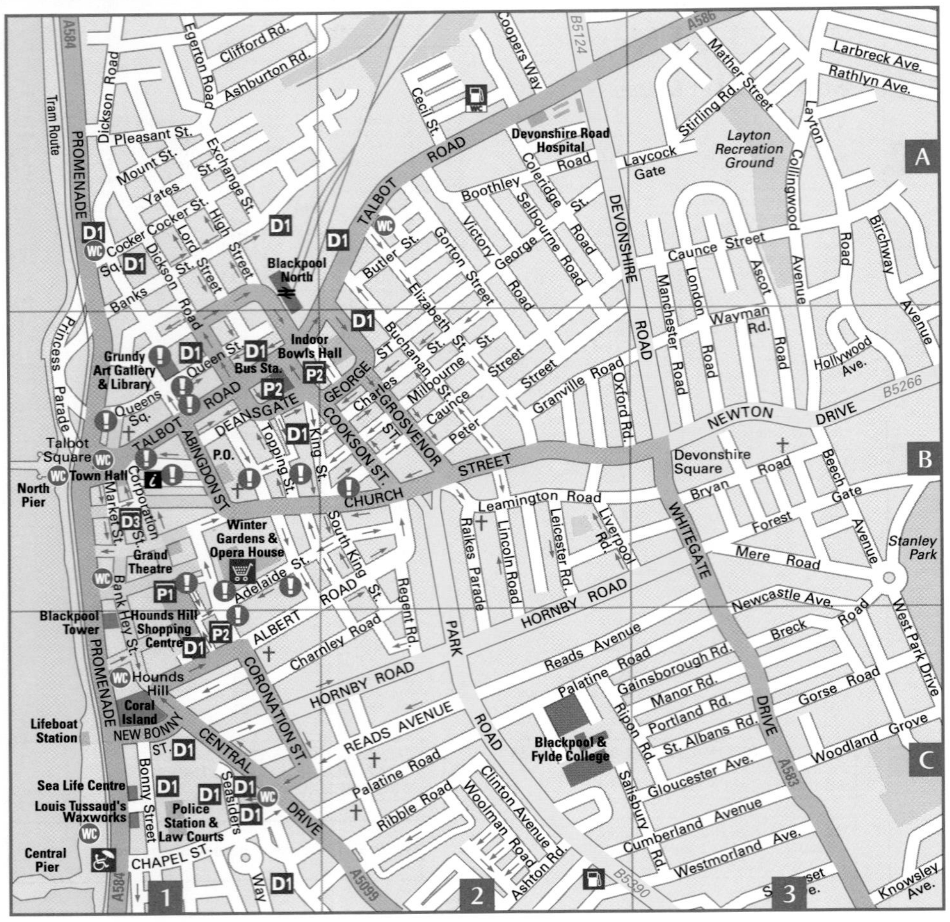

BLACKPOOL

0 300 yds
0 300m

INDEX TO STREET NAMES

Abingdon Street	B1
Adelaide Street	B1
Albert Road	C1
Ascot Road	A3
Ashburton Road	A1
Ashton Road	C2
Bank Hey Street	B1
Banks Street	A1
Beech Avenue	B3
Birchway Avenue	A3
Bonny Street	C1
Boothley Road	A2
Breck Road	C3
Bryan Road	B3
Buchanan Street	B2
Butler Street	A2
Caunce Street	B2/A3
Cecil Street	A2
Central Drive	C1
Chapel Street	C1
Charles Street	B2
Charnley Road	C1
Church Street	B2
Clifford Road	A1
Clifton Street	B1
Clinton Avenue	C2
Cocker Square	A1
Cocker Street	A1
Coleridge Road	A2
Collingwood Avenue	A3
Cookson Street	B2
Coopers Way	A2
Coronation Street	C1
Corporation Street	B1
Cumberland Avenue	C3
Deansgate	B1
Devonshire Road	A2
Devonshire Square	B3
Dickson Road	A1
Egerton Road	A1
Elizabeth Street	A2
Exchange Street	A1
Forest Gate	B3
Gainsborough Road	C2
George Street	B2/A2
Gloucester Avenue	C3
Gorse Road	C3
Gorton Street	A2
Granville Road	B2
Grosvenor Street	B2
High Street	A1
Hollywood Avenue	B3
Hornby Road	C1
Hounds Hill	C1
King Street	B1
Knowsley Avenue	C3
Larbreck Avenue	A3
Laycock Gate	A3
Layton Road	A3
Leamington Road	B2
Leicester Road	B2
Lincoln Road	B2
Liverpool Road	B2
London Road	A3
Lord Street	A1
Manchester Road	A3
Manor Road	C3
Market Street	B1
Mather Street	A3
Mere Road	B3
Milbourne Street	B2
Mount Street	A1
New Bonny Street	C1
Newcastle Avenue	B3
Newton Drive	B3
Oxford Road	B2
Palatine Road	C2
Park Road	C2
Peter Street	B2
Pleasant Street	A1
Portland Road	C3
Princess Parade	B1
Promenade	A1/C1
Queens Square	B1
Queen Street	B1
Rathlyn Avenue	A3
Reads Avenue	C2
Regent Road	B2
Ribble Road	C2
Ripon Road	C2
St. Albans Road	C3
Salisbury Road	C3
Seasiders Way	C1
Selbourne Road	A2
Somerset Avenue	C3
South King Street	B2
Stirling Road	A3
Talbot Road	B1/A2
Talbot Square	B1
Topping Street	B1
Victory Road	A2
Wayman Road	B3
Westmorland Avenue	C3
West Park Drive	B3
Whitegate Drive	B3/C3
Woodland Grove	C3
Woolman Road	C2
Yates Street	A1

TOURIST INFORMATION ☎ 01253 478222
1 CLIFTON STREET,
BLACKPOOL, FY1 1LY

COUNCIL OFFICE ☎ 01253 477477
TOWN HALL, TALBOT SQUARE,
BLACKPOOL, FY1 1NA

HOSPITAL A & E ☎ 01253 300000
VICTORIA HOSPITAL, WHINNEY HEYS ROAD,
BLACKPOOL, FY3 8NR

WEB-SITE www.blackpool.gov.uk

BOURNEMOUTH

0 400 yds
0 400m

INDEX TO STREET NAMES

Ascham Road	A3
Avenue Road	B1
Bath Road	C2
Beechey Road	A3
Bennett Road	A3
Bourne Avenue	B1
Braidley Road	B2
Branksome Wood Road	B1
Cavendish Road	A2
Central Drive	A1
Charminster Road	A2
Christchurch Road	B3
Cotlands	B3
Dean Park Road	B2
Dunbar Road	A2
Durley Chine Road	C1
Durley Chine Road South	C1
Durley Road	C1
East Avenue	A1
East Overcliff Drive	C3
Elgin Road	A1
Exeter Road	C2
Gervis Place	C2
Gervis Road	C3
Grove Road	C3
Hinton Road	C2
Holdenhurst Road	B3
Knyveton Road	B3
Lansdowne Road	A2
Leven Avenue	A1
Little Forest Road	A1
Lowther Road	A3
Madeira Road	B2
Malmesbury Park Road	A3
Manor Road	A3
Methuen Road	A3
Meyrick Road	B3
Milton Road	A2
Old Christchurch Road	B2
Ophir Road	A3
Oxford Road	B3
Pier Approach	C2
Poole Hill	C1
Portchester Road	A3
Priory Road	C1
Queen's Road	B1
Richmond Hill	B2
Russell Cotes Road	C2
St. Augustin's Road	A2
St. Anthony's Road	A2
St. Leonard's Road	A3
St. Michael's Road	C1
St. Pauls' Road	B3
St. Peter's Road	B2
St. Stephen's Road	B1
St. Swithun's Road	B3
St. Swithun's Road South	B3
St. Valerie Road	A2
St. Winifred's Road	A2
Stewart Road	A3
Surrey Road	B1
The Lansdowne	B3
The Square	B2
The Triangle	B1
Tregonwell Road	C1
Undercliff Drive	C3
Wellington Road	A2
Wessex Way	B1/A3
West Cliff Promenade	C1
West Cliff Road	C1
West Hill Road	C1
West Overcliff Drive	C1
West Promenade	C1
Westover Road	C2
Wimborne Road	B2

TOURIST INFORMATION ☎ 0906 802 0234
WESTOVER ROAD,
BOURNEMOUTH, BH1 2BU

COUNCIL OFFICE ☎ 01202 451451
TOWN HALL, BOURNE AVENUE,
BOURNEMOUTH, BH2 6DY

HOSPITAL A & E ☎ 01202 303626
ROYAL BOURNEMOUTH HOSPITAL,
CASTLE LANE EAST, BOURNEMOUTH, BH7 7DW

WEB-SITE www.bournemouth.gov.uk

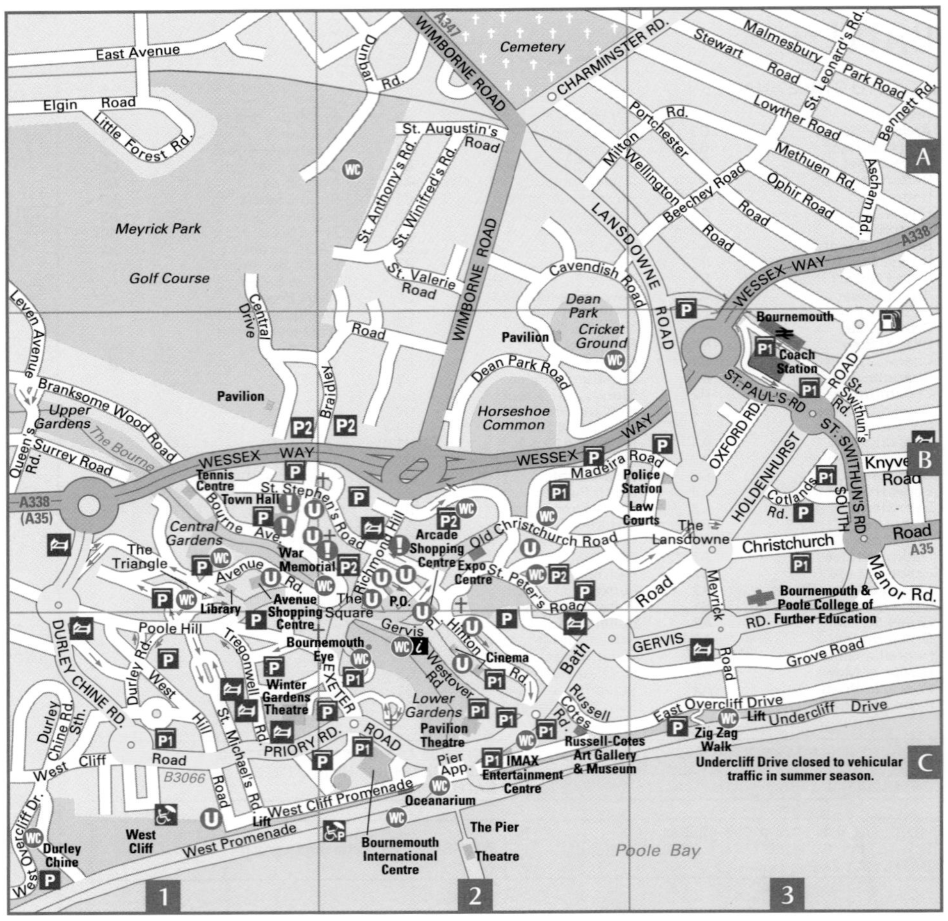

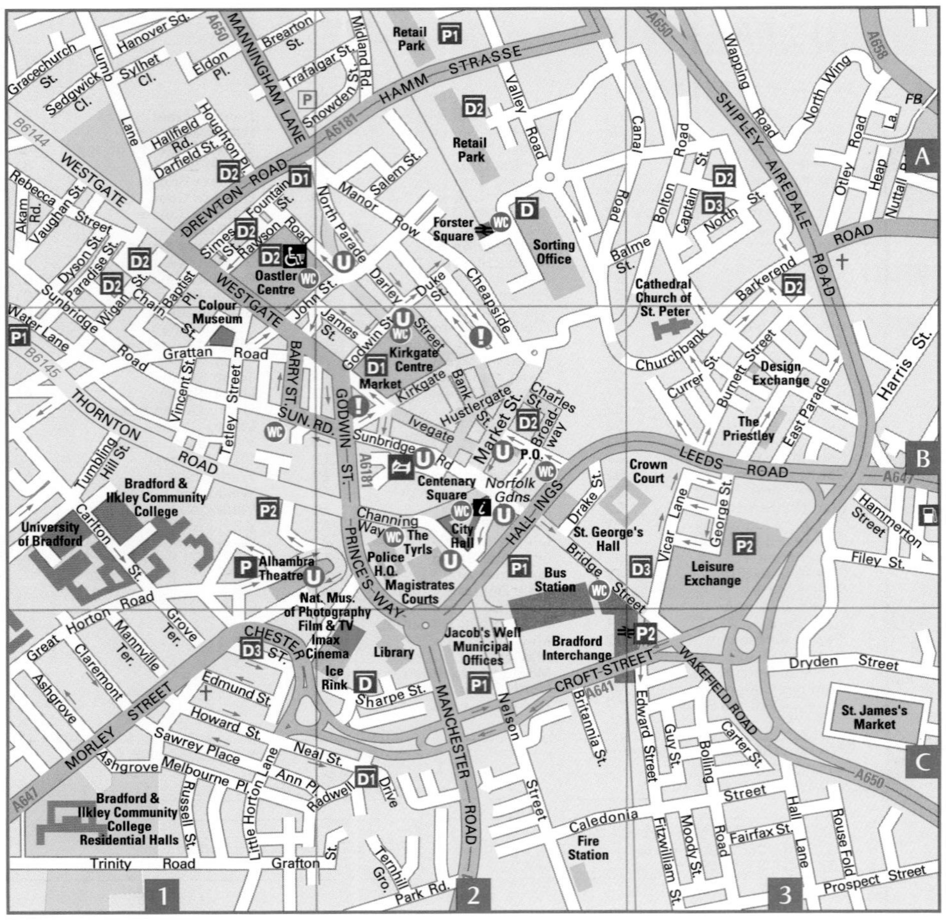

BRADFORD

0 200 yds
0 200m

INDEX TO STREET NAMES

Akam Road	A1
Ann Place	C1
Ashgrove	C1
Balme Street	A2
Bank Street	B2
Baptist Place	A1
Barkerend Road	A3
Barry Street	B1
Bolling Road	C3
Bolton Road	A3
Brearton Street	A1
Bridge Street	B2
Britannia Street	C2
Broadway	B2
Burnett Street	B3
Caledonia Street	C2
Canal Road	A2
Captain Street	A3
Carlton Street	B1
Carter Street	C3
Chain Street	A1
Charles Street	B2
Cheapside	B2
Chester Street	C1
Churchbank	B3
Claremont	C1
Croft Street	C2
Currer Street	B3
Darfield Street	A1
Darley Street	A2
Drake Street	B2
Drewton Road	A1
Dryden Street	C3
Duke Street	A2
Dyson Street	A1
East Parade	B3
Edmund Street	C1
Edward Street	C3
Eldon Place	A1
Fairfax Street	C3
Filey Street	B3
Fitzwilliam Street	C3
Fountain Street	A1
George Street	B3
Godwin Street	B2
Gracechurch Street	A1
Grafton Street	C1
Grattan Road	B1
Great Horton Road	C1
Grove Terrace	C1
Guy Street	C3
Hall Ings	B2
Hall Lane	C3
Hallfield Road	A1
Hamm Strasse	A2
Hammerton Street	B3
Hanover Square	A1
Harris Street	B3
Heap Lane	A3
Houghton Place	A1
Howard Street	C1
Hustlergate	B2
Ivegate	B2
James Street	B2
John Street	B1
Kirkgate	B2
Leeds Road	B3
Little Horton Lane	C1
Lumb Lane	A1
Manchester Road	C2
Manningham Lane	A1
Mannville Terrace	C1
Manor Row	A2
Market Street	B2
Melbourne Place	C1
Midland Road	A2
Moody Street	C3
Morley Street	C1
Neal Street	C1
Nelson Street	C2
North Parade	A2
North Street	A3
North Wing	A3
Nuttall Road	A3
Otley Road	A3
Paradise Street	A1
Park Road	C2
Prince's Way	B2
Prospect Street	C3
Radwell Drive	C1
Rawson Road	A1
Rebecca Street	A1
Rouse Fold	C3
Russell Street	C1
Salem Street	A2
Sawrey Place	C1
Sedgwick Close	A1
Sharpe Street	C2
Shipley Airedale Road	A3
Simes Street	A1
Snowden Street	A1
Sunbridge Road	A1
Sylhet Close	A1
Ternhill Grove	C2
Tetley Street	B1
Thornton Road	B1
Trafalgar Street	A1
Trinity Road	C1
Tumbling Hill Street	B1
Valley Road	A2
Vaughan Street	A1
Vicar Lane	B3
Vincent Street	B1
Wakefield Road	C3
Wapping Road	A3
Water Lane	B1
Westgate	A1
Wigan Street	B1

TOURIST INFORMATION ☎ 01274 433678
CITY HALL, CENTENARY SQUARE,
BRADFORD, BD1 1HY

COUNCIL OFFICE ☎ 01274 752111
CITY HALL, CHANNING WAY,
BRADFORD, BD1 1HY

HOSPITAL A & E ☎ 01274 542200
BRADFORD ROYAL INFIRMARY, DUCKWORTH
LANE, BRADFORD, BD9 6RJ

WEB-SITE www.bradford.gov.uk

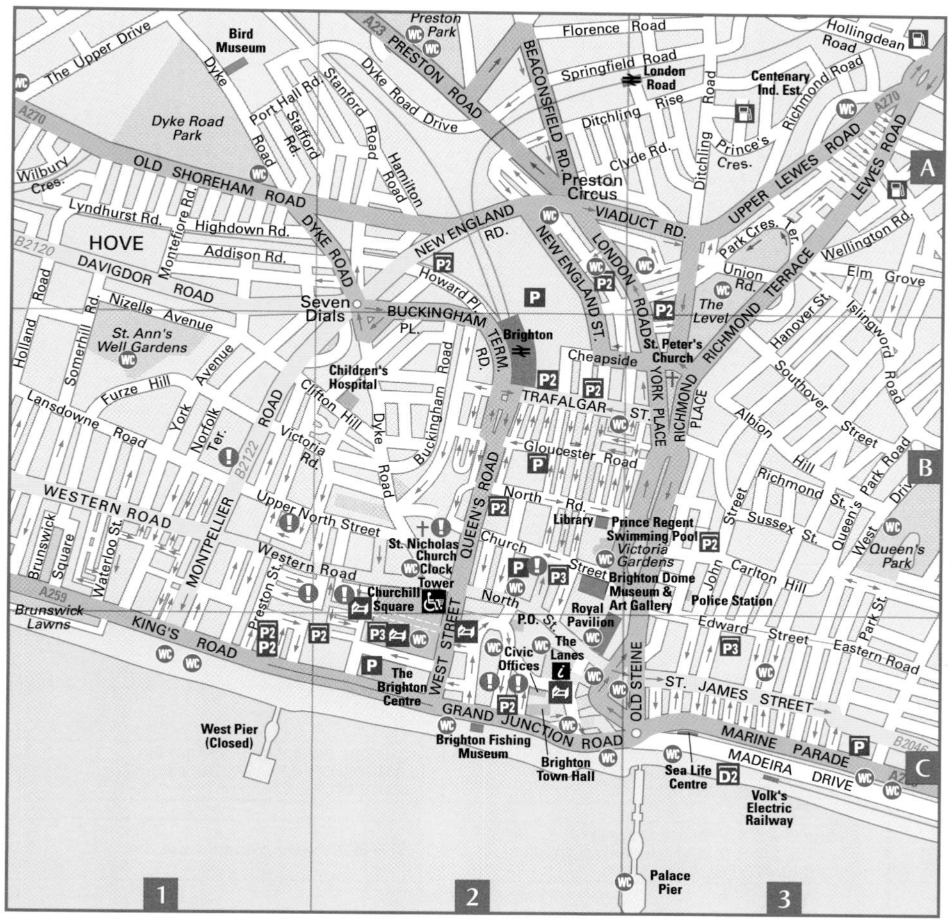

BRIGHTON

0 200 yds
0 200m

INDEX TO STREET NAMES

Addison Road	A1
Albion Hill	B3
Beaconsfield Road	A2
Brunswick Square	B1
Buckingham Place	A2
Buckingham Road	B2
Carlton Hill	B3
Cheapside	B2
Church Street	B2
Churchill Square	C2
Clifton Hill	B1
Clyde Road	A2
Davigdor Road	A1
Ditchling Rise	A2
Ditchling Road	A3
Dyke Road	B2
Dyke Road Drive	A2
Edward Street	C3
Elm Grove	A3
Florence Road	A2
Freshfield Road	C3
Furze Hill	B1
Gloucester Road	B2
Grand Junction Road	C2
Hamilton Road	A2
Hanover Street	B3
Highdown Road	A1
Holland Road	B1
Hollingdean Road	A3
Howard Place	A2
Islingword Road	A3
John Street	B3
King's Road	C1
Lansdowne Road	B1
Lewes Road	A3
London Road	A2
Lyndhurst Road	A1
Madeira Drive	C3
Marine Parade	C3
Montefiore Road	A1
Montpelier Road	B1
New England Road	A2
New England Street	A2
Nizells Avenue	A1
Norfolk Terrace	B1
North Road	B2
North Street	B2
Old Shoreham Road	A1
Old Steine	C3
Park Crescent Terrace	A3
Park Street	B3
Port Hall Road	A1
Preston Circus	A2
Preston Road	A2
Preston Street	C1
Prince's Crescent	A3
Queen's Park Road	B3
Queen's Road	B2
Richmond Place	B3
Richmond Road	A3
Richmond Street	B3
Richmond Terrace	B3
St. James's Street	C3
Somerhill Road	B1
Southover Street	B3
Springfield Road	A2
Stafford Road	A1
Stanford Road	A2
Sussex Street	B3
Terminus Road	B2
The Lanes	C2
The Upper Drive	A1
Trafalgar Street	B2
Union Road	A3
Upper Lewes Road	A3
Upper North Street	B1
Viaduct Road	A2
Victoria Road	B1
Waterloo Street	B1
Wellington Road	A3
West Drive	B3
West Street	C2
Western Road	B1
Wilbury Crescent	A1
York Avenue	B1
York Place	B3

TOURIST INFORMATION ☎ 0906 711 2255
10 BARTHOLOMEW SQUARE,
BRIGHTON, BN1 1JS

COUNCIL OFFICE ☎ 01273 290000
KING'S HOUSE, GRAND AVENUE,
HOVE, BN3 2LS

HOSPITAL A & E ☎ 01273 696955
ROYAL SUSSEX COUNTY HOSPITAL, EASTERN
ROAD, BRIGHTON, BN2 5BE

WEB-SITE www.brighton-hove.gov.uk

BRISTOL

0 200 yds
0 200m

INDEX TO STREET NAMES

Alfred Hill	A1
Anchor Road	C1
Avon Street	B3
Baldwin Street	B1
Bath Road	C3
Bond Street	A2
Bridge Street	B2
Bristol Bridge	B2
Broadmead	A2
Broad Quay	B1
Broad Street	B2
Broad Weir	A3
Canon's Road	C1
Canon's Way	C1
Castle Street	B3
Charles Street	A2
Cheese Lane	B3
Christmas Steps	A1
Church Lane	B3
College Green	B1
Colston Avenue	B1
Colston Street	B1
Corn Street	B1
Counterslip	B2
Dale Street	A3
Eugene Street	A1
Fairfax Street	A2
Frogmore Street	B1
Harbour Way	C1
High Street	B2
Horfield Road	A1
Houlton Street	A3
John Street	B2
King Street	B1
Lewins Mead	A1
Lower Castle Street	A3
Lower Maudlin Street	A2
Marlborough Street	A2
Marsh Street	B1
Merchant Street	A2
Nelson Street	A2
Newfoundland Street	A3
Newgate	B2
New Street	A3
North Street	A2
Old Bread Street	B3
Old Market Street	B3
Park Row	B1
Park Street	B1
Passage Street	B3
Penn Street	A3
Perry Road	B1
Pipe Lane	B1
Portwall Lane	C2
Prewett Street	C2
Prince Street	C1
Prince Street Bridge	C1
Queen Charlotte Street	B2
Queen Square	C1
Queen Street	B3
Redcliffe Backs	C2
Redcliffe Bridge	C2
Redcliffe Parade	C2
Redcliff Hill	C2
Redcliff Mead Lane	C3
Redcliff Street	B2
Redcross Street	A3
River Street	A3
Rupert Street	A1
St. Michael's Hill	A1
St. Nicholas Street	B2
St. Thomas Street	B2
Small Street	B1
Somerset Street	C3
Southwell Street	A1
Station Approach Road	C3
Straight Street	B3
Surrey Street	A3
Temple Back	B3
Temple Gate	C3
Temple Street	B2
Temple Way	C3
Terrell Street	A1
The Grove	C1
The Haymarket	A2
The Horsefair	A2
Thomas Lane	B2
Trenchard Street	B1
Tyndall Avenue	A1
Union Street	A2
Unity Street	B1
Unity Street	B3
Upper Maudlin Street	A1
Victoria Street	B2
Wapping Road	C1
Water Lane	B3
Wellington Road	A3
Welsh Back	B2
Wilder Street	A2
Wine Street	B2

TOURIST INFORMATION ☎ 0906 711 2191
THE ANNEXE, WILDSCREEN WALK,
HARBOURSIDE, BRISTOL, BS1 5DB

COUNCIL OFFICE ☎ 0117 922 2000
THE COUNCIL HOUSE, COLLEGE GREEN,
BRISTOL, BS1 5TR

HOSPITAL A & E ☎ 0117 923 0000
BRISTOL ROYAL INFIRMARY,
MARLBOROUGH STREET, BRISTOL, BS2 8HW

WEB-SITE www.bristol-city.gov.uk

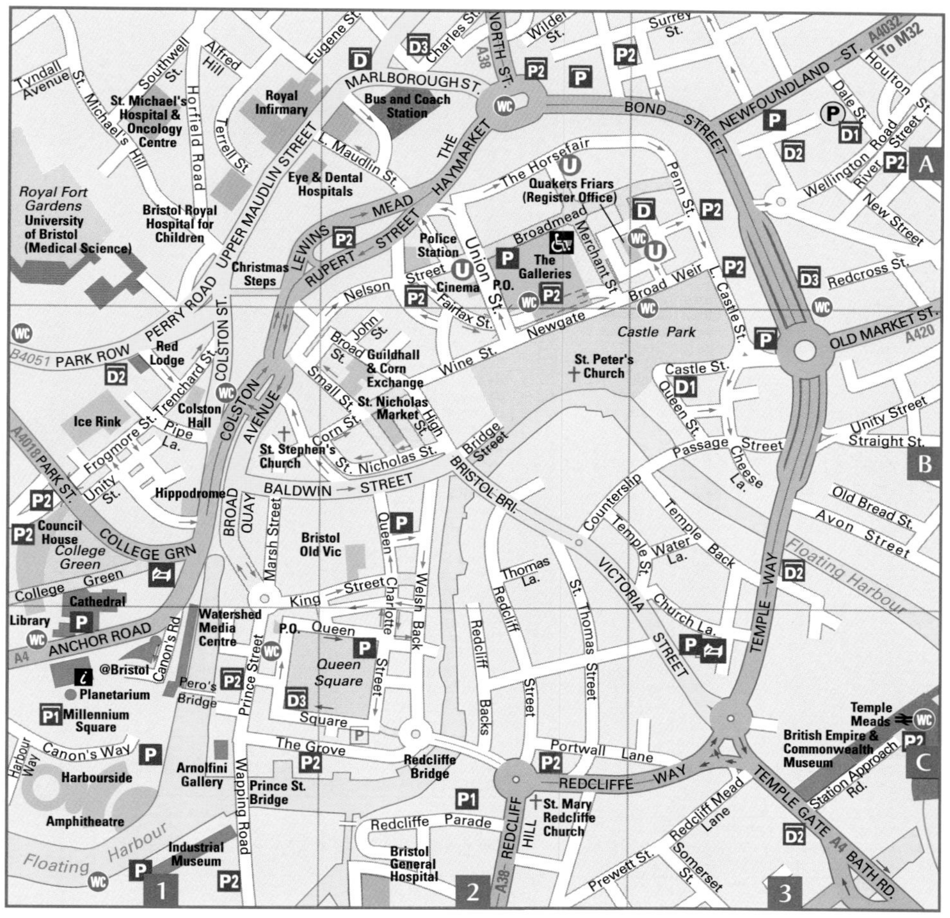

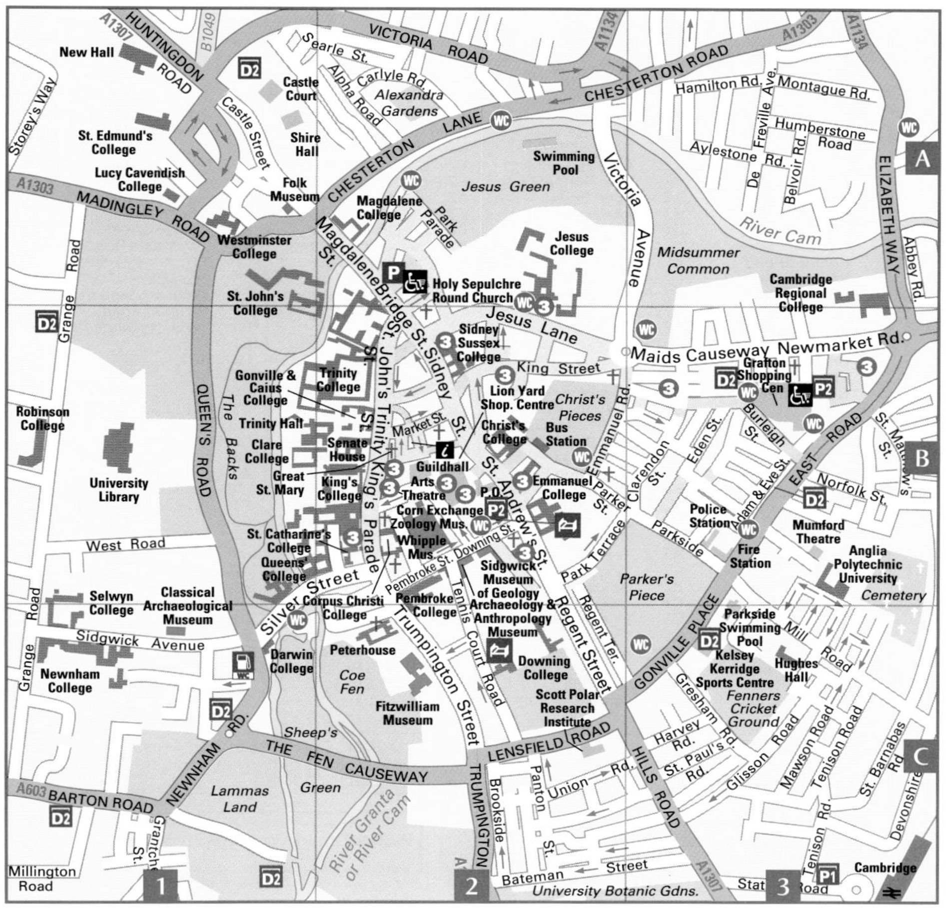

CAMBRIDGE

0 400 yds
0 400m

INDEX TO STREET NAMES

Adam and Eve Street	B3
Alpha Road	A2
Aylestone Road	A3
Barton Road	C1
Bateman Street	C2
Belvior Road	A3
Brookside	C2
Burleigh Street	B3
Carlyle Road	A2
Castle Street	A1
Chesterton Lane	A2
Chesterton Road	A2
Clarendon Street	B3
De Freville Avenue	A3
Devonshire Road	C3
Downing Street	B2
East Road	B3
Eden Street	B3
Elizabeth Way	A3
Emmanuel Road	B2
Fen Causeway, The	C1
Glisson Road	C3
Gonville Place	C3
Granchester Street	C1
Grange Road	B1
Gresham Road	C3
Hamilton Road	A3
Harvey Road	C3
Hills Road	C3
Humberstone Road	A3
Huntingdon Road	A1
Jesus Lane	B2
King's Parade	B2
King Street	B2
Lensfield Road	C2
Madingley Road	A1
Magdalene Bridge Street	A2
Maids Causeway	B3
Market Street	B2
Mawson Road	C3
Millington Road	C1
Mill Road	C3
Montague Road	A3
Newmarket Road	B3
Newnham Road	C1
Norfolk Street	B3
Panton Street	C2
Parker Street	B2
Park Parade	A2
Parkside	B3
Park Terrace	B2
Pembroke Street	B2
Queen's Road	B1
Regent Street	B2
Regent Terrace	B2
St. Andrew's Street	B2
St. Barnabas Road	C3
St. John's Street	B2
St. Matthew's Street	B3
St. Paul's Road	C3
Searce Street	A1
Sidgwick Avenue	C1
Sidney Street	B2
Silver Street	C1
Station Road	C3
Storey's Way	A1
Tenison Road	C3
Tennis Court Road	B2
Trinity Street	B2
Trumpington Road	C2
Trumpington Street	C2
Union Road	C2
Victoria Avenue	A2
Victoria Road	A2
West Road	B1

TOURIST INFORMATION ☎ 01223 322640
WHEELER STREET, CAMBRIDGE,
CAMBRIDGESHIRE, CB2 3QB

COUNCIL OFFICE ☎ 01223 457000
THE GUILDHALL, MARKET SQUARE,
CAMBRIDGE, CB2 3QJ

HOSPITAL A & E ☎ 01223 245151
ADDENBROOKE'S HOSPITAL, HILLS ROAD,
CAMBRIDGE, CB2 2QQ

WEB-SITE www.cambridge.gov.uk

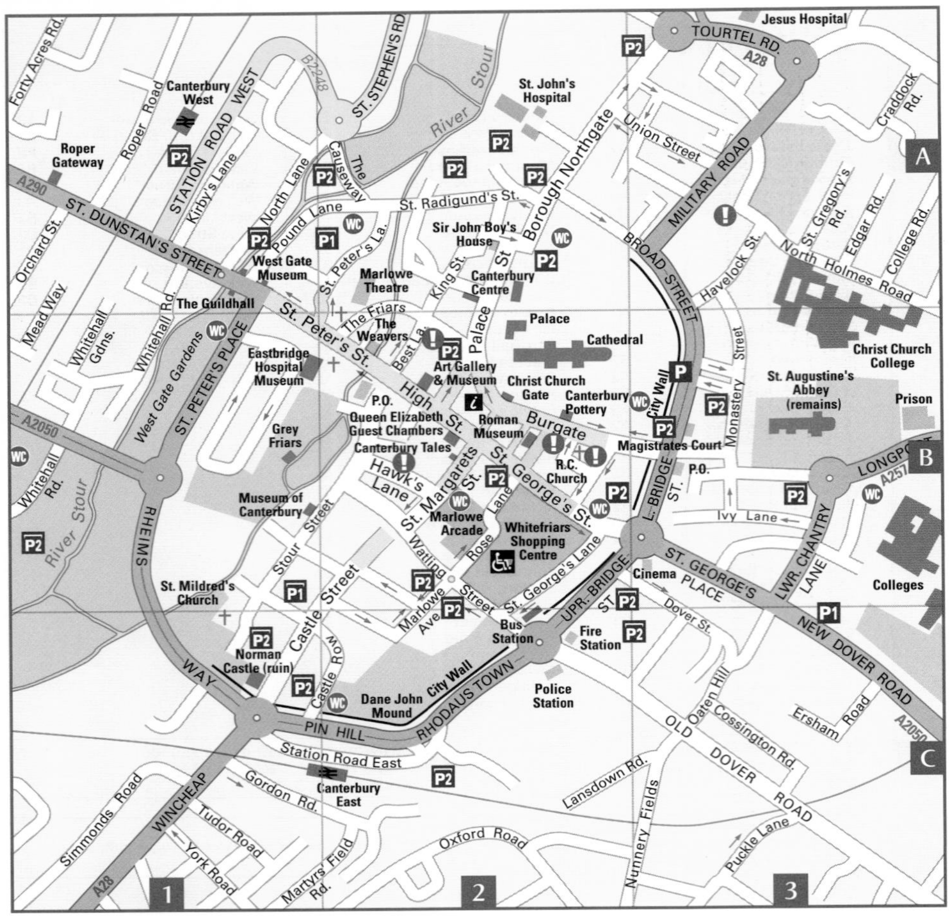

CANTERBURY

0 200 yds
0 200m

INDEX TO STREET NAMES

Best Lane	B2
Borough Northgate	A2
Broad Street	A3
Burgate	B2
Castle Row	C1
Castle Street	C1
College Road	A3
Cossington Road	C3
Craddock Road	A3
Dover Street	B3
Edgar Road	A3
Ersham Road	C3
Forty Acres Road	A1
Gordon Road	C1
Havelock Street	A3
Hawk's Lane	B2
High Street	B2
Ivy Lane	B3
King Street	A2
Kirby's Lane	A1
Lansdown Road	C2
Longport	B3
Lower Bridge Street	B3
Lower Chantry Lane	B3
Marlowe Avenue	C2
Martyrs' Field Road	C1
Mead Way	B1
Military Road	A3
Monastery Street	B3
New Dover Road	C3
North Holmes Road	A3
North Lane	A1
Nunnery Fields	C3
Oaten Hill	C3
Old Dover Road	C3
Orchard Street	A1
Oxford Road	C2
Palace Street	B2
Pin Hill	C1
Pound Lane	A1
Puckle Lane	C3
Rheims Way	B1
Rhodaus Town	C2
Roper Road	A1
Rose Lane	B2
St. Dunstan's Street	A1
St. George's Lane	B2
St. George's Place	B3
St. George's Street	B2
St. Gregory's Road	A3
St. Margarets Street	B2
St. Peter's Lane	A2
St. Peter's Place	B1
St. Peter's Street	A1
St. Radigund's Street	A2
St. Stephen's Road	A2
Simmonds Road	C1
Station Road East	C1
Station Road West	A1
Stour Street	B1
The Causeway	A2
The Friar's	B2
Tourtel Road	A3
Tudor Road	C1
Union Street	A3
Upper Bridge Street	C2
Watling Street	B2
Whitehall Gardens	B1
Whitehall Road	B1
Wincheap	C1
York Road	C1

TOURIST INFORMATION ☎ 01227 766567
34 ST. MARGARET'S STREET,
CANTERBURY, KENT, CT1 2TG

COUNCIL OFFICE ☎ 01227 862000
COUNCIL OFFICES, MILITARY ROAD,
CANTERBURY, CT1 1YW

HOSPITAL A & E ☎ 01227 766877
KENT & CANTERBURY HOSPITAL, ETHELBERT
ROAD, CANTERBURY, CT1 3NG

WEB-SITE www.canterbury.gov.uk

CARDIFF

0 400 yds
0 400m

INDEX TO STREET NAMES

Adam Street	C3
Albany Road	A3
Allerton Street	C1
Arran Place	A3
Arran Street	A3
Basil Place	A2
Bedford Street	A3
Boulevard de Nantes	B2
Bridge Street	C2
Brook Street	C1
Bute Street	C2
Bute Terrace	C2
Castle Street	B1
Cathays Terrace	A2
Cathedral Road	B1
Celerity Drive	C3
Central Link	C3
Charles Street	B2
Churchill Way	B3
City Road	A3
Clare Road	C1
Clare Street	B1
Claude Road	A3
Coburn Street	A2
College Road	B2
Colum Road	A1
Corbett Road	A2
Cornwall Street	C1
Cottrell Road	A3
Cowbridge Road East	B1
Craddock Street	C1
Craiglee Drive	C3
Croft Street	A3
Crwys Road	A2
Cyfartha Street	A3
De Burgh Street	B1
Despenser Street	C1
Duke Street	B2
Dumfries Place	B3
Ellen Street	C3
Elm Street	A3
Fanny Street	A2
Fitzhamon Embankment	C1
Flora Street	A2
Glossop Road	B3
Gordon Road	A3
Greyfriars Road	B2
Hamilton Street	B1
Harriet Street	A2
Herbert Street	C3
High Street	B2
Hirwain Street	A2
Keppoch Street	A3
Kingsway	B2
Lewis Street	B1
Longcross Street	B3
Maindy Road	A1
Mardy Street	C1
Mark Street	B1
Merches Gardens	C1
Merthyr Street	A2
Meteor Street	B3
Mill Lane	C2
Minny Street	A2
Miskin Street	A2
Moira Place	B3
Moira Terrace	B3
Moy Road	A3
Museum Avenue	A2
Neville Street	B1
Newport Road	B3
Newport Road Lane	B3
Ninian Park Road	C1
North Road	A1
Oxford Lane	B3
Park Grove	B2
Park Place	A2
Park Street	C2
Partridge Road	A3
Penarth Road	C2
Pendyris Street	C1
Pitman Street	B1
Planet Street	B3
Queen Street	B2
Rhymney Street	A2
Richard Street	A2
Richmond Road	A3
Ryder Street	B1
St. Mary Street	C2
St. Peters Street	B3
Salisbury Road	A2
Schooner Way	C3
Senghennydd Road	A2
Stafford Road	C1
Strathnairn Street	A3
Stuttgarter Strasse	B2
Taffs Mead Embankment	C2
Talbot Street	B1
Thesiger Street	A2
The Parade	B3
The Walk	A3
Tudor Street	C1
Tyndall Street	C3
Wedmore Road	C1
Wells Street	C1
West Grove	B3
Westgate Street	B2
Windsor Place	B2
Windsor Road	B3
Wood Street	C2
Woodville Road	A2
Wordsworth Avenue	C3
Working Street	B2
Wyeverne Road	A2

TOURIST INFORMATION ☎ 029 2022 7281
CARDIFF VISITOR CENTRE, 16 WOOD STREET,
CARDIFF, CF10 1ES

COUNCIL OFFICE ☎ 029 2087 2087
THE HELP CENTRE, MARLAND HOUSE, CENTRAL
SQUARE, CARDIFF, CF10 1EP

HOSPITAL A & E ☎ 029 2074 7747
CARDIFF UNIVERSITY OF WALES HOSPITAL,
HEATH PARK, CARDIFF, CF14 4XW

WEB-SITE www.cardiff.gov.uk

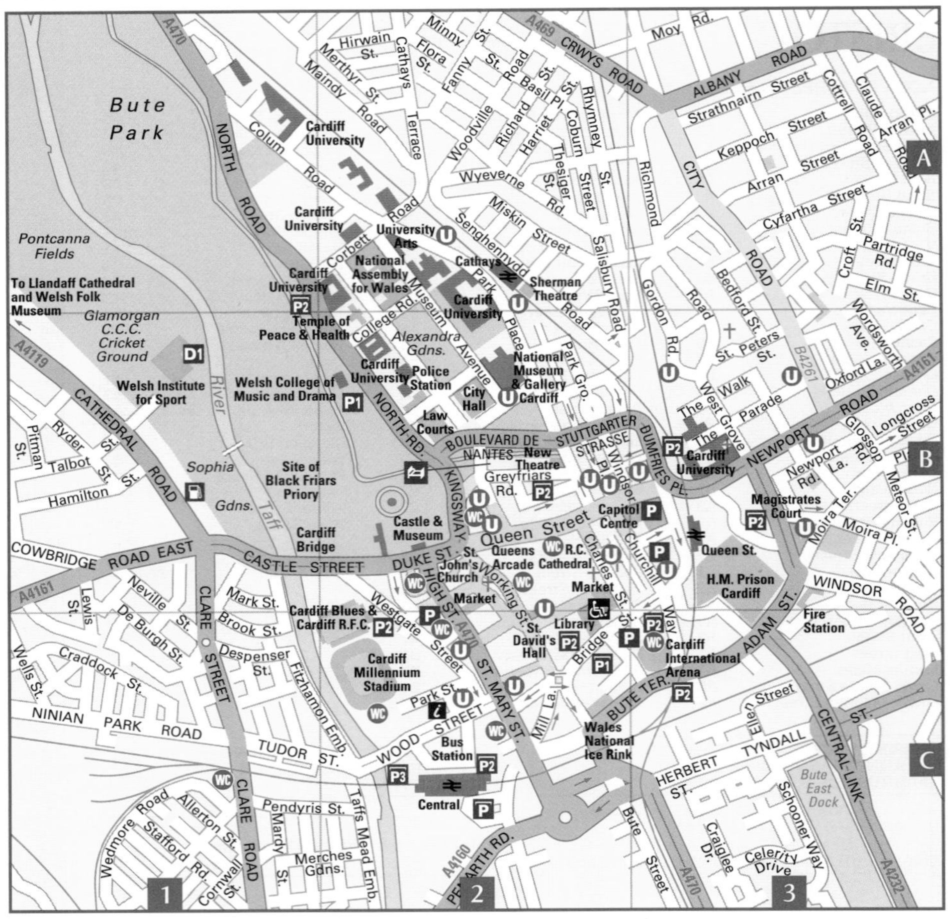

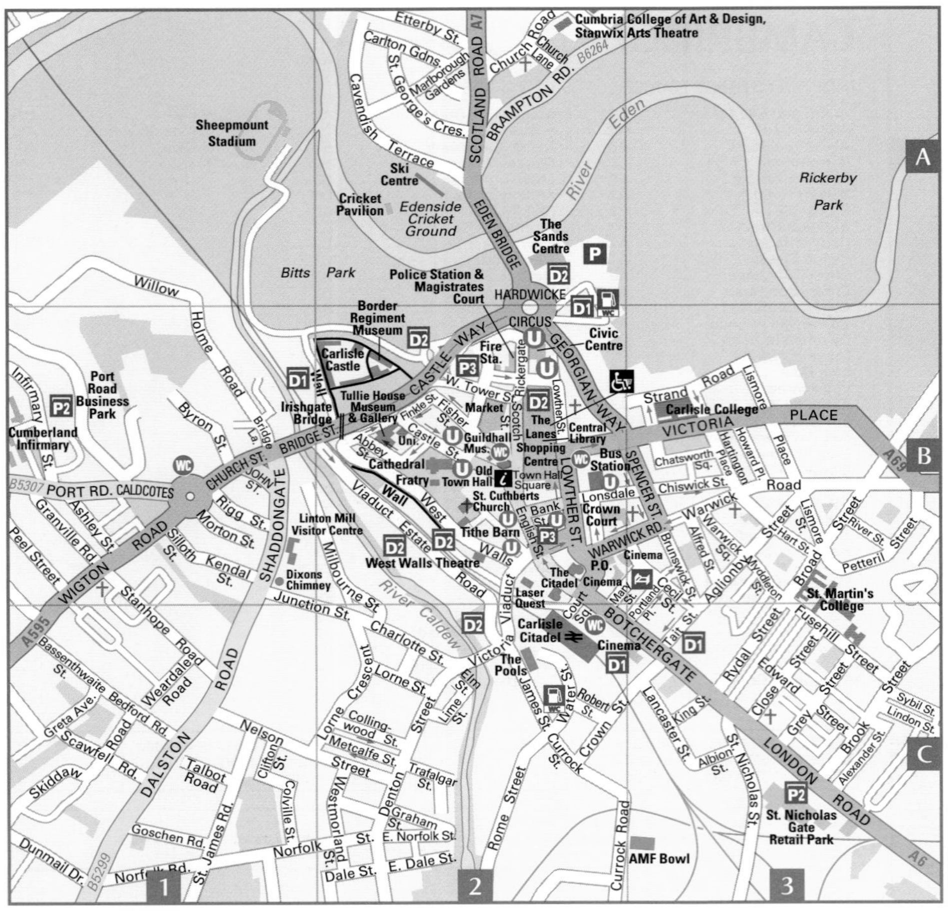

CARLISLE

0 400 yds
0 400m

INDEX TO STREET NAMES

Abbey Street	B2
Aglionby Street	B3
Albion Street	C3
Alexander Street	C3
Alfred Street	B3
Ashley Street	B1
Bank Street	B2
Bassenthwaite Street	C1
Bedford Road	C1
Botchergate	C2
Brampton Road	A2
Bridge Lane	B1
Bridge Street	B1
Broad Street	B3
Brook Street	C3
Brunswick Street	B3
Byron Street	B1
Caldcotes	B1
Carlton Gardens	A2
Castle Street	B2
Castle Way	B2
Cavendish Terrace	A2
Cecil Street	B3
Charlotte Street	C2
Chatsworth Square	B3
Chiswick Street	B3
Church Lane	A2
Church Road	A2
Church Street	B1
Clifton Street	C1
Close Street	C3
Collingwood Street	C2
Colville Street	C1
Crown Street	C2
Currock Road	C2
Currock Street	C2
Dale Street	C2
Denton Street	C2
Dunmail Drive	C1
East Dale Street	C2
East Norfolk Street	C2
Eden Bridge	A2
Edward Street	C3
Elm Street	C2
English Street	B2
Etterby Street	A2
Finkle Street	B2
Fisher Street	B2
Fusehill Street	C3
Georgian Way	B2
Goschen Road	C1
Graham Street	C2
Granville Road	B1
Greta Avenue	C1
Grey Street	C3
Hardwicke Circus	A2
Hart Street	B3
Hartington Place	B3
Howard Place	B3
Infirmary Street	B1
James Street	C2
John Street	B1
Junction Street	B1
Kendal Street	B1
King Street	C3
Lancaster Street	C3
Lime Street	C2
Lindon Street	C3
Lismore Place	B3
Lismore Street	B3
London Road	C3
Lonsdale	B2
Lorne Crescent	C2
Lorne Street	C2
Lowther Street	B2
Marlborough Gardens	A2
Mary Street	B2
Metcalfe Street	C2
Milbourne Street	B2
Morton Street	B1
Myddleton Street	B3
Nelson Street	C1
Norfolk Road	C1
Norfolk Street	C1
Peel Street	B1
Petteril Street	B3
Port Road	B1
Portland Place	C3
Rickergate	B2
Rigg Street	B1
River Street	B3
Robert Street	C2
Rome Street	C2
Rydal Street	C3
St. George's Crescent	A2
St. James Road	C1
St. Nicholas Street	C3
Scawfell Road	C1
Scotch Street	B2
Scotland Road	A2
Shaddongate	B1
Silloth Street	B1
Skiddaw Road	C1
Spencer Street	B3
Stanhope Road	B1
Strand Road	B3
Sybil Street	C3
Tait Street	C3
Talbot Road	C1
Trafalgar Street	C2
Viaduct Estate Road	B2
Victoria Place	B3
Victoria Viaduct	C2
Warwick Road	B2
Warwick Square	B3
Water Street	C2
Weardale Road	C1
West Tower Street	B2
West Walls	B2
Westmorland Street	C2
Wigton Road	B1
Willow Holme Road	A1

TOURIST INFORMATION ☎ 01228 625600
OLD TOWN HALL, GREEN MARKET,
CARLISLE, CA3 8JD

COUNCIL OFFICE ☎ 01228 817200
CARLISLE CITY COUNCIL, THE CIVIC CENTRE,
CARLISLE, CA3 8QG

HOSPITAL A & E ☎ 01228 523444
CUMBERLAND INFIRMARY, NEWTOWN ROAD,
CARLISLE, CA2 7HY

WEB-SITE www.carlisle-city.gov.uk

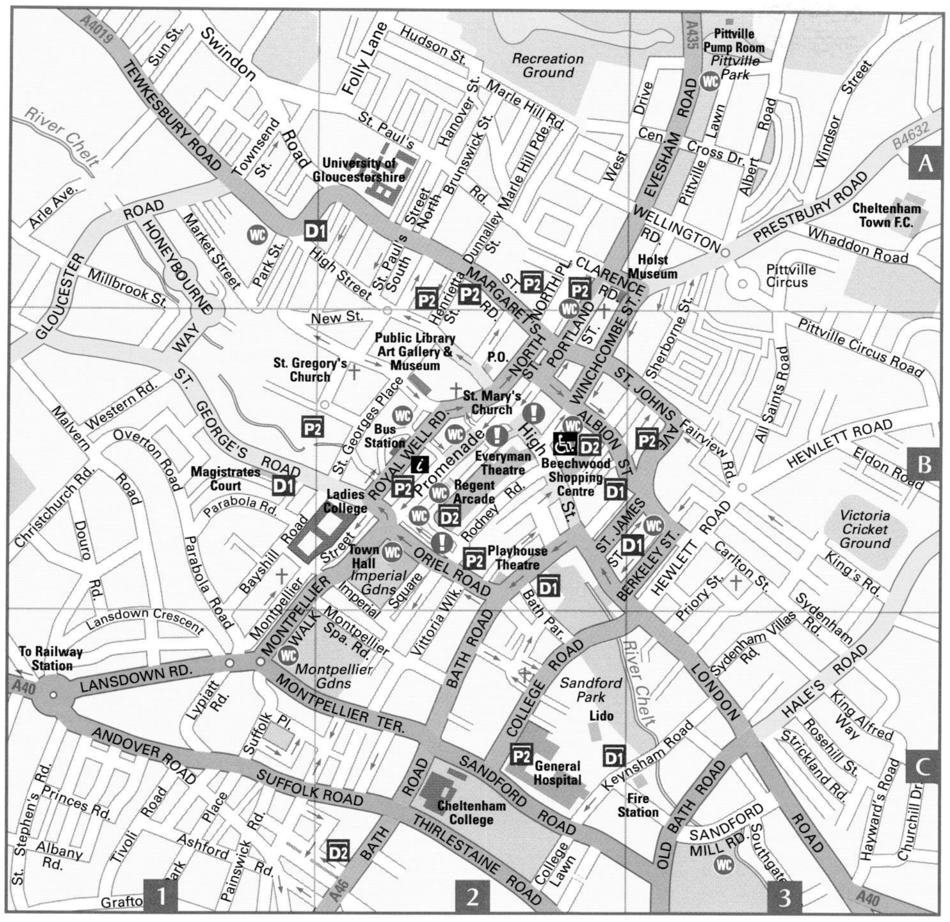

CHELTENHAM

0 300 yds
0 300m

INDEX TO STREET NAMES

Albany Road	C1	King Alfred Way	C3	St. George's Road	B1
Albert Road	A3	King's Road	B3	St. James Street	B2
Albion Street	B2	Lansdown Crescent	C1	St. Johns Avenue	B2
All Saints Road	B3	Lansdown Road	C1	St. Margaret's Road	A2
Andover Road	C1	London Road	C3	St. Paul's Road	A2
Arle Avenue	A1	Lypiatt Road	C1	St. Paul's Street North	A2
Ashford Road	C1	Malvern Road	B1	St. Paul's Street South	A2
Bath Parade	B2	Market Street	A1	St. Stephen's Road	C1
Bath Road	C2	Marle Hill Parade	A2	Sandford Mill Road	C3
Bayshill Road	B1	Marle Hill Road	A2	Sandford Road	C2
Berkeley Street	B2	Millbrook Street	A1	Sherborne Street	B3
Brunswick Street	A2	Montpellier Spa Road	B2	Southgate Drive	C3
Carlton Street	B3	Montpellier Street	C1	Strickland Road	C3
Central Cross Drive	A3	Montpellier Terrace	C1	Suffolk Place	C1
Christchurch Road	B1	Montpellier Walk	C1	Suffolk Road	C1
Churchill Drive	C3	New Street	A2	Sun Street	A1
Clarence Road	A2	North Place	B2	Swindon Road	A1
College Lawn	C2	North Street	B2	Sydenham Road	B3
College Road	C2	Old Bath Road	C3	Sydenham Villas Road	C3
Douro Road	B1	Oriel Road	B2	Tewkesbury Road	A1
Dunnally Street	A2	Overton Road	B1	Thirlestaine Road	C2
Eldon Road	B3	Painswick Road	C1	Tivoli Road	C1
Evesham Road	A3	Parabola Road	B1	Townsend Street	A1
Fairview Road	B3	Park Place	C1	Vittoria Walk	C2
Folly Lane	A2	Park Street	A1	Wellington Road	A3
Gloucester Road	B1	Pittville Circus	A3	West Drive	A2
Grafton Road	C1	Pittville Circus Road	B3	Western Road	B1
Hale's Road	C3	Pittville Lawn	A3	Whaddon Road	A3
Hanover Street	A2	Portland Street	B2	Winchcombe Street	B2
Hayward's Road	C3	Prestbury Road	A3	Windsor Street	A3
Henrietta Street	B2	Princes Road	C1		
Hewlett Road	B3	Priory Street	C3		
High Street	A2	Promenade	B2		
Honeybourne Way	B1	Rodney Road	B2		
Hudson Street	A2	Rosehill Street	C3		
Imperial Square	B2	Royal Well Road	B2		
Keynsham Road	C2	St. George's Place	B2		

TOURIST INFORMATION ☎ 01242 522878
77 PROMENADE, CHELTENHAM,
GLOUCESTERSHIRE, GL50 1PJ

COUNCIL OFFICE ☎ 01242 262626
MUNICIPAL OFFICES, PROMENADE,
CHELTENHAM, GL50 1PP

HOSPITAL A & E ☎ 08454 222222
CHELTENHAM GENERAL HOSPITAL,
SANDFORD ROAD, CHELTENHAM, GL53 7AN

WEB-SITE www.cheltenham.gov.uk

CHESTER

0 200 yds
0 200m

INDEX TO STREET NAMES

Bath Street	B3	Grosvenor Road	C1	St. John Street	B2
Bedward Row	B1	Grosvenor Street	C1	St. Martins Way	A1
Black Diamond Street	A2	Handbridge	C2	St. Oswalds Way	A2
Black Friars	C1	Hoole Road	A2	St. Werburgh Street	B2
Bold Square	B2	Hoole Way	A2	Seller Street	B3
Boughton	B3	Hunter Street	B1	Sibell Street	A3
Bouverie Street	A1	King Street	B1	Souter's Lane	C2
Bridge Street	B2	Leadworks Lane	B3	Stanley Street	B1
Brook Street	A2	Lightfoot Street	A3	Station Road	A3
Canal Street	A1	Louise Street	A1	Steam Mill Street	B3
Castle Drive	C1	Love Street	B2	Talbot Street	A2
Charles Street	A2	Lower Bridge Street	C2	The Bars	B3
Cheyney Road	A1	Lower Park Road	C3	The Groves	C2
Chichester Street	A1	Mill Street	B3	Trafford Street	A2
City Road	B3	Milton Street	A2	Union Street	B2
City Walls Road	B1	Newgate Street	B2	Upper Northgate Street	A1
Commonhall Street	B1	Nicholas Street	B1	Vicar's Lane	B2
Cornwall Street	A2	Nicholas Street Mews	B1	Victoria Crescent	C3
Crewe Street	A3	Northern Pathway	C3	Victoria Place	B2
Cuppin Street	C1	Northgate Avenue	A2	Victoria Road	A1
Dee Hills Park	B3	Northgate Street	B1	Walker Street	A3
Dee Lane	B3	Nun's Road	C1	Walpole Street	A1
Deva Terrace	B3	Old Dee Bridge	C2	Walter Street	A2
Duke Street	C2	Pepper Street	C2	Watergate Street	B1
Eastgate Street	B2	Phillip Street	A3	Water Tower Street	B1
Edinburgh Way	C3	Prince's Avenue	A3	Weaver Street	B1
Egerton Street	A2	Princess Street	B1	White Friars	C1
Elizabeth Crescent	C3	Queen's Avenue	A3	York Street	B2
Foregate Street	B2	Queen's Drive	C3		
Forest Street	B2	Queen's Park Road	C2		
Francis Street	A3	Queen's Road	A3		
Frodsham Street	B2	Queen Street	B2		
Garden Lane	A1	Raymond Street	A1		
George Street	A2	Russel Street	B3		
Gloucester Street	A2	St. Anne Street	A2		
Grey Friars	C1	St. George's Crescent	C3		
Grosvenor Park Terrace	B3	St. John's Road	C3		

TOURIST INFORMATION ☎ 01244 402111
TOWN HALL, NORTHGATE STREET,
CHESTER, CHESHIRE, CH1 2HJ

COUNCIL OFFICE ☎ 01244 324324
THE FORUM,
CHESTER, CH1 2HS

HOSPITAL A & E ☎ 01244 365000
COUNTESS OF CHESTER HOSPITAL, HEALTH PK,
LIVERPOOL ROAD, CHESTER, CH2 1UL

WEB-SITE www.chestercc.gov.uk

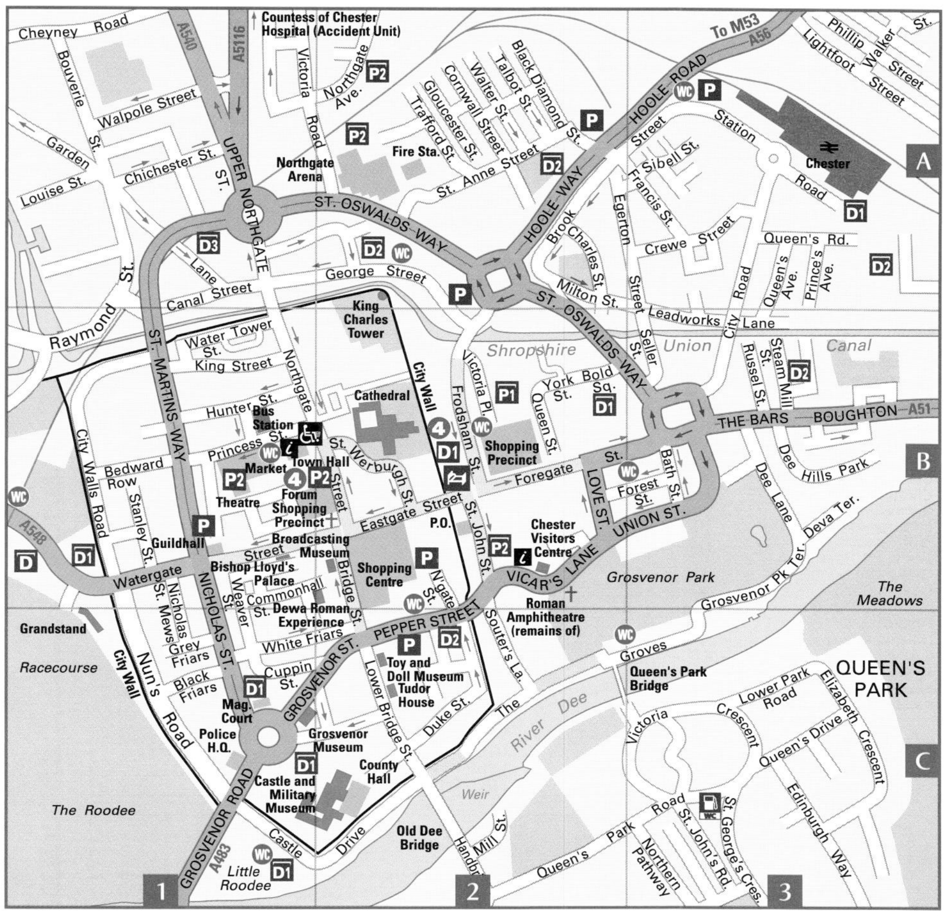

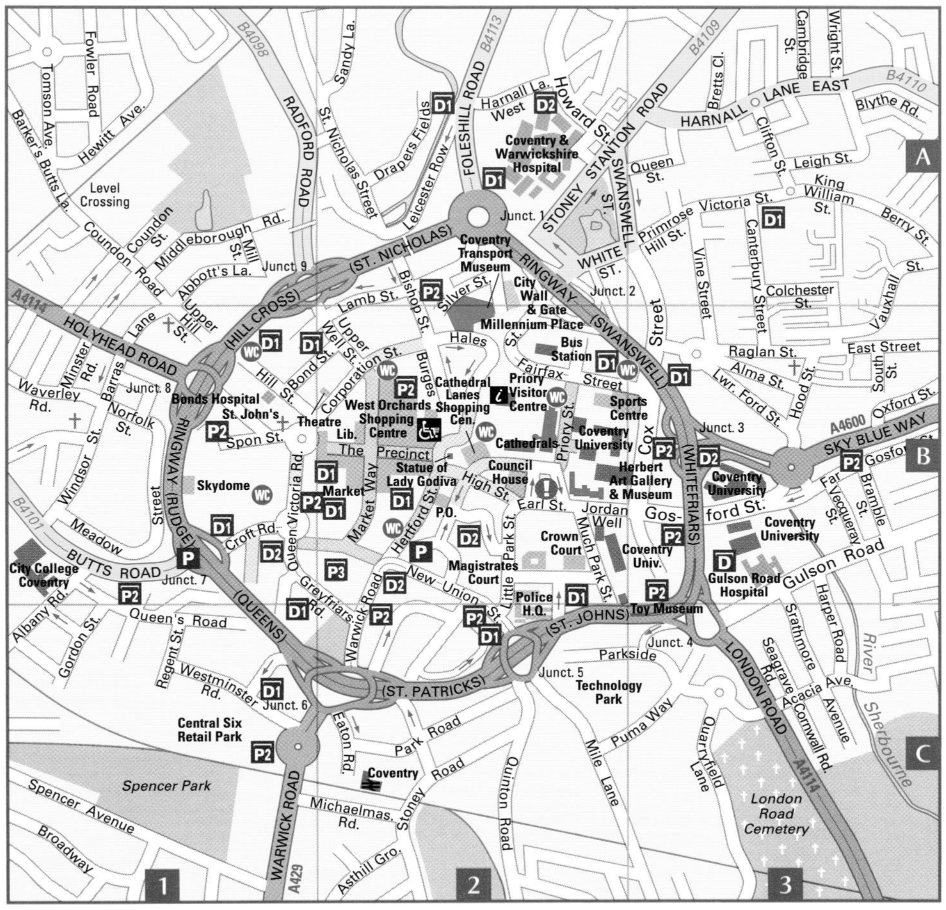

COVENTRY

0 500 yds
0 500m

INDEX TO STREET NAMES

Abbott's Lane	A1	Gulson Road	B3	Puma Way	C2	Vecqueray Street	B3
Acacia Avenue	C3	Hales Street	B2	Quarryfield Lane	C3	Victoria Street	A3
Albany Road	C1	Harnall Lane East	A3	Queen's Road	C1	Vine Street	A3
Alma Street	B3	Harnall Lane West	A2	Queen Street	A3	Warwick Road	C1
Asthill Grove	C2	Harper Road	B3	Queen Victoria Road	B1	Waveley Road	B1
Barker's Butts Lane	A1	Harper Street	B2	Quinton Road	C2	Westminster Road	C1
Barras Lane	B1	Hertford Street	B2	Radford Road	A1	White Street	A2
Berry Street	A3	Hewitt Avenue	A1	Raglan Street	B3	Windsor Street	B1
Bishop Street	A2	High Street	B2	Regent Street	C1	Wright Street	A3
Blythe Road	A3	Hill Street	B1	Ringway Hill Cross	B1		
Bond Street	B1	Holyhead Road	B1	Ringway Queens	B1		
Bramble Street	B3	Hood Street	B3	Ringway Rudge	B1		
Bretts Close	A3	Howard Street	A2	Ringway St. Johns	C2		
Broadway	C1	Jordan Well	B2	Ringway St. Nicholas	A2		
Burges	B2	King William Street	A3				
Butts Road	B1	Lamb Street	B2	Ringway St. Patricks	C2		
Cambridge Street	A3	Leicester Row	A2	Ringway Swanswell	B2		
Canterbury Street	A3	Leigh Street	A3	Ringway Whitefriars	B3		
Clifton Street	A3	Little Park Street	C2	St. Nicholas Street	A2		
Colchester Street	A3	London Road	C3	Sandy Lane	A2		
Cornwall Road	C3	Lower Ford Street	B3	Seagrave Road	C3		
Corporation Street	B2	Market Way	B2	Silver Street	A2		
Coundon Road	A1	Meadow Street	B1	Sky Blue Way	B3		
Coundon Street	A1	Michaelmas Road	C1	South Street	B3		
Cox Street	B3	Middleborough Road	A1	Spencer Avenue	C1		
Croft Road	B1			Spon Street	B1		
Drapers Fields	A2	Mile Lane	C2	Srathmore Avenue	C3		
Earl Street	B2	Mill Street	B1	Stoney Road	C2		
East Street	B3	Minster Road	A1	Stoney Stanton Road	A2		
Eaton Road	C2	Much Park Street	B2				
Fairfax Street	B2	New Union Street	B2	Swanswell Street	A2		
Far Gosford Street	B3	Norfolk Street	B1	The Precinct	B2		
Foleshill Road	A2	Oxford Street	B3	Tomson Avenue	A1		
Fowler Road	A1	Park Road	C2	Trinity Street	B2		
Gordon Street	C1	Parkside	C2	Upper Hill Street	B1		
Gosford Street	B3	Primrose Hill Street	A3	Upper Well Street	B2		
Greyfriars Road	B1	Priory Street	B2	Vauxhall Street	B3		

TOURIST INFORMATION ☎ 024 7622 7264
BAYLEY LANE, COVENTRY,
WEST MIDLANDS, CV1 5RN

COUNCIL OFFICE ☎ 024 7683 3333
COUNCIL HOUSE, EARL STREET,
COVENTRY, CV1 5RR

HOSPITAL A & E ☎ 024 7622 4055
COVENTRY & WARWICKSHIRE HOSPITAL,
STONEY STANTON ROAD, COVENTRY, CV1 4FH

WEB-SITE www.coventry.gov.uk

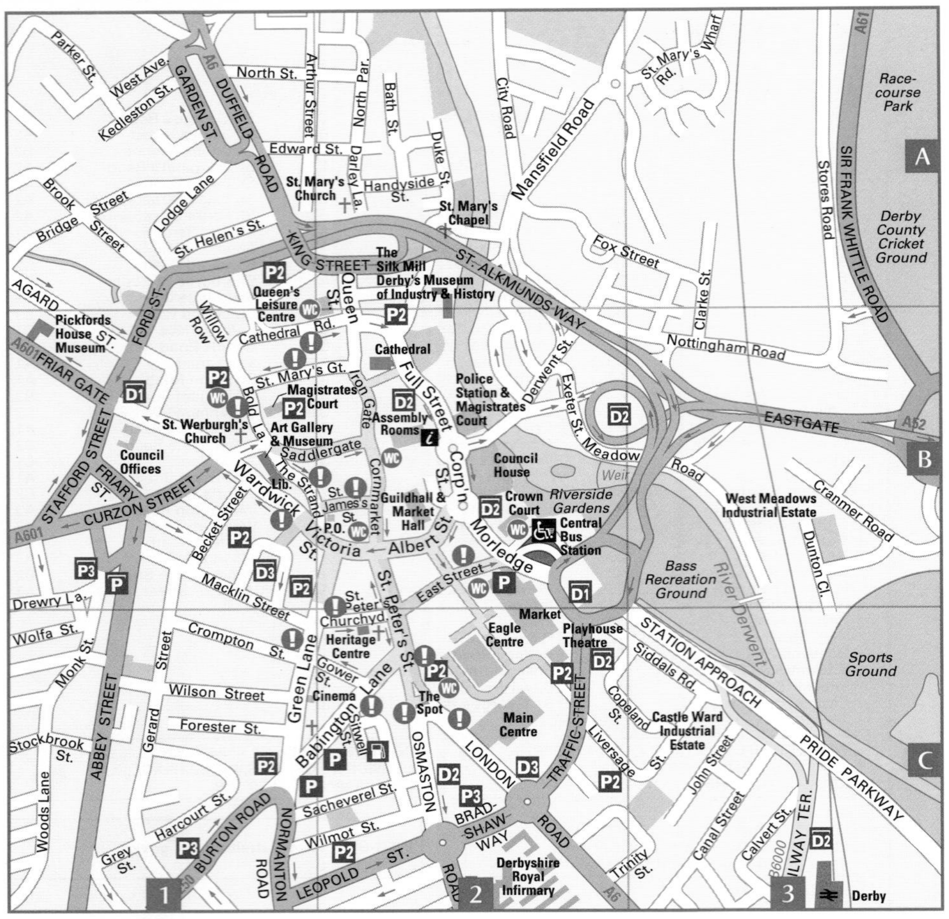

DERBY

0 300 yds
0 300m

INDEX TO STREET NAMES

Street	Grid	Street	Grid	Street	Grid
Abbey Street	C1	Friary Street	B1	St. Mary's Gate	B1
Agard Street	A1	Full Street	B2	St. Mary's Wharf Road	A3
Albert Street	B2	Garden Street	A1	St. Peter's Churchyard	C2
Arthur Street	A1	Gerard Street	C1	St. Peter's Street	B2
Babington Lane	C1	Gower Street	C2	Siddals Road	C3
Bath Street	A2	Green Lane	C1	Sir Frank Whittle Road	A3
Becket Street	B1	Grey Street	C1	Sitwell Street	C2
Bold Lane	B1	Handyside Street	A2	Stafford Street	B1
Bradshaw Way	C2	Harcourt Street	C1	Station Approach	B3
Bridge Street	A1	Iron Gate	B2	Stockbrook Street	C1
Brook Street	A1	John Street	C3	Stores Road	A3
Burton Road	C1	Kedleston Street	A1	The Strand	B1
Calvert Street	C3	King Street	A1	Traffic Street	C2
Canal Street	C3	Leopold Street	C1	Trinity Street	C2
Cathedral Road	B1	Liversage Street	C2	Victoria Street	B1
City Road	A2	Lodge Lane	A1	Wardwick	B1
Clarke Street	B3	London Road	C2	West Avenue	A1
Copeland Street	C2	Macklin Street	B1	Willow Row	B1
Cornmarket	B2	Mansfield Road	A2	Wilmot Street	C1
Corporation Street	B2	Market Place	B2	Wilson Street	C1
Cranmer Road	B3	Meadow Road	B2	Wolfa Street	C1
Crompton Street	C1	Monk Street	C1	Woods Lane	C1
Curzon Street	B1	Morledge	B2		
Darley Lane	A2	Normanton Road	C1		
Derwent Street	B2	North Parade	A2		
Drewry Lane	B1	North Street	A1		
Duffield Road	A1	Nottingham Road	B3		
Duke Street	A2	Osmaston Road	C2		
Dunton Close	B3	Parker Street	A1		
Eastgate	B3	Pride Parkway	C3		
East Street	B2	Queen Street	A2		
Edward Street	A1	Railway Terrace	C3		
Exeter Street	B2	Sacheverel Street	C1		
Ford Street	B1	Saddlergate	B2		
Forester Street	C1	St. Alkmunds Way	A2		
Fox Street	A2	St. Helen's Street	A1		
Friar Gate	B1	St. James Street	B2		

TOURIST INFORMATION ☎ 01332 255802
ASSEMBLY ROOMS, MARKET PLACE,
DERBY, DE1 3AH

COUNCIL OFFICE ☎ 01332 293111
THE COUNCIL HOUSE, CORPORATION STREET,
DERBY, DE1 2FS

HOSPITAL A & E ☎ 01332 347141
DERBYSHIRE ROYAL INFIRMARY,
LONDON ROAD, DERBY, DE1 2QY

WEB-SITE www.derby.gov.uk

DOVER

0 500 yds
0 500m

INDEX TO STREET NAMES

Street	Grid	Street	Grid
Astor Avenue	B1	Longfield Road	B1
Barton Road	A1	Maison Dieu Road	B2
Beaconsfield Avenue	A1	Marine Parade	B2
Beaconsfield Road	A1	Mayfield Avenue	A1
Belgrave Road	B1	Military Road	B2
Biggin Street	B2	Mount Road	C1
Bridge Street	B2	Napier Road	A1
Brookfield Avenue	A1	Noah's Ark Road	B1
Buckland Avenue	A1	Northbourne Avenue	B1
Cannon Street	B2	North Military Road	B1
Canons Gate Road	B2	Old Charlton Road	A2
Castle Avenue	A2	Old Folkestone Road	C1
Castle Hill Road	B2	Oswald Road	A1
Castle Street	B2	Park Avenue	A2
Cherry Tree Avenue	A1	Pencester Road	B2
Citadel Road	C1	Priory Hill	B1
Clarendon Place	B1	St. Radigund's Road	A1
Clarendon Street	B1	Salisbury Road	A2
Connaught Road	A2	Snargate Street	C2
Coombe Valley Road	B1	South Road	B1
Dover Road	A3	Stanhope Road	A2
Durham Hill	B2	The Viaduct	C2
Eaton Road	B1	Tower Street	B1
Edred Road	B1	Townwall Street	B2
Elms Vale Road	B1	Union Street	C2
Folkestone Road	B1	Upper Road	A3
Frith Road	A2	York Street	B2
Godwyne Road	B2		
Green Lane	A1		
Guston Road	A2		
Heathfield Avenue	A1		
High Street	B2		
Hillside Road	A1		
Jubilee Way	A3		
Ladywell	B2		
Limekiln Street	C2		
London Road	A1		

TOURIST INFORMATION ☎ 01304 205108
OLD TOWN GAOL, BIGGIN STREET,
DOVER, CT16 1DL

COUNCIL OFFICE ☎ 01304 821199
WHITE CLIFFS BUSINESS PARK,
DOVER, CT16 3PJ

HOSPITAL A & E ☎ 01227 766877
KENT & CANTERBURY HOSPITAL,
ETHELBERT ROAD, CANTERBURY, CT1 3NG

WEB-SITE www.dover.gov.uk

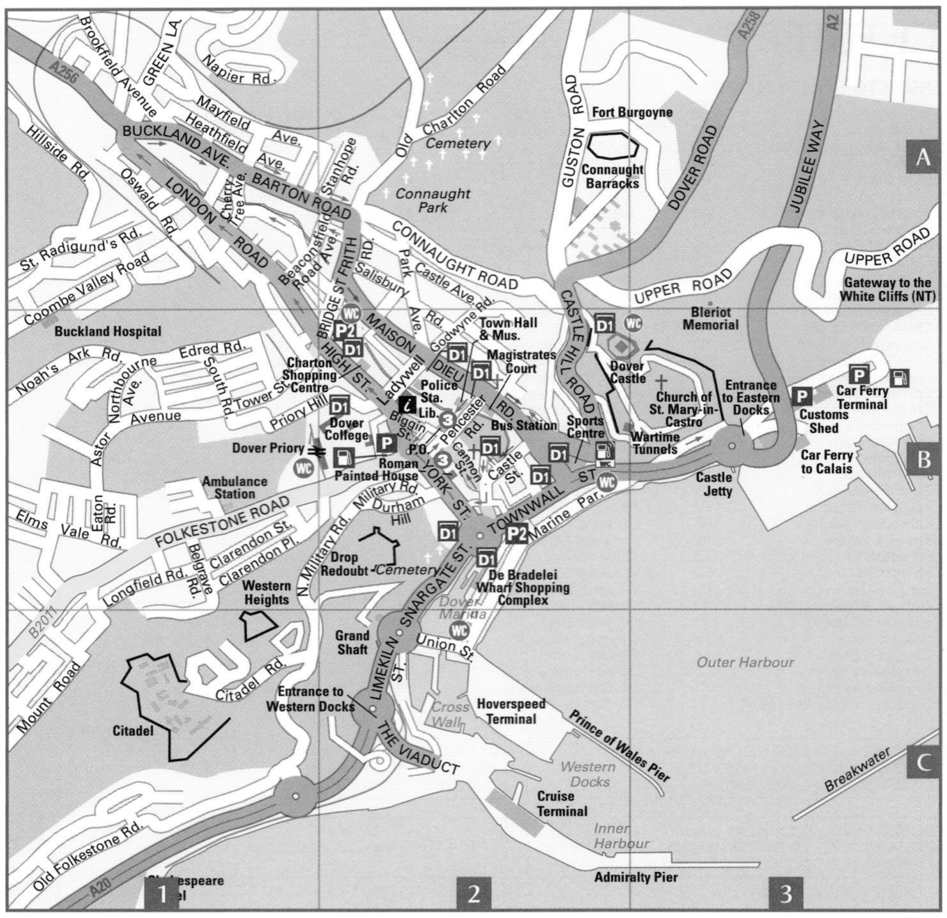

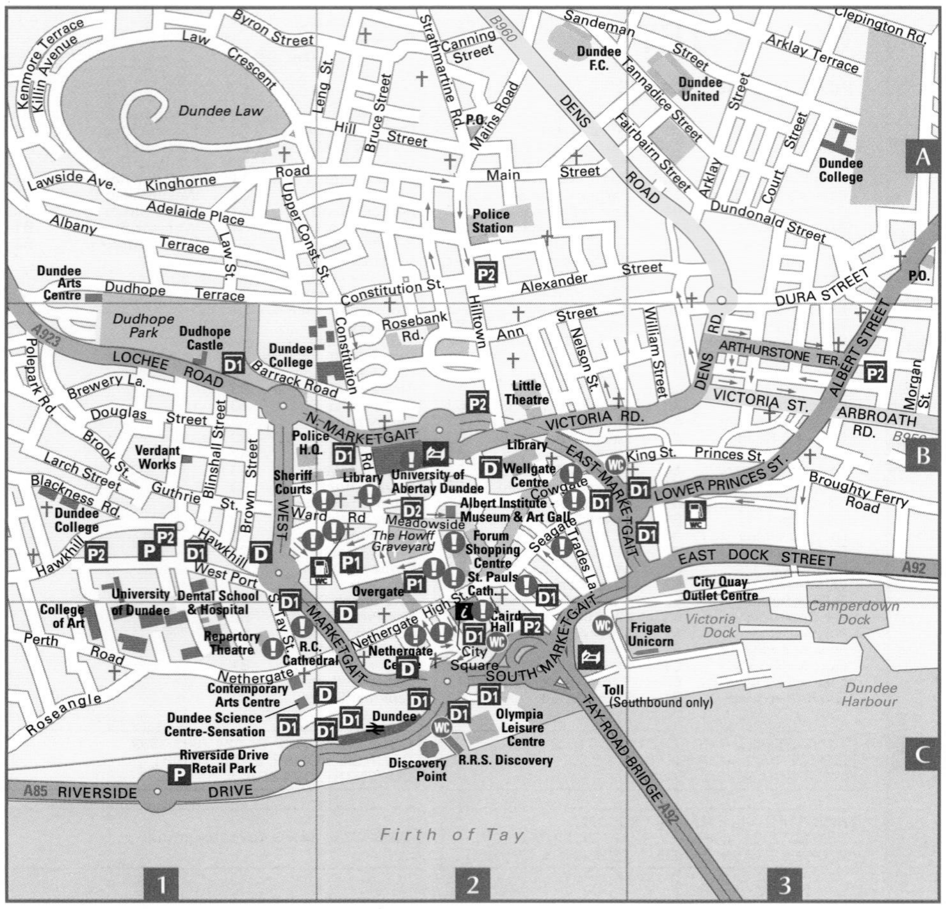

DUNDEE

0 400 yds
0 400m

INDEX TO STREET NAMES

Street	Grid	Street	Grid	Street	Grid
Adelaide Place	A1	High Street	C2	Victoria Street	B3
Albany Terrace	A1	Hill Street	A2	Ward Road	B1
Albert Street	B3	Hilltown	A2	West Marketgait	B1
Alexander Street	A2	Kenmore Terrace	A1	West Port	B1
Ann Street	B2	Killin Avenue	A1	William Street	B3
Arbroath Road	B3	Kinghorne Road	A1		
Arklay Street	A3	King Street	B2		
Arklay Terrace	A3	Larch Street	B1		
Arthurstone Terrace	B3	Law Crescent	A1		
Barrack Road	B1	Lawside Avenue	A1		
Blackness Road	B1	Law Street	A1		
Blinshall Street	B1	Leng Street	A1		
Brewery Lane	B1	Lochee Road	B1		
Brook Street	B1	Lower Princes Street	B3		
Broughty Ferry Road	B3	Mains Road	A2		
Brown Street	B1	Main Street	A2		
Bruce Street	A1	Meadowside	B2		
Byron Street	A1	Morgan Street	B3		
Canning Street	A2	Nelson Street	B2		
City Square	C2	Nethergate	C1		
Clepington Road	A3	North Marketgait	B1		
Constitution Road	B2	Perth Road	C1		
Constitution Street	A2	Polepark Road	B1		
Court Street	A3	Princes Street	B3		
Cowgate Street	B2	Riverside Drive	C1		
Dens Road	A2	Roseangle	C1		
Douglas Street	B1	Rosebank Road	B2		
Dudhope Street	B1	Seagate	B2		
Dudhope Terrace	A1	South Marketgait	C2		
Dundonald Street	A3	South Tay Street	C1		
Dura Street	B3	Strathmartine Road	A2		
East Dock Street	B3	Tannadice Street	A2		
East Marketgait	B2	Tay Road Bridge	C2		
Fairbairn Street	A2	Trades Lane	B2		
Guthrie Street	B1	Upper Constitution Street	A1		
Hawkhill	B1	Victoria Road	B2		

TOURIST INFORMATION ☎ 01382 527527
21 CASTLE STREET,
DUNDEE, DD1 3AA

COUNCIL OFFICE ☎ 01382 434800
CITY CHAMBERS, 21 CITY SQUARE,
DUNDEE, DD1 3BD

HOSPITAL A & E ☎ 01382 660111
NINEWELLS HOSPITAL, NINEWELLS ROAD,
DUNDEE, DD1 9SY

WEB-SITE www.dundeecity.gov.uk

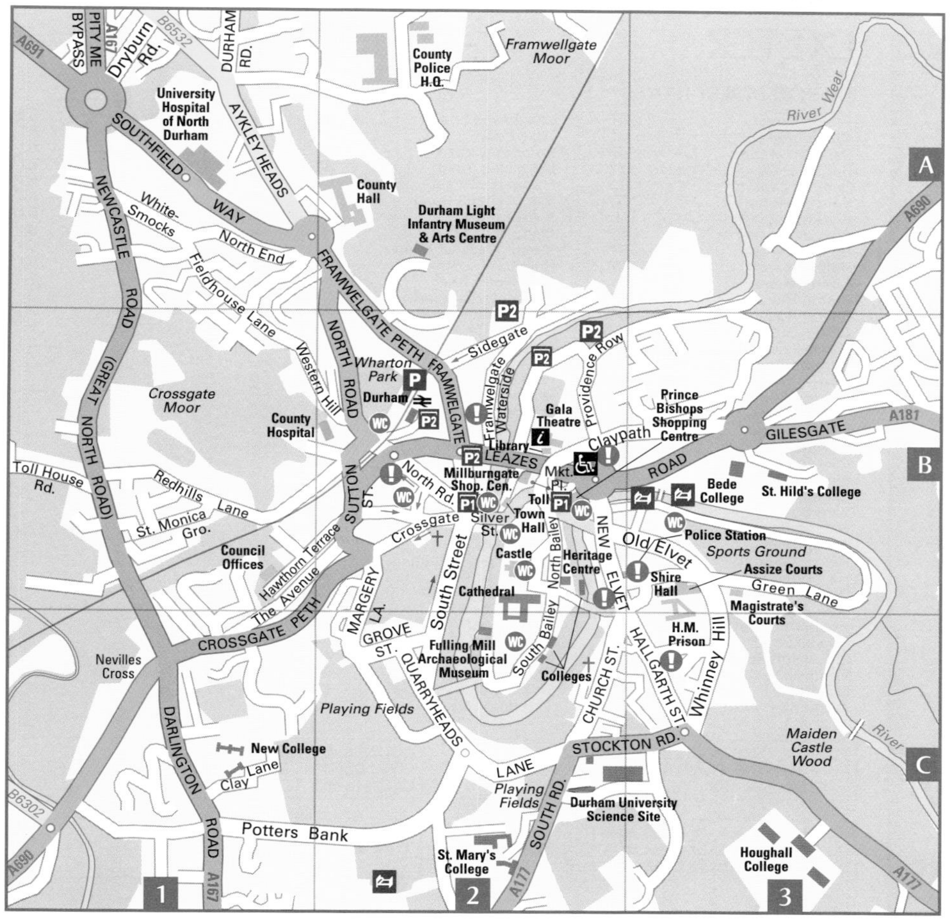

DURHAM

0 400 yds
0 400m

INDEX TO STREET NAMES

Aykley Heads	A1	South Bailey	C2
Church Street	C2	South Road	C2
Clay Lane	C1	South Street	C2
Claypath	B2	Southfield Way	A1
Crossgate	B2	Stockton Road	C2
Crossgate Peth	C1	Sutton Street	B2
Darlington Road	C1	The Avenue	C1
Dryburn Road	A1	Toll House Road	B1
Durham Road	A1	Western Hill	B1
Fieldhouse Lane	A1	Whinney Hill	C3
Framwelgate	B2	Whitesmocks	A1
Framwelgate Peth	A2		
Framwelgate Waterside	B2		
Gilesgate	B3		
Great North Road	A1		
Green Lane	B3		
Grove Street	C2		
Hallgarth Street	C3		
Hawthorn Terrace	B1		
Leazes Road	B2		
Margery Lane	C2		
Market Place	B2		
Millburngate Bridge	B2		
Newcastle Road	A1		
New Elvet	B2		
North Bailey	B2		
North End	A1		
North Road	B2		
Old Elvet	B3		
Pity Me Bypass	A1		
Potters Bank	C1		
Quarryheads Lane	C2		
Providence Row	B2		
Redhills Lane	B1		
St. Monica Grove	B1		
Sidegate	B2		
Silver Street	B2		

TOURIST INFORMATION ☎ 0191 384 3720
MARKET PLACE, DURHAM,
COUNTY DURHAM, DH1 3NJ

COUNCIL OFFICE ☎ 0191 386 4567
COUNTY HALL,
DURHAM, DH1 5UB

HOSPITAL A & E ☎ 0191 333 2333
DRYBURN HOSPITAL, NORTH ROAD,
DURHAM, DH1 5TW

WEB-SITE www.durhamcity.gov.uk

EASTBOURNE

0 200 yds
0 200m

INDEX TO STREET NAMES

Arlington Road	B1	Hartington Place	B3	Watts Lane	A1
Arundel Road	A2	High Street	A1	Whitley Road	A1
Ashford Road	B2/B3	Hyde Gardens	B2	Willingdon Road	A1
Avondale Road	A3	King Edward's Parade	C2	Winchcombe Road	A3
Bedfordwell Road	A2	Langney Road	B3		
Belmore Road	A3	Lewes Road	A2		
Blackwater Road	C2	Marine Parade	B3		
Borough Lane	A1	Mark Lane	B2		
Bourne Street	B3	Meads Road	C1		
Carew Road	A1/A2	Melbourne Road	A3		
Carlisle Road	C1	Mill Gap Road	A1		
Cavendish Avenue	A3	Mill Road	A1		
Cavendish Place	B3	Moat Croft Road	A1		
College Road	C2	Moy Avenue	A3		
Commercial Road	B2	Ratton Road	A1		
Compton Place Road	B1	Royal Parade	B3		
Compton Street	C2	Saffrons Park	C1		
Cornfield Terrace	B2	Saffrons Road	B1		
Denton Road	C1	St. Anne's Road	A1		
Devonshire Place	B2	St. Leonard's Road	B2		
Dittons Road	B1	Seaside	B3		
Dursley Road	B3	Seaside Road	B3		
Enys Road	A2	Selwyn Road	A1		
Eversfield Road	A2	Silverdale Road	C2		
Fairfield Road	C1	South Street	B2		
Firle Road	A3	Southfields Road	B1		
Furness Road	C2	Station Parade	B2		
Gaudick Road	C1	Susan's Road	B3		
Gilbert Road	A3	Sydney Road	B3		
Gildredge Road	B2	Terminus Road	B2		
Gorringe Road	A2	The Avenue	B2		
Grand Parade	C3	The Goffs	A1		
Grange Road	C2	Trinity Trees	B3		
Grassington Road	C2	Upper Avenue	A2		
Grove Road	B2	Upperton Lane	B2		
Hartfield Road	A2	Upperton Road	A1		

TOURIST INFORMATION ☎ 0906 711 2212
3 CORNFIELD ROAD,
EASTBOURNE, BN21 4QL

COUNCIL OFFICE ☎ 01323 410000
EASTBOURNE BOROUGH COUNCIL, TOWN HALL,
GROVE ROAD, EASTBOURNE BN21 4UG,

HOSPITAL A & E ☎ 01323 417400
EASTBOURNE DISTRICT GENERAL HOSPITAL,
KING'S DRIVE, EASTBOURNE, BN21 2UD

WEB-SITE www.eastbourne.gov.uk

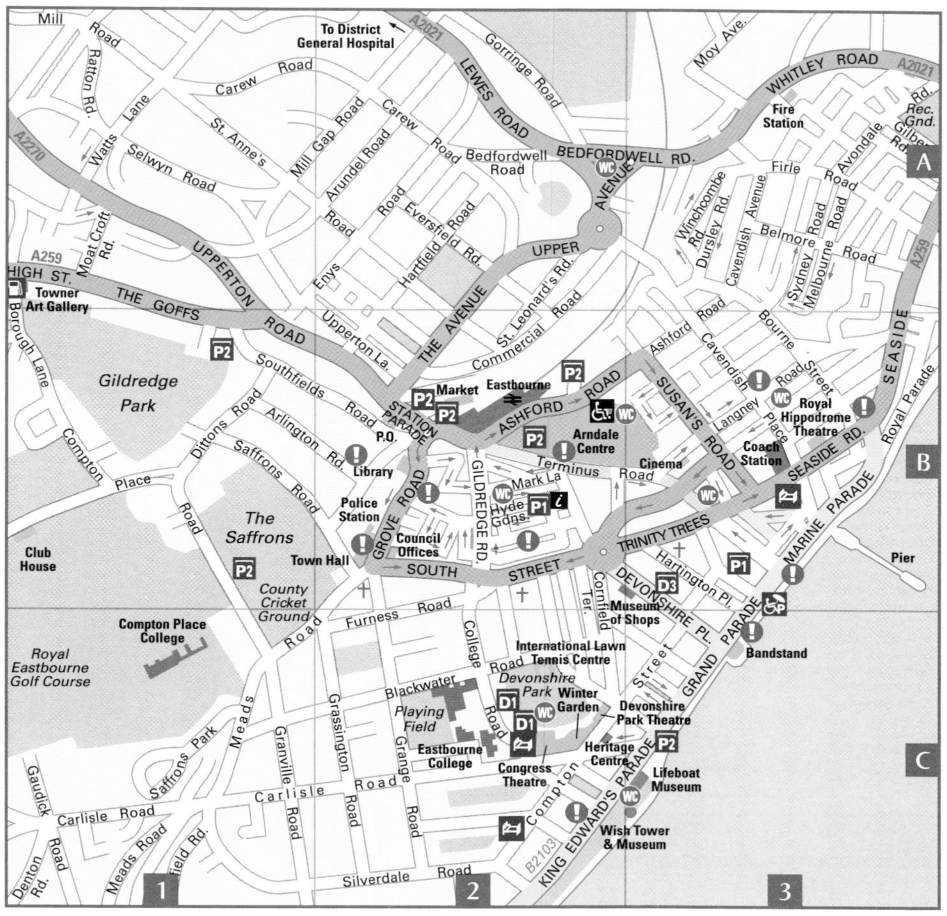

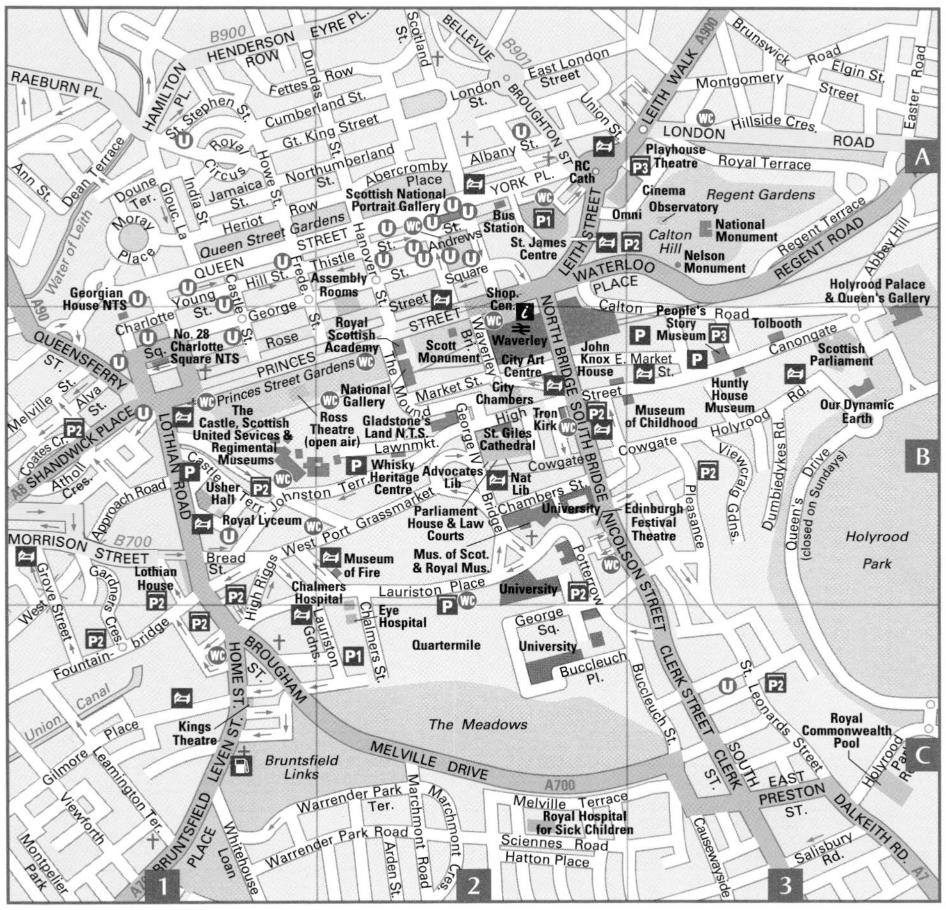

EDINBURGH

0 400 yds
0 400m

INDEX TO STREET NAMES

Abbey Hill	A3	Eyre Place	A2	London Street	A2	Thistle Street	A2
Abercromby Place	A2	Fettes Row	A1	Lothian Road	B1	Union Street	A2
Albany Street	A2	Fountainbridge	C1	Marchmont Road	C2	Viewforth	C1
Alva Street	B1	Frederick Street	A2	Marchmont Crescent	C2	Viewcraig Gardens	B3
Ann Street	A1	Gardners Crescent	B1	Market Street	B2	Warrender Park Terrace	C1
Arden Street	C2	George IV Bridge	B2	Melville Drive	C2	Warrender Park Road	C1
Atholl Crescent	B1	George Square	C2	Melville Street	B1	Waterloo Place	A2
Bellevue	A2	George Street	B1	Melville Terrace	C2	Waverley Bridge	B2
Bread Street	B1	Gilmore Place	C1	Montgomery Street	A3	West Approach Road	C1
Brougham Street	C1	Gloucester Lane	A1	Montpelier Park	C1	West Port	B1
Broughton Street	A2	Grassmarket	B2	Moray Place	A1	Whitehouse Loan	C1
Brunswick Road	A3	Great King Street	A1	Morrison Street	B1	Young Street	A1
Bruntsfield Place	C1	Grove Street	B1	Nicolson Street	B2	York Place	A2
Buccleuch Place	C2	Hamilton Place	A1	North Bridge	A2		
Buccleuch Street	C3	Hanover Street	A2	Northumberland Street	A1		
Calton Road	B3	Hatton Place	C2				
Canongate	B3	Henderson Row	A1	Pleasance	B3		
Castle Street	A1	Heriot Row	A1	Potterrow	B2		
Castle Terrace	B1	High Riggs	B1	Princes Street	B1		
Causewayside	C3	High Street	B2	Queen's Drive	B3		
Chalmers Street	C2	Hill Street	A1	Queensferry Street	B1		
Chambers Street	B2	Hillside Crescent	A3	Queen Street	A1		
Charlotte Square	B1	Holyrood Park Road	C3	Raeburn Place	A1		
Clerk Street	C3	Holyrood Road	B3	Regent Road	A3		
Coates Crescent	B1	Home Street	C1	Regent Terrace	A3		
Cowgate	B2	Howe Street	A1	Rose Street	B1		
Cumberland Street	A1	India Street	A1	Royal Circus	A1		
Dalkeith Road	C3	Jamaica Street	A1	Royal Terrace	A3		
Dean Terrace	A1	Johnston Terrace	B1	St. Andrew's Square	A2		
Doune Terrace	A1	Lauriston Gardens	C2	St. Leonards Street	C3		
Dumbiedykes Road	B3	Lauriston Place	B2	St. Stephen Street	A1		
Dundas Street	A1	Lawnmarket	B2	Salisbury Road	C3		
Easter Road	A3	Leamington Terrace	C1	Sciennes Road	C2		
East London Street	A2	Leith Street	A2	Scotland Street	A2		
East Market Street	B2	Leith Walk	A3	Shandwick Place	B1		
East Preston Street	C3	Leven Street	C1	South Bridge	B2		
Elgin Street	A3	London Road	A3	The Mound	B2		

TOURIST INFORMATION ☎ 0131 473 3800
INFORMATION CENTRE, 3 PRINCES STREET,
EDINBURGH, EH2 2QP

COUNCIL OFFICE ☎ 0131 200 2000
CITY CHAMBERS, HIGH STREET,
EDINBURGH, EH1 1YJ

HOSPITAL A & E ☎ 0131 536 1000
ROYAL INFIRMARY OF EDINBURGH,
1 LAURISTON PLACE, EDINBURGH, EH3 9YW

WEB-SITE www.edinburgh.gov.uk

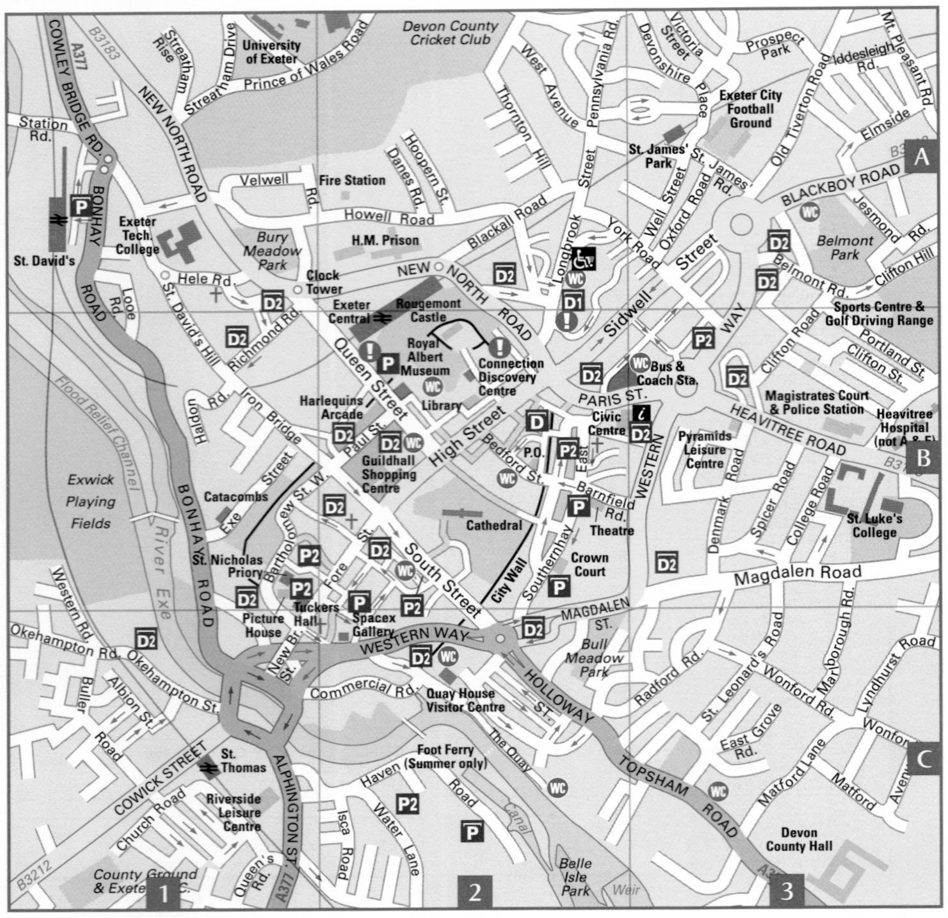

EXETER

0 400 yds
0 400m

INDEX TO STREET NAMES

Albion Street	C1
Alphington Street	C1
Barnfield Road	B2
Bartholomew Street West	B1
Bedford Street	B2
Belmont Road	A3
Blackboy Road	A3
Blackall Road	A2
Bonhay Road	B1
Buller Road	C1
Church Road	C1
Clifton Hill	A3
Clifton Road	B3
Clifton Street	B3
College Road	B3
Commercial Road	C2
Cowick Street	C1
Cowley Bridge Road	A1
Danes Road	A2
Denmark Road	B3
Devonshire Place	A3
East Grove Road	C3
Elmside	A3
Exe Street	B1
Fore Street	B2
Haldon Road	B1
Haven Road	C2
Heavitree Road	B3
Hele Road	A1
High Street	B2
Holloway Street	C2
Hoopern Street	A2
Howell Road	A2
Iddesleigh Road	A3
Iron Bridge	B1
Isca Road	C2
Jesmond Road	A3
Longbrook Street	A2
Looe Road	A1
Lyndhurst Road	C3
Magdalen Road	B3
Magdalen Street	C2
Marlborough Road	C3
Matford Avenue	C3
Matford Lane	C3
Mount Pleasant Road	A3
New Bridge Street	C1
New North Road	A1/A2
Okehampton Road	C1
Okehampton Street	C1
Old Tiverton Road	A3
Oxford Road	A3
Paris Street	B2
Paul Street	B2
Pennsylvania Road	A2
Portland Street	B3
Prince of Wales Road	A1
Prospect Park	A3
Queen's Road	C1
Queen Street	B2
Radford Road	C3
Richmond Road	B1
St. David's Hill	A1
St. James' Road	A3
St. Leonard's Road	C3
Sidwell Street	B2
Southernhay East	B2
South Street	B2
Spicer Road	B3
Station Road	A1
Streatham Drive	A1
Streatham Rise	A1
The Quay	C2
Thornton Hill	A2
Topsham Road	C2
Velwell Road	A1
Victoria Street	A3
Water Lane	C2
Well Street	A3
West Avenue	A2
Western Road	B1
Western Way	B2
Wonford Road	C3
York Road	A2

TOURIST INFORMATION ☎ 01392 265700
CIVIC CENTRE, PARIS STREET,
EXETER, EX1 1RP

COUNCIL OFFICE ☎ 01392 277888
CIVIC CENTRE, PARIS STREET,
EXETER, EX1 1JN

HOSPITAL A & E ☎ 01392 411611
ROYAL DEVON & EXETER HOSPITAL (WONFORD),
BARRACK ROAD, EXETER, EX2 5DW

WEB-SITE www.exeter.gov.uk

FOLKESTONE

0 200 yds
0 200m

INDEX TO STREET NAMES

Alder Road	B2
Archer Road	B3
Bathurst Road	B1
Beatty Road	A3
Black Bull Road	B2
Bournemouth Road	B2
Bouverie Road West	C1
Bradstone Road	B2
Broadfield Road	B1
Broadmead Road	B2
Brockman Road	B2
Canterbury Road	A3
Castle Hill Avenue	C2
Cheriton Gardens	C2
Cheriton Road	B1/B2
Cherry Garden Avenue	A1
Christ Church Road	C2
Churchill Avenue	A2
Clifton Crescent	C1
Coniston Road	A1
Coolinge Road	B2
Cornwallis Avenue	B1
Dawson Road	B2
Dixwell Road	C1
Dolphins Road	A2
Dover Hill	A3
Dover Road	A3
Downs Road	A2
Earles Avenue	C1
Foord Road	B2
Godwyn Road	C1
Grimston Avenue	C1
Grimston Gardens	C1
Guildhall Street	B2
Guildhall Street North	B2
Harbour Way	B3
High Street	C3
Hill Road	A3
Ivy Way	A3
Joyes Road	A3
Linden Crescent	B2
Links Way	A1
Lower Sandgate Road	C1
Lucy Avenue	A1
Manor Road	C2
Marine Parade	C2
Marshall Street	A3
Mead Road	B2
Park Farm Road	A2
Pavilion Road	B2
Radnor Bridge Road	B3
Radnor Park Avenue	B1
Radnor Park Road	B2
Radnor Park West	B1
Sandgate Hill	C1
Sandgate Road	C2
Shorncliffe Road	B1
Sidney Street	B3
The Leas	C2
The Stade	C3
The Tram Road	B3
Tontine Street	B3
Turketel Road	C1
Tyson Road	A3
Wear Bay Crescent	B3
Wear Bay Road	A3
Westbourne Gardens	C1
Wingate Road	A2
Wood Avenue	A3
Wilton Road	B1

TOURIST INFORMATION ☎ 01303 258594
HARBOUR STREET, FOLKESTONE,
KENT, CT20 1QN

COUNCIL OFFICE ☎ 01303 850388
CIVIC CENTRE, CASTLE HILL AVENUE,
FOLKESTONE, CT20 2QY

HOSPITAL A & E ☎ 01233 633331
WILLIAM HARVEY HOSPITAL, KENNINGTON RD,
WILLESBOROUGH, ASHFORD, TN24 OLZ

WEB-SITE www.shepway.gov.uk

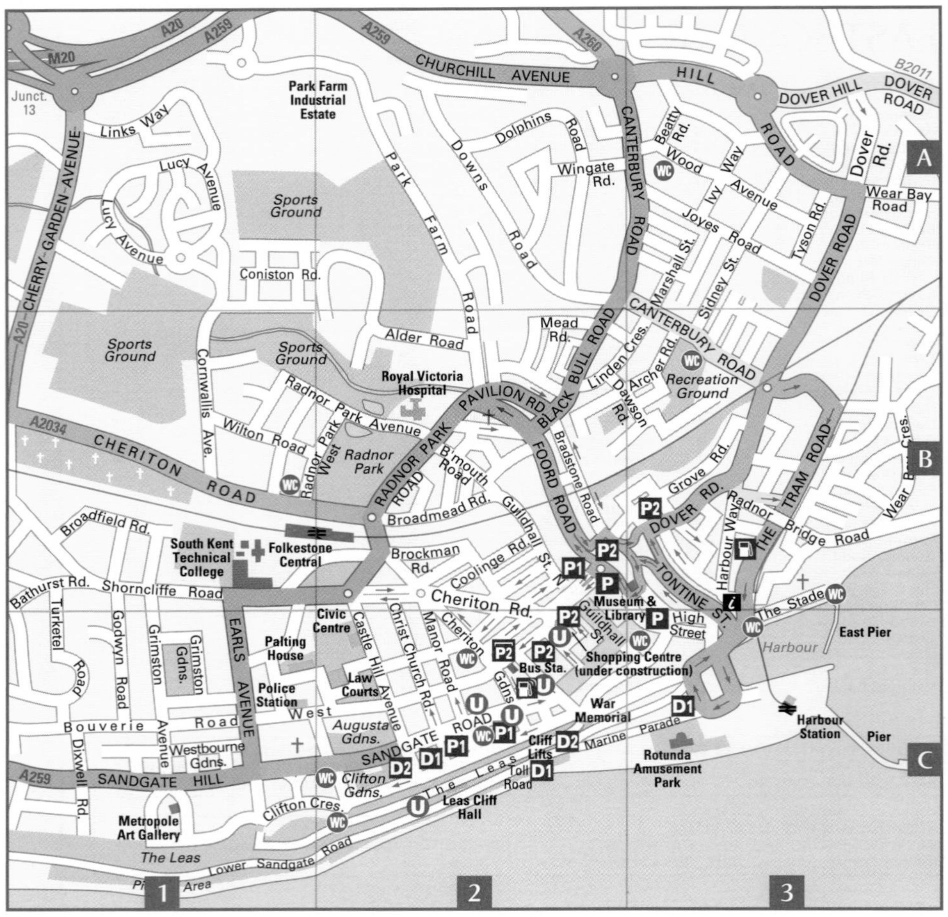

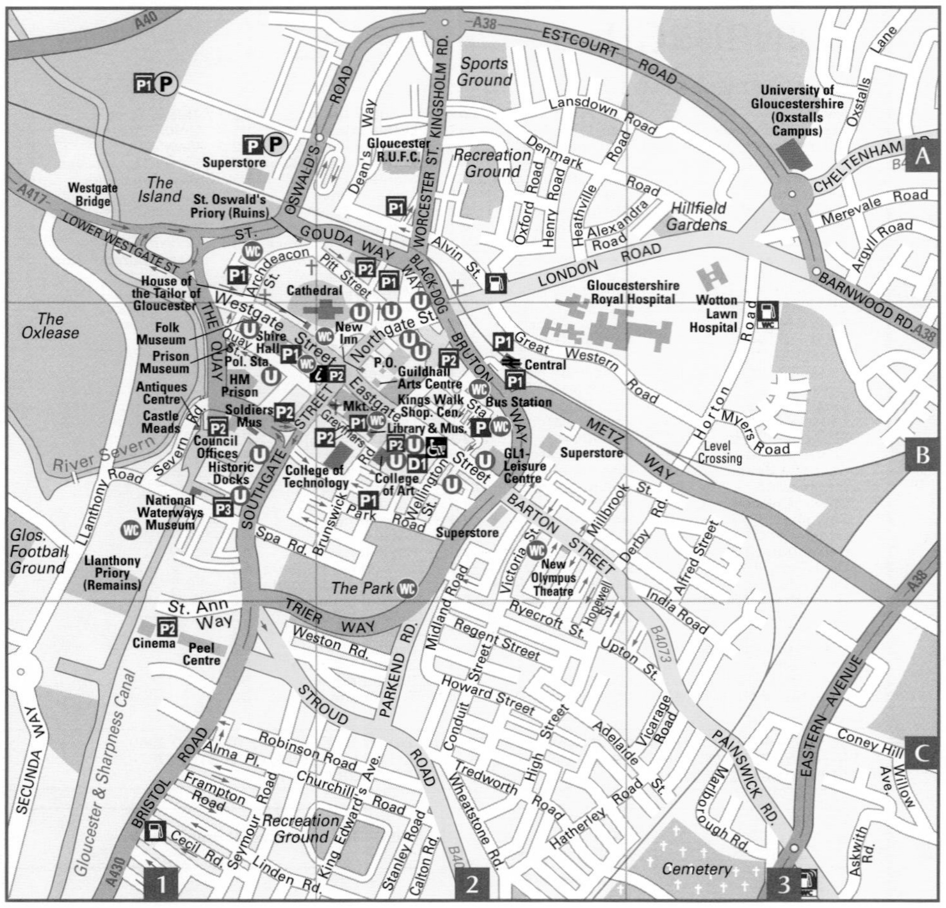

GLOUCESTER

0 500 yds
0 500m

INDEX TO STREET NAMES

Adelaide Street	C2
Alexandra Road	A2
Alfred Street	B3
Alma Place	C1
Alvin Street	A2
Archdeacon Street	A1
Argyll Road	A3
Askwith Road	C3
Barnwood Road	A3
Barton Street	B2
Black Dog Way	A2
Bristol Road	C1
Brunswick Road	B2
Bruton Way	B2
Calton Road	C2
Cecil Road	C1
Cheltenham Road	A3
Churchill Road	C1
Conduit Street	C2
Coney Hill Road	C3
Dean's Way	A2
Denmark Road	A2
Derby Road	B2
Estcourt Road	A2
Eastern Avenue	C3
Eastgate Street	B2
Frampton Road	C1
Gouda Way	A1
Great Western Road	B2
Greyfriars	B2
Hatherley Road	C2
Heathville Road	A2
Henry Road	A2
High Street	C2
Hopewell Street	C2
Horton Road	B3
Howard Street	C2
India Road	B3
King Edward's Avenue	C2
Kingsholm Road	A2
Lansdown Road	A2
Linden Road	C1
Llanthony Road	B1
London Road	A2
Lower Westgate Street	A1
Marlborough Road	C3
Merevale Road	A3
Metz Way	B2
Midland Road	C2
Millbrook Street	B2
Myers Road	B3
Northgate Street	B2
Oxford Road	A2
Oxstalls Lane	A3
Painswick Road	C3
Park Road	B2
Parkend Road	C2
Pitt Street	A2
Quay Street	B1
Regent Street	C2
Robinson Road	C1
Ryecroft Street	C2
St. Ann Way	C1
St. Oswald's Road	A1
Secunda Way	C1
Severn Road	B1
Seymour Road	C1
Southgate Street	B1
Spa Road	B1
Stanley Road	C2
Station Road	B2
Stroud Road	C1
The Quay	B1
Tredworth Road	C2
Trier Way	C1
Upton Street	C2
Vicarage Road	C3
Victoria Street	B2
Wellington Street	B2
Westgate Street	A1
Weston Road	C1
Wheatstone Road	C2
Willow Avenue	C3
Worcester Street	A2

TOURIST INFORMATION ☎ 01452 396572
28 SOUTHGATE STREET, GLOUCESTER,
GLOUCESTERSHIRE, GL1 2DP

COUNCIL OFFICE ☎ 01452 522232
COUNCIL OFFICES, NORTH WAREHOUSE,
THE DOCKS, GLOUCESTER, GL1 2EP

HOSPITAL A & E ☎ 01452 528555
GLOUCESTER ROYAL HOSPITAL
GREAT WESTERN RD, GLOUCESTER, GL1 3NN

WEB-SITE www.gloucester.gov.uk

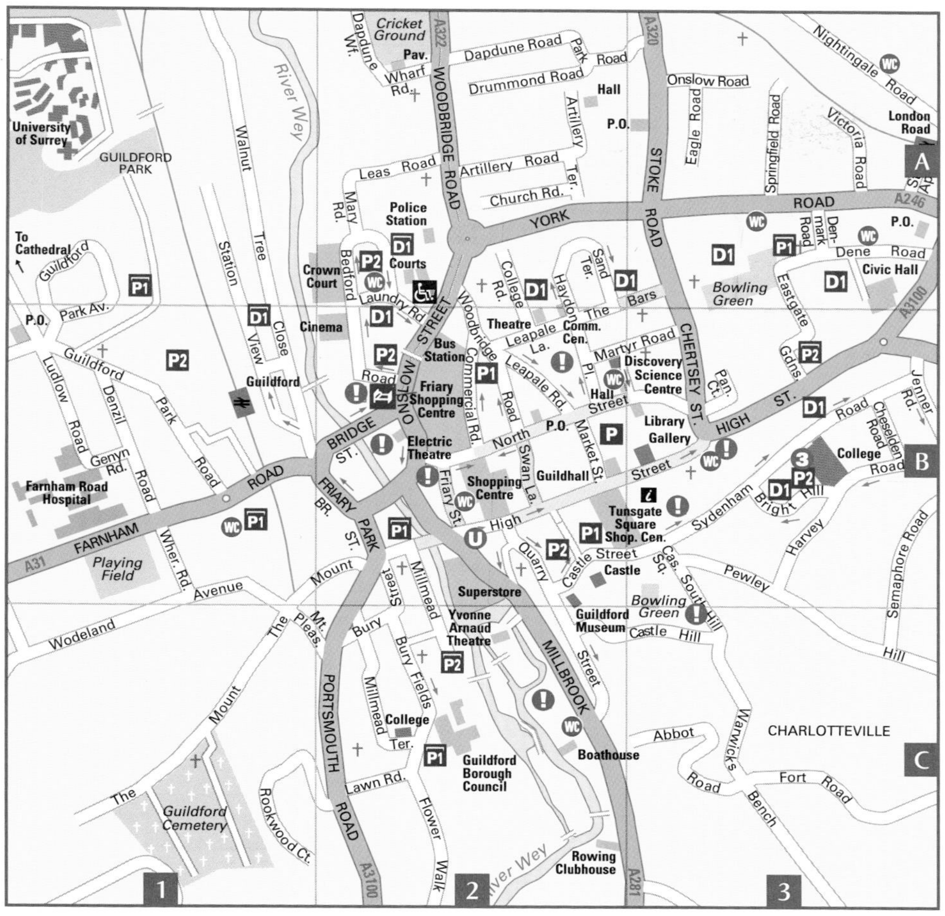

GUILDFORD

0 200 yds
0 200m

INDEX TO STREET NAMES

Abbot Road	C3
Artillery Road	A2
Artillery Terrace	A2
Bedford Road	A2
Bridge Street	B2
Bright Hill	B3
Bury Fields	C2
Bury Street	C2
Castle Hill	C3
Castle Square	B3
Castle Street	B2
Chertsey Street	A3
Cheselden Road	B3
Commercial Road	B2
Dapdune Road	A2
Dapdune Wharf	A2
Dene Road	A3
Denmark Road	A3
Denzil Road	B1
Drummond Road	A2
Eagle Road	A3
Eastgate Gardens	A3
Farnham Road	B1
Flower Walk	C2
Fort Road	C3
Friary Bridge	B2
Friary Street	B2
Genyn Road	B1
Guildford Park Avenue	A1
Guildford Park Road	B1
Harvey Road	B3
Haydon Place	A2
High Street	B2/B3
Laundry Road	A2
Lawn Road	C2
Leap Lane	B2
Leas Road	A2
Ludlow Road	B1
Market Street	B2
Martyr Road	B2
Mary Road	A2
Millbrook	C2
Millmead	B2
Millmead Terrace	C2
Mount Pleasant	C1
Nightingale Road	A3
North Street	B2
Onslow Road	A3
Onslow Street	B2
Pannells Court	B3
Park Road	A2
Park Street	B2
Pewley Hill	B3
Portsmouth Road	C2
Quarry Street	B2
Rookwood Court	C1
Sand Terrace	A2
Semaphore Road	C3
South Hill	B3
Springfield Road	A3
Station Approach	A3
Station View	A1
Stoke Road	A3
Swan Lane	B2
Sydenham Road	B3
The Bars	B2
The Mount	C1
Victoria Road	A3
Walnut Tree Close	A1
Warwicks	C3
Wharf Road	A2
Wherwell Road	B1
Wodeland Avenue	C1
Woodbridge Road	A2
York Road	A2

TOURIST INFORMATION ☎ 01483 444333
14 TUNSGATE,
GUILDFORD, GU1 3QT

COUNCIL OFFICE ☎ 01483 505050
GUILDFORD BOROUGH COUNCIL, MILLMEAD HOUSE, MILLMEAD, GUILDFORD, GU2 4BB

HOSPITAL A & E ☎ 01483 571122
ROYAL SURREY COUNTY HOSPITAL, EGERTON ROAD, GUILDFORD, GU2 7XX

WEB-SITE www.guildford.gov.uk

HARROGATE

0 150 yds
0 150m

INDEX TO STREET NAMES

Ainsty Road	A3
Albert Street	B2
Alexandra Road	A2
Arthington Avenue	B2
Beech Grove	C1
Belford Road	B2
Bower Road	A2
Bower Street	B2
Cambridge Street	B2
Cavendish Avenue	C3
Chelmsford Road	B2
Cheltenham Mount	A2
Chudleigh Road	A3
Clarence Drive	B1
Claro Road	A3
Cold Bath Road	C1
Commercial Street	A2
Coppice Drive	A1
Cornwall Road	B1
Crescent Gardens	B1
Dragon Avenue	A2
Dragon Parade	A2
Dragon Road	A2
Duchy Road	A1
East Parade	B2
East Park Road	B2
Franklin Mount	A2
Franklin Road	A2
Gascoigne Crescent	A3
Glebe Avenue	B1
Glebe Road	C1
Grove Park Terrace	A3
Grove Road	A2
Harcourt Drive	B3
Harcourt Road	A3
Heywood Road	C1
Hollins Road	A1
Homestead Road	B2
James Street	B2
Kent Road	A1
King's Road	B1
Knaresborough Road	B3
Lancaster Road	C1
Leeds Road	C2
Lime Grove	A3
Lime Street	A3
Mayfield Grove	A2
Montpellier Hill	B1
Montpellier Street	B1
Mowbray Square	A3
North Park Road	B3
Oatlands Drive	C3
Otley Road	C1
Oxford Street	B2
Park Chase	A3
Park Drive	C2
Park Parade	B3
Park Road	C1
Park View	B2
Parliament Street	B1
Princes Villa Road	B2
Providence Terrace	A2
Queen Parade	B3
Queen's Road	C1
Raglan Street	B2
Regent Avenue	A3
Regent Grove	A3
Regent Parade	A3
Regent Street	A3
Regent Terrace	A3
Ripon Road	A1
Robert Street	C2
St. James Drive	C3
St. Mary's Walk	C1
Skipton Road	A3
South Park Road	C2
Springfield Avenue	A1
Spring Grove	A1
Spring Mount	A1
Station Avenue	B2
Station Parade	B2
Stray Rein	C2
Stray Walk	C3
Studley Road	A2
Swan Road	B1
The Grove	A3
Tower Street	C2
Trinity Road	C2
Valley Drive	B1
Victoria Avenue	B2
Victoria Road	C1
West End Avenue	C1
West Park	B2
Woodside	B2
York Place	C2
York Road	B1

TOURIST INFORMATION ☎ 01423 537300
ROYAL BATHS ASSEMBLY ROOMS, CRESCENT RD, HARROGATE, NORTH YORKSHIRE, HG1 2RR

COUNCIL OFFICE ☎ 01423 500600
COUNCIL OFFICES, CRESCENT GARDENS
HARROGATE, HG1 2SG

HOSPITAL A & E ☎ 01423 885959
HARROGATE DISTRICT HOSPITAL, LANCASTER PARK ROAD, HARROGATE, HG2 7SX

WEB-SITE www.harrogate.gov.uk

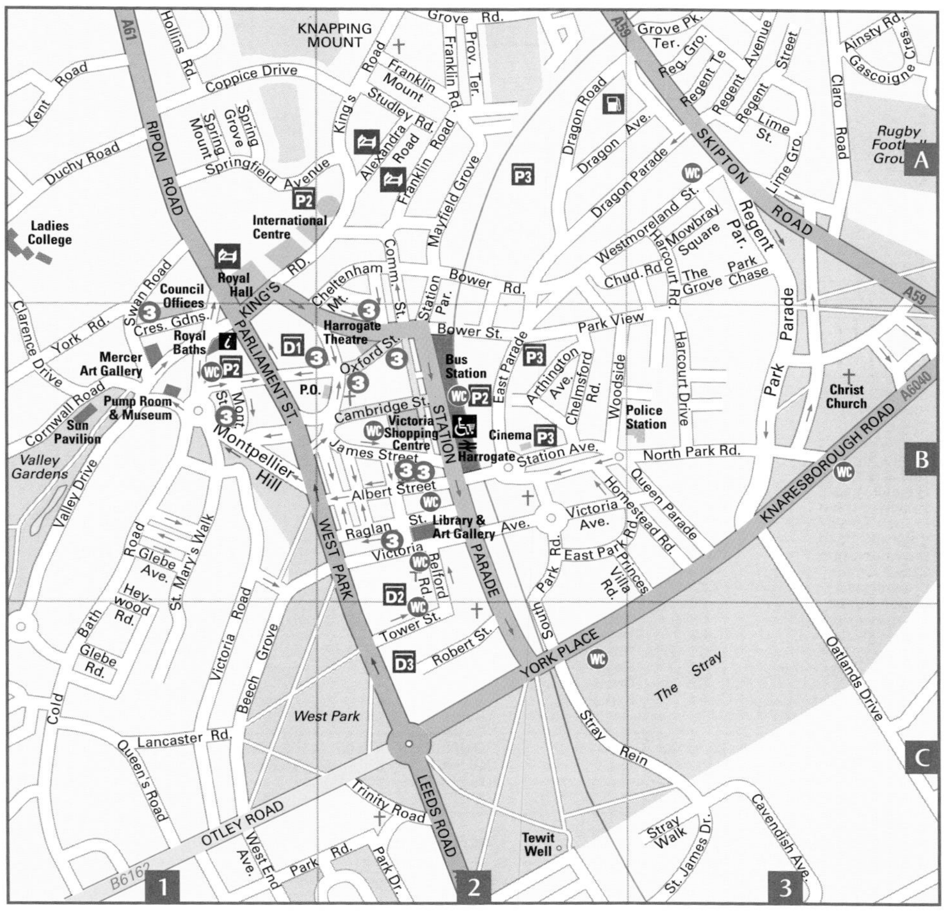

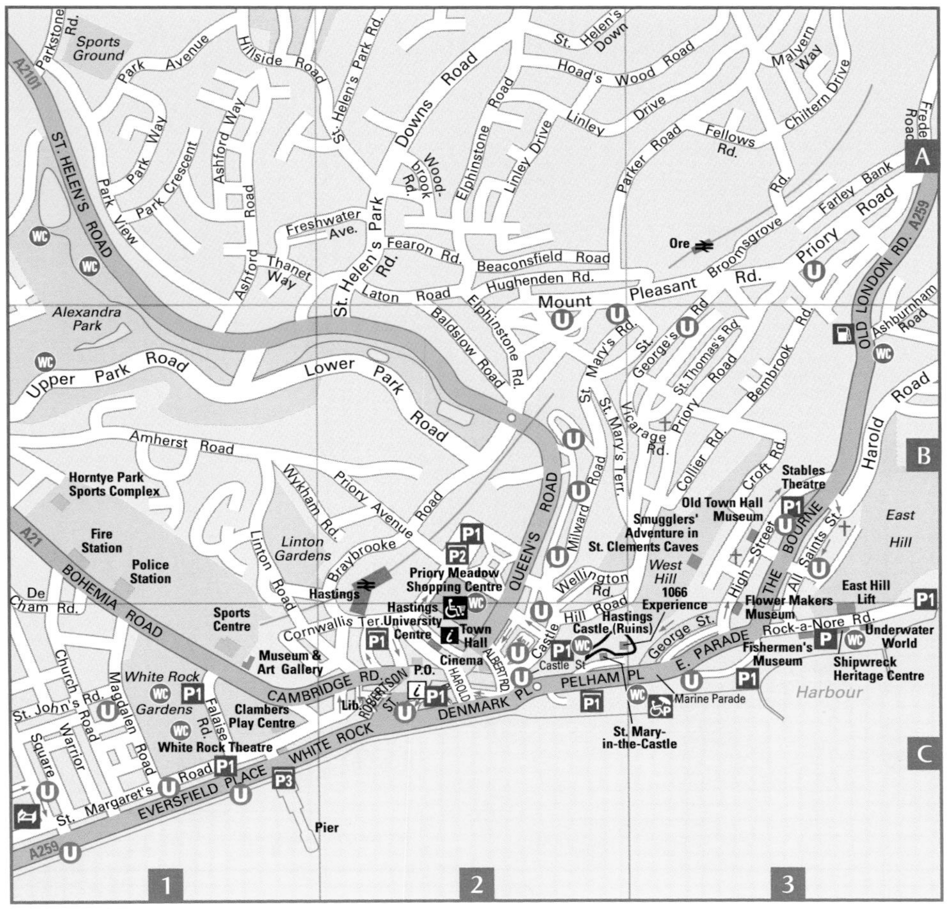

HASTINGS

0 500 yds
0 500m

INDEX TO STREET NAMES

Albert Road	C2
All Saints Street	B3
Amherst Road	B1
Ashburnham Road	B3
Ashford Road	A1
Ashford Way	A1
Baldslow Road	B2
Beaconsfield Road	A2
Bembrook Road	B3
Bohemia Road	B1
Braybrooke Road	B2
Broomsgrove Road	A3
Cambridge Road	C1
Castle Hill Road	C2
Castle Street	C2
Chiltern Drive	A3
Church Road	C1
Collier Road	B3
Cornwallis Terrace	C1
Croft Road	B3
De Cham Road	C1
Denmark Place	C2
Downs Road	A2
East Parade	C3
Elphinstone Road	A2
Eversfield Place	C1
Falaise Road	C1
Farley Bank	A3
Fearon Road	A2
Fellows Road	A3
Frederick Road	A3
Freshwater Avenue	A1
George Street	C3
Harold Place	C2
Harold Road	B3
High Street	B3
Hillside Road	A1
Hoad's Wood Road	A2
Hughenden Road	A2
Laton Road	A2
Linley Drive	A2
Linton Road	B1
Lower Park Road	B1
Magdalen Road	C1
Malvern Way	A3
Marine Parade	C3
Milward Road	B2
Mount Pleasant Road	A2
Old London Road	B3
Park Avenue	A1
Park Crescent	A1
Park View	A1
Park Way	A1
Parker Road	A2
Parkstone Road	A1
Pelham Place	C2
Priory Avenue	B2
Priory Road	B3
Queen's Road	B2
Robertson Street	C2
Rock-a-Nore Road	C3
St. George's Road	B3
St. Helen's Down	A2
St. Helen's Park Road	B2
St. Helen's Road	A1
St. John's Road	C1
St. Margaret's Road	C1
St. Mary's Road	B2
St. Mary's Terrace	B2
St. Thomas's Road	B3
Thanet Way	A1
The Bourne	B3
Upper Park Road	B1
Vicarage Road	B2
Warrior Square	C1
Wellington Road	B2
White Rock	C1
Woodbrook Road	A2
Wykeham Road	B1

TOURIST INFORMATION ☎ 01424 781111
QUEENS SQUARE, PRIORY MEADOW,
HASTINGS, TN34 1TL

COUNCIL OFFICE ☎ 01424 781066
HASTINGS BOROUGH COUNCIL, TOWN HALL, QUEENS ROAD, HASTINGS, TN34 1QR

HOSPITAL A & E ☎ 01424 755255
CONQUEST HOSPITAL, THE RIDGE,
ST. LEONARDS-ON-SEA, TN37 7RD

WEB-SITE www.hastings.gov.uk

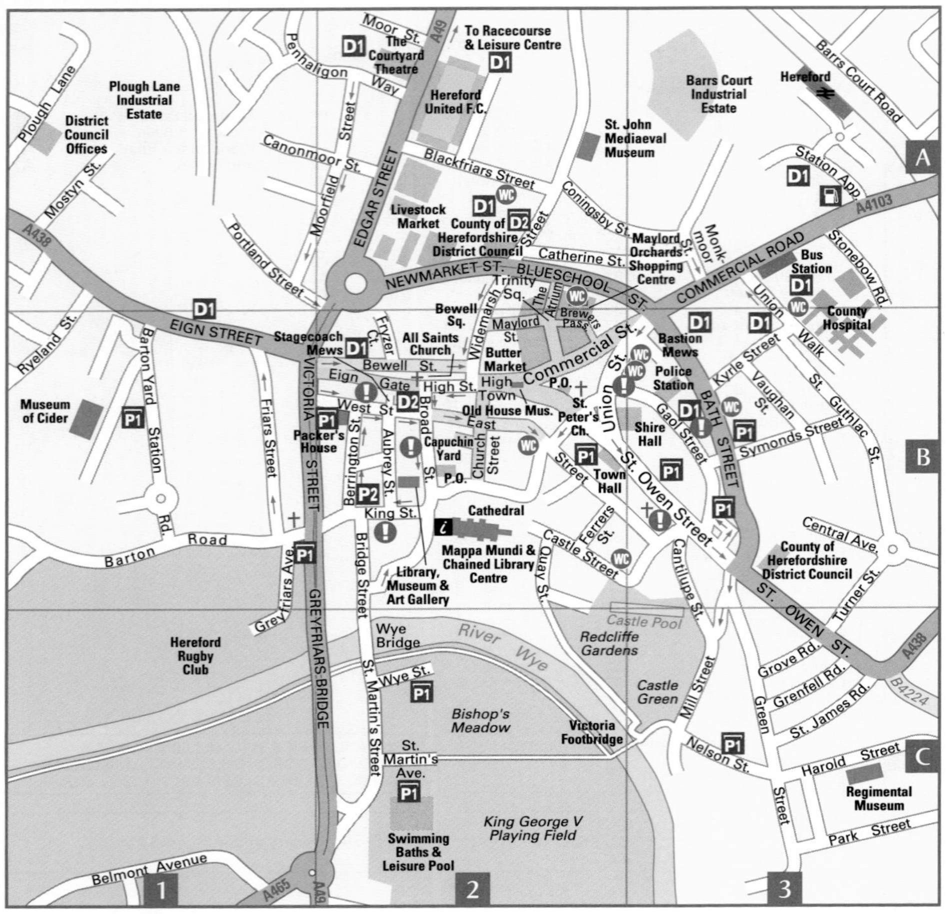

HEREFORD

0 250 yds
0 250m

INDEX TO STREET NAMES

Aubrey Street	B2
Barrs Court Road	A3
Barton Road	B1
Barton Yard	B1
Bath Street	B3
Belmont Avenue	C1
Berrington Street	B2
Bewell Street	B2
Blackfriars Street	A2
Blueschool Street	A2
Brewers Passage	B2
Bridge Street	B2
Broad Street	B2
Canonmoor Street	A1
Cantilupe Street	B3
Castle Street	B2
Catherine Street	A2
Central Avenue	B3
Church Street	B2
Commercial Road	A3
Commercial Street	B2
Coningsby Street	A2
East Street	B2
Edgar Street	A2
Eign Gate	B2
Eign Street	B1
Ferrers Street	B2
Friars Street	B1
Fryzer Court	B2
Gaol Street	B3
Green Street	C3
Grenfell Road	C3
Greyfriars Avenue	C1
Greyfriars Bridge	C2
Grove Road	C3
Harold Street	C3
High Street	B2
High Town	B2
King Street	B2
Kyrle Street	B3
Maylord Street	B2
Mill Street	C3
Monkmoor Street	A3
Moorfield Street	A1
Moor Street	A2
Mostyn Street	A1
Nelson Street	C3
Newmarket Street	A2
Park Street	C3
Penhaligon Way	A1
Plough Lane	A1
Portland Street	A1
Quay Street	B2
Ryeland Street	B1
St. Guthiac Street	B3
St. James Road	C3
St. Martin's Avenue	C2
St. Martin's Street	C2
St. Owen Street	B3
Station Approach	A3
Station Road	B1
Stonebow Road	A3
Symonds Street	B3
The Atrium	A2
Turner Street	C3
Union Street	B2
Union Walk	A3
Vaughan Street	B3
Victoria Street	B1
West Street	B2
Widemarsh Street	B2
Wye Street	C2

TOURIST INFORMATION ☎ 01432 268430
1 KING STREET,
HEREFORD, HR4 9BW

COUNCIL OFFICE ☎ 01432 260456
COUNCIL OFFICES, THE TOWN HALL,
ST. OWEN STREET, HEREFORD, HR1 2PJ

HOSPITAL A & E ☎ 01432 355444
HEREFORD COUNTY HOSPITAL,
UNION WALK, HEREFORD, HR1 2ER

WEB-SITE www.hereford.gov.uk

INVERNESS

0 300 yds
0 300m

INDEX TO STREET NAMES

Abban Street	A1
Academy Street	B2
Alexander Place	B2
Anderson Street	A2
Ardconnel Street	C2
Ardconnel Terrace	B3
Ardross Place	B2
Ardross Street	C1
Argyle Street	C3
Argyle Terrace	C3
Attadale Road	B1
Bank Street	B2
Baron Taylor's Street	B2
Benula Road	A1
Bishop's Road	C1
Bridge Street	B2
Broadstone Park	C3
Bruce Gardens	C1
Burnett Road	A3
Carse Road	A1
Castle Road	B2
Castle Street	B2
Celt Street	B1
Chapel Street	A2
Charles Street	B3
Church Street	B2
Columba Road	C1
Crown Avenue	B3
Crown Circus	B3
Crown Road	B3
Crown Street	C3
Culduthel Road	C2
Denny Street	C3
Dochfour Drive	C1
Douglas Row	A2
Duffy Drive	C2
Duncraig Street	B1
Eastgate	B3
Fairfield Road	B1
Friars Bridge	A1
Friars Lane	B2
Friars Street	B2
Gilbert Street	A1
Glebe Street	A2
Glenurquhart Road	C1
Grant Street	A1
Greig Street	B1
Harbour Road	A2
Harrowden Road	A1
Haugh Road	C2
High Street	B2
Hill Street	B3
Hontly Place	A1
Huntly Street	B1
Innes Street	A2
Kenneth Street	B1
Kingsmills Road	B3
King Street	B1
Leys Drive	C3
Lindsay Avenue	C1
Lochalsh Road	A1
Longman Road	A2
Maxwell Drive	C1
Mayfield Road	C2
Midmills Road	B3
Millburn Road	B3
Montague Row	B1
Muirfield Road	C3
Nelson Street	A1
Ness Bank	C2
Ness Bridge	B2
Ness Walk	C2
Old Edinburgh Road	C2
Park Road	C1
Perceval Road	B1
Planefield Road	B1
Queensgate	B2
Rancemore Road	B1
Riverside Street	A2
Ross Avenue	B1
Shore Street	A2
Smith Avenue	C1
Southside Place	C3
Southside Road	C3
Stephens Street	B3
Strother's Lane	B2
Telford Road	A1
Telford Street	A1
Tomnahurich Street	C1
Union Road	C3
Union Street	B2
View Place	C2
Walker Road	A2
Waterloo Bridge	A2
Wells Street	B1
Young Street	B2

TOURIST INFORMATION ☎ 01463 234353
CASTLE WYND,
INVERNESS, IV2 3BJ

COUNCIL OFFICE ☎ 01463 702000
COUNCIL OFFICES, GLENURQUHART ROAD,
INVERNESS, IV3 5NX

HOSPITAL A & E ☎ 01463 704000
RAIGMORE HOSPITAL, OLD PERTH ROAD,
INVERNESS, IV2 3UJ

WEB-SITE www.highland.gov.uk

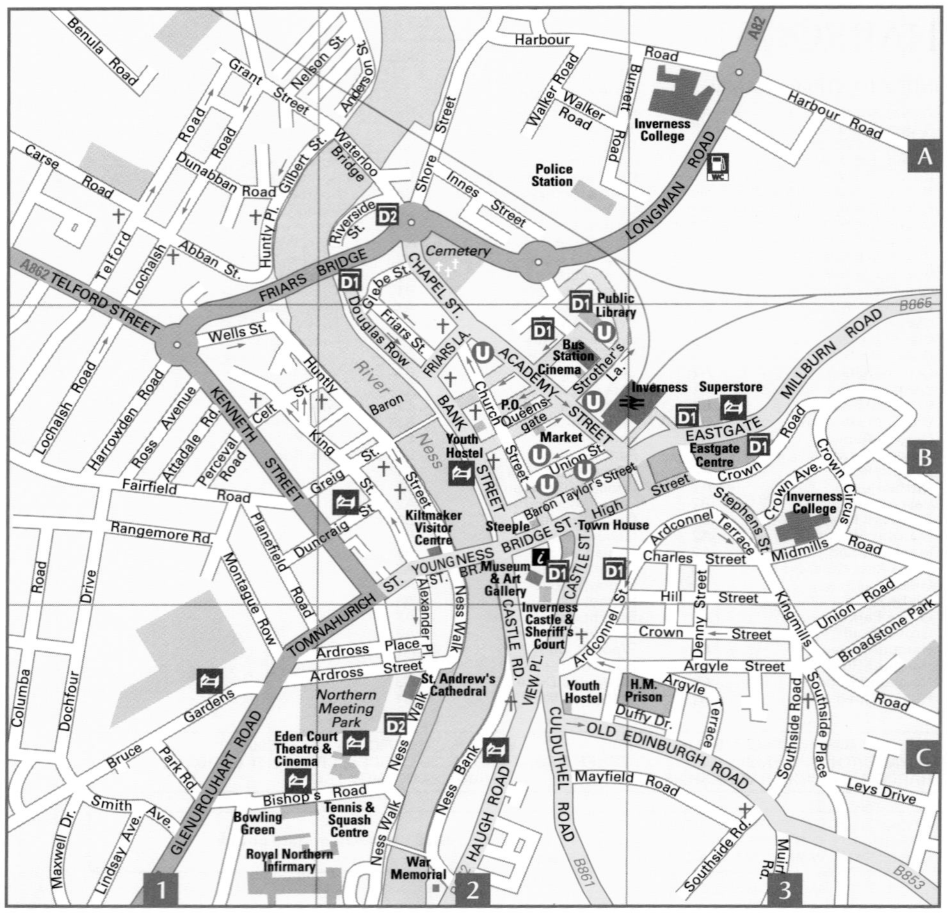

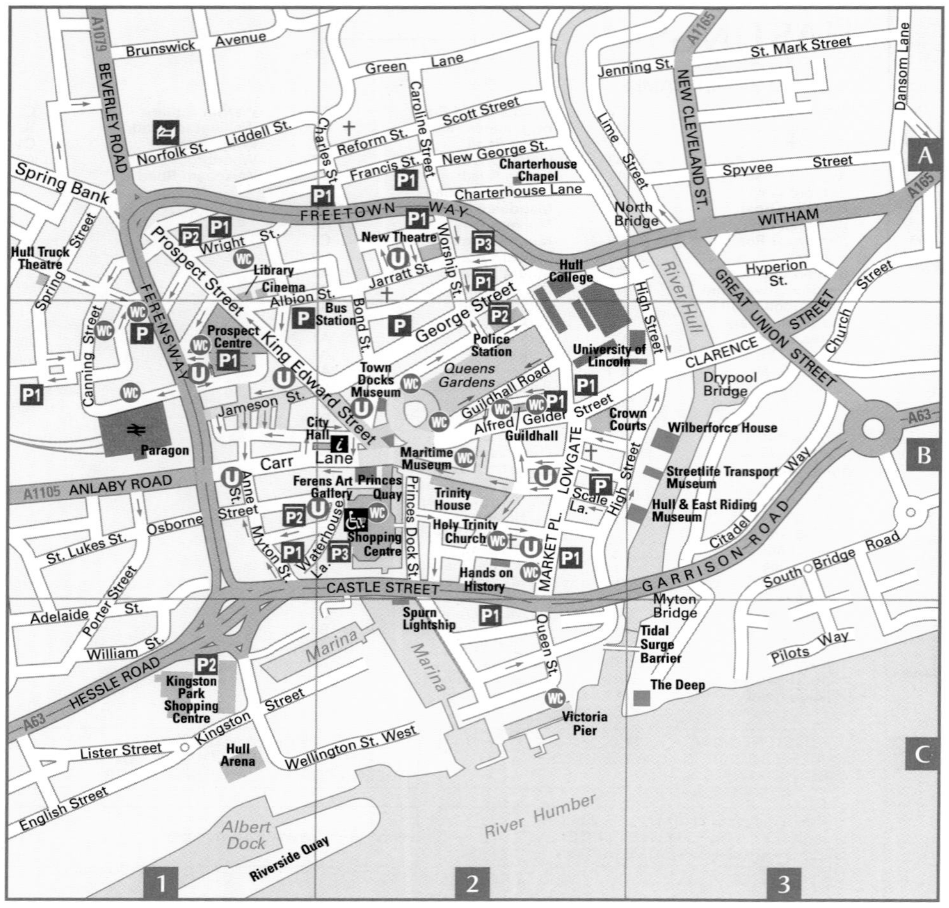

KINGSTON UPON HULL

0 300 yds
0 300m

INDEX TO STREET NAMES

Adelaide Street	C1
Albion Street	B1
Alfred Gelder Street	B2
Anlaby Road	B1
Anne Street	B1
Beverley Road	A1
Bond Street	B2
Brunswick Avenue	A1
Canning Street	B1
Caroline Street	A2
Carr Lane	B1
Castle Street	B2
Charles Street	A2
Charterhouse Lane	A2
Church Street	B3
Citadel Way	B3
Clarence Street	B3
Cleveland Street	A3
Dansom Lane	A3
English Street	C1
Ferensway	A1
Francis Street	A2
Freetown Way	A1
Garrison Road	B3
George Street	B2
Great Union Street	A3
Green Lane	A2
Guildhall Road	B2
Hessle Road	C1
High Street	A3
Hyperion Street	A3
Jameson Street	B1
Jarratt Street	A2
Jenning Street	A2
King Edward Street	B1
Kingston Street	C1
Liddell Street	A1
Lime Street	A2
Lister Street	C1
Lowgate	B2
Market Place	B2
Myton Street	B1
New Cleveland Street	A3
New George Street	A2
Norfolk Street	A1
North Bridge	A2
Osborne Street	B1
Pilots Way	C3
Porter Street	C1
Princes Dock Street	B2
Prospect Street	A1
Queen Street	C2
Reform Street	A2
St. Lukes Street	B1
St. Mark Street	A3
Scale Lane	B2
Scott Street	A2
Scott Street Bridge	A2
South Bridge Road	B3
Spring Bank	A1
Spring Street	B1
Spyvee Street	A3
Waterhouse Lane	B1
Wellington Street West	C1
William Street	C1
Witham	A3
Worship Street	A2
Wright Street	A1

TOURIST INFORMATION ☎ 01482 223559
1 PARAGON STREET,
KINGSTON UPON HULL, HU1 3NA

COUNCIL OFFICE ☎ 01482 300300
GUILDHALL, ALFRED GELDER STREET,
KINGSTON UPON HULL, HU1 2AA

HOSPITAL A & E ☎ 01482 328541
HULL ROYAL INFIRMARY, ANLABY ROAD,
KINGSTON UPON HULL, HU3 2JZ

WEB-SITE www.hullcc.gov.uk

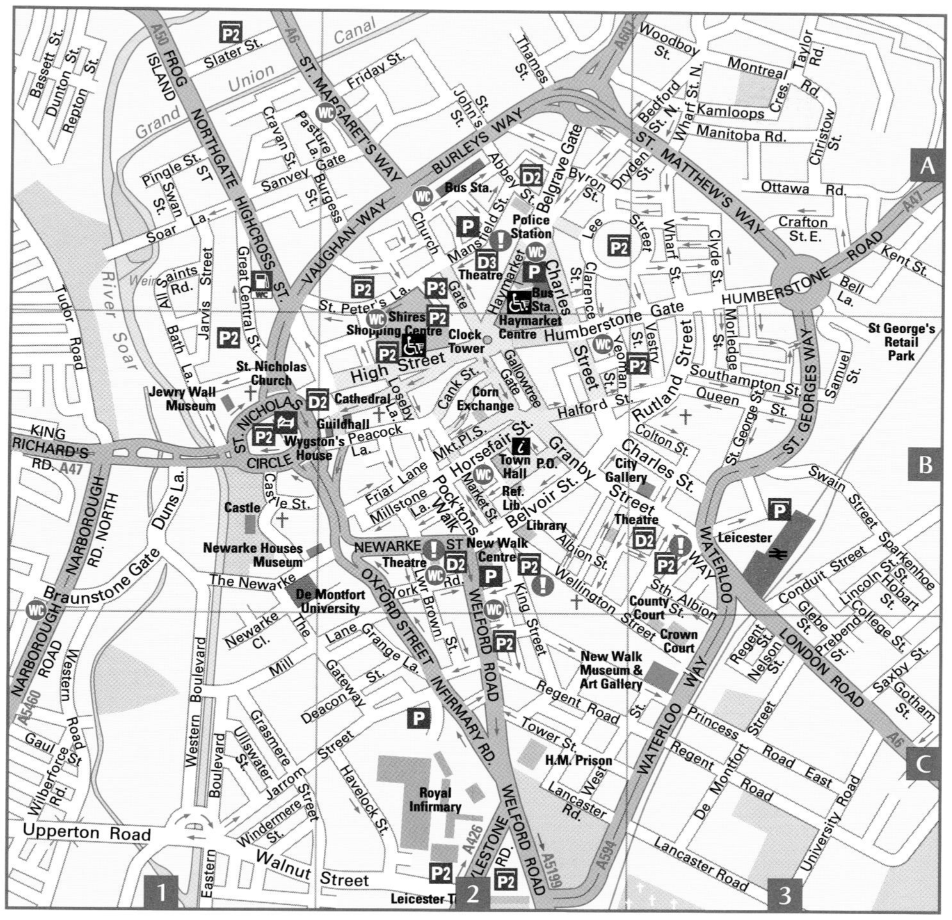

LEICESTER

0 200 yds
0 200m

INDEX TO STREET NAMES

Abbey Street A2
Albion Street B2
All Saints Road B1
Aylestone Road C2
Bassett Street A1
Bath Lane B1
Bedford Street North A3
Belgrave Gate A2
Bell Lane A3
Belvoir Street B2
Braunstone Gate B1
Burgess Street A2
Burleys Way A2
Byron Street A2
Cank Street B2
Castle Street B1
Charles Street B3
Christow Street A3
Church Gate A2
Clarence Street A2
Clyde Street A3
College Street B3
Colton Street B3
Conduit Street B3
Crafton Street East A3
Cravan Street A1
De Montfort Street C3
Deacon Street C2
Dryden Street A2
Duns Lane B1
Dunton Street A1
Eastern Boulevard C1
Friar Lane B2
Friday Street A2
Frog Island A1
Gallowtree Gate B2
Gaul Street C1
Glebe Street B3
Gotham Street C3
Granby Street B2
Grange Lane C2
Grasmere Street C1
Great Central Street A1
Halford Street B2
Havelock Street C2
Haymarket A2
High Street B2
Highcross Street A1
Hobart Street B3
Horsfair Street B2
Humberstone Gate B2
Humberstone Road A3
Infirmary Road C2
Jarrom Street C2
Jarvis Street B1
Kamloops Crescent A3
Kent Street A3
King Richard's Road B1
King Street B2
Lancaster Road C2
Lee Street A2
Lincoln Street B3
London Road C3
Loseby Lane B2
Lower Brown Street B2
Manitoba Road A3
Mansfield Street A2
Market Place South B2
Market Street B2
Mill Lane C1
Millstone Lane B2
Montreal Road A3
Morledge Street B3
Narborough Road C1
Narborough Road North B1
Nelson Street C3
Newarke Close C1
Newarke Street B2
Northgate Street A1
Ottawa Road A3
Oxford Street B2
Pasture Lane A1
Peacock Lane B2
Pocklingtons Walk B2
Prebend Street C3
Princess Road East C3
Pringle Street A1
Queen Street B3
Regent Road C2
Regent Street C3
Repton Street A1
Rutland Street B3
Samuel Street B3
Sanvey Gate A1
Saxby Street C3
Slater Street A1
Soar Lane A1
South Albion Street B3
Southampton Street B3
Sparkenhoe Street B3
St. George Street B3
St. George's Way B3
St. John's Street A2
St. Margaret's Way A1
St. Matthew's Way A3
St. Nicholas Circle B1
St. Peter's Lane A2
Swain Street B3
Swan Street A1
Taylor Road A3
Thames Street A2
The Gateway C1
The Newarke B1
Tower Street C2
Tudor Road A1
Ullswater Street C1
University Road C3
Upperton Road C1
Vaughan Way A1
Vestry Street B3
Walnut Street C1
Waterloo Way C3
Welford Road B2
Wellington Street B2
West Street C2
Western Boulevard C1
Western Road C1
Wharf Street A3
Wharf Street North A3
Wilberforce Road C1
Windermere Street C1
Woodboy Street A3
Yeoman Street B2
York Road B2

TOURIST INFORMATION ☎ 0116 299 4444
7-9 EVERY STREET, TOWN HALL SQUARE, LEICESTER, LE1 6AG

COUNCIL OFFICE ☎ 0116 254 9922
COUNCIL OFFICES, NEW WALK CENTRE, WELFORD PLACE, LEICESTER, LE1 6ZG

HOSPITAL A & E ☎ 0116 254 1414
LEICESTER ROYAL INFIRMARY, INFIRMARY SQUARE, LEICESTER, LE1 5WW

WEB-SITE www.leicester.gov.uk

LINCOLN

0 200 yds
0 200m

INDEX TO STREET NAMES

Alexandra Terrace B1
Baggholme Road B3
Bailgate A2
Beaumont Fee B2
Beevor Street C1
Brayford Way C1
Brayford Wharf North B1
Broadgate B2
Broadway A2
Bruce Road A3
Burton Road A1
Canwick Road C2
Carholme Road B1
Carline Road A1
Carr Street B1
Cheviot Street B3
Church Lane A2
Clasketgate B2
Croft Street B2
Cross Street C2
Curle Avenue A3
Drury Lane B2
East Gate B2
Firth Road C1
George Street C3
Great Northern Terrace C2
Greetwell Close A3
Greetwell Road B3
Gresham Street B1
Hampton Street B1
Harvey Street B1
High Street C2
John Street B3
Langworthgate A2
Lee Road A3
Lindum Road B2
Lindum Terrace B3
Long Leys Road A1
Mainwaring Road A3
Mill Road A1
Milman Road B3
Monks Road B3
Monson Street C2
Moor Street B1
Mount Street A1
Nettleham Road A2
Newland B1
Newland Street West B1
Newport A2
Northgate A2
Orchard Street B1
Pelham Bridge C2
Portland Street C2
Portland Street C2
Pottergate B2
Queensway A3
Rasen Lane A2
Richmond Road B1
Ripon Street C2
Rope Walk C1
Rosemary Lane B2
Ruskin Avenue A3
Saltergate B2
Sewell Road B3
Silver Street B2
Sincil Bank C2
Spa Road C3
St. Anne's Road B3
St. Giles Avenue A3
St. Mark Street C2
St. Mary's Street C2
St. Rumbold Street B2
Stamp End C3
Steep Hill B2
The Avenue B1
Tritton Road C1
Union Row B2
Upper Lindum Street B3
Upper Long Leys Road A1
Vere Street A2
Vine Street B3
Waterside North C2
Waterside South C2
West Parade B1
Westgate A2
Wigford Way B2
Wilson Street A1
Winn Street B3
Wragby Road B3
Yarborough Road A1

TOURIST INFORMATION ☎ 01522 873213
9 CASTLE HILL, LINCOLN, LN1 3AA

COUNCIL OFFICE ☎ 01522 881188
CITY HALL, BEAUMONT FEE, LINCOLN, LN1 1DD

HOSPITAL A & E ☎ 01522 512512
LINCOLN COUNTY HOSPITAL, GREETWELL ROAD, LINCOLN, LN2 5QY

WEB-SITE www.lincoln.gov.uk

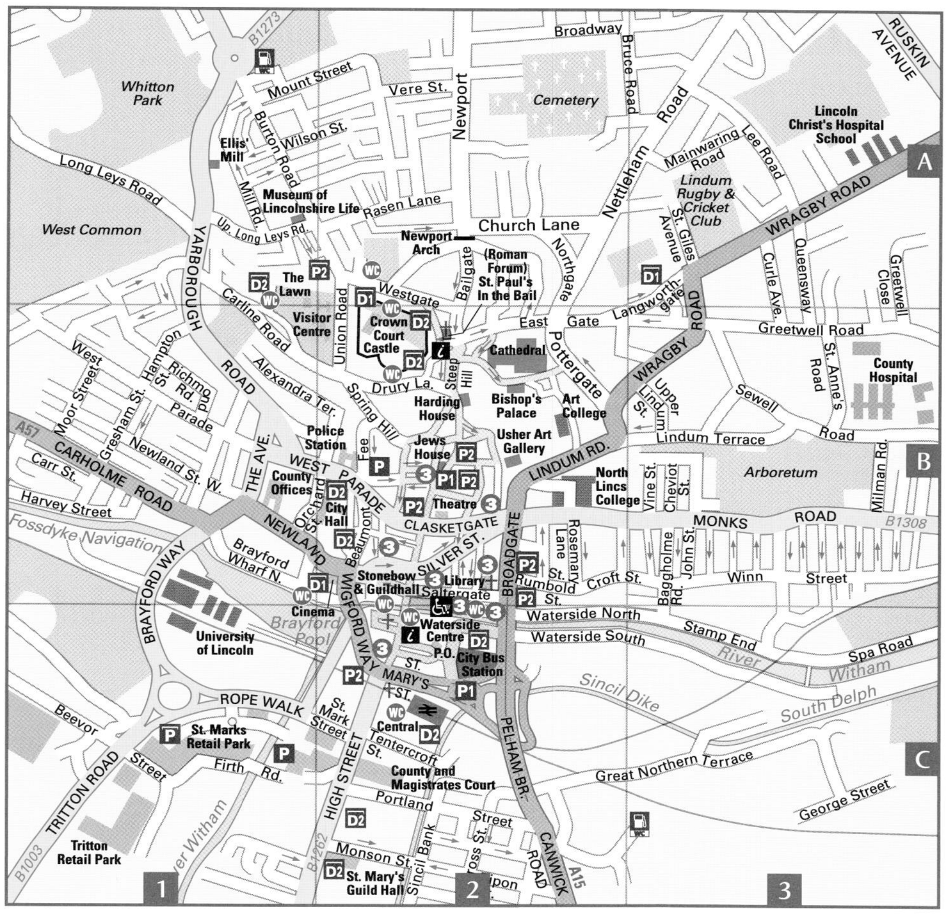

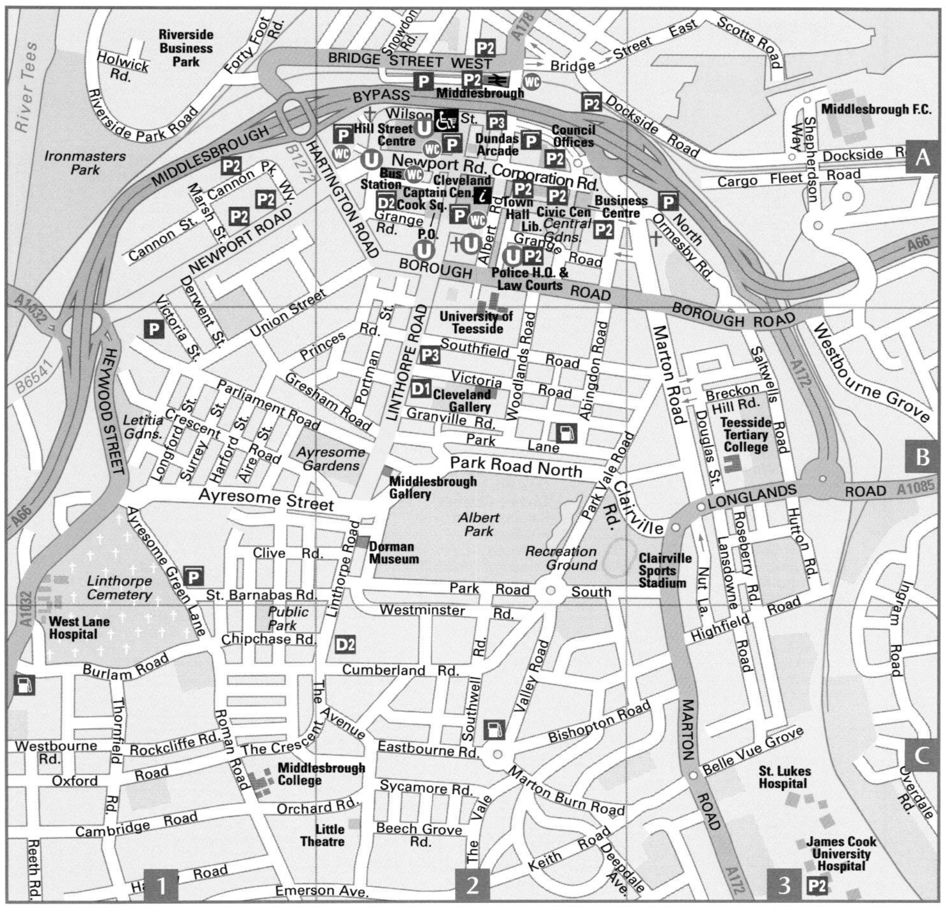

MIDDLESBROUGH

0 400 yds
0 400m

INDEX TO STREET NAMES

Abingdon Road B2
Aire Street B1
Albert Road A2
Ayresome Green Lane B1
Ayresome Street B1
Beech Grove Road C2
Belle Vue Grove C3
Bishopton Road C2
Borough Road A2/C3
Breckon Hill Road B3
Bridge Street East A2
Bridge Street West A2
Burlam Road C1
Cambridge Road C1
Cannon Park Way A1
Cannon Street A1
Cargo Fleet Road A3
Chipchase Road C1
Clairville Road B2
Clive Road B1
Corporation Road A2
Crescent Road B1
Cumberland Road C2
Deepdale Avenue C2
Derwent Street A1
Dockside Road A2/A3
Douglas Street B3
Eastbourne Road C2
Emerson Avenue C2
Forty Foot Road A1
Grange Road A2
Granville Road B2
Gresham Road B1
Harford Street B1
Harrow Road C1
Hartington Road A1
Heywood Street B1
Highfield Road C3
Holwick Road A1
Hutton Road B3
Ingram Road B3
Keith Road C2
Lansdowne Road B3
Linthorpe Road C2
Longford Street B1
Longlands Road B3
Marsh Street A1
Marton Burn Road C2
Marton Road B3/C3
Newport Road A1/A2
North Ormesby Road A3
Nut Lane B3
Orchard Road C1
Overdale Road C3
Oxford Road C1
Park Lane B2
Park Road North B2
Park Road South B2
Park Vale Road B2
Parliament Road B1
Portman Street B2
Princes Road B1
Reeth Road C1
Riverside Park Road A1
Rockcliffe Road C1
Roman Road C1
Roseberry Road B3
Saltwells Road B3
Scotts Road A3
Sheperdson Way A3
Snowdon Road A2
Southfield Road B2
Southwell Road C2
St. Barnabas Road B1
Surrey Street B1
Sycamore Road C2
The Avenue C2
The Crescent C1
The Vale C2
Thornfield Road C1
Union Street B1
Valley Road C2
Victoria Road B2
Victoria Street A1
Westbourne Grove B3
Westbourne Road C1
Westminster Road C2
Wilson Street A2
Woodlands Road B2

TOURIST INFORMATION ☎ 01642 243425
99-101 ALBERT ROAD, MIDDLESBROUGH, TS1 2PA

COUNCIL OFFICE ☎ 01642 245432
MUNICIPAL BUILDINGS, PO BOX 99A, RUSSELL STREET, MIDDLESBROUGH, TS1 2QQ

HOSPITAL A & E ☎ 01642 617617
NORTH TEES GENERAL HOSPITAL, HARDWICK ROAD, STOCKTON-ON-TEES, TS19 8PE

WEB-SITE www.middlesbrough.gov.uk

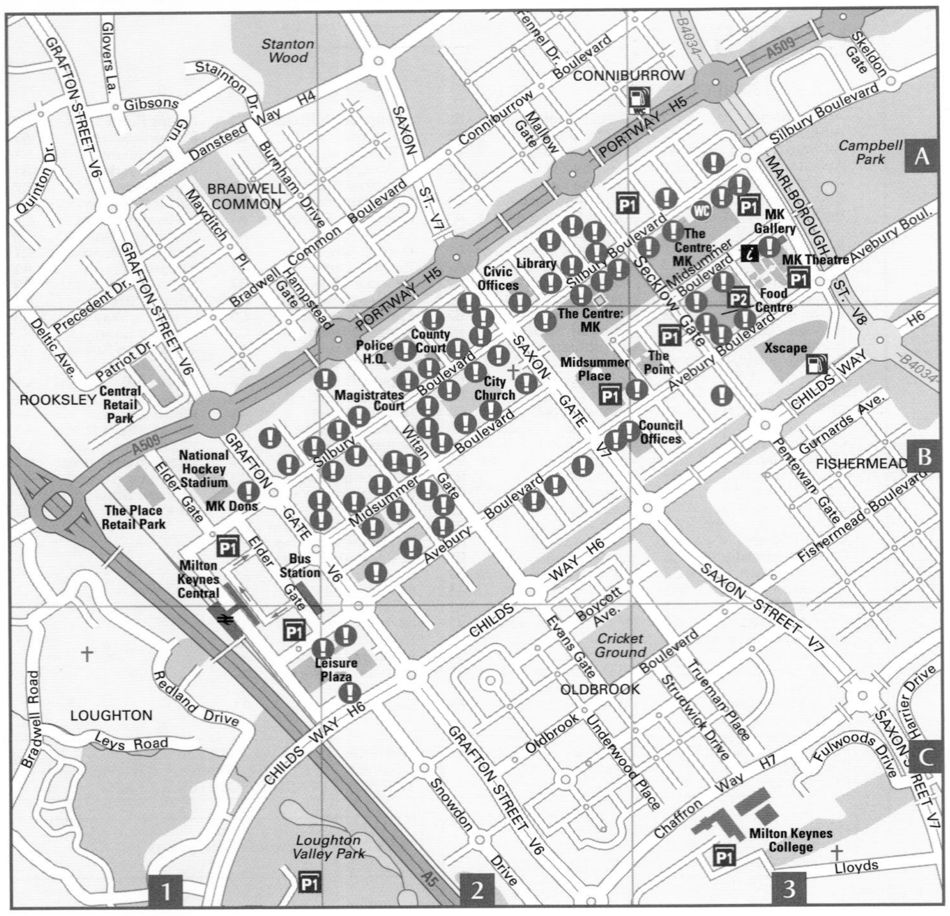

MILTON KEYNES

0 400 yds
0 400m

INDEX TO STREET NAMES

Avebury Boulevard	B2/A3
Boycott Avenue	C2
Bradwell Common Boulevard	A1
Bradwell Road	C1
Burnham Drive	A1
Chaffron Way	C3
Childs Way	C1/B3
Conniburrow Boulevard	A2
Dansteed Way	A1
Deltic Avenue	B1
Elder Gate	B1
Evans Gate	C2
Fennel Drive	A2
Fishermead Boulevard	B3
Fulwoods Drive	C3
Gibsons Green	A1
Glovers Lane	A1
Grafton Gate	B1
Grafton Street	A1/C2
Gurnards Avenue	B3
Hampstead Gate	A1
Harrier Drive	C3
Leys Road	C1
Lloyds	C3
Mallow Gate	A2
Marlborough Street	A3
Mayditch Place	A1
Midsummer Boulevard	B2/A3
Oldbrook Boulevard	C2
Patriot Drive	B1
Pentewan Gate	B3
Portway	B2/A3
Precedent Drive	B1
Quinton Drive	A1
Redland Drive	C1
Saxon Gate	B2
Saxon Street	A2/C3
Secklow Gate	A3
Silbury Boulevard	B2/A3
Skeldon Gate	A3
Snowdon Drive	C2
Stainton Drive	A1
Strudwick Drive	C3
Trueman Place	C3
Underwood Place	C2
Witan Gate	B2

TOURIST INFORMATION ☎ 01908 558300
MARGARET POWELL SQUARE, 890 MIDSUMMER BOULEVARD, MILTON KEYNES, MK9 3QA

COUNCIL OFFICE ☎ 01908 691691
CIVIC OFFICES, 1 SAXON GATE EAST, MILTON KEYNES, MK9 3HQ

HOSPITAL A & E ☎ 01908 660033
MILTON KEYNES GENERAL HOSPITAL, STANDING WAY, EAGLESTONE, MILTON KEYNES, MK6 5LD

WEB-SITE www.mkweb.co.uk

NEWCASTLE UPON TYNE

0 400 yds
0 400m

INDEX TO STREET NAMES

Albert Street	B3
Ancrum Street	A1
Argyle Street	B3
Askew Road	C3
Barrack Road	A1
Barras Bridge	A2
Bath Lane	B1
Bigg Market	B2
Blackett Street	B2
Byron Street	A3
Chester Street	A3
City Road	B3
Claremont Road	A2
Clarence Street	B3
Clayton Street	B2
Clayton Street West	C1
Corporation Street	B1
Coulthards Lane	C3
Crawhall Road	B3
Dean Street	B2
Diana Street	B1
Elswick East Terrace	C1
Eskdale Terrace	A3
Essex Close	C1
Falconar Street	A3
Forth Banks	C2
Forth Street	C1
Gallowgate	B1
Gateshead Highway	C3
George Street	C1
Gibson Street	B3
Grainger Street	B2
Grantham Road	A3
Grey Street	B2
Hanover Street	C2
Hawks Road	C3
Helmsley Road	A3
High Street	C3
Hillgate	C3
Howard Street	B3
Hunters Road	A1
Ivy Close	C1
Jesmond Road	A3
Jesmond Road West	A2
John Dobson Street	B2
Kelvin Grove	A3
Kyle Close	C1
Lambton Street	C3
Mansfield Street	B1
Maple Street	C1
Maple Terrace	C1
Market Street	B2
Melbourne Street	B3
Mill Road	C3
Neville Street	C1
New Bridge Street	B3
Newgate Street	B2
Northumberland Road	B2
Northumberland Street	A2
Oakwellgate	C3
Orchard Street	C2
Oxnam Crescent	A1
Park Terrace	A2
Percy Street	B2
Pilgrim Street	B2
Pipewellgate	C2
Pitt Street	B1
Portland Road	A3
Portland Terrace	A3
Pottery Lane	C1
Quarryfield Road	C3
Quayside	C3
Queen Victoria Road	A2
Railway Street	C1
Redheugh Bridge	C1
Richardson Road	A1
Rye Hill	C1
St. James Boulevard	C1
St. Mary's Place	A2
St. Thomas Street	A2
Sandyford Road	A2/A3
Scotswood Road	C1
Skinnerburn Road	C2
South Shore Road	C3
Stanhope Street	B1
Starbeck Avenue	A3
Stodart Street	A3
Stowell Street	B1
Strawberry Place	B1
Summerhill Grove	B1
Swing Bridge	C2
The Close	C2
Tyne Bridge	C3
Union Street	B3
Warwick Street	A3
Wellington Street	B1
West Street	C3
Westgate Road	B1
Westmorland Road	C1
Windsor Terrace	A2
York Street	B1

TOURIST INFORMATION ☎ 0191 277 8000
132 GRAINGER STREET, NEWCASTLE UPON TYNE, NE1 5AF

COUNCIL OFFICE ☎ 0191 232 8520
CIVIC CENTRE, BARRAS BRIDGE, NEWCASTLE UPON TYNE, NE99 1RD

HOSPITAL A & E ☎ 0191 273 8811
NEWCASTLE GENERAL HOSPITAL, WESTGATE ROAD, NEWCASTLE UPON TYNE, NE4 6BE

WEB-SITE www.newcastle.gov.uk

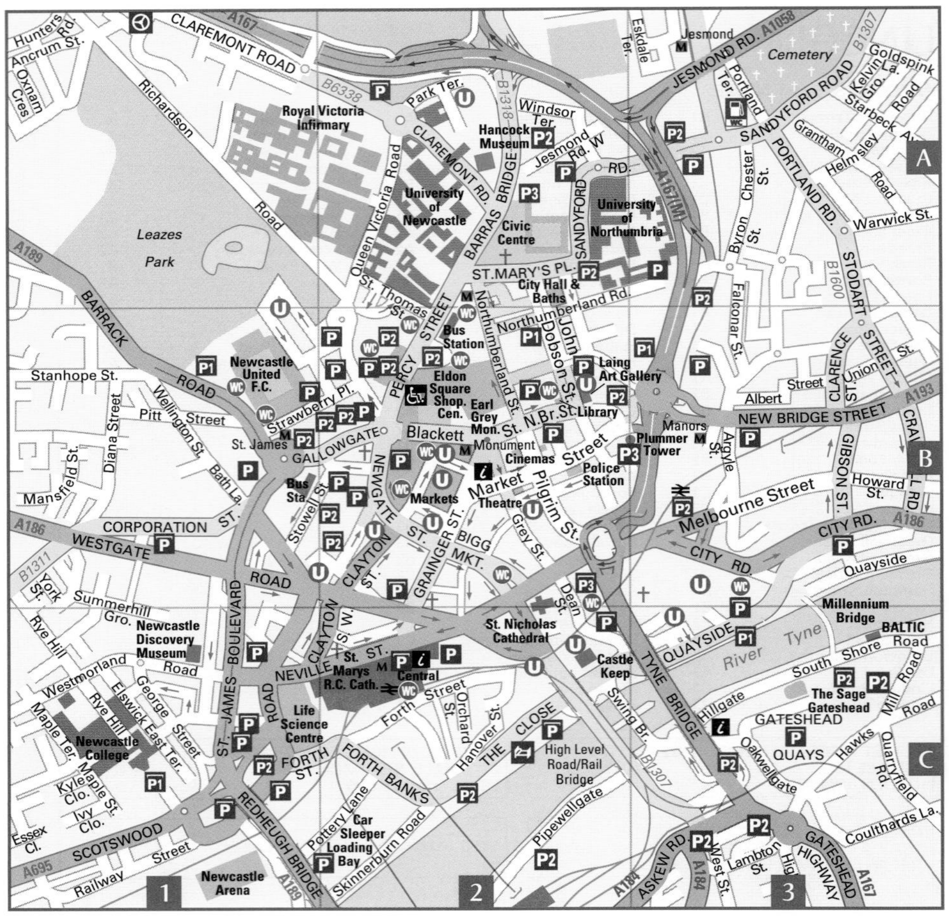

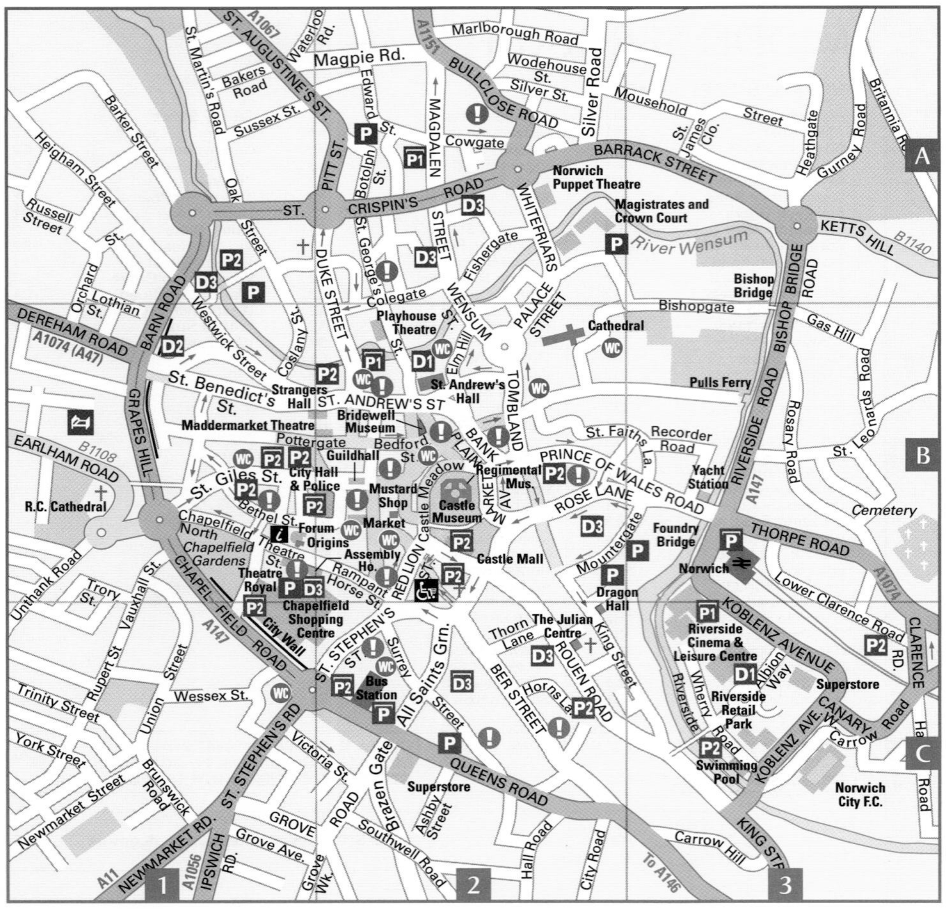

NORWICH

0 400 yds
0 400m

INDEX TO STREET NAMES

Albion Way	C3
All Saints Green	C2
Ashby Street	C2
Bakers Road	A1
Bank Plain	B2
Barker Street	A1
Barn Road	B1
Barrack Street	A2
Bedford Street	B2
Ber Street	C2
Bethel Street	B1
Bishopbridge Road	B3
Bishopgate	B3
Botolph Street	A2
Brazen Gate	C2
Britannia Road	A3
Brunswick Road	C1
Bullclose Road	A2
Canary Way	C3
Carrow Hill	C3
Carrow Road	C3
Castle Meadow	B2
Chapel Field Road	B1
Chapelfield North	B1
City Road	C2
Clarence Road	C3
Colegate	A2
Coslany Street	B1
Cowgate	A2
Dereham Road	B1
Duke Street	A2
Earlham Road	B1
Edward Street	A2
Elm Hill	B2
Fishergate	A2
Gas Hill	A3
Grapes Hill	B1
Grove Avenue	C1
Grove Road	C1
Grove Walk	C1
Gurney Road	A3
Hall Road	C2
Hardy Road	C3
Heathgate	A3
Heigham Street	A1
Horns Lane	C2
Ipswich Road	C1
Ketts Hill	A3
King Street	C2
Koblenz Avenue	C3
Lothian Street	A1
Lower Clarence Road	B3
Magdalen Street	A2
Magpie Road	A2
Market Avenue	B2
Marlborough Road	A2
Mountergate	B2
Mousehold Street	A3
Newmarket Road	C1
Newmarket Street	C1
Oak Street	A1
Orchard Street	A1
Palace Street	B2
Pitt Street	A2
Pottergate	B1
Prince of Wales Road	B2
Queens Road	C2
Rampant Horse Street	B2
Recorder Road	B3
Red Lion Street	B2
Riverside	C3
Riverside Road	B3
Rosary Road	B3
Rose Lane	B2
Rouen Road	C2
Rupert Street	C1
Russell Street	A1
St. Andrew's Street	B2
St. Augustine's Street	A1
St. Benedict's Street	B1
St. Crispin's Road	A1
St. Faiths Lane	B2
St. George's Street	A2
St. Giles Street	B1
St. James Close	A3
St. Leonards Road	B3
St. Martin's Road	A1
St. Stephen's Road	C1
St. Stephen's Street	C2
Silver Road	A2
Silver Street	A2
Southwell Road	C2
Surrey Street	C2
Sussex Street	A1
Theatre Street	B1
Thorn Lane	C2
Thorpe Road	B3
Tombland	B2
Trinity Street	C1
Trory Street	B1
Union Street	C1
Unthank Road	C1
Vauxhall Street	C1
Victoria Street	C1
Wensum Street	A2
Wessex Street	C1
Westwick Street	A1
Wherry Road	C3
Whitefriars	A2
Wodehouse Street	A2
York Street	C1

TOURIST INFORMATION ☎ 01603 727927
THE FORUM, MILLENNIUM PLAIN, NORWICH, NR2 1TF

COUNCIL OFFICE ☎ 01603 212212
CITY HALL, ST. PETER'S STREET, NORWICH, NR2 1NH

HOSPITAL A & E ☎ 01603 286286
NORFOLK & NORWICH UNIVERSITY HOSPITAL, COLNEY LANE, NORWICH, NR4 7UY

WEB-SITE www.norwich.gov.uk

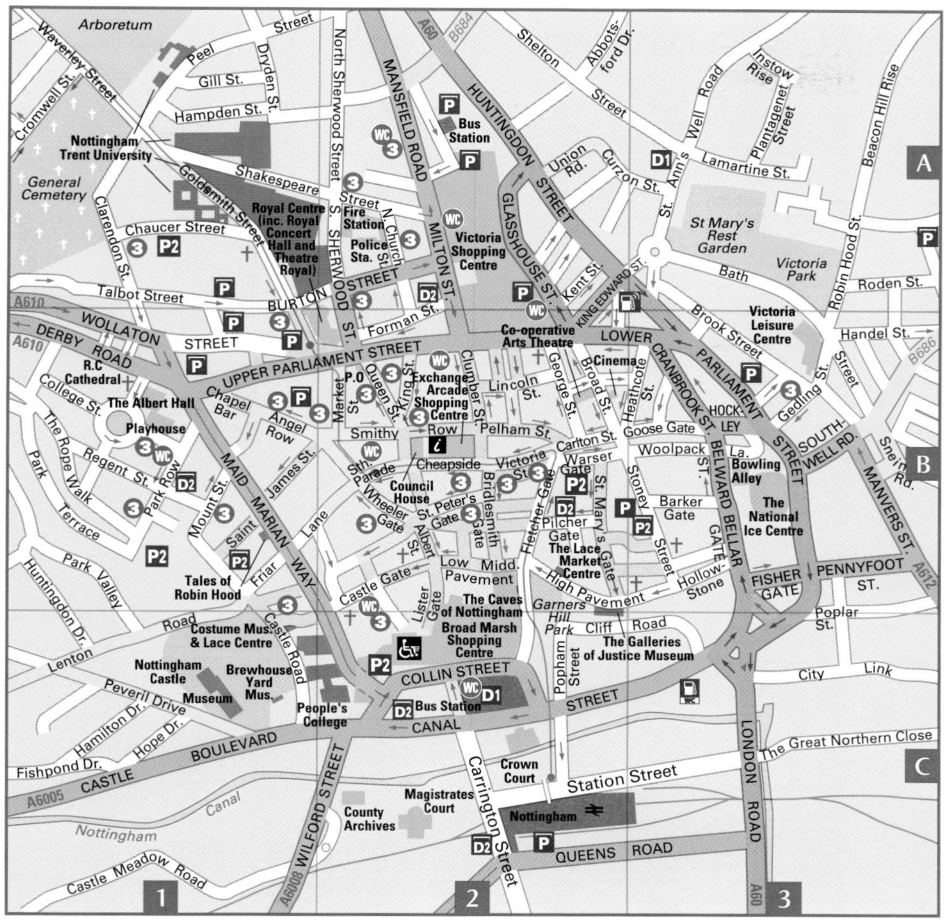

NOTTINGHAM

0 400 yds
0 400m

INDEX TO STREET NAMES

Abbotsford Drive	A2
Albert Street	B2
Angel Row	B1
Barker Gate	B3
Bath Street	A3
Beacon Hill Rise	A3
Bellar Gate	B3
Belward Street	B3
Bridlesmith Gate	B2
Broad Street	B2
Brook Street	A3
Burton Street	A1
Canal Street	C2
Carlton Street	B2
Carrington Street	C2
Castle Boulevard	C1
Castle Gate	B2
Castle Meadow Road	C1
Castle Road	C1
Chapel Bar	B1
Chaucer Street	A1
Cheapside	B2
City Link	C3
Clarendon Street	A1
Cliff Road	C2
Clumber Street	B2
College Street	B1
Collin Street	C2
Cranbrook Street	B3
Cromwell Street	A1
Curzon Street	A2
Derby Road	B1
Dryden Street	A1
Fisher Gate	B3
Fishpond Drive	C1
Fletcher Gate	B2
Forman Street	B2
Friar Lane	B1
Gedling Street	B3
George Street	B2
Gill Street	A1
Glasshouse Street	A2
Goldsmith Street	A1
Goose Gate	B3
Hamilton Drive	C1
Hampden Street	A1
Handel Street	B3
Heathcote Street	B2
High Pavement	C2
Hockley	B3
Hollowstone	B3
Hope Drive	C1
Huntingdon Drive	B1
Huntingdon Street	A2
Instow Rise	A3
Kent Street	A2
King Edward Street	B2
King Street	B2
Lamartine Street	A3
Lenton Road	C1
Lincoln Street	B2
Lister Gate	C2
London Road	C3
Low Pavement	B2
Lower Parliament Street	B2
Maid Marian Way	B1
Mansfield Road	A2
Manvers Street	B3
Market Street	B2
Middle Pavement	B2
Milton Street	A2
Mount Street	B1
North Church Street	A2
North Sherwood Street	A2
Park Row	B1
Park Terrace	B1
Park Valley	B1
Peel Street	A1
Pelham Street	B2
Pennyfoot Street	B3
Peveril Drive	C1
Pilcher Gate	B2
Plantagenet Street	A3
Popham Street	C2
Poplar Street	B3
Queens Road	C2
Queen Street	B2
Regent Street	B1
Robin Hood Street	A3
Roden Street	A3
St. Ann's Well Road	A3
St. James Street	B1
St. Mary's Gate	B2
St. Peter's Gate	B2
Shakespeare Street	A1
Shelton Street	A2
Smithy Row	B2
Sneinton Road	B3
South Parade	B2
South Sherwood Street	A2
Southwell Road	B3
Station Street	C2
Stoney Street	B3
Talbot Street	A1
The Great Northern Close	C3
The Rope Walk	B1
Union Road	A2
Upper Parliament Street	B1
Victoria Street	B2
Warser Gate	B2
Waverley Street	A1
Wheeler Gate	B2
Wilford Street	C1
Wollaton Street	B1
Woolpack Lane	B3

TOURIST INFORMATION ☎ 0115 915 5330
1-4 SMITHY ROW,
NOTTINGHAM, NG1 2BY

COUNCIL OFFICE ☎ 0115 915 5555
THE GUILDHALL, SOUTH SHERWOOD STREET,
NOTTINGHAM, NG1 4BT

HOSPITAL A & E ☎ 0115 924 9924
QUEENS MEDICAL CENTRE, UNIVERSITY HOSP,
DERBY ROAD, NOTTINGHAM, NG7 2UH

WEB-SITE www.nottinghamcity.gov.uk

OXFORD

0 400 yds
0 400m

INDEX TO STREET NAMES

Albert Street	A1
Banbury Road	A2
Beaumont Street	B1
Becket Street	B1
Blackhall Road	A2
Botley Road	B1
Broad Street	B2
Canal Street	A1
Cattle Street	B2
Cornmarket	B2
Cowley Place	C3
Folly Bridge	C2
George Street	B1
Great Clarendon Street	A1
Hart Street	A1
High Street	B2
Hollybush Row	B1
Holywell Street	B2
Hythe Bridge Street	B1
Iffley Road	C3
Juxon Street	A1
Keble Road	A2
Kingston Road	A1
Littlegate Street	C2
Longwall Street	B3
Magdalen Bridge	B3
Manor Road	B3
Mansfield Road	A3
Marlborough Road	C2
Merton Street	C2
Mill Street	B1
Museum Road	A2
Nelson Street	B1
New Road	B1
Norham Gardens	A2
Observatory Street	A1
Oxpens Road	C1
Paradise Street	B1
Park End Street	B1
Parks Road	A2
Plantation Road	A1
Queen Street	B2
Rewley Road	B1
Richmond Road	B1
Rose Place	C2
St. Aldate's	C2
St. Bernards Road	A1
St. Cross Road	A3
St. Ebbe's Street	C2
St. Giles	A2
St. Thomas' Street	B1
South Parks Road	A2
Speedwell Street	C2
Thames Street	C2
Trinity Street	C1
Turl Street	B2
Walton Crescent	A1
Walton Street	A1
Walton Well Road	A1
Woodstock Road	A1

TOURIST INFORMATION ☎ 01865 726871
15-16 BROAD STREET,
OXFORD, OX1 3AS

COUNCIL OFFICE ☎ 01865 249811
PO BOX 10,
OXFORD, OX1 1EN

HOSPITAL A & E ☎ 01865 741166
JOHN RADCLIFFE HOSPITAL, HEADLEY WAY,
HEADINGTON, OXFORD, OX3 9DU

WEB-SITE www.oxford.gov.uk

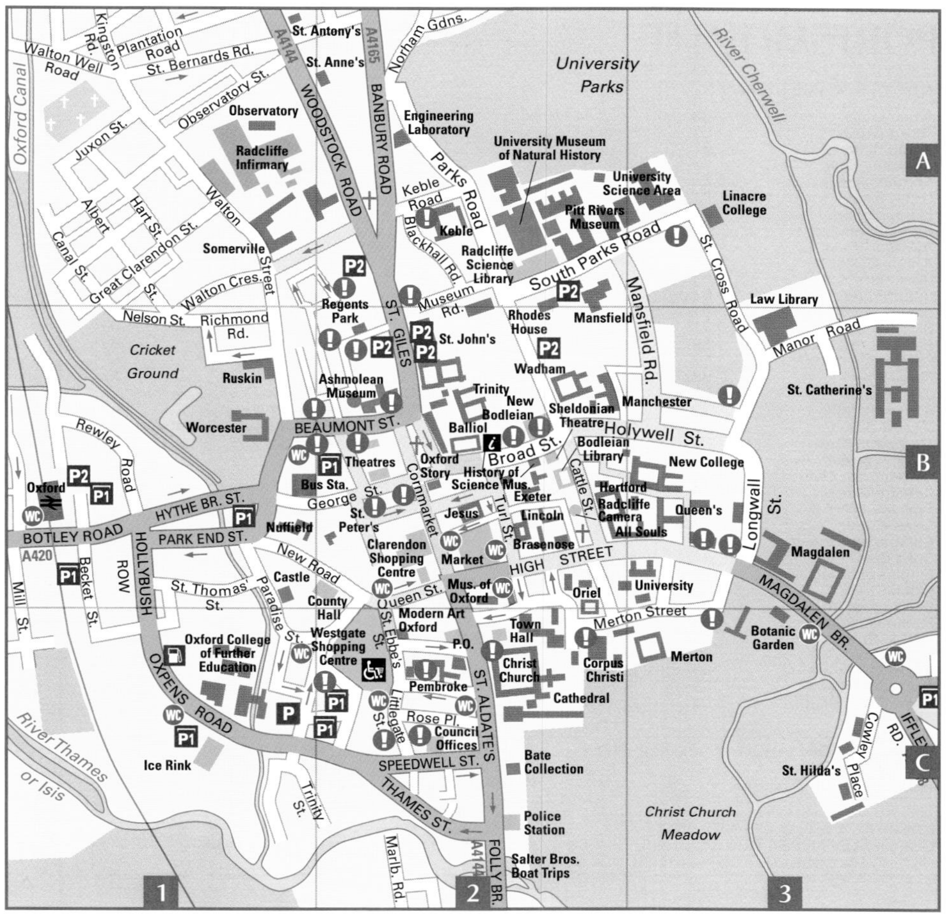

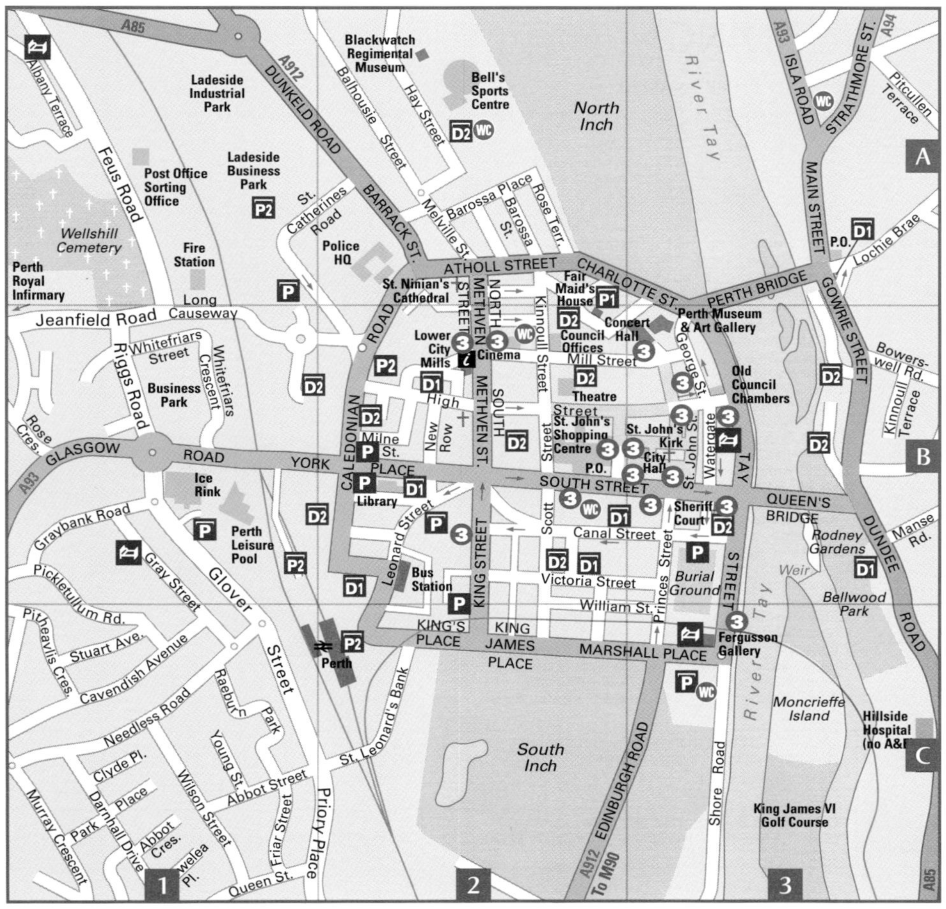

PERTH

0 300 yds
0 300m

INDEX TO STREET NAMES

Abbot Crescent	C1
Abbot Street	C1
Albany Terrace	A1
Atholl Street	A2
Balhousie Street	A2
Barossa Place	A2
Barossa Street	A2
Barrack Street	A2
Bowerswell Road	B3
Caledonian Road	B2
Canal Street	B2
Cavendish Avenue	C1
Charlotte Street	A2
Clyde Place	C1
Darnhall Drive	C1
Dundee Road	B3
Dunkeld Road	A1
Edinburgh Road	C2
Feus Road	A1
Friar Street	C1
George Street	B3
Glasgow Road	B1
Glover Street	B1
Gowrie Street	A3
Gray Street	B1
Graybank Road	B1
Hay Street	A2
High Street	B2
Isla Road	A3
Jeanfield Road	B1
King's Place	C2
King James Place	C2
King Street	B2
Kinnoull Street	A2
Kinnoull Terrace	B3
Knowelea Place	C1
Leonard Street	B2
Lochie Brae	A3
Long Causeway	A1
Main Street	A3
Manse Road	B3
Marshall Place	C2
Melville Street	A2
Mill Street	B2
Milne Street	B2
Murray Crescent	C1
Needless Road	C1
New Row	B2
North Methven Street	A2
Park Place	C1
Perth Bridge	A3
Pickletullum Road	B1
Pitcullen Terrace	A3
Pitheavlis Crescent	C1
Princes Street	C3
Priory Place	C2
Queen Street	C1
Queens Bridge	B3
Raeburn Park	C1
Riggs Road	B1
Rose Crescent	B1
Rose Terrace	A2
St. Catherines Road	A1
St. John Street	B3
St. Leonard's Bank	C2
Scott Street	B2
Shore Road	C3
South Methven Street	B2
South Street	B2
Strathmore Street	A3
Stuart Avenue	C1
Tay Street	B3
Victoria Street	B2
Watergate	B3
Whitefriars Crescent	B1
Whitefriars Street	B1
William Street	B2
Wilson Street	C1
Young Street	C1
York Place	B1

TOURIST INFORMATION ☎ 01738 450600
LOWER CITY MILLS, WEST MILL STREET,
PERTH, PH1 5QP

COUNCIL OFFICE ☎ 01738 475000
PERTH & KINROSS COUNCIL,
2 HIGH STREET, PERTH, PH1 5PH

HOSPITAL A & E ☎ 01738 623311
PERTH ROYAL INFIRMARY,
TAYMOUNT TERRACE, PERTH, PH1 1NX

WEB-SITE www.pkc.gov.uk

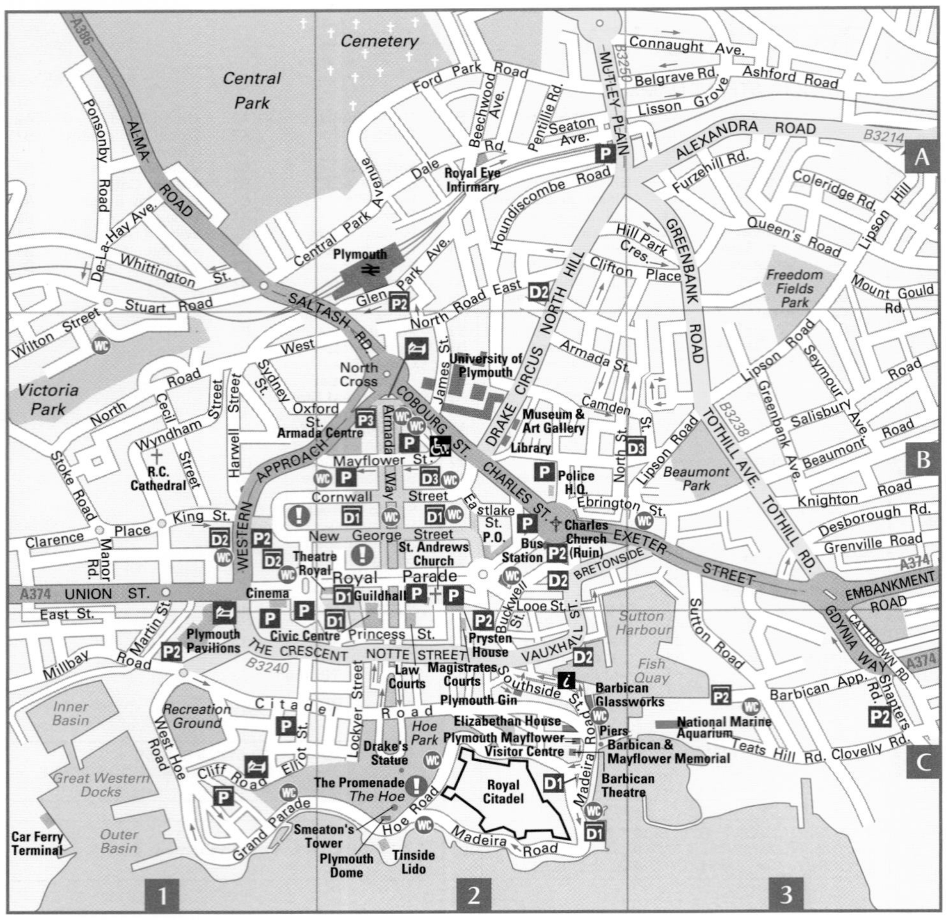

PLYMOUTH

0 400 yds
0 400m

INDEX TO STREET NAMES

Alexandra Road	A3	Gdynia Way	C3	Royal Parade	B2
Alma Road	A1	Glen Park Avenue	A2	Salisbury Road	B3
Armada Street	B3	Grand Parade	C1	Saltash Road	A1
Armada Way	B2	Greenbank Avenue	B3	Seaton Avenue	A2
Ashford Road	A3	Greenbank Road	A3	Seymour Avenue	B3
Barbican Approach	C3	Grenville Road	B3	Southside Street	C2
Beaumont Road	B3	Harwell Street	B1	Stoke Road	B1
Beechwood Avenue	A2	Hill Park Crescent	A2	Stuart Road	A1
Belgrave Road	A3	Hoe Road	C2	Sutton Road	B3
Bretonside	B2	Houndiscombe Road	A2	Sydney Street	B1
Buckwell Street	B2	James Street	B2	Teats Hill Road	C3
Camden Street	B2	King Street	B1	The Crescent	C1
Cattledown Road	C3	Knighton Road	B3	Tothill Avenue	B3
Cecil Street	B1	Lipson Hill	A3	Tothill Road	B3
Central Park Avenue	A1	Lipson Road	B3	Union Street	B1
Charles Street	B2	Lisson Grove	A3	Vauxhall Street	C2
Citadel Road	C1	Lockyer Street	C2	West Hoe Road	C1
Clarence Place	B1	Looe Street	B2	Western Approach	B1
Cliff Road	C1	Madeira Road	C2	Whittington Street	A1
Clifton Place	A2	Manor Road	B1	Wilton Street	B1
Clovelly Road	C3	Martin Street	C1	Wyndham Street	B1
Cobourg Street	B2	Mayflower Street	B2		
Coleridge Road	A3	Millbay Road	C1		
Connaught Avenue	A3	Mount Gould Road	A3		
Cornwall Street	B2	Mutley Plain	A2		
Dale Road	A2	New George Street	B1		
De-La-Hay Avenue	A1	North Cross	B2		
Desborough Road	B3	North Hill	B2		
Drake Circus	B2	North Road East	B2		
East Street	C1	North Road West	B1		
Eastlake Street	B2	North Street	B2		
Ebrington Street	B2	Notte Street	C2		
Elliot Street	C1	Oxford Street	B1		
Embankment Road	B3	Pentillie Road	A2		
Exeter Street	B2	Ponsonby Road	A1		
Ford Park Road	A2	Princess Street	C2		
Furzehill Road	A3	Queen's Road	A3		

TOURIST INFORMATION ☎ 01752 304849
ISLAND HOUSE, 9 THE BARBICAN,
PLYMOUTH, PL1 2LS

COUNCIL OFFICE ☎ 01752 668000
CIVIC CENTRE, ARMADA WAY,
PLYMOUTH, PL1 2EW

HOSPITAL A & E ☎ 01752 777111
DERRIFORD HOSPITAL, DERRIFORD ROAD,
CROWNHILL, PLYMOUTH, PL6 8DH

WEB-SITE www.plymouth.gov.uk

PORTSMOUTH

0 500 yds
0 500m

INDEX TO STREET NAMES

Albany Road	C3	Gunwharf Road	C1	St. James Road	C2
Albert Grove	C3	Hampshire Terrace	C2	St. James Street	B2
Alfred Road	B2	Havant Street	B1	St. Paul's Road	C2
Anglesea Road	B2	High Street	C1	St. Thomas's Street	C1
Arundel Street	B3	Holbrook Road	A3	Somers Road	B3
Astley Street	C2	Hope Street	A2	Southsea Terrace	C2
Bailey's Road	C3	Hyde Park Road	B3	Station Street	B3
Bellevue Terrace	C2	Isambard Brunel Road	B2	Stone Street	C2
Belmont Street	C3	Kent Road	C2	Sultan Road	A3
Bishop Street	A1	Kent Street	A1	Sussex Street	C2
Blackfriars Road	B3	King Charles Street	C1	The Hard	B1
Bradford Road	B3	King's Road	C2	Turner Road	A3
Britain Street	B1	King's Terrace	C2	Unicorn Road	A2
Broad Street	C1	King Street	C2	Upper Arundel Street	B3
Burnaby Road	B2	Lake Road	A3	Victoria Road North	C3
Cambridge Road	C2	Landport Terrace	C2	Warblington Street	C1
Canal Walk	B3	Lombard Street	C1	Watts Road	A3
Castle Road	C2	Margate Road	C3	White Hart Road	C1
Church Road	A3	Market Way	A2	Wingfield Street	A3
Church Street	A3	Melbourne Place	B2	Winston Churchill Avenue	B2
Clarendon Street	A3	Museum Road	C2	York Place	B2
College Street	B1	Nelson Road	A3		
Commercial Road	B2	Norfolk Street	C2		
Cottage Grove	C3	Northam Street	B3		
Crasswell Street	A3	Outram Road	C3		
Cross Street	A1	Pain's Road	C3		
Cumberland Street	A1	Paradise Street	B3		
Duke Crescent	A3	Park Road	B2		
Edinburgh Road	B2	Pembroke Road	C1		
Eldon Street	C2	Penny Street	C1		
Elm Grove	C3	Queen's Crescent	C3		
Flathouse Road	A3	Queen Street	B1		
Fyning Street	A3	Raglan Street	B3		
Green Road	C2	Railway View	B3		
Greetham Street	B3	St. Andrews Road	C3		
Grosvenor Street	C3	St. Edward's Road	C2		
Grove Road South	C3	St. George's Road	B1		

TOURIST INFORMATION ☎ 023 9282 6722
THE HARD,
PORTSMOUTH, PO1 3QJ

COUNCIL OFFICE ☎ 023 9282 2251
CIVIC OFFICES, GUILDHALL SQUARE,
PORTSMOUTH, PO1 2BG

HOSPITAL A & E ☎ 023 9228 6000
QUEEN ALEXANDRA HOSPITAL, SOUTHWICK
HILL ROAD, COSHAM, PORTSMOUTH, PO6 3LY

WEB-SITE www.portsmouth.gov.uk

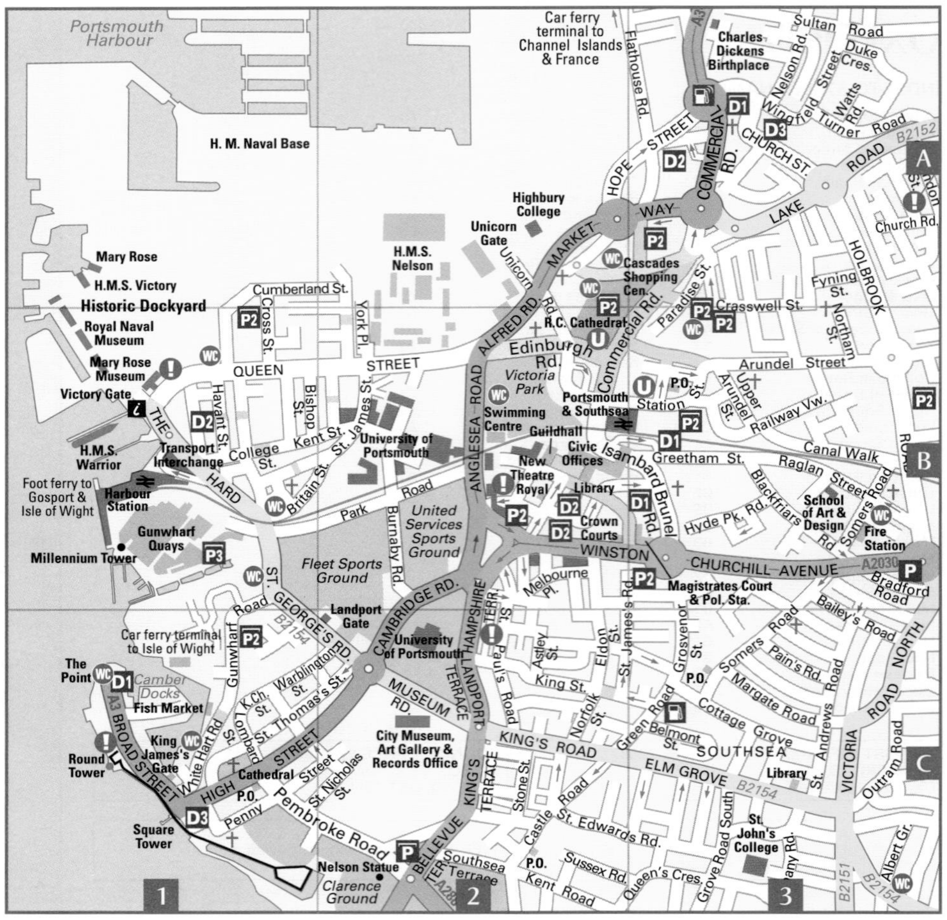

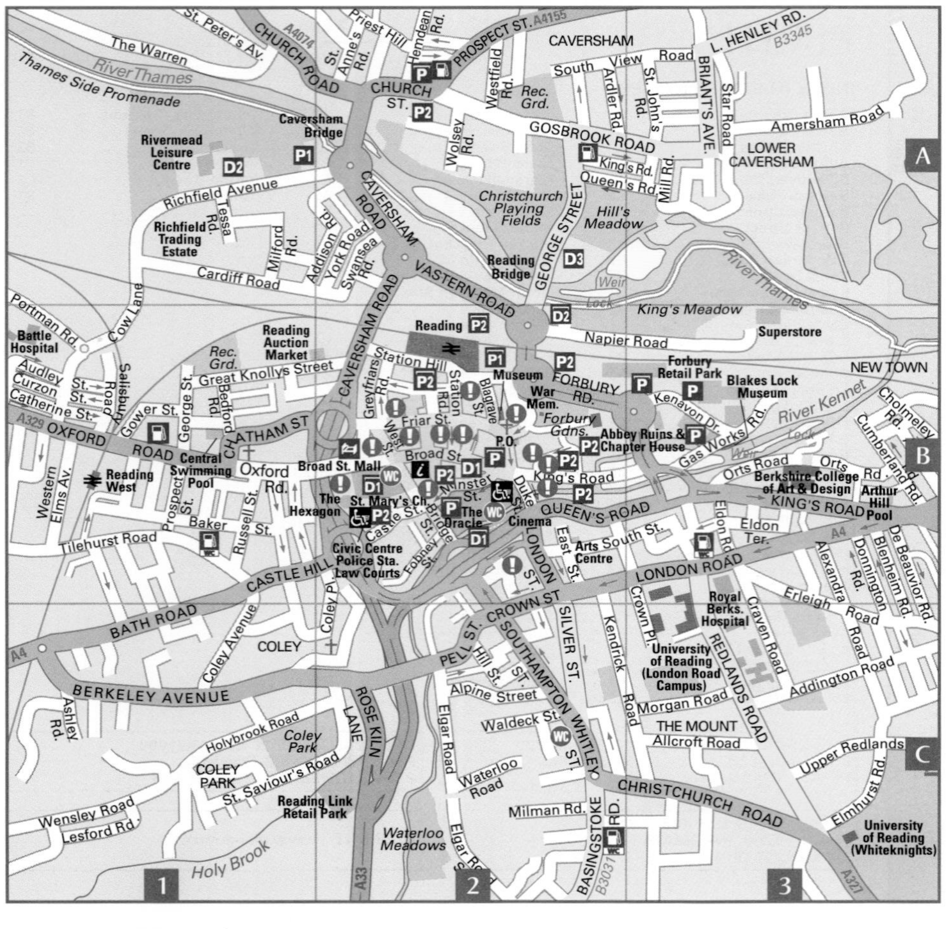

READING

0 500 yds
0 500m

INDEX TO STREET NAMES

Addington Road	C3	Cumberland Road	B3	Mill Road	A3	The Warren	A1
Addison Road	A1	Curzon Street	B1	Milford Road	A1	Tilehurst Road	B1
Alexandra Road	B3	De Beauvoir Road	B3	Milman Road	C2	Upper Redlands Road	C3
Allcroft Road	C3	Donnington Road	B3	Minster Street	B2	Vastern Road	A2
Alpine Street	C2	Duke Street	B2	Morgan Road	C3	Waldelk Street	C2
Amersham Road	A3	East Street	B2	Napier Road	B2	Waterloo Road	C2
Amity Road	B3	Eldon Road	B2	Orts Road	B3	Wensley Road	C1
Ardler Road	A2	Eldon Terrace	B3	Oxford Road	B1	Western Elms Avenue	B1
Ashley Road	C1	Elgar Road	C2	Pell Street	C2	Westfield Road	A2
Audley Street	B1	Elgar Road South	C2	Portman Road	A1	West Street	B2
Baker Street	B1	Elmhurst Road	C3	Priest Hill	A2	Whitley Street	C2
Basingstoke Road	C2	Erleigh Road	B3	Prospect Street *Caversham*	A2	Wolsey Road	A2
Bath Road	C1	Fobney Street	B2	Prospect Street *Reading*	B1	York Road	A2
Bedford Road	B1	Forbury Road	B2	Queen's Road *Caversham*	A2		
Berkeley Avenue	C1	Friar Street	B2	Queen's Road *Reading*	B2		
Blagrave Street	B2	Gas Work Road	B3	Redlands Road	C3		
Blenheim Road	B3	George Street *Caversham*	A2	Richfield Avenue	A1		
Briant's Avenue	A3	George Street *Reading*	B1	Rose Kiln Lane	C2		
Bridge Street	B2	Gosbrook Road	A2	Russell Street	B1		
Broad Street	B2	Gower Street	B1	St. Anne's Road	A2		
Cardiff Road	A1	Great Knollys Street	B1	St. John's Road	A3		
Castle Hill	B1	Greyfriars Road	B2	St. Mary's Butts	B2		
Castle Street	B2	Hemdean Road	A2	St. Peters Avenue	A1		
Catherine Street	B1	Hill Street	C2	St. Saviours Road	C1		
Caversham Road	B2	Holybrook Road	C1	Silver Street	C2		
Chatham Street	B2	Kenavon Drive	B3	South Street	B2		
Cheapside	B2	Kendrick Road	C2	Southampton Street	C2		
Cholmeley Road	B3	King's Road *Caversham*	A2	South View Road	A2		
Christchurch Road	C2	King's Road *Reading*	B2	Star Road	A3		
Church Road	A1	Lesford Road	C1	Station Hill	B2		
Church Street	A2	London Road	B3	Station Road	B2		
Coley Avenue	C1	London Street	B2	Swansea Road	A2		
Coley Place	B2	Lower Henley Road	A3	Tessa Road	A1		
Cow Lane	B1						
Craven Road	B3						
Crown Place	B3						
Crown Street	C2						

TOURIST INFORMATION ☎ 0118 956 6226
CHURCH HOUSE, CHAIN STREET,
READING, RG1 2HX

COUNCIL OFFICE ☎ 0118 939 0900
CIVIC CENTRE, CIVIC OFFICES, (OFF CASTLE ST.)
READING, RG1 7TD

HOSPITAL A & E ☎ 0118 987 5111
ROYAL BERKSHIRE HOSPITAL, LONDON ROAD,
READING, RG1 5AN

WEB-SITE www.reading.gov.uk

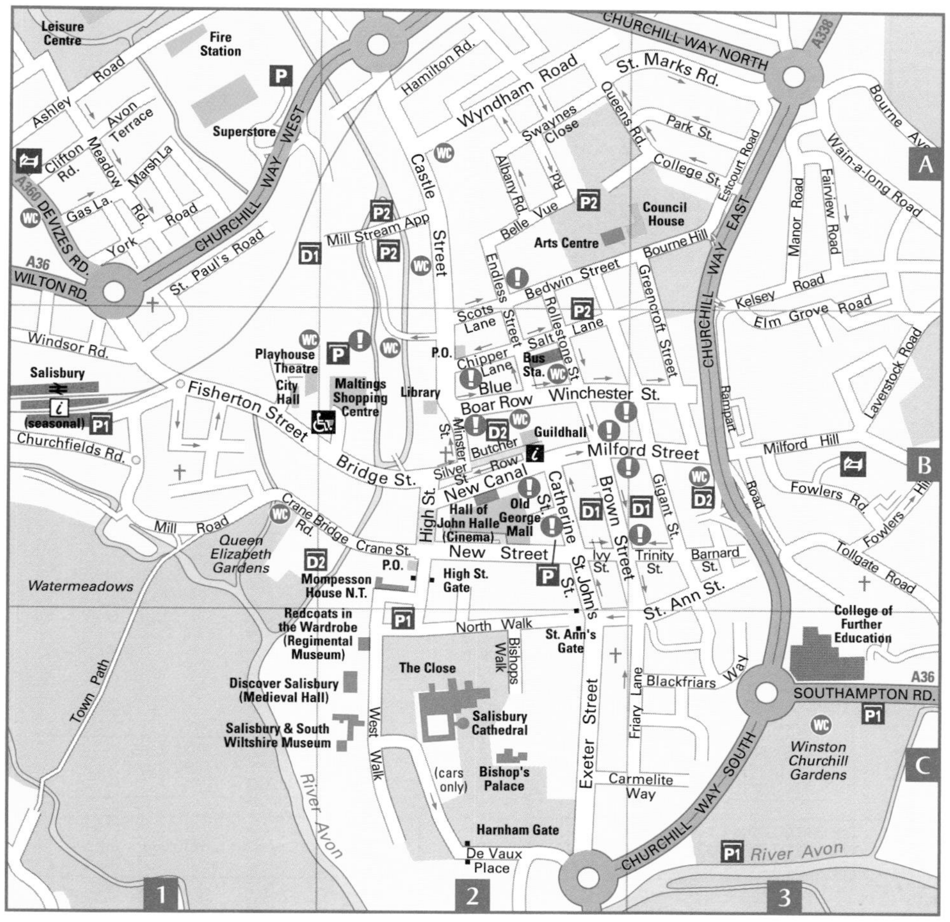

SALISBURY

0 200 yds
0 200m

INDEX TO STREET NAMES

Albany Road A2
Ashley Road A1
Avon Terrace A1
Barnard Street B3
Bedwin Street A2
Belle Vue Road A2
Bishops Walk C2
Blackfriars Way C3
Blue Boar Row B2
Bourne Avenue A3
Bourne Hill A3
Bridge Street B2
Brown Street B2
Butcher Row B2
Carmelite Way C2
Castle Street A2
Catherine Street B2
Chipper Lane B2
Churchfields Road B1
Churchill Way East B3
Churchill Way North A2
Churchill Way South C2
Churchill Way West A1
Clifton Road A1
College Street A3
Crane Bridge Road B1
Crane Street B2
De Vaux Place C2
Devizes Road A1
Elm Grove Road B3
Endless Street A2
Estcourt Road A3
Exeter Street C2
Fairview Road A3
Fisherton Street B1
Fowlers Hill B3
Fowlers Road B3
Friary Lane C3
Gas Lane A1
Gigant Street B3
Greencroft Street A3
Hamilton Road A2
High Street B2
Ivy Street B2
Kelsey Road A3
Laverstock Road B3
Manor Road A3
Marsh Lane A1
Meadow Road A1
Milford Hill B3
Milford Street B2
Mill Road B1
Millstream Approach A2
Minster Street B2
New Canal B2
New Street B2
North Walk C2
Park Street A3
Queens Road A2
Rampart Road B3
Rollestone Street B2
St. Ann Street C3
St. John's Street B2
St. Marks Road A2
St. Paul's Road A1
Salt Lane B2
Scots Lane B2
Silver Street B2
Southampton Road C3
Swaynes Close A2
Tollgate Road B3
Trinity Street B3
Wain-a-long Road A3
West Walk C2
Wilton Road A1
Winchester Street B2
Windsor Road B1
Wyndham Road A2
York Road A1

TOURIST INFORMATION ☎ 01722 334956
FISH ROW,
SALISBURY, SP1 1EJ

COUNCIL OFFICE ☎ 01722 336272
THE COUNCIL HOUSE, BOURNE HILL,
SALISBURY, SP1 3UZ

HOSPITAL A & E ☎ 01722 336262
SALISBURY DISTRICT HOSPITAL, ODSTOCK ROAD,
SALISBURY, SP2 8BJ

WEB-SITE www.salisbury.gov.uk

SCARBOROUGH

0 400 yds
0 400m

INDEX TO STREET NAMES

Aberdeen Walk B2
Albion Road C2
Ashville Avenue B1
Avenue Road C1
Belmont Road C2
Candler Street B1
Castle Road A2
Castle Road B2
Chatsworth Gardens A1
Columbus Ravine B1
Commercial Street C1
Cross Street B2
Dean Road B1
Eastborough B2
Esplanade C2
Falconers Road B2
Falsgrave Road C1
Foreshore Road B2
Franklin Street B1
Friargate B2
Friarsway B2
Garfield Road B1
Gladstone Road B1
Gladstone Street B1
Gordon Street B1
Grosvenor Road C2
Highfield C1
Hoxton Road B1
Longwestgate B3
Manor Road C1
Marine Drive A3
Mayville Avenue B1
Moorland Road A1
New Queen Street A2
Newborough B2
North Marine Road A2
North Street B2
Northstead Manor Drive A1
Northway B1
Norwood Street B1
Oak Road C1
Peasholm Crescent A1
Peasholm Drive A1
Peasholm Road A1
Prince of Wales Terrace C2
Princess Street B3
Prospect Road B1
Queen Street B2
Queen's Parade A2
Raleigh Street B1
Ramshill Road C2
Roscoe Street C1
Rothbury Street B1
Royal Albert Drive A2
Royal Avenue C2
St. James Road C1
St. John's Avenue C1
St. John's Road C1
St. Thomas Street B2
Sandside B3
Seamer Road C1
Stepney Road C1
Tollergate A2
Trafalgar Road A1
Trafalgar Square A2
Trafalgar Street West B1
Trinity Road C1
Valley Bridge Parade C2
Valley Bridge Road B2
Valley Bridge C2
Valley Road C1
Vernon Road B2
Victoria Park Mount A1
Victoria Road C1
Victoria Street B2
West Street C2
Westborough C1
Westbourne Grove C1
Westover Road C1
Westwood Road C1
Westwood C2
Weydale Avenue A1
Wykeham Street C1

TOURIST INFORMATION ☎ 01723 373333
UNIT 3, PAVILION HOUSE, VALLEY BRIDGE ROAD,
SCARBOROUGH, YO11 1UZ

COUNCIL OFFICE ☎ 01723 232521
TOWN HALL, ST NICHOLAS STREET,
SCARBOROUGH, YO11 2HG

HOSPITAL A & E ☎ 01723 368111
SCARBOROUGH GENERAL HOSPITAL,
WOODLANDS DRIVE, SCARBOROUGH, YO12 6QL

WEB-SITE www.scarborough.gov.uk

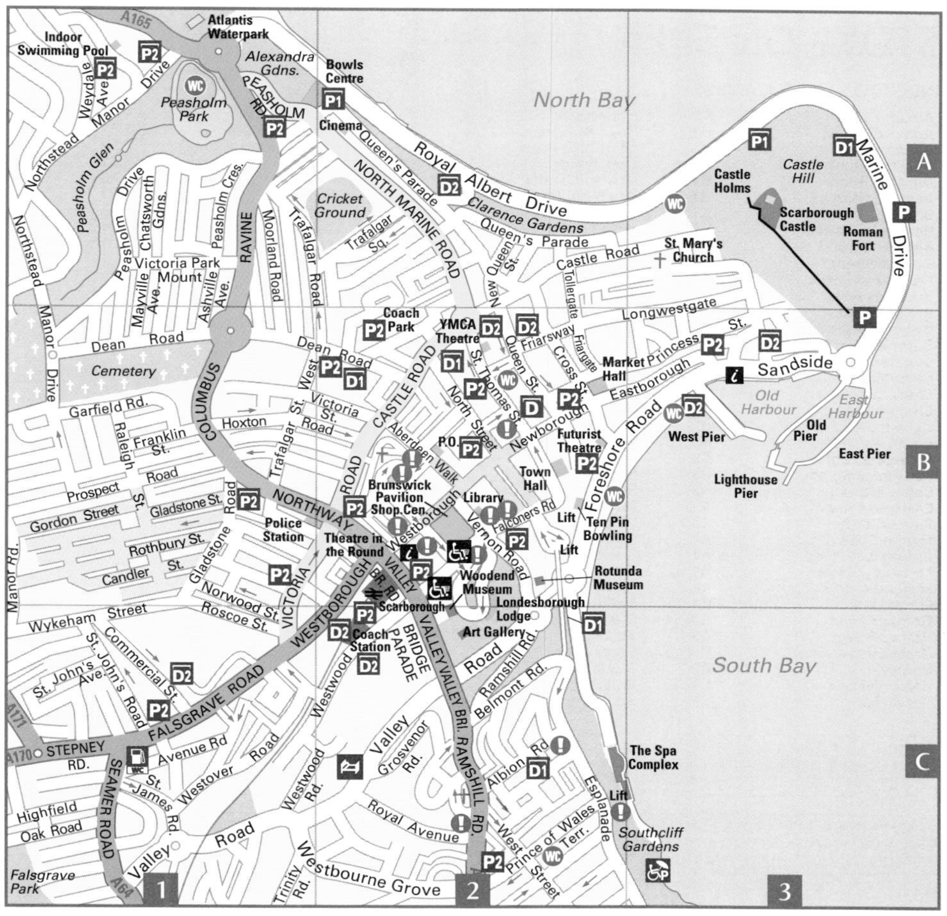

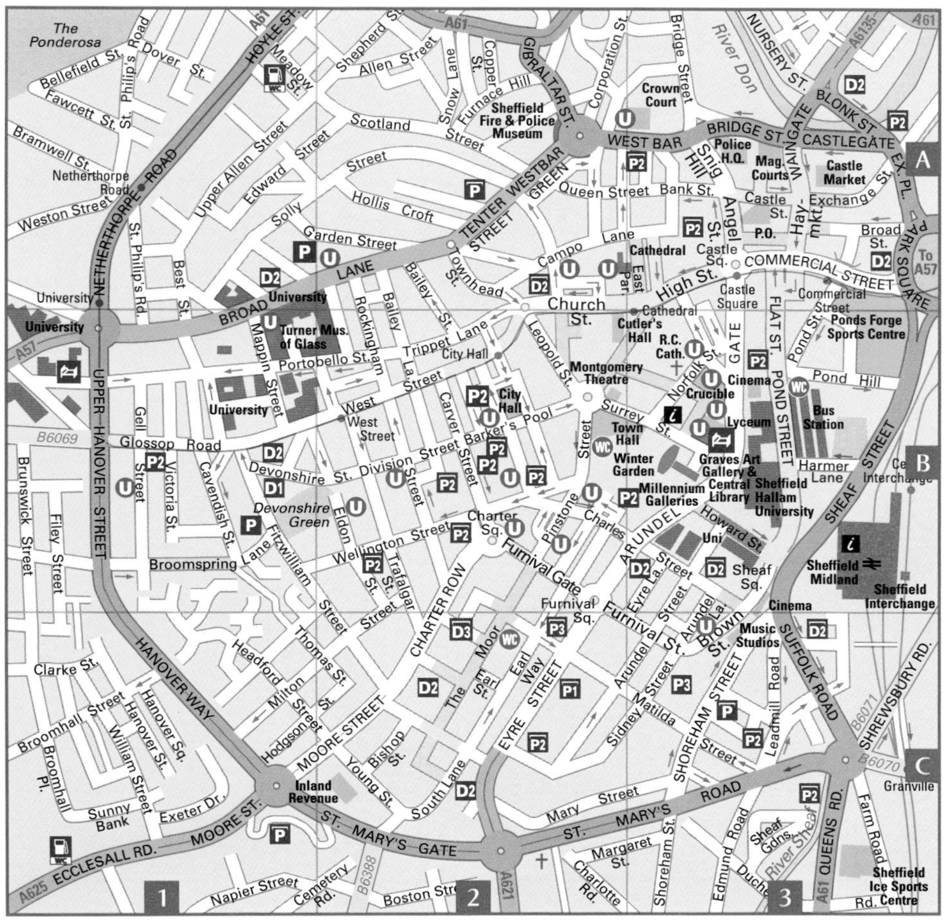

SHEFFIELD

0 300 yds
0 300m

INDEX TO STREET NAMES

Allen Street A2
Angel Street A3
Arundel Gate B2
Arundel Lane C3
Arundel Street C2
Bailey Lane A2
Bailey Street A2
Bank Street A3
Barker's Pool B2
Bellefield Street A1
Best Street A1
Bishop Street C2
Blonk Street A3
Boston Street C2
Bower Street A2
Bramwell Street A1
Bridge Street A3
Broad Lane A2
Broad Street A3
Broomhall Street C1
Broomhall Place C1
Broomspring Lane B1
Brown Street C3
Brunswick Street B1
Campo Lane A2
Carver Street B2
Castle Square A3
Castle Street A3
Castlegate A3
Cavendish Street B1
Cemetery Road C1
Charles Street B2/B3
Charlotte Road C2
Charter Row C2
Charter Square B2
Church Street A2
Clarke Street C1
Commercial Street A3
Copper Street A2
Corporation Street A2
Devonshire Street B1
Division Street B2
Dover Street A1
Duchess Road C3
Earl Street C2
Earl Way C2
East Parade A3
Ecclesall Road C1
Edmund Road C3
Edward Street A1
Eldon Street B2
Exchange Street A3
Exeter Drive C1
Eyre Lane C2
Eyre Street C2
Farm Road C3
Fawcett Street A1
Filey Street B1
Fitzwilliam Street B1
Flat Street A3
Furnace Hill A2
Furnival Gate B2
Furnival Square B2
Furnival Street B2
Garden Street A1
Gell Street B1
Gibraltar Street A2
Glossop Road B1
Hanover Square C1
Hanover Street C1
Hanover Way C1
Harmer Lane B3
Haymarket A3
Headford Street C1
High Street A3
Hodgson Street C1
Hollis Croft A2
Howard Street B3
Hoyle Street A1
Leadmill Road C3
Leopold Street B2
Mappin Street B1
Margaret Street C2
Mary Street C2
Matilda Street C3
Meadow Street A1
Milton Street C1
Moore Street C1
Napier Street C1
Nethergthorpe Road A1
Norfolk Street B3
Nursery Street A3
Pinstone Street B2
Pond Hill B3
Pond Hill B3
Pond Street B3
Portobello Street B1
Queen Street A2
Queens Road C3
Rockingham Street B2
St. Mary's Gate C2
St. Mary's Road C2
St. Philip's Road A1
Scotland Street A2
Sheaf Gardens C3
Sheaf Square B3
Sheaf Street B3
Shepherd Street A2
Shoreham Street C3
Shrewsbury Road C3
Sidney Street C2
Snig Hill A3
Snow Lane A2
Solly Street A1
South Lane C2
Spring Street A2
Suffolk Road C3
Sunny Bank C1
Surrey Street B2
Tenter Street A2
The Moor C2
Thomas Street C1
Townhead Street A2
Trafalgar Street B2
Trippet Lane B2
Upper Allen Street A1
Upper Hanover Street B1
Victoria Street B1
Waingate A3
Wellington Street B2
West Bar A2
West Street B2
Westbar Green A2
Weston Street A1
William Street C1
Young Street C2

TOURIST INFORMATION ☎ 0114 221 1900
1 TUDOR SQUARE,
SHEFFIELD, S1 2LA

COUNCIL OFFICE ☎ 0114 272 6444
TOWN HALL, SURREY STREET,
SHEFFIELD, S1 2HH

HOSPITAL A & E ☎ 0114 243 4343
NORTHERN GENERAL HOSPITAL, HERRIES ROAD,
SHEFFIELD, S5 7AU

WEB-SITE www.sheffield.gov.uk

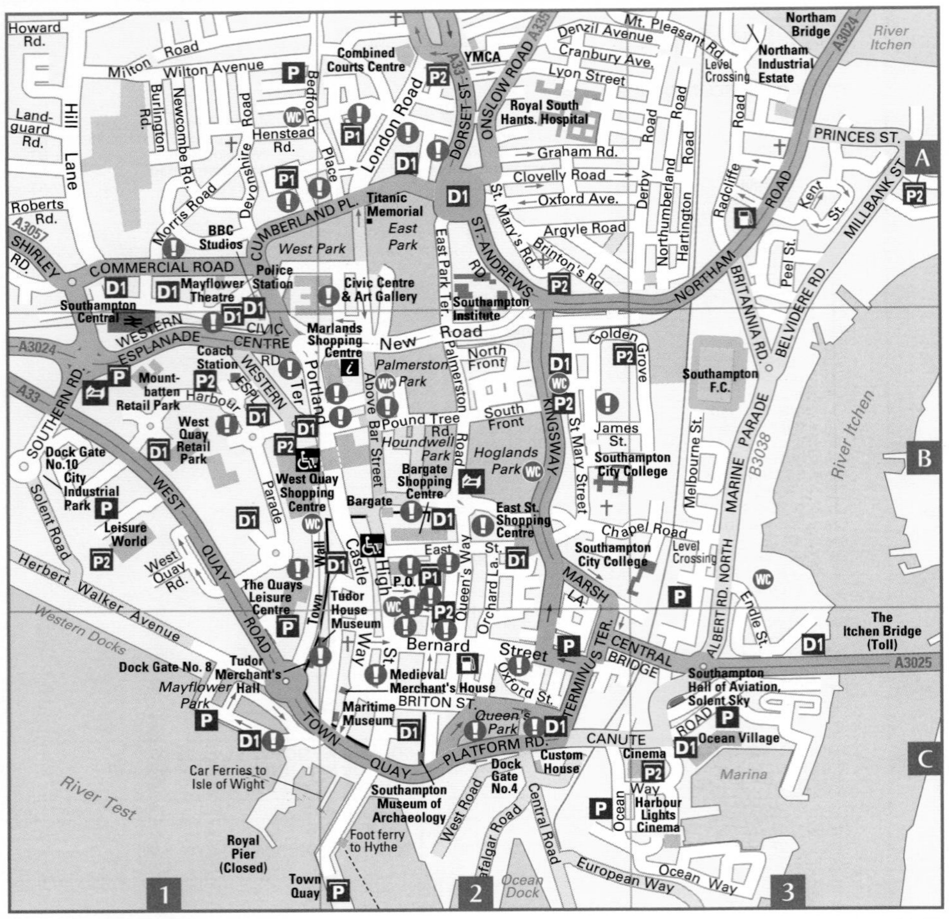

SOUTHAMPTON

0 400 yds
0 400m

INDEX TO STREET NAMES

Above Bar Street	B2
Albert Road North	C3
Argyle Road	A2
Bedford Place	A1
Belvidere Road	B3
Bernard Street	C2
Brintons Road	A2
Britannia Road	A3
Briton Street	C2
Burlington Road	A1
Canute Road	C2
Castle Way	B2
Central Bridge	C2
Central Road	C2
Chapel Road	B2
Civic Centre Road	B1
Clovelly Road	A2
Commercial Road	A1
Cranbury Avenue	A2
Cumberland Place	A1
Denzil Avenue	A2
Derby Road	A3
Devonshire Road	A1
Dorset Street	A2
East Park Terrace	A2
East Street	B2
Endle Street	B3
European Way	C2
Golden Grove	B2
Graham Road	A2
Harbour Parade	B1
Hartington Road	A3
Henstead Road	A1
Herbert Walker Avenue	B1
High Street	B2
Hill Lane	A1
Howard Road	A1
James Street	B2
Kent Street	A3
Kingsway	B2
Landguard Road	A1
London Road	A2
Lyon Street	A2
Marine Parade	B3
Marsh Lane	B2
Melbourne Street	B3
Millbank Street	A3
Milton Road	A1
Morris Road	A1
Mount Pleasant Road	A3
Newcombe Road	A1
New Road	B2
Northam Road	A3
North Front	B2
Northumberland Road	A3
Ocean Way	C2
Onslow Road	A2
Orchard Lane	C2
Oxford Avenue	A2
Oxford Street	C2
Palmerston Road	B2
Peel Street	A3
Platform Road	C2
Portland Terrace	B1
Pound Tree Road	B2
Princes Street	A3
Queen's Way	C2
Radcliffe Road	A3
Roberts Road	A1
St. Andrews Road	A2
St. Mary's Road	A2
St. Mary Street	B2
Shirley Road	A1
Solent Road	B1
Southern Road	B1
South Front	B2
Terminus Terrace	C2
Town Quay	C1
Trafalgar Road	C2
West Quay Road	B1
West Road	C2
Western Esplanade	B1
Wilton Avenue	A1

TOURIST INFORMATION ☎ 023 8083 3333
9 CIVIC CENTRE ROAD,
SOUTHAMPTON, SO14 7FJ

COUNCIL OFFICE ☎ 023 8022 3855
CIVIC CENTRE, CIVIC CENTRE ROAD,
SOUTHAMPTON, SO14 7LY

HOSPITAL A & E ☎ 023 8077 7222
SOUTHAMPTON GENERAL HOSPITAL, TREMONA RD, SHIRLEY, SOUTHAMPTON, SO16 6YD

WEB-SITE www.southampton.gov.uk

STOKE-ON-TRENT

0 500 yds
0 500m

INDEX TO STREET NAMES

Albion Street	A2
Ashford Street	B2
Avenue Road	B2
Aynsley Road	B2
Bedford Road	B2
Bedford Street	B1
Belmont Road	A1
Beresford Street	B2
Berry Hill Road	B3
Boon Avenue	C1
Botteslow Street	A3
Boughey Road	C2
Broad Street	A2
Bucknall New Road	A3
Bucknall Old Road	A3
Cauldon Road	B2
Cemetery Road	B1
Church Street	C2
Clough Street	A1
College Road	B2
Commercial Road	A3
Copeland Street	C2
Dewsbury Road	C3
Eagle Street	A3
Eastwood Road	A3
Elenora Street	C2
Etruria Road	A1
Etruria Vale Road	A1
Etruscan Street	B1
Festival Way	A1
Forge Lane	A1
Garner Street	B1
Glebe Street	C2
Greatbatch Avenue	C1
Hanley	A2
Hartshill Road	C1
Hill Street	C1
Honeywall	C1
Howard Place	B2
Ivy House Road	A3
Leek Road	C2
Lichfield Street	A3
Liverpool Road	C2
Lordship Lane	C2
Lytton Street	C2
Manor Street	C3
Marsh Street	A2
Newlands Street	B2
North Street	B1
Old Hall Street	A2
Oxford Street	C1
Parliament Row	A2
Potteries Way	A2
Potters Way	A3
Prince's Road	C1
Quarry Avenue	C1
Quarry Road	C1
Queen's Road	C1
Queensway	B1
Rectory Road	B2
Regent Road	B2
Richmond Street	C1
Ridgway Road	B2
Seaford Street	B2
Shelton New Road	B1
Shelton Old Road	C1
Snow Hill	B2
Stafford Street	A2
Station Road	C2
Stoke	C2
Stoke Road	C2
Stone Street	C1
Stuart Road	B3
Sun Street	A2
The Parkway	B2
Trentmill Road	B3
Victoria Road	B3
Warner Street	A2
Waterloo Street	A3
Wellesley Street	B2
Wellington Road	A3
West Avenue	C1
Westland Street	C1
Yoxall Avenue	C1

TOURIST INFORMATION ☎ 01782 236000
POTTERIES SHOPPING CENTRE, QUADRANT RD,
STOKE-ON-TRENT, ST1 1RZ

COUNCIL OFFICE ☎ 01782 234567
TOWN HALL, CIVIC CENTRE, GLEBE STREET,
STOKE-ON-TRENT, ST4 1RN

HOSPITAL A & E ☎ 01782 715444
UNI. HOSPITAL OF NORTH STAFFORDSHIRE,
PRINCE'S ROAD, STOKE-ON-TRENT, ST4 7LN

WEB-SITE www.stoke.gov.uk

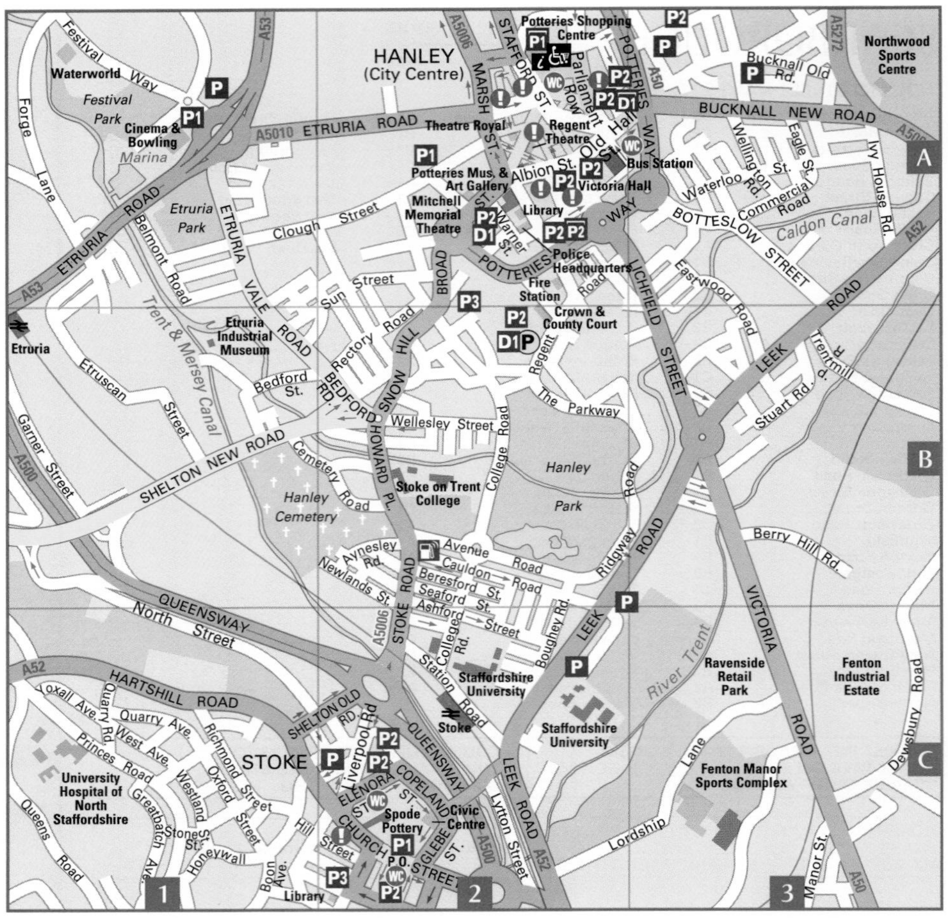

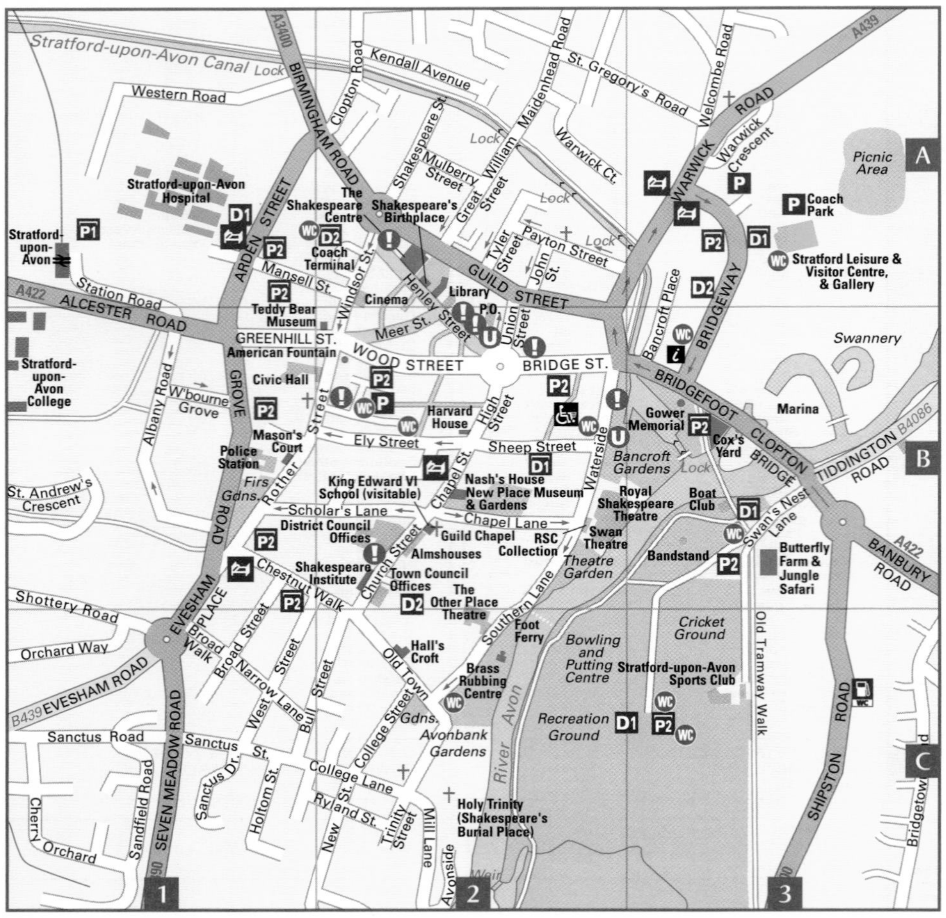

STRATFORD-UPON-AVON

0 500 yds
0 500m

INDEX TO STREET NAMES

Albany Road	B1
Alcester Road	A1
Arden Street	A1
Avonside	C2
Banbury Road	B3
Bancroft Place	B3
Birmingham Road	A1
Bridgefoot	B3
Bridge Street	B2
Bridgeway	B3
Bridgetown Road	C3
Broad Street	C1
Broad Walk	C1
Bull Street	C1
Chapel Lane	B2
Chapel Street	B2
Cherry Orchard	C1
Chestnut Walk	B1
Church Street	B2
Clopton Bridge	B3
Clopton Road	A2
College Lane	C2
College Street	C2
Ely Street	B2
Evesham Place	C1
Evesham Road	C1
Great William Street	A2
Greenhill Street	B1
Grove Road	B1
Guild Street	A2
Henley Street	A2
High Street	B2
Holtom Street	C1
John Street	A2
Kendall Avenue	A2
Maidenhead Road	A2
Mansell Street	A1
Meer Street	B2
Mill Lane	C2
Mulberry Street	A2
Narrow Lane	C1
New Street	C2
Old Town	C2
Old Tramway Walk	C3
Orchard Way	C1
Payton Street	A2
Rother Street	B1
Ryland Street	C2
St. Andrews Crescent	B1
St. Gregory's Road	A2
Sanctus Drive	C1
Sanctus Road	C1
Sanctus Street	C1
Sandfield Road	C1
Scholar's Lane	B1
Shakespeare Street	A2
Sheep Street	B2
Shipston Road	C3
Shottery Road	B1
Seven Meadow Road	C1
Southern Lane	C2
Station Road	A1
Swan's Nest Lane	B3
Tiddington Road	B3
Trinity Street	C2
Tyler Street	A2
Union Street	B2
Warwick Court	A2
Warwick Crescent	A3
Warwick Road	A3
Waterside	B2
Welcombe Road	A3
Westbourne Grove	B1
Western Road	A1
West Street	C1
Windsor Street	B2
Wood Street	B2

TOURIST INFORMATION ☎ 01789 293127
BRIDGEFOOT,
STRATFORD-UPON-AVON, CV37 6GW

COUNCIL OFFICE ☎ 01789 267575
COUNCIL OFFICES, ELIZABETH HOUSE,
CHURCH ST, STRATFORD-UPON-AVON, CV37 6HX

HOSPITAL A & E ☎ 01926 495321
WARWICK HOSPITAL, LAKIN ROAD,
WARWICK, CV34 5BW

WEB-SITE www.stratford.gov.uk

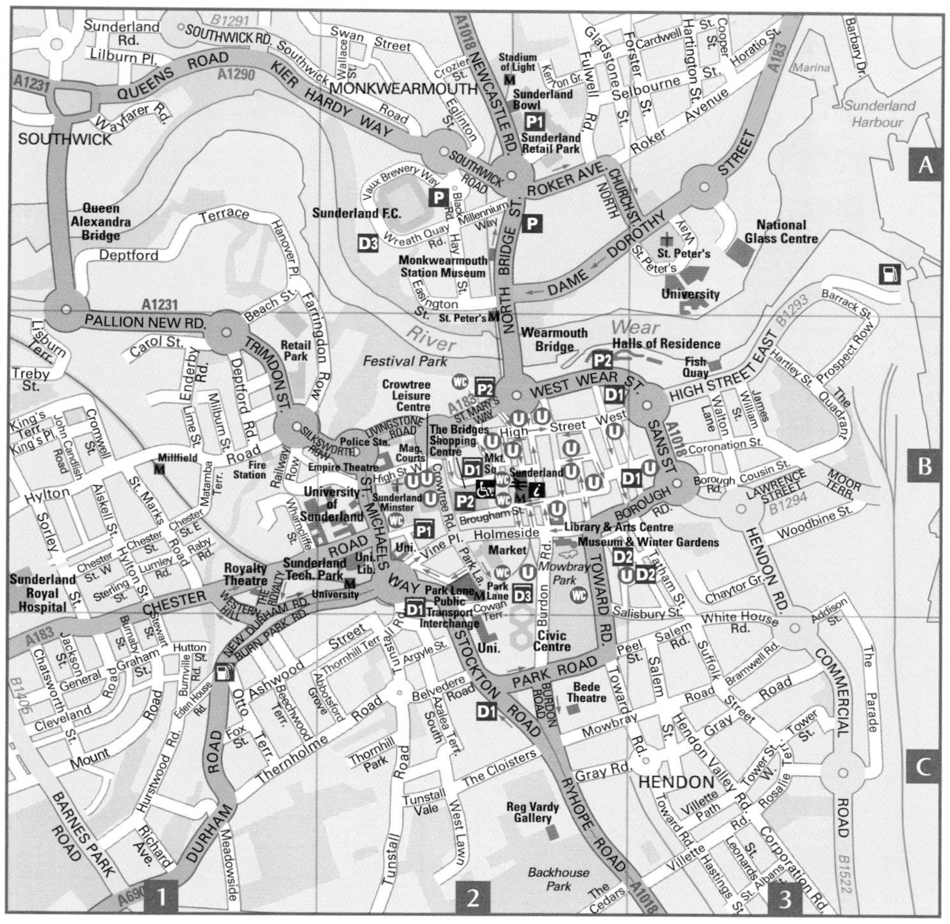

SUNDERLAND

0 400 yds
0 400m

INDEX TO STREET NAMES

TOURIST INFORMATION ☎ 0191 553 2000
50 FAWCETT STREET,
SUNDERLAND, SR1 1RF

COUNCIL OFFICE ☎ 0191 553 1000
SUNDERLAND CITY COUNCIL, CIVIC CENTRE,
BURDON ROAD, SUNDERLAND, SR2 7DN

HOSPITAL A & E ☎ 0191 565 6256
SUNDERLAND DISTRICT GENERAL HOSPITAL,
KAYLL ROAD, SUNDERLAND, SR4 7TP

WEB-SITE www.sunderland.gov.uk

SWANSEA

0 500 yds
0 500m

INDEX TO STREET NAMES

TOURIST INFORMATION ☎ 01792 468321
PLYMOUTH STREET,
SWANSEA, SA1 3QG

COUNCIL OFFICE ☎ 01792 636000
COUNTY HALL, OYSTERMOUTH ROAD,
SWANSEA, SA1 3SN

HOSPITAL A & E ☎ 01792 702222
MORRISTON HOSPITAL, HEOL MAES EGLWYS,
MORRISTON, SWANSEA, SA6 6NL

WEB-SITE www.swansea.gov.uk

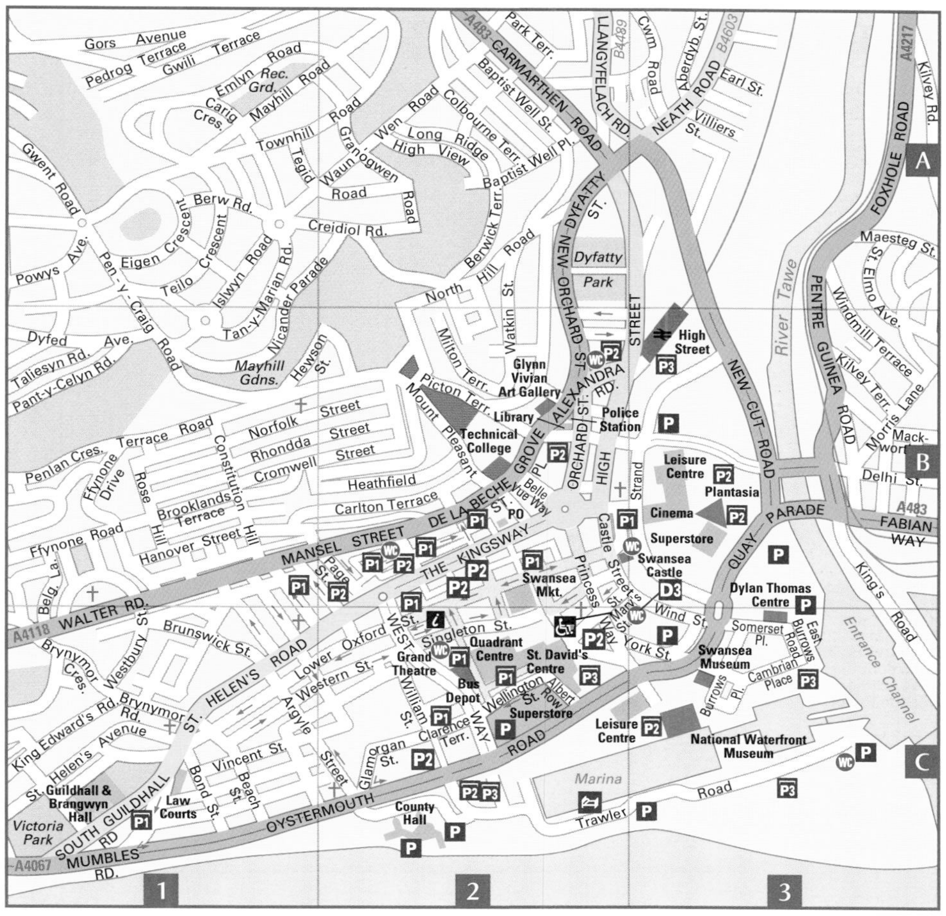

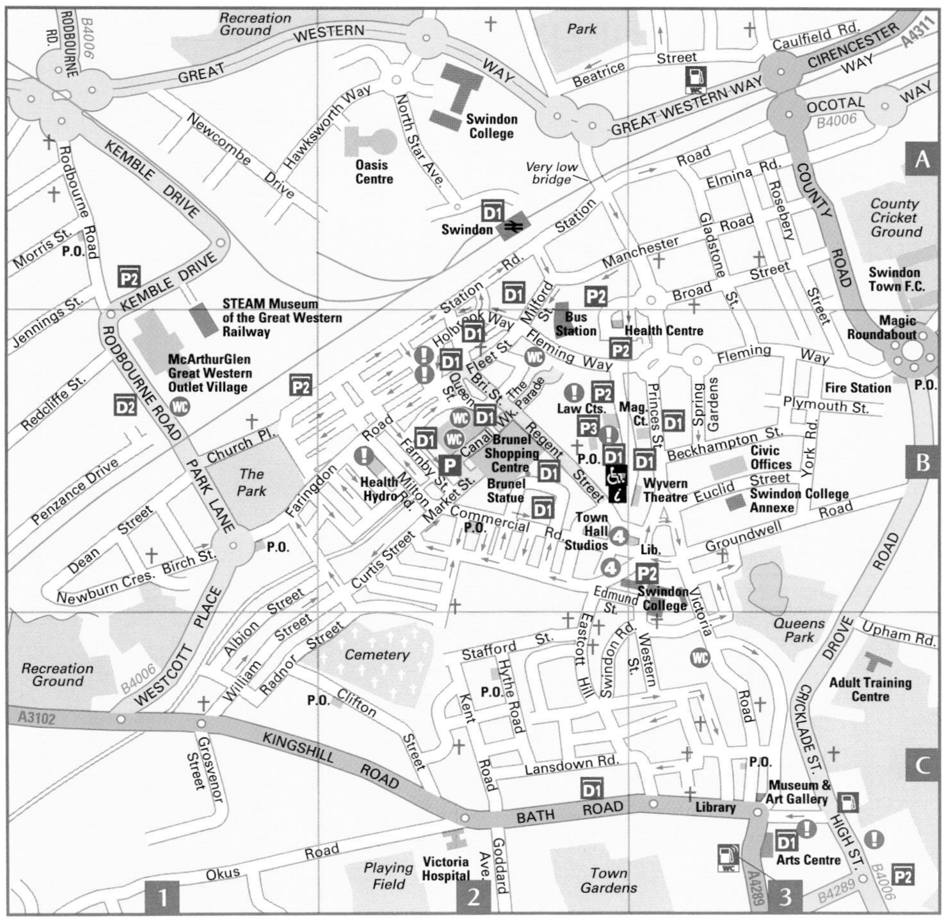

SWINDON

0 400 yds
0 400m

INDEX TO STREET NAMES

TOURIST INFORMATION ☎ 01793 530328
37 REGENT STREET,
SWINDON, SN1 1JL

COUNCIL OFFICE ☎ 01793 463725
CIVIC OFFICES, EUCLID STREET,
SWINDON, SN1 2JH

HOSPITAL A & E ☎ 01793 604020
THE GREAT WESTERN HOSPITAL,
MARLBOROUGH ROAD, SWINDON, SN3 6BB

WEB-SITE www.swindon.gov.uk

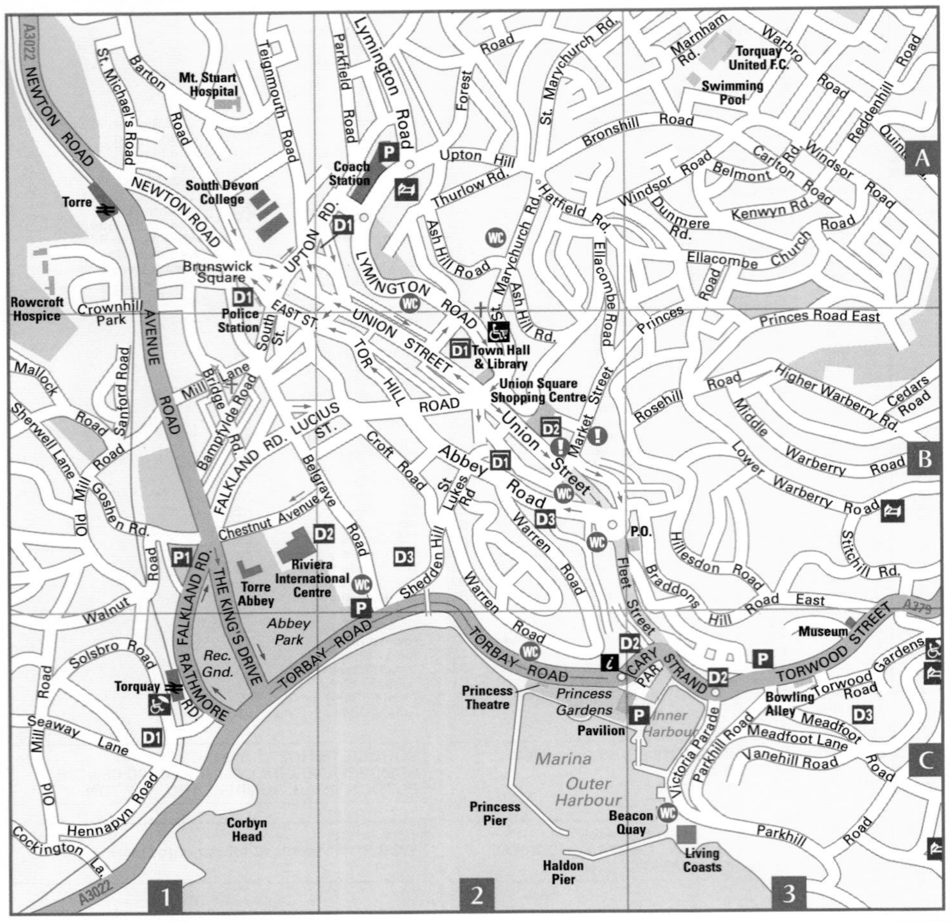

TORQUAY

0 400 yds
0 400m

INDEX TO STREET NAMES

Street	Grid	Street	Grid	Street	Grid
Abbey Road	B2	Marnham Road	A3	Vanehill Road	C3
Ash Hill Road	A2	Meadfoot Lane	C3	Victoria Parade	C3
Avenue Road	B1	Meadfoot Road	C3	Walnut Road	C1
Bampfylde Road	B1	Middle Warberry Road	B3	Warbro Road	A3
Barton Road	A1	Mill Lane	B1	Warren Road	B2
Belgrave Road	B1	Newton Road	A1	Westhill Road	A2
Belmont Road	A3	Old Mill Road	B1	Windsor Road	A3
Braddons Hill Road East	B3	Old Mill Road	C1		
Bridge Road	B1	Parkfield Road	A2		
Bronshill Road	A2	Parkhill Road	C3		
Brunswick Square	A1	Prince's Road	B3		
Carlton Road	A3	Princes Road East	B3		
Cary Parade	C3	Quinta Road	A3		
Cedars Road	B3	Rathmore Road	C1		
Chestnut Avenue	B1	Reddenhill Road	A3		
Cockington Lane	C1	Rosehill Road	B3		
Croft Road	B2	Sanford Road	B1		
Crownhill Park	A1	Seaway Lane	C1		
Dunmere Road	A3	Shedden Hill	B2		
East Street	A1	Sherwell Lane	B1		
Ellacombe Church Road	A3	Solsbro Road	C1		
Ellacombe Road	A2	South Street	B1		
Falkland Road	B1	St. Lukes Road	B2		
Falkland Road	B1	St. Marychurch Road	B2		
Fleet Street	B2	St. Michael's Road	A1		
Forest Road	A2	Stitchill Road	B3		
Goshen Road	B1	Strand	C3		
Hatfield Road	A2	Teignmouth Road	A1		
Hennapyn Road	C1	The King's Drive	B1		
Higher Warberry Road	B3	Thurlow Road	A2		
Hillesdon Road	B3	Tor Hill Road	B2		
Kenwyn Road	A3	Torbay Road	C1		
Lower Warberry Road	B3	Torwood Gardens Road	C3		
Lucius Street	B1	Torwood Street	C3		
Lymington Road	A2	Union Street	B2		
Mallock Road	B1	Upton Hill	A2		
Market Street	B2	Upton Road	A1		

TOURIST INFORMATION ☎ 01803 297428
VAUGHAN PARADE,
TORQUAY, TQ2 5JG

COUNCIL OFFICE ☎ 01803 201201
TOWN HALL, CASTLE CIRCUS,
TORQUAY, TQ1 3DR

HOSPITAL A & E ☎ 01803 614567
TORBAY DISTRICT GENERAL HOSPITAL,
NEWTON ROAD, TORQUAY, TQ2 7AA

WEB-SITE www.torbay.gov.uk

WATFORD

0 200 yds
0 200m

INDEX TO STREET NAMES

Street	Grid	Street	Grid
Addiscombe Road	B1	Muriel Avenue	C2
Albert Road North	A1	New Road	C3
Albert Road South	A1	New Street	B2
Aynho Street	C1	Park Avenue	A3
Banbury Street	C1	Park Avenue	B1
Beechen Grove	A1/B3	Queens Road	A2/B2
Brightwell Road	C1	Radlett Road	A3
Brocklesbury Close	A3	Rickmansworth Road	B1
Bushey Hall Road	B3	Rosslyn Road	A1
Cardiff Road	C2	Shaftesbury Road	A3
Cassio Road	B1	Souldern Street	C1
Chester Road	B1	St. James Road	C2
Church Street	B2	St. Johns Road	A1
Clarendon Road	A2	St. Pauls Way	A3
Clifton Road	C1	Stephenson Way	B3
Cross Street	A2	Sutton Road	A2
Dalton Way	C3	The Avenue	A1
Durban Road East	B1	The Broadway	B2
Ebury Road	A3	The Hornets	C1
Estcourt Road	A2	The Parade	A1
Exchange Road	B1	Upton Road	B1
Farraline Road	C1	Vicarage Road	C1/B2
Fearnley Street	B1	Water Lane	B3
George Street	B2	Waterfields Way	B3
Harwoods Road	C1	Watford Field Road	C2
Hempsted Road	A1	Wellstones	B2
High Street	A1/B2	Whippendell Road	B1
King Street	B2	Wiggenhall Road	C2
Lady's Close	B2	Willow Lane	C1
Lammas Road	C2		
Liverpool Road	C1		
Loates Lane	B2		
Lord Street	B2		
Lower High Street	B3		
Market Street	B1		
May Cottages	C2		
Merton Road	B1		

TOURIST INFORMATION ☎ 01727 864511
TOWN HALL, MARKET PLACE,
ST ALBANS, AL3 5DJ

COUNCIL OFFICE ☎ 01923 226400
WATFORD COUNCIL, TOWN HALL,
WATFORD, WD17 3EX

HOSPITAL A & E ☎ 01923 244366
WATFORD GENERAL HOSPITAL, VICARAGE ROAD,
WATFORD, WD18 0HB

WEB-SITE www.watford.gov.uk

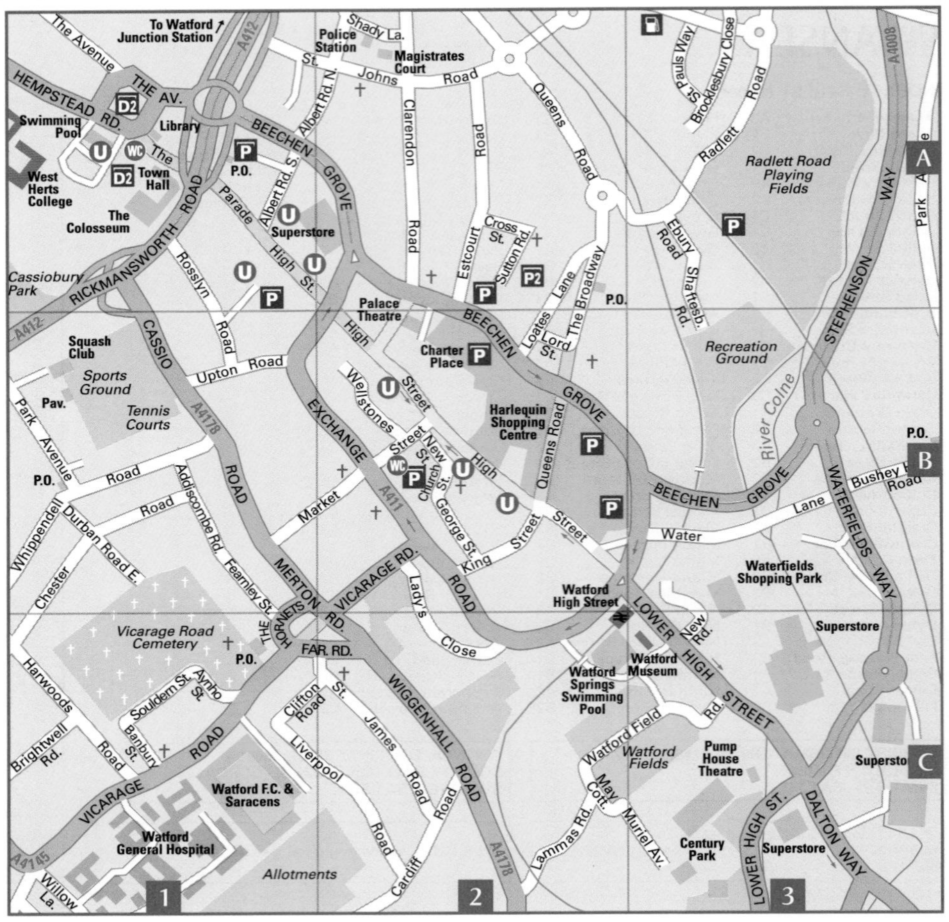

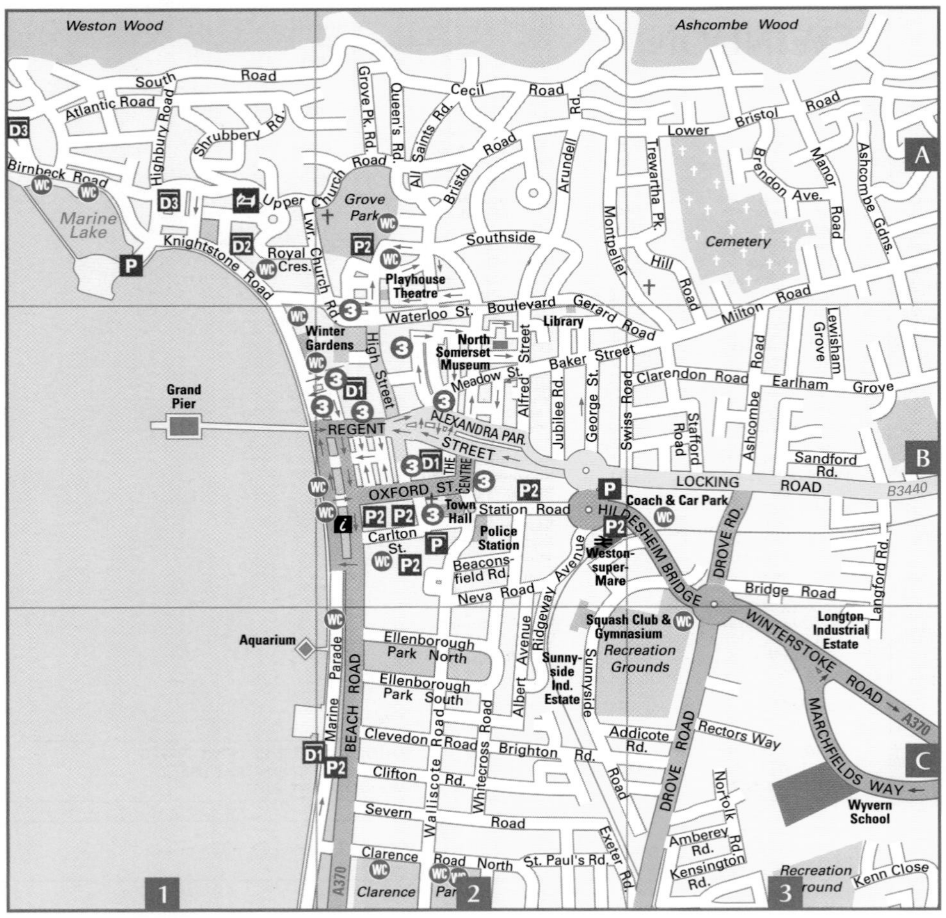

WESTON-SUPER-MARE

0 400 yds
0 400m

INDEX TO STREET NAMES

Street	Grid	Street	Grid	Street	Grid
Addicote Road	C2	Jubilee Road	B2	Walliscote Road	C2
Albert Avenue	C2	Kenn Close	C3	Waterloo Street Boulevard	B2
Alexandra Parade	B2	Kensington Road	C3	Whitecross Road	C2
Alfred Street	B2	Knightstone Road	A1	Winterstoke Road	C3
All Saints Road	A2	Langford Road	B3		
Amberey Road	C3	Lewisham Grove	B3		
Arundell Road	A2	Locking Road	B3		
Ashcombe Gardens	A3	Lower Bristol Road	A3		
Ashcombe Road	B3	Lower Church Road	A1		
Atlantic Road	A1	Manor Road	A3		
Baker Street	B2	Marchfields Way	C3		
Beach Road	C2	Marine Parade	C2		
Beaconsfield Road	B2	Meadow Street	B2		
Birnbeck Road	A1	Milton Road	B3		
Brendon Avenue	A3	Montpelier	A2		
Bridge Road	B3	Neva Road	B2		
Brighton Road	C2	Norfolk Road	C3		
Bristol Road	A2	Oxford Street	B2		
Carlton Street	B2	Queen's Road	A2		
Cecil Road	A2	Rectors Way	C3		
Clarence Road North	C2	Regent Street	B2		
Clarendon Road	B3	Ridgeway Avenue	C2		
Clevedon Road	C2	Royal Crescent	A1		
Clifton Road	C2	St. Paul's Road	C2		
Drove Road	C3	Sandford Road	B3		
Earlham Grove	B3	Severn Road	C2		
Ellenborough Park North	C2	Shrubbery Road	A1		
Ellenborough Park South	C2	South Road	A1		
Exeter Road	C2	Southside	A2		
George Street	B2	Stafford Road	B3		
Gerard Road	A2	Station Road	B2		
Grove Park Road	A2	Sunnyside Road	C2		
High Street	B2	Swiss Road	B3		
Highbury Road	A1	The Centre	B2		
Hildesheim Bridge	B2	Trewartha Park	A3		
Hill Road	A3	Upper Church Road	A1		

TOURIST INFORMATION ☎ 01934 888800
BEACH LAWNS,
WESTON-SUPER-MARE, BS23 1AT

COUNCIL OFFICE ☎ 01934 888888
TOWN HALL, WALLISCOTE GROVE ROAD,
WESTON-SUPER-MARE, BS23 1UJ

HOSPITAL A & E ☎ 01934 636363
WESTON GENERAL HOSPITAL, GRANGE ROAD,
UPHILL, WESTON-SUPER-MARE, BS23 4TQ

WEB-SITE www.n-somerset.gov.uk

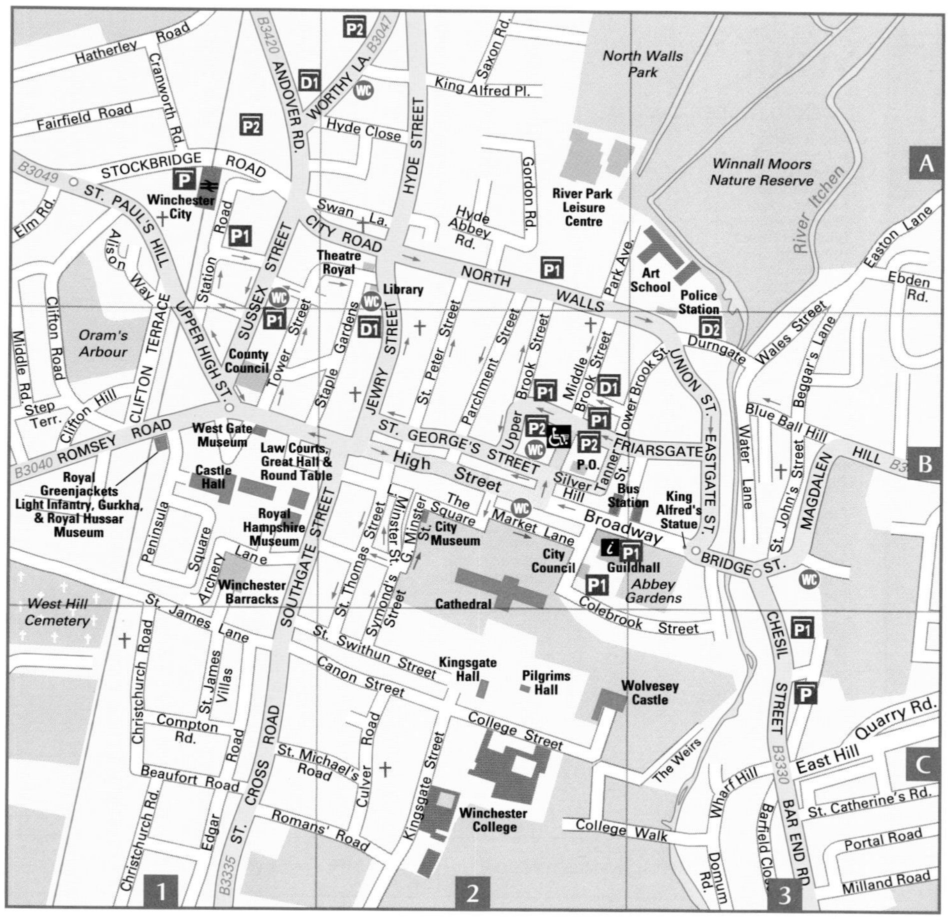

WINCHESTER

0 500 yds
0 500m

INDEX TO STREET NAMES

Alison Way	A1
Andover Road	A1
Archery Lane	B1
Bar End Road	C3
Barfield Close	C3
Beaufort Road	C1
Beggar's Lane	B3
Blue Ball Hill	B3
Bridge Stret	B3
Broadway	B2
Canon Street	C2
Chesil Street	C3
Christchurch Road	C1
City Road	A1
Clifton Hill	B1
Clifton Road	A1
Clifton Terrace	B1
Colebrook Street	B2
College Street	C2
College Walk	C2
Compton Road	C1
Cranworth Road	A1
Culver Road	C2
Domum Road	C3
Durngate	B3
East Hill	C3
Eastgate Street	B3
Easton Lane	A3
Ebden Road	A3
Edgar Road	C1
Elm Road	A1
Fairfield Road	A1
Friarsgate	B2
Gordon Road	A2
Great Minster Street	B2
Hatherley Road	A1
High Street	B2
Hyde Abbey Road	A2
Hyde Close	A2
Hyde Street	A2
Jewry Street	B2
King Alfred Place	A2
Kingsgate Street	C2
Little Minster Street	B2
Lower Brook Street	B2
Magdalen Hill	B3
Market Lane	B2
Middle Brook Street	B2
Middle Road	B1
Milland Road	C3
North Walls	A1
Parchment Street	B2
Park Avenue	A2
Peninsula Square	B1
Portal Road	C3
Quarry Road	C3
Romans' Road	C1
Romsey Road	B1
St. Catherine's Road	C3
St. Cross Road	C1
St. George's Street	B2
St. James Lane	B1
St. James Villas	C1
St. John's Street	B3
St. Michael's Road	C1
St. Paul's Hill	A1
St. Peter Street	B2
St. Swithun Street	C2
St. Thomas Street	C2
Saxon Road	A2
Silver Hill	B2
Southgate Street	C1
Staple Gardens	B2
Station Road	A1
Step Terrace	B1
Stockbridge Road	A1
Sussex Street	B1
Swan Lane	A2
Symond's Street	C2
Tanner Street	B2
The Square	B2
Tower Street	B1
Union Street	B3
Upper Brook Street	B2
Upper High Street	B1
Wales Street	B3
Water Lane	B3
Wharf Hill	C3
Worthy Lane	A1

TOURIST INFORMATION ☎ 01962 840500
GUILDHALL, BROADWAY, WINCHESTER
HAMPSHIRE, SO23 9LJ

COUNCIL OFFICE ☎ 01962 840222
CITY OFFICES, COLEBROOK STREET,
WINCHESTER, SO23 9LJ

HOSPITAL A & E ☎ 01962 863535
ROYAL HAMPSHIRE COUNTY HOSPITAL,
ROMSEY ROAD, WINCHESTER, SO22 5DG

WEB-SITE www.winchester.gov.uk

WINDSOR

0 400 yds
0 400m

INDEX TO STREET NAMES

Adelaide Square	C3
Albert Street	B1
Alexandra Road	C2
Alma Road	B2/C2
Arthur Road	B2
Barry Avenue	A2
Bexley Street	B2
Bolton Avenue	C2
Bolton Crescent	C2
Bolton Road	C2
Bulkeley Avenue	C1
Castle Hill	B3
Charles Street	B2
Clarence Road	B1
Clarence Street	B2
College Crescent	C1
Dagmar Road	B2
Datchet Road	A3
Frances Road	C2
Goslar Way	B1
Goswell Road	B2
Green Lane	B1
Grove Road	B2
Helston Lane	B1
High Street (Eton)	A2
High Street (Windsor)	B3
Imperial Road	C1
King Edward VII Avenue	A3
Kings Road	C3
Meadow Lane	A2
Mill Lane	A1
Osborne Road	C2
Oxford Road	B2
Park Street	B3
Parsonage Lane	B1
Peascod Street	B2
Peel Close	C1
Princess Avenue	C1
Romney Lock Road	A3
St. Leonards Road	C2
St. Marks Road	B2
Sheet Street	B3
South Meadow Lane	A2
Springfield Road	C1
Stovell Road	A1
Thames Street	A3
The Long Walk	C3
Upcroft	C1
Vansittart Road	B2
Victoria Street	B2
Victor Road	C2
Westmead	C1
Windsor & Eton Relief Road	B1
York Avenue	C1
York Road	C1

TOURIST INFORMATION ☎ 01753 743900
24 HIGH STREET,
WINDSOR, SL4 1LH

COUNCIL OFFICE ☎ 01753 810525
COUNCIL OFFICES, YORK HOUSE, SHEET STREET,
WINDSOR, SL4 1DD

HOSPITAL A & E ☎ 01753 633000
WEXHAM PARK HOSPITAL, WEXHAM STREET,
SLOUGH, SL2 4HL

WEB-SITE www.rbwm.gov.uk

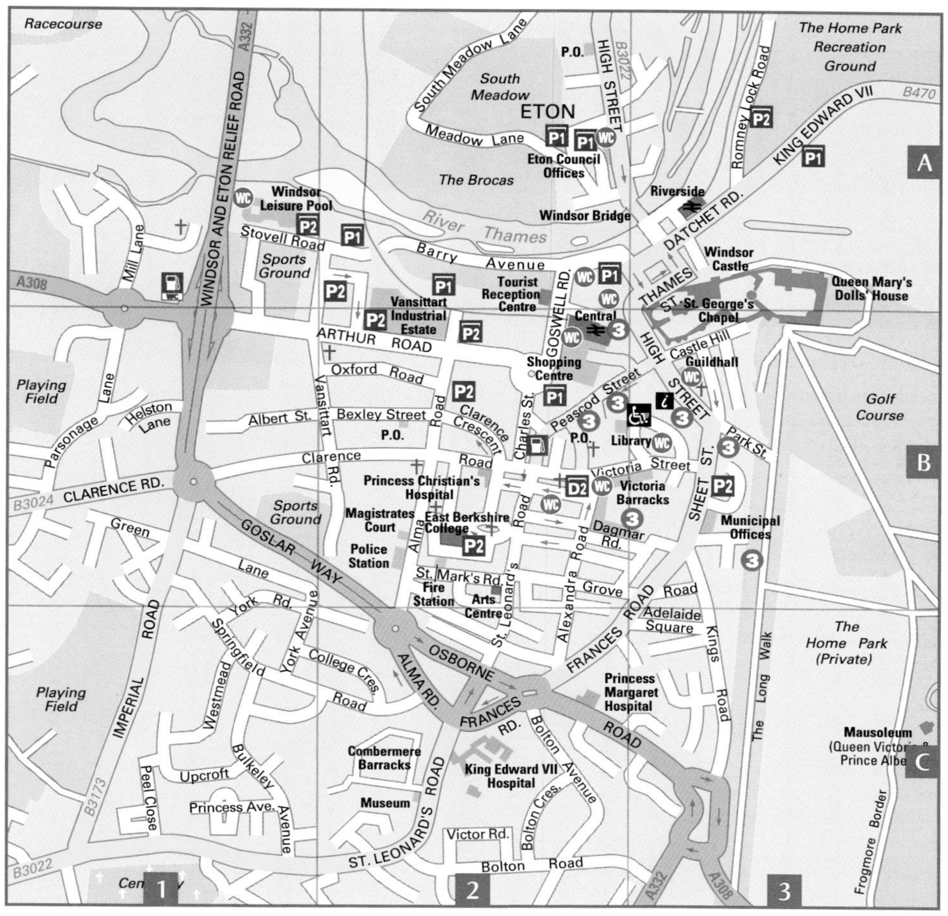

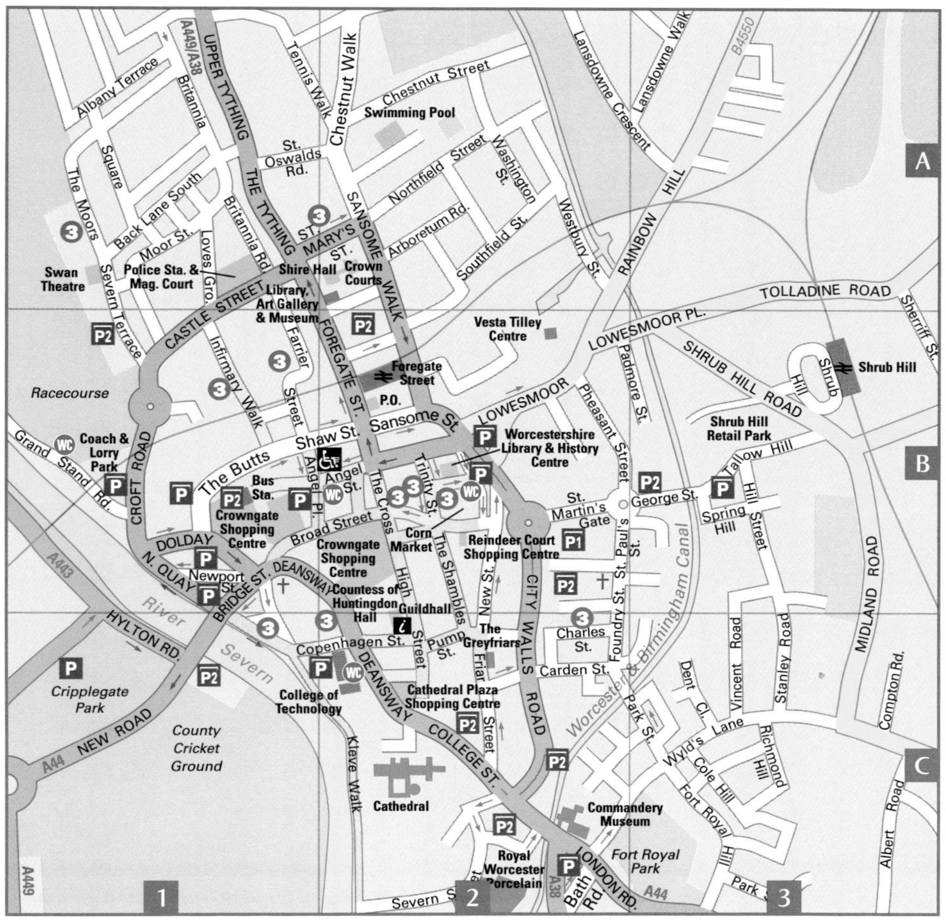

WORCESTER

0 200 yds
0 200m

INDEX TO STREET NAMES

Albany Terrace	A1
Albert Road	C3
Angel Place	B1
Angel Street	B2
Arboretum Road	A2
Back Lane South	A1
Bath Road	C2
Bridge Street	B1
Britannia Road	A1
Britannia Square	A1
Broad Street	B1
Carden Street	C2
Castle Street	B1
Charles Street	C2
Chestnut Street	A2
Chestnut Walk	A2
City Walls Road	B2
Cole Hill	C3
College Street	C2
Compton Road	C3
Copenhagen Street	C1
Croft Road	B1
Deansway	B1
Dent Close	C3
Dolday	B1
Farrier Street	B1
Foregate Street	B2
Fort Royal Hill	C3
Foundry Street	C2
Friar Street	C2
George Street	B3
Grand Stand Road	B1
High Street	B2
Hill Street	B3
Hylton Road	B1
Infirmary Walk	B1
Kleve Walk	C2
Lansdowne Crescent	A2
Lansdowne Walk	A3
London Road	C2
Loves Grove	A1
Lowesmoor	B2
Lowesmoor Place	B2
Midland Road	C3
Moor Street	A1
Newport Street	B1
New Road	C1
New Street	B2
Northfield Street	A2
North Quay	B1
Padmore Street	B2
Park Street	C2
Park Street	C3
Pheasant Street	B2
Pump Street	C2
Rainbow Hill	A2
Richmond Hill	C3
St. Martin's Gate	B2
St. Mary's Street	A1
St. Oswalds Road	A1
St. Paul's Street	B2
Sansome Street	B2
Sansome Walk	A2
Severn Street	C2
Severn Terrace	A1
Shaw Street	B1
Sherriff Street	A3
Shrub Hill	B3
Shrub Hill Road	B3
Sidbury	C2
Southfield Street	A2
Spring Hill	B3
Stanley Road	C3
Tallow Hill	B3
Tennis Walk	A1
The Butts	B1
The Cross	B2
The Moors	A1
The Shambles	B2
The Tything	A1
Tolladine Road	A3
Trinity Street	B2
Upper Tything	A1
Vincent Road	C3
Washington Street	A2
Westbury Street	A2
Wyld's Lane	C3

TOURIST INFORMATION ☎ 01905 726311
THE GUILDHALL, HIGH STREET,
WORCESTER, WR1 2EY

COUNCIL OFFICE ☎ 01905 723471
THE GUILDHALL, HIGH STREET,
WORCESTER, WR1 2EY

HOSPITAL A & E ☎ 01905 763333
WORCESTER ROYAL INFIRMARY, RONKSWOOD
HOSPITAL, NEWTOWN ROAD, WR5 1HN

WEB-SITE www.cityofworcester.gov.uk

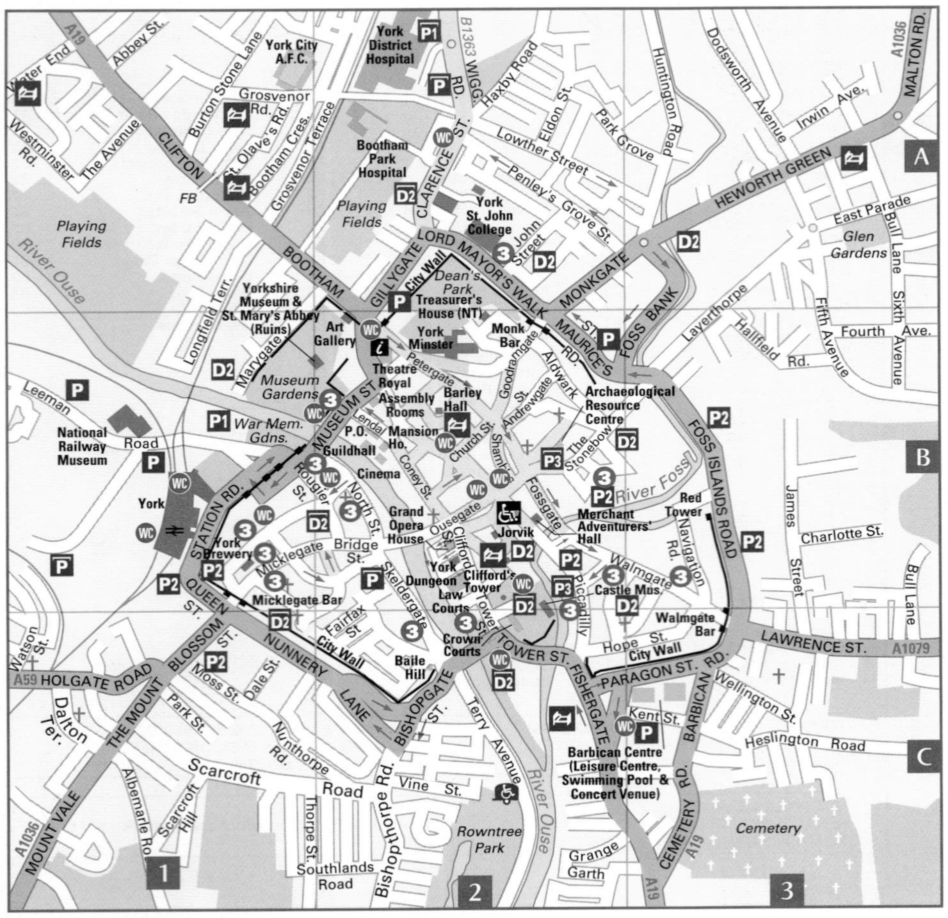

YORK

0 400 yds
0 400m

INDEX TO STREET NAMES

TOURIST INFORMATION ☎ 01904 621756
THE DE GREY ROOMS, EXHIBITION SQUARE,
YORK, YO1 7HB

COUNCIL OFFICE ☎ 01904 613161
THE GUILDHALL,
YORK, YO1 9QN

HOSPITAL A & E ☎ 01904 631313
YORK DISTRICT HOSPITAL, WIGGINTON ROAD,
YORK, YO31 8HE

WEB-SITE www.york.gov.uk

Directory of Services

Accommodation

Accommodation Access Codes Descriptions

We recommend when booking any accommodation you check that your specific requirements can be accommodated prior to confirming a reservation.

The symbols shown will enable people with disabilities to make an informed choice about where they can go on holiday in the UK.

National Accessible Scheme (launched 2002 reviewed 2005)

Assessments conducted since April 2002 will denote accessibility with the following symbols to indicate the level of access available. Properties displaying these signs will have been assessed on or after April 2002.

- Typically suitable for a person with sufficient mobility to climb a flight of steps but would benefit from fixtures and fittings to aid balance.
- Typically suitable for a person with restricted walking ability and for those that may need to use a wheelchair some of the time.
- Typically suitable for a person who depends on the use of a wheelchair and transfers unaided to and from a wheelchair in a seated position.
- Typically suitable for a person who depends on the use of wheelchair and transfers to and from the wheelchair in a seated position. They also require personal/mechanical assistance to aid transfer (e.g. carer/hoist).

National Accessible Scheme (pre 2002)

Assessments conducted prior to 2002 will denote accessibility with the following symbols to indicate the level of access available. Properties displaying these signs will have been assessed prior to April 2002.

- Accessible to a wheelchair user travelling independently.
- Accessible to a wheelchair user travelling with assistance.
- Accessible to someone with limited mobility, but able to walk a few paces and up a maximum of three steps.

Self Assessed Accessibility

Typically these properties have not been inspected by an approved body and are classified as self accessed. However, some properties will have been awarded a lower level of accessibility, but have undertaken additional work to achieve the higher standard of accessibility as suggested by the inspector.

- Accessible to a wheelchair user travelling independently
- Accessible to a wheelchair user travelling with assistance
- Accessible to someone with limited mobility, but able to walk a few paces and up a maximum of three steps.

Welcome to Tourism for All UK

Tourism for All UK (TFA UK) is the main information source for people with mobility, sight or hearing difficulties who wish to enjoy travel and holidays in the UK. TFA UK is a national registered charity providing information to the public, publications and guides, advice to the travel industry, and a reservations service.

tourismforall

TFA UK works with the national tourist board, Visit Britain, to provide quality assured, inspected accessible accommodation through the National Accessible Scheme. There are over 400 properties from hotels to Bed and Breakfast who are members of the scheme. To order a comprehensive guide or access other guides and information leaflets, including accessible accommodation in a range of countries, visit our website

www.tourismforall.org.uk

or call the information line on

0845 124 9971

www.tourismforall.org.uk

Page ref.	Town/Name	Services
74 C4	**Abbotsinch Ramada Glasgow Airport** Marchburn Drive, T 0141 8402200	SCO H
85 P10	**Aberdeen Aberdeen Patio Hotel** Beach Boulevard, T 01224 633339	SCO H
85 P10	**Aberdeen Arkaig Guest House** 43 Powis Terrace, T 01224 638872	SCO GH
85 N10	**Aberdeen Britannia Hotel** Malcolm Rd, T 01224 409988	SCO H
85 P10	**Aberdeen Cocket Hat Lodge Inn** North Anderson Dr, T 01224 695684	SCO
85 P10	**Aberdeen Copthorne Hotel** 122 Huntly St, T 01224 630404	SCO H
85 P10	**Aberdeen Ewood House** Kings Gate, T 01224 648408	SCO
85 P10	**Aberdeen Express By Holiday Inn** Chapel St, T 01224 623500	SCO H
85 P10	**Aberdeen Hillhead Halls** Uni of Aberdeen, T 01224 272660	SCO SC
85 P10	**Aberdeen Hillhead Halls** Uni of Aberdeen, T 01224 272662	SCO
85 P10	**Aberdeen Marcliffe At Pitfodels** Pitfodels,, T 01224 861000	SCO H
85 P9	**Aberdeen Mrs Haggart** Dyce, T 01224 704210	SCO SC
85 P10	**Aberdeen Northern Hotel** Gt Northern Rd, T 01224 483342	SCO H
85 N9	**Aberdeen Speedbird Inn** Argyll Rd, Dyce, T 01224 772884	SCO H
85 P10	**Aberdeen Thistle Altens** Soutarhead Rd, T 01224 723101	SCO H
85 N9	**Aberdeen Thistle Apt Hotel** Argyll Rd, T 01224 640233	SCO H
85 P10	**Aberdeen Woolmanhill Flats** John St, T 01224 262141	SCO SC
75 K2	**Aberdour Aberdour Hotel** 38 High St, T 01383 860325 www.aberdourhotel.co.uk	SCO H
37 F6	**Aberdyfi Hillside Village** Balkan Hill, T 01654 767522	CYMRU
80 D6	**Aberfeldy Balhomais Farm** Perthshire, T 01887 829692	SCO
80 D6	**Aberfeldy Balhomais Pine Chalet** Aberfeldy, T 01887 829692	SCO SC
80 D5	**Aberfeldy Ballinduin Steading** Strathtay, T 01887 840460 www.ballinduinsteading.co.uk	SCO SC
80 D6	**Aberfeldy Drumcroy Lodges** Mairns of Murthly, T 01887 820978	SCO SC
80 C6	**Aberfeldy Loch Tay Lodges** Acharn, T 01887 830209	SCO SC
80 C6	**Aberfeldy Loch Tay Lodges** Remony, T 01887 830209	SCO
80 D6	**Aberfeldy Novar** 2 Home St, T 01887 820779	SCO
80 D5	**Aberfeldy The Bunkhouse** Glassie Farm, T 01887 820265	SCO HOS
80 D6	**Aberfeldy The Ghillies Cottage** Farleyer Field Hse, T 01887 829 553	SCO SC
80 D5	**Aberfeldy The Schoolhouse** Tombuie, T 02894 462217	SCO SC
80 D5	**Aberfeldy Tomvale** Tom of Cluny, T 01887 820171	SCO SC
80 D5	**Aberfeldy Tomvale** Tom of Cluny, T 01887 820171 www.tomvale.co.uk	SCO B&B
80 A10	**Aberfoyle Covenanters Inn** Duckray Rd, T 01877 382347	SCO
80 A10	**Aberfoyle Crannaig House** Trossachs Rd, T 01877 382276	SCO B&B
79 R10	**Aberfoyle Forest Hills Hotel** Kinlochard, T 01877 387277	SCO H

Accommodation Key **Country:** GB England SCO Scotland CYMRU Wales NI Northern Ireland **Venue type:** H Hotel B&B Bed & Breakfast INN Inn SC Self Catering L Lodge HOS Hostel GH Guest House

Page ref.	Town/Name	Services
80 A10	Aberfoyle Rob Roy Hotel Stirlings, T 01877 382245	SCO H
74 D1	Aberfoyle Rowan & Oak Cots Trossachs Park, T 01877 382614	SCO
28 C7	Abergavenny Lower Green Farm Llanfair Green, T 01873 821219 www.lower-green.fsnet.co.uk	CYMRU SC
28 C6	Abergavenny Pandy Caravan Site Pandy, T 01873 890370	CYMRU
47 H5	Abergele Bron-y-wendon Park Wern Rd, Llanddulas, T 01492 512903 www.northwales-holidays.co.uk	CYMRU
47 H5	Abergele Dolhyfryd Lodge Hotel Rhuddlan Rd, T 01745 826505	CYMRU
47 H5	Abergele Ty Mawr Holiday Park Towyn Rd, Towyn, T 01745 832079	CYMRU
84 G6	Aberlour Templar's Cottage Kinermony Ltd, T 01340 871286	SCO
80 G9	Abernethy Gattaway Farm Perthshire, T 01738 850746 www.smoothhound.co.uk/hotels/gattaway.html	SCO B&B
80 E9	Aberuthven Kilrymont 8 Loanfoot Park, T 01764 662660	SCO B&B
36 E7	Aberystwyth Beachside Camping Clarach Bay, T 01970 623361	CYMRU
37 F6	Aberystwyth Cambrian Coast Ynyslas, Borth, T 01970 871233	CYMRU
36 E7	Aberystwyth Glan Y Mor Park Clarach Bay, T 01970 828900	CYMRU
37 F7	Aberystwyth Llety Gwyn Hotel Llanbadarn Fawr, T 01970 623965	CYMRU
36 E7	Aberystwyth Ocean View Park Clarach Bay, T 01970 623361	CYMRU
21 J2	Abingdon Kingfisher Barn Rye Farm, T 01235 527590	GB
68 E1	Abington Days Inn Welcome Break M74/A7, T 01864 502782	SCO L
68 E1	Abington Welcome Break Abington A74/M74, J13, T 0800 7314466	SCO
85 K11	Aboyne Birse Lodge Hotel Charleston Rd, T 013398 862253	SCO
85 K11	Aboyne Chesterton House Formaston Park, T 013398 86740	SCO B&B
86 B8	Achiltibuie The Steading Reiff, T 01854 622416	SCO SC
83 J7	Achmore Soluis Mu Thuath Braeintra, T 01599 577219	SCO GH
83 J5	Achnasheen Loch Torridon Hotel Torridon, T 01445 791242	SCO H
83 J2	Achnasheen Mellon Charles Aultbea, T 01445 731382	SCO SC
83 K2	Achnasheen Rocklea Little Grinard, Laide, T 01445 731459	SCO
49 H5	Alderley Edge Alderley Edge Hotel Macclesfield Rd, T 01625 583033	GB
74 B2	Alexandria De Vere Cameron House Loch Lomond, T 01389 755565	SCO H
85 L9	Alford Craich Cottage Tough, T 01975 562584	SCO SC
53 H5	Alford Half Moon Hotel 25-28 West St, T 01507 463477	GB
53 H4	Alford Yew Tree Cottage Maltby le Marsh, T 01507 450267	GB
51 G7	Alfreton The Boundary Lodge Broadmeadows, T 01773 819 066	GB
75 G1	Alloa Orchard Lodge Tullibody Rd, T 01259 226400	SCO SC
84 A4	Alness The Lodge Dalmore, T 01349 830618	SCO
71 H2	Alnwick Bog Mill Farm Cottage Bog Mill Farm, T 01665 604529	GB
71 H2	Alnwick Craster Pine Lodges 9 West End, Craster, T 01665 576286	GB
71 G3	Alnwick Village Farm Shilbottle, T 01665 575591	GB
49 G7	Alsager Alsager Campus Manchester Met Uni, T 01270 500661	GB
61 J2	Alston Greycroft Middle Park, The Raise, T 01434 381383	GB
75 G1	Alva Boll Holiday Cottages Brook St, T 01259 769638	SCO SC
80 H6	Alyth Airlie Mount Holidays 2 Albert St, T 01828 632986	SCO
80 H6	Alyth The Reed & The Toftin Lairdie Lowes, T 01828 632547	SCO SC
60 E6	Ambleside Birch Knoll Borrans Rd, Nr Waterhead, T 015394 31733	GB
60 E7	Ambleside Hawkshead Holidays Hawkshead, T 01625 828624	GB
60 E6	Ambleside Kirkstone Foot Hotel Kirkstone Pass Rd, T 015394 32232	GB
60 E6	Ambleside Nationwide Borrans Close, T 01446 771311 www.groomsholidays.org.uk Tranquil setting with beautiful secluded garden. Twin, 2 singles, double sofa bed & z bed. Bed linen. TV, video, washer/dryer, central heating, wheel in shower, mobile hoist, electric profiling bed.	GB SC
60 E6	Ambleside Rothay Manor Rothey Bridge, T 01539 433605 www.rothaymanor.co.uk	GB H
60 E6	Ambleside Rowanfield Guest House Kirkstone Rd, T 015394 33686	GB
60 E6	Ambleside The Larches Cumb, T 015394 32321	GB
46 B3	Amlwch Beudygwyn Farm Holidays Carreglefn, T 01407 711433	CYMRU
81 L10	Anstruther 25 High Street Fife, T 01333 310189	SCO
81 L10	Anstruther Lobster Pot Cottage 30 East Green, T 01333 340640 www.lobster-pot.co.uk	SCO SC
79 L6	Appin Appin House Apartments Argyll, T 01631 730207	SCO SC
79 M5	Appin Holly Tree Hotel Kentallen, T 01631 740292	SCO
79 L6	Appin Rhugarbh Croft Argyll, T 01631 730309	SCO
61 H4	Appleby Glebe Hayloft & Stable Glebe House, Bolton, T 017683 61125	GB
79 J9	Ardmaddy Ardmaddy Castle Cottages Argyll, T 01852 300353	SCO SC
78 G6	Aros Arlabeag Isle of Mull, T 01680 300441	SCO
79 Q10	Arrochar Innischonian House Tarbet, T 01301 702726	SCO
79 P10	Arrochar Village Inn Main St, T 01301 702279	SCO INN
12 C6	Arundel Mill Lane House Slindon, T 01243 814440	GB
40 D1	Ashbourne Dove Farm Ellastone, T 01335 324 357	GB
50 E7	Ashbourne Grange Holidays Kirk Ireton, T 01335 370880	GB SC
50 D7	Ashbourne Ilam Hall Yh Ilam Hall, Ilam, T 0870 770 5876	GB
40 E1	Ashbourne Lake View Bradley, T 01335 370577	GB
40 D1	Ashbourne Mona Villas B & B Church Ln, Mayfield, T 01335 343773	GB
50 D7	Ashbourne The Cot By The Pond Beechenhill Farm, Ilam, T 01335 310274 www.beechenhill.co.uk	GB SC
40 D2	Ashbourne The Courtyard Alkmonton, T 01335 330187	GB
15 F3	Ashford Ashford Intl Hotel Simone Weil Ave, T 01233 219988	GB
71 H5	Ashington Woodhorn Grange Queen Elizabeth II C Pk, T 01670 862332	GB
69 K1	Ashkirk Burnfoot Holiday Cottage Borders, T 01750 32205	SCO SC
69 K1	Ashkirk Synton Mains Farm The Davis Partnersip, T 01750 32388	SCO
40 E6	Atherstone Hipsley Farm Cottage Hipsley Ln, Hurley, T 01827 872437	GB
65 J5	Auchencairn Balcary Bay Hotel By Castle Douglas, T 01556 640217	SCO H
80 E10	Auchterarder Duchally Estate By Gleneagles, T 01764 663071	SCO SC
80 E9	Auchterarder Greystanes Western Rd, T 01764 664239	SCO B&B
80 E9	Auchterarder The Gleneagles Hotel Perthshire, T 01764 662231	SCO IR
81 J7	Auchterhouse Cas Tay Old Whisky Rd, T 0182626 237	SCO
84 D5	Auldearn Covenanters' Inn High St, T 01667 452456	SCO INN
68 E5	Auldgirth Lochmailing Holidays D & G, T 01387 740212	SCO
84 C9	Aviemore Avielochan Fm Cots Avielochan Farm, T 01479 810846	SCO SC
84 C9	Aviemore Aviemore Bunkhouse Dalfaber Rd, T 01479 811181 www.aviemore-bunkhouse.com	SCO HOS
84 D9	Aviemore Aviemore Holidays 113 Dalnabay, T 01479 810499	SCO SC
84 C9	Aviemore Aviemore Yh 25 Grampian Rd, T 01786 891400	SCO HOS
84 D10	Aviemore Cairngorm Lodge Glenmore, T 01786 891400	SCO HOS
84 C9	Aviemore Freedom Inn Aviemore Centre, T 01479 810781	SCO
84 C9	Aviemore High Range Chalets Highld, T 01479 810636	SCO SC
84 C9	Aviemore Lochside Cottage & Outlook Avielochan Farm, T 01479 810846	SCO
84 C9	Aviemore Logie 16 Craig Na Gower Ave, T 01479 810318	SCO
84 C9	Aviemore Macdonald Academy Aviemore Highland Resort, T 01479 810781	SCO L
84 C9	Aviemore Pine Bank Chalets Dalfaber Rd, T 01479 810000	SCO SC
84 C9	Aviemore Ravenscraig Guest House 141 Grampian Rd, T 01479 810278	SCO GH
84 C9	Aviemore Silverglades Holidays Highld, T 01479 810165	SCO SC
84 C9	Aviemore Waverley 35 Strathspey Ave, T 01479 811226	SCO B&B
84 A5	Avoch Inverleod Toll Rd, T 01381 621595	SCO B&B
67 H2	Ayr Alt-na-craig Hollybush, T 01292 560555	SCO B&B
67 J1	Ayr Enterkine Country House Annbank, T 01292 521608	SCO H
67 H1	Ayr Fairfield House Hotel 12 Fairfield Rd, T 01292 267461	SCO H
67 H2	Ayr Farden Chalet Farden Farmhouse, Hollybush, T 01292 560255	SCO SC
67 H1	Ayr Horizon Hotel Esplanade, T 01292 264384	SCO H
67 H1	Ayr Kildonan Hotel 27 Queens Terrace, T 01292 285122	SCO
67 H1	Ayr Miller House 36 Miller Rd, T 01292 282016	SCO GH
67 H1	Ayr Quality Station Hotel Burns Statue Square, T 01292 263268	GB
67 H2	Ayr South Lodge Doonside Estate, Alloway	SCO
67 H2	Ayr Springwater Chalets Ltd Dalrymple, T 01292 560343	SCO SC
50 D6	Bakewell Bolehill Farm Cottage Monyash Rd, T 01629 812359	GB
50 E5	Bakewell Croft Country House Hotel Great Longstone, T 01629 640278	GB
50 D6	Bakewell Haddon Grove Farm Cottage Monyash Rd, T 01629 813551	GB
37 J2	Bala Bryncelyn Holiday Park Llandderfel, T 01678 530212	CYMRU
37 J2	Bala Crynierth Caravan Park Cefn Ddwysarn, T 024 76694995	CYMRU
79 M5	Ballachulish Ballachulish Hotel Argyll, T 01855 811606 www.ballachulishhotel.com	SCO H
79 M5	Ballachulish Isles of Glencoe Argyll, T 01855 821582 www.islesofglencoe.co.uk	SCO H
84 H11	Ballater Bonn-na Coille 8 Braemar Rd, T 01339 755414	SCO SC
85 J11	Ballater Crannach Apartments Cambus o'May, T 013397 55892	SCO
84 G11	Ballater Crathie Holidays The Manse Courtyard, Crathie, T 01339 742100 www.crathieholidays.org.uk	SCO SC

Page ref.	Town/Name	Services
84 H11	Ballater Darroch Learg Hotel Braemar Rd, T 01339 755443	SCO H
84 H11	Ballater Glenernan Guest House 37 Braemar Rd, T 013397 53111 www.glenernanguesthouse.com	SCO GH
80 F2	Ballater Mar Lodge Braemar, T 0131 243 9352	SCO SC
84 H11	Ballater Moorside Guest House 26 Braemar Rd, T 01339 755492	SCO GH
84 G8	Ballindalloch Easter Corrie Tomnavoulin, T 01807 590241 www.eastercorrie.com	SCO SC
84 F9	Ballindalloch Tomintoul Yh Tomintoul, T 01786 891400	SCO HOS
74 B2	Balloch Anchorage Guest House 31 Balloch Rd, T 01389 753336	SCO GH
74 B2	Balloch Heathpete 24 Balloch Rd, T 01389 752195	SCO
83 Q7	Balnain Lochletter Lodges Highld, T 01456 476313	SCO SC
80 A8	Balquhidder Lochside Cottages Muirlaggan, T 01877 384219 www.lochsidecottages.co.uk	SCO SC
89 Q2	Baltasound The Baltasound Hotel Shetland, T 01957 711334	SCO H
77 K7	Bamburgh Point Cottages 39 The Wynding, T 0191 266 2800	GB
31 F4	Banbury Dovehouse Barn The Old Manor, Cropredy, T 01295 750235	GB
85 M11	Banchory Bridge of Bennie Cottage North Deeside Rd, T 01330 824288 www.cottageguide.co.uk & www.visitscotland.com	SCO SC

Page ref.	Town/Name	Services
85 M11	Banchory Crofter's Wayside Inn Lochton of Durris, T 01330 844543	SCO
85 L11	Banchory Home Farm North Inchmarlo, T 01330 822622	SCO SC
85 L11	Banchory Tor-na-coille Hotel Inchmarlo Rd, T 01330 822242	SCO
46 D5	Bangor British Hotel High St, T 01248 364911	CYMRU
37 F4	Barmouth The Sandpiper 7 Marine Parade, T 01341 280318	CYMRU
36 E4	Barmouth Trawsdir Caravans Park Llanaber, T 01341 280611	CYMRU
62 A4	Barnard Castle Hauxwell Cottage Marwood, T 01833 695022	GB
6 E2	Barnstaple Bracken House Hotel Bratton Fleming, T 01598 710320	GB
6 E1	Barnstaple Twitchen Farm Challacombe, T 01598 763568	GB
88 B8	Barra Northbay House Balnabodach, T 01871 890255	SCO SC
18 D5	Barry Fontygary Parks Ltd Rhoose, T 01446 710386	CYMRU
24 C2	Basildon Campanile Hotel Pipps Hill, T 01268 530810	GB

Page ref.	Town/Name	Services
21 K7	**Basingstoke Audleys Wood House Hotel** Alton Rd, T 01256 817555	GB
21 K6	**Basingstoke Hilton National** Old Common Rd, Black Dam, T 01256 460460	GB
20 A5	**Bath Carfax Hotel** Great Pulteney St, T 01225 462089 www.carfaxhotel.co.uk	GB H

Elegant city centre hotel, with WC lift to main floors, bedroom with WC-friendly toilet/shower, car park, dining room, lounge and a 5 Diamond rating.

Page ref.	Town/Name	Services
20 A5	**Bath Hilton Bath City** Walcot St, T 01225 463411	GB
20 A5	**Bath The Abbey Hotel** North Parade, T 01225 461603	GB
75 H4	**Bathgate Holiday Inn Express** Starlaw Rd, T 01506 650650	SCO
8 D4	**Beaminster Lewesdon Farm** Lewesdon Fm, Stoke Abbott, T 01308 868270	GB
8 D4	**Beaminster Riverside** Mosterton, T 023 8077 1729	GB
8 D4	**Beaminster Stable Cottage** Meerhay Manor, T 01308 862305	GB
74 D3	**Bearsden Kilmardinny Estate** Milngavie Rd, T 0141 943 1310	SCO SC
83 R6	**Beauly Dunsmore Lodges** Highld, T 01463 782424	SCO SC
83 R6	**Beauly Knoydart** Windhill, T 01463 782353	SCO
83 R6	**Beauly Lyndale** Station Rd, T 01463 783672	SCO
46 E5	**Beaumaris Bulkeley Hotel** Castle St, T 01248 810415	CYMRU
46 E5	**Beaumaris The Bulkeley Hotel** Castle St, T 01248 810415	CYMRU
6 C5	**Beaworthy Anglers Paradise** Winsford, Halwill, T 01409 221559	GB
6 B6	**Beaworthy Blagdon Farm Holidays** Ashwater, T 01409 211509 www.blagdon-farm.co.uk Award winning 5-star, fully accessible holiday cottages. In-door hydrotherapy pool, licensed bar, fishing lake.	GB H
45 J7	**Beccles Stringers Woodlands** Northgreen, Stoven, T 01502 575828	GB
32 E3	**Bedford Highfield Farm** Highfield Farm, Tempsford Rd, Sandy, T 01767 682332 www.highfield-farm.co.uk Highfield is marvellously situated on the Bedfordshire / Cambridgeshire borders. A1 and M1 nearby. "Acorn" cottage is designed to give every comfort to those disabled guests who wish to cater for themselves. All doors in Acorn are > 2'9", rooms are on the level, kitchen is usable by a person in a wheelchair and disabled Parking. B&B facilities also available.	GB B&B
77 K7	**Belford Outchester Farm Cottage** Ross Farm, T 01668 213228 www.rosscottages.co.uk	GB SC
75 F4	**Bellshill Hilton Strathclyde** Pheonix Crescent, T 01698 395500	SCO H
11 H6	**Bembridge Bembridge Coast Hotel** Isle of Wight, T 01983 873931	GB
87 P7	**Berriedale Kingspark Llama Farm** Highld, T 01593 751202	SCO
77 H6	**Berwick-upon-Tweed Felkington Farm** Felkington Farm, T 01289 387220	GB
77 H5	**Berwick-upon-Tweed Meadow Hill** Duns Rd, T 01289 306325	GB
47 F7	**Betws-y-coed Plas Hall Manor Hotel** Pont-y-pant, T 01690 750206 www.visitwales.com/	CYMRU H
59 G6	**Beverley Beverley Cottages** Carr View, Tickton, T 01964 543857	GB
59 F6	**Beverley Rudstone Walk Cottage** Rudstone Walk Fm, S.Cave, T 01430 422230	GB
23 H4	**Bexleyheath Marriott Hotel** 1 Broadway, T 020 8298 1000	GB
31 G5	**Bicester Pimlico Farm Cottage** Pimlico Farm, Tusmore, T 01869 810306	GB
75 J7	**Biggar Cormiston Cottage** Cormiston Rd, T 01899 220200	SCO B&B
75 H7	**Biggar Crossridge Country Cottage** Crossridge House, T 01555 880589	SCO SC
75 J7	**Biggar Lyne Cottage** Causeway End, T 01899 220141	SCO
75 K7	**Biggar The Glenholm Guest House** The Glenholm Centre, Broughton, T 01899 830408 www.glenholm.co.uk	SCO GH
12 D4	**Billingshurst Forte Trvlodge 5 Oaks** Five Oaks, T 08700 850 950	GB

Page ref.	Town/Name	Services
25 J5	**Birchington Crown Inn** Ramsgate Rd, Sarre, T 01795 542170	GB
25 J5	**Birchington Little Brooksend Farm** Brooksend, T 01843 841656	GB
40 C7	**Birmingham Copthorne** Paradise Circus, T 0121 200 2727	GB
40 D7	**Birmingham Hilton Birmingham Metropole** Nec, T 0121 780 4242	GB
40 C7	**Birmingham Jurys Inn Birmingham** 245 Broadst www.jurysdoyle.com	GB H
40 D6	**Birmingham Lyndhurst Hotel** 135 Kingsbury Rd, Erdington T 0121 373 5695	GB B&B
40 C7	**Birmingham Marriott Hotel** Hagley Rd, Five Ways, T 0870 400 7280	GB
40 C7	**Birmingham Novotel** 70 Brdst, T 0121 643 2000	GB
40 D7	**Birmingham Novotel Birmingham Airport** Birmingham Intl Airpt, T 0121 782 7000	GB
40 C7	**Birmingham Quality Norfolk Hotel** 267 Hagley Rd, T 0121 454 8071	GB
40 C7	**Birmingham Thistle Birmingham City** St Chads, Queensway, T 0870 333 9126	GB
89 B5	**Birsay Barony Hotel** Orkney, T 01856 721327	SCO
62 B3	**Bishop Auckland Bradley Burn Cottage** Wolsingham, T 01388 527285	GB
62 B4	**Bishop Auckland Swallows Nest** Cockfield, T 01388 718251	GB
33 J6	**Bishop's Stortford Warish Hall Farm** Warish Hall Farm, Takeley	GB
74 C3	**Bishopton Mar Hall** Mar Estate, T 0141 812 9999	SCO H
84 B4	**Black Isle Autumn Gold** Blablair, T 01381 622315	SCO B&B
56 C6	**Blackburn Mytton Fold Hotel** Whalley Rd, Langho, T 01254 240662 www.myttonfold.co.uk	GB H
56 B7	**Blackburn Shalom** 531b Livesey Branch Rd, T 01254 209032	GB
80 D10	**Blackford Blackford Hotel** Moray St, T 01764 682497	SCO H
80 D9	**Blackford Easterton Farm Cottage** Easterton Farm, T 01764 682268	SCO SC
55 G6	**Blackpool Burbage Holiday Lodge** Queens Promenade, Bispham, T 01253 356657	GB
55 G6	**Blackpool Hilton Blackpool** North Promenade, T 01253 623434	GB
55 G5	**Blackpool Norbreck Castle Hotel** Queens Promenade, T 01253 352341	GB
55 G6	**Blackpool Shellard Hotel** 18-20 Dean St, T 01253 342679	GB
55 G6	**Blackpool The Bond Hotel** South Shore, T 01253 341218	GB
66 D1	**Blackwaterfoot Lochside Guesthouse** Isle of Arran, T 01770 860276	SCO
18 E1	**Blaenau Lamb House** West Side, Blaina, T 01495 290179	CYMRU
37 G2	**Blaenau Ffestiniog Old Mill Farmhouse** Trawsfynydd, T 01766 540397	CYMRU
80 G4	**Blairgowrie Clackavoid Cottage** Glenshee, T 01250 882306	SCO SC
80 G6	**Blairgowrie Enochdhu** Rosemount Pk, T 01250 883379	SCO
80 G6	**Blairgowrie Holmrigg** Wester Essendy, T 01250 884309	SCO B&B
80 G6	**Blairgowrie Kinloch House Hotel** Perthshire, T 01250 884237	SCO
9 H4	**Blandford Forum Luccombe Farm** Milton Abbas, T 01258 880558	GB
75 H2	**Bo'ness Richmond Park Hotel** Linlithgow Rd, T 01506 823213	SCO
84 D9	**Boat of Garten Corronich** Highld, T 01479 831357	SCO
84 D9	**Boat of Garten Loch Garten Lodges** Loch Garten Rd, T 01309 672051	SCO
47 H5	**Bodelwyddan Bodelwyddan Castle Hotel** Denbighs, T 01745 585088	GB
4 A5	**Bodmin Churchtown** Lanlivery, T 01208 872148	GB
12 C7	**Bognor Regis Aldwick Hotel** Aldwick Rd, Aldwick, T 01243 821945	GB
12 C7	**Bognor Regis Beech Lodge** Felpham, T 01446 771311 www.groomsholidays.org.uk	GB SC

Spectacular sea views. 1 double, 3 twins, 1 single. Access via lift. TV, video, dishwasher, washer/dryer, central heating, garden/patio. Ceiling track hoist, wheel in shower, electric profiling bed.

Page ref.	Town/Name	Services
12 C7	**Bognor Regis Farrell House** 27 Nelson Road, T 01446 771311 www.groomsholidays.org.uk	GB SC

A peaceful setting just a walk from beautiful beaches. 2 twins, 1 single, 1 triple. TV, washer/dryer, central heating, garden, electric ceiling & mobile hoist, wheel in shower, electric profiling bed.

Page ref.	Town/Name	Services
17 F2	**Boncath Clynfyw Country Centre** Clynfyw, Abercych, Aber Cych, T 01239 841236 www.clynfyw.co.uk	CYMRU SC
75 G3	**Bonnybridge Antonine Wall Cottage** Bonnyside House, Bonnyside Rd, T 01324 811875 www.antoninewallcottages.co.uk	SCO SC
23 F2	**Borehamwood Elstree Moat House** Barnet By Pass, T 020 8214 9988	GB
88 B6	**Bornish Arnabhal** 5 Gerraidh Bhailteas, T 01878 710371	SCO
37 F6	**Borth Aberlei Farm Cottages** Ynyslas, T 01970 871233	CYMRU
4 A1	**Boscastle The Old Coach House** Tintagel Rd, T 01840 250398 www.old-coach.co.uk	GB
43 F2	**Boston Comfort Inn Boston** Bicker Bar, T 01205 820118	GB
10 B5	**Bournemouth Belvedere Hotel** Bath Rd, T 01202 297556	GB
10 B5	**Bournemouth Connaught Hotel** West Hill Rd, West Cliff, T 01202 298020	GB
10 B5	**Bournemouth Durley Hall Hotel** 7 Durley Chine Rd, T 01202 751000	GB
10 B5	**Bournemouth Durlston Court Hotel** Gervis Rd, East Cliff, T 01202 316316	GB
10 B5	**Bournemouth E Anglia Best Western** 6 Poole Rd, T 01202 765163	GB
10 C5	**Bournemouth Elstead Hotel** Knyveton Rd, T 01202 293071	GB
10 B5	**Bournemouth Highcliff Marriott** West Cliff, T 01202 557702	GB
10 B5	**Bournemouth Kings Langley Hotel** 1 West Cliff Rd, T 01202 557349	GB
10 B5	**Bournemouth Norfolk Royale Hotel** Richmond Hill, T 01202 551521	GB
10 C5	**Bournemouth Shelley Villa Hotel** 22 Wilfred Rd, Boscombe, T 01202 302400	GB
10 C5	**Bournemouth Wood Lodge Hotel** 10 Manor Rd, East Cliff, T 01202 290891	GB
60 F7	**Bowness-on-Windermere Deloraine** Helm Rd, T 015394 45557	GB
60 F7	**Bowness-on-Windermere Belsfield Hotel** Kendall Rd, T 01539 442448	GB
12 B7	**Bracklesham Bay Tamarisk** Farm Rd, T 01446 771311 www.groomsholidays.org.uk	GB SC

A lovely seaside setting. 2 twins, ensuite, 1 single, 1 z bed. Bed linen, TV video, dishwasher, washer/dryer, central heating, patio, electric & mobile hoist, wheel in shower, electric profiling bed.

Page ref.	Town/Name	Services
22 B5	**Bracknell Coppid Beech Hotel** John Nike Way, T 01344 303333	GB
20 A5	**Bradford-on-Avon Church Farm Cottage** Winsley, T 01225 722 246	GB
57 F6	**Bradford Acresgreen Bungalow** Thornton, T 01274 834262	GB
57 G6	**Bradford Novotel Bradford** Merrydale Rd, T 01274 683 683	GB
89 M6	**Brae Drumquin Guest House** Shetland, T 01806 522621	SCO
84 F11	**Braemar Braemar Lodge Hotel** Glenshee Rd, T 013397 41627	SCO SC

Accommodation Key — **Country:** GB England, SCO Scotland, CYMRU Wales, NI Northern Ireland — **Venue type:** H Hotel, B&B Bed & Breakfast, INN Inn, SC Self Catering, L Lodge, HOS Hostel, GH Guest House

Page ref.	Town/Name	Services
84 F11	**Braemar** The Invercauld Arms Hotel Invercauld Rd	SCO H
75 G6	**Braidwood** The Tower of Hallbar Braidwood Rd, T 0845 0900194	SCO SC
70 A7	**Brampton** Courtyard Cottages Warren Bank, Station Rd, T 016977 41818	GB
28 A7	**Brecon** Abercynafon Lodge Talybont on Usk, T 01874 676342	CYMRU
28 A5	**Brecon** Anchorage Caravan Park Bronllys, T 01874 711246	CYMRU
27 K5	**Brecon** Bishops Meadow Lodge Hay Rd, T 01874 610000	CYMRU
27 K6	**Brecon** Brynich Caravan Park Powys, T 01874 623325	CYMRU
27 K6	**Brecon** Castle of Brecon Hotel Castle Square, T 01874 624611	CYMRU
27 K6	**Brecon** Pencelli Cstle Caravan Park Pencelli, T 01874 665451	CYMRU
27 K5	**Brecon** Plough & Harrow Inn Felin Fach, T 01874 622709	CYMRU
24 C3	**Brentwood** Forte Travelodge A127, East Horndon, T 01277 810819	GB
75 F1	**Bridge of Allan** Lynedoch 7 Mayne Ave, T 01786 832178 www.lynedoch.com	SCO B&B
75 F1	**Bridge of Allan** The Queen's Hotel Henderson St, T 01786 833268	SCO H
80 G5	**Bridge of Cally** Bridge of Cally Hotel Perthshire, T 01250 886231	SCO INN
80 G5	**Bridge of Cally** Glen Albyn Perthshire, T 01250 886352	SCO B&B
85 P9	**Bridge of Don** Aberdeen Quality Hotel Aberdeen Exhib Cc, T 01224 706707	SCO
18 C3	**Bridgend** Coed Y Mwstwr Hotel Coychurch, T 01656 860621	GB
18 B4	**Bridgend** Glamorgan Holiday Hotel The Square, Porthcawl, T 01656 785375	CYMRU
72 B4	**Bridgend** Mulindry Cottages Isle of Islay, T 01496 810397	SCO
18 B4	**Bridgend** Rest Convalescent Home Rest Bay, Porthcawl, T 01656 772066	GB
18 C3	**Bridgend** Welcome Break Sarn Park M4, J36, T 0800 731 4466	CYMRU
39 G7	**Bridgnorth** Bulls Head Cottages Chelmarsh, T 01746 861469	GB
39 F6	**Bridgnorth** Haven Pasture Underton, T 01746 789632	GB
39 F7	**Bridgnorth** The Malthouse Wheathill, T 01952 433298	GB
8 C1	**Bridgwater** Apple View Temple Farm, Chedzoy, T 01278 423201	GB
8 B1	**Bridgwater** Blackmore Farm Cannington, T 01278 653442	GB
59 J3	**Bridlington** Marton Grange Marton C Sewerby, T 01262 602034	GB
8 C5	**Bridport** Blackmore Farmhouse Whitchurch Canonicorum, T 01297 489639	GB
8 D6	**Bridport** Burton Cliff Hotel Burton Bradstock, T 01308 897205	GB
8 C5	**Bridport** Conway Bungalow Bettiscombe, T 01308 868313	GB
8 C5	**Bridport** The Poplars Wood Fm Park, Charmouth, T 01297 560697	GB
13 G6	**Brighton** De Vere Grand Hotel King's Rd, T 01273 321188	GB
13 G6	**Brighton** Hilton Metropole Kings Rd, T 01273 775432	GB
13 G6	**Brighton** Quality Hotel West St, T 01273 220033	GB
13 G6	**Brighton** Thistle Brighton Kings Rd, T 01273 206700	GB
13 G6	**Brighton** University of Brighton Milthras House, Lewes Rd, T 01273 643167/8 www.brighton.ac.uk	GB SC
19 K3	**Bristol** Aztec Hotel Aztec West, Almondsbury, T 01454 201090	GB
19 J4	**Bristol** Bristol Marriott Royal College Green, T 0117 925 5100	GB
19 K6	**Bristol** Greyfield Farm Cottage Greyfield Fm, Greyfield Rd, High Littleton, T 01761 471132 www.greyfieldfarm.com	GB SC
19 J4	**Bristol** Novotel Bristol Centre Victoria St, T 0117 976 9988	GB
19 J5	**Bristol** Woodbarn Farm Denny Ln, Chew Magna, T 01275 332599	GB
82 G8	**Broadford** Corriegorm Beag Bayview Crescent, T 01471 822515 www.gpuknet.co.uk/cgb	SCO SC
82 G8	**Broadford** Corriegorm Beag Bay View Cr, T 01471 822517	SCO
82 G8	**Broadford** Earsary 7-8 Harrapool, T 01471 822697	SCO SC
82 F8	**Broadford** Sea Drift Ard Dorch, T 01471 822531	SCO SC
82 G8	**Broadford** Seaview Guest House Main St, T 01471 820308	SCO GH
82 G8	**Broadford** Skye Boat House 6 Strollamus, T 01582 768091	SCO SC
10 E4	**Brockenhurst** Balmer Lawn Hotel Lyndhurst Rd, T 01590 623116	GB
10 E4	**Brockenhurst** Careys Manor Hotel Hants, T 01590 623551	GB
10 D4	**Brockenhurst** Watersplash Hotel The Rise, T 01590 622344	GB
73 J7	**Brodick** A'chir Strathwhillan, T 01770 302331	SCO SC
73 J7	**Brodick** Auchrannie Country House Isle of Arran, T 01770 302234	SCO H
73 J7	**Brodick** Belvedere Guest House Alma Rd, T 01770 302397	SCO B&B
73 J7	**Brodick** Strathwhillan House Isle of Arran, T 01770 302331	SCO
73 J7	**Brodick** Vane Cottage Glen Cloy, T 01770 302219	SCO SC
29 J1	**Bromsgrove** Hilton Bromsgrove Birmingham Rd, T 0121 447 7888	GB
87 M9	**Brora** Glenaveron Golf Rd, T 01408 621 601	SCO B&B
87 M9	**Brora** Selkie Bed & Breakfast Harbour Rd, T 01408 621717	SCO B&B
87 M9	**Brora** Tigh Fada & The Eyrie 18 Golf Rd, T 01408 621 332	SCO SC
55 F1	**Broughton In Furness** Kepplewray Cumb, T 01229 716936 www.kepplewray.org.uk	GB H
81 K7	**Broughty Ferry** Kingennie Lodges Kingennie, T 01382 350777	SCO
23 G1	**Broxbourne** Cheshunt Marriott Halfhide Ln, Turnford, T 01992 451245	GB
9 F1	**Bruton** Discove Farm Holiday Cottage Dropping Ln, T 01749 812284 www.discove-farm.co.uk	GB SC
74 D1	**Buchlyvie** Upper Gartinstarry Stirlings, T 01360 850309	SCO
85 J4	**Buckie** 10 Great Eastern Road Banffshire, T 01542 831277	SCO SC
85 J4	**Buckie** The Bungalow 81 High St, T 01542 832367	SCO B&B
6 A5	**Bude** Kennacott Court Widemouth Bay, T 01288 362000	GB
6 A5	**Bude** Sharlands Farm Marhamchurch, T 01288 361322	GB
7 J7	**Budleigh Salterton** Lemprice Farm Yettington, T 01395 567037	GB
27 K3	**Builth Wells** Caer Beris Manor Powys, T 01982 552601	CYMRU
27 K3	**Builth Wells** Pencerrig Gardens Llandrindod Rd, T 01982 553226	CYMRU
78 E8	**Bunessan** Salachran Ardtun, T 01786 472900 www.salachran.info	SCO SC
78 E8	**Bunessan** Tigh Shee Ardton, T 01681 700541	SCO SC
84 F4	**Burghead, Elgin** Curlew Cottage 15 Granary St, T 01343 831114	SCO SC
22 C3	**Burnham** Burnham Beeches Hotel Grove Rd, T 01628 429955	GB
19 F6	**Burnham-on-Sea** Yew Tree House Hurn Ln, Berrow, T 01278 751382	GB
56 D6	**Burnley** Comfort Friendly Hotel Keirby Walk, T 01282 427611	GB
56 B2	**Burton In Lonsdale** Brentwood Farm Cottage Barnoldswick Ln, T 015242 62155	GB
40 D4	**Burton Upon Trent** The Moat Town Hill, Yoxall, T 01543 472210	GB
33 K1	**Bury St Edmunds** Best Western Beck Row, Mildenhall, T 01638 713223 www.smoke-house.co.uk	GB H
50 C5	**Buxton** Alison Park 3 Temple Rd, T 01298 22473	GB
50 D5	**Buxton** Cressbrook Hall Cottage Cressbrook, T 01298 871289	GB
50 D5	**Buxton** The Bungalow Millers Dale, T 01298 27778	GB
50 D6	**Buxtongton** Dairy Cottage Newhaven, Hartington, T 01629 636 268	GB
46 D6	**Caernarfon** Brynteg Park Llanrug, T 01286 873100	CYMRU
46 C7	**Caernarfon** Dinlle Caravan Park Gwynd, T 01492 623355	CYMRU
46 D7	**Caernarfon** Plas Baladeulyn Natile Penygroes, T 01286 880676	CYMRU
46 D6	**Caernarfon** Royal Victoria Hotel Llanberis, T 01286 870253	CYMRU
46 C7	**Caernarfon** The Ozanam Centre Tan Yr Allt, T 01286 881568	CYMRU
47 J4	**Caernarfon** The Stables Hotel Llanwnda, T 01286 830711	CYMRU
46 D6	**Caernarfon** Ty'n Rhos Country House Llanddeiniolen, T 01248 670489	CYMRU
46 C7	**Caernarfon** White Tower Park Llandwrog, T 01286 830649	CYMRU
78 E6	**Calgary** Treshnish Cottages Treshnish Point, T 01688 400249	SCO SC
80 B10	**Callander** Old Rectory Guest House Leny Rd, T 01877 339215	SCO GH
80 B10	**Callander** Roman Camp Hotel Main St, T 01877 330003	SCO H
80 B10	**Callander** The Crags Hotel 101 Main St, T 01877 330257	SCO GH
80 B10	**Callander** The Knowe Ancaster Rd, T 01877 330076	SCO GH
80 B10	**Callander** The Priory Bracklinn Rd, T 01877 330001	SCO
80 B10	**Callander** Trossachs Backpackers Invertrossachs Rd, T 01877 331200	SCO HOS
33 H3	**Cambridge** Crowne Plaza Downing St, T 01223 464466	GB
33 H3	**Cambridge** Winged Fellowship Bridget's Hostel, T 01223 311416	GB
4 A2	**Camelford** Mayrose Farm Helstone, T 01840 213509	GB
73 F7	**Campbeltown** Ifferdale Farm Cottage Ifferdale, Saddell, T 01583 431666	SCO
40 B5	**Cannock** Roman Way Hotel Hatherton, T 01543 572121	GB
15 G2	**Canterbury** Delightful B & B Pilgrims Way, T 01227 764799	GB
15 G2	**Canterbury** Ebury Hotel 65-67 New Dover Rd, T 01227 768433	GB
15 G2	**Canterbury** Kingsmead House 68 St Stephen's Rd, T 01227 760132	GB
15 G3	**Canterbury** Slippery Sam's Cottage Stone St, Petham, T 01227 700044	GB
15 G2	**Canterbury** Yew Tree Park Stone St, Petham, T 01227 700306	GB
80 F6	**Caputh** Western Caputh Hstl Manse Rd, T 01738 710449	SCO HOS
18 E4	**Cardiff** Copthorne Cardiff Culverhouse Cross, T 02920 599100	CYMRU
18 E4	**Cardiff** Novotel Cardiff Atlantic Wharf, T 02920 475 000	CYMRU
18 D4	**Cardiff** Parc Coed Machen Country Cottage St Brides-super-Ely, T 01446 760684	CYMRU
16 E1	**Cardigan** Brondesbury Lodge Heol Derw, T 01239 615427	CYMRU
17 F1	**Cardigan** Canllefaes Ganol Cottage Penparc, T 01239 613712	CYMRU
26 B3	**Cardigan** Ffynon Wen Guest House Aberporth, T 01239 810312	CYMRU
17 F1	**Cardigan** Gorslwyd Farm Tan-y-groes, T 01239 810593	CYMRU
17 G1	**Cardigan** Penbontbren Farm Hotel Glynarthen, T 01239 810248	CYMRU
16 E1	**Cardigan** The Gwbert Hotel Gwbert On Sea, T 01239 612638	CYMRU
17 F1	**Cardigan** The Stables Llechryd, T 01239 87777	CYMRU
16 E1	**Cardigan** Trenewydd Farm Cottage St Dogmaels, T 01239 612370	CYMRU
60 E1	**Carlisle** 7 Hether Drive Lowry Hill, T 01228 527242	GB
70 A6	**Carlisle** Arch View Bewhead, Roadhead, T 016977 48213	GB
69 K6	**Carlisle** Bessiestown Farm Catlowdy, Longtown, T 01228 577219	GB
60 F1	**Carlisle** County Hotel 9 Botchergate, T 01228 531316	GB
60 E2	**Carlisle** Green View Lodges Welton, Nr Dalston, T 016974 76230 www.green-view-lodges.com	GB SC
70 B7	**Carlisle** Holmhead Farm Hadrians Wall, Greenhead, T 016977 47402 www.holmhead.com	GB SC
60 E2	**Carlisle** Monkhouse Hill Sebergham, T 016974 76254	GB
60 E1	**Carlisle** Newfield Grange Hotel Newfield Drive, Kingstown, T 01228 819926	GB
17 J3	**Carmarthen** Cwmtwrch Farm Hotel Nantgaredig, T 01267 290238	CYMRU
17 K3	**Carmarthen** Hamdden Llety Mieri Golden Grove, T 01558 823059	CYMRU
56 B2	**Carnforth** Riverside Lodge Ingleton, T (015242) 41359	GB
55 H2	**Carnforth** The Stables Lindeth Rd, Silverdale, T 01524 702121	GB
55 H2	**Carnforth** Willowfield Hotel The Promenade, Arnside, T 01524 761354	GB
81 L7	**Carnoustie** Carlogie House Hotel Carlogie Rd, T 01241 853185	SCO
73 G7	**Carradale** Dunvalanree Portrigh Bay, T 01583 431226	SCO H
84 C8	**Carrbridge** The Cottage 8 Bogroy, T 0131 445 1251	SCO
69 F6	**Carrutherstown** Hetland Hall Hotel D & G, T 01387 840201	SCO H
65 H5	**Castle Douglas** Barncrosh Farm D & G, T 0155 6680 216	SCO
65 H3	**Castle Douglas** Craigadam Lodge D & G, T 01556 650233	SCO SC
65 H4	**Castle Douglas** Douglas House B&B 63 Queen St, T 01556 503262	SCO B&B
65 J4	**Castle Douglas** Redcastle House Haugh of Urr, T 01556 660475	SCO SC
65 F5	**Castle Douglas** Rusko Holidays Gatehouse of Fleet, Kirkcudbrightshire, T 01557 814215 www.ruskoholidays.co.uk	SCO SC

Beautiful 4 star cottage set amid magnificent Scottish scenery, near accessible beaches, hills and historic town – the perfect place to relax.

Page ref.	Town/Name	Services
30 D3	**Charlecote** Charlecote Pheasant Hotel Warwks, T 01789 279954	GB
23 F7	**Charlwood** Russ Hill Hotel Russ Hill, T 01293 862171	GB
19 H6	**Cheddar** The Heathers Westfield Ln, Draycott, T 01934 744187	GB
24 D1	**Chelmsford** Boswell House Hotel 118 Springfield Rd, T 01245 287587	GB
30 C6	**Cheltenham** Chester House Hotel Bourton-on-the-water, T 01451 820286	GB
29 J6	**Cheltenham** Hunting Butts Swindon Ln, T 01242 524982	GB
29 J6	**Cheltenham** Prestbury House Hotel The Burgage, Prestbury, T 01242 529533	GB
19 H2	**Chepstow** Cwrt-y-gaer Wolvesnewton, T 01291 650700	CYMRU
48 D7	**Chester** Carden Park Hotel & Spa Ches, T 01829 731000	GB

Page ref.	Town/Name	Services
48 D6	**Chester Comfort Inn Chester** 74 Hoole Rd, T 01244 327542	GB
48 D6	**Chester Dene Hotel** Hoole Rd, T 01244 321165	GB
48 D6	**Chester Green Bough Hotel** 60 Hoole Rd, T 01244 326241	GB
48 D6	**Chester Rowton Hall Hotel** Whitchurch Rd, Rowton, T 01244 335262	GB
48 D6	**Chester The Chester Grosvenor** Eastgate, T 01244 324024	GB
51 F5	**Chesterfield Abbeydale Hotel** Cross St, T 01246 277849	GB
51 F6	**Chesterfield Holestone Moor Barns** Holestone More Fm, Holestone More, Ashover, T 01246 591263 www.hmbarns.co.uk	GB SC
12 B6	**Chichester Cornerstones** Brookside Close, Runcton, T 01243 839096	GB
12 B6	**Chichester Crouchers Bottom Hotel** Birdham Rd, Apuldram, T 01243 784995	GB
12 B7	**Chichester St Andrews Lodge** Chichester Rd, Selsey, T 01243 606899	GB
12 B7	**Chichester St Catherines** 25 Clayton Rd, Selsey, T 020 8959 2848	GB
20 C4	**Chippenham The Parlour** Middle Farm, Stanley, T 01249 650339	GB
30 E6	**Chipping Norton Cleeves Farm** Over Norton, T 01608 645019	GB
38 A2	**Chirk Plas Owen Hotel** Glynceiriog, Llangollen, T 01691 718707	CYMRU
71 H5	**Choppington The Swan** Nthumb, T 01670 826060	GB
6 E4	**Chulmleigh Moortown Farm** Chawleigh, T 01491 577745	GB
38 D6	**Church Stretton Botvyle Farm Cottage** Shrops, T 01694 722869	GB
38 E6	**Church Stretton Gilberries Farm** Wall-under-heywood, T 01694 771253	GB
38 D6	**Church Stretton Jinlye** All Stretton, T 01694 723243	GB
38 E6	**Church Stretton The Crispen Cottage** Stone Acton Rd, Wallbank, T 01694 771319	GB
20 D1	**Cirencester Stratton House Hotel** Gloucester Rd, T 01285 651761	GB
20 E1	**Cirencester The Swan Hotel** Bibury, T 01285 740695	GB
35 F7	**Clacton On Sea Groomshill** 8 Holland Road, T 01446 771311 www.groomsholidays.org.uk	GB SC

In a quiet area of this famous seaside resort, ideal for town centre & beach. 3 twin bedrooms & 2 bed, wheel in shower, mobile hoist, electric profiling bed, TV, video, washer/dryer, central heating.

Page ref.	Town/Name	Services
16 D3	**Clarbeston Road Ivy Court Cottage** Ivy Court, Llysyfran, T 01437 532473	CYMRU
19 J1	**Clearwell Tudor Farmhouse Hotel** High St, T 01594 833046 www.tudorfarmhousehotel.co.uk	H

3 Star 13th Century converted farmhouse in pretty & idyllic village with AA 2 Rosette Restaurant and 22 en-suite bedrooms. Ideally located to explore the valley & forest of Dean.

Page ref.	Town/Name	Services
53 G2	**Cleethorpes Tudor Terrace Guest House** 11 Bradford Ave, T 01472 600800	GB
56 D5	**Clitheroe Higher Gills Farm** Rimington, T 01200 445370	GB
74 C3	**Clydebank Beardmore Hotel** Beardmore St, T 0141 951 6000	SCO H
60 C3	**Cockermouth Irton House Farm** Isel, T 01768 776380 www.disabledholiday.net	
60 C4	**Cockermouth Simonscales Mill** Simonscales Mill, T 01900 822594	GB
60 C3	**Cockermouth The Pheasant Inn** Bassenthwaite Lake, T 017687 76234	GB
34 D6	**Colchester Holiday Inn** Eight Ash Green, T 01206 767740	GB
34 C6	**Colchester Riverside Lodge** Earls Colne, T 01787 223487	GB
34 E6	**Colchester Rose & Crown** East St, T 01206 866677	GB
77 H4	**Coldingham Dunlaverock** Coldingham Bay, T 01890 771450	SCO GH
77 G6	**Coldstream Little Swinton Cottage** Little Swinton, T 01890 882173 www.littleswinton.co.uk	SCO SC
28 E7	**Coleford Dryslade Farm** English Bicknor, T 01594 860259 www.drysladefarm.co.uk	GB B&B
29 F7	**Coleford Speech House Hotel** Forest of Dean, T 01594 822607	GB
19 J1	**Coleford Wyndham Arms Hotel** The Cross, Clearwell, T 01594 833666	CYMRU
69 F6	**Collin Travelodge Dumfries** A75 Annan Rd, T 07775 846074	SCO
47 G4	**Colwyn Bay Ashmount Hotel** College Ave, Rhôs-on-Sea, T 01492 544582	CYMRU
47 G4	**Colwyn Bay Beachmount** 67 Colwyn Ave, T 01492 549314	CYMRU
47 G5	**Colwyn Bay Edelweiss Hotel** Off Lawson Rd, T 01492 532314	CYMRU
47 G5	**Colwyn Bay Holcombe Hotel** 9 Grosvenor Rd, T 01492 530423	CYMRU
47 G5	**Colwyn Bay Hwylfa Ddafydd Farm** Tan Y Graig Rd, T 01492 516965	CYMRU
47 G4	**Colwyn Bay Northwood Hotel** 47 Rhos Rd, Rhôs-on-Sea, T 01492 549931	CYMRU
8 B5	**Colyton Smallicombe Farm** Northleigh, T 01404 831310 www.smallicombe.com	GB B&B
8 B5	**Colyton Whitwell Farm Cottages** Colyford, T 01297 553803	GB
7 K6	**Colyton Wiscombe Linhaye Farm** Southleigh, T 01404 871342	GB
80 C8	**Comrie Drumearn Cottage** The Ross, T 01764 670030	SCO B&B
49 H6	**Congleton Sandhole Farm** Hulme Walfield, T 01260 224419	GB
79 K7	**Connel, Oban Wide Mouthed Frog** Dunstaffnage Marina, T 01631 567005 www.widemouthedfrog.com	SCO H

Restaurant with rooms with ground floor bedrooms for blue badge holders.

Page ref.	Town/Name	Services
83 R5	**Conon Bridge Kinkell House** Easter Kinkell, T 01349 861270	SCO
62 A2	**Consett Grouse Bungalow** Waskerley, T 0191 301 6719	GB
83 Q5	**Contin Hideaway** Craigdarroch Drive, T 01997 421127	SCO B&B
47 F5	**Conwy Conwy Touring Park** Bwlch Mawr, Lolyn Park, T 01492 592856	CYMRU
47 F6	**Conwy The Lodge Hotel** Tal-y-bont, T 01492 660766	CYMRU
13 G3	**Copthorne Copthorne Effingham** W Susx, T 01342 714994	GB
13 G3	**Copthorne Copthorne Gatwick** W Susx, T 01342 714971	GB
77 H7	**Cornhill on Tweed Coach House** Crookham, T 01890 820293	GB
80 H6	**Coupar Angus Red House Hotel** Station Rd, T 01828 628500	SCO H
41 F7	**Coventry Hilton National** Walsgrave Triangle, T 02476 603000	GB
30 E1	**Coventry Ibis Hotel Coventry** Abbey Rd, Whitley, T 024 7663 9922	GB
41 F7	**Coventry Novotel Coventry** J3 of M6, Exhall, T 02476 365000	GB
18 C4	**Cowbridge Jane Hodge Hotel** Trerhyngyll, Vale of Glamorgan, T 0171 452 2000 www.groomsholidays.org.uk	CYMRU

Set in the beautiful Vale of Glamorgan, with a fully equipped leisure centre, free to all guests; includes a multi-gym, hydrotherapy swimming pool, sauna, Jacuzzi, indoor bowls, children's play area.

Page ref.	Town/Name	Services
11 F5	**Cowes New Stable Cottage** Little Thorness Fm, T 01282 445444	GB
67 J2	**Coylton Finlayson Arms Hotel** 24 Hillhead, T 01292 570298	SCO INN
49 G6	**Cranage Padgate Guest House** Twemlow Ln, T 01477 534291	GB
38 D7	**Craven Arms Robin's Nest** Strefford, T 01588 672383	GB
38 D7	**Craven Arms Swallows Nest** Strefford, T 01588 672 383	GB
38 D7	**Craven Arms The Gables** Broome, T 01588 660667	GB
28 D1	**Craven Arms Upper Onibury Cottage** Upper Onibury, T 01584 856206	GB
23 F7	**Crawley Forte Travelodge Gatwick** Lowfield Heath, T 0800 850950	GB
7 G5	**Crediton Creedy Manor** Long Barn, T 01363 772684	GB
7 G5	**Crediton Welland Down Farm** Devon, T 01363 775928	GB
7 F4	**Crediton White Witches** Hele Barton, Black Dog, T 01884 860278	GB
49 G7	**Crewe Hunters Lodge Hotel** Sydney Rd, T 01270 583440	GB
49 G6	**Crewe The Old Vicarage Hotel** Cranage, Holmes Chapel, T 01477 532041	GB
79 Q8	**Crianlarich Crianlarich Yh** Station Rd, T 01786 891400	SCO HOS
36 D2	**Criccieth Llanystumdwy Park** Llanystumdwy, T 01766 522855	CYMRU
80 B8	**Crieff Achray House Hotel** St Fillans, T 01764 685 231	SCO H
80 D8	**Crieff Ardo Howe** 31 Burrell St, T 01764 652825	SCO GH
80 D8	**Crieff Caberfeidh** Highland Cr, T 01764 654859	SCO
80 D8	**Crieff Comely Bank Guest House** 32 Burrell St, T 01764 653409	SCO GH
80 E8	**Crieff Fendoch Guest House** Sma' Glen, T 01764 653446	SCO GH
80 D8	**Crieff Murraypark Hotel** Connaught Terrace, T 01764 653731	SCO H
80 E8	**Crieff Tuchethill House** Dollerie, T 01764 653188	SCO B&B
45 G1	**Cromer Cliftonville Hotel** Seafront, Runton Rd, T 01263 512543	GB
45 F1	**Cromer The Links Country Park Hotel** Sandy Ln, West Runton, T 01263 838383	GB
23 G5	**Croydon Hilton National** Waddon Way, Purley Way, T 020 8680 3000	GB
16 D2	**Crymmych Salutation Inn** Felindre Farchog, T 01239 820564	CYMRU
7 K4	**Cullompton Hemyock Castle** Hemyock, T 01823 680745	GB
83 R1	**Culrain Carbisdale Castle Yh** Highld, T 01786 891400	SCO HOS
75 F3	**Cumbernauld Dovecote Travel Inn** South Muirhead Rd, T 01236 725339	SCO
75 F3	**Cumbernauld Innkeeper's Lodge** 1 Auchenkilns Park, T 01236 795 861 www.innkeeperslodge.com	SCO H
81 J9	**Cupar Rathcluan** Carslogie Rd, T 01334 650000	SCO
81 K9	**Cupar Rockmount Cottage** Dura Den Rd, Pitscottie, T 01334 828164	SCO
81 J8	**Cupar St Andrews Country Cottage** Fife, T 01382 330318	SCO SC
19 F2	**Cwmbran Parkway Hotel** Cwmbran Drive, T 01633 871199	CYMRU
67 G3	**Dailly Brunston Castle Resort** Ayrshire, T 01465 811589	SCO
65 J4	**Dalbeattie Bellevue B & B** Port Rd, T 01556 611833	SCO B&B
65 J5	**Dalbeattie Clonyard House Hotel** Colvend, T 01556 630372	SCO H
65 J5	**Dalbeattie Kippford Holiday Park** D & G, T 01556 620636	SCO SC
76 B4	**Dalkeith Glenarch House** Melville Rd, Eskbank, T 0131 6631478	SCO GH
79 N8	**Dalmally Cruachan Guest House** Argyll, T 01838 200496	SCO
67 H2	**Dalrymple Kirkton Inn** 1 Main St, T 01292 560241	SCO INN
62 C5	**Darlington Blackwell Grange Hotel** Blackwell Grange, T 01325 509955	GB
62 B5	**Darlington East Greystone Farm Cottages** East Greystone Farm Cottages, Gainford, T 01325 730236 www.holidayfarmcottages.co.uk	GB SC

Two quality barn conversions; one level. Set in open countryside with lovely views, peaceful and relaxing. Ideal location for local amenities, attractions; The Dales .

Page ref.	Town/Name	Services
62 C6	**Darlington Quality Scotch Corner** Scotch Corner, T 01748 850900	GB
23 J4	**Dartford Hilton Dartford Bridge** Masthead Close, Crossways, T 01322 284444	GB
23 J5	**Dartford Thistle Brands Hatch** Brands Hatch, T 01474 854900 www.thistlehotels.com/brandshatch	GB H
5 J5	**Dartmouth The Dairy** Browns Fm Cottages, Capton, Dittisham, T 01803 712556 www.brownsfarmcottages.co.uk	GB SC
31 G3	**Daventry Bee Close House** Little Freston, T 01327361641	GB
89 E7	**Deerness Deersound Cottage** Halley Rd, T 01856 741331	SCO SC
47 J5	**Denbigh Bryn Glas Hotel** Trefnant, T 01745 730868	CYMRU
70 A2	**Denholm, Hawick Dunrovin** Dean Rd, T 01450 870466	SCO SC
41 F2	**Derby Midland Hotel** Midland Rd, T 01332 345892	GB
44 D4	**Dereham Dairy Farmhouse** Rawhall Ln, Bittering, T 01362 687687	GB
44 D4	**Dereham Greenbanks Country Hotel** Swaffham Rd, Wendling, T 01362 687742 www.greenbankshotel.co.uk	GB HOS
44 E3	**Dereham Moor Farm Stable Cottage** Moor Farm, Foxley	GB
78 F5	**Dervaig Corrieyairack** Isle of Mull, T 01899 220473	SCO SC
20 C6	**Devizes Abbotts Ball Farm** Potterne, T 01380 721 661	GB
20 C6	**Devizes Longwater** Lower Rd, Erlestoke T 01380 830095	GB B&B
84 A4	**Dingwall Western Brae Lodges** Highld, T 01349 877609	SCO SC
76 D2	**Dirleton Station House** Station Rd, T 01620 890512	SCO B&B
45 F7	**Diss Shelfanger Hall** Shelfanger, T 01379 642094	GB
37 F4	**Dolgellau George Iii Hotel** Penmaenpool, T 01341 422525	CYMRU
37 F4	**Dolgellau Graig Wen** Arthog, T 01341 250482	CYMRU
36 E5	**Dolgellau Pentre Bach Cottage** Llwyngwril, T 01341 250294 www.pentrebach.com	CYMRU SC
37 G4	**Dolgellau Royal Ship Hotel** Queens Square, T 01341 422209	CYMRU
75 H1	**Dollar Arndean Cottages** Blairingone, T 01259 743525	SCO SC

Accommodation Key | Country: GB England SCO Scotland CYMRU Wales NI Northern Ireland | Venue type: H Hotel B&B Bed & Breakfast INN Inn SC Self Catering L Lodge HOS Hostel GH Guest House

Page ref.	Town/Name	Services
51 J3	**Doncaster** Mount Pleasant Hotel Rossington, T 01302 868219	GB
9 G5	**Dorchester** Higher Waterston Farm Cottage Piddlehinton, T 01305 848208	GB
9 F5	**Dorchester** Lower Burton Farmhouse Dorset	GB
8 E6	**Dorchester** Tamarisk Farm Cottage West Bexington, T 01308 897784	GB
9 F5	**Dorchester** The Lodge Cottages Cerne Abbas, T 01300 341831	GB
22 E7	**Dorking** Bulmer Farm Holmbury St Mary, T 01306 730210	GB
22 E6	**Dorking** Burford Bridge Hotel Box Hill, T 01306 884561	GB HOS
22 E6	**Dorking** Denbies B&B London Rd, T 01306 876616 www.denbieswineestate.com	GB B&B
22 E7	**Dorking** Forte Travelodge Reigate Rd, T 0800 850950	GB
22 E6	**Dorking** Juniper Hall Centre Box Hill, T 1306 883849	GB
84 B1	**Dornoch** Castle Park Cottage Proncy, T 01862 810940	SCO
84 B1	**Dornoch** Cluaine Lodge Evelix, T 01862 810276	SCO SC
84 B2	**Dornoch** Dornoch Castle Hotel Castle St, T 01862 810216	SCO H
84 C2	**Dornoch** Dornoch Hotel Grange Rd, T 01862 810351	GB
84 C1	**Dornoch** Fourpenny Cottage Skelbo, T 01862 810727	SCO
89 B5	**Dounby** Lochland Chalets Orkney, T 01856 771340	SCO SC
7 F7	**Drewsteignton** Clifford Lodge Clifford Bridge, T 01647 24445	GB
59 F3	**Driffield** Life Hill Farm Sledmere, T 01377 236224	GB
59 G4	**Driffield** The Bell Market Place, T 01377 256661	GB
64 B7	**Drummore** Harbour Row D & G, T 01776 840631	SCO SC
83 R8	**Drumnadrochit** Clunebeg Lodge Clunebeg Estate, T 01456 450387 www.clunebeg.com	SCO GH
83 R8	**Drumnadrochit** Woodlands East Lewiston, T 01456 450356	SCO GH
74 B1	**Drymen** Rowardennan Yh Rowardennan, T 01786 891400	SCO HOS
40 B7	**Dudley** Copthorne Merry Hill Brierley Hill, T 01384 482882	GB
84 H6	**Dufftown, Keith** Parkmore Farm Banffshire, T 01340 820072	SCO SC
82 H7	**Duirinish** Duirinish Chalets Highld, T 01599 544268	SCO
46 C4	**Dulas** Minffordd Caravan Park Penrhoslligwy, T 01248 410678	CYMRU
7 H3	**Dulverton** Northmoor House & Lodge Northmoor, T 01398 323720	GB
65 K3	**Dumfries** Cairnyard House Beeswing, T 01387 730218	SCO
65 K3	**Dumfries** Cairnyard Lodges Beeswing, T 01387 730218	SCO SC
65 K3	**Dumfries** Dumfries & Galloway Coll Moat Hall, Herries Ave, T 01387 265621	SCO
65 K3	**Dumfries** Hazeldean Guest House 4 Moffat Rd, T 01387 266178	SCO GH
68 E5	**Dumfries** Midtown Cottage Parkgate, T 01387 860661	SCO
65 K3	**Dumfries** Netherfield Lochanhead, T 01387 730217	SCO B&B
65 K3	**Dumfries** Nunland Holidays Crocketford Rd, T 01387 730214	SCO SC
65 K3	**Dumfries** Orchard House 298 Annan Rd, T 01387 252612	SCO
65 K3	**Dumfries** Pine Chalet Beeswing	SCO
68 E4	**Dumfries** Stockman's Cottage Ae, T 01387 860648 www.gubhill.co.uk	SCO SC
65 K3	**Dumfries** Torbay Lodge 31 Lovers Walk, T 01387 253922	SCO GH
68 E5	**Dumfries** Wallamhill House Kirkton, T 01387 248249	SCO B&B
76 E3	**Dunbar** Goldenstones Hotel Queens Rd, T 01368 862356	SCO H
80 C10	**Dunblane** Hilton Dunblane Hydro Perthshire, T 01786 822551	GB
80 C10	**Dunblane** Mossgiel Doune Rd, T 01786 824325	SCO
75 F1	**Dunblane** Stable Cottage Row House, T 01786 841200	SCO SC
81 J7	**Dundee** Alcorn Guest House 5 Hyndford St, T 01382 668433	SCO
81 J7	**Dundee** Days Inn Dundee Strathmore Ave, T 01382 826000	SCO L
81 K7	**Dundee** Fishermans Tvn Broughty Ferry, T 01382 775941	SCO H
81 K7	**Dundee** Hilton Dundee Earl Grey Place, T 01382 229271	SCO
81 J7	**Dundee** Longforgan Coaching Inn Longforgan, T 01382 360386	SCO
81 J8	**Dundee** Seabraes Hall Roseangle, T 01382 573050	SCO SC
81 K7	**Dundee** Uni of Abertay Dundee Bell St, T 01382 308059	SCO SC
81 J8	**Dundee** West Park Villas West Park Rd, T 01382 344039	SCO
75 J2	**Dunfermline** Best Western Keavil Hotel Crossford, T 01383 736258	SCO H
75 J2	**Dunfermline** Bruce Street 29-35 Bruce St, T 01383 840041	SCO H
75 K2	**Dunfermline** Clarke Cottage Guest House 139 Halbeath Rd, T 01383 735935	SCO GH
75 K2	**Dunfermline** Garvock House Hotel St John's Drive, Transy, T 01383 621067 www.garvock.co.uk	SCO H
75 K2	**Dunfermline** Pitbauchlie House Hotel Aberdour Rd, T 01383 722282	SCO H
80 F6	**Dunkeld** 2 Burnmouth Road Little Dunkeld, T 01382 320237	SCO
80 F6	**Dunkeld** Hilton Dunkeld House Perthshire, T 01350 727771	GB
73 K3	**Dunoon** Dhailling Lodge 155 Alexandra Parade, T 01369 701253	SCO GH
73 K4	**Dunoon** Egmont Shore Rd, Toward, T 0141 639 3129	SCO SC
73 K3	**Dunoon** Lyall Cliff Hotel East Bay, T 01369 702041	SCO
73 K3	**Dunoon** Moncrief 133 Alexandra Parade, T 01369 707945	SCO
73 K2	**Dunoon** Stronchullin Holiday Cottage Ardentinny, T 01369 810246	SCO SC
73 K2	**Dunoon** The Anchorage Shore Rd, Ardnadam, T 01369 705108	SCO
76 E4	**Duns** Cranshaws Smiddy Berwickshire, T 01361 890277	SCO
77 F4	**Duns** Greenhope Cottage Ellemford, T 01361 890242	SCO SC
68 D5	**Dunscore** Lochmederie D & G, T 01387 870625	SCO
62 C2	**Durham** Durham Marriott Hotel Old Elvet, T 0191 386 6821	GB
62 D2	**Durham** Ramside Hall Hotel Carrville, T 0191 386 5282	GB
62 C2	**Durham** Saint Aidan's College Uni of Durham, T 0191 374 3269	GB
62 C2	**Durham** The Bracken Hotel Shincliffe, T 0191 386 2966	GB
62 C2	**Durham** Waterside Elvet Waterside, T 0191 378 0636	GB
85 N9	**Dyce** Aberdeen Marriott Hotel Farburn, T 01224 770011	SCO
85 N9	**Dyce** Dyce Skean Dhu Hotel Farburn Terrace, T 01224 723101	SCO H
85 N9	**Dyce** The Beaches 112 Victoria St, T 01224 722249	SCO
36 E3	**Dyffryn Ardudwy** Byrdir Gwynd, T 01341 247200	CYMRU
36 E3	**Dyffryn Ardudwy** Murmur Yr Afon Gwynd, T 01341 247353	CYMRU
36 E3	**Dyffryn Ardudwy** Ystumgwern Farm Gwynd, T 01341 247249	CYMRU
76 D6	**Earlston** The Smithy House Legerwood, T 01896 84518	SCO
44 D3	**East Dereham** Blackhall Barn Yarrow Ln, North Elmham, T 01362 683527	GB
74 E5	**East Kilbride** Hilton Stewartfield Way, T 01355 236300	SCO
74 E5	**East Kilbride** Stakis E Kilbride Stewartfield Way, T 01355 236300	SCO
13 K7	**Eastbourne** Congress Hotel 31-41 Carlisle Rd, T 01323 732118	GB
13 K7	**Eastbourne** Heatherdene Hotel 26-28 Elms Ave, T 01323 723598	GB
13 K7	**Eastbourne** Langham Hotel Royal Parade, T 01323 731451	GB
13 K7	**Eastbourne** The Grand Hotel King Edwards Parade, T 01323 412345	GB
82 D5	**Edinbane** Shorefield Isle of Skye, T 01470 582444	SCO
76 A3	**Edinburgh** 3 Keith Row M Lothian, T 0131 343 1354	SCO
76 A3	**Edinburgh** 5 Inverleith Row T 0131 5581653	SCO
76 A4	**Edinburgh** Aalpha Laurels 320 Gilmerton Rd, T 0131 666 2229	SCO GH
76 A4	**Edinburgh** Abbey Lodge Hotel 137 Drum St, Gilmerton, T 0131 6649548	SCO GH
76 A3	**Edinburgh** Airport City Central 30/2 Eyre Crescent, T 07950 018865	SCO SC
76 B3	**Edinburgh** Ardgarth Guest House 1 St Mary's Place, Portobello, T 0131 669 3021 www.ardgarth.com	SCO GH
76 A3	**Edinburgh** Averon Guest House 44 Gilmore Place, T 0131 229 9932	SCO
76 A3	**Edinburgh** Best Western Edi City 79 Lauriston Place, T 0131 622 7979	SCO
76 A3	**Edinburgh** Best Western Hotel 79 Lauriston Place, T 0131 622 7979	SCO H
75 K3	**Edinburgh** Birchtree Cottage 1 Barnton Grove, T 0131 339 3611	SCO
76 A4	**Edinburgh** Brae Lodge Guest House 30 Liberton Brae, T 0131 672 2876	SCO GH
76 A3	**Edinburgh** Budget Backpackers 37-39 Cowgate, T 0131 226 6351	SCO HOS
76 A3	**Edinburgh** Caledonian Hilton Hotel Princes St, T 0131 222 8888	SCO H
76 A3	**Edinburgh** Canon Court 20 Canonmills, T 0131 474 7000	SCO
75 K3	**Edinburgh** Edinburgh Marriott 111 Glasgow Rd, T 0870 400 7293	SCO H
76 A3	**Edinburgh** Express Holiday Inn 16-22 Picardy Place, T 0131 5582300	SCO H
76 A3	**Edinburgh** Glenfield Guest House 21 West Mayfield, T 0131 6629242	SCO
76 A3	**Edinburgh** Hilton Belford 69 Belford Rd, T 0131 332 2545	SCO
75 K3	**Edinburgh** Hilton Edinburgh Airport Edinburgh Intl Airpt, T 0131 519 4400	SCO H
76 A3	**Edinburgh** Holiday Express Inn Britannia Way, Ocean Drive, T 0131 5554422	SCO H
76 A3	**Edinburgh** Holiday Inn Corstorphine Rd, T 0870 400 9026	SCO H
76 A3	**Edinburgh** Holiday Inn Edi-north 107 Queensferry Rd, T 0131 332 2442	SCO H
76 A3	**Edinburgh** Holyrood Aparthotel Holyrood, T 0131 524 3200	SCO
76 A3	**Edinburgh** Hotel Ceilidh-donia 14-16 Marchhall Crescent, T 0131 667 2743	SCO H
76 A3	**Edinburgh** Hotel Ibis Edinburgh 6 Hunter Square, T 0131 2407000	SCO
75 K3	**Edinburgh** Innkeepers Lodge 114-116 St Johns Rd, T 0131 334 8235	SCO INN
76 A3	**Edinburgh** Intl Guest House 37 Mayfield Gardens, T 0131 667 2511 www.accommodation-edinburgh.com	SCO GH
76 A3	**Edinburgh** Jurys Inn Edinburgh 43 Jeffrey St, T 0131 200 3300	SCO H
76 A3	**Edinburgh** Kelly's Guest House 3 Hillhouse Rd, T 0131 332 3894 www.kellysguesthouse.cx	SCO GH
76 B3	**Edinburgh** Kings Manor Hotel 100 Milton Rd East, T 0131 669 0444 www.kingsmanor.com	SCO H
76 A3	**Edinburgh** Lindsay Guest House 108 Polwarth Terrace, T 0131 337 1580	SCO GH
76 B3	**Edinburgh** Melville Guest House 2 Duddingston Crescent, T 0131 6697856	SCO GH
76 A3	**Edinburgh** Napier University West Bryson, Blackfriars, T 0131 455 4427	SCO SC
76 A3	**Edinburgh** Napier University Wrights House, Bruntsfield, T 0131 455 4545	SCO
75 K3	**Edinburgh** Norton House Hotel Ingliston, T 0131 333 1275	GB
76 A3	**Edinburgh** Novotel Centre 80 Lauriston Place, T 0131 656 3500	SCO H
76 A3	**Edinburgh** Posthouse Edinburgh Corstorphine Rd, T 0870 4009026	SCO
76 A3	**Edinburgh** Premier Travel Inn 1 Morrison Link, T 0870 238 3319 www. premiertravelinn.com	SCO H
76 A3	**Edinburgh** Ramada Mount Royal 53 Princes St, T 0131 225 7161	SCO H
76 A3	**Edinburgh** Royal Garden Apartments Queen St, T 0131 220 1613	SCO
76 A3	**Edinburgh** Sheraton Grand Hotel 1 Festival Square, T 0131 229 9131	SCO
76 A3	**Edinburgh** St Christophers Inn Market St, T 01753 647603	SCO HOS
75 K3	**Edinburgh** The Trefoil Centre Gogarbank, T 0131 339 3148	SCO
76 A3	**Edinburgh** Thistle Edinburgh 107 Leith St, T 0141 3323311	SCO H
76 A4	**Edinburgh** Travel Lodge South Dreghorn Link, T 0131 441 4296	SCO
76 A3	**Edinburgh** Western Manor House Hotel 92 Corstorphine Rd, T 0131 5387490 www.westernmanorhousehotel.co.uk	SCO H
77 F7	**Ednam** Plumbrae's Barn Cliftonhill, T 01573 225028	SCO SC
81 L4	**Edzell** Kelvingrove Dunlappie Rd, T 01356 648316	SCO B&B
22 D4	**Egham** Runnymede Hotel Windsor Rd, T 01784 436171	GB
22 C4	**Egham** Savill Court Hotel Englefield Green, T 01784 434355	GB
84 G4	**Elgin** Moraydale 276 High St, T 01343 546381	SCO
84 G4	**Elgin** Torr House Hotel 8 Moss St, T 011343 542661	SCO
81 K10	**Elie** Red Tile Cottage 64 High St, T 01333 330219	SCO SC
81 K10	**Elie** The Stable The Park, Bank Street, T 01333 330219	SCO
33 H1	**Ely** Rosendale Lodge Witchford, T 01353 667700	GB
74 C3	**Erskine** Erskine Bridge Hotel Renfrews	SCO H
48 B6	**Ewloe** St Davids Park Hotel St Davids Park, T 01244 520800	CYMRU
6 E6	**Exeter** Beer Farm Okehampton, T 01837 840 265	GB
7 H6	**Exeter** Buckerell Lodge Hotel Topsham Rd, T 01392 221111	GB
7 F6	**Exeter** Clifford Barton Cottage Drewsteignton, T 01647 24763	GB
7 H6	**Exeter** Coach House Farm Moor Ln, Broadclyst, T 01392 461254	GB
7 J7	**Exeter** Couchayes Couches Ln, Woodbury, T 01395 233483	GB
6 D5	**Exeter** Higher Cadhan Farm Jacobstowe, Oakhampton, T 01837 851 647	GB
7 H6	**Exeter** Hue's Piece Paynes Farm, Broadclyst, T 01392 466720	GB
35 G1	**Eye** Alpha Cottages The St, Horham, T 01379 384424	GB
34 E2	**Eye** The Netus Wickham Skeith, T 01449 766275	GB
77 H4	**Eyemouth** Alemill Holiday Cottage Berwickshire, T 01890 771676	SCO SC
75 H3	**Falkirk** Ashbank Redding, T 01324 716649	SCO
80 H10	**Falkland** The Burgh Lodge Back Wynd, T 01337 858358	SCO HOS
3 F5	**Falmouth** Broadmead Hotel Kimberley Park Rd, T 01326 315704	GB
3 F5	**Falmouth** Trevaylor Hotel 8 Pennance Rd, T 01326 313041	GB
11 G4	**Fareham** Solent Hotel Rookery Ave, Whiteley, T 01489 880000	GB
11 G4	**Fareham** Travelrest Avenue House Hotel 22 The Ave, T 01329 232175	GB

Page ref.	Town/Name	Services
22 B7	**Farnham** Audubon House 73a Lodge Hill Rd, T 01252 715589	GB
84 A7	**Farr** Dalvourn Holidays Dalvourn Farm, T 01808 521467 www.dalvourn.com	SCO SC
25 G5	**Faversham** Shepherd Neame Ltd 17 Court St, T 01795 533380	GB
35 G5	**Felixstowe** Dorincourt Guest House 41 Undercliff Rd West, T 01394 270447	GB
35 H5	**Felixstowe** Merlin's Den 9 College Green, T 01394 282213 Self-catering annexe of owner's home with breakfast supplies provided daily. Just minutes from two miles of promenade and close to local shops.	GB SC
89 Q3	**Fetlar** Tigh Sith, Society of Our Lady of the Isles Aithness, T 01957 733200	SCO
89 C6	**Finstown** Lynwood Maitland Place, T 01856 761786	SCO B&B
74 E2	**Fintry** Culcreuch Castle Culcreuch Castle, T 01360 860555	SCO H
16 D2	**Fishguard** Gellifawr Pontfaen, T 01239 820343	CYMRU
15 H3	**Folkestone** Garden Lodge Canterbury Rd, Densole, T 01303 893147	GB
13 H3	**Forest Row** Hindleap Warren Wych Cross, T 01342 822625	GB
80 F9	**Forgandenny** Battledown B & B Off Station Rd, T 01738 812471	SCO B&B
84 E5	**Forres** Tulloch Holiday Lodges Rafford, T 01309 673311 www.tullochlodges.com	SCO SC
84 D4	**Forres** Woodpecker Cottage Kintessack, T 01309 641351	SCO
79 M4	**Fort William** Ardgour House Ardgour, Clovullin, T 01855 841311	SCO
79 M3	**Fort William** Clan Macduff Hotel Achintore Rd, T 01397 702341	SCO H
79 N3	**Fort William** Craig Nevis West Belford Rd, T 01397 702023	SCO GH
79 M3	**Fort William** Croit Anna Hotel Highld, T 01397 702268	SCO
79 N3	**Fort William** Cuil-na-sithe Lochyside, T 01397 702 267	SCO B&B
79 N3	**Fort William** Lochan Cottage Lochyside, T 01397 702695	SCO GH
79 M4	**Fort William** Lodge On The Loch Creag Dhu, Onich, T 01855 821237	SCO
79 N3	**Fort William** Mossfield Holiday Apartments Lochyside, T 01397 706061	SCO
79 M4	**Fort William** The Inn At Ardgour Ardgour, T 01855 841225	SCO H
79 N3	**Fort William** Underwater Centre Highld, T 01397 703786	SCO
79 N3	**Fort William** Woodland House Torlundy, T 01397 701698	SCO
22 B6	**Frimley** One Oak Toby Hotel Portsmouth Rd, T 01276 691939	GB
82 H3	**Gairloch** Dunedin 42 Strath, T 01445 712050	SCO B&B
82 H3	**Gairloch** Willow Croft Big Sand, T 01445 712448	SCO SC
76 D7	**Galashiels** Borders Centre Netherdale, T 01896 892270	SCO SC
76 D7	**Galashiels** College of Textiles Netherdale, T 01896 753474	SCO
76 C7	**Galashiels** Ettrickvale 33 Abbotsford Rd, T 01896 755224	SCO B&B
76 C7	**Galashiels** Thornielee Vale Near Clovenfords, T 01896 850634	SCO
36 D1	**Garn-Dolbenmaen** Hen Ysgol Bwlch Derwin, Pant Glas, T 01286 660701	CYMRU
71 H7	**Gateshead** Newcastle Marriott Metro Centre, T 0191 493 2233	GB
23 F7	**Gatwick** Le Meridien Gatwick Gatwick Airport, T 01293 567070	GB
23 F7	**Gatwick** London Gatwick Hilton Gatwick Airport, T 01293 518080	GB
65 H5	**Gelston** Rose Cottage D & G, T 01556 502513	SCO SC
9 G2	**Gillingham** Top Stall Fifehead Magdalen, T 01258 820022	GB
24 D5	**Gillingham** YHA Capstone Farm 377 Capstone Rd, T 01634 400788	GB
67 F5	**Girvan** Couthie Neuk Colmonell, T 01465 881234	SCO SC
66 E5	**Girvan** Downanhill Cottage Ballantrae, T 01465 831368	SCO SC
66 E5	**Girvan** Glenapp Castle Ballantrae, T 01465 831212	SCO H
45 F7	**Gissing** Bluebell Cottage Malthouse Fmcottages, T 1381 677512	GB SC
45 F7	**Gissing** Rose Cots Malthouse Fm Holiday Cottages, T 01379 677512 www.norfolkcottages.net	GB SC
74 D4	**Glasgow** Artto Hotel 37-39 Hope St, T 0141 248 2480	SCO H
74 D4	**Glasgow** Bewleys Hotel Glasgow 110 Bath St, T 0141 3530800	SCO H
74 D4	**Glasgow** Cairncross House 20 Kelvinhaugh Place, T 0141 3303110	SCO SC
74 D4	**Glasgow** Campanile Glasgow Tunnel St, T 0141 2877700	SCO H
74 D4	**Glasgow** Carlton George Hotel 44 West George St, T 0141 353 6373	SCO H
74 D4	**Glasgow** Fraser Suites Glasgow No 1-19 Albion St, T 0141 553 4288 www.fraserhospitality.com Scotland's largest luxury serviced apartment's complex, stay one night or longer in the merchant city. The new alternative to Htls, with more space, independence and facilities	SCO SC
74 D4	**Glasgow** Glasgow Guest House 56 Dumbreck Rd, T 0141 427 0129	SCO
74 D4	**Glasgow** Glasgow Hilton 1 William St, T 0141 204 5555	SCO H
74 D4	**Glasgow** Glasgow Marriott 500 Argyle St, T 0141 226 5577	SCO H
74 D4	**Glasgow** Glasgow Moat House Congress Rd, T 0141 306 9988	SCO H
74 D4	**Glasgow** Granada Lodge J20 of M8, 251 Paisley Rd, T 01525 878328	SCO
74 D4	**Glasgow** Holiday Inn 161 West Nile St, T 0141 352 8300	SCO H
74 D4	**Glasgow** Holiday Inn Glasgow W Bothwell St, T 0870 400 9032	SCO H
74 D4	**Glasgow** Ibis Hotel Glasgow 220 West Regent St, T 0141 225 6000	SCO H
74 D4	**Glasgow** Millennium Glasgow Hotel George Square, T 0141 332 6711	SCO H
74 D4	**Glasgow** Milton Hotel & Spa 27 Washington St, T 0141 222 2929	SCO H
74 D4	**Glasgow** Novotel Glasgow Centre 181 Pitt St, T 0141 222 2775	SCO H
74 C3	**Glasgow** Patio Hotel Clydebank Bus Pk, Clydebank, T 0141 951 1133	SCO
74 D4	**Glasgow** Posthouse Glasgow City Bothwell St, T 0870 400 9032	SCO
74 D4	**Glasgow** Quality Central Hotel Gordon St, T 0141 221 9680	GB
74 E4	**Glasgow** The Knowes 32 Riddrie Knowes, T 0141 770 5213	SCO SC
74 E4	**Glasgow** The Knowes 32 Riddrie Knowes, T 0141 770 5213 www.sol.co.uk/t/theknowes	SCO B&B
74 D4	**Glasgow** Thistle Glasgow 36 Cambridge St, T 0141 332 3311	SCO
74 D4	**Glasgow** Travel Lodge Glasgow 251 Paisley Rd, T 0141 4203882	SCO
74 D4	**Glasgow** Travelodge Central 11 Hill St, T 0141 3331515	SCO
74 D4	**Glasgow** Tulip Inn Glasgow 80 Ballater St, T 0141 429 4233 www.tulipinnglasgow.co.uk	SCO H
8 E1	**Glastonbury** Highlands Studio 21 Rowley Rd, T 01458 834587	GB
85 J11	**Glen Tanar, Aboyne** Glen Tanar Est Brooks House, T 013398 86451/86305	SCO SC
83 P7	**Glen Urquhart** Millness Croft Cottage Corrimony, T 01456 459090	SCO SC
78 H4	**Glenborrodale** Cluain Grianach Laga Bay, T 01223 360887	SCO SC
79 M4	**Glencoe** Creag Mhor Hotel Onich, T 01855 821379	SCO
64 C5	**Glenluce** Craw's Nest Bungalow Kilfillan, T 0121 378 1844	SCO
83 P9	**Glenmoriston** Binnilidh Mhor Dalchreichart, T 01320 340258	SCO SC
16 C2	**Goodwick** Fishguard Bay Hotel Quay Rd, T 01348 873571	CYMRU
76 B4	**Gorebridge** Ivory House 14 Vogrie Rd, T 01875 820755	SCO GH
76 B4	**Gorebridge** Newbyres Cottage 8 Hunterfield Rd, T 01875 821268	SCO
11 G5	**Gosport** West Wind Guest House Lee on the Solent, T 023 9255 2550	GB
74 A3	**Gourock** Spinnaker Hotel 121 Albert Rd, T 01475 633107	SCO H
55 H2	**Grange-over-Sands** Netherwood Hotel Fallowfield, Lindale Rd, T 015395 32552	GB
75 H2	**Grangemouth** Leapark Hotel 130 Bo'ness Rd, T 01324 486733	SCO H
42 C2	**Grantham** Kings Hotel North Parade, T 01476 590800	GB
42 C2	**Grantham** Marriott Hotel Swingbridge Rd, T 01476 593000	GB
84 E8	**Grantown-on-Spey** Craiglynne Hotel Woodlands Terrace, T 01479 872597	SCO
84 E8	**Grantown-on-Spey** Kinross House Guest House Woodside Ave, T 01479 872042	SCO
84 E8	**Grantown-on-Spey** Dunallan House Woodside Ave, T 01479 872140	SCO GH
84 E8	**Grantown-on-Spey** Holmhill House Woodside Ave, T 01479 873977	SCO GH
84 E8	**Grantown-on-Spey** Kinross Guest House Woodside Ave, T 01479 872042	SCO GH
84 D8	**Grantown-on-Spey** Muckrach Lodge Hotel Dulnain Bridge, T 01479 851257	SCO H
74 A3	**Greenock** Express By Holiday Inn Cartsburn, T 01475 786666	SCO H
74 A3	**Greenock** Tontine Hotel 6 Ardgowan Square, T 01475 723316	SCO H
69 J7	**Gretna** Hunters Lodge Hotel Annan Rd, T 01461 338214	SCO
69 J7	**Gretna** The Gables Hotel 1 Annan Rd, T 01461 338300	SCO H
69 J7	**Gretna** The Garden House Hotel Sarkfoot Rd, T 01461 337621	SCO H
69 J7	**Gretna** The Willows Loanwath Rd, T 01461 337996	SCO B&B
69 J7	**Gretna Green** Days Inn D & G, T 01461 337566	SCO L
69 J7	**Gretna Green** Welcome Break D & G, T 0800 731 4466	SCO
53 F2	**Grimsby** Millfields 53 Bargate, T 01472 356068	GB
53 F3	**Grimsby** Willow Lakes Ashby Cum Fenby, T 01472 824429	GB
45 K5	**Gt Yarmouth** Burlington Palm Crt Hotel North Dr, T 01493 844568	GB
45 J4	**Gt Yarmouth** Horse & Groom Motel Main Rd (A149), Rollesby, T 01493 740624	GB
22 C7	**Guildford** Guildford Ymca Ltd Bridge St, T 01483 532555	GB
89 N9	**Gulberwick** Virdafjell Shurton Brae, T 01595 694336	SCO B&B
76 C2	**Gullane** Hopefield House Main St, T 01620 842191	SCO
76 D3	**Haddington** Maitlandfield House 24 Sidegate, T 01620 826513	SCO H
13 K5	**Hailsham** Conquerors Herstmonceux, T 01323 832446	GB
35 H1	**Halesworth** School Farm Cottage Church Rd, Cratfield, T 01986 798844	GB
47 K5	**Halkyn** Forte Travelodge Unit 1228, A55, T 01352 780952	CYMRU
29 H3	**Hallow** The New Cottage Greenhill Ln, T 01905 640953	GB
75 F5	**Hamilton** Roadchef Lodge Lanarks, T 01698 891904	SCO
10 D5	**Hampshire** Smuglers View New Milton, T 01446 771311 www.groomsholidays.org.uk	GB SC

Basic, comfortable double and twin bedroom chalets, sited at Naish Holiday Village with plenty of activities for all. TV, lounge/diner, fitted kitchen, patio, wheel in shower, commode chair.

Page ref.	Town/Name	Services
37 F2	**Harlech** Hotel Maes Y Neuadd Talsarnau, T 01766 780200	CYMRU
37 F2	**Harlech** The Estuary Motel Talsarnu Village, T 01766 771155	CYMRU
33 H7	**Harlow** Swallow Churchgate Hotel Churchgate St Village, T 01279 420246	GB
88 F9	**Harris** Carminish House 1a Strond, T 01859 520400	SCO B&B
57 J4	**Harrogate** Azalea Court Hotel 56-58 Kings Rd, T 01423 560424	GB
57 H3	**Harrogate** Brimham Rocks Cottage Fellbeck, T 01765 620284	GB
57 H3	**Harrogate** Dinmore Cottages Burnt Yates, T 01423 771711	GB
57 G3	**Harrogate** Greengarth Pateley Bridge, T 01423 711688	GB
57 J4	**Harrogate** Harrogate Moat House Kings Rd, T 01423 849988	GB
57 J3	**Harrogate** Nidd Hall Hotel Nidd, T 01423 771598	GB
57 H3	**Harrogate** Old Spring Wood Lodges Hartwith Bk, Summer Bdge, T 01423 780279	GB
57 H4	**Harrogate** Swallow St George Hotel Ripon Rd, T 01423 561431	GB
57 H3	**Harrogate** The Boar's Head Hotel Ripley, T 01423 771888	GB
12 C3	**Haslemere** Lythe Hill Hotel Petworth Rd, T 01428 651251	GB
14 D7	**Hastings** Grand Hotel Grand Parade, St Leonards-on-Sea, T 01424 428510 www.grandhotelhastings.co.uk	GB H
16 C4	**Haverfordwest** Dreenhill Farm Dale Rd, T 01437 764494	CYMRU
16 B4	**Haverfordwest** Keeston Hill Cottage Keeston, T 01437 710440	CYMRU
16 B4	**Haverfordwest** Millmoor Farm Cottage Broad Haven, T 01437 781507	CYMRU
16 A3	**Haverfordwest** Ocean Haze Hotel St David's, T 01437 720826	CYMRU
16 B4	**Haverfordwest** Rosemoor Cottage Walwyns Castle, T 01437 781326	CYMRU
16 A3	**Haverfordwest** Tretio C & C Park Tretio, St Davids, T 01437 781359	CYMRU
56 D1	**Hawes** Old Station House Hardraw Rd, T 01969 667785	GB
70 A2	**Hawick** Caldy Cottage Parkdaill, T 01450 850246	SCO
70 A2	**Hawick** Cherry Cottage & Quince Cottage Bonchester Bridge, T 01450 860678	SCO
70 A2	**Hawick** Quince & Cherry Cottage Bonchester Bridge, T 01450 860678	SCO
70 A2	**Hawick** Stable Cottage Kirkton, T 01896 822411	SCO SC
69 K2	**Hawick** Whitchester Guest House Roxburghs, T 01450 377477	SCO GH
11 J5	**Hayling Island** Seagazers 2 Eastoke Ave, T 023 9246 2975	GB
11 J5	**Hayling Isld** Lakeside Resort Fishery Ln, T 02392 463976	GB
13 J4	**Heathfield** Iwood B&B Mutton Hall Ln, T 01435 863918	GB
13 K4	**Heathfield** Spicers B&B 21 Spicers Cottages, Cade Street, T 01435 866363 www.spicersbb	GB B&B
22 D4	**Heathrow** Renaissance Hotel Bath Rd, T 020 8897 6363	GB
74 B2	**Helensburgh** Drumfork Farm Dunbartonshire, T 01436 672329	SCO
74 B2	**Helensburgh** Rsr Braeholm East Montrose St, T 01436 671880	SCO L
87 N8	**Helmsdale** Kindale House 5 Lilleshall St, T 01431 821415	SCO GH

Accommodation Key — Country: GB England, SCO Scotland, CYMRU Wales, NI Northern Ireland. Venue type: H Hotel, B&B Bed & Breakfast, INN Inn, SC Self Catering, L Lodge, HOS Hostel, GH Guest House

Page ref.	Town/Name	Services
87 N8	**Helmsdale** Navidale House Hotel Navidale, T 01431 821258	SCO
2 C6	**Helston** Penzance Road Lodge Ashton, T 01736 763217	GB
22 D1	**Hemel Hempstead** Bobsleigh Inn Hempstead Rd, Bovingdon, T 01442 833276	GB
22 A3	**Henley-on-Thames** Stonor Arms Hotel Stonor, T 01491 638866	GB
22 A4	**Henley-on-Thames** Holmwood Binfield Heath, T 0118 947 8747	GB
28 D5	**Hereford** Anvil Cottage Grafton, T 01432 268689	GB
28 E5	**Hereford** Holme Lacy House Hotel Holme Lacy, T 01432 870870	GB
28 C5	**Hereford** The Neville Arms Abbey Dore, T 01981 240319	GB
25 H5	**Herne Bay** The South Wing Gothic House, 36 Ave Rd, T 01227 366862	GB
70 B5	**Hexham** Calvert Trust Kielder Kielder Water, T 01434 250232 www.calvert-trust.org.uk We provide outdoor activities, care and relaxation for people with disabilities, their families and friends. Fully accessible centre + self catering chalets.	GB SC
70 D5	**Hexham** Conheath Cottage Bellingham, T 01434 220250	GB
70 C7	**Hexham** Gibbs Hill Farm Cottage Bardon Mill, T 01434 344030	GB
70 C7	**Hexham** Montcoffer B&B Montcoffer, Bardon Mill, T 01434 344138 www.montcoffer.co.uk	GB B&B
61 L1	**Hexham** Old Byre Rye Hill Farm, Slaley, T 01434 673259	GB
70 C5	**Hexham** Rose Cottage Falstone, T 0191 285 4643	GB
13 F4	**Hickstead** Forte Travelodge A23, Jobs Ln, T 08700 850 950	GB
19 G7	**Highbridge** Merry Farm Merry Ln, Basonbridge, T 01278 783655	GB
41 G6	**Hinckley** Hanover Intl Hotel A5, T 01455 631122	GB
6 B4	**Holsworthy** Jay Lodge Bradworthy, T 01409 241719	GB
6 A4	**Holsworthy** Lympscott Farm Bradworthy, T 01409 241607	GB
44 E1	**Holt** The Pheasant Hotel The Coast Rd, Kelling, T 01263 588382	GB
47 K4	**Holywell** Talacre Beach Camping Station Rd, Talacre, T 01745 858000	CYMRU
30 D1	**Honiley** Honiley Court Hotel Warwks, T 01926 484234	GB
7 K5	**Honiton** Garden Lodge Broadhembury, T 01404 841403	GB
22 A6	**Hook** Hanover Intl Hotel Nately Scures, T 01256 764161	GB
23 F7	**Horley** Holiday Inn Gatwick Povey Cross Rd, T 0870 400 9030	GB
23 F7	**Horley** Langshott Manor Langshott, T 01293 786680	GB
23 F7	**Horley** Massetts Lodge 28 Massetts Rd, T 01293 783200	GB
23 F7	**Horley** Masslink House 70 Massetts Rd, T 01293 785798	GB
23 F7	**Horley** Thistle Gatwick Brighton Rd, T 01293 786992	GB
23 J3	**Hornchurch** Palms Hotel Southend Arterial Rd, T 01708 346789	GB
45 J3	**Horsey** The Old Chapel Horsey Corner, T 01493 393498	GB
22 D4	**Hounslow** London Heathrow Hilton T4, Heathrow Airpt, T 020 8759 7755	GB
89 C9	**Hoy** Stromabank Orkney, T 01856 701494	SCO H
50 D1	**Huddersfield** Hilton National J24 of M62, Ainley Top, T 01422 375431	GB
59 G7	**Hull** Campanile Hotel Freetown Way, T 01482 325530	GB
59 H7	**Hull** Kingstown Hotel Hedon, T 01482 890461	GB
59 J7	**Hull** Little Weghill Farm Preston, T 01482 897650	GB
59 G6	**Hull** Ramada Jarvis Hull Grange Park Ln, Willerby, T 01482 656488	GB
21 G5	**Hungerford** Littlecote House Hotel Littlecote, T 01488 682509	GB
44 A1	**Hunstanton** Caley Hall Motel Old Hunstanton, T 01485 533486	GB
33 F1	**Huntington** Huntington Marriott Kingfisher Way, T 01480 446000	GB
85 J6	**Huntly** Drumdelgie House Cairnie, T 01466 760368	SCO
85 K6	**Huntly** Forbes Arms Hotel Miltown of Rothiemay, T 01466 711248	SCO
85 L7	**Huntly** Tanaree & Dykeside Logie Newton, T 01464 841229	SCO
6 D1	**Ilfracombe** Cresta Hotel Torrs Park, T 01271 863742	GB
6 D1	**Ilfracombe** Harbourside Hotel Larkstone Terrace, T 01271 862231	GB
6 D1	**Ilfracombe** Sunnymeade Hotel Dean Cross, West Down, T 01271 863668 www.sunnymeade.co.uk A small, comfortable country Htl in N Devon between golden sandy beaches & close to Exmoor, 10 rooms, 4 on the ground floor with wheelchair access-wheel in or walk in showers. Award winning home cooked local Devon produce.	GB H
73 K4	**Inellen** Blanacuil Shore Rd, T 01369 870502	SCO
80 F8	**Inveralmond** Holiday Inn Express 200 Dunkeld Rd, T 01738 636666	SCO L
79 M10	**Inveraray** Fin Ro Cottage Crombies Land	SCO SC
79 M9	**Inveraray** Loch Fyne Hotel Newtown, T 0131 554 7173	SCO H

Page ref.	Town/Name	Services
79 M10	**Inveraray** Loch Fyne Hotel Newtown, T 01499 302748	SCO
74 A3	**Inverclyde** Howard Johnson Hotel Cartsburn, Greenock, T 01475 786666	SCO
81 J7	**Invergowrie, Dundee** Swallow Hotel Kingsway West, T 01382 641122	SCO H
74 A3	**Inverkip** The Foresters Station Rd, T 01475 521433	SCO B&B
83 Q9	**Invermoriston** Lann Dearg Studios Lann Dearg, Dalcataig, T 01456 459083	SCO SC
84 A6	**Inverness** Aberfeldy Lodge 11 Southside Rd, T 01463 231120	SCO
84 A6	**Inverness** Avalon Guest House 79 Glenurquhart Rd, T 01463 239075	SCO GH
84 B6	**Inverness** Copperfield Culloden Rd, Westhill, T 01463 792251	SCO GH
84 B6	**Inverness** Drumossie Park Cottage Drumossie Brae, T 01463 224127	SCO B&B
84 A6	**Inverness** Glen Mhor Hotel 9-12 Ness Bank, T 01463 234308	SCO H
84 A6	**Inverness** Holiday Inn Express Stoneyfield, T 01463 732700	SCO L
84 A6	**Inverness** Inverness Marriott Culcabock Rd, T 01463 237166	SCO H
84 A6	**Inverness** Inverness Millburn Yh Victoria Drive, T 01786 891400	SCO HOS
84 A6	**Inverness** Kingsmills Hotel Culcabock Rd, T 01463 237166	SCO
84 B6	**Inverness** Links View Blackpark Farm, Westhill, T 01463 790620	SCO SC
84 B6	**Inverness** Lodge At Daviot Mains Daviot, T 01463 772215	SCO B&B
84 A6	**Inverness** Lodge Park 9 Lodge Park, T 01463 221535	SCO
84 A6	**Inverness** Mardon 37 Kenneth St, T 01463 231005	SCO
84 A6	**Inverness** Moyness House 6 Bruce Gardens, T 01463 233836	SCO
84 A6	**Inverness** Ramada Jarvis Inverness Church St, T 01463 235181	SCO H
84 A6	**Inverness** Rookery Nook 56 Culcabock Ave, T 01463 237085	SCO SC
84 A6	**Inverness** Silverwells Guest House 28 Ness Bank, T 01463 232113	SCO GH
85 M8	**Inverurie** Strathburn Hotel Burghmuir Drive, T 01467 624422	SCO H
35 G3	**Ipswich** Blacksmiths Cottage Hall Farm, Hall Ln, Otley, T 01473 890766	GB
35 F4	**Ipswich** Ipswich County Hotel London Rd, Copdock, T 01473 209988	GB
35 G4	**Ipswich** Marriott Courtyard The Havens, T 01473 272244	GB
35 F4	**Ipswich** Novotel Ipswich Greyfriars Rd, T 01473 232400	GB
34 E4	**Ipswich** Odds & Ends House 131 High St, Hadleigh, T 01473 822032	GB
34 E4	**Ipswich** Stable Cottages Chattisham Pl, Chattisham, T 01473 652210	GB
35 F4	**Ipswich** Swallow Belstead Brook Belstead Rd, T 01473 684241	GB
74 B7	**Irvine** The Gailes Lodge Marine Drive, Gailes, T 01294 204040	SCO L
74 B7	**Irvine** Thistle Irvine 46 Annick Rd, T 0141 332 3311	SCO H
66 E1	**Isle of Arran** Strathconan Glenashdale, Whiting bay, T 01586 830323 www.arranselfcatering.com	SCO SC
88 B8	**Isle of Barra** Northbay House Balnabodach, T 01871 890255	SCO B&B
88 G7	**Isle of Harris** Ardhasaig House 9 Ardhasaig, T 01859 502066	SCO H
88 G6	**Isle of Harris** Lewis & Harris Yca Ardvourlie, T 01859 502502	SCO HOS
78 D8	**Isle of Iona** Finlay Ross Martyr's Bay, T 01505 704000	SCO B&B
78 D8	**Isle of Iona** Iona Hostel Lagandorain, T 01681 700 642	SCO HOS
72 B4	**Isle of Islay** Blackpark Croft Bridgend, T 01496 810376	SCO SC
72 B5	**Isle of Islay** The Old Stables Shore St, Bowmore, T 01496 810414	SCO
72 A4	**Isle of Islay** Coull Farm Cottage Kilchoman, Bruichladdich, T 01496 850317	SCO SC
72 C4	**Isle of Islay** Craigard Holidays Ballygrant, T 01496 810728 www.craigard-islay.co.uk	SCO SC
72 B5	**Isle of Islay** Laggan View Glenegadale, Port Ellen, T 01704 663316	SCO SC
88 D2	**Isle of North Uist** Redburn House Lochmaddy, T 0208 6927271	SCO B&B
82 H8	**Isle of Skye** Kyleakin Yh Kyleakin, T 01786 891400	SCO HOS
5 G5	**Ivybridge** Venn Farm Cottage Ugborough, T 01364 73240	GB
70 B1	**Jedburgh** Allerton House Oxnam Rd, T 01835 869633 www.allertonhouse.co.uk We strive to meet all of your wishes and needs with special facilities catering to children, complimentary indoor swimming just steps down the road, accommodation meeting all disability requirements and countless ways to pamper yourself for that special get-away. Allerton House offers elegant accommodation and affordable luxury.	SCO H
70 B1	**Jedburgh** Birchover Honeyfield Drive, T 01835 862887	SCO
70 B1	**Jedburgh** Crailing Old School Roxburghs, T 01835 850382	SCO B&B
70 B2	**Jedburgh** Hundalee House Borders, T 01835 863011	SCO
57 F5	**Keighley** Beeches Toby Bradford Rd, T 01535 610611	GB
84 H7	**Keith** Braehead Villa Braehead Terrace, Dufftown, T 01340 320461 www.visit-dufftown-scotland.co.uk Bed & Breakfast. Full Disabled Facilities. Private Parking on the Whisky Trail.	SCO B&B

Page ref.	Town/Name	Services
77 F7	**Kelso** Craignethan House Jedburgh Rd, T 01573 224818	SCO B&B
70 D1	**Kelso** Craignethan House Jedburgh Rd, T 01573 224818	SCO
77 F7	**Kelso** Cross Keys Hotel 36-37 The Square, T 01573 223303	SCO H
77 F7	**Kelso** Edenmouth Farm Roxburghs, T 01890 830391	SCO B&B
77 F7	**Kelso** Edenmouth Farm Roxburghs, T 01890 830391	SCO
77 F7	**Kelso** Garden Bank Cliftonhill, Ednam, T 01573 225028	SCO
77 F7	**Kelso** Ingleston House Abbey Row, T 01573 225800	SCO GH
76 E7	**Kelso** Lime Avenue Cottage Nenthorn Ave, Nenthorn, T 01573 24446	SCO
76 E7	**Kelso** Roxburgh Newtown Farm Roxburghs, T 01573 450250	SCO SC
75 K1	**Kelty** Benarty Steading Cottage Benarty House, T 01383 830235	SCO
60 F7	**Kendal** Avondale Silver St, Staveley, T 015394 45713	GB
60 F7	**Kendal** Greenbank Crosthwaite, T 015395 68598	GB
60 D4	**Keswick** Derwentwater Hotel Portinscale, T 01768 772538	GB
60 E4	**Keswick** Scales Farm Gueststhouse Scales, Threlkeld, T 01768 779660	GB
32 B1	**Kettering** Kettering Park Hotel Kettering Parkway, T 01536 416666	GB
34 D3	**Kettlebaston** Rector's Retreat The Old Convent, T 01449 741557	GB
29 H1	**Kidderminster** The Granary Hotel Heath Ln, Shenstone, T 01562 777535	GB
29 G1	**Kidderminster** The Little Houses Organs Hill Farm, Rock, T 01299 266435	GB
66 E1	**Kildonan** Island Properties Shore Road, T 01770 820624	SCO SC
16 D5	**Kilgetty** Hanbury Lodge Jeffreston, T 01834 811212	CYMRU
80 A7	**Killin** Breadalbane House Main St, T 01567 820134	SCO GH
80 A7	**Killin** Dall Lodge House Hotel Main St, T 01567 820217	SCO
80 A7	**Killin** Garden Cottage Lyon St, T 01567 820476	SCO
80 B7	**Killin** Greenacre Aberfeldy Rd, T 01567 820466	SCO
80 A7	**Killin** Killin Highland Lodges Perthshire, T 01764 685448	SCO SC
80 A7	**Killin** The Shieling Aberfeldy Rd, T 01567 820334	SCO
74 C6	**Kilmarnock** Fenwick Hotel Fenwick, T 01560 600 478	SCO H
74 C6	**Kilmarnock** Fenwick Hotel Fenwick, T 01560 600478	GB
74 C7	**Kilmarnock** Forte Travelodge Kilmarnock By Pass, T 01563 573810	SCO
74 C7	**Kilmarnock** Park Hotel Rugby Park, T 01563 545999	SCO H
20 A6	**Kilmersdon** The Creamery Batch Farm, T 01373 812337	GB
73 K2	**Kilmun** Kilmun Hotel Shore Rd, T 01369 840418	SCO
74 A6	**Kilwinning** High Smithstone Farm High Smithstone Fm, T 01294 552361	SCO SC
80 G7	**Kinclaven** Ballathie House Hotel Perthshire, T 01250 883268	SCO H
84 C10	**Kincraig** Loch Insh Chalets Highld, T 01540 651272	SCO SC
85 M5	**King Edward** Blackton Farm Banffshire, T 01888 551205	SCO
44 C4	**Kings Lynn** Cherry Tree Cottage Back Ln, Castle Acre, T 01760 755000	GB
44 D4	**Kings Lynn** Holmdene Farm Beeston, T 01328 701284	GB
44 A3	**Kings Lynn** Park House Sandringham, T 01485 543000	GB H
84 C11	**Kingcraig** Ballintean Bungalow Ballintean, Glenfeshie, T 01540 651352	SCO
44 B3	**Kings Lynn** Ffolkes Arms Hotel Lynn Rd, Hillington, T 01485 600210	GB
5 J6	**Kingsbridge** Beeson Farm Cottage Beeson Farm, Beeson, T 01548 581270 www.beesonhols.co.uk	GB SC
5 H6	**Kingsbridge** Stancombe Manor Sherford, T 01548 531634	GB
28 B3	**Kington** Offa's Dyke Lodge Gladestry, T 01544 370341	CYMRU
84 B10	**Kingussie** Arden House Newtonmore Rd, T 01540 661369	SCO GH
84 B10	**Kingussie** Avondale Guest House Newtonmore Rd, T 01540 661731	SCO
84 C10	**Kingussie** Birker Cottage Insh, T 01540 661069	SCO SC
84 B10	**Kingussie** Hermitage Guest House Spey St, T 01540 662137	SCO GH
84 B10	**Kingussie** Laggan Cottage Highld, T 01540 661558 www.yates128.freeserve.co.uk/cottage Holiday cottage in Cairngorm National Park with accessible ground floor facilities for up to 2 persons. Bedrooms upstairs for a further four mobile guests. Private car park.	SCO SC
84 C10	**Kingussie** Lagganlia Centre Kincraig, T 01540 661265	SCO SC
84 B10	**Kingussie** The Auld Poor House Highland, T 01540 661558 www.auldpoorhouse.co.uk Four Star Bed & Breakfast in Cairngorm National Park; accessible ground-floor en-suite room and access to lounge-Dining facilities via a stair lift. Private car park.	SCO SC
80 B5	**Kinloch Rannoch** Dunalastair Hotel The Square, T 01882 632323	SCO H

Page ref.	Town/Name	Services
86 E4	Kinlochbervie Horseshoe Cottage Oldshoremore, T 01971 521729	SCO SC
83 L4	Kinlochewe Cromasaig Highld, T 01445 760234	SCO
83 K3	Kinlochewe Loch Maree Hotel Talladale, Loch Maree, T 01445 760288	SCO
79 N4	Kinlochleven Blackwater Hostel Lab Rd, T 01855 831253	SCO HOS
80 G10	Kinross Lomond Country Inn Main St, Kinnesswood, T 01592 840253	SCO
61 J6	Kirkby Stephen Coldbeck Cottage Ravenstonedale, T 015396 23230	GB
61 J6	Kirkby Stephen Leases Smardale, T 017683 71198	GB
61 J6	Kirkby Stephen The Black Swan Hotel Ravenstonedale, T 015396 23204	GB
61 J6	Kirkby Stephen The Fat Lamb Crossbank, Ravenstonedale, T 015396 23242	GB
76 A2	Kirkcaldy Kingswood Hotel Kinghorn Rd, Burntisland, T 01592 872329 www.kingswoodhotel.co.uk	SCO H
76 A1	Kirkcaldy Scotties B&B 213 Nicol St, T 01592 268596 www.scottiesbandb.co.uk	SCO B&B
75 K3	Kirkliston Crannog New Liston Rd, T 0131 333 4621	SCO B&B
80 F5	Kirkmichael The Log Cabin Hotel Glen Derby, T 01250 881288	SCO H
80 F4	Kirkmichael The Log Cabin Hotel Glen Derby, T 01250 881288	SCO
69 H7	Kirkpatrick Fleming The Mill Grahamshill, T 01461 800344	SCO L
89 D6	Kirkwall Buttquoy Park Orkney	SCO SC
89 D6	Kirkwall Eastbank House East Rd, T 01856 870179	SCO GH
89 D6	Kirkwall Highbury Villas East Rd, T 01856 8471049	SCO
89 D6	Kirkwall Kirkwall Yh Old Scapa Rd, T 01786 891400	SCO HOS
89 D7	Kirkwall Lav'rockha Guest House Inganess Rd, T 01856 876103	SCO GH
81 J3	Kirriemuir Brandy Burn House Glen Clova, T 01575 550231	SCO SC
81 J4	Kirriemuir Glenprosen Cottages Balnaboth, Glenprosen, T 01575 540 302	SCO SC
81 J5	Kirriemuir Pearsie Lodge Pearsie, T 01575 540234	SCO SC
81 J3	Kirriemuir Steading Bunkhouse Glen Clova Htl, T 01575 550350	SCO HOS
81 J5	Kirriemuir Tipperwhig & Brankam Purgavie Farm, T 01575 560364	SCO SC
81 J5	Kirriemuir Welton of Kingoldrum Kingoldrum, T 01575 574743	SCO
38 A7	Knighton Tack Barn Beguildy, T 01547 510682	GB
28 B1	Knighton The Knighton Hotel Broad St, T 01547 520530	CYMRU
49 G4	Knutsford Premier Lodge Hoo Green, Mere, T 0787 960 4019	GB
82 F7	Kyle of Lochalsh Isle of Raasay Hotel Raasay, T 01478 660222	SCO H
86 E8	Lairg Birchbank Activity Lodge Knockan, Elphin, T 01854 666203	SCO
86 H6	Lairg Invermudale Annexe Altnaharra, T 01549 411250	SCO SC
86 H9	Lairg Lochview Lochside, T 01549 402578	SCO B&B
73 J7	Lamlash Lilybank Shore Rd, T 01770 600230	SCO GH
17 J1	Lampeter Bryn Castell Llanfair Rd, T 01570 422447	CYMRU
55 H4	Lancaster Lancaster House Hotel Green Ln, T 01524 844822	GB
56 C3	Lancaster New Inn Hotel Clapham, T 01524 251203	GB
55 H4	Lancaster Thurnham Mill Hotel Thurnham, T 01524 752852	GB
55 J4	Lancaster Travelodge Lancaster Bay Horse, T 01524 791775	GB
27 J4	Langammarch Wells Hillview Powys, T 01591 620711	CYMRU
69 J5	Langholm The Reiver's Rest 81 High St, T 01387 381343	SCO
8 D2	Langport Hay Loft & Stables Muchelney Ham, T 01458 253113	GB
73 K4	Largs Seger Property Mgnt 15 Killburn Court, T 01475 686369	SCO SC
75 F5	Larkhall Shawlands Hotel Ayr Rd, T 01698 791111	SCO L
4 C2	Launceston Waterloo Farm North Petherwin, T 01566 785386	GB
88 K4	Laxdale Laxdale Bunkhouse Laxdale Ln, T 01851 706966	SCO HOS
30 E2	Leamington Spa The Beeches Warwks, T 01926 612487	GB
79 K6	Ledaig Isle of Eriska Hotel Argyll, T 01631 720371	SCO H
29 G5	Ledbury The Old Kennels Farm Bromyard Rd, T 01531 635024	GB
57 H6	Leeds Hilton National - City Neville St, T 0113 244 2000	GB
57 H6	Leeds Holiday Inn Crowne Plaza Wellington St, T 0113 2442 200	GB
57 H6	Leeds Novotel Leeds Centre Whitehall Quay, T 0113 242 6446	GB
57 J6	Leeds Thorpe Park Hotel & Spa Thorpe Park, T 0113 264 1000	GB
57 H6	Leeds Weetwood Hall Otley Rd, Headingley, T 0113 230 6000	GB

Page ref.	Town/Name	Services
50 C7	Leek Larks Rise Bottom House, T 01538 304 350	GB
50 C7	Leek Swainsley Farm Butterton, T 01298 84530	GB
41 H4	Leicester Field Head Hotel Markfield Ln, Markfield, T 01530 245454	GB
41 H5	Leicester Holiday Inn Leics 29 St Nicholas Circle, T 0116 253 1161	GB
41 H5	Leicester The Red Cow Leicester Forest East, T 0116 238 7878	GB
41 H6	Leicester Time Out Hotel Enderby Rd, Blaby, T 0116 278 7898	GB
28 D3	Leominster Bramlear Barons Cross Rd, T 01568 613 406	GB
89 N8	Lerwick Craigmore Upper Baila, T 01595 695567	SCO
89 N8	Lerwick Glen Orchy Guest House 20 Knab Rd, T 01595 692031	SCO GH
89 N8	Lerwick Laebrak Gulberwick, T 01595 880231	SCO
89 N9	Lerwick Laebrak Gulberwick, T 01595 880231	SCO SC
89 N8	Lerwick Self-catering Shetland Inches, Bells Rd, T 01595 695354 www.selfcateringshetland.com	SCO SC
89 N8	Lerwick Shetland Hotel Holmsgarth Rd, T 01595 695515	SCO H
89 N8	Lerwick Whinrig 12 Burgh Rd, T 01595 693554	SCO
88 F9	Leverburgh Am Bothan Leverb'gh Am Bothan, T 01859 520251	SCO HOS
88 K4	Lewis Dolly's B & B 33 Aignish, Point, T 01851 870755	SCO B&B
88 L1	Lewis The Cross Inn Cross Ness, T 01851 810152	SCO INN
62 B7	Leyburn Eastfield Lodge Hotel St Matthews Terrace, T 01969 623196	GB
57 G1	Leyburn Foal Barn Spennithorne, T 01969 622580	GB
62 B7	Leyburn Golden Lion Hotel Market Place, T 01969 622161	GB
57 F1	Leyburn High Green House Thoralby, T 01969 663420	GB
23 H6	Limpsfield Arawa 58 Granville Rd, T 01883 714104	GB
52 C5	Lincoln Cliff Farm Cottage Cliff Farm, North Carlton, T 01522 730475 www.cliff-farm-cottage.co.uk	GB SC
52 E6	Lincoln Mill Lane Cottage 70 Mill Ln, Woodhall Spa, T 01526 353101 www.skegness.net/woodhallspa.htm	GB SC
75 H3	Linlithgow Arden House Belsyde, T 01506 672172	SCO B&B
4 C4	Liskeard Ducks Ditty Holiday Bungalow Cornwall	GB

Bungalow on quiet site. 'Away from it all', yet close to many attractions/amenities. Sleeps up to 5 in 1 double, 1 twin, 1 single. Details on website.

Page ref.	Town/Name	Services
4 C4	Liskeard Rosecraddoc Holidays Rosecraddoc, T 01579 344997	GB
4 C4	Liskeard Rosecraddoc Manor Cornwall, T 01502 500500	GB
4 C5	Liskeard Well Meadow Cottage Duloe, T 01503 220251	GB
28 E5	Little Dewchurch The Granary Henclose Farm, T 01432 840826	GB
12 D6	Littlehampton Bracken Lodge Guest House 43 Church St, T 01903 723174	GB
48 C4	Liverpool Campanile Hotel Queens Dock, T 0151 709 8104	GB
48 C4	Liverpool Greenbank Sports Acady Greenbank Ln, T 0151 280 7757	GB
48 C4	Liverpool Yha Liverpool Intl Tabley St, T 0151 709 8888	GB
75 J4	Livingston Ramada Jarvis Almondview, T 01506 431222	SCO H
46 E7	Llanberis Pen Y Pass Yh Nant Gwynant, T 01286 870428	CYMRU
17 K3	Llandeilo Maerdy Cottages Taliaris, T 01550 777448	CYMRU

Stable Cottage is totally wheelchair accessible. Set in the beautiful Talley Valley on the northwest edge of Brecon Beacons. Open all year. Phone for brochure.

Page ref.	Town/Name	Services
17 K3	Llandeilo Plough Inn Rhosmaen, T 01558 823431	CYMRU
27 G5	Llandovery Erwlon Caravan Park Brecon Rd, T 01550 720332	CYMRU
27 G4	Llandovery Rhandirmwyn Camping Rhandirmwyn, T 01550 760257	CYMRU
27 K2	Llandrindod Wells Bell Inn Llanyre, T 01597 823959	CYMRU
27 K1	Llandrindod Wells Bwlch Farm Llananno, T 01597 840366	CYMRU
27 K2	Llandrindod Wells Guidfa House Cross Gates, T 01597 851241	CYMRU
27 K2	Llandrindod Wells Hotel Metropole Temple St, T 01597 823700	CYMRU
28 A3	Llandrindod Wells The Nant Barn Hundred House, T 01982 570246	CYMRU
47 F4	Llandudno Ambassador Hotel Grand Promenade, T 01492 876886	CYMRU
47 F4	Llandudno Bay Court Hotel North Parade, T 01492 877356	CYMRU
47 F4	Llandudno Clarence Hotel Gloddaeth St, T 01492 860193	CYMRU
47 F4	Llandudno Dunoon Hotel Gloddaeth St, T 01492 860787	CYMRU
47 F4	Llandudno Epperstone Hotel 15 Abbey Rd, T 01492 878746	CYMRU
47 F4	Llandudno Esplanade Hotel Glan Y Mor Parade, T 01492 860300	CYMRU
47 F4	Llandudno Evans Hotel 1 Charlton St, T 01492 860784	CYMRU
47 F4	Llandudno Four Oaks Hotel The Promenade, T 01492 876506	CYMRU
47 F4	Llandudno Grafton Hotel Craig-y-don Parade, T 01492 876814	CYMRU
37 F7	Llandudno Marlborough Hotel South Parade, T 01492 875846	CYMRU
47 F4	Llandudno Ravenhurst Hotel West Shore, T 01492 875525	CYMRU
47 F4	Llandudno Rbs Belmont Hotel 21 North Parade, T 01492 877770 www.royalblindsociety.org.uk	CYMRU H
47 F4	Llandudno Royal Hotel Church Walks, T 01492 876476	CYMRU
47 G4	Llandudno Sharaton Craigside, T 01492 544440	CYMRU
47 F4	Llandudno West Shore Hotel West Parade, T 01492 876833 www.groomsholidays.org.uk	CYMRU

Situated at the foot of the Great Orme with magnificent views across Conwy Bay. A comfortable friendly hotel where service is foremost. All rooms are ensuite and have tea and coffee making facilities.

Page ref.	Town/Name	Services
26 C3	Llandysul Caravan Club Cardigan, Llwynhelyg, T 01545 560029	CYMRU
17 G1	Llandysul Pilbach Caravan Park Rhydlewis, T 01239 851434	CYMRU
46 E5	Llanfairfechan Aber Falls Hotel Abergwyngregyn, T 01248 680579	CYMRU
27 J4	Llangammarch Wells Lake Country House Powys, T 01591 620202	CYMRU
46 C4	Llangefni Treysgawen Hall Capel Coch, T 01248 750750	CYMRU
38 B1	Llangollen Bryn Howel Hotel Bryn Howel, T 01978 860331	CYMRU
38 B1	Llangollen Eirianfa Park Berwyn Rd, T 01978 860919	CYMRU
47 G6	Llanrwst Glan Y Borth Holidays Betws Rd, T 01492 641543	CYMRU
18 C5	Llantwit Major Acorn Caravan Park Ham Ln South, T 01446 794024	CYMRU
27 H4	Llanwrtyd Wells Abernant Lake Hotel Station Rd, T 01591 610250	GB
76 A4	Loanhead Aaron Glen Guest House 7 Nivensknowe Rd, T 0131 440 1293	SCO GH
74 B1	Loch Lomond Culag Lochside Guest House Luss, T 01436 860248	SCO B&B
83 M2	Lochbroom Taigh A'braoin 1a Letters, T 01560 484 003	SCO SC
88 C4	Lochcarnan Orasay Inn S Uist, T 01870 610298	SCO
83 J7	Lochcarron Lochview, Ardach Allt A Chuirn, T 01520 722511	SCO
80 B8	Lochearnhead Earnknowe Cottage Perthshire, T 01567 830238 www.earnknowe.co.uk	SCO SC
80 A8	Lochearnhead Muirlaggan Balquhidder, T 01877 384219	SCO
73 G2	Lochgilphead Empire Travel Ldg Union St, T 01546 602381	SCO L

Accommodation Key — Country: GB England, SCO Scotland, CYMRU Wales, NI Northern Ireland. Venue type: H Hotel, B&B Bed & Breakfast, INN Inn, SC Self Catering, L Lodge, HOS Hostel, GH Guest House

Page ref.	Town/Name	Services
79 K10	**Lochgilphead** Galley of Lorne Inn Main St, Ardfern, Arbyle, T 01852 500284 www.galleyoflorne.co.uk	SCO H
86 C7	**Lochinver** Ard Na Mara 102 Achmelvich, T 01571 844250	SCO SC
86 C7	**Lochinver** Glendarroch House Baddidarroch, T 01431 821207	SCO SC
86 C7	**Lochinver** Mountview 70 Baddidarrach, T 01571 844648 www.mountview-lochinver.co.uk	SCO SC
69 F5	**Lochmaben** Ardbeg Cottage 19 Castle St, T 01387 811855	SCO B&B
69 F5	**Lochmaben** The Crown Hotel 8 Bruce St, T 01387 811750	SCO INN
74 B5	**Lochwinnoch** East Lochhead Cottage East Lochhead, T 01505 842610	SCO SC
69 H6	**Lockerbie** Carik Cottage Waterbeck, T 01461 600 652	SCO B&B
69 H6	**Lockerbie** Courtyard Restaurant Eaglesfield, T 01461 500215	SCO
69 G4	**Lockerbie** Dinwoodie Lodge Hotel Johnstone Bridge, T 01576 470289	SCO
69 G5	**Lockerbie** Dryfesdale House Hotel Dryfebridge, T 01576 202427	SCO H
23 F4	**London** Baden Powell House Queen's Gate, S Kensington, T 020 7584 7031	GB
23 G3	**London** Bonnington In Bloomsbury 92 Southampton Row, T 020 7242 2828	GB
23 F4	**London** Chelsea Village Hotel Stamford Bridge, Fulham Rd, T 020 7565 1400	GB
23 F3	**London** Churchill Intercontinental Portman Square, T 020 7486 5800	GB
23 F3	**London** Clive Hotel Primrose Hill Rd, T 020 7586 2233	GB
23 F4	**London** Conrad Intl London Chelsea Harbour, T 020 7823 3000	GB
23 F4	**London** Copthorne Tara Scarsdale Place, Kensington, T 020 7937 7211	GB
23 G4	**London** Days Hotel 54 Kennington Rd, Waterloo, T 0207 922 1331 www.dayshotellondonwaterloo.co.uk	GB H
23 F3	**London** Hendon Hall Country Hotel Ashley Ln, Hendon, T 020 8203 3341	GB
23 G3	**London** Hilton Islington 53 Upper St, Islington, T 020 7354 7777	GB
23 G3	**London** Holiday Inn Kings Cross 1 Kings Cross Rd, T 020 7833 3900	GB
23 F3	**London** Hotel Ibis Euston 3 Cardington St, Euston, T 020 7388 7777	GB
23 F3	**London** Lancaster Gate Lancaster Gate, T 020 7402 4272	GB
23 G3	**London** London Bridge Hotel 8/18 London Bridge St, T 020 7855 2200	GB
23 F3	**London** Mayfair Intercontinental Stratton St, T 020 7629 7777	GB
23 G3	**London** Mercure City Bankside 75-79 Southwark St, T 020 7902 0800	GB
23 G3	**London** Novotel City South Southwark Bridge Rd, T 020 7089 0400	GB
23 G4	**London** Novotel Greenwich 173-185 Greenwich High Rd, T 020 8312 6800	GB
23 F3	**London** Novotel London Euston 100 - 110 Euston Rd, T 020 7666 9000	GB
23 H3	**London** Novotel London Excel Royal Victoria Dock, T 020 7540 9700	GB
23 F4	**London** Novotel London West 1 Shortlands, Hammersmith, T 020 8741 1555	GB
23 G3	**London** Novotel Tower Bridge 10 Pepys St, T 020 7265 6000	GB
23 G4	**London** Novotel Waterloo 113 Lambeth Rd, T 020 7793 1010	GB
23 F4	**London** Sheraton Park Tower 101 Knightsbridge, T 020 7235 8050	GB
23 F3	**London** The Berners Hotel 10 Berners St, T 020 7666 2000	GB
23 F3	**London** The Columbia Hotel 95-99 Lancaster Gate, T 020 7402 0021	GB
23 F3	**London** The Stafford Hotel St James's Place, T 020 7493 0111	GB
23 G3	**London** Thistle City Barbican Central St, Clerkenwell, T 020 7251 1565	GB
23 F3	**London** Thistle Marble Arch Bryanston St, Marble Arch, T 020 7629 8040	GB
23 F3	**London** Westland Hotel 154 Bayswater Rd, T 020 7229 9191	GB
77 G5	**Longformarcus** Kintra Ha' Gifford Rd, T 01361 890660	SCO
4 B5	**Looe** Bocaddon Holiday Cottages Bocaddon, Lanreath, T 01503 220192	GB
4 C5	**Looe** Bucklawren Farm St Martins, T 01503 240738	GB
4 C5	**Looe** Penvith Cottages St Martins By Looe, T 01483 277894 www.penvithcottages.co.uk	GB SC
84 G3	**Lossiemouth** Ceilidh B&B 34 Clifton Rd, Froghall, T 01343 815848 www.scottish-info.com/scotland/ceilidh.htm Our single en-suite has been classified for unaided wheelchair access users. It has direct access from the car park, a level entry shower, with stool and bars at W.C. There is also a bed leaver available. SASLI associate interpreter, holding deaf awareness and BSL stage3 Certificates on site. Assistance dogs welcome with prior notice.	SCO B&B
4 B5	**Lostwithiel** Hartswheal Barn Saint Winnow, T 01208 873419	GB
41 H4	**Loughborough** Quality Friendly Hotel New Ashby Rd, T 01509 211800	GB
53 G4	**Louth** The Beaumont Hotel Victoria Rd, T 01507 605005	GB
45 K7	**Lowestoft** Four Winds Retreat Kessingland, T 01502 740044	GB
45 K6	**Lowestoft** Hotel Victoria Kirkley Cliff, T 01502 574433	GB
45 K6	**Lowestoft** Ivy House Country Hotel Ivy Ln, Oulton Broad, T 01502 501353 www.ivyhousecountryhotel.co.uk Beautiful gardens. Peaceful location. Most rooms ground floor – 2 with wheel-in shower rooms. Private car park – 5 accessible bays. AA 2 rosettes. Special diets happily catered for.	GB H
28 E1	**Ludlow** The Feathers Hotel Bull Ring, T 01584 875261	GB
74 B2	**Luss** Blairglas Dunbartonshire, T 01389 850278	SCO B&B
74 B2	**Luss** Loch Lomond Hideaways Argyll, T 01436 860267	SCO SC
41 J7	**Lutterworth** Hothorpe Hall Ltd Theddingworth, T 01858 880257	GB
19 K1	**Lydney** Cider Press Cottage Westleigh Villa, St Swithens Rd, Oldcroft T 01594 510285	GB SC
19 J1	**Lydney** Cinderhill Cottage St Briavels, T 01594 530393	GB
19 K1	**Lydney** The Fountain Inn Fountain Way, Parkend, T 0870 7522236	GB
10 D5	**Lymington** Gothic Cottage Everton, T 01590 645941	GB
10 E5	**Lymington** Passford House Hotel Mount Pleasant Ln, T 01590 682398	GB
10 D5	**Lymington** The Nurse's Cottage Station Rd, Sway, T 01590 683402 www.nursescottage.co.uk	GB H
55 G7	**Lytham St Annes** Chadwick Hotel South Promenade, T 01253 720061	GB
55 G6	**Lytham St Annes** Club Pontin's Blackpool Holiday Centre, T 08706 010472	GB
49 J6	**Macclesfield** Lower House Cottage Wildboarclough, T 01260 227229	GB
49 J6	**Macclesfield** Strawberry Duck Bullgate Ln, Bosley, T 01260 223591	GB
49 J6	**Macclesfield** The Old Byre Leek Rd, Bosley, T 01260 273650	GB
49 J5	**Macclesfield** White House Manor The Village, Prestbury, T 01625 829376	GB
37 F6	**Machynlleth** Penmaendyfi House Cwrt, Pennal, T 01654 791616 www.penmaendyfi.co.uk	CYMRU B&B
37 G5	**Machynlleth** Warren Parc Penegoes, T 01654 702054	CYMRU
75 H3	**Maddiston** Avon Glen Apartments Melons Place, Melons Pl Farm, T 01324 621341	SCO SC
22 B4	**Maidenhead** Holiday Inn Manor Ln, T 01628 623444	GB
14 D3	**Maidstone** Apple Pye Cottage Bramley Knowle Fm, Eastwood Rd, Ulcombe, T 01580 720770 www.bramleyknowlefarm.co.uk	GB SC
14 C2	**Maidstone** Hilton Maidstone Bearsted Rd, T 01622 734322	GB
14 D2	**Maidstone** The Dog & Bear Hotel The Square, Lenham, T 01622 858219	GB
34 D7	**Maldon** Five Lakes Hotel Tolleshunt Knights, T 01621 868888	GB
58 E2	**Malton** The Old Post Office Thorpe Bassett, T 01944 758047	GB
29 G4	**Malvern** De Vere Farm Cottages Park Farm, Old Colwall, T 01684 540474	GB
29 G5	**Malvern** Mutlows Farm Cottages Drake St, Welland, T 01684 310878	GB
49 H3	**Manchester** Comfort Friendly Inn Hyde Rd, West Gorton, T 0161 220 8700	GB
49 H3	**Manchester** Holiday Inn Crowne Plaza Peter St, T 0161 236 3333	GB
49 H3	**Manchester** Le Meridien Victoria & Albert Hotel Water St, T 0161 832 1188	GB
49 H3	**Manchester** Luther King House Brighton Grove, Wilmslow Rd, T 0161 224 6404	GB
49 H3	**Manchester** Novotel 21 Dickinson St, T 0161 235 2200	GB
49 G2	**Manchester** Novotel West Worsley Brow, Worsley, T 0161 799 3535	GB
49 H4	**Manchester** Radisson Sas Hotel Manchester Airport, T 0161 490 5000	GB
49 H3	**Manchester** Renaissance Hotel Blackfriars St, T 0161 835 2555	GB
49 H3	**Manchester** Thistle Manchester Piccadilly Gardens, T 0161 228 3400	GB
49 H4	**Manchester** Waterside Hotel Wilmslow Rd, Didsbury, T 0161 445 0225	GB
49 H3	**Manchester** Yha Manchester Liverpool Rd, Castlefield, T 0161 839 9960	GB
16 D6	**Manorbier** Yha Manorbier Manorbier, T 01834 871803	CYMRU
25 K4	**Margate** Ferndale Hotel Cliftonville, T 01843 229192	GB
25 K4	**Margate** Lonsdale Court Hotel Cliftonville, T 01843 221053	GB
6 A5	**Marhamchurch Nr. Bude** Swallow Cottage Sharlands Farm, T 01288 361322	GB
46 D4	**Marianglas** Home Farm Caravan Park Anglesey, T 01248 410614	CYMRU
39 F2	**Market Drayton** Mickley House Tern Hill, T 01630 638505	GB
52 D3	**Market Rasen** Pelham Arms Farm Claxby Moor, T 01673 828261	GB
80 H10	**Markinch** Balbirnie House Hotel Balbirnie Park, T 01592 610066	SCO H
22 B3	**Marlow** Granny Anne's 54 Seymour Park Rd, T 01628 473086	GB
50 E7	**Matlock** Honeysuckle Cottage Grange Mill, T 01629 650368	GB
50 E6	**Matlock** Nether End Darley Dale, T 01629 732 131	GB
67 G2	**Maybole** Brewhouse Culzean Castle, T 0131 243 9352	SCO SC
67 G2	**Maybole** Royal Artillery Cottage Culzean Castle, T 0131 2265922	SCO
76 D7	**Melrose** Dryburgh Abbey Hotel Scottish Borders, T 01835 822261	SCO H
76 D7	**Melrose** East Faldonside Lodge Borders, T 01896 756389	SCO SC
70 A1	**Melrose** Easter Cottage Lilliesleaf, T 01835 870281	SCO B&B
76 D7	**Melrose** Eildon Holiday Cottage Dingleton Mains, T 01896 823258	SCO SC
76 D7	**Melrose** Eildon Holiday Cottage Dingleton Mains, T 01896 823258	SCO
76 D7	**Melrose** Waverley Castle Hotel Skirmish Hill, T 01896 822244	GB
45 F2	**Melton Constable** Wood Farm Cottage Plumstead Rd, Edgefield, T 01263 587347	GB
27 K7	**Merthyr Tydfil** Nant Ddu Lodge Hotel Cwm Taf, Cwmtaf, T 01685 379111	CYMRU
18 D1	**Merthyr Tydfil** Tregenna Hotel Park Terrace, T 01685 723627	CYMRU
63 F5	**Middlesbrough** Quality Hotel Tad Centre, Ormesby Rd, T 01642 203000	GB
49 G6	**Middlewich** Forge Mill Farm Cottage Forge Mill Fm, Warmingham, T 01270 526204	GB
54 E2	**Millom** Yha Duddon Estuary Borwick Rails, T 01229 773937 www.duddonyha.org.uk	GB HOS
73 K5	**Millport** Cathedral of The Isles The College, T 01475 530353	SCO GH
74 C3	**Milton** Milton Inn Dumbarton Rd, T 01389 761401	SCO INN
32 B5	**Milton Keynes** Hilton National Kents Hill Park, T 01908 694433	GB
32 B5	**Milton Keynes** Novotel Saxon St, Heelands, T 01908 322 212	GB
32 B5	**Milton Keynes** Quality Friendly Hotel Monks Way, Two Mile Ash, T 01908 561666	GB
74 E3	**Milton of Campsie** The Pavilion Upper Woodburn, T 01236 823249	SCO SC
73 H1	**Minard** Minard Castle Argyll, T 01546 886272	SCO B&B
7 J1	**Minehead** Primrose Hill Holidays Wood Ln, Blue Anchor, T 01643 821200 www.primrosehillholidays.co.uk	GB SC
7 H1	**Minehead** Promenade Hotel The Esplanade, T 01446 771311 www.groomsholidays.org.uk	GB H

With its unrivalled seafront location you can enjoy picturesque views of the harbour and coastline from the prize-winning gardens and conservatory, whilst sampling one of its famous cream teas.

Page ref.	Town/Name	Services
7 J1	**Minehead** The Langbury Blue Anchor Bay, Near, T 01643 821375	GB
53 G6	**Miningsby** Stamford Farmhouse Lincs, T 01507 588682	GB
69 F3	**Moffat** Black Bull Hotel Churchgate, T 01683 220206	SCO H
69 F3	**Moffat** Burnock Water Haywood Rd, T 01683 221329	SCO
69 F3	**Moffat** Lochhouse Farm Retreat Beattock, T 01683 300451	SCO B&B
48 B6	**Mold** Beaufort Park Hotel New Brighton, T 01352 758646	CYMRU
48 B6	**Mold** Forte Travelodge A55, Northop Hall, T 01244 816473	CYMRU
48 B6	**Mold** Holiday Inn Garden Court Gateway Services, T 01244 550011	CYMRU
68 C4	**Moniaive** Glenluiart Holidays Glenluiart House, T 01848 200331	SCO
81 L7	**Monifieth** Panmure Hotel Tay St, T 01382 532911	SCO H
38 C6	**Montgomery** Daisy Camping Snead, Churchstoke, T 01588 620471	CYMRU
81 P3	**Montrose** 36 Queen Street Gourdon	SCO
81 N5	**Montrose** Best Western Links Hotel Mid Links, T 01674 671000 www.linkshotel.com	SCO H
81 N3	**Montrose** Brawliemuir Farm Johnshaven, T 01561 362453	SCO SC
55 H3	**Morecambe** Eden Vale Flats 338 Marine Rd, T 01524 415544	GB
55 H3	**Morecambe** Lothersdale Hotel Central Promenade, T 01524 416404	GB
30 D5	**Moreton-in-Marsh** Treetops London Rd, T 01608 651036	GB
71 G4	**Morpeth** Beacon Hill Farm Longhorsley, T 01670 780900	GB
71 G3	**Morpeth** Dene House Farm Cottage Longframlington, T 01665 570549	GB
71 G4	**Morpeth** Linden Hall Hotel Longhorsley, T 01670 500000	GB
71 H5	**Morpeth** Longhirst Hall Longhirst, T 01670 791348	GB

Page ref.	Town/Name	Services
71 H3	**Morpeth The Byers** Old Helsay, Warkworth, T 01665 712952	GB
70 E3	**Morpeth The Byre Vegetarian B&B** Harbottle, Nr. Rothbury T 01669 650476	GB B&B
71 H3	**Morpeth Warkworth House Hotel** Warkworth, T 01665 711276	GB
71 F3	**Morpeth Whitton Farmhouse Hotel** Whitton, Rothbury, T 01669 620811	GB
75 F5	**Motherwell Holiday Express Inn** Strathclyde Park, T 01698 858585	SCO L
75 F5	**Motherwell Moorings Hotel** 114 Hamilton Rd, T 01698 258131	SCO H
75 F5	**Motherwell The Alona Hotel** Strathclyde Pk, T 01698 333777	SCO H
83 R6	**Muir-of-Ord Hillview Park** Highld, T 01463 870787	SCO B&B
83 N5	**Muir-of-Ord Strathkyle** Milton, Strathconon, T 01997 477285	SCO SC
84 A5	**Munlochy Anwoth** Littleburn Rd, T 01463 811674	SCO
76 B4	**Musselburgh Carberry Centre** Carberry Tower, T 0131 665 3135	SCO GH
76 B3	**Musselburgh Moir Lodge** 28 Linkfield Rd, T 0131 6532827	SCO
84 C5	**Nairn Burnside Lodge** Geddes, T 01667 454635	SCO SC
84 C5	**Nairn Claymore House Hotel** 45 Seabank Rd, T 01667 453731	SCO H
84 C5	**Nairn Greenlawns** 13 Seafield St, T 01667 452738	SCO
84 D5	**Nairn Hiddenglen Holidays** Laikenbuie, Grantown Rd, T 01667 454630 www.hiddenglen.co.uk	SCO SC
84 C5	**Nairn Napier** 60 Seabank Rd, T 01667 453330 www.napier-nairn.co.uk	SCO B&B
84 D5	**Nairn Tree Tops & Kestrels Nest** Laikenbuie, Grantown Rd, T 01667 454630	SCO
84 C5	**Nairn Windsor Hotel** 16 Albert St, T 01667 453108	SCO H
49 F7	**Nantwich Peacock** 221 Crewe Rd, T 01270 624069	GB
49 F7	**Nantwich Rookery Hall** Main Rd, Worleston, T 01270 610016	GB
16 D4	**Narberth Highl'd Grange Farm Guest House** Robeston Wathen, T 01834 860952	CYMRU
16 E4	**Narberth Noble Court** Redstone Rd, T 01834 861191	CYMRU
16 E4	**Narberth Plas Hyfryd Hotel** Moorfield Rd, T 07834 869006	CYMRU
34 D5	**Nayland Gladwins Farm** Harpers Hill, T 01206 262261	GB
48 D7	**Near Malpas Tilston Lodge** Tilston, T 01829 250223	GB
18 A2	**Neath Cwmbach Cottages** Cadoxton, T 01639 639825	CYMRU
76 E7	**Nenthorn Burnbrae Holidays** Burnbrae, T 01573 225570	SCO SC
84 E8	**Nethy Bridge Ailanbeg Cottage** Ailanbeg Lodge, T 01479 821363	SCO
84 E8	**Nethy Bridge Fhuran Forest Cottage** Badan Fhuaran www.lazyduck.co.uk	SCO HOS
84 E8	**Nethybridge Badanfhuarain Cottage** Badanfhuarain, T 01479 821642	SCO
84 E9	**Nethybridge Dell of Abernethy Cottage** Highld, T 01479 821643	SCO SC
84 E8	**Nethybridge Fhuarain Forest Cottage** Highld, T 01479 821642	SCO SC
84 E8	**Nethybridge Nethybridge Hotel** Highld, T 01479 821203	SCO H
84 E8	**Nethybridge Osprey & Red Kite** Dirdhu Court, T 01330 844344	SCO SC
68 B3	**New Cumnock Ashmark Farm Cottage** Ashmark Farm, Afton Rd, T 01290 338304 www.ashmarkfarm.co.uk	SCO SC
75 G6	**New Lanark New Lanark Mill Hotel** Lanarks, T 01555 667200	SCO H
10 D5	**New Milton St Ursula** 30 Hobart Rd, T 01425 613515	GB B&B
26 C3	**New Quay Quay West Resort** New Rd, T 01545 560477	CYMRU
21 H5	**Newbury Hilton Newbury Centre** Pinchington Ln, T 01635 529000	GB
21 H4	**Newbury Hilton Newbury North** J13 of M4, Oxford Rd, T 01635 247010	GB
71 H7	**Newcastle Copthorne** The Close, Quayside, T 0191 222 0333	GB
71 H7	**Newcastle Hilton Newcastle** Silverlink, Coast Rd, T 0191 202 9955	GB
71 H7	**Newcastle Novotel Newcastle** Ponteland Rd, Kenton, T 0191 214 0303	GB
70 D4	**Newcastle Redesdale Arms Hotel** Rochester, Otterburn, T 01830 520668	GB
71 G6	**Newcastle Airport Britannia Hotel** Woolsington, T 0191 401 9988	GB
17 F1	**Newcastle Emlyn Cenarth Falls** Cenarth, T 01239 710345	CYMRU
70 A6	**Newcastleton Bailey Mill** Bailey, T 016977 48617	GB
29 G5	**Newent The Old Winery** Welsh House Ln, Dymock, T 01531 890824	GB
29 G6	**Newent Windmill Annexe** Castle Tump, T 01531 890428	GB
13 H6	**Newhaven The Brighton Motel** Peacehaven, T 01273 583736	GB
33 K2	**Newmarket Heath Court Hotel** Moulton Rd, T 01638 667171	GB
74 D7	**Newmilns Loudoun Mains Holidays** Loudoun Mains, T 01560 321246	SCO
29 F7	**Newnham Swan House** High St, T 01594 516504	GB

Page ref.	Town/Name	Services
19 F2	**Newport Cwmcarn Forest Drive** Cwmcarn, T 01495 272001	CYMRU
39 G3	**Newport Harper Adams Agric'l Col** Shrops, T 01952 820280	GB
19 G3	**Newport Hilton Newport** Chepstow Rd, Langstone, T 01633 413737	GB
16 E3	**Newport Llwyngwair Manor Park** Newport, T 01446 774845	CYMRU
16 D2	**Newport Newport Yh** Lower St Mary's St, T 01239 820080	CYMRU
3 F2	**Newquay Chynoweth Lodge Hotel** 1 Eliot Gardens, T 01637 876684	GB
7 F7	**Newton Abbot Budleigh Farm** Moretonhampstead, T 01647 440835	GB
7 G7	**Newton Abbot High Hazel** Hennock, Bovey Tracey, T 01344 291377	GB
5 H3	**Newton Abbot New Cottage Farm** Poundsgate, Ashburton, T 01364 631421	GB
5 J3	**Newton Abbot Sampsons Thatch Hotel** Preston, T 01626 354913	GB
5 H3	**Newton Abbot The Pine Lodge** Buckland in the Moor, T 01803 663650	GB
5 H3	**Newton Abbot Wooder Manor** Widecombe in the Moor, T 01364 621 391	GB
62 C4	**Newton Aycliffe Redworth Hall** Redworth, T 01388 770600	GB
64 E5	**Newton Stewart Courtyard Cottage** East Kirkland, T 01988 402266	SCO
64 E6	**Newton Stewart East Culkae Farm House** Sorbie, T 01988 850214	SCO B&B
64 D5	**Newton Stewart Killiemore Lodge** Kirkcowan, T 01671 830213	SCO
64 E6	**Newton Stewart Old School Cottage** Pouton Farm, Garlieston, T 01988 600646	SCO
64 B5	**Newton Stewart Rowantree Guesthouse** 38 Main St, Glenluce, T 01581 300244	SCO
84 B11	**Newtonmore Craigower Lodge** Golf Course Rd, T 08450 505052	SCO HOS
84 A11	**Newtonmore Crubenbeg Farm Steadings** Highld, T 01540 673 566	SCO
84 A11	**Newtonmore Crubenbeg House** Falls of Truim, T 01540 673300 www.crubenbeghouse.com	SCO GH
38 A7	**Newtown Cilthrew Farm** Pentre, Kerry, T 01686 670667	CYMRU
38 A6	**Newtown Pen-y-gelli** Wern-ddu Ln, T 01686 628292	CYMRU
80 H6	**Newtyle Kinpurnie** North St, T 01828 650500	SCO SC
85 P10	**Nigg Gordon Hotel** Wellington Rd, T 01224 873012	SCO
76 D2	**North Berwick Beehive Cottage** Kingston, T 01620 894785	SCO
76 D2	**North Berwick Manora** South Hamilton Rd, T 01620 893935	SCO SC
84 A6	**North Kessock Bramble Cottage** Drumsmittal Croft, T 01463 731455	SCO
89 G2	**North Ronaldsay N Ronaldsay Bird Obs** Orkney, T 011857 633200	SCO
89 G2	**North Ronaldsay Observatory Guest House** Orkney, T 011857 633200	SCO GH
45 G2	**North Walsham Dairy Farm Cottage** Dilham, T 01692 535178	GB
45 G2	**North Walsham The Wolery** Bradfield Rd, Swafield, T 01692 403332	GB
62 D7	**Northallerton Lovesome Hill Farm** Lovesome Hill, T 01609 772311	GB
62 D7	**Northallerton Sundial Hotel** Darlington Rd, T 01609 780525	GB
31 J3	**Northampton Hilton Northampton** 100 Watering Ln, Collingtree, T 01604 700666	GB
31 J3	**Northampton Marriott Hotel** Eagle Drive, T 01604 768700	GB
31 H2	**Northampton Rye Hill Cottage** Holdenby Rd, East Haddon, T 01604 770990	GB
88 B8	**Northbay Airds Guest House** 244 Bruernish, T 01871 890720	SCO B&B
45 G5	**Norwich Beeches Hotel** 2-6 Earlham Rd, T 01603 621167	GB
44 D7	**Norwich Berwick Cottage** School Ln, East Harling, T 01787 372343	GB
45 F3	**Norwich Burgh House Cottages** Burgh House, Aylsham, T 01263 733567	GB
45 H4	**Norwich Eagle Cottage** Ferry Rd, Horning, T 01692 630297 www.norfolk-broads.co.uk	GB SC
45 G4	**Norwich Elm Farm Country House** 55 Norwich Rd, St Faiths, T 01603 898366	GB
45 G2	**Norwich Green Farm Hotel** Thorpe Market, T 01263 833602	GB
45 H4	**Norwich Hall Farm Cottages** Horning, T 01692 630385	GB
45 G4	**Norwich Hilton Norwich** Norwich Airport, T 01603 410544	GB
45 F3	**Norwich Holly Cottage** Burgh Rd, Aylsham, T 01263 733567	GB
45 G4	**Norwich Marriott Sprowston** Wroxham Rd, T 01603 410871	GB
45 F6	**Norwich Oakbrook House** Frith Way, Great Moulton, T 01379 677359 www.oakbrookhouse.co.uk	GB B&B
45 G4	**Norwich Old Rectory** Crostwick, T 01603 738513	GB
45 F2	**Norwich Owl & Harvest Cottages** Church Farm, Wickmere, T 01263 577332	GB
45 G4	**Norwich Ramada Jarvis Norwich** 121-131 Boundary Rd, T 01603 787260	GB
45 F1	**Norwich Roman Camp Inn** Holt Rd, Aylmerton, T 01263 838291	GB
45 F3	**Norwich Rookery Farm** Church St, Reepham, T 01603 871847	GB

Page ref.	Town/Name	Services
45 G4	**Norwich Spixworth Hall Cottage** Grange Farm, Spixworth, T 01603 898190	GB
45 H5	**Norwich Sunnybank** 3 Pound Ln, Blofield, T 01603 713986	GB
45 H4	**Norwich The Hideaway & Pondside** Blofield Heath, T 01603 715052	GB
41 H2	**Nottingham Holiday Inn Garden Crt** Castle Marina Park, T 0115 993 5000	GB
41 H1	**Nottingham Nottingham Gateway Hotel** Nuthall Rd, T 0115 979 4949	GB
41 G2	**Nottingham Novotel** Bostock Ln, Long Eaton, T 0115 946 5111	GB
69 G4	**Nr Lockerbie Courtyard Cottage** Johnston Bridge, T 01461 40800	SCO SC
31 H2	**Nr Northampton Courtyard Daventry** High St, Flore, T 01327 349022	GB
41 G5	**Nuneaton Bosworth Firs** Mrkt Bosworth, T 01455 290727	GB
42 C4	**Oakham Barnsdale Lodge Hotel** Rutland Water, Exton, T 01572 724 678	GB
79 K8	**Oban Cologin Country Chalets** Lergas Glen, T 01631 564501	SCO SC
79 K9	**Oban Eleraig Highland Chalets** Kilninver, T 018522 00225	SCO
79 L7	**Oban Falls of Lora Hotel** Connel Ferry, T 01631 710483 www.fallsoflora.com	SCO H
79 K9	**Oban Melfort Pier & Harbour** Kilmelford, T 01852 200333	SCO SC
79 K8	**Oban Oban Caledonian Hotel** Station Square, T 01631 563133 www.obancaldeonian.com	SCO H
79 K7	**Oban Oban Yh** Esplanade, T 01786 891400	SCO HOS
79 K9	**Oban Pier North** Melfort, Kilmelford, T 01852 200333	SCO
79 K7	**Oban The Kimberley Hotel** Dalriach Rd, T 01631 571115	SCO H
79 K9	**Oban The Pier North** Melfort, Kilmelford, T 01852 200333	SCO
79 L7	**Oban Tigh Grianach** North Connel, T 01631 710288	SCO SC
6 C7	**Okehampton Old Chapel** Portgate, Lewdown, T 01566 783401	GB
6 D6	**Okehampton Week Farm Holidays** Bridestowe, T 01837 861221 www.weekfarmonline.com	GB B&B
32 B3	**Olney The Old Stone Barn** Home Farm, Warrington, T 01234 711655	GB
79 M4	**Onich, Fort William Birchbrae** Highld, T 01855 821261 www.birchbrae.com	SCO SC
48 D1	**Ormskirk Beaufort Hotel** High Ln, Burscough, T 01704 892655	GB
89 C7	**Orphir Buxa Farm Chalets** Westrow Lodge, T 01856 811360	SCO SC
89 C7	**Orphir Waterside House** Houton Bay, T 01856 811320	SCO B&B
38 B3	**Oswestry The Coach House** Llanyblodwel, T 01691 828038	GB
21 J1	**Oxford Acorn Guest House** 260 - 262 Iffley Rd, T 01865 247998	GB
30 E6	**Oxford Banbury Hill Farm Cottage** Banbury Hill Farm, Charlbury, T 01608 810314	GB
21 J1	**Oxford Hawkwell House Hotel** Church Way, Iffley Village, T 01865 749988	GB
21 J1	**Oxford Westwood Country Hotel** Hinksey Hill Top, T 01865 735408	GB
74 C4	**Paisley Ardgowan Town House Hotel** 94 Renfrew Rd, T 0141 889 4763	SCO H
74 C4	**Paisley Holiday Inn Express** St Andrews Drive, T 0131 553 4422	SCO H
74 C4	**Paisley Travel Inn Glasgow Airport** Whitecart Rd, T 0141 842 1563	SCO
76 A6	**Peebles Courtyard Cottages** Winkston Farmhouse, T 017217 21264	SCO SC
76 A6	**Peebles Cringletie House Hotel** Edinburgh Rd, T 01721 725750 www.cringletie.com	SCO H

The only AA Top 200 Hotel in the Scottish Borders. A rural and tranquil retreat with friendly service. Dining is a feast. Well worth a visit!

Page ref.	Town/Name	Services
76 A7	**Peebles Glentress Hotel** Innerleithen Rd, T 01721 720100	SCO H
76 A6	**Peebles Horse Shoe Inn** Eddleston, T 01721 730225	SCO
76 A6	**Peebles Skerryvore** 66 Edinburgh Rd, T 01502 501 515	SCO
16 D6	**Pembroke Rosedene Guest House** Hodgeston, T 01646 672586 www.rosedeneguesthouse.co.uk	CYMRU B&B
16 C6	**Pembroke Stackpole Trust** Stackpole Home Farm, T 01646 661425	CYMRU
16 C5	**Pembroke Dock Cleddau Bridge Hotel** Port of Pembroke, T 01646 685961	CYMRU
61 G4	**Penrith Forte Travelodge** A66, Redhills, T 01768 866958	GB
60 F4	**Penrith Knotts Mill Lodge** Watermillock, Ullswater, T 017684 86699	GB

Accommodation Key Country: GB England SCO Scotland CYMRU Wales NI Northern Ireland Venue type: H Hotel B&B Bed & Breakfast INN Inn SC Self Catering L Lodge HOS Hostel GH Guest House

Page ref.	Town/Name	Services
60 E3	**Penrith Mosedale House** Mosedale, Mungrisdale, T 017687 79371	GB
60 F3	**Penrith Newton Rigg College** Cumbria Campus, T 01768 863791	GB
61 G3	**Penrith Norcroft Guesthouse** Graham St, T 01768 862365	GB
60 E5	**Penrith Patterdale Hall Estate** Glenridding, T 017684 82308	GB
61 H6	**Penrith Primrose Lodge** Primrose Cottage, Orton Rd, Tebay, T 01539 624 7941 www.primrosecottagecumbria.co.uk Specially built bungalow - 2 bedrooms & 2 bathrooms (1 is a large wheel in) for disabled guests. www.primrosecottagecumbria.co.uk	GB
61 G6	**Penrith Shap Wells Hotel** Shap, T 01931 716628	GB
60 F3	**Penrith Uni of Central Lancs** Cumbria Campus, T 01768 863791	GB
60 F4	**Penrith Waterside House** Watermillock, T 017684 86038	GB
34 C4	**Pentlow Fiddlesticks** Pentlow Ridge, Pinkuah Ln, T 01787 280154	GB
46 D4	**Pentraeth Bryn Tirion Hotel** Red Wharf Bay, T 01248 852366	CYMRU
2 A5	**Penzance Swallows End** Bosworlas, T 01736 787011	GB
2 B6	**Penzance The Queens Hotel** The Promenade, T 01736 362371	GB
2 B6	**Penzance Treverven House** St Buryan	GB
80 G8	**Perth Arisaig Guest House** 4 Pitcullen Crescent, T 01738 628240	SCO GH
80 G8	**Perth Cherrybank Inn** 210 Glasgow Rd, T 01738 624349	SCO INN
80 G8	**Perth Cherrybank Inn** 210 Glasgow Rd, T 01738 624349	SCO
80 G8	**Perth Glencarse Hotel** Glencarse, T 01738 860206	SCO
80 F8	**Perth Huntingtower Hotel** Crieff Rd, T 01738 583771	SCO H
80 G8	**Perth Isle of Skye Hotel** Queensbridge, 18 Dundee Rd, T 01738 624471	SCO
80 F8	**Perth Orchard Cottage** Huntingtower, T 01738 620783/444849	SCO SC
80 G8	**Perth Petra's B & B** 4 Albany Terrace, T 01738 563050	SCO B&B
80 G8	**Perth Quality Station Hotel** Leonard St, T 01738 624141	GB
80 G8	**Perth Sunbank House Hotel** 50 Dundee Rd, T 01738 624882	SCO H
80 G8	**Perth Tower View Coach Houses** Kinfauns, T 01738 446577	SCO SC
42 D6	**Peterborough Haycock Hotel** Wansford, T 01780 782223	GB
43 F6	**Peterborough Hotel Formule 1** Boongate, T 01733 894400	GB
42 E6	**Peterborough Marriott** Lynch Wood, T 01733 371111	GB
42 D7	**Peterborough Oundle Cottage Breaks** 30 Market Place, Oundle, T 01832 273 531	GB
85 P5	**Peterhead Greenbrae Farmhouse** Longside, T 01779 821051	SCO B&B
85 R6	**Peterhead Invernettie Guest House** South Rd, T 01779 473530	SCO GH
11 H2	**Petersfield Dunvegan Cottage** Frogmore Ln, East Meon, T 01730 823213	GB
12 C5	**Petworth The Old Railway Stn** Coultershaw Bridge, T 01798 342346	GB
63 H7	**Pickering Beech Farm Cottages** Wrelton	GB
58 E1	**Pickering Easthill Farm House** Thornton Dale, T 01751 474561	GB
58 D1	**Pickering Keld Head Farm Cottage** Keld Head, T 01751 473974	GB
63 J7	**Pickering Manor Farm Holidays** Newton-on-Rawcliffe, T 01751 472601	GB
63 J7	**Pickering Moonpenny Cottage** Levisham, T 01751 460311	GB
63 H7	**Pickering Rawcliffe House Farm** Stape, T 01751 473292 www.rawcliffehousefarm.com	GB SC
75 G2	**Pirnhall, Stirling Barn Lodge** Croftside, T 01786 813591	SCO L
80 E5	**Pitlochry Craigmhor Lodge** 27 West Moulin Rd, T 01796 472123	SCO
80 E5	**Pitlochry Arrochar** Well Brae, T 01796 472239	SCO SC
80 E5	**Pitlochry Atholl Villa Guesthouse** 29/31 Atholl Rd, T 01796 473820	SCO GH
80 E5	**Pitlochry Briar Cottage** Well Brae, T 01796 473678	SCO
80 E5	**Pitlochry Burnside Apartments** 19 West Moulin Rd, T 01796 472203	SCO
80 E5	**Pitlochry Craigatin House & Courtyd** 165 Atholl Rd, T 01796 472478	SCO GH
80 E5	**Pitlochry Craiglyn** 50 West Moulin Rd, T 01796 472065	SCO SC
80 E5	**Pitlochry Craigvrack Hotel** 38 West Moulin Rd, T 01796 472399	SCO H
80 E5	**Pitlochry Cuil-an-Daraich** Logierait, T 01796 482750	SCO GH
80 E5	**Pitlochry Dalshian Chalets** Old Perth Rd, T 01796 473080 www.dalshian-chalets.co.uk	SCO SC
80 B5	**Pitlochry Dunalastair Holidays** Dunalastair Est, T 01882 632314	SCO SC
80 E5	**Pitlochry East Haugh House Hotel** East Haugh, T 01796 473121	SCO H
80 E5	**Pitlochry Fishers Hotel** 75-79 Atholl Rd, T 0131 554 7173	SCO H
80 E5	**Pitlochry Green Park Hotel** Clunie Bridge Rd, T 01796 473248	SCO H
80 D4	**Pitlochry Loch Tummel Inn** Strathtummel, T 01882 634272	SCO

Page ref.	Town/Name	Services
80 E5	**Pitlochry Logierait Pine Lodges** Logierait, T 01796 482253	SCO SC
80 E5	**Pitlochry Oakburn Holidays** Lower Oakfield, T 01796 472080	SCO SC
80 E5	**Pitlochry Pitlochry Hydro Hotel** Knockard Rd, T 01796 472666	GB
80 E5	**Pitlochry The Old Mill Inn** Mill Ln, T 01796 474020	SCO
80 E5	**Pitlochry The Well House** 11 Toberargan Rd, T 01796 472239	SCO GH
83 J7	**Plockton Plockton Hotel** Harbour St, T 01599 544274	SCO H
5 F5	**Plymouth Boringdon Hall Hotel** Colebrook, Plympton, T 01752 344455	GB
5 F5	**Plymouth Campanile Hotel** Longbridge Rd, T 01752 601087	GB
5 F4	**Plymouth Coll of St Mark** Derriford Rd, Derriford, T 01752 777188	GB
4 E5	**Plymouth Copthorne Hotel Plymouth** Armada Centre, Armada Way, T 01752 224161	GB
4 E5	**Plymouth Haddington House Apartments** 40 & 42 Haddington Rd, T 01752 767 730	GB
5 F5	**Plymouth Hotel Ibis Plymouth** Longbridge Rd, T 01752 601087	GB
5 F5	**Plymouth Kitley House Hotel** Kitley Estate, Yealmpton, T 01752 881 555	GB
4 E5	**Plymouth New Continental Hotel** Millbay Rd, T 01752 220782	GB
5 F5	**Plymouth Novotel Plymouth** Marsh Mills, T 01752 221422	GB
5 F5	**Plymouth Traine Farm** Wembury, T 01752 862264	GB
75 H3	**Polmont Inchyra Grange Hotel** Grange Rd, T 01324 711911	SCO
18 A1	**Pontardawe Treehaven** Rhyd-y-fro, T 01792 830174	CYMRU
19 F1	**Pontypool Rhiw Ffranc Farm Apartments** Pentwyn, Abersychan, T 01495 775069	CYMRU
10 B6	**Poole Haven Hotel** Banks Rd, Sandbanks, T 01202 707333	GB
9 J5	**Poole Rockley Park** Chalet No 73, Hamworthy, T 01446 771311 www.groomsholidays.org.uk	GB SC

Located on a fun filled holiday park, sandy beaches & spectacular views over the bay. Double, twin, 2 sofa beds (all bed linen) TV, video, microwave, mobile hoist, wheel in shower, shower chair.

Page ref.	Town/Name	Services
9 J5	**Poole Sandford Park** Chalet No A22, T 01392 446777	GB
83 J1	**Poolewe Foura** Cove, T 01445 781236	SCO
83 J2	**Poolewe Innes Maree** Highld, T 01445 781454	SCO
18 A3	**Port Talbot Aberavon Beach Hotel** Princess Margaret Way, T 01639 884949 www.aberavonbeach.com	CYMRU H
18 A3	**Port Talbot Ty'n Y Caeau House** Margam Village, T 01639 883897	CYMRU
36 E2	**Porthmadog Garreg Goch Park** Morfa Bychan, T 01766 512210	CYMRU
36 E2	**Porthmadog Greenacres Park** Morfa Bychan, T 01766 512781	CYMRU
64 A5	**Portpatrick Braefield Guest House** Braefield Rd, T 01776 810255	SCO GH
64 A5	**Portpatrick Portpatrick Hotel** Heugh Rd, T 01776 810333	SCO H
64 A5	**Portpatrick The Fernhill Hotel** Heugh Rd, T 01776 810220	SCO H
82 E6	**Portree Brescalan Cottage** 3 Borve, T 01470 532425 www.brescalan.co.uk	SCO SC
82 F7	**Portree Croft** 16 Sconser, T 01478 650231	SCO
82 E6	**Portree Cuillin Hills Hotel** Isle of Skye, T 01478 612003	SCO H
82 D5	**Portree Edinbane Self Catering** Upper Edinbane, T 01470 582221	SCO
82 E6	**Portree No 6** No 6 Achachork, Highland, T 01478 613 167	SCO SC
82 E6	**Portree Viewfield House Hotel** Isle of Skye, T 01478 612217	SCO H
82 E6	**Portree Woodvale Cottage** Penifiler, T 01478 612235	SCO
11 H4	**Portsmouth Hilton National** Eastern Rd, Farlington, T 02392 219111	GB
85 P9	**Potterton The Byre** Butterywells Farm, T 01358 742673	SCO SC
47 K4	**Prestatyn Presthaven Sands** Shore Rd, Gronant, T 01745 856471	CYMRU
47 J4	**Prestatyn Tan Y Don Caravan Park** 263 Victoria Rd, T 01745 853749	CYMRU

Page ref.	Town/Name	Services
47 J4	**Prestatyn Traeth Ganol Hotel** 41 Beach Rd West, T 01745 853594	CYMRU
56 B5	**Preston Gibbon Bridge Hotel** Chipping, T 01995 61456	GB
55 J7	**Preston Novotel Preston** Walton Summit, T 01772 313331	GB
55 J6	**Preston Swallow Hotel** Samlesbury, T 01772 877351	GB
67 H1	**Prestwick Golf View Hotel** 17 Links Rd, T 01292 671234	SCO GH
36 D2	**Pwllheli Afonwen Cottages** Afonwen Fm House, T 01766 810939	CYMRU
36 C3	**Pwllheli Cim Farm** Bwlch Tocyn, Abersoch, T 01691 622436	CYMRU
36 C3	**Pwllheli Deucoch Touring Site** Sarn Bach, Abersoch, T 01758 713293	CYMRU
36 C2	**Pwllheli Gwynfryn Farm** Gwynd, T 01758 612536	CYMRU
36 C2	**Pwllheli Rhosfawr Caravan Park** Rhosfawr, T 01766 810545	CYMRU
36 C2	**Pwllheli Rhosydd** 26 Glan Cymerau, T 01758 612956	CYMRU
36 B3	**Pwllheli Rhydolion** Langian, T 01758 712342	CYMRU
36 B3	**Pwllheli The Cottage & Farmhouse** Mynytho, T 01758 713563	CYMRU
36 D2	**Pwllheli Y Beudy & Ysgubor** Chwilog, T 01766 810259	CYMRU
19 G1	**Raglan Harvest Home** Hill Farm, Bryngwyn, T 01291 690007	CYMRU
80 H8	**Rait, Perth Fingask Cottages** Fingask Castle, T 01821 670777	SCO SC
21 K5	**Reading Hanover Intl Hotel** Pingewood, T 0118 950 0885	GB
22 A5	**Reading Millennium Madejski Hotel** J11/M4, T 0118 925 3500	GB
22 A4	**Reading Renaissance Reading Hotel** Oxford Rd, T 0118 958 6222	GB
63 G4	**Redcar Falcon Hotel** 13 Station Rd, T 01642 470617	GB
30 B2	**Redditch Campanile Hotel** Winyates Green, T 01527 510710	GB
23 F6	**Redhill Innkeepers Lodge** Redstone Hill, T 01737 768434	GB
23 F6	**Redhill The Harlequin** Warwick Quadrant, T 01737 773721	GB
2 D4	**Redruth Trengove Farm Cottages** Cot Rd, Illogan, T 01209 843 008	GB
89 D6	**Rendall Widefirth Cottages** Orkney, T 01856 761028 www.orkney-selfcatering.com	SCO SC
27 J2	**Rhayader Wyeside Caravan Park** Aberystwyth Rd, T 01597 810183	CYMRU
86 E4	**Rhiconich Sealladh-ard-innis** Rhiconich Htl, T 01971 521224	SCO
74 B2	**Rhu Ardencaple Hotel** Shore Rd, T 0131 653 5353	SCO
74 A2	**Rhu Rosslea Hall Hotel** Ferry Rd, T 01436 820684	SCO
47 J4	**Rhyl Harborne House** 70 West Parade, T 01745 334251	CYMRU
47 J4	**Rhyl Sandy Shores Guest House** 48 River St, T 01745 351989	CYMRU
62 B6	**Richmond Mount Pleasant Farm** Whashton, T 01748 822784	GB
10 C4	**Ringwood Candlesticks Lodge** 136 Christchurch Rd, T 01425 427587	GB
57 J3	**Ripon Byre Cottage & Swallow Cottage** Littlethorpe, T 01765 677419	GB
57 H3	**Ripon Fountains Cottage** Fountains Abbey Est, T 0870 458 4422	GB
57 H3	**Ripon Lacon Hall Cottages** Lacon Hall, Sawley, T 01765 620658	GB
49 H1	**Rochdale Oakenrod House Hotel** 269 Bury Rd, T 01706 42115	GB
28 E6	**Ross-on-Wye Merton House Holidays** Edde Cross St, T 01989 563252	GB
76 A4	**Roswell Hunter Holiday Cottage** Whitehill Estate, T 0131 440 2082	SCO SC
51 G3	**Rotherham Best Western Elton** Main St, Bramley, T 01709 545681	GB
51 H3	**Rotherham Campanile Hotel** Hellaby Ind Est, T 01709 700255	GB
51 H3	**Rotherham Hellaby Hall** Old Hellaby Ln, Hellaby, T 01709 702701	GB
51 G3	**Rotherham Swallow Hotel** West Bawtry Rd, T 01709 830630	GB
73 J4	**Rothesay The Boat House** Battery Pl, T 01700 502696	SCO GH
79 P2	**Roy Bridge The Stronlossit Inn** Highld, T 0800 015 5321	SCO INN
13 J3	**Royal Tunbridge Wells Spa Hotel** Mount Ephraim, T 01892 520331	GB
48 E4	**Runcorn Campanile Hotel** Lowlands Rd, T 01928 581771	GB
69 G7	**Ruthwell Kirklands Hotel** D & G, T 01387 870284	SCO
14 D5	**Rye Woodlands** Whitebread Ln, Beckley, T 01797 260486	GB
14 D5	**Rye Woodlands Rye** Woodlands, Whitebreaed Ln, Beckley	GB
33 K4	**Saffron Walden Whitensmere Farm Cottage** Whitensmere Farm, Ashdon, T 01799 584244	GB
78 G6	**Salen Ard Mhor House** Pier Rd, T 01680 300255	SCO GH
10 C2	**Salisbury Byways House** 31 Fowlers Rd, T 01722 328364	GB
10 C2	**Salisbury Grasmere House Hotel** 70 Harnham Rd, T 01722 338388 www.grasmerehotel.com	GB H
10 B1	**Salisbury Hens View-fishing Logde** Hanging Langford, T 01722 790365	GB

Page ref.	Town/Name	Services
10 C2	**Salisbury Rose & Crown Hotel** Harnham Rd, Harnham, T 01722 399955	GB
10 C2	**Salisbury The Old Stables** Bridge Farm, Lower Rd, Britford, T 01722 349002 www.old-stables.co.uk	GB SC
10 C1	**Salisbury Webster's** 11 Hartington Rd, T 01722 339779	GB
4 D4	**Saltash St Mellion Intl Cc** St Mellion, T 01579 351351	GB
63 H5	**Saltburn-by-the-Sea Ellerby Hotel** Ellerby, T 01947 840342	GB
63 J5	**Saltburn-by-the-Sea The Firs** Runswick Bay, T 01947 840433	GB
49 G6	**Sandbach Saxon Cross Hotel** J17 of M6, T 01270 763281	GB
15 J2	**Sandwich The Old Dairy** Updown Park Farm, Eastry, T 01843 841656	GB
15 J2	**Sandwich The Old Dairy** Updown Park Farm, Eastry, T 01843 841656	GB
68 C3	**Sanquhar Newark** D & G, T 01659 50263	SCO B&B
68 C3	**Sanquhar Nith Riverside Lodges** Blackaddie House Htl, T 01659 50270	SCO
16 E5	**Saundersfoot Merlewood Hotel** St Brides Hill, T 01834 812421	CYMRU
16 E5	**Saundersfoot Saundersfoot Bay** Broadfield, T 01834 812284	CYMRU
16 E5	**Saundersfoot Smugglers Cottage** The Strand, T 01348 837742	CYMRU
35 H2	**Saxmundham Bluebell & Bertie** Park Farm, Sibton, T 01728 668324 www.farmstayanglia.co.uk/parkfarm	GB SC
35 J2	**Saxmundham Crown At Westleton** Westleton, T 01728 648777	GB
35 J2	**Saxmundham Rose Farm Barns** Rose Farm, Middleton, T 01728 648456	GB
89 N9	**Scalloway Hildasay Guest House** Upper Scalloway, T 01595 880822	SCO
63 K7	**Scarborough Cober Hill** Newlands Rd, Cloughton, T 01723 870310	GB
59 G1	**Scarborough Holiday Lodge** 33 Valley Rd, T 01723 363537	GB
63 K7	**Scarborough The Grainary** Harwood Dale, T 01723 870026	GB
80 G8	**Scone Glebe Cottage** Burnside House, T 01738 551268	SCO SC
80 G8	**Scone Perth Airport Skylodge** Perth Airport, T 01738 555700	SCO L
77 K7	**Seahouses Lynbank & Dalfaber** 151 Main St, T 01665 721066	GB
61 H7	**Sedbergh Cobble Holidays** Bainbridge Rd, T 015396 21000	GB SC
58 B7	**Selby Lund Farm Cottages** Lund Farm, Gateforth, T 01757 228775	GB
69 K1	**Selkirk Ale Cottage** Ashkirk, T 01750 32205	SCO
69 H2	**Selkirk Crook Cottage & Elspinhope** Ettrick Valley, T 01750 62259	SCO SC
69 H2	**Selkirk Crook Cottage & Elspinhope** Ettrick Valley, T 01750 62259	SCO
69 K1	**Selkirk Philipburn Hotel** Lingle Rd, T 01750 20747	SCO
69 K1	**Selkirk Synton Mains Farm** Ashkirk, T 01750 32388	SCO SC
76 C7	**Selkirk West Lodge** Yarrowford	SCO
12 B7	**Selsey Seagulls** Bill Point, Oval Ln, T 01446 771311 www.groomsholidays.org.uk	GB SC

Superb views across the channel. 3 twins, bed linen, TV video, dishwasher, washing machine, garden, sea facing patio, central heating, electric ceiling hoists, wheel in shower, electric profiling bed.

Page ref.	Town/Name	Services
9 H3	**Shaftesbury Hartgrove Farm** Hartgrove, T 01747 811830	GB
9 H2	**Shaftesbury The Coppleridge Inn** Elm Hill, Motcombe, T 01747 851980	GB
11 G6	**Shanklin Laramie** Howard Rd, T 01983 862905	GB
11 G6	**Shanklin Luccombe Hall Hotel** Luccombe Rd, T 01983 862719	GB
51 F4	**Sheffield Novotel Sheffield** Arundel Gate, T 0114 278 1781	GB
51 F4	**Sheffield Sheffield Marriott** Kenwood Rd, T 0114 2583811	GB
51 F4	**Sheffield Uni of Sheffield** Hounsfield Rd, T 0114 222 8803	GB
19 K7	**Shepton Mallet Leigh Holt** Burnt House Farm, Waterlip, T 01749 880280 www.burnthousefarmbandb.com	GB SC
9 F3	**Sherborne Monks Barn** Bishops Down, T 01282 445444	GB
30 D5	**Shipston on Stour The Cottage** Little Wolford, T 01608 684223	GB
73 J7	**Shiskine Derneneach Farm House** Douglas Park, T 01770 302505	SCO
38 D5	**Shrewsbury Lyth Hill House** Lyth Hill, T 01743 874660	GB
38 D3	**Shrewsbury Newton Meadows Cottage** Wem Rd, Harmer Hill, T 01939 290346 www.virtual-shropshire.co.uk/newton	GB SC
9 F7	**Sidmouth Anchor House** 3 Holland Rd, T 01446 771311 www.groomsholidays.org.uk	GB SC

A large attractive, 6 bedroom (wheelchair access to 3 via lift) centrally heated house. Sleeps up to 10. Mobile hoist, wheel in shower, electric profiling bed. TV, video, dishwasher, washer/dryer.

Page ref.	Town/Name	Services
82 D5	**Skeabost Bridge Auchendinny Guest House** Treaslane, T 01470 532470	SCO
82 E6	**Skeabost Bridge Taigh Na H-aibhne** Crepigill, T 0131 3326622	SCO SC
53 J6	**Skegness Chatsworth Hotel** North Parade, T 01754 764177	GB
53 J6	**Skegness Fountaindale Hotel** 69 Sandbeck Ave, T 01754 762731	GB
53 J5	**Skegness Kings Chalet Park** Trunch Lane, Chapel St Leonards, T 01446 771311 www.groomsholidays.org.uk	GB SC

A delightful chalet on the relaxed King's Chalet Park surrounded by unspoilt beaches & picturesque villages. Double, twin & bunk beds, bed linen. TV, wheel in shower, mobile electric hoist, commode.

Page ref.	Town/Name	Services
53 J6	**Skegness Saxby Hotel** 12 Saxby Ave, T 01754 763905	GB
56 E4	**Skipton Cawder Hall Cottages** Cawder Ln, T 01756 791579	GB
56 E4	**Skipton Craven Heifer Inn** Grassington Rd, T 01756 792521	GB
56 E2	**Skipton Dalegarth Cottage** 9 Dalegarth, Buckden, T 01756 760877	GB
57 F4	**Skipton Devonshire Arms House Hotel** Bolton Abbey, T 01756 710441 www.devonshirehotels.co.uk	GB H
56 E4	**Skipton Greenbank** Stirton, T 01756 793716	GB
56 E5	**Skipton Hanover Intl Hotel** Keighley Rd, T 01756 700100	GB
56 E2	**Skipton High Fold** Kettlewell, T 01756 760390	GB
56 E3	**Skipton River House Hotel** Malham, T 01729 830315	GB
57 F3	**Skipton The Barn** Grassington, T 01274 561546	GB
22 C4	**Slough Copthorne Slough** Cippenham Ln, T 01753 516222	GB
20 D2	**South Cerney Lakeside** South Cerney, Glos, T 01446 771311 www.groomsholidays.org.uk	GB SC

Basic compact chalets set in lovely lakeside surroundings on a lively site with plenty to offer. 1 double & 1 twin bedroom. Bed linen, TV, microwave, wheel in shower & commode chair. Private patio.

Page ref.	Town/Name	Services
51 G7	**South Normanton Swallow Hotel** J28 of M1, T 01773 812000	GB
75 K3	**South Queensferry Priory Lodge** 8 The Loan, T 0131 331 4345	SCO GH
89 D8	**South Ronaldsay Taftshurie B&B** Grimness, T 01856 831323	SCO B&B
88 B5	**South Uist Crossroads** Stoneybridge, T 01870 620321	SCO B&B
48 C5	**South Wirral Woodcote Hotel** 3 Houton Rd, Hooton, T 0151 327 1542	GB
30 E3	**Southam Knightcote Farm Cottage** Knightcote, T 01295 770637	GB
11 H2	**Southampton Beacon Hill Farm** Beacon Hill Ln, Exton, T 023 80829724	GB
11 G3	**Southampton Botley Parkk Hotel** Boorley Green, Botley, T 01489 780888	GB
11 F3	**Southampton Novotel** West Quay Rd, T 02380 330550	GB
11 F3	**Southampton Novotel** West Quay Rd, T 02380 330 550	GB
48 C1	**Southport Royal Clifton Hotel** Promenade, T 01704 533771	GB
48 C1	**Southport Sandy Brook Farm** Scarisbrick, T 01704 880337	GB
48 C1	**Southport Scarisbrick Hotel** 239 Lord St, T 01704 543000	GB
35 J1	**Southwold Newlands Country House** 72 Halesworth Rd, Reydon, T 01502 722164	GB
79 P2	**Spean Brdge Distant Hills Guest House** Roybridge Rd, T 01397 712452	SCO GH
79 N2	**Spean Bridge Dreamweavers** Mucomir, T 01397 712 548	SCO B&B
79 P2	**Spean Bridge Old Pines** Restaurant With Rooms, T 01397 712324	SCO
79 P2	**Spean Bridge Old Pines Hotel** Gairlochy Rd, T 01397 712324	SCO H
79 P2	**Spean Bridge The Heathers** Invergloy Halt, T 01397 712077	SCO GH
77 G4	**St Abbs Westwood House** Houndwood, T 01361 850232	SCO
81 L9	**St Andrews Balmashie Cottage** Fife, T 01334 880666	SCO SC
81 K9	**St Andrews Cauldside Farmhouse** Fife, T 01334 477011	SCO
81 K8	**St Andrews Milton Lea** By Balmullo, T 01334 839144	SCO
81 L9	**St Andrews Pitmilly West Lodge** Kingsbarns, T 01334 880581	SCO B&B
81 K9	**St Andrews Rufflets Country Hotel** Strathkinness Low Rd, T 01334 472594	SCO H
81 L9	**St Andrews The Old Station** Stravithie Bridge, T 01334 880505	SCO
4 A5	**St Austell Carlyon Bay Hotel** Sea Rd www.carlyonbay.com	GB H
3 G3	**St Austell Poltarrow Farm** St Mewan, T 01726 67111	GB
16 A3	**St Davids Hendre Eynon Park** Pembrks, T 01437 720474	CYMRU
48 E3	**St Helens Hilton St Helens** Linkway West, T 01744 453444	GB
3 J5	**St Martins The Dower Flat** Sausmarez Manor www.sausmarezmanor.co.uk	GB SC
2 C1	**St Marys Porthlow Farm** Isles of Scilly, T 01720 422636	GB
3 J5	**St Peter Port Albany Apartments** Queens Rd www.albanyselfcatering.com	GB SC
48 E3	**St Helens Haydock Thistle Hotel** Penny Ln, Haydock, T 01942 272000	GB
82 E4	**Staffin Gairloch View** 3 Digg, T 01470 562718	SCO B&B
42 D5	**Stamford Garden House Hotel** St Martins, T 01780 763359	GB
62 B1	**Stanley Oak Tree Inn** Tantobie, T 01207 235445	GB
81 J10	**Star of Markinch Granny Annexe** C/o Roseville, East End, T 01592 751220	SCO SC
33 F6	**Stevenage Novotel Stevenage** Knebworth Park, T 01438 346100	GB
75 G1	**Stirling Cambria Guest House** 141 Bannockburn Rd, T 01786 814603	SCO GH
75 G1	**Stirling Cambria Guest House** 141 Bannockburn Rd, T 01786 814603	SCO
75 F1	**Stirling Hawthorn Cottage** West Drip Farm, T 01786 472523 www.westdripfarm.com	SCO SC
75 G1	**Stirling Holiday Inn Express** Springkerse Bus Pk, T 01786 449922	SCO H
74 E1	**Stirling North Mid Frew Cottage** Thornhill, T 01786 870479	SCO SC
75 G1	**Stirling Stirling Centre** Uni of Stirling, T 01786 451666	SCO H
75 F1	**Stirling Stirling Yh** St John St, T 01786 891400	SCO HOS
10 D1	**Stockbridge Fifehead Manor** Middle Wallop, T 01264 781565	GB
49 H4	**Stockport County Hotel Bramhall** Bramhall, T 0161 455 9988	GB
49 H3	**Stockport Saxon Holme Hotel** Wellington Rd North, T 0161 432 2335	GB

Page ref.	Town/Name	Services
49 J4	**Stockport** Travel Inn Stockport Buxton Rd, T 0161 480 2968	GB
40 C1	**Stoke-on-Trent** Church Grange Alton, T 01889 507525	GB
40 C1	**Stoke-on-Trent** Foxtwood Cottage Foxt Rd, Froghall, T 01538 266 160	GB
49 H7	**Stoke-on-Trent** The Manor House Audley Rd, Alsager, T 01270 884000	GB
40 C1	**Stoke-on-Trent** Jay's Barn Bradley in the Moors, T 01889 507444	GB
40 B2	**Stone** Stone House Hotel Staffs, T 01785 815531	GB
75 F6	**Stonehouse** Thorndale Manse Rd, T 01698 791133	SCO
75 F6	**Stonehouse** Thorndale Guest House Manse Rd, T 01698 791133	SCO GH
88 K4	**Stornoway** Columba Place Isle of Lewis, T 01851 702778	SCO
34 E2	**Stowmarket** Coda Cottages Dandy Corner, Cotton, T 01449 780076	GB
67 H3	**Straiton** Balbeg House Balbeg, T 01655 770665	SCO SC
64 B6	**Stranraer** Bridge Cottage Killumpha, Port Logan, T 01776 860243	SCO
66 D6	**Stranraer** Corsewall Lighthouse Hotel Kirkcolm, T 01776 853220 www.lighthousehotel.co.uk	SCO H
30 C3	**Stratford-upon-Avon** Penshurst Guesthouse 34 Evesham Place, T 01789 205259	GB
30 D3	**Stratford-upon-Avon** Falcon Hotel Chapel St, T 01789 279953	GB
30 D3	**Stratford-upon-Avon** Grosvenor Hotel Warwick Rd, T 01789 269213	GB
30 D3	**Stratford-upon-Avon** Welcombe Hotel Warwick Rd, T 01789 295252	GB
30 C3	**Stratford-upon-Avon** Stratford Victoria Arden St, T 01789 271000	GB
30 C4	**Stratford-upon-Avon** Church Farm Dorsington, T 01789 720275	GB
30 D3	**Stratford-upon-Avon** East Bank House 19 Warwick Rd, T 01789 292758	GB
74 E7	**Strathaven** Drumboy Lodge Drumclog, T 01357 440544	SCO SC
75 F6	**Strathaven** Springvale Hotel 18 Lethame Rd, T 01357 521131	SCO H
82 H5	**Strathcarron** Innis Mhor Ardheslaig, T 01520 755339	SCO
83 Q5	**Strathpeffer** Achilty Hotel Achilty, Contin, T 01997 421355	SCO
83 R5	**Strathpeffer** Coul House Hotel Contin, T 01997 421487	SCO
83 Q5	**Strathpeffer** Strathpeffer Hotel Highld, T 01997 421200	SCO
83 J7	**Stromeferry** Soluis Mu Thuath House Braeintra, Achmore, T 01599 577219	SCO
71 K7	**Sunderland** Marriott Queens Parade, Seaburn, T 0191 529 2041	GB
71 J7	**Sunderland** Quality Hotel Witney Way, Boldon, T 0191 519 1999	GB
23 F5	**Sutton** Holiday Inn Sutton Gibson Rd, T 020 8770 1311	GB
40 E6	**Sutton Coldfield** Lea Marston Hotel Haunch Ln, Lea Marston, T 01675 470468	GB
40 D6	**Sutton Coldfield** Moor Hall Hotel Four Oaks, T 0121 308 3751	GB
44 C5	**Swaffham** Glebe Bungalow 8a Princes St, T 01760 722764	GB
10 B6	**Swanage** The Pines Hotel Burlington Rd, T 01929 425211	GB
17 J6	**Swansea** Gowerston Caravan Park Gowerton, T 01792 873050	CYMRU
17 K6	**Swansea** Hilton National Phoenix Way, T 01792 310330	CYMRU
27 H7	**Swansea** Maes Y Gwernen Hotel School Rd, Abercraf, T 01639 730218	CYMRU
17 H7	**Swansea** Pitton Cross Caravan Park Pitton Cross, Rhossili, T 01792 390593	CYMRU
17 K6	**Swansea** Riverside Caravan Park Morriston, T 01792 775587	CYMRU
17 K6	**Swansea** Swansea Marriot Hotel Maritime Quarter, T 01792 642020	CYMRU
20 E3	**Swindon** Hilton National J16, M4, Lydiard Fields, T 01793 881777	GB
20 E3	**Swindon** The Madison Inn Stratton St Margaret, T 01793 831333	GB
86 H3	**Talmine** Cloisters Church Holme, T 01847 601286	SCO
86 H3	**Talmine** Post Office Flat Highld, T 01847 601250	SCO SC
89 E7	**Tankerness** Sebay Mill Holiday Apartments Orkney, T 01856 872281	SCO SC
88 G7	**Tarbert** Avalon 12 West Side, T 01859 502334	SCO
88 F9	**Tarbert, Nr** Cabhalan Cottage 1 Quidinish, T 01463 712661	SCO
48 E6	**Tarporley** The Swan 50 High St, T 01829 733838	GB
48 E7	**Tarporley** Wild Boar Hotel Whitchurch Rd, Beeston, T 01829 260309	GB
8 C2	**Taunton** Buzzards View Curry Mallet, T 01823 480436	GB
8 C2	**Taunton** Holly Farm Stoke St Gregory, T 01823 490828	GB

Page ref.	Town/Name	Services
7 K2	**Taunton** Redlands House Trebles Holford, Combe Florey, T 01823 433159 www.escapetothecountry.co.uk	GB B&B

Quiet country location. Accessible Courtyard Room has own entrance and small cooking/eating area for simple meals in. Second upstairs room in house. Owner is wheelchair user.

Page ref.	Town/Name	Services
7 K1	**Taunton** Stilegate B&B Staple Close, West Quantoxhead, T 01984 639119 www.stilegate.co.uk	GB B&B
8 B3	**Taunton** The Spinney Curland, T 01460 234362	GB
79 M8	**Taynuilt** Roineabhal Country House Kilchrenan, T 01866 833207	SCO B&B
79 M8	**Taynuilt** Tigh An Daraich Bridge of Awe, T 01866 822693	SCO SC
5 K3	**Teignmouth** Cliffden Hotel Dawlish Rd, T 01626 770052	GB
5 K3	**Teignmouth** Front Flat Trevimider, Hermosa Rd, T 01626 775623	GB
39 F4	**Telford** Church Farm Cottages Rowton, Wellington, T 01952 770381 www.virtual-shropshire.co.uk/churchfarm	GB SC
39 G5	**Telford** Holiday Inn Ironbridge St Quentin Gate, T 01952 527000	GB
39 F5	**Telford** Ironbridge Yha Coalport, T 0870 7705882	GB
39 F5	**Telford** Old Rectory Stirchley Village, T 01588 660245	GB
39 F5	**Telford** Telford Country Hotel Great Hay, Sutton Hill, T 01952 429977	GB
9 G3	**Templecombe** Fountain Inn Motel High St, Henstridge, T 01963 362722	GB
16 E5	**Tenby** Atlantic Hotel The Esplanade, S.Beach, T 01834 842881	CYMRU
16 E5	**Tenby** Clarence House Hotel The Esplanade, T 01834 844371	CYMRU
16 D5	**Tenby** Greenhills Country Hotel St Florence, T 01834 871291/01834 871738 www.greenhillshotel.co.uk	CYMRU H
16 E5	**Tenby** Heywood Lodge Hotel Heywood Ln, T 01834 842684	CYMRU
16 D5	**Tenby** Milton Manor Hotel Milton, T 01646 651398	CYMRU
14 D4	**Tenterden** Little Silver Hotel Ashford Rd, St Michaels, T 01233 850321	GB
20 B2	**Tetbury** Hunters Hall Kingscote, T 01453 860393	GB
29 H5	**Tewkesbury** Puckrup Hall Hotel Puckrup, T 01684 296200	GB
44 E5	**Thetford** Chestnut Barn Annexe Southburgh, T 01953 851042	GB
57 K1	**Thirsk** Doxford House Sowerby, T 01845 523238	GB
57 K1	**Thirsk** Mowbray Stable Cottage Stockton Rd, South Kilvington, T 01845 522605	GB SC
68 D4	**Thornhill** Templand Cottages Templand Mains, T 01848 330775 www.templandcottages.co.uk Lovely fully-equipped farm cottages around landscaped courtward & gardens. Unspoilt area with stunning views and wildlife. Small indoor pool/sauna.	SCO SC
87 Q2	**Thurso** Castle Arms Hotel Mey, T 01847 851244	SCO
87 R2	**Thurso** Creag-na-mara East Mey, T 01847 851850	SCO B&B
87 N3	**Thurso** Forss House Hotel Forss, T 01847 861201	SCO H
87 P3	**Thurso** Weigh Inn Hotel Burnside, T 01847 893722	SCO H
73 H3	**Tighnabruich** Airy Cottage Carnethy, Kames, T 01563 829356	SCO SC
7 G4	**Tiverton** South Coombe Cottage Witheridge, T 01884 860302	GB
7 J3	**Tiverton** The Barn Huntsham, T 01398 361519 www.huntshambarn.co.uk	GB B&B
7 H4	**Tiverton** Tiverton Hotel Blundells Rd, T 01884 256120	GB
78 F5	**Tobermory** Cill-mhoire Dervaig, T 01688 400445	SCO SC
78 F5	**Tobermory** Druimard Country House Dervaig, T 01688 400345	SCO H
78 G5	**Tobermory** Highland Cottage Breadalbane St, T 01688 302030	SCO H
78 G5	**Tobermory** Tobermory Hotel 53 Main St, T 01688 302091 www.thetobermoryhotel.com	SCO H
23 K7	**Tonbridge** Goldhill Mill Cottage Goldhill Mill, Golden Green, T 01732 851626 www.goldhillmillcottages.com	GB SC
23 J7	**Tonbridge** Vauxhaul Premier Lodge Pembury Rd, T 01732 773111	GB

Page ref.	Town/Name	Services
5 K4	**Torquay** Babbacombe 1 Park Rd, St Marychurch, T 01446 771311 www.groomsholidays.org.uk	GB SC

A spacious apartment, a short walk from a delightful resort. 1 double bedroom, 2 double sofa beds. Bed linen. TV, video, washer/dryer, central heating, bath & wheel in shower, mobile electric hoist.

Page ref.	Town/Name	Services
5 J4	**Torquay** Fairmount House Hotel Herbert Rd, Chelston, T 01803 605446	GB
5 K4	**Torquay** Frognel Hall Higher Woodfield Rd, T 01803 298 339	GB
5 K4	**Torquay** Manderville 18 Thurlow Rd, T 01803 313336	GB
5 K4	**Torquay** Oddicombe Hall Hotel Babbacombe Downs Rd, T 01803 313457	GB
5 K4	**Torquay** The Corbyn Torbay Rd, T 01803 215595	GB
5 K4	**Torquay** Villa Capri Daddyhole Rd, Meadfoot, T 01803 297959	GB
5 K4	**Torquay** Vomero Holiday Apartments Stitchill Rd, T 01803 293470	GB
67 H1	**Troon** Piersland House Hotel 15 Craigend Rd, T 01292 314747	SCO H
74 B7	**Troon** South Beach Hotel South Beach, T 01292 312033	SCO H
3 F4	**Truro** Alverton Manor Cornwall	GB
3 G4	**Truro** Trenona Farm Holidays Trenona Farm, Ruan High Lns, T 01872 501339 www.trenonafarmholidays.co.uk	GB SC
3 F5	**Truro** Willows Barn & Owl Cottage Portscatho, T 01872 580150	GB
80 C5	**Tummel Bridge** Kynachan Loch Hotel Perthshire, T 01389 713713	SCO H
23 K7	**Tunbridge Wells** Ramada Jarvis 8 Tonbridge Rd, Pembury, T 01892 823567	GB
67 G3	**Turnberry** Westin Turnberry Ayrshire, T 01655 331000	SCO IR
85 M5	**Turriff** Delgatie Castle Aberdeens, T 01888 563479	SCO SC
85 N5	**Turriff** Garden Cottage New Byth, T 01888 544230	SCO SC
85 M6	**Turriff** Stonefolds Farm Cottage Fyvie, T 01651 891267	SCO SC
46 D4	**Tyn-Y-Gongl** Bryn Meirion Lodge Amlwch Rd, Benllech, T 01248 853118 www.brynmeirionlodge.co.uk	CYMRU B&B
36 E5	**Tywyn** Corbett Arms Hotel Corbetts Square, T 01654 710264	CYMRU
37 F5	**Tywyn** Eisteddfa Abergynolwyn, T 01654 782385	CYMRU
36 E5	**Tywyn** Pant Y Neuadd Aberdyfi Rd, T 01654 711393	CYMRU
37 F5	**Tywyn** Ynysmaengwyn Park Gwynd, T 01654 710684	CYMRU
13 H4	**Uckfield** Whitehouse Farm Horney Common, Nutley, T 01825 712377	GB
83 M1	**Ullapool** Dromnan Guest House Garve Rd, T 01854 612333	SCO GH
83 M1	**Ullapool** Hillview 10 Moss Rd, T 01854 612093	SCO SC
83 M1	**Ullapool** Royal Hotel Garve Rd, T 01854 612181	GB
55 F1	**Ulverston** Bark Cottage The Meadows, Lowick Green, T 01229 885416	GB SC
6 D3	**Umberleigh** Country Ways High Bickington, T 01769 560503	GB
89 P2	**Unst** Gardiesfauld Yh Uyeasound, T 01957 755212	SCO HOS
75 J3	**Uphall** Coille-mhor House Houston Mains, T 01506 854044	SCO
73 K4	**Upper Skelmorlie** The Smiddy 4 Golf Course Rd, T 01475 522480	SCO SC
11 F7	**Ventnor** Atherfield Green Farm Chale, T 01983 551420	GB
89 N11	**Virkie** Lighthousekeeper's House Sumburgh Head, T 01387 372240	SCO
3 G1	**Wadebridge** The Olde House Chapel Amble, T 01208 813219	GB
3 G1	**Wadebridge** Tzitzikama Lodge Rock Rd, Rock, T 01208 862839	GB
51 F1	**Wakefield** Hotel Campanile Monckton Rd, T 01924 201054	GB
21 K3	**Wallingford** George Hotel High St, T 01491 836665	GB
89 L8	**Walls** Burrastow House Shetland, T 01595 809307	SCO GH
40 B6	**Walsall** Quality Friendly Hotel Bentley, T 01922 724444	GB
23 H1	**Waltham Abbey** Marriott Hotel Old Shire Ln, T 01992 717170	GB
35 G6	**Walton On The Naze** Bufo Villae 31 Beatrice Rd, T 01255 672644	GB
9 H6	**Wareham** Kemps Country House Hotel East Stoke, T 01929 462563	GB

Page ref.	Town/Name	Services
9 J7	**Wareham Kingston Courtyard** Corfe Castle, T 01929 481066	GB
9 H6	**Wareham The Old Granary** West Holme Farm, T 01929 552972	GB
49 F4	**Warrington Holiday Inn Garden Crt** Woolston, T 01925 838779	GB
49 F5	**Warrington Tall Trees Lodge** Lower Whitley, T 01928 790824	GB
49 F4	**Warrington The Hanover Intl Hotel** Stretton Rd, Stretton, T 01925 730706	GB
30 D2	**Warwick Hilton National** A429 Stratford Rd, T 01926 499555	GB
30 C2	**Warwick Woodside** Langley Rd, Claverdon, T 01926 842446	GB
7 J1	**Watchet Roseville** Longville, 48A Brendon Rd, T 01282 445096 www.country-holidays2006.co.uk	GB SC
82 C5	**Waternish Auld Alliance Cottage** 33 Lochbay, T 01470 592363	SCO SC
82 C5	**Waternish Greenbank** Isle of Skye, T 01470 592369	SCO SC
82 C5	**Waternish Stein Inn** Waternish, T 01470 592362	SCO INN
32 C1	**Wellingborough Tudor Gate Hotel** Finedon, T 01933 680408	GB
19 J7	**Wells St Mary's Lodge** St Mary Mead, Long Street, Crosscombe, T 01749 342157 www.st-marys-lodge.co.uk	GB SC
19 H7	**Wells Swallow Barn** Double-gate Farm, Godney, T 01458 832217	GB
38 B4	**Welshpool Bank Farm Caravan Park** Middletown, T 01938 570526	CYMRU
37 K4	**Welshpool Brynllys** Llanerfyl, T 01938 820347	CYMRU
38 A5	**Welshpool Madog's Wells Farm** Llanfair Caereinion, T 01938 810446	CYMRU SC
38 A5	**Welshpool Upper Brithdir Farm** Berriew, T 01686 640263	CYMRU
8 B1	**Wembdon Ash-wembdon Farm Cottage** Hollow Ln, T 01278 453 097	GB
22 E3	**Wembley Hilton National** Empire Way, T 020 8902 8839	GB
75 J5	**West Calder Crosswoodhill Farm** West Lothian, T 01501 785205	SCO SC
22 D4	**West Drayton Excelsior Hotel Heathrow** Bath Rd, T 020 8759 6611	GB
22 D4	**West Drayton Holiday Inn Crowne Plaza** Stockley Rd, T 01895 445555	GB
22 D4	**West Drayton Novotel Heathrow** Junction 4 M4, Cherry Ln, T 01895 431431	GB
4 E5	**West Hoe Osmond Guest House** 42 Pier St, T 01752 229705	GB
75 K6	**West Linton Mill Cottage** Damside, Romanno Bridge, T 01968 660887	SCO SC
75 K6	**West Linton Netherby Cottage** Romanno Bridge, T 01968 661194	SCO
23 H6	**Westerham Roadchef Lodge** Clacket Ln, M25 Motorway, T 01959 565577	GB
19 G6	**Weston-super-Mare Hope Farm Cottage** Brean Rd, Lympsham, T 01934 750506	GB
19 G5	**Weston-super-Mare Kinclaven** 5 Park Place, T 07071 223345	GB
19 G6	**Weston-super-Mare Moorlands** Hutton, T 01934 812283	GB
89 D2	**Westray Holm View** Papa, T 01857 644211	SCO SC
89 D3	**Westray The Kilnmans Cottage** Trenabie Mill, T 01857 677447	SCO SC
87 P3	**Weydale, Thurso Curlew Cottage** Hilliclay Mains, T 01847 895638	SCO SC
8 E6	**Weymouth Gorwell Farm Cots** Abbotsbury, T 01305 871401	GB
75 H4	**Whitburn Hilcroft Hotel** East Main St, T 01501 740818	SCO H
63 J6	**Whitby Captain Cook's Haven** Larpool Ln, T 01723 501899	GB
63 G5	**Whitby Fowl Green Farm** Commondale	GB
63 J6	**Whitby Groves Dyke Cottage** Groves Bank, Sleights, T 01947 811404 www.grovesdyke.co.uk	GB SC
63 G6	**Whitby Millinder House** Westerdale, T 01282 445444	GB
63 J6	**Whitby The Beacon Guest House** Goathland, T 01947 896409	GB
83 Q9	**Whitebridge Wildside Highld Lodges** Highld, T 01456 486373	SCO SC
73 G6	**Whitefarland Byre Cottage** Sunny Oaks, T 01770 850247	SCO
64 E7	**Whithorn The Smiddy** Glasserton, T 01560 482363	SCO
66 E1	**Whiting Bay Grange House Hotel** Shore Rd, T 01770 700263	SCO
66 E1	**Whiting Bay Sandbraes Lodge** Isle of Arran, T 01770 700235	SCO SC
17 F4	**Whitland Homeleigh Country Cottage** Red Roses, T 01834 831765 www.homeleigh.org	CYMRU SC

Page ref.	Town/Name	Services
16 E4	**Whitland Latchygors Cottage** Llanfallteg, T 01994 240460	CYMRU
16 E4	**Whitland Pantglas Farm Park** Tavernspite, T 01834 831618	CYMRU
71 J6	**Whitley Bay Marlborough Hotel** The Promenade, T 0191 251 3628	GB
71 J6	**Whitley Bay York House Hotel** 30 Park Parade, T 0191 252 8313	GB
20 A1	**Whitminster Whitminster House Cottage** Whitminster House, T 01452 740204	GB
87 R3	**Wick Dunroamin** South Keiss, T 01955 631283	SCO
87 R4	**Wick Ryrie** 24 Lindsay Drive, T 01955 603001	SCO
48 E4	**Widnes Everglades Park Hotel** Derby Rd, T 0151 495 2040	GB
48 E4	**Widnes Hillcrest Hotel** Cronton Ln, T 0151 424 1616	GB
48 E2	**Wigan Quality Hotel Lancs Manor** East Pimbo, Skelmersdale, T 01695 720401	GB
49 H4	**Wilmslow Dean Bank Hotel** Adlington Rd, T 01625 524268	GB
10 B4	**Wimborne Grange Holiday Cottage** Grange, T 01202 884426 www.grangeholidaycottages.co.uk	GB SC
11 F1	**Winchester Harestock Lodge Hotel** Harestock Rd, T 01962 881870	GB
11 F1	**Winchester Lainston House Hotel** Sparsholt, T 01962 863588	GB
60 F7	**Windermere Burn How Gard'n House Hotel** Bowness-on-Windermere, T 015394 46226	GB
60 F7	**Windermere Burnside Hotel** Bowness-on-Windermere, T 015394 42211	GB
60 F6	**Windermere Cheshire Home** Holehird, Patterdale Rd, T 015394 42500	GB
60 F7	**Windermere Hawksmoor** Lake Rd, T 015394 42110	GB
60 F7	**Windermere Lindeth Howe House Hotel** Longtail Hill, T 015394 45759	GB
60 F7	**Windermere Linthwaite House Hotel** Bowness-on-Windermere, T 015394 88600	GB
48 C4	**Wirral Thornton Hall Hotel** Thornton Hough, T 0151 336 3938	GB
43 G5	**Wisbech Common Right Barns** Wisbech St Mary, T 01945 410424	GB
43 J5	**Wisbech Crown Lodge Hotel** Downham Rd, Outwell, T 01945 773391	GB
21 G1	**Witney Ducklington Farm** Coursehill Ln, Ducklington, T 01993 772175	GB
21 G1	**Witney Springhill Bed Farm** Cogges, T 01993 704919	GB
21 G1	**Witney Swallow's Nest** Springhill Farm, Cogges, T 01993 704919	GB
32 C5	**Woburn The Bedford Arms** George St, T 01525 290441	GB
22 D6	**Woking Wheatsheaf Hotel** Chobham Rd, Horsell, T 01483 773047	GB
22 B5	**Wokingham Hilton St Anne's Manor** London Rd, T 01189 772550	GB
40 B6	**Wolverhampton Novotel** Union St, T 01902 871100	GB
35 G2	**Woodbridge Boundary Farm** Saxtead Rd, Framlingham, T 01728 621026	GB
35 G4	**Woodbridge Grove House** 39 Grove Rd, T 01394 382202	GB
35 G2	**Woodbridge St Peter's View** Monk Soham, T 01728 685358	GB
52 E6	**Woodhall Spa Kirkstread Old Mill** Tattershall Rd	GB
52 E6	**Woodhall Spa Wayside Cottage** Main St, Horsington, T 01526 353101 www.skegness.net/woodhallspa.htm	GB SC
6 C1	**Woolacombe The Cleeve House** North Morte Rd, Mortehoe, T 01271 870719 www.cleevehouse.co.uk	GB H
77 H7	**Wooler Westnewton Estate** Westnewton, T 01668 216077	GB
70 E1	**Wooler Wooler Yh** 30 Cheviot St, T 01668 281365	GB
29 G3	**Worcester Crumplebury Farmhouse** Whitbourne, T 01886 821534	GB
29 F4	**Worcester Hidelow House Cottage** Acton Green, Acton Beauchamp, T 01886 884547 www.hidelow.co.uk	GB SC

Page ref.	Town/Name	Services
29 G2	**Worcester Old Yates Cottages** Old Yates Farm, Abberley, T 01299 896500	GB
29 G2	**Worcester The Riseling** Stanford Bridge, T 01886 853438	GB
29 H4	**Worcester Willow Bank House** Upton upon Severn, T 01527 543485	GB
51 H5	**Worksop Browns** The Old Orchard Cottage, Holbeck, T 01909 720 659 www.brownsholbeck.co.uk	GB B&B
51 J5	**Worksop Clumber Park Hotel** Clumber Park, Near, T 01623 835333	GB
12 E6	**Worthing Beach Hotel** Marine Parade, T 01903 234001	GB

Page ref.	Town/Name	Services
12 E6	**Worthing Berkeley Hotel** 86-95 Marine Parade, T 01903 820000	GB
12 E6	**Worthing Kingsway Hotel** 117 Marine Parade, T 01903 237542	GB
12 E6	**Worthing Manor Guest House** 100 Broadwater Rd, T 01903 236028 www.manorworthing.com	GB B&B
12 E6	**Worthing The Lantern Hotel** 54 Shelley Rd, T 0845 450 0227	GB
12 E6	**Worthing The Windsor Hotel** 14-20 Windsor Rd, T 01903 239655	GB
48 C7	**Wrexham Corner House Farm** Parkside, Rossett, T 01829 270452	CYMRU
38 C1	**Wrexham Forte Travelodge** Wrexham By Pass, Rhostyllen, T 01978 3655705	CYMRU
38 C1	**Wrexham James Caravan Park** Ruabon, T 01978 820148	CYMRU
45 H4	**Wroxham Broomhill** Station Rd, Hoveton, T 020 7452 2145 www.groomsholidays.org.uk	GB SC

By the picturesque River Bure, in a lovely setting, each delightful apartment sleeps 8. Bed linen, TV Video, washer/dryer, central heating, wheel in shower, mobile hoist, lift, electric profiling bed.

Page ref.	Town/Name	Services
45 F5	**Wymondham Wymondham Consort Hotel** 28 Market St, T 01953 606721	GB
6 E7	**Yelverton Headland Warren Farm** Headland Warren, Postbridge, T 01822 88206	GB
5 F4	**Yelverton Midway** The Crescent, Crapstone, T 01752 733221	GB
5 F4	**Yelverton Overcombe Hotel** Horrabridge, T 01822 853501	GB
58 C1	**York Angel Cottage** Wheatfield, Oswaldkirk, T 01439 788493	GB
58 D3	**York Blacksmiths Arms Inn** Westow, T 01653 618365	GB
58 B4	**York Clifton Bridge Hotel** Water End, Clifton, T 01904 610510	GB
58 D1	**York Dove Court** Salton, T 01751 431697	GB
57 K4	**York Gill House Farm** Long Marston, T 01904 738379	GB
58 C4	**York Heworth Court Hotel** 76 Heworth Green, T 01904 425156	GB
58 C4	**York Hilton York** 1 Tower St, T 01904 648111	GB
58 E5	**York Lakeside Lodges** Pocklington, T 01759 306585	GB
58 D1	**York Moorland & Heather Cottage** Hutton-le-Hole, T 01751 417743	GB
58 C4	**York Novotel York** Fishergate, T 01904 611 660	GB
58 C4	**York Novotel York** Fishergate, T 01904 611660	GB
58 B4	**York Ramada Jarvis York** Shipton Rd, Skelton, T 01904 670222	GB
58 B4	**York Savages Hotel** Clifton, T 01904 610818	GB
58 D1	**York The Cornmill** Kirkbymoorside, T 01751 432000	GB
58 B4	**York The Grange Hotel** 1 Clifton, T 01904 644744	GB
58 B2	**York Thornton Lodge Farm** Easingwold, T 01347 821306	GB
58 D4	**York Wolds View Holiday Cottage** Mill Farm, Yapham, T 01759 302172	GB
58 B5	**York York Lakeside Lodges** Moor Ln, T 01904 702346 www.yorklakesidelodges.co.uk	GB SC

Accessories

Page ref.	Town/Name
19 G3	**Newport Global Leather** T 01264 352000 **www.GL100.com**

Globaleather™

New Style Leather Blue Badge & Timer Display Wallet "Warp Free" so the wallet will not distort if displayed in the direct sun light. No need to remove the timer from the timer from the plastic pocket to make adjustments.

Page ref. Town/Name Services

Adaptations

31 J7 **Aylesbury** DS & P Mobility Electronics
Westcott Venture Park, Trostre Ind Pk, T 01296 658508
www.dsp-mobilityelectronics.com

49 J3 **Bredbury** Jeff Gosling Hand Controls Ltd (WC)
Hollingworth Crt, Stockport Rd West, T 0161 430 2151
www.jeffgosling.com

Manufacturer and installer of vehicle adaptations for the disabled driver/passenger. National Dealer Network for Hand Controls.

81 L10 **Cellardyke** Techmobility
12 John St, Teddington, Fife, T 01333 313932
www.techmobility.co.uk
Mobile Service throughout Scotland

34 C6 **Coggeshall** Techmobility
Purley Farm Barns, off Colne Road, Essex, T 01376 564499
www.techmobility.co.uk
Manufacturer and Installers of All types of Vehicle Adaptations

76 A3 **Edinburgh** PL Mobility
4B Granton Square, T 0131 551 6010
www.Plmobility.com

PL Mobility
-puts you in control-

PL Mobility offers quality vehicle adaptations for wheelchair users, their carers and people with any degree of disability. A wide range of equipment and the latest technology means that cars can be adapted to suit your individual needs- with safety and reliability guaranteed

22 D1 **Hemel Hempstead** Steering Developments
Unit 5, East Man Way, T 01442 212918
www.steeringdevelopments.co.uk
Vehicles and wheelchairs working together

32 C6 **Leighton Buzzard** P B Conversions
Unit 6 Acacia Close, Cherrycourt Way, T 01525 850588
www.pbconversions.co.uk

PB Conversions *giving you freedom*

Specialist in vehicle adaptations. Suppliers of Hand Controls, Voice Controls, Infra Red Systems, Left for Accelerators and Drive from the Wheelchair vehicles. 15 Years Experience and 3 year warranty on PBC products.

21 H5 **Newbury** Gowrings Mobility
Bone Lane, Newbury 0845 608 8020
www.gowringsmobility.co.uk

gowrings mobility

40 C6 **Walsall** Sirus Automotive Ltd
Unit 3 Frederick Street, T 01922 647755
www.sirusautomotive.com

33 F7 **Welwyn Garden City** Brig-Ayd Controls
56a Bridge Road East, T 01707 322322
www.brig-aydcontrols.co.uk

Bathroom Equipment

22 E4 **London** C & B Systems
Crest House, 102 Church Road, Teddington T 0208 614 1428
www.c-bsystems.co.uk
Suppliers of grabrails, showers and santrary ware.

Charity

22 D1 **Chipperfield** British Motor Sports Association for the Disabled
T: 01923 265577
www.justmobility.co.uk/bmsad/
Providing advice and assessments on all aspects of Motor Sport for disabled people.

23 G3 **Disability Now**
6 Market Road, Lower Holloway, T 0207 7619 7323
www.disabilitynow.org.uk

DN disabilitynow

Disability Now. National newspaper on disability www.disabilitynow.org.uk

45 F1 **Sherringham** Break Charity
Davison House, Montague Road, T 01263 822161
www.break-charity.org
Break provides holidays for people with special needs. For many families Break is a lifeline.

Consumer Research & (Disability) Information

29 H7 **Gloucester** Guide Information Service
T 01452 331131
www.guide-information.org.uk
Guide Disability Information for Gloucestershire. Free & Confidential Information on support services (local & national) transport, equipment, benefits, funding, mobility and lots more.

23 G3 **Ricability**
30 Angel Gate, City Road, T 0207 427 2468
www.ricability.org.uk
Independent research charity that publishes unbiased consumer guides for older and disabled people.

Employment & self employment for diabled people

Association of Disabled Professionals (ADP)
T 01204 431638
www.adp.org.uk
Supporting disabled people with work issues. Enquiries and Mentoring by disabled people on the telephone, email, fax about employment and self employment issues.

Exhibitions

75 J3 **Edinburgh** Mobility Roadshow Ltd
Royal Highland Centre, Ingliston, T 0870 770 3222
www.mobilityroadshow.co.uk
Mobility Roadshow : 5 & 6 April 2006 If you have a mobility, you can't afford to miss this unique event.

20 C2 **Swindon** Mobility Roadshow Ltd
Kemble Airfield, T 0870 770 3222
www.mobilityroadshow.co.uk
Mobility Roadshow : 8-10 June 2006 If you have a mobility, you can't afford to miss this unique event.

Forum of Mobility Centres

The Forum of Mobility Centres is a charitable network of 17 independent Mobility Centres which aim to help people achieve independent mobility as drivers, passengers and wheelchair users providing personal assessments and useful information on a range of services. There is now a new National Information Service on 0800 559 3636, offering advice on driving, adaptations and the location of Forum Mobility Centres.

14 C2 **Aylesford** Dart Driving Assessment & Advice Service
Cobtree Ward, Preston Ward Hospital, London Road, T 01622 795719

90 H3 **Belfast** Northern Ireland Mobility Centre
Disability Action, Portside Bus Pk, T 028 9029 7880
www.disabilityaction.org

30 B1 **Birmingham** Regional Driving Assessment Centre
Rednal Road, West Midlands, T 0121 627 8228

47 J5 **Bodelwyddan** North Wales Mobility & Driving Assessment Service
North Wales Resources Centre, Glan Clwyd Hospital, Denbighs, T 01745 584858

19 K4 **Bristol** Mobility Service of the Disabled Living Centre
The Vassall Centre, Gill Ave, Fishponds, Avon, T 0117 965 9353
www.dlcbristol.org

18 E4 **Cardiff** South Wales Mobility & Driving Assessment Service
Rookwood Hospital, Fairwater Rd, Llandaff, T 029 2055 5130

23 F5 **Carshalton** Queen Elizabeth's Foundation Mobility Centre
Damson Way, Fountain Drive, Surrey, T 020 8770 1151
www.qefd.org/mobilitycentre

22 B5 **Crowthorne** Mobility Advice & Vehicle Information Service (MAVIS)
Crowthorne Bus Est, Old Wokingham Rd, Berks, T 01344 661000
www.dft.gov.uk/access/mavis

41 F2 **Derby** Derby Regional Mobility Centre
Kingsway Hospital, Kingsway, T 01332 371929
www.drmc.uk.com

76 A3 **Edinburgh** Scottish Driving Assessment Service
Astley Ainslie Hospital, Grange Loan, T 0131 537 9192

57 H6 **Leeds** William Merritt Disabled Living Centre & Mobility Service
St. Mary's Hospital, Green Hill Rd, Armley, T 0113 305 5288
www.williammerrittleeds.org

71 H7 **Newcastle Upon Tyne** Mobility Centre
Reg'l Neurological Rehab'n, Hunters Road, T 0191 219 5694
www.nap.nhs.uk/snrs/index.html

21 J1 **Oxford** Oxford Driving Assessment Service
Oxford Centre for Enablement, Headington, T 01865 227600

44 C7 **Thetford** Kilverstone Mobility Assessment Centre
2 Napier Place, Norfolk, T 01842 753029
www.kmacmobil.org.uk

2 E4 **Truro** Cornwall Mobility Centre
Tehidy House, Royal Cornwall Hospital, Cornwall, T 01872 254920
www.cornwallmobilitycentre.co.uk

33 F7 **Welwyn Garden City** Hertfordshire Action on Disability Mobility
The Woodside Centre, The Commons, T 01707 324 581
www.hadnet.org.uk
Associate Members

48 E1 **Wigan** Wrightington Mobility Centre
Wrightington Hospital, Hall Lane, Appley Bridge, T 01257 256409

Holidays Tour Operator

London Access Africa!
Wheelchair accessible holidays in South Africa, T 0208 851 3065
www.accessafrica.co.uk

Access Africa .co.uk

We offer wheelchair accessible accommodation, tours and safaris in South Africa for the adventurous disabled traveller! Experience Africa in comfort with Access Africa!

Mobility Aids

22 B2 **Great Kingshill** Cowal Mobility Aids Limited
Cowal Court, Heath End Road, Bucks, T 01494 714400
www.cowalmobility.co.uk
Modifications to vehicles for the disable drivers.

Mobility Supplies/Products

Age Concern Enterprises
T:0800 77 22 66
www.aidcall-alarms.co.uk

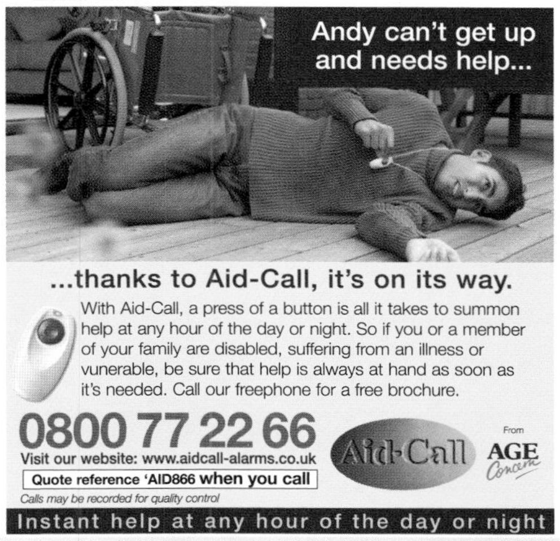

Andy can't get up and needs help...
...thanks to Aid-Call, it's on its way.
With Aid-Call, a press of a button is all it takes to summon help at any hour of the day or night. So if you or a member of your family are disabled, suffering from an illness or vulnerable, be sure that help is always at hand as soon as it's needed. Call our freephone for a free brochure.
0800 77 22 66
Visit our website: www.aidcall-alarms.co.uk
Quote reference 'AID866 when you call
Calls may be recorded for quality control
Aid-Call
From AGE Concern
Instant help at any hour of the day or night

Seven days a week and 365 days a year. Aid-Call brings peace of mind, both for the independent -minded and their families. Our alarms are used by a broad spectrum of people and ages, and by no means are all the users elderly. Knowing help is at your fingertips - 24 hours a day, seven days a week and 365 days a year- means everyone can relax and stop worrying.

55 G6 **Blackpool** Access Disability
55 Coronation St, T 0800 169 9212
www.accessdisability.co.uk

www.accessdisability.co.uk

POSITIVE ABOUT CHANGE...

Making Blackpool Accesible

Wheelchair / Scooter Hire & Sales.We also stock a large range of Mobility Products, Ramps, Induction Loops, Grab Rails, Stair Lifts and Much More.

Page ref. Town/Name Services

49 G1 Bolton RDK Mobility
190 Tonge Moor Road T:0800 107 5118
www.rdkmobility.co.uk

RDK Mobility
UK's No1 Mobility Centre

RDK Mobility supply Scooters, Power-Chairs, Wheelchairs, Walkers, Stairlifts, Walkin-Baths, Power Bath/patent Leg Lifter, Bathlifts, Showers, Adjustable-Beds, Riser/Recliners, Hoists, Widefit-Shoes, General Aids. Call 0800 107 5118 for a catalogue.

6 C2 Braunton Braunton Mobility Centre
Cross Tree Centre, Chaloners Road, T 01271 814577
www.braunton-mobility.toucansurf.com

BRAUNTON MOBILITY CENTRE
TELEPHONE 01271 814577
For all your Mobility needs including hire equipment

Probably the friendliest Mobility centre in Devon. Most products include free delivery. Free home demos & advice. We supply scooters, walkers, powerchairs, wheelchairs, beds, showerchairs and numerous other aids. A one stop shop for all your mobility needs. We also hire scooters & wheelchairs by the day/week or sometimes longer.

13 G6 Brighton Clearwell Mobility
110 Warren Rd, Woodingdean, T 01273 692244
www.clearwellmobility.co.uk
Shop open Mon-Sat 9-5pm. Wheelchair & Scooter Hire.

2 D4 Camborne Mobility Markets Ltd
Unit E-3, Formal Business Park, T 0800 0378 011
www.mobility-markets.co.uk
Small friendly business offering a wide range of products, we provide personal service, quality and real people to speak to when you call.

8 C4 Chard Batricar Independent Mobility
43 Ayishayes Rd, T 0500 974975
www.batricar.co.uk
Suppliers & manufactures of mobility vehicles, walking aids, manual & powered whelchairs & care products

84 G4 Elgin City Mobility
10b Chanonry St, T 01343 559720

For all your mobility requirements

City MOBILITY	City MOBILITY
46a Seafield Road, Longman Industrial Estate, Inverness, IV1 1SG	10b Chanonry Street, Chanonry Industrial Estate, Elgin, IV30 6NF
Tel: 01463 250850 Fax: 01463 250950	Tel/Fax: 01343 559720
e-mail: citymobility@caleystream.co.uk	e-mail: citymobility@caleystream.co.uk

For all your mobility requiremnets.

22 E3 Harrow Mobility World Ltd
78-80 Station Rd, T 0870 740 7772
www.mobilityworld.co.uk
Access, Mobility, Bathing, Care, Bed & Chair, Comfort, Household, Dining etc.

7 K6 Honiton Carmobility
Durham Way, Heath Park Ind Est, T 01404 44470
www.carmobility.co.uk

84 A6 Inverness City Mobility
46-A Seafield Rd, T 01463 250 850

For all your mobility requirements

City MOBILITY	City MOBILITY
46a Seafield Road, Longman Industrial Estate, Inverness, IV1 1SG	10b Chanonry Street, Chanonry Industrial Estate, Elgin, IV30 6NF
Tel: 01463 250850 Fax: 01463 250950	Tel/Fax: 01343 559720
e-mail: citymobility@caleystream.co.uk	e-mail: citymobility@caleystream.co.uk

For all your mobility requiremnets.

17 J6 Llanelli LTC Mobility
Unit 1 & 3a, Llanelli Workshops, Trostre Ind Park
T 01554 773608

23 G3 London Ridley Electronics Ltd
66a Capworth\St, Leyton, T 020 8558 7112
www.ridleyelect.co.uk

RIDLEY ELECTRONICS LIMITED

Designers and manufactures of equipment for people with disabilities.

23 F2 London Independent Living Company
11 Hale Lane, Mill Hill, T 020 8931 6000
www.independent-living.co.uk

Sales / Hire / Repair: Wheelchairs, Walkers, Mobility Scooters, Electric Rise Recline Chairs, Bathroom & Toilet Aids, Home Nursing Equipment, Wide Fitting Footwear, Incontinent Products, Daily Living Aids.

49 F7 Nantwich Ableworld
39 Beam St, T 01270 626971
www.ableworld.co.uk

18 A2 Neath L T C Mobility (Skewen)
Dynevor Place, Skewen
T 017 928 16564

5 J3 Newton Abbot Mobility South West
5-A Milber Trading Estate, T 0800 073 0276
www.mobilitysouthwest.co.uk
Stairlifts, Bathlifts, Gadgets & Aids.

76 A4 Penicuik (Nr) Pentland Mobility
Nine Mile Barn, Midlothian T 01968 679888
www.pentlandmobility.co.uk

PENTLAND MOBILITY LTD

We have over 25 years of experience, suppying the Medical Proffession we know that quality and service are paramount and as such strive to source the best available products at competitive prices. call for a brochure or to arrange a test drive. Incl the all terrain 'Tramper' exclusive to Pentland.

22 C3 Slough Mobility Supplies.com
136 Lower Cippenham Lane, Cippenham Village, T 01628 663132
www.mobility.supplies.com
Lowest Prices with highest service on Stairlifts, Bathlifts, Scooters, Wheechairs, Rise & Reeling Chairs, Adjustable Beds, Walking & Daily Living Aids etc.

40 B3 Stafford Ambucare Mobility & Nursing Equipment
Westgate St, Bellasis Street, T 01785 225900
Suppliers of a wide range of mobility and nursing equipment.

20 B1 Stroud Batricar Independent Mobility
61 Ryelands Rd, Stonehouse, T 0500 974975
www.batricar.co.uk
Suppliers & manufactures of mobility vehicles, walking aids, manual & powered whelchairs & care products

Team Hybrid Ltd
T 01329 830117
www.teamhybrid.co.uk

The Viper Power Cycle: Offering performance and reliability giving you the confidence to travel without fear of breaking down.
The Coyote Hand Cycle: Turn your wheelchair into a hand cycle in 30 seconds. Regain your freedom, get out in fresh air and get a good upper body & cardio vascular workout

29 J5 Tewkesbury Event Mobility Charitable Trust
8 Bayliss Rd, Kemerton
www.eventmobility.org.uk

Event Mobility Charitable Trust

Provision of electric scooters & manual wheelchairs at events throughout the UK. Advance bookings can be made to guarantee a scooter on arrival at an event. Visit our website for a form or send a SAE and a programme & booking form will be sent to you.

19 G5 Weston-super-Mare Avon Independence Ltd
21-23 Meadow St, T 08003285302
www.avonindependence.co.uk
2000 sq. feet shop selling all kinds of Mobility products.

40 A6 Wolverhampton Wolverhampton Mobility
210 Newhampton Rd, T 01902 744824
www.mobilityaid.co.uk
Service and repair to wheelchairs, powerchairs and scooters

Mobility Vehicle Servicing

29 H7 Gloucester Wheel-Ability
32 Herbert St, T 01452 414968
www.wheel-ability.co.uk
Service and repair to wheelchairs, powerchairs and scooters.

Motability Dealers

49 G4 Altrincham Evans Halshaw — FORD
258 Manchester Rd, T 0161 929 0365
www.evanshalshaw.com

21 G7 Andover Approach Andover — VAUXHALL
Newbury Rd, T 01264 324233
www.approach.co.uk

49 J3 Ashton-under-Lyne Evans Halshaw — FORD
Manchester Rd, T 0161 330 0121
www.evanshalshaw.com

90 G2 Ballymena Lindsay Ford Boucher Rd — FORD
Larne Rd, Pennybridge Ind Est, NI, T 028 2566 1727
www.lindsayford.co.uk
Ford Motability specialists, All models available. Ford KA, Fiesta, Fuson, Focus, Focus CMAX, Mondeo and Galaxy all available- some models nil advance.

90 H3 Bangor Lindsay Ford Bangor — FORD
3 Balloo Park, Balloo Industrial Estate, NI, T 028 9147 4700
www.lindsayford.co.uk
Ford Motability specialists, All models available. Ford KA, Fiesta, Fuson, Focus, Focus CMAX, Mondeo and Galaxy all available- some models nil advance.

90 H3 Belfast Lindsay Ford Belfast — FORD
15 Boucher Rd, NI, T 028 9087 8700
www.lindsayford.co.uk
Ford Motability specialists, All models available. Ford KA, Fiesta, Fuson, Focus, Focus CMAX, Mondeo and Galaxy all available- some models nil advance.

90 H3 Belfast Lindsay Ford Belfast — FORD
391-397 Upper Newtonards Road, NI, T 028 9065 4687
www.lindsayford.co.uk
Ford Motability specialists, All models available. Ford KA, Fiesta, Fuson, Focus, Focus CMAX, Mondeo and Galaxy all available- some models nil advance.

14 C7 Bexhill Birchwood Servicing — FORD
Beeching Road, T 08450 543014
www.birchwoodford.co.uk

23 H5 Bromley Bristol Street Bromley — FORD
93 Masons Hill, T 0208 8249 9000
www.bristolstreet.co.uk/bromley
Bristol Street Bromley for all your Motability needs, new Ford cars available with no deposit or advance payment.

24 D1 Chelmsford Mercedes of Chelfsford — MERCEDES
White Hard Lane, Springfield, T 01245 399399
www.mercedes-benzofchelmsford.co.uk

90 F1 Coleraine Lindsay Ford Coleraine — FORD
80-82 Bushmills Rd, NI, T 028 7035 5921
www.lindsayford.co.uk
Ford Motability specialists, All models available. Ford KA, Fiesta, Fuson, Focus, Focus CMAX, Mondeo and Galaxy all available- some models nil advance.

90 G3 Craigavon Lindsay Ford Craigavon — FORD
Highfield Heights, Highfield Road, NI, T 028 3834 2424
www.lindsayford.co.uk
Ford Motability specialists, All models available. Ford KA, Fiesta, Fuson, Focus, Focus CMAX, Mondeo and Galaxy all available- some models nil advance.

75 K2 Dundermline Park Dunfermline — RENAULT
Halbeath Interchange, Unit 3, T 01383 556100
www.parks.uk.com

13 K7 Eastbourne Birchwood Servicing — FORD
Lottbridge Drove, T 08450 543012
www.birchwoodford.co.uk

75 K3 Edinburgh Evans Halshaw — VAUXHALL
Cultins Rd, Off Calder Road, Sighthill
T 0131 453 4411

5 K1 Exeter NHM Ltd — CHEVROLET
10 Turnsham Road, T 01392 490780

Fiat Auto UK Ltd — FIAT
T 0845 606 6619
www.fiat.co.uk

AUTONOMY Mobility program FIAT

Mobility Scheme for Blue Badge Holders, Discounts on new cars. Available through all FIAT dealers for the location of your nearest dealer call our number.

71 H7 Gateshead Jennings Ford — FORD
Eslington Park, Dunston, T 0191 4607464
www.jennings-ford.co.uk

74 D4 Glasgow Henry Brothers — BMW
Kyle St, T 0141 333 0088
www.henrybrosbmw.co.uk

Mobility Dealer Key: Wheelchair accessible public toilet; Home Visits; MOT on site; PIE Maps Available Here

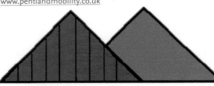

Page ref.	Town/Name	Services
50 C3	**Glossop Evans Halshaw** Brookfield, T 01457 863 311 www.evanshalshaw.com	FORD
42 C2	**Grantham Ilkeston Co-op Motor Group** Tollemache Rd, South, Spittlegate Level, T 01476 567 675 www.ilkestoncoopcars.co.uk	CITROËN

Page ref.	Town/Name	Services
13 J5	**Halland Birchwood Servicing** Eastbourne Road, T 08450 543013 www.birchwoodford.co.uk	FORD
35 F4	**Ipswich Lancaster Ipswich** Ranelagh Road, T 01473 718383 www.lancasterchryslerjeep.co.uk	CHRYSLER JEEP
35 F4	**Ipswich Mercedes Benz of Ipswich** Ranelagh Road, T 01473 232232 www.mercedes-benzofipswich.co.uk	MERCEDES
41 G6	**Leicester Paynes Garage** 1 Walting St, Hinckley, T 01455 237777 www.paynes-garages.co.uk	FORD
24 E3	**Leigh on Sea Lancaster Chrysler Jeep** 15 Stephenson Road 01702 522227 www.lancasterchryslerjeep.co.uk	JEEP
24 E3	**Leigh on Sea Mercedes of Southend** Stephenson Road, T 01702 311311 www.mercedes-benzofsouthend.co.uk	MERCEDES
90 G3	**Lisburn Lindsay Ford Lisburn** 18-20 Market Place, NI, T 028 9267 3121 www.lindsayford.co.uk Ford Motability specialists, All models available. All Ford and Mazda models available under Motability scheme, nil advance payment available on selected models.	FORD
90 G3	**Lisburn Lindsay Mazda Lisburn** 18-20 Market Place, NI, T 028 9260 0200 www.lindsaymazda.co.uk Mazda Motability specialists, All models available. All Ford and Mazda models available under Motability scheme, nil advance payment available on selected models.	MAZDA
23 F4	**London Dees of Wimbledon** 67 Plough Lane, T 020 8946 9000 www.dees.co.uk	FORD

Page ref.	Town/Name	Services
49 H3	**Manchester Evans Halshaw** 660 Chester Way, T 0161 872 2201 www.evanshalshaw.com	FORD
63 F4	**Middlesbrough Evans Halshaw** Cambridge Rd, Cargo Fleet Lane, T 01642 253666 www.evanshalshaw.co.uk	FORD
63 F4	**Middlesbrough Jennings Ford** Cargo Fleet Lane, T 01642 240055 www.jennings-ford.co.uk	FORD
23 F5	**Mitcham Morden Volkswagen** 145 Modern Rd, T 0208 685 5512	VOLKSWAGEN
71 H5	**Morpeth Jennings Ford** Woopies Lane, Choppineton Road, T 01670 519611 www.jennings-ford.co.uk	FORD
18 A2	**Neath Neath Car Sales** Neath Rd, Briton Ferry, T 01639 822445 www.ncsrenault.co.uk	RENAULT

Page ref.	Town/Name	Services
90 G2	**Newton Abbey Lindsay Ford Mallusk** 31 Mallusk Rd, NI, T 028 9083 7700 www.lindsayford.co.uk Ford Motability specialists, All models available. All Ford and Mazda models available under Motability scheme, nil advance payment available on selected models.	FORD
90 G2	**Newton Abbey Lindsay Mazda Mallusk** 31 Mallusk Rd, NI, T 028 9084 7940 www.lindsaymazda.co.uk Mazda Motability specialists, All models available. All Ford and Mazda models available under Motability scheme, nil advance payment available on selected models.	MAZDA
49 F5	**Northwich Evans Halshaw** Chesterway, T 01606 338 888 www.evanshalshaw.com	FORD
49 J2	**Oldham OMC Ford** Manchester Road, Werneth, T 0161 287 4141 www.omcford.co.uk	FORD
49 H1	**Rochdale OMC Ford** Manchester Rd, Castleton, T 01706 654424 www.omcford.co.uk A newly established dealership, that offers a very personal service in the selling and maintaining of Mobility Vehicles.	FORD
10 C1	**Salisbury Approach Andover** Brunel Rd, Churchfields, T 01722 323522 www.approach.co.uk	VAUXHALL
71 J7	**South Shields Jennings Ford** New Castle Rd, Newcastle, T 0191 4276 666 www.jennings-ford.co.uk	FORD
62 E5	**Stockton Jennings Ford** Yarm Rd, T 01642 632200 www.jennings-ford.co.uk	FORD
14 D7	**St. Leonards on Sea Birchwood Servicing** Sedlescombe Road North, T 08450 543015 www.birchwoodford.co.uk	FORD

Page ref.	Town/Name	Services
40 A1	**Stoke-on-Trent Cumbo** Waterloo Rd, Burslem, T 01782 828000 www.cumbo.co.uk A family run business offering friendly and professional service to all our customers.	CHRYSLER
62 D1	**Sunderland Jennings Ford** North Hylton Rd, T 0191 549 1111 www.jennings-ford.co.uk	FORD
62 C1	**Washington Jennings Ford** Parsons Rd, District 2, T 0191 4167700 www.jennings-ford.co.uk	FORD

Rentals (Car)

Page ref.	Town/Name	Services
52 C2	**Scunthorpe Amvale** 298 Queensway, Yorks, T 01724 864 399 www.amvale.com Providers of WAV's, people carrier and minibuses.	

Retail

Page ref.	Town/Name	Services
57 J6	**ASDA** ASDA House, Gt. Wilson, T 0845 300 1111 www.asda.co.uk	

Shopmobility

Shopmobility schemes operate throughout the UK, and are often self-funding by either charitable organisations, local authorities or managed by a local shopping centre.

The schemes aims to promote equality of access and to encourage independence of people with disabilities (permanent or temporary), through the provision of mobility equipment such as scooters, wheelchairs and power chairs.

All schemes shown meet the demanding quality service standards of the National Federation of Shopmobility UK

www.shomobilityuk.org

Shopmobility scheme that meet the criteria set down by the Department of Transport.

1. The scheme should be open to all people with a disability, whether temporary or permanent, regardless of their place of residence.
2. The scheme should have available both manual and powered wheelchairs/scooters.
3. (a) Car parking should be available at no more than 40 metres.
   (b) Car parking should be provided for Blue Badge Holders and non Blue Badge holders who use the scheme.
4. The scheme should operate for a period of at least 4 hours on normal shopping days, excluding Sundays and bank holidays. Individual schemes should publicise their own opening and closing times.

Page ref.	Town/Name	Services
36 E7	**Aberystwyth Ceredigion Mobile Shopmobility** The Portacabin, Bath St Car Park T 01239811150	WC
49 G4	**Altrincham Trafford Access Grp** Trafford Shopmobility & Access Group, 19 Regent Rd T 0161 929 1714	WC
21 G7	**Andover Andover Shopmobility** Bus Station, West Street, T 01264 352000 www.btinternet.com/shopmo.andover	
15 F3	**Ashford Ashford Shopmobility** Vicarage Lane Car Park, Vicarage Lane, T 01233 650063 www.shopmobilityashford.co.uk	WC
49 J3	**Ashton-under-Lyne Ashton-under-Lyne Shopmobility** Old Cross St, T 0161 339 9500	WC
8 B5	**Axminster Axminster Shopmobility** Launch Pad, Leacombe, Lyme Close, T 01297 34684	WC
32 B7	**Aylesbury Aylesbury Shopmobility** Civic Centre Car Park, Exchange St, T 01296 336725 www.aylesburyvaledc.gov.uk	WC
90 G2	**Ballymena Shopmobility Ballymena Ltd** The Tower Centre, Wellington St, T 02825 638 822	WC
31 F4	**Banbury Castle Quay Shopmobility** South Car Park, Castle Quay Shopping Centre T 01295 252722	
90 H3	**Bangor Bangor Shopmobility** The Arcade, 5559 High Street, T 028 91 456586	WC
23 H3	**Barking Barking & Dagenham Shopmobility** 51 Ripple Rd, T 0208 252 5340 www.shopmobility.org.uk	WC
51 F2	**Barnsley Barnsley Shopmobility** Albert St East, T 01226 786006	
6 D2	**Barnstaple North Devon Shopmobility** The Shopmobility Centre, Albert Lane, T 01271 328866 www.northdevontransport.com	
55 F3	**Barrow in Furness Furness Shopmobility** Oldham St Car Park, School Street, T 01229 434039	WC
24 D3	**Basildon Eastgate Shopmobility** Eastgate Business Centre, Southernham, T 01268 533644 www.eastgateshoppingcentre.com	
21 K6	**Basingstoke Basingstoke Shopmobility** Church St, T 01256 476066 www.shopmobilitybasingstoke.org Hire of both powered and manual wheelchairs together with the powered scooters. Manual wheelchairs and highweight scooters. Power chair available for holidays.	WC
20 A5	**Bath Bath Shopmobility** 4 Railway St, T 01225 481744	WC
32 D4	**Bedford Bedford Shopmobility** 1 The Howard Centre, Horne Lane, T 01234 348000	WC
90 H3	**Belfast Belfast Shopmobility** 2 Queen St, T 028 90 808090	WC
40 C7	**Birmingham Birmingham Shopmobility** Snow Hill Railway Station, 7 Colmore Row, T 0121 236 8980 www.birminghamshopmobility.org	WC
55 G6	**Blackpool South Shore Shopmobility** 300 Lytham Rd, South Shore, T 01253 349 427	
12 C7	**Bognor Regis Bognor Regis Shopmobility** Old Fire Station, Town Hall, Belmont St Car Park T 01243 830077	WC
49 G2	**Bolton Bolton Shopmobility** The Archways, Le Mans Crescent, T 01204 392946 www.comco.org	WC
10 C5	**Bournemouth Boscombe Shopmobility** Sovereign Centre, Boscombe, T 01202 399700	WC
57 G6	**Bradford The Oastler Centre** W Yorks, T 01274 754076	WC
18 C4	**Bridgend Bridgend Shopmobility** Lev F Car Park RHIW, Water St, T 0165666792 Monday-Saturday 9am - 5pm	WC
18 C4	**Bridgend Bridgend Shopmobility** Bridgend Borough CC, Rhiw Car Park, Water St T 01656 667 992	
8 B1	**Bridgwater Bridgwater Shopmobility** 52 CLARE St, T 01278 434254	WC
13 G6	**Brighton Brighton & Hove Shopmobility** Grenville St, T 01273 323 239	WC
19 J4	**Bristol Bristol Shopmobility** 26 Castle Gallery, The Galleries, Broadmead T 0117 922 6342	WC
5 K5	**Brixham Brixham Shopmobility** c/o Barclays Bank, Central Car Park, T 01803 521771	WC
40 E3	**Burton upon Trent Burton upon Trent Shopmobility** Unit 35a, Octagon Shopping Centre, Park St T 01283 515 191	WC
49 H1	**Bury Bury Shopmobility** 34 Minden Parade, T 0161 764 9966 www.bshopmobility.freeserve.co.uk	WC
34 C2	**Bury St Edmunds Bury St Edmunds Shopmobility** St Edmundsbury BC, Old Bus Shelter, Angel Hill T 01284 757 175	WC
22 B5	**Camberley Camberley Shopmobility** Ian Goodchild Centre, Knoll Rd, T 01276 707676 www.surreyheath.gov.uk	WC
33 H3	**Cambridge Cambridge Shopmobility** Park St Car Park, T 01223 457 452 www.cambridge.gov.uk/shopmo/shopmo.htm	WC
15 G2	**Canterbury Canterbury Shopmobility** 14 Gravel Walk, T 01227 459889	
18 E4	**Cardiff Cardiff Shopmobility** Oxford Arcade Car Park, Bridge Street, T 029 20 399355	WC
60 F1	**Carlisle Carlisle Shopmobility** L2, Lanes Car Park, Lowther St, T 01228 625950	
90 H2	**Carrickfergus Shopmobility Carrickfergus** 10c High St, T 02893 368415 www.shopmobilitycarrickfergus.com	
24 D5	**Chatham Chatham Shopmobility** Brook MS Car Park, Solomans Rd	WC
24 D1	**Chelmsford Chelmsford Shopmobility** Market Rd Public Convenience, T 01245 250467	WC
24 D1	**Chelmsford Meadows Shopping Centre** 45-47 High St, T 01245 357097 www.meadowsshopmobility.org.uk	WC
29 J6	**Cheltenham Shopmobility Cheltenham** Level 1, Beechwood Shopping Centre, High St, T 01242 255333 www.cheltenham.gov.uk/shopmobility	
51 F5	**Chesterfield Chesterfield Shopmobility** Multi Storey Car Pk, New Beetwell St, T 01246 559331	
48 E1	**Chorley Chorley & South Ribble Shopmobility** Unit 1, Flat Iron Car Park, Clifford St T 01257 260 888	WC
35 F7	**Clacton-on-Sea Clacton & Tendring Shopmobility** 114 Pier Ave, T 01255 435566	WC
34 D6	**Colchester Colchester Shopmobility** 15 Queen St, T 01206 505 256 www.ccvs.org	WC
47 G5	**Colwyn Bay Conwy Community Transport** 44 Sea View Rd, T 01492 533 822	

Page ref.	Town/Name	Services
30 E1	**Coventry** Coventry Shopmobility Barracks Car Park, Upper Precinct, T 024 76 832020	WC, Shopmobility
13 F3	**Crawley** Crawley Shopmobility County Mall, Station Way, Crawley, T 01293 522852	WC
49 G7	**Crewe** Crewe Shopmobility Victoria St Car Park, Adjacent to Asda, T 01270 580031	WC
23 G5	**Croydon** Croydon Shopmobility Whitgift Car Park, Wellesley Rd	WC
19 F2	**Cwmbran** Cwmbran Shopmobility 32 Gwent Square, T 01633 874 686	WC
62 C5	**Darlington** Darlington Association on Disability 20-22 Horsemarket, T 01325 489 999 www.darlingtondisability.org	WC, Shopmobility
31 G2	**Daventry** Daventry Shopmobility New St, T 01327 312555	WC, Shopmobility
41 F2	**Derby** Derby Shopmobility Coach Park, Derby Bus Station, Moreledge T 01332 200320	WC
57 H7	**Dewsbury** Dewsbury Shopmobility Kirklees Met Council, Social Services, T 01924 325070	WC
62 C2	**Durham** Durham Shopmobility Prince Bishop's Shopping Centre, T 0191 386 8556	WC, Shopmobility
13 K7	**Eastbourne** Eastbourne Shopmobility Eastbourne Arndale Centre, Terminus Rd, T 01323 439585	WC
11 F3	**Eastleigh** Eastleigh Shopmobility Unit 2, Swan Centre, Wells Place, T 023 80 902402	WC, Shopmobility
43 J7	**Ely** Ely Shopmobility Ely Museum, The Old Gaol, Market Street T 01353 666655 Open: Thursday, Friday and Saturday 10.30am - 1pm and 2pm - 4pm	WC
23 F5	**Epsom** Epsom & Ewell Shopmobility Ashley Centre Car Park, Ashley Avenue, T 01372 727086	WC
30 B4	**Evesham** Evesham Riverside Shopmobility Multi Storey Car Park, Bridge St, T 01386 49230	WC
7 H6	**Exeter** Exeter Shopmobility Deck F, King William St Car Park, T 01392 494001 www.exetercta.co.uk	WC, Shopmobility
11 G4	**Fareham** Fareham Shopmobility Multi-Storey Car Park, T 01329 282929	WC, Shopmobility
11 G4	**Fareham** Fareham Shopmobility Multi-Storey Car Park, Osborne Road, T 01329 282929	WC
71 H7	**Gateshead** Gateshead Shopmobility Units 1 Gateshead SC, Trinity Sq, T 0191 4779888	WC
71 H7	**Gateshead** Metrocentre Shopmobility T & W, T 0191 460 5299	WC
29 H7	**Gloucester** Gloucester Shopmobility 1 Hampden Way, T 01452 302 871	WC
58 D7	**Goole** Coalition Shopmobility The Courtyard, Boothferry Road, T 01405 837113 www.coalition-goole.demon.co.uk	WC, Shopmobility
11 H5	**Gosport** Gosport Shopmobility Gosport Shopmobility, Bus Stn, South St, T 02392 502692	WC
23 J4	**Grays** Lakeside Shopping Shopmobility West Thurrock Way, T 01708 869933	WC, Shopmobility
23 J4	**Greenhithe** Bluewater Shopmobility Lower Thames Walk, Bluewater Shopping Centre T 01322 427 427	Shopmobility
22 C7	**Guildford** Guildford Shopmobility Level 3, Bedford Rd Car Park, T 01483 453993	WC
57 F7	**Halifax** Calderdale Shopmobility, Halifax Calderdale Shopmobility, 9A - 13 George St T 01422 344040	WC
33 H7	**Harlow** Harlow Shopmobility Post Office Rd, T 01279 419 196 www.harlowcentre.com	WC, Shopmobility
22 E3	**Harrow** Harrow Shopmobility St George's Centre, St Ann's Road, T 0208 427 1200	Shopmobility
63 F3	**Hartlepool** Hartlepool Shopmobility Middleton Grange Shopping Centre, T 01429 861777	WC, Shopmobility
14 D7	**Hastings** Hastings Shopmobility Priory Meadows Shopping Centre, Queens Rd T 01424 447847	WC, Shopmobility
23 F1	**Hatfield** Hatfield Shopmobility The Bill Salmon Centre, 88 Town Centre, T 01707 262 731	WC
11 J4	**Havant** Havant Shopmobility 47 Market Parade, T 02392 455444	WC, Shopmobility
22 D1	**Hemel Hempstead** Hemel Hempstead Shopmobility Blue Car Park, Marlowes Centre, T 01442 259 259	WC, Shopmobility
22 B2	**High Wycombe** High Wycombe Shopmobility Level 2, Newland Car Park, Newland Street, T 01494 472277 www.communigate.co.uk/bucks	Shopmobility
41 G6	**Hinckley** Hinckley Shopmobility L2 Car Pk, Britannia Cente, T 01455 633920	WC
32 E5	**Hitchin** Hitchin Shopmobility Waitrose Supermarket, Bedford Rd, T 01462 423 399	WC
7 H6	**Honiton** Honiton Shopmobility 29-31 New St, T 0140446529	WC
22 E4	**Hounslow** Hounslow Shopmobility Level 3B Treaty Centre Car Park, High St T 020 8570 3343	WC, Shopmobility
50 D1	**Huddersfield** Huddersfield Shopmobility L1 Car Park, Kingsgate Shopping Centre, T 01484 559006	WC
50 D1	**Huddersfield** Huddersfield Shopmobility Gateway to Care, 2 Market St, T 01484 416666	WC, Shopmobility
59 G7	**Hull** Kingston upon Hull Shopmobility Car Park L2, Princes Quay Shopping Centre, T 01482 225686	WC
23 H3	**Ilford** Redbridge Shopmobility Exchange Mall Car Park, High Rd, T 020 8478 6864	WC, Shopmobility
41 G1	**Ilkeston** Ilkeston Shopmobility Shopmobility Centre, High St, T 0115 932 4956 www.erewash.gov.uk/shopmobility	WC, Shopmobility
35 F4	**Ipswich** Ipswich Shopmobility Buttermarket Shopping Centre, St. Stephens Ln T 01473 222 225	WC, Shopmobility
3 J7	**Jersey** St Helier Shopmobility Lower Ground Floor, Sand St Car Park, St Helier T 01534 739 672	
61 G7	**Kendal** Kendal & South Lakes Shopmobility Car Park L3, Westmorland Shopping Centre T 01539 740 933	WC, Shopmobility
32 B1	**Kettering** Kettering Shopmobility Wadcroft Car Park, Off Commercial Road, T 01536412886	WC, Shopmobility
44 A3	**Kings Lynn** West Norfolk Shopmobility Baker Lane Car Park, T 01553 770310	WC
22 E5	**Kingston upon Thames** Kingston upon Thames Shop. Eden Walk Car Park, Union Street, T 020 8547 1255	WC, Shopmobility
30 E2	**Leamington Spa** Leamington Spa Shopmobility Level 4 Royal Priors Car Park, Park St, T 01926 470 450	WC, Shopmobility
22 E6	**Leatherhead** Leatherhead Shopmobility Level 2, Swan Centre, Leret Way, T 01372 362400	WC
29 G5	**Ledbury** Individual Living Mobility Scheme St. Katherines Car Park, T 01531 636001	WC, Shopmobility
57 H7	**Leeds** White Rose Shopmobility White Rose Shopping Centre, Dewsbury Rd T 0113 277 3636	WC, Shopmobility
49 F3	**Leigh** Wigan Wigan Shopmobility Leigh Market Hall, Spinning Gate, T 01942 777 985	WC, Shopmobility
28 D3	**Leominster** Leominster Shopmobility 6 Morris Mews, T 01568 616755	WC, Shopmobility
23 G4	**Lewisham** Lewisham Shopmobility 29 Molesworth St, T 020 8297 2735	WC, Shopmobility
40 D5	**Lichfield** Lichfield Shopmobility Multi Storey Car Park, Castle Dyke, T 01543 308998	WC, Shopmobility
52 C5	**Lincoln** Lincoln Area DialaRide The Bus Station, Melville Street, T 01522 514 477	WC
90 G3	**Lisburn** Lisburn Shopmobility Bow St Mall, Antrim Road, T 028 92 677557	WC
12 D6	**Littlehampton** Littlehampton Shopmobility Bradbury Centre, St Martins Lane, T 01903 733004	WC, Shopmobility
48 C3	**Liverpool** Liverpool Shopmobility St George's Way, St John's Centre, T 0151 7070877	
23 F3	**London** Brent Cross Shopping Centre Brent Cross, Hendon, T 020 8457 4070	WC, Shopmobility
23 F3	**London** Camden Shopmobility 29a Pratt St, Camden, T 020 7482 5503	WC, Shopmobility
23 G3	**London** Waltham Forest Shopmobility Selborne Walk Shopping Centre, Walthamstow T 020 8520 3366	WC
23 F4	**London** Wandsworth Shopmobility 45 Garratt Lane, Wandsworth, T 020 8875 9585 www.wandsworthcommunitytransport.org.uk	WC, Shopmobility
23 G2	**London** Wood Green Shopmobility Wood Green Shopmobility, High Rd, Wood Green T 0208 881 5402	WC, Shopmobility
41 H4	**Loughborough** Loughborough Shopmobility Loughborough Town Hall, Market Place, T 01509 634 706 www.charnwood.gov.uk	Shopmobility
45 K6	**Lowestoft** Lowestoft Shopmobility Lowestoft Station, Denmark Road, T 01502 588 857	WC, Shopmobility
32 D6	**Luton** Luton Shopmobility L3 Market CarPark, Arndale Centre, T 01582738936 Open Monday-Friday 9:00 am- 4:30 pm. Escort service available, booking required, holiday wheelchair loan available.	WC, Shopmobility
32 D6	**Luton** Luton Shopmobility Level 3, Market Car Park, Arndale Centre, T 01582 738 936 www.lutonshopmobility.co.uk	WC, Shopmobility
22 B3	**Maidenhead** Maidenhead Shopmobility Nicholsons Car Park, The Broadway, T 01628 543038 www.shopmobility.org	WC, Shopmobility
14 C2	**Maidstone** Charterwood Mobility Unt19, Newnham Court Village, Bearsted, T 01622 631511	
14 C2	**Maidstone** Maidstone Shopmobility Chequers Centre Management Office, Pads Hill T 01622 678777	WC, Shopmobility
49 H3	**Manchester** Manchester Shopmobility Barbirolli Mall, Lower Arndale Centre, T 0161 839 4060	Shopmobility
49 G3	**Manchester** Manchester Trafford Centre Scootamart, 35 Festival Village, T 0161 747 8046 www.scootamart.com	Shopmobility
42 A7	**Market Harborough** Market Harborough Shopmobility HDC Offices, Adam & Eve Street, T 01858 410864	WC, Shopmobility
22 B3	**Marlow** Marlow Shopmobility Court Garden, Pound Lane, T 01628 405218	WC
18 D1	**Merthyr Tydfil** Merthyr Tydfil Shopmobility St Tydfil Square, T 01685 373237	WC, Shopmobility
62 E4	**Middlesbrough** Middlesbrough Shopmobility 1st Floor Car Park, Hillstreet, T 01642254545 www.middlesbroughshopmobility.co.uk Wheelchair, scooter hire scheme available.	WC, Shopmobility
49 F7	**Nantwich** Nantwich Shopmobility Ableworld, 39 Beam Street, T 01270 626971	WC
18 A2	**Neath** Neath Shopmobility High St Car Park, T 01639637372 Shopmobility services available at the Gnoll Park	WC, Shopmobility
56 D6	**Nelson** Nelson Shopmobility Marsden Resource Centre, Rigby Street, T 01282 692 502	WC
21 H5	**Newbury** Newbury Shopmobility 1 Bolton Place, Northbrook Street, T 01635 523 854 www.volunteerwestberks.org.uk Free scheme open Mon-Sat 9.30-4pm. Wheelchairs, scooters and power chairs.	WC, Shopmobility
71 J7	**Newcastle** South Shields Shopmobility 35 Mile End Rd,, South Shields, T 01914546286 www.southsheildsshopmobility.org.uk Service call available, Opening hours 10pm -4pm Mon-Sat. Long term loan available on manual wheelchairs.	WC, Shopmobility
71 H7	**Newcastle upon Tyne** Newcastle upon Tyne Shop. Eldon Sq Shopping Centre, Eldon Court, Off Percy St T 0191 261 6176	WC, Shopmobility
19 G3	**Newport** Newport Shopmobility 193 Upper Dock St, T 01633 673 845	WC
90 G4	**Newry** Newry Shopmobility Buttercrane Shopping Centre, Buttercrane Quay T 028 3025 6062	WC
5 J3	**Newton Abbot** Newton Abbot Shopmobility Multi Storey Car Park, Sherborne Road, T 01626 335 775	WC
90 H2	**Newtown Abbey** Newtown Abbey Shopmobility Mobility Plus, Ferbro Buildings, Antrim Rd T 028 90 838088	WC
31 J2	**Northampton** Northampton Shopmobility Greyfriars Car Park, Greyfriars, T 01604 233 714	WC, Shopmobility
49 F5	**Northwich** VRDS Northwich Shopmobility The Information Centre, 1 The Arcade, T 01606 353525 www.vrds.org.uk	
45 G5	**Norwich** Norwich Shopmobility 2 Castle Mall, T 01603 766 430	WC, Shopmobility
41 H1	**Nottingham** Arnold Shopmobility Croft Rd Car Park, Arnold, T 0115 966 1331	WC, Shopmobility
41 H2	**Nottingham** Beeston Shopmobility Multi storey Car Pk, Styring St, Beeston T 0115 917 3788	WC, Shopmobility
51 H6	**Nottingham** Mansfield Shopmobility Walkden St Car Park, Mansfield, T 01623 655222	WC
41 H2	**Nottingham** Notts Broad Marsh Shopmobility St Nicholas Centre, Stanford Street, T 0115 915 3888	WC, Shopmobility
41 H2	**Nottingham** West Bridgford Shopmobility Bridgford Rd Car Pk, Bridgford Rd, T 0115 981 5451	WC
41 F6	**Nuneaton** Nuneaton & Bedworth Shopmobility Ropewalk Multi Storey Car Park, Coton Rd T 02476 325 908	
90 F3	**Omagh** Omagh Shopmobility Omagh Volunteer Bureau, Drumragh Ave, T 028 82240772	
90 F2	**Orchard Street** Derry Shopmobility Shopmobility Foyle, Foyleside Shopping Centre T 02871 368623	WC
48 D2	**Ormskirk** West Lancashire Shopmobility Two Saints Place, Park Road, T 01695 570055	WC, Shopmobility
38 B3	**Oswestry** Oswestry Shopmobility Oswestry Community Action, Oswald Rd, T 01691 656882	WC
21 J1	**Oxford** Oxford Shopmobility Westgate Multi-storey Car Park, Norfolk St T 01865 248 737	WC
21 J1	**Oxford** Templars Square Shopping Centre 129 Pound Way, Cowley, T 01865 748867	WC
21 J3	**Oxon** Bicester Shopmobility Crown Walk, Bicester, T 01869 320132 www.cherwelldc.gov.uk/environment	WC, Shopmobility
5 J4	**Paignton** Paignton Shopmobility Victoria Car Park, Garfield Road, T 01803 521 771	WC, Shopmobility
61 G3	**Penrith** Eden Shopmobility The Resource Centre, Sandgate, T 01768 895 438	WC, Shopmobility
42 E6	**Peterborough** Peterborough Shopmobility Level 11, Queensgate Centre Car Park, T 01733 313 133	WC, Shopmobility
42 E6	**Peterborough** Serpentine Green Shopmobility Serpentine Green Shopping Centre, Hampton, T 01733 896 479 www.serpentinegreen.net	WC
4 E5	**Plymouth** Plymouth Shopmobility Mayflower East Car Park, Mayflower St, T 01752 600 633 www.plymshopmobilityct.fsnet.co.uk	WC, Shopmobility
10 B5	**Poole** Poole Shopmobility Multi Storey Car Park, Kingland Cr, T 01202 661 770	WC, Shopmobility
18 A2	**Port Talbot** Port Talbot Shopmobility Unit 43, Aberafan Shopping Centre, T 01639 637372 Shopmobility services available at Afan Forest Park and at Margam Park.	WC, Shopmobility
55 J7	**Preston** The Mobility Centre 28 Friargate, T 01772 204 667	WC, Shopmobility
22 A4	**Reading** Oracle Shopmobility The Oracle Shopping Centre, T 0118 9659008	WC
22 A4	**Reading** Reading Shopmobility Broad St Mall, T 0118 9310000	WC, Shopmobility
63 G4	**Redcar** Redcar Shopmobility 2 Pybus Place, The Esplanade, T 01642 498894	WC, Shopmobility
30 B2	**Redditch** Redditch Shopmobility Car Park 3, Kingfisher Centre, T 01527 69922	WC, Shopmobility
23 F6	**Redhill** Redhill Shopmobility The Belfry Shopping Centre, T 01737 772718	WC, Shopmobility
51 K4	**Retford** Retford/Bassetlaw Shopmobility Chancery Lane Car Park, Retford Nottingham T 01777 705 432	WC, Shopmobility
49 H1	**Rochdale** Rochdale Borough Shopmobility Unit 3, Bus Station Concourse, Smith St, T 01706 865 986 www.rochdaleshopmobility.co.uk	WC
23 J3	**Romford** Havering Shopmobility The Brewery, Waterloo Road, T 01708 722 570	WC, Shopmobility
48 E4	**Runcorn** Halton Lea Shopmobility Halton Disability Services, 102 River Walk T 01928 717445	WC
10 C1	**Salisbury** Salisbury Shopmobility 3B Priory Square, The Maltings, T 01722 3288068	WC, Shopmobility
10 C1	**Salisbury** Salisbury Shopmobility 3B Priory Square, The Maltings, T 01722 328068	WC, Shopmobility
59 G1	**Scarborough** Scarborough Shopmobility 5 Somerset Terrace, T 01723 369910 www.shopmobility.ik.com 10am-4pm Monday to Saturday. Located at the rear of Brunswick Shopping Centre.	WC, Shopmobility
51 F3	**Sheffield** Meadowhall Shopmobility Management Suite, Meadowhall Centre, T 0845 600 6800	WC, Shopmobility
38 D4	**Shrewsbury** Shrewsbury Shopmobility Raven Meadows MS Car Park, T 01743 236900	Shopmobility
48 D2	**Skelmersdale** West Lancashire Shopmobility Concourse Shopping Centre, Southway, Southway T 01695 570055	WC, Shopmobility
22 C4	**Slough** Slough Shopmobility Alpha St North, T 01753 691133 www.home.btconnect.com/outandabout	WC, Shopmobility
30 C1	**Solihull** Solihull Shopmobility 19 Drury Lane, T 0121 711 8701 www.solihull.gov.uk/about/shopmobility	WC
11 F3	**Southampton** Southampton Shopmobility 7 Castle Way, T 023 80 631263 NB: Car park is solely for the use of shopmobility service customers; not just blue badge holders	WC, Shopmobility
11 F3	**Southampton** WestQuay Shopmobility Podium Car Park L2, Harbour Parade, T 023 8063 6100	WC
48 C1	**Southport** Southport Shopmobility Link Tulketh St, T 01704 546 654 www.southportshopmobility.co.uk	WC, Shopmobility

Shopmobility Key | WC Wheelchair accessible public toilet

Page ref.	Town/Name	Services
22 E1	**St Albans St Albans Shopmobility** Drover's Way Car Pk, (off Catherine St), T 01727 819339	WC
48 E3	**St Helens St Helens Shopmobility** Chalon Way Multi Storey Car Park, T 01744 613 388	WC
40 B3	**Stafford Stafford Shopmobility** Broad St, T 01785 619456	WC
22 D4	**Staines Staines Shopmobility** Two Rivers Retail Park, Mustard Mill Rd T 01784 459 416	WC ♿
33 F6	**Stevenage Stevenage Shopmobility** 15 Queensway, T 01438 350300 www.lineone.net/stevenageshopmobility	WC
49 H3	**Stockport Stockport Shopmobility** Level 2, Merseyway Car Park, T 0161 666 1100	♿
62 E5	**Stockton-on-Tees Stockton-on-Tees Shopmobility** 3-5 Bridge Rd, T 01642 605 676 www.stocktonshopmobility.co.uk	WC ♿
40 A1	**Stoke-on-Trent Stoke-on-Trent Shopmobility** Potteries Shopping Centre Car Park, Hanley T 01782 233333	WC ♿
30 D3	**Stratford-upon-Avon Stratford Shopmobility** Sheep St Rear Access, T 01789 414534 www.stratford-dc.gov.uk	♿
62 D1	**Sunderland Sunderland Shopmobility** The Bridges Shopping Centre, Upp Market Sq T 0191 514 3337	WC
23 F5	**Sutton Sutton Shopmobility** 3rd Floor, St Nicholas Centre, St Nicholas Way T 020 87700691	♿
40 D6	**Sutton Coldfield Sutton Coldfield Shopmobility** Gracechurch Shopping Centre, 210A Parade, T 0121 355 1112 www.themall.co.uk/gracechruch	WC ♿
40 E4	**Swadlincote South Derbyshire Shopmobility** 10 West St, T 01283 210 770	WC ♿
17 K6	**Swansea Swansea Shopmobility** Unit 12, St David's Shopping Centre, T 01792 461 785	WC ♿
20 E3	**Swindon Swindon Shopmobility** Wyvern Multi-storey Car Park, Islington St T 01793 512621	WC ♿
8 B2	**Taunton Taunton Shopmobility** Old Market Shoppers Car Park, Paul St, T 01823 327900	WC ♿
5 K3	**Teignmouth Teignmouth Shopmobility** Quay Office, Quay Rd Car Park, T 01626 777775 www.teignmouth-devon.com	WC ♿
29 J5	**Tewkesbury Event Mobility** 8 Bayliss Rd, Kemerton, T 01368 725 391 www.eventmobility.org.uk Event Mobility loans electric scooters and manual wheelchairs at events countrywide. For a programme and advance booking form send a S.A.E. to Event Mobility, 8 Bayliss Rd, Kemerton, Tewkesbury, Glos GL20 7JH or view www.eventmobility.org.uk	
7 H4	**Tiverton Mid Devon Shopmobility** Phoenix Lane Multi Storey Car Park, T 01884 242099 www.tdcta.org.uk	WC ♿
5 K4	**Torquay Torquay Shopmobility** 1 Lymington Rd, T 01803 380982	WC ♿
13 J3	**Tunbridge Wells Tunbridge Wells Shopmobility** 125A Royal Victoria Place, T 01892 544355	♿
18 D1	**Tydfil Shopmobility Merthyr Tydfil** St. Tydfil Square, T 01685 373237	WC ♿
22 D3	**Uxbridge Hillingdon Shopmobility (Uxbridge)** Car Park L2, Chimes Shopping Centre, High St, T 01895 271510	
57 J7	**Wakefield Wakefield Shopmobility** Ridings Shopping Centre, T 01924 787788	WC ♿
40 C6	**Walsall Walsall Shop Mobility** 71 Hillary St, T 01922 860653	
9 J6	**Wareham LifeWheels Mobility Centre** St Johns Hill, T 01929 552 623 www.wddt.org.uk	WC
20 B7	**Warminster Warminster Shopmobility** CAB Building, Central Car Park, T 01985 217 438 www.communigate.co.uk/wilts/wsm	WC ♿
49 F3	**Warrington Birchwood Shopmobility** Birchwood Shopping Centre, Dewhurst Rd, T 01925 822 411	
48 E4	**Warrington Shopmobility Warrington** C.I.L, Beaufort Street, T 01925 231941 www.disabilitypartnership.org.uk	WC ♿
32 B2	**Wellingborough Wellingborough Shopmobility** 1 Orient Way, T 01933 228844	WC
40 C6	**West Bromwich Sandwell Shopmobility** Grd Flr Multi Storey Car Pk, Sandwell SC T 0121 553 1943	WC ♿
48 E2	**Wigan Wigan Shopmobility** Mesnes Terrace Car Park, Mesnes Terrace, T 01942 776070	WC ♿
11 F2	**Winchester Winchester Shopmobility** Upper Parking, The Brooks Shopping Centre T 01962 842 626	WC
22 C4	**Windsor Windsor Shopmobility** Peascod Place, off Bachelors Acre, T 01753 622 330	WC ♿
49 F6	**Winsford VRDS Winsford Shopmobility** The Dingle Centre, High Street, T 01606 557550 www.vrds.org.uk	
48 C4	**Wirral Birkenhead Shopmobility** Cavenoish Entreprise Centre, Brassey St T 0151 647 6162	WC ♿
48 C3	**Wirral Liscard Shopmobility** Liscard Crescent, Wallasey, T 0151606 4665	WC ♿
22 D6	**Woking Woking Shopmobility** Level 1 The Peacocks Centre, Victoria Way T 01483 776 612	WC ♿
22 B5	**Wokingham Wokingham Town Mobility** Volunteer Centre, Old Social Club, Elms Rd T 0118 9770332	
40 B6	**Wolverhampton Wolverhampton Shopmobility** 12 Cleveland St, T 01902 556021 www.wolverhampton.gov.uk	WC ♿
29 H3	**Worcester Worcester Shopmobility** Friary Walk, Crowngate Cen, T 01905 610523	WC ♿
51 H5	**Worksop Bassetlaw Shopmobility** Priory Centre, Bridge Place, T 01909 479070	WC ♿
12 E6	**Worthing Worthing Shopmobility** Worthing Shopmobility, Liverpool Gardens T 01903 820980	WC ♿
48 C7	**Wrexham Wrexham Shopmobility** Wrexham Bus Station, King Street, T 01978 312 390	WC ♿
49 H4	**Wythenshawe Wythenshawe Shopmobility** The Forum Centre, Poundswick Lane, T 0161 490 2103	
58 C4	**York Shopmobility York** L2, Piccadilly Car Pk, Coppergate Centre, T 01904 679 222 www.shopmobilityyork.org.uk	WC

Tolls

19 J3 Aust Severn Bridge & Second Severn Crossing (M4/M48: North of Bristol)
Severn River Crossing Plc, Bridge Access Rd, T 01454 635000
www.severnbridge.co.uk
Exemption for Blue Badge holders. You should show your badge at the toll booth to qualify for the exemption.

40 C6 Birmingham M6 Motorway (Birmingham Toll)
T 0870 850 6262
www.m6toll.co.uk
The Mobility Exemption Pass is for the sole use on the M6 Toll and Allows free passage of the nominated vehicle only. If you think you may be eligible for a Mobility Exemption Pass, you must apply to Midland Express Limited as no other evidence of disability (e.g. a Blue Badge) can be accepted. Organisations, recognised by the Secretary of State for Transport, which operate a vehicle for the carriage of disabled people can also use the motorway free of charge by applying in advance for a Mobility Exemption Pass.

19 J4 Bristol Clifton Suspension Bridge (B3124: West of Bristol)
Bridge Master, Clifton Suspension Bridge, Leigh Woods, T 0117 973 2122
www.clifton-suspension-bridge.org.uk
If you receive the higher rate mobility component of the Disability Living Allowance you can get an annual ticket (priced £1.00)

23 J4 Dartford Dartford Tunnel & Dartford Bridge (River Thames)
T 01322 221603
www.feta.gov.uk
If you are exempt from the payment of Vehicle Excise Duty (road tax), you can get an exemption. Regular users making a minimum of 4 journeys per week can get an exemption card.

81 K8 Dundee Tay Road Bridge (Newport-on-Tay - Dundee)
Exemption for Blue Badge holders. You should show your badge at the toll booth.

59 G7 Hessle Humber Bridge (Near Hull)
The Humber Bridge Board, Ferriby Rd, T 01482 647161
www.humberbridge.co.uk
Exemption for those who receive the higher rate of the mobility component of the Disability Living Allowance and who are exempt from the payment of Vehicle Excise Duty (road tax). Exemption vouchers are issued to the disabled person for use when crossing the bridge in their tax-exempt vehicle. Full details, including an application form are available can be found on the website.

71 H7 Howdon Tyne Tunnel (Near Newcastle)
Tyne Tunnel, T 0191 262 4451
www.twpta.gov.uk
Exemption for those exempt from the payment of Vehicle Excise Duty (road tax).

48 C3 Liverpool Mersey Tunnel (Liverpool - Birkenhead)
Mersey Tunnels, Georges Dock Building, Pier Head, T 0151 236 8602
www.merseytravel.gov.uk/information_tunnel_concessionary-travel.html
Concessions are available to individuals who are in receipt of the highest rate of Disability Living Allowance, or, if too old, the highest rate of Care Allowance. Full eligibility criteria and conditions of use are available can be found on the website. A 'Fast Tag' which can be shown at toll booths must be obtained in advance.

21 K4 Pangbourne Whitchurch Bridge (B471: Pangbourne - Whitchurch)
The Whitchurch Bridge Company, The Toll House, Whitchurch Bridge
www.whitchurchonthames.com/bridge.html
Exemption for Blue Badge holders.

4 E5 Plymouth Tamar Bridge (A38) & Torpoint Ferry (A374)

11 F3 Southampton Itchen Bridge (A3025: Woolston - Southampton)
Itchen Bridge, Woolston, T 023 8043 1040
Concessions available for invalid carriages or those exempt from the payment of Vehicle Excise Duty (road tax).

4 E5 Torpoint Tamarbridge
Torpoint Ferry Office, 2 Ferry Street, T 01752 812233
www.tamarbridge.org.uk
Free vouchers are available for individuals who: receive the higher rate of the mobility component of the Disability Living Allowance; receive War Pensioners Mobility Supplement; are exempt from the payment of Vehicle Excise Duty (road tax); and are registered blind. Please note that: An advance application for free vouchers must be made.

28 B4 Whitney-on-Wye Whitney-on-Wye Bridge (B4350: Whitney - Hay-on-Wye)
Blue Badge holders can cross at half price.

Travel Planning and Leisure

76 E3 Dunbar John Muir's Birth Place.
126 High Street, E Lothian, T 01368 865 899
www.jmbt.org.uk
Discover a Scottish hero and father of the conservation movement through our interactive exhibitions - Diary Extract, Poetic Writings, Touch Screen Computer & Yosemite film

National Disability Arts Forum
59 Lime St, T 0191 261 1628
www.artsaccessuk.org

ArtsAccessUK

Your online reference point for access information on the whole of the UK arts and culture sector.

National Rail
T 08457 48 49 50
www.nationalrail.co.uk
For train times, prices and to book assistance.

Transport Direct
www.transportdirect.info

Connecting People to Places

Britain's new free online journey planner covering travel by car and public transport, including accessibility information.

Used Wheelchair Accessible Vehicle Sales

Grimsby Amvale Limited
Estate Rd No.7, South Humberside Ind Est, T 01472 355700
www.amvale.com
Providers of wav's, people carrier and minibuses.

Wheelyboat Trust

12 C4 Petworth The Wheelyboat Trust
North Lodge, Burton Park, West Sussex, T 01798 342222
www.wheelyboats.org

Wheelchair accessible Wheelyboats provide disabled people with independent and hassle-free access to fishing, nature watching and pleasure boating at venues all over the UK. Great for families and friends too, standard Wheelyboats accommodate four people while the 20' stretch version can accommodate up to ten. For more information about a particular Wheelyboat venue, visit www.wheelyboats.org or telephone 01798 342222.

Useful Contacts

Blue Badge Network
Tel/Fax: 01384 257001
www.bluebadgenetwork.org.uk

Disability Rights Commission (DRC)
Tel: 08457 622633 Minicom: 08457 622644
www.drc.org.uk

Disabled Drivers' Association/ Disabled Drivers' Motor Club
Tel: 0870 770 3333 or 01832 734 724
www.dda.org.uk & www.ddmc.org.uk

Disabled Persons Transport Advisory Committee (DPTAC)
Tel: 020 7944 8011 Minicom: 020 7944 3277
www.dptac.gov.uk

Holiday Care/Tourism for All Holidays Ltd
Tel: 0845 124 9971 Minicom: 0845 124 9976
www.holidaycare.org.uk

Mobility and Inclusion Unit
The Department for Transport
Tel: 020 7944 6550 Minicom: 020 7944 3277
www.dft.gov.uk

National Parking Adjudication Service
Tel: 0161 242 5252
www.parking-appeals.gov.uk

Northern Ireland Department for Regional Development
Tel: 028 6634 3700 Minicom: 028 6634 3749
www.roadsni.gov.uk/BlueBadge/bbadge.htm

Scottish Executive Blue Badge Policy Section
Tel: 0131 244 0869

Shopmobility Key — WC Wheelchair accessible public toilet

Index to place names in Britain

In this index place names are followed by a page number and a grid reference. The place can be found by searching that grid square. Where more than one place has the same name, each can be distinguished by the abbreviated county or unitary authority name shown after the place name. A list of abbreviations used for these names is shown to the right.

Aber.	Aberdeenshire
Arg. & B.	Argyll & Bute
B'burn.	Blackburn with Darwen
B'pool	Blackpool
B. & H.	Brighton & Hove
B. & N.E.Som.	Bath & North East Somerset
B.Gwent	Blaenau Gwent
Beds.	Bedfordshire
Bourne.	Bournemouth
Brack.F.	Bracknell Forest
Bucks.	Buckinghamshire
Caerp.	Caerphilly
Cambs.	Cambridgeshire
Carmar.	Carmarthenshire
Cere.	Ceredigion
Chan.I.	Channel Islands
Ches.	Cheshire
Cornw.	Cornwall
Cumb.	Cumbria
D. & G.	Dumfries & Galloway
Darl.	Darlington
Denb.	Denbighshire
Derbys.	Derbyshire
Dur.	Durham
E.Ayr.	East Ayrshire
E.Dun.	East Dunbartonshire
E.Loth.	East Lothian
E.Renf.	East Renfrewshire
E.Riding	East Riding of Yorkshire
E.Suss.	East Sussex
Edin.	Edinburgh
Falk.	Falkirk
Flints.	Flintshire
Glas.	Glasgow
Glos.	Gloucestershire
Gt.Lon.	Greater London
Gt.Man.	Greater Manchester
Gwyn.	Gwynedd
Hants.	Hampshire
Hart.	Hartlepool
Here.	Herefordshire
Herts.	Hertfordshire
High.	Highland
Hull	Kingston upon Hull
I.o.A.	Isle of Anglesey
I.o.M.	Isle of Man
I.o.S.	Isles of Scilly
I.o.W.	Isle of Wight
Inclyde	Inverclyde
Lancs.	Lancashire
Leic.	Leicester
Leics.	Leicestershire
Lincs.	Lincolnshire
M.K.	Milton Keynes
M.Tyd.	Merthyr Tydfil
Med.	Medway
Mersey.	Merseyside
Middbro.	Middlesbrough
Midloth.	Midlothian
Mon.	Monmouthshire
N.Ayr.	North Ayrshire
N.E.Lincs.	North East Lincolnshire
N.Lan.	North Lanarkshire
N.Lincs.	North Lincolnshire
N.P.T.	Neath Port Talbot
N.Som.	North Somerset
N.Yorks.	North Yorkshire
Norf.	Norfolk
Northants.	Northamptonshire
Northumb.	Northumberland
Nott.	Nottingham
Notts.	Nottinghamshire
Ork.	Orkney
Oxon.	Oxfordshire
P. & K.	Perth & Kinross
Pembs.	Pembrokeshire
Peter.	Peterborough
Plym.	Plymouth
Ports.	Portsmouth
R. & C.	Redcar & Cleveland
R.C.T.	Rhondda Cynon Taff
Read.	Reading
Renf.	Renfrewshire
Rut.	Rutland
S'end	Southend
S'ham.	Southampton
S.Ayr.	South Ayrshire
S.Glos.	South Gloucestershire
S.Lan.	South Lanarkshire
S.Yorks.	South Yorkshire
Sc.Bord.	Scottish Borders
Shet.	Shetland
Shrop.	Shropshire
Slo.	Slough
Som.	Somerset
Staffs.	Staffordshire
Stir.	Stirling
Stock.	Stockton-on-Tees
Stoke	Stoke-on-Trent
Suff.	Suffolk
Surr.	Surrey
Swan.	Swansea
Swin.	Swindon
T. & W.	Tyne & Wear
Tel. & W.	Telford & Wrekin
Thur.	Thurrock
V. of Glam.	Vale of Glamorgan
W'ham	Wokingham
W. & M.	Windsor & Maidenhead
W.Berks.	West Berkshire
W.Dun.	West Dunbartonshire
W.Isles	Western Isles (Na h-Eileanan an Iar)
W.Loth.	West Lothian
W.Mid.	West Midlands
W.Suss.	West Sussex
W.Yorks.	West Yorkshire
Warks.	Warwickshire
Warr.	Warrington
Wilts.	Wiltshire
Worcs.	Worcestershire
Wrex.	Wrexham

▼ A

▼ B

▼D

Dudleston Heath 38 C2
Dudley T. & W. 71 H6
Dudley W.Mid. 40 B6
Dudley Port 40 B6
Dudlow's Green 49 F4
Dudsbury 10 B5
Duffield 41 F1
Duffryn 18 B2
Dufftown 84 H7
Duffus 84 F4
Dufton 61 H4
Duggleby 58 E3
Duiar 84 F7
Duinish 80 B4
Duirinish 82 H7
Duisky 79 M3
Duke End 40 E7
Dukestown 28 A7
Dukinfield 49 J3
Dulas 46 C4
Dulcote 19 J7
Dulford 7 J5
Dull 80 D6
Dullatur 75 F3
Dullingham 33 K3
Dullingham Ley 33 K3
Dulnain Bridge 84 D8
Duloe Beds. 32 E2
Duloe Cornw. 4 C5
Dulsie 84 D6
Dulverton 7 H3
Dulwich 23 G4
Dumbarton 74 B3
Dumbleton 30 B5
Dumcrieff 69 G3
Dumfin 74 B2
Dumfries 65 K3
Dumgoyne 74 D2
Dummer 21 J7
Dunalastair 80 C5
Dunan Arg. & B. 73 K3
Dunan High. 82 F8
Dunans 73 J1
Dunball 19 G7
Dunbar 76 E3
Dunbeath 87 P6
Dunblane 80 C10
Dunbog 80 H9
Dunbridge 10 E2
Duncanston Aber. 85 K8
Duncanston High. 83 R5
Dunchideock 7 G7
Dunchurch 31 F1
Duncote 31 H3
Duncow 68 E5
Duncryne 74 C2
Duncton 12 C5
Dundee 81 K7
Dundee Airport 81 J8
Dundon 8 D1
Dundon Hayes 8 D1
Dundonald 74 B7
Dundonnell 83 L2
Dundraw 60 D2
Dundreggan 83 P9
Dundrennan 65 H6
Dundridge 11 G3
Dundry 19 J5
Dunearn 76 A2
Dunecht 85 M10
Dunfermline 75 J2
Dunfield 20 E2
Dunford Bridge 50 D2
Dungate 14 E2
Dungavel 74 E7
Dungworth 50 E3
Dunham 52 B5
Dunham Town 49 G4
Dunham Woodhouses 49 G4
Dunham-on-the-Hill 48 D5
Dunhampton 29 H2
Dunholme 52 D5
Dunino 81 L9
Dunipace 75 G2
Dunkeld 80 F6
Dunkerton 20 A6
Dunkeswell 7 K5
Dunkeswick 57 J5
Dunkirk Ches. 48 C5
Dunkirk Kent 15 F2
Dunk's Green 23 K6
Dunlappie 81 L4
Dunley Hants. 21 H6
Dunley Worcs. 29 G2
Dunlop 74 C6
Dunloskin 73 K3
Dunmere 4 A4
Dunmore Arg. & B. 73 F4
Dunmore Falk. 75 G2
Dunn Street 24 D5
Dunnabie 69 H5
Dunnet 87 Q2
Dunnichen 81 L6
Dunning 80 F9
Dunnington E.Riding 59 H4
Dunnington Warks. 30 B3
Dunnington York 58 C4
Dunnockshaw 56 D7
Dunoon 73 K3
Dunragit 64 B5
Dunrostan 73 F2
Duns 77 F5
Duns Tew 31 F6
Dunsa 50 E5
Dunsby 42 E3
Dunscore 68 D5
Dunscroft 51 J2
Dunsdale 63 G5
Dunsden Green 22 A4
Dunsfold 12 D3
Dunsford 7 G7
Dunshalt 80 H9
Dunshill 29 H5
Dunsland Cross 6 C5
Dunsley N.Yorks. 63 J5
Dunsley Staffs. 40 A7
Dunsmore 22 B1
Dunsop Bridge 56 B4
Dunstable 32 D6
Dunstall 40 D3
Dunstall Green 34 B2
Dunstan 71 H2
Dunstan Steads 71 H1
Dunster 7 H1
Dunston Lincs. 52 D6
Dunston Norf. 45 G5
Dunston Staffs. 40 B4
Dunston Heath 40 B4
Dunston Hill 71 H7
Dunstone Devon 5 H3
Dunstone Devon 5 F5
Dunsville 51 J2
Dunswell 59 G6
Dunsyre 75 J6
Dunterton 4 D3
Duntisbourne Abbots 20 C1
Duntisbourne Leer 20 C1
Duntisbourne Rouse 20 C1
Duntish 9 F4
Duntocher 74 C3
Dunton Beds. 33 F4
Dunton Bucks. 32 B6
Dunton Norf. 44 C2
Dunton Bassett 41 H6
Dunton Green 23 J6
Dunton Wayletts 24 C2
Dunure 67 G2
Dunure Mains 67 G2
Dunvant 17 J6
Dunvegan 82 C6
Dunwich 35 J1
Durdar 60 F1
Durgan 2 E6
Durgates 13 K3
Durham 62 C2
Durham Tees Valley Airport 62 D5
Durisdeer 68 D3
Durleigh 8 B1
Durley Hants. 11 G3
Durley Wilts. 21 F5
Durley Street 11 G3
Durlow Common 29 F5
Durnamuck 83 L1
Durness 86 G3
Durno 85 M8
Duror 79 L5
Durrants 11 J4
Durrington W.Suss. 12 E6
Durrington Wilts. 20 E7
Dursley 20 A2
Dursley Cross 29 F7
Durston 8 B2
Durweston 9 H4
Duston 31 J2
Duthil 84 D8
Dutlas 28 B1
Duton Hill 33 K6
Dutson 6 B7
Dutton 48 E5
Duxford 33 H4
Dwygyfylchi 47 F5
Dwyran 46 C6
Dyce 85 N9
Dyfatty 17 H5
Dyffryn Bridgend 18 B2
Dyffryn I.o.A. 46 A5
Dyffryn Pembs. 16 C2
Dyffryn V. of Glam. 18 D4
Dyffryn Ardudwy 36 E3
Dyffryn Castell 37 G7
Dyffryn Ceidrych 27 G6
Dyffryn Cellwen 27 H7
Dyke Devon 6 B3
Dyke Lincs. 42 E3
Dyke Moray 84 D5
Dykehead Angus 81 J4
Dykehead N.Lan. 75 G5
Dykehead Stir. 74 D1
Dykends 80 H5
Dylife 37 H6
Dymchurch 15 G5
Dymock 29 G5
Dyrham 20 A4
Dysart 76 B1
Dyserth 47 J5

▼E

Eachwick 71 G6
Eadar dha Fhadhail 88 F4
Eagland Hill 55 H5
Eagle 52 B6
Eagle Barnsdale 52 B6
Eagle Moor 52 B6
Eaglescliffe 62 E5
Eaglesfield Cumb. 60 B4
Eaglesfield D. & G. 69 H6
Eaglesham 74 D5
Eaglethorpe 42 D6
Eagley 49 G1
Eairy 54 B6
Eakley 32 B3
Eakring 51 J6
Ealand 51 K1
Ealing 22 E3
Eamont Bridge 61 G4
Earby 56 E5
Earcroft 56 B7
Eardington 39 G6
Eardisland 28 D3
Eardisley 28 C4
Eardiston Shrop. 38 C3
Eardiston Worcs. 29 F2
Earith 33 G1
Earl Shilton 41 G6
Earl Soham 35 G2
Earl Sterndale 50 C6
Earl Stonham 35 F3
Earle 70 E1
Earlestown 48 E3
Earley 22 A4
Earlham 45 F5
Earlish 82 D4
Earls Barton 32 B2
Earls Colne 34 C6
Earl's Common 29 J3
Earl's Court 23 F4
Earl's Croome 29 H4
Earl's Green 34 E2
Earlsdon 30 E1
Earlsferry 81 K10
Earlsford 85 N7
Earlsheaton 57 H7
Earlston 76 D7
Earlswood Mon. 19 H2
Earlswood Surr. 23 F7
Earlswood Warks. 30 C1
Earnley 12 B7
Earnshaw Bridge 55 J7
Earsairidh 88 B9
Earsdon 71 J6
Earsdon Moor 71 G4
Earsham 45 H7
Earsham Street 35 G1
Earswick 58 C4
Eartham 12 C6
Earthcott Green 19 K3
Easby 63 F6
Easdale Arg. & B. 79 J9
Easdale (island) Arg. & B. 79 J9
Easebourne 12 B4
Easenhall 31 F1
Eashing 22 C7
Easington Bucks. 31 H7
Easington Dur. 62 E2
Easington E.Riding 53 G1
Easington Northumb. 77 K7
Easington Oxon. 21 K2
Easington R. & C. 63 H5
Easington Colliery 62 E2
Easington Lane 62 D2
Easingwold 58 B3
Easole Street 15 H2
Eassie 81 J6
East Aberthaw 18 D5
East Acton 23 F3
East Allington 5 H6
East Anstey 7 G3
East Anton 21 G7
East Appleton 62 C7
East Ardsley 57 J7
East Ashey 11 G6
East Ashling 12 B6
East Ayton 59 F1
East Barkwith 52 E4
East Barming 14 C2
East Barnby 63 J5
East Barnet 23 F2
East Barsham 44 D2
East Beckham 45 F2
East Bedfont 22 D4
East Bergholt 34 E5
East Bierley 57 G7
East Bilney 44 D4
East Blatchington 13 H7
East Boldon 71 J7
East Boldre 10 E4
East Bolton 71 G2
East Bower 8 C1
East Brent 19 G6
East Bridge 35 J2
East Bridgford 41 J1
East Buckland 6 E2
East Budleigh 7 J7
East Burnham 22 C3
East Burra 89 M9
East Burrafirth 89 M7
East Burton 9 H6
East Butsfield 62 B2
East Butterleigh 7 H5
East Butterwick 52 B2
East Calder 75 J4
East Carleton 45 F5
East Carlton Northants. 42 B7
East Carlton W.Yorks. 57 H5
East Chaldon 9 G6
East Challow 21 G3
East Charleton 5 H6
East Chelborough 8 E4
East Chiltington 13 G5
East Chinnock 8 D3
East Chisenbury 20 E6
East Clandon 22 D6
East Claydon 31 J6
East Coker 8 E3
East Compton Dorset 9 H3
East Compton Som. 19 K7
East Coombe 7 G5
East Cornworthy 5 J5
East Cottingwith 58 D5
East Cowes 11 G5
East Cowick 58 C7
East Cowton 62 D6
East Cramlington 71 H6
East Cranmore 19 K7
East Creech 9 J6
East Darlochan 66 A1
East Dean E.Suss. 13 J7
East Dean Hants. 10 D2
East Dean W.Suss. 12 C5
East Dereham 44 D4
East Down 6 D1
East Drayton 51 K5
East Dundry 19 J5
East Ella 59 G7
East End E.Riding 59 H6
East End E.Riding 59 J7
East End Essex 25 G1
East End Hants. 21 H5
East End Hants. 10 E5
East End Herts. 33 H6
East End Kent 14 D4
East End Kent 25 F4
East End M.K. 32 C4
East End N.Som. 19 H4
East End Oxon. 30 E7
East End Poole 9 J5
East End Som. 19 J6
East End Suff. 35 F5
East End Suff. 35 F3
East Farleigh 14 C2
East Farndon 42 A7
East Ferry 52 B3
East Firsby 52 D4
East Fleetham 71 H1
East Fortune 76 D3
East Garston 21 G4
East Ginge 21 H3
East Goscote 41 J4
East Grafton 21 F5
East Green Suff. 35 J2
East Green Suff. 33 K3
East Grimstead 10 D2
East Grinstead 13 G3
East Guldeford 14 E5
East Haddon 31 H2
East Hagbourne 21 J3
East Halton 52 E1
East Ham 23 H3
East Hanney 21 H2
East Hanningfield 24 D1
East Hardwick 51 G1
East Harling 44 D7
East Harlsey 62 E7
East Harnham 10 C2
East Harptree 19 J6
East Hartford 71 H6
East Harting 11 J3
East Hatch 9 J2
East Hatley 33 F3
East Hauxwell 62 B7
East Haven 81 L7
East Heckington 42 E1
East Hedleyhope 62 B2
East Hendred 21 H3
East Herrington 62 D1
East Heslerton 59 F2
East Hewish 19 H5
East Hoathly 13 J5
East Holme 9 H6
East Horndon 24 C3
East Horrington 19 J7
East Horsley 22 D6
East Horton 77 J7
East Howe 10 B5
East Huntspill 19 G7
East Hyde 32 E7
East Ilsley 21 H3
East Keal 53 G6
East Kennett 20 E5
East Keswick 57 J5
East Kilbride 74 E5
East Kimber 6 C6
East Kirkby 53 G6
East Knapton 58 E2
East Knighton 9 H6
East Knowstone 7 G3
East Knoyle 9 H1
East Kyloe 77 J7
East Lambrook 8 D3
East Langdon 15 J3
East Langton 42 A6
East Langwell 87 K9
East Lavant 12 B6
East Lavington 12 C5
East Layton 62 B5
East Leake 41 H3
East Learmouth 77 G7
East Leigh Devon 7 F5
East Leigh Devon 7 F4
East Leigh Devon 5 H5
East Leigh Devon 5 G5
East Lexham 44 C4
East Lilburn 71 F1
East Linton 76 D3
East Liss 11 J2
East Lockinge 21 H3
East Looe 4 C5
East Lound 51 K2
East Lulworth 9 H6
East Lutton 59 F3
East Lydford 8 E1
East Lyn 7 F1
East Lyng 8 C2
East Malling 14 C2
East Malling Heath 23 K6
East Marden 12 B5
East Markham 51 K5
East Martin 10 B3
East Marton 56 E4
East Meon 11 H2
East Mere 7 H4
East Mersea 34 E7
East Molesey 22 E5
East Moor 57 J7
East Morden 9 J5
East Morriston 76 E6
East Morton 57 G5
East Ness 58 C2
East Newton 59 J6
East Norton 42 A5
East Oakley 21 J6
East Ogwell 5 J3
East Orchard 9 H3
East Ord 77 H5
East Panson 6 B6
East Parley 10 C5
East Peckham 23 K7
East Pennard 8 E1
East Portlemouth 5 H7
East Prawle 5 H7
East Preston 12 D6
East Pulham 9 G4
East Putford 6 B4
East Quantoxhead 7 K1
East Rainton 62 D2
East Ravendale 53 F3
East Raynham 44 C3
East Rigton 57 J5
East Rolstone 19 G5
East Rounton 62 E6
East Row 63 J5
East Rudham 44 C3
East Runton 45 G1
East Ruston 45 H3
East Saltoun 76 C4
East Shefford 21 G4
East Sleekburn 71 H5
East Somerton 45 J4
East Stockwith 51 K3
East Stoke Dorset 9 H6
East Stoke Notts. 42 A1
East Stour 9 H2
East Stourmouth 25 J5
East Stratton 21 J7
East Street 8 E1
East Studdal 15 J3
East Suisnish 82 F7
East Taphouse 4 B4
East Thirston 71 G4
East Tilbury 24 C4
East Tisted 11 J1
East Torrington 52 E4
East Town 19 K7
East Tuddenham 44 E4
East Tytherley 10 D2
East Tytherton 20 C4
East Village 7 G5
East Wall 38 E6
East Walton 44 B4
East Wellow 10 E2
East Wemyss 76 B1
East Whitburn 75 H4
East Wickham 23 H4
East Williamston 16 D5
East Winch 44 A4
East Winterslow 10 D1
East Wittering 11 J5
East Witton 57 G1
East Woodburn 70 E5
East Woodhay 21 H5
East Woodlands 20 A7
East Worldham 11 J1
East Worlington 7 F4
East Yell 89 P3
East Youlstone 6 A4
Eastacott 6 E3
Eastbourne 13 K7
Eastbrook 18 E4
Eastburn E.Riding 59 F4
Eastburn W.Yorks. 57 F5
Eastbury Herts. 22 E2
Eastbury W.Berks. 21 G4
Eastby 57 F4
Eastchurch 25 F4
Eastcombe Glos. 20 B1
Eastcombe Som. 7 K2
Eastcote Gt.Lon. 22 E3
Eastcote Northants. 31 H3
Eastcote W.Mid. 30 C1
Eastcott Cornw. 6 A4
Eastcott Wilts. 20 D6
Eastcourt 20 C2
Eastdown 5 J6
Eastend 30 E6
Easter Ardross 84 A3
Easter Balmoral 84 G11
Easter Buckieburn 75 F2
Easter Compton 19 J3
Easter Drummond 83 Q9
Easter Ellister 72 A5
Easter Fearn 84 A2
Easter Howlaws 77 F6
Easter Kinkell 83 R5
Easter Lednathie 81 J4
Easter Poldar 74 E1
Easter Skeld 89 M8
Easter Suddie 84 A5
Eastergate 12 C6
Easterhouse 74 E4
Easterton 20 D6
Eastertown 19 G6
Eastfield Bristol 19 J4
Eastfield N.Lan. 75 G4
Eastfield N.Yorks. 59 G1
Eastfield Hall 71 H3
Eastgate Dur. 61 L3
Eastgate Lincs. 42 E4
Eastgate Norf. 45 F3
Easthall 33 F6
Eastham Mersey. 48 C4
Eastham Worcs. 29 F2
Easthampstead 22 B5
Easthampton 28 D2
Easthaugh 44 E4
Eastheath 22 B5
Easthope 38 E6
Easthorpe Essex 34 D6
Easthorpe Leics. 42 B2
Easthorpe Notts. 51 K7
Easthwaite 60 C6
Eastington Devon 7 F5
Eastington Glos. 30 C7
Eastington Glos. 20 A1
Eastleach Martin 21 F1
Eastleach Turville 21 F1
Eastleigh Devon 6 C3
Eastleigh Hants. 11 F3
Eastling 14 E2
Eastmoor Derbys. 51 F5
Eastmoor Norf. 44 B5
Eastnor 29 G5
Eastoft 52 B1
Eastoke 11 J5
Easton Cambs. 32 E1
Easton Cumb. 69 K6
Easton Cumb. 60 D1
Easton Devon 7 F7
Easton Dorset 9 F7
Easton Hants. 11 G1
Easton I.o.W. 10 E6
Easton Lincs. 42 C3
Easton Norf. 45 F4
Easton Som. 19 J7
Easton Suff. 35 G3
Easton Wilts. 20 B4
Easton Grey 20 B3
Easton Maudit 32 B3
Easton on the Hill 42 D5
Easton Royal 21 F5
Easton-in-Gordano 19 J4
Eastrea 43 F6
Eastriggs 69 H7
Eastrington 58 D6
Eastry 15 J2
East-the-Water 6 C3
Eastville 19 K4
Eastwell 42 A3
Eastwick 33 H7
Eastwood Notts. 41 G1
Eastwood S'end 24 E3
Eastwood S.Yorks. 51 G3
Eastwood W.Yorks. 56 E7
Eastwood End 43 H6
Eathorpe 30 E1
Eaton Ches. 49 H6
Eaton Ches. 48 E6
Eaton Leics. 42 A3
Eaton Norf. 45 G5
Eaton Norf. 44 A2
Eaton Notts. 51 K5
Eaton Oxon. 21 H1
Eaton Shrop. 38 E6
Eaton Shrop. 38 C7
Eaton Bishop 28 D5
Eaton Bray 32 C6
Eaton Constantine 39 F5
Eaton Ford 32 E3
Eaton Hall 48 D6
Eaton Hastings 21 F2
Eaton Socon 32 E3
Eaton upon Tern 39 F3
Eaves Green 40 E7
Ebberston 58 E1
Ebbesborne Wake 9 J2
Ebbw Vale 18 E1
Ebchester 62 B1
Ebdon 19 G5
Ebford 7 H7
Ebley 20 B1
Ebnal 38 D1
Ebrington 30 C4
Ebsworthy Town 6 D6
Ecchinswell 21 H6
Ecclaw 77 F4
Ecclefechan 69 G6
Eccles Gt.Man. 49 G3
Eccles Kent 24 D5
Eccles Sc.Bord. 77 F6
Eccles Green 28 C4
Eccles Road 44 E6
Ecclesfield 51 F3
Ecclesgreig 81 N4
Eccleshall 40 A3
Eccleshill 57 G6
Ecclesmachan 75 J3
Eccles-on-Sea 45 J3
Eccleston Ches. 48 D6
Eccleston Lancs. 48 E1
Eccleston Mersey. 48 D3
Eccup 57 H5
Echt 85 M10
Eckford 70 C1
Eckington Derbys. 51 G5
Eckington Worcs. 29 J4
Ecton Northants. 32 B2
Ecton Staffs. 50 C7
Edale 50 D4
Eday 89 E4
Edburton 13 F5
Edderside 60 C2
Edderton 84 B2
Eddington 21 G5
Eddleston 76 A6
Eden Park 23 G5
Eden Vale 62 E3
Edenbridge 23 H7
Edenfield 49 G1
Edenhall 61 G3
Edenham 42 D3
Edensor 50 E5
Edentaggart 74 B1
Edenthorpe 51 J2
Edern 36 B2
Edgarley 8 E1
Edgbaston 40 C7
Edgcote 31 G4
Edgcott Bucks. 31 H6
Edgcott Som. 7 G2
Edgcumbe 2 E5
Edge Glos. 20 B1
Edge Shrop. 38 C5
Edge End 28 E7
Edge Green Ches. 48 D7
Edge Green Gt.Man. 48 E3
Edge Green Norf. 44 E7
Edgebolton 38 E3
Edgefield 44 E2
Edgehead 76 B4
Edgeley 38 E1
Edgerley 38 C4
Edgerton 50 D1
Edgeworth 20 C1
Edginswell 5 J4
Edgmond 39 G4
Edgmond Marsh 39 G3
Edgton 38 C7
Edgware 23 F2
Edgworth 49 G1
Edinample 80 B8
Edinbane 82 D5
Edinburgh 76 A3
Edinburgh Airport 75 K3
Edinchip 80 A8
Edingale 40 E4
Edingley 51 J7
Edingthorpe 45 H2
Edingthorpe Green 45 H2
Edington Som. 8 C1
Edington Wilts. 20 C6
Edistone 6 A3
Edith Weston 42 C5
Edithmead 19 G7
Edlaston 40 D1
Edlesborough 32 C7
Edlingham 71 G3
Edlington 53 F5
Edmondsham 10 B3
Edmondsley 62 C2
Edmondstown 18 D2
Edmondthorpe 42 B4
Edmonstone 89 E5
Edmonton Cornw. 3 G1
Edmonton Gt.Lon. 23 G2
Edmundbyers 62 A1
Ednam 77 F7
Ednaston 40 E1
Edney Common 24 C1
Edra 80 A9
Edrom 77 G5
Edstaston 38 E2
Edstone 30 C2
Edvin Loach 29 F3
Edwalton 41 H2
Edwardstone 34 D4
Edwardsville 18 D2
Edwinsford 17 K2
Edwinstowe 51 J6
Edworth 33 F4
Edwyn Ralph 29 F3
Edzell 81 M4
Efail Isaf 18 D3
Efail-fâch 18 A2
Efailnewydd 36 C2
Efailwen 16 E3
Efenechtyd 47 K7
Effingham 22 E6
Effirth 89 M7
Efflinch 40 D4
Efford 7 G5
Egbury 21 H6
Egdean 12 C4
Egdon 29 J3
Egerton Gt.Man. 49 G1
Egerton Kent 14 E3
Egerton Forstal 14 D3
Egerton Green 48 E7
Egg Buckland 4 E5
Eggborough 58 B7
Eggerness 64 E6
Eggesford Barton 6 E4
Eggington 32 C6
Egginton 40 E3
Egglescliffe 62 E5
Eggleston 61 L4
Egham 22 D4
Egham Wick 22 C4
Egilsay 89 D5
Egleton 42 B5
Eglingham 71 G2
Eglinton 74 B6
Egloshayle 4 A3
Egloskerry 4 C2
Eglwys Cross 38 D1
Eglwys Fach 37 F6
Eglwys Nunydd 18 A3
Eglwysbach 47 G5
Eglwys-Brewis 18 D5
Eglwyswrw 16 E2
Egmanton 51 K6
Egmere 44 D2
Egremont 60 B5
Egton 63 J6
Egton Bridge 63 J6
Egypt 21 H7
Eigg 78 F2
Eight Ash Green 34 D6
Eilanreach 83 J9
Eildon 76 D7
Eilean Bhearnaraigh 88 E9
Eilean Iarmain 82 G9
Eilean Leodhais 88 J3
Eilean Scalpaigh 88 H8
Eilean Shona 78 H3
Einacleit 88 G5
Eiriosgaigh 88 B7
Eisteddfa Gurig 37 G7
Elan Village 27 J2
Elberton 19 K3
Elborough 19 G6
Elburton 5 F5
Elcho 80 G8
Elcombe 20 E3
Elder Street 33 J5
Eldernell 43 G6
Eldersfield 29 G5
Elderslie 74 C4
Eldon 62 C4
Eldrick 67 G5
Eldroth 56 C3
Eldwick 57 G5
Elemore Vale 62 D2
Elerch 37 F7
Elford Northumb. 77 K7
Elford Staffs. 40 D4
Elford Closes 33 J1
Elgin 84 G4
Elgol 82 F9
Elham 15 G3
Elie 81 K10
Elilaw 70 E3
Elim 46 B4
Eling Hants. 10 E3
Eling W.Berks. 21 J4
Eliock 68 D3
Elishader 82 E4
Elishaw 70 D4
Elkesley 51 J5
Elkington 31 H1
Elkstone 29 J7
Elland 57 G7
Elland Upper Edge 57 G7
Ellary 73 F3
Ellastone 40 D1
Ellbridge 4 E4
Ellel 55 H4
Ellemford 77 F4
Ellenborough 60 B3
Ellenhall 40 A3
Ellen's Green 12 D3
Ellerbeck 62 E7
Ellerby 63 H5
Ellerdine 39 F3
Ellerdine Heath 39 F3
Ellerker 59 F7
Ellerton E.Riding 58 D5
Ellerton N.Yorks. 62 C7
Ellerton Shrop. 39 G3
Ellerton Abbey 62 A7
Ellesborough 22 B1
Ellesmere 38 C2
Ellesmere Park 49 G3
Ellesmere Port 48 D5
Ellingham Hants. 10 C4
Ellingham Norf. 45 H6
Ellingham Northumb. 71 G1
Ellingstring 57 G1
Ellington Cambs. 32 E1
Ellington Northumb. 71 H4
Ellington Thorpe 32 E1
Elliot's Green 20 A7
Ellisfield 21 K7
Ellistown 41 G4
Ellon 85 P7
Ellonby 60 F3
Ellough 45 J7
Ellough Moor 45 J7
Elloughton 59 F7
Ellwood 19 J1
Elm 43 H5
Elm Park 23 J3
Elmbridge 29 J2
Elmdon Essex 33 H5
Elmdon W.Mid. 40 D7
Elmdon Heath 40 D7
Elmers End 23 G5
Elmer's Green 48 D2
Elmesthorpe 41 G6
Elmhurst 40 D4
Elmley Castle 29 J4
Elmley Lovett 29 H2
Elmore 29 G7
Elmore Back 29 G7
Elmscott 6 A3
Elmsett 34 E4
Elmstead Essex 34 E6
Elmstead Gt.Lon. 23 H4
Elmstead Market 34 E6
Elmstone 25 J5
Elmstone Hardwicke 29 J6
Elmswell E.Riding 59 F4
Elmswell Suff. 34 D2
Elmton 51 H5
Elphin 86 E8
Elphinstone 76 B3
Elrick 85 N10
Elrig 64 D6
Elrigbeag 79 N9
Elsdon 70 E4
Elsecar 51 F2
Elsenham 33 J6
Elsfield 31 G7
Elsham 52 D1
Elsing 44 E4
Elslack 56 E5
Elson Hants. 11 H4
Elson Shrop. 38 C2
Elsrickle 75 J6
Elstead 22 C7
Elsted 12 B5
Elsthorpe 42 D3
Elstob 62 D4
Elston Lancs. 55 J6
Elston Notts. 42 A1
Elstone 6 E4
Elstow 32 D4
Elstree 22 E2
Elstronwick 59 J6
Elswick 55 H6
Elsworth 33 G2
Elterwater 60 E6
Eltham 23 H4
Eltisley 33 F3
Elton Cambs. 42 D6
Elton Ches. 48 D5
Elton Derbys. 50 E6
Elton Glos. 29 G7
Elton Gt.Man. 49 G1
Elton Here. 28 D1
Elton Notts. 42 A2
Elton Stock. 62 E5
Elton Green 48 D5
Elvanfoot 68 E2
Elvaston 41 G2
Elveden 34 C1
Elvingston 76 C3
Elvington Kent 15 H2
Elvington York 58 D5
Elwick Hart. 62 E3
Elwick Northumb. 77 K7
Elworth 49 G6
Elworthy 7 J2
Ely Cambs. 33 J1
Ely Cardiff 18 E4
Emberton 32 B4
Embleton Cumb. 60 C3
Embleton Hart. 62 E4
Embleton Northumb. 71 H1
Embo 84 C1
Embo Street 84 C1
Emborough 19 K6
Embsay 57 F4
Emerson Park 23 J3
Emery Down 10 D4
Emley 50 E1
Emmington 22 A1
Emneth 43 H5
Emneth Hungate 43 J5
Empingham 42 C5
Empshott 11 J1
Empshott Green 11 J1
Emsworth 11 J4
Enborne 21 H5
Enborne Row 21 H5
Enchmarsh 38 E6
Enderby 41 H6
Endmoor 55 J1
Endon 49 J7
Endon Bank 49 J7
Enfield 23 G2
Enfield Wash 23 G2
Enford 20 E6
Engine Common 19 K3
Englefield 21 K4
Englefield Green 22 C4
Englesea-brook 49 G7
English Bicknor 28 E7
English Frankton 38 D3
Englishcombe 20 A5
Enham Alamein 21 G7
Enmore 8 B1
Ennerdale Bridge 60 B5
Enniscaven 3 G3
Ennochdhu 80 F4
Ensdon 38 D4
Ensis 6 D3
Enson 40 B3
Enstone 30 E6
Enterkinfoot 68 D3
Enterpen 62 E6
Enton Green 22 C7
Enville 40 A7
Eolaigearraidh 88 B8
Eoropaidh 88 L1
Epney 29 G7
Epperstone 41 J1
Epping 23 H1
Epping Green Essex 23 H1
Epping Green Herts. 23 F1
Epping Upland 23 H1
Eppleby 62 B5
Eppleworth 59 G6
Epsom 23 F5
Epwell 30 E4
Epworth 51 K2
Epworth Turbary 51 K2
Erbistock 38 C1
Erbusaig 82 H8
Erchless Castle 83 Q6
Erdington 40 D6
Eredine 79 L10
Eriboll 86 G4
Ericstane 69 F2
Eridge Green 13 J3
Eriff 67 K3
Erines 73 G3
Erisey Barton 2 E7
Eriskay 88 B7
Eriswell 34 B1
Erith 23 J4
Erlestoke 20 C6
Ermington 5 G5
Ernesettle 4 E4
Erpingham 45 F2
Erringden Grange 56 E7
Errogie 83 R8
Errol 80 H8
Erskine 74 C3
Ervie 66 D7
Erwarton 35 G5
Erwood 27 K4
Eryholme 62 D6
Eryrys 48 B7
Escart 73 G4
Escart Farm 73 G5
Escomb 62 B4
Escrick 58 C5
Esgair 17 G3
Esgairgeiliog 37 G5
Esgyryn 47 G5
Esh 62 B2
Esh Winning 62 B2
Esher 22 E5
Eshott 71 H4
Eshton 56 E4
Eskadale 83 Q7
Eskbank 76 B4
Eskdale Green 60 C6
Eskdalemuir 69 H4
Eskham 53 G3
Esknish 72 B4
Esperley Lane Ends 62 B4
Esprick 55 H6
Essendine 42 D4
Essendon 23 F1
Essich 84 A7
Essington 40 B5
Eston 63 F5
Etal 77 H7
Etchilhampton 20 D5
Etchingham 14 C5
Etchinghill Kent 15 G4
Etchinghill Staffs. 40 C4
Etherdwick Grange 59 J6
Etherley Dene 62 B4
Ethie Mains 81 M6
Eton 22 C4
Eton Wick 22 C4
Etteridge 84 A11
Ettiley Heath 49 G6
Ettington 30 D4
Etton E.Riding 59 F5
Etton Peter. 42 E5
Ettrick 69 H2
Ettrickbridge 69 J1
Ettrickhill 69 H2
Etwall 40 E2
Eudon George 39 F7
Euston 34 C1
Euxton 48 E1
Evanstown 18 C3
Evanton 84 A4
Evedon 42 D1
Evelix 84 B1
Evenjobb 28 B2
Evenley 31 G5
Evenlode 30 D6
Evenwood 62 B4
Evenwood Gate 62 B4
Everbay 89 F5
Evercreech 9 F1
Everdon 31 G3
Everingham 58 E5
Everleigh 21 F6
Everley 59 F1
Eversholt 32 C5
Evershot 8 E4
Eversley 22 A5
Eversley Cross 22 A5
Everthorpe 59 F6
Everton Beds. 33 F3
Everton Hants. 10 D5
Everton Mersey. 48 C3
Everton Notts. 51 J3
Evertown 69 J6
Eves Corner 25 F2
Evesbatch 29 F4
Evesham 30 B4
Evie 89 C5
Evington 41 J5
Ewart Newtown 77 H7
Ewden Village 50 E3
Ewell 23 F5
Ewell Minnis 15 H3
Ewelme 21 K2
Ewen 20 D2
Ewenny 18 C4
Ewerby 42 E1
Ewerby Thorpe 42 E1
Ewhurst E.Suss. 14 C5
Ewhurst Surr. 22 D7
Ewhurst Green 12 D3
Ewloe 48 C6
Ewloe Green 48 B6
Ewood 56 B7
Ewood Bridge 56 C7
Eworthy 6 C6
Ewshot 22 B7
Ewyas Harold 28 C6
Exbourne 6 E5
Exbury 11 F4
Exceat 13 J7
Exebridge 7 H3
Exelby 57 H1
Exeter 7 H6
Exeter Airport 7 H6
Exford 7 G2
Exfords Green 38 D5
Exhall Warks. 30 C3
Exhall Warks. 41 F7
Exlade Street 21 K3
Exminster 7 H7
Exmouth 7 J7
Exnaboe 89 M11
Exning 33 K2
Exton Devon 7 H7
Exton Hants. 11 H2
Exton Rut. 42 C4
Exton Som. 7 H2
Exwick 7 H6
Eyam 50 E5
Eydon 31 G4
Eye Here. 28 D2
Eye Peter. 43 F5
Eye Suff. 35 F1
Eye Green 43 F5
Eyemouth 77 H4
Eyhorne Street 14 D2
Eyke 35 H3
Eynesbury 32 E3
Eynort 82 D8
Eynsford 23 J5
Eynsham 21 H1
Eype 8 D5
Eyre 82 E5
Eythorne 15 H3
Eyton Here. 28 D2
Eyton Shrop. 38 C7
Eyton on Severn 38 E5
Eyton upon the Weald Moors 39 F4
Eywood 28 C3

▼F

Faccombe 21 G6
Faceby 62 E6
Fachwen 46 D6
Facit 49 H1
Faddiley 48 E7
Fadmoor 58 C1
Faebait 83 Q5
Faifley 74 D3
Fail 67 J1
Failand 19 J4
Failford 67 J1
Failsworth 49 H2
Fair Isle 89 K10
Fair Oak Devon 7 J4
Fair Oak Hants. 11 F3
Fair Oak Hants. 21 J5
Fair Oak Green 21 K5
Fairbourne 37 F4
Fairburn 57 K7
Fairfield Derbys. 50 C5
Fairfield Gt.Man. 49 J3
Fairfield Kent 14 E5
Fairfield Mersey. 48 B4
Fairfield Stock. 62 E5
Fairfield Worcs. 29 J1
Fairford 20 E1
Fairgirth 65 J5
Fairhaven 55 G7
Fairhill 75 F5
Fairholm 75 F5
Fairley 85 N10
Fairlie 74 A5
Fairlight 14 D6
Fairmile Devon 7 J6
Fairmile Surr. 22 E5
Fairmilehead 76 A4
Fairnington 70 B1
Fairoak 39 G2
Fairseat 24 C5
Fairstead 34 B7
Fairwarp 13 H4
Fairwater 18 E4
Fairy Cross 6 C3
Fairyhill 17 H6
Fakenham 44 D3
Fala 76 C4
Fala Dam 76 C4
Falahill 76 B5
Faldingworth 52 D4
Falfield 19 K2
Falin-Wnda 17 G1
Falkenham 35 G5
Falkirk 75 G3
Falkland 80 H10
Falla 70 C2
Fallgate 51 F6
Fallin 75 G1
Falmer 13 G6
Falmouth 3 F5
Falsgrave 59 G1
Falstone 70 C5
Fanagmore 86 D5
Fancott 32 D6
Fangdale Beck 63 F7
Fangfoss 58 D4
Fankerton 75 F2
Fanmore 78 F6
Fanner's Green 33 K7
Fans 76 E6
Far Cotton 31 J3
Far Forest 29 G1
Far Gearstones 56 C1
Far Green 20 A1
Far Moor 48 E2
Far Oakridge 20 C1
Far Royds 57 H6
Far Sawrey 60 E7
Farcet 43 F6
Farden 28 E1
Fareham 11 G4
Farewell 40 C4
Farforth 53 G5
Faringdon 21 F2
Farington 55 J7
Farlam 61 G1
Farlary 87 K9
Farleigh N.Som. 19 J5
Farleigh Surr. 23 G5
Farleigh Hungerford 20 B6
Farleigh Wallop 21 K7
Farlesthorpe 53 H5
Farleton Cumb. 55 J1
Farleton Lancs. 55 J3
Farley Derbys. 50 E6
Farley Shrop. 38 C5
Farley Staffs. 40 C1
Farley Wilts. 10 D2
Farley Green Suff. 34 B3
Farley Green Surr. 22 D7
Farley Hill 22 A5
Farleys End 29 G7
Farlington 58 C3
Farlow 39 F7
Farm Town 41 F4
Farmborough 19 K5
Farmcote 30 B6
Farmington 30 C7
Farmoor 21 H1
Farmtown 85 K5
Farnborough Gt.Lon. 23 H5
Farnborough Hants. 22 B6
Farnborough W.Berks. 21 H3
Farnborough Warks. 31 F4
Farnborough Street 22 B6
Farncombe 22 C7
Farndish 32 C2
Farndon Ches. 48 D7
Farndon Notts. 51 K7
Farne Islands 77 K7
Farnell 81 M5
Farnham Dorset 9 J3
Farnham Essex 33 H6
Farnham N.Yorks. 57 J3
Farnham Suff. 35 H3
Farnham Surr. 22 B7
Farnham Common 22 C3
Farnham Green 33 H6
Farnham Royal 22 C3
Farningham 23 J5
Farnley N.Yorks. 57 H5
Farnley W.Yorks. 57 H6
Farnley Tyas 50 D1
Farnsfield 51 J7
Farnworth Gt.Man. 49 G2
Farnworth Halton 48 E4
Farr High. 87 K3
Farr High. 84 A7
Farr High. 84 C10
Farraline 83 R8
Farringdon 7 J6
Farrington Gurney 19 K6
Farsley 57 H6
Farthing Corner 24 E5
Farthing Green 14 D3
Farthinghoe 31 G5
Farthingstone 31 H3
Farthorpe 53 F5
Fartown 50 D1
Farway 7 K6
Fascadale 78 G3
Faslane 74 A2
Fasnakyle 83 P8
Fassfern 79 M3
Fatfield 62 D1
Faugh 61 G1
Fauldhouse 75 H4
Faulkbourne 34 B7
Faulkland 20 A6
Fauls 38 E2
Faulston 10 B2
Faversham 25 G5
Fawdington 57 K2
Fawdon 71 H7
Fawfieldhead 50 C6
Fawkham Green 23 J5
Fawler 30 E7
Fawley Bucks. 22 A3
Fawley Hants. 11 F4
Fawley W.Berks. 21 G3
Fawley Chapel 28 E6
Faxfleet 58 E7
Faxton 31 J1
Faygate 13 F3
Fazakerley 48 C3
Fazeley 40 E5
Fearby 57 G1
Fearnan 80 C6
Fearnbeg 82 H5
Fearnhead 49 F3
Fearnmore 82 H4
Fearnoch Arg. & B. 73 J3
Fearnoch Arg. & B. 73 H2
Featherstone Staffs. 40 B5
Featherstone W.Yorks. 57 K7
Featherstone Castle 70 B7
Feckenham 30 B2
Feering 34 C6
Feetham 61 L7
Feizor 56 C3
Felbridge 13 G3
Felbrigg 45 G2
Felcourt 23 G7
Felden 22 D1
Felhampton 38 D7
Felindre Carmar. 27 G6
Felindre Carmar. 17 J3
Felindre Carmar. 17 G2
Felindre Carmar. 17 K2
Felindre Cere. 26 E3
Felindre Powys 38 A7
Felindre Powys 28 A6
Felindre Swan. 17 K5
Felinfach Cere. 26 E3
Felinfach Powys 27 K5
Felinfoel 17 J5
Felingwmisaf 17 J3
Felingwmuchaf 17 J3
Felixkirk 57 K1
Felixstowe 35 H5
Felixstowe Ferry 35 H5
Felkington 77 H6
Felldownhead 6 B7
Felling 71 H7
Felmersham 32 C3
Felmingham 45 G3
Felpham 12 C7
Felsham 34 D3
Felsted 33 K6
Feltham 22 E4
Felthamhill 22 E4
Felthorpe 45 F4
Felton Here. 28 E4
Felton N.Som. 19 J5
Felton Northumb. 71 G3
Felton Butler 38 C4
Feltwell 44 B6
Fen Ditton 33 H2
Fen Drayton 33 G2
Fen End 30 D1
Fen Street Norf. 44 D6
Fen Street Norf. 34 E1
Fen Street Suff. 34 D1
Fen Street Suff. 35 F2
Fenay Bridge 50 D1
Fence 56 D6
Fence Houses 62 D1
Fencott 31 G7
Fendike Corner 53 H6
Fenham 77 J6
Fenhouses 43 F1
Feniscowles 56 B7
Feniton 7 K6
Fenn Street 24 D4
Fenni-fach 27 K6
Fenny Bentley 50 D7
Fenny Bridges 7 K6
Fenny Compton 31 F3
Fenny Drayton 41 F6
Fenny Stratford 32 B5
Fenrother 71 G4
Fenstanton 33 G2
Fenton Cambs. 33 G1
Fenton Lincs. 52 B5
Fenton Lincs. 52 B7
Fenton Northumb. 77 H7
Fenton Notts. 51 K4
Fenton Stoke 40 A1
Fenton Barns 76 D2
Fenwick E.Ayr. 74 C6
Fenwick Northumb. 71 F6
Fenwick Northumb. 77 J6
Fenwick S.Yorks. 51 H1
Feochaig 66 B2
Feock 3 F5
Feolin 72 D4
Feolin Ferry 72 C4
Feorlan 66 A3
Feorlin 73 H1
Ferguslie Park 74 C4
Feriniquarrie 82 B5
Fern 81 K4
Ferndale 18 C2
Ferndown 10 B4
Ferness 84 D6
Fernham 21 F2
Fernhill Heath 29 H3
Fernhurst 12 B4
Fernilea 82 D7
Fernilee 50 C5
Fernybank 81 L3
Ferrensby 57 J3
Ferrindonald 82 G10
Ferring 12 D6
Ferry Hill 62 C3
Ferrybridge 57 K7
Ferryden 81 N5
Ferryhill 62 C3
Ferryside 17 G4
Fersfield 44 E7
Fersit 79 Q3
Ferwig 16 E1
Feshiebridge 84 C10
Fetcham 22 E6
Fetlar 89 Q3
Fetterangus 85 P5
Fettercairn 81 M3
Feus of Caldhame 81 M4
Fewcott 31 G6
Fewston 57 G4
Ffairfach 17 K3
Ffair-Rhos 27 G2
Ffaldybrenin 17 K1
Ffarmers 17 K1
Ffawyddog 28 B7
Ffestiniog 37 G1
Ffordd-las Denb. 47 K6
Ffordd-las Powys 28 B5
Fforest 17 J5
Fforest-fach 17 K6
Ffostrasol 17 G1
Ffos-y-ffin 26 D2
Ffridd Uchaf 46 D7
Ffrith Denb. 47 J4
Ffrith Flints. 48 B7
Ffrwdgrech 27 K6
Ffynnon 17 G4
Ffynnon Taf 18 E3
Ffynnongroyw 47 K4
Fibhig 88 H3
Fiddington Glos. 29 J5
Fiddington Som. 19 F7
Fiddleford 9 H3
Fiddler's Green Glos. 29 J6
Fiddler's Green Here. 28 E5
Fiddler's Green Norf. 44 C4
Fiddler's Green Norf. 44 E6
Fiddlers Hamlet 23 H1
Field 40 C2
Field Broughton 55 G1
Field Dalling 44 E2
Field Head 41 G5
Fife Keith 85 J5
Fifehead Magdalen 9 G2
Fifehead Neville 9 G3
Fifehead St. Quintin 9 G3
Fifield Oxon. 30 D7
Fifield W. & M. 22 C4
Fifield Bavant 10 B2
Figheldean 20 E7
Filby 45 J4
Filey 59 H1
Filgrave 32 B4
Filham 5 G5
Filkins 21 F1
Filleigh Devon 6 E3
Filleigh Devon 7 F4
Fillingham 52 C4
Fillongley 40 E7
Filmore Hill 11 H2
Filton 19 K4
Fimber 58 E3
Finavon 81 K5
Fincham 44 A5
Finchampstead 22 A5
Finchdean 11 J3
Finchingfield 33 K5
Finchley 23 F2
Findern 41 F2
Findhorn 84 E4
Findochty 85 J4
Findon Aber. 85 P11
Findon W.Suss. 12 E6
Findon Mains 84 A4
Findon Valley 12 E6
Finedon 32 C1
Finegand 80 G4
Fingal Street 35 G1
Fingerpost 29 G1
Fingest 22 A2
Finghall 57 G1
Fingland Cumb. 60 D1
Fingland D. & G. 69 H3
Fingland D. & G. 68 C2
Finglesham 15 J2
Fingringhoe 34 E6
Finkle Street 51 F3
Finlarig 80 A7
Finmere 31 H5
Finnart Arg. & B. 74 A1
Finnart P. & K. 80 A5
Finney Hill 41 G4
Finningham 34 E2
Finningley 51 J3
Finnygaud 85 L5
Finsbury 23 G3
Finstall 29 J1
Finsthwaite 55 G1
Finstock 30 E7
Finstown 89 C6
Fintry Aber. 85 M5
Fintry Stir. 74 E2
Finwood 30 C2
Fionnphort 78 D8
Fir Tree 62 B3
Firbank 61 H7
Firbeck 51 H4
Firby N.Yorks. 57 H1
Firby N.Yorks. 58 D3
Firgrove 49 J1
Firs Lane 49 F2
Firsby 53 H6
Firsdown 10 D1
Firth 89 N5
Fishbourne I.o.W. 11 G5
Fishbourne W.Suss. 12 B6
Fishburn 62 D3
Fishcross 75 H1
Fisherford 85 L7
Fisher's Pond 11 F2
Fisher's Row 55 H5
Fishersgate 13 F6
Fisherstreet 12 C3
Fisherton High. 84 B5
Fisherton S.Ayr. 67 G2
Fisherton de la Mere 9 J1
Fishguard 16 C2
Fishlake 51 J1
Fishleigh Barton 6 D3
Fishley 45 J4
Fishnish 78 H6
Fishpond Bottom 8 C5
Fishponds 19 K4
Fishpool 49 H2
Fishtoft 43 G1
Fishtoft Drove 43 G1
Fishtown of Usan 81 N5
Fishwick Lancs. 55 J6
Fishwick Sc.Bord. 77 H5
Fiskerton Lincs. 52 D5
Fiskerton Notts. 51 K7
Fitling 59 J6
Fittleton 20 E7
Fittleworth 12 D5
Fitton End 43 H4
Fitz 38 D4
Fitzhead 7 K3
Fitzroy 7 K3
Fitzwilliam 51 G1
Fiunary 78 H6
Five Acres 28 E7
Five Ash Down 13 H4
Five Ashes 13 J4
Five Bridges 29 F4
Five Houses 11 F6
Five Lanes 19 H2
Five Oak Green 23 K7
Five Oaks Chan.I. 3 K7
Five Oaks W.Suss. 12 D4
Five Roads 17 H5
Five Turnings 28 B1
Five Wents 14 D2
Fivehead 8 C2
Fivelanes 4 C2
Flack's Green 34 B7
Flackwell Heath 22 B3
Fladbury 29 J4
Fladdabister 89 N9
Flagg 50 D6
Flamborough 59 J2
Flamstead 32 D7
Flamstead End 23 G1
Flansham 12 C6
Flanshaw 57 J7
Flasby 56 E4
Flash 50 C6
Flashader 82 D5
Flask Inn 63 K6
Flaunden 22 D1
Flawborough 42 A1
Flawith 57 K3
Flax Bourton 19 J5
Flax Moss 56 C7
Flaxby 57 J4
Flaxholme 41 F1
Flaxlands 45 F6
Flaxley 29 F7
Flaxpool 7 K2
Flaxton 58 C3
Fleckney 41 J6
Flecknoe 31 G2
Fledborough 52 B5
Fleet Hants. 22 B6
Fleet Hants. 11 J4
Fleet Lincs. 43 G3
Fleet Hargate 43 G3
Fleetville 22 E1
Fleetwood 55 G5
Fleggburgh 45 J4
Flemingston 18 D4
Flemington 74 E5
Flempton 34 C2
Fletchersbridge 4 B4
Fletchertown 60 D2
Fletching 13 H4
Flete 5 G5
Fleur-de-lis 18 E2
Flexbury 6 A5
Flexford 22 C6
Flimby 60 B3
Flimwell 14 C4
Flint 48 B5
Flint Cross 33 H4
Flint Mountain 48 B5
Flintham 42 A1
Flinton 59 J6
Flint's Green 30 D1
Flishinghurst 14 C4
Flitcham 44 B3
Flitholme 61 J5
Flitton 32 D5
Flitwick 32 D5
Flixborough 52 B1
Flixton Gt.Man. 49 G3
Flixton N.Yorks. 59 G2
Flixton Suff. 45 H7
Flockton 50 E1
Flockton Green 50 E1
Flodden 77 H7
Flodigarry 82 E3
Flood's Ferry 43 G6
Flookburgh 55 G2
Flordon 45 F6
Flore 31 H2
Flotta 89 C8
Flotterton 71 F3
Flowton 34 E4
Flushdyke 57 H7
Flushing Cornw. 3 F5
Flushing Cornw. 2 E6
Fluxton 7 J6
Flyford Flavell 29 J3
Foals Green 35 G1
Fobbing 24 D3
Fochabers 84 H5
Fochriw 18 E1
Fockerby 52 B1
Fodderletter 84 F8
Fodderty 83 R5
Foddington 8 E2
Foel 37 J4
Foelgastell 17 J4
Foggathorpe 58 D6
Fogo 77 F6
Fogorig 77 F6
Fogwatt 84 G5
Foindle 86 D5
Folda 80 G4
Fole 40 C2
Foleshill 41 F7
Folke 9 F3
Folkestone 15 H4
Folkingham 42 D2
Folkington 13 J6
Folksworth 42 E7
Folkton 59 G2
Folla Rule 85 M7
Follifoot 57 J4
Folly Dorset 9 G4
Folly Pembs. 16 C3
Folly Gate 6 D6
Fonmon 18 D5
Fonthill Bishop 9 J1
Fonthill Gifford 9 J1
Fontmell Magna 9 H3
Fontmell Parva 9 H3
Fontwell 12 C6
Font-y-gary 18 D5
Foolow 50 D5
Footherley 40 D5
Foots Cray 23 H4
Force Forge 60 E7
Force Green 23 H6
Forcett 62 B5
Forches Cross 7 F5
Ford Arg. & B. 79 K10
Ford Bucks. 22 A1
Ford Devon 6 C3
Ford Devon 5 H6
Ford Devon 5 G6
Ford Glos. 30 B6
Ford Mersey. 48 C3
Ford Midloth. 76 B4
Ford Northumb. 77 H7

▼G

▼H

Haddington E.Loth. 76 D3
Haddington Lincs. 52 C6
Haddiscoe 45 J6
Haddon 42 E6
Hade Edge 50 D2
Hademore 40 D5
Hadfield 50 C3
Hadham Cross 33 H7
Hadham Ford 33 H6
Hadleigh Essex 24 E3
Hadleigh Suff. 34 E4
Hadleigh Heath 34 D4
Hadley Tel. & W. 39 F4
Hadley Worcs. 29 H2
Hadley End 40 D3
Hadley Wood 23 F2
Hadlow 23 K7
Hadlow Down 13 J4
Hadnall 38 E3
Hadspen 9 F1
Hadstock 33 J4
Hadston 71 H4
Hadzor 29 J2
Haffenden Quarter 14 D3
Hafod Bridge 17 K2
Hafod-Dinbych 47 G7
Hafodunos 47 G6
Hafodyrynys 19 F2
Haggate 56 D6
Haggbeck 69 K6
Haggersta 89 M8
Haggerston Gt.Lon. 23 G3
Haggerston Northumb. 77 J6
Haggrister 89 M5
Haggs 75 F3
Hagley Here. 28 E4
Hagley Worcs. 40 B7
Hagnaby Lincs. 53 G6
Hagnaby Lincs. 53 H5
Hague Bar 49 J4
Hagworthingham 53 G6
Haigh 49 F2
Haighton Green 55 J6
Hail Weston 32 E2
Haile 60 B6
Hailes 30 B5
Hailey Herts. 33 G7
Hailey Oxon. 21 K3
Hailey Oxon. 30 E7
Hailsham 13 J6
Hainault 23 H2
Haine 25 K5
Hainford 45 G4
Hainton 52 E4
Haisthorpe 59 H3
Hakin 16 B5
Halam 51 J7
Halbeath 75 K2
Halberton 7 J4
Halcro 87 Q3
Hale Cumb. 55 J2
Hale Gt.Man. 49 G4
Hale Halton 48 D4
Hale Hants. 10 C3
Hale Surr. 22 B7
Hale Bank 48 D4
Hale Barns 49 G4
Hale Nook 55 G5
Hale Street 23 K7
Hales Norf. 45 H6
Hales Staffs. 39 G2
Hales Green 40 D1
Hales Place 15 G2
Halesgate 43 G3
Halesowen 40 B7
Halesworth 35 H1
Halewood 48 D4
Half Way Inn 7 J7
Halford Devon 5 J3
Halford Shrop. 38 D7
Halford Warks. 30 D4
Halfpenny 55 J1
Halfpenny Green 40 A6
Halfway Carmar. 17 K2
Halfway Carmar. 17 J5
Halfway Powys 27 H5
Halfway S.Yorks. 51 G4
Halfway W.Berks. 21 H5
Halfway Bridge 12 C4
Halfway House 38 C4
Halfway Houses Kent 25 F4
Halfway Houses Lincs. 52 B6
Halghton Mill 38 D1
Halifax 57 F7
Halistra 82 C5
Halket 74 C5
Halkirk 87 P4
Halkyn 48 B5
Hall 74 C5
Hall Cross 55 H7
Hall Dunnerdale 60 D7
Hall Green Ches. 49 H7
Hall Green Lancs. 55 H7
Hall Green W.Mid. 40 D7
Hall Grove 33 F7
Hall of the Forest 38 B7
Halland 13 J5
Hallaton 42 A6
Hallatrow 19 K6
Hallbankgate 61 G1
Hallen 19 J3
Hallfield Gate 51 F7
Hallglen 75 G3
Hallin 82 C5
Halling 24 D5
Hallington Lincs. 53 G4
Hallington Northumb. 70 E6
Halliwell 49 F1
Halloughton 51 J7
Hallow 29 H3
Hallow Heath 29 H3
Hallrule 70 A2
Halls 76 E3
Halls Green Essex 23 H1
Hall's Green Herts. 33 F6
Hallsands 5 J7
Hallthwaites 54 E1
Hallwood Green 29 F5
Hallworthy 4 B2
Hallyne 75 K6
Halmer End 39 G1
Halmond's Frome 29 F4
Halmore 19 K1
Halmyre Mains 75 K6
Halnaker 12 C6
Halsall 48 C1
Halse Northants. 31 G4
Halse Som. 7 K3
Halsetown 2 C5
Halsham 59 J7
Halsinger 6 D2
Halstead Essex 34 C5
Halstead Kent 23 H5
Halstead Leics. 42 A5
Halstock 8 E4
Halsway 7 K2
Haltemprice Farm 59 G6
Haltham 53 F6
Haltoft End 43 G1
Halton Bucks. 32 B7
Halton Halton 48 E4
Halton Lancs. 55 J3
Halton Northumb. 70 E7
Halton Wrex. 38 C2
Halton East 57 F4
Halton Gill 56 D2
Halton Green 55 J3
Halton Holegate 53 H6
Halton Lea Gate 61 H1
Halton Park 55 J3
Halton West 56 D4
Haltwhistle 70 C7
Halvergate 45 J5
Halwell 5 H5
Halwill 6 C6
Halwill Junction 6 C6
Ham Devon 8 B4
Ham Glos. 19 K2
Ham Glos. 29 J6
Ham Gt.Lon. 22 E4
Ham High. 87 Q2
Ham Kent 15 J2
Ham Plym. 4 E5
Ham Shet. 89 H9
Ham Som. 8 B2
Ham Som. 8 B3
Ham Wilts. 21 G5
Ham Common 9 H2
Ham Green Here. 29 G4
Ham Green Kent 24 E5
Ham Green Kent 14 D5
Ham Green N.Som. 19 J4
Ham Green Worcs. 30 B2
Ham Hill 24 C5
Ham Street 8 E1
Hambleden 22 A3
Hambledon Hants. 11 H3
Hambledon Surr. 12 C3
Hamble-le-Rice 11 F4
Hambleton Lancs. 55 G5
Hambleton N.Yorks. 58 B6
Hambridge 8 C2
Hambrook S.Glos. 19 K4
Hambrook W.Suss. 11 J4
Hameringham 53 G6
Hamerton 32 E1
Hamilton 75 F5
Hamlet Devon 7 K6
Hamlet Dorset 8 E4
Hammer 12 B3
Hammerpot 12 D6
Hammersmith 23 F4
Hammerwich 40 C5
Hammerwood 13 H3
Hammond Street 23 G1
Hammoon 9 H3
Hamnavoe Shet. 89 M9
Hamnavoe Shet. 89 N4
Hamnavoe Shet. 89 N5
Hamnish Clifford 28 E3
Hamp 8 B1
Hampden Park 13 K6
Hamperden End 33 J5
Hampnett 30 C7
Hampole 51 H2
Hampreston 10 B5
Hampstead 23 F3
Hampstead Norreys 21 J4
Hampsthwaite 57 H4
Hampton Devon 8 B5
Hampton Gt.Lon. 22 E5
Hampton Kent 25 H5
Hampton Peter. 42 E6
Hampton Shrop. 39 G7
Hampton Swin. 20 E2
Hampton Worcs. 30 B4
Hampton Bishop 28 E5
Hampton Fields 20 B2
Hampton Heath 38 D1
Hampton in Arden 40 E7
Hampton Loade 39 G7
Hampton Lovett 29 H2
Hampton Lucy 30 D3
Hampton on the Hill 30 D2
Hampton Poyle 31 G7
Hampton Wick 22 E5
Hamptworth 10 D3
Hamsey 13 H5
Hamstall Ridware 40 D4
Hamstead 10 E5
Hamstead Marshall 21 H5
Hamsteels 62 B2
Hamsterley Dur. 62 B3
Hamsterley Dur. 62 B1
Hamstreet 15 F4
Hamworthy 9 J5
Hanbury Staffs. 40 D3
Hanbury Worcs. 29 J2
Hanbury Woodend 40 D3
Hanby 42 D2
Hanchurch 40 A1
Handa Island 86 D5
Handale 63 H5
Handbridge 48 D6
Handcross 13 F3
Handforth 49 H4
Handley Ches. 48 D7
Handley Derbys. 51 F6
Handley Green 24 C1
Handsacre 40 C4
Handside 33 F7
Handsworth S.Yorks. 51 G4
Handsworth W.Mid. 40 C6
Handwoodbank 38 D4
Handy Cross 22 B2
Hanford Dorset 9 H3
Hanford Stoke 40 A1
Hanging Bridge 40 D1
Hanging Houghton 31 J1
Hanging Langford 10 B1
Hangingshaw 69 G5
Hanham 19 K4
Hankelow 39 F1
Hankerton 20 C2
Hankham 13 K6
Hanley 40 A1
Hanley Castle 29 H4
Hanley Child 29 F2
Hanley Swan 29 H4
Hanley William 29 F2
Hanlith 56 E3
Hanmer 38 D2
Hannah 53 H5
Hannington Hants. 21 J6
Hannington Northants. 32 B1
Hannington Swin. 20 E2
Hannington Wick 20 E2
Hanslope 32 B4
Hanthorpe 42 D3
Hanwell Gt.Lon. 22 E3
Hanwell Oxon. 31 F4
Hanwood 38 D5
Hanworth Gt.Lon. 22 E4
Hanworth Norf. 45 F2
Happisburgh 45 H2
Happisburgh Common 45 H3
Hapsford 48 D5
Hapton Lancs. 56 C6
Hapton Norf. 45 F6
Harberton 5 H5
Harbertonford 5 H5
Harbledown 15 G2
Harborne 40 C7
Harborough Magna 31 F1
Harbost 88 L1
Harbottle 70 E3
Harbourneford 5 H4
Harbridge 10 C3
Harbridge Green 10 C3
Harburn 75 J4
Harbury 30 E3
Harby Leics. 42 A2
Harby Notts. 52 B5
Harcombe 7 K6
Harcombe Bottom 8 C5
Harden W.Mid. 40 C5
Harden W.Yorks. 57 F6
Hardendale 61 G5
Hardenhuish 20 C4
Hardgate Aber. 85 M10
Hardgate N.Yorks. 57 H3
Hardham 12 D5
Hardhorn 55 G6
Hardingham 44 E5
Hardingstone 31 J3
Hardington 20 A6
Hardington Mandeville 8 E3
Hardington Marsh 8 E4
Hardington Moor 8 E3
Hardley 11 F4
Hardley Street 45 H5
Hardmead 32 C4
Hardraw 61 K7
Hardstoft 51 G6
Hardway Hants. 11 H4
Hardway Som. 9 G1
Hardwick Bucks. 32 B7
Hardwick Cambs. 33 G3
Hardwick Lincs. 52 B5
Hardwick Norf. 45 G6
Hardwick Northants. 32 B2
Hardwick Oxon. 21 G1
Hardwick Oxon. 31 G6
Hardwick S.Yorks. 51 G4
Hardwick W.Mid. 40 C6
Hardwick Village 51 J5
Hardwicke Glos. 29 J6
Hardwicke Glos. 29 G7
Hardwicke Here. 28 B4
Hardy's Green 34 D6
Hare Green 34 E6
Hare Hatch 22 B4
Hare Street Herts. 33 G6
Hare Street Herts. 33 G6
Hareby 53 G6
Harecroft 57 F6
Hareden 56 B4
Harefield 22 D2
Harehill 40 D2
Harehills 57 J6
Harehope 71 F1
Harelaw 75 H6
Hareplain 14 D4
Harescough 61 H2
Harescombe 29 H7
Haresfield 29 H7
Hareshaw N.Lan. 75 G4
Hareshaw S.Lan. 74 E6
Harestock 11 F1
Harewood 57 J5
Harewood End 28 E6
Harford Devon 5 G5
Harford Devon 7 G6
Hargate 45 F6
Hargatewall 50 D5
Hargrave Ches. 48 D6
Hargrave Northants. 32 D1
Hargrave Suff. 34 B3
Hargrave Green 34 B3
Harker 69 J7
Harkstead 35 F5
Harlaston 40 E4
Harlaxton 42 B2
Harle Syke 56 D6
Harlech 36 E2
Harlequin 41 J2
Harlescott 38 E4
Harlesden 23 F3
Harleston Devon 5 H6
Harleston Norf. 45 G7
Harleston Suff. 34 E2
Harlestone 31 J2
Harley S.Yorks. 51 F3
Harley Shrop. 38 E5
Harleyholm 75 H7
Harlington Beds. 32 D5
Harlington Gt.Lon. 22 D4
Harlosh 82 C6
Harlow 33 H7
Harlow Hill 71 F7
Harlthorpe 58 D6
Harlton 33 G3
Harlyn 3 F1
Harman's Cross 9 J6
Harmby 57 G1
Harmer Green 33 F7
Harmer Hill 38 D3
Harmondsworth 22 D4
Harmston 52 C6
Harnage 38 E5
Harnham 10 C2
Harnhill 20 D1
Harold Hill 23 J2
Harold Park 23 J2
Harold Wood 23 J2
Haroldston West 16 B4
Haroldswick 89 Q1
Harome 58 C1
Harpenden 32 E7
Harpford 7 J6
Harpham 59 G3
Harpley Norf. 44 B3
Harpley Worcs. 29 F2
Harpole 31 H2
Harprigg 56 B1
Harpsden 22 A3
Harpswell 52 C4
Harpur Hill 50 C5
Harpurhey 49 H2
Harracott 6 D3
Harrietfield 80 E7
Harrietsham 14 D2
Harringay 23 G3
Harrington Cumb. 60 A4
Harrington Lincs. 53 G5
Harrington Northants. 31 J1
Harringworth 42 C6
Harris 82 D11
Harris Green 45 G6
Harriseahead 49 H7
Harriston 60 C2
Harrogate 57 J4
Harrold 32 C3
Harrop Fold 56 C5
Harrow 22 E3
Harrow Green 34 C3
Harrow on the Hill 22 E3
Harrow Weald 22 E2
Harrowbarrow 4 E3
Harrowden 32 D4
Harrowgate Hill 62 C5
Harry Stoke 19 K4
Harston Cambs. 33 H3
Harston Leics. 42 B2
Harswell 58 E5
Hart 62 E3
Hartburn 71 F5
Hartest 34 C3
Hartfield 13 H3
Hartford Cambs. 33 F1
Hartford Ches. 49 F5
Hartford Som. 7 H3
Hartford End 33 K7
Hartfordbridge 22 A6
Hartforth 62 B6
Hartgrove 9 H3
Harthill Ches. 48 E7
Harthill N.Lan. 75 H4
Harthill S.Yorks. 51 G4
Hartington 50 D6
Hartington Hall 71 F5
Hartland 6 A3
Hartland Quay 6 A3
Hartlebury 29 H1
Hartlepool 63 F3
Hartley Cumb. 61 J6
Hartley Kent 24 C5
Hartley Kent 14 C4
Hartley Northumb. 71 J6
Hartley Green 40 B3
Hartley Mauditt 11 J1
Hartley Wespall 21 K6
Hartley Wintney 22 A6
Hartlington 57 F3
Hartlip 24 E5
Hartoft End 63 H7
Harton N.Yorks. 58 D3
Harton Shrop. 38 D7
Harton T. & W. 71 J7
Hartpury 29 H6
Hartrigge 70 B1
Hartshead 57 G7
Hartshill 41 F6
Hartshorne 41 F3
Hartsop 60 F5
Hartwell Bucks. 31 J7
Hartwell E.Suss. 13 H3
Hartwell Northants. 31 J3
Hartwith 57 H3
Hartwood 75 G5
Harvel 24 C5
Harvington Worcs. 30 B4
Harvington Worcs. 29 H1
Harwell Notts. 51 J3
Harwell Oxon. 21 H3
Harwich 35 G5
Harwood Dur. 61 K3
Harwood Gt.Man. 49 G1
Harwood Northumb. 71 F4
Harwood Dale 63 K7
Harwood on Teviot 69 K3
Harworth 51 J3
Hasbury 40 B7
Hascombe 22 D7
Haselbech 31 J1
Haselbury Plucknett 8 D3
Haseley 30 D2
Haseley Knob 30 D1
Haselor 30 C3
Hasfield 29 H6
Hasguard 16 B5
Haskayne 48 C2
Hasketon 35 G3
Hasland 51 F6
Hasland Green 51 F6
Haslemere 12 C3
Haslingden 56 C7
Haslingden Grane 56 C7
Haslingfield 33 H3
Haslington 49 G7
Hassall 49 G7
Hassall Green 49 G7
Hassell Street 15 F3
Hassendean 70 A1
Hassingham 45 H5
Hassocks 13 G5
Hassop 50 E5
Hasthorpe 53 H6
Hastigrow 87 Q3
Hastingleigh 15 F3
Hastings E.Suss. 14 D7
Hastings Som. 8 C3
Hastingwood 23 H1
Hastoe 22 C1
Haswell 62 D2
Haswell Plough 62 D2
Hatch Beds. 32 E4
Hatch Hants. 21 K6
Hatch Beauchamp 8 C2
Hatch End 22 E2
Hatch Green 8 C3
Hatching Green 32 E7
Hatchmere 48 E5
Hatcliffe 53 F2
Hatfield Here. 28 E3
Hatfield Herts. 23 F1
Hatfield S.Yorks. 51 J2
Hatfield Broad Oak 33 J7
Hatfield Heath 33 J7
Hatfield Peverel 34 B7
Hatfield Woodhouse 51 J2
Hatford 21 G2
Hatherden 21 G6
Hatherleigh 6 D5
Hathern 41 G3
Hatherop 20 E1
Hathersage 50 E4
Hathersage Booths 50 E4
Hathershaw 49 J2
Hatherton Ches. 39 F1
Hatherton Staffs. 40 B4
Hatley St. George 33 F3
Hatt 4 D4
Hattingley 11 H1
Hatton Aber. 85 Q7
Hatton Derbys. 40 E3
Hatton Gt.Lon. 22 E4
Hatton Lincs. 52 E5
Hatton Shrop. 38 D6
Hatton Warks. 30 D2
Hatton Warr. 48 E4
Hatton Heath 48 D6
Hatton of Fintray 85 N9
Haugh 53 H5
Haugh Head 71 F1
Haugh of Glass 85 J7
Haugh of Urr 65 J4
Haugham 53 G4
Haughhead 74 E3
Haughley 34 E2
Haughley Green 34 E2
Haughley New Street 34 E2
Haughton Ches. 48 E7
Haughton Notts. 51 J5
Haughton Powys 38 C4
Haughton Shrop. 39 F6
Haughton Shrop. 38 E4
Haughton Shrop. 38 C3
Haughton Staffs. 40 A3
Haughton Green 49 J3
Haughton Le Skerne 62 D5
Haultwick 33 G6
Haunton 40 E4
Hauxton 33 H3
Havannah 49 H6
Havant 11 J4
Haven 28 D3
Havenstreet 11 G5
Havercroft 51 F1
Haverfordwest 16 C4
Haverhill 33 K4
Haverigg 54 E2
Havering Park 23 H2
Havering-atte-Bower 23 J2
Haversham 32 B4
Haverthwaite 55 G1
Haverton Hill 62 E4
Haviker Street 14 C3
Havyat 8 E1
Hawarden 48 C6
Hawbridge 29 J4
Hawbush Green 34 B6
Hawcoat 55 F2
Hawes 56 D1
Hawe's Green 45 G6
Hawick 70 A2
Hawkchurch 8 C4
Hawkedon 34 B3
Hawkenbury Kent 13 J3
Hawkenbury Kent 14 D3
Hawkeridge 20 B6
Hawkerland 7 J7
Hawkes End 40 E7
Hawkesbury 20 A3
Hawkesbury Upton 20 A3
Hawkhill 71 H2
Hawkhurst 14 C4
Hawkinge 15 H3
Hawkley 11 J2
Hawkridge 7 G2
Hawkshead 60 E7
Hawkshead Hill 60 E7
Hawksheads 55 H3
Hawksland 75 G6
Hawkswick 56 E2
Hawksworth Notts. 42 A1
Hawksworth W.Yorks. 57 G5
Hawksworth W.Yorks. 57 H6
Hawkwell Essex 24 E2
Hawkwell Northumb. 71 F6
Hawley Hants. 22 B6
Hawley Kent 23 J4
Hawley's Corner 23 H6
Hawling 30 B6
Hawnby 58 B1
Haworth 57 F6
Hawstead 34 C3
Hawstead Green 34 C3
Hawthorn Dur. 62 E2
Hawthorn Hants. 11 H1
Hawthorn R.C.T. 18 D3
Hawthorn Wilts. 20 B5
Hawthorn Hill Brack.F. 22 B4
Hawthorn Hill Lincs. 53 F7
Hawthorpe 42 D3
Hawton 51 K7
Haxby 58 C4
Haxey 51 K2
Haxted 23 H7
Haxton 20 E7
Hay Green 43 J4
Hay Mills 40 D7
Hay Street 33 G6
Haydock 48 E3
Haydon Dorset 9 F3
Haydon Swin. 20 E3
Haydon Bridge 70 D7
Haydon Wick 20 E3
Hayes Gt.Lon. 22 D3
Hayes Gt.Lon. 23 H5
Hayes End 22 D3
Hayfield Derbys. 50 C4
Hayfield Fife 76 A1
Haygrove 8 B1
Hayhillock 81 L6
Hayle 2 C5
Hayling Island 11 J4
Haymoor Green 49 F7
Hayne 7 H4
Haynes 32 E4
Haynes Church End 32 D4
Haynes West End 32 D4
Hay-on-Wye 28 B4
Hayscastle 16 B3
Hayscastle Cross 16 C3
Hayton Cumb. 61 G1
Hayton Cumb. 60 C2
Hayton E.Riding 58 E5
Hayton Notts. 51 K4
Hayton's Bent 38 E7
Haytor Vale 5 H3
Haytown 6 B4
Haywards Heath 13 G4
Haywood Oaks 51 J7
Hazel End 33 H6
Hazel Grove 49 J4
Hazel Street 13 K3
Hazelbank 75 G6
Hazelbury Bryan 9 G4
Hazeleigh 24 E1
Hazeley 22 A6
Hazelhurst 49 G1
Hazelside 68 D1
Hazelslack 55 H2
Hazelslade 40 C4
Hazelwood Derbys. 41 F1
Hazelwood Gt.Lon. 23 H5
Hazlefield 65 H6
Hazlehead Aberdeen 85 N10
Hazlehead S.Yorks. 50 D2
Hazlemere 22 B2
Hazlerigg 71 H6
Hazleton 30 B7
Heacham 44 A2
Head Bridge 6 E4
Headbourne Worthy 11 F1
Headcorn 14 D3
Headingley 57 H6
Headington 21 J1
Headlam 62 B5
Headless Cross 30 B2
Headley Hants. 12 B3
Headley Hants. 21 J5
Headley Surr. 23 F6
Headley Down 12 B3
Headley Heath 30 B1
Headon 51 K5
Heads Nook 61 F1
Heady Hill 49 H1
Heage 51 F7
Healaugh N.Yorks. 62 A7
Healaugh N.Yorks. 58 B5
Heald Green 49 H4
Heale Devon 6 E1
Heale Som. 8 C2
Healey Lancs. 49 H1
Healey N.Yorks. 57 G1
Healey Northumb. 62 A1
Healey W.Yorks. 57 H7
Healeyfield 62 A2
Healing 53 F1
Heamoor 2 B5
Heaning 60 F7
Heanor 41 G1
Heanton Punchardon 6 D2
Heanton Satchville 6 D4
Heap Bridge 49 H1
Heapey 56 B7
Heapham 52 B4
Hearn 12 B3
Hearthstane 69 G1
Heasley Mill 7 F2
Heast 82 G9
Heath Cardiff 18 E3
Heath Derbys. 51 G6
Heath W.Yorks. 51 F1
Heath and Reach 32 C6
Heath End Derbys. 41 F3
Heath End Hants. 21 J5
Heath End Hants. 21 H5
Heath End Surr. 22 B7
Heath Hayes 40 C4
Heath Hill 39 G4
Heath House 19 H7
Heath Town 40 B6
Heathbrook 39 F3
Heathcote Derbys. 50 D6
Heathcote Shrop. 39 F3
Heathencote 31 J4
Heather 41 F4
Heathfield Devon 5 J3
Heathfield E.Suss. 13 J4
Heathfield N.Yorks. 57 G3
Heathfield Som. 7 K3
Heathrow Airport 22 D4
Heathton 40 A6
Heatley 49 G4
Heaton Lancs. 55 H3
Heaton Staffs. 49 J6
Heaton T. & W. 71 H7
Heaton W.Yorks. 57 G6
Heaton Moor 49 H3
Heaton's Bridge 48 D1
Heaverham 23 J6
Heaviley 49 J4
Heavitree 7 H6
Hebburn 71 J7
Hebden 57 F3
Hebden Bridge 56 E7
Hebden Green 49 F6
Hebing End 33 G6
Hebron Carmar. 16 E3
Hebron Northumb. 71 G5
Heck 69 F5
Heckfield 22 A5
Heckfield Green 35 F1
Heckfordbridge 34 D6
Heckingham 45 H6
Heckington 42 E1
Heckmondwike 57 H7
Heddington 20 C5
Heddon-on-the-Wall 71 G7
Hedenham 45 H6
Hedge End 11 F3
Hedgerley 22 C3
Hedging 8 C2
Hedley on the Hill 62 A1
Hednesford 40 C4
Hedon 59 H7
Hedsor 22 C3
Heeley 51 F4
Heighington Darl. 62 C4
Heighington Lincs. 52 D6
Heightington 29 G1
Heights of Brae 83 R4
Heilam 86 G4
Heisker Islands 88 A2
Heithat 69 G5
Heiton 77 F7
Hele Devon 6 D1
Hele Devon 7 H5
Hele Devon 6 B6
Hele Devon 5 H3
Hele Som. 7 K3
Hele Torbay 5 K4
Hele Bridge 6 D5
Hele Lane 7 F4
Helebridge 6 A5
Helensburgh 74 A2
Helford 2 E6
Helhoughton 44 C3
Helions Bumpstead 33 K4
Hell Corner 21 G5
Hellaby 51 H3
Helland Cornw. 4 A3
Helland Som. 8 C2
Hellandbridge 4 A3
Hellesdon 45 G4
Hellidon 31 G3
Hellifield 56 D4
Hellingly 13 J5
Hellington 45 H5
Helmdon 31 G4
Helmingham 35 F3
Helmington Row 62 B3
Helmsdale 87 N8
Helmshore 56 C7
Helmsley 58 C1
Helperby 57 K3
Helperthorpe 59 F2
Helpringham 42 E1
Helpston 42 E5
Helsby 48 D5
Helsey 53 J5
Helston 2 D6
Helstone 4 A2
Helton 61 G4
Helwith 62 A6
Helwith Bridge 56 D3
Hem 38 B5
Hemborough Post 5 J5
Hemel Hempstead 22 D1
Hemerdon 5 F5
Hemingbrough 58 C6
Hemingby 53 F5
Hemingfield 51 F2
Hemingford Abbots 33 F1
Hemingford Grey 33 F1
Hemingstone 35 F3
Hemington Leics. 41 G3
Hemington Northants. 42 D7
Hemington Som. 20 A6
Hemley 35 G4
Hemlington 62 E5
Hemp Green 35 H2
Hempholme 59 G4
Hempnall 45 G6
Hempnall Green 45 G6
Hempriggs House 87 R5
Hempstead Essex 33 K5
Hempstead Med. 24 D5
Hempstead Norf. 45 J3
Hempstead Norf. 45 F2
Hempsted 29 H7
Hempton Norf. 44 D3
Hempton Oxon. 31 F5
Hemsby 45 J4
Hemswell 52 C3
Hemswell Cliff 52 C4
Hemsworth 51 G1
Hemyock 7 K4
Henbury Bristol 19 J4
Henbury Ches. 49 H5
Henderland 65 J3
Hendersyde Park 77 F7
Hendham 5 H5
Hendon Gt.Lon. 23 F3
Hendon T. & W. 62 D1
Hendraburnick 4 B2
Hendre Bridgend 18 C3
Hendre Gwyn. 36 C2
Hendreforgan 18 C3
Hendy 17 J5
Heneglwys 46 C5
Henfield S.Glos. 19 K4
Henfield W.Suss. 13 F5
Henford 6 B6
Hengherst 14 E4
Hengoed Caerp. 18 E2
Hengoed Powys 28 B3
Hengoed Shrop. 38 B2
Hengrave 34 C2
Henham 33 J6
Heniarth 38 A5
Henlade 8 B2
Henley Dorset 9 F4
Henley Shrop. 28 E1
Henley Som. 8 D1
Henley Som. 8 D4
Henley Suff. 35 F3
Henley W.Suss. 12 B4
Henley Corner 8 D1
Henley Park 22 C6
Henley-in-Arden 30 C2
Henley-on-Thames 22 A3
Henley's Down 14 C6
Henllan Carmar. 17 G1
Henllan Denb. 47 J6
Henllan Amgoed 16 E3
Henllys 19 F2
Henlow 32 E5
Hennock 7 G7
Henny Street 34 C5
Henryd 47 F5
Henry's Moat 16 D3
Hensall 58 B7
Henshaw 70 C7
Hensingham 60 A5
Henstead 45 J7
Hensting 11 F2
Henstridge 9 G3
Henstridge Ash 9 G3
Henstridge Bowden 9 F2
Henstridge Marsh 9 G2
Henton Oxon. 22 A1
Henton Som. 19 H7
Henwood 4 C3
Heogan 89 N8
Heol Senni 27 J6
Heolgerrig 18 D1
Heol-y-Cyw 18 C3
Hepburn 71 F1
Hepburn Bell 71 F1
Hepple 70 E3
Hepscott 71 H5
Hepthorne Lane 51 G6
Heptonstall 56 E7
Hepworth Suff. 34 D1
Hepworth W.Yorks. 50 D2
Hepworth South Common 34 D1
Herbrandston 16 B5
Hereford 28 E4
Heriot 76 B5
Herm 3 J5
Hermiston 75 K3
Hermitage D. & G. 65 H4
Hermitage Dorset 9 F4
Hermitage Sc.Bord. 70 A4
Hermitage W.Berks. 21 J4
Hermitage W.Suss. 11 J4
Hermitage Green 49 F3
Hermon Carmar. 17 G2
Hermon I.o.A. 46 B6
Hermon Pembs. 17 F2
Herne 25 H5
Herne Bay 25 H5
Herne Common 25 H5
Herne Pound 23 K6
Herner 6 D3
Hernhill 25 G5
Herodsfoot 4 C4
Herongate 24 C2
Heron's Ghyll 13 H4
Heronsgate 22 D2
Herriard 21 K7
Herringfleet 45 J6
Herring's Green 32 D4
Herringswell 34 B2
Herringthorpe 51 G3
Hersden 25 H5
Hersham Cornw. 6 A5
Hersham Surr. 22 E5
Herstmonceux 13 K5
Herston 89 D8
Hertford 33 G7
Hertford Heath 33 G7
Hertingfordbury 33 G7
Hesket Newmarket 60 E3
Hesketh Bank 55 H7
Hesketh Lane 56 B5
Heskin Green 48 E1
Hesleden 62 E3
Hesleyside 70 D5
Heslington 58 C4
Hessay 58 B4
Hessenford 4 D5
Hessett 34 D2
Hessle 59 G7
Hest Bank 55 H3
Hester's Way 29 J6
Hestley Green 35 F2
Heston 22 E4
Heswall 48 B4
Hethe 31 G6
Hethelpit Cross 29 G6
Hetherington 70 D6
Hethersett 45 F5
Hethersgill 69 K7
Hethpool 70 D1
Hett 62 C3
Hetton 56 E4
Hetton-le-Hole 62 D2
Heugh 71 F6
Heugh-head 84 H9
Heveningham 35 H1
Hever 23 H7
Heversham 55 H1
Hevingham 45 F3
Hewas Water 3 G4
Hewell Grange 30 B2
Hewell Lane 30 B2
Hewelsfield 19 J1
Hewelsfield Common 19 J1
Hewish N.Som. 19 H5
Hewish Som. 8 D4
Hewood 8 C4
Heworth 58 C4
Hewton 6 D6
Hexham 70 E7
Hextable 23 J4
Hexthorpe 51 H2
Hexton 32 E5
Hexworthy 5 G3
Hey 56 D5
Hey Houses 55 G7
Heybridge Essex 24 C2
Heybridge Essex 24 E1
Heybridge Basin 24 E1
Heybrook Bay 4 E6
Heydon Cambs. 33 H4
Heydon Norf. 45 F3
Heydour 42 D2
Heyop 28 B1
Heysham 55 H3
Heyshaw 57 G3
Heyshott 12 B5
Heyside 49 J2
Heytesbury 20 C7
Heythrop 30 E6
Heywood Gt.Man. 49 H1
Heywood Wilts. 20 B6
Hibaldstow 52 C2
Hibb's Green 34 C3
Hickleton 51 G2
Hickling Norf. 45 J3
Hickling Notts. 41 J3
Hickling Green 45 J3
Hickling Heath 45 J3
Hickstead 13 F4
Hidcote Bartrim 30 C4
Hidcote Boyce 30 C4
High Ackworth 51 G1
High Angerton 71 F5
High Bankhill 61 G2
High Beach 23 H2
High Bentham 56 B3
High Bickington 6 D3
High Birkwith 56 C2
High Blantyre 74 E5
High Bonnybridge 75 G3
High Borgue 65 G5
High Bradfield 50 E3
High Bradley 57 F5
High Bransholme 59 H6
High Bray 6 E2
High Bridge 60 E2
High Brooms 23 J7
High Bullen 6 D3
High Burton 57 H1
High Buston 71 H3
High Callerton 71 G6
High Casterton 56 B2
High Catton 58 D4
High Close 62 B5
High Cogges 21 G1
High Common 45 F7
High Coniscliffe 62 C5
High Crompton 49 J2
High Cross Hants. 11 J2
High Cross Herts. 33 G7
High Cross W.Suss. 13 F5
High Easter 33 K7
High Ellington 57 G1
High Entercommon 62 D6
High Ercall 38 E4
High Etherley 62 B4
High Ferry 43 G1
High Flatts 50 E2
High Garrett 34 B6
High Gate 56 E7
High Grange 62 B3
High Green Norf. 45 F5
High Green Norf. 44 D4
High Green Norf. 44 D5
High Green S.Yorks. 51 F3
High Green Suff. 34 C2
High Green Worcs. 29 H4
High Halden 14 D4
High Halstow 24 D4
High Ham 8 D1
High Harrington 60 B4
High Harrogate 57 J4
High Hatton 39 F3
High Hauxley 71 H3
High Hawsker 63 K6
High Heath Shrop. 39 F3
High Heath W.Mid. 40 C5
High Hesket 61 F2
High Hesleden 62 E3
High Hoyland 50 E1
High Hunsley 59 F6
High Hurstwood 13 H4
High Hutton 58 D3
High Ireby 60 D3
High Kelling 44 E2
High Kilburn 58 B2
High Kingthorpe 58 E1
High Knipe 61 G5
High Lane Derbys. 41 G1
High Lane Gt.Man. 49 J4
High Lane Worcs. 29 F2
High Laver 23 J1
High Legh 49 G4
High Leven 62 E5
High Littleton 19 K6
High Lorton 60 C4
High Marishes 58 E2
High Marnham 52 B5
High Melton 51 H2
High Moor 51 G4
High Newton 55 H1
High Newton-by-the-Sea 71 H1
High Nibthwaite 60 D7
High Offley 39 G3
High Ongar 23 J1
High Onn 40 A4
High Park Corner 34 E6
High Roding 33 K7
High Shaw 61 K7
High Spen 71 G7
High Stoop 62 B2
High Street Cornw. 3 G3
High Street Kent 14 C4
High Street Suff. 35 J3
High Street Suff. 35 H2
High Street Suff. 35 J1
High Street Suff. 34 C4
High Street Green 34 E3
High Throston 62 E3
High Town 40 B4
High Toynton 53 F6
High Trewhitt 71 F3
High Wham 62 B4
High Wigsell 14 C5
High Woolaston 19 J2
High Worsall 62 D6
High Wray 60 E7
High Wych 33 H7
High Wycombe 22 B2
Higham Derbys. 51 F7
Higham Kent 24 D4
Higham Lancs. 56 D6
Higham S.Yorks. 51 F2
Higham Suff. 34 B2
Higham Suff. 34 E5
Higham Dykes 71 G6
Higham Ferrers 32 C2
Higham Gobion 32 E5
Higham on the Hill 41 F6
Higham Wood 23 K7
Highampton 6 C5
Highams Park 23 G2
Highbridge Hants. 11 F2
Highbridge Som. 19 G7
Highbrook 13 G3
Highburton 50 D1
Highbury 19 K7
Highclere 21 H5
Highcliffe 10 D5
Higher Alham 19 K7
Higher Ansty 9 G4
Higher Ashton 7 G7
Higher Ballam 55 G6
Higher Blackley 49 H2
Higher Brixham 5 K5
Higher Cheriton 7 K5
Higher Combe 7 H2
Higher Folds 49 F2
Higher Gabwell 5 K4
Higher Green 49 G3
Higher Halstock Leigh 8 E4
Higher Kingcombe 8 E5
Higher Kinnerton 48 C6
Higher Muddiford 6 D2
Higher Nyland 9 G2
Higher Prestacott 6 B6
Higher Standen 56 C5
Higher Tale 7 J5
Higher Thrushgill 56 B3
Higher Town Cornw. 4 A4
Higher Town I.o.S. 2 C1
Higher Walreddon 4 E3
Higher Walton Lancs. 55 J7
Higher Walton Warr. 48 E4
Higher Wambrook 8 B4
Higher Whatcombe 9 H4
Higher Wheelton 56 B7
Higher Whiteleigh 4 C1
Higher Whitley 49 F4
Higher Wincham 49 F5
Higher Woodhill 49 G1
Higher Woodsford 9 G6
Higher Wraxall 8 E4
Higher Wych 38 D1
Highfield E.Riding 58 D6
Highfield N.Ayr. 74 B5
Highfield Oxon. 31 G6
Highfield S.Yorks. 51 F4
Highfield T. & W. 62 B1
Highfields Cambs. 33 G3
Highfields Northumb. 77 H5
Highgate E.Suss. 13 H3
Highgate Gt.Lon. 23 F3
Highgreen Manor 70 D4
Highlane Ches. 49 H6
Highlane Derbys. 51 G4
Highlaws 60 C2
Highleadon 29 G6
Highleigh Devon 7 H3
Highleigh W.Suss. 12 B7
Highley 39 G7
Highmead 17 J1
Highmoor Cross 21 K3
Highmoor Hill 19 H3
Highnam 29 G7
Highstead 25 J5
Highsted 25 F5
Highstreet 25 G5
Highstreet Green Essex 34 B5
Highstreet Green Surr. 12 C3
Hightae 69 F6
Highter's Heath 30 B1
Hightown Hants. 10 C4
Hightown Mersey. 48 B2
Hightown Green 34 D3
Highway 20 D4
Highweek 5 J3
Highwood 29 F2
Highwood Hill 23 F2
Highworth 21 F2
Hilborough 44 C5
Hilcote 51 G7
Hilcott 20 E6
Hilden Park 23 J7
Hildenborough 23 J7
Hildenley 58 D2
Hildersham 33 J4
Hilderstone 40 B2
Hilderthorpe 59 H3
Hilfield 9 F4
Hilgay 44 A6
Hill S.Glos. 19 K2
Hill Warks. 31 F2
Hill Worcs. 29 J4
Hill Brow 11 J2
Hill Chorlton 39 G2
Hill Common 45 J3
Hill Cottages 63 H7
Hill Croome 29 H4
Hill Deverill 20 B7
Hill Dyke 43 G1
Hill End Dur. 62 A3
Hill End Fife 75 J1
Hill End Glos. 29 H5
Hill End Gt.Lon. 22 D2
Hill End N.Yorks. 57 F4
Hill Green 33 H5
Hill Head 11 G4
Hill Houses 29 F1
Hill Mountain 16 C5
Hill of Beath 75 K2
Hill of Fearn 84 C3
Hill Ridware 40 C4
Hill Row 33 H1
Hill Side 50 D1
Hill Street 10 E3
Hill Top Hants. 11 F4
Hill Top S.Yorks. 51 G3
Hill Top S.Yorks. 50 E4
Hill View 9 J5
Hill Wootton 30 E2
Hillam 58 B7
Hillbeck 61 J5
Hillberry 54 C6
Hillborough 25 J5
Hillbutts 9 J4
Hillclifflane 40 E1
Hillend Fife 75 K2
Hillend Midloth. 76 A4
Hillend N.Lan. 75 G4
Hillend Swan. 17 H6
Hillend Green 29 G6
Hillersland 28 E7
Hillesden 31 H6
Hillesley 20 A3
Hillfarrance 7 K3
Hillfoot End 32 E5
Hillhead Devon 5 K5
Hillhead S.Ayr. 67 J1
Hilliard's Cross 40 D4
Hillingdon 22 D3
Hillington Glas. 74 D4
Hillington Norf. 44 B3
Hillmorton 31 G1
Hillockhead 84 H10
Hillowton 65 H4
Hillpound 11 G3
Hill's End 32 C5
Hills Town 51 G6
Hillsborough 51 F3
Hillsford Bridge 7 F1
Hillside Aber. 85 P11
Hillside Angus 81 N4
Hillside Shet. 89 N6
Hillside Worcs. 29 G2
Hillswick 89 L5
Hillway 11 H6
Hillyfields 10 E3
Hilmarton 20 D4
Hilperton 20 B6
Hilsea 11 H4
Hilston 59 J6
Hilton Cambs. 33 F2
Hilton Cumb. 61 J4
Hilton Derbys. 40 E2
Hilton Dorset 9 G4
Hilton Dur. 62 B4
Hilton Shrop. 39 G6
Hilton Staffs. 40 C5
Hilton Stock. 62 E5
Hilton of Cadboll 84 C3
Himbleton 29 J3
Himley 40 A6
Hincaster 55 J1
Hinchley Wood 22 E5
Hinckley 41 G6
Hinderclay 34 E1
Hinderton 48 C5
Hinderwell 63 H5
Hindford 38 C2
Hindhead 12 B3
Hindley Gt.Man. 49 F2
Hindley Northumb. 62 A1
Hindley Green 49 F2
Hindlip 29 H3
Hindolveston 44 E3
Hindon Som. 7 H1
Hindon Wilts. 9 J1
Hindringham 44 D2
Hingham 44 E5
Hinksford 40 A7
Hinstock 39 F3
Hintlesham 34 E4
Hinton Glos. 19 K1
Hinton Hants. 10 D5
Hinton Here. 28 C5
Hinton Northants. 31 G3
Hinton S.Glos. 20 A4
Hinton Shrop. 38 D5
Hinton Admiral 10 D5
Hinton Ampner 11 G2
Hinton Blewett 19 J6
Hinton Charterhouse 20 A6
Hinton Martell 10 B4
Hinton on the Green 30 B4
Hinton Parva Dorset 9 J4
Hinton Parva Swin. 21 F3
Hinton St. George 8 D3
Hinton St. Mary 9 G3
Hinton Waldrist 21 G2
Hinton-in-the-Hedges 31 G5
Hints Shrop. 29 F1
Hints Staffs. 40 D5
Hinwick 32 C2
Hinxhill 15 F3
Hinxton 33 H4
Hinxworth 33 F4
Hipperholme 57 G7
Hipsburn 71 H2
Hipswell 62 B7
Hirnant 37 K3
Hirst 71 H5
Hirst Courtney 58 C7
Hirwaen 47 K6
Hirwaun 18 C1
Hiscott 6 D3
Histon 33 H2
Hitcham Bucks. 22 C3
Hitcham Suff. 34 D3
Hitchin 32 E6
Hither Green 23 G4
Hittisleigh 7 F6
Hittisleigh Barton 7 F6
Hive 58 E6
Hixon 40 C3
Hoaden 15 H2
Hoaldalbert 28 C6
Hoar Cross 40 D3
Hoarwithy 28 E6
Hoath 25 J5
Hobarris 28 C1
Hobbister 89 C7
Hobbles Green 34 B3
Hobbs Cross 23 H2
Hobbs Lots Bridge 43 G5
Hobkirk 70 A2
Hobland Hall 45 K5
Hobson 62 B1
Hoby 41 J4
Hockerill 33 H6
Hockering 44 E4
Hockerton 51 K7
Hockley 24 E2
Hockley Heath 30 C1
Hockliffe 32 C6
Hockwold cum Wilton 44 B7
Hockworthy 7 J4
Hoddesdon 23 G1
Hoddlesden 56 C7
Hodgehill 49 H6
Hodgeston 16 D6
Hodnet 39 F3
Hodnetheath 39 F3
Hodsoll Street 24 C5
Hodson 20 E3
Hodthorpe 51 H5
Hoe 44 D4
Hoe Gate 11 H3
Hoff 61 H5
Hoffleet Stow 43 F2
Hoggard's Green 34 C3
Hoggeston 32 B6
Hoggrill's End 40 E6
Hogha Gearraidh 88 B1
Hoghton 56 B7
Hognaston 50 E7
Hogsthorpe 53 J5
Holbeach 43 G3
Holbeach Bank 43 G3
Holbeach Clough 43 G3
Holbeach Drove 43 G4
Holbeach Hurn 43 G3
Holbeach St. Johns 43 G4
Holbeach St. Marks 43 G2
Holbeach St. Matthew 43 H2
Holbeck 51 H5
Holbeck Woodhouse 51 H5
Holberrow Green 30 B3
Holbeton 5 G5
Holborough 24 D5
Holbrook Derbys. 41 F1
Holbrook Suff. 35 F5
Holburn 77 J7
Holbury 11 F4
Holcombe Devon 5 K3
Holcombe Gt.Man. 49 G1
Holcombe Som. 19 K7
Holcombe Burnell Barton 7 G6
Holcombe Rogus 7 J4
Holcot 31 J2
Holden 56 C5
Holden Gate 56 D7
Holdenby 31 H2
Holdenhurst 10 C5
Holder's Green 33 K6
Holders Hill 23 F3
Holdgate 38 E7
Holdingham 42 D1
Holditch 8 C4
Hole 7 K4
Hole Park 14 D4
Hole Street 12 E5
Holehouse 50 C3
Hole-in-the-Wall 29 F6
Holford 7 K1
Holgate 58 B4
Holker 55 G2
Holkham 44 C1
Hollacombe Devon 6 B5
Hollacombe Devon 7 G5
Hollacombe Town 6 E4
Holland Ork. 89 D2
Holland Surr. 23 H6
Holland Fen 43 F1
Holland-on-Sea 35 F7
Hollandstoun 89 G2
Hollee 69 H7
Hollesley 35 H4
Hollicombe 5 K4
Hollingbourne 14 D2
Hollingbury 13 G6
Hollingrove 13 K4
Hollington Derbys. 40 E2
Hollington E.Suss. 14 C6
Hollington Staffs. 40 C2
Hollingworth 50 C3
Hollins 51 F5
Hollins Green 49 F3
Hollins Lane 55 H4
Hollinsclough 50 C6
Hollinwood Gt.Man. 49 J2
Hollinwood Shrop. 38 E2
Hollocombe 6 E4
Hollow Meadows 50 E4
Holloway 51 F7
Hollowell 31 H1
Holly Bush 38 D1
Holly End 43 H5
Holly Green 22 A1
Hollybush Caerp. 18 E1
Hollybush E.Ayr. 67 H2
Hollybush Worcs. 29 G5
Hollyhurst 38 E1
Hollym 59 K7
Hollywater 12 B3
Hollywood 30 B1
Holm 69 H4
Holm of Drumlanrig 68 D4
Holmbridge 50 D2
Holmbury St. Mary 22 E7
Holmbush 13 F3
Holme Cambs. 42 E7
Holme Cumb. 55 J2
Holme N.Lincs. 52 C2
Holme N.Yorks. 57 J1
Holme Notts. 52 B7
Holme W.Yorks. 50 D2
Holme Chapel 56 D7
Holme Hale 44 C5
Holme Lacy 28 E5
Holme Marsh 28 C3
Holme next the Sea 44 B1
Holme on the Wolds 59 F5
Holme Pierrepont 41 J2
Holme St. Cuthbert 60 C2
Holme-on-Spalding-Moor 58 E6
Holmer 28 E4
Holmer Green 22 C2
Holmes 48 D1
Holmes Chapel 49 G6
Holme's Hill 13 J5
Holmesfield 51 F5
Holmeswood 48 D1
Holmewood 51 G6
Holmfield 57 F7
Holmfirth 50 D2
Holmhead D. & G. 68 C5
Holmhead E.Ayr. 67 K1
Holmpton 59 K7
Holmrook 60 B6
Holmside 62 C2
Holmsleigh Green 8 B4
Holmston 67 H1
Holmwrangle 61 G2
Holne 5 H4
Holnest 9 F4
Holnicote 7 H1
Holsworthy 6 B5
Holsworthy Beacon 6 B5
Holt Dorset 10 B4
Holt Norf. 44 E2
Holt Wilts. 20 B5
Holt Worcs. 29 H2
Holt Wrex. 48 D7
Holt End Hants. 11 H1
Holt End Worcs. 30 B2
Holt Fleet 29 H2
Holt Heath Dorset 10 B4
Holt Heath Worcs. 29 H2
Holt Wood 10 B4
Holtby 58 C4
Holton Oxon. 21 K1
Holton Som. 9 F2
Holton Suff. 35 J1
Holton cum Beckering 52 E4
Holton Heath 9 J5
Holton le Clay 53 F2
Holton le Moor 52 D3
Holton St. Mary 34 E5
Holtspur 22 C3
Holtye 13 H3
Holtye Common 13 H3
Holway 8 B2
Holwell Dorset 9 F3
Holwell Herts. 32 E5
Holwell Leics. 42 A3
Holwell Oxon. 21 F1
Holwell Som. 20 A7
Holwick 61 L4
Holworth 9 G6
Holy Cross 29 J1
Holy Island I.o.A. 46 A5
Holy Island Northumb. 77 K6
Holy Island (island) Northumb. 77 K6
Holybourne 22 A7
Holyfield 23 G1
Holyhead 46 A4
Holymoorside 51 F6
Holyport 22 B4
Holystone 70 E3
Holytown 75 F4
Holywell Cambs. 33 G1
Holywell Cornw. 2 E3
Holywell Dorset 8 E4
Holywell E.Suss. 13 J7
Holywell Flints. 47 K5
Holywell Northumb. 71 J6
Holywell Green 50 C1
Holywell Lake 7 K3
Holywell Row 34 B1
Holywood 68 E5
Hom Green 28 E6
Homer 39 F5
Homersfield 45 G7
Homington 10 C2
Homore 88 B5
Honey Hill 25 H5
Honey Street 20 E5
Honey Tye 34 D5
Honeyborough 16 C5
Honeybourne 30 C4
Honeychurch 6 E5
Honicknowle 4 E5
Honiley 30 D1
Honing 45 H3
Honingham 45 F4
Honington Lincs. 42 C1
Honington Suff. 34 D1
Honington Warks. 30 D4
Honiton 7 K5
Honley 50 D1
Hoo Med. 24 D4
Hoo Suff. 35 G3
Hoo Green 49 G4
Hoo Meavy 5 F4
Hood Green 51 F2
Hood Hill 51 F3
Hooe E.Suss. 13 K6
Hooe Plym. 5 F5
Hooe Common 13 K5
Hook Cambs. 43 H6
Hook E.Riding 58 D7
Hook Gt.Lon. 22 E5
Hook Hants. 22 A6
Hook Hants. 11 G4
Hook Pembs. 16 C4
Hook Wilts. 20 D3
Hook Green Kent 13 K3
Hook Green Kent 24 C5
Hook Green Kent 24 C4
Hook Green Kent 23 J4
Hook Norton 30 E5
Hook-a-Gate 38 D5
Hooke 8 E4
Hookgate 39 G2
Hookway 7 G6
Hookwood 23 F7
Hoole 48 D6
Hooley 23 F6
Hoop 19 J1
Hooton 48 C5
Hooton Levitt 51 H3
Hooton Pagnell 51 G2
Hooton Roberts 51 G3
Hop Pole 42 E4
Hopcrofts Holt 31 F6
Hope Derbys. 50 D4
Hope Devon 5 G7
Hope Flints. 48 C7
Hope Powys 38 B5
Hope Shrop. 38 C5
Hope Staffs. 50 D7
Hope Bagot 28 E1
Hope Bowdler 38 D6
Hope End Green 33 J6
Hope Mansell 29 F7
Hope under Dinmore 28 E3
Hopehouse 69 H2
Hopeman 84 F4
Hope's Green 24 D3
Hopesay 38 C7
Hopkinstown 18 D2
Hopley's Green 28 C3
Hopsford 41 G7
Hopstone 39 G6

► Lam - Lon

Lamarsh 34 C5
Lamas 45 G3
Lamb Corner 34 E5
Lamb Roe 56 C6
Lambden 77 F6
Lamberhurst 13 K3
Lamberhurst Quarter 13 K3
Lamberton 77 H5
Lambfell Moar 54 B5
Lambley Northumb. 61 H1
Lambley Notts. 41 J1
Lambourn 21 G4
Lambourn Woodlands 21 G4
Lambourne End 23 H2
Lambs Green 13 F3
Lambston 16 C4
Lambton 62 C1
Lamellion 4 C4
Lamerton 4 E3
Lamesley 62 C1
Lamington 75 H7
Lamlash 73 J7
Lamloch 67 K4
Lamonby 60 F3
Lamorna 2 B6
Lamorran 3 F4
Lampert 70 B6
Lampeter 17 J1
Lampeter Velfrey 16 E4
Lamphey 16 D5
Lamplugh 60 B4
Lamport 31 J1
Lamyatt 9 F1
Lana Devon 6 B6
Lana Devon 6 B5
Lanark 75 G6
Lanarth 2 E6
Lancaster 55 H3
Lanchester 62 B2
Lancing 12 E6
Landbeach 33 H2
Landcross 6 C3
Landerberry 85 M10
Landewednack 2 E7
Landford 10 D3
Landican 48 B4
Landimore 17 H6
Landkey 6 D2
Landmoth 62 E7
Landore 17 K6
Landrake 4 D4
Landscove 5 H4
Landshipping 16 D4
Landulph 4 E4
Landwade 33 K2
Landywood 40 B5
Lane Bottom 56 D6
Lane End Bucks. 22 B2
Lane End Cumb. 60 C7
Lane End Derbys. 51 G6
Lane End Dorset 9 H5
Lane End Hants. 11 G2
Lane End Here. 29 F7
Lane End Kent 23 J4
Lane End Wilts. 20 B7
Lane Ends Derbys. 40 E2
Lane Ends Gt.Man. 49 J3
Lane Ends Lancs. 56 C6
Lane Ends N.Yorks. 56 E5
Lane Green 40 A5
Lane Head Dur. 62 B5
Lane Head Dur. 62 A4
Lane Head Gt.Man. 49 F3
Lane Head W.Yorks. 50 D2
Lane Heads 55 H6
Lane Side 56 C7
Laneast 4 C2
Lane-end 4 A4
Laneham 52 B5
Lanehead Dur. 61 K2
Lanehead Northumb. 70 C5
Lanesend 16 D5
Lanesfield 40 B6
Laneshawbridge 56 E5
Langar 42 A2
Langbank 74 B3
Langbar 57 F4
Langbaurgh 63 F5
Langcliffe 56 D3
Langdale End 63 K7
Langdon Cornw. 4 C1
Langdon Cornw. 6 B7
Langdon Beck 61 K3
Langdon Hills 24 C3
Langdon House 5 K3
Langford Beds. 32 E4
Langford Essex 24 E1
Langford Notts. 52 B7
Langford Oxon. 21 F1
Langford Budville 7 K3
Langham Essex 34 E5
Langham Norf. 44 E1
Langham Rut. 42 B4
Langham Suff. 34 D2
Langham Moor 34 E5
Langho 56 B6
Langholm 69 J5
Langland 17 K7
Langlands 65 G5
Langlee 70 B2
Langleeford 70 E1
Langley Ches. 49 J5
Langley Derbys. 41 G1
Langley Essex 33 H5
Langley Glos. 30 B6
Langley Gt.Man. 49 H2
Langley Hants. 11 F4
Langley Herts. 33 F6
Langley Kent 14 C2
Langley Northumb. 70 D7
Langley Oxon. 30 E7
Langley Slo. 22 D4
Langley Som. 7 J3
Langley W.Suss. 12 B4
Langley Warks. 30 C2
Langley Burrell 20 C4
Langley Corner 22 D3
Langley Green Derbys. 40 E2
Langley Green W.Suss. 13 F3
Langley Green Warks. 30 D2
Langley Heath 14 D2
Langley Marsh 7 J3
Langley Mill 41 G1
Langley Moor 62 C2
Langley Park 62 C2
Langley Street 45 H5
Langney 13 K6
Langold 51 H4
Langore 4 C2
Langport 8 D2
Langrick 43 F1
Langrick Bridge 43 F1
Langridge B.& N.E.Som. 20 A5
Langridge Devon 6 D3
Langridgeford 6 D3
Langrigg 60 C2
Langrish 11 J2
Langsett 50 E2
Langshaw 76 D7
Langshawburn 69 H3
Langside 74 D4
Langstone Hants. 11 J4
Langstone Newport 19 G2
Langthorne 62 C7
Langthorpe 57 J3
Langthwaite 62 A6
Langtoft E.Riding 59 G3
Langtoft Lincs. 42 E4
Langton Dur. 62 B5
Langton Lincs. 53 G5
Langton Lincs. 53 F6
Langton N.Yorks. 58 D3
Langton by Wragby 52 E5
Langton Green Kent 13 J3
Langton Green Suff. 35 F1
Langton Herring 9 F6
Langton Long Blandford 9 H4
Langton Matravers 9 J7
Langtree 6 C4
Langtree Week 6 C4
Langwathby 61 G3
Langwell House 87 P7
Langwith 51 H5
Langworth 52 D5
Lanivet 4 A4
Lank 4 A3
Lanlivery 4 A5
Lanner 2 E4
Lanoy 4 C3
Lanreath 4 B5
Lansallos 4 B5
Lansdown 20 A5
Lanteglos 4 A2
Lanteglos Highway 4 B5
Lanton Northumb. 77 H7
Lanton Sc.Bord. 70 B1
Lanvean 3 F2
Lapford 7 F5
Laphroaig 72 B6
Lapley 40 A4
Lapworth 30 C1
Larach na Gaibhre 73 F3
Larachbeg 78 H6
Larbert 75 G2
Larbreck 55 H5
Larden Green 48 E7
Larg 64 D3
Largie 85 L7
Largiemore 73 H2
Largoward 81 K10
Largs 74 A5
Largybaan 66 A2
Largybeg 66 E1
Largymore 66 E1
Lark Hall 33 J3
Larkfield 74 A3
Larkhall 75 F5
Larkhill 20 E7
Larklands 41 G1
Larling 44 D7
Larriston 70 A4
Lartington 62 A5
Lasborough 20 B2
Lasham 21 K7
Lashbrook 6 C5
Lashenden 14 D3
Lassington 29 G6
Lassintullich 80 C5
Lassodie 75 K1
Lasswade 76 B4
Lastingham 63 H7
Latchford 49 F4
Latchingdon 24 E1
Latchley 4 E3
Lately Common 49 F3
Lathbury 32 B4
Latheron 87 P6
Latheronwheel 87 P6
Latimer 22 D2
Latteridge 19 K3
Lattiford 9 F2
Latton 20 D2
Lauchentyre 65 F5
Lauder 76 D6
Laugharne 17 G4
Laughterton 52 B5
Laughton E.Suss. 13 J5
Laughton Leics. 41 J7
Laughton Lincs. 42 D2
Laughton Lincs. 52 B3
Laughton en le Morthen 51 H4
Launcells 6 A5
Launcells Cross 6 A5
Launceston 6 B7
Launde Abbey 42 A5
Launton 31 H6
Laurencekirk 81 N3
Laurieston D.& G. 65 G4
Laurieston Falk. 75 H3
Lavendon 32 C3
Lavenham 34 D4
Laverhay 69 G4
Lavernock 18 E5
Laversdale 69 K7
Laverstock 10 C1
Laverstoke 21 H7
Laverton Glos. 30 B5
Laverton N.Yorks. 57 H2
Laverton Som. 20 A6
Lavister 48 C7
Law 75 G5
Lawers 80 B7
Lawford Essex 34 E5
Lawford Som. 7 K2
Lawhitton 6 B7
Lawkland 56 C3
Lawkland Green 56 C3
Lawley 39 F5
Lawnhead 40 A3
Lawrence Weston 19 J4
Lawrenny 16 D5
Lawshall 34 C3
Lawshall Green 34 C3
Lawton 28 D3
Laxdale 88 K4
Laxey 54 D5
Laxfield 35 G1
Laxford Bridge 86 E5
Laxo 89 N6
Laxton E.Riding 58 D7
Laxton Northants. 42 C6
Laxton Notts. 51 K6
Laycock 57 F5
Layer Breton 34 D7
Layer de la Haye 34 D7
Layer Marney 34 D7
Layham 34 E4
Laymore 8 C4
Layter's Green 22 C2
Laytham 58 D6
Layton 55 G6
Lazenby 63 F4
Lazonby 61 G3
Lea Derbys. 51 F7
Lea Here. 29 F6
Lea Lincs. 52 B4
Lea Shrop. 38 C7
Lea Shrop. 38 D5
Lea Wilts. 20 C3
Lea Bridge 51 F7
Lea Green 29 F2
Lea Marston 40 E6
Lea Town 55 H6
Lea Yeat 56 C1
Leac a' Li 88 G8
Leachd 73 J1
Leachkin 84 A6
Leadburn 76 A5
Leaden Roding 33 J7
Leadenham 52 C7
Leaderfoot 76 D7
Leadgate Cumb. 61 J2
Leadgate Dur. 62 B1
Leadgate Northumb. 62 B1
Leadhills 68 D2
Leadingcross Green 14 D2
Leafield 30 E7
Leagrave 32 D6
Leake Commonside 53 G7
Leake Hurn's End 43 H1
Lealands 13 J5
Lealholm 63 H6
Lealt Arg.& B. 72 E1
Lealt High. 82 F4
Leam 50 E5
Leamington Hastings 31 F2
Leamington Spa 30 E2
Leamoor Common 38 D7
Leanach 73 J1
Leargybreck 72 D3
Leasgill 55 H1
Leasingham 42 D1
Leason 17 H6
Leasowe 48 B3
Leat 6 B7
Leatherhead 22 E6
Leathley 57 H5
Leaton Shrop. 38 D4
Leaton Tel.& W. 39 F4
Leaveland 15 F2
Leavenheath 34 D5
Leavening 58 D3
Leaves Green 23 H5
Leavesden Green 22 E1
Lebberston 59 G1
Lechlade 21 F2
Leck 56 B2
Leckford 10 E1
Leckfurin 87 K4
Leckgruinart 72 A4
Leckhampstead Bucks. 31 J5
Leckhampstead W.Berks. 21 H4
Leckhampstead Thicket 21 H4
Leckhampton 29 J7
Leckie 74 E1
Leckmelm 83 M2
Leckuary 73 G1
Leckwith 18 E4
Leconfield 59 G5
Ledaig 79 L7
Ledburn 32 B6
Ledbury 29 G5
Ledgemoor 28 D3
Ledicot 28 D2
Ledmore 86 E8
Ledsham Ches. 48 C5
Ledsham W.Yorks. 57 K7
Ledston 57 K7
Ledstone 5 H6
Ledwell 31 F6
Lee Arg.& B. 78 F8
Lee Devon 6 C1
Lee Hants. 10 E3
Lee Lancs. 55 J4
Lee Shrop. 38 D2
Lee Brockhurst 38 E3
Lee Chapel 24 C3
Lee Clump 22 C1
Lee Mill Bridge 5 F5
Lee Moor 5 F4
Leebotten 89 N10
Leebotwood 38 D6
Leece 55 F3
Leeds Kent 14 D2
Leeds W.Yorks. 57 H6
Leeds Bradford International Airport 57 H5
Leedstown 2 D5
Leegomery 39 F4
Leek 49 J7
Leek Wootton 30 D2
Leekbrook 49 J7
Leeming N.Yorks. 57 H1
Leeming W.Yorks. 57 F6
Leeming Bar 57 H1
Lee-on-the-Solent 11 G4
Lees Derbys. 40 E2
Lees Gt.Man. 49 J2
Leeswood 48 B7
Leftwich 49 F5
Legars 77 F6
Legbourne 53 G4
Legerwood 76 D6
Legsby 52 E4
Leicester 41 H5
Leicester Forest East 41 H5
Leigh Dorset 9 F4
Leigh Dorset 10 B5
Leigh Gt.Man. 49 F2
Leigh Kent 23 J7
Leigh Shrop. 38 C5
Leigh Surr. 23 F7
Leigh Wilts. 20 D2
Leigh Worcs. 29 G3
Leigh Beck 24 E3
Leigh Common 9 G2
Leigh Delamere 20 B4
Leigh Green 14 E4
Leigh Park 11 J4
Leigh Sinton 29 G3
Leigh upon Mendip 19 K7
Leigh Woods 19 J4
Leigham 5 F5
Leighland Chapel 7 J2
Leigh-on-Sea 24 E3
Leighterton 20 B2
Leighton N.Yorks. 57 G2
Leighton Powys 38 B5
Leighton Shrop. 39 F5
Leighton Som. 20 A7
Leighton Bromswold 32 E1
Leighton Buzzard 32 C6
Leinthall Earls 28 D2
Leinthall Starkes 28 D2
Leintwardine 28 D1
Leire 41 H7
Leirinmore 86 G3
Leiston 35 J2
Leith 76 A3
Leitholm 77 F6
Lelant 2 C5
Lelley 59 J6
Lemington 71 G7
Lempitlaw 77 F7
Lemsford 33 F7
Lenchwick 30 B4
Lendalfoot 67 F4
Lenham 14 D2
Lenham Heath 14 E3
Lenie 83 R8
Lenimore 73 G6
Lennel 77 G6
Lennox Plunton 65 G5
Lennoxtown 74 E3
Lent Rise 22 C3
Lenton Lincs. 42 D2
Lenton Nott. 41 H2
Lenton Abbey 41 H2
Lentran 83 R6
Lenwade 44 E4
Lenzie 74 E3
Leochel-Cushnie 85 K9
Leominster 28 D3
Leonard Stanley 20 B1
Leorin 72 B6
Lepe 11 F5
Lephinchapel 73 H1
Lephinmore 73 H1
Leppington 58 D3
Lepton 50 E1
Lerryn 4 B5
Lerwick 89 N8
Lesbury 71 H2
Lescrow 4 B5
Leslie Aber. 85 K8
Leslie Fife 80 H10
Lesmahagow 75 G7
Lesnewth 4 B1
Lessingham 45 H3
Lessness Heath 23 H4
Lessonhall 60 D1
Leswalt 64 A4
Letchmore Heath 22 E2
Letchworth Garden City 33 F5
Letcombe Bassett 21 G3
Letcombe Regis 21 G3
Leth Meadhanach 88 B7
Letham Angus 81 L6
Letham Falk. 75 G2
Letham Fife 81 J9
Lethanhill 67 J2
Letheringham 35 G3
Letheringsett 44 E2
Lettaford 7 F7
Letter Finlay 83 N11
Letterfearn 83 J8
Lettermore 87 J5
Lettershaws 68 D1
Letterston 16 C3
Lettoch 84 F7
Letton Here. 28 C1
Letton Here. 28 C4
Letty Green 33 F7
Letwell 51 H4
Leuchars 81 K8
Leumrabhagh 88 J6
Leurbost 88 J5
Leusdon 5 H3
Levedale 40 A4
Level's Green 33 H6
Leven E.Riding 59 H5
Leven Fife 81 J10
Levencorroch 66 E1
Levenhall 76 B3
Levens 55 H1
Levens Green 33 G6
Levenshulme 49 H3
Levenwick 89 N10
Leverburgh 88 F9
Leverington 43 H4
Leverstock Green 22 D1
Leverton 43 G1
Leverton Lucasgate 43 H1
Leverton Outgate 43 H1
Levington 35 G5
Levisham 63 J7
Levishie 83 Q9
Lew 21 G1
Lewannick 4 C2
Lewcombe 8 E4
Lewdown 6 C7
Lewes 13 H5
Leweston 16 C3
Lewisham 23 G4
Lewiston 83 R8
Lewistown 18 C3
Lewknor 22 A2
Leworthy 6 E2
Lewson Street 25 F5
Lewth 55 H6
Lewtrenchard 6 C7
Ley 4 B4
Ley Green 32 E6
Leybourne 23 K6
Leyburn 62 B7
Leyland 55 J7
Leylodge 85 M9
Leymoor 50 D1
Leys 81 J7
Leysdown-on-Sea 25 G4
Leysmill 81 M6
Leysters 28 E2
Leyton 23 G3
Leytonstone 23 G3
Lezant 4 D3
Lezerea 2 D5
Lhanbryde 84 G4
Libanus 27 J6
Libberton 75 H6
Libbery 29 J3
Liberton 76 A4
Lichfield 40 D5
Lickey 29 J1
Lickey End 29 J1
Lickfold 12 C4
Liddaton Green 6 C7
Liddesdale 79 J5
Liddington 21 F3
Lidgate Derbys. 51 F5
Lidgate Suff. 34 B3
Lidgett 51 J6
Lidlington 32 C5
Lidsey 12 C6
Lidsing 24 D5
Lidstone 30 E6
Lieurary 87 N3
Liff 81 J7
Lifton 6 B7
Liftondown 6 B7
Lightcliffe 57 G7
Lighthorne 30 E3
Lighthorne Heath 30 E3
Lightwater 22 C5
Lightwood 40 B1
Lightwood Green Ches. 39 F1
Lightwood Green Wrex. 38 C1
Lilbourne 31 G1
Lilburn Tower 71 F1
Lilleshall 39 G4
Lilley Herts. 32 E6
Lilley W.Berks. 21 H4
Lilliesleaf 70 A1
Lilling Green 58 C3
Lillingstone Dayrell 31 J5
Lillingstone Lovell 31 J4
Lillington Dorset 9 F3
Lillington Warks. 30 E2
Lilliput 10 B6
Lilly 6 D2
Lilstock 7 K1
Lilyhurst 39 G4
Limbury 32 D6
Lime Side 49 J2
Limefield 49 H1
Limehurst 49 J2
Limekilnburn 75 F5
Limekilns 75 J2
Limerigg 75 G3
Limerstone 11 F6
Limington 8 E2
Limpenhoe 45 H5
Limpley Stoke 20 A5
Limpsfield 23 H6
Limpsfield Chart 23 H6
Linaclate 88 B4
Linbriggs 70 D3
Linby 51 H7
Linchmere 12 B3
Lincluden 65 K3
Lincoln 52 C5
Lincomb 29 H2
Lincombe Devon 5 H5
Lincombe Devon 5 H6
Lindal in Furness 55 F2
Lindale 55 H1
Lindean 76 C7
Lindfield 13 G4
Lindford 12 B3
Lindisfarne 77 K6
Lindley 57 H5
Lindores 80 H9
Lindow End 49 H5
Lindridge 29 F2
Lindsaig 73 H3
Lindsell 33 K6
Lindsey 34 D4
Lindsey Tye 34 D4
Linfitts 49 J2
Linford Hants. 10 C4
Linford Thur. 24 C4
Linford Wood 32 B4
Lingague 54 B6
Lingards Wood 50 C1
Lingdale 63 G5
Lingen 28 C2
Lingfield 23 G7
Lingley Green 48 E4
Lingwood 45 H5
Linhope 69 K3
Linicro 82 D4
Linkend 29 H5
Linkenholt 21 G6
Linkhill 14 D5
Linkinhorne 4 D3
Linksness 89 B7
Linktown 76 A1
Linley Shrop. 38 C6
Linley Shrop. 39 F6
Linley Green 29 F3
Linlithgow 75 J3
Linlithgow Bridge 75 H3
Linn of Muick Cottage 81 J2
Linnels 70 E7
Linney 16 B6
Linshiels 70 D3
Linsiadar 88 H4
Linsidemore 83 R1
Linslade 32 C6
Linstead Parva 35 H1
Linstock 60 F1
Linthwaite 50 D1
Lintlaw 77 G5
Lintmill 85 K4
Linton Cambs. 33 J4
Linton Derbys. 40 E4
Linton Here. 29 F6
Linton Kent 14 C2
Linton N.Yorks. 56 E3
Linton Sc.Bord. 70 C1
Linton W.Yorks. 57 J5
Linton-on-Ouse 57 K3
Lintzford 62 B1
Linwood Hants. 10 C4
Linwood Lincs. 52 E4
Linwood Renf. 74 C4
Lionacleit 88 B4
Lional 88 L1
Lionel 88 L1
Liphook 12 B3
Lipley 39 G2
Liscard 48 C3
Liscombe 7 G2
Liskeard 4 C4
L'Islet 3 J5
Lismore 79 K7
Liss 11 J2
Liss Forest 11 J2
Lissett 59 H4
Lissington 52 E4
Liston 34 C4
Lisvane 18 E3
Liswerry 19 G3
Litcham 44 C4
Litchborough 31 H3
Litchfield 21 H6
Litherland 48 C3
Litlington Cambs. 33 G4
Litlington E.Suss. 13 J6
Little Abington 33 J4
Little Addington 32 C1
Little Alne 30 C2
Little Altcar 48 C2
Little Amwell 33 G7
Little Ann 21 G7
Little Asby 61 H6
Little Aston 40 C6
Little Atherfield 11 F7
Little Ayton 63 F5
Little Baddow 24 D1
Little Badminton 20 B3
Little Ballinluig 80 E5
Little Bampton 60 D1
Little Bardfield 33 K5
Little Barford 32 E3
Little Barningham 45 F2
Little Barrington 30 D7
Little Barrow 48 D6
Little Barugh 58 D2
Little Bavington 70 E6
Little Bealings 35 G4
Little Bedwyn 21 F5
Little Beeby 41 J5
Little Bentley 35 F6
Little Berkhamsted 23 F1
Little Billing 32 B2
Little Birch 28 E5
Little Bispham 55 G5
Little Blakenham 35 F4
Little Bloxwich 40 C5
Little Bollington 49 G4
Little Bookham 22 E6
Little Bourton 31 F4
Little Bowden 42 A7
Little Bradley 33 K3
Little Brampton 38 C7
Little Braxted 34 C7
Little Brechin 81 L4
Little Brickhill 32 C5
Little Bridgeford 40 A3
Little Brington 31 H2
Little Bromley 34 E6
Little Broughton 60 B3
Little Budworth 48 E6
Little Burdon 62 D5
Little Burstead 24 C2
Little Burton 59 H5
Little Bytham 42 D4
Little Canford 10 B5
Little Carlton Lincs. 53 G4
Little Carlton Notts. 51 K7
Little Casterton 42 D4
Little Catwick 59 H5
Little Catworth 32 D1
Little Cawthorpe 53 G4
Little Chalfield 20 B5
Little Chalfont 22 C2
Little Chart 14 E3
Little Chesterford 33 J4
Little Chesterton 31 G6
Little Cheverell 20 C6
Little Clacton 35 F7
Little Clanfield 21 F1
Little Clifton 60 B4
Little Coates 53 F2
Little Comberton 29 J4
Little Common 14 C7
Little Compton 30 D5
Little Corby 61 F1
Little Cornard 34 C5
Little Cowarne 29 F3
Little Coxwell 21 F2
Little Crakehall 62 C7
Little Cransley 32 B1
Little Crawley 32 C4
Little Creaton 31 J1
Little Cressingham 44 C6
Little Crosby 48 C2
Little Crosthwaite 60 D4
Little Cubley 40 D2
Little Dalby 42 A4
Little Dewchurch 28 E5
Little Ditton 33 K3
Little Doward 28 E7
Little Down 21 G6
Little Downham 43 J7
Little Drayton 39 F2
Little Driffield 59 G4
Little Dunham 44 C4
Little Dunkeld 80 F6
Little Dunmow 33 K6
Little Durnford 10 C1
Little Easton 33 K6
Little Eaton 41 F1
Little Eccleston 55 H6
Little Ellingham 44 E6
Little End 23 J1
Little Everdon 31 G3
Little Eversden 33 G3
Little Fakenham 34 D1
Little Faringdon 21 F1
Little Fencote 62 C7
Little Fenton 58 B6
Little Finborough 34 E3
Little Fransham 44 D4
Little Gaddesden 32 C7
Little Garway 28 D6
Little Gidding 42 E7
Little Glemham 35 H3
Little Glenshee 80 E7
Little Gorsley 29 F6
Little Gransden 33 F3
Little Green Cambs. 33 F4
Little Green Notts. 42 A1
Little Green Suff. 34 E1
Little Green Suff. 34 E1
Little Green Wrex. 38 D1
Little Grimsby 53 G3
Little Gringley 51 K4
Little Gruinard 83 K2
Little Habton 58 D2
Little Hadham 33 H6
Little Hale 42 E1
Little Hallingbury 33 H7
Little Hampden 22 B1
Little Haresfield 20 B1
Little Harrowden 32 B1
Little Haseley 21 K1
Little Hatfield 59 H5
Little Hautbois 45 G3
Little Haven Pembs. 16 B4
Little Haven W.Suss. 12 E3
Little Hay 40 D5
Little Hayfield 50 C4
Little Haywood 40 C3
Little Heath 41 F7
Little Hereford 28 E2
Little Hockham 44 D6
Little Horkesley 34 D5
Little Hormead 33 H6
Little Horsted 13 H5
Little Horton 20 D5
Little Horwood 31 J5
Little Houghton 32 B3
Little Hucklow 50 D5
Little Hulton 49 G2
Little Hungerford 21 J4
Little Hutton 57 K2
Little Idoch 85 M6
Little Irchester 32 C2
Little Keyford 20 A7
Little Kimble 22 B1
Little Kineton 30 E3
Little Kingshill 22 B2
Little Langdale 60 E6
Little Langford 10 B1
Little Laver 23 J1
Little Lawford 31 F1
Little Leigh 49 F5
Little Leighs 34 B7
Little Lever 49 G2
Little Ley 85 L9
Little Linford 32 B4
Little Linton 33 J4
Little London Bucks. 31 H7
Little London E.Suss. 13 J5
Little London Essex 33 H6
Little London Hants. 21 G7
Little London Hants. 21 K6
Little London I.o.M. 54 C5
Little London Lincs. 43 H3
Little London Lincs. 43 F3
Little London Lincs. 53 G5
Little London Lincs. 52 E4
Little London Norf. 43 J3
Little London Norf. 44 B6
Little London Oxon. 21 J1
Little London Powys 37 K7
Little London Suff. 34 E3
Little London W.Yorks. 57 H6
Little Longstone 50 D5
Little Lyth 38 D5
Little Malvern 29 G4
Little Maplestead 34 C5
Little Marcle 29 F5
Little Marland 6 D4
Little Marlow 22 B3
Little Marsden 56 D6
Little Massingham 44 B3
Little Melton 45 F5
Little Milford 16 C4
Little Mill 19 G1
Little Milton 21 K1
Little Missenden 22 C2
Little Musgrave 61 J5
Little Ness 38 D4
Little Neston 48 B5
Little Newcastle 16 C3
Little Newsham 62 B5
Little Oakley Essex 35 G6
Little Oakley Northants. 42 B7
Little Odell 32 C3
Little Offley 32 E6
Little Onn 40 A4
Little Orton Cumb. 60 E1
Little Orton Leics. 41 F5
Little Ouse 44 A7
Little Ouseburn 57 K3
Little Overton 38 C1
Little Packington 40 E7
Little Parndon 33 H7
Little Paxton 32 E2
Little Petherick 3 G1
Little Plumpton 55 G6
Little Plumstead 45 H4
Little Ponton 42 C2
Little Posbrook 11 G4
Little Potheridge 6 D4
Little Preston 31 G3
Little Raveley 43 F7
Little Ribston 57 J4
Little Rissington 30 C7
Little Rollright 30 D5
Little Ryburgh 44 D3
Little Ryle 71 F2
Little Ryton 38 D5
Little Salkeld 61 G3
Little Sampford 33 K5
Little Saxham 34 C2
Little Scatwell 83 P5
Little Shelford 33 H3
Little Shrawardine 38 C4
Little Silver 7 H5
Little Singleton 55 G6
Little Smeaton N.Yorks. 51 H1
Little Smeaton N.Yorks. 62 D6
Little Snoring 44 D2
Little Sodbury 20 A3
Little Sodbury End 20 A3
Little Somborne 10 E1
Little Somerford 20 C3
Little Soudley 39 G3
Little Stainforth 56 D3
Little Stainton 62 D5
Little Stanney 48 D5
Little Staughton 32 E2
Little Steeping 53 H6
Little Stoke 40 B2
Little Stonham 35 F3
Little Street 43 J7
Little Stretton Leics. 41 J6
Little Stretton Shrop. 38 D6
Little Strickland 61 G5
Little Stukeley 33 F1
Little Sugnall 40 A2
Little Sutton 48 C5
Little Swinburne 70 E6
Little Tarrington 29 F4
Little Tew 30 E6
Little Tey 34 C6
Little Thetford 33 J1
Little Thornage 44 E2
Little Thornton 55 G5
Little Thorpe 62 E2
Little Thurlow 33 K3
Little Thurlow Green 33 K3
Little Thurrock 24 C4
Little Torboll 84 B1
Little Torrington 6 C4
Little Tosson 71 F3
Little Totham 34 C7
Little Town Cumb. 60 D5
Little Town Lancs. 56 B6
Little Town Warr. 49 F3
Little Twycross 41 F5
Little Urswick 55 F2
Little Wakering 25 F3
Little Walden 33 J4
Little Waldingfield 34 D4
Little Walsingham 44 D2
Little Waltham 34 B7
Little Warley 24 C2
Little Washbourne 29 J5
Little Weighton 59 F6
Little Welland 29 H5
Little Welnetham 34 C2
Little Wenham 34 E5
Little Wenlock 39 F5
Little Whittington 70 E7
Little Wilbraham 33 J3
Little Wishford 10 B1
Little Witcombe 29 J7
Little Witley 29 G2
Little Wittenham 21 J2
Little Wittingham Green 35 G1
Little Wolford 30 D5
Little Woodcote 23 F5
Little Wratting 33 K4
Little Wymington 32 C2
Little Wymondley 33 F6
Little Wyrley 40 C5
Little Wytheford 38 E4
Little Yeldham 34 B5
Littlebeck 63 J6
Littleborough Devon 7 G4
Littleborough Gt.Man. 49 J1
Littleborough Notts. 52 B4
Littlebourne 15 H2
Littlebredy 8 E6
Littlebury 33 J5
Littlebury Green 33 H5
Littledean 29 F7
Littleferry 84 C1
Littleham Devon 6 C3
Littleham Devon 7 J7
Littlehampton 12 D6
Littlehempston 5 J4
Littlehoughton 71 H2
Littlemill E.Ayr. 67 J2
Littlemill High. 84 D5
Littlemoor Derbys. 51 F6
Littlemoor Dorset 9 F6
Littlemore 21 J1
Littlemoss 49 J3
Littleover 41 F2
Littleport 43 J7
Littlestead Green 22 A4
Littlestone-on-Sea 15 F5
Littlethorpe 57 J3
Littleton Ches. 48 D6
Littleton Hants. 11 F1
Littleton Som. 8 D1
Littleton Surr. 22 D5
Littleton Drew 20 B3
Littleton Panell 20 D6
Littleton-on-Severn 19 J2
Littletown Dur. 62 D2
Littletown I.o.W. 11 G5
Littlewick Green 22 B4
Littlewindsor 8 D4
Littleworth Glos. 30 C5
Littleworth Oxon. 21 G2
Littleworth S.Yorks. 51 J3
Littleworth Staffs. 40 C4
Littleworth Worcs. 29 H4
Littley Green 33 K7
Litton Derbys. 50 D5
Litton N.Yorks. 56 E2
Litton Som. 19 J6
Litton Cheney 8 E5
Liurbost 88 J5
Liverpool 48 C3
Liverpool John Lennon Airport 48 D4
Liversedge 57 H7
Liverton Devon 5 J3
Liverton R.& C. 63 H5
Liverton Street 14 D3
Livingston 75 J4
Livingston Village 75 J4
Lixwm 47 K5
Lizard 2 E7
Llaingarreglwyd 26 D3
Llaingoch 46 A4
Llaithddu 37 K7
Llampha 18 C4
Llan 37 H5
Llan Ffestiniog 37 G1
Llanaber 37 F4
Llanaelhaearn 36 C1
Llanaeron 26 D2
Llanafan 27 F1
Llanafan-fawr 27 J3
Llanafan-fechan 27 J3
Llanallgo 46 D4
Llanarmon 36 D2
Llanarmon Dyffryn Ceiriog 38 A2
Llanarmon-yn-Ial 47 K7
Llanarth Cere. 26 D3
Llanarth Mon. 28 C7
Llanarthney 17 J3
Llanasa 47 K4
Llanbabo 46 B4
Llanbadarn Fawr 36 E7
Llanbadarn Fynydd 27 K1
Llanbadarn-y-garreg 28 A4
Llanbadoc 19 G1
Llanbadrig 46 B3
Llanbeder 19 G2
Llanbedr Gwyn. 36 E3
Llanbedr Powys 28 B6
Llanbedr Powys 28 A4
Llanbedr-Dyffryn-Clwyd 47 K7
Llanbedrgoch 46 D4
Llanbedrog 36 C2
Llanbedr-y-cennin 47 F6
Llanberis 46 D7
Llanbethery 18 D5
Llanbister 28 A1
Llanblethian 18 C4
Llanboidy 17 F3
Llanbradach 18 E2
Llanbryn-mair 37 H5
Llancadle 18 D5
Llancarfan 18 D4
Llancayo 19 G1
Llancynfelyn 37 F6
Llandafal 18 E1
Llandaff 18 E4
Llandaff North 18 E4
Llandanwg 36 E3
Llandawke 17 F4
Llanddaniel Fab 46 C5
Llanddarog 17 H4
Llanddeiniol 26 E1
Llanddeiniolen 46 D6
Llandderfel 37 J2
Llanddeusant Carmar. 27 G6
Llanddeusant I.o.A. 46 B4
Llanddew 27 K5
Llanddewi 17 H7
Llanddewi Rhydderch 28 C7
Llanddewi Skirrid 28 C7
Llanddewi Velfrey 16 E4
Llanddewi Ystradenni 28 A2
Llanddewi-Brefi 27 F3
Llanddewi'r Cwm 27 K4
Llanddoged 47 G6
Llanddona 46 D5
Llanddowror 17 F4
Llanddulas 47 H5
Llanddwywe 36 E3
Llanddyfnan 46 D5
Llandefaelog Fach 27 K5
Llandefaelog-tre'r-graig 28 A6
Llandefalle 28 A5
Llandegfan 46 D5
Llandegla 47 K7
Llandegley 28 A2
Llandegveth 19 G2
Llandegwning 36 B2
Llandeilo 17 K3
Llandeilo Abercywyn 17 G4
Llandeilo Graban 27 K4
Llandeilo'r-Fan 27 H5
Llandeloy 16 B3
Llandenny 19 H1
Llandevaud 19 H2
Llandevenny 19 H3
Llandinabo 28 E6
Llandinam 37 K7
Llandissilio 16 E3
Llandogo 19 J1
Llandough V. of Glam. 18 E4
Llandough V. of Glam. 18 C4
Llandovery 27 G5
Llandow 18 C4
Llandre Carmar. 17 K1
Llandre Carmar. 16 E3
Llandre Cere. 37 F7
Llandrillo 37 K2
Llandrindod Wells 27 K2
Llandrinio 38 B4
Llandudno 47 F4
Llandudno Junction 47 F5
Llandudoch 16 E1
Llandwrog 46 C7
Llandybie 17 K4
Llandyfaelog 17 H4
Llandyfan 17 K4
Llandyfriog 17 G1
Llandyfrydog 46 C4
Llandygai 46 D5
Llandygwydd 17 F1
Llandyrnog 47 K6
Llandyry 17 H5
Llandysilio 38 B4
Llandyssil 38 A6
Llandysul 17 H1
Llanedeyrn 19 F3
Llanedy 17 J5
Llaneglwys 27 K5
Llanegryn 37 F5
Llanegwad 17 J3
Llaneilian 46 C3
Llanelian-yn-Rhos 47 G5
Llanelidan 47 K7
Llanelieu 28 A5
Llanellen 28 C7
Llanelli 17 J5
Llanelltyd 37 G4
Llanelly 28 B7
Llanelly Hill 28 B7
Llanelwedd 27 K3
Llanelwy 47 J5
Llanenddwyn 36 E3
Llanengan 36 B3
Llanerfyl 37 K5
Llaneuddog 46 C4
Llanfachraeth 46 B4
Llanfachreth 37 G3
Llanfaelog 46 B5
Llanfaelrhys 36 B3
Llanfaenor 28 D7
Llanfaes I.o.A. 46 E5
Llanfaes Powys 27 K6
Llanfaethlu 46 B4
Llanfaglan 46 C6
Llanfair 36 E3
Llanfair Caereinion 38 A5
Llanfair Clydogau 27 F3
Llanfair Dyffryn Clwyd 47 K7
Llanfair Talhaiarn 47 H5
Llanfair Waterdine 28 B1
Llanfairfechan 46 E5
Llanfair-Nant-Gwyn 16 E2
Llanfair-Orllwyn 17 G1
Llanfairpwllgwyngyll 46 D5
Llanfairynghornwy 46 B3
Llanfair-yn-neubwll 46 B5
Llanfallteg 16 E4
Llanfaredd 27 K3
Llanfarian 26 E1
Llanfechain 38 A3
Llanfechell 46 B3
Llanfendigaid 36 E5
Llanferres 47 K6
Llanfflewyn 46 B4
Llanfigael 46 B4
Llanfihangel Crucornau 28 C6
Llanfihangel Glyn Myfyr 37 J1
Llanfihangel Nant Bran 27 J5
Llanfihangel Rhydithon 28 A2
Llanfihangel Rogiet 19 H3
Llanfihangel Tal-y-llyn 28 A6
Llanfihangel-ar-arth 17 H1
Llanfihangel-nant-Melan 28 A3
Llanfihangel-uwch-Gwili 17 H3
Llanfihangel-y-Creuddyn 27 F1
Llanfihangel-yng-Ngwynfa 37 K4
Llanfihangel-yn-Nhywyn 46 B5
Llanfihangel-y-pennant Gwyn. 36 E1
Llanfihangel-y-pennant Gwyn. 37 F5
Llanfilo 28 A5
Llanfoist 28 B7
Llanfor 37 J2
Llanfrechfa 19 G2
Llanfrothen 37 F1
Llanfrynach 27 K6
Llanfwrog Denb. 47 K7
Llanfwrog I.o.A. 46 A4
Llanfyllin 38 A4
Llanfynydd Carmar. 17 J3
Llanfynydd Flints. 48 B7
Llanfyrnach 17 F2
Llangadfan 37 K4
Llangadog 27 G6
Llangadwaladr I.o.A. 46 B6
Llangadwaladr Powys 38 A2
Llangaffo 46 C6
Llangain 17 G4
Llangammarch Wells 27 J4
Llangan 18 C4
Llangarron 28 E6
Llangasty-Talyllyn 28 A6
Llangathen 17 J3
Llangattock 28 B7
Llangattock Lingoed 28 C7
Llangattock-Vibon-Avel 28 D7
Llangedwyn 38 A3
Llangefni 46 C5
Llangeinor 18 C3
Llangeitho 27 F3
Llangeler 17 G2
Llangelynin 36 E5
Llangendeirne 17 H4
Llangennech 17 J5
Llangennith 17 H6
Llangenny 28 B7
Llangernyw 47 G6
Llangian 36 B3
Llangiwg 18 A1
Llangloffan 16 C2
Llanglydwen 16 E3
Llangoed 46 E5
Llangoedmor 16 E1
Llangollen 38 B1
Llangolman 16 E3
Llangorse 28 A6
Llangorwen 37 F7
Llangovan 19 H1
Llangower 37 J2
Llangrannog 26 C3
Llangristiolus 46 C5
Llangrove 28 E7
Llangua 28 C6
Llangunllo 28 B1
Llangunnor 17 H3
Llangurig 27 J1
Llangwm Conwy 37 J1
Llangwm Mon. 19 H1
Llangwm Pembs. 16 C5
Llangwnadl 36 B2
Llangwyfan 47 K6
Llangwyllog 46 C5
Llangwyryfon 27 F1
Llangybi Cere. 27 F3
Llangybi Gwyn. 36 D1
Llangybi Mon. 19 G2
Llangyfelach 17 K6
Llangynhafal 47 K6
Llangynidr 28 A7
Llangyniew 38 A5
Llangynin 17 F4
Llangynllo 17 G1
Llangynog Carmar. 17 G4
Llangynog Powys 37 K3
Llangynwyd 18 B3
Llanhamlach 27 K6
Llanharan 18 D3
Llanharry 18 D3
Llanhennock 19 G2
Llanhilleth 19 F1
Llanidloes 37 J7
Llaniestyn 36 B2
Llanigon 28 B5
Llanilar 27 F1
Llanilid 18 C3
Llanishen Cardiff 18 E3
Llanishen Mon. 19 H1
Llanllawddog 17 H3
Llanllechid 46 E6
Llanlleonfel 27 J3
Llanllugan 37 K5
Llanllwch 17 G4
Llanllwchaiarn 38 A6
Llanllwni 17 H1
Llanllyfni 46 C7
Llanllywel 19 G2
Llanmadoc 17 H6
Llanmaes 18 C5
Llanmartin 19 G3
Llanmerewig 38 A6
Llanmihangel 18 C4
Llan-mill 16 E4
Llanmiloe 17 F5
Llanmorlais 17 J6
Llannefydd 47 H5
Llannerch Hall 47 J5
Llannerch-y-medd 46 C4
Llannerch-y-Môr 47 K5
Llannon Carmar. 17 J5
Llan-non Cere. 26 E2
Llannor 36 C2
Llanover 19 G1
Llanpumsaint 17 H3
Llanreithan 16 B3
Llanrhaeadr 47 J6
Llanrhaeadr-ym-Mochnant 38 A3
Llanrhian 16 B2
Llanrhidian 17 H6
Llanrhyddlad 46 B4
Llanrhystud 26 E2
Llanrothal 28 D7
Llanrug 46 D6
Llanrumney 19 F3
Llanrwst 47 F6
Llansadurnen 17 F4
Llansadwrn Carmar. 17 K2
Llansadwrn I.o.A. 46 D5
Llansaint 17 G5
Llansamlet 17 K6
Llansanffraid 26 E2
Llansanffraid Glan Conwy 47 G5
Llansannan 47 H6
Llansannor 18 C4
Llansantffraed 28 A6
Llansantffraed-Cwmdeuddwr 27 J2
Llansantffraed-in-Elwel 27 K3
Llansantffraid-ym-Mechain 38 B3
Llansawel Carmar. 17 K2
Llansawel N.P.T. 18 A2
Llansilin 38 B3
Llansoy 19 H1
Llanspyddid 27 K6
Llanstadwell 16 C5
Llansteffan 17 G4
Llanstephan 28 A4
Llantarnam 19 G2
Llanteg 16 E4
Llanthony 28 B6
Llantilio Crossenny 28 C7
Llantilio Pertholey 28 C7
Llantood 16 E1
Llantrisant I.o.A. 46 B4
Llantrisant Mon. 19 G2
Llantrisant R.C.T. 18 D3
Llantrithyd 18 D4
Llantwit Fardre 18 D3
Llantwit Major 18 C5
Llantysilio 38 A1
Llanuwchllyn 37 H3
Llanvaches 19 H2
Llanvair-Discoed 19 H2
Llanvapley 28 C7
Llanvetherine 28 C7
Llanveynoe 28 C5
Llanvihangel Crucorney 28 C6
Llanvihangel Gobion 19 G1
Llanvihangel-Ystern-Llewern 28 D7
Llanvithyn 18 D4
Llanwarne 28 E6
Llanwddyn 37 K4
Llanwenog 17 H1
Llanwern 19 G3
Llanwinio 17 F3
Llanwnda Gwyn. 46 C7
Llanwnda Pembs. 16 C2
Llanwnnen 17 J1
Llanwnog 37 K6
Llanwonno 18 D2
Llanwrda 27 G5
Llanwrin 37 G5
Llanwrthwl 27 J2
Llanwrtyd 27 H4
Llanwrtyd Wells 27 H4
Llanwyddelan 37 K5
Llanyblodwel 38 B3
Llanybri 17 G4
Llanybydder 17 J1
Llanycefn 16 E3
Llanychaer Bridge 16 C2
Llanycil 37 J2
Llanycrwys 17 K1
Llanymawddwy 37 H4
Llanymddyfri 27 G5
Llanymynech 38 B3
Llanynghenedl 46 B4
Llanynys 47 K6
Llan-y-pwll 48 C7
Llanyre 27 K2
Llanystumdwy 36 D2
Llanywern 28 A6
Llawhaden 16 D4
Llawndy 47 K4
Llawnt 38 B2
Llawr-y-dref 36 B3
Llawryglyn 37 J6
Llay 48 C7
Llechcynfarwy 46 B4
Llecheiddior 36 D1
Llechfaen 27 K6
Llechryd Caerp. 18 E1
Llechryd Cere. 17 F1
Llechrydau 38 B2
Lledrod Cere. 27 F1
Lledrod Powys 38 B3
Llethrid 17 J6
Llidiad-Nenog 17 J2
Llidiardau 37 H2
Llithfaen 36 C1
Lloc 47 K5
Llong 48 B6
Llowes 28 A4
Lloyney 28 B1
Llundain-fach 26 E3
Llwydcoed 18 C1
Llwydiarth 37 K4
Llwyn M.Tyd. 27 K7
Llwyn Shrop. 38 B7
Llwyncelyn 26 D3
Llwyn-croes 17 H3
Llwyndafydd 26 C3
Llwynderw 38 B5
Llwyndyrys 36 C1
Llwyneinion 38 B1
Llwyngwril 36 E5
Llwynhendy 17 J6
Llwyn-Madoc 27 J3
Llwynmawr 38 B2
Llwyn-onn 26 D3
Llwyn-y-brain Carmar. 16 E4
Llwyn-y-brain Carmar. 27 G5
Llwyn-y-groes 26 E3
Llwynypia 18 C2
Llynclys 38 B3
Llynfaes 46 C5
Llysfaen 47 G5
Llyswen 28 A5
Llysworney 18 C4
Llys-y-frân 16 D3
Llywel 27 H5
Load Brook 50 E4
Loanhead 76 A4
Loans 74 B7
Lobb 6 C2
Lobhillcross 6 C7
Loch a Charnain 88 C4
Loch Baghasdail 88 B7
Loch Choire Lodge 87 J6
Loch Eil Outward Bound 79 M3
Loch Head D.& G. 64 D6
Loch Head D.& G. 67 J4
Loch na Madadh 88 D2
Loch Sgioport 88 C5
Lochailort 79 J2
Lochaline 78 H6
Lochans 64 A5
Locharbriggs 68 E5
Lochawe 79 N8
Lochboisdale 88 B7
Lochbuie 78 H8
Lochcarron 83 J6
Lochdhu Hotel 87 N5
Lochdon 79 J7
Lochearnhead 80 A8
Lochee 81 J7
Lochend High. 87 Q3
Lochend High. 83 R7
Locheport 88 C2
Locheuphort 88 C2
Lochfoot 65 K3
Lochgair 73 H1
Lochgarthside 83 R9
Lochgelly 75 K1
Lochgilphead 73 G2
Lochgoilhead 79 P10
Lochgoyn 74 D6
Lochhill E.Ayr. 67 K2
Lochhill Moray 84 G4
Lochinch Castle 64 B4
Lochinver 86 C7
Lochlea 74 C7
Lochmaben 69 F5
Lochmaddy 88 D2
Lochore 75 K1
Lochportain 88 D1
Lochranza 73 H5
Lochside Aber. 81 N4
Lochside High. 86 G4
Lochside High. 87 L6
Lochton 67 G5
Lochuisge 79 J5
Lochurr 68 C5
Lochussie 83 Q5
Lochwinnoch 74 B5
Lockengate 4 A4
Lockerbie 69 G5
Lockeridge 20 E5
Lockerley 10 D2
Lockhills 61 G2
Locking 19 G6
Lockington E.Riding 59 F5
Lockington Leics. 41 G3
Lockleywood 39 F3
Locks Heath 11 G4
Locksbottom 23 H5
Locksgreen 11 F5
Lockton 58 E1
Loddington Leics. 42 A5
Loddington Northants. 32 B1
Loddiswell 5 H6
Loddon 45 H6
Lode 33 J2
Loders 8 D5
Lodsworth 12 C4
Lofthouse N.Yorks. 57 G2
Lofthouse W.Yorks. 57 J7
Loftus 63 H5
Logan D.& G. 64 A6
Logan E.Ayr. 67 K1
Loganlea 75 H4
Loggerheads 39 G2
Logie Coldstone 85 J10
Logierait 80 E5
Login 16 E3
Lolworth 33 G2
Lonbain 82 G5
Londesborough 58 E5
London 23 G3
London Apprentice 4 A6
London Beach 14 D4
London City Airport 23 H3
London Colney 22 E1
London Gatwick Airport 23 F7
London Heathrow Airport 22 D4
London Luton Airport 32 E6
London Minstead 10 D3
London Stansted Airport 33 J6
Londonderry 57 H1
Londonthorpe 42 C2
Londubh 83 J2
Long Ashton 19 J4
Long Bank 29 G1
Long Bennington 42 B1
Long Bredy 8 E5
Long Buckby 31 H2
Long Clawson 42 A3
Long Common 11 G3
Long Compton Staffs. 40 A3
Long Compton Warks. 30 D5
Long Crendon 21 K1
Long Crichel 9 J3
Long Dean 20 B4
Long Downs 2 E5
Long Drax 58 C7
Long Duckmanton 51 G5
Long Eaton 41 G2
Long Gill 56 C4
Long Green Ches. 48 D5
Long Green Essex 34 D6
Long Green Worcs. 29 H5
Long Hanborough 31 F7
Long Itchington 31 F2
Long Lane 39 F4
Long Lawford 31 F1
Long Load 8 D2
Long Marston Herts. 32 B7
Long Marston N.Yorks. 58 B4
Long Marston Warks. 30 C4
Long Marton 61 H4
Long Meadowend 38 D7
Long Melford 34 C4
Long Newnton 20 C2
Long Preston 56 D4
Long Riston 59 H5
Long Stratton 45 F6
Long Street 31 J4
Long Sutton Hants. 22 A7
Long Sutton Lincs. 43 H3
Long Sutton Som. 8 D2
Long Thurlow 34 E2
Long Whatton 41 G3
Long Wittenham 21 J2
Longbenton 71 H7
Longborough 30 C6
Longbridge Plym. 5 F5
Longbridge W.Mid. 30 B1
Longbridge Warks. 30 D2
Longbridge Deverill 20 B7
Longburgh 60 E1
Longburton 9 F3
Longcliffe 50 E7
Longcombe 5 J5
Longcot 21 F2
Longcroft 75 F3
Longcross Devon 4 E3
Longcross Surr. 22 C5
Longden 38 D5
Longdon Staffs. 40 C4
Longdon Worcs. 29 H5
Longdon Green 40 C4
Longdon upon Tern 39 F4
Longdown 7 G6
Longfield 24 C5
Longfield Hill 24 C5
Longfleet 10 B5
Longford Derbys. 40 E2
Longford Glos. 29 H6
Longford Gt.Lon. 22 D4
Longford Shrop. 39 F2
Longford Tel.& W. 39 G4
Longford W.Mid. 41 F7
Longforgan 81 J8
Longformacus 76 E5
Longframlington 71 G3
Longham Dorset 10 B5
Longham Norf. 44 D4
Longhirst 71 H5
Longhope Glos. 29 F7
Longhope Ork. 89 C8
Longhorsley 71 G4
Longhoughton 71 H2
Longlands Cumb. 60 D3
Longlands Gt.Lon. 23 H4
Longlane Derbys. 40 E2
Longlane W.Berks. 21 H4
Longlevens 29 H7
Longley 50 D2
Longley Green 29 G3
Longmanhill 85 M4

M

Moor End Beds. 32 D3
Moor End Beds. 32 C6
Moor End Cumb. 55 J2
Moor End E.Riding 58 E6
Moor End Lancs. 55 G5
Moor End N.Yorks. 58 B6
Moor End W.Yorks. 57 F7
Moor Green W.Mid. 40 C7
Moor Green Wilts. 20 B5
Moor Head 57 G6
Moor Monkton 58 B4
Moor Row 60 B5
Moor Side Cumb. 55 F2
Moor Side Lancs. 55 H6
Moor Side Lancs. 55 H6
Moor Side Lincs. 53 F7
Moor Street 24 E5
Moorby 53 F6
Moorcot 28 C3
Moordown 10 B5
Moore 48 E4
Moorend 60 E1
Moorends 51 J1
Moorfield 50 C3
Moorgreen Hants. 11 F3
Moorgreen Notts. 41 G1
Moorhall 51 F5
Moorhampton 28 C4
Moorhouse Cumb. 60 E1
Moorhouse Notts. 51 K6
Moorland 8 C1
Moorlinch 8 C1
Moorsholm 63 G5
Moorside Dorset 9 G3
Moorside Gt.Man. 49 J2
Moorside W.Yorks. 57 H6
Moorthorpe 51 G1
Moortown I.o.W. 11 F6
Moortown Lincs. 52 D3
Moortown Tel. & W. 39 F4
Morar 82 G11
Morborne 42 E6
Morchard Bishop 7 F5
Morcombelake 8 D5
Morcott 42 C5
Morda 38 B3
Morden Dorset 9 J5
Morden Gt.Lon. 23 F5
Morden Park 23 F5
Mordiford 28 E5
Mordington Holdings 77 H5
Mordon 62 D4
More 38 C6
Morebath 7 H3
Morebattle 70 C1
Morecambe 55 H3
Morefield 83 M1
Moreleigh 5 H5
Morenish 80 B7
Moresby Parks 60 A5
Morestead 11 G2
Moreton Dorset 9 H6
Moreton Essex 23 J1
Moreton Here. 28 E2
Moreton Mersey. 48 B4
Moreton Oxon. 21 K1
Moreton Staffs. 40 D2
Moreton Staffs. 39 G4
Moreton Corbet 38 E3
Moreton Jeffries 29 F4
Moreton Mill 38 E3
Moreton Morrell 30 E3
Moreton on Lugg 28 E4
Moreton Paddox 30 E3
Moreton Pinkney 31 G4
Moreton Say 39 F2
Moreton Valence 20 A1
Moretonhampstead 7 F7
Moreton-in-Marsh 30 D5
Morfa Carmar. 17 J4
Morfa Cere. 26 C3
Morfa Bychan 36 E2
Morfa Glas 18 B1
Morfa Nefyn 36 B1
Morgan's Vale 10 C2
Morganstown 18 E3
Mork 19 J1
Morland 61 G4
Morley Derbys. 41 F1
Morley Dur. 62 B4
Morley W.Yorks. 57 H7
Morley Green 49 H4
Morley St. Botolph 44 E6
Mornick 4 D3
Morningside Edin. 76 A3
Morningside N.Lan. 75 G5
Morningthorpe 45 G6
Morpeth 71 H5
Morrey 40 D4
Morridge Side 50 C7
Morrilow Heath 40 B2
Morriston S.Ayr. 67 G3
Morriston Swan. 17 K6
Morristown 18 E4
Morston 44 E1
Mortehoe 6 C1
Morthen 51 G4
Mortimer 21 K5
Mortimer West End 21 K5
Mortimer's Cross 28 D2
Mortlake 23 F4
Morton Derbys. 51 G6
Morton Lincs. 42 D3
Morton Lincs. 52 B3
Morton Lincs. 52 B6
Morton Notts. 51 K7
Morton S.Glos. 19 K2
Morton Shrop. 38 B3
Morton Bagot 30 C2
Morton on the Hill 45 F4
Morton Tinmouth 62 B4
Morton-on-Swale 62 D7
Morvah 2 B5
Morval 4 C5
Morvich High. 83 K8
Morvich High. 87 K9
Morvil 16 D2
Morville 39 F6
Morwellham 4 E4
Morwenstow 6 A4
Morwick Hall 71 H3
Mosborough 51 G4
Moscow 74 C6
Mosedale 60 E3
Moselden Height 50 C1
Moseley W.Mid. 40 C7
Moseley W.Mid. 40 B6
Moseley Worcs. 29 H3
Moses Gate 49 G2
Moss S.Yorks. 51 H1
Moss Wrex. 48 C7
Moss Bank 48 E3
Moss Houses 49 H5
Moss Nook 49 H4
Moss Side Gt.Man. 49 H3
Moss Side Lancs. 55 G6
Moss Side Mersey. 48 C2
Mossat 85 J9
Mossbank 89 N5
Mossblown 67 J1
Mossburnford 70 B2
Mossdale 65 G3
Mossend 75 F4
Mossgiel 67 J1
Mossley Ches. 49 H6
Mossley Gt.Man. 49 J2
Mossley Hill 48 C4
Mosspaul Hotel 69 J4
Moss-side 84 C5
Mosstodloch 84 H4
Mossy Lea 48 E1
Mosterton 8 D4
Moston Gt.Man. 49 H2
Moston Shrop. 38 E3
Moston Green 49 G6
Mostyn 47 K4
Motcombe 9 H2
Mothecombe 5 G6
Motherby 60 F4
Motherwell 75 F5
Mottingham 23 H4
Mottisfont 10 E2
Mottistone 11 F6
Mottram in Longdendale 49 J3
Mottram St. Andrew 49 H5
Mouldsworth 48 E5
Moulin 80 E5
Moulsecoomb 13 G6
Moulsford 21 J3
Moulsham 24 D1
Moulsoe 32 C4
Moulton Ches. 49 F6
Moulton Lincs. 43 G3
Moulton N.Yorks. 62 C6
Moulton Northants. 31 J2
Moulton Suff. 33 K2
Moulton V. of Glam. 18 D4
Moulton Chapel 43 F4
Moulton St. Mary 45 J5
Moulton Seas End 43 G3
Mount Cornw. 2 E3
Mount Cornw. 4 B4
Mount Kent 15 G3
Mount W.Yorks. 50 D1
Mount Ambrose 2 E4
Mount Bures 34 D5
Mount Charles 4 A5
Mount Hawke 2 E4
Mount Manisty 48 C5
Mount Oliphant 67 H2
Mount Pleasant Ches. 49 H7
Mount Pleasant Derbys. 41 F1
Mount Pleasant Derbys. 40 E4
Mount Pleasant E.Suss. 13 H5
Mount Pleasant Flints. 48 B5
Mount Pleasant Gt.Lon. 22 D2
Mount Pleasant Hants. 10 E5
Mount Pleasant Norf. 44 D6
Mount Pleasant Suff. 34 B4
Mount Sorrel 10 B2
Mount Tabor 57 F7
Mountain 57 F6
Mountain Ash 18 D2
Mountain Cross 75 K6
Mountain Water 16 C3
Mountbenger 69 J1
Mountblow 74 C3
Mountfield 14 C5
Mountgerald 83 R4
Mountjoy 3 F2
Mountnessing 24 C2
Mounton 19 J2
Mountsorrel 41 H4
Mousa 89 N10
Mousehole 2 B6
Mouswald 69 F6
Mow Cop 49 H7
Mowden 62 C5
Mowhaugh 70 D1
Mowsley 41 J7
Mowtie 81 P2
Moxley 40 B6
Moy High. 79 R2
Moy High. 84 B7
Moylgrove 16 E1
Muasdale 72 E6
Much Birch 28 E5
Much Cowarne 29 F4
Much Dewchurch 28 D5
Much Hadham 33 H7
Much Hoole 55 H7
Much Hoole Town 55 H7
Much Marcle 29 F5
Much Wenlock 39 F5
Muchalls 85 P11
Muchelney 8 D2
Muchelney Ham 8 D2
Muchlarnick 4 C5
Muchra 69 H2
Muchrachd 83 N7
Muck 78 F3
Mucking 24 C3
Muckle Roe 89 M6
Muckleford 9 F5
Mucklestone 39 G2
Muckleton 38 E3
Muckletown 85 K8
Muckley 39 F6
Muckley Corner 40 C5
Muckton 53 G4
Mudale 86 H6
Muddiford 6 D2
Muddles Green 13 J5
Muddleswood 13 F5
Mudeford 10 C5
Mudford 8 E3
Mudgley 19 H7
Mugdock 74 D3
Mugeary 82 E7
Mugginton 40 E1
Muggintonlane End 40 E1
Muggleswick 62 A2
Mugswell 23 F6
Muie 87 J9
Muir of Fowlis 85 K9
Muir of Ord 83 R5
Muirdrum 81 L7
Muiredge 76 B1
Muirhead 74 E4
Muirhouses 75 J2
Muirkirk 68 B1
Muirmill 75 F2
Muirton 80 G8
Muirton of Ardblair 80 G6
Muker 61 L7
Mulbarton 45 F5
Mulben 84 H5
Mull 78 G7
Mullacott Cross 6 D1
Mullion 2 D7
Mullion Cove 2 D7
Mumby 53 J5
Munderfield Row 29 F3
Munderfield Stocks 29 F3
Mundesley 45 H2
Mundford 44 C6
Mundham 45 H6
Mundon 24 E1
Munerigie 83 N10
Mungasdale 83 K1
Mungoswells 76 C3
Mungrisdale 60 E3
Munlochy 84 A5
Munnoch 74 A6
Munsley 29 F4
Munslow 38 E7
Murchington 6 E7
Murcott Oxon. 31 G7
Murcott Wilts. 20 C2
Murdostoun 75 G5
Murieston 75 J4
Murkle 87 P3
Murlaggan 83 L11
Murrell Green 22 A6
Murrow 43 G5
Mursley 32 B6
Murston 25 F5
Murthly 80 F7
Murton Cumb. 61 J4
Murton Dur. 62 D2
Murton Northumb. 77 H6
Murton Swan. 17 J7
Murton York 58 C4
Musbury 8 B5
Muscliff 10 B5
Musselburgh 76 B3
Mustard Hyrn 45 J4
Muston Leics. 42 B2
Muston N.Yorks. 59 G2
Mustow Green 29 H1
Mutford 45 J7
Muthill 80 D9
Mutley 4 E5
Mutterton 7 J5
Muxton 39 G4
Mybster 87 P4
Myddfai 27 G5
Myddle 38 D3
Myddlewood 38 D3
Mydroilyn 26 D3
Myerscough College 55 H6
Myerscough Smithy 56 B6
Mylor 3 F5
Mylor Bridge 3 F5
Mynachdy 18 E4
Mynachlog-ddu 16 E2
Myndtown 38 C7
Mynydd Fechell 46 B3
Mynydd Llandygai 46 E6
Mynydd-bach Mon. 19 H2
Mynydd-bach Swan. 17 K6
Mynyddygarreg 17 H5
Mynytho 36 C2
Mytchett 22 B6
Mytholm 56 E7
Mytholmroyd 57 F7
Mythop 55 G6
Myton-on-Swale 57 K3
Mytton 38 D4

▼N

Naast 83 J2
Nab's Head 56 B7
Na-Buirgh 88 F8
Naburn 58 B5
Nackington 15 G2
Nacton 35 G4
Nadderwater 7 G6
Nafferton 59 G4
Nailbridge 29 F7
Nailsbourne 8 B2
Nailsea 19 H4
Nailstone 41 G5
Nailsworth 20 B2
Nairn 84 C5
Nancegollan 2 D5
Nancekuke 2 D4
Nancledra 2 B5
Nanhoron 36 B2
Nannau 37 G3
Nannerch 47 K6
Nanpantan 41 H4
Nanpean 3 G3
Nanstallon 4 A4
Nant Peris 46 E7
Nant-ddu 27 K7
Nanternis 26 C3
Nantgaredig 17 H3
Nantgarw 18 E3
Nant-glas 27 J2
Nantglyn 47 J6
Nantgwyn 27 J1
Nantlle 46 D7
Nantmawr 38 B3
Nantmel 27 K2
Nantmor 37 F1
Nantwich 49 F7
Nantycaws 17 H4
Nant-y-derry 19 G1
Nant-y-dugoed 37 J4
Nantyffyllon 18 B2
Nantyglo 28 A7
Nant-y-Gollen 38 B3
Nant-y-groes 27 K2
Nant-y-moel 18 C2
Nant-y-Pandy 46 E5
Naphill 22 B2
Napley Heath 39 G2
Nappa 56 D4
Napton on the Hill 31 F2
Narberth 16 E4
Narborough Leics. 41 H6
Narborough Norf. 44 B4
Narkurs 4 D5
Nasareth 36 D1
Naseby 31 H1
Nash Bucks. 31 J5
Nash Here. 28 C2
Nash Newport 19 G3
Nash Shrop. 29 F1
Nash V. of Glam. 18 C4
Nash Street 24 C5
Nassington 42 D6
Nasty 33 G6
Nateby Cumb. 61 J6
Nateby Lancs. 55 H5
Nately Scures 22 A6
Natland 55 J1
Naughton 34 E4
Naunton Glos. 30 C6
Naunton Worcs. 29 H5
Naunton Beauchamp 29 J3
Navenby 52 C7
Navestock 23 J2
Navestock Side 23 J2
Navidale 87 N8
Nawton 58 C1
Nayland 34 D5
Nazeing 23 H1
Neacroft 10 C5
Neal's Green 41 F7
Neap House 52 B1
Near Sawrey 60 E7
Nearton End 32 B6
Neasden 23 F3
Neasham 62 D5
Neat Enstone 30 E6
Neath 18 A2
Neatham 22 A7
Neatishead 45 H3
Nebo Cere. 26 E2
Nebo Conwy 47 G7
Nebo Gwyn. 46 C7
Nebo I.o.A. 46 C3
Necton 44 C5
Nedd 86 D6
Nedderton 71 H5
Nedging 34 D4
Nedging Tye 34 E4
Needham 45 G7
Needham Market 34 E3
Needham Street 34 B2
Needingworth 33 G1
Needwood 40 D3
Neen Savage 29 F1
Neen Sollars 29 F1
Neenton 39 F7
Nefyn 36 C1
Neighbourne 19 K7
Neilston 74 C5
Neithrop 31 F4
Nelson Caerp. 18 E2
Nelson Lancs. 56 D6
Nelson Village 71 H6
Nemphlar 75 G6
Nempnett Thrubwell 19 J5
Nenthall 61 J2
Nenthead 61 J2
Nenthorn 76 E7
Neopardy 7 F6
Nerabus 72 A5
Nercwys 48 B6
Neriby 72 B4
Nerston 74 E5
Nesbit 77 H7
Nesfield 57 F5
Ness 48 C5
Nesscliffe 38 C4
Neston Ches. 48 B5
Neston Wilts. 20 B5
Nether Alderley 49 H5
Nether Auchendrane 67 H2
Nether Barr 64 E4
Nether Blainslie 76 D6
Nether Broughton 41 J3
Nether Burrow 56 B2
Nether Cerne 9 F5
Nether Compton 8 E3
Nether Dalgliesh 69 H3
Nether Dallachy 84 H4
Nether Edge 51 F4
Nether End 50 E5
Nether Exe 7 H6
Nether Glasslaw 85 N5
Nether Haugh 51 G3
Nether Heage 51 F7
Nether Heselden 56 D2
Nether Heyford 31 H3
Nether Kellet 55 J3
Nether Kinmundy 85 Q6
Nether Langwith 51 H5
Nether Loads 51 F6
Nether Moor 51 F6
Nether Padley 50 E5
Nether Poppleton 58 B4
Nether Silton 62 E7
Nether Skyborry 28 B1
Nether Stowey 7 K2
Nether Wallop 10 E1
Nether Wasdale 60 C6
Nether Wellwood 68 B1
Nether Welton 60 E2
Nether Westcote 30 D6
Nether Whitacre 40 E6
Nether Winchendon 31 J7
Nether Worton 31 F6
Netheravon 20 E7
Netherbrae 85 M5
Netherburn 75 G6
Netherbury 8 D5
Netherby Cumb. 69 J6
Netherby N.Yorks. 57 J5
Nethercott 31 F6
Netherend 19 J1
Netherfield E.Suss. 14 C6
Netherfield Notts. 41 J1
Netherfield S.Lan. 75 F6
Netherhall 74 A4
Netherhampton 10 C2
Netherhay 8 D4
Netherland Green 40 D2
Netherley 85 N11
Nethermill 69 F5
Netherseal 40 E4
Nethershield 67 K1
Netherstreet 20 C5
Netherthird D. & G. 65 H5
Netherthird E.Ayr. 67 K2
Netherthong 50 D2
Netherthorpe 51 H4
Netherton Angus 81 L5
Netherton Ches. 48 E5
Netherton Devon 5 J3
Netherton Hants. 21 G6
Netherton Mersey. 48 C2
Netherton N.Lan. 75 F5
Netherton Northumb. 70 E3
Netherton Oxon. 21 H1
Netherton P. & K. 80 G5
Netherton S.Lan. 75 H5
Netherton W.Mid. 40 B7
Netherton W.Yorks. 50 E1
Netherton W.Yorks. 50 D1
Netherton Worcs. 29 J4
Netherton Burnfoot 70 E3
Netherton Northside 70 E3
Nethertown Cumb. 60 A6
Nethertown Staffs. 40 D4
Netherwitton 71 G4
Netherwood D. & G. 65 K3
Netherwood E.Ayr. 68 B1
Nethy Bridge 84 E8
Netley Abbey 11 F4
Netley Marsh 10 E3
Nettlebed 21 K3
Nettlebridge 19 K7
Nettlecombe Dorset 8 E5
Nettlecombe I.o.W. 11 G7
Nettlecombe Som. 7 J2
Nettleden 32 D7
Nettleham 52 D5
Nettlestead Kent 23 K6
Nettlestead Suff. 34 E4
Nettlestead Green 23 K6
Nettlestone 11 H5
Nettlesworth 62 C2
Nettleton Lincs. 52 E2
Nettleton Wilts. 20 B4
Nettleton Hill 50 C1
Netton Devon 5 F6
Netton Wilts. 10 C1
Neuadd Cere. 26 D3
Neuadd I.o.A. 46 B3
Neuadd Powys 27 J4
Nevendon 24 D2
Nevern 16 E1
Nevill Holt 42 B6
New Abbey 65 K4
New Aberdour 85 N4
New Addington 23 G5
New Alresford 11 G1
New Alyth 80 H6
New Arley 40 E7
New Arram 59 G5
New Ash Green 24 C5
New Balderton 52 B7
New Barn 24 C5
New Belses 70 A1
New Bewick 71 F1
New Bolingbroke 53 G7
New Boultham 52 C5
New Bradwell 32 B4
New Brancepeth 62 C2
New Bridge D. & G. 65 K3
New Bridge Devon 5 H3
New Brighton Flints. 48 B6
New Brighton Hants. 11 J4
New Brighton Mersey. 48 C3
New Brighton W.Yorks. 57 H7
New Brighton Wrex. 48 B7
New Brinsley 51 G7
New Broughton 48 C7
New Buckenham 44 E6
New Byth 85 N5
New Cheriton 11 G2
New Cross Cere. 27 F1
New Cross Gt.Lon. 23 G4
New Cumnock 68 B2
New Deer 85 N6
New Duston 31 J2
New Earswick 58 C4
New Edlington 51 H3
New Elgin 84 G4
New Ellerby 59 H6
New Eltham 23 H4
New End 30 B2
New England 42 E5
New Farnley 57 H6
New Ferry 48 C4
New Galloway 65 G3
New Gilston 81 K10
New Greens 22 E1
New Grimsby 2 B1
New Hartley 71 J6
New Haw 22 D5
New Heaton 77 G7
New Hedges 16 E5
New Herrington 62 D1
New Hinksey 21 J1
New Holland 59 G7
New Houghton Derbys. 51 H6
New Houghton Norf. 44 B3
New Houses 56 D2
New Hunwick 62 B3
New Hutton 61 G7
New Hythe 14 C2
New Inn Carmar. 17 H2
New Inn Mon. 19 H1
New Inn Torfaen 19 F2
New Invention Shrop. 28 B1
New Invention W.Mid. 40 B5
New Lanark 75 G6
New Lane 48 D1
New Lane End 49 F3
New Leake 53 H7
New Leeds 85 P5
New Lodge 51 F2
New Longton 55 J7
New Luce 64 B4
New Mains 75 G7
New Malden 23 F5
New Marske 63 G4
New Marton 38 C2
New Mill Cornw. 2 B5
New Mill Herts. 32 C7
New Mill W.Yorks. 50 D2
New Mill End 32 E7
New Mills Cornw. 3 F3
New Mills Derbys. 50 C4
New Mills Glos. 19 K1
New Mills Mon. 19 J1
New Mills Powys 37 K5
New Milton 10 D5
New Mistley 35 F5
New Moat 16 D3
New Ollerton 51 J6
New Orleans 66 B2
New Oscott 40 C6
New Park Cornw. 4 B2
New Park N.Yorks. 57 H4
New Pitsligo 85 N5
New Polzeath 3 G1
New Quay 26 C2
New Rackheath 45 G4
New Radnor 28 B2
New Rent 61 F3
New Ridley 71 F7
New Road Side 56 E5
New Romney 15 F5
New Rossington 51 J3
New Row Cere. 27 G1
New Row Lancs. 56 B6
New Sawley 41 G2
New Shoreston 77 K7
New Silksworth 62 D1
New Swannington 41 G4
New Totley 51 F5
New Town Beds. 32 E4
New Town Cere. 16 E1
New Town Dorset 9 J3
New Town Dorset 9 J4
New Town E.Loth. 76 C3
New Town E.Suss. 13 H4
New Town Glos. 30 B5
New Tredegar 18 E1
New Tupton 51 F6
New Ulva 73 F2
New Valley 88 K4
New Village 51 H2
New Walsoken 43 H5
New Waltham 53 F2
New Winton 76 C3
New World 43 G6
New Yatt 30 E7
New York Lincs. 53 F7
New York T. & W. 71 J6
Newall 57 H5
Newark Ork. 89 G3
Newark Peter. 43 F5
Newark-on-Trent 52 B7
Newarthill 75 F5
Newball 52 D5
Newbarn 15 G4
Newbarns 55 F2
Newbattle 76 B4
Newbiggin Cumb. 61 F4
Newbiggin Cumb. 61 H4
Newbiggin Cumb. 61 G2
Newbiggin Cumb. 55 F3
Newbiggin Cumb. 60 B7
Newbiggin Dur. 61 L4
Newbiggin N.Yorks. 57 F1
Newbiggin N.Yorks. 61 L7
Newbiggin Northumb. 70 E7
Newbiggin-by-the-Sea 71 J5
Newbigging Angus 81 K7
Newbigging S.Lan. 75 J6
Newbiggin-on-Lune 61 J6
Newbold Derbys. 51 F5
Newbold Leics. 41 G4
Newbold on Avon 31 F1
Newbold on Stour 30 D4
Newbold Pacey 30 D3
Newbold Verdon 41 G5
Newborough I.o.A. 46 C6
Newborough Peter. 43 F5
Newborough Staffs. 40 D3
Newbottle Northants. 31 G5
Newbottle T. & W. 62 D1
Newbourne 35 G4
Newbridge Caerp. 19 F2
Newbridge Cornw. 2 B5
Newbridge Cornw. 4 D4
Newbridge E.Suss. 13 H3
Newbridge Edin. 75 K3
Newbridge Hants. 10 D3
Newbridge I.o.W. 11 F6
Newbridge N.Yorks. 58 E1
Newbridge Oxon. 21 H1
Newbridge Pembs. 16 C2
Newbridge Wrex. 38 B1
Newbridge Green 29 H5
Newbridge on Wye 27 K3
Newbridge-on-Usk 19 G2
Newbrough 70 D7
Newbuildings 7 F5
Newburgh Aber. 85 P8
Newburgh Fife 80 H9
Newburgh Lancs. 48 D1
Newburgh Sc.Bord. 69 J1
Newburn 71 G7
Newbury Som. 19 K6
Newbury W.Berks. 21 H5
Newbury Wilts. 20 B7
Newbury Park 23 H3
Newby Cumb. 61 G4
Newby Lancs. 56 D5
Newby N.Yorks. 63 F5
Newby N.Yorks. 56 C2
Newby N.Yorks. 59 G1
Newby Bridge 55 G1
Newby Cote 56 C2
Newby Cross 60 E1
Newby East 61 F1
Newby West 60 E1
Newby Wiske 57 J1
Newcastle Bridgend 18 B4
Newcastle Mon. 28 D7
Newcastle Shrop. 38 B7
Newcastle Emlyn 17 G1
Newcastle International Airport 71 G6
Newcastle upon Tyne 71 H7
Newcastleton 69 K5
Newcastle-under-Lyme 40 A1
Newchapel Pembs. 17 F2
Newchapel Stoke 49 H7
Newchapel Surr. 23 G7
Newchurch Carmar. 17 G3
Newchurch I.o.W. 11 G6
Newchurch Kent 15 F4
Newchurch Lancs. 56 D7
Newchurch Lancs. 56 D6
Newchurch Mon. 19 H2
Newchurch Powys 28 B3
Newchurch Staffs. 40 D3
Newcott 8 B4
Newcraighall 76 B3
Newdigate 22 E7
Newell Green 22 B4
Newenden 14 D5
Newent 29 G6
Newerne 19 K1
Newfield Dur. 62 C3
Newfield Dur. 62 C1
Newfound 21 J6
Newgale 16 B3
Newgate 44 E1
Newgate Street 23 G1
Newhall Ches. 39 F1
Newhall Derbys. 40 E3
Newham 71 G1
Newham Hall 71 G1
Newhaven 13 H6
Newhey 49 J1
Newholm 63 J5
Newhouse 75 F4
Newick 13 H4
Newingreen 15 G4
Newington Edin. 76 A3
Newington Kent 15 G4
Newington Kent 24 E5
Newington Notts. 51 J3
Newington Oxon. 21 K2
Newington Bagpath 20 B2
Newland Cumb. 55 G2
Newland Glos. 19 J1
Newland Hull 59 G6
Newland N.Yorks. 58 C7
Newland Oxon. 30 E7
Newland Worcs. 29 G4
Newlandrig 76 B4
Newlands Cumb. 60 E3
Newlands Essex 24 E3
Newlands Northumb. 62 A1
Newlands Sc.Bord. 70 A4
Newland's Corner 22 D7
Newlands of Geise 87 N3
Newlyn 2 B6
Newmachar 85 N9
Newmains 75 G5
Newman's End 33 J7
Newman's Green 34 C4
Newmarket Suff. 33 K2
Newmarket W.Isles 88 K4
Newmill Aber. 81 N2
Newmill Moray 85 J5
Newmill Sc.Bord. 69 K2
Newmillerdam 51 F1
Newmiln 80 G7
Newmilns 74 D7
Newney Green 24 C1
Newnham Glos. 29 F7
Newnham Hants. 22 A6
Newnham Herts. 33 F5
Newnham Kent 14 E2
Newnham Northants. 31 G3
Newnham Bridge 29 F2
Newnham Paddox 41 G7
Newport Cornw. 6 B7
Newport Devon 6 D2
Newport E.Riding 58 E6
Newport Essex 33 J5
Newport Glos. 19 K2
Newport High. 87 P7
Newport I.o.W. 11 G6
Newport Newport 19 G3
Newport Norf. 45 K4
Newport Pembs. 16 D2
Newport Som. 8 C2
Newport Tel. & W. 39 G4
Newport Pagnell 32 B4
Newport-on-Tay 81 K8
Newpound Common 12 D4
Newquay 3 F2
Newquay Cornwall Airport 3 F2
Newsbank 49 H6
Newseat 85 M7
Newsells 33 G5
Newsham Lancs. 55 J6
Newsham N.Yorks. 62 B5
Newsham N.Yorks. 57 J1
Newsham Northumb. 71 J6
Newsholme E.Riding 58 D7
Newsholme Lancs. 56 D4
Newsome 50 D1
Newstead Northumb. 71 G1
Newstead Notts. 51 H7
Newstead Sc.Bord. 76 D7
Newthorpe N.Yorks. 57 K6
Newthorpe Notts. 41 G1
Newtoft 52 D4
Newton Arg. & B. 73 J1
Newton Bridgend 18 B4
Newton Cambs. 43 H4
Newton Cambs. 33 H4
Newton Cardiff 19 F4
Newton Ches. 48 E7
Newton Ches. 48 E5
Newton Cumb. 55 F2
Newton D. & G. 69 G4
Newton Derbys. 51 G7
Newton Gt.Man. 49 J3
Newton Here. 28 C2
Newton Here. 28 E3
Newton Here. 28 C5
Newton High. 84 B6
Newton High. 83 R5
Newton High. 84 B4
Newton Lancs. 56 B4
Newton Lancs. 55 J2
Newton Lancs. 55 G6
Newton Lincs. 42 D2
Newton N.Ayr. 73 H5
Newton Norf. 44 C4
Newton Northants. 42 B7
Newton Northumb. 71 F7
Newton Northumb. 70 E3
Newton Notts. 41 J1
Newton Pembs. 16 B3
Newton Pembs. 16 C5
Newton S.Glos. 19 K2
Newton S.Lan. 75 H7
Newton Sc.Bord. 70 B1
Newton Shrop. 38 D2
Newton Som. 7 K2
Newton Staffs. 40 C3
Newton Suff. 34 D4
Newton Swan. 17 K7
Newton W.Loth. 75 J3
Newton W.Yorks. 57 K7
Newton Warks. 31 G1
Newton Wilts. 10 D2
Newton Abbot 5 J3
Newton Arlosh 60 D1
Newton Aycliffe 62 C4
Newton Bewley 62 E4
Newton Blossomville 32 C3
Newton Bromswold 32 C2
Newton Burgoland 41 F5
Newton by Toft 52 D4
Newton Ferrers 5 F6
Newton Flotman 45 G6
Newton Green 19 J2
Newton Harcourt 41 J6
Newton Kyme 57 K5
Newton Longville 32 B5
Newton Mearns 74 D5
Newton Morrell N.Yorks. 62 C6
Newton Morrell Oxon. 31 H6
Newton Mountain 16 C5
Newton Mulgrave 63 H5
Newton of Leys 84 A7
Newton on the Hill 38 D3
Newton on Trent 52 B5
Newton Poppleford 7 J7
Newton Purcell 31 H5
Newton Regis 40 E5
Newton Reigny 61 F3
Newton St. Cyres 7 G6
Newton St. Faith 45 G4
Newton St. Loe 20 A5
Newton St. Petrock 6 C4
Newton Solney 40 E3
Newton Stacey 21 H7
Newton Stewart 64 E4
Newton Tony 21 F7
Newton Tracey 6 D3
Newton under Roseberry 63 F5
Newton Underwood 71 G5
Newton upon Derwent 58 D5
Newton Valence 11 J1
Newton with Scales 55 H6
Newtonairds 68 D5
Newtongrange 76 B4
Newtonhill 85 P11
Newton-le-Willows Mersey. 48 E3
Newton-le-Willows N.Yorks. 57 H1
Newtonmore 84 B11
Newton-on-Ouse 58 B4
Newton-on-Rawcliffe 63 J7
Newton-on-the-Moor 71 G3
Newtown Bucks. 22 C1
Newtown Ches. 48 E7
Newtown Cornw. 4 C3
Newtown Cornw. 2 C6
Newtown Cumb. 70 A7
Newtown Derbys. 49 J4
Newtown Devon 7 G3
Newtown Devon 7 J6
Newtown Dorset 8 D4
Newtown Glos. 19 K1
Newtown Gt.Man. 48 E2
Newtown Gt.Man. 49 G2
Newtown Hants. 11 H3
Newtown Hants. 21 H5
Newtown Hants. 10 D3
Newtown Hants. 10 E2
Newtown Hants. 11 G3
Newtown Here. 29 F4
Newtown Here. 28 D3
Newtown High. 83 P10
Newtown I.o.M. 54 C6
Newtown I.o.W. 11 F5
Newtown Northumb. 71 F3
Newtown Northumb. 71 F1
Newtown Oxon. 22 A3
Newtown Powys 38 A6
Newtown R.C.T. 18 D2
Newtown Shrop. 38 D2
Newtown Som. 8 B1
Newtown Som. 8 B3
Newtown Staffs. 49 J6
Newtown Staffs. 50 C6
Newtown Staffs. 40 B5
Newtown Wilts. 9 J2
Newtown Wilts. 21 G5
Newtown Linford 41 H5
Newtown St. Boswells 76 D7
Newtown Unthank 41 G5
Newtown-in-Saint-Martin 2 E6
Newtyle 80 H6
Newyears Green 22 D3
Neyland 16 C5
Nibley Glos. 19 K1
Nibley S.Glos. 19 K3
Nibley Green 20 A2
Nicholashayne 7 K4
Nicholaston 17 J7
Nidd 57 J3
Nigg Aberdeen 85 P10
Nigg High. 84 C3
Nightcott 7 G3
Nilig 47 J7
Nimlet 20 A4
Nine Ashes 23 J1
Nine Elms 20 E3
Nine Mile Burn 75 K5
Ninebanks 61 J1
Ninemile Bar 65 J3
Nineveh 29 F2
Ninfield 14 C6
Ningwood 11 F6
Nisbet 70 B1
Niton 11 G7
Nitshill 74 D4
Nizels 23 J6
No Man's Heath Ches. 38 E1
No Man's Heath Warks. 40 E5
No Man's Land 4 C5
Noah's Ark 23 J6
Noak Hill 23 J2
Noblehill 65 K3
Noblethorpe 50 E2
Nobottle 31 H2
Nocton 52 D6
Noddsdale 74 A4
Nogdam End 45 H5
Noke 31 G7
Nolton 16 B4
Nolton Haven 16 B4
Nomansland Devon 7 G4
Nomansland Wilts. 10 D3
Noneley 38 D3
Nonington 15 H2
Nook Cumb. 69 K6
Nook Cumb. 55 J1
Norbreck 55 G5
Norbury Ches. 38 E1
Norbury Derbys. 40 D1
Norbury Gt.Lon. 23 G4
Norbury Shrop. 38 C6
Norbury Staffs. 39 G3
Norbury Common 38 E1
Norbury Junction 39 G3
Norchard 16 D6
Norcott Brook 49 F4
Nordelph 43 J5
Norden Dorset 9 J6
Norden Gt.Man. 49 H1
Nordley 39 F6
Norham 77 H6
Norland Town 57 F7
Norley 48 E5
Norleywood 10 E5
Norlington 13 H5
Norman Cross 42 E6
Normanby N.Lincs. 52 B1
Normanby N.Yorks. 58 D1
Normanby R. & C. 63 F5
Normanby by Stow 52 B4
Normanby le Wold 52 E3
Normanby-by-Spital 52 D4
Normandy 22 C6
Norman's Bay 13 K6
Norman's Green 7 J5
Normanston 45 K6
Normanton Derby 41 F2
Normanton Leics. 42 B1
Normanton Lincs. 42 C1
Normanton Notts. 51 K7
Normanton Rut. 42 C5
Normanton W.Yorks. 57 J7
Normanton le Heath 41 F4
Normanton on Soar 41 H3
Normanton on Trent 51 K6
Normanton-on-the-Wolds 41 J2
Normoss 55 G6
Norrington Common 20 B5
Norris Green 4 E4
Norris Hill 41 F4
Norristhorpe 57 H7
North Acton 23 F3
North Anston 51 H4
North Ascot 22 C5
North Aston 31 F6
North Baddesley 10 E3
North Ballachulish 79 M4
North Balloch 67 H4
North Barrow 9 F2
North Barsham 44 D2
North Benfleet 24 D3
North Bersted 12 C6
North Berwick 76 D2
North Boarhunt 11 H3
North Bovey 7 F7
North Bradley 20 B6
North Brentor 6 C7
North Brewham 9 G1
North Bridge 12 C3
North Buckland 6 C1
North Burlingham 45 H4
North Cadbury 9 F2
North Cairn 66 D6
North Camp 22 B6
North Carlton Lincs. 52 C5
North Carlton Notts. 51 H4
North Cave 58 E6
North Cerney 20 D1
North Chailey 13 G4
North Charford 10 C3
North Charlton 71 G1
North Cheriton 9 F2
North Chideock 8 D5
North Cliffe 58 E6
North Clifton 52 B5
North Cockerington 53 G3
North Coker 8 E3
North Collafirth 89 M4
North Common S.Glos. 19 K4
North Common Suff. 34 D1
North Connel 79 L7
North Coombe 7 G5
North Cornelly 18 B3
North Corner 19 K3
North Cotes 53 G2
North Cove 45 J7
North Cowton 62 C6
North Crawley 32 C4
North Cray 23 H4
North Creake 44 C2
North Curry 8 C2
North Dalton 59 F4
North Deighton 57 J4
North Dell 88 K1
North Duffield 58 C6
North Elkington 53 F3
North Elmham 44 D3
North Elmsall 51 G1
North End Bucks. 32 B6
North End Dorset 9 H2
North End E.Riding 59 H4
North End E.Riding 59 H5
North End E.Riding 59 J6
North End Essex 33 K7
North End Hants. 11 G2
North End Hants. 10 C3
North End Leics. 41 H4
North End N.Som. 19 H5
North End Norf. 44 E6
North End Northumb. 71 G3
North End Ports. 11 H4
North End W.Suss. 12 E5
North End W.Suss. 12 C6
North Erradale 82 H2
North Fambridge 24 E2
North Ferriby 59 F7
North Frodingham 59 H4
North Gorley 10 C3
North Green Norf. 45 G7
North Green Suff. 35 H1
North Green Suff. 35 H2
North Green Suff. 35 H2
North Grimston 58 E3
North Halling 24 D5
North Harby 52 B5
North Hayling 11 J4
North Hazelrigg 77 J7
North Heasley 7 F2
North Heath W.Berks. 21 H4
North Heath W.Suss. 12 D4
North Hill 4 C3
North Hillingdon 22 D3
North Hinksey 21 H1
North Holmwood 22 E7
North Houghton 10 E1
North Huish 5 H5
North Hykeham 52 C6
North Johnston 16 C4
North Kelsey 52 D2
North Kessock 84 A6
North Killingholme 52 E1
North Kilvington 57 K1
North Kilworth 41 J7
North Kingston 10 C4
North Kyme 52 E7
North Lancing 12 E6
North Lee 22 B1
North Lees 57 J2
North Leigh 30 E7
North Leverton with Habblesthorpe 51 K4
North Littleton 30 B4
North Lopham 44 E7
North Luffenham 42 C5
North Marden 12 B5
North Marston 31 J6
North Middleton Midloth. 76 B5
North Middleton Northumb. 71 F1
North Molton 7 F3
North Moreton 21 J3
North Mundham 12 B6
North Muskham 51 K7
North Newbald 59 F6
North Newington 31 F5
North Newnton 20 E6
North Newton 8 B1
North Nibley 20 A2
North Oakley 21 J6
North Ockendon 23 J3
North Ormesby 63 F5
North Ormsby 53 F3
North Otterington 57 J1
North Owersby 52 D3
North Perrott 8 D4
North Petherton 8 B1
North Petherwin 4 C2
North Pickenham 44 C5
North Piddle 29 J3
North Plain 69 G7
North Pool 5 H6
North Poorton 8 E5
North Quarme 7 H2
North Queensferry 75 K2
North Radworthy 7 F2
North Rauceby 42 D1
North Reston 53 G4
North Rigton 57 H5
North Rode 49 H6
North Roe 89 M4
North Ronaldsay 89 G2
North Runcton 44 A4
North Sandwick 89 P3
North Scale 54 E3
North Scarle 52 B6
North Seaton 71 H5
North Shields 71 J7
North Shoebury 25 F3
North Side 43 F6
North Skelton 63 G5
North Somercotes 53 H3
North Stainley 57 H2
North Stainmore 61 K5
North Stifford 24 C3
North Stoke B. & N.E.Som. 20 A5
North Stoke Oxon. 21 K3
North Stoke W.Suss. 12 D5
North Stoneham 11 F3
North Street Hants. 11 H1
North Street Kent 15 F2
North Street Med. 24 E4
North Street W.Berks. 21 K4
North Sunderland 77 K7
North Tamerton 6 B6
North Tawton 6 E5
North Third 75 F2
North Thoresby 53 F3
North Tidworth 21 F7
North Togston 71 H3
North Town Devon 6 D5
North Town Hants. 22 B6
North Town W. & M. 22 B3
North Tuddenham 44 E4
North Uist 88 C1
North Walsham 45 G2
North Waltham 21 J7
North Warnborough 22 A6
North Watten 87 Q4
North Weald Bassett 23 H1
North Wembley 22 E3
North Wheatley 51 K4
North Whilborough 5 J4
North Wick 19 J5
North Widcombe 19 J6
North Willingham 52 E4
North Wingfield 51 G6
North Witham 42 C3
North Wootton Dorset 9 F3
North Wootton Norf. 44 A3
North Wootton Som. 19 J7
North Wraxall 20 B4
North Wroughton 20 E3
North Yardhope 70 E3
Northacre 44 D6
Northall 32 C6
Northall Green 44 D4
Northallerton 62 D7
Northam Devon 6 C3
Northam S'ham. 11 F3
Northampton 31 J2
Northaw 23 F1
Northay Devon 8 C4
Northay Som. 8 B3
Northbay 88 B8
Northbeck 42 D1
Northborough 42 E5
Northbourne Kent 15 J2
Northbourne Oxon. 21 J3
Northbridge Street 14 C5
Northbrook Hants. 11 G1
Northbrook Oxon. 31 F6
Northchapel 12 C4
Northchurch 22 C1
Northcote Manor 6 E4
Northcott 6 B6
Northcourt 21 J2
Northedge 51 F6
Northend B. & N.E.Som. 20 A5
Northend Bucks. 22 A2
Northend Warks. 30 E3
Northfield Hull 59 G7
Northfield Sc.Bord. 77 H4
Northfield Som. 8 B1
Northfield W.Mid. 30 B1
Northfields 42 D5
Northfleet 24 C4
Northhouse 69 K3
Northiam 14 D5
Northill 32 E4
Northington Glos. 20 A1
Northington Hants. 11 G1
Northlands 53 G7
Northleach 30 C7
Northleigh Devon 7 K6
Northleigh Devon 6 E2
Northlew 6 D6
Northmoor 21 H1
Northmoor Green 8 C1
Northmuir 81 J5
Northney 11 J4
Northolt 22 E3
Northop 48 B6
Northop Hall 48 B6
Northorpe Lincs. 43 F2
Northorpe Lincs. 52 B3
Northorpe Lincs. 42 D4
Northover Som. 8 E2
Northover Som. 8 D1
Northowram 57 G7
Northport 9 J6
Northrepps 45 G2
Northton 88 E9
Northway Glos. 29 J5
Northway Som. 7 K3
Northwich 49 F5
Northwick S.Glos. 19 J3
Northwick Som. 19 G7
Northwick Worcs. 29 H3
Northwold 44 B6
Northwood Gt.Lon. 22 D2
Northwood I.o.W. 11 F5
Northwood Kent 25 K5
Northwood Mersey. 48 D3
Northwood Shrop. 38 D2
Northwood Green 29 G7
Northwood Hills 22 E2
Norton Glos. 29 H6
Norton Halton 48 E4
Norton Herts. 33 F5
Norton I.o.W. 10 E6
Norton Mon. 28 D6
Norton N.Som. 19 G5
Norton N.Yorks. 58 D2
Norton Northants. 31 H2
Norton Notts. 51 H5
Norton Powys 28 C2
Norton S.Yorks. 51 H1
Norton S.Yorks. 51 F4
Norton Shrop. 38 E5
Norton Shrop. 39 G5
Norton Shrop. 38 D7
Norton Stock. 62 E4
Norton Suff. 34 D2
Norton Swan. 17 K7
Norton V. of Glam. 18 B4
Norton W.Mid. 40 A7
Norton W.Suss. 12 C6
Norton W.Suss. 12 B7
Norton Wilts. 20 B3
Norton Worcs. 29 H3
Norton Worcs. 30 B4
Norton Bavant 20 C7
Norton Bridge 40 A2
Norton Canes 40 C5
Norton Canon 28 C4
Norton Disney 52 B7
Norton Ferris 9 G1
Norton Fitzwarren 7 K3
Norton Green Herts. 33 F6
Norton Green I.o.W. 10 E6
Norton Green Stoke 49 J7
Norton Hawkfield 19 J5
Norton Heath 24 C1
Norton in Hales 39 G2
Norton in the Moors 49 H7
Norton Lindsey 30 D2
Norton Little Green 34 D2
Norton Malreward 19 K5
Norton Mandeville 23 J1
Norton St. Philip 20 A6
Norton Subcourse 45 J6
Norton Wood 28 C4
Norton Woodseats 51 F4
Norton-Juxta-Twycross 41 F5
Norton-le-Clay 57 K2
Norton-sub-Hamdon 8 D3
Norwell 51 K6
Norwell Woodhouse 51 K6
Norwich 45 G5
Norwich Airport 45 G4
Norwick 89 Q1
Norwood End 23 J1
Norwood Green Gt.Lon. 22 E4
Norwood Green W.Yorks. 57 G7
Norwood Hill 23 F7
Norwood Park 8 E1
Noseley 42 A6
Noss Mayo 5 F6
Nosterfield 57 H1
Nosterfield End 33 K4
Nostie 83 J8
Notgrove 30 C6
Nottage 18 B4
Notting Hill 23 F3
Nottingham 41 H1
Nottingham East Midlands Airport 41 G3
Nottington 9 F6
Notton W.Yorks. 51 F1
Notton Wilts. 20 C5
Nottswood Hill 29 G7
Nounsley 34 B7
Noutard's Green 29 G2
Nowton 34 C2
Nox 38 D4
Noyadd Trefawr 17 F1
Nuffield 21 K3
Nun Monkton 58 B4
Nunburnholme 58 E5
Nuneaton 41 F6
Nuneham Courtenay 21 J2
Nunney 20 A7
Nunnington Here. 28 E4
Nunnington N.Yorks. 58 C2
Nunnington Park 7 J3
Nunnykirk 71 F4
Nunsthorpe 53 F2
Nunthorpe Middbro. 63 F5
Nunthorpe York 58 B4
Nunton 10 C2
Nunwick N.Yorks. 57 J2
Nunwick Northumb. 70 D6
Nup End 33 F7
Nupend 20 A1
Nursling 10 E3
Nursted 11 J2
Nurton 40 A6
Nutbourne W.Suss. 12 D5
Nutbourne W.Suss. 11 J4
Nutfield 23 G6
Nuthall 41 H1
Nuthampstead 33 H5
Nuthurst W.Suss. 12 E4
Nuthurst Warks. 30 C1
Nutley E.Suss. 13 H4
Nutley Hants. 21 K7
Nutwell 51 J2
Nyadd 75 F1
Nyetimber 12 B7
Nyewood 11 J2
Nymet Rowland 7 F5
Nymet Tracey 7 F5
Nympsfield 20 B1
Nynehead 7 K3
Nythe 8 D1
Nyton 12 C6

▼O

Oad Street 24 E5
Oadby 41 J5
Oak Cross 6 D6
Oak Tree 62 D5
Oakamoor 40 C1
Oakbank 75 J4
Oakdale Caerp. 18 E2
Oakdale Poole 10 B5
Oake 7 K3
Oaken 40 A5
Oakenclough 55 J5
Oakengates 39 G4
Oakenholt 48 B5
Oakenshaw Dur. 62 C3
Oakenshaw W.Yorks. 57 G7
Oakerthorpe 51 F7
Oakes 50 D1
Oakfield I.o.W. 11 G5
Oakfield Torfaen 19 F2
Oakford Cere. 26 D3
Oakford Devon 7 H3
Oakfordbridge 7 H3
Oakgrove 49 J6
Oakham 42 B5
Oakhanger 11 J1
Oakhill 19 K7
Oakington 33 H2
Oaklands Conwy 47 G7
Oaklands Herts. 33 F7
Oakle Street 29 G7
Oakley Beds. 32 D3
Oakley Bucks. 31 H7
Oakley Fife 75 J2
Oakley Hants. 21 J6
Oakley Oxon. 22 A1
Oakley Poole 10 B5
Oakley Suff. 35 F1
Oakley Green 22 C4
Oakley Park 37 J7
Oakridge Lynch 20 C1
Oaks 38 D5
Oaks Green 40 D2
Oaksey 20 C2
Oakshaw Ford 70 A6
Oakshott 11 J2
Oakthorpe 41 F4
Oaktree Hill 62 D7
Oakwoodhill 12 E3
Oakworth 57 F6
Oare Kent 25 G5
Oare Som. 7 G1
Oare Wilts. 20 E5
Oasby 42 D2
Oatfield 66 A2
Oath 8 C2
Oathlaw 81 K5
Oatlands 57 J4
Oban 79 K8
Obley 28 C1
Oborne 9 F3
Obthorpe 42 D4
Occlestone Green 49 F6
Occold 35 F1
Occumster 87 Q6
Ochiltree 67 K1
Ochr-y-foel 47 J5
Ochtertyre P. & K. 80 D8
Ochtertyre Stir. 75 F1
Ockbrook 41 G2
Ockeridge 29 G2
Ockham 22 D6
Ockle 78 G3
Ockley 12 E3
Ocle Pychard 28 E4
Octon 59 G2
Odcombe 8 E3
Odd Down 20 A5
Oddingley 29 J3
Oddington 31 G7
Oddsta 89 P3
Odell 32 C3

Putsborough 6 C1
Puttenham Herts. 32 B7
Puttenham Surr. 22 C7
Puttock End 34 C4
Putts Corner 7 K6
Puxton 19 H5
Pwll 17 H5
Pwllcrochan 16 C5
Pwlldefaid 36 A3
Pwll-glas 47 K7
Pwllgloyw 27 K5
Pwllheli 36 C2
Pwll-Mawr 19 F4
Pwllmeyric 19 J2
Pwll-trap 17 F4
Pwll-y-glaw 18 A2
Pye Corner Herts. 33 H7
Pye Corner Kent 14 D3
Pye Corner Newport 19 G3
Pye Green 40 B4
Pyecombe 13 F5
Pyle Bridgend 18 B3
Pyle I.o.W. 11 F7
Pyleigh 7 K2
Pylle 9 F1
Pymore Cambs. 43 H7
Pymore Dorset 8 D5
Pyrford 22 D6
Pyrford Green 22 D6
Pyrton 21 K2
Pytchley 32 B1
Pyworthy 6 B5

Q

Quabbs 38 B7
Quadring 43 F2
Quadring Eaudike 43 F2
Quainton 31 J6
Quarff 89 N9
Quarley 21 F7
Quarndon 41 F1
Quarr Hill 11 G5
Quarrier's Village 74 B4
Quarrington 42 D1
Quarrington Hill 62 D3
Quarry Bank 40 B7
Quarrybank 48 E6
Quarrywood 84 F4
Quarter 75 F5
Quatford 39 G6
Quatt 39 G7
Quebec 62 B2
Quedgeley 29 H7
Queen Adelaide 43 J7
Queen Camel 8 E2
Queen Charlton 19 K5
Queen Dart 7 G4
Queen Oak 9 G1
Queen Street 23 K7
Queenborough 25 F4
Queen's Bower 11 G6
Queen's Head 38 C3
Queensbury Gt.Lon. 22 E3
Queensbury W.Yorks. 57 G6
Queensferry Edin. 75 K3
Queensferry Flints. 48 C6
Queenzieburn 74 E3
Quemerford 20 D5
Quendale 89 M11
Quendon 33 J5
Queniborough 41 J4
Quenington 20 E1
Quernmore 55 J3
Queslett 40 C6
Quethiock 4 D4
Quick's Green 21 J4
Quidenham 44 E7
Quidhampton 21 J6
Quidinish 88 F9
Quina Brook 38 E2
Quine's Hill 54 C6
Quinhill 73 F5
Quinton Northants. 31 J3
Quinton W.Mid. 40 B7
Quinton Green 31 J3
Quintrell Downs 3 F2
Quixhill 40 D1
Quoditch 6 C6
Quoig 80 D8
Quoisley 38 E1
Quorn 41 H4
Quorndon 41 H4
Quothquan 75 H7
Quoyloo 89 B5

R

Raasay 82 F6
Raby 48 C5
Rachan 75 K7
Rachub 46 E6
Rackenford 7 G4
Rackham 12 D5
Rackheath 45 G4
Racks 69 F6
Rackwick Ork. 89 B8
Rackwick Ork. 89 D3
Radbourne 40 E2
Radcliffe Gt.Man. 49 G2
Radcliffe Northumb. 71 H3
Radcliffe on Trent 41 J2
Radclive 31 H5
Radcot 21 F2
Raddington 7 J3
Radernie 81 K10
Radford B.&N.E.Som. 19 K6
Radford Nott. 41 H1
Radford Oxon. 31 F6
Radford W.Mid. 41 F7
Radford Semele 30 E2
Radipole 9 F6
Radlett 22 E1
Radley 21 J2
Radley Green 24 C1
Radmore Green 48 E7
Radnage 22 A2
Radstock 19 K6
Radstone 31 G4
Radway 30 E4
Radway Green 49 G7
Radwell Beds. 32 D3
Radwell Herts. 33 F5
Radwinter 33 K5
Radyr 18 E3
Raechester 70 E5
Rafford 84 E5
Ragdale 41 J3
Ragged Appleshaw 21 G7
Raglan 19 H1
Ragnall 52 B5
Rain Shore 49 H1
Rainford 48 D2
Rainham Gt.Lon. 23 J3
Rainham Med. 24 E5
Rainhill 48 D3
Rainhill Stoops 48 E3
Rainow 49 J5
Rainsough 49 G2
Rainton 57 J2
Rainworth 51 H7
Raisbeck 61 H6
Raise 61 J2
Rait 80 H8
Raithby Lincs. 53 G6
Raithby Lincs. 53 G4
Rake 12 B4
Raleigh's Cross 7 J2
Ram 17 J1
Ram Alley 21 F5
Ram Lane 14 E3
Ramasaig 82 B6
Rame Cornw. 2 E5
Rame Cornw. 4 E6
Rampisham 8 E4
Rampside 55 F3
Rampton Cambs. 33 H2
Rampton Notts. 52 B5
Ramsbottom 49 G1
Ramsbury 21 F4
Ramscraigs 87 P7
Ramsdean 11 J2
Ramsdell 21 J6
Ramsden 30 E7
Ramsden Bellhouse 24 D2
Ramsden Heath 24 D2
Ramsey Cambs. 43 F7
Ramsey Essex 35 G5
Ramsey I.o.M. 54 D4
Ramsey Forty Foot 43 G7
Ramsey Heights 43 F7
Ramsey Island Essex 25 F1
Ramsey Island Pembs. 16 A3
Ramsey Mereside 43 F7
Ramsey St. Mary's 43 F7
Ramsgate 25 K5
Ramsgate Street 44 E2
Ramsgill 57 G2
Ramsholt 35 H4
Ramshorn 40 C1
Ramsnest Common 12 C3
Ranais 88 K5
Ranby Lincs. 53 F5
Ranby Notts. 51 J4
Rand 52 E5
Randwick 20 B1
Rangemore 40 D3
Rangeworthy 19 K3
Ranish 88 K5
Rankinston 67 J2
Rank's Green 34 B7
Ranmoor 51 F4
Rannoch School 80 A5
Ranscombe 7 H1
Ranskill 51 J4
Ranton 40 A3
Ranton Green 40 A3
Ranworth 45 H4
Rapness 89 E3
Rapps 8 C3
Rascarrel 65 H6
Rash 56 B1
Rashwood 29 J2
Raskelf 57 K2
Rassau 28 A7
Rastrick 57 G7
Ratagan 83 K9
Ratby 41 H5
Ratcliffe Culey 41 F6
Ratcliffe on Soar 41 G3
Ratcliffe on the Wreake 41 J4
Ratford Bridge 16 B4
Ratfyn 20 E7
Rathen 85 P4
Rathillet 81 J8
Rathmell 56 D3
Ratho 75 K3
Ratho Station 75 K3
Rathven 85 J4
Ratley 30 E4
Ratling 15 H2
Ratlinghope 38 D6
Ratsloe 7 H6
Rattar 87 Q2
Ratten Row Cumb. 60 E2
Ratten Row Lancs. 55 H5
Rattery 5 H4
Rattlesden 34 D3
Rattray 80 G6
Raughton Head 60 E2
Raunds 32 C1
Ravenfield 51 G3
Ravenglass 60 B7
Raveningham 45 H6
Raven's Green 35 F6
Ravenscar 63 K6
Ravensdale 54 C4
Ravensden 32 D3
Ravenshaw 56 E5
Ravenshayes 7 H5
Ravenshead 51 H7
Ravensmoor 49 F7
Ravensthorpe Northants. 31 H1
Ravensthorpe W.Yorks. 57 H7
Ravenstone Leics. 41 G4
Ravenstone M.K. 32 B3
Ravenstonedale 61 J6
Ravenstruther 75 H6
Ravensworth 62 B6
Raw 63 K6
Rawcliffe E.Riding 58 C7
Rawcliffe York 58 B4
Rawcliffe Bridge 58 C7
Rawdon 57 H6
Rawmarsh 51 G3
Rawnsley 40 C4
Rawreth 24 D2
Rawridge 8 B4
Rawson Green 41 F1
Rawtenstall 56 D7
Rawyards 75 F4
Raydon 34 E5
Raylees 70 E4
Rayleigh 24 E2
Raymond's Hill 8 C5
Rayne 34 B6
Rayners Lane 22 E3
Raynes Park 23 F5
Reach 33 J2
Read 56 C6
Reading 22 A4
Reading Green 35 F1
Reading Street 14 E4
Reagill 61 H5
Rearquhar 84 B1
Rearsby 41 J4
Rease Heath 49 F7
Reaveley 71 F2
Reawick 89 M8
Reay 87 M3
Reculver 25 J5
Red Ball 7 J4
Red Bull 49 H7
Red Dial 60 D2
Red Hill Hants. 11 J3
Red Hill Warks. 30 C3
Red Lodge 33 K1
Red Lumb 49 H1
Red Oaks Hill 33 J5
Red Point 82 H4
Red Post Cornw. 6 A5
Red Post Devon 5 J4
Red Rail 28 E6
Red Rock 48 E2
Red Roses 17 F4
Red Row 71 H4
Red Street 49 H7
Red Wharf Bay 46 D4
Redberth 16 D5
Redbourn 32 E7
Redbourne 52 C3
Redbrook Glos. 28 E7
Redbrook Wrex. 38 E1
Redbrook Street 14 E4
Redburn High. 83 R4
Redburn High. 84 D6
Redburn Northumb. 70 C7
Redcar 63 G4
Redcastle Angus 81 M5
Redcastle High. 83 R6
Redcliff Bay 19 H4
Reddingmuirhead 75 H3
Reddish 49 H3
Redditch 30 B2
Rede 34 C3
Redenhall 45 G7
Redesmouth 70 D5
Redford Angus 81 L6
Redford Dur. 62 A3
Redford W.Suss. 12 B4
Redgrave 34 E1
Redhill Aber. 85 M10
Redhill N.Som. 19 H5
Redhill Notts. 41 H1
Redhill Surr. 23 F6
Redhill Aerodrome & Heliport 23 F7
Redhouse 73 G4
Redhouses 72 B4
Redisham 45 J7
Redland Bristol 19 J4
Redland Ork. 89 C5
Redlingfield 35 F1
Redlynch Som. 9 G1
Redlynch Wilts. 10 D2
Redmarley D'Abitot 29 G5
Redmarshall 62 D4
Redmile 42 A2
Redmire 62 A7
Redmoor 4 A4
Rednal 38 C3
Redpath 76 D7
Redruth 2 D4
Redscarhead 76 A6
Redshaw 68 D1
Redstone Bank 16 E4
Redwick Newport 19 H3
Redwick S.Glos. 19 J3
Redworth 62 C4
Reed 33 G5
Reed End 33 G5
Reedham 45 J5
Reedley 56 D6
Reedness 58 D7
Reepham Lincs. 52 D5
Reepham Norf. 44 E3
Reeth 62 A7
Regaby 54 D4
Regil 19 J5
Regoul 84 C5
Reiff 86 B8
Reigate 23 F6
Reighton 59 H2
Reinigeadal 88 H7
Reiss 87 R4
Rejerrah 2 E3
Releath 2 D5
Relubbus 2 C5
Relugas 84 D6
Remenham 22 A3
Remenham Hill 22 A3
Rempstone 41 H3
Rendcomb 30 B7
Rendham 35 H2
Rendlesham 35 H3
Renfrew 74 D4
Renhold 32 D3
Renishaw 51 G5
Rennington 71 H2
Renton 74 B3
Renwick 61 G2
Repps 45 J4
Repton 41 F3
Rescobie 81 L5
Rescorla 4 A5
Resipole 79 J4
Resolis 84 A4
Resolven 18 B1
Respryn 4 B4
Reston 77 G4
Restormel 4 B4
Reswallie 81 L5
Reterth 3 G2
Retew 3 G3
Retford 51 K4
Rettendon 24 D2
Rettendon Place 24 D2
Retyn 3 F3
Revesby 53 F6
Revesby Bridge 53 G6
Rew 5 H3
Rew Street 11 F5
Rewe Devon 7 H6
Rewe Devon 7 G6
Reybridge 20 C5
Reydon 35 J1
Reydon Smear 35 K1
Reymerston 44 E5
Reynalton 16 D5
Reynoldston 17 H7
Rezare 4 D3
Rhadyr 19 G1
Rhandirmwyn 27 G4
Rhayader 27 J2
Rhedyn 36 B2
Rhemore 78 G5
Rhenigidale 88 H7
Rheola 18 B1
Rhes-y-cae 47 K6
Rhewl Denb. 38 A1
Rhewl Denb. 47 K6
Rhewl Shrop. 38 C2
Rhian 86 H8
Rhicarn 86 C7
Rhicullen 84 A3
Rhidorroch 83 M1
Rhifail 87 K5
Rhigos 18 C1
Rhiston 38 B6
Rhiw 36 B3
Rhiwargor 37 J3
Rhiwbina 18 E3
Rhiwbryfdir 37 F1
Rhiwderin 19 F3
Rhiwinder 18 D3
Rhiwlas Gwyn. 46 D6
Rhiwlas Gwyn. 37 J2
Rhiwlas Powys 38 B2
Rhode 8 B1
Rhodes Minnis 15 G3
Rhodesia 51 H5
Rhodiad-y-brenin 16 A3
Rhodmad 26 E1
Rhonadale 73 F7
Rhonehouse 65 H5
Rhoose 18 D5
Rhos Carmar. 17 G2
Rhos N.P.T. 18 A1
Rhos Common 38 B4
Rhôs Lligwy 46 C4
Rhosaman 27 G7
Rhoscolyn 46 A5
Rhoscrowther 16 C5
Rhosesmor 48 B6
Rhos-fawr 36 C2
Rhosgadfan 46 D7
Rhos-goch I.o.A. 46 C4
Rhosgoch Powys 28 A4
Rhos-hill 16 E1
Rhoshirwaun 36 A3
Rhoslan 36 D1
Rhoslefain 36 E5
Rhosllanerchrugog 38 B1
Rhosmaen 17 K3
Rhosmeirch 46 C5
Rhosneigr 46 B5
Rhosnesni 48 C7
Rhôs-on-Sea 47 G4
Rhossili 17 H7
Rhosson 16 A3
Rhostrehwfa 46 C5
Rhostryfan 46 C7
Rhostyllen 38 C1
Rhos-y-bol 46 C4
Rhos-y-brithdir 38 A3
Rhosycaerau 16 C2
Rhos-y-garth 27 F1
Rhos-y-gwaliau 37 J2
Rhos-y-llan 36 B2
Rhos-y-mawn 47 G6
Rhos-y-Meirch 28 B2
Rhu 74 A2
Rhuallt 47 J5
Rhubodach 73 J3
Rhuddall Heath 48 E6
Rhuddlan 47 J5
Rhue 83 M1
Rhulen 28 A4
Rhunahaorine 73 F6
Rhuthun 47 K7
Rhyd Gwyn. 37 F1
Rhyd Powys 37 J5
Rhydaman 17 K4
Rhydargaeau 17 H3
Rhydcymerau 17 J2
Rhyd-Ddu 46 D7
Rhydding 18 A2
Rhydgaled 47 H6
Rhydlanfair 47 G7
Rhydlewis 17 G1
Rhydlios 36 A2
Rhydlydan Conwy 47 G7
Rhydlydan Powys 37 K6
Rhydolion 36 B3
Rhydowen 17 H1
Rhyd-Rosser 26 E2
Rhydspence 28 B4
Rhydtalog 48 B7
Rhyd-uchaf 37 H2
Rhyd-wen 37 J3
Rhyd-wyn 46 B4
Rhyd-y-ceirw 48 B7
Rhyd-y-clafdy 36 C2
Rhydycroesau 38 B2
Rhydyfelin Cere. 26 E1
Rhydyfelin R.C.T. 18 D3
Rhyd-y-foel 47 H5
Rhyd-y-fro 18 A1
Rhyd-y-groes 46 D6
Rhydymain 37 H3
Rhydymwyn 48 B6
Rhyd-yr-onnen 37 F5
Rhyd-y-sarn 37 F1
Rhydywrach 16 E4
Rhyl 47 J4
Rhymney 18 E1
Rhyn 38 C2
Rhynd 80 G8
Rhynie Aber. 85 J8
Rhynie High. 84 C3
Ribbesford 29 G1
Ribchester 56 B6
Ribigill 86 H4
Riby 52 E2
Riccall 58 C6
Riccarton 74 C7
Richards Castle 28 D2
Richings Park 22 D4
Richmond Gt.Lon. 22 E4
Richmond N.Yorks. 62 B6
Richmond S.Yorks. 51 G4
Rich's Holford 7 K2
Rickarton 81 P2
Rickerscote 40 B3
Rickford 19 H6
Rickinghall 34 E1
Rickleton 62 C1
Rickling 33 H5
Rickling Green 33 J6
Rickmansworth 22 D2
Riddell 70 A1
Riddings 51 G7
Riddlecombe 6 E4
Riddlesden 57 F5
Ridge Dorset 9 J6
Ridge Herts. 23 F1
Ridge Wilts. 9 J1
Ridge Green 23 G7
Ridge Lane 40 E6
Ridgebourne 27 K2
Ridgeway 51 G4
Ridgeway Cross 29 G4
Ridgeway Moor 51 G4
Ridgewell 34 B4
Ridgewood 13 H4
Ridgmont 32 C5
Riding Gate 9 G2
Riding Mill 71 F7
Ridley 24 C5
Ridleywood 48 C7
Ridlington Norf. 45 H2
Ridlington Rut. 42 B5
Ridsdale 70 E5
Riechip 80 F6
Rievaulx 58 B1
Rift House 62 E3
Rigg 69 H7
Riggend 75 F4
Rigmaden Park 56 B1
Rigsby 53 H5
Rigside 75 G7
Riley Green 56 B7
Rileyhill 40 D4
Rilla Mill 4 C3
Rillaton 4 C3
Rillington 58 E2
Rimington 56 D5
Rimpton 9 F2
Rimswell 59 K7
Rinaston 16 C3
Ring o' Bells 48 D1
Ringford 65 G5
Ringinglow 50 E4
Ringland 45 F4
Ringles Cross 13 H4
Ringmer 13 H5
Ringmore Devon 5 G6
Ringmore Devon 5 K3
Ring's End 43 H5
Ringsfield 45 J7
Ringsfield Corner 45 J7
Ringshall Herts. 32 C7
Ringshall Suff. 34 E3
Ringshall Stocks 34 E3
Ringstead Norf. 44 B1
Ringstead Northants. 32 C1
Ringwood 10 C4
Ringwould 15 J3
Rinloan 84 G10
Rinsey 2 C6
Ripe 13 J6
Ripley Derbys. 51 F7
Ripley Hants. 10 C5
Ripley N.Yorks. 57 H3
Ripley Surr. 22 D6
Riplingham 59 F6
Ripon 57 J2
Rippingale 42 E3
Ripple Kent 15 J3
Ripple Worcs. 29 H5
Ripponden 50 C1
Risabus 72 B6
Risbury 28 E3
Risby E.Riding 59 G6
Risby Suff. 34 B2
Risca 19 F2
Rise 59 H5
Riseden 14 C4
Risegate 43 F3
Riseholme 52 C5
Riseley Beds. 32 D2
Riseley W'ham 22 A5
Rishangles 35 F2
Rishton 56 C6
Rishworth 50 C1
Risinghurst 21 J1
Risley Derbys. 41 G2
Risley Warr. 49 F3
Risplith 57 H3
Rispond 86 G3
Rivar 21 G5
Rivenhall 34 C7
Rivenhall End 34 C7
River Kent 15 H3
River W.Suss. 12 C4
River Bank 33 J2
River Bridge 19 G7
Riverford Bridge 5 H4
Riverhead 23 J6
Riverside 18 E4
Riverton 6 E2
Riverview Park 24 C4
Rivington 49 F1
Roa Island 55 F3
Roach Bridge 55 J7
Road Green 45 G6
Road Weedon 31 H3
Roade 31 J3
Roadhead 70 A6
Roadside High. 87 P3
Roadside Ork. 89 F3
Roadside of Kinneff 81 P3
Roadwater 7 J2
Roag 82 C6
Roast Green 33 H5
Roath 18 E4
Roberton S.Lan. 68 E1
Roberton Sc.Bord. 69 K2
Robertsbridge 14 C5
Robertstown 18 D1
Robertstown 57 G7
Robeston Cross 16 B5
Robeston Wathen 16 D4
Robeston West 16 B5
Robin Hood Derbys. 50 E5
Robin Hood Lancs. 48 E1
Robin Hood W.Yorks. 57 J7
Robin Hood Doncaster Sheffield Airport 51 J3
Robin Hood's Bay 63 K6
Robinhood End 34 B5
Robins 12 B4
Roborough Devon 6 D4
Roborough Plym. 5 F4
Roby 48 D3
Roby Mill 48 E2
Rocester 40 D2
Roch 16 B3
Roch Bridge 16 B3
Roch Gate 16 B3
Rochdale 49 H1
Roche 3 G2
Rochester Med. 24 D5
Rochester Northumb. 70 D4
Rochford Essex 24 E2
Rochford Worcs. 29 F2
Rock Cornw. 3 G1
Rock Northumb. 71 H2
Rock Worcs. 29 G1
Rock Ferry 48 C4
Rockbeare 7 J6
Rockbourne 10 C3
Rockcliffe Cumb. 69 J7
Rockcliffe D.&G. 65 J5
Rockcliffe Cross 69 J7
Rockfield Arg.&B. 73 G5
Rockfield High. 84 D2
Rockfield Mon. 28 D7
Rockford 10 C4
Rockhampton 19 K2
Rockhead 4 A2
Rockingham 42 B6
Rockland All Saints 44 D6
Rockland St. Mary 45 H5
Rockland St. Peter 44 D6
Rockley 20 E4
Rockside 72 A4
Rockwell End 22 A3
Rockwell Green 7 K4
Rodborough 20 B1
Rodbourne 20 C3
Rodbridge Corner 34 C4
Rodd 28 C2
Roddam 71 F1
Rodden 9 F6
Rode 20 B6
Rode Heath 49 H7
Rodeheath 49 H6
Rodel 88 F9
Roden 38 E4
Rodhuish 7 J2
Rodington 38 E4
Rodington Heath 38 E4
Rodley 29 G7
Rodmarton 20 C2
Rodmell 13 H6
Rodmersham 25 F5
Rodmersham Green 25 F5
Rodney Stoke 19 H6
Rodsley 40 E1
Rodway 19 F7
Roe Cross 49 J3
Roe Green 33 G5
Roecliffe 57 J3
Roehampton 23 F4
Roesound 89 M6
Roffey 12 E3
Rogart 87 K9
Rogate 12 B4
Rogerstone 19 F3
Roghadal 88 F9
Rogiet 19 H3
Rokemarsh 21 K2
Roker 62 E1
Rollesby 45 J4
Rolleston Leics. 42 A5
Rolleston Notts. 51 K7
Rollestone 20 D7
Rolleston-on-Dove 40 E3
Rolston 59 J5
Rolstone 19 G5
Rolvenden 14 D4
Rolvenden Layne 14 D4
Romaldkirk 61 L4
Romanby 62 D7
Romannobridge 75 K6
Romansleigh 7 F3
Romesdal 82 E5
Romford Dorset 10 B4
Romford Gt.Lon. 23 J3
Romiley 49 J3
Romney Street 23 J5
Romsey 10 E2
Romsley Shrop. 39 G7
Romsley Worcs. 29 J1
Rona 82 G5
Ronachan 73 F5
Ronague 54 B6
Ronnachmore 72 B5
Rood End 40 C7
Rookhope 61 L2
Rookley 11 G6
Rookley Green 11 G6
Rooks Bridge 19 G6
Rook's Nest 7 J2
Rookwith 57 H1
Roos 59 J6
Roose 55 F3
Roosebeck 55 F3
Roosecote 55 F3
Rootham's Green 32 D3
Rootpark 75 H5
Ropley 11 H1
Ropley Dean 11 H1
Ropley Soke 11 H1
Ropsley 42 C2
Rora 85 Q5
Rorrington 38 C5
Rose 2 E3
Rose Ash 7 F3
Rose Green Essex 34 D6
Rose Green W.Suss. 12 C7
Rose Hill 13 H5
Roseacre Kent 14 C2
Roseacre Lancs. 55 H6
Rosebank 75 G6
Rosebrough 71 G1
Rosebush 16 D3
Rosecare 4 B1
Rosecliston 3 F3
Rosedale Abbey 63 H7
Roseden 71 F1
Rosehearty 85 P4
Rosehill 38 D4
Roselands 13 K6
Rosemarket 16 C5
Rosemarkie 84 B5
Rosemary Lane 7 K4
Rosemount P.&K. 80 G6
Rosemount S.Ayr. 67 H1
Rosenannon 3 G2
Rosenithon 3 F6
Rosepool 16 B4
Rosevean 4 A5
Roseville 40 B6
Rosewell 76 A4
Roseworth 62 E4
Rosgill 61 G5
Roshven 79 J3
Roskhill 82 C6
Roskorwell 2 E6
Rosley 60 E2
Roslin 76 A4
Rosliston 40 E4
Rosneath 74 A2
Ross D.&G. 65 G6
Ross Northumb. 77 K7
Ross P.&K. 80 C8
Ross Priory 74 C2
Rossdhu House 74 B2
Rossett 48 C7
Rossett Green 57 J4
Rosside 55 F2
Rossington 51 J3
Rossmore 10 B5
Ross-on-Wye 29 F6
Roster 87 Q6
Rostherne 49 G4
Rosthwaite Cumb. 60 D5
Rosthwaite Cumb. 55 F1
Roston 40 D1
Rosudgeon 2 C6
Rosyth 75 K2
Rothbury 71 F3
Rotherby 41 J4
Rotherfield 13 J3
Rotherfield Greys 22 A3
Rotherfield Peppard 22 A3
Rotherham 51 G3
Rothersthorpe 31 J3
Rotherwick 22 A6
Rothes 84 G6
Rothesay 73 J4
Rothienorman 85 M7
Rothiesholm 89 F5
Rothley Leics. 41 H4
Rothley Northumb. 71 F5
Rothney 85 L8
Rothwell Lincs. 52 E3
Rothwell Northants. 42 B7
Rothwell W.Yorks. 57 J7
Rotsea 59 G4
Rottal 81 J4
Rotten Row Bucks. 22 A3
Rotten Row W.Mid. 30 C1
Rottingdean 13 G6
Rottington 60 A5
Roud 11 G6
Roudham 44 D7
Rough Close 40 B2
Rough Common 15 G2
Rougham Norf. 44 C3
Rougham Suff. 34 D2
Rougham Green 34 D2
Roughburn 79 Q2
Roughlee 56 D5
Roughley 40 D6
Roughton Lincs. 53 F6
Roughton Norf. 45 G2
Roughton Shrop. 39 G6
Round Bush 22 E2
Roundbush Green 33 J7
Roundham 8 D4
Roundhay 57 J6
Roundstreet Common 12 D4
Roundway 20 D5
Rous Lench 30 B3
Rousay 89 C4
Rousdon 8 B5
Rousham 31 F6
Rousham Gap 31 F6
Routenburn 73 K4
Routh 59 G5
Rout's Green 22 A2
Row Cornw. 4 A3
Row Cumb. 55 H1
Row Cumb. 61 H3
Row Heath 35 F7
Row Town 22 D5
Rowanburn 69 K6
Rowardennan Lodge 74 B1
Rowarth 50 C4
Rowbarton 8 B2
Rowberrow 19 H6
Rowde 20 C5
Rowden 6 E6
Rowen 47 F5
Rowfields 40 D1
Rowfoot 70 B7
Rowhedge 34 E6
Rowhook 12 E3
Rowington 30 D2
Rowland 50 E5
Rowland's Castle 11 J3
Rowlands Gill 62 B1
Rowledge 22 B7
Rowlestone 28 C6
Rowley Devon 7 F4
Rowley Dur. 62 A2
Rowley Shrop. 38 C5
Rowley Park 40 B3
Rowley Regis 40 B7
Rowly 22 D7
Rowner 11 G4
Rowney Green 30 B1
Rownhams 10 E3
Rowrah 60 B5
Rowsham 32 B7
Rowsley 50 E6
Rowstock 21 H3
Rowston 52 D7
Rowthorne 51 G6
Rowton Ches. 48 D6
Rowton Shrop. 38 C4
Rowton Tel.&W. 39 F4
Roxburgh 77 F7
Roxby N.Lincs. 52 C1
Roxby N.Yorks. 63 H5
Roxton 32 E3
Roxwell 24 C1
Royal British Legion Village 14 C2
Royal Leamington Spa 30 E2
Royal Oak 48 D2
Royal Tunbridge Wells 13 J3
Roybridge 79 P2
Roydon Essex 33 H7
Roydon Norf. 44 E7
Roydon Norf. 44 B3
Roydon Hamlet 23 H1
Royston Herts. 33 G4
Royston S.Yorks. 51 F1
Royton 49 J2
Rozel 3 K6
Ruabon 38 C1
Ruaig 78 B6
Ruan Lanihorne 3 F4
Ruan Major 2 D7
Ruan Minor 2 E7
Ruanaich 78 D8
Ruardean 29 F7
Ruardean Hill 29 F7
Ruardean Woodside 29 F7
Rubery 29 J1
Ruckcroft 61 G2
Ruckinge 15 F4
Ruckland 53 G5
Rucklers Lane 22 D1
Ruckley 38 E5
Rudbaxton 16 C3
Rudby 62 E6
Rudchester 71 G7
Ruddington 41 H2
Ruddlemoor 4 A5
Rudford 29 G6
Rudge 20 B6
Rudgeway 19 K3
Rudgwick 12 D3
Rudhall 29 F6
Rudheath 49 F5
Rudley Green 24 E1
Rudloe 20 B5
Rudry 18 E3
Rudston 59 G3
Rudyard 49 J7
Rufford 48 D1
Rufforth 58 B4
Ruffside 61 L1
Rugby 31 G1
Rugeley 40 C4
Ruishton 8 B2
Ruislip 22 D3
Ruislip Gardens 22 D3
Ruislip Manor 22 E3
Rum 82 D11
Rumbling Bridge 75 J1
Rumburgh 45 H7
Rumford 3 F1
Rumleigh 4 E4
Rumney 19 F4
Rumwell 7 K3
Runcorn 48 E4
Runcton 12 B6
Runcton Holme 44 A5
Rundlestone 5 F3
Runfold 22 B7
Runhall 44 E5
Runham Norf. 45 J4
Runham Norf. 45 K5
Runnington 7 K3
Runsell Green 24 D1
Runshaw Moor 48 E1
Runswick Bay 63 J5
Runtaleave 80 H4
Runwell 24 D2
Ruscombe Glos. 20 B1
Ruscombe W'ham 22 A4
Rush Green Gt.Lon. 23 J3
Rush Green Herts. 33 F6
Rushall Here. 29 F5
Rushall Norf. 45 F7
Rushall W.Mid. 40 C5
Rushall Wilts. 20 E6
Rushbrooke 34 C2
Rushbury 38 E6
Rushden Herts. 33 G5
Rushden Northants. 32 C2
Rushford Devon 4 E3
Rushford Norf. 44 D7
Rushlake Green 13 K5
Rushmere 45 J7
Rushmere St. Andrew 35 G4
Rushmoor 22 B7
Rushock 29 H1
Rusholme 49 H3
Rushton Ches. 48 E6
Rushton Northants. 42 B7
Rushton Shrop. 39 F5
Rushton Spencer 49 J6
Rushwick 29 H3
Rushy Green 13 H5
Rushyford 62 C4
Ruskie 80 B10
Ruskington 52 D7
Rusko 65 F5
Rusland 55 G1
Rusper 13 F3
Ruspidge 29 F7
Russ Hill 23 F7
Russell Green 34 B7
Russell's Green 14 C6
Russell's Water 22 A2
Russel's Green 35 G1
Rustall 13 J3
Rustington 12 D6
Ruston 59 F1
Ruston Parva 59 G3
Ruswarp 63 J6
Rutherend 74 E5
Rutherford 76 E7
Rutherglen 74 E4
Ruthernbridge 4 A4
Ruthin Denb. 47 K7
Ruthin V. of Glam. 18 C4
Ruthrieston 85 P10
Ruthven Aber. 85 K6
Ruthven Angus 80 H6
Ruthven High. 84 B11
Ruthvoes 3 G2
Ruthwaite 60 D3
Ruthwell 69 F7
Ruyton-XI-Towns 38 C3
Ryal 71 F6
Ryal Fold 56 B7
Ryall Dorset 8 D5
Ryall Worcs. 29 H4
Ryarsh 23 K6
Rydal 60 E6
Ryde 11 G5
Rydon 6 B5
Rye 14 E5
Rye Foreign 14 D5
Rye Harbour 14 E6
Rye Park 23 G1
Rye Street 29 G5
Ryebank 38 E2
Ryeford 29 F6
Ryehill 59 J7
Ryhall 42 D4
Ryhill 51 F1
Ryhope 62 E1
Rylands 41 H2
Rylstone 56 E4
Ryme Intrinseca 8 E3
Ryther 58 B6
Ryton Glos. 29 G5
Ryton N.Yorks. 58 D2
Ryton Shrop. 39 G5
Ryton T.&W. 71 G7
Ryton-on-Dunsmore 30 E1

S

Sabden 56 C6
Sabden Fold 56 D6
Sackers Green 34 D5
Sacombe 33 G7
Sacombe Green 33 G7
Sacriston 62 C2
Sadberge 62 D5
Saddell 73 F7
Saddington 41 J6
Saddle Bow 44 A4
Sadgill 61 F6
Saffron Walden 33 J5
Sageston 16 D5
Saham Hills 44 D5
Saham Toney 44 C5
Saighdinis 88 C2
Saighton 48 D6
St. Abbs 77 H4
St. Agnes 2 E3
St. Albans 22 E1
St. Allen 3 F3
St. Andrews 81 L9
St. Andrews Major 18 E4
St. Anne 3 K4
St. Anne's 55 G7
St. Ann's 69 F4
St. Ann's Chapel Cornw. 4 E3
St. Ann's Chapel Devon 5 G6
St. Anthony 3 F5
St. Anthony-in-Meneage 2 E6
St. Anthony's Hill 13 K6
St. Arvans 19 J2
St. Asaph 47 J5
St. Athan 18 D5
St. Aubin 3 J7
St. Audries 7 K1
St. Austell 4 A5
St. Bees 60 A5
St. Blazey 4 A5
St. Blazey Gate 4 A5
St. Boswells 76 D7
St. Brelade 3 J7
St. Breock 3 G1
St. Breward 4 A3
St. Briavels 19 J1
St. Brides 16 B4
St. Brides Major 18 B4
St. Bride's Netherwent 19 H3
St. Brides Wentlooge 19 F3
St. Bride's-super-Ely 18 D4
St. Budeaux 4 E5
St. Buryan 2 B6
St. Catherine 20 A5
St. Catherines 79 N10
St. Clears 17 F4
St. Cleer 4 C4
St. Clement Chan.I. 3 K7
St. Clement Cornw. 3 F4
St. Clether 4 C2
St. Colmac 73 J4
St. Columb Major 3 G2
St. Columb Minor 3 F2
St. Columb Road 3 G3
St. Combs 85 Q4
St. Cross South Elmham 45 G7
St. Cyrus 81 N4
St. Davids Fife 75 K2
St. David's P.&K. 80 E8
St. David's Pembs. 16 A3
St. Day 2 E4
St. Decumans 7 J1
St. Dennis 3 G3
St. Denys 11 F3
St. Dogmaels 16 E1
St. Dogwells 16 C3
St. Dominick 4 E4
St. Donats 18 C5
St. Edith's Marsh 20 C5
St. Endellion 3 G1
St. Enoder 3 F3
St. Erme 3 F4
St. Erney 4 D5
St. Erth 2 C5
St. Erth Praze 2 C5
St. Ervan 3 F1
St. Eval 3 F2
St. Ewe 3 G4
St. Fagans 18 E4
St. Fergus 85 Q5
St. Fillans 80 B8
St. Florence 16 D5
St. Gennys 4 B1
St. George Bristol 19 K4
St. George Conwy 47 H5
St. Georges N.Som. 19 G5
St. George's Tel.&W. 39 G4
St. George's V. of Glam. 18 D4
St. Germans 4 D5
St. Giles in the Wood 6 D4
St. Giles on the Heath 6 B6
St. Harmon 27 J1
St. Helen Auckland 62 B4
St. Helena 45 F4
St. Helen's E.Suss. 14 D6
St. Helens I.o.W. 11 H6
St. Helens Mersey. 48 E3
St. Helier Chan.I. 3 J7
St. Helier Gt.Lon. 23 F5
St. Hilary Cornw. 2 C5
St. Hilary V. of Glam. 18 D4
St. Hill 13 G3
St. Ibbs 32 E6
St. Illtyd 19 F1
St. Ippollitts 32 E6
St. Ishmael 17 G5
St. Ishmael's 16 B5
St. Issey 3 G1
St. Ive 4 D4
St. Ives Cambs. 33 G1
St. Ives Cornw. 2 C4
St. Ives Dorset 10 C4
St. James South Elmham 45 H7
St. John Chan.I. 3 J6
St. John Cornw. 4 E5
St. John's I.o.M. 54 B5
St. John's Surr. 22 C6
St. John's Worcs. 29 H3
St. John's Chapel Devon 6 D3
St. John's Chapel Dur. 61 K3
St. John's Fen End 43 J4
St. John's Hall 62 A3
St. John's Highway 43 J4
St. John's Kirk 75 H7
St. John's Town of Dalry 68 B5
St. Judes 54 C4
St. Just 2 A5
St. Just in Roseland 3 F5
St. Katherines 85 M7
St. Keverne 2 E6
St. Kew 4 A3
St. Kew Highway 4 A3
St. Keyne 4 C4
St. Lawrence Cornw. 4 A4
St. Lawrence Essex 25 F1
St. Lawrence I.o.W. 11 G7
St. Leonards Bucks. 22 C1
St. Leonards Dorset 10 C4
St. Leonards E.Suss. 14 D7
St. Leonards Grange 11 F5
St. Leonard's Street 23 K6
St. Levan 2 A6
St. Lythans 18 E4
St. Mabyn 4 A3
St. Madoes 80 G8
St. Margaret South Elmham 45 H7
St. Margarets Here. 28 C5
St. Margarets Herts. 33 G7
St. Margarets Wilts. 21 F5
St. Margaret's at Cliffe 15 J3
St. Margaret's Hope 89 D8
St. Mark's 54 B6
St. Martin Chan.I. 3 J5
St. Martin Chan.I. 3 K7
St. Martin Cornw. 4 C5
St. Martin Cornw. 2 E6
St. Martin's I.o.S. 2 C1
St. Martins P.&K. 80 G7
St. Martin's Shrop. 38 C2
St. Mary 3 J7
St. Mary Bourne 21 H6
St. Mary Church 18 D4
St. Mary Cray 23 H5
St. Mary Hill 18 C4
St. Mary Hoo 24 D4
St. Mary in the Marsh 15 F5
St. Marychurch 5 K4
St. Mary's I.o.S. 2 C1
St. Mary's Ork. 89 D7
St. Mary's Airport 2 C1
St. Mary's Bay 15 F5
St. Mary's Croft 64 A4
St. Mary's Grove 19 H5
St. Maughans Green 28 D7
St. Mawes 3 F5
St. Mawgan 3 F2
St. Mellion 4 D4
St. Mellons 19 F3
St. Merryn 3 F1
St. Mewan 3 G3
St. Michael Caerhays 3 G4
St. Michael Church 8 C1
St. Michael Penkevil 3 F4
St. Michael South Elmham 45 H7
St. Michaels Fife 81 K8
St. Michaels Kent 14 D4
St. Michaels Worcs. 28 E2
St. Michael's on Wyre 55 H5
St. Minver 3 G1
St. Monans 81 L10
St. Neot 4 B4
St. Neots 32 E2
St. Newlyn East 3 F3
St. Nicholas Pembs. 16 C2
St. Nicholas V. of Glam. 18 D4
St. Nicholas at Wade 25 J5
St. Ninians 75 F1
St. Osyth 35 F7
St. Ouen 3 J6
St. Owen's Cross 28 E6
St. Paul's Cray 23 H5
St. Paul's Walden 32 E6
St. Peter 3 J7
St. Peter Port 3 J5
St. Peter's 25 K5
St. Petrox 16 C6
St. Pinnock 4 C4
St. Quivox 67 H1
St. Ruan 2 E7
St. Sampson 3 J5
St. Saviour Chan.I. 3 H5
St. Saviour Chan.I. 3 K7
St. Stephen 3 G3
St. Stephens Cornw. 4 E5
St. Stephens Cornw. 6 B7
St. Stephens Herts. 22 E1
St. Teath 4 A2
St. Thomas 7 H6
St. Tudy 4 A3
St. Twynnells 16 C6
St. Veep 4 B5
St. Vigeans 81 M6
St. Wenn 3 G2
St. Weonards 28 D6
St. Winnow 4 B5
St. y Nyll 18 D4
Saintbury 30 C5
Salachail 79 M5
Salcombe 5 H7
Salcombe Regis 7 K7
Salcott 34 D7
Sale 49 G3
Sale Green 29 J3
Saleby 53 H5
Salehurst 14 C5
Salem Carmar. 17 K3
Salem Cere. 37 F7
Salem Gwyn. 46 D7
Salen Arg.&B. 78 G6
Salen High. 78 H4
Salendine Nook 50 D1
Salesbury 56 B6
Saleway 29 J3
Salford Beds. 32 C5
Salford Gt.Man. 49 H3
Salford Oxon. 30 D6
Salford Priors 30 B3
Salfords 23 F7
Salhouse 45 H4
Saline 75 J1
Salisbury 10 C2
Salkeld Dykes 61 G3
Sallachy High. 86 H9
Sallachy High. 83 K7
Salle 45 F3
Salmonby 53 G5
Salperton 30 B6
Salph End 32 D3
Salsburgh 75 G4
Salt 40 B3
Salt Hill 22 C3
Salt Holme 62 E4
Saltaire 57 G6
Saltash 4 E5
Saltburn 84 B3
Saltburn-by-the-Sea 63 G4
Saltby 42 B3
Saltcoats Cumb. 60 B7
Saltcoats N.Ayr. 74 A6
Saltcotes 55 G7
Saltdean 13 G6
Salterbeck 60 A4
Salterforth 56 D5
Saltergate 63 J7
Salterswall 49 F6
Saltfleet 53 H3
Saltfleetby All Saints 53 H3
Saltfleetby St. Clements 53 H3
Saltfleetby St. Peter 53 H4
Saltford 19 K5
Salthaugh Grange 59 J7
Salthouse 44 E1
Saltley 40 C7
Saltmarshe 58 D7
Saltney 48 C6
Salton 58 D1
Saltrens 6 C3
Saltwick 71 G6
Saltwood 15 G4
Salvington 12 E6
Salwarpe 29 H2
Salwayash 8 D5
Sambourne 30 B2
Sambrook 39 G3
Samlesbury 56 B6
Sampford Arundel 7 K4
Sampford Brett 7 J1
Sampford Courtenay 6 E5
Sampford Moor 7 K4
Sampford Peverell 7 J4
Sampford Spiney 5 F3
Samuelston 76 C3
Sanaigmore 72 A3
Sancreed 2 B6
Sancton 59 F6
Sand 19 H7
Sand Hutton 58 C4
Sandaig Arg.&B. 78 A6
Sandaig High. 82 H10
Sandal Magna 51 F1
Sanday 89 G3
Sandbach 49 G6
Sandbank 73 K2
Sandbanks 10 B6
Sandend 85 K4
Sanderstead 23 G5
Sandford Cumb. 61 J5
Sandford Devon 7 G5
Sandford Dorset 9 J6
Sandford I.o.W. 11 G6
Sandford N.Som. 19 H6
Sandford S.Lan. 75 F6
Sandford Shrop. 38 E2
Sandford Shrop. 38 C3
Sandford Orcas 9 F2
Sandford St. Martin 31 F6
Sandford-on-Thames 21 J1
Sandgarth 89 E6
Sandgate 15 H4
Sandgreen 65 F5
Sandhaven 85 P4
Sandhead 64 A5
Sandhills Dorset 9 F3
Sandhills Dorset 8 E4
Sandhills Surr. 12 C3
Sandhills W.Yorks. 57 J6
Sandhoe 70 E7
Sandholme E.Riding 58 E6
Sandholme Lincs. 43 G2
Sandhurst Brack.F. 22 B5
Sandhurst Glos. 29 H6
Sandhurst Kent 14 C5
Sandhurst Cross 14 C5
Sandhutton 57 J1
Sandiacre 41 G2
Sandilands 53 J4
Sandiway 49 F5
Sandleheath 10 C3
Sandling 14 C2
Sandlow Green 49 G6
Sandness 89 K7
Sandon Essex 24 D1
Sandon Herts. 33 G5
Sandon Staffs. 40 B3
Sandown 11 H6
Sandplace 4 C5
Sandquoy 89 G3
Sandridge Devon 5 J5
Sandridge Herts. 32 E7
Sandridge Wilts. 20 C5
Sandringham 44 A3
Sandrocks 13 G4
Sandsend 63 J5
Sandside 55 H1
Sandsound 89 M8
Sandtoft 51 K2
Sanduck 7 F7
Sandway 14 D2
Sandwell 40 C7
Sandwich 15 J2
Sandwick Cumb. 60 F5
Sandwick Shet. 89 N10
Sandwick W.Isles 88 K4
Sandwith 60 A5
Sandy Beds. 32 E4
Sandy Carmar. 17 H5
Sandy Bank 53 F7
Sandy Haven 16 B5
Sandy Lane W.Yorks. 57 G6
Sandy Lane Wilts. 20 C5
Sandy Lane Wrex. 38 D1
Sandy Way 11 F6
Sandycroft 48 C6
Sandygate Devon 5 J3
Sandygate I.o.M. 54 C4
Sandyhills 65 J5
Sandylands 55 H3
Sandypark 7 F7
Sandyway 28 D6
Sangobeg 86 G3
Sankyn's Green 29 G2
Sannaig 72 D4
Sanndabhaig 88 K4
Sannox 73 J6
Sanquhar 68 C3
Santon Bridge 60 C6
Santon Downham 44 C7
Sapcote 41 G6
Sapey Common 29 G2
Sapiston 34 D1
Sapperton Derbys. 40 D2
Sapperton Glos. 20 C1
Sapperton Lincs. 42 D2
Saracen's Head 43 G3
Sarclet 87 R5
Sardis 16 C5
Sarisbury 11 G4
Sark 3 K5
Sarn Bridgend 18 C3
Sarn Powys 38 B6
Sarn Bach 36 C3
Sarn Meyllteyrn 36 B2
Sarnau Carmar. 17 G4
Sarnau Cere. 26 C3
Sarnau Gwyn. 37 J2
Sarnau Powys 38 B4
Sarnau Powys 27 K5
Sarnesfield 28 C3
Saron Carmar. 17 K4
Saron Carmar. 17 G2
Saron Gwyn. 46 D6
Saron Gwyn. 46 C7
Sarratt 22 D2
Sarre 25 J5
Sarsden 30 D6
Sartfield 54 C4
Satley 62 B2
Satron 61 L7
Satterleigh 6 E3
Satterthwaite 60 E7
Sauchen 85 L9
Sauchie 75 G1
Sauchrie 67 H2
Saughall 48 C5
Saughall Massie 48 B4
Saughtree 70 A4
Saul 20 A1
Saundby 51 K4
Saundersfoot 16 E5
Saunderton 22 A1
Saunton 6 C2
Sausthorpe 53 G6
Saval 86 H9
Savalbeg 86 H9
Saverley Green 40 B2
Savile Town 57 H7
Sawbridge 31 G2
Sawbridgeworth 33 H7
Sawdon 59 F1
Sawley Derbys. 41 G2
Sawley Lancs. 56 C5
Sawley N.Yorks. 57 H3
Sawston 33 H4
Sawtry 42 E7
Saxby Leics. 42 B4
Saxby Lincs. 52 D4
Saxby All Saints 52 C1
Saxelbye 41 J3
Saxham Street 34 E2
Saxilby 52 B5
Saxlingham 44 E2
Saxlingham Green 45 G6
Saxlingham Nethergate 45 G6
Saxlingham Thorpe 45 G6
Saxmundham 35 H2
Saxon Street 33 K3
Saxondale 41 J2
Saxstead 35 G2
Saxtead Green 35 G2
Saxtead Little Green 35 G2
Saxthorpe 45 F2
Saxton 57 K6
Sayers Common 13 F5
Scackleton 58 C2
Scadabhagh 88 G8
Scaftworth 51 J3
Scagglethorpe 58 E2
Scaitcliffe 56 C7
Scalasaig 72 B1
Scalby E.Riding 58 E7
Scalby N.Yorks. 59 G1
Scaldwell 31 J1
Scale Houses 61 G2
Scaleby 69 K7
Scalebyhill 69 K7
Scales Cumb. 60 E4
Scales Cumb. 55 F2
Scalford 42 A3
Scaling 63 H5
Scalloway 89 M9
Scalpay W.Isles 88 H8
Scalpay (island) W.Isles 88 H8
Scamblesby 53 F5
Scampston 58 E2
Scampton 52 C5
Scaniport 84 A7
Scapa 89 D7
Scapegoat Hill 50 C1
Scarborough 59 G1
Scarcewater 3 G3
Scarcliffe 51 G6
Scarcroft 57 J5
Scardroy 83 N5
Scarfskerry 87 Q2
Scargill 62 A5
Scarinish 78 B6
Scarisbrick 48 C1
Scarning 44 D4
Scarrington 42 A1
Scarrowhill 61 G1
Scarth Hill 48 D2
Scarthingwell 57 K6
Scartho 53 F2
Scaur D.&G. 65 J3
Scaur D.&G. 65 J5
Scawby 52 C2
Scawby Brook 52 C2
Scawton 58 B1
Scayne's Hill 13 G4
Scealascro 88 G5
Scethrog 28 A6
Schaw 67 J1
Scholar Green 49 H7
Scholes S.Yorks. 51 F3
Scholes W.Yorks. 57 J6
Scholes W.Yorks. 50 D2
Scholes W.Yorks. 57 G7
School Green 49 F6
School House 8 C4
Schoose 60 B4
Sciberscross 87 K9
Scilly Isles 2 C1
Scissett 50 E1
Scleddau 16 C2
Sco Ruston 45 G3
Scofton 51 J4
Scole 35 F1
Scone 80 G8
Sconser 82 F7
Scopwick 52 D7
Scoraig 83 L1
Scorborough 59 G5
Scorrier 2 E4
Scorriton 5 H4
Scorton Lancs. 55 J5
Scorton N.Yorks. 62 C6
Scot Hay 40 A1
Scotby 60 F1
Scotch Corner 62 C6
Scotforth 55 H4
Scothern 52 D5
Scotland 42 D2
Scotland End 30 E5
Scotland Street 34 D5
Scotlandwell 80 G10
Scotnish 73 F2
Scots' Gap 71 F5
Scotston 80 E6
Scotstown 79 K4
Scotswood 71 H7
Scott Willoughby 42 D2
Scotter 52 B2
Scotterthorpe 52 B2
Scottlethorpe 42 D3
Scotton Lincs. 52 B3
Scotton N.Yorks. 62 B7
Scotton N.Yorks. 57 J4
Scottow 45 G3
Scoulton 44 D5
Scounslow Green 40 C3
Scourie 86 D5
Scousburgh 89 M11
Scouthead 49 J2
Scrabster 87 P2
Scrafield 53 G6
Scrainwood 70 E3
Scrane End 43 G1
Scraptoft 41 J5
Scratby 45 K4
Scrayingham 58 D4
Scredington 42 D1
Scremby 53 H6
Scremerston 77 J6
Screveton 42 A1
Scriven 57 J4
Scronkey 55 H5
Scrooby 51 J3
Scropton 40 D2
Scrub Hill 53 F7
Scruton 62 D7
Sculthorpe 44 C2
Scunthorpe 52 B1
Scurlage 17 H7
Sea 8 C3
Sea Mills 19 J4
Sea Palling 45 J3
Seaborough 8 D4
Seaburn 71 K7
Seacombe 48 B3
Seacroft Lincs. 53 J6
Seacroft W.Yorks. 57 J6
Seadyke 43 G2
Seafield Arg.&B. 73 F2
Seafield S.Ayr. 67 H1
Seafield W.Loth. 75 J4
Seaford 13 H7
Seaforth 48 C3
Seagrave 41 J4
Seagry Heath 20 C3
Seaham 62 E2

▼T

Index to place names in Ireland

In this index place names are followed by a page number and a grid reference. The place can be found by searching that grid square. Where more than one place has the same name, each can be distinguished by the abbreviated county name shown after the place name. A list of abbreviations used for these names is shown to the right.

Banbr.	Banbridge	*S.Dub.*	South Dublin
Kilk.	Kilkenny	*Water.*	Waterford
N.Down	North Down	*Wexf.*	Wexford
N.Tipp.	North Tipperary		

Have your say

If you have any general comments about this Guide or about Blue Badge parking, we would like to hear from you. If there are specific areas not covered by this atlas which you would like to see added, please let us know.

Help required

We have worked hard to compile comprehensive and accurate information in this map but we know how quickly things can change. We would appreciate notifications of any changes in particular classifications of car parks, petrol stations, or changes in the local parking rules.

Blue Badge Parking Newsletter

We aim to supply by post a quarterly information newsletter specifically on Blue Badge parking, holiday accommodation ideal for Blue Badge Holders, and the latest on useful places of interest to visit. If you want to be sent this free publication, please register with us. All our contact details are listed below.

Free Online Mapping Service for Blue Badge Holders

We have created a dedicated free online mapping service at: www.parkingforbluebadges.com

This site will keep the content in the atlas up to date and additional valuable street or area content will be added.

For information on getting more involved with this site either to add data, or to get a direct linkage or using the map as a location map for your site, please contact us directly.

To have this link through icon on your website, let us know.

Purchase Maps

To purchase this and other PIE guides, including the London Blue Badge Parking Guide or other Blue Badge related items visit our shop at www.thePIEguide.com/shop, or call us on **0870 444 5434** or email us at **sales@thePIEguide.com.**

Resellers and Distributors

To resell this and other PIE Guides, please contact PIE directly on **0870 444 5434** or email **sales@thePIEguide.com.**

PIE Contact Details:

Address:
The Bridge 12-16 Clerkenwell Road, London, EC1M 5PQ
Tel: 0870 444 5434
Web site:
www.parkingforbluebadges.com

About Us

PIE (Public Information Exchange) produces customised map-based products for different community groups, including motorbike and scooter riders; mums and toddlers; and lorry drivers etc. Our publications also include guides to coach parking, quality ladies toilets, regional motorbike riding maps, coffee shops and WIFI hotspots, the White Van Guide to cafes and much more. If you require a customised map, please let us know.

Would you like to see more in depth information in your area? To nominate a part of the UK that would particularly benefit from a PIE Guide, please get in touch, and let us know where and why. Equally, if you are interested in supporting or sponsoring our next national PIE Guide, please get in touch.